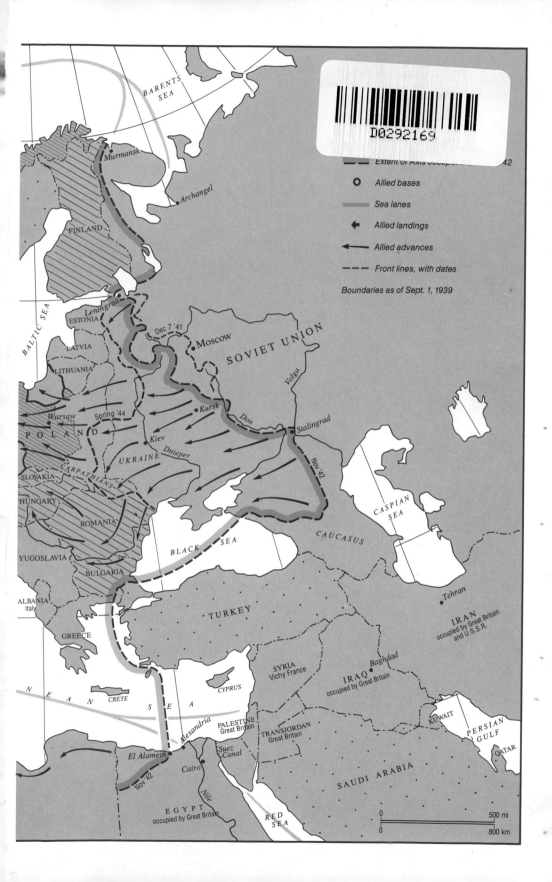

BARENTS SEA

•Murmansk

•Archangel

FINLAND

Extent of Axis occup........ 42

O   Allied bases

▬▬   Sea lanes

◄   Allied landings

◄—— Allied advances

- - - Front lines, with dates

Boundaries as of Sept. 1, 1939

BALTIC SEA

Leningrad
ESTONIA
Dec 7 '41   •Moscow   SOVIET UNION
LATVIA
LITHUANIA
Volga

Warsaw   Spring '44   •Kursk   Don
P O L A N D   •Stalingrad
                •Kiev
CARPATHIANS   Dnieper   Nov '42
UKRAINE
SLOVAKIA

HUNGARY
ROMANIA   CASPIAN
                                      SEA
YUGOSLAVIA
BULGARIA   BLACK   SEA   CAUCASUS

ALBANIA
Italy   •Tehran
GREECE   TURKEY   IRAN
                                    occupied by Great Britain
                                    and U.S.S.R.

N   SYRIA
E A N   CRETE   S E A   Vichy France   IRAQ •Baghdad
                CYPRUS   occupied by Great Britain

                    Alexandria   PALESTINE   KUWAIT   PERSIAN
El Alamein   •Cairo   Great Britain   TRANSJORDAN   GULF
        Nov '42   Suez   Great Britain   QATAR
                        Canal

    E G Y P T   SAUDI ARABIA
    occupied by Great Britain   Nile   RED
                            SEA

                0   500 mi
                0   800 km

To Daddy
Christmas 1987

This is one war Book
I'm sure you haven't read —
I'd like to read it when you
finish (about Nov. '88) —
Hope you enjoy it — We
all love you —

Yogi, Gail, Will,
Brett, Sam —

DELIVERED FROM EVIL

Books by Robert Leckie

HISTORY

Delivered from Evil
The Wars of America: Updated and Revised, 1609–1980
American and Catholic: The Catholic Church in the U.S.
Challenge for the Pacific: The Struggle for Guadalcanal
With Fire and Sword (edited with Quentin Reynolds)
Strong Men Armed: U.S. Marines Against Japan
Conflict: The History of the Korean War
The March to Glory: 1st Marine Division's Breakout from Chosin

AUTOBIOGRAPHY

Helmet for My Pillow
Lord, What a Family!

BELLES LETTRES

These Are My Heroes: A Study of the Saints
Warfare: A Study of War
A Soldier-Priest Talks to Youth

FICTION

Ordained
Marines!
The Bloodborn
Forged in Blood
Blood of the Seventeen Fires

FOR YOUNGER READERS

The Battle for Iwo Jima
The Story of Football
The Story of World War Two
The Story of World War One
The War in Korea
Great American Battles
The World Turned Upside-Down
1812: The War Nobody Won
The Big Game
Keeper Play
Stormy Voyage

DELIVERED

1817

FROM EVIL

The Saga of World War II

Robert Leckie

HARPER & ROW, PUBLISHERS, New York
Cambridge, Philadelphia, San Francisco, Washington
London, Mexico City, São Paulo, Singapore, Sydney

DELIVERED FROM EVIL. Copyright © 1987 by Robert Leckie. All rights reserved. Printed in the United States of America. No part of this book may be used or reproduced in any manner whatsoever without written permission except in the case of brief quotations embodied in critical articles and reviews. For information address Harper & Row, Publishers, Inc., 10 East 53rd Street, New York, N.Y. 10022. Published simultaneously in Canada by Fitzhenry & Whiteside Limited, Toronto.

FIRST EDITION

Designer: Lydia Link
Maps by George Colbert
Copyeditor: Ann Finlayson
Indexer: Auralie Logan

Library of Congress Cataloging-in-Publication Data

Leckie, Robert.
  Delivered from evil.

  Includes index.
  1. World War, 1939–1945. I. Title.
D743.L43 1987   940.53   86–46305
ISBN 0–06–015812–3

87 88 89 90 91 RRD 10 9 8 7 6 5 4 3 2 1

To Glennis S. Rickert, M.D.

Witty Friend and Wise Physician

Contents

PART VI. 1943

PART VII. 1944

Maps

———◆◆———

GREENLAND
occupied by U.S.
Julianehaab

DENMARK STRAIT

NORTH
ATLANTIC
OCEAN

Reykjavik
ICELAND
occupied by U.S.

NORWEGIAN
SEA

NORWAY

SWED

Scapa Flow

NORTH
SEA

DENMARK

IRELAND

GREAT
BRITAIN

Elbe

Berlin

London

June 6 '44

NETH.

BELG.

GERMANY

Paris

FRANCE

Vichy

SWITZ.

ITALY

June 6 '4

Marseilles
Aug 15 '44

Rome

Anzio
Jan 22 '44

Saler

PORTUGAL

SPAIN

Sept 9 '43

MADEIRA
Portugal

M E D

I T

Nov 8 '42

Gibraltar

Nov 8 '42

E

SICILY

July 10 '43

CANARY IS.
Spain

Nov 8 '42
Oran

Algiers

Tunis

Malta

R

A

Casablanca
MOROCCO
Vichy France

TUNISIA

Tripoli

ALGERIA
Vichy France

RIO DE ORO
Spain

LIB
Italy

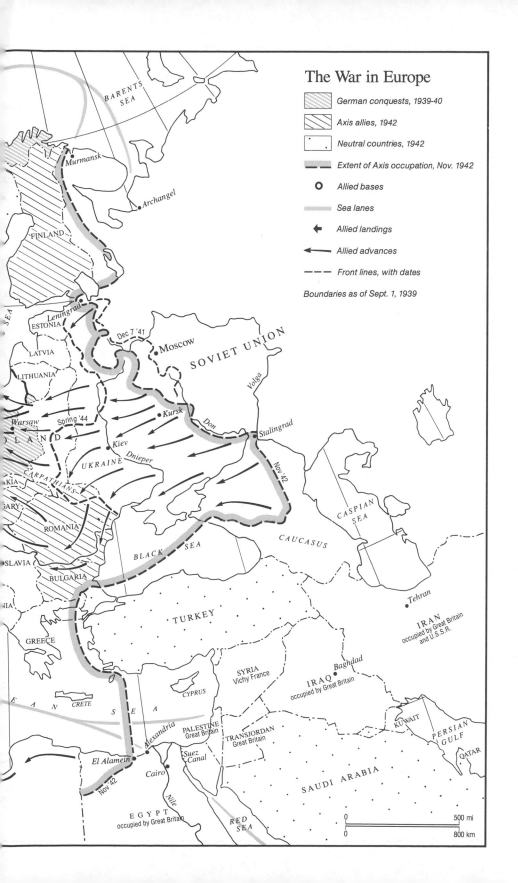

The War in Europe

- German conquests, 1939-40
- Axis allies, 1942
- Neutral countries, 1942
- Extent of Axis occupation, Nov. 1942
- O Allied bases
- Sea lanes
- ← Allied landings
- ← Allied advances
- --- Front lines, with dates

Boundaries as of Sept. 1, 1939

BARENTS SEA

Murmansk

Archangel

FINLAND

SEA

Leningrad
ESTONIA
Dec 7 '41
Moscow

SOVIET UNION

LATVIA

LITHUANIA

Volga

Warsaw
Spring '44
Kursk
Don
Stalingrad

OLAND

Kiev
Dnieper
UKRAINE
Nov '42

CARPATHIANS

KIA

CASPIAN SEA

GARY

ROMANIA

CAUCASUS

SLAVIA

BLACK SEA

BULGARIA

Tehran

GREECE

TURKEY

IRAN
occupied by Great Britain
and U.S.S.R.

NIA

SYRIA
Vichy France
CYPRUS
IRAQ Baghdad
occupied by Great Britain

CRETE

E
A
N
S
E
A

PALESTINE
Great Britain
TRANSJORDAN
Great Britain

KUWAIT

PERSIAN GULF

QATAR

El Alamein
Nov '42
Cairo
Alexandria
Suez Canal

SAUDI ARABIA

EGYPT
occupied by Great Britain

Nile

RED SEA

0   500 mi

0   800 km

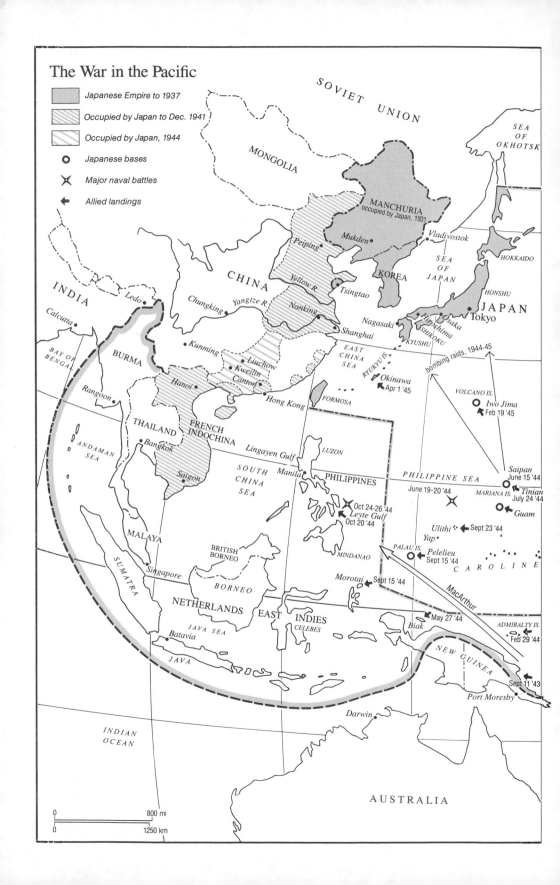

The War in the Pacific

- Japanese Empire to 1937
- Occupied by Japan to Dec. 1941
- Occupied by Japan, 1944
- ○ Japanese bases
- ✕ Major naval battles
- ← Allied landings

SOVIET UNION

MONGOLIA

SEA OF OKHOTSK

MANCHURIA
occupied by Japan, 1931

Peiping

Mukden

Vladivostok

HOKKAIDO

CHINA

Yellow R

Tsingtao

KOREA

SEA OF JAPAN

HONSHU

JAPAN

Tokyo

INDIA

Ledo

Chungking

Yangtze R

Nanking

Nagasaki

Osaka

Hiroshima

SHIKOKU

KYUSHU

Calcutta

BAY OF BENGAL

BURMA

Kunming

Liuchow

Kweilin

Canton

Shanghai

EAST CHINA SEA

RYUKYU IS.

Okinawa
Apr 1 '45

bombing raids, 1944-45

Rangoon

THAILAND

Hanoi

FRENCH INDOCHINA

Hong Kong

FORMOSA

VOLCANO IS.

○ Iwo Jima
← Feb 19 '45

ANDAMAN SEA

Bangkok

Lingayen Gulf

LUZON

PHILIPPINE SEA

Saipan
June 15 '44

Saigon

SOUTH CHINA SEA

Manila

PHILIPPINES

June 19-20 '44

✕ Tinian
July 24 '44

MARIANA IS.

○ Guam

MALAYA

SUMATRA

Singapore

BRITISH BORNEO

MINDANAO

✕ Oct 24-26 '44
← Leyte Gulf
Oct 20 '44

Ulithi

Yap

← Sept 23 '44

PALAU IS.

Peleliu
Sept 15 '44

C A R O L I N E

NETHERLANDS EAST INDIES

BORNEO

CELEBES

Morotai ← Sept 15 '44

MacArthur

Batavia

JAVA SEA

JAVA

← May 27 '44

Biak

ADMIRALTY IS.

← Feb 29 '44

NEW GUINEA

Sept 11 '43

Darwin

Port Moresby

INDIAN OCEAN

AUSTRALIA

0		800 mi
0	1250 km	

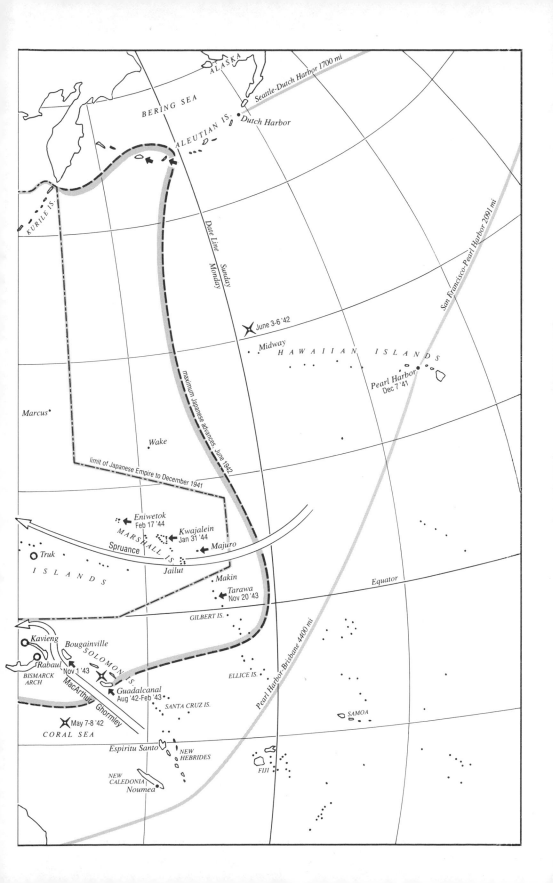

ALASKA

BERING SEA

Seattle-Dutch Harbor 1700 mi

ALEUTIAN IS.   • Dutch Harbor

KURILE IS.

Date Line

Sunday
Monday

San Francisco–Pearl Harbor 2091 mi

✠ June 3-6 '42

• Midway   H A W A I I A N   I S L A N D S

Pearl Harbor
Dec 7 '41

Marcus•

maximum Japanese advances June 1942

Wake

limit of Japanese Empire to December 1941

Eniwetok
Feb 17 '44

Kwajalein
Jan 31 '44

M A R S H A L L   I S .

Spruance   ← Majuro

Truk

I S L A N D S   Jaluit

Makin

Tarawa
Nov 20 '43

Equator

GILBERT IS.

Kavieng

Bougainville

SOLOMON IS.

Pearl Harbor–Brisbane 4400 mi

Rabaul
Nov 1 '43

BISMARCK
ARCH.

MacArthur Ghormley

ELLICE IS.

✠
← Guadalcanal
Aug '42-Feb '43

SANTA CRUZ IS.

SAMOA

✠ May 7-8 '42

CORAL SEA

Espiritu Santo

NEW
HEBRIDES

FIJI

NEW
CALEDONIA
Noumea

PART ONE

1919–1938

1. 1919: Versailles

AT ELEVEN O'CLOCK IN THE MORNING of the eleventh day of the eleventh month of the year 1918 the guns of the Great War began to fall silent. At dusk, a sickle moon arose. Its faint light fell on no-man's-land where bloated rats splashed in shell holes filled with water, searching for corpses to feed upon. The little moon shone on those silent dark heaps of rubble that once were towns and cities, making crooked silhouettes of broken church crosses and toppled Gothic towers. Darkness brought crowds of singing, shouting soldiers into no-man's-land to caper among the cruel black lace of the barbed wire. They exchanged prisoners or swapped German sausage for American cigarettes or French cognac. Bonfires were lighted. Rockets and Very flares trailing their long red tails were fired at the brightening wisp of yellow, shining palely now on the obsidian seas silently rolling over fleets of sunken ships and armies of drowned men and untold stores of treasure lost forever. Soon complete silence engulfed those gouged and gutted farmlands that had become the battlefields, and the sickle moon, having reached its zenith, slowly began its descent—while beneath it the cataclysm that had convulsed the world came shuddering to a stop.

Three weeks later, on December 4, 1918, President Woodrow Wilson of the United States of America sailed for the peace conference in Paris. He sailed with high hopes, buoyant in the belief that the noble principles embodied in his famous "fourteen points" would produce a peace between equals and lead to formation of a League of Nations empowered to keep that peace.

Woodrow Wilson came to Europe as though he were peace incarnate. No conquering Caesar entering Rome followed by captive kings "to grace in chains his chariot wheels" ever received a more tumultuous triumph. For Wilson was not just another conqueror, of whom this tortured continent had seen a surfeit, but a savior *without* a sword. Everywhere he went he seemed to the frenzied, cheering populace to embody the aspirations of suffering humanity.

"No one has heard such cheers," one correspondent wrote. "I, who heard them in the streets of Paris, can never forget them in all my life. I saw Foch pass, Clemenceau pass, Lloyd George, generals, returning troops, banners, but Wilson heard from his carriage something different, inhuman or superhuman."

Such adulation could not fail to convince Thomas Woodrow Wilson, the idealist, the "professor in politics," that it was he who would be the architect of peace and that once again his Fourteen Points were to be its keystone. At least at first, his ears still echoing to that thunderous applause, he could not entertain the opposite suspicion: that he was to be party not to a peace among equals but

3

to a vengeful Carthaginian ultimatum imposed by the victor on the vanquished.*

Certainly there had been an abundance of words and deeds suggesting that the latter course was to be the real one. In Britain, Prime Minister David Lloyd George had secured a delay in the conference to take advantage of the rise in popularity given him by the Armistice, successfully campaigning for reelection on such merciful slogans as "Hang the Kaiser!" or "Make 'em pay!" With similar compassion, Winston Churchill rose in the House of Commons on March 3, 1919, to declare:

"We are holding all our means of coercion in full operation or in immediate readiness for use. We are enforcing the blockade with vigour. We have strong armies ready to advance at the shortest notice. Germany is very near starvation. The evidence I have received from the officers sent by the War Office all over Germany shows, first of all, the great privation which the German people are suffering, and, secondly, the great danger of a collapse of the entire structure of German social and national life under the pressure of hunger and malnutrition. Now is therefore the time to settle."

The blockade of which Churchill spoke, and the hunger and suffering resulting from it, had already caused the deaths of 800,000 German noncombatants during the last two years of the war, and it was not to be lifted until the Treaty of Versailles was signed and the Allies had gained a trading head start. Moreover, "now" was indeed "the time to settle," as Churchill's colleagues well knew. To torment the Germans further would be to drive them with the fury of despair into the arms of the devil: the Bolshevik menace which at that time terrified all Europe.

Wilson's idealism, then, was in no way acceptable to the other members of the Big Four—Lloyd George, Premier Georges Clemenceau of France, and Premier Vittorio Orlando of Italy—if it was not indeed a major sticking point with them. All of them considered the American to be naive and obviously unacquainted with the "practical" give-and-take of European power politics. They were also irked by the lone hand which Wilson had played with the enemy during the final months of the war, and they were indeed intensely jealous of his worldwide popularity. So they had negotiated secret treaties, sharing out the spoils in a way which, though customary, was not exactly compatible with the Fourteen Points. They also excluded the defeated nations from the conference, the surest sign that the "peace" was to be a capitulation, and relegated those smaller Allied nations, for whose rights the war had supposedly been fought, to the sidelines.

*In brief, the Fourteen Points were: (1) open peace covenants, openly arrived at; (2) freedom of the seas; (3) removal of trade barriers; (4) arms reduction; (5) adjusting of colonial claims; (6) Russian territory evacuated and restored; (7) Belgian territory evacuated and sovereignty restored; (8) French territory restored and the Alsace-Lorraine question settled; (9) Italian frontiers adjusted; (10) division of Austria-Hungary; (11) redrawing of Balkan boundaries; (12) Turkish control only of their own peoples; (13) establishment of an independent Poland; (14) formation of a "general association of nations."

Finally, in the hearts of Georges Clemenceau and his countrymen there throbbed a horrible ache for revenge, a yearning for a hard peace that would humble and hobble Germany for good and all.

It is indeed difficult to fault the French. Twice within the memory of many living Frenchmen the German nation had hurled itself upon its western neighbor. In 1871, Bismarck's harsh terms had torn from France the province of Alsace and part of Lorraine, the birthplace of Joan of Arc, and extracted a brutal, astronomical indemnity for the day of $1 billion. During 1914–18, no nation had suffered as much as the French. The country's manhood had been bled white, and a terrible mutiny among the soldiers had almost brought France to her knees and robbed her of her sacred honor. Much of the countryside was in ruins, the ports were obsolete, and the railroads worn out. In 1918, the vengeful General Ludendorff, aware that Germany could not win, had with deliberate spite wrecked France's northern mines in order to cripple a trade rival. A merciful lifting of the blockade imposed for the same reason on such an enemy seemed to Clemenceau to make a mockery of compassion. But when he tried to make this clear to Wilson, inviting him to visit the mines, the American refused, on those very grounds that he did not wish to be influenced against the Germans. His reply infuriated the Tiger of France and only deepened his conviction that he was dealing with a starry-eyed visionary who fancied himself the second Messiah. "Mr. Wilson bores me with his Fourteen Points," Clemenceau growled. "Why, Almighty God has only ten!"

Mr. Wilson, however, was not so ingenuous. By then, the echoing cheers had begun to fade in his ears, and he clearly saw the course upon which his colleagues were embarked. He knew European geography and history and was deeply aware of the difficulties of redrawing the borders of a continent constantly divided by war and dissension since it had emerged from the Dark Ages. He saw that much of the Carthaginian peace that Clemenceau was preparing was consonant with many of his Fourteen Points, such as national self-determination, and that to block his colleagues was also to endanger that League of Nations which was the keystone of the Points and the soul of his policy. That was his mistake. He made his concessions to save the League, but in his defense it must be observed that one of the League's functions was to review the decisions made at Paris.

Still, to be fair to Wilson, he could not have been so impolitic as to take up the cudgels for the late enemy when the common man everywhere was calling for his head. Nor could he simply have walked out of the conference, as he at one time seems to have considered, and thus leave much of Europe exposed to the Communist menace. Nor was he entirely to blame for the futile attempt to settle Europe's problems on the basis of national determination, for nationalism was by then the very real mental fashion of the men of "advanced ideas." Even before the war, British thinker Norman Angell had written: "Political nationalism has become, for the European of our age, the most important thing in the world, more important than civilization, humanity, decency, kindness, pity; more important than life itself." As votaries of this new religion, the Allied leaders decided to carve the multinational Austro-Hungarian Empire into separate national states.

They created the separate states of Austria and Hungary, a new republic of Czechoslovakia, and, by joining some Slavic areas to Serbia, the new nation of Yugoslavia. Poland was revived as an independent state and given a "corridor" through Germany to the once-German city of Danzig (now Gdańsk, Poland) on the Baltic, while Romania was almost doubled in size at the expense of Hungary. Unfortunately, the peoples within these new boundaries did not coincide in language or race, and where there had once been a common market in Middle Europe, there were now trade barriers erected by each of the succession states. Each new nation also included minorities quick to demand self-determination, or minorities such as the German-speaking residents of Czechoslovakia and Poland, who had allegiance elsewhere. Unhappily, their race and language were like a string that a valorous but fanatic German corporal named Adolf Hitler would one day use to yank both them and their new homeland into Germany. Thus strategically vital Central Europe was cut up into a crowd of quarreling states unable to make common cause together, and Austria, once the central nervous system when it was an empire, was left a weakling with neither ports nor markets, whose only salvation lay in union with Germany. This, of course, was not to be.

Germany was to stay weak. The country was to be stripped of all its overseas colonies, to admit war guilt as a basis for later reparation, to lose land for the Polish Corridor and the other buffer states ringing it round, to permit demilitarization west of the Rhine, and to be disarmed of all but enough troops to police the interior. Undoubtedly, the terms of the new Versailles Treaty were not nearly so harsh as what a victorious Germany might have dictated. But they were nonetheless Carthaginian, certain, as Germany's own Treaty of Versailles had been certain, to produce another and probably more terrible cataclysm, granting the growth of weaponry and the spread of industrialization. But even worse than these deliberate shackles was the monster sin of omission by which the Allies had ignored the economic problems that had caused the conflict just ended.

One of Wilson's Fourteen Points was to call for the removal of all economic barriers, but he and his colleagues completely ignored this, causing the British economist John Maynard Keynes to comment: "The fundamental economic problems of a Europe starving and disintegrating before their eyes was the one question on which it was impossible to arouse the interest of the Four." He added:

The future life of Europe was not their concern; its means of livelihood was not their anxiety. Their preoccupations, good and bad alike, related to frontiers and nationalities, to the balance of power, to imperial aggrandisements, to the future enfeeblement of a strong and desperate enemy, to revenge, and to the shifting by the victors of their unbearable financial burdens on to the shoulders of the defeated.

Eventually, Lloyd George perceived the danger, and on March 25, 1919, he circulated a memorandum, part of which read:

You may strip Germany of her colonies, reduce her armaments to a mere police force and her navy to that of a fifth-rate power; all the same, in the end, if she feels that she has been unjustly treated in the peace of 1919, she will find means of exacting retribution from her conquerors. The maintenance of peace will . . . depend upon there being no causes of exasperation constantly stirring up the spirit of patriotism, of justice or of fair play to achieve redress. . . . For these reasons I am, therefore, strongly averse to transferring more Germans from German rule to the rule of some other nation than can possibly be helped. I cannot conceive any greater cause of future war than that the German people, who have certainly proved themselves one of the most vigorous and powerful nations in the world, should be surrounded by a number of small states, many of them consisting of people who have never previously set up a stable government for themselves, but each of them containing large masses of Germans clamouring for reunion with their native land.

There could hardly have been a more accurate forecast, and yet the warning was ignored. On May 7, 1919, the terms were read to a German delegation led by Count Ulrich von Brockdorff-Rantzau. Shocked, Brockdorff angrily attacked the Allies for continuing the blockade and insisted that the Fourteen Points were binding on all who signed the Armistice, after which he refused to sign the treaty. Then the German press published the terms. The German people were aghast. A bitter outcry against the treaty arose.

Back in Paris, one of those who were shocked by the terms was Herbert Hoover, the American engineer who had become famous for feeding war victims. Unable to sleep, he rushed outside his hotel to walk the dark streets in dismay. Later, before he became president of the United States, he wrote: "It seemed to me the economic consequences alone would pull down all Europe and thus injure the United States."

But the Allies would not budge, and a despairing Germany knew that it must sign. The blockade was strangling the country and the Communists had taken to the streets. On Saturday, June 28, a new German delegation—Dr. Herman Muller and Dr. Johannes Bell—arrived at the Palace of Versailles. They were led to a point outside the great doorway into the Hall of Mirrors, the very same glittering room in which a humiliated France had heard Wilhelm I proclaimed as the first German emperor. Forming a lane into the hall were two facing files of soldiers in the gorgeous uniforms of the *Garde Républicaine.* They held naked sabers before their eyes. The Germans stared at them morosely. Beneath the plumed and gleaming Achilles helmets, every face was twisted in open hatred and contempt.

Inside the hall, the Allied leaders sat at a long table. In their center was Georges Clemenceau, crouched in his chair like a yellowish gnarled gnome.

"*Faites entrer les Allemands,*" he rasped, his coal-black eyes glittering. "Show in the Germans!"

With a flash and click the guardsmen sheathed their sabers. Dr. Muller and Dr. Bell were conducted to their chairs. Then they arose. With downcast eyes they approached the small table on which the treaty lay. They signed. Outside the palace, crashing cannon signaled to a jubilant Paris that the detestable Boche had at last been paid back. Inside the hall, the Allies signed: Wilson, Lloyd George, Orlando, finally Clemenceau. Turning, the Tiger of France felt his hand seized by former Premier Paul Painlevé, who congratulated him.

"Yes," murmured Clemenceau, his eyes softening and brimming with tears, "it is a beautiful day."

2. The League of Nations

BUT IT HAD NOT BEEN A BEAUTIFUL DAY: not for France, nor for its allies; nor for Germany nor its allies; nor for the world. Rather, it had been a very black day indeed. Because of the war and the treaty, all European balance was destroyed; and because Europe was the center of world trade as well as the headquarters for all but two of the world's empires, so also was world balance destroyed.

Three of these empires—the German, Austrian, and Turkish—simply vanished. A fourth, the Russian, having exchanged the whip of the Cossack for the goad of the commissar, was already engaged in recovering the land lost to Germany, while crushing the last remnants of White Russian resistance and preparing the Red Army for the forthcoming invasion of Poland. A fifth, and once the most powerful, Great Britain, had sunk from the status of world banker and arbiter to that of a debtor nation whose voice and counsel no longer carried special weight. A sixth, the French, was reduced to the status of a second-rate power whose multiparty system was made for chaos. A seventh, the United States of America, was retreating into isolationism, while preparing to embark on that "noble experiment" of Prohibition. The eighth and newest, Italy, having received as war booty the South Tyrol, Trieste, Rhodes and the Dodecanese Islands, calmly seized Fiume (now Rijeka, Yugoslavia) and then retired from its forage, sulking because it could not also grab islands off the coasts of Dalmatia and Albania. Only the ninth, Japan, was satisfied. Because of a casualty rate of .002 percent—that is, 300 dead and 907 wounded—Japan had emerged as the dominant power in the Far East and been given a collection of German islands, which, contrary to League of Nations regulations for these "mandated" isles, it promptly began to fortify and to use for bases to expand its sea power in the Western Pacific.

Of all these arrivals and departures, the most shattering were the coming of the Russian Revolution and the passing of the Pax Britannica. Although the new masters of Russia had yet to consolidate themselves before they could begin to spread their Marxist doctrine of atheistic materialism throughout the world, the old balance of power embodied in the Pax Britannica was definitely dead. Because

Britain had felt compelled to field a huge conscript army in a continental land war, it forever lost control of that balance of power by which it had traditionally prevented wars from becoming worldwide. Perhaps this was inevitable, granting the industrialization of other nations and the quickening race for markets, granting also the acceleration of only a few nations with land-mass-plus-population toward the exclusive rank of superpower; and probably the wonder of it all was that this seafaring island race for a hundred years had been able even to check Europe's fratricidal tendencies. However that may be, something had to replace the Pax Britannica. To Woodrow Wilson, the League of Nations would fill the vacuum. He was as certain of this as he was positive that the United States would ratify the treaty and accept the Covenant of the League.

Unfortunately, Woodrow Wilson seemed to be able to alienate certain people without even trying. Before sailing for Europe, he had angered the Republican opposition by calling for a Democratic sweep in the midterm election of 1918. Then he had neglected to name any high-ranking Republican to the peace delegation. Finally, he had defied Republican senators who opposed making the League Covenant part of the treaty. "When that Treaty comes back," he had said, "gentlemen on this side will find the Covenant not only in it, but so many threads of the Treaty tied to the Covenant that you cannot dissect the Covenant from the Treaty without destroying the whole vital structure." Much as this decision to make warp and woof of Treaty and Covenant was then hailed as a triumph of Wilsonian statecraft, in fact his intransigence doomed both.

President Wilson mistook his countrymen's ebullient enthusiasm for the World War, a conflict which he personally entered with great reluctance ("There is such a thing as a man's being too proud to fight"), as proof that they were at last ready to accept world responsibility. But they were not. It would take another much crueler conflagration to rid themselves of the notion that a war is like a football game: When the game is over and victory is yours, it's time to celebrate. That was what was happening. The Torrid Twenties were at hand, and many, many Americans, either ignoring Prohibition or actually taking up drink in defiant resentment of the Volstead Act's arrogant intrusion into their private lives, had beaten their swords into cocktail shakers and were dancing deeper and deeper into the ostrich hole of isolation. Moreover, apathy was giving way to disillusion. The time of the "debunkers" had also arrived with their oh-so-palatable myths that 126,000* Americans had died and 334,000 had been wounded "to pull England's chestnuts out of the fire" or to rescue the big American banks from an Allied defeat that would mean default on their enormous debts. And had they not won "the war to end wars"? What, then, was this talk about a League of Nations to prevent *future* wars? Many Americans bitterly believed they had been deliberately deceived and they vowed never again to ignore George Washington's warning against involvement in "the broils of Europe." To these people, the

---

*Actual battle deaths were 55,000, but death from other causes, chiefly from the postwar flu epidemic, raised the total to this figure.

wearying labyrinthine way of foreign policy seemed to wind up the hill of Sisyphus. Thus, Wilson did not have, as he fervently believed, his countrymen on his side. Moreover, when he returned home he found himself ranged against Senator Henry Cabot Lodge of Massachusetts, a suave, scholarly and powerful Republican leader who had no difficulty in arousing opposition to the League, "this evil thing with a holy name."

Lodge hated Wilson with an implacable hatred. Even though he personally favored creation of a world organization, he wanted nothing born of the brain of Thomas Woodrow Wilson. So Lodge moved to bury the treaty by hobbling it with reservations and hamstringing it with debate. Lodge was not only supported by all that was reactionary in America, including resurgent isolationism, but by many internationalists who believed that Wilson had betrayed his own principles for the League. The *New Republic* abandoned its allegiance to Wilson with the dire prophecy: "The European politicians who with American complicity have hatched this inhuman monster, have acted either cynically, hypocritically or vindictively, and their handiwork will breed future cynicism, hypocrisy, and vindictiveness in the minds of future generations."

Though shaken, Wilson refused to accept this Cassandra cry and vowed to take his cause to the people. In September of 1919 he began to stump the country. "I can predict with absolute certainty," he declared, "that within another generation there will be another world war if the nations of the world do not concert the method by which to prevent it." But Wilson's power to move the masses was gone. Passionate and eloquent as ever, he spoke to unheeding audiences. On the night of September 25, he suffered a nervous collapse followed by a stroke. Slowly, with drawn blinds, the presidential train reversed its course to carry a paralyzed chief executive back to Washington. For two months Wilson lay in the White House unable to move, seen only by his physician, his secretary and his family. He could barely scrawl an indecipherable signature on the few documents brought to him by his wife or his secretary, Joseph Tumulty.

For the first time in American history the problem foreseen by the Constitution arose: "In the case of . . . inability to discharge the powers and duties of the said office, the same shall devolve on the Vice President." But when Secretary of State Robert Lansing attempted to implement this proviso, he met a furious rebuff from Tumulty. Moreover, dim-witted Vice President Thomas R. Marshall, famous for that penetrating epigram, "What this country needs is a good five-cent cigar," was literally terrified that "the same should devolve" on him. Eventually, Wilson recovered his mental powers but not his health. His pride he could never lose, and when defeat of the League appeared certain, he rejected all calls for compromise with the fierce reply: "Let Lodge compromise! Better a thousand times to go down fighting than to dip your colors to dishonorable compromise."

This from that statesman who in Paris had made a creed of compromise. On November 19, 1919, the League was rejected in the Senate, and again a year later.

"We had a chance to gain the leadership of the world," said a sorrowing

Woodrow Wilson. "We have lost it, and soon we shall be witnessing the tragedy of it all."

It has been said that American abstention was the chief rock upon which the League of Nations foundered; and yet, even with the United States a member, it is difficult to see what the League could have done to prevent war or remove injustices or restrain a predatory nation. The real rock that sank the League was the problem faced by any world organization committed to keeping the peace: How do you punish a sovereign state?

To do so, a world organization must be sovereign to the errant state, and no state, however just and righteous, has yet to surrender an iota of its sovereignty, let alone been willing to accept a judgment of errancy. To impose its will, then, the League needed force; and it had none. It was a policeman without a pistol, a judge dependent for his power of persuasion on the writ of international law or the thrust of public opinion, neither of which has been known to dissuade any government determined to follow a certain course. So the League sank into a noble futility, becoming a debating society invoking empty sanctions against the new breed of international predators spawned by the Treaty of Versailles.

Not even Woodrow Wilson could have envisioned that "the tragedy of it all" was so close at hand, or that it could so completely engulf mankind. Of predictions of another world war there was then a surfeit; and yet, no one foresaw that the death of the dynasties and the end of the empires was to be so quickly succeeded by the day of the dictator.

3. Benito Mussolini

BENITO MUSSOLINI, the undoubted father of that authoritarian nationalism called fascism, entered the world on July 29, 1883, in the little lost village of Predappio on the Romagna, a poverty-stricken district of central Italy slanting away into the Apennines. The big iron double bedstead on which he was born had been forged by his blacksmith father, and on the wall above it hung two portraits symbolic of the dichotomy that was to divide the lustily squalling infant's childhood. The one, a portrait of the Virgin Mary, had been hung there by his mother, Rosa, the twenty-five-year-old schoolmistress of Predappio, who was, like all of the village women and indeed of the district itself, a devout Catholic; the other, of Giuseppi Garibaldi, the revolutionary liberator of Sicily, had been nailed there by his father, Alessandro, at twenty-eight a Socialist so ardent and so locally renowned that he was under constant police surveillance and needed a permit to travel the seven miles to neighboring Forlì to fetch the doctor. Throughout Benito's childhood, these two creeds were to vie for possession of his head and heart. Where Rosa sought to consecrate the child to the Blessed Mother and dress him in Mary blue until his confirmation, Alessandro countered by naming him after Benito Juárez, the Mexican revolutionary who had executed the Emperor Maximilian.

The Mussolinis were as poor as their neighbors. They lived in a three-room apartment in a dilapidated tenement. Benito shared a straw sleeping mat with his younger brother, Arnaldo, in a cubbyhole that was also the kitchen.

On Sundays Rosa took Benito to the ninth-century church of San Cassiano, where he became an unwilling and then an unwelcome worshipper. By the time he was eight, because of his proclivity for pinching his neighbors and talking in a loud voice when the Mass was in progress, he was banned from the church. In revenge, he shinnied up an adjacent tree to pelt both celebrant and congregation with small stones and acorns. By the time he was nine, Rosa had begun to despair of her oldest child: taciturn, solitary, a leader of a gang of thieving urchins, always at odds with authority, fierce, possessed of a demonic energy and a macabre sense of humor. Not even Benito's voracious reading and his appetite for learning could convince his mother that she could control him or save him from a bad end.

Nine years later, it appeared that Rosa had won, for she had succeeded in enrolling Benito in a school conducted by Salesian fathers in Faenza, twenty miles away. Oddly enough, it was the anticlerical Alessandro who drove his son in the donkey cart to the priests' school. But that was probably so that he could get him alone and warn him: "Pay attention to what they teach you, especially the geography and history—but don't let them stuff your head with nonsense about God and the saints." Nodding grimly, Benito replied: "Don't worry, Papa—I know there's no such person as God."

The Salesians, however, disagreed—and they proceeded to try to beat the Almighty into the unbowed head of their stubborn and rebellious pupil. They never succeeded, nor could they have, granting Benito's fierce resentment of a system that divided the students into classes according to wealth. Benito was at the bottom, and his always active inferiority complex was not assuaged by the kitchen scraps fed him and his fellow paupers. These were the bitterest years of Benito Mussolini's life. He was always in trouble, always being disciplined, always being punished. All he had to do to escape chastisement was to ask forgiveness, but this he would not do; his proud spirit could never beg for pardon. At last, after he threw an inkpot at a teacher who had hit him with a ruler, the fathers decided to expel him. Only Rosa's tearful intervention saved him—but for what? More war between himself and his teachers, until, in the summer of 1894, he stabbed a fellow pupil in the buttocks with a pocketknife and that was the end at Faenza.

Benito came home immensely proud of his reputation as a rebel who had challenged and—in his view—bested the Church. Alessandro greeted his eleven-year-old son as a full-fledged hero, a prodigy of socialism who would one day be heard from in Italy. He gave Benito books to read: Bakunin, Zola, Victor Hugo.

The theme of the oppressed struggling valiantly against the injustice of a world of priests and capitalists sank deep into Benito's mind. The boy also practiced public speaking in his room. Once, Rosa heard what seemed to her a stream of gibberish and she rushed into his room in fright, only to find Benito standing in the center bellowing away at the four walls. Benito grinned at the fear on his mother's face, at the unspoken doubt of his sanity, reassuring her with the remark: "I am preparing for the day when all Italy trembles at my words."

That was enough for Rosa. She enrolled Benito in a Forlì secular school, Forlimpopoli Secondary Modern College. At once, he resumed his vendetta with authority; his brawling and bullying continued, and after a particularly brutal fistfight he was asked to leave, then pardoned. But on two other occasions he was suspended and sent home for ten days: once for impertinence and once for stabbing a classmate. Although Benito Mussolini was later fond of describing himself as having headed his class, he was in fact a mediocre student who inspired only fear in his fellow students and was not well liked. The boy did have some gifts, however, playing the trombone in the school band, and at the age of seventeen delivering a speech in the local theater to commemorate Verdi.

By then, also, Benito had discovered in himself an insatiable lust for women. As regularly as his mother attending Mass, he made his Sunday visits to the brothels of Forlì, where he made love like a bull in a pasture. In his autobiography, he described his style: "I caught her on the stairs, throwing her into a corner behind a door, and made her mine. When she got up weeping and humiliated she insulted me by saying I had robbed her of her honor and it is not impossible she spoke the truth. But I ask you, what kind of honor can she have meant?"

On July 8, 1901, a few weeks prior to his eighteenth birthday, Benito Mussolini was graduated from Forlimpopoli with an elementary schoolteacher's certificate. His parents were overjoyed. Rosa advised him to apply for the post of secretary to the Predappio village council, but that body, having had a surfeit of anticlerical Mussolinis, was least of all inclined toward this bohemian intellectual, this local "crazy man" with his black cape turning green with age, his unshaven chin and unbrushed hair, and his huge shabby black umbrella, which he carried to and from the library at Forlì where he read "all those books."

At eighteen, Mussolini had matured physically. He had reached his full height of five feet six inches and was already remarkable for his commanding head and his broad low brow, piercing black eyes, wide mouth and jutting square jaw. Because of his great head, he gave the impression of physical strength. Yet, if he were to remove his outer garments, it would be seen that his shoulders were thin, his arching chest a pouting pigeon's breast and his arms and legs spindly. However, like Napoleon, he could strike fear into men twice his size with a direct glance from those astonishing eyes. This trait became more apparent when, in 1902, he took a substitute teacher's job at three dollars a week in Gualtieri, one hundred miles to the east in the province of Reggio Emilia. Although the village administration was Socialist and inclined to indulge him in his radical beliefs, he nevertheless charmed few villagers with his life-style.

Mussolini bathed at dawn, standing stark naked in the Po. He walked barefoot from the river to the school, dangling his shoes from a stick held over his shoulder, like a hobo with his bindle. His fondness for drink and cards did not delight Gualtieri's parents, nor did his liaison with a lady whose husband was away on military service. When his appointment expired in June 1902, it was not renewed—and Mussolini decided to migrate to Switzerland.

He was leaving Italy to escape military service, importunate mistresses and bad debts that included his unpaid rent. He left without going home to say good-bye, and when he learned at the border that his father had been arrested and jailed, he kept going. Alessandro served six months in prison. During that time Rosa continued to scrape and scrimp to send money to Benito.

He needed it. He arrived in Switzerland with less than a dollar in his pocket. He finally found a job as a bricklayer's assistant at 35 centimes an hour, earning 20 francs for sixty hours work—and then, with his shoes gone and his hands broken and bleeding, he quit. Even so, his employer angrily hurled his pay at him as "stolen money."

Moving on to Lausanne, he finally came up against complete destitution, his only possession a nickel medallion of Karl Marx. He was starving. His hatred of the rich and comfortable now became obsessional. Yet he must feed himself, and to do so he snatched bread from a peasant family's table, running to wolf it down crouched in the wooden box beneath a bridge where he lived. Eventually, he was arrested as a vagrant. A few days prior to his nineteenth birthday, he was sent to jail.

Freed, he chanced on a group of Italian Socialists in a Lausanne café. Benito Mussolini had not been aware that there was a large body of expatriate Italian workers in Switzerland, most of them in the building trades. They hated their employers. Their loathing of the exploiters of mankind, the managers of the means of livelihood, complemented Mussolini's. He had found his opportunity. His command of language, his ability to put their enmity and their grievances into coherent form, soon held them spellbound. Within four months of his arrival, he was elected secretary of their Italian Trade Union of Bricklayers and Bricklayers' Assistants.

Now Mussolini was able to put to use the lessons learned from childhood in his father's school for hate. The Church, the King, the Army, the Government, the established Order, even Christ himself, all these devils drawn from the litany of the afflictors of mankind chanted to him over all those years by Alessandro were now his targets as he appeared at union meetings and strike demonstrations, screeching, screaming, bellowing with his great head thrown back and his square jaw sawing the air, his small dainty hands cupped like paws above his head and clawing away as though these imagined enemies were truly before him in flesh and blood.

Like all demagogues, Mussolini had an unerring eye for the dramatic gesture, the single stroke that would sway a hesitant crowd his way. Debating a Lausanne pastor, he drew from his pocket a cheap nickel watch borrowed in advance and said: "It is now 3:30 P.M. If God exists, I give him five minutes to strike me dead." God Himself only knows how ancient and enduring this cheap trick is, but it had the predictable result. Shocked, stilled and hushed, the crowd watched Mussolini with narrowed eyes. When he snapped his watch shut and turned on the abashed clergyman with a triumphant leer, a roar burst from the audience. *"Duce! Duce! Duce!"* they cried. "Leader! Leader! Leader!" It was but the isolated cry of a few hundred poor workingmen, but it was prophetic of the waves of thunder that would one day go washing across that famous balcony on the Palazzo Venezia.

For all his popularity among a crowd of illiterate bricklayers, Benito Mussolini still cut a sorry figure in Lausanne. He could obtain only menial work— butcher's boy, fortune teller, delivery boy, sculptor's assistant—spending his nights studying French and German with his feet stuck in a box of sawdust to keep them warm. The Swiss police watched him carefully, twice jailing him and escorting him from the country, only to find him returned through a different canton.

Mussolini had few male friends at this time; in fact, he seldom did. His companions were among the Russian and Polish émigré women who tried to satisfy his lust. More perceptive than the men, perhaps because they were more intimate, some of them came to realize with misgivings that Mussolini's hatred of injustice sprang not from a love of the oppressed but from his deep sense of inferiority.

In July of 1903, after two more arrests as an agitator, he was finally expelled from Switzerland. The Italian police who received him immediately opened a dossier on "this impulsive and violent" young man, and set a watch on him. They soon lost him, however, for Mussolini, aware that men of his age were still due for military service in January 1904, escaped again to Switzerland. He did not dodge the draft out of cowardice (he would later prove his bravery), but because he refused to fight for a regime he detested, a truly conscientious objection for which in later years as dictator he would have people shot.

Early in 1904 he spent several months in France, by his own account walking all the way to Paris, where he was arrested yet again. For a time, he visited in Germany and Austria, but was ultimately back in Switzerland, speaking and writing in the same atheistic, anticlerical, antisocial vein. It was not long before he had been publicly denounced as an enemy of society, and in Italy he was tried in absentia and found guilty of desertion.

But Italy declared an amnesty for deserters, and at the age of twenty-one he returned home, resigned to a tour of military service. In January 1905, he joined the 10th Bersaglieri, a regiment of elite troops famous for moving everywhere in double time, their rifles held at high port, the green plumes in their round cocked hats waving, and even their bandsmen tootling away ahead of them on the run.

While Mussolini was in Verona Barracks in February of that year, his mother died of meningitis at the age of forty-six. Weeping, professing great grief for the passing of a woman whose heart he had pierced like a thorn, Mussolini applied for an early release from service. He was refused, and forced to serve the entire eighteen months. He did so with discretion, preaching sedition to his fellow soldiers with great circumspection, and actually staying clear of the guardhouse until his discharge.

His old passion for fame and power returned, but he was frustrated once again to find himself an impecunious ($2.50 a week) second-grade teacher in the mountain town of Tolmezzo, near the Austrian border. Here, his old bad habits —wine, women and cards—resurfaced, joined by a macabre penchant for ghost games in the ruins of the local castles or parties in the cemetery enlivened by his speeches to the dead. At Tolmezzo, his latest mistress, a woman older than he, gave him venereal disease, and he proved a miserable teacher only able to control his pupils by bribing them with candy. For this, together with his preaching to priests to burn their soutanes and put on worker's clothes, the parents of his students kept them home. When his contract expired, it was not renewed.

Undaunted, Mussolini rejoined his father, who had been forced to move from the apartment in Predappio to make way for the new schoolmistress and had found a new home near the village. Here for a few months he studied French and Latin, and in November 1907 passed an examination in French enabling him to teach in secondary schools and granting him the coveted title of "Professor." He tried for the same qualification in German, but failed. Eventually he was back editing a Socialist newspaper, *La Lima* (The Rasp), in Oneglia on the Italian Riviera, where he had obtained still another teaching post. This was perhaps the calmest period of Mussolini's life, and yet, four months after he began in Oneglia, he was again unemployed. For the third straight time, his contract was not renewed.

Benito Mussolini rejoined his father, who was operating a wine shop in Forlì. Alessandro was by then nearly paralyzed. He had sold his forge, taken a common-law wife named Anna Guidi, and opened the *taverna*. Benito helped his father, and so did Anna's daughter, the pretty, blond, nineteen-year-old Rachele.

Rachele adored Benito. She did not, like many others in Forlì, mock him for his bohemian appearance. Nevertheless, although she did not resist his advances, she did not submit to him; and Mussolini, preparing to take an editor's job in the Austrian town of Trento, promised to marry her upon his return. Rachele laughed in gentle derision. She knew that Socialists who married in the Church were expelled from the party.

In February 1909, Mussolini set to work editing *L'Avvenire* (The Future) with typical bombast and indifference to the laws of libel. Eleven times his paper was confiscated and six times he went to jail. Seven months later, he was expelled for attempting to "incite violence against the authorities."

Back to Forlì he trudged, seeking Rachele. He found her outside of town in the home of her sister. "I want Rachele to be the mother of my children," he told the aghast sister. "But tell her to hurry, I'm pushed for time." Rachele came clattering eagerly down the stairs, clutching a piggy-bank, which Benito broke into with glee. Bundling her clothes in a shawl, not even bothering to comb her hair, Rachele seized Benito's arm and followed him outside into the pouring rain.

The unmarried couple moved into a broken-down apartment in Forlì. Mussolini, now twenty-six, threw himself into his most ambitious project: reorganizing the federation of Socialist clubs in Forlì electoral district and editing a Socialist weekly, *La Lotta di Classe* (The Class Struggle). Although the offices of *La Lotta di Classe* were in his bedroom and the paper itself rarely sold 500 copies, Mussolini was overjoyed. *He* was the newspaper: editor, reporter, copy reader and circulation manager. He could say what he pleased. Thus, the opportunity for revilement of Church and State was unrivaled. Mussolini's obscene jests about the consecrated Host appalled even some Socialists. But if the Church had no power to restrain him, the army did; when he broke the law by advising soldiers of "this criminal organization" to disobey their officers, he was put in jail briefly. Yet his happiness probably would have been complete, had he not been so poor. Although his salary of $25.00 a month was more than twice as much as he had ever earned, he was always broke. When his first child, Edda, was born in September 1910, Mussolini had just enough money to buy a cheap wooden cradle and carry it home to their tiny bedroom.

It was at this time that he swore off strong drink. Coming home late one morning wild-eyed drunk on cognac, he smashed every piece of crockery in the apartment. When he awoke, Rachele screamed: "If you ever come home like that again, I'll kill you!" Laying his hand on his little daughter's head, he swore off spirits forever. And he kept his word.

And why not? Life had become too fast, too fascinating to be wasted in tippling. Benito Mussolini's name was now a household word on the Romagna. He was somebody going somewhere, even being hailed as an original thinker, which, in truth, he was not. Avid reader though he was, much of it was superficial. "Nine pages of a book is enough to understand it," he would say. "The first three, the last three, and the three in the middle."

What Mussolini really sought in his reading was ideas that would be adaptable to his own attitudes. Like Lenin inventing the myth of the Russian proletariat, when in fact none existed, in order to invoke Marx as the patron saint of Bolshevism, Mussolini turned to advocates of violence such as Georges Sorel and Friedrich Nietzsche. His opportunity to put his faith into action came in 1911, when Italy launched its colonial war on Turkey.

"Before conquering Turkey, let Italians conquer Italy!" he thundered. "Bring water to parched Puglia, justice to the South and education everywhere. On to the streets for the General Strike!"

The strike, however, was brief and much less bloody than Mussolini had desired. Though he led his followers in tearing up trolley and railroad lines in order to disrupt the movement of troops, though many shops in Forlì were boarded up and the factories idled, a single charge by a troop of cavalry wielding naked sabers brought the "general strike" to a close with only a few minor casualties. Mussolini, to his huge delight, was taken captive and placed on trial for "instigation to delinquency." With typical showmanship, he turned the courtroom into a stage. "If you acquit me," he told his judges, "you will give me pleasure; if you condemn me, you will do me honor."

They honored him with a year in Forlì jail, a sentence later reduced to five months. He came out a hero, and nine months later, hailed as the Duce of Italian Socialists, he was elected to the party's National Executive Committee and given the editorship of its foremost daily, the Milan-based *Avanti!* (Forward!).

Now he had a real audience, and his belligerent, boasting, abusive style of journalism succeeded in raising *Avanti!*'s circulation from 28,000 to 100,000, while recruiting thousands of new members for a Socialist Party barely numbering a million followers. With Rachele and Edda left behind in Forlì (probably on purpose), Milan gave Mussolini the freedom to indulge his sexual appetite. One of his mistresses, Ida Dalser, presented him with the only illegitimate child he ever acknowledged. But in 1915 he abandoned both mother and child, condemning them to a miserable existence from which, in 1937, he "rescued" the mother by confining her to a mental hospital. Another woman was red-haired Margherita Sarfatti, a wealthy Milanese who was *Avanti!*'s art critic. She was also quite unbeautiful, a trait shared by all of Mussolini's women with the exception of Donna Rachele and, much, much later, the famous Clara Petacci. Margherita survived into the Fascist era, even becoming Mussolini's official biographer, until she finally fell victim to his anti-Jewish legislation. By the fall of 1914, however, Mussolini had little time to spare for amorous adventure, being engaged in defending himself against the bitter attacks of his Socialist comrades, who accused him of betraying the party.

War clouds had by then gathered over Europe, but on July 29, five days before World War I erupted, Mussolini had with other members of the Socialist Executive Committee signed an antiwar manifesto condemning this coming "capitalist conflict" and demanding that Italy remain neutral. Inexplicably, about two months later, he had sent *Avanti!* to press with a leading article committing socialism to Italy's entry into the war on the Allied side. His associates were stunned, dumbfounded; but then on November 15, 1914, they were choking with rage when a new newspaper, *Il Popolo d'Italia* (The People of Italy), appeared on the streets with the name of Benito Mussolini on its masthead. "He who has steel has bread!" the former famous pacifist cried. "A revolution is an idea which has found bayonets!" Within an hour this fiery first edition was sold out, and within nine days Benito Mussolini was on trial for his Socialist life.

It took place in Milan's famous Teatro del Popolo. The theater was packed with infuriated Socialists. Mussolini appeared and they raised a thunderous chant: "*Chi paga?* Who's paying?" He strode down the aisle to a tumult of catcalls and hisses. To either side of him was a waving forest of brandished fists. He ducked his head to avoid the blows aimed at him. Again, the great cry arose, "*Chi paga?*", seeming to shake the glittering crystal prisms hanging from the great chandelier overhead. Mussolini ascended the stage, to be struck by a shower of small coins. "Judas, there's your blood money!" a woman screamed. Others shouted, "Traitor!" "Sellout!"

Mussolini's efforts to speak were drowned in an explosion of whistles, boos and obscenities. He sidestepped a flying chair, brushed aside more coins. "If you proclaim that I am unworthy," he began, his voice barely audible above that storm of sound, and with one voice his accusers thundered: "YES!"

Enraged, Benito Mussolini seized a glass. Holding it aloft, he crushed it in his hand until the blood ran down his sleeve. It was a gesture that in the old days might have quelled the angriest of crowds, but this massive jury of his peers merely laughed in derision. Mussolini gave up. Pale and trembling, he descended from the stage and strode grimly up the aisle. "You have not heard the last of me," he shouted.

Indeed, they had not. In the ensuing weeks, *Il Popolo d'Italia* thundered louder and louder for war. Why? Why had Mussolini turned his coat? For money? Probably not. More likely he probably could not bear to sit passively on the sidelines while there was a war going on. A massive struggle such as World War I offered more scope for his peculiar talents. Even if he did accept money from the big landowners to found his own paper, it was not for wealth itself—to which he would always remain indifferent—but for the power, prestige and privilege that his own newspaper would give him. More money was forthcoming from France and probably Britain, both anxious to bring Italy into the war on the Allied side. So the strident voice of *Il Popolo d'Italia* calling for intervention became more shrill and insistent. Soon he had a national audience, millions hailing him as their Duce, taking to the streets to shout for war, battling with those who still screamed for peace. Frequently, Mussolini was himself a victim of the *pacifisti,* staggering home to Rachele—who was now in Milan—with his hat stove in and his clothing torn. On April 12, he led a prowar demonstration in Rome, and was arrested and jailed. He was out in eight hours, never again to hear prison doors swing shut behind him. On May 24, 1915, he achieved his heart's desire: Italy, promised rich plunder in the secret Treaty of London, declared war on Austria. Four months later, Benito Mussolini was back in the gray-green uniform of the Bersaglieri.

Again, why? Why was Italy's most famous interventionist editor, the adored Duce, going off to war with a private's rifle on his shoulders? Surely, he could have had his pick of commissions; been given a desk in the office of propaganda; perhaps even made chief of propaganda. But Mussolini wanted none of this. He wanted to *serve*. Combat, coming home a war hero, suited his dreams of destiny. And he did see action, seventeen months of it, high up in the snow-crested Alps. He became a model soldier, actually seeming embarrassed when soldiers, even officers, clambered into his trench to shake the hand of *Il Popolo*'s editor. He suffered as only a common soldier can: scourged by Austrian shellfire banging and spanging off the rocks, mingling whispering rock splinters with the shrapnel whistling around his ears; so cold in zero-degree weather, which froze his boots to the floor of the trenches; so hungry that when the enemy artillery pinned down the food convoys, he, like his comrades, gnawed on his straw-covered wine bottle; soaked in the spring thaw by weeks of rain compelling him to bail out his trench

with his boots—and always in his nostrils the stench of the dead and on his flesh
the filthy lice. Still, he accepted it all without complaint, bent over his notepaper
almost nightly beneath the faint flickering light of a sardine-oil lamp to scribble
the war diary published weekly in *Il Popolo.* Eventually, inevitably, he became
Italy's best-known private soldier. When he was made corporal, it was a time for
celebration among his millions of followers; even his marriage to Rachele in a civil
ceremony—an odd gesture from this excommunicated Socialist—was an event to
be remembered. So, above all, was that dreadful day in February 1917 when, on
the front line high in the Carso, that icy limestone ridge north of the Adriatic,
Benito Mussolini was given up for dead.

He had been one of twenty men test-firing a howitzer. Surprisingly, none of
these veteran soldiers was alarmed by the gun barrel glowing redder and redder.
At last it burst with a horrible roar, instantly killing four men and hurling
Mussolini about fifteen feet. At the hospital, the surgeons counted forty-four
shrapnel wounds in his body, some as big as a man's fist. Within a single month,
Mussolini endured twenty-seven operations, some without anesthesia. His
wounds were packed with searing alcohol swabs to prevent gangrene. "I wanted
to howl like a crazy wolf," he said after his recovery.

Back at *Il Popolo,* Mussolini made himself the common soldier's prophet.
With the full fury of his passionate energy, he hurled himself upon the Socialist
opposition clamoring for an end to the war, raising its red flag inscribed with the
party slogan, "Not another winter in the trenches." Now as devoutly prowar as
he had been belligerently pacifist, Mussolini countered with the cry: "Stand to the
finish!" He wrote hundreds of letters to his old comrades in the trenches, signing
himself: "Your old Bersagliere, almost sawed in half."

Consciously or unconsciously, Mussolini was appealing to those millions of
disenchanted, disillusioned soldiers who returned home after the war to find
themselves mocked and spat upon like so many traitors. Woodrow Wilson's
refusal to honor the secret Treaty of London, his refusal even to allow Premier
Orlando to attend his meetings with Clemenceau and Lloyd George, had dashed
Italy's dreams of building its own imperium on the ruins of the fallen Austrian
and Turkish empires. A howl of rage convulsed the peninsula. Six hundred
thousand Italians had died and almost 1.5 million had been wounded—to say
nothing of a war debt of 12 billion lire—for Trento and Trieste? With perfect
illogic, the stay-at-homes—especially the millions of service-deferred workers—
turned against those who had fought this detestable war. War cripples had their
crutches kicked from under them, other soldiers were set upon by gangs of
civilians who beat them and tore their medals from their breasts.

Now it was the Socialists who had opposed the war whose star was rising.
From excoriating soldiers, they turned to vilifying the Church and the monarchy.
Churches were burst into and altars draped with the red flag of Communism. The
portrait of little King Victor Emmanuel was replaced with a photograph of Lenin.
Growing bolder, the Socialists—now numbering 1.2 million card-carrying mem-
bers and millions more who supported them—compelled Premier Francesco Nitti

to grant amnesty to 150,000 deserters. Now it was the war veterans who gave a low growl of outrage.

Benito Mussolini at once sensed their bitterness. On March 23, 1919, a rainy Sunday, he met with a handful of followers in a shabby little hall on Milan's Piazza San Sepolcro to form the Fascist Party. The name was taken from the Roman *fasces,* a bundle of elm rods grouped around an ax with the blade projecting which was carried before a magistrate to symbolize his power over life and death. Although Mussolini boasted in *Il Popolo* that 120 people had been present at the meeting, there were actually only fifty-four. One of *Il Popolo*'s reporters in the next room covering a trade meeting had added the names of seventy Lombardy milk wholesalers. Mussolini declared: "We will defend our dead even if we dig trenches in the squares and streets."

His words ignited a train of powder that went flashing across the boot of Italy. Fascist Party chapters were organized everywhere. A Fascist uniform was adopted, based chiefly on that of the *Arditi,* the Italian army elite sworn to kill or die to defend Italy. A tight-fitting black shirt was worn above gray-green breeches and puttees, with a black fezlike cap with a black tassel. Adopted also was the battle cry *"A noi!"*—"To us!"—and the meaningless battle chant, *"Eja, eja, alala!"* said to be the war cry of Aeneas and his Trojans.

Gibbering nonsense that this might seem to be, it was very effective. The year 1920 arrived and found Italy a land divided and teetering on the brink of civil war. The Socialists and Communists, it appeared, had by far the upper hand. Workers of every description rallied to the red flag. Strike after strike was called. Prison warders forced a raise out of the government by threatening to turn loose every criminal in their charge if it were denied. Postal workers poured sulfuric acid into the letter boxes, and each night in Rome disgruntled electricians caused a blackout, which produced bedlam everywhere, especially in the hospitals. Railroad men made a travesty of the timetables, gleefully slamming on the brakes if an army officer or a priest boarded the train, competing with each other to see who could delay his train the longest. The undoubted victor in this antigovernment contest was a train from Turin arriving in Rome 400 hours or nearly seventeen days late. Finally, 600,000 metalworkers staged a coup by seizing hundreds of factories from Milan to Naples, holding them idle for a month.

Unfortunately, no one but the Fascists seemed able or eager to defeat this deliberate campaign to detonate the social structure of Italy in order to make straight the way of the Soviet state. Thus, to the Fascist skull-and-crossbones banners were drawn the best and the worst of Italian society. Priests, poets and philosophers joined pimps, pornographers and toughs in violent attacks upon the Socialist enemy. Every Fascist, it seemed, had a gun or a knife; few were without the familiar *manganello,* the nineteen-inch bludgeon with which they beat their victims, or the bottles of castor oil with which they dosed them half a pint at a time. Universal now was the motto, *"Me ne frego!"* ("I don't give a damn!"), which a wounded Fascist had scrawled on his bandages, while from the lips of massed marchers burst the thunderous wartime song of the shock troops,

Giovinezza, or *Youth.* Night after night in city after city Fascist "action squads" carried the battle to the Socialists, and because their dedication to Mussolini-style violence was absolute, they almost always won. In desperation, the Socialists appealed to the police for protection, only to find the pistols of the law pointed at their own heads. In Trieste, for instance, when Fascists stormed the offices of a Socialist newspaper, an appeal for police help brought truckloads of officers rushing to the scene—to arrest the Socialists.

Mussolini was winning support everywhere. General Armando Diaz, army commander in chief, ordered copies of *Il Popolo* to be distributed free to every soldier in his command. Bankers and bishops, industrialists and even the Masons casting aside their customary secrecy openly hailed *Il Duce* as the savior of Italy in the face of the Bolshevik menace. More important, they poured gold into Mussolini's coffers so that by the fall of 1921, he had a war chest of 24 million lire and was ready to make his move for power.

Mussolini's plan was to march on Rome, to force the king to dismiss the government of Premier Luigi Facta and to replace it with himself and his Fascists. Even though *Il Duce* had by then raised his own Fascist militia, he had no desire to provoke a civil war that would pit this illegal, ill-trained force against the regular army. He intended to bluff, not bleed. As dress rehearsal, he ordered attacks on a number of cities. The first on September 21 was Ravenna, seized by 3,000 men under Italo Balbo. Next, on May 12, 1922, came Ferrara, overwhelmed at every critical point by 63,000 Fascists while Balbo held the prefect at gunpoint. Finally, Bologna fell to 20,000 men who held it for five days. Mussolini now knew —and so did the king, Premier Facta, and the Socialists—that a city could be seized and held.

In response, the Socialists called a general strike for August 1922. When Facta's government made no attempt to break the strike, despite a warning from Mussolini, the Fascist blackshirts moved in to keep the railways running and to burn at least a hundred Socialist headquarters down to the ground. Now, with the strike broken and the stunned Socialists thoroughly cowed, was the time to make the great gamble. On October 24, at the Fascist Congress in Naples, the magic word went out: Rome.

It thrilled and sent springing into action 40,000 blackshirts from the foggy cold Dolomites on the Austrian border to sunny Sicily 1,000 miles to the south. On foot, on plow horses, on bicycles, by captured train, in donkey carts and rickety trucks and horse-drawn carriages, they began converging on the Eternal City. They were a ragtag, bobtail army indeed, runaway farm boys and veterans from as long ago as the Battle of Adowa (1896) mingling with those who were truly the lame, the halt and the blind, as well as the working and professional classes from a hundred different cities; miserable in the rains that fell that momentous October 27, suffering hunger and a dozen other different hardships from the deficiencies of an amateurish logistics and command system organized by such "generals" as twenty-six-year-old Italo Balbo, red-bearded and lisping and known affectionately as Iron Beard by his adoring followers. Some of them carried modern firearms, but most were armed with hunting rifles or farm implements, clubs and knives and rusty old swords, and whatever obsolete muskets or artillery that could be plundered from museums and ancient arsenals broken into along the line of march.

Although King Victor Emmanuel was not exactly an admirer of the Fascists, he did dislike them much less than the Socialists, who never ceased to mock him either openly in Parliament or with satires and caricature in their newspapers. Actually, the little king disliked almost everyone and everything except his statuesque Queen Elena, his priceless coin collection and the throne he had inherited as the last decrepit scion of the ancient and faineant House of Savoy. Twisted in outlook since youth by his diminutive stature—even his practice of wearing iron weights to bed had failed to stretch him to more than five feet in height—he was a dedicated misanthrope and miser, unashamed to review his troops in patched and faded uniforms if it would save a few more lire for the enormous fortune he had stashed safely away in a London bank. But though the blackshirts marching jubilantly on Rome were confident of his indulgence, Victor Emmanuel was not so sure of them. His qualms were not assuaged when he asked General Diaz, "What will the army do?" and was told: "Your Majesty, the army will do its duty —but it would be better not to put them to the test." Nor did he like it when Premier Facta came to tell him he wanted to fight the Fascists, that Mussolini was bluffing. Trembling, the king said petulantly: "I won't form a government while there's violence in Italy—I can't and I won't." Next Facta suggested declaring a state of siege. The king shook his head. "The only thing resulting from a state of siege is civil war. What is called for here is that one of us must sacrifice himself." To the amazement of Victor Emmanuel, the normally humorless Facta bowed and replied with splendid irony: "It is not necessary, Your Majesty, to indicate which one of us that will be."

So Facta resigned, and eventually, on October 29, as city after city fell to the blackshirts, while their numbers were augmented hourly by swarms of recruits climbing aboard their hijacked trains and swaying trucks, joining in the endless choruses of *Giovinezza* and chanting *"Viva Mussolini! Viva Mussolini!"*, the frightened little king sat down in the Quirinale and dictated the telegram that went to the Duce, sitting sweating in *Il Popolo*'s offices in Milan: "HM the King begs you to proceed to Rome as soon as possible as he wishes to entrust you with the task of forming a Cabinet."

That night, as a cold rain swept through the central railway station in Milan, thousands of shouting Fascists bent their bodies into the wind to watch as a short man in a gray raincoat, his own great head lowered against the downpour, strode into a waiting train to take his place by a window, blowing kisses as he chugged out of sight, headed for Rome and the beginning of the Fascist Era.

Benito Mussolini did not immediately enshackle the Italian nation in Fascist chains. He had not desired absolute power, and he was very much aware that although his cabinet was full of Fascists, he must deal with a constitutional monarch and a legally elected Parliament. King Victor Emmanuel, of course, had not filled many of his premiers with fear; they had frequently ignored or "forgotten" the constitutional requirement to consult with him before acting in an emergency. Surprisingly, Premier Mussolini was far more deferential, probably because he needed the king as an ally or at least a neutral observer in his drive against the Italian left. He was not as courteous to those leftists in Parliament but rather curt and even contemptuous. Appearing before the Chamber of Deputies on November 16, he declared in a cold voice: "I could have turned this drab gray hall into a bivouac for my blackshirts, and made an end of Parliament." Gazing nervously around them at the blackshirts ostentatiously cleaning their fingernails with their daggers, the Socialists shifted uneasily on their benches. "It was in my power to do so," *Il Duce* went on, "but it was not my wish." He paused dramatically, and added: "At least not yet." Another pause. "The Chamber must understand that I can dissolve it—in two days or two years. I claim full powers." Not surprisingly, they were given to him.

He did not use these powers immediately, hurling himself instead into a one-man campaign to reform the government and industry of Italy. Early each morning he made the rounds of the government offices, dropping his card like an ominous threat onto the desks of absent bureaucrats. Eventually, he fired 35,000 civil servants. He also merged the blue-shirted Nationalists with his Fascists and abolished the King's Guard, which he replaced with his own militia sworn in allegiance to himself, not the king. His most famous feat, of course, was to make the laggard Italian trains run on time, while he came close to solving unemployment by the simple course of putting the able-bodied jobless into the army.

But the showdown with the Socialists and their dwindling Communist allies could not be avoided. It came in 1924, after the Fascists claimed 64 percent of the popular vote and an overwhelming majority in the chamber. The result, however, was challenged by the Socialist deputy, Giacomo Matteotti. In a biting, detailed, documented indictment delivered in the chamber among howling, hissing Fascists, he demonstrated that the elections had been rigged. Mussolini arose and strode from the chamber in a white-faced fury. Outside, he cannoned into Giovanni Marinelli, administrative secretary of the Fascist Party. "If you weren't a bunch of cowards," *Il Duce* shouted, "no man would have delivered a speech like that!" Marinelli interpreted Mussolini's remark to mean that he wanted Matteotti eliminated. To kill him, of course, would be too dangerous. Instead, Marinelli decided to discredit him. He knew that the deputy had evidence that he was accepting bribes from an American oil company. To silence him, Marinelli decided to kidnap Matteotti and torture him into admitting that he had masterminded the systematic assassination of Fascist officials. But the three Fascist thugs he hired for this purpose bungled the job and killed Matteotti.

If Marinelli was appalled, Mussolini was incredulous and aghast. He sensed immediately that once the deputy's body was found—and it was soon uncovered in a shallow grave outside the city—it would be instantly concluded that he was Matteotti's murderer. It was. Accusation, invective and vituperation howled around *Il Duce*'s head. A typical incident occurred at a banquet in Mussolini's honor. As he unfolded his napkin, a note fluttered onto his plate, reading: "You are Matteotti's murderer—prepare for the handcuffs." Glancing nervously at the king beside him, he saw that Victor Emmanuel was reading a similar note, which he silently handed him. It said: "Your Majesty, Matteotti's murderer sits next to you—give him up to justice."

In a frenzy to be rid of the rope tightening around his own neck, Mussolini ordered a thorough investigation. A wave of arrests among ranking Fascist officials was followed by a stunning series of resignations. Now his own followers joined the Socialists in demanding his head. Only the king and his managing mother, Queen Margherita, remained loyal to him. Mussolini was given the coveted Collar of the Annunciation, a glittering and superbly beautiful decoration of gold-linked jewels which the House of Savoy had awarded only twenty times in six centuries. With it came the right to call the king "cousin." And Cousin Victor stood staunchly by *Il Duce*'s side throughout the Socialist storm.

But fiercer winds were to blow, this time from his fellow Fascists. On New Year's Eve of 1924, thirty-three militia chiefs burst into Mussolini's huge office, gathering menacingly around him and the terrified ministers with whom he had been conferring. Even Mussolini was shaken, glancing up uneasily at their leader, Aldo Tarabella, a tiny, snarling terrier of a man weighing less than ninety pounds. In Tarabella's hard blue northern eyes he could read the unspoken message: a Fascist dictatorship.

"The prisons are full of Fascists," Tarabella cried. "They're putting fascism on trial, and you don't want to take responsibility for the revolution."

Il Duce's eyes flashed. "The body they threw between my feet prevents me from walking."

Tarabella's lips curled. "What kind of a revolutionary chief are you, to be frightened by a corpse? You must make up your mind to shoot the chiefs of the opposition!"

Mussolini's square jaw worked and his cheeks blanched. "I do not want to be imposed upon," he said. "I will *not* be imposed upon."

Jeering openly, the militia chiefs stomped from the room through the open door, which Tarabella, with deliberate contempt, slammed in *Il Duce*'s face. Slightly more than a year later, Benito Mussolini signed the decree abolishing all political opposition. Matteotti's murderers were tried, convicted and sentenced to a token six years in prison, from which, two months later, an amnesty freed them to emerge as Fascist heroes. Decree followed decree, the most important among them the annulling of all passports to prevent the flight of "wanted" members of the opposition and the closing of the civil service to all but Fascists.

Italy was now a totalitarian state.

Although Benito Mussolini had become the Western world's first dictator since a Roman mob murdered Cola di Rienzo in the fourteenth century, he was not immediately pilloried or vilified by the press or chanceries of Europe. Probably this was because of the perception that he had indeed done much good in Italy, and seemed to be continuing to do so. His achievements were astonishing, especially in communications, where he built 400 new bridges, 4,000 miles of new roads and 600 telephone exchanges, sent mighty ocean liners steaming across the Atlantic in record-breaking time, and launched the celebrated Rome-Chicago flight of twenty-five airplanes under the command of Marshal Italo Balbo. He waged successful war against Sicily's entrenched Mafia, putting 400 top mafiosi in prison and reducing Palermo Province's annual murder rate from 278 to twenty-five. Most spectacular of all, he drained the Pontine Marshes, turning this huge malarial swamp into a productive home for 3,000 well-stocked farms serving three new towns. To this and more was added the stunning diplomatic triumph by which anticlerical Benito Mussolini, son and grandson of anticlerics, priest-baiter, antichrist, satyr insatiate, and sacrilegious profaner of the sacraments, concluded the famous Lateran Treaty with the Vatican. Under it, the Fascist government agreed to pay the papacy $50 million in cash and government bonds as an indemnity for the lost papal states. Existence of an independent Vatican state with the pope as its ruler was confirmed, and Roman Catholicism became Italy's official religion. In return, the Vatican recognized the Kingdom of Italy with Rome as its capital and agreed to remain outside all temporal dispute within it. The Lateran Treaty was indeed a masterpiece of diplomacy, and its author was hailed extravagantly throughout Catholic Italy and somewhat more calmly elsewhere in the world.

But by then Benito Mussolini was accustomed to the accolade. Great man after great man had made the pilgrimage to the Palazzo Chigi to grasp the hand of this wonder-worker with the charming smile and mellifluous voice. Even so prodigious a revolutionary as Mohandas Gandhi saw him and lamented: "Unfortunately, I am no superman like Mussolini." The American financial wizard Otto Kahn declared, "The world owes him a debt of gratitude." Winston Churchill came to Rome to shake his hand and congratulate him on crushing the Communist menace. "He is the one giant figure in Europe," cried the Archbishop of Canterbury, and Thomas Edison found him "the greatest genius of the modern age."

Many others unable to make the pilgrimage wrote to him in adulation, often imploring him to send them an autographed photograph of himself. From Germany came a gushing encomium from the thirty-seven-year-old leader of a not very large or well-known political group called the National Socialists. He too wanted such a memento of Mussolini's esteem. But *Il Duce* took the letter and wrote across it in the bold and flourishing hand with which he signed his decrees: "Request refused."

The rejected suppliant was Adolf Hitler.

4. Adolf Hitler

ADOLF HITLER, the malevolent genius who became the second dictator to rise among postwar Europe's despairing, disillusioned masses, was of only slightly less humble origins than Benito Mussolini. Hitler's father was born Alois Schicklgruber, the illegitimate son of an Austrian woman named Maria Anna Schicklgruber and an unknown father. Later a man named Johann Nepomuk Huttler, who had taken young Alois into his home, died and left him a small sum if he would change his name to Huttler. So Alois Schicklgruber became Alois Hitler (one of many variations of the name in northern Austria). He had been apprenticed as a cobbler, but at the age of seventeen he left his native village of Strones bound for Vienna and "something better" in life. He found it at the age of seventeen as a very junior customs official in the Austrian Ministry of Finance.

Although Alois Hitler's lack of education limited his future, he could at least rise to the rank of inspector. Because he was by then an imposing physical presence—broad-shouldered, bullet-headed, ramrod straight in his resplendent customs uniform, his thick mustaches curled in the style of Emperor Franz Josef —he could also expect a certain amount of status as well as a pleasant life in the company of the drinking companions and willing chambermaids whom he met in the inns where he lived during his slow ascent up the bureaucratic ladder. Alois had a succession of wives, or mistresses becoming wives, one bastard son also named Alois, and a legitimate daughter named Angela. His last wife was Klara Polzl, the pretty granddaughter of Johann Nepomuk Huttler. She gave him six more children. Of these, her obvious favorite was the boy Adolf.

Adolf Hitler was born at Branau-am-Inn at six o'clock in the evening of April 20, 1889. Two days later he was baptized in the Catholic church. Sickly at first, Adolf gradually shook off his infirmities and became a healthy baby. Perhaps it was because he survived, as her first three children had not, that Klara indulged him in every whim and desire, making of him a *Muttersöhnchen,* a spoiled, noisy, mischievous Mama's boy. Adolf returned this affection by adoring his mother. Conversely, he came to hate his stern, authoritarian father, staying out of his way as much as possible and dreading to hear that shrill summoning whistle. Three years after Adolf's birth, Alois received his first major promotion, to the position of Higher Customs Officer at Passau across the German border. Here, too, on March 23, 1893, Klara gave birth to a fifth child, a boy named Edmund.

A week later, Alois was transferred again, this time to a higher post in Linz. Because the presence of the new baby made it impossible to take up new lodgings, the father moved on to Linz, leaving Klara with the family in Passau. It was during this period that Adolf became extremely fond of his little brother, and fonder still of his mother, in whose indulgent love he might now bask with no interference from his father. However, like all paradises, the Passau period came to an end—the family was shocked to learn that Alois had resigned from the customs service and had bought a farm in the village of Hafeld, about thirty miles southwest of Linz.

Like a true peasant, Alois had responded to the call of the land; yet, no matter how industriously he worked among his orchards and bees, the farm did not pay, simply because it was unproductive land. In the meantime, Adolf, at six years old, went to school with his twelve-year-old sister, Angela, in the nearby village of Fischlham. A teacher named Mittermaier remembered Adolf as a lively and bright youngster who stood at the head of his class, and both children as neat and orderly, obviously the product of a disciplined home. Adolf still fitted that description after Alois sold the farm and moved the family to Lambach, halfway between Linz and Salzburg.

Lambach was a medieval town, boasting a great Benedictine monastery founded in the eleventh century, as well as many other beautiful churches. Adolf was enrolled in the monks' school, once again doing well and immediately falling under the Church's spell. Ritual fascinated him, especially the sound of the black-robed monks singing Latin hymns or of the massed male voices chanting plainsong, and it was from this that his lifelong love of opera probably derived. He was also enchanted by the elegance and color of the service of the altar, of the shiny silk or satin vestments or the glittering gold of the chalices and spiky monstrances, watching with drawn breath while the solemn movements of the Mass were carried out amid the splendor of Byzantine architecture. Here again was born another love—of architecture—and it may be speculated that all of this contributed to Adolf Hitler's near mystical understanding of how the masses may be moved: by massed singing, by music, by the substitution of military splendor and might for ecclesiastical awe and mystery, and above all, by the power of reiteration, as he was to learn from those daily recitals of the litanies. So impressed, the young Adolf Hitler thought often and long of becoming a monk and perhaps rising to the power and authority of an abbot, who ruled his community like a king. At this monastery also, young Adolf Hitler discovered the swastika that was to become the symbol of the Nazi Party he was to forge. It was included in the coat of arms of Abbot Theodorich von Hagen, who presided at the monastery in the middle of the nineteenth century. In German a swastika is a *Hakenkreuz* (crooked cross), and apparently the abbot's family regarded the word *Haken* as a pun on their own name, Hagen. Actually, this gentle little joke was only a small part of the abbot's escutcheon, but the boyish Adolf Hitler who saw and remembered it would turn it into his own crooked cross, the black spider's legs of which would sprawl across half the civilized globe.

Although life at Lambach was serene and pleasant, Alois Hitler again bought more land, this time in the little village of Leonding outside Linz. While Alois set up his beehives once more, Adolf with the other children went to the local

Volksschule, where he again did well. A year later, Edmund, who was now six, died of measles.

The death of his brother snapped something inside the soul of the ten-year-old Adolf Hitler. From a happy, good-natured, cocky, fun-loving boy to whom studies came easy, he was transformed into a morose, moody, brooding, nervous child to whom, now shorn of his self-assurance, study had become a bore and detestation. Driven even deeper into his soul now was the dichotomy dividing it between love and adulation of his mother and hatred and fear of his father. Klara became the epitome of womankind, a reincarnated Virgin Mary to whom henceforth all women would be compared and found wanting; while Alois was the forbidding father figure, living symbol of that repressive authority and power which Adolf Hitler now detested and against which he would forever rebel, until, of course, he came to possess it himself.

Between these two extremes lay the self into which the anguished youth inevitably retreated. Bereft of his brother, rejected by those teachers whom he had alienated; misunderstood, as he thought, by an unsympathetic father, he took solace from himself alone. Rejecting his books, he turned to drawing under what was to be a lifelong delusion that he had talent. After two poor years—1900 and 1901—at the *Realschule* in Linz, the equivalent of a modern four-year high school, he told his father that he would give up his studies to become an artist. Alois was appalled. His oldest son, Alois, had become a ne'er-do-well and all the others except Angela and the mouselike Paula, the youngest, were dead. The family fortunes depended on the seemingly gifted Adolf, and here he was at the age of twelve a failure in school who was telling his father that he would study no more but take up painting instead.

"Artist, no!" Alois thundered, according to Hitler's account in *Mein Kampf.* "Never as long as I live!"

To his father's "Never!" Hitler writes, he responded with his own "Nevertheless!" This, of course, is an exaggeration. The "old man's" word was still law in the patriarchal Austrian manner. Adolf remained in school.

But he did so only reluctantly, retreating deeper into himself, into fantasy, and then, after he had discovered in his father's tiny library magazines describing and picturing the Franco-Prussian War of 1870, into a delightfully stirring world of battles and bugle calls. Here were *men!* Here were not those insipid, bloodless asses who sat at the head of his classroom trying to cram his head with useless knowledge. Here were gods in gleaming helmets astride huge prancing stallions wielding flashing sabers and *doing things* for the Fatherland. "From this time onward," he wrote, "I became more and more excited about everything in any way connected with war, or for that matter with soldiering." When he came upon the works of the popular writer Karl May, adventure stories full of fierce, painted Red Indians galloping across the American plains, his excitement and love of combat, however vicarious, was boundless. One of Adolf Hitler's professors has described him as he was at this time:

I well remember the gaunt, pale-faced boy who shuttled backwards and forwards between Linz and Leonding. He was definitely gifted, but only in a one-sided way, for he was lacking in self-control, and to say the least he was regarded as argumentative, willful, arrogant and bad-tempered, and he was notoriously incapable of submitting to school discipline. Nor was he industrious. If he had been, he would have achieved much better results with his undoubted ability.

He reacted with ill-concealed hostility whenever a teacher reproved him or gave him some advice. At the same time he demanded the unqualified subservience of his fellow-pupils, fancying himself in the role of a leader, and of course playing many small harmless pranks, which is not unusual among immature youngsters. He seemed to be infected with the stories of Karl May and the Redskins.

On January 3, 1901, Alois Hitler died. His death left his shocked son, who was just three months short of his thirteenth birthday, as the nominal head of the family. It was the steadfast Klara, however, who assumed responsibility. Moreover, she was far from destitute. She would receive half her husband's pension until her death and each of the children was entitled to a smaller one. The house in Leonding was substantial and mortgaged only at a quarter of its value. Indeed, with no Alois to take the patriarch's customary lion's share of the family income, there was even enough money to send Adolf to a boys' home at Linz during weekdays. However, if Klara hoped that this indulgence would produce an improvement in Adolf's schoolwork, she was mistaken. Instead of improving, he grew worse.

The change that had come over him after his brother's death had caused Adolf Hitler to fall out of love with the Church. Typically, he now hated the ancient institution whose psychological insights he would eventually make his own. Adolf Hitler could never leave a love and let it live. Psychopathic egotist that he was, he would, if he could, have avenged any affront however slight with murder. Now he must kill the thing he had loved, and he went about it by an unmerciful baiting of those priest-teachers who would allow it.

For the remainder of his three years at the Linz *Realschule,* there was no improvement in Adolf's marks or his manners. At the end of his third year, he was given a passing grade only on the condition that he would not return to the school.

Still, Klara did not despair. She entered Adolf in the *Realschule* at Steyr, a small industrial town twenty-five miles southeast of Linz. He stayed at a boarding house there. Adolf was now fifteen, a typical adolescent, as a drawing of him by a classmate shows. He is scrawny, pasty-faced and flat-chested, certainly no fine physical specimen, and beneath his thick nose is a faint line of mustache. His chin is sharp, as though lifted for the blows his obvious arrogance can provoke, and his forehead recedes. Across it falls the familiar unruly forelock of thick brown hair. In this face there is a shocking expression of calculated insolence.

These twin characteristics—arrogance and insolence—would never leave

Adolf Hitler, and at Steyr, as elsewhere, they succeeded in alienating his teachers to the extent that they made it known to Adolf that he could never hope to advance into an *Oberrealschule*. But they gave him his certificate, or diploma, probably out of pity for his mother. Adolf took the certificate and went out to celebrate the end to classroom drudgery in wine. He got drunk, awakening the next morning lying face down on a country road in a puddle of puke, filthy, penniless and suffering from that splitting headache typical of a youth's first hangover. Worse, his certificate was missing! At first, he thought of telling his mother that it had been blown from his hands on the train, but the mistress of his boarding house persuaded him to return to the *Realschule* to ask for another.

It was a mistake. The director already had the certificate in hand. It had been used for toilet paper and torn twice in two. Obviously, this was Master Hitler's method of showing his disdain for formal education. But the director did not join in the joke. Brandishing the stained and quartered document, he gave Adolf a dressing-down that convulsed his body with waves of humiliation, one that he literally never forgot. And that was the end of Adolf Hitler's school days. Henceforth, at the age of sixteen, he would draw upon himself.

In June of 1905, Klara Hitler sold the house in Leonding and moved her little family—herself, Adolf and Paula, for Angela had married—to an apartment in Linz. Here began Hitler's salad days. He became a dilettante, a dabbler in art, literature and architecture, laying siege to the well-stocked Linz library or sketching the handful of stately buildings still standing to remind the city of its medieval magnificence. Sometimes, as he strolled its streets, he amused himself by redesigning it to his own taste; or else he would cross the bridge over the Danube and climb the little mountain known as the Postlingberg. But above all, Adolf adored the opera; and it was at the opera house where he met August Kubizek, perhaps his only real friend ever. From Kubizek comes a description of how the sound and fury of Hitler's favorite composer, Richard Wagner, could transport him into ecstasy.

When he listened to the music of Wagner, he was transformed. His violence left him, he became quiet, submissive, tractable. His gaze lost its restlessness, and his daily preoccupations were as though they had never been. His own destiny, however heavily it weighed upon him, no longer appeared to have any importance. He no longer felt lonely, an outlaw, a man kicked around by society. He was in a state of intoxicated ecstasy. Willingly he allowed himself to be carried away into a legendary world more real to him than the world he saw around him every day. . . . He was transported into the blessed regions of German antiquity, which was for him the ideal world, the highest goal of all his endeavors.

Hitler's dream of becoming a giant in art and architecture was shattered in October 1907, when the Vienna Academy of Fine Arts found his test drawings "unsatisfactory"—and two months later his mother died of cancer. The one being in the world whom Adolf truly loved without stint or reservation was gone. He walked behind her coffin to the frozen cemetery at Leonding as though he were the corpse. "In all my career," wrote Dr. Eduard Bloch, the Jewish physician who attended Klara, "I have never seen anyone so prostrate with grief as Adolf Hitler."

A few weeks later—in January 1908—owning hardly more than the clothes on his back, carrying a framed photograph of his mother, Adolf Hitler set out for Vienna.

He was at first reasonably happy in Vienna. He was still receiving a small pension from the government, as well as a stipend from his mother's estate, and because he was frugal and had no vices he could make do on bread and milk and a tiny boarding-house room littered with sketches and stinking of kerosene. Above all he possessed that pearl of great price which his fiercely independent spirit craved the most: absolute freedom. He could go to the opera once and sometimes twice a week and his ticket to the Hof Library was like a passport to the accumulated wisdom of the world. He read voraciously: books on mythology (his favorite subject), philosophy, the scores and librettos of operas as well as histories of music and architecture. He did not systematically consume these intellectual feasts but rather gobbled them. Later in life, echoing Mussolini, he would say that one needed to read only one third of a book to understand it: the beginning, middle and end. Nevertheless, because of his incredibly retentive memory, his mind was so crammed with facts on these subjects that he could discourse for hours.

Already, Hitler's burning, bulging blue eyes and his hoarse, rasping voice, together with his knack of repetition—the phrases falling on his hearer's mind like the measured blows of a hammer—had the power to hold people spellbound. Rebuke he could not stand. The slightest contradiction sent him into paroxysms of rage. If he could not bully people into agreeing with him, then he turned charmer, trying to persuade his stubborn listener with honeyed courtesy and smiling deference. Failing that, the demons that dwelt within him would begin to howl once more.

From his friend August Kubizek come many insights into the Hitler of this time. Kubizek describes him as pacifist, anticlerical and antimonarchical, but with as yet no really strong political preference. In his personal habits he was abstemious and neat, never masturbated and detested dirty jokes. He worshipped sexual purity in both men and women, despising homosexuals as well as ladies of easy virtue. Because of his aloofness and proud bearing, he was apparently attractive to women. But he chose none of them, probably because none could compete with Klara Hitler.

Hitler's anti-Semitism first surfaced when he told Kubizek of how he had turned witness against a Handelee, one of those East European Jews who wore long kaftans and lived by begging or selling knickknacks in the street. A policeman had caught this man begging, and when he asked for witnesses, Hitler volunteered to accompany him to the police station. Apparently, his hatred of authority was waived in the interest of a higher hatred of Jews. Although Kubizek was astounded at the time (Hitler had always professed a great admiration for Jewish musicians and composers), he was aghast a few days later when Hitler calmly declared, "I have joined the Anti-Semitic League and I have also put your name down." Kubizek said nothing, not wishing to engage in futile debate with his fiery friend; and soon that mismatched friendship would come to an end. In November 1908, Hitler suddenly vanished from the room he shared with August Kubizek. No one knew why or where he had gone.

Adolf Hitler had suffered the terrible blow that was to leave him down and out in a cold and friendless Vienna: for the second time the Academy of Fine Arts had rejected him, refusing even to allow him to take the examination for admission.

Although Hitler survived the winter of 1908–09 in Vienna, the succeeding bitterly cold winter nearly finished him. By September 1909, the money from his mother's bequest ran out and he could no longer afford lodging. He took to the streets, begging there, sleeping in doorways and cheap coffee houses. No one befriended him. As the weather worsened, his shoes were torn to pieces on the icy pavement, his feet became blistered and frostbitten, and his hands were covered with chilblains. He had no overcoat or hat, and rain and snow had worn his single blue suit threadbare and bleached it lilac. His hair was uncut and uncombed and he had grown a shaggy dark beard. Hunger gnawed at his belly like a family of rats. At last, he lined up with other pathetic wretches at the Asylum for the Shelterless, applying for a five-day ticket. It was granted. He was given a bath, his clothing was disinfected and he was assigned an iron cot with two thin sheets, instructed to use his clothes as a pillow. Each morning and evening, he received a slim ration of bread and soup. During the day he was expected to look for work. He tried shoveling snow and applied for a grave-digger's job, but he was too weak for either. Neither could he carry travelers' luggage at the railroad station, for to lift or walk rapidly caused him too much pain. To live, he crept from shelter to shelter, begging food from the various religious orders that ran them. But his mind was still nimble and he quickly learned the trick of "borrowing" the tickets of those who moved out of the Asylum before their five-day stay ended. In this way, he was able to spend seven weeks there, and then, just as it appeared that he would at last be thrown out on the streets again, he discovered the Männerheim (Men's Home).

Whereas the Asylum had been a doss house for the desperately poor, the Männerheim was more like a huge YMCA operated for the benefit of single men barely able to support themselves. Though it looked like a prison and was run like a monastery, Adolf Hitler found that being admitted there was like moving from hell to heaven. For a small weekly stipend he was given a cubicle with an iron bed and sheets and blankets, and the privileges of eating well-cooked meals in a huge dining room or using the reading room, writing room, showers and a laundry. Drinking was forbidden, the cubicles were cordoned off during the day, and a Männerheim lodger was expected to be clean, reasonably well-dressed and well-mannered. The last three requirements were next to impossible for Adolf Hitler. He was always dirty, his hair and his beard unkempt; he wore cast-off clothing—a derby hat and a knee-length coat, gray trousers and patched shoes —all of which were filthy and greasy, especially the single shirt which he wore until it was stiff with grime. When he washed it, Männerheim lodgers would joke: "Hitler washed his shirt today—there will be fine weather tomorrow."

As for decent manners, he had become in the spring of 1910 passionately interested in politics, given to impromptu speeches in the Männerheim lounge, ranting in his customary frenzy, alienating many of his fellow lodgers. To bait him, they invited him to speak on politics, and while he was speaking someone would tie his coattails to a bench. Immediately, someone else would bluntly contradict him. At once, Hitler flew into his usual frenzy, advancing in fury on his tormentors, brandishing the T-square he always carried—and dragging the bench with him. It was a droll spectacle, which invariably collapsed the occupants of the lounge with laughter and brought the supervisor hurrying into the room with a threat to expel Hitler.

To support himself, Hitler painted colored postcards. They were not originals, rather traced from existing cards and then filled in with watercolors. To give them an antique look, he sometimes held them near the fire until they turned brownish or sepia. Usually he painted two or three postcards a day, just about enough to pay his weekly lodging bill. To him, his gaudy little copies were the works of a misunderstood genius which would one day be of great value. And so he passed three lost years in the Männerheim, devouring newspapers, living off corn pudding and margarine with an occasional cream cake in a cheap coffee shop to celebrate a holiday, dabbling in the occult or half-baked "sciences" such as telepathy, phrenology, graphology and physiognomy, calling down fire and brimstone on the heads of the Jews, the Catholic Church and the Austro-Hungarian Empire; remembering every insult, every burst of derisive laughter or scornful sneer that his presence or his wild prophecies could provoke, cherishing them, actually, treasuring them, storing them up, as though to nourish the horrible ache for revenge still swelling in his heart. Then, just as he teetered on the abyss of demented despair into which one thousand days of the Männerheim's organized hopelessness could easily plunge a man, he was abruptly and inexplicably rescued by his half-forgotten half brother in England.

Alois Hitler the younger was the illegitimate son of Alois Senior and Franziska Matzelsberger, being legitimized after his father married Franziska and his sister Angela was born. Both were reared by Klara Hitler. Good for nothing all his youth, Alois left home at the age of sixteen and by the time he was twenty he had been twice imprisoned for theft. At that time he wrote to Klara asking for help. Back came a letter ostensibly from his stepmother but in his brother Adolf's handwriting: "To steal and be caught means that you are not even a good thief. In that case my advice to you is to go and hang yourself." Apparently the rebuke struck home. Alois never forgot or forgave his brother, a grudge that was most unusual in a man so good-humored. For Alois was an amiable amoralist, fond of a full glass and a fine lass, ready to steal or betray at the drop of a coin. To him, indeed, the only crime in stealing was to be caught.

Leaving Germany, Alois became a waiter in Paris, plied the same trade in Dublin, married a young Irish actress named Bridget Dowling in London and drifted on to Liverpool, where he opened a small restaurant. He sold the restaurant and became a part-time waiter and part-time salesman of safety razors, then just becoming popular. He dreamed of cornering the safety-razor market, and in this euphoric mood he sent a round-trip railroad ticket to Liverpool to his sister, now Angela Raubal. She was to set up his Central European branch. This was in 1912. In November of that year he and Bridget went down to the railroad station to welcome Angela. But the person who stepped off the train was Adolf.

Alois was astounded and Bridget shocked by the appearance of this pale, gaunt, shifty-eyed young man who arrived without luggage and glanced furtively about him like a fugitive. He immediately seized Alois by the arm and began whispering wildly in German. Bridget guessed that he was explaining how he came to have Angela's ticket, but she never did learn how.

Adolf Hitler was a fugitive from Austrian justice, a fact that explained his furtive manner. He was a draft dodger, what Europeans described as a deserter. He had avoided military service by using the birth certificate of his dead brother Edmund, six years younger than he. He should have offered himself for conscription when he was twenty, on April 20, 1909, but took refuge in the Asylum instead. During his stay at the Männerheim he was technically a deserter liable to arrest. It is likely that he left that place because he had discovered the police on his trail, and that he sought refuge with Angela Raubal. Angela, who was caring for the witless Paula as well as rearing her beautiful young daughter, Geli, had already through lawsuit compelled Adolf to assign his pension to her. When he arrived at her home and found her in possession of the ticket from Alois, he probably threw this up to her, and then appealed to her to "save" him from the police by giving him the ticket. Like Benito Mussolini, Adolf Hitler was no physical coward, and he would soon prove his bravery. But with the Europe of that time gone mad with militarism, it did not take a very perceptive man to see the war clouds gathering; and Hitler, again like *Il Duce,* had no wish to be the cannon fodder of a monarchy he despised.

So he remained "on the lam" in Liverpool for four or five months, a shadowy figure who haunted the docks, learning little English and making no English friends, sponging without a qualm off the brother he detested, showing an interest only in the marvelous British machinery, which opened their bridges and loaded their ships. From this experience he gained an abiding respect for English technology. And then he returned to Vienna, to the Männerheim, where he celebrated his twenty-fourth birthday. A month later, again just a few steps ahead of the police, he migrated to Munich, the city that he loved in the country that he idolized. Once again, he rented a small room and resumed the life of a recluse, painting by day, reading by night, living on bread and sausage and seldom venturing forth except to perform household chores that earned him a discount on his rent. "He camped in his room like a hermit," his landlady recalled, "with his nose stuck in those thick, heavy books." It was here that the Austrian police finally found him, and on January 12, 1914, he received a summons to present himself for military service at Linz.

Adolf Hitler was now in deep trouble. If he did not comply, he would be turned over to the Austrian police under an extradition treaty between the two countries. In Austria, he could expect to be convicted of desertion and sentenced to a year in prison and fined 2,000 kronen—a substantial sum—after which he would still have to do his military duty. So he sat down with a lawyer friend and concocted a long, discursive, mendacious alibi, offered in groveling, breast-beating style that he, as the son of a customs official, knew full well would satisfy the bureaucrats in the Austrian Consulate. In sum, he was a poor, starving artist, so destitute and so preoccupied in his desire to bring lasting fame upon his Fatherland that he simply forgot his military obligation. He was believed, and escaped punishment, being sent instead to Salzburg for medical examination. The report stated: "Unfit for combatant and auxiliary duty, too weak. Unable to bear arms."

Relieved but outwardly still repentant, Adolf Hitler returned to his hermitage in Munich, from which the war he dreaded was soon to pluck him.

On August 1, 1914, Germany declared war on Russia, thus setting Europe ablaze in the conflagration first known as the Great War. Germany's declaration was read to a huge cheering crowd gathered on the Odeonsplatz in Munich. Hitler was among them, and a photograph taken at the time shows him in the center of the throng, jubilant and joining in the singing of Germany's great patriotic song, "The Watch on the Rhine." Two days later he petitioned the King of Bavaria for permission to join a Bavarian regiment.

Jubilant? Singing? This pacifist, draft-dodging hater of imperialist war wanted to march off to one—*singing?* True. For Hitler in his profound love for Germany believed that the war just beginning would make it *the* world power, and that Austria—the homeland that he hated so passionately—would cease to exist and become a German province. Fitting punishment for the cause of all his misery, Hitler believed, and his elation was boundless when King Ludwig granted his petition. On August 16, he was enrolled in the 16th Bavarian Reserve Infantry, or List Regiment, after its commander, Colonel List. He became a courier, or dispatch runner. When his regiment entrained for the Belgian front in late October of that year, he was one of eight or ten stationed at regimental headquarters.

Dispatch runners carried messages from headquarters to the fighting front. They went in pairs, on the assumption that if one were killed, the other would get through. Although Hitler in later years liked to describe himself as a "front-line soldier," this was not true. His billet was always at least a mile from the front. He slept in comfort, almost always out of range of enemy artillery, and he ate cooked meals. Although he was frequently in great danger, his life in no way approached the distillate of pure misery and terror endured by Benito Mussolini.

But he was a good soldier, courageous and resolute, careful and determined. His exploits won him every medal available to a German enlisted man, and although he never rose above the rank of acting corporal, he also never put in for promotion, apparently content to be a courier. After two years of unending combat duty, his luck ran out: Within one week he was wounded twice, the first a mere shell splinter in the face, the second a far more serious shell fragment in the thigh, which caused his evacuation back to Germany. Recovered, he was given a pass to Berlin, where he was dismayed to hear people talking defeatism. It was the same in Munich, where his suspicions of Jewish treason were revived. He believed that they were plotting against the central government. Unable to bear such "treachery," he volunteered for combat and rejoined his old regiment on March 1, 1917. Hitler was immediately appalled by the despair in the hollow, sunken eyes of his old comrades.

His Männerheim mood returned. He sat apart, morose, brooding, suddenly leaping to his feet in rage to denounce the "hidden enemies" of the Reich, whom he quickly identified as Jews and their capitalist lackeys. He received no mail and sent none out, always refusing to share the delicacies from home offered to him, content to stuff himself with bread and jam washed down by endless cups of tea. Then, on the night of October 13, 1918, in trenches south of Ypres, Adolf Hitler was blinded in an enemy gas attack.

In the hospital at Pasewalk near Stettin (now Szczecin, Poland), Hitler was told that he would never see again. He sank into a deep depression, characterized by fits of weeping and long periods of withdrawal. His world had ended. He would never paint or draw again, and Germany lay prostrate despite his own sacrifices and those of millions of his comrades. Worse, the sailors who had mutinied at Kiel were spreading across the country, preaching revolution and waving the red flag. The danger of Germany turning Bolshevik was the shock that restored a purpose to Hitler's life, and with that, his health. Gradually, his sight returned, and on November 21, ten days after the Armistice, he made his way to Munich, where the Bavarian Socialist Republic had been proclaimed. Hitler was still in the army, quartered in the barracks of the List Regiment, and he watched in dismay as the Socialist Republic gave way to a Soviet Republic and a Red Army was formed. All of the leaders of both governments—Socialist or Communist— were Jews! Once again the denunciatory wrath flowed from his lips, and he only escaped execution at the hands of the Red Guards who had come to arrest him by threatening them with a loaded carbine. It was only natural that when a rightist movement was formed in Munich, Hitler joined it. After rightist forces stormed Munich, he became an undercover agent for them, "fingering" at least ten comrades who were executed as Communists.

As a reward, he was sent to an indoctrination course conducted by the army at the University of Munich. Here he learned about the Germans' destiny as the "master race" and about the "interest slavery" imposed on Germany by the international banking community—chiefly the Jewish financiers of England, France and the United States, those detested democracies that had imposed the hateful, humiliating Treaty of Versailles on a prostrate Fatherland—and here also he discovered that he was a natural orator. When a soldier arose to challenge an economics professor's description of Jewish finance, Hitler destroyed him with a devastating flow of argument—not necessarily logical—delivered with an air of authority and in such an insistent, querulous, rasping tone that it held the class transfixed. At this moment Adolf Hitler sensed his power over men in the mass. From a student, he became a teacher, so respected at the university that when his commanding officer received from an agent named Adolf Gemlich a request for an explanation of the proper attitude to take with the Jews, it was he who was delegated to make the reply.

In his letter, written at the age of thirty in September of 1919, can be seen Adolf Hitler's program for the destruction of the race he despised. But it contains no foaming, frenzied outburst of irrational hatred characteristic of his Männerheim style. Here instead his ideas are set forth in a cold, calculating, methodical manner. Well might any Jew with a knowledge of history, reading this, have thanked God that the author was a mere nobody, a faceless corporal without the slightest chance of putting his proposals into practice. For here is outlined the entire "legal" apparatus for carrying out a pogrom in the efficient German fashion. Phrases such as "elimination of their privileges," "ruthless intervention" or "deliberate removal" are but sinister adumbrations of the concentration camps and the "final solution."

In this fateful year following the end of World War I Adolf Hitler had found his voice, and in the twin "sellouts" to the Jews and at Versailles the poles of his political power-to-be. Now all he needed was an organization.

Anton Drexler was a toolmaker in the Munich railroad yard, a workingman —the son and grandson of workingmen—who believed with a passion in that glorious and inevitable day when the working class would at last be freed from bondage to the wealthy. He was a tall, spare man, as undistinguished as his dab of mustache and rimless glasses. But he did found the German Workers' Party, later to become the *Nationalsozialistische Deutsche Arbeiterpartei,* or National Socialist German Workers' Party, eventually abbreviated to Nazi. Drexler's party was one of dozens formed in Munich during the final dark days of the war and after. It was fiercely loyal to the war effort, hating strikers, Jews, Bolsheviks, war malingerers and profiteers. Like most political parties in Munich, it met in a beer hall, a grimy, tiny, ill-lighted place called the Sterneckherbräu. Here, on September 12, 1919, came Corporal Adolf Hitler, sent there by his military superiors to report on the party's activities.

There were only twenty-five members present, a typical cross-section of workers, soldiers, would-be writers, merchants and pseudo-intellectuals. Hitler, sent to observe, became instead the speaker of the evening, jumping to his feet to annihilate a speaker who had suggested that Bavaria secede from Germany and unite with Austria. Nevertheless, he was bored with the German Workers Party, only reluctantly accepting a pamphlet that Drexler eagerly pressed upon him as he took his leave. Unable to sleep in the List Regiment barracks that night, he read Drexler's manifesto. It astonished him. The shy railway worker's ideas were so much his own! Still he did not immediately join Drexler's party, dismayed that his "frightful, frightful little club" possessed a total wealth of 7 marks, 50 pfennigs. When he did join on January 1, 1920—Member #55, Executive Committee Member #7—it was with the intention of destroying the party and reshaping it to his own ends.

Soon, Hitler was the party's chief recruiter, gaining many converts in the List Barracks, chief among them Rudolf Hess, a gallant officer and later flier who had been studying philosophy and geopolitics at the University of Munich. Other than being credited with the idea of *Lebensraum,* or living space, to be seized in European Russia, Hess had no talents or skills. But he was indeed devoted to Hitler, whom he regarded as the greatest son of the German race and whose alter ego he quickly became. For this, Hess would be rewarded with the title of deputy leader of the Nazi Party.

Another prize, albeit an unsavory one, was Ernst Roehm, chief of staff of the military governor of Munich. Roehm was a chubby, red-faced little man who had been wounded three times in the war and had half his nose shot away. During the party's early days he was the one man able to negotiate with Hitler on equal terms. Roehm organized and commanded the infamous *Sturmabteilungen* (Storm Troops), the dreaded SA or "brownshirts," who formed Hitler's private army and won the battle of the streets against the Communists and other political opposition. In the SA Ernst Roehm was able to indulge his fondness for handsome young men.

In February 1920, Hitler and Drexler drew up the party's "epochal program" with its twenty-five points. He was given the opportunity to proclaim these at a mass meeting at the Hofbrauhaus attended by a record-breaking 2,000 people. Not all of them were Hitler's friends and there were numerous Communists present, as well as the inevitable observer from the Munich police.

According to this reporter, Hitler's speech provoked a "fearful uproar." He attacked the Berlin government, blaming it for the hunger spreading throughout Germany and the flood of inflated paper marks that was drowning the economy. He denounced the Jews, of course, and attacked every other party, with the predictable result that everyone was eventually shouting and brandishing fists. "There was often so much tumult," wrote the police reporter, "that I believed that any moment they would all be fighting." To Hitler, that night was to mean "a wolf had been born, destined to hurl itself on the herds of seducers and deceivers of the people." From that night on also, the party was his.

Adolf Hitler never again spoke to mere handfuls. During sixteen meetings in 1920, the Munich police carefully finger-counted crowds ranging from 1,200 to 3,500 persons. They also detailed the astonishingly successful techniques of this meteoric new demagogue. Hitler loved violence, believing that a speech accompanied by some violent act would be more vividly remembered. Thus, he welcomed hecklers, who gave his burly bodyguards the chance to plow into the throng with fists flying. He knew, of course, from his church-school days the power of reiteration; and thus as the litany of curses fell from his lips in calculated repetition, the large halls he favored would echo and reecho with the rising roars of his listeners. Hitler had made a science of rousing audiences to a frenzy. He studied the beer halls for their acoustics, their colors, the best places from which to speak or to make entrances and exits. He deliberately arrived late, keeping his audiences in suspense, and then suddenly bursting in on them from some completely unexpected point—like a Messiah coming on a cloud—marching purposefully to the rostrum with his face fixed and frozen, preceded and followed by platoons of watchful bodyguards.

His speeches began falteringly. His voice was muted, his head slowly swiveling while the bulging blue eyes raked the audience for that sign of eager restlessness which was his cue to rouse them into frenzy. Then his voice rose querulously, he spat out his accusations and charges like bullets, pausing at the proper moment for the thunderous cries of *"Sieg Heil! Sieg Heil!"* (To Victory!) to go reverberating around the room. When he finished, he was near exhaustion. His face was white, his hair was plastered against his skull, and his clothing was wet with sweat. But he had once again demonstrated that the National Socialist German Workers Party was his—and that he was the party.

By then Hitler had also introduced the swastika as the party emblem. At first, it was not exactly what he wanted, but eventually it would emerge as the most fearful flag, with its crooked black cross imposed upon a blood red field within a white circle. He wrote that the new flag "was wonderfully suited for the young movement, and it was as young and new as the movement . . . it was like a blazing torch."

Hitler was now obsessed by a pair of related ideas: one was the power of a putsch (coup d'état) to seize control of a government, the other the necessity of ruling without mercy. He had been in Berlin during the absurd five-day "rule" of "Chancellor" Wolfgang Kapp, an army creature who was such a prodigy of futility that he could not proclaim martial law because no one would lend his daughter a typewriter to type out his proclamation. Hitler also saw soldiers of a *Freikorps*—one of those private armies of left and right that had become the curse of Germany—club a boy to his knees for jeering at them, then stomp the life out of him with their boots. Next, the soldiers machine-gunned a crowd of innocent civilians who had protested. Hitler admired this pitiless use of power. One day he would have his own private army, and he began forming it by putting his bodyguards in uniform: swastika armbands, ski caps, knee breeches and thick woolen socks with gray jackets. They were the forerunners of the storm troops, the dreaded SA and SS. In 1921, Hitler arrogated to himself the title *Unser Führer* (Our Leader) which he later depersonalized into *Der Führer* (*The* Leader). He was now the unabashed dictator of the Nazi Party, answerable to no one, not even for what happened to the funds which the paid attendance at his speeches sent flowing into the party treasury.

Like Benito Mussolini, Adolf Hitler cared for money only as a means to his end of power. He lived quietly and obscurely in two miserable bare rooms that would be his home until 1929, always scornful of the pleasures and possessions that were the obsession of his latest and most valued recruit, Hermann Goering. In 1922 when he joined the party, Goering was still a handsome hero, the legendary ace of Baron von Richthofen's famous Flying Circus. Eventually he would become fat and vicious, fond of violence, addicted to morphine, adorning his face with makeup and his figure with those jewels in which he took a childish delight. Hitler was overjoyed to receive Goering into the party, giving him command of the SA brownshirts which, by December 1922, had grown to a force of about 600 men. For his part, Goering saw in the Nazi Party the opportunity to satisfy his cravings for power, wealth and violence. But his new command brought him into inevitable conflict with Captain Ernst Roehm's Reich War Flag group. Nevertheless, the two commanders were in step with each other when, in November 1923, Adolf Hitler launched his famous Beer-Hall Putsch.

Hitler was now convinced that the infant Weimar Republic was on the verge of collapse and the time for his push for power had come. He had just returned from the village of Bayreuth, sacred to the memory of his idol, Richard Wagner, and there had been anointed by the great composer's widow and children as though he were indeed Odin descended from Valhalla to save the German Reich. His head also had been turned by interviews with foreign journalists, indicating that he was now an international figure, and he had secured the allegiance of all of Munich's right-wing armies. Even more important, he had received the support of Erich Ludendorff, the most revered man in Germany, the great quartermaster general who had been the virtual ruler of the nation during the last two years of the war. Ludendorff's head was as full of Wagnerian fancies as Hitler's, and he had spent his declining, if not degenerating, years in his estate outside Munich attempting to commune with the demigods of Teutonic mythology. With such forces, Hitler proposed nothing less than the arrest of the Munich government and proclaiming his own, after which he would march on Berlin and seize total power.

On November 8, Hitler learned that the ruling triumvirate of Munich had called a meeting of 3,000 officials for that night at the Bürgerbräukeller. He rode there in a bright red touring car, dressed in a tightly belted trench coat, his hands in his pockets with one of them grasping a loaded revolver. His armed storm troopers and Hermann Goering followed in trucks. Hitler waited for them to burst into the hall and cow the screaming, terrified officials with machine guns.

Delivered from Evil

Then he came inside, jumped onto a table, drew his revolver, and fired two shots in the air.

"Silence!" he screamed.

As the noise subsided, Goering in a steel coal-scuttle helmet joined Hitler and together they forced their way up to the speaker's platform where the chiefs of Munich sat in silent trepidation.

"The National Revolution has begun!" Hitler shouted. "Six hundred armed men are occupying the hall. No one may leave. The barracks of the Reichswehr* and the police have been occupied. The Reichswehr and the police have joined the swastika flag! The Bavarian government is deposed! The Reich government is deposed!"

These were lies. The truth was that about sixty storm troopers were in the hall. No one had been deposed and no one had gone over to Hitler. Still, *Der Führer*'s air of authority gave weight to his words, and in a louder voice he announced that he would take over the government, and Ludendorff, "who will soon be here," would command the Reichswehr. Next, Hitler took off his trench coat, revealing a black frock coat and trousers, the traditional garb of office worn by the three men he was menacing with his pistol. It was a mistake. The coat was too big and the pants were baggy. With his little dab of mustache and his big pistol, Hitler did indeed look like Charlie Chaplin, or at least the little man on a wedding cake. When his bodyguard rushed up with a stein of beer, which *Der Führer* drained while still waving his pistol, setting it down with a loud thump and sigh of satisfaction, wiping the foam from his mustache, the putsch had sunk to the level of comic opera. One of the "captured" officials did indeed mutter, "Let us play out the comedy."

Then Ludendorff arrived: tall, soldierly, wearing a brown hunting jacket and an alpine hat, but still easily the most commanding presence in the hall. Everyone, including Hitler and his leaders, deferred to him with obsequious bows. But the quartermaster general was not enchanted when he found that *Der Führer* was planning to become the new dictator, a position which he rather fancied himself. Nevertheless, he accepted command of the Reichswehr, while the three captive officials, submitting to the logic flowing from the muzzle of Hitler's pistol, also agreed to join the new government. A message from Roehm arrived informing Hitler that he had seized the War Ministry. Elated, Hitler sent out a party to destroy the printing presses of the opposition Social Democrats' newspaper and another under Rudolf Hess to arrest Social Democrats and Jews.

Hitler next went to the barracks of the engineers and infantry to persuade them to surrender. They refused. Returning to the hall, he found that his three captured officials had vanished. Presumably, they were preparing a counterstroke. They were. Hitler, meanwhile, spent most of the night rushing about Munich to make fiery speeches. In a word, he was acting like the naive, incompetent adventurer that he was. If it was fatuous for him to believe that he could seize

*Name (Imperial Defense) by which the German armed forces were known 1919–1935.

Bavaria's capital city without the assistance of the Reichswehr stationed there, it was downright stupid to think that his untrained rabble could overcome these professional soldiers. Worse, from Munich he would march on Berlin, again with a rabble-in-arms, without transport or artillery or cavalry or plan of attack or friendly forces within the city. A measure of Adolf Hitler's incompetence at the time was that the 2,000 rifles issued his storm troopers were not equipped with firing pins, thus making them less effective than cap pistols. Nevertheless, in the morning, after a brief restless nap, he led 3,000 armed men from the Bürgerbräukeller toward the center of town, where he hoped to join forces with Roehm at the War Ministry.

Awaiting them at the Odeonsplatz were the police and soldiers of the Reichswehr. They were under orders to stop *Der Führer,* even if it meant killing him and Ludendorff. Both men were at the head of their "troops." Hitler wore his trench coat. He was deathly pale. His breath came quickly as he sought to remain abreast of the tall general striding purposefully ahead. Goering and other Nazi leaders were behind them, urging on their men, who were now singing and waving their weapons. The approach narrowed, reducing the column from eight to four abreast. . . . On they came . . . closer. . . .

At a distance of about sixty feet, someone fired. History does not know who, but the shot provoked a volley from the police. As instructed, they fired into the street, sending a shower of splinters from the paving stones into the oncoming mob. Goering fell with two splinters in the groin. There were answering shots. Policemen fell. A man with whom Hitler had linked arms was instantly killed, and Hitler slumped to the ground, landing so heavily on his shoulder that he dislocated it and believed himself wounded. Now the stunned throng of Nazis ran for cover or for safety. But Erich Ludendorff still strode straight ahead, his hands thrust casually into the pockets of his brown jacket. The police and soldiers parted ranks deferentially and the quartermaster general passed calmly through them, returning to his estate to resume communion with the Valkyrie and vanishing forevermore from the pages of history.

Adolf Hitler, meanwhile, was running for his life. His putsch had been put down with a loss of eighteen Nazis killed and about 100 wounded, with three policemen killed. Although Hitler found refuge in the suburban home of a friend, he was taken captive a few days later. He was brought to trial on February 26, 1924, convicted and sentenced to five years in the Landsberg fortress.

Hitler spent only nine months in prison, if his baronial sojourn in the Landsberg may be so described. True enough, he did have a cell, but it was one crowded with visitors or piled high with the gifts that flowed into it. Fruit, flowers, wine, beer, hams and sausages, candy, cakes—even oil paintings—arrived at the prison from the legions of Hitler's admirers, many of them women. *Der Führer* used these gifts to bribe his warders and to seduce them so that they shouted "Heil Hitler!" and saluted whenever he came into their presence. Hitler might have been staying at a luxury hotel, or better, enjoying a retreat among the old retainers of his estate. He rose at 6:00, bathed, breakfasted, answered his voluminous mail with uncensored letters of his own, addressed his fellow Nazi prisoners at midmorning, lunched with them seated like a lord at the head of the table, conversing affably on the subjects of art, literature, automobiles or the leading men of the day, quaffed his beloved strong English tea at midday, finishing with a light supper of herring or sausage and a liter of beer, with perhaps a post-prandial stroll along "Hitler's Walk" with some favored Nazi visitor.

Most of Hitler's time in the Landsberg was spent writing *Mein Kampf* (My Struggle), dictating it to Rudolf Hess, who had been given a convenient prison sentence to act as secretary to his adored Führer. The book is both an account of Hitler's life and a blueprint for the destruction of Judeo-Christian civilization and the conquest of the world. Robert Payne, one of Hitler's better biographers, has rightly compared *Mein Kampf* to Machiavelli's *The Prince.* In its disdain for morality and the sanctity of human life, it is just as chilling—and just as seminal. All those terrible demons that dwelt within Hitler—hatred of the Jews, contempt for humanity, belief in the German superman, the need for tearing *Lebensraum* or living space out of the hide of the despicable Slavs—are here set free to howl. Most impressive of all is Hitler's penetrating analysis of the uses of propaganda, and he was probably history's greatest exponent of this modern technique. He had learned from his days in the monastery school the irresistible power of repetition on mediocre minds. The rising-falling chant of the Church's litany—the praise of God and His saints—was to be perverted to serve Hitler's catalog of lies. Again and again he makes the point that the minds of the masses are soggy, sodden, absolutely incapable of prolonged retention, like a bog surrendering a footprint almost as quickly as it receives it. Thus, skilled propaganda must confine itself to a few points, beating them into the mass-man's brain—again and again, repeat and repeat—with the relentless rhythm of a metronome.

Eventually, *Mein Kampf* was to sell 5 million copies in eleven different languages. Although it became the bible of the Nazi Party, it was largely ignored in Germany and was probably unread by those world leaders whose countries Hitler had targeted for conquest. The greatest pity is that right until the very end, Adolf Hitler was derided and denigrated as a raving madman—as though the world were so weak and frail that it could be convulsed by an idiot—rather than being perceived as a malevolent genius possessed of a first-class mind.

At ten o'clock in the morning of December 20, 1924, when the gates of the Landsberg swung open for Adolf Hitler, he was free to use that mind once more.

When Hitler returned to Munich, the Nazi Party was scarcely more than an empty name. There was no office, no treasury, no newspaper (the *Völkischer Beobachter* had been confiscated), not even a typewriter. Even Hitler himself—the soul of the party—seemed subdued.

The change, of course, was due to Hitler's realization that he had bungled the Beer-Hall Putsch, and his vow never again to attempt to seize power by force of arms. Instead, he would bring down the Weimar Republic by legal subversion, while building a mass movement and intimidating the opposition by street terror. By February 1925, he had recovered his confidence, opening his campaign in a speech before 2,000 people in the Bürgerbräukeller. It was vintage Hitler, so successful that the Bavarian government immediately revoked his license to speak. The revocation lasted until May 1927, during which period Hitler wrote articles for the *Völkischer Beobachter,* relicensed by a provincial government whose persistent permissiveness was to prove fatal to the entire country. Hitler also used this hiatus from the speaker's hall to strengthen the party with such notable recruits as Joseph Goebbels, Heinrich Himmler and Martin Bormann.

Goebbels was the son of a Rhineland workingman. He was small—barely five feet tall—and thin; black-haired and dark-eyed, with high cheekbones, a long thin nose and a wide mouth. A clubfoot and a pronounced limp added to his unprepossessing appearance, as well as to the inferiority complex that was to express itself in his contempt for the human race and his hatred of the Jews. Yet, when Goebbels spoke, his deep, musical voice and his sharp, biting wit could charm whomever he sought to persuade. His failure as a novelist and dramatist deepened his grudge against humanity and the established order, while whetting his appetite for success anywhere. He found his opportunity in the Nazi Party, where he was easily the most intellectual member, affectionately known to *Der Führer* as "the little doctor." He would also receive from Hitler the mantle of master propagandist for the Nazi regime, and as minister of culture he would create the myth of the messianic Führer, while satisfying his lust for women among the actresses and starlets who submitted to his sexual blackmail. Goebbels was also a leading contributor to the evolution of the "final solution of the Jewish question."

Although the "final solution" was born in the brain of Hitler and given expression by Goebbels, its execution was left to a mouselike little man with a minotaur's appetite for human flesh and blood. Heinrich Himmler was born in Munich in 1900, the son of a pious and authoritarian schoolmaster who had once been tutor to the Crown Prince of Bavaria. Toward the end of World War I he served as a cadet officer in a Bavarian regiment and afterward studied agriculture. Himmler worked for a while selling fertilizer, until his dreams of military glory led him to join one of Munich's many rightist military formations. He was at Ernst Roehm's side as his standard-bearer during the Beer-Hall Putsch. In 1927, Himmler left politics for chicken farming. Failing there, he returned to the Nazi Party and in 1929 was appointed head of Hitler's personal bodyguard, the black-shirted *Schutzstaffel* (Defense Echelon), the infamous SS. At the time, only about 200 men comprised this evil elite—physical specimens so splendid that a single cavity could disqualify an applicant for admission—but under Himmler the SS would expand into an omnipresent, omnipotent state within the Nazi state itself. And Heinrich Himmler would become Reichsführer SS, chief of the dreaded Gestapo (secret police), commander of the Waffen-SS and minister of the interior —in all these titles the second most powerful man in Germany.

Small and shy, exquisitely courteous in his demeanor, this little gray monster could not have frightened a nursery—and yet he was to order the torture and death of millions of innocent people. He was a hypochondriac and a faint heart, almost passing out when a hundred Jews were executed for his benefit near the Soviet front. From this experience, and presumably to spare his queasy stomach further shocks, he ordered "the more humane means" of murder by poison gas in chambers disguised as shower rooms. He also created a special SS pseudo-science whereby every imaginable kind of painful experiment was made on the living flesh of "inferior human beings"; that is, criminals, cripples, the deformed, Gypsies, Jews and Slavs.

Himmler would one day find himself in unequal competition with Martin Bormann, that short, squat, silent, crafty and brutal murderer who became *Der Führer*'s private secretary. Hailed by Hitler as "my most loyal party comrade," Bormann was known to those who hated and feared him as their chief's "brown eminence." From being Hitler's secretary, Bormann eventually became his master in all but title. He catered to his every personal want with doglike devotion, and with careful cunning was able to exploit his every weakness to the increase of his own power. No one came to see *Der Führer* without Bormann's approval, for it was he who drew up his appointment schedule. When visitors did appear, the Brown Eminence was always hovering nearby, able to squelch any report or proposal that might endanger his own schemes or disturb the world of fantasy into which Hitler ultimately withdrew. Above all, Martin Bormann possessed a matchless skill for undermining some rival he had marked for destruction.

It was with such men, then—with Rudolf Hess and Ernst Roehm, Joseph Goebbels and Hermann Goering, Heinrich Himmler and Martin Bormann—and with hundreds like them that Adolf Hitler sought to rebuild his shattered Nazi Party.

Party records show that the number of dues-paying members increased slowly: in 1925, 27,000; in 1926, 49,000; in 1927, 72,000; in 1928, 108,000. Even from these probably inflated figures, it appeared that the Nazi Party was dying. Outside Bavaria, it had scarcely any influence at all, and the elections of May 1928 seemed to deliver its death blow. Hitler's party received only 810,000 votes, or 2.6 percent of the total. It had done much better four years earlier, receiving 1.918 million in the spring voting and 907,300 in the winter. *Der Führer* was at the head of a party holding only twelve out of the Reichstag's 491 seats, while the despicable Communists held fifty-four.

What had happened? Hitler well knew. Germany was prospering. The economic genius Dr. Hjalmar Schacht had put an end to inflation, and unemployment was declining. The French army, which had moved into the Ruhr when Germany threatened to halt reparations payments, had been withdrawn. The revered Field Marshal Paul von Hindenburg had become president at the age of seventy-seven and his patriarchal presence seemed to give the German people a sense of stability. Worse for Hitler, the Communists had been decisively repudiated in the elections of 1925. All of Adolf Hitler's bugaboos were dead and buried. True, the Jewish whipping boy remained, but well-fed Germans with steady jobs were not at the moment searching for a scapegoat. Scapegoats, of course, were the stuff of which revolutions could be made; without them, Hitler would have to resort to a putsch once more—this time against a satisfied German people. Hitler needed a disaster or catastrophe of the first order to bring angry, discontented mobs crowding back into his beer halls and rathskellers, and in the Great Depression of 1929 he got one.

The year 1929 was critical in many ways for Adolf Hitler. In spite of the electoral reverses of the previous year, he had become the darling of the wealthy and the ennobled of Germany. Both were under the delusion that the spellbinder from Munich would support a revival of the Hohenzollern dynasty, and both poured money into his coffers. Hitler was now immensely rich, and he began to spend money lavishly. He left his dingy rooms with their threadbare carpets and rented a princely apartment in one of Munich's most affluent districts. With this came a new Mercedes-Benz (*Der Führer* loved big, fast cars), a second secretary, a pair of servants, and, for companionship, the beautiful daughter of his half sister, Angela.

No one had paid much attention when Hitler had had himself appointed guardian of Angela ("Geli") Raubal, but when this twenty-one-year-old blue-eyed brunette came to live with her uncle and occupied the bedroom next to his, Nazi eyebrows shot up like exclamation points. Geli Raubal was strikingly beautiful. She was gay and outgoing and charmingly ingenuous. Hitler was obviously infatuated with her, taking her everywhere with him, flying into a rage if anyone became especially attentive to her. Finding her in the arms of his faithful chauffeur, he fired him on the spot.

Whether or not they were intimate is not known. Despite all the psychiatric nonsense that has been written about Hitler—as the chronic masturbator, the unrequited impotent psychopath, the sexless sadist—and despite his own inclination to put women on a pedestal, he was completely normal in his sexual appetites, merely sublimating them through his ferocious political activity. But there seems no doubt that his beautiful niece was the one woman he really loved. He did draw her in the nude, producing obscene drawings that were stolen and then bought back from a blackmailer. It was also said that he whipped her with his bull-hide whip. Hitler's close friend, Ernst ("Putzi") Hanfstaengl, the authority for these allegations, also claimed that Geli once said to someone else: "My uncle is a monster. You would never believe the things he makes me do." Unfortunately, Hanfstaengl was an inveterate liar who also disliked Geli. All that can be said beyond doubt is that this beautiful girl so fond of male attention did live in luxury with her powerful uncle for two years, and that, as the servants have testified, she frequently was the object of those vile, screaming rages which soon would earn Hitler the nickname "Carpet-Chewer." On the night of September 18, 1931, one of these rages was provoked by a heated argument between them. Geli wanted something—what, no one knows— and Hitler refused to give it to her. He bellowed at her in a fury, and then rushed downstairs to the limousine waiting to take him to Nuremberg for a speech that night. Geli ran to the balcony and Hitler shouted up to her, "For the last time, *No!*" Then the Mercedes roared away.

Oddly calm and controlled, Geli Raubal went to her room, locked herself in, telephoned a girlfriend for an idle chat, wrote a few letters, and at midnight shot herself through the heart with her uncle's revolver.

Geli Raubal's suicide shattered Adolf Hitler and brought him close to taking his own life. He lived in seclusion for weeks, unable to eat or sleep or to conduct party affairs. His associates had to watch him closely, forcing him to surrender the revolver he always carried with him. Meantime, the party moved swiftly to hush the scandal. But the opposition Socialist newspaper, the *Münchner Post,* published articles suggesting that the suicide was the result of Hitler's refusal to allow her to go to Vienna to marry a young man there. The articles said her body was bruised and her nose broken. There was, of course, no testimony supporting these charges, especially not from the servants who broke down the door and found the body. The *Völkischer Beobachter* indignantly denied the allegations.

There still persists to this day, however, the unproved theory that Hitler drove Geli Raubal to her death. Much is made of the fact that the Catholic Church gave Geli a Christian burial in her native Austria. Normally, the Church will not bury a suicide in consecrated ground, maintaining that self-destruction is the final act of despair, the last rejection of the grace of God. Only if it is believed that the suicide was involuntary, either forced upon the subject or the result of mental derangement, will this prohibition be lifted. But neither the priest who buried Geli Raubal nor his bishop ever gave an explanation of why the exception was made.

Unfortunately, in the writing of history the less that is known the wider and more lurid the speculation. But there are only two facts known in the death of Geli Raubal: She killed herself with her uncle's pistol and no one knows why.

Adolf Hitler was to make a cult of Geli Raubal. The room in which she had killed herself was kept exactly as she had left it, decorated daily with fresh flowers. A life-size painting of her would be installed at Obersalzberg and a bust of her given a place of honor in the new Chancellery in Berlin. Wherever Hitler went, he carried Geli's picture with him, along with the photograph of his mother.

Meanwhile, *Der Führer* recovered, buoyed by the rising tide of misery that was flooding Germany and lifting his Nazi Party ever higher toward power. The Depression triggered by the Wall Street stock market crash of October 29, 1929, had had worse effect on Germany than on the rest of the industrial world, if only because it was living on loans more than any other nation. Unemployment soared: from 1.32 million in September 1929 to 3 million in 1930, 5.668 million in 1931, and 6.128 million in 1932. Hitler's hoarse, rasping voice preaching hatred of Jews and Communists was once more heard in crowded beer halls and rathskellers. In the election of 1930 his party polled 6.409 million votes, compared to 810,000 in 1928, and held 107 Reichstag seats compared to a previous twelve. The Communists also gained, holding seventy-seven seats. Germany was being polarized between right and left, and at this juncture the hideous street war between the Nazis and the Communists began.

Ultimately, Hitler's brownshirts won, chiefly because they were better organized and on fire to avenge the "martyrdom" of their comrade, Horst Wessel. Actually, Horst Wessel was a pimp who lived off the takings of his mistress, a prostitute. He was killed in a dispute over her, but the ever-alert Goebbels, scenting a propaganda coup, quickly put it out that the Reds had murdered him. So the infuriated brownshirts took to the streets singing their famous "Horst Wessel Song": "For the last time the rifle is loaded. . . . Soon Hitler banners will wave over the barricades. . . ." The song was also sung at the closing of all Nazi meetings, and eventually history's first hymn to a panderer was woven into the warp and woof of Nazi mythology, along with the swastika, the arm's length salute and the greeting "Heil Hitler!"

Gradually, however, some of the brownshirts became disenchanted with National Socialism. Former Communists, they had believed that the Nazis were socialistic. Now, they saw that they had been exploited by Hitler in his thrust for power, and the Berlin SA rose in revolt. They sacked the Berlin party headquarters and sent Goebbels fleeing for his life. Only *Der Führer* was able to calm them. Still, he felt uneasy about these ruffians whom he used and despised. They were alienating the army and the police, both of whom he needed. The answer was a telegram to Ernst Roehm, in Bolivia as a military instructor, asking him to come home and take command. Roehm did, effectively organizing and disciplining the SA, and also taking command of the SS, much to the dismay of Heinrich Himmler.

Meanwhile, the tide of misery was rising higher. Nearly 20 million Germans were living at the starvation level. They believed this malevolent mystic when he blamed the Jews and the Communists and the greedy bankers of the democracies for their travail. They eagerly accepted his triune credo of race, sacrifice and heroism as a call to German greatness. As the winter elections of 1932 approached, Hitler and Goebbels organized a singularly vicious campaign against the aging President von Hindenburg. They derided him as stupid, senile and politically naive. Hindenburg got 49.6 percent of the vote and Hitler 30.1, the remaining 20 percent going to the other candidates. It was 0.4 percent short of the absolute majority needed to govern, and another election was held. In this Hindenburg received 53 percent and Hitler almost 37 percent. The old man still held the presidency, but Hitler and the Nazis now made it impossible for anyone to govern. Hindenburg tried to persuade Hitler to accept the post of vice chancellor, but *Der Führer* wanted all or nothing. Reluctantly, with deep misgivings, Hindenburg gave in. On January 30, 1933, Adolf Hitler was sworn in as chancellor of Germany. "And now, gentlemen," Hindenburg cried, almost wistfully, "forward with God!"

Unfortunately, not only for Germany but also for the world, *Herr Gott* was Adolf Hitler.

5. America Before Roosevelt

WHILE THE DICTATORS STRUTTED and rattled their sabers, the democracies slept —none more soundly or serenely than the United States of America. "Back to normalcy!" cried President Harding, cheerfully inane as ever, by which he meant back to the womb of isolationism. However, Harding, unlike Wilson, had not misjudged the mood of his countrymen. They did indeed desire to withdraw from the world, to crawl back into that wide, warm womb from which they had ventured forth, so it seemed to them, with such disastrous results.

"Never again!" became the watchword of a postwar America in which the debunker was hailed as a true prophet. Many of these writers and preachers who sounded the tocsin, "War is the bunk," had actually served in the trenches and had sincerely echoed Mr. Wilson's crusading cry that this was "the war to end all wars." Such patent nonsense is, of course, no more possible than a peace that makes all men peaceful, but it was nevertheless devoutly and deeply believed. And when that same war ended in a bloody stalemate, these same prophets concluded that all wars end that way, moving from this illogical premise—which ignored all prior American history—to the even more irrational conclusion that war solves nothing and is never efficacious. The only solutions, then, were pacifism —and above all isolationism.

Under the three presidents who held office during the Republican ascendancy of 1920–33, isolationism became the keystone of American foreign policy. It was first given expression by Harding when he declared that the nation needed "not submergence in internationality but sustainment in triumphant nationality," and it was this position that helped him to defeat the internationalist Democrat James M. Cox in 1920. Unfortunately, Warren Gamaliel Harding could easily challenge Millard Fillmore for the crown of presidential ineptitude. Like his "big, bow-wow style of oratory"—of which sham Augustan prose the above quotation is a polysyllabic sample—he was himself large, impressive and shallow. His easy morals and vulgar tastes have been celebrated by Alice Roosevelt Longworth, who wrote, after a visit to the White House that had once been her home, that she went upstairs to find that "trays with bottles containing every imaginable brand of whiskey stood about" in "a general atmosphere of waistcoat unbuttoned, feet on the desk, and spittoon alongside." If she had looked downstairs she might have seen Harding's young mistress slipping in the back door and hiding in the cloakroom.

In 1923, with his administration shaken by financial scandals, Harding sought to recover his diminishing popularity through a cross-country speaking tour. Returning from Alaska, he fell painfully ill of what was believed to have been tainted crabmeat, and on the night of August 3 he died of apoplexy.

But isolationism still lived in the political credo of Calvin Coolidge, who became the fifth vice president to move up to the White House. Coolidge has entered American history as a colorless country lawyer whose political career was "a shining example of what inertia could do for a man of patience." His remark "The business of America is business" is frequently advanced as proof of his dullness. Actually, he was an extremely witty man from whose lips wisecracks fell with effortless ease. But Coolidge had long ago learned that Americans of that day did not "cotton" to wise guys, and he had deliberately adopted a safer public pose of bovine solemnity. It worked, and in 1924 Silent Cal was reelected. Unfortunately, it was in his administration that isolationism began to share control of American foreign policy with its ostrich twin, pacifism.

The American Committee for the Outlawry of War was organized in 1921 by the wealthy Chicago lawyer Salmon O. Levinson. He drew to his standard politicians, clergymen and intellectuals of all description. One of them wrote with supreme naiveté: "Humanity is not helpless. This is God's world! We can outlaw this war system just as we outlawed slavery and the saloon." After which, presumably, crime and disease would be marched to the wall. Nevertheless, the Kellogg-Briand Pact, so called after the U.S. secretary of state and the French foreign minister, was signed in Paris on August 27, 1928, with great solemnity and pomp and—at least outwardly—profound cries of gratitude to Almighty God. Under the treaty, the signatory nations renounced war as an instrument of policy and promised to solve all disputes among them "by pacific means." The world's press was ecstatic, and the American poet Robert Underwood Johnson wrote:

> Lift up your heads, ye peoples,
> The miracle has come.
> No longer are ye helpless,
> No longer are ye dumb.

Of the sincerity of the statesmen who signed this so-called epochal document there can be no doubt. Of their perspicacity, of their understanding of human nature, something less may be said. To list the fifteen original signatories is to call the roll of most of the combatants of World War II: Germany, France, Great Britain, the United States, Japan, Canada, Australia, New Zealand, South Africa, Belgium, India, Italy, Ireland, Poland and Czechoslovakia. Later, thirty-one more nations, including the Soviet Union, signed the pact.

Kellogg-Briand bound no one. It was an exercise in noble futility, in peace by wishing. It employed no sanctions and set up no procedure or apparatus for settling international disputes. Worse, it chloroformed the democracies and sent them happily off to sleep convinced that the big bad wolf of war had been banned from the front door. In fact, by late 1928, when it was signed, pacifism-isolationism had become so thoroughly American that it was not even an issue in the presidential contest between Herbert Hoover, the Republican, and the Democrat, Alfred E. Smith, the first Catholic to be nominated for President. What was an issue was Smith's Catholicism. The electorate was told by Republican politicians and Protestant clergymen alike that America's traditional Protestantism was at stake, or fed such absurdities as the warning that if Smith were elected the Pope would bastardize all their children.* Hoover took no part in this outpouring of bigotry; he won without needing it.

Herbert Hoover was eminently unqualified to be president. His reputation was that of a highly successful engineer and a competent administrator who had fed wartime Europe's hungry masses. But this is only to say that—like a soldier —he had dealt all his life in imperatives, and knew little of the art of harmonizing the conflicting interest in a great pluralist society such as the United States. He was no politician. Worse, during his first year in office the stock market collapse triggered the Great Depression, which made domestic problems take precedence over foreign ones. Moreover, Hoover was crippled by an ingrained isolationism —he believed that the systems of the Old World and the New World were hopelessly irreconcilable—and by the doctrinal pacifism of his Quaker faith. He regarded all forms of violence with horror. Thus, the State Department had only the carrot and no stick with which to conduct foreign policy. When Japan invaded China in 1931, opening what it euphemistically called "the China incident" to maintain the myth of a nonwar, Hoover ruled out any threat of the use of force to restrain it. Instead, he called for "moral condemnation," whatever that means. The United States simply would not recognize any changes in China conflicting with either Kellogg-Briand or the American Open Door policy there. Japan feared moral censure about as much as a wolf fears a shepherd's whistle, and since there was no shepherd's stick in evidence, it went merrily ahead with the plundering of the Chinese province of Manchuria. A discouraged League of Nations also declined the Japanese challenge.

Hoover's administration was not only pacifist and isolationist, it was openly antimilitarist, as was most of the country. Officers on duty in Washington were cautioned to wear civilian clothes and to put on their uniforms only for parades or other military occasions. The academic community derided military history as "drum and trumpet hoopla" and all cadets or reserve officer students were mocked as modern Yankee Doodles with pimples on the brain. When Gen. Douglas MacArthur, army chief of staff, submitted his proposed budget to the Senate Armed Forces Committee, he was asked—with a leer and a giggle— "What do you need all that toilet paper for?"

But then it appeared that the beginning of the end of pacifist-isolationism had arrived in the presidential year of 1932 when Hoover was defeated by the fervent internationalist Franklin Delano Roosevelt.

*After his defeat, Al Smith jokingly told some of his intimates that he had sent a one-word telegram to the Holy Father, which said: "Unpack!"

6. Franklin Delano Roosevelt

IF THERE IS SUCH A PERSON as an American aristocrat, Franklin Delano Roosevelt was one. In birth and breeding he differed from the dictators in the way that the rule of law differs from the reign of force.

Roosevelt was the descendant of one Claes Marenszen van Rosenvelt, who arrived in New Amsterdam from Holland around 1648. His father was James Roosevelt, a tall, handsome, blue-eyed man with muttonchop whiskers and a flair for adventure. He had known Sam Houston and marched with Garibaldi. A graduate of Union College and Harvard Law School, he made some excellent investments in coal and railroads, which enabled him to live the life of privilege and possession of the typical Hudson River squire. He went abroad regularly to the watering places of Germany or as a guest in the country houses of Britain. He bred trotters on his Hyde Park estate and was fond of a glass and a good cheroot. He always kept $500 in gold available and he owned a private railroad car which took him to the balls and cotillions of nearby New York City. He differed from other descendants of the Hudson Valley wellborn only in that he, almost alone among them, was a registered Democrat.

James Roosevelt's first wife, Rebecca, died in 1876, leaving him with only one child: James Roosevelt Roosevelt, nicknamed "Rosy." Four years later, James met Sara Delano at a dinner party in New York City. He was then fifty-two, and she was only twenty-six, the same age as his son, and her father was an old friend. Still this tall, handsome girl returned the love of her distinguished suitor, and they were married in the fall of 1880. On Monday, January 30, 1882, James Roosevelt observed in his diary: "At quarter of nine my Sallie had a splendid large baby boy. He weighs 10 lbs without clothes."

The baby was named Franklin Delano Roosevelt and he would be an only child, not quite spoiled by the affection lavished on him by his adoring parents. He grew into a spirited, lively boy who would one day be taller than his father. He was obedient to his strong-willed parents, and yet sturdy enough to rebel against the long hair and velvet suits in which his mother kept him. Franklin was athletic, given to swimming, fishing or boating on the broad Hudson, skating on it in winter or skimming over the snow-covered roads in the little Russian sleigh built for Napoleon III and brought back from the Paris Exposition of 1872 by his father. During the summer the family fled the suffocating heat of the Hudson Valley for the cool breezes of Campobello, an island off the New Brunswick coast. There Franklin learned to handle a sailboat in rough water; or at the Delano house at Fairhaven, Massachusetts, he would ship aboard one of the numerous whaleboats off his grandfather's dock. From the Hudson, the Atlantic and Buzzard's Bay he derived his undying love of ships. But he was also an avid reader, and at the age of nine had begun his famous stamp collection. His education was by tutors, German ones when he was vacationing with his father in the Black Forest, a Frenchwoman named Jeanne Rosat-Sandos at Hyde Park.

The winter of 1887 was spent in Washington, where James took his little boy to the White House to visit President Cleveland. After the Roosevelts rose to go, the president put his hand on Franklin's head and said: "I am making a strange wish for you. It is that you may never be president of the United States."

It was not until 1896 that young Franklin went away to school: to the Reverend Endicott Peabody's famous institution at Groton, Massachusetts, the most exclusive school in America. Peabody was passionately dedicated to the ideal of producing Christian gentlemen of high moral character and sound education. To do so, as he admitted, he was sometimes "a bit of a bully." But he was so successful that applications for Groton usually were filed at birth. Peabody remembered young Roosevelt as a "quiet, satisfactory boy of more than ordinary intelligence, taking a good position in his Form but not brilliant. . . . We all liked him. So far as I know that is true of the masters and boys alike."

It is likely that Roosevelt's charm was a defense mechanism. Older than those in the form, come from a solitary life without experience of formal education, he might have adopted the mask of geniality to protect an inner reserve. Throughout his life those who knew FDR would remark on the enormous affability, garrulity even, which was like a shield protecting his private person. Eleanor Roosevelt would say of her husband's life at Groton: "He knew things that they didn't; they knew things he didn't. He felt left out. It gave him sympathy for people who are left out."

Young Roosevelt was still inconspicuous when he entered Harvard in 1900. He was dismayed not to be admitted to Porcellian, the exclusive club which had welcomed all other Roosevelts, and had to accept a lesser club. Nevertheless, he enjoyed himself in Cambridge, made many lasting friendships and was studious enough to take his degree in three years. While there, he shocked his widowed mother (James died in December 1900)—who had taken a house in Boston to be near her only son—by informing her that he had fallen in love with Eleanor Roosevelt, a fifth cousin once removed, who was nineteen years old. He wanted an early marriage.

Until her engagement to Franklin, Eleanor Roosevelt had led a sad and solitary life. She had seen her father (Teddy Roosevelt's only brother) and two uncles die of drink and self-indulgence. Her mother was a beautiful but severe woman who had called her young daughter "Granny" because "She is such a funny child, so old-fashioned." By such remarks, as though disclaiming responsibility for her daughter's lack of beauty, Anna Hall Roosevelt made Eleanor keenly aware of it, even after Anna died of diphtheria when Eleanor was eight. But now Eleanor had a taste of happiness and she assured her prospective mother-in-law: "It is impossible for me to tell you how I feel toward Franklin. I can only say that my one great wish is always to prove worthy of him."

The engagement was announced in December 1904, after Franklin had entered Columbia Law School, and the wedding took place on March 17, 1905. The Reverend Mr. Peabody came down from Groton to perform the ceremony and "Uncle Teddy" came out from the White House to give away the bride. "Well, Franklin," President Theodore Roosevelt said to the bridegroom, "there's nothing like keeping the name in the family."

Two years later FDR passed the New York Bar examinations, after which the young couple took a belated honeymoon in Europe. Upon their return Eleanor gave birth to the first of six children (one died in infancy) and meekly accepted the role of a dutiful daughter-in-law imposed on her by the strong-willed Sara Roosevelt.

As early as 1907 when he became a clerk in a Wall Street law firm specializing in thwarting the antitrust laws, Franklin Roosevelt had calmly announced to a friend that he wanted to enter politics and intended to become president of the United States. In this he was encouraged by his cousin who *was* president, resisting, meanwhile, TR's attempts to make a Republican of him. Three years later, bored by the "good life" and the snobbery and worship of money among the people of his class, he took his first step in the "betrayal" of them and ran as a Democratic candidate for the State Senate. FDR found that he loved the rough-and-tumble of campaigning. Far from being repelled by the sham camaraderie of political picnics with their beer and clambakes and hot dogs and baby kissing, he took to it like a local fire chief. He was not a good orator at first, chiefly because of the long and exasperating pauses between his sentences. Once he overcame this defect, he improved. His charming, straightforward manner and masculine good looks pleased his audiences. The magic of the Roosevelt name in Dutchess County also helped, and Franklin Delano Roosevelt became only the second Democrat since the Civil War to go to Albany from that district.

In the beginning FDR was not a very popular member of the Democratic delegation. His ardent conservatism was acceptable, because of his obviously sincere dedication to the cause. But his haughty Harvard-Groton manner, his gold pince-nez and his habit of throwing back his head to look down his nose put the stamp of an unspeakable snob on this tall, thin, indubitably arrogant young senator. He was particularly obnoxious to the New York Irish from the Tammany Hall machine. They called him an "awful, arrogant fellow," and branded his ideas "the silly conceits of a political prig." He did not endear himself to Boss Charles Murphy when he led a rebellion against Tammany's hand-picked candidate for the U.S. Senate nor when, in 1912, he sided with Woodrow Wilson in his successful bid for the Democratic nomination and the presidency in 1912. That sweep returned Roosevelt to the State Senate.

But then on Wilson's inaugural day Roosevelt met his newfound friend, Josephus Daniels of North Carolina, in a hotel lobby. Daniels was Wilson's choice for secretary of the navy, and he asked FDR: "How would you like to come with me as assistant secretary of the navy?" Roosevelt's sailor eyes beamed. "How would I like it? How would I *like* it? I'd rather have that place than any other position in public life!" So Daniels cleared the appointment with New York's two senators: O'Gorman the Democrat said FDR was acceptable but Elihu Root the Republican countered: "You know the Roosevelts, don't you? Whenever a Roosevelt rides, he wishes to ride in front."

Franklin Delano Roosevelt was only thirty-one when he came to Washington. His ballooning self-confidence born of early electoral successes bordered on the bumptious, and he early conceived a contempt for the man who brought him there. To him, Josephus Daniels was a landlubber who couldn't tell a bulkhead from an overhead, a ridiculous country editor whose old-fashioned ideas and style of dress made him "the funniest looking hillbilly I have ever seen." Fortunately for Roosevelt, he was roundly rebuked by Interior Secretary Franklin Lane, who told him that he should be ashamed of himself, that if he could not be loyal to his chief he should resign. FDR dropped his parodies and comical imitations of Daniels and instead began to study him, to learn that knowing ships and the sea could not compare to Daniels' skill in getting Congress to grant his navy the needed appropriations. From derision FDR's attitude changed to one of admiration.

But he was still the arrogant, supremely confident patrician when, in 1914, he broke with Tammany Hall to run against Boss Murphy's candidate for the U.S. Senate. Roundly beaten in the primaries, a sobered Roosevelt realized that his career would be better served if he befriended the New York City machine instead of alienating it, and so he dropped his plans to build an upstate anti-Tammany movement and smoked the peace pipe with Murphy. At this time also, Franklin Delano Roosevelt met and fell in love with his wife's social secretary.

Lucy Mercer could trace her pedigree to two distinguished Maryland colonial families, among them the Carrolls of Carrollton, the wealthiest of American families during the Revolution. From them she derived her Catholicism, although the money that she might also have inherited was squandered by her father, a dashing Marine Corps officer. Nevertheless, when Lucy arrived in Washington in 1913—beautiful and charming, pedigreed but penniless—she was gladly welcomed into the capital's social whirl.

To support herself she accepted a part-time position as Eleanor Roosevelt's social secretary. She met FDR and saw much of him socially as well. A lovely young woman such as herself was always in demand at Washington dinner parties, and Lucy was also a welcome guest at the Roosevelt table. During the summer of 1916 when Mrs. Roosevelt was at Campobello with the children, a romance bloomed between Franklin and Lucy. It was encouraged by Alice Roosevelt, the daughter of Uncle Teddy, who often invited the couple to dinner or tea. By the following summer, Eleanor seems to have suspected her husband's infidelity, showing great reluctance to take herself off to Campobello again, going only upon his repeated insistence and the pleas of her children. In 1918, FDR came down with pneumonia, and while he was ill, Eleanor discovered letters from

Lucy in his correspondence. She confronted him with the evidence and threatened to divorce him unless he never saw Lucy again; also offering to maintain a semblance of the marriage for the sake of the children, but again without Lucy. Sara Roosevelt next issued her own ultimatum: If Franklin wanted Lucy, he would get no money from his mother. A penniless politician, as Roosevelt well knew, has rather a dim future, but in those days a divorced politician had no future at all. Still, he seems to have been willing to sacrifice all for Lucy.

Lucy, however, was a devout Catholic who could not or would not marry a divorced man, and after she wed the older, wealthy, and widowed Winthrop Rutherfurd, the affair seemed to have come to an end.

In 1941 Lucy accompanied her ailing husband to Washington for medical treatment. A mutual friend arranged a White House meeting but Lucy refused to go. Shortly afterward her husband died. FDR sent Lucy a note of condolence, she replied—and the relationship was quietly resumed. When Eleanor was away on her many travels, Lucy dined at the White House, where Anna Roosevelt Boettiger took her mother's place as hostess. Her daughter's complicity in the affair magnified Eleanor Roosevelt's bitterness over her husband's infidelity. Rejected in childhood and youth, she had once again been cruelly rebuffed in her maturity.

It is probable that the Mercer affair, which seemed to have ended, was a watershed in the lives of the Roosevelts. For her part, Mrs. Roosevelt became determined to carve out a career for herself independent of her husband, and she became renowned and respected throughout America, eventually the most famous of First Ladies. Franklin, generally regarded in 1918 as a handsome, fun-loving social butterfly who was also a political lightweight, seemed to change overnight into a serious and dedicated aspirant to the presidency. His disappointment in seeming to have lost his beloved Lucy probably had as much to do with this sobering metamorphosis as the dreadful poliomyelitis that struck him down in the summer of 1921.

By 1921, Franklin Delano Roosevelt had become a national figure. His decision to remain on friendly terms with Boss Murphy, while not openly embracing all that allegiance to Tammany Hall implied, had led him to second the nomination of Alfred E. Smith at the Democratic Presidential Convention in San Francisco. He dutifully voted for Smith seven times until the New Yorker dropped out of the hunt. He was then inclined to support William G. McAdoo, Wilson's choice, over Gov. James M. Cox of Ohio, the candidate of the city machines. After Boss Murphy agreed to back Roosevelt for the vice presidency, the Cox-Roosevelt ticket was chosen—but was sharply defeated in November by Warren G. Harding. Nevertheless, FDR's tireless campaigning and stirring oratory had guaranteed that at thirty-nine years of age his was the most promising career in the country.

The following summer FDR spent at Campobello with his family. On August 10 he took his sons sailing. Seeing a forest fire, they went ashore to help fight it. When FDR returned to his cottage, he felt a chill and went to bed. In the morning he found that his left leg dragged and could not support his weight. By nightfall he had severe pain in his back and legs and a temperature of 102 degrees. Eventually, his illness was diagnosed as polio. His fever sank to 100 degrees, but he was paralyzed from the waist down. He never regained muscular power below the waist; by the end of October he was just able to sit up in bed with assistance.

For all the pain and exhaustion and depression that his ordeal caused him, and the suffering which it inflicted on his family, Franklin Roosevelt remained doggedly determined to pursue his political career. In this he was supported by Eleanor, who at last confronted her mother-in-law anxious only for her son's recovery and rehabilitation. The family struggle ended with Eleanor and Franklin triumphant. But FDR would never walk again unassisted. Although he learned to handle canes and leg braces—"my irons," as he called them—he still needed an attendant. To rise from a chair he had to seize the attendant's shoulder.

Franklin Roosevelt never accepted the status of a lifelong cripple. He fought constantly against his limitations, frequently inventing devices that would give him greater freedom of action. One of these was a contraption fitted to the forward davit of his houseboat enabling him to be lowered into the Hudson to swim. In the fall of 1924 when he discovered Warm Springs, Georgia, he swam in the pools daily in the hopeful delusion that their medicinal waters might restore power to his atrophied limbs. Through swimming he developed powerful arms, chest and shoulders, and was able to compete with full-bodied swimmers. He loved the buoyancy that water gave him.

Four years at Warm Springs taught Franklin Roosevelt many things. Association with the rural South opened his eyes to rural poverty. His own suffering and correspondence with other polio victims deepened his sympathy for the underprivileged. His fight against this crippling disease gave him an understanding of the nation's health problems, while his founding of the March of Dimes, which provided the funds for the research that ultimately conquered the disease, increased his faith in concerted action against the ills of mankind. His natural resilience and optimism never deserted him, nor did his charm and personal magnetism. His disability was never a drain on his enormous energy, nor did it interfere with the performance of his public duties after he was elected governor of New York State in 1928 and president of the United States in 1932.

He moved about in a wheelchair until he was confronted by staircases, whereupon he was carried up and down them. On airplanes he was assisted by a special ramp or lift so that he could be wheeled or swung aboard. When on vacation at Warm Springs, Georgia, he drove an open Ford with hand controls. The long flowing boat cloak which he affected probably was chosen to conceal his wheelchair when he posed for photographers, and his jests usually sufficed to deflect attention from his wasted legs. Among reporters and photographers assigned to him there was a gentleman's agreement not to refer to or photograph his useless limbs or to show him as a helpless cripple. Thus, few Americans other than those in public life or the Fourth Estate ever knew that Franklin Delano

Roosevelt was paralyzed from the waist down.

As a man, to quote Oliver Wendell Holmes, Franklin Roosevelt did not possess a first-rate intellect but rather a first-rate temperament. His warm and outgoing nature did not permit too much introspection or reflection, so that he was never a theorist in the class of Jefferson or Lincoln. But he was a whole human being, full of joy and vitality, responsive to the needs of his fellowman and sustained by a simple but deep religious faith.

As the "gentleman's agreement" might suggest, Roosevelt was immensely popular with the press, and famous for the long cigarette holder sticking jauntily from his clenched teeth—a stage prop eventually to be rivaled by Winston Churchill's cigar and the pipe of Joseph Stalin—and the good-humored lift of his belligerent jaw. Capable of deep loyalty, he was also an implacable hater, and it was well said of him: "He never forgot a friend or forgave a foe." He was also an astute politician, capable of remarkable and instantaneous reading of the public pulse, able to reach the people directly through such mediums as the intimate radio talks he called Fireside Chats. In 1932, FDR had muted his internationalism considerably; indeed, economic paralysis at home was and had to be his chief concern when he uttered that electrifying inaugural sentence: "First of all, let me assert my firm belief that the only thing we have to fear is fear itself." Eventually, however, the ruthless march of the dictators would draw his eyes outward again. Even as he took the oath of office, Adolf Hitler was embarked on a campaign to suppress parliamentary rule in Germany.

7. The Rise of Fascism

AT NINE O'CLOCK ON THE NIGHT of February 27, 1933, the dome of the Reichstag, the parliamentary building in the center of Berlin, began to glow. Soon the glow turned to a fiery red, windows burst with a tinkling shower of broken glass, and black smoke poured out of them. The Reichstag was on fire! Within minutes, the night silence was broken by the clanging of fire engines careening through the streets and the sky was crisscrossed with searchlight beams and the streams of water playing against the Reichstag. In the flickering light of the flames, Hermann Goering could be seen running toward the burning building. Sweat poured from his bloated body and his chest heaved with the unfamiliar exertion. Still, he had enough wind to shout himself hoarse with cries against the Communists. They had set the Reichstag afire, he yelled, as a signal for a Red uprising. They must be made to pay!

Reporters crowded around Goering, asking him how he knew that the Communists were responsible. He gave several different explanations, none supported by evidence, and the police quickly dispersed the newsmen. Later, a demented, three-quarters-blind Dutchman named Marinus van der Lubbe was found wandering in Bismarck Hall behind the Reichstag. Goering quickly pounced upon this scapegoat, announcing that incriminating Communist documents were found upon his person. No one took him seriously, since it was plain that van der Lubbe was incapable of any coordinated physical movement. Nevertheless, he was executed.

Actually, the Communists were in hiding at the time and had no reason to burn down the Reichstag. But even as Goering bellowed out his accusations, thousands of Prussian police assisted by thousands more of Hitler's blackshirts and brownshirts began combing the city for Communists. Within a week, 4,000 of them were rounded up and thrown into prison, and Hitler had rid himself of his most dangerous external rival in time for the March elections, in which the Nazis gained 44 percent of the vote and 288 seats in the Reichstag. Now Hitler was ready to move against his most dangerous internal enemy.

Ernst Roehm had done rather too fine a job with the SA. By the time Hitler had been named chancellor, he had reorganized it and raised its strength to 600,000 men. A year later, it stood at 3 million—larger than the Wehrmacht, as Germany's armed forces came to be called. Roehm had grown so in power that he dreamed of commanding the Wehrmacht as well. Like Goering, this pig-faced swaggerer was a habitual drunkard who, when in his cups, could not conceal either his ambition or his contempt for his colleagues—even *Der Führer.* Inevitably, he alienated them all—and especially *Der Führer,* who suspected Roehm of plotting against him with General Kurt von Schleicher, the former chancellor. The generals and admirals of the Wehrmacht also desired the end of Roehm and the curbing of the SA.

But Hitler made no move; rather, with customary cunning he began to heap honors upon his old comrade. At Party Day in Nuremburg in 1933, Ernst Roehm stood beside *Der Führer* in the place of honor. In January of 1934, Hitler wrote a letter of fulsome praise to Roehm, which was published in all the party newspapers. Whatever suspicions Roehm might have had were now allayed and Hitler was content to wait for the opportune moment before he struck. It came in June 1934, when Roehm announced that on doctor's orders he was retiring to Wiessee in the Bavarian Lakes for a rest. Roehm also issued an order to the SA, assuring his men that their numbers would never be reduced. Hitler was infuriated. Aware that the SA would begin its annual leave on July 1, Hitler calculated that Roehm would be at his weakest on June 30 or July 1. On June 29 Hitler flew in his private plane to Godesberg. He was joined by Goebbels, who warned him of an impending mutiny in the SA.

Throughout that stormy night, while the German Maidens of Godesberg stood bravely outside the Hotel Dreesen in the pouring rain to serenade their Führer, Adolf Hitler received a stream of messages by telephone, telegraph and special courier. Himmler called to warn him that the SA had scheduled a meeting for the following day. A bulletin from Munich said the uprising was already under way there. Hitler became excited, exalted even. He would fly to Munich at once to put down the rebellion and seize Roehm. But there were no rebellions. The messages and bulletins were all carefully fabricated by Himmler, not so much to deceive Hitler as to hurry him along a course he had already chosen.

At four o'clock in the morning Hitler arrived at the Brown House in Munich, where he summoned the SA leaders into his presence. He confronted them in a towering rage. "Traitors!" he screamed, tearing off their insignia and placing them under arrest. Now it was Roehm's turn.

About a hundred of Hitler's personal bodyguards, all heavily armed and led by Sepp Dietrich, *Der Führer*'s most trusted officer, were already en route to Wiessee in trucks. Hitler met them outside town. Riding in an armored car and protected by six other cars and the truckloads of soldiers, he made for Roehm's chalet. According to the official version, Hitler stormed into the lobby, overpowered the surprised guards and burst into Roehm's room to find him lying naked in bed with a nude boy beside him. What seems more likely (of the homosexual orgies taking place in Wiessee there can be no doubt) is that Hitler waited for Dietrich and his soldiers to take charge of the hotel before he confronted Roehm and placed him under arrest. Meanwhile, all over Germany in the hideous slaughter that was to be known as the Night of the Long Knives, SA leaders and Adolf Hitler's enemies—private and public, real or imagined—old friends of the early days, veterans of the Beer-Hall Putsch, fellow prisoners in the Landsberg, co-conspirators and old collaborators, churchmen, generals and politicians, as well as the enemies of Himmler, Goering, Goebbels and others, were being put to death. Sometimes the end was merciful, as when General von Schleicher and his young wife were summarily shot to death; at other times it was bestial, as when seventy-three-year-old Gustav von Kahr, the man who had suppressed the Beer-Hall Putsch, was hacked to death with pickaxes. How many were murdered is still not known, certainly hundreds.

Late the following afternoon, Adolf Hitler arrived by air in Berlin. He was greeted by Goering and Himmler, who silently handed him a sheaf of frayed papers bearing the names of those marked for death. Hitler stood between his henchmen, going slowly down the list with a careful finger. Sometimes he looked up questioningly, at which point he would receive hurriedly whispered explanations why this or that victim had not yet been caught and killed.

In the case of Wilhelm Schmidt, a well-known music critic, there was no explanation, merely a mumbled apology. Schmidt had been practicing on his cello when the SS killers burst into his house and dragged him away from his wife and three children, taking him to Dachau where he was tortured and shot. But it was the wrong Wilhelm Schmidt, not the Munich press chief whom Hitler hated and wanted killed. Angrily tossing his head, Hitler gave orders that Schmidt's widow be given a pension. Then, suddenly lifting his eyes to the darkening sky, he shook his head like a man recovering from a blow. But it was not from shock at the size of the death list in his hand, it was from jubilation. Almost to a man, his enemies were gone! But then he bit his lip. Ernst Roehm was still alive.

At ten o'clock next morning, having discussed Roehm's fate with Goebbels and Goering, Hitler gave the order to kill his old friend. To save face, however, he instructed the guards at Stadelheim Prison to give Roehm a loaded revolver so that he could kill himself. Roehm refused. He stood in his cell, naked to the waist, taunting his executioners.

"If Adolf wants to kill me," he snarled, "let him do his own dirty work."

The answer was a machine-gun burst fired through the bars of his cell. *"Mein Führer,"* Ernst Roehm moaned, sinking to the floor with the blood pouring from his hairy chest. *"Mein Führer."*

Adolf Hitler's last enemy was gone, and a month later the last obstacle to his assumption of complete power was removed with the death on August 2, 1934, of President von Hindenburg. Hitler immediately decided to abolish the office of president. Within three hours of Hindenburg's death, he proclaimed himself Führer and Reich chancellor. He was now the chief of the state, the party and the armed forces. His power was greater even than that of Benito Mussolini, whom he had already met and with whom he would eventually forge an alliance. To make it absolute he ordered all his generals and admirals to take a personal oath of loyalty to him. It was administered the same day, and went:

"I swear before God to give my unconditional obedience to Adolf Hitler, Führer of the Reich of the German People, Supreme Commander of the Wehrmacht, and I pledge my word as a brave soldier to observe this oath always, even at peril of my life."

Next, Rudolf Hess told the nation: "By this oath we again bind our lives to a man, through whom—this is our belief—superior forces act in fulfillment of Destiny. Do not seek Adolf Hitler with your brains; all of you will find him with the strength of your hearts. Adolf Hitler is Germany and Germany is Adolf Hitler. Germany is our God on earth." All over Germany the masses roared back: "Heil Hitler!"

And still the democracies slept.

Perhaps it would be fairer and more accurate to say that the democracies were "distressed" rather than slumbering. The Depression that had begun in the United States spread throughout the industrialized world, trailing that wake of misery that was to be Adolf Hitler's good fortune. In Great Britain during 1930–31, unemployment tripled from 1 million to nearly 3 million. British financial credit all but vanished. So did the traditional iron nerve of that steady seafaring island race. In 1933, the young students of the Oxford Union adopted the infamous Joad Resolution, introduced by a professor of that name, which declared: "That this House will in no circumstances fight for its King or Country." Such pacifism impressed Mussolini, who remarked: "These men are not made of the same stuff as Francis Drake and the other magnificent English adventurers who created the Empire. They are, after all, the tired sons of a long line of rich men—and they will lose their Empire." Britain was also distracted by the abdication of King Edward VIII in order to marry the twice-divorced American, Mrs. Wallis Warfield Simpson. This dilemma divided and distracted Britain as had no event since the General Strike of 1926. From this internal preoccupation of 1936, the English turned to another but more joyous one in 1937: the coronation of Edward's brother as King George VI. But the successive governments of Ramsay MacDonald, Stanley Baldwin and Neville Chamberlain were marked by a spirit of timidity and inertia.

France also was distracted by the Depression and by the recurrent crises endemic to its multiple-party system. A series of political vendettas ultimately brought the right and the left into open battling on the streets. Eventually, the Popular Front, a leftist coalition of Radical Socialists, Socialists and Communists, was formed under the Socialist Léon Blum. It reduced the working week from forty-eight hours to forty, while the dictators were raising theirs, with no corresponding deduction in wages. This was supposed to lower unemployment, but actually increased it. Blum's introduction of compulsory arbitration of wage disputes and nationalization of banks and the munitions industry also proved to be unsuccessful experiments for which the nation would pay, and their failure toppled Blum's government. Another leftist government also fell and Édouard Daladier became the next premier. Daladier was the son of a baker who had served in the trenches and won his officer's bars there. He became a history teacher and then a legislator who was boosted up the political ladder by a wealthy and titled mistress, the Marquise de Crussol. Sophisticated Parisians often wondered aloud what the marquise saw in Édouard Daladier—a big, florid-faced, sloppy and clumsy man.

Paul Reynaud, the leader of Daladier's conservative opposition, was also his opposite in other ways. Where Daladier had been a poor provincial, Reynaud had been born into one of the wealthy families that still ruled France. Short at five feet two inches, he was a dapper and athletic man, cocky, as small men often are, and highly cultivated. Paul Reynaud also had help from a ladyfriend, the influential, wealthy and ambitious Countesse Hélène de Portes. Such was France and its leaders of the middle thirties, a quarreling congeries of right and left, of labor and capital, of Church and anticleric, of militarist and pacifist, all so absorbed in their mutual hostility that they did not seem to feel the heat of the volcano building beneath their feet.

Early in 1935 it became clear that Benito Mussolini sought to begin building his new Roman Empire by seizing the helpless kingdom of Ethiopia on the east coast of Africa. Fifty members of the League of Nations, led by Britain, did little to prevent the aggression. Anthony Eden, Britain's minister for League of Nations affairs, told the assembly that the invasion could be stopped by cutting off Mussolini's oil supplies. But the ministers demurred. So deep was the horror of war dwelling in the hearts of most of them that they imposed instead deliberately ineffectual sanctions on materials that Italy either possessed in quantity or did not need to make war. Britain alone might have deterred *Il Duce*. The British fleet was based in Alexandria in four times the strength of the Italian navy, and could easily have turned back the Italian troop transports making for the Suez Canal, or even destroyed them if it came to a fight; but Prime Minister Stanley Baldwin in his own sincere desire for peace feared to take any action that might provoke a war. Even the stirring appeals of Emperor Haile Selassie of Ethiopia failed to move these fainthearted ministers. The slender, black-bearded emperor's calm and quiet dignity, his brave refusal to submit to Mussolini's territorial demands, earned for "the Lion of Judah" worldwide admiration, but elicited from the League only a moral condemnation of Italy.

Such empty censure seemed to *Il Duce* a guarantee of noninterference, and on October 3 he ordered 200,000 Italian troops, with 50,000 pack horses and 10,000 trucks, to invade Ethiopia from the Italian colonies of Eritrea and Somalia. The Ethiopians were brave but poorly trained, and only a fifth of Haile Selassie's 250,000-man army possessed modern weapons, including 16,000 rifles and 600 machine guns secretly supplied them by Adolf Hitler. *Der Führer* wanted to confront a weakened Italy when he moved against Austria.

Italian air power was decisive. *Il Duce* had 400 aircraft, while Haile Selassie had only thirteen, of which but eight took off, and these without arms. The emperor's troops were also stricken and demoralized when Marshal Rodolfo Graziani sprayed them with phosgene and mustard gas. Nevertheless, the Italians soon stopped singing, saving their breath to stagger along mule tracks and stream beds weighed down by 50-pound packs and their weapons in temperatures as high as 140 degrees. But they kept advancing, chiefly because 30,000 Italian engineers had managed to build thirteen bridges and 300 miles of new roads. En route, the Ethiopians struck at them repeatedly in misguided mass attacks; they would have done better by adopting the tactics of guerrilla warfare, harassing tactics in which they excelled, and which, joined to the enemy's ordeals of terrain and weather, would certainly have eroded their numbers and will to fight. By May of 1936, the capital at Addis Ababa was under siege and Emperor Haile Selassie had fled aboard a British warship. On the warm night of May 9 a perspiring Benito Mussolini appeared on the balcony of the Palazzo Venezia. Silver trumpets pealed and a twenty-one gun salute was followed by an even more thunderous roar from the throng that crowded the plaza with eagerly upturned faces.

"Blackshirts of the revolution," *Il Duce* cried, "Italian men and women, at home and throughout the world, hear me. . . . Italy has at last her Empire . . . a Fascist Empire."

Still the League of Nations did not move, even when, in 1937, Emperor Haile Selassie entered the assembly to be greeted by the whistles, boos and obscene jeers of Fascist journalists in the balcony. At last the sight of the Lion of Judah gazing at them with quiet contempt moved Nicolas Titulescu of Romania to leap to his feet with the infuriated cry: "*À la porte les sauvages!* Throw the savages out!" They were indeed removed—none too gently—and that was the extent of the League's chastisement of Italy. At home, the journalists were decorated by Benito Mussolini, along with those generals glorying in a war that had taken a so-called first-rate modern army seven grueling months to subdue a backward, fourth-rate kingdom. But *Il Duce* had not only shown the world how ineffectual the League of Nations was, but also how decadent the democracies had become, a demonstration that was not lost upon his "friend" in Berlin.

That same year the coal-rich, German-speaking Saar voted 90 percent to return from France to Germany. Next, Hitler repudiated all the terms of the Treaty of Versailles and openly created his new air force, the Luftwaffe (Air Weapon). In the spring of 1936 he mounted the biggest bluff of his career: His troops marched into the demilitarized zone of the Rhineland. They were received with great rejoicing, but the news of their arrival caused widespread consternation in France and Great Britain. Hitler himself was terrified. As he admitted later: "The forty-eight hours after the march into the Rhineland were the most nerve-racking in my life. If the French had then marched into the Rhineland, we would have had to withdraw with our tail between our legs, for the military resources at our disposal would have been wholly inadequate for even a moderate resistance."

France, possessor of the largest army in the world, backed by Britain, commanding the most powerful navy, blustered and postured. In wrath, the French appealed to the League of Nations and all their allies. Foreign Minister Pierre-Étienne Flandin warned the British: "It is your last chance. If you do not stop Germany now, all is over." Brave words indeed, but perhaps they were a screen for the French habit of taking counsel from British pacifism. France *could* have stopped Hitler on its own. But when *Der Führer,* who actually could field no more than four brigades, threatened to send in six divisions—that is, a factor of about 90 to 8—the democracies collapsed. "After all," remarked Lord Lothian, summing up the British position, "they're only going into their own back yard." Back yard, yes; but now the French city of Strasbourg was once more under German guns, and the parade of German demands had only begun.

In that same year in Spain, Generalissimo Francisco Franco raised the standard of revolt against the leftist Republican government. Thus began the savage and bloody Spanish Civil War, in which both Hitler and Mussolini and Premier Stalin of the Soviet Union seized the opportunity to train their troops in real combat. *Der Führer* and *Il Duce* both sent men and arms to Franco, while the Soviets subverted the Loyalist cause and eventually took it over. Although the democracies were generally sympathetic to the Loyalists, they once again stood still, fearing to provoke World War II. They adopted a position of strict neutrality.

"Neutrality" was also by then an albatross hanging around the neck of Franklin Delano Roosevelt. In 1934, the "revelations" of the Nye Committee, headed by the isolationist Senator Gerald Nye, seemed to demonstrate on the basis of highly specious evidence that America entered World War I "to save the skins of American bankers who had bet too boldly on the outcome of the war." This was a ridiculous simplification of what was at best an arguable claim. But it was also exactly what the country wanted to hear, and because Nye's charges seemed to give a scholarly or scientific cast to the debunking movement, he appeared to have proved that wars were fought to fatten profiteers and munitions makers. Nye's widely publicized hearings inspired neutrality legislation, which placed an embargo on arms to all belligerents, ordered all belligerents who bought arms in America to pay for them on delivery and transport them in their own ships (cash and carry), banned loans to belligerents and forbade American citizens to travel on belligerent ships.

Such a law passed in 1917 would certainly have prevented American entry into World War I; but in 1936 and after, it merely assured the dictators that the Anglo-French alliance could not count on American assistance. In the meantime, Franco triumphed in Spain and the Japanese drove ever deeper into China. The United States did no more than protest when the Japanese with contemptuous deliberation sank the American gunboat *Panay* in the Yangtze River. Only the prospect of being denied American scrap iron and oil compelled the Japanese to apologize and pay an indemnity.

Even Franklin Roosevelt was submitting to an antimilitarism born of pacifism and isolationism. When Congress cut the army's budget, he concurred, ignoring the pleas of Secretary of War George Dern and General MacArthur. Both men came to the White House to make personal, emotional appeals. Dern warned that it would be a "fatal error" to stint national defense while Nazi Germany was obviously rearming and Japan was growing more daring. FDR, who did not enjoy being lectured, replied with a characteristic tongue lashing that left Dern white and trembling. Now MacArthur lost his temper.

"When we lose the next war, Mr. President," he cried, "and the last American boy lying in the mud with an enemy bayonet through his belly and an enemy foot on his dying throat spits out his last curses, I want the name not to be MacArthur, but Roosevelt!"

FDR turned livid. His massive shoulders heaved and his big hands grasping his desk were white-knuckled as he struggled to come erect on his paralyzed legs.

"You must not talk that way to the president!" he roared.

MacArthur stood up, apologized, and offered his resignation. Turning, he walked stiffly toward the door. Behind him he heard Roosevelt, exercising his amazing self-control, remark in a friendly tone: "Don't be foolish, Douglas. You and the budget must get together on this."

Outside the White House, Dern gleefully exclaimed to MacArthur: "You've saved the army." The chief of staff didn't answer. He was vomiting on the White House steps.

MacArthur had indeed saved the army, and the other services as well: after this confrontation Roosevelt became more openly concerned with national defense and the dictators.

In 1937, FDR called for a "quarantine" against aggressor nations. If international lawlessness was not checked, he warned, "Let no one imagine that America will escape, that America may expect mercy, that this Western Hemisphere will not be attacked." Americans, however, were still not listening. Instead, they heeded the relentless isolationist call that came thrumming out of the Midwest. Powerful groups such as the America First Committee, organized by Col. Robert McCormick, publisher of the influential *Chicago Tribune,* and many Midwestern industrialists, clergymen and politicians preached the doctrine that America was blessed by two great oceans serving as moats and must never again cross either to fight. Nor were many Americans especially outraged by the activities of the pro-Nazi German-American Bunde that drilled in SS-like uniforms up and down the Eastern Seaboard.

No one, that is, but the Jews of North America, horrified by what was happening to their brethren in Germany. Hitler had begun to take his vengeance in 1933. At Nazi instigation, a wave of violent anti-Jewish demonstrations erupted, to be followed by an official decree banning Jews from public employment and from the medical and legal professions. Admission of Jews to the universities was also restricted. In September 1935, Hitler published his Nuremberg Laws, stripping Jews of their civil rights and establishing degrees of Jewishness. A "full Jew" was one with four non-Aryan grandparents; a first degree "mixed breed" had two non-Aryan grandparents; a second degree "mixed breed" had one. Full Jews were deprived of German citizenship and forbidden to marry Aryans. They became less than slaves and anyone with a grievance against them might satisfy it without fear of punishment or restraint. To the Nazis merely to be Jewish was a crime. There was no escaping retribution; no act of renunciation was possible. Probably the most famous demonstration of this inescapable fate concerned the German-Jewish philosopher Edith Stein. She became a Catholic nun, taking refuge in a convent in Holland. There she was hunted down, seized and sent to die in the concentration camp at Auschwitz.

Gradually the pogrom against the German Jews escalated, culminating on November 9, 1938, in *Kristallnacht,* or Night of Broken Glass, so called because of the shattering of thousands of Jewish shops across the country. Two days earlier, a seventeen-year-old Polish Jew named Herschel Grynszpan had walked into the German embassy in Paris and fired fatal shots at Ernst von Rath, a youthful third secretary. Actually, Rath had little or no admiration for Hitler, yet when he died of his wounds, *Der Führer* pounced upon his death as the signal to unleash the pogrom he had been preparing. Hordes of angry mobs smashed shop windows, pouring into thousands of stores to loot them and then burn them down. Synagogues went up in flames. Jews were hunted down and butchered. In less than twenty hours, damage estimated at 23 million marks had been done and an unknown number of Jews murdered.

By the end of 1938, Hitler had attained all the objectives of his program: the complete exclusion of German Jews from public life. Under his pressure, Italy and Hungary also enacted anti-Semitic laws. The only alternative left to these Jews was to accept the policy of forced emigration and leave the country.

Christianity also felt Hitler's wrath. A faith preaching brotherhood of man under the fatherhood of God was anathema to a leader preaching the gospel of faith in himself and racial supremacy. Therefore Protestants and Catholics were also persecuted as well, and the campaign against the Catholic clergy became notorious for its obscene cunning. Hitler did not strike at the body of Catholicism, but at its soul. Priests and nuns were hauled into court to face false and foul charges, which a lackey press dutifully circulated around the country. Ultimately, however, as war approached and Hitler realized that almost all the men he would need for his armies were Christians, the campaign against their faith was quietly dropped.

Nevertheless, his pogroms and persecutions had so horrified and sickened the outside world that many hitherto-closed eyes were opened, and many of the best minds and noblest souls of Germany were driven out of the country, to the eventual benefit of the democracies in which they sought refuge and also to the detriment of a German people consequently left ever firmer in the grip of the monster. It was astonishing how this race "of poets and philosophers" had been enchanted by a Machiavellian spellbinder. It was as though his own baleful nature had come into communion with some dark barbaric spirit still slumbering beneath the veneer of a civilized people. Hitler himself sometimes sensed the malign power he possessed, or that possessed him. Albert Speer, his architect and eventually the Nazi industrial czar, has told how he sat with Hitler at Obersalzberg, silently watching twilight darken into night. Suddenly Hitler spoke, musingly: "There are two possibilities for me: To win through with all my plans, or to fail. If I win, I shall be one of the greatest men in history. If I fail, I shall be condemned, despised and damned."

8. Germany Expands

THE YEAR 1938 was fateful for Europe and the world. Only nineteen years previously Prime Minister David Lloyd George of Britain had warned his Versailles colleagues of the folly of ringing Germany round with small buffer states, some of them with no experience of self-government, all of them containing large masses of Germans. Here was the racial tie, like an unseverable umbilical cord, with which Hitler might draw these states inside his Third Reich, and in 1938 he began to seize it to launch his program of *Anschluss,* or annexation.

The techniques would become familiar. Nazi agents inside the target countries were to excite the *Anschluss* aspirations of the German communities, to undermine the existing government, with no small assistance from German radio broadcasts, and to create the crisis that would give Hitler his excuse for the takeover.

Hitler had tried a coup in Austria three years earlier, when about 150 Austrian Nazis in army uniforms invaded the Chancellery, murdered Chancellor Engelbert Dollfuss and tried to proclaim a Nazi state. They were captured, eleven were hanged and most of the rest given long prison sentences. In February 1938, however, Hitler relied more upon himself than foreign agents. First he secured from Benito Mussolini a promise that he would not interfere in the subversion of his northern neighbor. Next, Austrian Chancellor Kurt von Schuschnigg was invited to Obsersalzberg. To his incredulous dismay, Schuschnigg was treated like a captive, bullied, made to fear for his life and forced to sign a document tantamount to the surrender of his country to Germany. German troops then streamed over the border, and with Austria firmly in Hitler's fist, the people voted almost 100 percent for *Anschluss.*

Hitler now cast his covetous eye on the Sudetenland of western Czechoslovakia, an area inhabited by Germans. He announced that he would "protect" the Sudeten Germans against the "atrocities" of the Czech government. And here, at last, it seemed that the democracies had awakened to the danger. Prime Minister Neville Chamberlain of Great Britain telegraphed Hitler requesting a meeting. *Der Führer* agreed to meet him at Berchtesgaden. At sixty-nine years of age, never having flown in an airplane before, Chamberlain made the four-hour flight from London to Munich.

Neville Chamberlain was one of those rich men's sons who go into politics looking for something to do. With his long, lanky figure clad in statesman black, his protruding teeth and scraggly gray mustache, and the rolled black umbrella that he grimly grasped everywhere he went as though he were wielding Excalibur, he might be taken for the epitome of determined futility. He had risen to the top of the Conservative Party chiefly by quiet intrigue and loyal if undistinguished service. Chamberlain believed himself to be a master of foreign policy, conversant not only with the problems of Europe but those of the world. His overweening self-confidence suggested to him that he could solve them, and in this he fancied himself the great peacemaker destined to be honored and revered by posterity. This decent, well-meaning but self-deluded man also had one enormous defect: He trusted people and believed what they said. In dealing with an accomplished liar like Hitler, this was a fatal flaw.

Hitler greeted him, smiling broadly, the soul of charm. Chamberlain asked for a "man to man" talk. Hitler agreed. They withdrew to a private chamber, a bleak, sparsely furnished room. Hitler began to speak, his words punctuated by the rattle of the rain against the windowpane. Chamberlain listened politely. Then his eyebrows rose. Hitler was shouting, pouring out a catalog of the crimes of Versailles. Two thirds through his speech, *Der Führer* exploded in rage. He became the legendary Carpet Chewer, screaming, pop-eyed, apoplectic, cursing the names of Czechoslovakia and its president, Dr. Eduard Beneš. Chamberlain was stunned. He had never seen a statesman rave before. Hitler again changed themes, conferring, this time, a purring accolade upon himself and Germany. Two hours and a half passed, and the sound of the rain and Hitler's voice still filled Chamberlain's ears. He had spoken scarcely half a dozen sentences. At last, after Hitler warned that if a world war were to erupt over Czechoslovakia, he wanted it to come now, while he was still young, Chamberlain interrupted to insist that the use of force must be excluded.

"Force!" Hitler repeated angrily. "Who speaks of force? Herr Beneš applies force against my country in the Sudetenland. Herr Beneš mobilized in May, not I. I shall not put up with this any longer! I shall settle this question in one way or another. I shall take matters in my own hands!"

Chamberlain was visibly alarmed. "If I have understood you aright," he said, "you are determined to proceed against Czechoslovakia in any case. If this is so, why did you let me come to Berchtesgaden? In the circumstances, it is best for me to return at once. Anything else now seems pointless."

Hitler was startled. He was unaccustomed to being corrected. He adopted a soothing tone and spoke of self-determination for the Sudeten Germans. Chamberlain said he could not discuss such a proposal without consulting his colleagues. He would return home immediately—Hitler looked up in dismay—but come back to Germany again—Hitler smiled in relief.

The British prime minister went home convinced that Hitler would invade Czechoslovakia to gain the Sudetenland, starting another world war if necessary. He did not realize that *Der Führer* was again bluffing the democracies, that he knew he was not yet strong enough to fight France, Britain and Czechoslovakia, possessor of the finest small army in Europe, easily held mountain defenses and the giant Skoda arsenal, second only to Germany's own Krupp works. Nor could he risk provoking the Soviet Union, the traditional power broker of Eastern Europe. But Neville Chamberlain still had his childlike trust in Hitler. "I got the impression that here was a man who could be relied upon to keep his word," he said, a few days after his own ordeal at the Berghof. He believed *Der Führer* when he said the Sudetenland was his last territorial claim in Europe, and in the interests of peace he was prepared to give it to him.

So were France and the U.S.S.R., Czechoslovakia's allies. The French were simply terrified of Hitler. Premier Daladier knew that for all its superiority in numbers, the French army was poorly trained and equipped, and its air force was a travesty. The Popular Front's shortened work week and nationalization of the munitions industry had done their debilitating work. Worse for France, the Spanish Civil War was winding down, with the tide turning in favor of Franco's forces. France, flanked on the Mediterranean by *Il Duce,* facing *Der Führer* in the east, would soon confront still a third Fascist dictator—*El Caudillo* (The Leader)—across the Pyrenees. What was needed was time, and the sellout of the Sudetenland would provide that time. The Soviets also informed a disillusioned and disheartened President Beneš that if France would not fight for Czechoslovakia, neither would they. There was nothing for this gallant, forsaken little country to do but bow its head and extend its arm for the amputation.

It took place at Munich on September 30, 1938. Chamberlain, Daladier, Hitler and Mussolini were present. The Soviet Union was not invited and the Czechs were there only to sign. A memorandum was drawn acceding to German demands on the Sudetenland, and it was this that the Czechs signed. "They wished," they said, "to register their protest before the world against a decision in which they had no part."

But the world wasn't listening. It heard instead only Hitler's renewed pledge to make no more territorial acquisitions and the cheers that greeted Neville Chamberlain upon his triumphal return to London. He read to the ecstatic crowd a pledge of everlasting Anglo-German friendship signed by himself and Hitler. Wielding his familiar umbrella with one hand, with the other he waved this document in the air, crying: "I believe it is peace for our time."

To some other members of his party it was rather "war for our time." Winston Churchill said, "We have sustained a total and unmitigated defeat,"* and Duff Cooper resigned as first lord of the Admiralty. In the main, however, Chamberlain was supported by both his party and his people. Meanwhile, Nazi agents were already at work subverting Czechoslovakia for the ultimate takeover. On March 15, 1939, Hitler entered Prague in triumph. Without firing a shot, merely by running a magnificent bluff, he had annexed an entire country together with its army and its arsenal and secured his southeastern flank. Nor was Hitler the only hyena gorging on the carcass. Within twenty-four hours Poland demanded from Czechoslovakia and received the frontier district of Teschen.

But *Der Führer* had already turned north, demanding and receiving from Lithuania the port of Memel on the Baltic. Next, Mussolini, jealous as the ignored junior partner of the newly formed Rome-Berlin Axis, seized the little state of Albania across the Adriatic Sea, prompting President Roosevelt to ask both Führer and Duce to promise not to take more land for the next ten or twenty-five years. "A result of infantile paralysis!" Mussolini sneered.

In truth, Roosevelt's own country did indeed seem paralyzed. That same year the spirit of pacifism-isolationism had culminated in the ludicrous Ludlow Amendment introduced in the House. It proposed a constitutional amendment making any declaration of war subject to a popular referendum! The prospect of a threatened democracy springing not to arms but to the ballot box must have seemed comical indeed to both Duce and Führer; and if the infamous Joad Resolution at Oxford was the work of silly boys under the influence of a pacifist professor, the Ludlow Amendment was the considered wisdom of an American representative. When it was returned to committee by a House vote of 209–188, it had fallen only 21 votes short of passage, halfway home to becoming the law of the land. Therefore, as much as America might deplore Axis excesses, as she had done with Japan, she was still not going to do anything about them. Her head was still in the sand and her heart was still in her mouth, and thus she convinced the dictators that she would stay out of any European war.

That war was assured when, on March 31, 1939, France and Britain guaranteed Poland against aggression.

Adolf Hitler was indubitably the chief cause of World War II. But it is also true that in the beginning, after he took power in 1933, he did not actively seek

*Winston Churchill's constant misuse of the verb "to sustain" probably accounts for today's widespread abuse of it as a synonym for receive or suffer.

it. He was only, in a sense, spurred along the war path by the collapse of opposition to him of the German General Staff, the "victory fever" that infected him after his early successes and inflated his ego and the complaisant, accommodating attitude of the Western Allies. Hitler's original and true purpose, announced in November 1937, was to obtain *Lebensraum,* that is, living space for Germany's expanding population. Without it, he believed, Germany would never be self-sufficient, especially in food. To buy food abroad would consume Germany's foreign exchange, and also make it dependent on foreign supply, which could be cut off in time of war. The thinly populated countries of Eastern Europe, often a prize of foreign conquering armies, included vast, fertile farmland.

Western statesmen generally misconstrued Hitler's expansion into the East —particularly into the abominated Soviet Union—as a diversion of danger from the West. They did not speak publicly of this view, but only in private conversations and in talks with Hitler himself. In November 1937, Lord Halifax, second in command of Neville Chamberlain's government, gave Hitler to understand that he would have a free hand in the East. In February 1938, Sir Neville Henderson, British ambassador in Berlin, gave much the same assurance. That same month, Anthony Eden resigned as foreign minister after Chamberlain's response to his protests was to advise him to "go home and take an aspirin." He was replaced by the Germanophilic Lord Halifax.

With such encouragement, Hitler prepared to implement his plans for *Lebensraum,* only to find them opposed by the General Staff. They protested his occupation of the Rhineland because they feared the French army; they were apprehensive of the risks of sending troops to Franco in the Spanish Civil War; and they were against his march into Austria. But these protests and objections were minimal in comparison to the solid wall of opposition erected by the generals against the move into Czechoslovakia. General Ludwig Beck, the chief of staff and a constant critic of Hitler's intuitive style of leadership, drafted a memorandum arguing that *Der Führer*'s aggressive *Lebensraum* program would lead to worldwide catastrophe and German ruin. Beck's objections were read to a conference of top generals, who approved them and then sent them to Hitler—who ignored them. Beck resigned, and became the chief architect of a generals' plot to overthrow Hitler. Because of the Czech capitulation, however, the conspiracy fell apart, leaving the generals in disarray and Hitler, now in complete command of the Wehrmacht, pluming himself on his own genius. "Most people have no imagination," he cried. "They are blind to the new, the surprising things. Even the generals are sterile. They are imprisoned in the coils of their technical knowledge. The creative genius stands always outside the circle of the experts."

Prior to his entry into Prague, Hitler had already turned to Poland with what seemed moderate demands: return of part of the port of Danzig and a free passage to East Prussia through the "Polish Corridor." They were refused. The Poles had an exaggerated idea of their own strength. Also at that time there had risen in the West an incredible spirit of euphoria. It was born of the belief that their rush to rearm, during the respite granted since Munich, had placed the dictators on the defensive. Chamberlain spoke privately of a new disarmament conference and said hopes for peace had never been so sanguine. It was then that Hitler invaded Czechoslovakia. Chamberlain was crushed, then outraged. On March 29, he sent Poland an offer of support against "any action which threatened Polish independence."

History may be searched for an about-face so complete and so fraught with consequence. Chamberlain had placed his country's fate in the hands of a foreign, faraway government, and one never celebrated for its stability. Colonel Joseph Beck, the Polish foreign minister, later admitted that he decided to accept the British offer between "two flicks of the ash" from the cigarette he was smoking. So casually do statesmen make decisions involving the life or death of millions!

Britain, of course, did realize that there was no way that the Western Allies could come to Poland's aid except through its neighbor, the U.S.S.R., though Chamberlain did make some half-hearted motions in that direction. But the Soviet Union quite understandably wanted no defensive arrangements except on its own typically stringent terms. Moreover, the nations of Eastern Europe have always regarded Russian reinforcement as a prelude to occupation. Thus, nothing came of these dilatory talks; and yet the Anglo-French guarantee of Poland remained in force.

It stunned and infuriated Hitler. Here, the Western Powers who had been so accommodating were now without warning openly hostile. And they were also rearming. If he waited, it might be too late. So he must quicken his steps! But to do so might bring the Soviet Union in against him and so ignite another world war: for Germany, another war on two fronts, dreaded *bête noire* of Hitler's dreams. It seemed also to Hitler that the cool calm Britain of history would never have embarked on such a provocative course without first having secured the Soviets' approval. So he must detach the U.S.S.R. from this supposed alliance, he must swallow his hatred and fear of communism and approach with a smile the one man in the world he despised as the scum of the earth.

Joseph Stalin.

9. Joseph Stalin

IOSIF VISSARIONOVICH DZHUGASHVILI (known to the world as Joseph Stalin) was the lowest born of all the dictators who tormented humanity in the first half of the twentieth century: the son of peasants, whose parents and all their ancestors within memory had been serfs owned by a local princely house. His birthplace was Gori in the province of Georgia.

Georgians are usually small, the male average being only a little more than five feet tall; Stalin at a full-grown five feet four inches was above average. Longevity was another astonishing characteristic: to live to a hundred years or more was not uncommon among Georgians.

Joseph Stalin was born on December 9, 1879, the fourth son of Vissarion Dzhugashvili and Ekaterina Geladze. But Soso, or "Little Joe," Joseph's Georgian nickname, was to be the family's only child, his three older brothers having died in infancy. Soso was also certainly legitimate, a status which could not be easily claimed by his oldest brother. When Ekaterina was a young and gorgeous red-haired servant, she was seduced by a prominent czarist official. She became pregnant, and when this began to be obvious, a "father" for the child was sought. He was found in Vissarion Dzhugashvili, a hard-drinking shoemaker from the village of Didi-Lilo. A shop in nearby Gori was bought for Vissarion; and it was here that he came to live with his pregnant bride.

When Vissarion was drunk, he would beat Soso, and also Ekaterina. Brutality was common among a class only recently released from debasing servitude. Soso, however, was not resigned to such abusive custom, and he came to hate his father; he was overjoyed when, in his fifth year, Vissarion went to live alone in the capital of Tiflis, some sixty miles away. Vissarion died in 1890, his end hastened by drink. Other details of his life are either unavailable or obviously fabricated, both certainly on the orders of his dictator son. Stalin was always ashamed of his father, and he probably also knew about the circumstances of his parents' marriage. Where he could, he suppressed or rewrote uncomplimentary facts.

Vissarion's departure left Ekaterina with the task of providing for Soso as well as raising him. She was more than equal to it, sewing, baking bread, working as a maid. She loved her only child dearly and dreamed of his being ordained someday in the Georgian Orthodox Church. She fed him well, keeping him neat and clean and warmly clothed in winter. Ekaterina often sang folk songs to her son, discovering to her delight that he had excellent pitch and shared her love for music.

Soso was growing into a strong and healthy boy when, at the age of seven, he fell seriously ill of smallpox, the dreaded killer of Georgia. Ekaterina prayed, promising the Lord that if the boy were spared, she would dedicate him to the Church. Soso did live, chiefly because of his health and stamina and his mother's devoted care. But he emerged with his face pockmarked for life. In the files of the Okhrana, the czarist secret police, he was called *Ryaboi,* "the Pockmarked One." Upon Soso's recovery, his mother set him to work learning the Russian language, a requirement for enrollment in the Gori theological school. When he was on his way to mastering it, he was accepted. To pay for his education, Ekaterina went to work at the school as a seamstress, laundress and charwoman.

Soso entered the Gori school just before his ninth birthday, both the physical and mental superior of his classmates. His love of swimming in the Gori rivers had given him a powerful, broad-shouldered torso, and he was already so at home in the water that no one in the school and few men in Gori could compete with him. But his short legs were thin and he had a curious way of walking, almost apelike, swinging his long arms and swaying. His face was narrow and elongated, covered with both pockmarks and freckles, with a long, thin nose and penetrating black eyes glinting with cunning. Like most of his classmates, he had thick black hair.

Sullen in mood, curt in speech, and always eager to pick a fight, he was far from being beloved; but because of his physical prowess (Soso became the school wrestling champion), he was respected and feared. Besides his pleasure in giving pain, he could laugh at the misfortunes of his fellows or sneer at their successes. To Soso, a friend was a person who submitted to his will. In games, he always insisted on being captain of his team and usually led it to victory.

Soso excelled in his studies, never coming to any class unprepared. He was also a voracious reader, who frequented a bookshop specializing in works forbidden by the school. After he had read Marx and Darwin, he became an avowed atheist.

Incredibly, three dictators—Mussolini, Hitler and Stalin—all three the sons of devout, doting mothers at whose knees they learned to recite their prayers, all three educated in church schools, and all emerged as atheists and persecutors of religion. But Soso was clever enough to shield his true beliefs from the Russian fathers who replaced the Georgian teachers in 1890, when he was eleven. Generally he had his teachers' esteem as a superior student, and his years at the theological school were formative and without major incident. There was one near-tragic accident: Soso fell beneath a horse-drawn carriage and lay close to death for some time. Blood poisoning complicated his condition, but again he survived: this time with a malformed left arm two to three inches shorter than the other. Stalin was always deeply conscious of this deformity, as he would be of his height when he joined the company of taller Russians and Europeans. When photographed with taller men, he always insisted on being taken seated and at an angle that would reduce the difference in height; and it was a rare picture that did not show him from his right side with his left arm behind his back.

Soso was six months short of fifteen when he left the Gori school with honors. After his vacation during the summer of 1894, he would enter the Tiflis Theological Seminary for six more years of study and eventually be ordained a priest.

Tiflis Theological Seminary was the most prestigious institution of learning in Transcaucasia. But this drab four-story building had also housed a hive of fiercely nationalistic Georgian students. Russian rectors had been beaten and murdered by them. Student strikes were not uncommon. From its portals issued a stream—not of Orthodox priests sworn to uphold the twin pillars of throne and altar on which the czarist system rested—but of fire-eating revolutionaries sworn to hack them both down. Until 1900, three hundred students had matriculated there, but only fifty were graduated. In 1901 there were only eleven graduates.

By 1905 the entire school counted a paltry forty students. Why had this religious institution—even more than the Jesuits turning out their Voltaires and James Joyces—been so signally consistent in producing the opposite of its purpose? Probably because of its dogmatic, domineering, spying, prying administration and because of its repressive prisonlike atmosphere.

The school day began at seven o'clock in the morning with church services often lasting three or four hours and ended with a strictly enforced five o'clock curfew. Reading newspapers or attending the theater were forbidden. Any writing even suggestively critical of czarism was prohibited, along with the works of Marx and Engels, Victor Hugo and Balzac, Dostoevsky and Tolstoy, Darwin and Thackeray or any thinker in whom the inquisitor might discover the tiniest evil seed of democracy or socialism. To be caught reading seditious literature was among the most serious offenses, and both rectors and inspectors spent more time prying open desks or lockers in search of it than they did in classrooms or in improving the curriculum. Finally, the food was abominable, so unnourishing as to produce much sickness and even death.

Into this dreadful regimen came fifteen-year-old Soso, a student so brilliant that the seminary granted him one of the half-scholarships allowed to only eighteen pupils. With this, Soso paid only half the cost of his education, clothing, food, books and school supplies. Almost immediately, he hated the place. He detested the monks and came to despise his fellow students. He felt deeply wounded by their jibes directed against his shortened left arm, his pockmarked face and his short stature. He hated the seminary as a symbol of that authority which he was gradually coming to regard as his oppressor. People who ruled over others were his enemies, not because of any altruistic hatred of despotism but because they possessed the power that *he* wanted.

Soso's hunger for power became evident very soon after he began his studies. A Marxist youth group of ten students including Soso had been secretly formed with a program designed to correspond to the six-year course of studies. Soso deliberately broke it up. His biting sarcasm and coarse comment made it impossible for the group to function, and after it had fallen apart Soso formed his own secret society "of parrots who repeated everything said by their little dictator." By this time Soso had also found a subtle but supremely efficient instrument of self-advancement: denunciation. Because the monks rightly suspected the students of constantly scheming and spreading seditious ideas throughout the seminary, they relied heavily upon a system of student spies. Soso saw clearly and quickly that an informer could ingratiate himself with the faculty. Denunciation was a wonderful vehicle for vengeance, for ridding oneself of a rival, for grubbing higher marks. He used it cleverly and constantly during his career at the seminary, as he would use it with rather more deadly effect in his climb to absolute power.

Stalin's official biographers have said that he became a conscious Marxist at the age of fifteen. This is not true. Soso did not move toward Socialist Democracy —as it was called then—until he was eighteen. During the intervening years at the seminary, his only cause was himself; himself and his personal vendetta with the authorities. Because he was often scorned, he withdrew into himself, forsaking the games and sports of which he had been so fond. His contacts with his classmates were confined to secret circulation of a handwritten anticzarist and antiadministration magazine. Otherwise, he read, read, read. His truly insatiable appetite for learning could not be satisfied by his teachers, bound as they were by an obscurantist curriculum and mentality. Actually, all that they could really give him were Church-related subjects, and this was all that he remembered in later years. Like the young Adolf Hitler, Soso did indeed love the liturgy, probably because he sang so well. All of his speeches and writings would be in the rising-falling, repetitive rhythms of the litany, like the monotonous clanging of the censer's chain.

Probably no other student in the seminary had his room or his desk or locker searched so often. Eventually, Soso's excursions into the forbidden *Deshavaya Biblioteka* (Cheap Library) got him into trouble. In 1896, he was caught reading Victor Hugo and sentenced to solitary confinement. A year later he was again apprehended with seditious literature, and this time punished by much longer imprisonment. It was in this last incarceration that Soso sank into despair, experiencing what the Spanish mystic St. John of the Cross has called "the dark night of the soul." Alone in that dank, dark cell he felt completely outcast—a social leper. Every hand was raised against him, and there was no escaping the persecution. Society, then, was doing this to him. Mankind, rotten, degenerate, depraved mankind, was his enemy. From this experience dates Joseph Stalin's association with what the world now calls Communism.

Shortly after his release, Soso met a young revolutionary named Lado Ketskhoveli. Lado was in hiding from the police. He had led the student strike at the seminary in 1893. Five or six years older than Soso, he seemed to have great leadership abilities and Soso admired him. In response, Lado shrewdly exploited the youth's bitterness. He provided Soso with illegal Marxist literature and introduced him to other young Marxists in Tiflis. He taught Soso the arts of agitation and propaganda and soon had him evangelizing students and workers in the city. Predictably, Soso's academic standing began to deteriorate. All of his free time between three and five was spent in such work in the city and his nights among the student cells. He became a favorite among the Tiflis railway workers and helped to organize their strike on December 14, 1898. The walkout was put down by police and Cossacks wielding whips and the flat of their sabers. Dozens of workers were wounded and jailed, although none was killed. Soso seemed to enjoy the bloodshed. It left him strangely calm and relaxed. A trait was emerging that was to mark him for the rest of his life. He loved bloodshed. Not his own, of course, because as Trotsky would remark years later, Stalin was not without courage, "but he used it economically." No. Stalin loved "the swish of whips and sabers." Three years later, in his first published article, he put forward the thesis that street demonstrations ending in bloodshed advanced the cause of communism. Whips and sabers would swish among workers and "curious onlookers" alike, "irrespective of age, sex and even class. Thereby, the whip lash is rendering us a great service, for it is hastening the revolutionisation of the 'curious onlookers.' It is being transformed from an instrument of taming into an instrument for rousing the people."

Soso had now found a movement through which he could sublimate his hatred. His declining standing in classroom and comportment was snowballing. He could not care less for the seminary or the priesthood, and he showed it.

On May 27, 1899, Iosif Vissarionovich Dzhugashvili was expelled from the Tiflis Theological Seminary. He was not quite nineteen. He had entered the seminary almost five years ago, intending to become a priest; but like so many seminarians before him, he came out instead a flaming revolutionary.

Much of Stalin's boyhood reading had been in Georgian nationalistic literature, and he had become fascinated by a legendary hero named Koba, "the Indomitable." He chose Koba for his pseudonym but did not really use it until he left the seminary and plunged into revolutionary activity. He did not, however, join his Tiflis colleagues immediately. From May 1899 to December 1899, there is an inexplicable seven-month gap in Stalin's career that is either skipped or glossed over by his official biographers. With good reason: An overwhelming weight of circumstantial evidence makes it almost undeniably certain that during that period Koba was being trained to be an agent of the Okhrana.

The Okhrana was a supremely efficient counterintelligence and counterespionage organization devoted to the czar and to the preservation of the czarist system. It had its agents planted in practically all the revolutionary organizations throughout the Russian Empire. Sometimes it had two, neither of whom knew of the existence of the other. If one were exposed, the other could continue to report. The Okhrana was so thorough that it regularly read Lenin's mail while he was in exile. If it were written in invisible ink—as it frequently was—the Okhrana would raise it to visibility and then reduce it again. Very little of the movements and plans of the eventual Father of the Revolution were unknown to the Okhrana. It could boast that, through its international network of agents, it knew before the American ambassador in St. Petersburg knew the details of the Treaty of Portsmouth which Theodore Roosevelt had negotiated in the New Hampshire city to end the Russo-Japanese War. As early as 1905 it was opening and reading U.S. Embassy mail, as well as the correspondence of other embassies. All this was due to the network of agents who either infiltrated revolutionary cells as bona fide comrades or who, under the guise of trustworthy employees, gained access to foreign secrets.

The Okhrana sought neither fervent patriots nor fiery revolutionaries to be agents. Rather, it looked for down-and-outers, men who were in despair, or frustrated, or hated society, or thirsted for revenge, or needed money or would do anything for money, or who had been caught in compromising situations. To maintain an agent's "cover" among colleagues who had become suspicious, the Okhrana would go so far as to arrest him, jailing or exiling him. Basic intelligence was a must: The Okhrana could not be bothered with stupid or illiterate peasants or workers. Other requirements were some education and youth. Older men were set in their ways and not so easily trained. It is doubtful whether many young men in the province of Georgia were as eminently qualified for the role of secret Okhrana agent as was Iosif Vissarionovich Dzhugashvili.

Without a degree, Koba seemed to have no future. With his fierce pock-marked face and deformed arm, the beard and sideburns he had grown and his rude manners, no bourgeois enterprise would have accepted him. Manual labor he detested, and he had no skills. Besides, he was penniless, hungry and largely friendless. His mother still living in Gori had not a kopeck to spare and his associates in the Tiflis Marxist circle also had only enough for themselves. Although it is possible to doubt that Koba became an Okhrana agent, all the signs point toward his complicity. Perhaps he salved his conscience by rationalizing that he would be in a position actually to *help* the revolution by passing along valuable inside information or tip-offs on impending raids. Thus, it is most likely that Koba spent his unexplained seven-month absence under the instruction of an officer from the Georgian Okhrana—among the best in the empire—who tutored him in the arts of betrayal and provocation. When his education was completed, an excellent cover was found for him as an employee of the Tiflis Geophysical Observatory. Here he was among devoted revolutionaries, fellow classmates and rebels from the Gori and Tiflis schools. Here he was not an observer-meteorologist as the official biographers state, but merely a bookkeeper earning a modest 20 rubles a month. Soon he was distributing illegal pamphlets and copies of Lenin's newspaper, *Iskra* (The Spark). Where or how he got them no one knew or cared. Next he organized an underground printing press, printing 700 inflammatory leaflets a day. He became a fiery orator. At the age of twenty he gave his first public speech at a May Day outing typically held in the country far from the eyes and ears of the police. "We have grown so strong," Koba trumpeted, "that next year we will be able to conduct our *Mayevka* not in mountain hollows, but on the main streets of Tiflis." This roar of the mouse raised quite a few eyebrows among the older, more experienced Marxists of Tiflis, all of whom deplored violence, preached a gradualist approach to the revolution and feared to expose themselves to identification. Koba's belligerence, along with the money for his *Iskra* copies and his printing press and paper, most likely came from the Okhrana. Both were suited to its objectives of cowing the workers and smoking out the city's top revolutionaries.

The moment to do so, however, was delayed until 1901 by the reluctance of the leaders to make a foolish move and by Koba's very junior status in the movement. By March of that year, however, Koba had learned the names and location of all the Tiflis chiefs, of those who were wanted and those heretofore unknown, of those who were sympathetic to the cause but not active, assisting it either with money or safe and secret meeting places.

On the night of March 21–22, the Okhrana arrested scores of prominent intellectuals and leaders—among them Lenin's disciple, Victor Kurnatovsky, who had unwisely befriended Koba—and more than fifty top worker-organizers. Shoe stores, taverns, libraries, newspaper offices, the observatory, and the homes of sympathizers coughed up much of the substructure's secret files as well as lists of important members. There was one exception: Koba. While this mammoth raid was going on, he was strolling the streets, gulping down the fresh spring air. He returned to his room in the observatory only after the police had searched it and found nothing. With admirable foresight—not to say forewarning—Koba had hidden his own seditious literature under rocks beside the Kura River. On that memorable strolling night when the underground apparatus of Tiflis was all but destroyed, he had not bumped into a single colleague or visited a single hangout. Yet, in the eyes of the Okhrana the raid had not been completely successful, for there were many leaders of the workers still at large.

This deficiency was rectified that same year when Koba fulfilled his promise to plant the Red flag in the streets of Tiflis. Excited and encouraged by him, some 2,000 workers battled police and Cossacks in the center of town. Koba was himself on the sidelines, safe from a chance bullet or the wrath of a Cossack unaware of his true allegiance. The demonstration was quickly squelched in blood. More than seventy leading workers were wounded or arrested. The hospitals and jails were full. It would be years before the workers' movement would recover. And Koba? He was exhilarated, eagerly looking forward to another demonstration the following year. Joseph Iremashvili, Koba's oldest friend, remarked: "I realized that the blood that had flowed during the demonstration had intoxicated him."

But Koba's days in Tiflis were numbered. His intrigues and slanders against the older party chiefs landed him before a party court, the first ever convened in Georgia to try a comrade. He was expelled. Undaunted, he moved on to Batum, an oil-refining center of some 35,000 people on the Black Sea. He arrived in November 1901, and immediately exhorted the workers to follow the example of their comrades in Tiflis. They did. During early March 1902, workers aroused by Koba's inflammatory oratory began to demonstrate. On March 7, thirty were arrested. But not Koba. Next day, Koba led 300 more in a march to Batum Prison, where they demanded the release of their comrades. They too were all arrested. But not Koba. On the following day, some 2,000 workers fought the police and Cossacks in the streets. Koba on the sidelines was once again a cheerleader. Fifteen workers died, fifty-four were wounded and over 500 more were arrested. But not Koba.

Still free and unscathed, he busied himself arranging a revolutionary funeral for the slain workers, and also in composing an elegiac for them. In his best liturgical style, he wrote: "All honor to you who have laid down your lives for the truth! All honor to the breasts that suckled you! All honor to you whose brows are adorned with the crown of martyrs, and who with pale and faltering lips breathed words of struggle in your hour of death! All honor to your shadows that hover over us and whisper in our ears, 'Avenge our blood!' "

But now suspicions began to form against Koba. Even Noi Zhordania, founder and chief of the Georgian movement, suspected that the young firebrand might be an agent provocateur. There was talk of trying him. Conveniently for him, with true Okhrana finesse, Koba at this point was arrested, jailed and sent into exile. After only a month in Siberia he "escaped," returning to Georgia in 1904 to resume his career. In this year also, he married his first wife, Ekaterina Svanidze, who came from his father's village of Didi-Lilo. The following year she gave birth to a son, Yakov.

But Koba was now so busy with party affairs that he had little time for home life, although he seems to have been happily married. He was rising in the Georgian party hierarchy, and in 1905 he traveled to the Bolshevik Conference in Finland as a Tiflis delegate. In 1906 he was in Stockholm for the Fourth Congress of the Social-Democratic Workers Party, and in 1907 traveled to London for the Fifth Congress.

Koba was now twenty-seven years of age. His record during those eight years as a revolutionary strains credulity and contradicts reality. Without funds, he supported himself and his wife and child, and traveled 23,000 unharassed miles through territory hostile to revolutionaries. Presumably during these travels he needed money to eat, buy clothing and pay for transportation and lodging. He obtained passports—so difficult and sometimes impossible for his colleagues to secure—with remarkable ease. Until he began his travels his revolutionary activity was of benefit to no one but the Okhrana; and when blood was shed, it satisfied only them and himself. It seems permissible to suggest that if he had not been a secret agent of the czar, then those eight years were either marvelously fortunate and charmed, or else curious and suspicious.

When Koba came to the London Conference of the Russian Social Democratic Labor Party in 1903, he was an unknown nobody. But then, to the surprise of almost everyone, Lenin obtained for him the title of consultative delegate. Why? First, Lenin was the leader of the Bolshevik section of the Communist Party. The Bolsheviks were in the majority and they sought forceful seizure of power. In the minority were the Mensheviks, who advocated a peaceful path to power in cooperation with the bourgeois. Georgia was overwhelmingly Menshevik. Koba, a Bolshevik, would help Lenin expand his foothold there. The second reason is that Lenin was badly in need of funds. His sources of money just prior to the London Conference had been drying up. These were the intelligence services of Japan, Germany and Austria, all of them, especially the Japanese during the Russo-Japanese War, eager to support anyone who would cripple the czar. By the time of the London Conference the entire party was dead broke, both sections having had to borrow money to provide return tickets for their comrades. Lenin had already met Koba in Berlin and had listened with hesitant approval to his scheme to replenish Bolshevik coffers by robbing the Imperial Bank in Tiflis. Now almost penniless in London, with the Mensheviks shutting off his illegal sources, Lenin turned in despair to Koba. His obtaining for him the title of consultative delegate was proof of this decision: Koba was utterly without power to contribute to the conference anything of a political, ideological or theoretical cast. He differed from the intellectual Lenin as a dagger differs from a book. And he knew that if he could deliver as he promised 300,000 rubles— about $2 million by today's standards—he would have climbed quite a few rungs up the Bolshevik ladder of leadership.

Just before Koba left for London for what turned out to be the turning point of his career, his wife Ekaterina died. He was heartbroken. His friend Iremashvili tells of meeting him at the graveyard following the Orthodox funeral rites:

"At the cemetery gate, Koba firmly pressed my hand, pointed to the coffin and said: 'She is dead and with her my last warm feelings for all human beings have died.' He placed his right hand over his heart: 'It is all so desolate here inside, so unspeakably desolate!' "

From the day he buried his wife, Joseph Stalin indeed lost the last vestiges of human feeling. His heart filled with the unalterably malicious hatred which his cruel father had begun to engender in him while he was still a child. Ruthless with himself, he became ruthless with all people.

After the funeral, Koba returned to Tiflis to organize the robbery of the Imperial Bank of Tiflis on Erevan Square: 300,000 rubles in cash, plus stocks and bonds. It was done with great bloodshed among the Cossack guards as well as scores of innocent people.

At first Lenin and his Bolsheviks regarded the robbery as a great success. But then, gradually, it seemed rather an unqualified disaster. The cash was in 500-ruble notes with known serial numbers. Bolshevik agents who tried to cash them were arrested, among them the future Soviet foreign minister, Maksim Litvinov. The stocks and bonds were not negotiable. Worse was the worldwide outrage provoked by the senseless slaughter of innocent civilians, even the whole-sale onslaught upon the police and Cossacks. Lenin's reputation was badly damaged, and for a time it seemed that the Bolsheviks were finished. Once again there appears the sinister trademark of the Okhrana: A bloody Communist coup turns out to be a crippling boomerang. Once again, where was Koba? Not even on the sidelines, but this time nowhere to be seen. He regarded himself as the "supreme commander" of the operation; the "field commander" was a young friend of Koba's from Gori, an extremely courageous but not overly bright Armenian youth named Semën Arshakovich Ter-Petrosyan. However, there can be no positive proof of provocation, any more than in previous incidents; when Stalin ordered the invasion of a stubborn Georgia in 1921, he destroyed the records that might prove it.

Nevertheless, this most notorious "expropriation" made Koba's fortune, if only because it brought him close to Lenin. Nor were there any more suspicious incidents to raise the eyebrows of the comrades. From 1907 until 1917, the year of the Russian Revolution, Koba was arrested five more times and given six more exiles. In all, he served out one exile, escaped five times and received one amnesty.

These were the credentials of a true Bolshevik, and none bore the Okhrana imprint. Evidently Koba had decided to take his chances with the Bolsheviks. He was now carefully climbing more rungs toward the pinnacle of power. When the Revolution did come, and after Lenin and his Bolsheviks eventually became the new masters of Russia, Comrade Koba was waiting with quiet expectation in the wings.

Koba was in exile in Siberia when the Revolution was begun in St. Petersburg in February 1917. By then he had started to call himself "Stalin" (Man of Steel), although in conversation his friends still referred to him as Koba. He hurried back to what was now called Petrograd, and in July insinuated himself deeper into Lenin's esteem by helping him to escape the agents of the Provisional Government and go into hiding in Finland. After Lenin returned and overthrew the Provisional Government in the October Revolution, he appointed Stalin a commissar in the first Bolshevik government. Eventually, he would become a member of the all-powerful Central Committee.

It seems that, except for Lenin, Stalin was still hated and distrusted by all who knew him, especially Leon Trotsky, who had come back from Canada to organize the Red Army. Because he was so repellent personally, he was shunned: for his crudeness, for his appearance in his rough blouse and short legs stuffed into felt boots, for his pockmarked face and drooping mustache and what Trotsky called his "yellow eyes" peering balefully about him, for the foul pipe he smoked habitually and would put out at no one's bidding, for his lack of humor, his wounding sarcasm, his halting, imperfect Russian. Of all these ugly traits, his crudeness was probably the most repulsive. His everyday speech was studded with scatology and obscenities. He abused even his mother, the one person besides his dead wife whom he appears to have loved. Once, in 1927, when he arrived in Tiflis and saw her waiting to greet him in the station, he exclaimed in an attempt at humor, "You here too, old whore?" To his friends being waited on by his daughter, Svetlana, he cried banteringly: "Well, my friends, who do you think is fucking her now?"

Stalin was also despised as an intellectual parrot incapable of generalizing on his own. True enough, he had been a bright boy and an omnivorous reader and had spent those five years at the seminary. But juvenile sharpness and undisciplined reading and the Orthodox Church's narrow curricula had in no way made him the equal of thinkers such as Lenin or Trotsky. To them and their disciples Stalin's stock of ideas was threadbare, most of them seeming to come from cheap Socialist pamphlets written for workingmen. Friendless as he always was, he would come alone to meetings deliberately late, sitting in solitary silence in the back of the room listening to the other speakers—far more skilled in oratory than himself—splitting their dialectical hairs or debating one another. At last, he would rise and offer a summation or critique, as though he were chairman of the meeting, always solving a dispute with some hackneyed quotation from Marx. Invariably, he took the position of the majority. After he embraced Leninism, he became the soul of orthodoxy, repeating the Master's ideas but rarely grasping Lenin's deeper insights. Yet Stalin's ability to hold his tongue and make no mistakes born of impatience or impetuosity was a powerful asset. He also possessed an iron nerve and imperturbable calm. When he was in jail and the prisoners were forced to run a gantlet of club-wielding soldiers, Stalin walked calmly between them reading a book.

Nevertheless, as Trotsky observed, Stalin could be very sparing of such courage. When he took command of the defense of Tsaritsyn against the White Army, he spent most of his time on the other side of the Volga, guarded by a rifle regiment and an armored train. In one instance, he arrested an entire district staff, who were forced aboard a barge, which was then sunk in the Volga. Anyone who opposed or challenged him was a "traitor" or a "White Guard plotter." He threw into battle a division formed of untrained recruits. They were immediately captured, and after they were freed, Stalin ordered their execution. By his excesses he lost 60,000 men and allowed an inferior White Army of 26,000 to surround the city. When Tsaritsyn was finally relieved by a cavalry division, Stalin was across the river poised for flight. Nevertheless, three years after the Revolution, Joseph Stalin ranked number four in the Party hierarchy, behind only Lenin, Trotsky and Bukharin. He had passed such recognized chieftains as Kamenev, Rykov and Tomsky.

How? Ordinarily any careerist seeking to rise to the top of a structured organization must be championed by a powerful patron. But by 1920, Lenin had grown extremely suspicious of Stalin. He warned one woman not to volunteer to work for Stalin: "Stalin is a vindictive person. Who knows unto which generation his vengeance will carry? And you have children." This from the mouth of the man who had "made" Stalin. But by 1920, the warning was already too late. Stalin was moving slowly but surely toward victory in what he cynically called "the battle for the throne." No committee was too small or ineffectual for him to chair. Some day, in some way, it would be of use. Inexorably, his load of administrative work grew larger and larger. His puppets were everywhere taking positions of power, replacing men who either disappeared or had been denounced.

Stalin also had help inside Lenin's own office. Nadya Alliluyeva, daughter of Sergei Alliluyev in whose house Stalin lived, worked there as a decoder of messages. Frequently she warned him of plots against him, which he was able to forestall. Stalin in 1920 was nearly twice as old as Nadya. Nadya was very pretty, graceful, gentle, rosy-cheeked. Nevertheless, he seduced her. She became pregnant. As a true Communist, her father had always upheld the principle of free love; however, when he found out about his daughter's condition, he remembered his bourgeois origins and demanded that Stalin marry Nadya. He did, and she gave him two children: Vassily and Svetlana.

Marriage did not deter Stalin from trying to possess any woman he desired, and men invited to dine with him always left their daughters at home and tried to excuse their wives—fearing the fate that befell Lazar Kaganovich.

In Stalin's presence, Kaganovich unwisely boasted of the beauty of his sixteen-year-old daughter, Maya. Stalin asked him to bring her with him to dinner at his dacha. With misgivings, Kaganovich obliged. After dinner he rose to leave, taking Maya's hand. "Let her stay a few days," Stalin said. She did, returning to her parents only after she had become pregnant. By this time, Stalin had become all-powerful. He had already taken his two greatest strides forward. On April 2, 1922, a plenum of the Central Committee elected Joseph Stalin General Secretary, or "Gensek." When the vote was announced, many delegates looked at each other in disbelief and dismay. An attempt was made to annul the election on the ground that the Congress had no authority to elect a general secretary. But Stalin had his allies, the powerful Comrades Kamenev and Zinoviev. They were out to block the autocratic Trotsky's march toward Lenin's chair by placing a general secretary in his path. What had they to fear from that crude dunce of a Koba? So the election was upheld and Stalin became the Gensek.

Here again was one of Stalin's great assets: the contempt in which he was held by his rivals. With such competition, who needed a champion? Trotsky in his ballooning self-esteem couldn't conceal his derision of "the gray blur," as he called Koba. Trotsky, Zinoviev, Kamenev and Bukharin all regarded him as a country cousin, ripe for the plucking by city slickers such as themselves. But those who thought they could use Stalin against Trotsky had fatally underestimated Koba's ambition, will and skill at empire building. Far from becoming his masters, they had been unwitting pallbearers at their own funeral. Stalin gradually expanded the powers of the Gensek. He gained more and more influence over the Party apparatus as well as the far-flung provincial parties. All the documents and directives pouring out of the Secretariat bore the signature "J. Stalin." Local leaders in the provinces, districts and capitals of the national republics were given the impression that "J. Stalin" possessed great personal power. Thus, while Lenin's health gradually declined, while all eyes were focused on the dashing, brilliant Trotsky as the obvious heir apparent, that dunce of a Koba like a giant octopus had spread his administrative tentacles throughout the Party.

Lenin died on January 21, 1924 (not of poison given him by Stalin, as has been charged). On May 22, the eve of the Thirteenth Congress, a plenum of the Central Committee was convened in the Kremlin. Lenin's Testament was read to the members. In it he asked that Stalin be removed from the General Secretariat because he was rude and abused his power. It was a bombshell, almost certain to settle the dictator's mantle around Trotsky's shoulders. Copies of the Testament were distributed to all present, and it was agreed that it should be read to all delegates of the Thirteenth Congress and also published. Stalin made no comment. Nor did he waste his breath cursing Lenin. Instead, that night agents of the GPU went careening around Moscow in high-powered automobiles, stopping at all the apartments and hotels housing members of the Central Committee to seize their copies of the Testament. It was never read to the Party members and never published; and Zinoviev saved Stalin's skin by assuring the Central Committee that the Gensek had changed his ways and was no longer the ugly creature described by Lenin.

Now the Soviet Union was in the hands of a triumvirate: Zinoviev, Kamenev and Stalin. Among them, they defeated Trotsky. Next, Stalin broke away from the other triumvirs and joined the right wing led by Bukharin, Rykov and Tomsky. Zinoviev and Kamenev then went over to Trotsky. But these three were no match for the Gensek, who had them expelled from the Party. Four years later, during 1928–29, he turned against Bukharin, Rykov and Tomsky. He was now alone atop that pinnacle of power which his ambitious and ruthless soul had coveted for decades. He was the dictator of all the Russias, more powerful and far more murderous and malevolent than all the czars before him, his commissars easily as rapacious and self-seeking as the ousted boyars of the czars. With such power, Stalin was now ready to seize the Cossack's fallen whip and flog his backward nation into the ranks of the advanced countries.

If Stalin had another passion to match his lust for power, it was his hatred of "backward" Russia. "We were beaten by the Mongols because we were backward," he said. "We were beaten by the Anglo-French because we were backward. We were beaten by the Japanese and the Germans because we were backward." In his eyes, this fixation on old ways and worn tools was symbolized by the Russian peasantry, particularly the well-to-do kulaks (literally "fists," used of comparatively prosperous peasants) of the Ukrainian breadbasket. In 1929, he decided to liquidate them and "expropriate" their lands to make way for the collectivization of agriculture. Officially, there were 1 million kulak farms. But this figure did not take into account that many of the kulaks had fought with the White Army, emigrating after its defeat. Many others, not wishing to sit still for execution, had sold their holdings and gone to live in the city. So the blows delivered by Central Committee agents fell not on the heads of all the kulaks as planned, but on many ordinary muzhiks (peasants). Any hard-working farmer, along with his family, could now be classified as a kulak. Soon the poorer peasants joined the sport of despoiling them. Neighbor robbed neighbor. Within a year, 3 million "kulaks" were torn from their lands. Some were shot, while others were dragged off to die in prisons or forced-labor camps. Some statisticians say that as many as 12 million peasants "disappeared" from the Ukraine during the pogrom. Nor does this take into account the millions who starved to death during the famine that followed the collectivization of the farms. The Soviet Union, which had been a grain-exporting nation under the czars, became, and still is, a grain-importing nation. Cattle production in the year 1985 still has to reach the czarist level of 1917.

Stalin next turned to the industrialization of the Soviet Union with the same ruthless vigor, but with rather less blood and agony. Instead, while he decreed the development of heavy industries on a gigantic scale, the toll was more in misery than in life. He transported 25 million muzhiks from the farms to the cities, pressing them into this procrustean bed to make workers of them. Their suffering was extreme, in severe shortages of consumer goods, in a harsh industrial discipline and in a brooding, despairing sense of loss at having been wrenched from their traditional way of life among the fields and streams and customs of rural Russia. Nevertheless, Stalin was much more successful in industrialization than in collectivization.

Joseph Stalin had never really concealed his pleasure in murder and vengeance. In 1923, he had said to Kamenev: "To choose the victim, to prepare the blow with care, to slake an implacable vengeance, and then go to bed . . . there is nothing sweeter in the world." Here was an echo of the credo of another supreme tormentor of men, Genghis Khan: "The greatest pleasure is to trample on the bodies of your enemies and to hear the lamentations of their women."

In the thirties, with Trotsky in exile and soon to perish with a Stalinist assassin's ax in his head, with all the other old Bolshevik enemies in disarray, Stalin began to clean house. He started by settling personal grudges. Among the first to go were his brother-in-law, Aleksei Svanidze, and his wife, who had raised Stalin's first son in their own home. His present wife's brother-in-law, Stanislav Redens, was arrested and imprisoned. Although tortured, he refused to sign the admission of guilt as "an enemy of the people" that Stalin customarily demanded to justify his executions. If the Gensek could not stand people more intelligent or talented than himself, he also abhorred a brave man. Redens's refusal to crack, even under such refinements of cruelty as electric shocks, upset Stalin. He couldn't sleep. He needed that all-important public "confession." At last, he just had Redens put quietly away. Now Stalin's wife became troublesome. She reproached him for murdering their friends. Nadya Alliluyeva also died. Mysteriously. Stalin put it out that she had killed herself, but Abel Yenukidze, a prominent Party leader, claimed that he had found her body with a strangler's finger marks still on her throat. This was unwise of Abel, because Cain-Stalin, as Trotsky called the Gensek, also put him away. There is not enough space in this chapter to list all of Stalin's personal victims—including Lenin's wife, Krupskaya, whom he probably poisoned.* Adolf Hitler's sudden swift butchery in the Night of the Long Knives was but a ripple of red in comparison to the river of blood that flowed in Stalin's U.S.S.R. for ten long years.

Twelve members of the first Soviet government lived to see the year 1937. Stalin killed eleven of them and he himself was the twelfth. During the height of his infamous "purge," of the 504 men elected to the Central Committee by four Congresses 1925 to 1934, Stalin killed 375. Thickening the stream of old Bolsheviks delivered to the torturers of the Lubyanka Prison were those veterans such as ambassadors and other far-away officials whom Stalin lured back to Moscow. Incredibly, only a few such as Stanislav Redens had the courage to face the reality: that Stalin could *never* be trusted. One old Georgian comrade who was being tortured to "confess" to a catalog of crimes, including being a "British spy," Stalin's favorite label for his special enemies, made the courageous reply: "I have known Stalin for thirty years. Stalin won't rest until he has butchered

*Alexander Solzhenitsyn's three-volume *Gulag Archipelago* gives a detailed look at the atrocities perpetrated in the forced-labor camps.

us all, beginning with the unweaned baby and ending with the blind great-grandmother."

Like a roll call of the heroes of communism, the chief Bolsheviks were marched to the wall: Zinoviev, Kamenev, Bukharin. . . . Then the military: the entire high command and almost all the senior officers, either to the wall or to prison camps. First and foremost, the cultivated, intelligent Marshal Tukhachevsky, the chief of staff—talented Tukachevsky, with his flair for the violin and, to Stalin, his insufferable military skill. Tukhachevsky was the kind of man who was anathema to Koba, and he liquidated him along with his unfortunate friends, his musical colleagues, his daughter. Of the five Soviet marshals, Stalin killed three; of the four fleet commanders, another three. When a friend of Marshal Semën Budënny remarked gloomily, "They're taking everybody, one after another," Budënny replied: "Don't worry, they won't touch us. They're only taking the smart ones." Indeed, the intelligent, the able, the experienced—some 82,000 of them—were swept away to make room for the inept, the fawning and the untrained. Teen-age shavetails with fuzzy cheeks were commanding battalions and captains in their early twenties led divisions. Like the cuckoo fouling its own nest, Stalin in his frenzy of hatred and revenge emasculated his armed forces; and this on the eve of the calamitous war that Marshal Tukhachevsky with remarkable foresight and accuracy had predicted Hitler would begin in the spring of 1941. But Stalin ignored this warning. Instead, he believed Hitler! Thus the most accomplished liar and murderer in the history of humanity put his faith in the word of his only living rival for supremacy in such skills, informing Hitler that he would indeed be delighted to discuss with him a new partition of Poland.

10. The German-Russian Nonaggression Pact

NO ONE IN AUTHORITY in the Allied camp suspected that Hitler would propose marriage to Stalin; indeed, Hitler's silence following the British guarantee of Poland was frequently misinterpreted as the collapse of a man whose bluff has been called. Neither British nor French intelligence had an inkling of the secret feelers going out from Berlin to Moscow.

The Allies actually were confident that they would not be attacked. It was generally believed that with the French army the best and biggest in the world, and the British navy, again the world's best and biggest, the Allies were unbeatable. France during that fateful summer of 1939, so far from seeming a frightened nation, appeared to be one joyfully celebrating a victory.

In Paris the first week of July was known as *la grande semaine,* the great week for partying. President Albert Lebrun gave a dinner for the young emperor and empress of Annam. U.S. Ambassador William Bullitt held a ball for the Yale Glee Club. British Ambassador Sir Eric Phipps's grand ball in the Charot mansion at Versailles was rained out, but the undaunted revelers were able to make do in the magnificent mansion given to Napoleon by Paul Borghese.

The last night of the racing season at Longchamps was a gala under the lights: 100,000 ecstatic ticket holders were serenaded by twenty-two orchestras and entertained by ballet dancers, wrestlers and vaudeville turns. That same night Lady Mendl regaled 750 guests with a circus complete with elephants, horses and other animals. Among many celebrities, Douglas Fairbanks and Mary Pickford, Eve Curie and the inevitable Duke and Duchess of Windsor were there.

Drinking and dancing until dawn bemused the distinguished guests at the Polish embassy. The Polish ambassador, Jules Lukasciewicz—"Luka," as he was known to his intimates—was delighted to see among his guests such notables as French Foreign Minister Georges Bonnet, Gen. Maurice Gustave Gamelin, chief of French armed forces, and Sir Leslie Hore-Belisha, Britain's secretary for war. Paul Reynaud also was present. Much of the talk that gay evening beneath a serene night sky was military. There was much chest thumping. The Allies not only had the best and biggest army and navy but their combined air forces were also the world's best. The high point of the evening was reached when the orchestra switched from playing polonaises to mazurkas. "Luka" pulled off his shoes and socks and led his guests through the dances. Fireworks illuminated the night. M. Reynaud glanced up at the slashed and crisscrossed sky. "It is scarcely enough to say that they are dancing on a volcano," he remarked grimly. "For what is an eruption of Vesuvius compared to the cataclysm that is forming under our very feet?" But the dancing went on until dawn.

On July 14, Bastille Day, the 150th anniversary of the storming of that prison-fortress by the Paris mob, the beginning of the French Revolution, 300,000 people gathered to see what was to be the greatest display of military might ever assembled.

From a distance on high came the murmur of many motors. The crowd gasped. An aerial armada was approaching with a growing roar, 315 planes of every description from the Anglo-French air forces thundering overhead at a speed of 175 mph.

Now came the tramp of marching feet. Thirty thousand soldiers, each man representative of a hundred more whom the French could put in the field, came marching up the Champs. Among them were the colorful warriors of the French empire: *tirailleurs* from Senegal, Madagascar and Vietnam, desert spahis riding Arabian horses, the bearded regulars of the French Foreign Legion striding along with axes in their hand. There were the cadets of the military academy at St.-Cyr, pink-cheeked beneath their white-plumed kepis; burly Zouaves in red pants, the *Chasseurs Alpins* with skis, ropes and rifles. Marching with them were their British brothers: the legendary foot guards—Grenadiers and Coldstream, Scots, Irish and Welsh—strutting behind the Royal Marine band. There were armored units, of course, but only medium tanks for fear the heavies would grind the

Europe, 1939–40

•••••• Partition line, German-Soviet
        Nonaggression Treaty, Aug. 1939

← German Landings in Norway, Apr. 9, 1940

Occupied by Germany

Occupied by U.S.S.R.

Boundaries as of Sept. 1, 1939

```
0                    300 mi
0                    500 km
```

ATLANTIC
OCEAN

Murmansk

Narvik

K
A
R
E
L
I
A

NORWAY

Gällivare

FINLAND

Namsos

*Lake
Ladoga*

Andalsnes

Trondheim

SWEDEN

Mannerheim Line

Helsinki

Leningrad

Bergen

Oslo

SOVIET
UNION

Orkney Is.
Scapa Flow

Stavanger

Stockholm

ESTONIA

Kristiansand

Skagerrak

NORTH
SEA

DENMARK

B
A
L
T
I
C

S
E
A

LATVIA

Memel

LITHUANIA

GREAT
BRITAIN

Copenhagen

*EAST
PRUSSIA*

Kiel

Danzig

Hamburg

Brest-Litovsk

London

Dunkirk

Berlin

Warsaw

English Channel

NETH.

P O L A N D

Lvov

Brest

BELG.

Rhine

RHINELAND

GERMANY

Teschen

LUX.

SUDETENLAND

Prague
BOHEMIA

Paris

FRANCE

*Maginot
Line*

MORAVIA

SLOVAKIA

Munich
Berchtesgaden

Vienna

HUNGARY

SWITZ.

A U S T R I A

Budapest

ROMANIA

Vichy

Lyon

Milan

Bucharest

Bordeaux

Belgrade

YUGOSLAVIA

BULGARIA

Marseilles

SPAIN

ITALY

Rome

ALBANIA
occupied by Italy,
1939

CORSICA

GREECE

SARDINIA

Naples

MEDITERRANEAN SEA

streets into rubble, and enormous guns still horse-drawn as in the last war. From all this rumble and roar, military muscle and might, it should be clear to Adolf Hitler, Premier Édouard Daladier suggested in a moving speech, that if he started a war it would be one he could not win.

Der Führer was delighted to learn that Premier Stalin was receptive to a discussion of a nonaggression pact. In August, Hitler sent his foreign minister, Joachim von Ribbentrop, on a secret journey to the Kremlin.

Joachim von Ribbentrop was the son of an army officer. The noble prefix preceding his name was fraudulent, a reflection on his snobbish, class-conscious, social-climbing nature. A student of languages, he switched to a business career, returning from Canada in 1914 to volunteer for the army. His career was remarkably undistinguished, yet he rose to the rank of lieutenant. At war's end, Ribbentrop went into the wine and liquor business. His marriage to Anneliese Henckle, daughter of Germany's largest champagne maker, gave him the entree into high society that he craved. Ribbentrop was a johnny-come-lately in the Nazi Party, entering it in 1932. But his opulent villa on the Lentzeallee was admirably suited to the secret conferences conducted by Hitler to form his first cabinet in 1933. *Der Führer* was quick to reward this loyalty.

The older Nazis detested this arrogant, vain, touchy and humorless upstart. Goering called him that "dirty little champagne peddler." Goebbels, his bitter enemy, remarked: "He bought his name, he married his money and he swindled his way into office." Ribbentrop's counterpart in Italy, Count Galeazzo Ciano, observed in his famous diary: "The *Duce* says you only have to look at his head to tell that he has a small brain." Ribbentrop was indeed incompetent, and it was he who assured Hitler that Britain would not oppose his policy of *Lebensraum*. Nevertheless, *Der Führer* maintained faith in his minister, perhaps because of his doglike devotion. Hitler rebuked his detractors, even insisting that in foreign affairs Ribbentrop was greater than Bismarck.

When Ribbentrop met Stalin in Moscow, the Soviet dictator was at his dissimulating best. Ribbentrop was delighted at his reception: smiles, a firm handclasp, a straightforward warm glance. There was no difficulty whatsoever in coming to an agreement, in forging the nonaggression pact which Stalin sought as fervently as Hitler. Although he did not regret his purges, Stalin knew how they had weakened his country. He had also changed his mind about the democracies. In 1938, he had privately and publicly made known his willingness to join France and Britain in defending Czechoslovakia. He was ignored. Then in 1939 he had been ignored again at the Munich sellout. He now distrusted the democracies. Where Hitler saw the pact as a guarantee of his eastern flank, Stalin regarded it as securing his western border. He believed the democracies would fight Germany and hoped that they would exhaust each other. Then, perhaps, he could wolf them all down. The prospect of no immediate war, at most an easy march into a prostrate Poland, pleased him. So he embraced Ribbentrop and spoke to him tenderly of his love for Hitler and the German people.

When Ribbentrop, who hated Britain because of his social rejection when he was there as an ambassador, remarked that the pact would stun London financiers, Stalin beamed and raised his glass. "I know how much the German nation loves its Führer," he said, "and I should therefore like to drink to his health." They clinked glasses and exchanged smiles. Ribbentrop was elated. He offered toasts to Stalin, to the U.S.S.R. and to German-Soviet relations. He even proposed that the pact include a preamble saluting the friendly relations between the two countries. At this, Stalin ceased to purr. He remembered Hitler's persecution of his Communists and became Koba again: "The Soviet government cannot suddenly present to the public assurances of friendship after they had been covered with pails of shit by the Nazi government for six years." There was a momentary silence, one of those awkward pauses in which, a Russian proverb says, an idiot is born; but then the bonhomie was resumed, and the pact was signed. When it was made public, it did not include the secret protocol by which Germany was to seize Lithuania and the Soviets to take Estonia and Latvia. Poland, of course, would be divided evenly. Thus, rape and ruin and ferocious massacre would not only afflict the long-suffering Poles but also the peoples of these three little helpless Baltic countries.

Unable to contain his eagerness to report to his master, Ribbentrop turned to leave the Kremlin. Stalin seized his arm and said: "The Soviet government takes the new pact very seriously. I can guarantee on my word of honor that the Soviet Union will not betray her partner." This time he meant it. Ribbentrop knew that he did. In a state of high excitement, he sent off his jubilant cablegram to *Der Führer.*

On the night of August 23, 1939, Adolf Hitler was at supper in the Berghof surrounded by his intimates. A note was handed to him. Hitler read it eagerly. He stared into space, flushed deeply in delight and began pounding the table so hard he rattled the glasses. "I have them!" he cried, his voice breaking in excitement. "I have them!" A moment later, he subsided, finishing his meal before announcing conclusion of the nonaggression pact. The effect was at first one of disbelief and then of jubilation. Two days later, Goebbels held a news conference to discuss the agreement. He reported to Hitler that night, and *Der Führer* again gathered his entourage together. "The sensation was fantastic!" he quoted Goebbels as saying. "And when the church bells began ringing outside, a British correspondent said: 'That is the death knell of the British Empire.' "

That night they all stood on the terrace of the Berghof to gaze across the valley toward the legendary Untersberg, where Charlemagne was said to await recall to life. In awed silence they watched the Northern Lights rising behind the mountain, bathing it in an eerie red light. Above it the sky actually shimmered in the colors of a rainbow. Someone whispered, "Götterdämmerung," a reference to the mythic Twilight of the Gods, the final struggle in which the German gods and all things are destroyed by the Powers of Evil. Now the red light had crept across the valley and was flickering on everyone's face and hands. "Looks like a good deal of blood," Hitler murmured to an adjutant. "This time we won't bring it off without violence."

Announcement of the German-Soviet Nonaggression Pact stupefied the Allies and shattered the rose-colored glasses they had only lately put on. France began mobilizing. Britain became the bulldog Britain of old, defiant and growling. A formal treaty with Poland was at once proclaimed. Orders were issued to man air and coastal defenses. Warning telegrams were sent to dominion governments and the colonies. All leave was canceled in the fighting services. The Admiralty issued warnings to all merchant shipping. The Admiralty also had a new first lord: Winston Churchill. Upon his return to the post he had held in World War I, the Admiralty signaled the fleet: "Winston is back." Churchill was also a member of the new War Cabinet formed by Chamberlain, a turn of events that caused much consternation in Germany. "Churchill in the Cabinet," Reichsmarschall Hermann Goering murmured in dismay. "That means that the war is really on. Now we shall have war with England."

Der Führer demurred. He believed Ribbentrop's assurance that Britain did not want war. Intelligence reports stated that the British General Staff would do all in its power to avoid a war. In its evaluation of the Polish army it predicted an early Polish collapse. Any attempt by the Allies to come to Poland's aid would be too late, and therefore hopeless. And Hitler was supremely confident that his Wehrmacht could strike quickly and decisively with its new blitzkrieg tactics.

In war it is axiomatic that the victors of the last war fight the new one with the tactics of the old. Having won, the victor is content with what won for him; but the vanquished wants to know why he lost. This was true of the Allies and the Germans after World War I. France expected to fight a defensive war and built its Maginot Line, a huge chain of mostly underground forts stretching from the Swiss border to a point just below Belgium. Britain anticipated another "economic war" based upon a blockade supported by "strategic bombing" of populations and industrial centers. The Germans, however, quickly saw that static or trench warfare had been their undoing and they conceived the *Blitzkrieg,* or lightning war. Many ingredients went into this martial mixture: the tactics of infiltration, which had almost succeeded in 1918, a study of the American Civil War with emphasis on the lightning campaigns of Stonewall Jackson and the realization that by welding guns to internal combustion engines—tanks and airplanes—technology had conferred an enormous advantage on the offense. Guns could now burst through or fly over fixed defenses. Finally, the Germans seized upon the very tactics that this radical change in warfare had called forth from the minds, not of defeated Germans, but victorious enemies: J. F. C. Fuller and B. H. Liddell Hart of Britain and Charles de Gaulle of France. This was to attack the "brains" rather than the "body" of the enemy forces. The "brains" were the commanding generals and staff officers in the rear areas of division, corps and army headquarters, the "body" was the soldiery manning the front with their weapons, supplies and transport. If the brains are destroyed, the body becomes demoralized, disorganized, much like (there is no better image) a chicken with its head cut off. Moreover, as Fuller advocated to Marshal Foch in his "Plan 1919" during the last war, the brains had to be attacked *before* the body.

The weapons to accomplish this were the tank and the airplane. The tank together with armored troop carriers would be formed into armored divisions which, supported by fighter planes and dive bombers, would break through the enemy front at selected points and roll into the enemy's command posts in the rear. After them would come the slower formations to mop up the leaderless and terrified foe. To this was added the coldly efficient tactic of next attacking the cities from the air to force the terror-stricken populations onto the highways, where they could again be strafed and bombed so that these arteries would become clogged with bodies and burning vehicles and thus present an impassable barrier to the retreating enemy.

For all of Hitler's frenzies and intuitive sudden stops and turns, much as some historians might dismiss him as an amateur or a "half-educated paranoic," he was indeed a military visionary. To the theory of paralyzing the enemy army's will to fight, he had added his own special touch of striking at the enemy *people's* will to fight. He had read how Sherman had done it in Georgia, and he would do the same in Europe—but *before* the war began.

"The enemy people must be demoralized and ready to capitulate, driven into moral passivity, before military action can even be thought of. . . . We shall have friends who will help us in the enemy countries. We shall know how to obtain such friends. Mental confusion, contradiction of feeling, indecisiveness, panic: These are our weapons."

There it was, war total and amoral, and humanity had indeed gone into a long, dark descent since the thirteenth century when the Lateran Council banned crossbows as being contrary to the laws of God and morality. Crossbows were indeed used, as has every weapon devised by the ingenious mind of man; and Adolf Hitler was also going to use everything he had. He was the only leader in Europe with a set purpose and the means to obtain it: *Lebensraum* and blitzkrieg.

So August of 1939 came to Europe as it had come in the fateful hot August of 1914. Battle lines were being drawn, armies were mobilizing, soldiers drilling, tanks went clanking through the streets, airplanes were parked in rows on the airfields, buildings were sandbagged, parks entrenched, sea coasts fortified and children were sent from the cities to the countryside along with animals from the zoos, to be followed by valuables removed from vaults and truckloads of irre- placeable files; and while the rectors of universities sought a safe place to bury their academic treasures and the pastors of churches and cathedrals removed their stained-glass windows and precious altar services to store them in cellars, gas masks were issued to civilians. War was coming, everyone knew it, but the only one who wanted it was Adolf Hitler. "I shall give a propagandist reason for starting the war, whether it is plausible or not," he told his generals. "The victor will not be asked, later on, whether he told the truth or not. In starting and waging a war it is not Right that matters, but Victory. Have no pity."

On the last night of August in the sleepy little German town of Gleiwitz on the Polish border (now Gliwice, Poland), a group of SS men in Polish uniforms seized the radio transmitter. They broadcast an alarm in Polish, saying that Gleiwitz was in Polish hands and the time had come for Poles to attack Germany. Outside they killed a prisoner from a concentration camp also dressed in a Polish uniform, leaving him sprawling on the ground as a "casualty." In a forest near Hohenspitzen other SS men machine-gunned a dozen more prisoners, draping their bodies over fences and fallen trees to make it appear that they had died attempting to invade Germany. They had hardly fallen before the sirens of arriving police cars could be heard, followed, of course, by reporters and photographers.

Next morning the German spearheads went crashing into Poland. Two days later, both France and Britain declared war on Germany. Adolf Hitler sat at his enormous desk in the Berlin Chancellery listening silently to an interpreter reading the Allied ultimatum. Von Ribbentrop stood at the window. When the reading was finished, Hitler remained silent, still, the muscles in his reddening cheeks beginning to move. In a fury of frustration he turned on Ribbentrop and screamed:

"What now?"

PART TWO

1939

11. September 1939: The Invasion of Poland

THE GERMAN PEOPLE did not share Hitler's enthusiasm for the war. From the start, they were in a somber mood. No cheering crowds formed quickly outside the Chancellery when Hitler's personal flag was run up the pole, as they used to do. Instead, the streets were quiet and empty. Germans who had lived through World War I realized what the future held, and their pessimism infected their younger countrymen. In early September, false air-raid alarms sent them scurrying to the shelters, where they sat in a combination of deep depression and numbed apprehension. Hitler was shocked by this reaction. It was on his mind when, twelve hours after the invasion began, he left Berlin by special train to tour the Polish front. En route, he was informed that a German submarine had torpedoed and sunk the British liner *Athenia,* with a loss of 112 lives, twenty-eight of whom were Americans. Remembering full well how unrestricted German submarine warfare had brought the United States into the last war, he immediately ordered his media to report that the liner had been sunk by the British. Winston Churchill, the first lord of the Admiralty, he said, had craftily planted a time bomb in his own ship's hold, hoping that by killing his own people and some Americans he could blame Germany, thus turning world opinion against it and bringing America into the war on his side. It was, of course, no more believed than the Gleiwitz "incident," but it did show that *Der Führer* was still in top form. Meanwhile, his train still rolled east toward the front.

Although none of the regiments marched off to war decorated with flowers as in 1914, the German troops were in the main in high spirits and enthusiastic. Wilhelm Pruller was such a soldier. He was an ardent, believing Nazi, an Austrian assigned to a machine-gun section. At four o'clock in the morning of that fateful September 1, 1939, he was with his unit two miles from the Polish border. Pruller's truck was parked in the rain within a hundred yards of a huge petroleum and munitions complex. He thought: *One grenade, and we've had it.* . . . His mind roved again to his reflections of the last few days, how the stupid, stubborn Poles had forced his beloved *Volksdeutsche* to go to war . . . how much he loved *Der Führer* . . . almost as much as his wife, Henny, and their daughter, Lore, back in Vienna. . . . The Poles haven't accepted our rightful demands, he thought bitterly; nor Russia's "centuries-old rights" either. How hateful the French and British were!

Pruller yawned and scratched himself. He and his comrades had not slept for nights. Nor bathed. Would they soon be lousy? His belly growled in hunger.

The rolling kitchens had been slow getting to the front. They'd had nothing but hot coffee. Suddenly, the order came to advance. His truck roared and lurched forward. The men were thrown off balance, cursing, reaching to secure their guns and ammunition. They also stopped telling dirty jokes, leaning eagerly ahead. At the border, Wilhelm Pruller told himself: *It is a wonderful feeling, now, to be a German.* The truck stopped. Tanks flowed past them in what seemed to be an endless column. Word came that Danzig had been occupied. The men shouted in glee. Their truck lurched forward once more.

"We've crossed the border," Pruller yelled. "We're in Poland!" Jubilant, the men shouted: *"Deutschland! Deutschland über alles!"*

Poland possessed an army of about 1.7 million men with which to halt about 800,000 German invaders. There was also a reservoir of about 800,000 reservists, none of whom had yet been activated. But Poland's army was obsolete. Most of its troops were foot soldiers and nearly 20 percent of its fighting strength was concentrated in twelve huge cavalry brigades. There was very little armor and few mechanized formations. Moreover, Poland's air force was inadequate, only about 450 airplanes to the 1,400 being flown by the Germans—and the country relied too much on the traditional and very real bravery of its soldiers and the distraction of a heavy Allied thrust from France into Germany. The French, however, sent out only a few desultory patrols toward Germany's Siegfried Line before retiring inside their own Maginot Line forts.

Poland was also disarmed by its huge frontier, about 3,500 miles in all. On the west, the stretch of 1,250 miles adjoining German territory had been expanded to 1,750 miles by the seizure of Czechoslovakia, which also left it exposed on the south. Thus, western Poland was like a huge bulge caught north and south in German jaws. The flat Polish plain also offered easy going for a mobile invader. This was minimized, however, by an imperfect road system running through frequent lakes and forests, although Hitler could not have chosen a better month for his blitzkrieg.

Worst of all for Poland was Marshal Edward Smigly-Rydz's decision to defend at the frontier in the west rather than east of Warsaw behind the Vistula-San river line. This was made out of economic and patriotic considerations: the Polish plain west of the river line contained most of the country's industry and those Silesian coalfields that had once been German. To abandon it would be to give up much industry and would stagger national pride. Also, Smigly-Rydz was supremely confident of his army's ability to stop the invaders.

But it couldn't. Within forty-eight hours the Luftwaffe destroyed the Polish air force. Caught by surprise on the ground, the Polish aircraft were strafed and bombed to pieces and few indeed were the Polish pilots who managed to scramble aloft for battle. Antiaircraft installations were also knocked out as the Germans seized complete control of the air. With this, their armored or panzer divisions were free to roll without fear of interference from the skies.

Roll they did, spearheading two huge German armies crashing down from the north and south. Almost immediately, their armor rumbled deep into the enemy rear, overrunning command posts to spread confusion as ordered, or striking at nerve centers to paralyze Polish communications. Radio stations, telegraph stations, bridges and tunnels, road and railway junctions as well as airfields were brought beneath the blazing guns of the blitzkriegers. Deeper and deeper they drove, making certain that none of the spearheading panzers would be cut off and chopped up piecemeal. Within two days the archaic, slow-moving Polish army was knocked brainless, leaving it with a wildly flailing body. Its vaunted heavy cavalry charged tanks—flesh against steel, sabers against shells— and went down in hideously bloody masses of screaming, neighing, kicking, twitching men and horses. The Polish soldiers fought with dogged bravery, earning the grudging admiration of their enemies. But within a week they were fragmented and leaderless. Their commanders seemed powerless to form a continuous front against the roaring flood of tanks flowing steadily eastward. Hastily erected defenses were brushed aside and their defenders left behind to be destroyed or imprisoned by the infantry and artillery following about twenty miles to the rear.

Meanwhile, the Luftwaffe was steadily chipping away at enemy communications behind the front. The same targets struck at by the tanks came under the bombs of screaming Stuka dive bombers falling from the skies beneath a protective umbrella of Messerschmitt fighter planes. Polish civilians were scourged by the policy of *Schrecklichkeit,* or "frightfulness," calculated to force them onto the roads and highways where their terrified masses would block Polish troop movement. Stukas with whistles in their wings fell screeching upon them, paratroopers were dropped onto the countryside to spread terror and sabotage while fighters flew at low levels to strafe the fugitives on the roads. The Luftwaffe also operated in an extremely dispersed way, in formations of a dozen or fewer rather than in the customary larger concentrations, and this contributed to Polish paralysis and confusion. Heavy German radio bombardment disguised as Polish transmissions helped to demoralize the rear. Both these factors deepened Polish disillusionment in their chief's fatuous belief that spiritual power could conquer firepower.

The efficient Germans carefully refrained from bombing bridges or highways required for their eastward advance. Wherever they went, they could count upon the assistance of some 2 million Germans living in the combat area. Thus, finger by finger, Poland's grasp upon its western vitals was being pried free of the salient, until, on the seventeenth day of the invasion, the Soviet Union struck from the east with a decisive stab in the back.

When the Soviets attacked, Hitler was still in Poland aboard his special train. With its offices and kitchens, radio transmitters and antiaircraft guns, the train was actually Hitler's headquarters. At night it was always drawn up outside a tunnel: Despite the fact that there was hardly a single Polish airplane aloft, *Der Führer* still had his unreasoning fear of bombs.

Nevertheless, he was enjoying his tour, learning much that could be used in future invasions. On September 5, he had visited the sector captured by the armored corps under General Heinz Guderian, a commander whom he came to admire. Hitler was astonished when Guderian showed him the blown bridges and the twisted wreckage of a Polish artillery battalion. "Our dive bombers did *that?*" he exclaimed. Guderian smiled and shook his head. "No, *mein Führer,* our panzers." Hitler was delighted. He had always put more faith in tanks than airplanes. Long ago, when he saw his first tank, he had exclaimed: "That's what I want! That's what I want!" Now he felt himself vindicated—again.

A few weeks later, however, when the U.S.S.R. entered the war, *Der Führer* was not so elated. Stalin would take half of Poland! It was part of the bargain, of course; yet it seemed a stiff price to pay for a secure eastern flank. Hitler still hated the Soviets with a passion. But now, with Poland collapsing so rapidly, France and Britain would surely see the futility of their position. He would be able to deal with them. And then . . . move farther east . . .

A police state's power to brainwash its people is almost incalculable. Wilhelm Pruller and his comrades were like blotting paper in the hands of Herr Doktor Goebbels's skillful propagandists. They soaked up every lie calculated to infuriate them. Hordes of unarmed Polish peasants were wreaking prodigies of atrocity on brave German soldiers, they were told. Here a motorcycle driver was murdered beside the vehicle he was repairing. There a squad of soldiers was attacked by an entire village, their eyes gouged out, emasculated and murdered. A Red Cross convoy of doctors and medics—180 soldiers strong—was ambushed and destroyed. Wilhelm Pruller believed every word. "Cowards, cowards they are," he wrote bitterly in his diary. "You can hardly get them to fight a decent fight. But they are very good at murdering. If an armed civilian crosses my path, I'll cut off his head with my own hands, I will." Although Pruller wrote of his grudging admiration for the tough, brave enemy, he could not conceal his contempt for the Polish people. They were dirty and backward (although he found the pigs and chickens, milk and bread that they gave him and his comrades very tasty), and with their dilapidated isbas (log cabins) and their unpaved cities, they were hardly better than primitive, miles beneath his own master race. Pruller was in fact so obsessed with this inculcated sense of superiority that he was stunned —almost desolated—when he was taken prisoner by the Poles.

For four days Pruller was led through forests and swamps by his captors, shot at by both sides: by Germans who saw the Polish uniforms around him, by Poles who saw the uniforms of himself and his friends. Gradually, his sense of superiority returned. He concluded that all the Polish officers were Jews. But then, he could not believe it when they treated him kindly, shared their food and promised him that he would not be harmed. "Many of them are actually human beings!" he wrote incredulously. On the fourth day of his captivity, a fog turned to rain. Pruller was again dispirited. But then he heard shots. He saw Poles running out of the woods with upraised hands. He was overjoyed. It must be Germans! But when he too ran from the woods, he saw that they were not. "*They are our Russian allies!*" he wrote. "I can't describe this moment," he continued. "I felt no joy. I didn't laugh. Or cry. Or weep. I wasn't touched at all. Only someone who rises from the dead can know this feeling."

The day after the Soviets invaded Poland, the Polish government and its high command sought sanctuary in Romania. Like a fleeing man shouting back encouragement over his shoulder, Marshal Smigly-Rydz sent a message to his troops imploring them to fight on. They did: the defense of Warsaw was magnificent. One hundred thousand troops and 800,000 civilians defied the blitzkriegers. Every thirty seconds the Warsaw radio broadcast the opening notes of Chopin's most famous and stirring *Polonaise** to tell the world that the Polish capital still lived. But it was gasping. By September 25, the Luftwaffe had left the city in a heap of rubble. For a week there had been no water, gas, electricity—or food. Starving Poles cut chunks of flesh from the bodies of dying horses. Those even more desperate crept among the 25,000 human bodies sprawled among the wreckage, searching for the warmer flesh. Enraged by this gallant resistance, Hitler ordered an escalation of the aerial bombardment. Round-the-clock saturation bombing began, until, on September 28, the Warsaw radio played Chopin's *Death March,* signifying that the end had come. Warsaw had been so hammered into dust that many of the dead were not uncovered until the following spring.

Von Ribbentrop flew to Moscow in a joyous mood. He was received with embraces and victory toasts. With his opposite number, Soviet Foreign Minister Vyacheslav Molotov—who was always under Stalin's instructions—Poland was split almost exactly down the middle.

Germany took most of the mines and factories, almost half of the 150,000 square miles of land, and 22 of the 35 million people. Russia took the rest, together with most of Poland's oil resources. In this, the wily Koba outwitted the self-esteeming champagne salesman. In exchange for much worthless (to him) territory, Stalin received a section of Poland abutting Romania and included the oil fields near Lwow (now L'vov, Soviet Union). Germany was left with no common border with Romania or access to its famous Ploesti oil fields. If Hitler wanted oil from the east, it would have to come over Soviet-controlled railroads and only if he was still friends with Stalin.

12. Fall 1939: Nuclear Fission, Scapa Flow, *Graf Spee,* Finland

IN WASHINGTON DURING the early days of 1939, while the isolationist Senator William E. Borah from Idaho was still assuring cheering audiences, "There is not going to be any war," a group of physicists met at Georgetown University. They listened in amazement and dismay to a report made by two brilliant European colleagues, Niels Bohr of Denmark and Enrico Fermi of Italy: German physicists

*In A-flat, Opus 53.

had succeeded in the splitting apart, or fission, of uranium atoms.

A month later at a meeting of the American Physical Society at Columbia University in New York City, Bohr and Fermi brought to their colleagues news that experimental confirmation had been made of the German results in both America and Denmark. Fermi went on to discuss the probability that each nucleus as it split would shoot out two or three subatomic particles. These, rattling around among uranium atoms, might produce further fissions: an explosive chain reaction. After the meeting, a reporter asked Fermi and Bohr if uranium 235 might not be used to make a bomb. Both scientists exchanged uneasy glances. Fermi answered hesitantly, "It has not yet been proved that a chain reaction would occur." He added that probably twenty-five years, perhaps fifty years, of research would be necessary to produce one. Fermi, of course, had exaggerated the difficulty. He was aware even then that experiments were being conducted at Columbia and in Paris that within a few days did conclusively prove that a chain reaction was possible. The Italian physicist, who would one day flee Mussolini's Italy to become an American citizen, wanted no publicity on American interest in fission. He wanted, indeed, to suppress publication of papers dealing with experiments in nuclear physics in the United States. Such information might prove invaluable to the dictators whom he detested. Fermi also hoped to interest the American government in supporting such work in America. He first approached the navy, which had the reputation of being more receptive to new ideas than the army. He was granted an interview scheduled for March 17. Two days before then, Hitler seized Czechoslovakia. Fermi's anxiety grew. He knew that Czechoslovakia contained the only considerable uranium deposits in Europe. However, in his imperfect English Fermi was unable to convey his apprehension to the pair of youthful lieutenant commanders who heard him out. With exasperating courtesy, they gave him the classic brush-off: Keep in touch.

Fermi was now on fire to reach someone high in government. He was aware that German scientists were politically sophisticated and could almost immediately communicate their discoveries to the top echelons. Americans were not. They could not care less about using their science to serve the military. Soon Fermi became convinced that the only person with the power to order governmental action was the president himself. He was joined in this belief by Leo Szilard, Edward Teller and Eugene Wigner, all of Hungary, and Victor Weisskopf of Austria. Foreigners like himself, all soon to be fugitives from the dictators too, they formed the "Fermi five." Eventually, Szilard took over the movement to warn America of the danger in Berlin. Szilard was delighted to find that Albert Einstein, the most famous fugitive of all, was deeply concerned about his native Germany's interest in fission. If there was any one scientist in America who had access to the presidential ear, it was Albert Einstein. In July, the Fermi Five approached Einstein and asked him to call upon Roosevelt. Einstein demurred. He was one of the world's greatest exponents of nonviolence. How could he put his name to development of the most violent weapon ever proposed? The Five argued: The chain reaction will come (Einstein doubted that this was possible);

in whose hands should it be? That was the question: not violence or nonviolence but *whose* violence? At last, Einstein agreed to sign a letter to the president. It was drafted by Szilard and Wigner and Einstein signed it. Now the problem was to find a man who could deliver it to FDR. Szilard's friend, Dr. Alexander Sachs, was chosen. Born in Russia and educated in science, sociology, philosophy and jurisprudence, Sachs had become a brilliant economist with an international reputation. More important, he was a confidant of the president's. On October 11, 1939, he entered the Oval Office and sat down opposite him.

"Mr. President," Sachs began with an impish grin, "I want you to know that I paid for my trip to Washington. I can't deduct it from my income tax. So won't you please pay attention?"

Roosevelt chuckled, and Sachs quickly explained his mission. To be certain that the contents of the letters he carried were actually communicated to the President, he read them aloud. First, Einstein's missive:

> . . . it may become possible to set up a nuclear chain reaction in a large mass of uranium, by which vast amounts of power and large quantities of new radiumlike elements would be generated. Now it appears almost certain that this could be achieved in the immediate future. . . . This new phenomenon would also lead to the construction of . . . extremely powerful bombs of a new type. . . . A single bomb of this type, carried by boat and exploded in a port, might very well destroy the whole port together with some of the surrounding territory. . . . In view of this situation you may think it desirable to have some permanent contact maintained between the Administration and the group of physicists working on chain reactions in America. One possible way of achieving this might be for you to entrust with this task a person who has your confidence and who could perhaps serve in an unofficial capacity.

Einstein's letter also observed that the Nazis had halted sales of Czechoslovakian uranium, but that a better supply was available in the Belgian Congo. A note from Szilard urged FDR to import large quantities of uranium-holding pitchblende from the Congo. Next was a note from Sachs himself warning of what would happen if Hitler became the world's sole possessor of atomic weapons. Roosevelt glanced up grimly.

"What you are after is to see the Nazis don't blow us up?"

"Precisely, Mr. President."

FDR pressed a button on his desk. His military aide, Brigadier General Edwin M. Watson, known as "Pa" for his benign appearance, came into the office. Roosevelt handed him the three missives.

"Pa, this requires action."

Although Hitler's scientists had indeed gained a head start on those of France, Britain and the United States in pursuit of the weapon that could make all others inadequate and obsolete, they were not as close to a solution as the Fermi Five believed. Most of their research was in the direction of obtaining sizable quantities of "heavy water," a slowing-down medium or "moderator" through which a chain reaction might be produced. Hitler himself was not as passionately devoted to atomic research as he might have been, his mystic, intuitive nature being more attuned to the "secret weapons" he was constantly and darkly boasting about. This kind of talk, intended to unnerve his enemies, actually did make them uneasy, but it had the reverse effect of speeding up experiment in the democracies.

In the fall of 1939, when Franklin Delano Roosevelt was setting the atomic-bomb program in motion, Hitler was infuriated by the refusal of France and Britain to accept his peace offers. He was particularly incensed that the British, Saxon "cousins" of the Germans, should make common cause against him with the decadent French. As November 8 approached, the sixteenth anniversary of the Beer-Hall Putsch in the Bürgerbräukeller in Munich, he prepared a vitriolic diatribe against these perfidious kin. He delivered it there before the Old Guard of the Nazi Party. It was not as long as usual because he had cut it to obtain time to catch his train back to Berlin. Nor did he tarry to drink beer with his old comrades as he usually did. Instead, he marched silently from the room, accompanied by his bodyguards and Heinrich Himmler.

Twelve minutes later a huge bomb planted in a pillar behind the speaker's platform exploded, killing seven persons and wounding sixty-three. Since all the party chieftains had departed with Hitler, these were only members of the rank and file. Thus, whoever had planted the bomb—and there were suspicions that it might have been an agent of Himmler's—had failed. Worse, the "miraculous" escape confirmed in Hitler's mind his concept of himself as the man of destiny, the superhuman being chosen by some supernatural power to lead Germany into its rightful place in the sun. "In all modesty I must say that I am irreplaceable," he told his generals two weeks later. "Neither a military nor a civilian person could replace me."

In truth, Adolf Hitler had reached the peak of his physical and mental powers in that late fall of 1939. He was fifty years old, but looked younger. There was no trace of gray in his hair, his complexion was ruddy, his blue eyes clear, his carriage erect and proud and his stride the quick, confident movement of a man in his prime. Throughout the world, of course, he was caricatured as a pasty-faced dumpling with a Charlie Chaplin mustache. There might have been some basis for this in the fact that he did not photograph well, but those close to him could testify to his truly impressive appearance, his dignity—when he was not enraged, of course—his obvious sense of his own power.

Hitler's private personality was vastly different from his public one. Gone were the shouts, the bluster, the threats, the burning eyes and abrasive voice calculated to arouse the masses. Rather, he could coo like a dove. Men who knew him spoke of his *süsse Stimme,* his sweet voice. Sometimes it was caressing. Man-to-man, when he wanted to be, he could be charming. The Hitler Maidens who came to the Berghof in busloads loved him. He listened graciously to their serenades, bowed to them, kissed their hands, spoke to them tenderly like a loving father.

Much of Hitler's public image was fashioned by Goebbels, who portrayed him as an ascetic who neither smoked nor drank nor ate meat nor sought the company of women. Such a legend was invaluable as portraying him—"the greatest German of all time"—as absolutely dedicated to the service of the people. In truth, he abstained only from tobacco. Otherwise, he drank beer and diluted wine, was very fond of Bavarian sausage and had possessed many women, before and after the death of Geli Raubal. Since 1932, however, Hitler had kept to one mistress: Eva Braun. Eva was a vivacious, athletic young girl of seventeen when Hitler met her in 1929. She was working for Heinrich Hoffmann, *Der Führer*'s official photographer. Probably because of this tenuous association with films, legend has it that she was a film star. But Eva was not beautiful, just gay, pleasant and fresh-faced. She was also fair-haired and blue-eyed, those "Nordic" features that Hitler prized so highly. She came to live with him in 1932. Eva and *Der Führer* were very formal, even distant, in the presence of his entourage. At bedtime, she retired first to their room and Hitler waited a discreetly decent interval before following. Occasionally, after dinner, they might hold hands. Otherwise they gave no sign of their relationship.

At mealtimes Hitler showed himself to be remarkably self-indulgent. Although the only meat he ate was sausages and he never ate fish, he was extremely fond of caviar. He loved the desserts made especially for him by his cook, Willy Kannenberg, an enormously fat man whose clowning could make *Der Führer* laugh. He doted on crystallized fruits and cream cakes, which he consumed in astonishing quantities and with a lip-smacking, finger-licking gusto that his guests pretended to ignore. Tea and coffee he drank drowned in cream and sugar: in effect, a syrup. After dinner, the guests retired to one of two sitting rooms to watch movies or listen to one of Hitler's interminable monologues, struggling to stay awake. Sometimes to relieve these boring evenings sparkling wine was passed around. After the fall of France it was champagne of low quality, Goering and his air marshals having appropriated the best.

Since Christmas of 1936, there had been present in Hitler's entourage a most unattractive and unwelcome member: Dr. Theo Morell. He had become Hitler's personal physician after he had been summoned by *Der Führer* on that festive day to cure him of eczema. "I had eczema on both legs," Hitler recalled. "It was so bad that I was covered in bandages and couldn't get my boots on even." Morell cured him, and also perceived that most of his powerful patient's stomach trouble was of hysterical origin and that he was a classic hypochondriac. Playing cleverly on these weaknesses, which in the beginning he knew how to cure, he earned *Der Führer*'s lasting gratitude.

Everyone else despised him. In his midfifties, Morell was short, fat, bald, with a round, full face, muddy complexion and brown eyes so nearsighted that he needed to wear Coca-Cola eyeglasses. One of Hitler's secretaries has described Morell's conduct during the soirées at the Berghof: "With his heavy, hairy hands clasped across a pudgy paunch, Morell would fight back his drowsiness. He had the odd characteristic that when he closed his eyes he did so from the bottom upward—it looked hideous behind the thick pebble glasses. . . . Sometimes Colonel von Below would give him a nudge, and he'd wake with a start and chuckle out loud in case *Der Führer* had told a joke."

It was at table that Morell won everyone's dislike. "He didn't eat," one observer said. "He munched like a pig at a trough." Another remarked: "Morell had an appetite as big as his belly, and he gave not only visual but audible expression of it." But to complain of the good doctor's overpowering body odors was to receive Hitler's instant rebuke. "I didn't hire Morell for his fragrance but to look after my health." This Morell did assiduously, to the gradual decline of Hitler's physical well-being. As it became clear to other physicians that Morell was a first-class quack, Hitler's attachment to him grew stronger. So did the size of Morell's medicine chest. He gave *Der Führer* every conceivable kind of pill, placebo or dragée, some to lift him up, others to calm him down, along with cold poultices and hot compresses, leeches and bacilli, and so many thousands of injections that he sometimes found it difficult to find an entry point for his needle on Hitler's scarred veins. Morell's masterpiece was the "daily cocktail" he injected into his patient: a mixture of glucose, Vitamultin and liver extract. While Hitler the hypochondriac thus made himself dependent on the ministrations of a charlatan, he issued his infamous euthanasia decree.

Although the order was dated September 1, 1939, it was actually made in early October, ostensibly to obtain hospital beds for wounded German soldiers. One third of the beds in German hospitals were then occupied by the aged, infirm or insane—and it was their beds that Hitler, the hater of weaklings, desired. Physicians were requested to fill out seemingly innocuous forms listing those under their care who were senile, feeble, criminally insane or of non-German blood. The doctors had no suspicion of how this information would be used, but soon after the forms were returned, executions by lethal injection began. Several thousand patients were murdered before their relatives began to ask questions.

All had received a form letter telling them that their relative had been transferred to another hospital and had died there. Because of the danger of contagion, their bodies had been cremated. People began comparing letters and quickly detected a pattern. News of the euthanasia program was spread in religious circulars, and protests were made, most of them by clergymen. More than this public clamor, the low number of casualties in Poland convinced Hitler that the beds were not really needed and the program was dropped. Furthermore, Hitler was now preoccupied with the war at sea, which he seemed to be winning.

Lieutenant Gunther Prien was considered one of the ablest young officers in the German U-Boat Command. In early September of 1939 he was summoned into the presence of Commodore Karl Doenitz, the submarine chief. Doenitz asked Prien if he thought he could penetrate the huge and heavily guarded British naval base at Scapa Flow in the Orkney Islands, Scotland, and attack the warships there. He told him to study the problem and come back with his answer. Prien returned.

"Yes or no?" Doenitz asked.

"Yes, sir."

"Have you thought it all out? Have you thought of Emsmann and Henning who tried the same thing in the First World War and never came back?"

"Yes, sir."

"Then get your boat ready."

Prien saluted and rejoined his crew. Toward the end of the month he was ready for his patrol, guiding his U-boat through the Kiel Canal and into the North Sea. His men were mystified. Funnel smoke had been sighted repeatedly, but the lieutenant had ordered no attack. This was unlike their popular and aggressive young skipper. On October 13, Prien sighted the Orkneys and took his boat down to the sea bed. Then he mustered his crew forward. "Tomorrow we go into Scapa Flow," he told them quietly, studying them carefully. With relief he saw their faces light up. They began joking, and Prien's confidence rose. That night all hands went to diving stations and the boat began to rise. Ballast pumps gasped and motors hummed. Prien studied the sky through his periscope. All clear. The boat surfaced. Everyone drew breath. Though there was a new moon the Northern Lights were beaming on the bay.

Nevertheless, Prien boldly stole into Scapa Flow. "It is disgustingly light," he wrote in his ship's log. "The whole bay is lit up." At first, he saw no ships. But then, turning to port: "Two battleships are lying there at anchor, and farther inshore, destroyers. Cruisers not visible, therefore attack the big fellows." Mechanically, Prien began giving the range, the depth for the torpedo runs. Torpedomen in the boat's bow stood tensely beside their tubes. "Fire!" Two torpedoes went gushing out the tubes toward the southern target, one toward the northern. Prien waited expectantly. Flames leaped from the northern ship, followed by the roar of an explosion. "About!" Prien cried eagerly. The boat swung around, its stern aimed at the enemy. Three more torpedoes went speeding silently away. Three more were loaded forward. Now there was a tremendous explosion, a roar and a rumbling. The harbor came to life. Destroyers started signaling. Cars sped along the road only a few hundred yards from Prien's submarine. The three other torpedoes were discharged.

Prien never knew their fate. Nor did he care. He was already withdrawing. He knew that with his primitive periscope he could not conduct night attacks while submerged. Nor could he maneuver unobserved on a bright night in a calm sea. Moreover, he was certain that he had been spotted by a car, which had stopped opposite him, turned around and gone speeding away. Finally, his tubes were empty, so he slid through the water toward the narrows with both engines at full speed ahead. At a quarter after two in the morning, Prien's boat slipped out of Scapa Flow and began to dive.

Sinking toward the bottom at about the same time inside Scapa Flow was the great British battleship, *Royal Oak.*

Stunning though Prien's feat had been to British pride, it was far from being the serious threat to British survival that magnetic mines—one of Hitler's "secret weapons"—had become. Some 56,000 tons of Allied shipping had been lost during the months of September and October 1939. The Admiralty at once suspected that the sinking had been caused by magnetic mines sown in the approaches to British ports by submarines and airplanes. A jubilant Hitler hinted darkly that this secret weapon—to which there was no counter—would bring Britain to its knees. At the Admiralty, Winston Churchill and his sea lords were deeply concerned. "Every day hundreds of ships went out of British harbours," he wrote, "and our survival depended on their movement." There seemed no way to obtain one of these deadly explosives, magnetically drawn to a ship by its steel structure.

Fortunately for Britain, a magnetic mine was found sunk in the mud off Shoeburyness on November 23. Now the secret weapon could be examined, and a means of neutralizing it devised. One development was the introduction of new methods of minesweeping and fuse provocation. A second, more effective, method was the device called degaussing. A ship was demagnetized by passing an electric cable around its hull. Eventually, all Allied warships and merchant vessels, as well as those of neutral shippers, were equipped with degaussing gear. Gradually, Germany's magnetic-mine warfare was brought under control, but at enormous cost in men and money: at its peak it required the services of 60,000 men. Even as the threat subsided, a new menace appeared in the form of German "sea wolves."

Under the Treaty of Versailles the Germans had been permitted to build three pocket battleships—the *Deutschland, Admiral Scheer* and *Admiral Graf Spee*—as well as two battle cruisers, *Scharnhorst* and *Gneisenau.* Hitler had no intention of challenging the Royal Navy with these ships; British tonnage outweighed the German by 2 million tons to 235,000. Rather, these ships were to be destroyers of Allied merchant shipping. They were also to riddle the British blockading line of armed merchant vessels and they had been expressly designed for these missions.

With masterly skill German naval architects had compressed a pocket battleship's six 11-inch* guns, thick armor and the engines to provide 26-knot speed for the allowable limit of 10,000 tons. Germany's 8-inch-gun cruisers were also more modern than their British counterparts. Thus it was with great apprehension that the Admiralty learned that the sea wolves had put to sea. *Deutschland* found the first victim: the armed merchant cruiser *Rawalpindi* on patrol between Iceland and the Faroes. *Rawalpindi* was merely a converted liner with a broadside of four old 6-inch guns, no match at all for the formidable *Deutschland.* Still her gallant commander, Captain Kennedy, gave battle. With slow, sure power *Deutschland* pounded *Rawalpindi* beneath the waves, including her skipper and 270 of the crew. Aroused, the British put an entire fleet to sea, but in the gloom and mists of a North Sea November, the Germans were able to return to port. All but one, and that one the best of them all: the *Graf Spee* under Captain Hans

*Inches in naval ordnance measure the diameter of a gun barrel, not the length of a shell.

Langsdorff, who had taken her into the South Atlantic, where, amid rising criticism of Churchill and the Admiralty, he had begun to attack shipping off the coast of South America. In two months, the *Graf Spee,* considered one of the most beautiful warships in the world, commanded by the chivalrous Captain Langsdorff, sank nine ships without taking a single life.

On December 13, 1939, a trio of British cruisers caught up with the German raider off Rio de Janeiro. They were the 8-inch-gun *Exeter* and the 6-inch-gun *Ajax* and *Achilles,* under Commodore H. Harwood. To Langsdorff's surprise, the outgunned British attacked. He returned fire, putting *Exeter* out of action. But not before she and her sisters had inflicted considerable damage on *Graf Spee.* More important, as Commodore Harwood had hoped, such impetuous tactics convinced Langsdorff that the British must be expecting help from heavier warships not far off. They were fighting a delaying action, he thought, and he broke off the engagement. But he was too badly hurt to return to Germany. Instead, he made for the neutral port of Montevideo in Uruguay. There he would receive temporary repairs before attempting to break through into the North Atlantic and make for Germany. But after *Graf Spee* entered the Plata River, he realized that Uruguayan public opinion was strongly pro-Allied. He could not persuade the authorities to allow him to remain in Montevideo more than seventy-two hours. In the meantime, British propaganda skillfully played upon his fears by planting reports in the local press that a powerful British fleet was in the vicinity. Langsdorff cabled his predicament to headquarters, asking permission to scuttle his ship if it became necessary, to save the lives of his crew. It was granted, and *Graf Spee* put to sea.

Outside the port, the British cruisers cleared for action. The sun was dipping below the horizon when an enormous flame flashed from *Graf Spee*'s midsection, followed by a vast, rolling double explosion. Black smoke temporarily obscured the pocket battleship. Another blast seemed to erupt beneath her, lifting her—and then dropping her back crumpled into the sea. The mainmast buckled in two and then the magazine blew up to hurl the great afterturret that had withstood British shells into the air. Flames now swept the dying ship. German sailors, scattered aboard tugs and other ships in the vicinity, stood rigidly at attention to give the Nazi salute with tears in their eyes. Three days later, on December 20, in a deliberate affront to Hitler, Captain Langsdorff wrapped himself in the old Imperial German flag and committed suicide.

With that, and with the French fleet in control of the Mediterranean, the first phase of sea warfare ended in favor of the Allies. In the meantime, the Soviet Union had invaded Finland.

Although Stalin was Hitler's ally, he still was anxious to safeguard the U.S.S.R.'s Baltic flank against any possible attack by his "friend." Under the secret protocol in the Nonaggression Pact, Hitler had agreed that the states of Lithuania, Estonia and Latvia should become Soviet "protectorates." These were the old-time buffer states of czarist Russia and Stalin was anxious to reclaim them.

He did it in simple, straightforward, strong-arm fashion. The target states were informed of Soviet demands and asked to send a plenipotentiary to Moscow. Upon arrival, he would be confronted by Foreign Minister Molotov. Under Stalin's instructions, Molotov would ask the abashed visitor to sign a mutual defense treaty. He would also be informed that shortly 100,000 Soviet troops would arrive on his borders to "keep the peace" and these forces would be billeted on his countrymen at their expense. If he demurred, he would be taken to Stalin, who would suggest to Molotov in a gently reproving tone that perhaps only 50,000 troops would suffice. Stalin would generously add that the official and his friends would also be able to remain in power. Grateful for having lessened his country's burden and saved his own neck, the plenipotentiary would sign. But Finland would not.

Stalin offered Finland 2,134 square miles if it would cede him 1,066 square miles. He only wanted some breathing space on the Karelian Isthmus, the link between the two countries above Leningrad, plus some Baltic bases. The Finns still demurred. Angry now, Stalin demanded that a delegation come to the Kremlin. Inside his office, he jabbed his finger at three red-circled dots on a map, and growled: "Do you need these islands?" Perplexed, the delegates peered at the map. They had never heard of the islands, but they stubbornly insisted that they wanted them. Centuries of contact with their powerful neighbor had taught them that if you begin to feed the Russian bear, he becomes insatiable. So Stalin broke off the talks, and the delegates returned home convinced that they had called his bluff. Responsible Finns disagreed and even a German military attaché warned a Finnish general to settle: "Otherwise nothing might remain of Finland but a tale of heroism." Stalin was not bluffing. But he was listening too eagerly to military advisers assuring him that he needed only his powerful air force and a few hundred thousand men for a quick conquest of Finland. Thus an unfailing prescription for war: One side believes it will not be attacked, the other believes that it won't have to fight.

Like Hitler faking the "Polish invasion" at Gleiwitz, Stalin complained that Finnish artillery had deliberately killed a Russian soldier. The Communist press accused the bloodthirsty Finns of preparing to attack the peace-loving U.S.S.R. Finland had only 4 million people compared to 180 million in Russia, and an army of 33,000 men with a handful of tanks and sixty aircraft opposing 1.5 million men with 9,000 tanks and 10,000 aircraft. Nevertheless, the Soviets invaded Finland "in self-defense" on November 30, 1939.

About 100,000 soldiers moving over five routes began what looked more like a circus coming to town than a serious invasion. Convinced by their own propaganda that they would be welcomed as "liberators," some battalions crossed the border marching behind brass bands. Other units waved banners and strewed leaflets. They came dressed in lightweight uniforms and with light equipment, believing, as Stalin did, that Finland would collapse within a few days. They believed this until they ran into the ferocious Finnish soldiery inside the Mannerheim Line.

Field Marshal Baron Carl Gustav Emil von Mannerheim commanded the Finnish army. At seventy-two, he was still sharp and spry. Born of a Swedish family in Russian-held Finland, he became a general in the czarist army. After the Revolution, he commanded Finland's anticommunist forces, earning a reputation as a skillful tactician while throwing off the Soviet yoke. For this, he was rewarded with near dictatorial powers, but was defeated in 1919 in an election for president. He retired then, returning to duty in the early 1930s to reorganize the country's armed forces and build its defenses.

The Mannerheim Line was primitive, but the Line's intrepid soldiers made it famous by their defense. It consisted of sixty-six concrete blockhouses with tank traps in between running across the Karelian Isthmus's eighty-eight-mile width. It had neither the sophisticated armaments and fortifications nor the facilities for living, fighting, and supplying of the more famous Maginot Line. It had only, as Marshal Mannerheim admitted, "the tenacity and courage of the soldiers" who held it.

They were indeed tenacious and courageous, and clever, too. They lured the Soviet spearheads deep into snow forests or onto frozen lakes. Then they struck, attacking this column, then another. Sometimes one formation would hit and hold the Soviet front while another slashed the rear. They fragmented the Soviet units and devoured them piecemeal. Finnish ski troopers clad in white swished over the white forest floors shooting up supplies, cutting up relief columns, picking off stragglers, and sometimes so completely isolating entire brigades that the Soviets were compelled to supply them by air.

Red Army soldiers, frostbitten and chattering in their thin clothing, were shattered by this reception. Although they had quickly shed the delusion that they would be welcomed, they still believed that they could win swiftly and easily. Vyaschlev Oreshin was a young soldier who marched into Finland ardently attached to his "army of revolution." He wrote: "Stern and relentless as the punishing hand of Nemesis, it will call such warmongers to account. It will drive them forth from their cafés and restaurants. It will drag them from their concert halls and compel them to [listen to] the majestic symphony of war." Within a week his bombast had evaporated, and he was writing: "Our casualties are heavy . . . more from frostbite than from enemy fire. The butchers are accustomed to fire carefully at our troops from the side of the road. We can't even put our nose out of the trenches. Our men have launched several attacks but have always been beaten back." They were also being surrounded and annihilated. At Christmas the Finns destroyed a large tank unit trying to break out of a ring of steel. An American correspondent named James Aldridge described the battlefield:

It was the most horrible sight I had ever seen. As if the men had suddenly turned to wax. There were two or three thousand Russians and a few Finns all frozen together in fighting attitudes. Some were locked together, their bayonets within each other's bodies, some were frozen with their arms crooked holding the hand grenades they were throwing. . . . Their fear was registered in their frozen faces. Their bodies were like statues of men throwing all of their muscles and strength into some work, but their faces recorded something between bewilderment and horror.

Finland's gallant resistance earned worldwide admiration. For a time, France and Britain considered coming to its side, and in the United States there were loud cheers for the only nation in World War I that had "paid its war debts." This was not actually true; what Finland had paid for was surplus property bought after the war was over, and the Finns were amused by this typical Yankee loyalty to "a good customer." They were not amused, however, when a still-isolationist America refused to lend them money to buy arms in Sweden. Hitler, meanwhile, was secretly delighted at the discomfiture of his ally, while Stalin was appalled. To break the Finnish will, he ordered a redoubling of the bombardment of cities, and in this he gave the first demonstration of a theory that had bemused some of the best military minds in the world.

This was the concept of "strategic bombing," which prescribed not only aerial destruction of an enemy's war plant but also the deliberate scourging of his civilian population through the bombing of cities. The latter, of course, is "frightfulness" and it is not a German idea at all. It was first formulated by the Italian General Giulio Douhet. He claimed that if a single city could be paralyzed with terror, the systematic bombardment of scores of cities could not fail to destroy communications, halt industrial production, produce lawlessness and send the terrified populations fleeing into the countryside. Then, said Douhet, "The time would soon come when, to put an end to horror and suffering, the people themselves, driven by the instinct of self-preservation, would rise up and demand an end to the war—this before their army and navy had time to mobilize at all."

Douhet's concept had powerful allure and led Britain to form the first independent flying service, the Royal Air Force (1918). In the United States, the army took its aircraft away from the Signal Corps and formed the Army Air Corps. Other nations made similar changes, and their navies also organized air arms. All of these were not, of course, dedicated solely to strategic bombing but also flew the wide range of tactical support and supply missions. It was tactical, not strategic, air that Hitler used against Poland. Flying artillery covered the panzers and was half of the blitzkrieg. The strategy of frightfulness in the cities helped, but was not decisive. But strategic airpower had made some notable converts, among them Hermann Goering in Germany and Gen. Billy Mitchell in the United States. With Douhet, they believed that wars of the future would be won from the sky, by airpower alone, and in their eagerness to embrace Douhet's simplistic solutions they were very much like the musician who described the universe as a harmony, and was thus, in Aristotle's caustic comment: "True to his art." Stalin, whether consciously or not, was also putting strategic bombing into practice when he tried to break Finland's will from the sky.

And he failed. Helsinki and other Finnish cities were bombed for two weeks, but instead of breaking Finland's resolve, the Soviet frightfulness only strengthened it. Ultimately, the Soviet Union had to resort to conquering Finland with an old-fashioned steamroller. Twenty-seven divisions* were massed opposite the Mannerheim Line backed up by artillery lined up hub to hub. On February 2, 1940, following a shattering bombardment, the Soviets attacked. For ten days, the doughty Finns held fast, but then, three days later, the Mannerheim Line was breached and the Soviets debouched onto the open plains. Here the tiny Finnish army could not contain them. On March 12, Finland accepted Stalin's terms.

The Finns had fought with consummate skill and courage. The Soviet soldiers fed so remorselessly into the crucible had also in the main been brave, though bewildered. Much of the steel in the Red Army spine was put there by the political commissars attached to every unit. They restored discipline among badly mauled formations or forced unwilling troops to obey orders to attack. Others were dissuaded from surrender by threats of reprisal against their families or warnings that their captors would torture and kill them. Such tactics sometimes boomeranged; occasionally men (and officers) took them seriously and preferred suicide to surrender. But the Russian soldiery did demonstrate that, under the commissar as well as under the czar, there was much sad truth in the peasant proverb: "Our only defense is the living breasts of our soldiers." Their commanders also showed that they had learned nothing of maneuver since the czars. Mass attack followed mass attack, each successive wave being mowed down like lead soldiers storming a hot stove. At some points, Soviet soldiers advanced into minefields hand in hand and singing, apparently indifferent to the explosions that were blowing them apart and the machine-gun fire that was scything them. Marshal von Mannerheim has written: "The fatalistic submission which characterized [their] infantry was astonishing. . . . Even if political terror played its part, the real explanation is to be found in the Russian people's hard struggle against nature, which in the course of ages has created a capacity for suffering and deprivation, a passive courage and a fatalism incomprehensible to Europeans. . . ."

Finland's stirring stand was also due to Soviet contempt for the Finns' ability, to the Red Army's inadequate supply and training of troops—most of whom were bad shots—and to the U.S.S.R.'s poor advanced planning. No thought had been given to the dreadful ordeal of the Finnish lakes-and-forest country and the cold that could drop to 50 degrees below zero. Most of the soldiers were not prepared to operate in such terrain and temperatures. Without compasses and unable to ski, they literally floundered to death. In all, upward of 200,000 Russians were killed against 25,000 Finns. The Soviet Union lost 1,600 tanks—one quarter of its armor—and 725 airplanes (975 if unverified kills were included) against sixty-one for the Finns. So the Soviet Union had won a Pyrrhic victory, while suffering an enormous loss in military prestige. More decisive in the history of World War II, Finland had shown Adolf Hitler that the Russian bear might be a very tame beast indeed.

---

*A division is the smallest military formation embracing all arms: infantry, artillery, engineers, pioneers, supply, transport, armor, etc. It usually numbers about 15,000 men, although Soviet and Japanese divisions were smaller.

PART THREE

1940

13. The Phony War

THERE WAS ONE MAN on whom Senator William E. Borah never quit: himself. The Lion of Idaho, as he liked to be called, had been not in the least discountenanced when his unfailing assurance to the American public, "There is not going to be any war," went unheeded by Adolf Hitler. When the fall of Poland was succeeded by a six-month lull in hostilities, the senator was quick to redeem himself and disqualify the conflict with the comment: "This is a phony war."

It was a label that stuck. Much of the world, and particularly people in the United States, like disgruntled spectators at a tame and bloodless prizefight, jeered at the Phony War in which the Anglo-French behind the Maginot Line quietly confronted the Germans behind their own Siegfried Line. It was not until December 1939 that the British Expeditionary Force suffered a casualty, while total French casualties killed and wounded on land, sea and air were 1,433. So far from bombing each other, the rival air forces spent their time showering enemy soldiers with propaganda leaflets. British Air Vice-Marshal Arthur Harris was incensed by this most unwarlike assignment and said bluntly that the leaflets would accomplish nothing more than to "supply the Continent's requirement for toilet paper. . . ." Soldiers on both sides adopted a live-and-let-live attitude and it was considered extremely unsporting for any soldier to take an unprovoked pot shot at a passive enemy. British soldiers, splendidly sardonic as always, sang:

> We're gonna hang out the washing on the Siegfried Line
> Have you any washing, mother dear?
> We're gonna hang out the washing on the Siegfried Line
> 'Cos the washing day is here.
> Whether the weather be wet or fine
> We'll just rub along without a care.
> We're gonna hang out the washing on the Siegfried Line—
> If the Siegfried Line's still there.

Nevertheless, during the Phony War there arose many harbingers of what the next five years would bring. In the United States, Franklin Roosevelt wrote a friendly letter to Winston Churchill, reminding him that they had both been high naval officials in the last war and still shared an interest in naval affairs. In his warmest chatty style, FDR suggested that they should keep in touch, using the diplomatic pouch to exchange personal letters. Churchill showed the lette. to Chamberlain, asking permission to answer it and promising that the prime minister would see whatever he wrote before it went out. Chamberlain granted his request, and the most famous correspondence of the war was begun. Although Chamberlain had never been an admirer of Churchill, considering him bull-headed, impetuous and prone to undertake daring but risky enterprises, he had come closer to him since Poland. He knew that Churchill now had the power to bring his government down, but had gallantly chosen not to do so. By then also, Roosevelt had begun to reflect quietly whether or not he should abide by the traditional two-term limitation begun by George Washington.

He had been stunned, of course, by the fall of Poland, but had been perhaps even more shaken by the solid isolationist phalanx in Congress, which had thwarted his every attempt to repeal the Neutrality Act. American sentiment was strongly in favor of following another dictum of George Washington's: "Avoid the broils of Europe." Although American sympathy was overwhelmingly pro-Allied, not too many understood as Roosevelt did that the Anglo-French needed American material support to survive. To them, even war itself was "un-American." Frank Leahy, the famous Notre Dame football coach, was roundly cheered when he said: "Football is America's substitute for war." Most difficult of all for Roosevelt in those days was the uncompromising attitude of Charles A. Lindbergh, the heroic aviator who had been first to conquer the Atlantic, and who, because of the tragic kidnap-murder of his baby boy, still was the recipient of a vast outpouring of sympathy. Lindbergh's father had been a congressman who had opposed American entry into World War I. His son, Charles, was like so many other Midwesterners whose Germanic and Slavic forebears had fled the Old World's compulsory military service, migrating to Middle America with their hearts full of hatred for war and the military. To these sincere and loyal Americans, pacifism or isolationism or a combination of both—if the words were not indeed interchangeable—was as native as the smell of corn or a nasal twang. Lindbergh insisted that to repeal neutrality was to open the gate on the road to war. In a Sunday-night broadcast he broke an eight-year silence to warn an enormous audience that if America went to war: "We must throw the entire resources of our entire nation into the conflict. Munitions alone will not be enough. We are likely to lose a million men, possibly several million—the best of American youth. We will be staggering under the burden of recovery the rest of our lives."

Lindbergh's speech provoked a blizzard of mail to fall on Congress: no fewer than a million letters all supporting his position. Polls also showed that from 80 to 90 percent of the American people wanted to "stay out of it." They also showed that the electorate was so adamant in its position that any attempt to persuade it otherwise might boomerang against the president. Roosevelt's indignation was boundless. He privately spoke of Lindbergh's "indiscretion" in accepting a medal from Goering, and hinted darkly that he might be a Nazi admirer. Vindictive as ever, FDR had this loyal and courageous, though probably mistaken, American removed from the rolls of the active reserve and ordered his income-tax returns to be audited. Nevertheless, FDR was now compelled to mute his open allegiance to the Allies; but he also began to think that if Europe were to be saved, it might be necessary for him to seek an unprecedented third term in the coming fall elections.

Meanwhile, the clever Dr. Joseph Goebbels seized upon the lull of the Phony War to crank up his propaganda mills. Concealed transmitters began foreign-language broadcasts that appeared to be from local stations. The Dutch were reminded of their Teutonic ancestry and in Belgium Flemings were incited to fight the Walloons. French *poilus*—the "hairy ones"—attracted to German stations because of their superior music, were told that the British would fight until the last Frenchman was dead, or in a propaganda ploy perhaps as old as warfare itself, warned that the officers who kept them on duty while they went on leave did so to get an uninterrupted crack at the *poilus'* wives and sweethearts.

There was a special treat for the British: Lord Haw-Haw. His real name was William Joyce. He had been born in the United States but raised in Ireland. Prior to the war he had been propaganda director for Britain's Fascist organization. Just before war began, he fled to Germany, where he was hired by Goebbels. Lord Haw-Haw was a hit in Britain. Polls showed that more than a quarter of the island's population listened to him every night. He seemed to know everything that was going on in Old Blighty. Village meetings, blackout accidents, troop movements and train delays, he knew all about them, serving them up in a lilting, honeyed Irish brogue salted with witticisms. In comparison to the bland, obviously censored broadcasts of the BBC, Lord Haw-Haw was a welcome relief, and his listeners were just as amused by his dire predictions of impending destruction for Perfidious Albion as they were by his barbed digs at the Colonel Blimps who ran the government. Although it has been said that William Joyce was a clever propagandist, the fact is that he dismayed or disturbed no one. After the war the British tried and executed him for treason.

Allied propaganda broadcasts probably were not as skillful as the Goebbels product, and they never reached the ears of the regimented German troops. They did better among civilians, who were quickly forbidden to listen to foreign broadcasts. They obeyed, at least during the early days of the Phony War. Else Wendel was one such loyal German who would never disobey a decree. Else worked as a secretary in the Strength Through Joy office. She was proud of having "the correct attitude" and had accepted without a murmur the severe rationing announced by Dr. Goebbels. An adult's weekly ration consisted of less than a quarter-pound of butter, less than half a pound of meat and only powdered milk. People had to scrounge for other edibles, which they hoarded like pack rats. They also scrambled for coal, which was in especially short supply. During that savagely cold winter, clothing became scarce. After Goebbels announced that it would be rationed, a flood of anxious buyers flowed through the clothing stores, cleaning out the shelves so thoroughly that the stores were closed for two months. People began to make their own clothes from whatever materials they could obtain, even patchwork cut from worn garments. They made wooden clogs, too, noisy and uncomfortable substitutes for rare leather footwear.

Such shortages were suffered in loyally sacrificial silence by citizens such as

Else Wendel. Each night after work, she sat shivering in her apartment with her coat on and the stove unlighted. She did this to conserve her meager supply so that at Christmas, when her children came home, the apartment would be warm. Else was lonely and sad without her two children. Her husband had collected the bonuses for having them, after which he divorced Else and left them with her. Else could not work and care for the children, so she farmed them out, one with a cousin, the other with an unrelated family, but she soon divined that this had not been a wise move. The families seemed to be deliberately turning her children against her. Weekend visits with them were strained and devoid of any sign of love. Else realized that the other families wanted her children for the extra food and clothing coupons that came with them. One weekend, Else's cousin refused to allow her son to go walking with her. Then she discovered that neither would be home with her for Christmas. To the cold that chilled Else's body was now added the sorrow that chilled her soul. She felt like echoing the sarcastic travesty on "Silent Night" being softly whispered by many Berliners:

> Silent night, holy night;
> All is calm, all is bright.
> Only the Chancellor stays on his guard
> Germany's future to watch and to ward.
> Leading our nation aright.

Austerity apparently was only for ordinary Germans. It never affected the life-style of the ruling Nazis, many of whom dwelt in opulence, even magnificence, until the end of the war. Hitler did not stint himself, much as Dr. Goebbels might mislead the public into believing that the greatest German of all times was suffering as they were. The champion in ostentation, of course, was Reichsmarschall Hermann Goering. There were legendary parties at Karinhall, Goering's country estate ninety miles from Berlin, which he had named after his deceased Swedish wife. Karinhall was in the national forest, of which Goering was the National Huntsman. He loved to hunt the deer, pheasant and other game stocked there, or to frolic in the bathtub with lion cubs from the zoo. There was also a small Greek temple containing Karin's ashes. When the door was opened, the lighting came on and a spotlight focused on a bust of Karin slowly revolving on a turntable. The mansion itself was packed with treasure: services of silver and gold, precious pottery studded with jewels, objets d'art, rare and beautiful china, wine cellars full of France's finest vintages, tapestries and paintings, among them the works of such artists as Rembrandt, Rubens and El Greco, gestures of "appreciation" from wealthy Jews he had helped to escape from Germany. Guests at Karinhall often gaped to see some of the world's most famous paintings that they had earlier seen in German museums adorning the walls. After France fell, Goering was the most prodigious plunderer of them all, sending home trainloads of loot.

The Reichsmarschall often appeared at his balls dressed in a uniform of white and gold, with a red sash around his ample waist almost as long as he was tall. His hands sparkled from all the rings on his pudgy fingers, while his chest gleamed with decorations. Goering had a childish love of jewelry. When he was depressed, his servants would bring him a crystal glass full of uncut diamonds. He would spread them on the table before him, arranging and rearranging them in different formations, laughing as they caught the light. His guests were also beautifully attired. They were mostly film and theater people from Vienna and Berlin. The ladies dressed in exciting and revealing gowns that the prudish Führer might have found shocking. But not Goering. The flashier the better for "Meyer," as he was later contemptuously called by bomb-weary Berliners after his famous remark: "If an enemy bomb ever falls on Berlin, then my name is Meyer." At his parties, guests were waited on by servants dressed in hunting breeches, they danced in the great hall to music played by some of the country's finest orchestras, or they rode over the immense estate in Goering's private railroad.

Meanwhile, the SS men in the private army of Goering's hated rival, Reichsführer-SS Heinrich Himmler, received amenities of a different order. In his concern for preserving the purity of Aryan blood, Himmler had thoughtfully opened a number of *Lebensborne* for his men. These were maternity homes for unwed mothers of Aryan heritage. Originally they were supported by dues from the SS men, but after the annexation of Austria were maintained by the money and property taken from the Jews. Gradually, the *Lebensborne* became unabashed places of copulation. An SS man could enter, find a suitable fräulein, bed her, impregnate her—and leave her to pass through the period of gestation in privacy. After the child was born, it would either be kept by the mother on a state subsidy or put out for adoption. The lady might repeat this process several times, not always with the same Fritz. What was important to Himmler was that the purity of the Aryan blood was being preserved, although it seems permissible to wonder if he did not also believe he had hit upon a marvelous recruiting stratagem.

Inevitably, word of these SS mating–lying-in places leaked out and a scandal seemed to be about to erupt. Much of this uneasiness had been provoked by publication at Christmas of an "Open Letter to an Unmarried Mother." Girls were urged to submit to soldiers going to the front out of sympathy and patriotism. Any offspring would be cared for by the state. The protests against the *Lebensborne* were quickly silenced, however, when the Reichsführer-SS personally put them on the Index Germanorum.

"Every war involves a tremendous letting of the best blood," Himmler said in a Phony War decree. "Beyond the boundaries of laws and customs . . . it will be a high duty of German women and girls of good blood to become the mothers, outside the bonds of marriage, and not irresponsibly but in the spirit of deep moral seriousness, of children of soldiers going on active service of whom fate alone knows whether they will come back again or die for Germany."

Stalemate still persisted on the Western Front. The golden moment for France to have penetrated the rickety, undermanned Siegfried Line to seize the vital industries of the Ruhr—Germany's Achilles heel—had long since passed.

France had been undone by its hopelessly outdated mobilization schedule and its reliance on old tactics and old weapons. This vast army so celebrated in the Western press was actually a conscript army, which could not go into action until the reservists had been called away from their civilian jobs. Next, the French believed that any offensive action must be preceded by a massive artillery bombardment, the old notion of a "can opener" that would breach enemy defenses. But the heavy artillery was in storage and would not be available for use until the sixteenth day of mobilization. By then, Poland was gone and the French sat still. Nevertheless, this untried army was still hailed as the world's greatest. Just before the war, when General Alphonse Georges had shown Winston Churchill the comparative strengths and quality of the French and German armies, Churchill had burst out admiringly: "But you are the masters!" Only a few know otherwise. For some years Paul Reynaud almost alone had warned of the danger of relying upon a slow-mobilizing conscript army rather than a mechanized force of professionals ready for instant combat. For this he earned the undying enmity not only of the leftist governments in power eager to economize on the older, cheaper system, but also of many generals content with their slow-motion army. So the myth of an Allied victory gained by the French army's holding action while the British navy twisted the economic screws of a sea blockade remained indestructible.

Many of the officers in the British Expeditionary Force (BEF) that landed in France were appalled at the unmilitary appearance and spirit of the French soldiery. General Sir Alan Brooke, who commanded one of the BEF's two corps, was deeply dismayed with what he saw. "Never have I seen anything more slovenly and badly turned out," he wrote. "Men unshaven, horses ungroomed, clothes and saddlery that did not fit, vehicles dirty, and complete lack of pride in themselves or their units. What shook me most, however, was the look in the men's faces, disgruntled and insubordinate looks, and, although ordered to give 'Eyes left,' hardly a man bothered to do so."

On March 20, 1940, one of the principal politicians responsible for this sorry state of the French army—Premier Édouard Daladier—fell from power. The fall of Finland had been his undoing. His successor was Paul Reynaud. But Reynaud had only squeaked into power, and his hold on it was so tenuous that he had great difficulty forming a cabinet. Loner and harsh military critic that he had been, he could not possibly survive too many confrontations. Daladier was insisting that he be given the War Ministry, a position Reynaud had planned to confer on his friend, Col. Charles de Gaulle. If Daladier were war minister that meant that General Gamelin and all the other military chiefs whom Reynaud had criticized would stay at their desks. So Reynaud offered Daladier the Foreign Ministry, which he refused. But if Daladier stayed out of the cabinet, that might mean that Reynaud would be out, too. So Daladier got what he wanted, which was the very opposite of what Reynaud wanted. De Gaulle, one of the theoretical fathers of the German blitzkrieg, stayed out of the government. Once again, the French politicians' capacity for hating one another had done its damage.

Meanwhile, Hitler had taken every advantage of the lull called the Phony War. He had steadily raised his industrial capacity toward the peak he believed he needed to invade France. He had not only moved his formations westward from Poland but had begun to train them in blitzkrieg tactics. More and more tanks and armored vehicles and airplanes were rolling off the assembly lines, while his artillery—mainly horse-drawn in Poland—was steadily being motorized. Obviously, Adolf Hitler did not intend to prolong the "Sitzkrieg," or sitdown war, now in effect. Obviously also, the Phony War was turning genuine, much to the surprise and perhaps even chagrin of the Lion of Idaho, whose pacifist roaring still reverberated across America. In his high tone of moral superiority Senator Borah had repeatedly infuriated Secretary of State Cordell Hull with his smug assurances that his own sources of information in Europe were more reliable than the State Department's. Who and where they were was never known. The lion-maned senator had fallen into the common error of wishful thinking. From this he had moved to the equally familiar blunder of mistaking the part for the whole. A lull is part of the whole war. Like a caesura in music, it is part of the composition, a standing-still before the dreadful, clanging, horrifying symphony of battle is renewed.

14. April–June 1940: Norway and Denmark

IT WAS THE BRITISH who first looked north toward neutral Norway, their anxious eyes falling on the Norwegian coastal waters down which vital iron ore from the Swedish iron mines was shipped to Germany. As early as September 19, 1939, Winston Churchill had proposed mining their neutral—and sympathetic— neighbor's territorial waters to halt this traffic. In a classic demonstration of the adage "You become what you fight," Churchill seems to have given no thought to the Hitlerian crime of neutrality violation which he was urging on the British Cabinet. Nor could he remember that his own Admiralty had rejected such a proposal at the end of the last war, because Commander in Chief Lord Beatty had found it "repugnant to the officers and men in the Grand Fleet" as well as "a crime as bad as any that the Germans have committed elsewhere." Fortunately, in 1939 the British Foreign Office felt the same way, and Churchill's proposal was shelved.

With the onset of the Russo-Finnish War it was revived again by Churchill, who has written: "I welcomed this new and favourable breeze as a means of achieving the major strategic advantage of cutting off the vital iron-ore supplies of Germany." Although his powerful pleading did not persuade the Cabinet to authorize an invasion, it did instruct the British chiefs of staff to "plan for a landing force at Narvik." Almost at the tip of Norway's northeastern coast, Narvik was a port with a railroad leading to the Swedish minefields at Gällivare. Ostensibly the purpose of landing a force there was to bring aid to embattled Finland; actually it would be to seize the Swedish iron mines. While the chiefs began to plan, Adolf Hitler was receiving a Norwegian visitor whose name was to go into the dictionaries of many languages as a synonym for traitor.

Vidkun Quisling was born in 1887, the son of Norwegian peasants. A brilliant student, he was graduated first in his class at the Norwegian military academy, and while still in his twenties had been sent to Petrograd as a military attaché. Quisling was much impressed by the Russian Communists, so much so that when he returned to Oslo he approached the Communist-oriented Labor Party with a proposal to set up a "Red Guard." It was rejected. With the careerist's indifference to the worthiness of a cause, he swung from extreme left to farthest right. He did not immediately become a Nazi, but after serving as minister of defense from 1931 to 1933, he founded his own Fascist party, the National Union, basing it on Nazi tactics and ideology. In Norway's democratic soil, Nazism was not a fertile seed. Quisling was unable even to get himself elected to Parliament. So he turned to Nazi Germany, going there first in 1933 in search of assistance and subsidies. Six years later—December 1939—he came back with plans for a Nazi coup in his homeland. He was taken to Adm. Erich Raeder, the German naval chief. Quisling told Raeder he had many sympathizers among the Norwegian military, outlining a takeover scheme based on the typical *Anschluss* tactics. Raeder was impressed, and brought Quisling into Hitler's presence. *Der Führer* was also impressed. He saw Quisling twice more, but because he was so depressed by the coincident loss of the *Graf Spee* he was reluctant to undertake any large new naval operation such as an amphibious invasion of Norway would require. However, said Hitler, if the British were really planning to invade the country, he would certainly try to beat them to it. Otherwise, he preferred a neutral Scandinavia. With a promise to provide him funds to build his own Nazi party and to combat British propaganda, Hitler bade his visitor farewell.

Der Führer was sincere when he spoke of keeping Norway neutral. He did not want to risk a major naval defeat at the hands of the Royal Navy. He was getting his iron ore on schedule, and would not move unless the Allies showed him that they planned to get there first. This they proceeded to do.

A broadcast by the belligerent Churchill called upon almost all the neutrals —Belgium, Holland, Norway, Denmark, Switzerland—to remember their duty under the covenant of the League of Nations and unite with the Allies "against aggression and wrong." The neutral presses raised a storm of protest, but the broadcast also raised Hitler's eyebrows. Next, on February 10, 1940, the German prisoner ship *Altmark,* carrying British captives from the South Atlantic to Germany, was sighted by British destroyers and chased into a Norwegian fjord.

Churchill ordered the *Cossack* to burst into these Norwegian waters and rescue the prisoners. She did, despite the presence of a pair of little Norwegian gunboats. Norway at once protested, but Hitler, judging others by himself, believed that it was outrage simulated to cover compliance with the British. A report from Quisling claiming that the action of the *Cossack* had been prearranged between Britain and Norway confirmed his suspicions. The *Altmark* affair, then, decisively changed *Der Führer*'s mind. He sent for Gen. Nikolaus von Falkenhorst and ordered him to command and plan for a Norwegian operation. "I am informed that the British intend to land there," he told him, "and I want to be there before them. The occupation of Norway by the British would be a strategic turning movement which would lead them into the Baltic, where we have neither troops nor fortifications. . . . The enemy would find himself in a position to advance on Berlin and break the backbone of our two fronts."

Hitler also wanted Norway for air and submarine bases on its west coast, to control the Skagerrak passage from the North Sea into the Baltic, to lie athwart Britain's sea communications to northern Russia when the time came to stab his latest ally in the back and, of course, to protect that vital ore traffic. There was another compelling—and to the Fermi Five in the United States—chilling reason: Norway possessed almost all the heavy water in the world. Pure heavy water, which German physicists sought in their pursuit of fission, could be obtained only through an extremely prolonged electrolytic process requiring enormous amounts of electricity. Hydroelectric power was abundant in Norway. By the spring of 1940, Norwegian scientists had already acquired nearly 100 pounds of heavy water. As Fermi and his friends knew, if the Nazis captured Norway, they would promptly order production increased as much as a hundredfold.

But as fast as Hitler moved, the Allies kept pace with him. France's Premier Daladier before his fall from power had even proposed a "sudden stroke" to be justified, again à la Hitler, by "propaganda to exploit the memory of the recent complicity of Norway in the *Altmark* incident." In Britain, plans had been firmed up to throw three divisions ashore at four points in Norway and to move rapidly on the Gällivare iron mines. It would take place March 20. But on March 13 Finland fell and the Allies were robbed of their excuse to invade. Still Churchill pressed for the invasion, as well as for another favorite project: the mining of Germany's rivers from the air. It was agreed that Norwegian coastal waters would be mined on April 5, followed by the four-point landings. But then another delay arose when the French War Committee objected to the river-mining operation because it would bring German retaliation on France alone. They were not concerned, though, for German retaliation on an Allied-occupied Norway. So the invasion date was moved three days ahead, to April 8. Hitler's D-day was April 9. On the morning of that date, jubilant Allied newspapers announced that on the preceding day Allied ships had mined the Norwegian coasts. But rejoicing quickly turned to chagrin when the morning radio reports began blaring news of German landings in Norway and an invasion of Denmark.

It had been a very close race, even a photo-finish, and Herr Hitler had come home in front by half a head.

Denmark was the first target, and the little kingdom was a sitting duck. At the capital of Copenhagen in the north, the harbor was free of ice and its defenders free from any fear of invasion. On the land border with Germany in the south, the bridges were unblown, the roads unmined and the soldiery unwilling to fight. At 4:10 in the morning, the invasion began.

In the south, there was no resistance to German armor rolling over the border. In the north, vital airfields the Germans needed to cover the impending invasion of Norway were swiftly seized, in some cases without a shot being fired. A German troopship successfully passed the harbor defenses without challenge and sent an assault battalion ashore. The citadel was assaulted and quickly fell. Now the Germans in their coal-scuttle steel helmets began marching on the royal palace. Early risers cycling to work were astounded to encounter these troops. At first it was believed that a motion picture was being filmed, until the Palace Guard opened fire and the Germans returned it. Inside the palace elderly King Christian was anxiously conferring with his hastily awakened cabinet. They heard rifle fire and the approach of German aircraft deliberately roaring in low to frighten the populace. King Christian at once ordered his guards to cease firing and surrendered his country.

Before dawn—in less than two hours—the swastika flag was waving triumphantly over Denmark.

The invasion of Norway went off almost as smoothly. A force of two battle cruisers, a pocket battleship, seven cruisers, fourteen destroyers, twenty-eight submarines, together with supporting supply ships and transports carrying 10,000 soldiers sailed right under the nose of the British to put formations of 2,000 men apiece ashore at Oslo and Kristiansand on the south coast and Bergen, Trondheim and Narvik on the west.

At Oslo, the capital, the German attackers nearly met disaster. The brand-new battle cruiser *Blücher* and the pocket battleship *Lützow* had entered the long Oslo fjord.* Both warships intended to bombard the port prior to an airborne assault on the airfield. Neither expected resistance, until the old Oscarborg naval fortress opened fire in the darkness. Its batteries sank *Blücher.* A thousand Germans perished, among them ranking army officers whose mission was to persuade King Haakon VII to surrender as his brother King Christian† had done in Denmark. Many of those who sank beneath the waves suffered a horrible death: freezing in icy water before help could reach them or dragged down by the suction

---

Lützow was the *Deutschland* renamed because Hitler feared to have a ship of that name sunk.
†Christian and Haakon were both sons of King Frederick VIII of Denmark. When Norway separated from Sweden (October 27, 1905), the Storting, Norway's Parliament, chose Haakon as monarch, and he reigned until his death in 1957.

of the sinking cruiser. Worst of all were the sailors caught in burning oil patches. They faced the horrible alternatives of diving beneath the blazing oil to drown or continue to swim through flames. Such sights and the loss of *Blücher* compelled the captain of *Lützow* to turn and flee.

At the Oslo airfield, meanwhile, the German attaché waited for German parachute troops who never came. The field was absolutely open, but King Haakon could have ordered its defense and held it ready for Allied aircraft. Instead, he had become convinced from reports that the invasion was too strong for him to attempt to halt the Germans immediately. With his cabinet and members of Parliament, together with twenty-three trucks loaded with gold, he sought temporary sanctuary inland. Shortly afterward a single Messerschmitt touched down at the Oslo airport. Then more roared in, ringing the field with their outward-thrusting wing guns until transports could ferry in troops. By noon two battalions of about 800 men each had landed. A band came in. Forming behind the band, the German soldiers goose-stepped into Oslo in a victory parade. Their own soldiers having melted into the snow-covered hills, the citizens of Oslo stood in anguished awe to see the hated Nazis come strutting and trumpeting into their capital.

Now Maj. Vidkun Quisling showed his mettle. He and his heralded fifth column had been of little or no use anywhere in the invasion, but once he saw that Oslo had fallen, he rushed into the city and seized the radio station to broadcast an announcement that the Germans had come to protect Norway from the British and that he was the new prime minister. Quisling's speech enraged the Norwegians and aroused their king. Haakon refused to acknowledge German control of his country or Quisling's personal appeals for confirmation in his post. Six days after Quisling proclaimed himself prime minister, the Nazis removed him from office, eventually sending a gauleiter into Norway to govern with customary Nazi brutality. Quisling himself survived until the end of the war, when Norway tried him for treason, convicting and executing him. He had not really been a very effective traitor.

Meanwhile, the king and government whom he had betrayed had been moving farther inland with Norway's gold reserve. The Nazis pretended to be anxious to negotiate with the king, actually trying to locate him so that two busloads of parachutists on his trail could capture him and his entourage. But the parachutists were stopped at a roadblock and dealt a bloody repulse. Haakon then moved on to an inn in the little village of Nybergsund. From there he authorized a radio appeal to his 3 million subjects to resist the invaders. The Germans were outraged. Late on April 11 the villagers of Nybergsund heard the murmur of many motors approaching. With a roar, the Luftwaffe warbirds swooped down with explosive and incendiary bombs. They machine-gunned those who tried to escape. In the diary of a Luftwaffe pilot later captured in Norway was found the exultant entry: "Nybergsund. *Oslo Regierung. Alles vernichtet.* Oslo government. Completely wiped out."

But it was not true. Haakon and his officials had also heard the dreadful hum of the approaching aircraft and had taken refuge in a nearby wood. There they had stood, knee-deep in snow, watching helplessly while an innocent village and its inhabitants vanished from the face of the earth. Now, Haakon faced a choice: He could either lead his government with its gold across the nearby border into Sweden, where aslyum would also mean internment, or trek onward to some safe Norwegian place to continue the resistance. For Haakon the decision was not difficult: he chose a march through the mountains, rallying the resistance en route, until he reached Åndalsnes on the northwest coast. There he halted to await succor by the British.

But Norway was now—along with Denmark, Austria, Czechoslovakia and Poland—a Nazi satellite.

Germany had not been quite so fortunate at sea. High on the North Sea near Narvik the British cruiser *Renown* fought the heavier *Gneisenau* and *Scharnhorst* in a brief, furious, salvo-for-salvo battle. A salvo from *Renown* staggered one of the Germans, but they were still successful in luring the British warship away from the landing areas. The German cruiser *Königsberg* was sunk by British aircraft, and British submarines sank seven smaller ships, scoring a torpedo hit on *Lützow* that carried away part of her propeller and stern.

Narvik, the key city so close to the Swedish iron mines, fell with surprising ease. Three German destroyers led five troopships into the harbor. Two Norwegian cutters which sought to intercept them were blown out of the water. A division of soldiers under General Eduard Dietl went ashore to seize and fortify strong points around the harbor. General Dietl announced to the Norwegians that he had come to protect them from the British. He summoned the garrison commander, a Quisling follower, who quickly surrendered. He commiserated with the mayor who had protested the needless bloodshed. "Sad, isn't it?" Dietl murmured. "I can assure you, gentlemen, that we do not wish any bloodshed. I am happy to inform you that Norway is now occupied peacefully in the name of the Führer."

But it was not that easy. That afternoon, five British destroyers under Captain B. A. W. Warburton-Lee appeared off Narvik. They learned from a pilot that ten German destroyers were inside the harbor and its fjords. Outnumbered two to one, the gallant Warburton-Lee nevertheless chose battle, signaling the Admiralty that he would attack "at dawn high water." True to his word, he led his flotilla into the harbor at first light April 10. British gunnery sank two enemy destroyers, damaged two more and put six merchant ships on the bottom. The Germans countered by sinking two Britishers and damaging a third, killing Warburton-Lee.

Three days later the 30,000-ton battleship *Warspite* led nine British destroyers into the harbor. General Dietl was astounded and appalled: astounded because he could not believe that any commander would risk such a huge warship in such narrow waters, appalled because *Warspite* and her nine little furies pounded everything German beneath the waves—warships, merchant ships and one submarine. Then the British sailed out to sea again, and this time Dietl was really astounded: With their firepower the enemy could have made a shambles of the port installations and sent him and his men scurrying into the mountains.

Dietl's report created near panic in Berlin. Karl Doenitz, the U-boat chief, was furious. His submarines had fired hundreds of torpedoes at the British ships and every single one had missed. In exasperation, Doenitz recalled them all to put them out of service until his torpedo experts could locate and correct what had caused their "fish" to misfire. Admiral Raeder was also depressed. His navy had barely missed being annihilated. He had lost four out of five capital ships and half his destroyer force, and it would be at least six months before the losses could be replaced.

For the first time Hitler lost his celebrated nerve, issuing an order for General Dietl to abandon Narvik. Also for the first time, the toadying twins of the OKW*—Generals Wilhelm Keitel and Alfred Jodl—stood up to Hitler after a braver colonel beneath them refused to send the order to retreat. Jodl finally persuaded Hitler to tear it up and send another commanding Dietl to hold Narvik to the last man.

How was it that the Royal Navy, the admiration of the seagoing world, operating in those North Sea waters which the Admiralty regarded as its own private pond, had failed to intercept and destroy a vastly inferior naval force embarked on that most difficult of all military operations, a seaborne invasion? In part, the extent of the sea space running about 800 miles from Oslo in the south to Narvik in the north, the nature of the Norwegian coast serrated as it was by so many fjords in which even capital ships might hide, and the mists and hazes of the weather all tended to favor the invaders. Perhaps more important to the Germans was the Admiralty's overweening confidence. On April 2, when General Gamelin urged Field Marshal Lord Ironside, chief of the British Imperial General Staff, to hasten the expeditionary force to Norway, Ironside replied: "With us the Admiralty is all-powerful; it likes to organize everything methodically. It is convinced that it can prevent any German landing on the west coast of Norway." In effect, it was really convinced that the Germans wouldn't dare.

But as early as April 7 British aircraft actually spotted the German forces sailing swiftly northward across the Skagerrak toward Norway. At once the Home Fleet was alerted to sail within an hour, while bombers were sent roaring aloft. They found the German ships and emptied their bomb bays on them. Not a single ship was hit in the war's first demonstration of the futility of sending high-altitude horizontal bombers after maneuvering warships. In Mitchell's famous demonstration of planes versus ships, his horizontal bombers had sunk warships *dead in the water,* like shooting fish in a barrel. To sink moving, maneuvering ships requires dive bombers hurtling down from the skies, or torpedo bombers skimming in low over the water; and since both these warbirds

*OKW—*Oberkommando der Wehrmacht,* the high command of the armed forces.

usually take off from aircraft-carrier decks, it is obvious that seapower had baptized airpower with salt water, just as it had done to firepower five centuries earlier. Unfortunately for Britain, on this momentous day its seapower was not being properly deployed.

It was twelve hours, not sixty minutes, before the Home Fleet debouched from Scapa Flow into the North Sea, and it did so without its aircraft carriers. Worse, the admirals in the Admiralty and those at sea were more concerned with catching and destroying the "big boys" in the German fleet than with intercepting the smaller troop-carrying warships. Thus anxious to bring Hitler's capital ships to battle, they lost sight of the possibility of an amphibious invasion of Norway. Indeed, Churchill and his sea lords had concluded that the German fleet was trying to break out of the North Sea into the Atlantic to fall upon Allied shipping. Hence, the Home Fleet in the beginning made no attempt to attack the enemy in midpassage but sailed northeast toward the Atlantic to head the Germans off. Churchill has admitted that he found it hard to believe that the German fleet was actually heading for Narvik, as a report from Copenhagen indicated. Instead, he and his admirals thought the land objective must have been Larvik, a port just west of Oslo at almost the farthest point south of Narvik. Of course, the Home Fleet did make a fairly rapid readjustment and did inflict considerable damage on the German navy, but by then the German soldiery was ashore and swiftly consolidating its holds on the port cities, from which it would shortly move through the valleys against the surprised Norwegian army.

The Luftwaffe provided invaluable assistance. Some 800 fighter planes and bombers simply demoralized the Norwegian people, while the 250 transport planes brought in reinforcements and material almost round-the-clock. The Messerschmitts and Stukas flying off newly seized airports in Denmark as well as Norway would have made it most difficult for the British to mount a counterinvasion. But none was forthcoming anyway. The Admiralty, having already boated troops, ordered its cruiser squadron at Rosyth "to march your soldiers ashore, even without their equipment, and join the fleet at sea." Similar orders were sent to troop-laden ships in the Clyde.

But the Norwegians cannot wholly escape blame, as Churchill has been at pains to point out. At the time, he wrote, their government was "chiefly concerned with the activities of the British." Distracted by the British and French mining of its waters, Norway did not think to mobilize until, many hours after being attacked, King Haakon authorized call-up letters to be sent out. Mobilization by mail with an enemy ashore! And the help that Norway anticipated from the Allies did not appear until a week later.

Political wrangling in Great Britain delayed the Allied counterinvasion of Norway. Churchill and the Military Coordinating Council wanted to send two divisions to Narvik, where a smaller British force had already landed but had not attacked. Admiral Lord Cork and Orrery had repeatedly urged Gen. P. J. Mackesy to strike, but Mackesy was a timid man who demurred with the overcautious commander's customary complaint that he didn't have enough troops. So Churchill was going to send him two more divisions. After all, Narvik was not only still the key to control of the iron-ore traffic, it would be an invaluable port into which men and material could be fed and on which airfields could be built to support the eventual reconquest of Norway. But the Joint Planning Committee insisted that the troops be sent to Trondheim in central Norway, as King Haakon in nearby Åndalsnes had requested. Haakon was now an ally, the committee argued, and his wishes should be honored. Churchill and the Council finally bowed to severe political pressure, and the expedition mounted out for Trondheim. But in midpassage Churchill divided the force and sent half to Trondheim and half to Narvik—not enough to take either objective.

The Allies planned to land above and below Trondheim: "Mauriceforce" to the north at Namsos, "Sickleforce" to the south at Åndalsnes. They would attack the city from both sides in a pincers movement.

At Åndalsnes, commanders were landed at one place and their men at another. The cables for their field telephones were en route to Narvik. Mortar ammunition and carriages for the Bren guns had been left behind in Britain. Instead of attacking Trondheim, Sickleforce was ordered to swing south to link up with the Norwegian army. But the British soldiers found they could not distinguish Norwegians from Germans except at close range, and were fired on by "friendly" soldiers. Without transport, they moved in commandeered cars and trucks driven by Norwegian civilians who spoke little English. Worse, their antitank shells could not penetrate German armor. Whole units were annihilated and hundreds of British soldiers were captured; some of them were flown to Berlin, where Hitler showed them off to the public. Captured plans of Britain's canceled Stavanger landing were seized upon by Goebbels as proof that the Allies intended to invade Norway first.

To the north of Namsos, Mauriceforce's situation was just as confused but more desperate. Its antiaircraft guns had gone to Narvik and the men had reindeer saddles but no skis. The French *Chasseurs Alpins* had their skis but the wrong straps for their boots, and their supply ship was too big to enter the harbor. Soon the Luftwaffe appeared and blasted Namsos into a pile of rubble. Mauriceforce, outnumbering the Germans two to one, was pinned down and scourged from the sky. At last it became clear that the Trondheim operation could not go forward, and on May 1 and 2 both forces were withdrawn. Germany was now in complete control of central and southern Norway.

High in the north at Narvik, General Mackesy was at last moving. His forces had been built to 25,000 men—British, Norwegian, and Polish soldiers, French *Chasseurs Alpins* and men of the French Foreign Legion—against 2,000 Austrian Alpine troops and the same number of German sailors commanded by General Dietl. Dietl made skillful use of his inferior force and the difficult terrain, assisted in his defense by Mackesy's creeping tactics. Still, Dietl feared he would lose northern Norway. He planned to evacuate his remaining troops by railroad to

Sweden. He had already lost 800 killed. His men were weary from constant fighting and lack of sleep and food. They were disgusted to see the bodies of their dead comrades thrown into sewers. They were near mutiny when, on May 28, they were driven out of Narvik. But the Allied victory was a hollow one, a mere face-saving gesture made to cheer the people of France and Britain already depressed by Allied setbacks in the Battle of France then raging.

On June 7 and 8, without notifying the Norwegian forces beforehand, the Allies withdrew, taking with them King Haakon with his government and his gold. Norway was now completely in German hands.

The fall of Norway was the downfall of Neville Chamberlain. To him as prime minister was ascribed the blame for that miserable, bloody fiasco, not to Winston Churchill, its true author. As first lord of the Admiralty, Churchill had planned and urged first the invasion of Norway, then the actual mining of its neutral waters, the spark that sent Hitler rocketing into action, and it was Churchill who had been involved in the repeated delays and changes of course that had robbed the Allied forces of both essential equipment and precious time, not to mention clearness of purpose and unity of action. Yet Chamberlain accepted the blame. He could easily have thrown Churchill to the wolves already howling outside his door, as another prime minister had done to Churchill in 1915. But he did not do so. He respected the first lord for his loyalty and propriety, and had found his fighting spirit and detailed knowledge of military affairs to be indispensable. So Neville Chamberlain faced the wolves alone.

On May 7 the debate on Norway began in the House of Commons. There were uniforms everywhere. Many of the members had served in Norway. Sir Roger Keyes arose. He wore a naval uniform plastered with six rows of ribbons and the Grand Cross of the Order of the Bath. In bitter tones he denounced Chamberlain's conduct of the war, excusing his friend Churchill. Leo Amery, another friend of Churchill's, got to his feet. He quoted Oliver Cromwell's angry words when, three centuries ago, he dismissed the Long Parliament. "You have sat here too long for any good you might be doing. Depart, I say, and let us have done with you. In the name of God, go!" A roar of approval rose from the benches of the Loyal Opposition. "Go!" they cried. "Go!" In the ensuing days Labour Party leaders joined the attack. Chamberlain was castigated for failing to form a national government from all the parties. It was now clear to Chamberlain that he, not his government, was the focal point of the criticism. He called upon Churchill to defend him. Churchill did so with customary mastery and balance, so that he not only failed to appear ludicrous in exonerating his chief from blame for wrongs he himself had committed, but he also produced a vote of confidence in the government—but it was only by 81 votes. Chamberlain knew that his days were numbered.

On May 10, the day when the Hitlerian thunderbolts were hurled against France, Belgium and Holland, Chamberlain summoned Churchill and Lord Halifax to 10 Downing Street. He sat opposite them, cool, unruffled, as though the fate of Europe were not at stake in the great battle then raging across the Channel. He told his visitors that only a national government could deal with this terrible crisis. He said he believed it was beyond his power to form such a coalition. The hostility of Labour had convinced him of this. There was a long pause. Lord Halifax, whom Chamberlain secretly preferred, began to speak. Churchill has described his words: "He said that he felt that his position as a peer, out of the House of Commons, would make it very difficult for him to discharge the duties of prime minister in a war like this. He would be held responsible for everything, but would not have the power to guide the assembly upon whose confidence the life of every government depended. He spoke for some minutes in this sense, and by the time he had finished it was clear that the duty would fall upon me—had in fact fallen on me." It had. Chamberlain departed to see the king, and soon from the palace came a call for Churchill. King George received him graciously. "I suppose you don't know why I have sent for you?" he asked coyly. In the same vein, Churchill replied: "Sir, I simply couldn't imagine why." The king laughed, and said: "I want to ask you to form a government," and Churchill accepted the invitation.

Twice, now, Winston Churchill had been first lord of the Admiralty. Twice he had failed, perhaps more disastrously this time than in 1915, when the Turks at Gallipoli turned back his effort to force the Dardanelles and so gain the Black Sea and communications with Russia. That repulse had cost him his office. This time the debacle at Norway which he had also authored had made him His Majesty's first minister.

15. Winston Churchill

WINSTON LEONARD SPENCER CHURCHILL was born November 30, 1874, the son of a handsome, dashing British lord and a beautiful, wealthy American heiress. Thus a fairy tale might begin, and yet, if ever a life were charmed or a career guided by some invisible hand, it was evident in the person of this incredible human being.

The child who was to be this man, to continue the fairy tale, entered life at Blenheim Castle, an enormous edifice of gold-colored stone given by a grateful Britain to Churchill's most illustrious ancestor, John Churchill, the first Duke of Marlborough—the greatest captain of his age, and the special hairshirt of King Louis XIV of France—who was, with the Duke of Wellington, one of the two greatest soldiers in British history.

Winston's father was Lord Randolph Churchill. Because he was a younger son, he did not inherit the dukedom, nor could his own courtesy title pass on to any of his children. Winston's mother was Jenny Jerome, whose father, Leonard Jerome, was a piratical New York financier so distinguished in those days of the Robber Barons that he was hailed as "the king of Wall Street." He was also a man of many pleasures, who had named his daughter after his current mistress, the Swedish singing star, Jenny Lind. It is not known what Jenny Jerome's mother thought of this selection. Jenny became an international beauty, who was cosseted and spoiled in the gilded salons of Europe. She was twenty when she met Lord Randolph, who proposed to her almost at once. They were married in April 1874, and seven months later Winston was born. Winston arrived in Blenheim two months early because, as he said later, he was eager to begin living in such a distinguished place, named as it was for Marlborough's first famous victory.

Lord and Lady Randolph at once consigned him to a nurse, hurrying away from Blenheim to renew their pursuit of pleasure. They seldom saw their children (another son, Jack, was born four years after Winston). Winston has said that the only time his mother noticed him was to scold him for being a nuisance. Yet, he wrote, "She shone for me like the Evening Star. I loved her dearly—but at a distance."

Lord Randolph was actually callous in his treatment of his son, frequently rude, sometimes brutal. Still Winston adored him and in later life wrote an adulatory biography of him, which failed to mention his many vices. Lord Randolph was a typical aristocratic dandy. He wore a curled mustache, violet waistcoats and tan shoes, an amber cigarette holder embossed with a huge diamond sticking jauntily from his mouth. He was called "the Champagne Charlie of politics," a calling in which he might have carved out a brilliant career had he not been so erratic and given to uncontrollable rages. Often his wrath fell on the head of his son, yet Winston continued to idolize his father. Lord Randolph was also subject to fits of deep depression, the "black dog" which also prowled like a sinister shadow at Winston Churchill's heels. His fondness for female flesh led him to an indiscreet union with a Blenheim housemaid from which liaison he contracted the syphilis that eventually drove him mad. Passing through conflicting moods of dejection and euphoria, of delusions of grandeur and maniacal rages, he finally died on January 24, 1895, at the age of forty-five. His wife was hardly better. She was said to have had at least two hundred lovers and, after the death of Lord Randolph, a pair of handsome but impecunious young husbands each possessing impeccable manners and the brains of an oyster.

Winston's childhood was not without warmth and affection, which he found in his nanny, a Mrs. Everest, whom he nicknamed "Womany." (Either in fact or in fiction, English nannies never seem to have first names.) Womany tried her utmost to discipline her willful charge, but with absolutely no success. *He* was a Churchill. While his parents were away, it was *his house*. Before he was five, the servants came to detest him for his hectoring, domineering manner.

At seven Winston was sent to St. George's, Ascot, a fashionable preparatory school notorious for its brutal discipline. Even those Victorians who firmly believed that to spare the rod was to spoil the child were shocked by a headmaster who beat his pupils so savagely that their blood spattered his study. Winston Churchill's flesh also yielded blood, but his will remained unbroken. Obdurate, he was always in trouble. Nor would he back down before any of the bigger schoolyard bullies. Like most smaller boys who are quick and brave and willing to take a punch, he believed that he had been sent by the Queen of Heaven to punish these bigger boys. But more often than not it is the smaller boys such as Winston who are the true bullies. His belligerence was soon a byword. Meanwhile, he read omnivorously but without guidance and remained at the bottom of his class. By way of another preparatory school, Winston entered Harrow at the age of thirteen. Again, he was an indifferent student, not actually lazy but interested only in those pursuits that caught his fancy. Thus he enjoyed the cadet corps, became a champion fencer, memorized a thousand lines from Macaulay's *Lays of Ancient Rome* and was well on his way to mastery of the English sentence. But for Latin and French he cared not a fig, writing English essays for those classmates who would do his Latin tasks.

Winston thought Harrow was a colossal bore. Like a true "interruptive interrupter," he sought to enliven his days by deliberately making trouble. So the headmaster took the rod to him more than any other boy, a habit that did not deter Winston from telling the headmaster how to run the school. Yet it was at Harrow that Winston Churchill began to evolve into what can only be described as a thoroughgoing jingoist. He had always, like the young Mussolini, the young Hitler, the young Stalin, been convinced that he was a man of destiny. But at Harrow he learned to place his faith in allegiance to his family, his sovereign, his class, his country (indubitably in that order) and to that British Empire which he considered a colonizing and civilizing power greater even than Rome. This was and always would be his credo, and these were the winged wheels of the fiery chariot of his ambition. But at Harrow, he was again a failure.

It was this very ambition—immodest and unashamed—that had caused many of his less flamboyant schoolmates to regard him as a beastly bounder, and his superior airs toward and sometimes derision of his teachers had earned him most unenviable marks. There was no way he could pass on to either Oxford or Cambridge, those ancient and noble institutions of learning which the British ruling classes had founded for their sons.

As he neared seventeen, his appearance was not without promise, even though his parents found him unprepossessing. He had reached his full height of five feet six and a half inches. He was stocky, with square shoulders matching his square belligerent jaw, his mouth was good-humored and generous, and beneath his crop of carroty red hair his deep-set blue eyes were capable of turning so coldly menacing that one fellow Harrovian, who had unwisely disputed the sidewalk with him, found them comparable to those of a wild boar. But his parents noticed only his faint lisp, his sloppiness, his willfulness, his invincible indifference to his tutors and his interest in only a few suitably aristocratic pastimes such as fox hunting or polo. Yet he did have one serious passion: the military. He was fond of drilling his cousins and his brother Jack. He built an outdoor castle complete with a drawbridge and a catapult, which he used to fling apples at cows. Above all, he loved to command his armies of toy soldiers, arranging them in formations to fit the campaigns of his famous ancestor.

It was this hobby that decided his career: Lord Randolph seeing his hopeless son at play with his lead soldiers suddenly suggested a military career. Winston agreed with great enthusiasm, but he needed three cracks at the entrance examination, plus the help of a London crammer, to be accepted finally in 1893 as a cadet at the British Military College at Sandhurst. Even so, he could only qualify for the cavalry, which had lower intellectual standards and higher financial requirements than the infantry. Lord Randolph was furious at the cost of getting Winston into only the second class at Sandhurst and the expensive prospects of keeping him there. He rebuked him for his "slovenly, happy-go-lucky, harum-scarum style of work" and his "idle, useless, unprofitable life." Winston apologized and promised to improve, unaware that his father's rages were the first symptoms of the dreadful disease that was sapping his life.

Cadet Churchill was happy at Sandhurst. He enjoyed the military life, especially the splendid scarlet-and-gold uniform that he wore. Because he was physically lazy, he detested drill and the Spartan regulations then common to most military schools. But he did love to ride, sometimes spending eight hours a day in the saddle, and becoming a topflight polo player. Although he professed an interest in the art of war, he received little intellectual instruction in that discipline. That was for infantry officer candidates, not the cavalry, whose twin duties were "to look smart in time of peace and get killed in war." The cavalry, moreover, suited Winston's ardent, impetuous nature. He never really got over being a subaltern of hussars, and although he embraced the machines of modern war —warships, airplanes and tanks—he thought of them as metallic steeds charging into the fray.

Winston's overpowering desire to see action led him to spend the autumn leave of 1895 in Spain's rebellious colony of Cuba. Trading upon the high-placed connections of his parents, and with typical brashness, he pulled enough strings to obtain a letter of introduction to the Spanish general in charge of destroying the insurgents. Next, in another maneuver that was to be typical, he wangled an assignment from the *Daily Graphic* to cover the conflict and also report on a new Spanish bullet. With a subaltern friend, he attached himself to a column pushing into the jungle, and to his immense delight was fired upon for the first time in his life on his twenty-first birthday. Little more action ensued, and Winston came home, bringing with him the beginning of a lifelong fondness for fine Havana cigars and the habit of taking a siesta. Through the refreshing medium of this hour-long afternoon nap, he remarked later, he was able to get a day-and-a-half's work out of every twenty-four hours.

In 1896 his 4th Hussars were posted to India for garrison duty. Bangalore bored him. There were no interesting people, no witty, combative conversationalists such as himself with whom to pass the dull off-duty hours, and the wearying, soul-destroying, seemingly senseless rounds of peacetime military duty were crushing his spirit. He tried to revive it with vigorous physical exercise, improving his polo game, which he played with zest and abandon, even though he had to strap up the right shoulder he had dislocated jumping ashore at Bombay. But he still yearned for intellectual exertion, to stock his mind with the mental furniture he already knew he would need in the future. He did not seek erudition for its own sake. He wanted facts, a world view, a knowledge of the panorama of mankind which would enable him to overwhelm and awe his opponents in the political arena he intended to enter. With great delight he discovered Macaulay and Gibbon, not only learning from them what had happened since the beginning of history but also assimilating some of that sonorous lofty style that was to lift his own career to the heights. He did this secretively, alone in his quarters during the long hot afternoons, afraid to arouse suspicions of being a "literary" or "brainy" officer among those comrades who passed the same hours drinking quinine-laced port or perusing *Ruff's Guide to the Turf.* Inevitably, his steadily increasing powers of expression and his expanding knowledge made him arrogant. He became bumptious toward his colleagues, those indolently lounging hussars who, true to their art, conceived of life as a checkerboard of rattling good chukkers and thundering great cavalry charges. They resented it, and one day throwing aside their copies of *Ruff's* they hurled themselves on him, pinned his struggling body to the ground and fixed him there by placing a large sofa on top of him. He squirmed free, only slightly abashed and still irrepressible, crying: "You can't keep me down like that!"

It was indeed not possible, ever; and Winston Churchill was "up" again in April of 1897 when he heard while on home leave that Gen. Sir Bindon Blood was organizing the Malakand Field Force to chastise the rebellious Pathans of Afghanistan. Caught between the hostile Russian and British empires, these rugged mountain tribesmen had declared their independence. Sir Bindon's "pheasant shoot," as he called the expedition, was intended to put them down again. Churchill hastened back to India, receiving permission to act as a war correspondent and officer. His dispatches back home might have been set to the music of "Rule Britannia," although they were celebrating little more than the customary slaughter of an ill-armed rabble. Oddly, Churchill, always magnanimous to a brave enemy, failed to mention either the dauntless courage and even military prowess of the Pathans, or the poor tactical skill of British commanders whom these fierce people sometimes repulsed. But there are no lines for the enemy in "Rule Britannia." Churchill was himself at least as brave as the foe. He fought foremost in all the small actions in which he was engaged. Once he made himself the lone rearguard of a rearguard action. In another engagement with the British pinned down, he boldly rode his gray pony up and down the line in full view of the enemy. "Foolish perhaps," he wrote to his mother, "but I play for high stakes and given an audience there is no act too daring or too noble." The audience, of course, was General Blood, who mentioned Churchill in his dispatches.

Churchill was overjoyed, but the book he wrote about the expedition infuriated rather than impressed his military superiors. He had criticized official policies, especially the neglect of wounded soldiers, and he was taken to task as a pink-cheeked glory hound who had the colossal cheek to lecture his betters. Although the book earned him the equivalent of two years' pay, it cost him a shot at the Tirah expedition to the Northwest Frontier in 1898. Nor did Lord Kitchener want this "swab" of a journalist along in the Sudan either, officer though he might be. But Churchill simply had to play a part in this glorious campaign, mounted to avenge the murder of Gen. Charles George ("Chinese") Gordon at Khartoum in 1885 during the Holy War by which the Mahdi (Messiah) won Sudanese independence. So he turned again to one of his mother's friends, Lady Jeune, a prominent society hostess, who persuaded the War Office to overrule Kitchener, and Churchill went along as a supernumerary officer in the 21st Lancers as well as a "swab" of a correspondent.

At the Battle of Omdurman, in which the Mahdi was defeated, Churchill participated in a wild cavalry charge, an assault upon an immensely superior enemy which was as foolish as Kitchener's decision to come out of an excellent defensive position to engage a foe being destroyed by superior British weaponry. Churchill, however, thought that Omdurman was a glorious victory. After it, he decided that he had had enough military honor and was now ready to enter politics. Resigning his commission, he returned home in the summer of 1899 to run in a by-election at Oldham in Lancashire. He was narrowly defeated.

He was dejected; but then bugles blared once more and the blaze of true battle beckoned again: in 1899 the Boer War began. Churchill at once secured a commission to cover it for the *Morning Post* at the enormous pay in those days of $1,250 a month plus expenses. Armed with cases of wine and cognac, to comfort and persuade, he took ship for South Africa.

Eager as always for action, he attached himself to an armored-train patrol propelled by an engine in its middle. It was ambushed by the Boers. Churchill soon found himself looking into the little round mouth of a Boer rifle muzzle.

Churchill's captors knew who he was and treated him kindly, although they were amused at his angry insistence on being freed as "a noncombatant." So he remained in a prisoner-of-war camp in Pretoria, until he and two other prisoners found a section of the camp wall invisible to the guards. One dark night Churchill was the first over it. He waited for the others. After an hour he heard someone whisper that the game was up, and he scurried off on his own.

Without a map, a compass or knowledge of the Boer language, but armed with a few bars of chocolate, plenty of money and an inexhaustible audacity, he walked down the road in darkness heading east away from the camp. He boarded a slow freight train, jumping off before dawn to spend the next day hiding in a grove of trees. He walked all the following night, finally in desperation knocking at the door of a house. To his relief, the owner was British. He fed the fugitive, and with the help of two English-born miners sent him on his way hidden in a freight car full of wool. Arriving safely in Portuguese East Africa, Churchill made for the British Consulate to obtain clean clothes and to telegraph the electrifying news of his daring escape to the *Morning Post*. He made skillful use of the Boers' delightful £25 reward for his person, "Dead or Alive," and became an overnight hero at home. In Durban, where he arrived by ship on December 23, 1899, he was hailed by a huge crowd in front of the Town Hall, delivering one of his carefully prepared "impromptu" speeches.

On the strength of his popularity, Churchill was able to persuade a reluctant high command to grant him a lieutenant's commission in the South African Light Horse. Once again he was the soldier-journalist, participating in and describing some of the fiercest fights of the war while the tide of battle flowed toward Pretoria. So it was that the boy-hero, the boy-master of words and the boy-director of dramatics was among the first into Pretoria, where he brought his incredible career to a predictable climax by tearing down the Boer *Vierkleur* (Four Colors) from the flagstaff and replacing it with the Union Jack.

Winston Churchill returned to England in triumph, and just in time for the October elections. Everywhere he went he was toasted and lionized, and the voters of Oldham who had so narrowly rejected him little more than a year earlier now flocked to his standard with enthusiasm. Churchill was now a member of Parliament. He was only a few weeks short of his twenty-sixth birthday, starting his new career at the same age as his hero, Napoleon. Almost from the moment of his maiden speech, which he found to be "a terrible, thrilling, yet delicious experience," he astounded and angered his Conservative colleagues by advocating a program of social reform that was actually far more Liberal than Tory.

Churchill could not care less. He liked making noise, wanted to be noticed, even if it meant ostracism among his own. In a remarkably perceptive flash of self-analysis, he had already told his mother that he cared less for the principles he professed than for the impression his words could make and the fame they could bring him. He amended this rare and astonishing confession by declaring that a great and noble cause could thrust him above himself and force him to fit his phrases to his facts rather than vice versa. Still, there was much of the demagogue in Winston Churchill. Superb orator that he was—perhaps the greatest of his age—he was an indifferent debater. He relied on his incredible memory more than spontaneous thought. All his speeches were written out in advance, honed and polished like a gem on a jeweler's lathe. But if his flow of eloquence were stopped, he would falter or be nonplussed. Interrogation put him off. Once in 1904 he lost the thread of an argument and his speech sputtered out in silence. Some members wondered if he were not going the way of his father. But Churchill thereafter never spoke without clutching a sheaf of notes.

Rhetoric not reason was the most powerful weapon in his oratorical arsenal. He practiced, practiced, practiced his art, thundering out his perorations in his bath or rehearsing them in a treehouse built in the branches of a great tree at his mother's home. Almost always, in the absence of that great cause of which he spoke, he argued for victory, to awe, to overwhelm or to crush an opponent. He did not argue for truth, perhaps because he confused himself with an earlier

Savior who had said that He was Truth itself. If truth happened to coincide with his objective, so much the better.

Churchill also was inclined to choose self-serving causes. In his early days as an MP, he was for limiting military expenditure; as first lord of the Admiralty, he was for expanding it; but after the war, he was against it again. As a young Conservative, he supported his party's program of erecting tarriff barriers to protect British manufactures against imports. But as it became increasingly clear to him that Prime Minister Arthur Balfour had no intention of promoting him, he decided that the main chance that he sought with all his ardor was in the Liberal camp. The Tories, he was certain, were moribund. Churchill, they thought, was a traitor. Thus, when the Conservatives in 1903 again raised the standard of protectionism, Churchill stumped the country denouncing it as "unspeakable humbug." He also spoke of his colleagues in highly offensive language. While he was speaking in March 1904, Tory backbenchers staged a mass walkout. Two months later Winston Churchill, now known as "the Blenheim rat," walked across the floor of the House into the Liberal Party.

Churchill's nose for the scent of success proved sound: Four years after joining the Liberals, his ceaseless calls for social justice brought him the office of president of the Board of Trade in the Liberal government formed by Herbert Henry Asquith. At thirty-three Churchill was a full-fledged Cabinet minister. But that great event ran a surprising second to another great occurrence of 1908: his marriage to Clementine Hozier.

"I married and lived happily ever afterwards," Winston Churchill wrote in his book *My Early Years.* That is not exactly true, if only because his was a true love, and as is well known, true love never runs smooth. In fact, Churchill once said to Franklin Roosevelt during a dispute: "Lovers' quarrels are a part of love." Nevertheless, the youthful new minister had chosen a remarkable woman indeed for his wife.

Clementine Hozier's mother was Lady Blanche, eldest daughter of the tenth Earl of Airlie, and Henry Hozier, an ordinary or at least undistinguished employee of Lloyds of London. It is likely that Hozier was not Clementine's true father; her mother had had many lovers before, during and after the marriage. Although Clementine's childhood had been seared by the quarrels and eventual separation of her parents—on one occasion Hozier tried to kidnap her—she had matured into a beautiful and clever woman. She was also fiercely independent. Before she met Churchill she had broken off two engagements, and might have done the same to him but for his dazzling style and passionate declarations of devotion. These did not match his later courtship, which seemed like the absentminded wooing of a man standing for reelection. He was late for his engagement party, at the wedding he stood in the vestry talking politics with Lloyd George and on the honeymoon he revised a book and wrote endless political letters.

Because they were such opposites the marriage was a success. Clementine was the one solid rock upon which Winston might make his shifting stands, and his was the one career to which she devoted her loyalty and courage. In spite of the Liberal label that he wore, Churchill was at heart a deep-dyed conservative, in Clementine's phrase, "The last man alive who believes in the divine right of kings," and because she was a thoroughgoing and unflinching liberal, it was inevitable that they should have arguments. But there was never a permanently wounding or divisive quarrel or a hint of infidelity. Churchill was not easy to get along with. He was spoiled and capricious and he chose his friends for their wit and originality, the more ribald and outrageous the better. He was also fond of gambling, particularly in the casinos of his beloved French Riviera. Clementine despised his salty friends and detested the Riviera. She also found it difficult to become reconciled to his extravagant style of life at Chartwell, the country house which he bought in 1922.

Long before he purchased and rebuilt this handsome manor in Kent—the Garden of England—Winston Churchill had become a thoroughgoing hedonist, a veritable glutton of every minor vice. His voluminous writing and extensive lecturing were rich in royalties and honorariums, and down the road there would be a bequest from a distant relative worth a princely $20,000 a year. Churchill bathed in this golden flood with a gay profligacy which might have seemed disgusting in another man, but seemed zestful in him, redeemed by both generosity and good taste. He bought strings of polo ponies and spent $2,000 a year on tack and polo gear alone. Parties and balls at Chartwell and the neighboring country houses of Kent were always gay and glittering in their laughing and bejeweled guests, rich in food, copious in wine and cognac and aromatic in those big Corona-Corona cigars that were becoming the Churchill trademark. When he spent Christmas with his family at Blenheim, he dined off gold plates served by powdered footmen all over six feet tall wearing maroon breeches and waistcoats, silk stockings and silver-buckled shoes.

All this was close to anathema to Clementine. She would have preferred a quieter life with her five children: Diana, Sarah, Randolph, Marigold and Mary. Conversely the noisy life was the *bon vivre* to her husband, and she wisely refrained from attempting to restrain him. No one could, of course, although Clementine did succeed in softening his "whiff of grapeshot" attitude toward striking workers or other recalcitrants, whom, with his characteristically military habit of mind, he frequently regarded as the enemy. She softly slipped a velvet glove over his iron fist, reminding him that besides the stick there was a carrot. Without her, Churchill would certainly have become a harsher man.

At the Board of Trade, Winston Churchill began to push for an astonishing program of social reform, which immediately drew the fire of the Conservatives. With Lloyd George he also took on the House of Lords, that "feudal assembly, a prejudiced Chamber, hereditary, non-elected, irresponsible, irremediable and all composed of one class and that class not the best class." At the end of 1909, when the Lords' refusal to accept the Commons' budget provoked the so-called Peers versus People election campaign, Churchill went flashing through the northwest spouting invective and vituperation. The Liberals won, and Asquith in gratitude promoted Churchill to home secretary.

In this post, Churchill's zeal for reform seemed to cool, and he showed a noticeable drift toward the right. Demonstrations of every order were rising against the Liberal government: from striking miners in Wales, from the "screaming sisterhood" of the Suffragettes, from militant Sinn Feiners in Ireland and from the embattled peers of the House of Lords. Churchill thought the Liberals' prescriptions for these disorders were too mild. His "whiff of grapeshot" philosophy was coming to the fore again. Churchill's temperament and talents were simply too hot for the Home Office. He needed an assignment in which his flair for invention and innovation joined to his unrivaled power of breaking down opposition could be put to good use. Asquith wisely gave it to him when he made him first lord of the Admiralty in October 1911.

Winston Churchill burst upon the Admiralty like a bomb. He happily badgered admirals and befriended lowly seamen. He loved to be taken roaring across harbors in gleaming launches and piped aboard mighty warships. He tried to revive the Nelsonian "band of brothers" spirit, visiting wardrooms and crews' quarters alike to produce, through his own personal magnetism, a new camaraderie. He also founded the Royal Naval Air Service and learned to fly in its rudimentary contraptions, which provided him with a new quota of accidents and close calls. Above all he was fond of the 4,000-ton Admiralty yacht, *Enchantress.* He spent months aboard her, visiting naval shipyards and docks, sailing into the Mediterranean each summer, supposedly on naval business but actually just to see the sights and to increase his influence with guests such as Prime Minister Asquith.

Eventually, however, his overbearing style began to erode his early popularity. Ordinary seamen and "snotties," as the Royal Navy so ungallantly calls its young officers, were not always enthralled to see the pink and plump first lord of the Admiralty go dashing gleefully about ship during target practice, elevating, deflecting and sighting the guns like a small boy with a new toy. Admirals did not relish being lectured by the first lord on their responsibilities, any more than senior officers delighted in being overruled by him on advice supplied by junior officers. Neither did his sharp tongue soothe the ruffled fur of old sea dogs. "Don't talk to me about naval tradition," he snapped to a pompous admiral, "it's nothing but rum, sodomy and the lash."

Nevertheless, this ignorant civilian, as he was sometimes called, made some vital changes in the British navy. First and most important, he introduced a class of fast and heavily armed battleships firing 15-inch guns that was to make the British fleet superior to the German in the coming war. Next, by switching from coal to oil he made the fleet faster and able to stay at sea longer. He also established the Naval War Staff over bitter opposition, and improved morale by raising pay, humanizing a brutal disciplinary code, rewarding officers of ability and making it possible to rise from the ranks. All these genuine and far-reaching achievements made the Royal Navy ready when World War I began; but alas for his reputation and his country, his bold but rash personality brought both to grief very early in that dreadful conflict.

It is not known exactly who first advanced the idea of forcing the Dardanelles. But it was indubitably Churchill who seized upon it with Napoleonic vision and ardor. The Dardanelles is the modern name for the ancient Hellespont, the strait between European and Asian Turkey, Germany's eastern ally in World War I. Turkish forts and troops guarded the Dardanelles, then and perhaps still the most strategically vital narrow waters in the world. Churchill's grandiose scheme was to force the Dardanelles with warships and an amphibious assault on the forts, capture Constantinople, knock Turkey out of the war, enter the Black Sea to rally Russia and turn the entire continent of Europe from the rear. This would not only win the war at a single stroke but capture vast colonial booty. It was a strategic maneuver on a continental scale, worthy of Napoleon Bonaparte. But its basic flaw was to ignore a naval axiom: A ship is a fool to fight a fort. The flat trajectory of naval ordnance is simply no match for the higher angle of land-based artillery, its armor is much more vulnerable and the problems of a fleet's exterior lines of supply and communication opposed to the fort's interior lines are equally daunting. Nevertheless, Churchill pressed for the Dardanelles operation and got it, with a resulting disaster, a bloody fiasco, for which he was then compelled to accept more of the blame than was his due, and it finished him at the Admiralty.

Churchill's fall from office was the most devastating blow of his career. Like his father before him, he sat for hours with his head in his hands, sunk in dejection while the Black Dog of despair trotted silently around his soul. Clementine thought he would die of grief, and he himself said: "Like a sea-beast fished up from the depths, or a diver too suddenly hoisted, my veins threatened to burst from the fall in pressure." Though out of office, Churchill was still in government, quick to demonstrate the futility of the murderous frontal assaults in France, pleading for conscription and suggesting development of a "land battleship" that was to become the tank. But the pain persisted, until a relative suggested that he might relieve it by taking up painting. To Churchill's great delight, he found that he was more than just a dauber. He was an indifferent draftsman and not much on composition, but he did have a feeling for color: bright, vibrant color. More, he had found a lifetime pursuit that could be balm for his bruised spirit.

There was also the stimulation of danger available across the Channel. He sought and was denied a commission as a brigadier general, and although chagrined, contented himself with a colonel's rank and command of the 6th Battalion, Royal Scots Fusiliers. In war, even in wet and miserable trench war, Churchill's gaiety returned. Clementine kept him well supplied with cognac and Corona-Coronas and battle was once again a lark. Upon the amalgamation of the 6th and 7th Scots Fusiliers, however, Churchill lost his command, returning to the Commons after a hundred days in the trenches.

Lloyd George, who succeeded Asquith as prime minister, always had doubts about the sincerity of Winston Churchill. In public he paid him great tribute, but in private he said he was a monster of egotism who would "make a drum of his mother's skin if he could use it to sound his own praises." Nevertheless the Welsh Wizard preferred not to have him for an enemy, and in July 1917 brought him into the War Cabinet as minister of munitions. After the Armistice, Churchill moved up to war secretary. But he still complained: "What is the use of being war secretary if there is no war?" From Bonar Law came the crushing reply: "If we thought there was going to be a war, we wouldn't appoint you war secretary." But there was a war, the savage conflict between the White Army and the Red Army in Russia. British troops were in Murmansk and Archangel, serving as guards of military supplies. Churchill wanted to enter the war to rid the world of "the plague bacillus of Bolshevism." But Lloyd George was not interested, nor were the other war-weary Allies. Actually, they were sick of army life and near mutiny, a disaster which Churchill avoided by a program of rapid demobilization, returning a million men to civilian life within a month.

In February 1921, Churchill moved from war secretary to the more amenable post of colonial secretary. But the year 1921 was not a happy one for Churchill. In April, Clementine's brother committed suicide. In June, Lady Randolph Churchill suffered a mortal hemorrhage after a fall made it necessary to amputate her leg. In August, his beloved red-haired daughter Marigold—fondly nicknamed "the Duckalilly"—died of septicemia. Her parents were inconsolable. Even Clementine was hardly comforted by the arrival of Mary a year later. A few weeks afterward a crisis in foreign affairs catapulted Lloyd George's government and Winston Churchill from power. At this point, Churchill collapsed with acute appendicitis. He was in the hospital while Clementine campaigned for him in his constituency, calmly ignoring the saliva spat upon her by housewives angered by her husband's contempt for women's rights. Churchill joined her, but was defeated. "In a twinkling of an eye," he remarked, "I found myself without an office, without a seat, without a party and without an appendix."

Winston Churchill saw clearly that his last defeat was also the doomsday of the Liberal Party. He was again leaning toward Conservatism, but he knew the Blenheim Rat could not expect a prodigal son's welcome. So he spent the next six months working on his monumental six-volume book *The World Crisis.* This bombastic work has been described as "The autobiography of Winston Churchill cleverly disguised as a history of the universe." The shot is right on the mark. *The World Crisis* is in truth a vast monologue written in a pretentious polysyllabic style. In the spring of 1923, however, renewed political warfare recalled him from his literary labors. Ostensibly still a Liberal, but with his heart back in its natural Tory home, he was defeated in an election which saw the Labour Party, assisted by the lackluster Liberals, take office for the first time. This so horrified Churchill that he ran his Conservative colors up the flagpole again, returning to Parliament in the Tory victory of 1924. Anyone can "rat," he said with a chuckle, "but it takes real skill to 're-rat.' "

In reward, Prime Minister Stanley Baldwin made him chancellor of the Exchequer, the highest Cabinet post. Churchill wept when Baldwin offered it to him, replying: "That fulfills my ambition. I still have my father's robe as chancellor. I shall be proud to serve you in this splendid office." Like his father, he cared little for high finance, acquiring a superficial knowledge of economics that failed to conceal his disdain for this modern—and to him—sham science. His only successes were to reduce taxes somewhat and increase pensions, but these were far overshadowed by his blunder in returning Britain to the gold standard. This had the effect of raising the value of the pound so that British exports became more expensive overseas and imports cheaper at home, thus harming British manufactures.

By the end of the twenties Winston Churchill had eclipsed even Lloyd George as a central figure in British affairs. But to the electorate he was beginning to seem slightly ridiculous, a relic from another age with his saber-rattling solutions and the rolling periods of his archaic language. Those MPs who had known him since Harrow complained that he was no different than he had been in 1900: still the eternal subaltern of hussars, still riding down the opposition with rhetoric, still sabering every problem to the ground. For his part, Churchill was disillusioned with the changes taking place. He despised enfranchised women as "flappers," detested the Labour MPs, whom he regarded as Bolsheviks in Savile Row clothing, and was dismayed and saddened by the class hatreds of the British workingmen, those "Russian wolves" howling at him and heckling him instead of tugging their forelocks like the trusty yeomen of yore. By 1929 he was ready to quit politics for good and retire to a life of writing and painting. In the May elections, he was at 10 Downing Street to hear the results. It was a Conservative massacre. Highball in hand, Churchill rose again and again to go out in the passage to stare morosely at the teletype machine tapping out its messages of defeat. In a cursing, foaming rage he tore the printed sheets off the rollers and, as one observer suggested, would have smashed the machine itself if the Labour victory had grown any bigger.

Winston Churchill was out of office once again.

Churchill spent the decade between his fall from office and the outbreak of World War II writing and lecturing. In 1939 he was back in Parliament, but he was generally regarded as a has-been, a freak from a remote past with no understanding of the present and no influence on the future. At sixty-five he was balding, heavy-jowled and portly. "Old Church's" fire, it seemed, was out.

But it still burned, even if the oratorical blaze that it usually fueled was replaced by a ten-year literary bonfire of amazing brilliance. He wrote incessantly, dictating to his secretaries in the morning while still in bed and finishing in the small hours in his study, his imagination inflamed and his tongue loosened by his customary quota of whiskies and cognacs. Whereas his warnings of approaching Armageddon were generally ignored in his own country, he became a prophet of high honor abroad. Canada and the United States lionized him. To the Canadians he extolled the might of the British Empire; to the Americans he spoke of the indissoluble unity of the English-speaking people. It was in New York in 1931 that it appeared that his incredible life was over. Sunk in thought, he automatically alighted from a limousine on the left side, as though the curb were there as it is in left-hand-drive Britain. But he had stepped instead into traffic and was instantly struck down. The impact nearly killed him, and his recovery was painfully slow.

Churchill next sailed for Europe and the battlefields made famous by his illustrious ancestor, for he was then at work on his four-volume *Marlborough.* What he saw in Germany disturbed him. This veteran of World War I quickly realized that the martial spirit had again seized the Teuton. He also was disgusted by Hitler's appeals to anti-Semitism, telling *Der Führer's* friend, Putzi Hanfstaengl: "Tell your boss from me that anti-Semitism may be a good starter, but it is a bad sticker." .

After Hitler's accession to power, Churchill began sounding the tocsin again. This time his warnings were not ignored as the wheezing of a decrepit old war-horse, but rather dismissed as the Cassandra-crying of a pathetic old bore. Almost alone in those years from 1933 to 1939, despised and derided, sustained only by his unfailing courage, which he knew to be the one virtue that redeems all others, Winston Churchill rang the alarm. He called for Britain to rearm. Only from strength could aggression be deterred. Kellogg-Briand was a fairy tale, disarmament was an invitation to be invaded—for what other purpose were the dictators rearming? Churchill, seemingly alone among British leaders, realized that when you disarm yourself, you doubly arm your enemy who hasn't; and he also knew that pacifism has caused more wars than its ugly sister, bellicism. Winston Churchill had found that great and noble cause, which could lift him above himself. To sustain him he had not only his leonine courage but his simple faith in the sturdy virtues that he believed had made Western civilization. Now that sacred edifice was menaced by a new Attila, the rule of law was about to be obliterated by the rule of violence. Steadily, with each new Hitlerian victory— the Rhineland, the Saar, Austria, the Sudetenland, Czechoslovakia—his voice grew more strident and irritating to those who believed in peace by wishing. But then came Poland . . . and Norway . . . and now he was the prime minister and that powerful, insistent voice was the only one now worth listening to. In his first and perhaps most famous speech on May 13, 1940, he said:

"I have nothing to offer you but blood, toil, tears and sweat. . . . You ask, what is our policy? I can say: It is to wage war by sea, land and air, with all our might and with all the strength that God can give us; to wage war against a monstrous tyranny, never surpassed in the dark, lamentable catalogue of human crime. That is our policy. You ask, what is our aim? I can answer in one word: It is victory, victory at all costs, victory in spite of all terror: victory however long and hard the road may be; for without victory, there can be no survival."

Here at last was a chief, here was a man made for war.

16. May 1940: Blitzkrieg in Holland, Belgium and France

ON JANUARY 10, 1940, there were 2 million German soldiers massed on the borders of France, Holland and Belgium. That same day staff Maj. Helmut Reinberger was ordered to take the Luftwaffe's top-secret plans for the invasion from Berlin to Cologne. He put them in his yellow briefcase and hurried to the railroad station, only to find to his dismay that his train had already left. Reinberger was desperate to get to Cologne on time. He decided to fly, hitching a ride in a Messerschmitt-108 piloted by his friend, Maj. Erich Honmann. Reinberger knew that it was forbidden to fly when carrying top-secret information. But he just could not risk being late, and he took the chance. He didn't know that Honmann had never flown an ME-108 before.

Heavy fog engulfed the fighter plane shortly after takeoff. Honmann became nervous. This was no weather for breaking in an unfamiliar aircraft. He came down to 600 feet, hoping to follow the Rhine to Cologne. But the river below was too narrow to be the Rhine! Where was he? He began fumbling with the instrument panel and unwittingly shut off the plane's fuel supply. It nosed over in a dive that took it between two trees, which sheared off the wings. The fuselage containing the majors and the yellow briefcase crashed on a ridge. An old peasant man hurried up to it. He spoke no German, and Major Reinberger in his bad French learned that they were in Belgium near the Dutch border. Horrified, he begged a box of matches from the peasant, emptied out his briefcase and set the papers on fire. Just then Belgian soldiers rode up on bicycles to capture the two majors and stamp out the fire. They took all to a control point, where Reinberger seized the papers and threw them into a stove. A Belgian officer reached into the fire and yanked them out, severely burning his hand. Now Reinberger tried to grab the officer's pistol to kill himself. He was restrained and the papers were taken to the Belgian army commander, who wrote in his log: "The veil has been torn away."

It may seem incredible that the Dutch and the Belgians did not immediately invite France and Britain to help defend their countries. But the fact is that the Allied habit of appeasement during the five years leading up to the war had compelled them to rethink their position and to adopt a policy of strict neutrality. In 1939, General Gamelin had asked the Dutch and Belgians to join Allied staff talks. They declined, asking "What possible advantage could there be in military talks at a time when England is not ready for war, France is in chaos and the Germans are rearmed?"

Neither King Leopold III of Belgium nor Queen Wilhelmina of Holland was a bold leader. Leopold at thirty-eight had been only five years on the throne, sitting there in the immense shadow of his father, Albert, the hero-king of World War I, who had eaten, slept and fought with his troops, joining the victorious Allies to push the Germans off Belgian soil. Leopold believed that strong ties with the Allies would only provoke a German invasion. Wilhelmina, much older and many more years a monarch, agreed. Holland had remained neutral in the earlier war and had not been scratched, and the country hoped, like the democracies before it, to obtain peace by wishing. But Holland had not been invaded then because the German plan to attack France had called for the violation of the neutrality of Belgium alone. The 1940 plan so dramatically revealed was definitely aimed at the Dutch as well.

The Dutch even refused to hold staff talks with the Belgians, fearing that even so little might give Hitler an excuse to invade. Both countries, however, were more realistic than the Allies in preparing their defense. They had larger armies per capita than Britain and spent more on defense. Holland also had plans to repel attack by opening the dikes and letting the sea flood the plains. In the sixteenth century, the Dutch had thwarted the Spanish Duke of Alva in this way. Four centuries later, they were going to drown the German blitzkrieg by pulling a few levers, and then, after the Dutch soldiery blew up the bridges and held roadblocks and vital road networks, the great bulk of the people would retreat into Fortress Holland, the heavily populated industrial sector of Amsterdam-Rotterdam-Utrecht-The Hague. It did not seem to occur to the Dutch that the twentieth century's airplanes and parachutists might move too fast for their fingers to reach the levers.

Hitler flew into a carpet-chewing rage when he heard that the secret was out. "It is things like this that can lose us the war!" he screamed. He ordered the majors' wives thrown into prison and had Goering fire the Western Front's air commander and his deputy. Eventually he calmed down, especially after it was demonstrated to him that Reinberger had probably destroyed enough of the plans to make the remainder useless. This conviction, however, was contradicted by reports of increasing Belgian and Dutch mobilization and Belgian orders commanding its troops not to resist Allied soldiers coming over the border. In an agony of indecision, *Der Führer* canceled the January invasions. He had begun to toy with the idea of invading Norway, especially after Admiral Raeder had informed him that war could not be waged without the vital iron-ore traffic down Norwegian waters. Moreover, Hitler had never really liked the invasion plan.

It was actually a slightly altered version of the old Schlieffen Plan of World War I. The only real change was to invade Holland in order to enter northern Belgium and join forces for the southward wheel on Paris. Hitler had suggested to his army chiefs, Franz Halder and Walther von Brauchitsch, a strike farther south through the Ardennes Forest in Belgium. They did not approve, claiming that the Ardennes was "impenetrable" for armor.

Lt. Gen. Erich von Manstein disagreed. Manstein had perhaps the most brilliant and innovative mind in the German army, although his abrasive person-

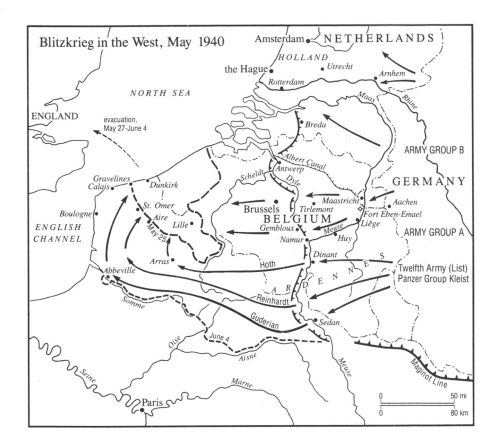

ality sometimes put him in bad odor with the higher-ups. He had been born the son of a general of artillery named Lewinski, but after he became orphaned, he was adopted by the wealthy, land-owning family whose name he bore. Manstein was a foremost exponent of mobile, armored warfare. He believed that ultimately it saved lives because of its speed. He could never forget the slaughter of Verdun in World War I, when a half million men died before this classic bloodbath of static warfare was finally stopped. He had always disliked the plan that Hitler eventually canceled. It seemed to him only a half-measure, like the Schlieffen Plan. Only decisive measures could conquer France and the Low Countries. In a memorandum, he proposed a strike through the Ardennes to the south joined to a feint in the north through the Low Countries. It was well known that the Anglo-French planned to move rapidly north to help defend Holland and Belgium if they were attacked. Manstein reasoned that if the Allies moved north to counter the feint, the major German strike to the south would fall in their rear and cut them off. Surrounded, they would have to surrender. For this southern route, Manstein deliberately chose the densely wooded Ardennes hill country:

first because it was considered impenetrable, secondly because armor could move through its rugged terrain without being observed from the air. Manstein gave his memorandum to his chief, General Gerd von Rundstedt, who forwarded it to Halder and Brauchitsch. They promptly buried it and it did not reach Hitler.

Nevertheless, *Der Führer* had not abandoned his notion of an attack farther south. But he had no precise plan such as Manstein's, which grew sharper and more daring each time he rewrote it. Every time he advanced it, however, Halder and Brauchitsch squelched it. Hitler's cancellation of the January invasion seemed to Manstein his last chance. He took his sixth memorandum to Brauchitsch, and in a heated confrontation accused him of defeatism. Two days later he was assigned to a remote district. But before he departed, he participated in war games in which he proved beyond doubt that a northern attack might be halted by stiff Allied opposition, while a southern thrust coupled to a northern feint could quickly win the war. Col. Rudolf Schmundt, Hitler's chief adjutant, saw Manstein at the games and came back to Hitler wild with enthusiasm for his plan. Manstein was summoned and "sold" the operation, which Hitler presented to his chiefs as his own and ordered them to execute as Plan Yellow. At this point, the German Army chiefs forgot their conviction that *Der Fuehrer* should be assassinated. In the glow of an anticipated brilliant conquest, they burned their moral standards and hoisted instead the Hitlerian oriflamme: VICTORY. They agreed with Manstein completely now, and especially liked his plan's ingenious feature of outflanking the Maginot Line.

La défense—that was the new French military fashion. The old one of *l'attaque* had long been discarded. It was *l'attaque,* Gamelin and his generals had ruefully agreed, that had caused the hideous French casualties in World War I. The offensive theories of Napoleon, which the Germans had turned against them in the Franco-Prussian War of 1870, had never been tested before by machine guns, barbed wire and massive entrenchments backed up by artillery. When the French made them their own again in 1914, brave *poilus* in horizon blue marched straight into the sausage machine. But it was *la défense* that had ultimately beaten the Germans, and it would do so again. Such was French military doctrine symbolized by the great Maginot Line, which War Minister André Maginot had begun in 1929. It stretched from Switzerland to Longwy just below the Ardennes in Belgium.

It cost a half-billion dollars—probably ten times that by 1980 standards—to build this gigantic complex. It consisted of an elaborate chain of huge underground forts six levels deep, each containing living quarters, kitchens, ammunition dumps, telephone systems, miniature railways, power stations, general supplies, water reserves and bombproof above-ground casements. These two-story massive buildings were truly indestructible, with concrete roofs more than eight feet thick. The guns were on the top floor, while on the first were the generators and magazines with troop quarters and stores. All of the casemate guns were sited in the direction from which the Boche were supposed to appear. But they also had interlocking fire, to strike at attackers upon a neighboring casemate or to take it under bombardment if it fell. Enormous underground reservoirs held the fuel, while water was tapped from deep wells. Formidable as the Maginot Line indubitably was, it was not a pleasant place for the troops. Living quarters were cramped and the *poilus* slept in three-tiered bunks. Their eyes burned from light-bulb glare and their ears rang from the constant hum of the machinery. Even worse was the stench: the septic tanks were neither well ventilated nor properly drained. It was so damp within these thousand-man forts that eventually the men had to sleep outside in tents, only entering the concrete buildings when on duty.

The Maginot Line was not, as popularly believed, a continuous line running west to the sea. It protected only the center of France's northeastern frontier, going only as far west as the Belgian border. It was not intended to be a Chinese Wall, but was meant to be a shield acting in concert with the sword of the French army. The Line would guard against attack from the east, forcing the invader into the open north to be cut down by the sword. Yet the tragedy of the Maginot is that it did become in the minds of the French a Chinese Wall. It was the subject of so much propaganda that the French people began to feel confident in its invincibility and to adopt that habit of defensive thinking, which was to base all upon the shield and allow the sword to rust.

The French army was rotten. It had never recovered from the shock of the last war, especially after details of the great mutiny of the *poilus* in 1917 were made public. Since 1936 it had been poorly armed and its will to fight weakened by the indifference and pacifism of the leftist Popular Front. Its high command had the world's worst communications system. From Generals Gamelin and Georges at the very top of the command structure on down to divisional level, there were many headquarters many miles apart and much bad blood between them. Supporting this was the world's worst air-force command system. Nominally, the chiefs of the Air Cooperation Forces Command gave the orders, but so did the Air High Command, the zone commanders and even the chiefs of lesser forces. Like French tanks, few French airplanes were equipped with radios.

This might have been because of General Gamelin's disdain for air power. He believed that rival air forces would destroy each other in the early battles, leaving the ultimate decision to be contested by land armies. Gamelin was not an armor enthusiast, either. When Col. Charles de Gaulle published his book *Toward a Professional Army* in 1933, Gamelin was among those who resented the criticism of conscription implied in the title. The army was then agitating for an extension of compulsory military service. It still believed in the "big battalions" made possible by universal conscription, and to show its displeasure with de Gaulle's contrary demand for a small, highly trained force of professionals, it decreed that in future all lectures or publications be approved by the high command. That effectively squelched all discussion of de Gaulle's controversial proposal and the book sold only 750 copies in France.

De Gaulle wanted to form his professionals into an armored mobile force that would protect the country during the dangerous first few days of a war when the reserves and conscripts were being called to duty. Such a force would have been invaluable in early September 1939, if France actually had wanted to succor Poland. Although the book made de Gaulle's reputation, his later acclaim as one of the early visionaries of the blitzkrieg was unearned. He did not even understand the value of the Luftwaffe as the blitzkrieg's lightning twin of the tank. His description of the costs of forming this force alienated many politicians already critical of the costs of the Maginot Line. Some of them asked sarcastically if de Gaulle's force would be stationed before or behind the Maginot. Meanwhile, the Socialists and Communists were horrified at the idea of a small elite force able to seize political power. Among the politicians, only Paul Reynaud heeded de Gaulle.

Finally, if the French army was rotten, the French nation was sick. France had been bled white in the last war and was further weakened by a falling birthrate produced by the death of 1.5 million virile soldiers and the practice of birth control. Political crises, political scandals, strikes, the vicissitudes of bloc government, personal vendettas, all these and more had conspired to weaken France's power. To many Frenchmen, democracy seemed a failure, or at least had not survived the Depression as well as the dictatorships. France was so flabby with fear of communism that many Frenchmen were actually prepared to accept fascism as the lesser of two evils.

Yet France was strangely confident as the chestnuts bloomed on the boulevards of Paris in that spring of 1940. Why not, with a powerful army of 800,000 front-line soldiers backed up by a trained reserve of 5.5 million men? Why not, with their magnificent Maginot Line to keep the detestable Boche at bay? Why not, with 102 divisions, mostly French, holding a broad front from Switzerland to the Channel? Who would think that France could be a soft overripe melon ready to burst upon a single blow?

On the night of May 9, 1940, Admiral Wilhelm Canaris informed the Dutch military attaché in Berlin that Holland would be invaded at dawn. Similar warning came from the Vatican. The Dutch considered themselves ready. Their hands were poised to pull the levers. to open the dikes and flood the lowlands.

Out of the predawn darkness dropped the German paratroopers, floating to earth alongside the dikes and canals. Some of them wore Allied uniforms or the uniforms of Dutch policemen, postmen or railway guards. They carried machine guns and radios and rubber boats for crossing the canals. Assisted by about thirty Dutch fifth columnists, they seized canal locks and water controls, secured un-blown bridges, and opened to the waiting panzer formations the fair prospects of a dry level plain.

Dutch positions were taken by guile. At Gennep, bridge guards watched with idle curiosity while Dutch policemen marched a handful of German prisoners over the bridge. A railroad train approached the bridge pushing a flatcar on which machine guns were mounted. The guards nonchalantly waved it by. It always appeared at this hour. They began to talk to the "policemen." Suddenly, with their "prisoners," they had guns in their hands and were mowing the guards down. Just as quickly, the machine guns on the flatbed were turned on the bridge's other defenders and one more vital passage fell to the blitzkriegers.

So the panzer divisions went swarming over the Lowlands, driving on the cities, while above them screeching Stukas swept the skies, even bombing Rotterdam, which had been declared an "open city." Gradually, the speed and number of the German columns slashing toward the cities and airfields demoralized the Dutch army. Airfields were a prime objective because they could be used to cover the attack on Belgium to the south. Most were taken from the air. First, bombers struck at medium levels to frighten Dutch antiaircraft gunners. Next came the bombers and strafing fighters to keep them underground. Other aircraft dropped fire bombs on the hangars to incinerate the Dutch air force. Then came the paratroops. "And so, when the defenders came up for air, they found themselves looking into the muzzles of tommy-guns."

At Rotterdam airport Dutch machine guns shot at German paratroopers, but many of them got through, and the airport quickly fell.

Some German pilots were incensed that the "treacherous Dutch" had fired at the paratroopers. One of them, Gottfied Leske, wrote: "It's a rotten, beastly business, shooting at defenseless parachutists. Typically Dutch. I think it isn't according to international law, anyway." But Leske thought it was great fun killing civilians during attacks on Antwerp. Some ran, others pedaled madly away on bicycles, mothers frantically pushed baby carriages. Leske and his cohorts swooped down to strafe them, pursuing them with streams of bullets even as they flung themselves into ditches. Leske was annoyed with one pilot who was reluctant to kill civilians. "They are our enemies, aren't they? One must kill his enemies! Who are we to decide whether to do or not to do? The Führer decides."

Only at The Hague were Canaris's warnings taken seriously. The airfields were well defended and sown with obstacles. At one of them, eleven of thirteen German transport planes were shot down. At the other two, runway obstacles wrecked German planes as they landed. Troops pouring out of them were massacred. The commander of the operation crash-landed in an open field. He had brought along his dress suit to call on Queen Wilhelmina to accept her surrender. Instead, he radioed headquarters and was told the attack on The Hague had been called off.

Nevertheless, Holland fell after five days of battle. For the most part, the Dutch had fought bravely. But *Schrecklichkeit* from the skies had paralyzed the civilian populace, too many dikes had stayed closed and too many canals and bridges remained open. The speed and timing of the German onslaught was simply overwhelming, and everyone was disarmed by the rumors and exaggerations flying about almost as thick as bullets. German soldiers dressed as nuns . . . messages and instructions written on billboards advertising Pecha chicory . . . sentries shot by Dutch traitors . . . millions of cotton puffs blossoming in the sky . . . tanks by the thousands roaring across the plain. . . . None of this was true. The Germans used only 4,000 parachutists, suffering a mere 180 casualties. To the south, Belgian confidence in concrete fortifications was also being shaken.

Belgium had constructed an eminently defensible position along the line of the Albert Canal. The bridges over the canal were guarded by the "invincible" Fort Eben-Emael. Adolf Hitler had for some time been studying the defenses of Eben-Emael. He concluded that it was truly impregnable—except for the roof. Only a handful of antiaircraft gunners held the roof. Hitler sent for Gen. Karl Student, commander of German airborne forces. He asked him if he thought he could take the fort with an airborne landing of a small elite force on the roof. After a day's thought, Student reported that he thought it would work. He began to train a handpicked force of only about eighty parachute-engineers. They practiced on a mock-up of the fort's roof, an exact replica of the armored cupolas, ventilation shafts, casemate embrasures and other openings into the fort below. Issued a new and secret highly intensive explosive, they took off in gliders and landed in darkness on the roof, completely surprising the gunners and killing them to a man. Below them, 1,000 Belgian soldiers stayed inside the fort. If they had sallied forth, they would certainly have overwhelmed the invaders, armed only with grenades and small arms. But they remained at their posts, while the Germans quickly destroyed big guns by dropping explosives down their muzzles, blew up exits and observation posts, feeding more explosives into ventilation shafts and gun slits and into ammunition elevators. Fort Eban-Emael surrendered in less than a day, and the unprotected bridges over the Albert Canal were seized by glider troops before they could be blown.

After the Maastricht Bridge in nearby Holland had been taken to outflank the canal on the Dutch side, a lodgement was found across it and a panzer division broke loose to envelop the entire Belgian position. The Belgian army was forced to fall back upon the French and British rushing north to the rescue with Polish formations that had escaped the first blitz. Very soon they were fighting not to save Belgium or Holland but themselves and France.

Gen. Heinz Guderian was known to his troops as "Hurrying Heinz." He was born at Kulm in Prussia in 1888, the son of an army officer, growing up in the military districts to which his father was assigned. Educated in various cadet schools and the military academy, he served as an officer in World War I. During that period his service with a telegraph battalion interested him in radio communication. Imaginative and innovative, he began to envision radio—then in its primitive stages—as an unrivaled means of directing troops in battle. He read translations of the theories of tank warfare advanced by Fuller and Liddell Hart and began to think of a revolutionary style of lightning warfare that ultimately was to emerge as the blitzkrieg. By 1931 he was the mechanical warfare expert of the Wehrmacht. Two years later, with Hitler in power, he impressed *der Führer* in a now-famous demonstration of the use of armored vehicles. With the German chancellor taking his side against the obstinate orthodoxy of the staff officers standing between himself and the German High Command, Guderian's rise was thereafter swift and his theories on the use of tanks supported by aircraft began to gain acceptance. Thus, by the fall of 1939, he became commander of all panzer formations and his controversial views were vindicated in the Polish campaign when his panzer corps smashed through all opposition.

After Hitler embraced Manstein's daring plan to traverse the dense Ardennes and fall in surprise on the Allied right flank, Hurrying Heinz was an obvious choice to lead one of three corps in the panzer group of eight armored divisions assembled for the operation. Overall command was given to Gen. Ewald von Kleist, much Guderian's senior. But Hurrying Heinz got the most powerful corps, the XIXth, with three divisions, and the shortest route to the River Meuse and the pivotal city of Sedan. He was on the left. In the middle was the Twelfth Corps with two divisions under Gen. Georg-Hans Reinhardt and on the right the XVth with two divisions led by Gen. Hermann Hoth. One of Hoth's divisions, the 7th, was commanded by an unknown general named Erwin Rommel. The entire force was to begin to move on May 10.

On May 10, the Allies put into execution General Gamelin's controversial Dyle-Breda Plan. This was to confront the Germans from the city of Breda in Holland south to the Dyle River in Belgium, while holding a fifty-mile stretch of the Meuse River. General Georges detested Gamelin's plan as a prescription for disaster. Georges had already demonstrated his contention that the Ardennes was far from "impenetrable." In maneuvers conducted in the summer of 1938, he had shown that seven French divisions pretending to be Germans, most of them motorized and with heavy armor, could move through the forests undetected to cross the Meuse and smash the "French" defenses there. The demonstration had been so devastating that Gamelin had suppressed all news of it. Gamelin advanced his Dyle-Breda Plan and named Georges to command the northeastern sector. This was to add insult to injury. Instead of only ten divisions in the north far from the vital Meuse crossings, there were now to be thirty, and this was to include two of the three new armored divisions, most of the motorized forces and the reliable British Expeditionary Force. Should Dyle-Breda succeed, Gamelin would be the hero; should it fail, Georges would be the heel. And Georges was certain that it would fail, for holding what he believed to be the decisive sector—that fifty-mile stretch of the Meuse—were the two worst units in the French army.

At first, it appeared that Gamelin, not Georges, was right. On May 12 in the Gembloux Gap between Huy and Tirlemont, German tanks engaged those of the French 1st Cavalry Corps. The forces were about equal in number, but the French heavy tanks were superior to the German heavies. Firing at long distance, hundreds of yards from each other, they fought the first big, pitched tank battle in history. It appeared that the French had won a victory, which gave the French First Army far to the south on the Allied right flank time to consolidate its position. Next morning Paris newspapers hailed the triumph. But also then, the German Stukas attacked the French armor, which had no air cover of its own. German tanks moving in packs picked off individual French tanks. German infantry with antitank guns knocked out more. Within two days more than 100 French armored vehicles were destroyed. Far worse, this tank battle to the north diverted Allied attention from the Ardennes. Adolf Hitler was so elated he almost wept. "They've fallen right into my trap!" he exulted.

There was as yet no action along the fifty-mile Meuse front, held by the French Ninth Army under Gen. André Corap and the French Second Army led by Gen. Charles Huntziger. Corap's troops were the men who had so disgusted Gen. Alan Brooke. Those in General Huntziger's Second Army were no better. Many of them were veterans of World War I, others were aging territorials.* The Ninth and Second were also heavily larded with units drawn from French colonies in North Africa and from as far away as Indo-China and Madagascar. Their officers in the main were men called out of retirement. Their artillery was largely horse-drawn and only half the required strength. Although the French liked to boast of their huge reserve of 5.5 million "trained" soldiers, most of them had spent only twelve indifferent months reluctantly exposed to a boring routine of drill that was more military than martial. Very few of these troops had spent much time deliberately subjected to that hardship and adversity which Napoleon called the school of the good soldier.

During that frigid winter of 1939–40, the period of the Phony War, these units had fallen into a routine that was a combination of boredom and bad habits. The officers, with the true Gallic flair for enjoying a fine meal, spent much of their time at mess. The *poilus* when on guard listened to the broadcasts of Monsieur Ferdonnet, "the traitor of Stuttgart," hired by Goebbels to discourage and divide the Allies. Ferdonnet liked to tell the *poilus* that their officers mistreated them and that they were foolish to fight for the overpaid English. When off-duty, the *poilus* quite simply got drunk. There was a free ration of wine, and also, for those troops embarking on a dangerous mission, a ration of *gnôl.* This was almost pure grain alcohol, a fiery liquid dealt out a half-pint at a time from gigantic basket bottles into the *poilu*'s *bidon,* or canteen, with a double ration going to those embarking on real danger. How the French arrived at the conclusion, shared by the Japanese, that alcohol hones a man's fighting instincts is not known. Drink certainly will make a man pugnacious, but also a pushover for an opponent whose reflexes are not slowed and skewed by such soporifics. Nevertheless, alcohol was issued freely and as drunkenness became prevalent, *salles de désethylation—* drunk tanks—were established.

Some of the men suspected that the wine and *gnôl* contained bromides, just as among the Americans it was widely believed that their food and drink was laced with saltpeter. The idea in all such suspicions is that the ingredient smug-

---

*Nonregulars similar to American reservists and National Guardsmen.

gled into a man's body makes him impotent. A French sociologist who studied the boredom on the French lines concluded:

Was it not this bromide which explained strange weaknesses which happened during a leave and thoroughly spoiled the long-awaited return of this or that conscript with his wife? Though a common subject for jokes, this was no minor problem. The soldier to whom this weakness happened felt his male dignity diminished, and he was secretly, though deeply, wounded. The frustrated wife imagined that her husband had been having far too good a time and wasting his forces in guilty love affairs.

The wives did have a complaint. They knew that villages near the fronts contained brothels and that their men had frequent leave to make use of them. They also despaired of the pittance paid them as dependents of soldiers, so little money that they frequently had to assume a lower living standard. In winter, the landlords often shut off the heat in their apartments, explaining that because men at the front were exempt from paying rent, they had no money to buy fuel. Complaints from shivering wives also helped to lower the *poilu*'s morale. Thus many of the troops of the "world's greatest army": soldiers of straw on whom an avalanche of fire was about to descend.

On the morning of May 9 a surprising number of German tourists on bicycles and in automobiles came over the border into the tiny neutral nation of Luxembourg. As night fell, they drew their concealed weapons and seized control of frontier crossings and bridges. At dawn, Luxembourgers could hear a rising roar of thousands of motors coming from the German border. Soon the panzer flood began to flow through the little country's picturesque hamlets and villages. No one opposed them. Little Luxembourg barely had time for a dying gasp.

Von Kleist's panzer group met no opposition until its right flank penetrated Belgium. Here Erwin Rommel's 7th Division encountered formidable obstacles that slowed its advance to less than two miles an hour. Forest trails and roads were heavily barricaded. Bridges were so expertly blown there was hardly a shard available to build new ones. At this rate, Rommel would never reach the Meuse on schedule. But the Belgian defenders had been ordered to withdraw. Rommel stepped up his advance, reaching the Ourthe next day. Here the French had destroyed a bridge, believing it would take the Germans two days to replace it. It took two hours, and Rommel's fast-moving tankers crossed it to surprise a French light tank division. By nightfall of May 12 his motorcycle spearheads had reached the Meuse crossings at three points: Dinant, Yvoir and Houx. But the crossings had been blown, and the French were on the cross-river heights in force.

At Houx, Rommel brought up his heavy tanks to bombard French pillboxes. Because the pillboxes had not been completely armored, they were easily knocked out. Rommel next put a rifle company aboard rubber boats and personally led the flotilla across the Meuse under heavy fire. Although the Germans had no antitank guns, their appearance frightened the French tanks away. Rommel clung to his tiny bridgehead throughout the night, and next day German engineers began building a pontoon bridge. It was completed by the following morning and fifteen tanks rolled over it.

The Meuse had been crossed.

Although Rommel had been first to cross the river obstacle, the true *Schwerpunkt,* or power punch, in the German plan resided in the three divisions led by Hurrying Heinz Guderian. He had fought in the Ardennes in the last war and believed that its high plateaus would be ideal for tank passage and its abundant foliage make excellent camouflage. He was right. His movement through Luxembourg was largely a matter of traffic control. His troops gaily waved their hats as they roared through. Later an Allied air attack was beaten off by antiaircraft gunners and Messerschmitt fighter planes. Thirteen bombers were destroyed. Not until May 12 did Guderian's spearhead meet any real opposition. Three times in one day Guderian came under aerial bombardment, but still he urged his panzers westward until on the 13th they, too, were on the Meuse. Across it was their objective: Sedan, the site of the decisive German victory in the Franco-Prussian War of 1870. Now it was up to the Luftwaffe.

Hitler had promised 1,500 fighters and bombers, almost all the operational strength of the Luftwaffe, for Plan Yellow. Von Kleist had wanted them to strike en masse, but Guderian had long ago provided that the attackers would come in waves. At the Luftwaffe, the commanders decided that Kleist's contrary orders had not arrived on time and followed Guderian's instructions. At 7:00 A.M. on May 14 the bombers appeared. They pounded the French positions for four hours. Then came the dreaded Stukas, falling from the sky with sirens screeching. Cheering Germans on the opposite bank watched the bombs describe their dreadful descending curves. Explosions of almost machine-gunlike rapidity sent shock waves rolling across the Meuse. Debris flew into the air and fell as though the heavens were raining steel and concrete. For hour after hour this concentrate of terror scourged those very troops least likely to endure it or to attempt to repel it: aging or half-trained reservists cowering in incomplete bunkers, artillerists with only a few shells to fire although French warehouses nearby were crammed with ammunition, antiaircraft gunners too dazed to dash to their guns to return the fire. There were few Allied planes aloft to menace this Luftwaffe aerial picnic. Those few that arrived saw the hopelessness of odds ranging as high as a 100 to 1 and turned to flee.

Now the Stukas also left, and the men of a German elite division clambered into rubber boats and began paddling toward Sedan. French fire raked them but they paddled doggedly on. Many of their comrades swam alongside them in full battle gear. They emerged dripping from the water to crawl up the opposite bank and rush the French bunkers. Here the French fought back bravely. Perhaps 70 percent of the attackers were killed or wounded. But they kept coming, eventually knocking out the bunkers with hand grenades. By dusk, six full German infantry battalions held a formidable bridgehead, and some soldiers had penetrated to La Marfée heights beyond. But still no tanks had crossed.

Guderian's bridgehead was definitely at the mercy of any heavy Allied counterattack, especially one including tanks or motorized artillery. But none came. Instead, the French began seeing tanks. Reports of German armor across the river began to fly from unit to unit, multiplied, of course, by heated imaginations. Commanders began to order withdrawals. Soon these retreats became routs. Terrified gunners and riflemen swept down the roads away from the front, hysterically crying, "Tanks! Tanks!" Some were firing their rifles wildly, as though the surrounding darkness were full of Germans. There were officers among them. Some *poilus* actually claimed to have *seen* these nonexistent tanks, so powerful is the action of terror upon the imagination. Worse, commanders at all levels pretended to have received written orders to withdraw, but were unable to produce them or to specify who had sent them. Nowhere was an attempt made to halt the panic, to turn the deserters around and to direct them back to their abandoned posts. Paralysis was also creeping up the chain of command, reaching even General Georges. He sat in his headquarters in a hotel's grand ballroom surrounded by silent, white-faced staff officers sitting slumped in their chairs, and he began to weep uncontrollably. There was nothing to be done, he sobbed, wringing his hands: the front had been penetrated and the Germans were over the Meuse.

But there was much that could have been done, if only there were someone bold and resolute enough to do it. On the following day—the 15th—the Allies still possessed enough men and material to erase the German bridgeheads. In General Corap's sector opposite Rommel, a French unit gave a minor check to the Germans by capturing forty motorcyclists. But then its commander retired, satisfied with this minuscule bag when he might have destroyed Rommel's tanks. Still Corap might have launched a strong counterblow by using two fine French colonial divisions and an armored division with 150 tanks. But by the time they were ordered to move against Rommel, it was too late, and when the tanks did come upon him, they were out of fuel.

General Huntziger opposing Guderian fared even worse. At first, his tanks engaged Guderian's and sent them reeling backward. But then there was no pursuit, no thrust for the jugular, and Guderian brought up a battalion of engineers who threw hollow charges under the French tracks and wheels and forced them back. More and more tanks crawled carefully over the bobbing pontoon bridges to come roaring to Guderian's aid. Allied air sought to sink the bridges. Ten Royal Air Force bombers surprised the bridge defenders, but what few hits they scored were with lightweight bombs. Twenty-eight French bombers tried next and were destroyed. Now the German antiaircraft gunners had found the range and were filling the sky with polka-dot black puffs. Eight hundred Luftwaffe fighters roared aloft. The Allies, attacking in small waves rather than in large ones or even in concentration, were massacred. It was the RAF's Black Day of the war. Of seventy-one bombers, only thirty-one returned. Fifty fighters were missing of the 250 sent aloft, and many survivors were cripples, which barely got back to base.

Now the French on the ground were naked to their tormentors from the skies. Again their terrified imagination multiplied the number of enemy tanks. General Gamelin contributed to this exaggeration when he issued an order: "The torrent of German tanks must finally be stopped." Guderian, in fact, did not have that much armor across the river. But he was not attacked. Instead, confused French rifle companies fought each other, artillery was abandoned, truck drivers ran their vehicles off the road and many soldiers ripped off their badges anticipating capture. At this point Heinz Guderian made his decisive decision to send his armor flying west "until the last drop of petrol."

Guderian had privately planned that upon crossing the Meuse he would plunge ahead so fast that no orders from above would overtake him. But once he had secured his bridgehead, he hesitated. Should he await reinforcements or race west with what he had? A subordinate decided him, quoting his own slogan: *"Klotzen' nicht kleckern"*—"Concentrate, don't disperse." So he decided to send two divisions plunging ahead while holding the third to guard Sedan. But then came orders from Kleist to halt all further advance. Dismayed, Guderian called the Panzer Group chief to say he could not agree to a halt. To do so would be to throw away all the surprise and success that had been gained. Kleist disagreed. A heated argument ensued. Finally, Kleist approved continuing the advance for another twenty-four hours.

Guderian's forces plunged westward again. By nightfall of the 16th—with Reinhardt on his right moving along a parallel road—he had penetrated fifty-five miles west of Sedan. Once again he was ordered to halt, this time by Hitler. The German High Command simply could not believe the ease of the Meuse crossings. They anticipated a heavy French counterattack on their left flank. Hitler agreed. So Kleist relayed the order to Guderian, and told him he was coming to see him next morning. At 7:00 A.M. the plane touched down and a tight-lipped, grim-faced Kleist alighted. Without greeting Guderian, he gave him a tongue-lashing for disobeying orders. Guderian was infuriated. ("He did not see fit to waste a word of praise on the performance of the troops.") He asked to be relieved of his command. Kleist agreed. But before Guderian's relief could take over, Col. Gen. Sigmund List, commander of the Twelfth Army following Guderian, came to Guderian's headquarters. He told Guderian that he should not resign, and issued the order: "Reconnaissance in force to be carried out." This was a ruse by which all the "forces" were indeed on "reconnaissance." Guderian's headquarters remained in place "so that it may be easily reached." This also was a deception. Guderian would not be there, nor could anyone reach him "easily" if only because "A wire was laid from there to my advanced headquarters, so that I need not communicate with my staff by wireless and my orders could therefore not be monitored by the wireless intercept units of the OKH and OKW." Whereupon, Hurrying Heinz took off. He did not stop until nightfall when he was seventy miles from Sedan, and did not stop again until three days later when he reached Abbeville on the Channel coast. The Allies had been cut in two and the most sweeping victory in all military history put in motion.

It was won chiefly by the intuitions of one man: Guderian. Quite literally he had pulled the German Army after him to victory. Much credit for Plan Yellow must go of course to Erich von Manstein, and much also to Hitler's visionary enthusiasm for it. But Guderian was the man on the spot. He sensed French hesitation and scented victory. He had seen the crushed and terrified French soldiery throw down their arms in piles which German tanks ground into pieces. Nor could the moment have been more opportune: Huntziger had concluded that the Germans were going to wheel left and race for Paris and he had therefore fallen farther south to the Maginot Line, while Corap in the north had retreated farther north. A hole some forty gaping miles wide had opened in the French line. Guderian did not know this, but he did sense that the moment for which he had spent decades preparing himself had finally come. Now was the time to prove his theories of the deep penetrations possible to armor. Guderian seized that moment, boldly stretching his obedience to hamstringing orders up to the very limit of insubordination. *But he had been right.*

On the morning of May 10 Premier Paul Reynaud wrote out his resignation. Hearing that war had begun, he destroyed it and sent a message to Gamelin: "The battle has begun. Only one thing counts: to win it." Gamelin tore up his own resignation and replied: "Only France counts."

Five days later Reynaud's telephone call awakened Winston Churchill at seven-thirty in the morning. Reynaud spoke in English and with great emotion. "We have been defeated." Churchill fell into shocked silence. Reynaud said again: "We are beaten. We have lost the battle."

Churchill replied, "Surely it can't have happened so soon?"

"The front is broken near Sedan," Reynaud said. "They are pouring through in great numbers, with tanks and armored cars."

Churchill sought to calm Reynaud. "All experience shows that the offensive will come to an end after a while. I remember the twenty-first of March, 1918. After five or six days they have to halt for supplies, and the opportunity for counterattack is presented. I learned all this at the time from the lips of Marshal Foch himself."

There was a silence, and then, again: "We are defeated. We have lost the battle."

Churchill said he would fly over and have a talk. He arrived at the Quai d'Orsay at dusk on the 16th and was ushered into the presence of Reynaud, Daladier and Gamelin. Reynaud seemed utterly dejected. Only that morning he had been given a postcard taken from the body of a slain officer. It said: "I am killing myself, M. le Premier, to let you know that all my men were brave, but one cannot send men to fight tanks with rifles." Everyone was standing. A small map stood on a student's easel and Gamelin used it to explain what had happened. Small like Reynaud, elegant, with a detached professorial air, the French war chief spent five minutes describing disaster and predicting approaching doom before a shocked and silent audience.

Churchill spoke. *"Ou est la masse de manoeuvre?"* he asked in his imperfect French. "Where is the strategic reserve?"

"Aucune," Gamelin replied, with a shrug and a shake of his head. "There isn't any."

Churchill stared at him in incredulity. He could not believe that the French reserve was gone. Gone! Difficult as it certainly was to defend the 500-mile Allied front, no commander worthy of the name would strip himself of his strategic reserve, those divisions to be rushed to the critical points to contain breakthroughs and drive the enemy back. But there weren't any. Gamelin had committed his all to his cumbersome Dyle-Breda Plan. The Maginot Line had been a colossal failure. The Germans had chosen not to break their heads against it but had simply gone around it. True, this was the very purpose of the Maginot, to act as a shield deflecting the enemy onto the northern plain, there to be cut down by the sword of the French army. But the Germans in the north had been a feint, and the true pulverizing blow had come out of the "impenetrable" Ardennes.

Gamelin began to speak again. He spoke of containing the "Sedan bulge." He had still not grasped the blitzkrieg's capacity for making swift and deep penetrations. He could not believe that an army could win a decisive battle without deploying the bulk of its forces, which was why he still envisaged a Sedan "salient." He was withdrawing eight or nine divisions from quiet sectors and from the Maginot to hammer at the flanks of this bulge. Eight or nine more were being brought over from Africa. Although twelve motorized German divisions following the panzers were guarding their own flanks as they drove between Huntziger's and Corap's disconnected armies, it did not seem likely that the Germans could maintain this corridor and still support the armor racing for the coast. He paused. Churchill looked out the window toward clouds of smoke rising past it. Below, in the gardens of the Quai d'Orsay, huge bonfires were burning, fed by wheelbarrows full of archives being dumped onto them by white-haired officials. Evidently, the French government was preparing to flee Paris. Evidently, Reynaud and Daladier did not place much faith in Gamelin's seemingly sound proposals to halt the German flood. Churchill asked the French war chief when and where he intended to strike the German flanks.

Gamelin replied, "Inferiority of numbers, inferiority of equipment, inferiority of method," and gave a helpless shrug of his shoulders.

At the head of his list he might have placed inferiority of leadership; and yet, it is unjust to blame the French alone. Winston Churchill standing there among these dejected and despairing French chieftains was acutely aware of his own country's tiny contribution to the Allied effort: only ten divisions and *not a single armored division.* He found it impossible to reject the French pleas for more RAF fighter squadrons. Even though he had come to the Quai d'Orsay prepared to offer four more squadrons, he realized that this would not be enough to revive his allies' fighting spirit. So he eventually obtained Cabinet permission to offer six more. This reduced total fighter strength for the defense of Britain to twenty-five squadrons, the very limit. But the offer did encourage Reynaud and Daladier.

Next day, Reynaud dismissed Gamelin and relieved Daladier as war minister, taking that portfolio himself and giving the former premier the Foreign Ministry. Gamelin was replaced by Gen. Maxime Weygand, commander of French forces in the Middle East. Weygand came from shadowy origins: It was said that he was either the illegitimate son of Maximilian of Mexico, or of a Brussels businessman, or of King Leopold II of Belgium. He had been a disciple of Marshal Foch in the last war. His ideas of how to fight the new war hardly differed from Gamelin's. He was seventy-four years old. After he arrived and saw the gravity of the situation, he remarked that if he had known it, he would never have left Syria.

Marshal Henri-Philippe Pétain became vice-president of the War Council. Pétain was revered throughout France as the hero of Verdun. He had settled the French army mutiny with a combination of sympathy, tact and firmness. He was eighty-four, but it was not senility that made him the worst possible choice, it was the convictions he harbored beneath his snowy locks. Pétain had concluded that Europe must inevitably fall under the hegemony of Adolf Hitler. He believed that if France submitted to Germany, it could become the first among a galaxy of satellite states. His spirit of defeatism was evident in his comment when he left Madrid for Paris:

"My country has been beaten and they are calling me back to make peace and sign an armistice."

17. May 1940: Enigma and Dunkirk

AFTER CUTTING THE ALLIES in two during his historic dash across northern France, Gen. Heinz Guderian's spearheads reached Abbeville on the Channel coast. He wheeled north, making for the Channel ports and the rear of the British Expeditionary Force, which was still in Belgium facing the frontal attacks of German infantry. On Guderian's right was Reinhardt's panzer corps. On May 22, Guderian cut off Boulogne, and on the following day Calais was also isolated. He entered Gravelines, only ten miles from Dunkirk, the last remaining port from which the embattled BEF might escape. Reinhardt's armor had kept abreast of him on the canal line Aire–St.-Omer–Gravelines. Both corps—five divisions strong—were now poised for the thrust that would seal the doom of the BEF. But then came an astonishing order from the high command: Halt and stay where you are. Enraged, frustrated, dismayed, Guderian and Reinhardt bombarded Kleist with protests and demands for explanations. Back came the reply: *Der Führer*'s orders.

It had been Adolf Hitler's personal intervention that halted his armor at this critical moment, and it was his first great mistake of the war. Why did he give the order? History does not know, probably never will know, exactly why. Even his topmost generals could not learn his reasons or divine his motives. Moreover, if he had given an explanation, it would probably be untrue, for great men are not fond of admitting their mistakes. Perhaps he could not have given a true reason if he had wanted to, granted his intuitive style of making decisions and his impulsiveness, his tendency to change direction like a weather vane.

It is clear, however, that Hitler had become increasingly nervous after Guderian swept west. He could not believe that the Allies could so obligingly fall into his trap, doubted the incredible ease of the panzers' advance, wondered fretfully about the enemy's lack of resistance. It was too good to be true—it could be a trap! On May 17, the day after French defense of the Meuse collapsed, General Halder observed in his diary: "Rather unpleasant day. The Führer is terribly nervous. Frightened by his own success, he is afraid to take any chance and so would rather pull the reins on us." That was the day Guderian was halted. Halder noted: ". . . Führer unaccountably keeps worrying about the south flank. He rages and screams that we are on the best way to ruin the whole campaign." It was only after Halder had convinced him that the infantry behind Guderian was providing its own flank guards that Hitler agreed to turn the armor loose again.

Hitler had himself served in Flanders during World War I and so had his other chief at the OKW, General Keitel. Both believed that the marshy terrain was dangerous for tanks. He had been advised by Field Marshal Gerd von Rundstedt, Kleist's superior officer, that there had been much loss of armor during the dash to the Channel, as much from wear and tear as from battle. Further losses in the canals and fens would greatly reduce the armor's effectiveness in the impending second phase of the Battle for France. Finally, as anticipated, Hermann Goering had provided the clincher: He assured Hitler that he could prevent a British escape: "My Luftwaffe will complete the encirclement and close the pocket at the coast from the air."

Some German generals believed there was a political reason for Hitler's order, that he wanted to assure the British of his peaceful intentions toward them. When Hitler visited Rundstedt's headquarters, officers there were astonished by his friendly attitude toward the British. He spoke of his admiration for the British Empire, which he compared to the Catholic Church, insisting that both were stabilizing influences in the world. All he wanted from Britain was that it should acknowledge German suzerainty on the continent. He would even offer to support Britain with troops if it should have difficulty within the Empire. Further, the return of Germany's lost colonies was not essential. Colonies were chiefly a matter of prestige, he said. They could not be held in war, and not many Germans wanted to settle in the tropics anyway.

Nevertheless, if Hitler actually was considering extending the olive branch to Britain, an earnest of his sincerity would be to refrain from harming the BEF. To do this he would have to have this quarter million Britons in his power. If they were to escape, that would only exalt their nation and renew its determination to fight on. But here at hand, in the BEF, was this excellent opportunity to express his deep desire for peace. Thus, it would seem that Goering's vain assurance of capturing this force might have been the determining factor in his decision to halt the panzers.

Whatever prompted it—Goering's promise, his own fear of the fens of Flanders, his desire to conserve his tanks for the next stroke, or a combination of some or all of these—his decision was to be one of the two mistakes that brought him down.

As early as May 19 the commander of the BEF, Lord Gort, had concluded that he might be forced to withdraw his forces into Dunkirk. But the British high command ordered him instead to move the BEF in a southwesterly direction, that is, to fight his way south to join French forces there. This conformed to Weygand's new plan, which was that the Northern Armies, rather than allow themselves to become surrounded, should fight their way south to the Somme. They were to hammer at the panzer divisions that had cut their communications. At the Somme, a new Allied line similar to the one drawn in the last war would be formed.

Nevertheless, on May 20 the British War Cabinet began to have disquieting reservations about the success of a fighting retreat to the Somme. Churchill thought that even if it were successful, large bodies of troops might be cut off or driven against the sea. He said that as a precautionary measure the Admiralty should be instructed to assemble a fleet of small vessels, which could sail to ports and inlets on the French coast. Control of what was to be called Operation Dynamo was given to Admiral Sir B. H. Ramsay. At Dover, Ramsay began to study "the emergency evacuation across the Channel of very large forces."

Hitler and his intelligence chiefs believed that they possessed the best and only unbreakable enciphering system in the world. It was called Enigma, after the *Enigma Variations* in which the British composer Sir Edward Elgar described his friends in musical cipher. The machine itself looked like a bulky portable typewriter measuring 7 by 11 by 13 inches. The letters on the keyboard were arranged like those on a typewriter, but there were no numbers or punctuation marks. On a deck behind the keyboard the twenty-six letters of the alphabet appeared in alphabetical order in three rows. When the operator at the keyboard punched a letter, one of the letters on the deck lighted up—but never the letter that the operator had punched. If the operator punched the same letter another time, yet a different letter on the deck lighted up.

While the operator worked, an assistant wrote down the letters as they appeared on the deck: a meaningless procession of letters. But then he transmitted them in Morse code by radio to a waiting recipient equipped with the same machine. He in turn typed these letters on his keyboard, whereupon they appeared on his deck in a meaningful message. The message, of course, could be intercepted; but the Germans believed it could not be decoded without use of the same machine. Even then the decoder would have to know what particular setting the sender had used on his machine that day. There were literally millions of possible settings, and as the war wore on the Germans began to change them every day. To British Intelligence, the problem of decoding Enigma messages without an Enigma machine of their own seemed insurmountable. Nevertheless, a team of brilliant mathematicians trained in cryptanalysis attacked it. One of them was a young genius named Alan Mathison Turing. He was an eccentric who had once changed all his money into silver, melting it down into ingots, which he buried and then forgot where he had buried them. He had also said: "A sonnet written by a machine will be better appreciated by another machine." In a variation of this theme, Turing and his colleagues set to work in the belief that a riddle created by one machine can be solved by another machine.

In this they were ably assisted by Polish cryptanalysts who had already been at work decoding the Enigma's messages. They had had modest success breaking some of the ciphers of the early Enigmas through use of their own machine called the Bombe, a combination of six Enigmas. As war neared, the Poles gave the British a Polish-constructed copy of the Enigma along with plans and drawings of the Bombe.

This formed the nucleus of decoding work begun under cover of a nonexistent Government Code and Cypher School located in a pseudo-Tudor-Gothic mansion called Bletchley Park outside the grim railroad-junction town of Bletchley, about fifty miles northwest of London. Most of the detection work took place in Hut 6. By the spring of 1940 Turing and his colleagues had built the first of what was destined to be a series of ever more complex machines designed to solve the Enigma riddle. It was a large copper-colored cupboard about six feet tall, which at first glance might appear to be an Oriental goddess. Working with this and from a vast bank of intercepted signals, the British cryptanalysts were able to discover a pattern and also some of Enigma's unsuspected idiosyncrasies. Standard procedures among the German operators also gave off valuable hints. Once all these clues were fed into the Bombe, this amazing machine was able to break the day's code. The material emerging came to be known by the code name Ultra.

It was on May 22, 1940, that the Bombe became operational and Admiral Ramsay received his first Ultra message. It was a triumph of such value that fear that the Germans might learn of the discovery rivaled the elation caused by the solution. After British Intelligence learned that an important meeting among four Luftwaffe generals was scheduled for May 26, it was decided not to bomb the site lest the Germans begin to suspect how the secret was discovered. But on May 25 the Bombe decoded a radio message confirming knowledge of Hitler's order to halt the panzers. This had been discovered earlier in some papers lost by a German officer. But these could have been a plant: Now the Bombe certified this crucial piece of information. Lord Gort decided not to join any more versions of the fighting retreat south and devoted all his energies to evacuating the BEF. Gort was also informed in an instruction from Anthony Eden, secretary of state for war: "It is obvious that you should not discuss the possibility of the move with the French or the Belgians."

Neither did Winston Churchill mention this gradually evolving plan to Premier Paul Reynaud when he visited him in London on May 26. Churchill endured but did not submit to Reynaud's renewed and passionate demands for more British air. He assured his French colleague of Britain's undying commitment to victory, hoping to strengthen Reynaud against those members of his cabinet—Pétain and the Naziphile Paul Baudouin—who were already calling for a separate peace. But shortly after Reynaud departed, Churchill confirmed the Admiralty order: "Operation Dynamo is to commence."

It may be argued that this piece of duplicity, if such it were, was typical of "perfidious Albion." Yet there was no other course. Weygand's plan was not succeeding and the Belgians were collapsing, their king obviously preparing to capitulate, which he did on May 28. No troops had been braver than the Belgians, and none as gallant in the way they sacrificed themselves to cover British movements. But Belgium was down from twenty divisions to ten, with its chief cities —Brussels, Ghent, Bruges and the mighty port of Antwerp—in German hands. Worse, at any moment Hitler might rescind his order and turn loose the roaring panzers once more. Finally, even more than an amphibious invasion, an amphibious evacuation under fire is the most difficult of all military operations. To risk the enemy gaining knowledge of the time and place would be the most supreme folly, its author, if it occurred, worthy of being forever damned and reviled. So the secret was kept from the Allies, and the BEF began its masterly fighting march to the sea.

Command was exercised by Gen. Alan Brooke, assisted by Generals Bernard Law Montgomery and Harold Alexander. Brooke worked tirelessly to cover the retreat: shifting units, plugging gaps, stiffening spines. He would never forget the sight of lunatics freed by the bombing of the asylum at Armentières standing beside the road in their brown corduroy suits, eyes shining in childish delight at the vast disorder of the retrograde movement, spittle dripping from their gaping mouths. Brooke himself felt he had reached the edge of sanity. "I had reached a stage when the receptive capacity of my brain to register disaster and calamities had become numbed by successive blows. It is a providence of nature that it should be so, otherwise there would be more mad people in the world." Eventually, the still unbroken survivors of the march to the sea entered Dunkirk. On May 27, the evacuation began.

Although the Admiralty had with great forethought rounded up the British, Belgian and Dutch coastal steamers and ferries which, in the main, would do most of the lifting of the men in Dunkirk, there were also needed hundreds of small craft—pleasure boats 30 to 100 feet in length—that could be used to ferry troops to the larger ships forced to stand hundreds of yards offshore by Dunkirk's gradually shelving beaches. How to collect them and organize them to the utmost efficiency in the few days remaining between the decision to evacuate and the actual sea-lift itself seemed an insurmountable task. Providentially, the Small Vessels Pool had already on May 14 notified the owners of such craft to forward "full particulars" of their vessel's capacity to the Admiralty. Although this notice, carried on the BBC news, has been advanced by the French as one of the "proofs" of Britain's early and unilateral decision to evacuate, this is not true. Information on the pleasure craft was needed for possible requisitioning of them as replacements for the wooden minesweepers and other harbor craft drawn off in the campaign against magnetic mines. Providentially this data was already in the Admiralty's hands when it was decided to evacuate Dunkirk on May 27.

That day dawned bright and clear, but it was a black one for the people of Dunkirk and those British soldiers who had not yet reached the beaches. The Luftwaffe rose early and firebombed the town. Buildings consumed by tongues of flame collapsed in a loud hissing and showers of sparks. Streets were turned into avenues of inferno. Thousands died, many suffocated to death as they lay trapped in buried cellars. By noon the last remnants of the BEF had staggered onto the twenty miles of beaches surrounding the town. They had abandoned all of their heavy equipment, keeping only their handguns and their packs stuffed with the half rations that were to sustain them through the ordeal. They joined the men already there, who for three, four, five days on end had endured the fiery lashing of the Luftwaffe.

But for the friendly warm sand upon which these battered and harried men stood or sat, they would have been mercilessly destroyed by the German bombardment. But the sand muffled the explosions. After the earlier raids the men had been astonished to discover how few had been killed or wounded. Lighter fragmentation bombs might have taken a heavier toll, but these heavy missiles buried themselves deep in the sand before erupting. A rocky beach also might have proved disastrous for the British. But the sand helped to save the BEF, and soon its doughty survivors were regarding the Stukas with contempt. They also searched the skies in vain for their own planes. Each time they saw smoke clouds spiraling upward from rescue ships stricken by the enemy, a bitterness welled up inside them, and they growled: "Where the bloody hell's the RAF?"

High overhead and out of sight the fighter planes of the RAF were fighting the Luftwaffe for control of the air. The entire Metropolitan Air Force of twenty-five squadrons—Britain's sacred reserve upon which its very survival depended—had taken to the air. Hour after hour, sometimes making four sorties a day, the British fighters hurled themselves against the German bombers. German formations numbering forty or fifty airplanes were attacked by squadrons half that number. Gradually, mastery of the air went to the British. Kills by the score soon were counted in the hundreds. But the embittered soldiers below them knew nothing of the critical battles raging above, and soon they lowered their anxious eyes from what seemed only hostile skies and directed them outward toward the sea.

Streaming across it came the most remarkable armada in the history of warfare. In all 887 vessels arrived, of which 655 were civilian, and they included boats of every size, shape and weight, wind-driven, oar-driven, motor-driven. There were motorboats and fishing boats, pleasure boats and whaleboats, lifeboats and fireboats; there were yachts and yawls and Channel ferries; passenger ships, tramp steamers, paddle wheelers, French ketches, Dutch shuyts, tugs towing barges, and one car ferry making its first voyage on the open sea. Destroyers dashed among them like shepherd dogs of the sea, herding the larger vessels offshore alongside a mile-long mole in the harbor, while the smaller craft rode the surf to the beaches.

On the mole, men lined up in groups of thirty or more to trot up the gangplanks of the larger ships. A strict discipline was enforced. Soldiers crazed by the bombing were shot to death lest they infect their steadier comrades with panic and so ruin the whole vast undertaking. Those on the beaches stood shoulder-high in the water to be hauled aboard the smaller boats bobbing like corks in the water. Their places were taken by men standing knee-deep behind them, whose stations were filled by those at the water's edge. With a strange calm and confidence the human waves rippled forward and the vast antheap gathered on the beaches began to shrink.

From the night of the 27th to the night of the 31st, the weather turned fair for the British and foul for the Germans. Pouring rain kept the Luftwaffe grounded. Continued fair skies might have meant catastrophe. On just one clear afternoon, the Luftwaffe sank three British destroyers, damaged seven more and put five large passenger ships on the bottom. Wet weather also immobilized the panzers. It made the marshes more dangerous, and the armor also needed time for regrouping and repair. The German navy, meanwhile, was still reeling from its chastisement at Norway and in no strength to challenge the British in the Channel.

The result has been called the Miracle of Dunkirk. In all, about 340,000 men were evacuated, of whom 198,000 were British and the rest French, Polish, and Belgian. The deliverance of Dunkirk had saved the flower of the British Army. The nucleus and structure for the British Army of the future had been preserved. They would form the cadres to be fleshed out by conscription. Just as important, ranking commanders such as Brooke, Montgomery and Alexander had been preserved, all to be field marshals, and Brooke to become chief of the Imperial General Staff. Officers who were lieutenants at Dunkirk would command battalions, captains would be colonels and even the "snotties" of the saving fleet would rise to command of ships. These men would soon be wielding every weapon to strike the Axis enemy everywhere. In a word, the BEF had been delivered at Dunkirk to turn in snarling defiance on the new Attila. Nevertheless, as Churchill warned Parliament: "Wars are not won by evacuations." He also, recalling Ferdinand Foch's famous fighting speech in front of Amiens, delivered a stirring peroration that inflamed the ardor of his countrymen and excited the admiration of all their Allies:

"We shall go on to the end. We shall fight in France, we shall fight in the seas and oceans, we shall fight with growing confidence and growing strength in the air, we shall defend our Island, whatever the cost may be. We shall fight on the beaches, we shall fight on the landing-grounds, we shall fight in the fields and in the streets, we shall fight in the hills; we shall never surrender; and even if, which I do not for a moment believe, this island or a large part of it were subjugated and starving, then our Empire beyond the seas, armed and guarded by the British Fleet, would carry on the struggle, until, in God's good time, the New World, with all its power and might, steps forth to the rescue and the liberation of the Old."

18. The Fall of France

"SAUVE QUI PEUT!" ("Run for your lives!" or, "Every man for himself!")

Sauve qui peut! became the battle cry of the "magnificent" French army. With lightning speed the Germans had broken through the so-called Weygand Line in the north and the armored columns began splitting off again, taking all the roads and driving for the Seine and Paris, for the Swiss frontier and victory.

In front of them they drove a demoralized French soldiery. Everywhere rifles were thrown down and hands thrown up. All across a stunned and sorrowing nation long lines of shamefaced French soldiers were herded into prison camps. Everywhere as resistance collapsed hoarse voices could be heard crying hysterically: *"Sauve qui peut!"*

Hans Habe, a young Hungarian novelist, had joined a foreign volunteer regiment and was fighting in the northeast in the province of Lorraine when the collapse began. His commanding officer asked him to return to a wood to guide two companies to the front. He took the main road to Châtillon. "This road offered an amazing spectacle. Everywhere I saw guns, knapsacks, tins of food, cartridge-cases in the ditch. Equipment worth hundreds of thousands of francs was strewn along the road: No one thought of picking it up. All these things had become too heavy for the infantrymen."

Habe and his friend came to a house where two terrified black colonials sat smoking. One of them was a corporal who understood French. He said he had nothing against the Germans. "Hitler no come Senegal," he kept repeating. "I no come Germany. I and Hitler no enemy." A German shell exploded nearby and everyone threw himself down. The other Senegalese cried in fright, "Shof ki poo! Shof ki poo!" He did not know its meaning, but he had heard the French shouting it in times of danger. At every explosion he wailed, "Shof ki poo! Shof ki poo!"

Eventually the Germans shortened the range. A shell crashed among Habe and the others. From the terrified colonial rose a hideous dying cry. Shrapnel had torn his back open. Blood bubbled on his lips. His thick pink tongue quivered in his mouth. "Shof ki poo!" he moaned with his expiring breath. "Shof ki poo!"

Hundreds of thousands of terrified civilians fleeing the northern front had clogged the roads to Paris. Haggard and staggering, they hobbled on, some of them with their feet bound up in string and cloth to replace worn-out shoes. They were covered with mud from flinging themselves into ditches upon the approach of enemy planes. Old men trundled their wrinkled wives along in wheelbarrows, mothers pushed prams, in which babies shared space with household goods. From stables, barns and garages had flowed an astonishing variety of conveyances: shiny new automobiles and ancient farm carts thick with dust, hay wains and lorries, tumbrils and bicycles—all stuffed or piled high with bedclothes and dinner plates, clocks and lanterns, hams and bottles of wine, pots and pans and wedding pictures, Bibles and bedsheets.

All along the roads the villages were burning. The fresh June air was redolent with the smell of smoke and full of drifting ash. Soldiers joined the southward-streaming throng. Officers in automobiles blew their horns trying to open a path. Cavalrymen tried to butt their horses through, but their mounts reared, sometimes toppling onto carts and wagons. Soldiers sank to the roadside in exhaustion or crawled into hundreds of abandoned vehicles to sleep. Always there rose the hurrying cry, *"Les Allemands!"* Always, the Germans were but a few miles to the rear. But no one saw them. "In one village," wrote Hans Habe, "a transport truck had run into a house wall; the dead soldiers hung out like marionettes with no one to guide their strings. The horn had been jammed, and blew without interruption, as though the dead driver and his dead passengers were impatient for the wall to move aside."

Into Paris streamed this miserable horde of displaced people, infecting the capital city with their fear. Twenty-six years earlier that famous ragtag Taxicab Army had rattled out of Paris carrying reinforcements to the Battle of the Marne, and a fighting general had vowed that he would fight until not a stone stood upon a stone in the beautiful City of Light; but now a frightened citizenry joined the refugee flood flowing south, following a government already fleeing for Tours.

At this juncture, *Il Duce* struck. "I need a few thousand dead so as to be able to attend the peace conference as a belligerent," he had said, and now, perceiving the mathematical certainty of an Axis victory which he also required, he declared war on France. In the United States, President Roosevelt took to the airwaves to declare: "The hand that held the dagger has struck it into the back of its neighbor."

The Soviet Union invaded the already subverted Baltic states of Lithuania, Latvia and Estonia. Stalin then tore two large chunks off Romania: Bessarabia, and the northern part of the province of Bucovina. He now had his armed forces firmly planted on the Baltic and at the mouths of the Danube.

In France, many soldiers paused in their flight to loot and carouse. Sergeant Hans Habe came into Ligny-en-Barrois in the Champagne district and found the town empty and the railroad station full of drunken soldiers. A freight train fifteen or twenty cars long stood on the railroad tracks. It was loaded with fine cognac and champagne. To reach the train, Habe had to wade through a field of broken glass and half-empty bottles. Soldiers crouched in the glass, smashing emptied bottles or flinging aside half-filled ones. Civilians were there, too. Habe saw a drunken old woman fall face downward on the broken glass, writhing there with her blood mingling with the ooze of cognac and champagne. Officers joined the frolic. Habe saw one of them go staggering through the glass field bent beneath a crate marked "Grand Marnier." Another group was playing ninepins with champagne bottles for targets. They bowled empty bottles at them, and when one was hit and exploded with a gush of white foam, they yelled and danced and kissed each other.

Everywhere, Habe heard officers crying: "Take what you find. If you can't take it with you, burn it. Don't leave anything for the Germans." Disgusted, he could not prevent his men from loading cognac and bottles of Grand Marnier onto their truck. In every village the same scenes were repeated. All the stores had been plundered. Soldiers staggered down the roads with their pockets bulging with bottles, shoes, toys. Few of the *poilus* wore their steel helmets; instead, they sported civilian hats they had stolen from the stores. Cheese factories had been cleaned out. Hundreds of wheels of Port du Salut, Roblechons or Roquefort lay on the roads. Vehicles drove over them so that the roads became smeared with cheese. Habe's truck entered Domrémy-la-Pucelle, the birthplace of Joan of Arc. In front of the house in which she was born, *poilus* paused to drink or urinate or quarrel over loot. Thus was France served in its dying days, and thus its sainted savior of another time of dishonor was saluted.

On June 11 Winston Churchill received a mournful message from Paul Reynaud. A deteriorating situation was now snowballing downhill. He called for a meeting of the Supreme Council at Briare near Orléans. Churchill flew over and was taken to the château there. Facilities were slightly better than primitive. The only telephone was in the lavatory, and it was poorly operated. Privacy was impossible while the telephone's users cursed the frequent delays and the necessity of shouted repetitions. The French and British premiers and their war chiefs met for dinner. Churchill urged the French to form a "Breton redoubt" in Brittany. He promised to keep them supplied until they could break out and recapture Metropolitan France. General Weygand replied that the situation was hopeless. Churchill next importuned the French to fight for Paris, citing the "enormous absorbing power of a house-to-house defense of a great city upon an invading army." He reminded Marshal Pétain of what Clemenceau had said in the last war: "I will fight in front of Paris, in Paris and behind Paris." Pétain replied with quiet dignity that in those days there was a mass of maneuver of sixty divisions, and now there was none.

General Weygand requested British reinforcements, insisting that every British air squadron should immediately be thrown into the battle. "Here," he said, "is the decisive point. Now is the decisive moment. It is therefore wrong to keep *any* squadrons back in England." Churchill replied: "This is not the decisive point and this not the decisive moment. That moment will come when Hitler hurls his Luftwaffe against Great Britain." Again urging the French to fight on —Weygand had mentioned a possible armistice—Churchill maintained that they could wear out a hundred German divisions. "Even if that were so," Weygand snapped, "they would still have another hundred to invade and conquer you. What would you do then?" Churchill's answer was that the best way to halt a German invasion was to drown as many as possible and knock the others on the head when they crawled ashore. Weygand smiled wanly. "At any rate I must admit that you have a very good anti-tank obstacle."

After dinner over coffee and cognac, Reynaud told Churchill that Pétain wanted France to seek an armistice. He had written a memorandum on the subject. "He has not handed it to me yet," Reynaud confided. "He is still ashamed to do it." Churchill was appalled. The French knew that they were lost, and still they had asked for Britain's fighter squadrons! Although he said nothing, Churchill had begun to think now of the French navy. If the Germans seized it, the combined fleets of Germany, Italy and France, and probably Japan, could become a formidable, even overpowering opponent for the Royal Navy, and for the United States Navy as well. In the morning he approached Admiral Jean-François Darlan, the French naval chief, and said: "Darlan, you must never let them get the French fleet." Darlan nodded. "There is no question about that. It would be contrary to naval tradition and to honor."

On that same morning General de Gaulle left for Brittany to investigate the possibility of forming a Breton Redoubt. Meanwhile, Churchill said his goodbye to Reynaud in the château garden. Pétain approached them slowly. "The old man looks buoyant this morning," Reynaud quipped. "There must be some bad news."

Churchill did not smile. With a heavy heart he returned to London convinced that France was preparing to surrender, that Britain now faced Hitler alone and must concentrate on its own defenses. Behind him he left a government divided against itself. Pétain was rapidly gaining powerful converts to his peace crusade. Reynaud stood gallantly against them, but except for de Gaulle and Georges Mandel, minister of the interior, he seemed surrounded by defeatists. He called for another meeting with Churchill.

The British prime minister made his last visit to France on June 13, accompanied by his advisers. Reynaud dropped a bombshell in his lap. The Council of Ministers believed that France could not carry on. Weygand had said that to do so would be to subject its people to deliberate extinction or enslavement by an evil power. France wished to be released from its solemn pledge not to make a separate peace. Churchill withdrew with his colleagues to consider this. He returned to say that the Anglo-French war aim remained the total defeat of Hitler. Britain could not then release France from its pledge. No reproaches would be leveled against the country, whatever it did, but Britain could not cooperate in a separate peace. Churchill urged Reynaud, who had appealed to President Roosevelt for American intervention on June 10, to make a new and final appeal to him. Reynaud did. Roosevelt replied:

Your message has moved me very deeply. As I have already stated to you and Mr. Churchill, this Government is doing everything in its power to make available to the Allied Governments the material they so urgently require, and our efforts to do still more are being redoubled. This is so because of our faith in and our support of the ideals for which the Allies are fighting.

The magnificent resistance of the French and British Armies has profoundly impressed the American people.

I am, personally, particularly impressed by your declaration that France will continue to fight on behalf of Democracy, even if it means slow withdrawal, even to North Africa and the Atlantic. It is most important to remember that the French and British Fleets continue in mastery of the Atlantic and other oceans, also to remember that vital materials from the outside world are necessary to all armies.

I am also greatly heartened by what Prime Minister Churchill said a few days ago about the continued resistance of the British Empire, and that determination would seem to apply equally to the great French Empire all over the world. Naval power in world affairs still carries the lessons of history, as Admiral Darlan well knows.

Roosevelt had gone a long way: too far for his own chances for an unprecedented third term if his message were made public. But that was just what Churchill and Reynaud wanted. Roosevelt had virtually declared war on the Axis. To make public his promises and assurances would surely dismay the Germans and lift the hearts of the French. But Roosevelt quite understandably refused permission to publish the message. He was having enough difficulty convincing his countrymen that the two-terms-only tradition set by George Washington should be abandoned. Publication of his message conceivably could deny him even the Democratic Party's nomination. Of course, he said it was the State Department that had the gravest reservations. Whichever or whoever, it seemed that Reynaud was finished—until Winston Churchill reached into his locker for his last shot.

To the French government now resident in Bordeaux came the prime minister's proposal for an Anglo-French union. If the two countries became one, France could not capitulate. Its government would sit in London. There would be a common citizenship for both peoples. All resources would be pooled. Reynaud embraced it with joy. But he had few supporters—de Gaulle, Jean Monnet, Georges Mandel. Pétain and his party considered it anathema. It was "a scheme to put France in tutelage and carry off her colonial empire." Pétain scoffed at the union as "fusion with a corpse." Weygand had convinced the aged marshal that

England also was lost. "In three weeks England will have her neck wrung like a chicken." Jean Ybarnegaray reflected the Council's obsessive fear of Communism when he said: "Better be a Nazi province. At least we know what that means." Reynaud replied with contempt: "I prefer to collaborate with my allies rather than my enemies." Georges Mandel asked: "Would you rather be a German district than a British dominion?"

The answer seemed to be yes. The cabinet voted, fourteen to ten, to seek an armistice. Reynaud said he would resign. It was now up to President Alfred Lebrun to decide whether or not he would accept the resignation. He spent the afternoon weeping on a sofa. The heads of both the Senate and the Chamber of Deputies advised Lebrun to keep Reynaud, fire Pétain and fight on from North Africa. Lebrun replied falteringly that his only wish was to save lives.

"In that case, I can't form a government," Reynaud told him contemptuously. "If you want such a policy, go and ask Marshal Pétain."

Lebrun did approach Pétain. Astonished to find that the marshal already had chosen his cabinet, the president nevertheless asked him to form a government. Paul Baudouin became the foreign minister. Without requesting terms, he asked Germany for an armistice.

France had fallen, and Britain now stood at bay alone.

19. Charles de Gaulle

SHORTLY BEFORE WINSTON CHURCHILL left France for the last time on June 13, 1940, he saw Charles de Gaulle standing silently beside a doorway. At six feet five inches, de Gaulle towered above the French leaders such as the diminutive Reynaud, Gamelin and Weygand, even above Churchill at five six and a half. The British chief stepped up to him. *"L'homme de destin,"* he said in a low voice. "Man of destiny." De Gaulle did not reply, but Churchill could perceive the anguish in his eyes. A few days later Churchill received a call from Maj. Gen. Sir Edward Spears, his liaison officer in France. Spears had been warned that de Gaulle had alienated too many of the Frenchmen now in power and he expressed his anxiety for his safety. A plan to rescue him was made. On the afternoon of June 17, de Gaulle went to his office in Bordeaux. He made a few appointments for the afternoon as a blind. Then he accompanied General Spears, who was going home, to the airfield. They walked out to a small airplane together and shook hands in farewell. Spears clambered aboard, and de Gaulle turned away—suddenly whirling to climb into the moving airplane and slam the door. French officials and police gaped in dismay at the fleeing plane, soon but a speck in the sky. Inside it rode Charles de Gaulle and the honor of France.

It is no exaggeration to say that Charles de Gaulle thought of himself as the living embodiment of French honor. For almost all of his conscious life, the word *l'honneur* had been like a credo to him and the love of France a religion. His family was one of the oldest in France, able to trace its origins back for more than five centuries to the great battlefield at Agincourt, where the first ancestor, Jehan de Gaulle, fought the British in 1415. Throughout the late Middle Ages the de Gaulles were members of the *petite noblesse d'épée,* the sword-bearing officer class. By the eighteenth century they had risen slightly to the rank of petite *noblesse de robe,* that is, lesser nobility without title or land. The family profession was now the law. Three generations of de Gaulles served the Bourbon monarchy as Crown lawyers. During the French Revolution, Jean-Baptiste-Philippe de Gaulle was imprisoned in the Bastille. His son, Julien-Philippe, veered the family away from law toward the writing and teaching of history. Julien-Philippe edited an official biography of Saint Louis and wrote a lengthy history of Paris. He had three sons, all scholars. Henri, the middle son, born in 1848, was the father of Charles de Gaulle. Henri was trained for the army, being wounded during the siege of Paris in the Franco-Prussian War of 1870. But he left the service for a more lucrative teaching position in Lille. There, in 1886, he met and married Jeanne Maillot-Delannoy, a second cousin on his mother's side. Four boys and a girl were born to them, and Charles was the second son.

He had sprung, then, from a family deeply rooted in French history and tradition, in the values of family and service, devoutly Catholic and intensely conservative. His father, a very tall man who had transmitted his height to his sons, was a stern but courteous teacher. Both his students and his family stood in awe of him. It was from Henri that Charles inherited his intelligence, and it was his father who trained him in a logical way of thinking, instilled in him a sense of history and by example showed him the path to high moral character. His mother was responsible for his passionate nature concealed beneath a cultivated mask of hauteur. Henri de Gaulle also imparted to all of his children—and to his students—his love for the French language, teaching them to use it properly and with elegance. Charles's own literary style, highly prized for its polish, was owed to him. Henri also taught his children to be patriotic. Charles wrote later: "An anxious concern about the fate of our country came as second nature to my three brothers, my sister and myself."

After the turn of the century this very private family moved from Lille to Paris, where Henri was overjoyed to receive the position of lay headmaster at the Jesuit College of the Immaculate Conception. After a change of government brought about the separation of church and state and the closing of Jesuit schools, Henri founded his own academy. But then the Jesuits were expelled from France, and Charles was sent to Belgium to continue his education under the black-robed sons of Saint Ignatius. By then the dominating quality of his character had appeared: his brothers and sister were almost as much in awe of him as of his father.

Once, he and his older brother Xavier were playing war, and Xavier decided that he wanted to be "King of France" rather than "Emperor of Germany." Charles was indignant. "Never! France is mine!"

Suddenly the youthful Charles de Gaulle became conscious of the growing quarrel between the chief powers of Europe: the Anglo-French and the German Empire. The saber-rattling Kaiser Wilhelm was challenging the British on the sea and France on land. France's endemic political pluralism seemed to Charles a corrosive force weakening the state, and he saw the Church and the army as the nation's only stabilizing influences. He decided to go into the army. He would enroll in the military academy at St.-Cyr. But he was an indifferent student, interested only in history and literature, relying more on his incredible memory than disciplined habits of study to get him through his classes. He trained and strengthened that memory by memorizing words backward, and even whole sentences. He memorized hundreds of lines of French poetry, all of *Cyrano de Bergerac,* and even lengthy passages from Greek plays. But he still did not know how to put his long nose to the grindstones of mathematics and science, so his father packed him off to preparatory school for two years. There he buckled down and passed into St.-Cyr.

Because the French army believed that before a man can give orders he must learn to take them, it required all officer candidates to serve one year as an enlisted man. De Gaulle chose the 33rd Infantry Regiment, in which he enlisted October 10, 1910. A year later he entered St.-Cyr on the outskirts of Paris. Here he became known as *la Grande Asperge* (the Big Asparagus) because of his height; and also as Cyrano because of his long nose. In response to this jest, he climbed onto a mess table to recite the whole of Rostand's famous play. He was graduated thirteenth in a class of 211, though his report stated: "Average in everything but height." On October 1, 1912, he was commissioned a sublieutenant, after which his request to return to the 33rd Infantry was granted. There his commanding officer was Col. Henri-Philippe Pétain.

At fifty-six years of age, Pétain was remarkably old for a colonel. He had gone slowly up the ladder of promotion because he was a theoretical gadfly whose constant criticism of the French military doctrine of *l'attaque*—like the irritating buzzing of that winged creature—had annoyed his superiors. But Pétain had remained in fine physical shape and was still a commanding presence who understood soldiers and knew how to lead them. His aloof and glacial manner often repelled younger officers, who were torn between twin fears of his reproachful silence and of his sarcasm when he chose to speak. De Gaulle was not so dismayed; actually, much of his own coldly superior style was adapted from Pétain. And Pétain thought very highly of de Gaulle, predicting a brilliant career for him.

In August 1914, during the early fighting in World War I, the Big Asparagus was leading a charge across a bridge in the Belgian town of Dinant when enemy machine-gun fire brought him down. He spent seven months in the hospital recovering from a severe leg wound. In February 1916, he was back with the 33rd Infantry at Verdun, the bloodiest battle of the war, perhaps of all time. In command was his old colonel and preceptor—Henri-Philippe Pétain—now a general. Pétain became "the hero of Verdun," idolized by a grateful French nation and, after he put down the French army mutiny with tact and firmness, worshiped by the French *poilu*. At Verdun, de Gaulle was now a captain. He was bayoneted in the thigh and an exploding grenade knocked him unconscious. He was believed dead. "Captain de Gaulle," the report said, "reputed for his great intellectual and moral worth . . . led his men in a fierce attack and savage hand-to-hand fight. . . . He fell in the fighting. A peerless officer in all respects." Actually, de Gaulle was a prisoner in Germany. He made five attempts to escape, each of them thwarted by his great height. At last he was sent to maximum security prison where he passed 120 days in solitary confinement within a dark cell. Such treatment did not improve his low estimate of the enemy.

After the Armistice, Captain de Gaulle returned to France, carrying a suitcase crammed with notes and reflections jotted down during thirty-two months of imprisonment. He was twenty-eight and a career of writing and lecturing on military matters appeared to lie ahead. But in April 1919, with Poland menaced by the Red Army commanded by Marshal Mikhail Tukhachevsky—a fellow captive in de Gaulle's prison camp—he chose instead to volunteer as a captain in the Polish 4th Division of chasseurs.

He did not leave immediately, however, and in June of that year he met Yvonne Mendroux, the daughter of a Calais biscuit manufacturer. Yvonne was only eighteen, shy and reserved, but much impressed by the tall haughty captain with the immaculate uniform and impeccable manners. She had already rejected a general's son because "traipsing from garrison town to garrison town was not for me." But de Gaulle did not appear to be a traipser. After their first meeting, they met again at the annual ball of the École Polytechnique at the Palace of Versailles. There, standing in his dress uniform, serenely superior amid the glitter and grandeur of Versailles, the cream of Parisian society swirling around him in silks and satins and precious stones, was Charles de Gaulle. He asked Yvonne for a dance, and after the sixth waltz Yvonne said to her brother: "Captain de Gaulle has just asked me to marry him. I said yes."

The engagement, however, was not to be announced until de Gaulle returned from Poland. He was with the 4th Division when it distinguished itself in the critical Battle of Warsaw, in one of the decisive battles of world history. Marshal Józef Piłsudski decisively defeated Tukhachevsky and sent the Bolshevik tide flowing back to Russia. De Gaulle was highly commended for his brave and intelligent handling of his battalion, and received Poland's highest military decoration: the *Ordo Virtuti Militari.*

Now he could come home to marry and take up that writing and lecturing career. At St.-Cyr he was assigned to lecture on nineteenth-century warfare, and astonished both his superiors and his students by a ringing denunciation of Napoleon. The Corsican conqueror, he said, left France "crushed, invaded, drained of blood and of courage, smaller than when he took control, condemned to accept bad frontiers the evils of which have never been redressed." De Gaulle had also become extremely critical of the new French military doctrine of *la défense,* a 180-degree turn away from the old and tragic dogma of *l'attaque.* Younger officers such as de Gaulle and some of his fellow students at the École Supérieure de Guerre, in which he had enrolled in 1922, believed that the tank would make the offense king again. Unfortunately, de Gaulle's criticism and arguments were always offered with an icy superiority that irritated his instructors, all of them senior officers. "A very developed personality," one of his reports went, "great confidence in himself. Could achieve excellent results if he admitted mistakes with a little better grace, and if he consented more easily to allow his point of view to be disputed."

At the École Supérieure there were only three grades; Very Good, Good and Passable. Only a Very Good could earn an officer a coveted appointment to the General Staff. De Gaulle's instructors were so incensed by his air of superiority and his *sang-froid* that they went to extreme lengths to cut the Big Asparagus down to size with only a Passable. But his treatment became a cause célèbre in the army. No less a person than Marshal Pétain, now inspector general of the army, intervened. Pétain came to the École to interview everyone concerned, from which he produced the judgment that his protégé—for such he had become—was worth far more than Passable. The school's commandant, however, refused to bow to Pétain's wishes and gave de Gaulle a mere Good, which, as he and his rejoicing instructors well knew, was not good enough for the General Staff. Instead, de Gaulle was posted to Germany. Before he left, he told his fellow students: "I will come back to this dirty hole only when I am commandant of it."

Come back he did, in April 1927, to give an unprecedented series of lectures to his old professors. The sweet revenge was not only his but also Marshal Pétain's, who still resented the Passable grade and wanted "to give a lesson to those professors that they will understand." The lectures were brilliant but far from successful, if only because the audience was glacially cool toward the lecturer, not even cowed by the presence of the great marshal himself on the dais.

Pétain's power and prestige ultimately broke the resistance to promoting de Gaulle. Soon he was a major, and in trouble again for attempting to stop men in his battalion from applying for transfers to other posts. He faced a trial that could end his career. Once again Pétain intervened—and no action was taken. De Gaulle next spent about two years in the Middle East, being posted back to Paris in 1931 to serve on the General Secretariat charged with preparation and organization of the nation for war. From 1932 to 1937—approximately the years of the rise of Adolf Hitler—de Gaulle served under no fewer than fourteen different governments, at last concluding that the French state was rotten and feeble. Politics had divided it and made it disjointed. There were good and sincere men in office, he said, even talented ones. "But the political game consumed them and paralyzed them."

It was in this capacity that Charles de Gaulle met Paul Reynaud, and it was then that his controversial book, *Toward a Professional Army,* was published.

Because of that book, much has been made of de Gaulle as one of the pioneers of tank warfare. Actually, he was not; certainly he was not an armored-warfare visionary in the class of Sir Basil Liddell Hart or J. F. C. Fuller. No German officer ever read him and especially not Heinz Guderian. He had no original ideas on the subject and nothing as developed or reflective as other theorists. But he was nevertheless thoroughly convinced of the impact armor would have on the battle of the future. This, combined with his heroic nature, his family traditions, his fierce love of France, his theories of leadership and his vast reading in military history, together with his enormous self-confidence and resolute courage in refusing to be intimidated by repeated warnings and rebukes from on high, uniquely equipped him for the Cassandra role that made him so hated. That he had not been heeded was not his fault or even unusual. What matters is that de Gaulle persisted in this course and because he did so was befriended by Paul Reynaud, becoming his private adviser, present at all those despairing conferences where his very bearing, the very anguish in his eyes brought him to the attention of the British prime minister. And thus the future leader of the Free French was spirited away from those headquarters of defeat and selfish dissent, his soul seared by his witness of that dreadful debacle he had been powerless to prevent.

20. June 1940: Hitler Enters Paris

THE SCALPS OF NINE COUNTRIES now hung from the war belt of Adolf Hitler: Austria, Czechoslovakia, Poland, Luxembourg, Norway, Denmark, Belgium, Holland, and France. Not even Napoleon had reigned over such a vast European empire. *Der Führer* was now truly *Herr Gott,* and it was as *Gott* himself that he planned to appear for the French capitulation.

It was to take place on June 21 in the same railroad car within that very forest of Compiègne where the German generals had surrendered to Marshal Foch almost twenty-two years earlier. The railroad car still stood in the clearing there. There also stood a statue of Marshal Foch. Another statue was of the German eagle being transfixed by the French sword. Letters of gold inscribed on a granite boulder said: *Here on the eleventh of November, 1918, succumbed the criminal pride of the German empire—vanquished by the free peoples it tried to enslave.*

With loving care Hitler drafted and redrafted the armistice terms in his headquarters at Brûly-de-Pêche, a small village just inside the Belgian frontier. He sent General Keitel running like an errand boy between the headquarters and the little village church in which his secretaries typed out his handwritten terms. From time to time Hitler strolled down the single village street to enter the church and watch the secretaries clattering away by candlelight. It was a scene he never forgot, the beginning of his vengeance, and he savored it. His terms were harsh. France was to be split in two, one part occupied by Germans, the other ruled by the French with the Pétain government's capital in Vichy. All Germans in France sought by Germany were to be handed over. French prisoners of war were to remain in captivity until the war was over. The French fleet would not be touched, Hitler promised, knowing full well he would seize it when the need and opportunity arose. Satisfied, Hitler took his sleeping pills and went to bed.

Next morning, because a fog made it impossible to fly, he drove to Compiègne in his armored Mercedes-Benz. With him were Hess, Goering, Raeder, Brauchitsch and Keitel. Ribbentrop came separately. Hitler wore an army cap, a double-breasted field-gray uniform and gleaming black leather jackboots. He strode among the forest's stately oaks and elms in exultation.

The honor guard supplied by the black-uniformed SS Leibstandarte Adolf Hitler was present. So was a regimental band. Nazi flags were draped over the statue of the transfixed eagle, although the statue of Foch remained untouched. Hitler went inside, followed by his entourage, all in dress uniform. They took their places, staring at the four empty chairs awaiting the French delegates. From outside came the sound of music, a stirring performance of "Deutschland über Alles." The French had arrived. They came in: General Huntziger; Vice-Admiral Le Luc; Air Force General Bergeret, representing the armed forces; and Léon Noel, the former French Ambassador to Poland, for the civil government. Hitler remained seated while his entourage rose to bow with swift frigidity. He stared impassively before him while Keitel read out the terms. Then he arose, gave the Nazi salute, stared each of the Frenchmen contemptuously in the eye and strode out. Outside the band again broke into "Deutschland über Alles."

The greatest moment in the life of Adolf Hitler had passed. Now he would satisfy a lifelong craving: He would see Paris.

As an architectural "artist" and a lover of the Baroque, Hitler had yearned for years to behold the City of Light's most magnificent buildings. He wanted especially to see the Opera House, which he regarded as second only to the Vienna Opera House. In his youth Hitler had seen colored postcards of the Paris Opera House and been delighted by them. In his library were books on the subject and a complete set of drawings.

Hitler arrived in Paris after dark on June 23. His visit was unheralded and he really did not need the extreme security precautions. As he had said, who would expect to find the master of Europe wandering around the Opera House at six o'clock in the morning? By his orders, the entire Opera House was lighted as though for a great performance. Followed by his entourage, he strode up the great ornamental stairway with shining eyes, pausing here and there either to deliver a lecture on the functions of stairways or to admire the Baroque ornamentation. He seemed to know his way about the Opera House better than the white-haired attendant who guided him. Coming to the proscenium box, Hitler stopped, puzzled. He asked the attendant what had happened to the salon that should be there. Startled, the attendant replied that it had been removed during renovations. *Der Führer*'s eyes twinkled in triumph. "You see how well I know my way about here." He was, however, a bit crushed when his guide with great dignity declined a huge 50-franc tip. Next Hitler visited the Madeleine, crossed the Place de la Concorde and drove along the Champs-Elysées to the Arc de Triomphe where an enormous Nazi flag waved over the Tomb of the Unknown Soldier. Then he visited the Invalides, gazing in rapture at the Tomb of Napoleon. "This is the finest moment of my life," he murmured. From there he hurried to the Panthéon, and then to the Sainte-Chapelle, where he was puzzled again. He did not know that the chapel's stained-glass windows had been removed for safekeeping and he wondered why this dark little building should be called the "jewel of Paris." Finally he drove to Montmartre, stepping from his armored car to gaze in admiration at the huge white dome of Sacré-Coeur. With true Gallic sang-froid, parishioners hurrying up the great steps to early Mass pretended not to recognize him. After four hours in Paris, the ruler of Europe left, never to return.

Adolf Hitler came back to a Germany that was—at least outwardly—over-joyed. His generals were euphoric, even ecstatic, for they knew that they were going to be promoted. Row upon row of them in medal-plastered tunics sat in the front seats of the packed Kroll Opera House when *Der Führer* delivered his victory speech. He spoke standing before a curtain of cloth of gold under a huge Nazi banner, tracing, as always, the two decades of German shame under the savage terms of Versailles, describing how he broke the chains one by one until Germany was at last not only free but the most powerful nation in the world. All he wanted now, he said, was peace with Britain and return of the lost colonies. Surprisingly, Hitler eschewed histrionics. His voice was calm; he did not strive for the thunderous bursts of applause that customarily went reverberating around the huge hall. His audience was hushed, reverent, even worshipful, crouching beneath him as though the gods that gave to Greece its divine Alexander and to Rome its divine Augustus had now conferred upon Germany the divine Adolf.

With unprecedented generosity *Der Führer* on that memorable night sol-emnly awarded no fewer than twelve field marshal's batons, and upon Hermann Goering he conferred the unparalleled new rank of Reichsmarschall—marshal of marshals. But then, upon *Der Führer*'s final "Heil!", the applause did come, bursting forth with a roar that seemed to shake the crystal chandeliers.

Britain, everyone present knew, was next.

Wilhelm Pruller had not seen action in the conquest of the Lowlands and France. He had missed Norway, too, although he had written in his diary then: "Dear God in Heaven, we thank Thee that we are Germans and still more that we are allowed to live in this gigantic epoch." While the blitzkrieg rolled west, he had filled his diary with martial bluster and fierce diatribes against Reynaud and Churchill. On June 10, however, he had the pleasure of sprinkling a little blood on his pages. His unit had found a German armored car lying on its side. A soldier lay beside it with a knife in his chest: dead. Another was also knifed, but still alive. He said black French prisoners had stabbed them. Pruller and his *Kameraden* immediately rounded up twenty black prisoners and shot them dead.

After this incident, Wilhelm was transferred to a camp in his native Austria. He listened to *Der Führer*'s victory speech on the radio there. When he heard the final "Heil!" his eyes filled with tears of pride. "We are aware of our strength!" he wrote. "We know that at the conclusion of this struggle will be the most glorious victory of history; we fear nothing, no one. For after all the Führer has said how incomparably we are armed for this last phase of the struggle. . . . But despite all this, once more the Führer has appealed to reason. As a soldier, as a human being, as victor! Once more he has given England and the world the possibility of ending this senseless battle. What a man!"

Remarkably enough, Else Wendel also felt "intoxicated" by the victories. It was now summer and she had forgotten the hardships of a brutal winter. She did feel a little sorry for the fallen nations, but, after all, "the strongest feeling of all was our pride in Germany, showing the world that the Treaty of Versailles, with its bitter humiliation, has been broken. I was proud to be German. I was also proud of Hitler. . . . He had put Germany back as a great nation of the world. Feverishly we waited the invasion of England."

But not everyone exulted in the pealing bells and the swirling flags. Ruth Andreas-Friedrich and her intellectual friends in Berlin were shocked and saddened by the string of victories. "Put out the flags, take in the flags," Ruth wrote in her diary.

Every window, every gable, every tower, all in a sea of swastika'd flags. Order for display of flags: 'As of today, for a period of one week.' Ringing of church bells: three days. Once again Christian tongues have to join in praising the bloody victory of arms. . . . Paris fell last Friday. When the report came over the radio, employees of the paper were all at lunch at the canteen. 'Hurrah!' comes a shout from a corner. Everyone winces. 'Hurrah!' again, but this time with noticeably less authority. One of our scrubwomen has jumped up, grabbed her glass and is cheering, 'Long live the Führer!' Icy silence at every table.

By September, the jubilation had given way to apprehension. Britain had not been invaded. Nobody sang "We sail against England!" any more. The war had not ended that summer as everyone had been promised. Older Germans who could remember the last war were in a somber mood: They knew another long and bitter war was ahead. The signing of the Tripartite Pact among Germany, Italy and Japan on September 27 evoked little enthusiasm. The cheering crowds were small, composed mostly of schoolchildren. Japan was very far away; few Germans could understand what help it could be to Germany. Many of them knew that the Japanese career of expansion in East Asia was bringing them into collision with the United States. Again Germans who could remember the last war recalled with trepidation how American intervention had tipped the scales. Hitler's frequent gibes at America distressed them, and they did not like his oft-quoted sneer: "I will never believe that Americans can fight like heroes." Some of them had fought Americans in Belleau Wood during World War I.

Food was again scarce in Germany. Sometimes grocery windows actually contained more food than the stores themselves. The victorious Germans had far fewer of the good things in life than the vanquished French. Hans Habe, who had been taken prisoner, soon learned how true that was. Because he feared he would be shot if it were learned that he was a Hungarian on the enemy's side, he had managed to pass himself off as Maurice Napier, a dead *poilu*. His fluency in both French and German quickly made him invaluable to the prison authorities. They also sent him on shopping errands in Nancy. The loyal French shopkeepers in that city withheld their goods from German officers, telling them they were out of stock. If they did sell, it was at outrageous prices. So the commandant decided that Habe with his flawless French should do their shopping, providing him with an ambulance, a "sick" soldier and a Red Cross armband to get him past the Elite Guard and to carry back his treasures. On his first mission they handed him their shopping list:

8 yards red silk
4 yards blue silk (sky blue if possible)
2 lbs. pepper
Soap (as much as possible)
Chocolate (as much as possible)
14 bottles of Eau de Cologne
6 bottles of perfume (only the genuine French article!)
5 bottles of hair tonic
5 wristwatches (gold or silver) for ladies

Hans Habe took the list with an inward smile. In the ambulance, the "sick" soldier and the armband, *Herr Kommandant* had unwittingly provided him with the means for escape.

21. Summer 1940: The U.S. Arms, Operation Sea-Lion, the French Fleet, the Battle of Britain

THE OUTBREAK OF WORLD WAR II did not shock America as its predecessor had done in 1914. This time Americans had seen the storm gather and break; and this time they declared: "We're staying out of it."

But Americans were far from neutral in thought as Woodrow Wilson had asked them to be in 1914. President Roosevelt was aware of this when he said: "This nation will remain a neutral nation, but I cannot ask that every American remain neutral in thought as well." Like FDR, the vast majority of Americans were openly for the Allies. Pro-Fascist organizations such as the German-American Bund were few, small and ineffectual.

Yet the Americans had no intention of intervening. Again unlike 1914, this generation had had experience of European war and was not eager to renew it. A poll taken at the time showed only 2.5 percent of the nation favored intervention. The disenchanted and disillusioned remainder told the Allies, in effect: "Last time we pulled you out of a hole, and the only thanks we got was to be called 'Uncle Shylock' when we asked you to pay back the money we loaned you. Now you're in trouble again because of the mess you made at Versailles. Well, we wish you well, but we're not coming over this time." Some idealistic young men went off to Canada to train for the Royal Air Force, but the bulk of a youth fed from the cradle on the horrors of war preferred the football fields to the battlefields of Europe.

Roosevelt believed that an Allied victory was essential to American security. He was convinced that the fate of democratic government was at stake. A German victory would leave an unarmed America alone in the world against the Axis Powers all-powerful in Europe and Asia. Fortunately for democracy, FDR was uniquely fitted to convert his countrymen to his belief that the Allies must be helped. Even as late as the fall of 1939, in the seventh year of his administration, he was still held in high esteem by the majority of Americans. His New Deal had not ended the Depression as it had promised, but it had done much to restore American self-respect. It had also revolutionized American political thought. Prior to FDR, debate focused on such matters as Prohibition, the war debt and law enforcement; after him, it took up the problems of Social Security, labor legislation or public housing. In addition to this social revolution, Roosevelt rescued the presidency from the desuetude into which it had sunk in the hands of his three predecessors, and he not only raised it to the position of dignity and power intended for it by Washington and Jackson and Lincoln, but also streamlined it into an instrument capable of standing the strain of modern government.

Why then, it may be asked, did not this powerful and able chief mobilize his nation's vast industrial and military resources to the point where America would dominate the world situation and bring an end to the war? The answer to that question, which might also have been asked of Woodrow Wilson, was that Roosevelt governed in a democracy. He could only lead the people as far as they wanted to be led, and his task, then, was to make them wish to advance to his own objective of a strengthened defense establishment and "all aid to the Allies short of war."

To do this, in September of 1939 FDR proclaimed a "limited national emergency," authorized an increase of 17,000 regulars in the army and raised the National Guard by 35,000 to its authorized strength of 200,000. The Army Air Corps had already been authorized to expand to 6,000 aircraft and 50,000 men. By European standards, these increases were minute, but they were all that the public was then ready to accept. Roosevelt never forgot that he was dealing with a public that was largely pacifist, he was always mindful of the public opinion polls, and he never jeopardized his overall objective by taking some indiscreet giant step that would put the isolationist hounds on his track. As it was, he was widely criticized as a hypocritical warmonger who was craftily nibbling away at American isolationist tradition, taking a nation to war against its will.

FDR's next step was to call for revision of Neutrality legislation, and Congress obliged in November of 1939 by repealing the arms embargo and placing the trade of all belligerents, whether for munitions or other supplies, on a cash-and-carry basis. The President told the nation that developing such a trade in munitions would help build national defense, and that by keeping it on a cash-and-carry basis the United States would avoid the kind of incidents at sea that had led to intervention in 1914. "There lies the road to peace!" he exclaimed.

There, rather, lay the road to war. FDR did not think so, because he still believed that the Allies were stronger than Hitler. But repeal of the arms embargo effected a deep breach in the isolationist wall, if it was not also an interventionist act. It favored the Allies because, through their control of the seas, they could buy all war material that they needed, while Germany could not; and implicit in it was the assurance that if the Allies proved weaker than Hitler, as they were, then other radical steps would be taken to prevent their collapse.

Isolationism waxed strong again with the onset of the Phony War and the corresponding "phony peace" in America. Presented with a war that was not a war, Americans refused to take it seriously, ignored the plight of the democracies and began to lose their temper at British interference with neutral trade. FDR's hands were so firmly tied that, in the words of his biographer Robert Sherwood, "It was the one crisis in Roosevelt's career when he was completely at a loss as to what action to take—a period of terrible, stultifying vacuum."

Ironically, Hitler's blitzkrieg in the Low Countries and France freed Roosevelt's hands. On May 16, 1940, he appeared before Congress to ask for 50,000 airplanes and a defense appropriation of $900 million. He did not, however, dare to ask for peacetime conscription. This bill had to await the fall of France and be introduced on the initiative of private citizens. France's fall also startled some isolationists, who became aware that a Luftwaffe based in the French colonial port of Dakar could raid Brazil. Air power had brought the Western Hemisphere within range of the broils of Europe, and this sobering thought raised some ostrich heads from the sands.

But only a few. Throughout 1940 the war of words between isolationists and interventionists raged unabated. The isolationists were a strange collection of bedfellows indeed. Native American Fascists, including such groups as Fritz Kuhn's German-American Bund, the Silver Shirts of William Dudley Pelley and the Ku Klux Klan, echoed the pacifist cries of German and Italian foreign agents. There were doctrinal pacifists such as the Socialist Norman Thomas and there were some, but not many, Italian- and German-Americans who sympathized with the lands of their origin or who admired *Il Duce* or *Der Führer*. Then there were the Communists vociferously following the Comintern's Party line that this was a "Bourgeois-Imperialist" war—until, of course, Hitler invaded Russia, whereupon the customary flip-flop was performed; not, however, without the soulsearching and agonizing which the Kremlin's abrupt twists and turns of policy always imposed upon its foreign followers and their fellow travelers. Yet, with few exceptions, the somersault was always executed. Such people mingled with sincere Americans who were isolationists by conviction, leaders such as Senators Burton K. Wheeler and Gerald P. Nye, newspaper tycoons Colonel Robert McCormick and William Randolph Hearst, Charles A. Lindbergh and the radical, right-wing radio priest, Father Charles E. Coughlin. Missing from this coterie was Senator Borah, who died on January 19, 1940.

The America First Committee, formed in September 1940, battled on even terms with the Committee to Defend America by Aiding the Allies, a group organized by William Allen White, a beloved small-town Kansas publisher with a national reputation. White's committee attracted such outstanding Americans as President James B. Conant of Harvard, publisher Henry Luce and Mrs. Dwight W. Morrow, Lindbergh's mother-in-law. From the American Jewish community, understandably anxious to bring down Hitler, came financial assistance and the support of its widespread influence in the press and radio.

Debate between these two groups was on fairly even terms. The America Firsters maintained that the nation could best defend itself on its own shores and should make itself so strong as to discourage any invasion, while their opponents argued that now was the time to intervene while Britain still held out as a free-world bastion and the British fleet still controlled the sea. At no time up until Pearl Harbor was this debate ever resolved. America remained hesitant, indecisive. A poll taken at this time showed only 7.7 percent favoring intervention. A Britain alone and at bay had increased interventionist sentiment by only 5 percent!

In the meantime, Franklin Delano Roosevelt had made what has been aptly called "the great commitment." In May of 1940, using his great powers, he had begun to transfer airplanes and equipment of the U.S. Army and Navy to the Allies. With that act neutrality was fitted for a shroud, and after Italy entered the war on Hitler's side, FDR made his action public. "In our American unity," he said, "we will pursue two obvious and simultaneous courses; we will extend to the opponents of force the material resources of this nation and, at the same time, we will harness and speed up the use of those resources in order that we ourselves in the Americas may have equipment and training equal to the task of every emergency and every defense."

In September, Roosevelt introduced a bill that called for establishment of the first peacetime draft in American history. It touched off a bitter and furious outcry from the America Firsters. Senator Wheeler cried that Bill 1776 would "plow under every fourth American boy." Isolationist women gathered outside the White House to kneel on the pavement to pray for defeat of the legislation. In New York, Representative Clare Hoffman waved a placard reading: "Kill

1776, Not Our Boys." Marchers paraded down Fifth Avenue holding an enormous banner proclaiming: "The Yanks Are Not Coming—Our Fight Is on the Sidewalks of New York." Nevertheless, Congress did pass what was called the Selective Service Act. An army of 1.4 million men was to be raised through a lottery draft. A blindfolded Secretary of War Henry Stimson drew numbers of men between the ages of twenty-one and twenty-eight out of a huge glass container. Surprisingly, the men so arbitrarily selected went off to the training camps without protest. They even sang:

> *Good-bye, dear, I'll be back in a year*
> *'Cause I'm in the Army, now.*
> *They took my number right out of a hat*
> *And there's not much a man can do about that.*

A huge air force and a two-ocean navy were also authorized, as Congress passed billion-dollar spending bills to raise aircraft production to 36,000 planes a year and to build new battleships and aircraft carriers. All this, however, was strictly for "hemisphere defense." Roosevelt continued to resist every appeal for direct intervention. He knew that the nation would not approve such a course. Moreover, 1940 was an election year, and he was seeking his precedent-shattering third term against the strong Republican dark-horse nominee, Wendell Willkie.

Nevertheless, "hemisphere defense" was going to call forth a giant war machine geared to a gargantuan war industry, and once it was in mesh, it would be able to roll in any corner of the world. Britain was then in need of destroyers and America had fifty over-age destroyers from the last war. On the other hand, America needed bases to defend the 300-mile-wide "security zone" which it and Latin-American countries had drawn around their coasts, and these the British possessed. So Britain got the destroyers and America got the bases—leased or otherwise granted—and with this single, severely criticized presidential act, FDR secured great strategical advantages for the U.S. Navy and came to the side of beleaguered Britain during its darkest hour.

In his blitzkriegs Adolf Hitler had been nearly flawless. Within a year he had conquered seven countries and evicted Britain from the Continent, as the Kaiser had not been able to do. But now he was to make mistakes, to slip and stumble in a fashion all but foreordained by the two great errors imbedded in his policy.

The first of these was made clear when, in August 1939, Britain rejected his offer of a negotiated peace based upon recognition of his conquests. Hitler could not understand that Britain would not allow him to establish hegemony over Europe. European hegemony had been possible only to the Roman Empire, which may be said to have organized Europe. Since Rome fell, the attempts of this or that conqueror to "unify" Europe by his own arms and under his own standard had bathed that continent in blood. It had not been and will not be possible, and Britain was the last nation to allow it.

Hitler's second error consisted of two parts. The first was the failure to realize that Britain was the center of gravity of the alliance against him; the second his inability to comprehend sea power. By defeating all the Allies but Britain, Hitler was like a hunter who shoots the cubs before the lioness. Still unconquered, Britain was free to fight on and to recruit new allies. Eventually, reluctantly, Hitler came to realize this and because of it he ordered the invasion of Britain. In so doing he again displayed his ignorance of sea power. The way to crush Britain was not the direct route of invasion, but the indirect one of attrition at sea. Hitler had the very weapon at hand, the U-boat, then being built in numbers and beginning to sortie from submarine pens located from the Arctic Ocean to the Spanish coast.

Although Hitler had not seized the French fleet, with Italy in the war, Britain was denied the direct sea route to Egypt through the Mediterranean. If Egypt were taken, all of North Africa would be in Axis hands. Shorn of the Suez Canal, without an overseas base within striking distance of Europe, strangled by the undersea blockade, Britain's plight would indeed be desperate—even hopeless. But Hitler and his generals were land-minded rather than sea-minded, they preferred annihilation to attrition, and thus instead of undermining their chief enemy, they chose to overwhelm her.

In his unbounded confidence, Hitler already had a plan for the elimination of the British people. Today it may sound fantastic—even comical—but Hitler was dead serious about it. In his ambivalence toward the British, his love had changed to hatred. A Germany army of occupation was to remain on British soil indefinitely and the United Kingdom would become a province of Germany. All British males between seventeen and forty-five would be deported to Germany as slave laborers. Younger ones would be trained in Heinrich Himmler's special schools for the racially impure. "The aim of this school," Himmler explained to Hitler, "should be to teach the pupil how to count up to a maximum of 500, how to write his name, that it is God's command that he should be obedient to Germans, honorable, industrious and brave. I regard reading as unnecessary." All the British intelligentsia and the Jews were to be liquidated. Nubile women would mate with the swains of the SS to produce a sturdy Anglo-German race. Younger ones would be trained for this privilege. Older ones would be allowed to live until they were no longer useful.

Reinhard Heydrich was the author of this plan. Execution of it was given to Colonel Professor Dr. Franz Six, a former dean of the faculty of political science at the University of Berlin.

The detail and precise instructions for this tragicomic scheme were the diametric opposite of the total lack of preparation for Operation Sea Lion, the code name for the invasion of Britain; and to examine the catalog of Sea Lion's deficiencies is to wonder if it was not after all a gigantic bluff. First, there was no plan, and in mid-July Hitler gave proof of his monstrous ignorance of amphibious warfare by ordering one to be prepared in thirty days. Second, there were no proper landing craft, proof again that Hitler must have commenced the war without reckoning on knocking out Britain. Third, barges and river boats had to be collected and converted into tank lighters, assault boats and vehicle ferries. Fourth, no soldier in the German Army had been trained in amphibious warfare and no officer had experience of it. Fifth, apart from the very severe limitations imposed by tides and weather, the sine qua non of success was control of the air. Sixth, even if the Luftwaffe knocked the RAF out of the sky, it probably could not prevent the mighty Royal Navy from attacking the invasion fleet. Seventh, to embark the first wave of about 100,000 men would require more than half of the 1.2 million tons of shipping that Germany had available for all its needs, and it would not be possible to concentrate this in a single staging area.

At the outset, the army and navy quarreled. The navy maintained that it would have to land the first two waves two days apart, because it had not enough ships. This was utterly rejected by General Halder, who snapped: "I might just as well put the troops that have been landed straight through the sausage machine." In reply, the naval chief of staff said that to attack on a broad front as the army proposed was to invite slaughter on the passage over. Eventually, it was agreed to cross the Channel at its narrowest point, with the troops sailing through a corridor formed by two thick minefields patrolled by submarines on either side, and the Luftwaffe providing cover overhead. Such was Sea Lion, a most fantastic and improbable sea monster indeed, and because neither of the squabbling services had any real faith in it, they ended by passing the baton to Reichsmarschall Hermann Goering.

The air supreme commander was delighted. Here was the opportunity at last to vindicate the Douhet theory of strategic bombing, to prove that a war could be won by aerial bombardment alone. Goering and his Luftwaffe would not only destroy the Royal Air Force but would bomb the stubborn British into submission.

Meanwhile, the British had turned their island into a bristling hedgehog ready to repel invasion from both sea and sky. Antiaircraft guns were in position, barrage balloons floated overhead, beaches were barricaded and fortified, buildings were sandbagged and lines of fortification were dug across beautiful golf courses and gardens. Men of the BEF who had lost their equipment at Dunkirk were rearmed—often with weapons of World War I vintage sent across the ocean by America—and a Civil Defense Service and a Home Defense Guard were organized. Everywhere firefighting squads, repair units and demolition platoons were organized, and as every person and penny in Britain were mobilized, with seemingly every able man and woman available on fire watch or air-raid alert, factories adopted round-the-clock schedules to turn out guns and airplanes. Thus that great British quality of rising to the occasion, of flourishing in adversity, had come to the fore again. Britain had not been successfully invaded since William the Conqueror came over in 1066, and in commemoration of the British determination to prevent any recurrence of that event, A. P. Herbert addressed a derisive verse to Hitler, which went:

Napoleon tried. The Dutch were on their way,
A Norman did it, and a Dane or two.
Some sailor-King may follow one fine day;
But not, I think, a low land-rat like you.

Finally, Churchill rose in Parliament to rally the island race with a stirring call to arms: "What General Weygand called the Battle of France is over. I expect that the Battle of Britain is about to begin. Upon this battle depends the survival of Christian civilisation. Upon it depends our own British life, and the long continuity of our institutions and our Empire. The whole fury and might of the enemy must very soon be turned on us. Hitler knows that he will have to break us in this island or lose the war. If we can stand up to him, all Europe may be free and the life of the world may move forward into broad, sunlit uplands. But if we fail, then the whole world, including the United States, including all that we have known and cared for, will sink into the abyss of a new Dark Age, made more sinister, and perhaps more protracted, by the lights of perverted science. Let us therefore brace ourselves to our duties, and so bear ourselves that, if the British Empire and its Commonwealth last for a thousand years, men will still say: 'This was their finest hour.' "

Churchill knew that Hitler was in a position to offer "the most tempting terms." He had learned of *Der Führer*'s astonishingly friendly remarks at Rundstedt's headquarters. He was aware that Hitler would be willing to let Britain and her empire alone. Such a peace would allow him freedom to seek his much-desired *Lebensraum* in the East. It could even be argued among those influential Britons willing to accept such terms that it was to everyone's benefit to allow the Nazis and the Communists to devour each other. Such a position, of course, ignored the consequences of what would happen if one or the other emerged the winner, gorged and grown more powerful on the spoils of victory. An object lesson of such a possibility was the present problem of the French fleet.

Churchill had been reflecting more and more on what to do about the French navy, the fourth largest in the world. Admiral Darlan had given him his word that the Germans would not get it. Churchill wondered about Darlan. Small like Reynaud at five feet two inches, the French naval chief was belligerent, as small men often are. He was also an extremely capable administrator who had worked hard to make the French navy powerful. Yet Darlan was an enigma. After he became the minister of marine in the Vichy government, he changed his mind about ordering his ships to sail to the safety of colonial harbors in North Africa. Why? Could it have been his ambition, for he was already well on his way to being Pétain's second in command? Or could he have had one of those legalist minds that make the pages of history such sorry reading? Did he find in the fact that he was minister of marine an obligation to obey the terms of the French surrender rather than the moral imperative to fight on against the Nazis? Perhaps Darlan had assimilated some of Pétain's defeatism and awe of the Nazis' naked power.

Whatever the reason, he did not give the order for the fleet to sail; and Churchill, mulling all this over, remembering that Darlan was an English hater whose great-grandfather had died under Nelson's guns at Trafalgar, while recognizing also that he was a German hater as well and much loath to see his ships sail beneath the swastika, at last decided that in June of 1940 standing at bay alone, Britain could not risk the seizure of such a powerful force by Hitler. With the sorrowful but not reluctant approval of his War Cabinet, Churchill moved to seize or immobilize the ships of his former ally himself.

Much of the French navy was in the British ports of Portsmouth and Plymouth: two battleships, four light cruisers, some submarines, seven destroyers and about two hundred smaller but valuable minesweeping and antisubmarine vessels. At Alexandria were a battleship, four cruisers and a number of smaller ships. This force was covered by a British battle squadron. At Oran at the other end of the Mediterranean were the *Dunkerque* and *Strasbourg,* battle cruisers much superior to *Gneisenau* and *Scharnhorst,* together with two battleships, several cruisers and a number of destroyers, submarines and other vessels. Seven cruisers were at Algiers, along with an aircraft carrier and two light cruisers. The great battleship *Jean Bart* was at Casablanca, unfinished, minus her guns and with no hope of being finished there. There were many other French ships in other ports, but these were the accessible ones that the British sought to seize or destroy.

In the early morning of July 3 the British took possession of all the warships at Plymouth and Portsmouth. Only three Britons and one Frenchman were killed. Many of the French sailors agreed to sail their ships with the British.

On the same day Vice Adm. Sir James Somerville sailed from Gibraltar at daylight with the battleships *Valiant* and *Resolution,* the battle cruiser *Hood,* the aircraft carrier *Ark Royal,* two cruisers and eleven destroyers. At 9:30 he was off Oran, where he sent Vice Adm. Marcel Gensoul in command there the following message:

(a) Sail with us and continue to fight for victory against the Germans and the Italians.

(b) Sail with reduced crews under our control to a British port. The reduced crews will be repatriated at the earliest moment.

If either of these courses is adopted by you, we will return your ships to France at the conclusion of the war, or pay full compensation if they are damaged meanwhile.

(c) Alternatively, if you feel bound to stipulate that your ships should not be used against the Germans or Italians . . . then sail with us with reduced crews to some French port in the West Indies—Martinique, for instance—where they can be demilitarized to our satisfaction, or perhaps entrusted to the United States and remain safe until the end of the war, the crews being repatriated.

If you refuse these fair offers, I must, with profound regret, require you to sink your ships within six hours.

Finally, failing the above, I have the orders of His Majesty's government to use whatever force may be necessary to prevent your ships from falling into German or Italian hands.

Admiral Gensoul replied that in no case would his ships be allowed to fall into German or Italian possession, and that he would meet force with force. Gensoul also forwarded the British ultimatum to the French Admiralty, where, it appears, Darlan deliberately omitted the West Indian proposal—by far the most acceptable—when he presented it to the Council of Ministers. At last Somerville, whose reluctance to strike at his former comrades had made both himself and his officers indecisive, opened fire at 5:45 P.M. A fierce, ten-minute bombardment ensued. The battleship *Brétagne* was blown up, *Dunkerque* ran aground, the battleship *Provence* was beached and *Strasbourg* escaped to gain sanctuary at Toulon.

At Alexandria the French commander agreed to empty his oil tanks, to disarm his guns and to repatriate some of his crews, while at Dakar on July 8 *Richelieu* was disabled by an aerial torpedo from one of *Ark Royal*'s airplanes. At Martinique the French ships there were immobilized and placed in the care of the United States.

This effective denial of French naval power to Hitler had been a grievous time for the men of both fleets. Duty and conscience dueled in the minds of everyone. Yet the French were not embittered. General de Gaulle was splendidly understanding. For Winston Churchill, the response of two afflicted French families in a village near Toulon was like a kiss of absolution. Both families had lost a sailor son at Oran. At a funeral for both attended by all the villagers the British Union Jack lay beside the French Tricolor.

A week after the bombardment at Oran—on July 10, 1940—Reichsmarschall Hermann Goering opened the aerial combat known as the Battle of Britain. For the first time in history a powerful air force was to attempt to bomb another nation into submission. But somehow the Reichsmarschall got his strategic warfare backward. The bomber is the instrument of strategic warfare. Yet Goering launched the Battle of Britain with fighter planes, believing that after his Messerschmitts had lured the RAF's Spitfires and Hurricanes into annihilating combat, the sky would belong to the bombers of the Luftwaffe. It did not occur to him that bombers escorted by fighters might first destroy the RAF on the ground as well as in the air. Further, Goering and his Luftwaffe generals did not seem to be aware of two decisive factors: the British secret weapon of radar, or radio location, by which they could learn of the German approach, their strength and location, and direct their fighters into the battle second by second; and the fact that the RAF had moved its fighter squadrons inland in a belt around London.

Moreover, the German squadrons based on the Channel had a tactical flying time of only eighty minutes. It took a half hour to cross into Britain and another to return, leaving the pilots only twenty minutes in which to accomplish their mission. They were also limited to an operational range of only 125 miles. That might be sufficient for defense but never enough for offense. Finally, slightly less than one tenth of all of Britain was within the selected attack sector. Thus the German fighter pilots were like a dog on a leash, able to attack only as far as the leash would permit.

Conversely, the RAF pilots had perhaps triple the tactical flying time available to their enemies, and were able to land within a few minutes for refueling or repair. This enabled them to fly more sorties. Also emergency landings made on airfields all over Britain saved many damaged aircraft. If British flyers were forced to bail out, they landed among friends and were soon returned to action. The Germans were taken prisoner. These advantages and handicaps, of course, were only a repetition in aerial combat of the odds that always favor the defense. What doubled these odds and greatly discouraged the German fighter pilots was radar.

Its success was truly astonishing. German fighter planes were detected even as they began to assemble over the Pas de Calais. Thereafter their every movement was faultlessly projected on the screens in British fighter-control centers all over the island. Fighter Command was almost always able to direct its flyers to the right position at the right time, whereas the Germans had to depend on their far inferior human eyesight to position themselves.

Still, Goering opened the battle with the utmost confidence. He had about 2,670 front-line aircraft against 1,475 for the RAF. His Messerschmitts were faster and had a faster rate of climb than the Spitfires and Hurricanes, but the British craft were more maneuverable and better armed. Thus in equipment it was a standoff. In flying skill the edge might have gone in the beginning to the Germans, through the experience gained in the Spanish Civil War and over Poland, Norway, the Low Countries and France. In numbers, of course, Germany had the advantage; but this was first canceled out by the tactical difficulties inherent in invasion and then reversed by radar. In spirit, however, the British were superbly superior. Napoleon said that in war the moral to the material is as three to one, and nowhere was this axiom more splendidly demonstrated than in the Battle of Britain.

These were the very youths of the generation which had passed the infamous Joad Resolution, and they took to the skies with a daring and tenacity that surprised the Germans. They had been disdained as effete, spineless hedonists. Nevertheless, assisted by Polish, French, Belgian, Czech and Canadian pilots, as well as some American volunteers, they fought with a bravery and skill that won the world's admiration and evoked Churchill's immortal accolade: "Never in the field of human conflict was so much owed by so many to so few."

John Beard was one of those few. One day in July Beard was in the leading flight of Hurricane fighter planes moving in four V formations of three planes each. They flew at 20,000 feet, the roar of their Merlin engines drowning all other sound, their wingtips dipping right-left, right-left. Beneath them London was invisible under a pall of smog. Sometimes the top of a barrage balloon glinted faintly below or the silver thread of the Thames came into view. Then Beard was flying over green fields and winding roads. Like his comrades, his head swiveled constantly, searching the sky for Germans, glancing into his rear-view mirror for the unwelcome sight of an enemy on his tail. Suddenly Beard heard the flight leader's voice in his earphones. *Germans!* Beard looked quickly toward his leader and saw the Heinkel bombers.

Orders came through the earphones. Twelve Hurricanes described a great circle to strike the enemy on their flank. *Right into the thick of them,* Beard thought. Then he nosed over with his comrades and dived on the unwary Germans. Almost at once, he got on the tail of a German. He took his hands from the throttle lever to get both hands on the stick. He steadied his Hurricane, like a soldier leveling his rifle. His thumb went to the gun button. Still the unsuspecting Heinkel flew on. *Why doesn't the fool move?* Beard thought. Instinctively he made the motions of the escape maneuver the German pilot should take. Then he pressed the gun button. Smoke curled from the eight machine guns in his wings. The Hurricane trembled in the recoil. The smell of cordite flowed into his cockpit, mingling with the stench of hot oil and the air compressors. Beard's burst lasted two seconds. He saw his bullets flash into the Heinkel. Roaring over him and turning away, Beard saw a red glow spreading inside his target. Flame licked out along its fuselage, and the Heinkel went spinning downward with pieces flying from it.

Beard pulled the stick back and climbed once more. Looking toward London, he saw a small formation of enemy bombers encircled by Messerschmitt fighters. He flew toward them, just as three flights of Spitfires stood on their tails beneath them, zooming up and outward with all guns chattering. To Beard's amazement, eight German bombers and fighters went plunging earthward in flames.

Beard turned away. He was over London again. Below was a labyrinth of winding streets and an area of green he knew to be Kensington Gardens. He caught a quick glimpse of the Round Pond where he had sailed boats as a child. But there was no time for nostalgia. A Dornier-17 bomber roared across his line of flight pursued by a Hurricane. But behind the Hurricane were two Messerschmitts. The Hurricane hadn't seen his pursuers and they hadn't seen Beard! Beard kicked the rudder and swung toward his prey. He reached for the gun button, adroitly placing his first burst just ahead of the nose of the first Messerschmitt, which flew right into it and fell apart. Turning toward the next German, Beard was astonished to see him execute a perfect half-Immelmann turn and speed away. But now there was no time to be lost in admiration: two Messerschmitts were on Beard's tail. He glanced quickly at his dashboard. He was almost out of fuel and had only a few bullets left. He dived and ran for home, just as the Germans did the same.

John Beard had had a good sortie.

Because many of Goering's flyers had given full rein to their disastrous habit of exaggerating their success, the Reichsmarschall believed that he had annihilated Britain's Fighter Command and he moved his attacks inland. Bombers struck at British airfields. Fighters were ordered to make low-level attacks. Once again the Luftwaffe suffered costly losses. The British airfields were well defended by both heavy and medium antiaircraft guns. Again radar alerted them to approaching enemy flights. Aerial cables were used to defend against the low-level attacks. The cables were fired by rockets, descending slowly to the lower levels by parachutes. Thus, many Messerschmitts were "clothes-lined." British aircraft parked on the fields were also cleverly camouflaged and widely dispersed, so that horizontal bombers often did little more damage than to convulse the airfield earth.

Such indifferent success fell far short of its objective. The Spitfires and Hurricanes were still snarling. Nevertheless, Goering next ordered daylight bombing of British industry and its vital shipping. The famous Junkers-87, or Stuka dive bomber, was the chief instrument of this attack, covered by Messerschmitts. But the Stukas proved too slow. The bombs slung under their bellies slowed their diving speed, which could reach only 150 miles per hour. The much speedier Messerschmitts were unable to follow them down and cover them. It was equally impossible to provide fighter cover at all the levels between dive and pull-out. Very quickly the RAF discovered that the diving Stukas were practically defenseless after they peeled out of formation to begin their lonely descent. Antiaircraft gunners easily tracked these slow targets looming steadily larger. Because the required altitude for a dive was between 10,000 and 15,000 feet, the Stukas attracted swarms of Spitfires and Hurricanes from both above and below. The Stuka, whether with one or two engines, was definitely the wrong bomber to attempt to vindicate Douhet's ideas. What was needed was a horizontal bomber with four engines, a long-range bomber such as would eventually appear in the HE-177 and such as was already wreaking havoc on British shipping, west of Ireland.

Finally, in his onslaught upon British industry and shipping, Goering seems not to have calculated the losses his Luftwaffe had to suffer by striking at the heart of British defenses. All the raids were against heavily defended and obvious targets. No attempt was made—indeed, none *could* have been made—to seek out soft spots or to change rhythm or direction, attacking now from here, now from there. And so, having failed to knock out Britain's Fighter Command or to cripple its industry and shipping, Goering shifted his sights to the British cities. He would destroy them, he would crush the people's will to fight, and he would raze London to the ground. This was the final step in the Douhet doctrine of strategic bombing, and Goering, having exceeded his original purpose of providing air cover for the invasion of Britain, was now attempting nothing less than bombing Britain into submission. On September 7 the dreadful "Blitz" of London began.

Sgt. Gottfried Leske was the Luftwaffe airman who had complained of the "treacherous" Dutch shooting "helpless" German paratroopers. His was one of the bombers that flew toward London on that memorable September 7. There were twenty in his flight. Above them roared their stubby ME fighter escorts. At 10,000 feet the air was soupy, but it improved as they approached the Channel. Leske and his comrades were in high spirits. The long-awaited all-out assault on the heart of the British Empire was beginning. *It is the beginning of the end,* Leske thought joyfully. *Today we will destroy the airfields, power plants, hangars and oil tanks of the enemy. Today we will smash Britain to pieces.*

Leske's bomber was heading for the airfield at Croydon. He grinned to see the forward planes' bombs falling from the opened bays. He was surprised that they did so little damage, merely making a few holes on the airfield; disappointed, too, when his own bombs were wasted. But then he had no time for reflection: The Hurricanes and Spitfires were diving on his formation in swarms. Then the MEs roared to the rescue and the dogfights began. Leske was relieved when his plane turned its nose for home.

But he was soon back again, this time over central London. The sky was clear, although dusk brought a light mist. Leske could still see the city, which seemed disorderly to him with its winding streets, but yet colorful. He delighted in the colors of the Thames estuary. He tried to fix the picture in his mind because he actually believed that he would never see London again. Here is Leske flying over London: "For a moment I thought it's really too bad that I've never been to London, and now never will be able to go there. Because today as I flew over the biggest city in the world, I knew with absolute certainty, as though I could foretell the future: This all will be destroyed. It will stand but for a few days more. Until the moment the Führer pronounces its death sentence. Then there will be nothing left but a heap of ruins."

For two whole months Leske saw London burning: burning in a thousand different places, burning up the Thames, burning up the docks, Westminster, the churches, the apartments, the homes, the theaters and libraries and museums. . . . Day after day Leske and his comrades flew over "dying London" to drop their bombs and with increasing frequency for many of them to go down in flames after them, and still the survivors stubbornly maintained their faith in myth, resolutely refusing to recognize reality. It was like "The Emperor's New Clothes." No one dared to say: "But London is still there."

And it was.

More than the soldiers guarding the beaches or the sailors on their ships or the pilots in their cockpits, the civilians in the cities bore the brunt of the Blitz. Richard Hillary, a fighter pilot, was in a London pub one night, on leave to recuperate from wounds suffered in action. His hands were bandaged. An air raid was in progress. Hillary cursed himself for a fool not to be down in a shelter. But when the cab driver who had brought him to the pub said, "We'd be better off underground tonight, sir, and no mistake," Hillary shrugged, and took a swig of his beer. "Nonsense! We couldn't be drinking this down there." A girl laughed.

. . . A huge detonation rocked the pub. Everyone dived for the floor. Hillary saw the fat barmaid sink out of sight before the floor rose up and struck him in the face. Then there was quiet. People picked themselves off the floor. An air-raid warden came in with a flashlight. "Anybody hurt?" Hillary replied, "I think there is somebody hurt behind the bar." But the barmaid had only received a cut on the head and was taken away on a stretcher.

Hillary and the cab driver went out to the street. The warden asked apologetically, "If you have nothing very urgent on hand, I wonder if you'd help here for a bit. You see, it was the house next to you that was hit, and there's someone buried in there." Hillary and the cabbie nodded. They strode to the collapsed building, a heap of splintered beams and bricks and mortar. They began to push and pull and heave the wreckage aside, Hillary having great difficulty because of his wounded hands. At last they saw the feet of a woman. They worked furiously. She became visible lying on a bed between two beams. She was still alive. But the baby she had clasped to her breast was not. The dead infant was passed back. An opening was made between the beams and the bed drawn out. It was a middle-aged woman who lay there in a shabby cotton nightgown drawn taut over her swollen belly. Her careworn face was blood-streaked and her eyes were squeezed shut. Hillary drew out his flask of brandy and held it to her lips. Most of the fluid flowed down her chin but some of it seeped through her clenched teeth. The woman opened her eyes and reached instinctively for her baby. Then she began to cry. Without sound or convulsion the tears ran down her cheeks. Then she looked at Hillary. "Thank you, sir," she said, taking his hand, and then: "I see they got you, too."

For two solid months the crowded capital on the Thames endured the agony of the Blitz. The Germans attacked by day and by night. As many as 320 bombers escorted by 600 fighters struck, or as few as a half dozen or even a lone wolf, gliding silently down to keep Londoners unnerved. Yet the British calmly dug themselves out of the ruins and doggedly went about the business of defending their island. They passed through a very great ordeal in which the fear of attack, the screaming of sirens, and the relentless rhythm of recurrent crisis were often more formidable than the hideous clang and crash of death and destruction which actually engulfed them. Yet they survived it. Their will to fight not only was not weakened, it was made stronger. In the end, Goering had to give up his gorgeous dream of victory by bombardment. By October 31 it had become a nightmare. No fewer than 1,733 aircraft had been lost by the Luftwaffe against 915 for the RAF. Operation Sea Lion was postponed until the spring of 1941, and then shelved altogether. Britain had won the Battle of Britain, the giant air battle for the skies above the island.* But beneath the surface of the surrounding seas it was losing the fight for its life.

*In the twelve months from June 1940 to June 1941, civilian casualties were 43,381 killed and 50,856 seriously injured for a total of 94,237.

22. Fall 1940: The U-Boat Peril, Italy Invades the Balkans

"THE ONLY THING THAT EVER really frightened me during the war," wrote Winston Churchill, "was the U-boat peril."

The fall of France had given Doenitz submarine bases from North Cape to the Bidassoa, and had thus doubled their cruising range. Moreover, Karl Doenitz, now an admiral, had earned the admiration of Hitler and had begun to get some —but not nearly all—of the big new U-boats he requested.

From his headquarters in Lorient on the Bay of Biscay, "Papa" Doenitz formed his undersea killers into wolf packs and sent them prowling into the North and South Atlantic in fanwise groups of eight to twenty. The moment any one submarine contacted a convoy, it radioed Doenitz and shadowed the enemy vessels while the admiral sent in all the other U-boats in the vicinity.

The wolves gathered at night. Rising silently to the surface, they slipped in among the ships of the convoy, fired their torpedoes, and then dived to escape the wrath of converging destroyers. Half an hour later, they might surface again to renew the attack, firing their deadly "fish" in the flickering light of burning victims. Their attacks continued throughout the night, and often during the following day from beneath the surface; and unless enemy counterattacks proved too effective, the wolf packs might hang on to a convoy for days on end.

To meet this renewal of the dreaded U-boat war, the Admiralty evolved new antisubmarine tactics and weapons. If the wolf packs launched night surface attacks, the escorting warships lighted the night with rockets, searchlights and star shells. Forced beneath the surface, the U-boats had to move more slowly and were exposed to blankets of depth charges. They could also be detected by new listening devices such as sonar, or asdic, as the British called it. Equipment housed in a steel bubble beneath a ship's hull listened for a U-boat's propellers or sent out echo-ranging "pings," which bounced off a U-boat's hull and returned. In defense, the Germans invented the *Pillenwerfer,* a device which shot out small gas bubbles that returned an echoing "ping" similar to those used in sonar. Thus they could confuse the sonar operators. Radar also was used in antisubmarine warfare, but only to detect surfaced submarines. "Huff-duff," a high-frequency direction finder, picked up U-boat messages to other submarines or to Doenitz, and through this information a bearing could be taken on the U-boats. Eventually, huff-duff would enable Allied aircraft to surprise surfaced submarines, sometimes catching the unfortunate crews sunning themselves on deck.

Most of these measures, of course, were the product of experience, coming only with the passage of time, and not soon enough to reduce the appalling losses that staggered Britain in the fall of 1940. Before France fell, Britain had been receiving about 1.2 million tons of cargo a week by sea. A month later, sinkings

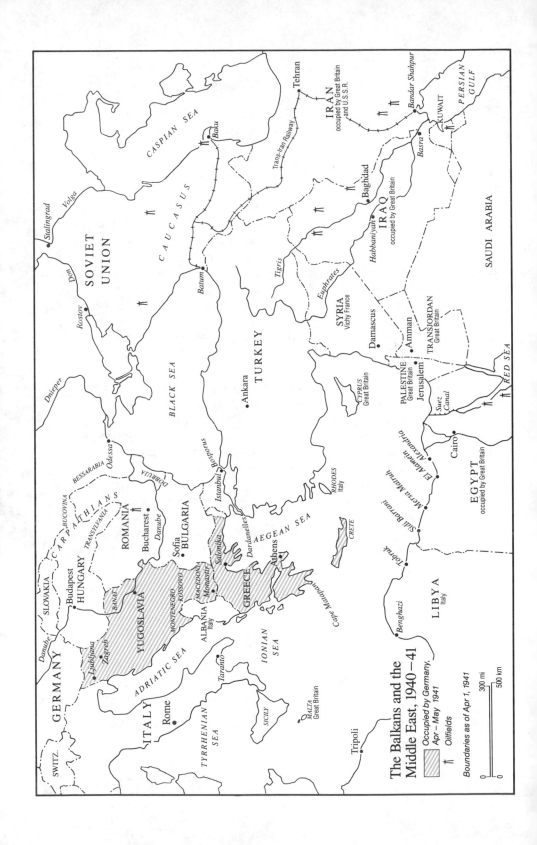

The Balkans and the
Middle East, 1940-41

☐ Occupied by Germany,
  Apr–May 1941
⚒ Oilfields

Boundaries as of Apr 1, 1941

SWITZ.

GERMANY

Rome
ITALY

Taranto

TYRRHENIAN
SEA

SICILY

MALTA
Great Britain

Tripoli

LIBYA
Italy

Benghazi

IONIAN
SEA

ADRIATIC SEA

SLOVAKIA

HUNGARY
Budapest

Danube

Ljubljana
Zagreb

BANAT

YUGOSLAVIA

MONTENEGRO
KOSSOVO

ALBANIA
Italy

MACEDONIA
Monastir

GREECE

Athens

AEGEAN SEA

CRETE

RHODES
Italy

Cape Matapan

CARPATHIANS
BUCOVINA

TRANSYLVANIA

ROMANIA
Bucharest

Danube

Sofia
BULGARIA

Salonika

Dardanelles

Istanbul Bosporus

BESSARABIA

DOBRUJA

Odessa

Dnieper

BLACK SEA

Ankara

TURKEY

CYPRUS
Great Britain

Tobruk

Sidi Barrani

Mersa Matruh

El Alamein
Alexandria

Cairo

EGYPT
occupied by Great Britain

Suez
Canal

RED SEA

PALESTINE
Great Britain
Jerusalem

TRANSJORDAN
Great Britain

Amman

SYRIA
Vichy France
Damascus

CAUCASUS

Batum

Baku

CASPIAN SEA

SOVIET
UNION

Stalingrad

Volga

Don

Rostov

Tehran

IRAN
occupied by Great Britain
and U.S.S.R.

Trans-Iran Railway

Baghdad

IRAQ
occupied by Great Britain

Habbaniyah

Tigris

Euphrates

SAUDI ARABIA

KUWAIT

Basra

Bandar Shahpur

PERSIAN
GULF

0   300 mi
0   500 km

brought this down to 750,000 tons. Within the ensuing two months losses soared far above the critical point reached during World War I. In October one wolf pack of only eight submarines caught an Atlantic convoy of thirty-four ships and sank twenty of them. By January of 1941 the arrival of ships in British ports was *less than half* of what it had been the previous year. During the first three months of 1941 no fewer than 142 ships were sunk, to say nothing of the number damaged.

Obviously, Britain was being strangled, and just as it began gasping for supplies, it found that it had no more money to buy them. Up until November 1940, Britain had paid for everything it received from America. In all, $4.5 billion had been disbursed and Britain had but $2 billion remaining, most of which was invested. Even if the country divested itself of all its gold and foreign assets, it could not hope to pay for more than one twentieth of the war material it needed. Britain, then, faced strategic bankruptcy. To avoid it, Churchill adopted the bold course of a frank appeal to his great friend across the sea. But first he must await the result of the American elections, which he did with great anxiety. Much as he respected Wendell Willkie, and appreciated Willkie's statement, "All of us— Republicans, Democrats and Independents—believe in giving aid to the heroic British people," he still preferred to deal with a man whom he had known since the days of World War I, when Roosevelt was assistant secretary of the Navy.

In the United States, the election brought out a record 50 million voters at the conclusion of a campaign distinguished by the invective poured upon Roosevelt's head by the isolationists. However, FDR won by 3 million votes, news that Churchill received with "indescribable relief." A month later the prime minister sent the President a 4,000-word letter outlining Britain's plight, its shipping losses, its faltering production and the exhaustion of its dollar supply. He asked, in effect, for two things: material and the safe delivery of that material. This was nothing less than to request that American industry and the American navy be placed at Britain's disposal, and Churchill, leaving to Roosevelt the details of how such an unprecedented course might be adopted, ended by saying: "If, as I believe, you are convinced, Mr. President, that the defeat of the Nazi and Fascist tyranny is a matter of high consequence to the people of the United States and to the Western Hemisphere, you will regard this letter not as an appeal for aid, but as a statement of the minimum action necessary to achieve our common purpose."

Churchill later said this was one of the most important letters he ever wrote, and he was right. Roosevelt was so impressed that he pondered the letter for a week, gradually evolving the revolutionary concept that came to be known as Lend-Lease. He explained to the country, "Now, what I am trying to do is eliminate the dollar sign," and he gave the famous illustration: "Suppose my neighbor's house catches fire and I have a length of garden hose four or five hundred feet away. If he can take my garden hose and connect it up with his hydrant, I may help him put out the fire. Now . . . I don't say to him before that operation, 'Neighbor, my hose cost me fifteen dollars; you have to pay me fifteen dollars for it.' No! . . . I don't want fifteen dollars—I want my garden hose back after the fire is over."

It was a homey and touching analogy, even if it did overlook the fact that the material to be lent or leased to the Allies would not, like the garden hose, be returned intact after the crisis had passed but was very likely to be destroyed in surmounting it. But the "garden hose" very neatly squelched the isolationists, even drowning the famous charge that Lend-Lease would "plow under every fourth American boy." Thus FDR received from Congress the power to lend or lease any war material to any government "whose defense the President deems vital to the defense of the United States." Ultimately, Lend-Lease would include the Soviet Union, China and the rest of the Allies, it would take 14 cents out of every dollar the United States spent to fight the war, and it would rise to a total outlay of $50 billion. Only about $8 billion came back in "reverse Lend-Lease," that is, food, equipment and services supplied by the Allies to American troops overseas. Of this, Britain contributed $2 billion and the Soviets nothing. The Communists claimed that they had made payment in blood, implying, therefore, that they alone had bled and suggesting that they be subsidized in defending themselves.

Still, what Churchill called "the most unsordid act in the history of any nation" probably did as much as any other factor to save Britain and doom the Axis. After it was passed, FDR turned to the second part of Churchill's appeal, safe delivery of the material, and in so doing he justified many of the isolationists' charges against him and held a wake for neutrality.

By then neutrality was hardly more than a convention. Axis consulates in America were closed down and Axis assets frozen. Now FDR began his Undeclared War against the U-boats. In April of 1941 he made an enormous expansion of the North Atlantic "security zone," advancing it roughly halfway across the ocean. West of this line, the U.S. Navy would defend American ships. They would also notify the British of any submarines they had located.

Inasmuch as Germany in 1941 could no more afford the free passage of arms across the Atlantic than it could in 1914, the Nazi government angrily protested. No matter, soon German and American warships were shooting at one another in the "war short of war." Next, in July American Marines took over occupation of Iceland from the British. Then, in August, FDR led his nation still closer to the Allied cause when, meeting secretly at sea with Winston Churchill, he proclaimed the Atlantic Charter and the Four Freedoms: freedom of speech, freedom of religion, freedom from want, freedom from fear. Here, in the charter, was the cornerstone of the United Nations, an attempt to ensure peace based upon pledges of no territorial aggrandizement, respect for national self-determination, equal access to world resources, economic collaboration and abandonment of the use of force in international life. Here also was another source of aggravation to isolationists, who demanded to know how much FDR had promised to Churchill. In fact, he made no binding commitments; but in September, angered by losses of American ships, he ordered the Navy to shoot Axis vessels on sight. Shortly afterward he asked Congress for armed merchantmen to trade with belligerents. Although the isolationists fought the proposal bitterly, the sinking of the destroyer *Reuben James* by a German submarine clinched the battle against them. In November 1941, the last of the neutrality restrictions was voted away.

The situation had now gone far beyond the delicate relationship existing between America and Germany in 1917. Now, with very little attempt at concealment, America was giving military assistance to Britain, and was preparing to arm the ships that were bringing Britain the lifeblood of war. If the United States was only de facto a British ally, it might have been de jure a German enemy, for it would seem that any nation using arms to help one side ought to expect the use of arms against it by the other. Yet Hitler held his hand. He had no desire to provoke the American eagle before he could dispose of the Russian bear.

Der Führer's war for *Lebensraum* had lost its masterly, timetable quality and had begun to become hit-and-miss and reactive. Hitler no longer controlled events but was improvising. First, his failure to invade Britain or to conquer it from the air made him lose sight of the fact that Britain was still his chief enemy. He might yet strangle it at sea or wreck the British Empire by evicting it from North Africa, the Middle East and East Africa. To do so probably would force Spain and Turkey into the war on the Axis side, deny Britain both the Suez and its last overseas base within striking distance of Europe, create the possibility of Asian hookup with the new Axis partner in Japan, and open up the easy southern route for the eventual invasion of Russia. Britain was very weak in these outposts, while Italian control of the Mediterranean would make possible an Italo-German concentration there. But Hitler failed to appreciate these promising possibilities. Instead, he turned away from Britain and prepared to attack the Soviet Union. It was a mistake of the first magnitude, and the pages of history show few more grave. Here was Britain still defiant and the United States manifestly preparing to come to its side, yet instead of maintaining the pressure on Britain, he chose to ease up and take on an entirely new enemy. He was like a man in a street fight turning from a battered but still strong opponent to take on a spectator just as strong.

Hitler had his reasons, of course, and they must have seemed compelling. To prepare for the prolonged struggle with Britain, he needed the resources of European Russia and he had to make sure of his eastern flank once and for all. Stalin had already made it plain that he would not give Hitler a free hand in the West without guarantees of Soviet bases in the Balkans. This Hitler would not agree to. Instead, he would destroy the U.S.S.R., after which the Wehrmacht would be reorganized with emphasis on the naval and air power required to subjugate Britain. Thus Hitler was running the risk of the two-front war he had sworn to avoid. He was very like "those fools of 1914," and no more than they could he escape the dilemma of German geography: landlocked, sandwiched between Frank and Slav. Better to have wooed the French than to make war on them. And so, if Hitler's great mistake was to attack the Soviets, a greater one was in going to war at all.

Before he moved against the Soviet Union, however, Hitler found it necessary to secure his own southern flank by seizing the Balkans.

The Balkans not only were strategically important in southeastern Europe, these always-quarreling states were also important sources of oil, minerals, grain, dairy products and meat. Through Turkey they provided a landward bridge to the Middle East as well. On the west were Yugoslavia and Greece and between them Italian-held Albania. On the east were Turkey, Bulgaria, Romania and Hungary.

Greece and Yugoslavia were both pro-Allies, both resenting Mussolini's seizure of their common neighbor, Albania, in 1939. Hungary was too close to Germany to make any profession of sympathy. Romania wanted only to be left alone, suspicious of its great neighbor, the U.S.S.R., which had already taken Bessarabia from her; distrustful of Hungary, which wanted Transylvania, wary of Bulgaria, from whom it had taken territory in the Second Balkan War in 1913. Turkey, though sympathetic to the Allies, had adopted a stance of strict neutrality.

Il Duce and *Der Führer* began a diplomatic offensive in the Balkans, backed, as was customary, by the threat of force. On August 30, 1940, under the so-called Vienna Awards, King Carol II of Romania was compelled to cede 3,000 square miles of southern Dobruja to Bulgaria, and 16,000 square miles of northern Transylvania to Hungary. Carol told his infuriated countrymen he had yielded to the Axis in order to forestall further land grabs by the Soviets. In response, the Romanians forced him to abdicate. He was succeeded by his son, Michael, who was promptly forced to entrust what was left of his country to a Fascist dictatorship under General Ion Antonescu. In October by special so-called invitation German and Italian troops entered Romania and enrolled that unhappy country in the Axis order. Hungary was next. Pressure, meanwhile, was being brought to bear on Bulgaria and Yugoslavia.

Only Greece resisted the Axis diplomatic blitz.

One reason Mussolini had joined Hitler in blitzing the Balkans was that he had found his partner's string of victories unbearable. When he learned of Hitler's plan to invade the Low Countries, he had ordered Count Ciano to warn Holland and Belgium. Hitler ostensibly blamed the betrayal on King Victor Emmanuel, whom he detested, but thereafter he kept his plans to himself. Still *Il Duce* complained to Ciano: "Hitler always faces me with a fait accompli. This time I'm going to pay him back in his own coin. He will find out from the papers that I have occupied Greece." On October 15, Mussolini called a war council in Rome. His lickspittle generals assured him of an easy conquest, boasting that their men were spoiling for a fight. *Il Duce* was delighted. A quick victory was exactly what he wanted to mollify his German colleague and to impress the world. What he had been told—and what he might have suspected—was empty, strutting braggadocio. In equipment and spirit the Italian Army was simply not ready for war, and never would be. Still Mussolini pressed upon Greece his deliberately arrogant demand that it should renounce the guarantee of its independence given by Britain in 1939. King George II and Prime Minister—rather, dictator—Joannes Metaxas indignantly refused. So *Il Duce* castigated Greece as an "unneutral" country secretly in alliance with Britain and began massing troops on the Albanian frontier. On October 28, 1940, the vanguard of 200,000 Italians poured across the border into Greece. That morning, a beaming Duce greeted the visiting Führer at the railroad station in Florence with the gleeful cry: "Führer, we are on the march!"

Hitler was disturbed, and then infuriated after he discovered that the Italian march was to the rear. Mussolini had calculated that the Greeks with only a few hundred antiquated airplanes, no mechanized equipment and few heavy weapons would never stand up to the legionaries of the New Rome. Moreover, the Metaxas Line of defense faced Bulgaria, not Albania. For several days Italian troops singing "Giovinezza," the Fascist hymn, sped down the narrow valleys of northern Greece. However, their hymns of victory soon turned to dirges. The Greek evzones, elite infantrymen, chosen for their familiarity with the mountains, took to the hills. Under Metaxas's direction, they waited until the Italians were extended from their supply bases and caught in the valleys. Then the evzones lobbed their mortar and artillery shells down upon the massed enemy. Day after day the Italians were forced backward, hampered by poor roads and heavy rains. Soon their retreat became a wild rout. The Greeks pursued them into Albania. Sixteen Greek divisions chased twenty-seven Italian divisions thirty miles inside Albania and penned them up in the mountains.

Mussolini's chagrin intensified after the British carrier *Illustrious* made a daring aerial strike on the Italian fleet in the harbor at Taranto, putting it out of action for six months. But far worse was yet to come across the Mediterranean in the Libyan desert, where the tank—the youngest and most hideous son of Mars —had dethroned the infantry as the Queen of Battle.

23. September 1940–January 1941: The Desert War

THE TANK HAD COME into being in World War I after Winston Churchill suggested developing a "land battleship." A secret study commission was formed, called the Water Commission to conceal its true purpose. But some of the stuffier members objected to being teased about sitting on the "W.C.," as the British call the toilet, and so the name was changed to the Water Tank Commission. Eventually it was shortened to "tank," and it was in this earthy way that this dreadnought of the earth got its name.

The tank had been invented to break the stalemate of trench warfare. It was a mobile armored gun, which could advance against machine-gun fire and crush the great networks of barbed wire strung through no-man's-land. The first tanks were slow because the emphasis was on armor, and long because they had to get over trenches. Such large slow targets soon became extremely vulnerable to artillery. Furthermore, no one in high command understood the capacity that this new weapon—if shortened and made much faster—would have for really deep penetration. So the tank ended World War I regarded as an infantry support weapon, just like the airplane. It was left to junior officers such as Fuller and Liddell Hart to develop the theories that so impressed Heinz Guderian.

Between the wars the British and French governments were loath to spend the money that these expensive new weapons required, and also reluctant because no one seemed to know how they should be used. Their professional armies had resumed a peacetime life-style centering on the cavalry. It seemed only natural that when faster but very light tanks were manufactured, they should go to the cavalry. However, mounted troops had done very little in the last war. Cavalry commanders began to fear that unless they adapted to armor, their dashing units with their truly great traditions would be disbanded. But the infantry which had done all the fighting was envious of the money going to the cavalry for this new arm. Opinion inevitably polarized: Tank extremists wanted armies of nothing else, infantry apologists wanted only heavy tanks able to move no faster than a foot soldier.

Vested interests also entered the dispute. Foot commanders with their swagger sticks and gleaming leather did not relish taking orders from tank commanders in oily overalls. They preferred to have the tanks subordinated to all other arms, acting only in a support role and never, ever to get beyond the range of their own artillery. It was this belief shared by the French high command that had caused France to collapse so quickly beneath the blitzkrieg.

The high cost of armor was a constant consideration. Liddell Hart's theories of "the expanding torrent," in which speedy tanks penetrate deep under the cover of wide-ranging aircraft, were simply too expensive to put into practice. Moreover, they were not needed to police the colonies, the almost exclusive mission of the Anglo-French professional armies between the wars. Only Hitler could afford them and want them. What France and Britain needed in their overseas possession was a speedy little lightweight tank mounting a single machine gun. It could chase horsemen, climb hills and deflect the low-velocity bullets of Indian and Arab rebels. That was what was required and that was what was manufactured.

Nevertheless, as Hitler came to power and began to rearm, the unthinkable prospect of another European war became thinkable again. Not only Germany but other armament-making countries began to produce fast as well as heavy tanks mounting artillery fired from a swiveling turret. But their use was still not clear-cut, at least among the professionals of the democracies, still not attuned to the Liddell Hart–Fuller theories. Only Guderian had listened to these prophets. But even his great success with armor never envisioned the unique warfare that would take place in the desert. Everyone still had a different answer to the question: How do you fight tanks? General Weygand in demanding Britain's fighter squadrons had insisted that airplanes should fight tanks. Churchill had countered that artillery, not air, fights tanks. But the truth is that every weapon can fight tanks, and in the desert's alternating hells of heat and cold tanks most of all fought tanks.

Desert warfare was born in World War II because the Western Desert was the western flank of Britain's enormous Middle East Command. Only Britain's own homeland took precedence over the Middle East in importance. The oilfields of the Persian Gulf nations contained those supplies that nourished not only British war-making capacity but its population and industry as well. Although it is commonly believed that the Desert War of 1940–43 was fought to keep open the British lifeline through the Mediterranean and the Suez Canal, the fact is that the Suez had at the time little world traffic. The war was fought with a lifeline in mind but primarily for lifeblood: oil.

Commanding this vast theater in 1940 was Gen. Sir Archibald Wavell, believed by many experts to have been Britain's finest soldier in the entire war. Archibald Percival Wavell was born to command, the son and grandson of generals. Born at Colchester on May 5, 1883, he entered Sandhurst in 1900 and was graduated at the top of his class a year later. Three days after his eighteenth birthday, Wavell was commissioned a subaltern in his father's old regiment, the famous Black Watch. He served with distinction in South Africa, saw action in India, and in 1908 entered the Staff College. He was then six months short of his twenty-sixth birthday and ten years younger than the average age of his associates. When he was graduated, he was only one of two officers to receive an A.

During World War I he was a staff officer, first as a liaison officer with Grand Duke Nicholas in Russia, and then as the Imperial General Staff's liaison officer with Field Marshal Sir Edmund Allenby in the Middle East. Allenby had the reputation of being something of a bully, but Wavell stood up to him. Suave and scholarly, a model of tact and poise, Wavell was nevertheless tenacious and not one to be dissuaded by a loud voice. After service in Silesia and occupied Germany, he was one of the few officers who took an interest in armored warfare, then very much in its infancy.

In June of 1939 Wavell came to Egypt to organize the newly created Middle East Command. It was a vast theater comprising nine countries and parts of two continents, covering an area 1,700 miles by 2,000. To defend it, Wavell had only a ragtag army of less than 40,000 men. He had sixty-four field guns and his one armored division was far below strength. Wavell had not only been directed to prepare war plans for the entire theater, but was also enjoined to consult with the

British naval and air commanders-in-chief and provide liaison with the French in Syria and North Africa. Consultations were also necessary with British ambassadors in Egypt and Iraq, the governor-general in the Sudan, the high commissioner for Palestine and Transjordan, the governors of Cyprus, Aden and British Somaliland, and the political agent in the Persian Gulf. To do this he had been assigned five officers.

It is doubtful that any other British commander of that day possessed Wavell's strategic grasp, his administrative ability, or the wit, the nerve and the leadership to do so much with so little. On his own he quickly made a survey of all Egyptian facilities such as ports and airfields in order to make Egypt a base for 300,000 men. When he was ordered in December 1939 to build such a base, his survey was complete and he had anticipated the command by six months. Next he ordered Gen. Howard ("Jumbo") Wilson to prepare a plan for the invasion of Italian Libya, with particular reference to the problems of supply in the desert. Wilson prepared a forward base at Mersa Matrûh, a little white village standing on the edge of the sea and at the end of the railroad and paved highway from Alexandria. In May and June, with Germany obviously overwhelming France, it became apparent to Wavell that Mussolini would probably like to add Britain's African colonies to his resuscitated Roman Empire. Looking eastward toward Ethiopia were 200,000 Italians under a viceroy, the Duke of Aosta. To defend there, Wavell pieced out his handful of troops along the rambling borders of Somaliland, Kenya and the Sudan. To the west stood *Il Duce*'s old Fascist comrade, Marshal Italo Balbo, with 300,000 men. To defend there, Wavell put most of his troops into the Western Desert Force and sent for Major General Richard O'Connor to command them.

Richard O'Connor was the best of choices. Bold and unorthodox in action, he was in his manner shy and unassuming. In appearance, he was small and neat as a bird, with large, slightly hooded, thoughtful eyes and a noble forehead. Some of his officers called him the Little Terrier because of his tenacity. After Mussolini declared war on France, O'Connor realized that his small, ill-equipped army now faced an enemy ten times as large. But in his quiet confidence he also realized that his opponent knew no more than he did about fighting in the desert.

The desert is like the sea. With one exception, there are no roads. But none are needed since virtually all the battleground provides smooth going for both wheeled and tracked vehicles. Neither are there towns and villages, except for a few inhabited places along the coast, and thus there are neither obstacles nor shelter nor people. Desert warfare is war in its purest form. Its only limitation is supply. Like a fleet on the barren sea, the armies of the equally arid desert cannot live off the land. All supplies—especially food, water and fuel—have to be imported.

The battleground on which this unique warfare was to be fought was a vast arena stretching 400 miles along the Mediterranean coast from El Alamein in Egypt to Derna (Darnah) in Libya. Its inland limits lay 150 miles south at the oases of Jarabub (Wahat Jaghbub) and Siwa. Behind them was the barrier of the Great Sand Sea, a scorching wasteland beneath a blazing sun. There was but one natural feature: an escarpment 500 feet high leading down to the sea from the plateau on which the battles were fought. It could not be traversed by wheeled vehicles and in most places not by tanks either. Thus, its three passes—Fûka, Halfaya and Sidi-Rezegh—were of the utmost importance.

Without natural features to guide on, navigation was as difficult as at sea; perhaps more so, because a mere map and compass was no substitute for a sextant. It was also extremely difficult to judge how far away the horizon was. A newcomer soon learned to keep a watchful eye on his fuel gauge and his odometer. At night it was even more difficult. In the absence of natural features, drivers were guided by artificial signposts: an empty can of rations, an abandoned fuel can, a helmet. But these could vanish almost as quickly as they appeared.

Often the bright blue sky appeared to be crisscrossed by plumes of sand rising behind tanks and trucks. Drivers approaching each other sought desperately to keep to windward to avoid the other vehicle's dust. Tanks cut deep ruts into the sand and sent up bigger plumes. Because there were so many vehicles careening across the battlefield, it sometimes seemed that half the surface of the desert was floating in the air. Sand penetrated a vehicle's every chink: it got into the carburetor or lay on the windshield. Truck drivers kept their windshield-wipers going to be able to see. Sandstorms whirling across the desert like yellowish opaque fogs could reduce visibility to a yard or two.

Every face was caked with sand clinging to the sweat oozing from every pore beneath that merciless sun. Sand clotted the corners of the eyes and many drivers wore sand goggles. Sand also penetrated the clothes to coat the hairy parts of the body. It made a matted paste of the hair on a man's head. Sweat pouring down the body make little rivulets in this coating. Because water on the desert was scarcer than gasoline, men simply had to accustom themselves to being dirty. A bath was a gift from the gods. On a gallon of water per man per day for all purposes, soldiers usually used most of it to quench their thirst or to make tea, reserving about a canteen cupful with which to shave, clean their teeth or wash their feet. What remained was strained and poured into the truck radiator. Many soldiers washed only a third of their bodies a day. Like soldiers aboard troop transports compelled to take salt-water showers, smearing their bodies with that wretched sticky "salt-water soap" that could never be washed off, a thunderstorm on the desert fell on these dirty troopers like a blessing. Thundering black clouds rolling off the escarpment sent tidal waves of sound washing across the sands and lifted the hearts of the soldiers of both sides. Shouting gleefully, they shucked their clothes and went capering about naked in the blissful cleansing rain. An hour later they were dirty again.

As it has been in every conflict since Agamemnon set sail for Troy, small defects made big differences. To the British, their four-gallon gasoline can was an abomination. At best, it was not a sieve; at worst, it leaked 30 percent of its contents between base and consumer. Since the truck convoys bringing gasoline reserves to the front needed 180,000 gallons a day themselves, the resulting loss was incalculable. To estimate how much was lost in men, tanks, trucks and supplies because of a gasoline shortage would be impossible, not to mention the number of ships and sailors lost bringing up more fuel to compensate for the vast gallonage that sank uselessly into the sands. British soldiers whose tanks were full loathed those leaking cans. They would be empty before the fuel tank was, intensifying the reek of gasoline in the process. "Heave the bastard!" they cried, flinging it over the side, and eagerly searching battlefield sites for one of those immensely superior German "Jerrycans."

British antitank guns were also markedly inferior to the German. The famous—and dreaded—88mm antiaircraft gun which had been adapted to desert warfare as an antitank gun could knock out a British tank at 3,000 yards. Conversely, the pitiful British 2-pounders* were effective at only 1,200 yards (if that), meaning that British tanks would be receiving hits from the Germans for 1,800 yards before they were within killing range themselves. The Dervishes Winston Churchill had fought in the Sudan hardly suffered from a greater inferiority in weapons.

For the British, however, there was always tea. "Brew up!" Nothing in the desert was so gladly welcomed as a steaming mug of strong black tea. Headquarters often despaired of the countless tons of gasoline consumed in bringing kettles to the boil. There were half-hearted attempts to put a stop to it, especially after armored formations lay immobile with empty fuel tanks while Tommies everywhere were brewing up on their sand-and-gasoline "stoves." These, actually nothing more than an empty ration can filled with sand into which gasoline was poured and ignited, were their most precious possession. But no one seriously wanted to put a stop to tea. One might as well put a stop to being British.

"Brew up!" also had a second, horrible connotation. It meant that an enemy tank had been set afire. Gunners peering eagerly through the telescopic sights that gave them a round view of the desert were rewarded when they saw their shells go flashing into the enemy's hide and the faintest beginning of that deadly red glow which would soon become a blaze. "Brew up!" they cried in exultation, like the fighter pilot crying, "Flamer!" when the enemy went spiraling toward earth in flames. Death in desert warfare could be a hideous, screaming, fiery end. Stricken tanks were quite literally crematories. Very few remains were found within their charred and burnt-out hulks.

So the tanks rolled back and forth across this barren land in which only Bedouins could survive, each side following almost identical routines. They rose at any time between midnight and four in the morning, some of them crawling stiffly off the truck and tank hoods on which they had slept, like Russian peasants on their stoves, cuddling against the engines for warmth during the cold of the desert night. Entering their vehicles, they moved into battle positions before first

---

*British land artillery is measured in pounds, that is, the weight of the projectile. Two pounds is the equivalent of 37 millimeters.

light, sustained by only a hard biscuit smeared with marmalade. It was in the predawn hour, like the last light of day, that the dimly lighted desert threw up its mirages, its queer distortions of shapes. Bushes looked like tanks, tanks looked like rows of trees and a herd of grazing camels could appear to be concentrations of enemy armor. Inside the tanks each driver sat with hands on the steering sticks and one foot poised over the gas pedal, his eyes glued to the narrow slit in front of him opening on the desert. The radio operator fiddled with his apparatus or cleaned the armor-piercing shells for the cannon, while the gunner squinted through his round O, testing his gun's traverse and checking the ammunition belts. Above them was the tank commander, standing upright in the turret or sitting there with dangling legs. Like a fighter pilot, his head swiveled constantly, searching the vast sand sea for movement or a shape against the horizon, constantly changing position to study his rear as well as his front. On the commander's chest was the microphone with which he kept in touch with his crew or his headquarters. Slowly the light of the rising sun stole across the desert floor. Soon the cooled sands were hot again. Shimmering heat waves could be seen. The sweat was coming again . . . orders . . . movement . . . blazing battle . . . death or the fear of death . . . tea taken with heads still swiveling and eyes still glued to the horizon . . . returning darkness. Once again they wrapped themselves in blankets or crawled back onto the hoods, gazing up at the gorgeous, glittering African night sky, at its brilliant moon, listening to the tiny sounds of vipers and scorpions scurrying among the rocks until, at last, they fell into restless sleep.

Gen. Richard O'Connor believed that his unfamiliarity with desert terrain could only be overcome by intensive night-and-day training. Armored maneuver was the key. His troops could not practice such tactics as night-leaguering enough. "Leaguer" is a derivative of *laager,* the camp encircled by wagons which the Dutch Boers used to repel the attacks of African tribes. It is itself a derivative of the circle of wagons used by the Teutonic tribes against the Romans or by settlers of the American West against Indians. At Mersa Matrûh, the circle was squared, the tanks assembling at night in a compact square with the thinner-skinned vehicles on the inside. From this they could move out swiftly into offensive formations. Under O'Connor, the men of the Western Desert Force could do it at night blindfolded.

O'Connor's method of studying ground was similar to Wellington's: a personal reconnaissance deep into enemy territory. Once he irritated one of his brigadiers by approaching one of his armored patrols from the west, i.e., the enemy's direction. "I did NOT like this," the brigadier wrote in his diary.

O'Connor soon realized that supply was the desert's biggest problem and that the truck—especially the three-tonner—was the solution. Like Nelson complaining that the phrase "lack of frigates" was written on his heart, O'Connor almost daily beseeched Wavell in Cairo for a flood of trucks. He also discovered how severely the desert punished motorized vehicles, especially tanks. In July 1940, he decided to withdraw his tanks to conserve them for a major battle. That appeared to be certain after France surrendered and the Italian forces watching Tunisia now about-faced to join the Tenth Army facing Egypt. Marshal Rodolfo Graziani commanded this force, Italo Balbo having come to an inglorious end when his own antiaircraft gunners shot him down. Graziani had done well against Ethiopia in 1936 fighting Haile Selassie's spear-wielding troops. But in 1940 he did not seem too eager to move against the British, who had already in early skirmishing established a moral superiority over his men. Graziani believed in building a firm base, including such amenities as a motorized brothel. *Il Duce* thundered at him throughout August. But still Graziani firmed his base. He told Mussolini his offensive should follow the German invasion of Britain, when the British in Egypt would be demoralized. After Operation Sea Lion was locked in a dry cage, he still dallied. On September 7 *Il Duce* ordered him to attack within two days or else, and six days later Graziani's grand offensive shrugged forward.

About 100,000 men attacked behind a heavy artillery barrage, which fell on empty British frontier posts. Moving slowly in a close-packed mass against no opposition, but stung constantly on the flanks by British units that vanished as suddenly as they appeared, Graziani's army advanced at the rate of twelve miles a day. Sixty miles into Egypt and still eighty miles from O'Connor at Mersa Matruh (Marsa Matrûh), Graziani halted at Sidi Barrâni. He erected a monument commemorating this glorious feat of arms and began firming his base again. Sometimes, however, the reluctant warrior's instinct for self-preservation can save him.

Graziani was right in marking time: O'Connor was waiting for him prepared to strike him suddenly and with all his armor. Now Wavell in Cairo took over. He knew that the Duke of Aosta's army in Ethiopia was the weaker of the two forces to either side of him. Powerful though it was, it was totally cut off from Italy and was wasting away. But before he could concentrate his inferior forces against Aosta, he had to deal with Graziani. If Graziani defeated O'Connor, *Il Duce* would own Egypt. So Wavell sent Brigadier Eric Dorman-Smith to O'Connor's command to see if an offensive against Graziani were feasible. Dorman-Smith reported back on October 22 that it was, whereupon Wavell drew from a desk drawer a directive ordering O'Connor to attack.

Because of Graziani's time-wasting approach, O'Connor was now much stronger and better prepared. His armored division was at full strength and equipped with heavy new "I" tanks, and he also had a full-strength Indian and Australian division and a brigade from New Zealand. But he was still heavily outnumbered by the Italian air force. Moreover, the daring plan he had conceived was strongly opposed by some of his commanders, and also by Dorman-Smith. Graziani's forces were concentrated in armed camps around Sidi Barrâni, "boxes" all out of supporting distance with each other. O'Connor believed he could exploit the gap between two large camps at Nibeiwa and Sofafi. His artillery would bombard Nibeiwa from the east with the objective of causing panic and confusion in the camp. Simultaneously the I tanks would attack Nibeiwa from the west, the Italian rear. Infantry following in trucks would drive to the northwest corner of the camp—where a concentration of vehicle tracks had led O'Connor to believe the area was not mined—and make an assault on foot. In other words, the starting point for the attack would be *inside* the Italian's lines, in their *rear.* O'Connor had ingeniously concluded that his forces inside the enemy's defenses would be safer from air attack. All depended, of course, upon the fact that the gap between the two big camps remained open and unpatrolled—penetrable. Much also depended upon making an approach march of sixty miles which would not so weaken O'Connor's troops that they could not fight a battle at its end. In those days, there was no life-sustaining equipment for armor such as tank-transporters or tank-towing vehicles. A tank moved on its own power. If it were halted or hit, it could not be immediately recovered for repair. To avoid the attrition of such a march, O'Connor established forward magazines of food, fuel, water and ammunition. Here was boldness backed by hard-headed logistics skill.

Daylight of December 9 dawned at Sidi Barrâni. There was a haze over the desert. Military routine was beginning in the Italian armed camps. Suddenly, from the direction of the sun came the thunder of artillery and a shower of shells began falling on Nibeiwa. In the ensuing furor when soldiers ran for their slit trenches or frantically pulled on their uniforms inside their tents, no one realized that the British armor and motorized infantry had slipped through the gap south of them, wheeled north toward the sea and was swinging west to attack that unmined northwest corner of their camp. Only when they heard the growling roar of the heavy I tanks were they aware of their peril. It was too late. The I tanks came upon twenty Italian mediums warming up outside the camp and shot them into blazing wrecks. They broke into the camp to fire on the men in the trenches and those swarming out of the tents. By half-past eight in the morning, it was all over at Nibeiwa, and by then O'Connor's fast-moving forces were attacking everywhere.

O'Connor now sent his troops moving against the two Tummar camps above Nibeiwa and closer to Sidi Barrâni. They moved out in a sandstorm. It blew into their eyes and clogged their gun mechanisms. But the Little Terrier urged them on, ranging over the battlefield in his staff car, calling for "offensive action" at every headquarters he visited. Tummar West fell just before sundown, and Tummar East capitulated early the next morning. Sidi Barrâni was next, taken in a dawn attack launched in a sandstorm on the 11th. That night, the Battle of Sidi Barrâni was over. O'Connor's British, Australian, New Zealand and Indian troops were the first to gaze upon the litter of a desert battlefield. All around them was the debris of defeat: food dumps, abandoned tanks and trucks as well as burnt-out ones, weapons of every caliber, piles of ammunition and blowing in the wind the paperwork of a beaten, fleeing army.

Sir Richard O'Connor's spoiling attack by which Wavell hoped to knock Graziani off balance had been turned into a major victory. In three days' fighting, O'Connor and his men removed the Italian threat to Egypt. They shattered two Italian corps, took 38,000 prisoners, including four generals, and captured seventy-three tanks and 237 guns, all accomplished at a loss of only 624 men killed, wounded or missing.

Although Italian fighting spirit has often been mocked, frequently justifiably, the Italian army at Sidi Barrâni for the most part fought bravely. The Italian gunners at Nibeiwa gallantly attacked the monster I tanks with machine guns and hand grenades and were all shot down. General Maletti, the camp commander, was killed while firing a machine gun still clad in his pajamas. That he was caught by surprise in his sleep testifies to the unorthodoxy of O'Connor's daring plan. To be awakened by shelling from the east, where the enemy was supposed to be, and then to be struck from the west where he was *not* supposed to be had been most unsettling.

O'Connor's next objective was the fortress of Bardia (Bardiyah) just across the Libyan frontier. Bardia was a little town perched on a tiny harbor and connected by paved road to Tobruk (Tobruq) and Benghazi (Banghazi). It was held by 45,000 men and 400 guns under Gen. "Electric Whiskers" Borgonzoli. Mussolini had already sent a dramatic message to Borgonzoli: "I have given you a difficult task, but one well suited to your courage and experience as an old and intrepid soldier—the task of defending Bardia to the last." In true Roman fashion, Borgonzoli replied: "I am aware of the honor and I have today repeated to my troops your message—simple and unequivocal. In Bardia we are and here we stay."

O'Connor thought differently, and for Bardia he had a plan entirely different from Sidi Barrâni. He was not a set-piece fighter. For each of his battles he had a fresh approach. Sidi Barrâni had shown gaps that could be exploited. Bardia was a fortress guarded by an eighteen-mile belt of modern defenses. Chief of these was an antitank ditch four feet deep and twelve feet wide, supported by barbed wire and minefields. O'Connor saw at once that in contrast to Nibeiwa the infantry here would have to precede the I tanks. They would have to secure a bridgehead beyond the antitank ditch, after which the ditch would be bridged and lanes cleared through the minefields. Then O'Connor's iron behemoths could go clanking into Bardia.

On the bitter cold night of January 2–3, 1941, all the British tanks with their exhaust baffles removed went roaring up and down the Bardia defenses to delude the Italians into thinking a powerful force of armor was coming against them. An hour after midnight Australian foot soldiers moved into their assembly areas. They were dressed for the cold, and loaded down with weapons, rations and ammunition. They also carried Italian wire-cutters and Bangalore torpedoes, lengths of pipe stuffed with explosive to be slipped underneath the barbed wire to blast a path through it. Just before dawn, every last gun that O'Connor possessed opened up on Bardia. The barrage not only pinned down the Italians, it distracted them while the Australians were busily clearing the barbed wire and opening avenues in the minefields. Soon they were taking prisoners. Then they had two lanes cleared. Together, now, the I heavies and the Australians went charging into Bardia. Again the Italians fought well and a dogfight ensued. During a lull in the battle, a British fleet bombarded the town while the RAF struck Italian airfields. But a renewed attack bogged down because of poor staff work, and it was not until the next morning that Bardia fell.

Once again O'Connor had won a stunning victory. Forty thousand Italians had been killed, wounded or captured, and the war booty included 400 guns, thirteen medium and 115 light tanks, plus 706 trucks—a boon to the truck-starved O'Connor. For the jaunty Australians there was the unexpected reward of captured Italian champagne in which they toasted their victory, bellowing their lilting marching song, "Waltzing Matilda."

> Once a jolly swagman camped by a billabong
> Under the shade of a coolibah tree
> And he sang as he watched and waited till his billy boiled—
> "You'll come a'waltzin' Matilda with me."

There were other less printable ditties sung in that inimitable Cockney accent and punctuated with gusts of ribald laughter and long swigs at the captured bubbly. For General O'Connor there was the even more intoxicating prospect of pursuit. The moment Bardia fell, his forewarned 7th Armored Division had gone racing for Tobruk.

General Wavell now faced a strategic problem. He had to maintain a balance between Libya to the west and Ethiopia to the east. He had already taken the 4th Indian Division from O'Connor for use in Eritrea, replacing it with the under-strength 6th Australian Division. Yet the Little Terrier had made excellent use of his Aussies, and Wavell now feared that O'Connor's victories might pull him into a mistake. There were still 80,000 Italians and 900 guns in Cyrenaica—the Roman name for eastern Libya—and another 90,000 with 500 guns in Tripolitania to the west. Tobruk was 200 miles away from O'Connor's base at Mersa Matrûh. That was a long and vulnerable supply line. A resourceful enemy could certainly cut it or at least shoot it up. But so far, the enemy had been anything but resourceful. O'Connor already had surrounded Tobruk and was poised to seize this most valuable supply port. So Wavell, like Rundstedt with Guderian, allowed O'Connor to pull him toward Tobruk.

O'Connor realized that he was at the end of his line of communications. To strike farther westward, he *had* to have Tobruk. Apart from its value as a port, it possessed a distillation plant and wells capable of producing 40,000 gallons of water a day. In the desert that was no mean possession. Tobruk seemed to O'Connor an easier nut to crack than Bardia. It had similar perimeter defenses more than twice as long but with many more gaps and held by fewer troops and guns. Altogether there were 32,000 men, 220 guns, and forty-five light and medium tanks under Gen. Petassi Manella. Once again O'Connor informed the commander of his armor that upon word of the fall of Tobruk, he was to speed inland for Mechili (Makhayla). Already in O'Connor's restless mind a plan for the eventual capture of Tripoli itself was evolving. Speed was still of the essence. He had news that Italian reinforcements were sailing for Tripoli. Most sobering of all was the threat of British aid to Greece. It had already reduced his aerial support, and at any moment Winston's Churchill's almost fatal fascination for peripheral operations could further erode his strength. O'Connor felt that he simply must seize Tripoli as quickly as possible, if only to make the prospect of the conquest of all Libya more palatable to Churchill than a Balkan adventure. With all Libya in British hands, the Axis would have no hope whatsoever of recovering it, Egypt would be safe and the precious oil would still flow to Britain from the Persian Gulf.

But first: Tobruk. At 5:40 on the morning of January 21, 1941, O'Connor launched a straight-out frontal assault. A preliminary concentration of artillery so dazed the defenders that they started to surrender before the attack began. In went the Australians, opening a gap in the perimeter so that the I tanks, now down to a mere dozen, could go lumbering through. The Italians fought back with tank counterattacks. But their armor was too thin-skinned, and by nightfall, the Italian artillery had fallen silent—probably to avoid counter-battery fire—and General Manella was a prisoner. A dawn charge overwhelmed the garrison and by early afternoon the troops were again drinking that delectable nectar—the wine of the enemy—and counting the booty. There were 25,000 prisoners, 208 guns, twenty-three medium tanks, 200 trucks, and enough canned food to feed more than 30,000 men for two months. Best of all, the port had been only slightly damaged—British ships were being unloaded there within three days—and those splendid wells were intact.

The Little Terrier was now on fire to take Benghazi, the important port to the west of the Gulf of Syrte (Sirte or Sidra). To do so would destroy the remaining Italian forces in Cyrenaica. On January 21 the chiefs of staff in London signaled that Benghazi was vital. For the first time, O'Connor had received strategic sanction for his advances. Before the enthusiasm of the chiefs could veer away to Greece again, he had to act promptly.

Between Tobruk and Benghazi stood the Jebel Akhdar, or Green Mountains. It was a fertile region, typically Mediterranean, but more like Greece or Italy than Africa. White farmhouses of the Italian settlers stood among broad fields of grain beneath green hillsides dotted with gray olive trees. It was a place of wine and water, a huge green oasis between the sea and half a continent of desert. Behind it, on the sea, was Benghazi.

Because the rugged hills of the Jebel Akhdar could not be penetrated by armor, it offered the Italians the opportunity to concentrate the defense of Benghazi at two strong points. The first, on the left flank, was the ancient city of Derna, a natural position of great strength lying in an enormous wadi twelve miles wide. The second, on the right, was the town of Mechili in the desert just below the Jebel Akhdar's eastern extremity. It was to Mechili that O'Connor had sent his lighter armor after Tobruk fell, hoping to find an opening there. But there was none. Mechili was as strongly held as Derna. Nevertheless, O'Connor, forever fearful of that dreaded signal ordering him to halt, perhaps even to withdraw or take away his army for shipment to Greece, resolved to smash open the Derna-Mechili gates to Benghazi. The Australians would push up the coast road on Derna while the armor would roll through Mechili, speeding across the desert to the coast road below Benghazi. Thus the Italians there and at Derna would be trapped between the Australians and the armor.

On January 24 the Australian infantry moved up from Tobruk toward Derna. Far below them, O'Connor prepared to hurl his armor at Mechili. But on the night of the 26th the Italians escaped through the Jebel Akhdar. O'Connor was dismayed. Why, it is difficult to understand; unless he had become accustomed to gorging himself on Italian booty and felt cheated of another such meal. For the way was now open for his turning movement on Benghazi, his drive to the coast road. Be that as it may, O'Connor could not move. The desert had exacted payment for his three victories. His armor was down to fifty medium and ninety-five light tanks, and there was not enough food, fuel and ammunition for a punishing desert march of 120 miles with a battle at its end. He had to sit down to wait for reinforcements and resupply. It looked like an ulcerous delay of two weeks. Nagged by his dread of being whistled off his prey, O'Connor could not abide it and begged Wavell for permission to proceed. It was granted. On February 4, with only fifty mediums and eighty lights, the 7th Armored Division roared away for Beda Fomm on the coast road.

The going was very rough: strewn boulders and soft sand. O'Connor following in his staff car wondered if Graziani had been right in declaring the desert below the Jebel Akhdar to be "impenetrable." To either side of the vehicle tracks he saw broken-down tanks. "My God," he said to Dorman-Smith, "do you think it's going to be all right?"

The going became easier until a sandstorm caused some units to become lost. Nevertheless by three that afternoon the armor reached Masus, halfway to the coast. Now came aerial reports that the Italian Tenth Army was retreating from Benghazi in force. The coast road was thronged with enemy transport driving south at great speed. They were making for Beda Fomm. If they reached it before the British, they could throw out a blocking force to the west to hold O'Connor at bay while the main body escaped to Tripoli. At once O'Connor sent armored cars to plug the gap. By noon the following day his armor followed by artillery was in Beda Fomm. A half hour later the first Italian trucks appeared from the north. By a margin of only thirty minutes O'Connor had closed his trap and the annihilating Battle of Beda Fomm was begun.

Again and again the Italian armor sought to break the British grip on their escape route. Again and again they were repulsed, sometimes wiped out. Once a column of trucks led by thirty tanks tried to penetrate the defenses of a rifle brigade. Momentarily, it appeared that they had broken through, until British artillery firing on the enemy mixed among its own men blew them away. Meanwhile, the Australians drove through Derna into the Italian rear. At nine o'clock in the morning of February 7, 1941, the Italian Tenth Army surrendered. When

O'Connor heard the news, he turned to Dorman-Smith and said:

"We'd better send a message to Archie. What shall we say?"

Dorman-Smith suggested that Wavell would appreciate a hunting metaphor. "Fox killed in the open?"

O'Connor was delighted and the message sent off. "Let's go forward to see how things are," he said. They drove toward the sea with the salt-scented air flowing through the staff car's open windows. The Little Terrier's calm gaze fell on herds of antelope parting to permit their passage. Buzzards flew overhead. Dorman-Smith asked O'Connor how it felt to be a completely successful commander. O'Connor reflected before he answered:

"I would never consider a commander completely successful until he had restored the situation after a serious defeat and a long retreat."

In his becomingly modest style O'Connor had in a single sentence expressed the essence of military wisdom. They drove on, passing a busload of Italian women standing amid the debris of battle under the watchful eye of a lone priest in a soutane. They came to the huge party at which the British with their New Zealand, Australian and Free French comrades were toasting their victory. O'Connor still wore his desert-stained campaign rig and except for his red-braided general's cap was hardly noticeable. He took a victory drink, sipping it absently in his birdlike manner, wondering how much Italian transport had been captured. It would be needed for the advance on Tripoli. One more leap and all Libya would be his. Then he drove to the Italian prisoner-of-war camp and asked to see the senior enemy general. Bergonzoli was brought to him, resplendent in his full dress uniform complete with spurs.

"I'm sorry you are so uncomfortable," O'Connor murmured apologetically. "We haven't had time to make proper arrangements."

Bergonzoli bowed politely. "Thank you very much. We do realize that you came here in a very great hurry."

O'Connor's hooded eyes flickered briefly at the unconscious irony in Bergonzoli's remark. He left the camp, eager to learn the extent of his booty. For the fourth time he counted it: 20,000 prisoners, 112 medium tanks, 216 guns, and 1,500 wheeled vehicles. But the fourth count was to be the last count. That long-dreaded signal had arrived from Cairo. Winston Churchill had ordered Wavell to halt O'Connor's westward advance and to withdraw the fighting units of his forces to Egypt in preparation for shipment to Greece.

Even as he crouched for the kill, Sir Richard O'Connor had been whistled off his prey.

PART FOUR

1941

24. January 1941: Libya

As First Lord of the Admiralty during both world wars, Winston Churchill had been a staunch proponent of the long-standing British policy of relying chiefly on its navy during war. The Royal Navy was not only the senior service, it was the superior service. Because of a fleet able to blockade an enemy coast, to sever his line of communications and to transport troops and supplies to those allies fighting on the continent, Britain was able to defeat both Louis XIV and Louis XV in the long Anglo-French struggle for colonial supremacy and to bring down Napoleon. When Horatio Nelson vanquished the French fleet at the so-called Battle of the Nile, he cut Napoleon's line of communications and forced him to leave Egypt. When Nelson won his greatest victory at Trafalgar, he made possible Waterloo and the Corsican conqueror's final defeat. For two centuries Britain's war chiefs abhorred the idea of fielding a large land army on the continent. They favored using small bodies of troops always transported by the navy to strike the enemy on his periphery. Or else their strategy was to invade from the sea to join friendly forces in an enemy country and arouse opposition to the ruling powers. This was doctrine, and Winston Churchill embraced it.

In World War I, however, Britain for the first time fielded a huge conscript army on the continent and suffered enormous losses in human life. The flower of British manhood sank into lifelessness in the blood-mixed mud of Flanders at Ypres . . . Passchendaele . . . these hideous battles with their horrible casualties were never forgotten by Winston Churchill. One day American generals wrangling with him over the invasion of Europe would find that they were not up against a willfully stubborn old man but rather Ypres and Passchendaele. Once these fears and convictions were joined to Churchill's flair for the dramatic—à la Gallipoli—and his emotional response to problems—it was perhaps inevitable that he should choose a peripheral adventure in Greece over O'Connor's almost guaranteed conquest of Libya.

Churchill's febrile imagination was now off and running toward the Balkans like a hound after a hare. Stimulated by the way the Greeks had repulsed the Italians, always drawn to the relatively low risk in lives of peripheral operations, he conceived of forming a powerful combination of Balkan states against Germany. As the British military historian Correlli Barnett has aptly observed: A Churchill he was indeed, but he was no Marlborough. This was no cold and calculated strategy taking into account the perils as well as the possibilities. Moreover, all the Balkan armies were primitive and Britain could spare very little to help them. Nevertheless, in January of 1941 Churchill tried to induce Gen.

Joannes Metaxas to accept British help. Metaxas declined, observing that the force offered would be sure to provoke German invasion and would not be strong enough to repel it. Metaxas suggested that it would be wiser for Britain to clean out Africa first. But then, on January 29, Metaxas unexpectedly died and Churchill was able to persuade his successor to accept his proposal. Most of O'Connor's valiant army was taken from him and shipped to Greece.

Maj. Gen. Richard O'Connor now faced a dilemma. In ten weeks he had advanced 500 miles and with a vastly inferior force had won four major battles while destroying an Italian army of ten divisions, capturing 130,000 prisoners, 400 tanks, thousands of wheeled vehicles, and two major fortresses, all at the astonishingly low cost of 476 killed, 1,225 wounded and 43 missing. His had indeed been a campaign for the textbooks, a model of originality, daring and speed. Now he was being ordered to give up his army just as he stood on the threshold of the climactic victory. Should he obey, or should he seize the initiative on his own, win his victory and present the British Cabinet with a fait accompli? Many generals before him had succumbed to such temptation. But O'Connor did not even consider it. It was not in his character to disobey. So a static Cyrenaica command was set up with inexperienced troops under the equally green Lieutenant General Sir Philip Neame. O'Connor went back to Egypt as commander of British troops there.

General Wavell did not consider this arrangement dangerous. He knew that a German lieutenant general named Erwin Rommel had arrived in Libya to take command of an Italo-German force. But his intelligence did not believe that Rommel would be able to advance before May, or at the earliest mid-April. It was a sound estimate, which neglected only one small detail: the character of Erwin Rommel. On March 31, Rommel attacked. He came on cautiously at first, but then, finding nothing really menacing before him, he speeded his advance. The untried General Neame and his raw troops both fell into confusion. Wavell sent O'Connor back to Libya to advise Neame. On April 6 Sir Richard, who had recently been knighted, was driving with Neame in a command tractor and was captured by Germans who had penetrated British lines. The finest of Britain's desert generals was lost and history was denied the stirring spectacle of two master tacticians dueling each other in that vast featureless wasteland made for maneuver.

By his great strategic blunder Winston Churchill had guaranteed that the Desert War would continue for two more years.

25. Spring 1941: The Balkans, Greece, Crete

IN THE SPRING OF 1941 Adolf Hitler became restless. His timetable for the invasion of the Soviet Union was approaching and the Balkans were still not entirely subdued. He could not launch the greatest military operation of his career without nailing down this unstable southern flank.

Hungary and Romania were satellites safely within the Axis orbit. On March 1, 1941, Bulgaria was also compelled to enter it, and on the following day German troops were in Sofia. In Greece there remained the thankless task of rescuing his blundering partner, Mussolini. There would be some benefits from this, however, since he could move from Greece to join the Vichy French in Syria and also pro-Axis forces in the oil-rich Persian Gulf. That was something for the future. For now, he had to deal with the last Balkan recalcitrant, Yugoslavia.

Yugoslavia was the largest Balkan state, three quarters the size of Italy with a population of 14 million. To coerce Yugoslavia, Hitler threatened an invasion by his troops in neighboring Bulgaria and Hungary. On March 25, 1941, Yugoslavia submitted, signing the Tripartite Pact to become the latest Nazi satellite. Germany agreed to respect Yugoslavia's sovereignty and territorial integrity and not to demand passage of German troops through its land.

Although it seemed to Hitler that his terms had been comparatively generous, the Yugoslav people themselves reacted with fury and defiance. In the Terrazia of Belgrade, the capital city, Yugoslavs publicly tore Hitler's picture into shreds and vowed they would not accept the Tripartite Pact. Two days later, on March 27, Gen. Dusan Simovic led a successful coup d'état. The leading members of the government were arrested and the regent, Prince Paul, was forced from the throne. Eighteen-year-old Prince Peter was proclaimed king, and a new government organized from all parties except those that had dealt with Hitler.

Hitler was enraged, and much of his wrath was directed against Mussolini. Like someone pulling a loose thread, *Il Duce*'s invasion of Greece was unraveling all *Der Führer*'s war plans for 1941. First, Italian losses in Greece and Africa had encouraged a Resistance movement in France. Next, they had suggested to Francisco Franco in Spain that it would be unwise to join such an unsteady coalition, and he chose to sit out the war instead. Now Hitler faced delay in attacking the Soviet Union because of this Yugoslav rebellion, undoubtedly encouraged in part by those same Italian losses. Hitler did not hesitate to inform *Il Duce* of his displeasure, and Mussolini, appropriately crestfallen, replied that he was sorry his letter to *Der Führer* informing him of his plans for Greece had not arrived in time. In fact, Mussolini had made sure that it would not arrive in time. His humility was only due to his having broken the military Eleventh Commandment: Thou shalt not lose. So Hitler was forced to come to Mussolini's assistance in Africa, to which he sent Lieutenant General Erwin Rommel with the first units of what was to be the famed Afrika Korps; and he detailed an army of half a million men for Greece. But first, he must conquer Yugoslavia and chastise those insolent citizens of Belgrade who had dared to deface the image of the Greatest German of All Times.

Belgrade had been declared an open city, which meant to Hitler nothing more than that it was probably lightly defended. Wave after wave of German bombers, flying in Operation Punishment, left the Terrazia a heap of smoldering rubble and killed 17,000 residents of Belgrade. Meanwhile, at 5:15 A.M. on April 6, 1,000 Luftwaffe planes and twenty divisions numbering 650,000 men swept into Yugoslavia. They struck at airfields, bridges, communications and vital services. Within a few hours Yugoslavia was without electricity, telephones or radio.

It was a remarkable campaign, well planned and well executed by Field Marshal Wilhelm List. The Germans came across mountainous terrain considered impassable for armor. One spearhead came out of Bulgaria's mountain passes to drive southward toward Greece. Others rolled across Yugoslavia to join the Italians in Albania. Another advanced from Hungary toward Zagreb, while still others moved southward from Romania to capture Belgrade. A campaign of terror was begun in the capital city. Civilians suspected of anti-Nazi attitudes were rounded up and machine-gunned to death while the bodies of partisans dangled from lampposts. It was over in eleven days. On April 17 the Yugoslav Army capitulated and King Peter fled to Britain. Yugoslavia was then carved into pieces with chunks going to Germany, Italy, Hungary and Bulgaria. What was left became a Nazi satellite. But a most unwilling one: guerrillas took refuge in the forests and mountains, from which they harassed the conquerors unmercifully. They were especially pitiless to the Italian troops, and many of these garrison soldiers yearned for the comparative safety of the front lines.

Some 56,000 troops, most of them Anzacs,* the pride of O'Connor's disbanded army, were shipped to Greece to engage a German army of a half million men. On March 27, 1941, they were approaching Cape Matapan at the southernmost point of the Grecian peninsula when an Italian naval force attempted to intercept them. At once the Royal Navy brought them to night battle. Using radar-directed guns flashing and booming in the darkness, the British sank the Italian cruisers *Fiume, Zara* and *Pola,* while damaging three destroyers and a battleship. British seamen boarding the *Pola* before she sank were astonished at the incredible disarray on her decks. Empty bottles were everywhere, together with bundles of clothing wrapped by seamen preparing to abandon ship. Italian sailors were sprawled on the decks in a drunken stupor. *Pola* had not fired a shot.

On the same day that he attacked Yugoslavia, Hitler sent his columns driving into Greece from Bulgaria. But they did not strike directly at the main

*Australian and New Zealand troops.

Greek forces in the Metaxas Line facing the Bulgarian mountain passes. They swerved westward, passed through southern Yugoslavia and debouched into the valley of the Vardar River. Within two days they had isolated three Greek divisions and captured Salonika, where the British-Anzacs had landed. Another flanking thrust was mounted farther westward through the Monastir Gap. This maneuver effectively cut off twelve of Greece's finest divisions facing the Italians at the Albanian border and also turned the flank of the British-Anzacs on Mount Olympus. Still the doughty Greeks fought on. "We'll throw them into the sea— the Baltic Sea!" they cried. Although the boast was backed by bravery, it was still empty. There were too many Germans, too many guns, too many Luftwaffe planes, too much professional skill.

The embattled British and Anzacs began a miserable, bloody retreat toward Athens. The roads were narrow and twisting, sometimes winding through steep ravines. It rained steadily. Beside the roads was the familiar debris of defeat: burning dumps, vehicles and houses, discarded clothing, dead mules and horses, abandoned ammunition and harness, hundreds of dilapidated Greek trucks or farm carts, British three-tonners, captured Italian tractors bogged down in the ditches riddled with bullets, burnt out or merely tipped over in bomb craters, and everywhere bundles and bundles of paper melting in the rain. Eventually the withdrawals became cavalcades of confusion. Greek soldiers and civilians mingled with the British and Anzacs. Greeks on horseback or on foot, in buses or private cars were mixed in with the military vehicles. Traffic was often bumper-to-bumper, and where the roads widened, trucks were double- or treble-parked while their weary drivers stole a nap. Roused by cursing officers and NCOs, the drivers sent their vehicles lurching forward again. Strafing Messerschmitts added to the confusion and produced more delays while everyone took to the hillsides for safety. There was little or no support from the RAF, if only because the Germans had seized all the airfields. Sometimes it took such retreating columns as many as twelve hours to cover fifteen miles.

Soon it became obvious that the British-Anzac force must get out of Greece as soon as possible. "You have done your best to save us," the Greek government cabled. "We are finished. But the war is not yet lost. Save as much as you can of your army to help win elsewhere." On April 23, the weary British-Anzacs reached the southern beaches, just as King George and his government took off for Britain. Fortunately, the next two nights were moonless. Under cover of darkness the troops were evacuated to waiting ships. By day big guns were blown apart, tanks were driven into the sea and stores of gasoline set on fire. When the Germans reached the beach at Kalamata, they found nothing but a mass of twisted, blackened wreckage.

Some 43,000 of the original force of 56,000 had been saved. Half of them returned to Egypt and the other half went to Crete, Hitler's next objective.

Adolf Hitler's conquest of the Balkans seemed to satisfy him. Field Marshal List's army had captured 90,000 Yugoslavs, 270,000 Greeks and 13,000 British-Anzacs, at a cost of only 5,000 Germans killed and wounded. These had been stunning and easy victories and they had secured his southern flank. He wanted no more diversions from the invasion of the U.S.S.R. It had been scheduled for early May, but now, heavy rains in East Prussia together with the Balkan delays had pushed the date back to late June. *Der Führer* was thus not very receptive when Gen. Kurt Student proposed an airborne invasion of the island of Crete.

As commander in chief of German airborne forces, Student had planned and executed the airborne phases of the conquest of Norway and was now on fire to seize this strategic island in the Mediterranean. Student took his enthusiasm to Reichsmarschall Goering, who, he knew, "was easy to enthuse," and Goering passed him on to Hitler. But *Der Führer* was still reluctant to undertake anything other than Barbarossa.

"It sounds all right," he said, "but I don't think its practicable."

Student was not discouraged. He pointed out that Crete could become an unsinkable aircraft carrier from which the Luftwaffe could protect Greece and strike British shipping supplying and reinforcing Libya and Egypt. At last Hitler consented. Student was overjoyed. He would use *all* the German airborne forces. Formidable as that may have sounded, it amounted to no more than one Parachute Division and one Glider Regiment, to which would be added a Mountain Division that had never been ferried by air before. Many of Student's parachutists were still in training.

Col. Karl von der Heydte was one of those regimental and battalion commanders who gathered in a sealed and shuttered room in the Hotel Bretagne in Athens on May 19. Von der Heydte was delighted when he saw the huge map of Crete on the wall. *So that's where we're going,* he thought. Cultivated man that he was, he knew that this celebrated "hundred-city" island was the site of the famed palace at Knossos. Crete was the source of many of the legends of antiquity. Zeus, the father of the Greek gods, was said to have been born there. It was from Crete that Icarus, the son of Daedalus, flew too close to the sun on wings of wax and feathers, until the heat melted the wax and Icarus fell into the sea. But then von der Heydte was disappointed after General Student outlined his plan and informed the commanders that they would take off that night. He was well aware that the hotel room was only a few yards from the foot of the Acropolis. He had so wanted to see Athens. "I felt like a child at the open door of a room full of toys and not being allowed to enter."

Maj. Gen. Sir Bernard Freyberg of New Zealand commanded on Crete. He had been personally chosen by Winston Churchill. During the twenties Churchill met this redoubtable soldier, then one of the few living men to hold a Victoria Cross, at a country house in Britain. He asked him to show him his many wounds. Freyberg stripped and the astonished Churchill counted twenty-seven separate scars and gashes. "Of course," Freyberg modestly explained, "you nearly always get two wounds for every bullet or splinter, because mostly they have to go out as well as in." The hero-worshipping prime minister never forgot this scene, and

Freyberg, who was to add three (or six) more wounds in World War II, became his choice for Crete.

Freyberg commanded about 27,000 British-Anzacs evacuated from Greece together with two Greek divisions of about the same number. He also had several heavy and light antiaircraft batteries, but less than a dozen tanks. Churchill was very nervous about Crete. He had urged that at least another dozen of the big I tanks should be sent there. He had also been informed that the Germans planned to surprise Crete from the air. But on May 5, Freyberg assured him: "Cannot understand nervousness; am not in the least anxious about airborne attack." Actually he was more worried about assault from the sea, which seems surprising inasmuch as the Germans had absolutely no flair for amphibious warfare and the Royal Navy was based in strength in Crete's great natural harbor at Suda Bay.

In the early-morning darkness of May 20, 1941, Colonel von der Heydte and his battalion were brought by trucks to the airfield. They covered their ears with their hands to shut out the deafening roar of 120 massed transports. Their whirling propellers raised clouds of dust through which the parachutists could see red sparks flashing from engine exhausts. NCOs waving pale green flashlights guided the men aboard the transports. Von der Heydte got in last. To his own surprise, he fell asleep. At dawn his adjutant awakened him.

"We are near Crete, sir."

The colonel arose from his seat and walked toward the open door. He could see Crete: "Still small, like a cliff rising out of the glittering sea to meet us." He glanced again and again at his watch. Now he could see the beaches, the narrow white ribbon of the surf . . . then the mountains . . . the transports "like giant birds trying to reach their eyries in the rocks."

"Prepare to jump!" cried the dispatcher seated beside the open door.

The parachutists rose from their bucket seats. They fastened their parachute hooks to the static line running down the center of thc cabin. The transport was losing altitude. Von der Heydte could feel the pressure in his ears.

"Ready to jump!"

The colonel was at the door in two strides. His men pressed into line behind him. Von der Heydte could see white puffs of cotton wool appearing as though by magic in the air outside. Ack-ack! As though floating beneath him was the village of Alikianós. He could see people in the streets staring upward. Others ran to their houses and vanished inside. Like enormous black vultures, the shadows of the transports flitted swiftly over the roofs of the houses. Von der Heydte could see a reservoir gleaming like a huge mirror. Above it white parachutes floated toward the earth. The colonel smiled: He knew these were dummies designed to draw fire away from the live parachutists.

"Go!"

Like a skier, Von der Heydte pushed downward and threw his arms outward as though reaching for the black swastika painted on the wing opposite him. The slipstream caught him and sent him swirling into space, the air roaring in his ears.

There came a sudden jerk and a giant hand squeezing the wind out of his lungs, and then, looking upward, he saw his parachute with its camouflage patchwork spreading open above him. "In relation to this giant umbrella, I felt small and insignificant."

About 3,500 German parachutists floated down from the skies above Crete. Most of them were killed. Even though the Luftwaffe had knocked out most of Freyberg's antiaircraft batteries, his British-Anzacs and Greeks took a fearful toll of the parachutists. Some fell into the sea where they became entangled in their rigging and drowned. Others, dangling helplessly in trees, were picked off by sharpshooters. Cretans wielding knives slaughtered many trapped in ravines or caught on the beaches. Because of a fear of prevailing winds blowing toward the sea, some transport pilots unloaded their human cargoes too far inland, sometimes inside enemy lines. Weapon-containers were dropped wide of the mark. Many of the gliders, unable to find suitable landing sites on mountainous Crete, crash-landed in the hills. Still they came on, gliders carrying a dozen to thirty soldiers each towed by ancient transports. As many as ten gliders were strung out behind each transport like kites on a string.

Some troops of the Mountain Division, together with the heavier weapons —antitank and antiaircraft guns, field artillery, and even tanks—were aboard torpedo boats and small Greek caiques attempting to reach Crete by sea. But Adm. Sir Andrew Cunningham ordered three cruisers and four destroyers to intercept this motley armada. They scattered it and sent 400 Mountain soldiers to the bottom. In retaliation, the Luftwaffe flew in land-based bombers and torpedo planes to succeed in "pulling a lot of hair" from the Royal Navy's scalp. The cruisers *Fiji* and *Gloucester* were sunk, along with three destroyers, including the *Kelly,* whose commander, Lord Louis Mountbatten, was fished alive from the sea. Shaken, Admiral Cunningham ordered his fleet to retire temporarily from Cretan waters.

On land, the Germans were still fighting to take Crete at all costs. They did pay dearly, but by the end of May they held the airfield at Máleme and had driven Freyberg's forces across the island to the tiny fishing village of Sphakia. Here— à la Dunkirk, à la Greece—the Royal Navy began its third evacuation of a beaten army within a year. Troops who were veterans of the Grecian withdrawal knew exactly what to do this time. They hid in caves by day and marched down to waiting destroyers by night for the 350-mile voyage to Egypt. But they also ran a fiery gauntlet of bombs and the Royal Navy was again scourged. It suffered 2,000 casualties of its own, losing a total of three cruisers, six destroyers and twenty-nine smaller vessels, while a battleship, four cruisers and seven destroyers were damaged.

Worse, the British nation was shocked. Here was the third straight defeat, following in the wake of disaster in Libya and Greece. Egypt itself was now menaced not only by the formidable Erwin Rommel and his growing Afrika

Korps but also by the Luftwaffe based on Crete. Cyprus, Malta, Syria, the Suez and, most ominous of all, the oil-rich Persian Gulf, seemed threatened. Such a grim prospect, together with a renewal of the aerial Blitz that spring, made May of 1941 seem darker even than May of 1940.

Nevertheless, Hitler had also paid a fearsome price. Germany suffered 17,000 casualties taking Crete. Its Parachute Division had been so brutally mauled it was never used again. Hitler was so upset by his losses that he never again attempted an airborne operation. Whenever he met General Student, he reminded him: "The day of parachute troops is over."

On the conquered island Colonel Baron von der Heydte was relaxing in a small villa near the coast which had once housed the British Consulate. He had come there with the remnants of his battalion, badly battered in the decisive battle for the village of Canea (Khania). With the immemorial intuition of all soldiers since Agamemnon he had sensed that the island had fallen when his adjutant awakened him to announce:

"The battle for Canea is over, sir. The fight for comfortable billets has now begun."

26. Spring 1941: The Middle East

THE INFLUENCE OF LUCK on war cannot be calculated. Napoleon believed in luck as much as in destiny—if the two terms are not actually interchangeable—and whenever he could he chose "lucky" colonels to command his regiments. Accident, then, seems to be far more decisive in war than design, and there is no more compelling illustration of this suggestion than Winston Churchill's failure to persuade the French to fight on from North Africa.

If they had, it is almost certain that Hitler would have pursued them there. Spain, hardly more than a long spit across the Straits of Gibraltar, would have been forced to follow him, or at least to allow passage of German troops across its territory. As a consequence, Gibraltar would have fallen, and because French colonial troops would never have been able to stand up to German panzers, the western end of the Mediterranean would have been closed to Britain. Even the supine spine of Graziani the Sleepwalker would have been stiffened and he would have been in Cairo by the end of 1940. The Suez would then have been lost to Britain, thus closing the other end of the Mediterranean. Syria and the Persian Gulf would have been open to Axis invasion and the Soviet Union's vulnerable southern flank in the Caucasus unmasked. Finally, Turkey could probably have been bullied into joining the Axis.

Luckily for Britain, the French chose not to fight on from North Africa and thus force Hitler to exclude them from the Mediterranean. Also fortunately for Britain, *Der Führer* was much too preoccupied with his plan for the invasion of the U.S.S.R. from the northwest to perceive the golden opportunity in such a course. But Admiral Raeder had seen it. Distrustful of Operation Sea Lion, Raeder had already on September 6, 1940, suggested that the best way to defeat Britain was to exclude it from the Mediterranean. Hitler had not listened. On September 16, at a meeting of the high command, Raeder was more specific. "The British have always considered the Mediterranean as the pivot of their world-empire," he said. "Italy is fast becoming the main target of attack. Britain always attempts to strangle the weaker. The Italians have not yet realized their danger when they refuse our help. *For this reason the Mediterranean question must be cleared up during the winter months* [all italics in original]. Gibraltar must be taken. The Suez Canal must be taken. It is doubtful if the Italians can accomplish this alone; support by German troops will be needed. An advance from Suez through Palestine and Syria as far as Turkey is necessary. If we reach that point Turkey will be in our power. *The Russian problem will then appear in a different light. Fundamentally, Russia is afraid of Germany. It is doubtful if an advance against Russia from the north will be necessary.* The question of North-West Africa is also of decisive importance. All indications are that Britain, with the help of Gaullist France, and possibly also of the U.S.A., wants to make this region a center of resistance and to set up air bases for an attack on Italy. *In this way Italy would be defeated.*"

Here was a masterly strategic prescription for strangling Britain before the United States could come to its side, as well as for taking the Soviets unawares on their vulnerable southern flank. Here was also a prescience of the path that the British ultimately *did* persuade the Americans to follow. Here was vast booty, the loss of which would destroy both Britain and the Soviet Union: the oil-rich Persian Gulf taken from Britain, the industry, oil and grain of the Caucasus wrenched away from the U.S.S.R. Most ominous of all for the Allies, the Axis had the *capacity* to carry out Raeder's plan. But even though the minutes of that meeting state, "The Führer agrees with the general line of thought," he did not adopt it. He was much too afraid of the sea and much too preoccupied with planning for Barbarossa. So luck had twice been with Winston Churchill: first, in the French decision to surrender; second, in Hitler's rejection of the Raeder suggestion. Then, preposterously enough, Lady Luck smiled a third time.

After the fall of France, British prestige sank to its lowest point in the Middle East. In Iraq, the Italian Legation in Baghdad became a center for disseminating Axis propaganda and fomenting anti-British feeling. In March 1941 the situation worsened when the pro-German Rashid Ali became prime minister and the pro-British regent, Emir Abdul Ilah, fled the country. Conscious of this threat to the Persian Gulf, Gen. Sir Claude Auchinleck, British commander in chief in India, at once sent a brigade to Basra, Iraq's main port on the Gulf. The men disembarked without opposition on April 18. Rashid Ali, who had counted on the protection of German aircraft, was chagrined.

Nevertheless, he gathered a force and marched against Habbaniyah, the British air force training base in the Iraqi desert. Eventually, a force of about 9,000 men with 50 guns was in position upon a plateau overlooking Habbaniyah. British aircraft flew in from Egypt and a battalion of infantry was flown in from India. Iraqi artillery began shelling the British positions and firing at their aircraft as they took off. On the first day, forty British were killed and wounded and twenty-two airplanes destroyed or disabled. Still, the British airmen persevered in taking off under intense artillery fire. Soon it was discovered that the Iraqi gunners abandoned their posts the moment enemy aircraft appeared overhead. One by one, their guns were blasted from the skies. After four days of such attacks the Iraqis withdrew. The British pursued. On May 30, they reached the outskirts of Baghdad, and Rashid Ali with his government took precipitate flight for Iran. Iraq was secured.

Next came Syria, one of the colonies of the French Empire that considered itself bound by the surrender terms. Syria was governed from Vichy. Its high commissioner and commander in chief of Vichy French forces there was General Dentz. But Dentz had been ordered by Admiral Darlan to allow German and Italian aircraft to land there. By the end of May there were 120 of them. From Syria, of course, the Axis could mount an attack on the Suez Canal as well as air raids on the great oil refineries at Abadan on the Persian Gulf. Luftwaffe planes flying from the Dodecanese were already hammering Egypt, and presumably, if Hitler decided to stretch out his hand, they could transport German airborne troops from their base in Crete. Meanwhile, since 1940 Syria had become filled with German agents seeking to arouse its Arab population against the British. Obviously, Britain had to forestall the Axis in Syria.

On June 8, a force under Gen. Harold Wilson, assisted by Free French troops, invaded Syria. It was hoped that the French, their former allies, would offer only token resistance, and then lay down their arms. But they resisted fiercely. Wavell in Egypt was forced to scrape up more troops from his already exhausted command. Finally, Damascus was captured by the Australians on the 21st, following a daring seaborne Commando raid behind enemy lines. Although General Dentz still commanded 24,000 men, four fifths of his air force was gone. He sued for an armistice, and Syria passed into Allied occupation.

Iran (Persia) followed. In August 1941, after Hitler's invasion of the U.S.S.R., a joint force of British and Soviet troops moved into Iran to prevent the pro-German Shah Riza Pahlevi from delivering it into Axis hands.

Thus had the back door to Eastern Europe and southern U.S.S.R. been slammed shut in the Axis's face, and it seemed that Hitler's last chance to follow Raeder's magisterial advice had gone a-glimmering. But *Der Führer* still possessed one ace in the hole in the Middle East: the commander of his Afrika Korps, who had already earned worldwide admiration as the masterly Desert Fox.

27. Erwin Rommel

IN MARCH OF 1941 British Intelligence issued a bulletin which said: "Detachments of a German expeditionary force under an obscure general, Rommel, have landed in North Africa."

Nothing could have betrayed British Intelligence's ignorance of German generals as succinctly and completely as this bulletin. Rommel, of course, was not as celebrated as, say, Rundstedt or Guderian, but he had been chief of Hitler's personal bodyguard and, as commander of the 7th Panzer Division in the fighting breakthrough of the Ardennes, had shown a daring and dash rivaling even Guderian's. In World War I his combat record had been merely incredible. The British, however, knew next to nothing about him simply because they relied on French Intelligence for profiles of German generals and those personal details that enable a commander to gauge his opponent. After the fall of France, however, such information was not available. The dossiers on Hitler's war chiefs remained on file in the French War Ministry, where, presumably, they were perused only by their subjects, either in delight or dismay, like men reading their own obituaries.

Subsequent reports on Rommel erroneously portrayed him as an ardent Nazi who had been chosen for North Africa through political pull. Indeed, the journalistic hacks of the Allied side were to satisfy the public craving for enemy monsters with a kind of bouillabaisse of unfounded conjecture and deliberate fabrication. Rommel was said to be variously a Free Corps bully, along with Goering, Hess, Roehm and Martin Bormann, the son of a laborer and one of the first of Hitler's head-breaking storm troopers, an NCO who rose from the ranks during World War I, and finally a policeman between the wars.

Where did all this palpable nonsense—not a word of it is true—originate? In the Nazi Propaganda Ministry. Why did Western journalists swallow it so eagerly and circulate it so assidiuously? Simple. It was good copy. Only Erwin Rommel seems to have been concerned about the truth, but when he protested indignantly to Propaganda, he was flabbergasted to receive the ingenuous reply: We thought we made you look good. From this experience, Rommel wisely drew a moral that he never forgot: Never trust a publicist.

The truth about Erwin Johannes Eugen Rommel is that he was born at noon on Sunday, November 15, 1891, at Heidenheim, a small town in the South German province of Württemberg, near the ancient city of Ulm. His father, also named Erwin Rommel, was a schoolmaster and the son of a schoolmaster. Both were mathematicians of distinction, and respected scholars. Herr Professor Rommel in 1886 married Helena von Luz, oldest daughter of the president of Württemberg. Four boys and one girl were born to them. One son, Manfred, died young; another, Karl, was crippled by malaria while serving as a pilot in Turkey and Persia during World War I; and a third, Bernhardt, mildly embarrassed this sober, proper family by becoming an opera singer. The daughter, Helena, became a teacher.

Erwin, the second son, according to his sister was "a very gentle and docile child. Small for his age, he had a white skin and hair so pale that we called him the 'white Teddy bear.' He spoke very slowly and only after reflecting for a long time. He was very good-tempered and amiable and not afraid of anyone. When other children used to run away from the chimney sweeps, with their black faces and top hats, he would go up solemnly and shake hands with them. We had a very sunny childhood, brought up by kind and affectionate parents who taught us their own love of nature. Before we went to school we used to play all day in the garden or in the fields and woods."

Rommel went to school in Aalen, to which the family moved in 1898 after Rommel Senior became director of the *Realgymnasium* there, that is, headmaster of a school in which "modern" subjects rather than classics were taught. Young Erwin was a poor student. Trying to catch up with his classmates, he lost his appetite and couldn't sleep. Then he lost interest. In rebuke, the schoolmaster said: "If Rommel ever shows us a dictation without a mistake, we will hire a band and go off for a day in the country." Stung, Erwin did compose a flawless dictation, but after it produced neither band nor holiday, he lost interest again. For years he remained a quiet little boy, as indifferent to games as to study.

In his teens, Erwin became friendly with a boy named Keitel (no relation to Hitler's lackey), and suddenly he blossomed. He studied hard and passed his examinations with good marks. He became athletic, bicycling and hiking in summer, skiing in winter. He and his friend built model airplanes, even a full-scale glider which they could never get aloft. They talked of studying engineering, a dream that Keitel realized. But Erwin's father opposed the idea. He was not exactly enthusiastic over his son's second thought of a military career.

There was no military tradition in the Rommel family, even though Rommel Senior had been a lieutenant of artillery. The army was almost the exclusive preserve of the Prussian Junkers, aristocrats born with a "von" before their name and silver spoons in their mouths, destined from that birth for a commission in the elite regiments and almost guaranteed accelerated promotion. But the Rommels, old and respectable Swabian stock though they were, were not the sort of fish to swim in that water. The most Erwin could hope for was to make major, ending his career as adjutant for some nameless regiment and retiring into anonymity and a modest pension. It is possible that Erwin thought: Yes, but if there's a war? The same could have been said of Napoleon: if there had been no French Revolution, retirement as an obscure and embittered major of artillery. So Erwin chose a military career.

On July 19, 1910, he joined the 124th Infantry Regiment as an "aspirant," that is, an enlisted man hoping to go on to a *Kriegsschule,* or war academy. Nine months later he was posted to the *Kriegsschule* in Danzig. There he met Lucie

Maria Mollin, daughter of a wealthy landowner in West Prussia, where the family, Italian in origin, had lived since the thirteenth century. Lucie had come to Danzig to study languages. They fell in love. Although they were not to announce their engagement for another four years, they never wavered in their devotion to each other. Theirs was to be a totally selfless union.

At Danzig, Rommel had to study hard. Classroom work never came as easily to him as the practical side of soldiering. But when he was graduated and commissioned at the end of January 1912, his marks were at least above average. Bidding good-bye to his "Dearest Lu," he returned to the 124th Infantry in Weingarten. Rommel even by German standards was short—about five feet six inches—but wiry and strong, with a fighter's nose and chin and a firm, broad, good-humored mouth. He excelled at drilling troops and was popular with the men. He was also extremely interested in the details of military organization. Not a talker but a listener, he was even-tempered and agreeable, willing, because he neither smoked nor drank and considered himself engaged, to swap duties with other pleasure-seeking subalterns eager for a night on the town. But he was no one's easy mark. NCOs quickly learned that the little lieutenant would not tolerate shabby soldiering. Although he was first and foremost a field soldier, in garrison he still liked his steel and leather to shine and his soldiers to snap and pop. Still, he had no distinctive flair or perception and was not original. Without a war, he would have had the mediocre career foreseen by his father.

In March 1914, as war clouds gathered over Europe, Rommel was assigned to a field artillery unit in Ulm. He enjoyed riding and turning out a smart battery. On July 31 he returned to barracks to find horses being bought and sold in the barrack square and orders for him to return to his regiment immediately. Next day his company drew field gear. That night their colonel clad in field gray mustered the regiment and read out the mobilization order. Jubilant, warlike shouts echoed and reechoed around the stone walls of the massive old monastery that served as a barracks. Erwin Johannes Eugen Rommel had found his war.

In combat—not to say war, for war is only the condition of hostility making combat possible—there are many officers and men who are naturally brave. To be brave is probably easier for an officer if only because his responsibility should stabilize him, and as he rises higher in the chain of command, his perspective enables him to understand, when it appears, the necessity for self-sacrifice. An enlisted man has no such gyroscope to maintain his equilibrium. He quite naturally feels he is too young to die. His bravery, his sacrifice of his own life to obey an order he does not comprehend is therefore that much finer. This is what Robert E. Lee meant when he cried, at the Battle of Antietam, "Such courage in ones so young is marvelous." Then there are brave soldiers who are impetuous and flamboyant, in which category Winston Churchill would probably belong. Next is the man of quiet courage who believes that bravery is but the simple duty of his calling, a commander such as Sir Richard O'Connor. Perhaps even higher—

and to suggest this is not to diminish the honor due to all forms of bravery—is the man who could have been a coward, who has conquered an inexplicable, uncontrollable fear because he prefers self-respect to shame. Sometimes such a man does show the white feather, and is thereafter so ashamed and remorseful that he cannot wait for the opportunity to redeem himself; and when he succeeds, he becomes the happiest of men—not because he has earned the approbation of his comrades, but because he has won back his own self-respect.

Finally, there is the man who is the pure fighting animal: clever, coldly calculating, ruthless, resourceful, decisive, tireless, almost above misery and pain —and possessed of a bravery so incredible that it might be a difference of kind rather than degree. This was Erwin Rommel. His exploits during World War I are so numerous and so diverse that to recite them all might become monotonous and a bore. But illustrative of all the qualities cited above was his first combat action on August 22, 1914.

His regiment was moving against the French near Longwy. Rommel was sent forward on horseback to reconnoiter the nearby village of Bleid. He had been patrolling for twenty-four hours and was so sick from food poisoning that he could barely keep to his saddle. Nevertheless, he went forward alone in a thick fog. Locating the village, he brought up his platoon. They were fired on. Choosing three men, Rommel went forward again. He found a footpath and followed it. It led to a road where, through the fog, he saw fifteen or twenty French *poilus.* What to do now, seeing himself so badly outnumbered? Go back and bring up his platoon? Send back a runner to bring up the platoon while he kept watch on the enemy? Or attack immediately, regardless of odds?

Rommel attacked. He and his three soldiers rushed forward shouting and firing from the hip. Some French fell, but the others broke and ran for cover. They opened fire from their concealment. Now Rommel's platoon, which he had trained to move up if its point were endangered, came forward. He armed half of his men with bundles of straw and posted the other half to cover them with gunfire. House by house, doors were kicked in and the lighted bundles hurled inside. *Poilus* rushing out of them were cut down and the French routed from the blazing village. Thus the independence, boldness and style of leadership that were to characterize Erwin Rommel. Always it would be he—not a subordinate —who would go forward to lead or reconnoiter, no matter how large or small the scale.

For his other exploits he was finally awarded the *Pour le Mérite,* a decoration usually reserved for senior generals, which, when awarded to junior officers, corresponded to the Medal of Honor. His final feat was against the Italians on the Austrian front. With six men roped together he swam the icy Piave at night to attack seven-strong the well-defended village of Longarone. He captured it by firing at it from different points in the darkness and in the morning walking in alone to order its surrender. After this, to his immense disgust, he was given a staff appointment which he held to the end of the war.

Rommel turned twenty-seven four days before the war ended. He was still a captain. He endured the hiss and spit aimed at officers in uniform during the postwar reaction in Germany, and the booing directed at his *Pour le Mérite* from a draft of "red" sailors he was ordered to train. As might be expected, he faced the sailors down and actually taught them how to goose-step. In 1921, he was posted to Stuttgart, where he remained an infantry captain for nine long years.

Such would seem a frustrating and boring climax to a career once so bright with promise. Rommel, however, thought he was lucky. Outside the army was the repugnant *Freikorps,* the boredom of business or the tedium of teaching. Inside it was the drill, critique and reflection which he enjoyed almost as much as the excitement of battle, and also the consolation of being with his beloved wife as well as duty in his native Württemberg. Rommel knew that the Treaty of Versailles limited the German Army to 100,000 men and 4,000 officers for the express and sole purpose of policing the interior. Only four thousand officers: to be chosen as one of them was fortunate indeed. But it had been no accident. General Hans von Seeckt, the commander in chief who would be known as "the man who made the next war," had been hand-picking a hard core of professionals around whom the German Army of the future would be built. By every imaginable means of subterfuge and pretense, Seeckt kept in being the entire apparatus for mobilization. Every one of the four thousand officers whom he had so carefully selected was absolutely aware that his mission was not the Versailles-mandated one of maintaining internal security but rather the creation and training of a new and even more formidable force out of the wreckage of the old. Thus, Captain Erwin Rommel was actually content, even delighted that he and his beloved Lu could take trips throughout Italy and Switzerland, could ride, ski, swim and go boating or mountain climbing. Happiness seemed complete when, on Christmas Eve, 1928, their only child, Manfred, was born after twelve years of marriage. Ten months later Rommel was posted to the Infantry School at Dresden as an instructor. His lectures there were published in a little book, *Infantry Attacks,* which was to have an enormous worldwide circulation. But it was still three more years before he made major.

That was the year—1933—when Hitler took power. Like most German officers Rommel had always been indifferent to politics, although he had despised the Nazis as a "set of scallywags" and said it was a pity that Hitler had surrounded himself with such people. Hitler he admired, regarding him as an idealist who would lead Germany out of its postwar misery and save the country from Communism. In this he was no different from almost all the members of the officer corps and 90 percent of the German people. He was not horrified but pleased to learn of the destruction of Ernst Roehm and the dissolution of his ruffianly brownshirts during the Night of the Long Knives. His was the attitude of the bulk of the German General Staff: Adolf Hitler was the new hope of Germany.

Rommel did not meet Hitler personally until 1935, when he was commanding a jaeger battalion at Goslar. *Der Führer* was coming to Goslar for a peasant festival. Rommel's battalion was to parade, but when he learned that his men were to be preceded by a column of detestable SS troops, he refused. This brought him into conference with Himmler, whom he despised, and Goebbels, whom he admired. It was agreed that a terrible mistake had been made, and Rommel's jaegers impressed Hitler, who personally congratulated Rommel.

Der Führer must have noticed his *Pour le Mérite,* for Rommel was next posted as a lieutenant colonel to help train the Hitler Youth. He came into conflict with their leader, Baldur von Schirach, a young, handsome, theatrical poetaster, and also an ardent Nazi who showered *Der Führer* with reams of flattering odes. Rommel objected that Schirach was stressing sport and military training too much and neglecting education and moral formation. He disliked turning teenagers into "little Napoleons" who scorned schools and studies. Schirach quickly decided that Rommel had to go, and he did.

But Adolf Hitler found it most difficult to forget blond and blue-eyed Germans, especially brave ones, and Rommel's next command, as a full colonel, was of the handpicked elite battalion which served as *Der Führer's* personal bodyguard.

Now close to Hitler but not intimate with him, Rommel began to make notes of his observations of him. Rommel was not a trained psychologist, of course, but he was practical and shrewd, and he understood men. It was Hitler's magnetic, almost hypnotic, power that impressed him most. Next was his faith in his own destiny; like Napoleon, he had a "star," some supernatural force that was guiding him in his mission to lead Germany "up to the sun." Rommel thought that Hitler's intuitive faculty was amazing, how he could sense who agreed and who disagreed with him, and would then set out to flatter the former for his perception or to charm or overwhelm the latter. In time, Rommel would come to distrust Hitler's intuitive handling of military affairs, but in 1938 it impressed him. So did his marvelous memory and his ability to grasp the root of the matter under discussion and to distill a solution from it. Finally, Rommel the brave was deeply impressed by Hitler's physical courage. True enough, he took pains for his personal safety, but no coward could ever have excited the admiration of a man such as Rommel. That was why he gave *Der Führer* such surprising advice when he was about to enter Prague in triumph in 1939.

"What would you do if you were in my place, Colonel?" Hitler asked.

"I should get into an open car," Rommel said, "and drive through the streets to the Hradcany without an escort."

Der Führer was mildly startled, if only because he knew the Czechs were in no mood to hail him as a liberator. Yet he followed Rommel's advice and made an enormous impression.

Although Rommel was not one of the early exponents of the lightning war, he saw it at work from the vantage of Hitler's headquarters in Poland. He divined at once the importance of close-up air support for ground forces and realized the revolution being made by the tank. Yet, for all the prestige that his association with *Der Führer* gave him, he chafed at a command far from the sound of guns, yearning for the excitement of battle, and he was overjoyed when he was named to command the 7th Panzer Division during the daring decisive thrust through the Ardennes in the Battle for France. He was still leading it during the climatic battles in the Cotentin Peninsula. Thus, he was a true panzer leader by the time Hitler called upon him in 1941 to rescue Mussolini's disintegrating African empire.

With typical thoroughness, Rommel began studying "the desert gallop," O'Connor's lightning campaign through Cyrenaica. He was particularly impressed by the masterly coordination of British armor, air and naval forces. He also began giving the men of his Afrika Korps special desert training in Germany. He had found on the Baltic a sandy peninsula corresponding to the terrain in the Libyan desert. There he worked out tactical and maintenance problems. His troops lived in deliberately overheated barracks and trained in artificial sandstorms with strictly rationed food, fuel and water. After their "hothouse" training, they began moving across the Mediterranean to Tripoli. The first units arrived in February 1941. Rommel landed on the 12th, eagerly sending out reconnaissance units to encourage the disheartened Italians at El Agheila. Reports that O'Connor had been halted by Wavell and his troops taken from him for shipment to Greece sent his spirits soaring. He communicated his confidence to his subordinates. "We *must* save Tripolitania from the attack of the British Army," he told them, clenching his fists. "We *will* hold them."

Guessing correctly that the British did not expect him to attack until May, or at the earliest mid-April, ignoring Hitler's instructions only to have plans prepared by April 20, Rommel attacked on March 31, and within a week he had swept away the weak Cyrenaica command set up by Wavell. On April 6, to Rommel's delight, O'Connor and Neame were captured. Rommel flew to Mechili in his Stork—a small aircraft similar to the Piper Cub—alighting with a broad and buoyant grin. He walked quickly up a rise to the command trucks of the captured British generals and went inside to speak to them, courteous and chivalrous as ever. Coming outside he made a minute inspection of these large, angular vehicles on caterpillar tracks. He watched his soldiers emptying them of their British gear. He saw a pair of huge sun-and-sand goggles—O'Connor's—and grinned again, stooping to retrieve them. "Booty—permissible, I take it, even for a general." Still smiling, he adjusted the goggles above the gold-braided rim of his peaked cap.

A new stage prop had been added to the memorabilia of World War II. A world familiar with Churchill's cigar and Stalin's pipe, the cigarette holder of FDR and Hitler's mustache and Mussolini's fez, would now instantly recognize the goggles of the Desert Fox.

28. The Battle of Hellfire Pass

WITHIN LESS THAN TWO WEEKS Rommel had driven the British back some 400 miles, almost to the eastern border of Cyrenaica and the western edge of Egypt. But the port city of Tobruk still was held by those Australians who would one day be famous as the "desert rats." Rommel understood full well that he could not risk deep advance with such a fortress athwart his line of communications. So he tried to take it. On April 13–14 he attempted to storm Tobruk and was beaten back. He failed again on April 16–17. Meanwhile, his troops were driving on Egypt, reaching the frontier on April 28. Sollum, at the base of the escarpment, and Fort Capuzzo were captured. For the third time, from April 30 to May 4, Rommel assaulted Tobruk and once again he was driven off. Now his forces at the frontier were almost out of fuel and a lull descended upon the desert war.

At this point Winston Churchill decided upon a bold initiative to destroy Rommel before he could grow stronger. A huge reinforcement of tanks for Egypt was gathered, thus drastically depleting Britain's reserves in the face of a possible cross-Channel spring invasion by Hitler. Furthermore, this precious convoy was sent through the Mediterranean over which the Luftwaffe had controlled the air since January. This would bring the tanks to General Wavell six weeks sooner. Such boldness was in sharp contrast to the timidity of Hitler and his chief of staff, Halder, who succeeded only in tabling a report that if Rommel were reinforced by four panzer divisions, he would certainly conquer Egypt. Mussolini had objected, being as reluctant to accept such a scale of German help as Hitler was unwilling to provide it. After all, Rommel had been sent to Libya only after the Italian defeat, and he was just supposed to hold Tripoli. That Rommel, being so far away from Germany as to consider himself holding an independent command, had actually done so much with so little had only convinced Halder that here was "a soldier gone stark mad." So the Axis forfeited the chance to drive Britain from the one place second in importance only to its homeland.

The five ships carrying 295 tanks to Wavell had passed through the Mediterranean under cover of misty weather. One ship struck a mine sailing through the Sicilian narrows and went down with fifty-seven tanks. The other four arrived safely in Alexandria on May 12 with 238 tanks. They were immediately assigned to Operation Battleaxe, the attack which Churchill hoped would gain a "decisive" victory in North Africa. Command of this operation was given to Maj. Gen. M. N. de la Beresford-Peirse, an unimaginative soldier who had never commanded armor. He hastily planned to launch a frontal attack on Rommel's position, forming a rough inverted triangle. Fort Capuzzo–Sollum was its upside-down base and Halfaya was its apex.

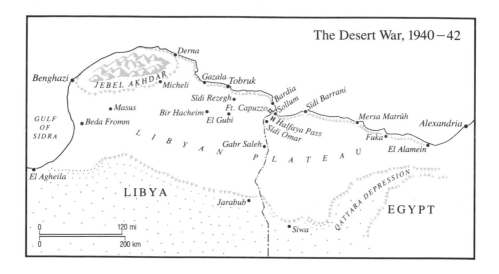

The Desert War, 1940–42

The main body of the armor and part of the infantry were to swing left toward Capuzzo while two separate forces were to make a frontal assault on Halfaya. It was through this vital pass that the coast road climbed from the sea to the escarpment. One British force was to strike the pass at the bottom, the other at the top. Once the breakthrough had been achieved, and the forward German armor destroyed, it would be exploited, in conjunction with the Tobruk garrison, as far as the Derna-Mechili line, about a hundred miles away.

It was at best an orthodox plan, defective mostly in that it lacked the overwhelming air and artillery support and numerical superiority almost always necessary for frontal assaults. Also, although the British would have a numerical superiority at the outset, they could not reinforce, whereas Rommel could call upon his 2nd Armored Division in Tobruk only eighty miles away. Rommel also realized that Halfaya Pass was "the crucial position in this battle." Accordingly, he dug in batteries of his new 88-mm guns there and at other forward posts.

To reach these positions, Beresford-Peirse's force made a thirty-mile approach march starting on the afternoon of June 14. The final bound of eight miles was made in bright moonlight in the early hours of the 15th, and the battle began with the right wing striking the outlying position at Halfaya Pass. Unfortunately, it had been decreed that the tanks could not attack until there was light enough for the artillery to start shooting, but the battery assigned to the right wing had become stuck in the sand. It was broad daylight when the thirteen big Matildas leading this assault began to move in. It was then that the 88s began barking with their high metallic voices. "They are tearing my tanks to pieces," the squadron commander radioed. Only one of the thirteen survived this massacre in what was to be known as Hellfire Pass.

Meanwhile, the center column spearheaded by a whole regiment of Matildas overwhelmed the defenders of Fort Capuzzo. There had been no 88s or antitank traps in their path, and they were able to beat off two counterattacks. On the left, however, a brigade of the medium Cruiser tanks attempting to turn Rommel's right flank had blundered into his antitank trap on the Hafid Ridge. Checked, they paused, resuming the advance in the afternoon, only to clank deeper into the trap. Upon the appearance of panzer units on their own left flank, they withdrew. By nightfall, the British had lost half of their tanks. Rommel's tank strength was almost intact, and with the arrival of his other panzer regiment from Tobruk, he held the initiative.

Next day Rommel hurled the whole of his 5th Light Division at the British left flank and counterattacked Capuzzo in the center. He was repulsed at Capuzzo by British holding well-chosen and concealed positions, but the effect of his assault was to unhinge the British plan to renew their assault that day. During the early-morning darkness of the third day, Rommel moved all of his mobile forces to the British left or desert flank, hoping thereby to sweep through Halfaya Pass to cut off the enemy retreat. But when the threat became manifest, Beresford-Peirse and his commanders hastily conferred and called for a precipitate retreat. Only the stubborn fighting qualities of the British tankmen at Capuzzo saved the infantry from destruction or captivity, and on the fourth day of Operation Battleaxe the British were back where they had started thirty miles to the east.

Defeat in the Battle of Hellfire Pass stunned Winston Churchill. He had taken the double risk of weakening home defenses and running the Luftwaffe gantlet in the Mediterranean, and was bitterly disappointed by renewed failure. He did not see that Battleaxe had been too hastily launched, nor did he grasp the lesson to be learned from it: that defense always catches up with offense. Prior to Battleaxe, the offense had reigned supreme. Since September 1939, the blitzkrieg had been unstoppable. Military fashion—as appealing to the mob as fashions of the mind or manners—had veered 180 degrees from defense to offense, especially when carried out by fast-moving armor supported by air. Just to attack, it had been assumed, was to gain the victory. But Battleaxe proved that even in country as open as the desert a mobile defense can be just as effective as mobility in attack. It all depends on an understanding of the weapons available and skill in using them—in a word, on the commander. As Napoleon said, "There are no bad regiments, only bad colonels." Erwin Rommel was no bad colonel.

Unfortunately—and unjustly—the conclusion that Battleaxe formed in the prime minister's mind was that it had been Wavell's fault. Churchill did not see —probably did not want to see—the impossible task given to the chief of the Middle East Command. He ignored Wavell's record: conquest of all of Italian East Africa at a cost to Mussolini of 200,000 prisoners, including the Duke of Aosta, viceroy of Ethiopia; another 200,000 captives taken by O'Connor while he conquered Cyrenaica; planning and conducting no fewer than six major campaigns between February and June 1941, never less than three at a time and in May five at a time. In two years in the Middle East Wavell had built a base from scratch, and if 1941 had been overshadowed by defeats in Greece, Crete and Cyrenaica, only Cyrenaica was his responsibility. Later, on reflection, Churchill with his customary generosity would acknowledge that Sir Archibald Wavell had been overloaded beyond the powers of any single soldier. But on June 21, 1941, he telegraphed Wavell that he was to be relieved by Sir Claude Auchinleck, commander in chief in India.

Next day Hitler attacked Russia.

29. Rudolf Hess and Operation Barbarossa

OPERATION BARBAROSSA was Adolf Hitler's typically flamboyant code name for the invasion of Russia. Barbarossa, or Redbeard, was the sobriquet of the German medieval conqueror, Emperor Frederick I. During the last few centuries of the Middle Ages, the peasants of Germany believed that Barbarossa lay with his knights in an enchanted sleep within a cave in the Kyffhäuser Mountains in Thuringia. One day they would awake and conquer Europe for Germany. Hitler fancied himself as the reincarnation of Barbarossa, and he would unite not only Europe but also Russia under the swastika flag.

Barbarossa was anathema to Rudolf Hess, the number 2 Nazi, because it raised in his mind the specter of another two-front war. Such a prospect had haunted the deputy Führer ever since Britain declared war on Germany. At that time, Hermann Goering had said to Hess in Hitler's presence: "We must fly to England, and I'll try to explain the situation." Hitler had shrugged. "It will be of no use, but if you can, try it." Both Hitler and Goering quickly forgot the idea. Hess didn't. He brooded on it as he sank quietly out of sight in Nazi Germany. True, he was always a member of Hitler's entourage at such important ceremonial occasions as the French surrender in Compiègne. Although he was no longer a regular at Hitler's table, he still arrived infrequently, accompanied by his own vegetarian cook. But few knowledgeable Nazis still spoke of him as *Der Führer*'s alter ego. Other Nazis—Goering, Goebbels, the rising young architect Albert Speer—absorbed Hitler's attention.

After the Luftwaffe was defeated in the Battle of Britain, Rudolf Hess's fear of a two-front war returned. He remembered having met and befriended the Duke of Hamilton during the 1936 Olympics. It occurred to him that he, Rudolf Hess, solely on his own, might fly to Britain and through the offices of Hamilton negotiate a peace with this stubborn island people. Three times he attempted to fly to Britain, but each time bad weather forced him back.

Hess was discouraged until, in May 1941, he became privy to the plans for

Barbarossa. Hess did not share Hitler's belief in an easy conquest of Russia, not with Britain still undefeated and the United States manifestly preparing to come to its side. A two-front war would bring not peace and prosperity to Germany but desolation and death. On the night of May 10, his plan to fly to Britain refreshed by his terror, he put on the uniform of a Luftwaffe lieutenant colonel and drove to Augsburg, where he handed a sealed letter for Hitler to his adjutant. Then he climbed into the cockpit of an ME-110 equipped with extra fuel tanks and took off for Scotland. Twice British fighters tried to intercept him, but both times he eluded them. Flying over Lanarkshire he crawled out of the cockpit and parachuted to earth. He landed within a few miles of the Duke of Hamilton's estate. A pitchfork-wielding farmer took him into custody. Hess told him that his name was Lieutenant Colonel Alfred Horn and that he wished to see the duke. He was taken to him. The astonished Hamilton at once put in a call to London, and Hess was soon under arrest.

British officials who interviewed Hess could hardly believe that the number 2 Nazi was actually in their hands. They listened in amazed silence while the Deputy Führer explained that he had come to make peace. Of course, there were certain terms: Churchill must go, and Germany's lost colonies must be returned. Hess also repeatedly scoffed at rumors of an imminent German invasion of Russia. He warned that if Britain did not make peace, Hitler would ring the island round with a pitiless blockade and starve the British into submission. Gradually, British incredulity gave way to the conviction that this was indeed Rudolf Hess, but that he was obviously half-mad and had no authority whatsoever. Instead of being saluted as a savior as he had expected, he was unceremoniously put in prison, where he stayed until the war ended. In the meantime his adjutant, Karl Heinz Pintsch, was delivering his letter to *Der Führer.*

Pintsch was extremely apprehensive when he arrived at the Berghof with Hess's letter. He knew that Hitler, like an oriental potentate, could be most unpleasant to bearers of bad tidings; and the letter, taken in the context of Hess's nervous manner and those extra fuel tanks, could hardly be anything else. The adjutant was trembling when he was ushered into Hitler's office. Silently, he handed him the letter. Hitler opened it and began to read: "*Mein Führer,* when you receive this letter I shall be in England. You can imagine that the decision to take this step has not been easy for me, since a man of forty has other ties in life than one of twenty. . . ."

Hitler's face worked convulsively, tears streamed down his cheeks and a cry of anguish broke from his lips. Rudolf Hess, his comrade-in-arms of the List Regiment; his selfless, faithful companion in the dark early days of street fighting; his unswerving second in the Beer-Hall Putsch, codefendant on trial, and then his fellow prisoner and amanuensis in the Landsberg. This man trusted above all others, his very shadow, staunch supporter during the Night of the Long Knives, Rudolf Hess, his closest friend, perhaps his only friend, had betrayed him! Suddenly *Der Führer*'s sobbing ceased. Hess knew all about Barbarossa. Judging his enemy by himself, as all ruthless men do, Hitler feared that under torture Hess would reveal the plans for the Soviet invasion. He could not believe that the British, unlike himself, did not have a policy of torturing prisoners. At once, he put in a call to Goering and told him of Hess's flight. "He must be shot down!" he screamed. Goering immediately called his fighter chief, Adolf Galland, and ordered him to take off with an entire wing. Galland was astonished. There were only ten minutes of daylight left, he told Goering, and no reports of enemy aircraft flying in.

"Flying *in!*" Goering repeated angrily. "What do you mean by flying in? You are supposed to stop an aircraft flying *out!* The deputy Führer has gone mad and is flying to England in an Me-110. He must be brought down!"

Galland put down the phone, wondering who was mad, Hess, Goering or himself. The order was certainly lunatic. There were at that moment many Me-110s aloft. How would anyone know which one Hess was flying? As a token, and to protect himself with the Reichsmarschall, he ordered each squadron leader to send up one or two planes and did not tell them why. In his mind he was certain that Hess could never make it to Britain. If he did, the Spitfires would take care of him. That was what Galland told Goering when he reported failure to intercept the deputy Führer, and thus he was again astonished two days later to see a party communication which read:

Party member Rudolf Hess recently managed to obtain an aircraft against the Führer's strict orders forbidding him to fly on account of an illness which had been growing worse for years. On May 10 at about 6 P.M. Hess took off from Augsburg on a flight from which he has not returned. . . . A preliminary check on the papers he left behind seems to indicate that he harbored the illusion that he could bring about a peace between Germany and England by a personal intervention through certain English acquaintances.

Like Adolf Galland, many Nazis who read this wondered: so Hess was mad. Was he the only one?

Adolf Hitler's fears that Rudolf Hess might give away the secret of the Russian invasion were gradually allayed. Although the British newspapers were full of the sensational defection, there was no hint of outright betrayal. Intelligence reports on Hess's condition merely stated that he was in prison and had not been tortured. So *Der Führer* went ahead with his plans for Operation Barbarossa. On June 14, he assembled in Berlin all the commanders of his army groups, armies and panzer groups to tell them of his reasons for the invasion. He told them that because he could not defeat Britain, he must win a complete victory on the continent. With the U.S.S.R. vanquished, Germany's position would then be unassailable, no matter what Britain or even the United States might do. His arguments were unconvincing. Most—perhaps all—of his field marshals and generals felt as Heinz Guderian thought: "So long as the war in the West was still undecided, any new undertaking must result in a war on two fronts; and Adolf Hitler's Germany was even less capable of fighting such a war than had been the Germany of 1914. The assembled company listened to Hitler's speech in silence and then, since there was to be no discussion, dispersed, still in silence and with heavy hearts."

What Guderian and the others should have known by then was that Barbarossa was a personal and private vendetta. Just as he had covered Beneš of Czechoslovakia with contumely, just as he had bullied Schuschnigg or punished Poland or chastised the residents of Belgrade, Hitler was operating out of his own mindless, boundless hatred. For the Slavs, he reserved a special contempt. Thus, he did not so much seek to conquer them as to eradicate them, put an eternal end to Russia. The only Russians permitted to live would be slaves. The vast area between Poland and the Urals would be one enormous German farm worked by Slavic slaves guarded by SS troops.

Lebensraum had been forgotten. Where the grain-rich Ukraine—the breadbasket of Russia—was to have been turned into German farmland to solve both problems of overpopulation and reliance on imported food, Hitler now wanted to turn it into an enormous complex of fortified strong points. Each fortress would be garrisoned by SS troops equipped with airfields, radio stations and panzer formations able to bring the blitzkrieg instantly to any point of insurrection. Thus his heart had conquered his head. *Lebensraum,* the perfectly reasonable excuse for seizing the Ukraine, had been replaced by *Schrecklichkeit.*

Only Russian slaves would survive. But Russian customs, language, books, art, music, universities and museums, in a word, Russian culture, would vanish. Anything worth preserving would be crated and shipped back to Germany. The Soviet population would be vastly reduced either by starvation or mass execution, and its millions of Jews would go the same way as those of Poland and other occupied countries. Communist Party members or anyone who had worked for the Soviet government would join the march to the wall.

All the great cities such as Moscow, Kiev and Leningrad would be leveled. Moscow would actually disappear, drowned to death. "In a few weeks we shall be in Moscow," *Der Führer* boasted to his frightened secretaries. "There is absolutely no doubt about it. I will raze this damned city to the ground and I will make an artificial lake to provide energy for an electric power station. The name of Moscow will vanish forever."

Hitler was convinced that he could conquer the U.S.S.R. in six months, perhaps less. "We have only to kick in the door," he said, "and the whole rotten structure will come crashing down." Some influential Nazis such as Goering, his apprehensive eye always on Britain, protested about the dangers of a second front, but the fat boy, as the German generals called him, had lost much prestige in the Battle of Britain. Grand Admiral Erich Raeder also objected, insisting that Britain should first be brought to its knees by U-boat warfare and the conquering strides of Rommel's Afrika Korps on the Suez and the Persian Gulf. But his advice was rejected too.

Goering and Raeder were right, of course. *Der Führer* was changing his line of direction, one of the cardinal sins if not the supreme sin of war, and he was doing it on a strategic scale. Britain was not only unbeaten but growing stronger, and in the United States its mighty friend—not to say ally—was obviously being guided to its side by Franklin Delano Roosevelt. To turn away from Britain thus renascent and thus supplied and sustained and to attack the unknown power of the Soviet Union—in its enormous population and dreadful winters alone a formidable enemy—was a mistake of a magnitude unrivaled in the history of warfare. Such a colossal blunder would not have been possible if Hitler had been open to criticism from his experts; but because he allowed no criticism and accepted advice only from toadies such as Keitel, he made this catastrophic miscalculation. It may be added that to err so decisively is almost a consequence of decision making in a closed society. In a free-speech society, where criticism abounds—not necessarily constructively—he who commands finds himself answerable to others and must listen to them.

But Hitler's faith in his military genius had become so swollen by his string of victories that it had crowded out of his mind virtually all the practical considerations. Chief among these, the Balkan diversion joined with the poor staging weather in East Prussia and Poland, had cost him five weeks delay, bringing him that much closer to the Russian winter. For another, his very career of conquest had begun to siphon off divisions needed for occupation duties. When he had blitzed the West in 1940, his rear or eastern flank had been secured by the Nonaggression Pact with the U.S.S.R. and therefore required only seven divisions to guard it. But in 1941, as he faced toward the East, he was compelled to leave behind him in the West forty-nine divisions holding the Atlantic Wall.

Nevertheless, the force which Hitler had gathered on the borders of Russia was undoubtedly the most formidable yet assembled. One hundred and fifty-four German divisions, eighteen Finnish (Finland again opposed the U.S.S.R., but this time as Germany's ally) and fourteen Romanian, together with detachments from Italy, Spain, Czechoslovakia and Hungary stood poised on a gigantic 1,800-mile front stretching from the Baltic to the Black Sea. Supporting them were 3,000 tanks and 2,400 airplanes. No wonder Hitler drastically reduced his estimate of the length of the war from six months to eight weeks.

Unfortunately for the Wehrmacht, Barbarossa was based on the same blitzing tactics of annihilation that had brought success everywhere but in Britain. The blitz had simply been unable to leap over Britain's natural antitank obstacle— the English Channel—and equally formidable natural obstacles awaited it in Russia: a land too vast and too poorly equipped with roads to permit the lightning war to function properly. Just as inhibiting, though not as well known, was German dependence on *wheeled* vehicles for its transport of troops and supplies.

The very nation that had perfected deep penetration through the use of armor supported by aircraft had overlooked the vital nature of tank *tracks*. What was really revolutionary about the tank was not its armor or its self-propelled gun but its tracks. A tank could move overland, off the smooth paved surface of a road. By laying its own track as it moved, it obviated the necessity of following a prefabricated track, i.e., a road. *Wheeled* vehicles can only move on roads. As Liddell Hart has observed, they only increase the marching pace. But tracked tanks gave a two-dimensional movement to warfare: They could traverse either roads or unpaved earth. Guderian had missed the vital point urged by Liddell Hart and others: *All* vehicles should be tracked. But in the panzer divisions of mid-1941 fewer than 300 vehicles—mostly tanks—were tracked, while nearly 3,000 were wheeled. This had not been a difficulty when the panzers were roaring over the superb road networks of the technically sophisticated West. But in the limitless distances of the Soviet Union with its scarcity of paved roads, it would prove a monumental deterrent. In the thaws and rains of spring these sandy trails (for they were hardly more) could become immobilizing morasses of mud; in winter they were frozen sheets of ice. Tracked vehicles could either traverse them or leave them to move overland, but wheeled ones either sank into the mud or skidded off the ice into snowbanks. So seemingly small a difference—but one as vital as the difference between the British longbow and the French lance—would have an enormous effect on world history. It would not, however, become immediately apparent, because by the summer rather than the spring of 1941 the Soviet roads were relatively dry.

Thus Hitler was still supremely confident in the power of the blitzkreig. He rejected all advice to concentrate his forces and move straight for Moscow, the center of Russian gravity. He clung stubbornly to the broad advance, dreaming of a mammoth double envelopment such as had never before been executed. Still intuitive, still believing blindly in his destiny to be a conqueror greater even than Alexander or Napoleon, he calmed his nervous General Staff with the cry: "When Barbarossa begins, the world will hold its breath!"

The world—the free world at least—did hold its breath in trepidation when the invasion began early on the Sunday morning of June 22, 1941. The flood of German iron took the Soviets completely by surprise. Both Churchill and Roosevelt had warned Stalin, but the Soviet dictator preferred to trust *Der Führer* to the very end.

In Moscow, Count Friedrich von der Schulenberg, the German ambassador to the Soviet Union, arrived at the Kremlin at six o'clock in the morning. Pale and perspiring, he handed Foreign Minister V. M. Molotov a note from the German government declaring war on Soviet Russia. Molotov took it, spat upon it and tore it up.

"I know it is war," he snarled. "Your aircraft have just bombed some ten open villages. Can it really be that we deserved this?" Schulenberg did not reply. He stood in apprehensive silence while Molotov rang for his secretary. When he arrived, Molotov snapped:

"Show this gentleman out through the back door."

30. Hitler Drives for Moscow

THREE HUGE GERMAN COLUMNS smashed into Russian territory. On the left, the Northern Army Group under Wilhelm von Leeb crossed the East Prussian frontier into Soviet-occupied Lithuania. In the middle, east of Warsaw, the Central Army Group commanded by Fëdor von Bock struck at both sides of the Soviet bulge into northern Poland. On the right, Gerd von Rundstedt's Southern Army Group swept into the Soviet front from southern Poland above the Carpathians. Between Bock in the center and Rundstedt in the south was a gap of some sixty miles formed by the western end of the Pripet Marshes. This opening had been left deliberately with the intent of gaining greater concentration and speed on sturdier going.

Almost everywhere the Germans' speed and concentration met with astonishing success. Despite an abysmal lack of intelligence on the Russian people and terrain, in the face of faulty maps and in spite of nonexistent roads and railways, the Germans burst through the flimsy Soviet defenses like a stunt cyclist through a paper hoop. The advance was so fast that the foot soldiers had a hard time keeping up with it. Twenty-five-mile marches in a single day were common. All across the face of western U.S.S.R. rose dense yellow clouds of dust kicked up by retreating Soviet columns and pursuing Germans. By July 2 the Luftwaffe had effectively shot the Soviet Air Force out of the skies; 150,000 Soviet soldiers, 1,200 tanks and 600 big guns had been captured. Chief of Staff Franz Halder wrote exultantly in his diary: "It is probably not an exaggeration to say that the campaign against Russia had been won in fourteen days." Although the Russian tanks clearly outnumbered those of the German invaders, they were notably inferior. Their air force was composed mostly of archaic crates, and the Luftwaffe pilots who shot them down pitied the gallant pilots who flew them. But the Russian soldier was still the brave, tough fighter of old. Even when encircled, the Russians stood their ground and fought. Nor was it easy to surround them. Staying shy of the roads over which the German motorized columns rolled, they kept to the trackless spaces between them, taking shelter in swamps and forests. If encircled, they could generally break out, moving by night through the forests, heading eastward to join forces with units deeper inside their homeland. Still, there was no question that the German attack had taken the U.S.S.R. completely unawares.

No attempt had been made to blow the bridges over the vital Bug River to the south of Brest-Litovsk on the western frontier, and the Germans poured over it. Many Soviet formations were caught unprepared in their camps and barracks. Perhaps 2,000 Soviet airplanes were destroyed on the ground. Again and again various headquarters received the signal: "We are being fired on. What shall we

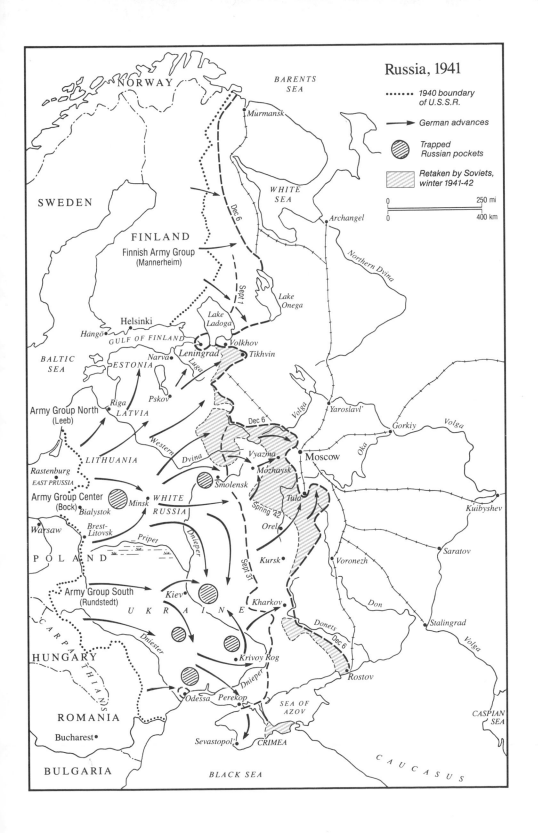

Russia, 1941

······· 1940 boundary of U.S.S.R.

→ German advances

Trapped Russian pockets

Retaken by Soviets, winter 1941-42

0 — 250 mi
0 — 400 km

NORWAY

BARENTS SEA

Murmansk

SWEDEN

WHITE SEA

Archangel

FINLAND

Finnish Army Group (Mannerheim)

Dec 6

Sept 1

Lake Onega

Northern Dvina

Helsinki

Hängö

GULF OF FINLAND

Lake Ladoga

Volkhov

Leningrad

Tikhvin

BALTIC SEA

ESTONIA

Narva

Luga

Pskov

Riga

Army Group North (Leeb)

LATVIA

Western Dvina

Dec 6

Vyazma

Volga

Yaroslavl'

Gorkiy

Volga

LITHUANIA

Rastenburg

EAST PRUSSIA

Army Group Center (Bock)

Minsk

Bialystok

WHITE RUSSIA

Smolensk

Mozhaysk

Moscow

Oka

Warsaw

Brest-Litovsk

Spring '42

Tula

Kuibyshev

Pripet

Dnieper

Sept 37

Orel

POLAND

Army Group South (Rundstedt)

Kiev

Kursk

Saratov

Voronezh

CARPATHIANS

UKRAINE

Kharkov

Don

Stalingrad

HUNGARY

Dniester

Krivoy Rog

Dnieper

Donets

Dec 6

Rostov

Volga

Odessa

Perekop

ROMANIA

Bucharest

SEA OF AZOV

CASPIAN SEA

BULGARIA

Sevastopol'

CRIMEA

BLACK SEA

CAUCASUS

do?" Back went the rebuke: "You must be insane! And why is your signal not in code?" The first orders from the Red Army high command were not issued until three hours after the invasion, and then they did not refer to a "war" but to "unprecedented aggression."

Premier Joseph Stalin simply could not believe that Hitler had betrayed him. He clung to the belief that the invasion was a wildcat action on the part of undisciplined German formations and that, if he were to respond with force, he might provoke a *real* war with Germany. Stalin during the first fateful week of the war was a stunned man. It was Molotov who took to the airwaves to denounce "the Fascist brigands covered with blood." It was Molotov who boldly predicted that Hitler would go down the way Napoleon went in 1812. Nevertheless, his bald announcement that there had been no declaration of war put his chief in a sorry light. For two years the Soviet media had been singing hymns to "the great and brilliant Stalin, thanks to whose intelligence our country has not known the horrors of war." To admit that the U.S.S.R. had without warning been pounced upon by the German predator, that it was engaged in another life-or-death struggle rivaling the Great Patriotic War against Napoleon, was to suggest that the Great Helmsman, the Grand Strategist of the Revolution, the Supreme Military Leader, had been taken down the garden path by the acting corporal from Austria.

There is no doubt that Stalin was then on the verge of a nervous breakdown. "All that the great Lenin created we have lost forever," he cried in a mood of despair. He locked himself in his study and refused to see anyone for days on end. For at least a week, Ambassador Ivan Maisky in Britain was powerless to reach him with Churchill's offers of aid. Though Stalin usually spoke frequently on the state radio, he had nothing to say to his country until July 3, a full eleven days after the outbreak of hostilities.

"Comrades, citizens, brothers and sisters, soldiers and sailors," he began in a slow and labored voice, "it is to you, my dear friends, to all of you, that I am speaking." Stalin had never spoken in such tones before, and would never do so again. He paused frequently. No call to arms could have been duller. Compared to the magnificent defiance and stirring rhythms of Winston Churchill's speeches, it was as water is to wine. Understandably enough, Stalin began by telling deliberate lies of how the German invader had been crushed; to have done otherwise, to have admitted that Hitler's legions were smashing into the U.S.S.R. at the rate of twenty-five to thirty miles a day might have had disastrous consequences. Stalin also attempted to justify his Nonaggression Pact by saying that it had given him almost two years to prepare for the present war. Then, falling into his familiar liturgical style, stressing and repeating the words "single" and "must," he called for his famous "scorched earth" policy. Not a single railway engine or coach must fall to the enemy; not a single pound of grain or a single gallon of gasoline; all cattle and corn that could not be carried away must be given to the state to transport to the rear; whatever valuables that could not be moved—presumably houses, barns, schools, any sort of shelter—must be destroyed. Detachments of guerrillas and saboteurs were to be formed to harry the Germans and wreck their communications. "They must be hounded and annihilated at every step, and all their measures frustrated." He referred to the aid offered the U.S.S.R. by Churchill and Roosevelt, and called for union with the once-despised democracies in the common fight for "freedom" against the enslaving hordes of fascism.

Immediately after this speech, Stalin became Koba again—searching for scapegoats to whom he could transfer blame. General after general was arrested and executed until it was feared that the bloody purges of 1937 were being renewed. This time, however, Stalin stopped short of emasculating his own forces. Nevertheless, the fear of his accusing finger was again great enough for General I. E. Petrov to remark, upon being appointed to a higher command: "So now they are going to shoot me, *too!*"

Having shot the generals whom he had publicly blamed for the failure to halt Hitler, Stalin turned energetically to the reorganization of the Red Army. Three major commands were created: the Northwestern, covering the Baltic and Leningrad; the Southwestern, guarding the Ukraine and Stalingrad; and the Western, protecting Moscow. The Western, the most important, went to Marshal Semën Timoshenko, and the others to Stalin's old Civil War cronies: the Northwestern to Marshal Klimint Voroshilov and the Southwestern to Marshal Semën Budënny. Each commander had a political commissar assigned to him: Nikolai Bulganin to Timoshenko, Andrei Zhdanov to Voroshilov and Nikita Khrushchev to Budënny. Political commissars were a standard feature of the Red Army, being assigned to every unit from top command down to company level. Stalin also personally assumed the office of defense commissar, replacing Timoshenko, and he chose Marshal Georgi Zhukov to be his troubleshooter at the front.

Now that he had recovered from his shock and been encouraged by the support of Churchill and Roosevelt, Stalin became a dedicated war lord. He spent almost all of his time in the operations room at the Supreme Headquarters set up in his Kremlin suite. Although the rest of the Soviet government was eventually moved to the comparative safety of Kuibyshev 500 miles to the east, Stalin remained in the Kremlin, completely absorbed in direction of the war. His General Staff was required to report to him three times during every twenty-four hours: by telephone between ten and eleven every morning and four and five in the afternoon and in person at nine or ten at night. The personal session could last until the small hours of the morning. The generals met in Stalin's huge main office overlooking the Moscow River. They worked at a long map table under portraits of Suvorov and Kutuzov, the two most famous soldiers in Russian history. That these two czarist heroes had been raised to the Communist altar beside icons of Marx and Lenin was suggestive of Stalin's shrewd appeal to Russian patriotism, to a people embattled rather than a proletariat at bay. It was not Communism versus Fascism—a battle cry about as inspiring as "Long live two-plus-two!"—but Holy Russia against the hordes of Germany, just as it had been Holy Russia against the Mongols, the Teutonic Knights, the Swedes and the Grande Armée of Napoleon. Every one of Stalin's orders of the day was to end with the cry: "Death to the German invader!"

Those orders were carefully formulated during each night session. Sometimes civilian experts were present at these briefings, along with members of the Politburo such as Molotov or Lavrenti Beria, chief of OGPU, Stalin's secret service, which had become more insidious and more dreaded than the Okhrana of the czars. Stalin paced up and down the office, puffing on his pipe, listening carefully to the advice of his experts. He had become a rapid learner and had clamped an extremely tight control over direction of the war. From time to time he went to his desk to knock out his pipe and fill the bowl with tobacco torn from two cigarettes. At last the text of the orders would be read aloud, corrected by Stalin down to the smallest detail, and then despatched to the various commands.

In the beginning Stalin had been extremely suspicious of Churchill. He had not forgotten Churchill's anti-Bolshevik zeal during the civil war, and had suspected him of secretly preparing to make a separate peace with Germany so that the two dictatorships might devour each other. But when Sir Stafford Cripps arrived from London, bringing with him a British military mission and a personal letter from the prime minister offering unlimited assistance, his attitude softened. An agreement was worked out between the two powers, and eventually a Soviet military mission flew to the United States with an enormous shopping list.

Stalin was not immediately able to reply to Churchill's letter. The U.S.S.R., it seemed, was collapsing. Smolensk had fallen and the Germans were less than 200 miles away. Well over 600,000 prisoners had been taken, among them Yakov (Yasha) Dzhugashvili, Stalin's only child by his first wife. He had joined the Red Army as a lieutenant of artillery and been immediately sent to the front. He told his astonished captors that he had no special privileges as Stalin's son, but that his father had said good-bye to him by telephone before he left. Stalin never wrote to his son or mentioned him while he was in prison (where he died), presumably because he had called upon all Russians not to surrender and regarded Yasha's capture as an embarrassment.

The generalissimo was also enraged by wholesale desertions from the Soviet ranks, especially among the Ukrainians, who welcomed the Germans until Hitler's wholesale deportation of hundreds of thousands of them to Germany as slave laborers convinced them that he was no liberator.

When Stalin did write to Churchill—on July 18—he made his first of many requests for a second front that he would repeat with increasingly bitter monotony over the years. He wanted it either in northern France or in Norway against the Finns, who had joined Hitler in order to recover the land lost to the Soviet Union in 1940.

"A frontier in Northern France," he wrote, "could not only divert Hitler's forces from the East, but would at the same time make it impossible for Hitler to invade Great Britain. The establishment of the front just mentioned would be popular with the British Army, as well as the whole population of southern England."

Churchill was outraged by this request:

Hitherto they had watched with stony composure the destruction of the front in France in 1940, and our vain efforts in 1941 to create a front in the Balkans. They had given important economic aid to Nazi Germany and had helped them in many minor ways. Now, having been deceived and taken by surprise, they were themselves under the flaming German sword. Their first impulse and lasting policy was to demand all possible succor from Great Britain and her Empire, the possible partition of which between Stalin and Hitler had for the last eight months beguiled Soviet minds. . . . They did not hesitate to appeal in urgent and strident terms to harassed and struggling Britain to send them the munitions of which her armies were so short. They urged the United States to divert to them the largest quantities of the supplies on which we were counting, and, above all, even in the summer of 1941 they clamoured for British landings in Europe, regardless of the risks, or cost, to establish a Second Front.

Churchill's ire was also aroused by the spectacle of the British communists executing another disgusting about-face. First they had denounced the "capitalist and imperialist war," until the Nonaggression Pact tucked them into bed with the "fascist murderers of the people," and now they were fiercely antifascist again, screaming, "Second Front, Now!" and scrawling the slogan all over Britain. Similar somersaults were turned in the United States. Churchill was aware of the ordeal through which the Russian people were passing, and he was sincerely eager to come to their side. But he knew that the generalissimo's ignorance of the complications of seaborne landings was even greater than *Der Führer*'s. To land and support a great army on a hostile coast is like moving a great city to battle across the unsteady surface of the sea. It requires that a superiority on the water and in the air be maintained at the invasion point, and it also demands vast armadas of landing craft—especially those carrying tanks, able to crawl up onto open beaches to unload their human cargoes or send the iron ones clanking inland. Such small vessels, sprung from Churchill's fertile brain, were already in development in Britain and the United States, but they were not yet anywhere near production. Indeed, the United States Marine Corps, eventually the world's master of the amphibious whip, was at that moment conducting landing maneuvers with the wooden Higgins boat, a clumsy craft that had to be swung out from ships on davits, into which combat-loaded Marines, climbing down swaying cargo nets, were compelled to jump and from which they would vault, weapons in hand, when they grounded themselves on the beach.

In his reply to Stalin, Churchill pointed out that without fighter cover it was not possible to land troops in Norway in the perpetual daylight prevailing at this time of year. Enough fighter protection from the air was simply not available. Nor was it feasible to go into a France now guarded by forty-nine German divisions with its coastal defenses being made stronger daily by Germany's resourceful Dr. Fritz Todt, minister of armaments and munitions. Moreover, Britain's resources were already being severely strained by the maritime Battle of the Atlantic and by those reverses in North Africa being regularly inflicted by Rommel. All that could be done for some time, Churchill wrote, was to send supplies on a large scale. To Stalin, with the Germans only 200 miles from Moscow, this was small comfort.

Within three weeks, Bock's Army Group Center with fifty-one divisions had come that close to the Soviet capital, having penetrated 450 miles beyond Białystok. Leeb's Army Group North was slicing through the Baltic states and advancing on Leningrad while Rundstedt's Army Group South was surging through the Ukraine toward its capital at Kiev.

By July 8, more than half of the 164 Soviet divisions identified thus far had been destroyed and half a million prisoners captured. Another 300,000 Soviets surrendered after Smolensk fell. Yet the very speed of the advance on such a broad front had spread the German forces thin, exposing them to counterattack on the flanks. This the Soviets began to do with great skill, sheltering in that sixty-mile gap in the Pripet Marshes and building reserves there until they were strong enough to strike at Rundstedt and slow his drive on Kiev. Moreover, the Germans, who had expected to encounter only 200 divisions, were astounded to identify no fewer than 360 by August 17. Finally, alarmed to discover that the Red Army was concentrating between Smolensk and Moscow, the General Staff urged Hitler to slow his flank advances, build up his center and go smashing away for Moscow. Thus they could break the back of the Red Army and seize the capital city before the Soviets could concentrate much further.

Der Führer refused. His eyes were fixed north and south on Leningrad and Stalingrad, the twin "holy cities of Communism." Their fall, he insisted, would cause a Soviet collapse. In the south also were the industry, oil and granaries he desired. Thus, Hitler allowed psychological and economic considerations to obscure war's true purpose: destruction of the enemy army.

By then, to be closer to the front, *Der Führer* had moved his headquarters to a forest in East Prussia near the town of Rastenburg, once a citadel of the Teutonic Knights. It was called the Wolf's Lair, a fitting name for this makeshift settlement of huts and bunkers set down in a gloomy damp forest. In summer, clouds of buzzing, biting mosquitoes made the nights hideous; in winter, raw gray mists swirled ghostlike through the pines. Summer or winter, it seemed that everyone had a cold. Hitler worked in a hut above a concrete underground bunker standing in the center of a complex of defense posts, checkpoints, barbed-wire entanglements and minefields. His personal safety was obviously still an obsession with him. In the Wolf's Lair Hitler often switched on the radio to listen to Goebbels' gloating announcement of the latest victory. As always, Hitler personally selected the musical fanfare preceding such bulletins. For the U.S.S.R. he had selected a few bars from Liszt's *Les Préludes.* "You'll hear that often in the future," he had boasted to Albert Speer. But the Liszt fanfare did not stir the German home front as had the other musical vaunts. It was not like the old days with their bloodless conquests, or even slightly bloody ones, in Poland, France, Norway and the Low Countries. There were too many casualties. Trains from the East were already arriving in Germany loaded with pine boxes.

Toward the end of August the German spearheads had begun to slow down. Resistance had become much stiffer. The Soviets had begun to cover their front with minefields. It was easily done, inasmuch as only the Germans kept to the roads. No one had anticipated the appallingly difficult terrain that the panzers were encountering. Tank movement was slowed as never before, held up by vast virgin forests, swamps, terrible roads and bridges too weak to support a tank. In the center the great motor highway leading to Moscow was the only thoroughfare that a Westerner would call a "road." A highway it was not. Moreover, the disastrous defect of wheeled transport was already apparent in the panzer units. Such vehicles could not abandon the miserable sandy trails and tracks to move overland, and when it rained for an hour or more the sand turned to mud. Columns as long as a hundred miles were stuck in the mud, unable to move until the sun came out and dried the trail. Passage through the swamps was even more difficult.

Dr. Heinrich Haape was a medical officer in an infantry battalion of Bock's Army Group Center moving on Moscow. The Germans were pursuing retreating Soviets through a swamp. A log bridge about six yards wide had been built through it. Haape's comrades were unable to move over it in daylight because it was raked by enemy machine-gun fire. So they crossed it at night. The logs rolled and sank beneath their feet; marsh gases gurgled to either side of them; they could smell the discharging methane. March discipline was in effect and no one spoke. Suddenly, coming faintly through the eerie silence, Haape heard ghostly cries. Soviet soldiers were trapped in the marsh, slowly sinking in its bottomless depths. Haape heard the screams of a Soviet soldier only a few yards from the bridge. "Surely we can help him," he whispered to his orderly. "How?" the orderly replied. "I don't like leaving any poor devil to a fate like that. But anybody who leaves these logs will get sucked in himself." Haape said nothing, quietly dropping out of the column, searching for a loose log. He found one. With the help of another soldier he wrenched it free and threw it toward the sinking Russian. Haape stood still, listening. The cries for help ceased. Haape could hear the man struggling toward the log. But then he shrieked in terror again. There was a loud, whooshing, gurgling sound. Haape felt his flesh crawl. Then all was quiet.

German reserves were now streaming toward the front in trainloads. Benno Zeiser was a rifleman on one of them. There were forty soldiers to a car. They went rattling across Poland with the sliding doors wide open. With other lowly privates, Zeiser stood in the back row craning his neck to view the countryside flashing past the heads of rows of NCOs seated at the open doors with legs dangling over the side. Although the men had been issued ample rations, sleeping and washing were problems. At night they slept fitfully on jolting steel floors. The air inside the closed wagon was close and foul with body odors. Sometimes the train stopped, and then the soldiers would scurry about—never too far from the train for fear of being left behind and tried as a deserter—in search of water to wash in. There were no latrines at the stops and the men merely opened their flies to "pump ship," in the German phrase, or squatted in lines with lowered trousers. If the train whistle blew, there were shrieks of dismay from men caught with their pants down. They raced for the moving freight cars tugging up their trousers on the run like men in a three-legged race.

In Poland, Zeiser was surprised to see women and children come crowding down to the railroad tracks begging for bread. Zeiser and his comrades threw it to them. As the train began to slow, the throngs grew larger. It stopped with a lurch and men unable to relieve themselves for hours jumped eagerly to the ground, yanking down their trousers and presenting the astounded Poles with rows of naked, functioning backsides. Shocked by this aberrant apparition, the screaming women herded their children to safety.

The train crossed into the U.S.S.R. at Przemyśl and Zeiser saw bombed-out cities for the first time. Chimneys stood like gaunt sentries among piles of rubble. Many buildings were sliced in two and Zeiser from the open side could see into bedrooms and offices like the layers in half a cake. In the U.S.S.R., the train finally stopped for good, and the soldiers alighted in full marching gear. Soon they were striding for the front. Ahead of him Zeiser saw what seemed an enormous brown serpent undulating toward him. From it issued a steady, subdued hum, like a beehive. Russian prisoners, six deep! Zeiser marveled how few German soldiers were needed to guard them. He couldn't even see the end of the column. Then he clutched at his nose, fighting against a terrible choking stench. It sickened him. He gasped for air but dared not remove his hand. It was as though he had scented the quintessential filth. *But these are not animals,* he thought, *these are men.* Quickly he and his comrades moved off the road to allow this foul column to pass. The prisoners were like scarecrows, bearded, emaciated, stumbling, wailing, muttering to themselves. Their gray-brown uniforms hung on them in folds. Occasionally a man broke ranks and was driven back into step by a blow of a rifle butt between the shoulder blades. A prisoner with blood-stained bandages around his head paused to beg bread from the horrified civilians beside the road. A whiplash across his shoulders changed his mind. Another, a giant of a man, stepped out of ranks to urinate. Beaten back into step, he could not contain himself and drenched the man in front of him. He didn't turn his head.

Starving wild dogs ran panting beside the column in search of food. Their ribs were visible against their taut skin like the strings of a harp. There was no food for the dogs within this flood of misery but the animals were soon food for the men. They begged Zeiser's comrades to shoot the dogs, making bang-bang gestures with their thumb-and-forefinger. The soldiers obliged. Howling like beasts, the Soviet prisoners fell on the stricken creatures, tearing them apart with their hands before they were even quite dead. The guards did not interfere, seeming to enjoy the sport. They watched while the prisoners lighted fires to roast stick-skewered pieces of dog flesh. Without fat it became quickly charred and stank horribly, but the prisoners wolfed it down. When they passed through a village, they swarmed eagerly over the garbage heap. Any scrap was edible, no matter how rotten. Once Benno Zeiser saw one of them roasting dried pig's dung.

The Soviets were probably even less gentle with their prisoners. Ivan Krylov, a high-ranking Soviet staff officer, was at the headquarters of a General Krassovsky when a prisoner was brought in. He was a slender man. His horn-rimmed spectacles and his fine, manicured hands suggested that he was a man of some cultivation. He had tried to escape, but a blow from a rifle butt dissuaded him. His head was swathed in bandages and blood trickled from his lips as he spoke. He had lost his front teeth and had difficulty talking. Commandant Fechner, who spoke German, interrogated him for General Krassovsky.

"Your name, rank and unit," Krassovsky barked, and Fechner quickly translated.

"Heinrich Fechner, company sergeant major, 147th Infantry Division."

Krassovsky grinned and looked at Commandant Fechner. "Fechner, eh? No relation of yours, I suppose, Comrade Fechner?"

The commandant smiled uneasily. Ivan Krylov, watching the prisoner intently, thought that he saw his eyelids flicker as though he understood Russian.

"What other units are there at Kriukov? Who commands them? What equipment have they?"

"I don't know."

Krassovsky's face hardened. "You mean you don't want to say."

"No. I really don't know."

"Do you speak Russian?"

"No."

"Do you understand Russian?"

"No."

"Good," Krassovsky snapped with a leer. "Tell him, Comrade Fechner, that we shall send him to Kharkov escorted by Cossacks."

The prisoner turned white. He didn't wait for Krassovsky's words to be translated. "Shoot me right away!" he pleaded in Russian.

"Oh, so that loosens your tongue, eh? You do speak Russian, after all. And almost without an accent. Where were you born?"

"Łódź."

"So you're not German at all. You're Polish."

"I was born in 1908. Łódź was in Russian hands, then."

"So much the worse for you. You're Russian, and you're fighting against us. You'll be hanged."

"Hang me, then, but don't turn me over to the Cossacks."

"Lieutenant Petrov, call Cossack Lieutenant Kromov."

The prisoner swayed. "Excellency," he pleaded, "I'll talk. I'll answer your questions."

He did, and very quickly. When the German attack struck at dawn, the Soviets were waiting for it.

Benito Mussolini was fast becoming disenchanted with Adolf Hitler. Embarrassed by his own defeats, the obviously aging Duce (his hair was now snow white) was bitterly envious of *Der Führer*'s victory string. On June 10, 1941, he said to his son-in-law, Count Galeazzo Ciano: "I've had my fill of Hitler. These conferences called by a ringing of a bell are not to my liking; the bell is rung when people call for their servants. And besides, what kind of conferences are these? For five hours I am forced to listen to a monologue which is quite fruitless and boring." On July 6, he said: "I now seriously ask whether an English victory would not be more desirable than a German victory." Nevertheless, when Hitler did ring the bell again in mid-August, Mussolini eagerly accepted his invitation to visit the Eastern front. The two dictators—rather, the two corporals—were flown in one of Hitler's enormous Kondor planes from the Wolf's Lair in Rastenburg toward the Ukraine.

Flying over Romania, the Italian corporal seized this marvelous opportunity to lecture the German corporal. He spoke movingly of the Emperor Trajan who had Romanized Romania. He recalled those astonishing Roman engineers who had thrown bridges over the southern reaches of the Danube, where even the Germans with modern equipment were having trouble. Perceiving that he was scoring points, the Italian corporal next requested the privilege of taking over the controls of the plane. With a triumphant gesture he settled into the pilot's seat, hummed a few bars from "Giovinezza," and landed the plane safely on the ground.

A huge motorcade formed behind the open car carrying the two corporals. The Italian corporal, his romantic spirit aroused by the sight of the countryside—the slim birches bending in the wind, the golden grain bowing to the breeze, the beautiful blond Ukrainian girls bringing flowers and sunflower seeds—began to wax eloquent on the subject of Russian literature. When he came to Tolstoy, the German corporal at last found his voice. *War and Peace,* he cried, was nothing but a boring recital of communist propaganda. Tolstoy was a czarist toady. He wished that they were both alive so that they could see what *he* would do with Russia. The unstoppable monologue was begun. Now it was the Italian corporal who glowered, glancing at his watch. Where had he erred?

Suddenly the entourage rounded a bend. A storm of cheers drowned out the German corporal. *Bersaglieri!* Again the face of the Italian corporal glowed. His old outfit, his own troops! He had sent them to the U.S.S.R. solely for propaganda purposes, but here they were, carrying the day for him—revving up their roaring motorcycles as they streaked past. Standing in the stirrups to let the wind stiffen the feathers flying from their burnished steel helmets, they raised their fists in the

Fascist salute. *"Duce!"* they bellowed. *"Duce! Duce! Duce!"* The Italian corporal arose with clenched fist to return the salute. He sat down, feeling cheerful again.

But again he had erred. He had fallen silent just long enough for the German corporal to renew his monologue, picking up the pieces where the Bersaglieri had broken them. The U.S.S.R. would fall before the onset of winter. In the spring he would resume his conquering march. He would be in the Urals, entering Persia, camping on the shores of the Caspian Sea. A gleam came into the Italian corporal's eye. This was the path Alexander had trod.

"E allora?" he burst out, interrupting. *"Piangeremo come Allessandro Magno per la luna?"*

The German corporal's bulging eyes clouded in disapproval of such rudeness. He glanced inquiringly at the Italian corporal's interpreter, Dr. Eugene Dollman, an Austrian. Dr. Dollman shifted uneasily, glancing at *Il Duce.* Falteringly, he translated:

"What then? Shall we weep for the moon like Alexander the Great?"

The German corporal stared at the Italian corporal as though he were mad, for he was now with great glee quoting gobbets of Giovanni Pascoli's famous poem on Alexander. Dr. Dollman was hard pressed to keep up with him. At last he finished telling *Der Führer* how Alexander, reaching the borders of the conquerable world, lifted his face to the moon and wept because he could not conquer her as well.

The Italian corporal nodded cheerfully. A correct translation. He smiled at his companion. It had become such a nice trip: Trajan . . . the Danubian bridges . . . flying the plane . . . the Bersaglieri . . . two busted monologues . . . And now he had shown himself to be a man of culture. The German corporal glared. Unaware that he was like a king conferring an accolade, he gave the Italian corporal a long, cold look.

31. The Birth of the Atom Bomb

ALTHOUGH PRESIDENT ROOSEVELT in October 1939 had shown himself deeply interested in the development of an atomic bomb, during the twenty-two months elapsing between then and July 1941, little progress had been made. At commercial and university laboratories all over America—and in Britain and France as well—experiments were being privately conducted on the elements U.235 and U.238 to see if either or both could produce the chain reaction necessary for such a bomb.

One of the difficulties contributing to this agonizingly slow and unorganized exploration was that at the time American nuclear physicists were largely unaccustomed to using their science to serve the military. The professors were especially reluctant. Traditional American suspicion of a large standing army as a threat to freedom had been compressed on campus into a distillate of distrust of the military itself, and sometimes outright hostility. Idealist scientists—particularly the younger ones—were horrified at the thought of contributing to the creation of such a monstrously devastating instrument of death and destruction. Those who worked during the thirties toward splitting the atom had been sincerely and selflessly dedicated to discovering an enormous source of energy for the good of mankind. When the uranium atom was successfully split in January 1939—releasing energy 3 million times greater than that which is liberated in the burning of coal—jubilation among these scientists was universal. But then it was realized that the split uranium atom also released energy 20 million times greater than the explosive force of TNT. Now there were doubts and reservations. Sincere men willing and eager to serve God and/or mankind had no wish to serve Mars.

Moreover, another revolutionary discovery had been made simultaneously with the discovery of fission, rendering it possible not only to tap a tremendous new source of power but also to devise the most devastating explosive the world had ever known. This discovery was that when the uranium atom splits, some of the neutrons in its nucleus are freed. Inasmuch as uranium could only be split by neutrons, this suggested the awesome possibility that once the first uranium atom was split, it would free other neutrons which would split other uranium atoms, which in turn would liberate more neutrons. Here was a chemical chain reaction similar to what happens when an ordinary fire is lighted by a match.

Here was a dilemma indeed for those troubled men of science fearful of perverting their calling to the destruction rather than the benefit of civilization. They did not realize as clearly as those refugee scientists from the Nazi and Fascist tyrannies—men such as Einstein, Teller, Fermi, Szilard and others—that the battle lines between freedom and slavery had already been drawn in the world. The refugees knew about the Kaiser Wilhelm Institute in Berlin with its hundreds of scientists commanded to construct an atomic bomb. They realized that it was no longer possible to be neutral, for to be neutral was actually to be negative. Such a crisis of conscience is not familiar to men accustomed to the imperatives of materialist research. Even when the gathering war clouds burst over Europe, many still hesitated. Their position was best expressed by Volney Wilson, a brilliant young scientist in the University of Chicago's Department of Physics. In 1940, Wilson was asked to calculate the probability of a chain reaction in ordinary uranium. He reported that it could probably be made to work, but then asked to be "taken off this job" because such force "is going to be too destructive." He added: "I don't want to have anything to do with it."

Such an attitude—sincere, honest and agonizing—was not uncommon in the early days of 1939. It helps to explain, along with the difficulty and expense of private research itself, the slowness of progress. After the war began, after the fall of one free country after another was succeeded by Hitler's satanic slaughters, more and more American scientists realized that between freedom and slavery there could be no middle ground.

In March 1940, experiments at the Universities of Minnesota and Columbia and at General Electric Company laboratories confirmed the existence in U.238 of what was called "a friendly cannibal." This so-called cannibal could swallow so many fast neutrons that there would not be enough left to produce a chain reaction. This meant that U.238 could not be used to make an atomic bomb, and since U.238 was the only type of uranium readily available in large amounts to everyone, that meant that no one could make the A-bomb. Not even the Nazis. So the cannibal in U.238 seemed friendly indeed. Civilization seemed to be spared the mushroom cloud.

But this eleventh-hour reprieve was actually only a respite. It was soon found that U.235 could be split by fast as well as slow neutrons. If U.235 could be separated in large quantities from U.238, it could be used to make an atomic bomb by bringing about an uncontrolled chain reaction with fast neutrons; or as a source of power 2 million times more powerful than gasoline through a controlled chain reaction with slow neutrons.

But where to get U.235 in sizable quantities? Scientists at the University of Minnesota and General Electric did produce samples of "pure" U.235—the first to exist on earth—and they "weighed" exactly one billionth and two billionths of a gram at Minnesota and one hundredth of a millionth of a gram at General Electric. They were of great use, however, in tests at Columbia confirming that U.235 could be split only by slow neutrons and U.238 by fast neutrons. It was soon shown that the friendly cannibal in U.238 made a chain reaction impossible; and to build a bomb using slow neutrons would require one of such enormous dimensions that no existing airplane could carry it. Later it was found that U.235 could be split by fast neutrons, if there were enough of them, to sustain a chain reaction.

If there were enough of them. That was the rub. To discover whether or not a fast-neutron chain reaction would be self-sustaining would require vast amounts of U.235. To obtain it might take millions of years of laboriously produced minute samples such as were made at Minnesota and General Electric, or else be produced in quantity by the construction of enormous plants costing billions of dollars, plants that might or might not do the job. Such a risk was not worth the cost.

Nevertheless, this apparent dead end did not discourage the physicists and chemists involved. Experiments continued all over America. At Columbia, work was begun on constructing an "exponential pile" seeking valuable information on which to base the building of more sophisticated atomic piles in which chain reactions might be produced. At the University of California under the supervision of Dr. Glenn Seaborg a group of young physicists and chemists, many in their twenties, began bombarding U.238 with neutrons of intermediate speed. They knew exactly what they were after: a new element unknown in nature—Number

94—for which Drs. Philip Abelson and Edwin McMillan had been searching. Seaborg obtained from these two scientists permission to continue their work, and with the cooperation of McMillan this new element was discovered and named plutonium.

Here was the breakthrough! Tests on this new child of uranium proved that it had the same fissionable properties as U.235, and that it was of at least equal and probably even greater efficiency. Almost as important, it could be produced in quantities large enough to make an atomic bomb.

A new age had been born, far more revolutionary than the ages preceding it. But all those great eras that had made revolutionary changes in the style of living—the Age of Bronze, the Iron Age, the Ages of Steam and Electricity—had been born as it were by accident, or at least by barely perceptible stages. The Atomic Age had been born by design. For the first time mankind—rather, all the great scientific minds of the Western world—had consciously set out to bend the forces of nature to its will, and had actually been present at the birth of the new age it had produced. For the first time also mankind had knowingly pulled out of the bottle a genie with a potential for good or evil on a cosmic scale. For its effect on World War II this discovery was summarized in a report from Professor Ernest Lawrence to the National Academy of Sciences. It included three significant paragraphs:

1. Uranium 238 would be available for energy production, thus increasing about one hundred-fold the total atomic energy obtainable from a given quantity of uranium.

2. Using Element 94 one may envisage preparation of chain reaction units for power purposes weighing perhaps a hundred pounds instead of a hundred tons, as probably would be necessary for units using natural uranium.

3. If large elements of Element 94 were available, it is likely that a chain reaction with fast neutrons could be produced. In such a reaction the energy would be released at an explosive rate which might be described as a "super bomb."

This report greatly accelerated the Atomic Bomb Project. On December 6, 1941, Dr. James Conant, president of Harvard University, with a sense of urgency in his voice, informed a small gathering of leading scientists that the Roosevelt administration now believed that "the possibility of obtaining atomic bombs for use in the present war was great enough to justify an 'all-out' effort."

At the time, of course, the date of December 6, 1941, was not significant. However, there had been disturbing reports of a vast increase in the production of heavy water in Nazi-occupied Norway, the Desert Fox had inflicted new reverses on the British Army in North Africa, German spearheads had driven to within sight of the onion spires of Moscow and there seemed no possibility of heading off war with Japan.

It was possible that the atomic bomb might not be made soon enough.

32. Operation Crusader: Duel in the Desert

GENERAL SIR CLAUDE AUCHINLECK was an imposing man, big and broad-shouldered, with light brown hair and fierce blue eyes set in a fighting face, a man of quiet confidence who gave the impression of great strength, both moral and physical. The Auk, as his men called him, was also an able and bold soldier, always willing to follow a novel or original course. In Norway in June 1940, he had attacked and seized Narvik just to convince the Germans that the Allies were there to stay. By this ruse not a single man was lost during the subsequent evacuation, even though the Germans controlled the air.

Auchinleck, however, like every senior officer in the British Army, knew nothing of armor. A second drawback was that he was a veteran of the Indian Army. Although the British Army and the Indian Army served together in India, mutual pride placed them almost worlds apart, like two different clubs pursuing a joint objective. British Army officers had a tendency to look down on those of the Indian Army as "frontier soldiers." The "Indians" resented this, believing that India had the space and the men in which to train soldiers, while Britain had neither. Whatever the merits of either position, the fact was that as an Indian Auchinleck knew very few of the officers of the British service and therefore was somewhat handicapped in selecting commanders. Under a prime minister as domineering as Winston Churchill, diplomacy would have served him better, and his stubborn refusal to launch an early offensive against Rommel got him in trouble at the start. Churchill wanted a "big victory"—and soon. He had already bullied his chief of staff, Sir John Dill, into relegating the undermanned Far East to priority number 3 after the Middle East, and he sought to do the same with Auchinleck by summoning him to Britain for consultation. In London, Auchinleck would not budge. Operation Crusader, as the new offensive was called, could not be launched before November 1. General Alan Cunningham, *his* choice, would command it, not General Wilson, Churchill's choice. Thus, in a clash of strong personalities, with Churchill already dissatisfied and Auchinleck already perhaps too sensitive to interference, was Crusader begun.

Lt. Gen. Sir Alan Cunningham seemed an excellent choice to command the new British Eighth Army forming in the desert. He came to North Africa much better known than Richard O'Connor had been. Within eight weeks he had destroyed the Italian Empire in East Africa, crushing and capturing the Duke of Aosta, viceroy of Ethiopia. His speed and dash—at one point he led his army in a 740-mile march—delighted the British public, and his conquests received far more publicity than O'Connor's.

Like O'Connor, Cunningham was a small man, but extremely handsome and charming. He spoke easily and well, although he seemed to have a slightly choleric temper. Unlike O'Connor, he found vast forces being assembled for his command, supported by a strong air force and the Mediterranean Fleet led by his own older brother, the redoubtable seadog, Sir Andrew. But like O'Connor again, when he arrived in the desert in August, he knew nothing about desert warfare or armor, and he had only two months in which to familiarize himself with such tactics and equipment whereas the Little Terrier had had six. Cunningham's ignorance was so deep that he did not know how to use a radiotelephone. Peccadillo that this may seem, it actually reflects a large defect. A sailor cannot sail his ship without a complete knowledge of its nomenclature. A soldier bursting into a munitions dump shouting for ammunition for "the guns" will get nothing if he cannot specify the caliber he needs. Similarly, a general in charge of a large specialized force such as an army of armor must know in intimate detail not only the nomenclature but also the operation of its equipment, as well as—and this is vital—its special language of command. Without it, his orders may be issued without assurance. This, of course, was not Cunningham's fault but rather the sin of the peacetime British Army. Still, it was most embarrassing for the commander of the Eighth Army to give orders to his teachers, and to have to learn it all within two months placed an almost intolerable strain on what turned out to be his frail health. Moreover, his seasoned armor commanders had returned to Britain, and the veteran tank officer who was to command his armored corps had been killed with some of his staff in an airplane crash. So Cunningham's armor commanders knew no more than he did.

Nevertheless, Eighth Army was now the rich man of the desert. To this force —which might better have been called Eighth "Colonial" Army, with its Australian, New Zealand, Indian and South African contingents—was flowing the produce of American and British factories. It now had four complete armored brigades, with a fifth shipped into Tobruk by sea. In the main, these units were equipped with the new Crusader tanks and the American Stuarts, called Honeys because of their superior speed and maneuverability. There were also four motorized infantry divisions, with a fifth in Tobruk, where the British 70th Division had relieved the Australian 9th.

Rommel, meanwhile, received very few reinforcements and no additional tank units. Barbarossa was soaking up all the Wehrmacht's available blood and iron. He had to pretend that a light division was a panzer division and to improvise an unmotorized infantry division from some extra artillery and infantry battalions. He still had three unreliable Italian divisions, plus three new small ones with obsolete equipment and a shortage of motor transport. These could only be used in static situations, and were actually a restraint on Rommel's freedom of movement. In the air Rommel possessed 120 German aircraft and 200 Italian, compared to 700 for Cunningham. In armor he was even more inferior: 174 German gun-armed tanks and 146 obsolete Italian of little value, against 710 gun-armed British tanks of which 200 were heavies. Thus Cunningham had a superiority of about 2 to 1 over Rommel as a whole and 4 to 1 over his German units. Rommel's chief asset was that two thirds of his antitank guns were the new long-barreled 50-mm cannon with about 70 percent better penetration than his old 37s. Thus his defense was no longer as dependent on his handful of 88s as it had been in Battleaxe.

Because some of the British forces did not arrive in the desert until mid-October, Auchinleck was compelled to postpone D-Day to November 15 to give them time to train. This irritated Churchill, who cabled: "It is impossible to explain to Parliament and the nation how it is our Middle East armies have had to stand for four and a half months without engaging the enemy." A further delay of three days pushed the timetable to November 18.

Long before then General Cunningham had completed his plan for Crusader. It was based on seeking and winning a decisive tank battle. Rommel's frontier defenses ran from Bardia through Sollum to Sîdi Omar and thence south to Gabr Saleh. The British armor under Gen. Willoughby Norrie was to attempt to get around the German right at Gabr Saleh. The infantry was to pin down the German left until the tank battle had been won. Then, in conjunction with the armor, it would defeat Rommel's infantry in the frontier defenses and drive for Tobruk. Cunningham's plan was odd in that he, the attacker, proposed to surrender the initiative to Rommel, the defender. At Gabr Saleh, the armor was to halt to await German reaction. General Norrie objected to this feature and for exactly that reason. He said Gabr Saleh had no military significance and there was no reason to believe that Rommel would attack there. Instead, he urged Cunningham to drive straight for Tobruk with the armor and thus force the Desert Fox to fight him. Cunningham replied that Rommel's reaction to his approach march would reveal what he planned to do. Norrie, however, was unconvinced, repeating his cogent argument with a force that merely unsettled but did not dissuade his chief.

So Crusader was saddled with an imperfect plan in which even its author now had little faith. On the night before the battle, Cunningham received a stirring message from Churchill: "For the first time British and Empire troops will meet the German with an ample supply of equipment in modern weapons of all kinds. The battle will affect the whole course of the war. Now is the time to strike the hardest blow yet struck for final victory, home and freedom. The Desert Army may add a page to history which will rank with Blenheim and Waterloo. The eyes of all nations are upon you. All our hearts are with you. May God uphold the right!"

Cunningham had not suspected that so much depended upon Crusader, and the realization imposed an additional strain on his already overwrought nerves. He was worried about Rommel. Would he attack at Gabr Saleh, or would he attack the infantry? Cunningham had always feared that the Desert Fox might try to enter the gap between the British armor on the left and its infantry on the right, and fall on the foot troops. To prevent this, he had posted one of his four armored brigades as an infantry flank guard, much to the dismay of Norrie.

While Cunningham lay on his cot in his command camper, rehearsing his fears and the chances for disaster, a splendid thunderstorm broke over the desert. Cunningham could see flashes of lightning and hear the rolling thunder. Pelting rain played against the steel sides and roof of his camper like handfuls of buckshot. Tomorrow, Cunningham thought morosely, the desert will be a quagmire. He tried to sleep, but with the eve-of-battle symptoms familiar to many officers and men in the Eighth Army—burning eyes, dry throat and queasy stomach—it was not quite possible.

The British movement next day was unopposed. Only the soggy desert slowed it, and after the sun dried the rain-dimpled sand, it grew speedier. By evening, General Cunningham's spearheads had taken possession of Gabr Saleh and the surrounding desert. Only a force of German armored cars had been observed during the advance. Cunningham was puzzled. Where was Rommel? The answer was that the Desert Fox was too preoccupied in preparing an assault on Tobruk to be concerned with what had been reported as a mere "reconnaissance in force." This had come from the screen of armored cars he placed between himself at Tobruk and the enemy. Next day the British wheeled right and drove toward the airfield on top of the escarpment at Sîdi Rezegh twelve miles southeast of Tobruk. This was the key to the British-held fortress. Meanwhile, two of Norrie's armored brigades had gotten into deep trouble, east and west.

In the east, the 4th Armored Brigade was chasing a German scouting unit when it was struck in the rear and badly mauled. In the west, the 22nd Armored Brigade filled with inexperienced riflemen, fancying itself the Light Brigade at Balaclava, made a gallant but foolish charge into heavily fortified Italian positions and lost forty of its 160 tanks. On the following day—the 20th—the 4th Armored Brigade now at Gabr Saleh was punished a second time by a German panzer division. But then, on the morning of the 21st, there were again no Germans on the Gabr Saleh front. Where was Rommel this time? He was moving on the British advanced force at the Sîdi Rezegh airfield. He had ordered his armored commander, Gen. Ludwig Cruewell, to take both panzer divisions and destroy the British. There now ensued a battle that was the essence of armored warfare in the desert.

It was fought with great bravery and dash by the soldiers of both sides, even the Italians, beneath clouds of dust or choking black smoke rising from thousands of blazing guns or burning vehicles, in sandstorms and rainstorms, soldier against soldier and tank against tank. Confusion was its common denominator. Conflicting reports, orders and counterorders, frequent communications breakdowns, all conspired to send battle groups roaring off in the wrong direction, either into an empty desert in pursuit of a nonexistent enemy or into surprising collision with an enemy unit in a place where it was not supposed to be. A misunderstood order or the sudden cry of "Tanks!" could cause a desert "flap," one of those precipitate, careening flights of hundreds of motor vehicles, some of them driven by naked soldiers caught in the blissful act of "having a bath." Fortunes changed hour-by-hour, so dramatically that at one point the British press could interpret General Cunningham's reports as indicative of a great victory, only to realize a few hours later that the Eighth Army confronted disaster. Even today it is not possible to follow the battle without the help of hourly situation maps. But it was at and around Sîdi Rezegh that most of the action took place.

Here, on the fourth day, the Germans cleverly pushed their wheeled 50-mm antitank guns ahead of their tanks and around the British flanks. Many of them were deployed in hollows. British tankers struck by these excellent weapons fancied that they had been hit by the only thing visible—a tank—never dreaming that the enemy was using his artillery in combination with his tanks. The compartmentalized British military mind simply could not conceive of artillery being used that way, and thus the havoc wrought by the concealed 50s had a redoubled psychological effect. The 7th Armored Brigade was down to twenty-eight tanks before the arrival of the 22nd Armored Brigade, which was in its turn chewed to pieces. Next day the battered 4th was again scourged. Thus, in detail, one after another, rather than en masse, the British fed their armor into the jaws of the Afrika Korps. As Rommel was to say later: "What difference does it make if you have two tanks to my one, when you spread them out and let me smash them in detail? You presented me with three brigades in succession." Crusader had become hideously unhinged, disjointed, even, and General Cunningham had lost control.

It was the 4th Armored Brigade that suffered most horribly on that dreadful fifth day. Major Robert Crisp, a famous South African cricket player, was in command of a troop moving up to Sîdi Rezegh. He was in his command tank, a Honey. Alongside him in another Honey was his friend, Tom Eynon. They drove to the west, toward the enemy. Suddenly they came to the edge of a long escarpment, halting with an abrupt lurch. Over the air Crisp heard Eynon exclaim: "Jesus Christ, Bob! What the hell is all this?"

Below the tracks of their tanks and straight ahead of them was an airfield, its outer boundaries marked by the litter of wrecked German and Italian fighter planes, its center a smoking heap of twisted and burning tanks. To Crisp's left the desert was empty, but to his right inside the depression he was astonished to see men at work digging slit trenches, planting mines, setting up antitank and field guns; even, incredibly, cooking a meal. Farther distant across the depression atop another escarpment were other figures, not quite so active. Crisp was puzzled. Who was who? The burning tanks, he was sure, were British Crusaders. But whose troops were these? He put in a call to his battalion headquarters, explaining the situation. Back came the reply: "Treat anything you see as enemy."

Both Crisp and Eynon were astounded. They were certain the troops below them were friendly; those farther away were enemy. In fact, Crisp was going to machine-gun them. "Browning, traverse right," he called to his gunner. "One, two thousand. Enemy infantry—" Crisp paused. Someone was banging on the side of the tank and shouting. Crisp looked down and saw a tall lean brigadier standing up in a little open car. He was not aware of it then, but he was looking at Jock Campbell, a legendary tank commander famous for his dash and daring.

"There's a Jerry attack coming in from the west," Campbell yelled. "We need you. Follow me."

Crisp drew breath sharply. "Sir, if you wait ten minutes, the whole brigade will be up."

"If you're there in ten minutes, you'll be in time. If you're there in fifteen, you'll be too late." Campbell settled down beside his fair-haired driver. "Follow me!"

Crisp went bouncing down the escarpment followed by Eynon. Crisp contacted his CO and explained what was happening. Then he was down among the grimy, weary Tommies, many of whom glanced up with a grin. They gave thumbs-up signs, cheering the little car leading the two tanks—its driver's blond head gleaming like the white plume of Navarre, the tall general holding aloft his blue-and-white pennant standing stiff in the wind. Soon they were on the smooth going of the airfield, in among the knocked-out Crusaders. When Crisp saw a few wrecked Germans, he felt better. Then they were on the edge of the airfield, and the deadly red-and-yellow flowers were blossoming around them . . . the explosions were in their ears, the tanks swaying in the concussions . . . the flying earth and shrieking shrapnel rattling against their sides. Ahead the little car vanished and reappeared among the deadly fountains and the smoke. Its flag never wavered. Suddenly, it stopped. Crisp's driver hit the brakes. Campbell jumped out and waved to the westward. Crisp stared ahead in horror. Perhaps 1,200 yards to his front he could make out the shapes of sixty or seventy iron monsters moving steadily toward him. Their cannon mouths flashed flame. Between them moved their infantry and Crisp caught the *brrrrt* of machine-gun fire. With another explanatory wave, Campbell jumped back into the little car, made an about-face, and doubled back the way he came, vanishing among the wrecked tanks. Crisp guessed that he was off for more reinforcements.

Now he looked around for Tom Eynon. He was coming over the airfield at top speed. He was almost abreast of Crisp, about 100 yards away, when suddenly he spun completely around, slewing up sand like a speedboat sloughing up water, and went racing back to vanish, like Campbell, among the derelict tanks. Crisp was incredulous. He knew his friend would not abandon him. Something must have happened.

It had. Eynon had seen the little car racing backward and was just about to line up alongside Crisp when his Honey swung completely around and sped off in the other direction. Eynon thought his driver was mad, until his operator yanked on his leg and yelled up to him that the driver had been hit. Then the tank stopped. Everyone but the driver piled out. Eynon tried to pull him out through the hatch, grasping him under the armpits to heave him free. To his horror, Eynon heard the Honey's gears engage. It lurched forward, knocking him backward and rolling over him. Before he lost consciousness, Eynon guessed what had happened: A German shell had killed the driver, and in his final convulsion he had reversed course until his foot clamped down on the clutch, staying there until Eynon tried to pull him out, when it slipped off and reengaged the gears. When Eynon came to in a German hospital, he realized that one of his legs had been snapped off at the hip.

Alone, now, Crisp stared at the steadily approaching Germans. "Cannon," he called to the gunner. "Twelve hundred. You see all those things coming toward you. They're Jerry tanks. Pick out one and stay on it till you knock it off. Get cracking!" Immediately the first shot burst out. Crisp watched its tracer following a long shallow curve. It struck one of the dark silhouettes but went bouncing into the air. Too far away, Crisp thought in disgust. Still, he kept the gun firing, if only to be doing something, knowing full well that he was easily within the German range. He wondered why he was not hammered by clouds of armor-piercing shells, suddenly realizing that his very immobility was probably puzzling the enemy. Behind him were the silhouettes of those wrecked Crusaders. Blending in among them, he realized, was the silhouette of his own Honey. Probably the Germans could not believe that a solitary tank was holding them up. They must have thought the derelict hulks were operable.

But then he changed his mind. The red fountains were playing about him again. He could smell and taste the acrid cordite. Creeping toward him with flaming guns were the Mark IIIs and Mark IVs. The Honey was taking hits, lurching. "I've got one, sir!" the gunner cried exultantly. Crisp grinned to see the black smoke curling up from a Mark III, watching in satisfaction while the enemy crew bailed out. He felt entitled to a bit of swagger and radioed his CO: "Hello JAGO, JAGO one calling. Seventy enemy tanks approaching western edge of airfield. Am engaging at thousand yards." Crisp's eyes came back to the line of tanks. They were only 800 yards away . . . Crisp looked behind him, searching the desert for signs of rescuing tanks charging forward with fluttering pennants. But then he saw his own artillery exploding among the Germans. "Gunner, cease fire!" he cried. "Driver, advance, turn about—go like hell!"

Back across the airfield sped the Honey . . . twenty miles an hour . . . thirty . . . Major Crisp exulted in his tank's speed, the fastest in the desert. But shells still burst around them. For concealment, the driver swerved left and right, raising his own screen of dust or dodging into the smoke of the shellbursts. Crisp radioed his CO, suggesting that he line up his tanks on the eastern edge of the escarpment, facing west toward the pursuing Germans. "I don't know my arse from my elbow, let alone east from west," the CO replied. But Crisp heard him give the order to move out. Approaching the escarpment, Crisp saw a huge, swirling cloud of dust. Within it he picked out the silhouette of British tanks. Then his Honey began to sputter. He smelled smoke. Behind him fumes were pouring out of the engine louvers. The Honey halted and Crisp cried: "Bail out!" Grabbing what personal possessions they could, Crisp and his crew jumped to the ground. They raced back among the shellbursts to the edge of the escarpment, wearily climbing up the slope.

Crisp saw his friend Harry Maegraith and asked why the battalion hadn't come to his aid. "What the hell happened to everybody?"

"You never saw such a foul-up! We got to the edge of the escarpment all right, and then nobody knew what to do or where to go. We were told to advance on the airfield and line up on you facing west. Then Fifth Tanks got mixed up with us, and between us we kicked up such a hell of a lot of dust that we couldn't see ten yards in any direction. We just went round and round with each other in circles. I don't think any of our tanks went into action."

Next, Crisp saw his CO, a study in exasperation. He told him that out of the regiment's eighty tanks, only four were serviceable. The rest were either lost or knocked out. Then Brig. Alex Gatehouse, the brigade commander, arrived, clambering out of his Honey in familiar black overalls. Gatehouse calmly announced that his headquarters had been captured by the Germans and that he wanted tanks to follow him to get it back. Undismayed to hear that only four were available, he drove off to his other regiment to muster a dozen and lead them into a wild donnybrook. But he didn't get his headquarters back.

Major Robert Crisp watched Gatehouse's Honey disappear into the dust, unhappily aware of his own pleasure in being "knocked out." He had had enough of gallant brigadiers for one day. "Jesus, sir," he exclaimed to his CO, "that brigadier will get a bloody V.C. for today's performance, but I wish to hell he had waited ten minutes."

Jock Campbell did get a Victoria Cross, the highest British decoration. His driver, in the class-conscious British Army's way of sharing out the glory, got nothing. So did Robert Crisp.

Two days later Erwin Rommel aimed a daring counterstroke at the British Eighth Army. He collected his armor and sent it careening eastward into his enemy's rear areas. He expected to disrupt communications to the extent that General Cunningham would call off the battle and retire behind the frontier wire. Then, in his own good time, Rommel would deal with Tobruk. There was also the possibility that his armor could go roaring right into Egypt in a daring raid that would at least unstring the nerves of Middle East Command's headquarters. Here was a bold plan, typical of Rommel, concocted in the midst of a wild battle.

What Rommel was intending to strike, of course, was the mind of Sir Alan Cunningham. He sensed Cunningham's confusion and indecision and was preparing to deliver the blow that would finally unnerve him. Rommel's instincts were correct. Sir Alan Cunningham was a spent man, indeed. He was on the verge of collapse, sustained only by a dogged courage and devotion to duty. But when he awoke on November 23 to read reports that out of Eighth Army's 450 cruiser tanks at least 300 had already been lost, he became intensely alive to the possibility that if Rommel were to attack again that day, he might soon have no cruisers at all. Beyond his own immediate danger lay the threat to Egypt and the Middle East. Convinced in his own mind that he should break off the battle, Cunningham sent an "urgent request" to Auchinleck to fly up at once to discuss the situation.

Auchinleck arrived, to the intense relief of Cunningham's generals who were doing all in their power to prevent a retreat. The Auk sat listening silently while Cunningham recited what to another less ardent chief would have sounded like a litany of defeat. With the intuition of a great general, Auchinleck sensed that Rommel was in as much trouble as Cunningham, perhaps worse with Tobruk still unvanquished behind him. He ordered the battle to continue and gave Cunningham the written command: "You will continue to attack the enemy relentlessly using all your resources even to the last tank." It was a great gamble, and Auchinleck knew that if it failed, Egypt might be lost. But by it he saved the Crusader operation. Auchinleck had also seen that Cunningham was at the end of his powers. He was determined to relieve him, and on the morning of November 26, Maj. Gen. Neil Ritchie, formerly deputy chief of staff of the Middle East Command, arrived at Eighth Army headquarters to replace Cunningham. Exhausted, Sir Alan went into a hospital where it was discovered that he had been suffering from severe overstrain.

The Auk had been right on both counts: on Cunningham's health and Rommel's strength. On the night that he ordered the battle to continue, the Desert Fox was down to 100 tanks, and his Afrika Korps was blundering about in as much confusion as the Eighth Army. The desert south of Sîdi Rezegh was like a foretaste of hell: swirling clouds of dust and smoke illumined pinkish by the flickering light of hundreds of burning tanks, trucks and guns. But it was then that Rommel delivered his counterstroke.

It was now, of course, not an indecisive mind that guided the forces opposing Rommel but one just as resolute as his own. Auchinleck had quietly assured Eighth Army's commanders: "He is making a desperate effort, but he will not get very far. That column of tanks simply cannot get supplies. I am sure of this." He was right again, but Rommel's spearheads still stormed eastward on a direct course for Eighth Army's headquarters. What was derisively dubbed "The Mersa Matrûh Sweepstakes" had already started. The supply troops and vehicles of Norrie's armor were in one vast flap, streaming eastward ahead of Rommel's on-charging armor, and some of them did not stop until they did reach Matrûh.

As usual, the Desert Fox was at the head of his forty-mile-long column, driving along in his Mammoth, the command vehicle he had taken from O'Connor. In the afternoon he visited what he mistakenly believed to be a captured British field hospital. He was surprised to see British officers still walking about and as many British wounded as there were Germans. The Germans, seeing him, gaped and sat up in bed at attention. The medical officer conducting him around seemed to think Rommel was a Polish general. "I think we'd better get out of this," Rommel whispered to his aide, turning to stride nonchalantly toward the Mammoth, giving a final salute to his captured soldiers before roaring off.

Just before dark, he passed through a gap in the frontier wire. He was in Egypt! As darkness fell, he decided to return to Libya but could not find the gap in the wire marking the opening in a minefield. With Generals Bayerlein and Cruewell he slept that night in the middle of an Indian division, slipping away at first light.

During that day Rommel thought he had a chance to capture Cunningham and his staff. Still east of the wire he joined the commander of one of his panzer divisions. Through his glasses he saw a group of British staff officers beside a staff car studying maps. "General Cunningham!" he exclaimed. "Go and take him!" Too impatient to await the arrival of tanks, Rommel shouted: "Never mind, I'll go and take them myself!" Pushing his goggles up over his cap brim, standing erect in a staff car, he roared off with three other unarmored cars and about twenty motorcycles. The British saw the cloud of dust moving toward them, jumped into their car and sped off.

Rommel also came close to capturing those supplies that Auchinleck was so confident he could not obtain. Cunningham flying over the battlefield was upset to see a tank battle going on beneath him. The Germans were on direct course of a vital supply base full of water needed by four divisions. Its capture would be a calamity. Fortunately, the panzers stopped fifteen miles short of the base. They also just missed two enormous dumps—each six miles square—stuffed with vitals: beans, bullets and black oil. If they had captured and supplied themselves from them, they might have gone on into Egypt. But they did not see them because they were so cleverly camouflaged and because the RAF kept German scout planes away from them. Gradually, however, Rommel's panzers ran out of steam. They spent more time foraging for fuel than in exploiting their breakthrough. More important, the British remained firm. During the night of November 26–27 they captured Sîdi Rezegh. Tobruk was relieved by British infantry, and Rommel decided that the time had come to hurry home. He had failed to recover the initiative. If he had succeeded, he would have brought off a master stroke. But even the general who contained him—Sir Claude Auchinleck—later admitted that his sudden eruption "came as a rude shock," and he was immensely relieved to learn that the Desert Fox was back on the defensive.

Maj. Gen. Neil Ritchie was the epitome of the between-wars British soldier. He was one of those men born into the gentry or the aristocracy who chose the military as one of the two callings of their caste—the other was politics—and because they had the private means to compensate for its low pay. To such officers the civilian world, the outside, was a repugnant place filled with cunning, brash, pushy, ruthless, selfish and ambitious men, while the military, "the inside," was an eminently satisfying sanctuary in which one encountered other high-principled men embued with the same qualities of modesty, manners, morality, chivalry, courage and a sense of duty. Occasionally one might meet a dedicated professional with a first-class mind such as Wavell, but on the whole professionalism on the German model was not to be encouraged. In such a corps an oil-stained, self-assertive wretch such as Guderian or Rommel would have been cut dead. A professional pose was thought to be bad form among men trained to studied casualness or bred on Ruff's and well-catered point-to-points.

Neil Ritchie was all this, and more: He was rich, he was very tall, very big and very handsome. He was easily one of the most commanding presences in the British Army, thorough, authoritative and possessed of a perhaps heavy sense of humor. Even though he seemed to have a high opinion of himself, it was just as difficult not to like him as it was not to suspect that he might be a little slow. In command of a huge army during a vital battle, he might resemble a mudder on a fast track. Auchinleck had chosen him because there was no time to fly a new army commander out from London, and because the generals commanding the Eighth Army's armor and infantry, though senior to Ritchie, were too valuable where they were. To remove them might upset the command structure. Auchinleck was aware that Ritchie was a staff officer whose last field command had been a battalion in France in World War I. Four years ago he had been but a major. For these reasons, Auchinleck had regarded his appointment as temporary, until the battle could be fought and won and a new chief be appointed. In the meantime, he, Auchinleck, would compensate for Ritchie's inexperience.

Fortunately for Ritchie and the Eighth Army, his defects were not immediately apparent, if only because Rommel's raid into Egypt had returned the initiative to the British. They had relieved Tobruk and captured Sîdi Rezegh. However, Rommel quickly expelled them from this burnt-over battleground and isolated Tobruk again, but at great cost to the Afrika Korps. It was worn out. Rommel's officers were recommending a general retreat from Cyrenaica. With characteristic obstinacy, Rommel refused. He planned still another dash to the frontier wire—until on December 4 he received word that he could not expect his armor to be replenished until the end of the month, when the Luftwaffe would be based in Sicily to cover Axis supply ships in the Mediterranean. The British, he knew, were steadily replenishing their armor, and the daily tank-to-tank battles in the area around El Adem were forcing him to fight a losing war of attrition.

On the twenty-first day of Crusader, Maj. Robert Crisp was leading his troops on a scouting movement to locate the 22nd Armored Brigade. Finding it, he prepared to rejoin his own outfit, only to be warned that the desert to the northeast which he had to cross was "unfriendly." Crisp moved out warily, watching the eastern sky turn red with the advent of day. Out of the mists emerged two shapes. Crisp halted his tanks and studied them through his binoculars. They flew no identifying pennants. Their turrets were clamped down and no antennae were in sight. Crisp thought they were Mark IIIs. He edged closer. They remained still, their backs to Crisp. He charged diagonally toward them at thirty miles an hour, believing that if they were Germans he would have the advantages of speed and angle. Still they did not move. Crisp returned to his tanks and gave them the thumbs-up signal to fire. The Honeys' guns blazed. Crisp saw four shots from his own Honey go into one of the other tanks. The crew bailed out, while the other tank roared off into the desert, turning and swinging its turret toward

Crisp as it did. It came racing toward Crisp and he thought: *That's fine. Now we'll get the bastard!* Then he saw that the tank was a Crusader and that there was an officer sitting on it waving a red flag.

In horror, Crisp realized what he had done. *He had knocked out one of his own tanks.* "Cease fire!" he called in anguish, scrambling down to the desert floor to run toward the stricken tank. "Don't let anybody be dead," he prayed aloud. "Don't let anybody be dead." A young officer screamed at him: "You bloody fool! You've killed my gunner!" Crisp glanced away in dread and despair. Soldiers had lowered a rope into the turret. *Maybe the gunner wasn't dead,* he thought hopefully. *Maybe he was only wounded.* The body that came out of the turret was limp. A youngster . . . red-headed . . . fair . . . freckled . . . with a lolling head and lifeless blue eyes looking straight into Crisp's own. If it had been his own son, Crisp's grief could not have been more excruciating, more soul-destroying.

Fortunately, he was called to his Honey to talk to headquarters. He climbed wearily into the turret. "Listen, Bob," the voice said, "I know what's happened there. It's not the first time and it won't be the last. You can't worry about that, now. You've got a job to do. There's a Jerry column crossing our front. You're to rejoin immediately. Get on with it." Crisp spoke dully into his microphone, "Driver, advance." The gears shifted, the motor roared and Robert Crisp drove away without another look.

General Auchinleck had arrived at General Ritchie's headquarters to "hold his hand," as he said later. Believing that Rommel had shot his bolt, he advised Ritchie to give him no rest. But the Desert Fox had a few shots left in his locker. He sent out two columns to rescue his frontier garrisons, one along the coast road and the other along the Trigh Capuzzo. Both were defeated. On December 4 he struck again at Tobruk. Backed by 88-mm guns brought right up to the attacking zone, the Germans very nearly cracked that hard nut. If Rommel had renewed the attack next day, he would have had a good chance of success. But it was on that night that he received word he would get no more heavy hardware for a month. Aware that the Eighth Army was about to attack him again, he began to withdraw. On the night of the 7th he was in full retreat. Except for a three-week epilogue, Crusader had ended in a British victory, won by their bulldog tenacity in battle and optimism in adversity. It certainly had not been achieved by skillful generalship in the field, where Erwin Rommel had carried off the palm, although Sir Claude Auchinleck's quiet confidence and intuitive perception of Rommel's difficulties may be said to have turned the tide.

During the ensuing three weeks Rommel fell back behind rear guards skillfully deployed to keep the pursuing British at bay. It was actually a fighting retreat, the most difficult of military maneuvers. A gallant Italian defense of El Gubi helped him to retire to Gazala, where he offered battle in a bluff that did not deceive his enemy. When the British tried to get around him, Rommel in a series of unruffled delaying actions fell all the way back to El Agheila. Here, aided by a surprise reinforcement that lifted his tank strength to seventy, within an extremely strong natural defensive position, he turned again to offer battle in earnest. This time, Auchinleck wisely advised Ritchie to let the Desert Fox go to ground, and in mid-January 1942, Crusader came to an end.

The great sand sea was silent again. The glittering night sky was breathtaking, and soldiers sprawled on their vehicle hoods for warmth could hear once more the small sounds of tiny creatures scuttling among the rocks. By day, tank retrievers looking like huge ants bearing off their prey crawled across the desert towing knocked-out vehicles to the centers for refitting and repair; for it is one of the great windfalls of victory to claim the enemy's damaged guns and gear as well as your own and to make them new again. Gradually the overcrowded hospitals began to discharge a stream of ambulatory wounded, and overworked doctors and nurses and other medical personnel at last could sink into that blissful sleep "that knits up the ravelled sleeve of care."

Major Robert Crisp lay in a hospital in Tobruk. He had been engaged in the pursuit of the retreating Axis forces when he came under fire. To his dismay he saw Harry Maegraith's tank take a direct hit. The turret flew open and Maegraith and his crew bailed out. They ran toward Crisp's tank and he directed the Honey toward them. He leaned down from his turret to call to Maegraith. "Okay, Harry?" Maegraith nodded, grinning. "Okay, Bob." Crisp spoke to his driver, "Advance. Hard left." CRAAAACK! There was an enormous clang beside his head and Crisp sank back into the tank unconscious. Maegraith was killed. Crisp's tank crew brought him back to headquarters. It was believed that the shrapnel inside his skull would finish him. At the hospital a surgeon, marveling that Crisp was still alive, removed a piece of rusty shrapnel about the size of a boy's marble. Then he was evacuated to Alexandria where the wound became infected, and it appeared, once more, that he was a goner. His temperature soared. With his body baking in an oven and his head in an inexorably turning red-hot vise, he was wheeled into the operating room. A nurse holding a notebook and pencil approached him. Just before the anesthesia blotted out his mind, she asked him, in a voice of deep compassion, for the name and address of his next of kin.

33. The Siege of Leningrad Begins

WHEN HITLER INVADED RUSSIA on June 22, 1941, the swiftest of his three columns was Army Group North on the left under Marshal Wilhelm Ritter von Leeb. Leeb's group swept through the Baltic States of Lithuania, Latvia and Estonia bound for Leningrad. After he took Leningrad, Leeb was scheduled to join the Finnish army north of the city and then wheel south to strike to the rear of Moscow while Rundstedt's Army Group Center attacked the Soviet capital's front. Leningrad was expected to fall quickly, and Hitler had scheduled a victory parade there for some time in July. But the city of Peter the Great proved to be surprisingly tough.

Peter had founded his capital city on May 16, 1703, locating it on a dismal marsh fronting the Gulf of Finland. Petrograd or St. Petersburg as it was then called—more affectionately "Piter" by the proud people who lived there—was deliberately intended by Peter and Catherine the Great, and all those Czar Alexanders and Nicholases who succeeded them, to possess an architectural grandeur and industrial power, a science and an art, rivaling the great cities of the west. Indeed, the westward-looking Peter called his imperial capital Russia's "window on the West," and its aristocracy spoke French not Russian. St. Petersburg disdained Moscow as backward and isolationist, while the southern city distrusted and hated St. Petersburg as the home of all that was innovative, compassionate—and dangerous.

St. Petersburg was dangerous indeed, the center of revolutionary activity in Russia. Its roll call of martyrs to the cause of democracy was as long as the litany of its giants of music and literature, of science and industrial innovation. In St. Petersburg was born the Decembrist movement which in 1825 sought to convert the czar to parliamentary government. It failed, and many of the noble young officers who embraced it were executed or exiled. Nevertheless, the roster of the martyrs to change grew longer, and among those shot was Alexander Ulyanov, the older brother of Nikolai Lenin.* Czarism also died, and it gasped its last in the uprising of the tormented people of St. Petersburg. It was replaced by an even more hideous form of tyranny, brought to a triumphant St. Petersburg by Lenin in April of 1917. He had arrived at the Finland Station from Switzerland in a special armored train provided by the German General Staff in the hope that he would lead Russia out of World War I. He did, but he also directed from St. Petersburg the Bolshevik Revolution, which culminated in formation of the Union of Soviet Socialist Republics and the rise of international communism. It was not long before the long-suffering Russian people realized that they had exchanged the whip of the czar for the goad of the commissar. Lenin also gave his own name to the City of Peter, and in March 1918 offered Leningrad the ultimate insult: fearing the approach of the German Army, he "temporarily" shifted the seat of Soviet government to Moscow, from which it never returned.

Adolf Hitler coveted Leningrad even more than Moscow. As the leader of Nazism's sacred crusade against Communism, he wished to crush the birthplace of that detestable creed; as "the greatest German of all time" he also desired to destroy the Russian capital, which Peter the Great had used as a base to extend Russian power over the Baltic Sea, that very body of water which for centuries the Germans had regarded as *their* sea, dominated by the military prowess of the Teutonic Knights or the commercial cunning of the cities of the Hanseatic

*Many Bolsheviks had assumed names. Lenin's real name was Vladimir Ilyich Ulyanov.

League. Hitler's plan for Leningrad was also more diabolical than his scheme to efface Moscow beneath a hydroelectric lake: He would simply starve the population to death. If the city surrendered, the Germans would not feed its people; if it held out, it would be encircled in a ring of steel cut off from all supplies and starved into submission.

Besides his psychological motives, *Der Führer* had good military cause to covet Leningrad. Once it fell, Marshal von Leeb's Army Group North could join the Finnish army in the Karelian Isthmus to the north and swoop south to turn Moscow from the rear. This would isolate the Soviet capital from the eastern republics to which it had been frantically transferring its heavy industry and cut her off from the flow of American supplies arriving at Murmansk and Archangel in the north. In the summer of 1941, the plan appeared foolproof. Leeb's forces had crashed easily through the Baltic States into the U.S.S.R., pausing only momentarily to regroup opposite Leningrad's outer defenses: the line of the Luga River running about seventy-five miles southwest of Leningrad. Both he and *Der Führer* were confident that the Luga Line would not only be easily pierced but that Leningrad itself was far from adequately defended.

Command in Leningrad was shared by Commissar Andrei Zhdanov and Marshal Klimint Voroshilov, although ultimate authority, according to communist custom, always was vested in the political commissar. Both Zhdanov and Voroshilov were the cronies and creatures of Joseph Stalin. Zhdanov was generally regarded as a brilliant organizer. Voroshilov was simply an old Bolshevik, a veteran of the Civil War and the conflict with Finland, but a mediocre general at best. Both men had shared the generalissimo's conviction that Hitler would not invade the Soviet Union in spite of intelligence clearly suggesting that the Wehrmacht was massing on the Baltic borders. Zhdanov was so confident that there would be no war that on July 19 he left Leningrad by train for his favorite holiday resort: Sochi on the Caucasian Black Sea coast. Here Stalin also had a villa, and it had been Zhdanov's custom to spend two or three weeks with him there. To both Zhdanov and Voroshilov the defenses of Leningrad appeared to be secure. The city was much safer in 1941 than it had been in 1939, when the frontier with Finland was only twenty miles to the north. Finnish forts commanded the entrance to the Gulf of Finland and ships of the Soviet Baltic Fleet entered those waters bound for their great base at Kronstadt at their peril.

By 1941, however, Stalin's incorporation of the Baltic states of Estonia, Latvia and Lithuania into the Soviet Union had pushed the frontiers 400 miles farther away and had given the Baltic Fleet bases 200 and 300 miles closer to Germany. Finland, after the winter war, had been stripped of her forts on the gulf island of Hangö and pushed above the Karelian Isthmus north of Leningrad. The city of Lenin, it seemed to Stalin and Zhdanov, was now a mighty fortress, a secure military bastion. No one noticed that Leningrad, like the unfortunate British base of Singapore, had all her guns sited seaward or toward Karelia and the Finnish frontier. It occurred to no one that if the Baltic Command in the west collapsed, Leningrad would be open to attack from the south and southwest, where there was deployed not one Soviet division, not a single regiment nor a military formation of any kind. After the first day of the invasion, with the Baltic Command already beginning to crack, the people of Leningrad panicked.

The moment Molotov announced that the Soviet Union was at war, women shoppers flocked to the grocery stores to buy everything in sight: butter, canned goods, lard, sugar, groats, flour, sausage, matches, salt. Like all other Soviets, Leningrad people had no faith in the government's ability to keep them fed and supplied. They had been through too many shortages and famines, starting with the Revolution. Savings banks were all but stormed. Unruly depositors shouted angrily that they wanted their money immediately. They took it in packets and promptly traded it for gold, jewelry, watches, rugs and samovars, knowing full well that paper money would soon become worthless and the value of this hard wealth would skyrocket. In midafternoon the banks closed, and when they re-opened two days later, there was a limit of withdrawals of 200 rubles per person per month. By the end of the day also the city was out of vodka. This too would in great part be hoarded.

The panic soon subsided, however, and the people of Leningrad, like the rest of the Soviet Union, rose up in patriotic anger. Troops paraded down the splendid Nevsky Prospekt singing:

> Rise up, mighty land,
> Rise up for the deadly battle. . . .
> Let noble anger
> Boil like a wave.
> We march to the People's War
> The Holy War.

In the first week of war an amazing 212,000 men, almost all of them untrained youths, signed up for the People's Volunteers. Some Leningraders saw in the approaching Germans liberation from the hated Stalinist despotism, but others were sophisticated enough to realize that the Nazis were capable of matching any terror. NKVD secret police were everywhere, hunting suspected spies or pro-German saboteurs. A strict curfew and a system of control points denied entry into the city to anyone but bona fide residents, and organizations of worker's vigilantes to guard railroad stations and sniff out criminals—together with a decree of death by shooting for any violation—produced a 60 percent reduction of crime within a few weeks. Robberies were off 95.6 percent and drunkenness 78 percent.

On June 27 Andrei Zhdanov returned to Leningrad. In his younger days Zhdanov had been a handsome man, with jet-black hair and beautiful dark eyes. But the long working hours of the men who served the nocturnal Stalin, his chain-smoking habit, the Kremlin's sumptuous ceremonial banquets and his practice of drinking endless cups of tea in the Russian manner—steaming hot with the sugar cubes inside his mouth—had combined to make him at forty-five on the eve of war a plump man whose sunken eyes looked out of a haggard face and whose ample belly bulged to either side of the belted blouse he constantly wore.

Zhdanov had been Stalin's right-hand man. He rose to power during the dreadful purges of the thirties, during which he served Stalin with great zeal. Shortly before the war, however, Zhdanov ran afoul of a conspiratorial troika composed of Molotov, Georgi Malenkov and Lavrenti Beria, the much-feared police chief. Malenkov seems to have been the leader. Like Zhdanov a plump man, he was one of Stalin's youngest secretaries. During the first days of the war when Stalin was in shock and unable to conduct the affairs of government, Malenkov with Molotov and Beria succeeded in placing the blame for the Soviet Union's disastrous foreign policy on the head of Zhdanov, even though Molotov was the foreign minister and his two fellow conspirators, along with Stalin, had zealously pursued that policy. Dethroned as Stalin's royal prince, Zhdanov was packed off to Leningrad.

In Leningrad Zhdanov worked himself almost into exhaustion. He had seen at once the need for a secondary line of defense on the Luga River, 75 miles southwest of the city. More than 30,000 Leningraders—almost all of them women wielding picks and shovels while wearing civilian dresses—were sent to the Luga to dig trenches, gun emplacements and tank traps. They worked day and night, in rain or sunshine, with little food and primitive housing, strafed and bombed by the Luftwaffe, tongue-lashed by the small group of army sappers who directed them. But they built the Luga Line, running 200 miles along the eastern shore of the broad marshy river, and after they had finished, they stumbled back to "Piter" on foot, their clothes in tatters, their feet bruised and their hands raw, their bodies caked with sweat-soaked dirt. Some of them did not return, buried where they fell under the bombs and bullets of the Luftwaffe.

Zhdanov's next concern was in the evacuation of nearly 400,000 children into the nearby countryside or to Yaroslavl' on the Volga River. Many of them were killed during their flight when the Nazis bombed their trains. Other unnumbered thousands were taken captive and sent to slave labor camps where they died. More fell victim to the Nazi terror scourging the outlying villages. Wherever the panzers rolled, in their wake were posters tacked up in village squares listing the various violations—dozens of them, and many of them trivial—for which the offender "will be immediately shot." The children had been sent from the city for fear that the Luftwaffe would strike Leningrad with the same blitz that it had hurled at London. This apprehension had also caused the Leningraders to collect all the city's art treasures from Peterhof palace, the Hermitage, the Winter Palace and other repositories and pack them aboard trucks to take them to safe sanctuaries out of reach of the Wehrmacht. One huge train of twenty-two freight cars pulled by two locomotives in tandem and protected by antiaircraft batteries on flatcars chugged out of Leningrad loaded with half a million paintings and other creations of such giants as Rembrandt, Velasquez, Van Dyck, El Greco and Da

Vinci. But there was no blitz on Leningrad, not for the first few months of the war.

Meanwhile, the energetic and resourceful Zhdanov had brought about the conversion of many of Leningrad's factories to war production. By July five factories were turning out artillery pieces and shells, eleven were making mortars, twelve producing tanks and armored cars, fourteen turning out flamethrowers and thirteen—including a toy factory and a stove plant—mass-producing hand grenades. By August Leningrad's distilleries had made a million Molotov cocktails, using either alcohol or gasoline. Nevertheless manufacture of munitions for the front was encountering steadily increasing difficulties, chief of them a scarcity of materials. An appeal to Moscow brought the blunt reply: "There are more important fronts than yours. Use your local resources." But these were drying up, and many Leningrad factories were being dismantled preparatory to being shipped to the Urals far out of the Wehrmacht's reach. There was also a shortage of factory workers, many of whom had been mobilized by the army or had joined the People's Volunteers. Those still at work were supposed to work three hours a day on fortifications after putting in an eleven-hour shift in their plant. But no one protested. Every able person in the city was devoting fourteen, sixteen or even eighteen hours a day to production or fortification. Leningrad was aroused, preparing for the worst but hoping for the best.

The Northwest Front defending Leningrad had all but collapsed. Zhdanov and Klimint Voroshilov knew that its broken, backpedaling armies could not turn and make a stand at the Luga. They were retreating, rather fleeing, much too rapidly. Panic, that great dissolver of discipline, had seized them. Sometimes soldiers fought with refugees who had clogged the highways from the Baltic and made even retreat difficult. Eighty thousand workmen employed building fortifications also were fleeing east. Mixed in with the soldiers and workers were peasants herding their cattle to safer fields or carrying away all their worldly possessions in ox carts, German agents, deserters and anticommunist farmers only too happy to trade blows with the enraged soldiery. In eighteen days of fighting the Northwest Front's three armies had been driven back 300 to 325 miles. Among them they had possessed well over 350,000 men, but by July 10 they were down to below 150,000. Their air support was gone, most of it lost in the first four hours of the war. They were down to fewer than 1,500 guns and mortars. Armored and mechanized divisions had lost so many tanks and vehicles that they had become mere rifle divisions. Some 10,000-man divisions were down to 2,000 soldiers. All of these Soviets reeling back before Army Group North's flood of tanks were exhausted. Even after they reached the sanctuary of the Luga Line, they were in no condition to fight. Maj. Gen. M. P. Pyadyshev, the brilliant tactician commanding there, realized that he could not depend on them. He also knew that he could not hold the Luga without trained men, of which there were few in Leningrad. Never a man to hesitate or take counsel from his fears, Pyadyshev called for the People's Volunteers.

These were the patriotic youths who had been signing up by the hundred thousand since the first day of war. The fact that they had no training disturbed but did not dismay Pyadyshev. At the least, they were bodies which could bar the Germans' path. Not all of them were so young. The great composer Dmitri Shostakovich was one of them. "Up to now I have known only peaceful work," he said. "Now I am ready to take up arms. Only by fighting can we save humanity from destruction." The actor Nikolai Cherkasov and the forty-six-year-old poet Vsevolod Rozhdestvensky also joined; but none of these famous men was assigned to combat duty. This was for the young with their hard bodies and high hearts.

They came out to the Luga in a flood, by train or truck, or on foot; marching over the dirt roads with the dust clouds billowing overhead, singing as only Russian soldiers can sing, their mighty choruses lifting the hearts of the peasants watching them pass through their villages, moving them to press upon them gifts of sausage or mugs of cider laced with vodka. The units of the People's Volunteers suffered horribly. Their officers, from platoon leaders up to division commanders, were just as inexperienced and inept as they were. Many of these youths were unarmed, waiting to seize a rifle falling from the lifeless fingers of their comrades. Others did not even know how to aim and fire a weapon. Frequently the volunteers broke and fled, but enough of them stood their ground with a stoicism that never ceased to amaze the Germans, shaking their faith in their own superior military prowess, which was real but could not put to flight an enemy inferior in everything but tenacity.

There were casualties among the high command as well, for Marshal Semën K. Timoshenko, the defense commissar, had begun to put the blame for Soviet defeat on those generals whose only crime had been to obey his orders. Timoshenko had also shared the belief that Germany would not attack and had issued orders strictly prohibiting his commanders from offering any sort of provocation to the Nazis. The highly regarded Gen. Dmitri Pavlov and his chief of staff, Maj. Gen. V. E. Klimovsky, were among the first to go to the wall. "What can I tell you about the situation?" the dumbfounded Pavlov said to the general who replaced him. "The stunning blows of the enemy caught our troops by surprise. We were not ready for battle. We were in peacetime conditions, carrying out exercises in our camps and firing ranges. And for this reason we suffered heavy losses, in air power, artillery and tanks—and in manpower, too." Next to be executed was the man who was the real hero of the Luga Line: M. P. Pyadyshev, the commander who had begun to fortify the river even before Zhdanov got back to Leningrad. Pyadyshev just vanished and was never heard from again. His execution was certain, but no one could say what his crime was.

Nevertheless, for all these appalling casualties and spiteful or stupid extermination of superior commanders, the Luga Line was holding. It delayed Army Group North from July 9 to August 8—more than four weeks—and it upset the Nazi timetable. Hitler's victory parade on Palace Square scheduled for mid-July had to be postponed and then postponed again. But the unequal contest between Soviet flesh and German steel could have only one ending: On the night of August 8 behind a thunderous bombardment that shook the earth like an erupting volcano, Leeb's panzers forced the Luga and routed the fought-out remnants of the Northwest Front and the riddled volunteers. Now there was no stopping the German tanks. The bulk of the defending Soviet forces were driven east, thus preventing them from retreating north to Leningrad and environs, where they might turn to confront Army Group North once more. A gap of a dozen miles was left open and the Nazi armor roared through it. On August 30 the Germans reached the Neva River in the vicinity of Ivanoskoye about a dozen miles southeast of Leningrad. The little railway station of Mga a few miles farther southeast was captured. The Nazi hold on Mga severed all rail connections between Leningrad and the rest of the Soviet Union—the mainland as it came to be called—and all the highways were also cut. Four days later the fall of Shlisselburg on Lake Ladoga to the east forged the last section of the iron ring being drawn around Leningrad on its landward front. Even though the Baltic Fleet had returned to Kronstadt there was no possibility of relief or rescue from the sea. Leningrad was encircled in a ring of steel, and Leeb in his headquarters at Gatchina to the southwest was now preparing for the final surge into the city itself.

The news from Leningrad gave Joseph Stalin a shock surpassed only by the invasion of the U.S.S.R. itself. He thought of abandoning the city, as Molotov, Malenkov and Beria had been urging him to do. They had accused Zhdanov and Voroshilov of putting up a poor defense, insisting that the city could not be held and to try to do so would be too costly, drawing off priceless resources needed for the defense of Moscow. They also hinted that Zhdanov-Voroshilov might be negotiating with the enemy. It was a nice touch beautifully timed: Stalin was already shaken by the mass defection of the Ukrainians.

He was also fearful that the Baltic Fleet would fall into Nazi hands, and he ordered his naval commissar and chief of staff—Adm. Nikolai Kuznetsov and Marshal Boris Shaposhnikov—to prepare instructions to scuttle it. Both men obeyed, but they sent the order back to Stalin unsigned. They were aware that Stalin was trying to transfer blame should a premature sinking of the ships turn out to be a disaster. That was why he delayed sending out the instruction under his own signature, desperately hoping for the improvement that would obviate it.

Eventually, Stalin decided that Leningrad would have to be abandoned, and he did send out the orders not only to mine the Baltic Fleet, but also the naval depots and all the great military installations, together with the chief structures of the city. He directly blamed Zhdanov and Voroshilov for Leningrad's predicament, but only Voroshilov was dismissed, to be replaced by Marshal Georgi Zhukov, Stalin's troubleshooter and "the savior of Moscow." Zhdanov was given one more chance, but he had to save the city very quickly. Only speedy salvation would change Stalin's mind, and if Leningrad fell, so would Zhdanov's head. No fault, of course, would be imputed to Zhukov.

Georgi Konstantinovich Zhukov exploded in Leningrad with the force of a magnetic mine. Here was a Slav of the Slavs, short, stocky, with thick Slavic features and a round Slavic skull, bright blue eyes and a sharp, bitter tongue. Sarcastic and profane, he was a driver, immediately applying to all his commanders the credo he had borrowed from an infantry officer addressing his men: "Our principle is this: If you retreat, I will kill you. If I retreat without orders, you kill me. And Leningrad will not be surrendered." This was now the Zhukov Principle. To it he added his own credo: Attack! Attack! Attack! It made no difference how weak the unit so ordered might be. If its men had no weapons or ammunition or had been battered for weeks, they must attack. If they disobeyed, they were shot.

To this persuasive psychological club was added probably the most destructive weapon in the Soviet arsenal: the Katyusha, the electrically fired multibarreled mortar that German soldiers called Stalin's Organs. If it did not rend, it at least terrified the enemy, with its hideous scream and fiery tails. When the missiles exploded, the air was filled with the rush of sound and the hiss of fire. The Katyusha was named for the Soviet soldier's favorite song of that name. Once during the savage fighting around Ligovo railroad station just southwest of the city, the Soviets were amazed to hear music. A band had struck up "Katyusha," and the men began to sing its sweet-sad lyrics:

> Katyusha came to the shore,
> To the very highest bank.
> She came to sing a song
> For the one she loved,
> For the one whose letter she kept. . . .

From the German side came a shout: "Play it again, Russ. Play it again!"

Katyusha did come again—again and again—her horrible hoarse voices mingling with the silent swift shells of the dreadnoughts of the Baltic Fleet and the Red Army's land-based artillery. It was this combination that wrought the most effective destruction among the Germans in the critical battle for the railway station at Ligovo. But the Nazis in their gray-green uniforms and coal-scuttle helmets kept attacking there and on the much-fought-over Pulkovo Heights. From this vantage all of Leningrad could be taken under fire by enemy gunners. War had washed up to the very southern edge of Leningrad. If the line Ligovo-Pulkovo-Kolpino were penetrated, the Germans could send their artillery crashing into the naked city and probably their panzers as well.

On September 17 Zhukov issued a general order to all commanders of the Forty-second and Forty-fifth Armies: Any withdrawal from this line would be punished with instant execution. But now the people and the defenders of Leningrad had a slogan of their own: "Leningrad is not afraid of death—death is afraid of Leningrad." On the night of September 18 the fiercest battle of the siege raged around the Klinovsky House at Ligovo. It was repeatedly taken by the Germans only to be lost again in Soviet counterattacks. Finally, the Germans were beaten back. The Ligovo-Kolpino line had been straightened out again. Neither side could claim decisive victory, however, for that fog of war which so often obscures which way the tide of battle is flowing had enshrouded the battlefield. But if Marshal Georgi Zhukov could not be sure that his defense would hold, Field Marshal Wilhelm Ritter von Leeb was beginning to doubt that he could maintain his offensive.

The aging Leeb was cracking under constant pressure from Hitler. Like Zhdanov and Voroshilov he was accused of dragging his feet. He was losing so much time! Time was precious now, with Bock's Army Group Center preparing for the kill at Moscow. It was not so much that Leeb was not conforming to Hitler's grand strategy of taking Leningrad and then joining the Finns in a southern drive to the rear of Moscow. Leeb's armor was badly needed at Moscow. On September 5 Hitler told Leeb to release it to the Moscow front as soon as possible. Because Leeb seemed to be advancing, General Halder agreed to let him keep it until the 12th. Then he was given another day. Next, two more . . . But on September 17 the Moscow front was adamant: The armor must come south, and the 6th Panzers began disengaging. Then the entire 41st Panzer Corps was ordered south. Although Leeb tried frantically to pierce the Ligovo-Kolpino line, he knew in his heart that he could not do it without the power of the panzers which had brought Army Group North up to the very edge of Leningrad. Although he did not know it yet, Zhukov had won. Leningrad had won. Now there came reports that the enemy was digging in, preparing winter quarters. Soon troops from Leningrad were on their way south to help hold Moscow. On the night of October 5, Stalin called Zhukov. He wanted to know what the situation was in Leningrad. Zhukov replied that the enemy was now on the defensive. Stalin said: "Turn your command over to your deputy and come to Moscow."

Early next morning Zhukov left Leningrad by air to take charge of the Battle for Moscow. Behind him, Commissar Andrei Zhdanov began preparing for the dreadful northern winter, unsuspecting that the Third Horseman of the Apocalypse—Famine—would be a far more formidable foe.

34. August 1941: Hitler Drives Southeast

IN WAR THE CHIEF OBJECTIVE is the enemy army. Destroy it, and the enemy's country and people are yours. Military history abounds with illustrations of this maxim. Most significant of them for Americans was the British failure to destroy George Washington's army. Again and again, Washington saved this vital little force. Again and again, he was outflanked by superior tacticians such as Sir William Howe and later Sir Henry Clinton. Always he got away to fight another day. As long as his little army remained unvanquished, the Revolution lived; and although it is today fashionable to belittle Washington as a general who never won a battle, the fact is that by declining decisive battle, by keeping his army in being, he ultimately—with the help of France, of course—wore down the British will to fight. Next in importance to the enemy's army is his capital, especially if it is a vital nerve center, the fall of which will cripple his communications and also strike an unnerving psychological blow.

In August of 1941 Adolf Hitler ignored both of these axioms by deciding to put both the Leningrad and Moscow operations on hold in order that a strengthened Army Group South could go smashing into the Ukraine and Crimea in all-out assault. *Der Führer* ordered this over the objections of those generals courageous and patriotic enough to oppose him. Col. Gen. Franz Halder, chief of the general Staff, was the most strenuous objector, and he was heartbroken when Hitler commanded him to be still. Nevertheless, Halder was present at a conference of Army Group South on August 23, where he renewed his arguments for driving on Moscow before the huge army concentrating in front of it could get any larger. Gen. Heinz Guderian was at this conference. He agreed with Halder that another attempt to change Hitler's mind should be made. He warned that an attack on Kiev, the Ukrainian capital, could lead to an unacceptable and perhaps disastrous winter campaign. Field Marshal von Bock, commander of Army Group Central, suggested that Guderian should accompany Halder back to the Wolf's Lair and as a general from the front warn *Der Führer* of the consequences of his decision. So Guderian flew back to Hitler's headquarters with Halder, and was immediately ordered to report to Field Marshal Walther von Brauchitsch, commander in chief of the army.

"I forbid you to mention the question of Moscow to the Führer," Brauchitsch said in greeting. "The operation to the south has been ordered. The problem now is simply how to carry it out. Discussion is pointless."

Guderian immediately asked to be sent back to his Panzer Group. To see Hitler under such conditions would be a waste of time. Brauchitsch demurred. He must see *Der Führer.* "But without mentioning Moscow!"

Guderian had little respect for Brauchitsch. He regarded him as only less loathsome than the toady twins—Keitel and Jodl—and was very much aware of the reason for his devotion to *Der Führer.* Hitler had persuaded Brauchitsch's first wife to agree to a divorce, and had even paid the divorce settlement costs. This left Brauchitsch free to marry the Nazi Charlotte Schmidt two months later. Her influence and his obligation to Hitler made him thereafter a weak and compliant sycophant. Guderian was no such fawning flatterer. He marched into the presence of Hitler, surrounded by Keitel, Jodl and others, to make a report on his command and await the proper opportunity to mention Moscow. It came when Hitler asked:

"In view of their past performance, do you consider that your troops are capable of making another great effort?"

"If the troops are given a major objective, the importance of which is apparent to every soldier—yes."

"You mean, of course, Moscow?" Hitler asked coldly.

"Yes, *mein Führer*. Since you have broached the subject, let me give you the reasons for my opinions."

Hitler nodded and Guderian began to speak. First and foremost, he said, the Soviet army concentrating before Moscow was the true objective. It had suffered severely in recent battles and could be beaten long before the onset of winter. Next Moscow, the real "holy city" of Holy Russia, was the true prize. It was the Soviet road, rail and communications center. It was the political solar plexus, it was an important industrial center, and its capture would have an enormous psychological effect on the Russian people and the world as well. The soldiers dreamed of taking Moscow, Guderian said, and were extremely enthusiastic over the prospect. Once Moscow was lost, the Soviets would have great difficulty moving troops south to fight in the Ukraine. Moreover, much time would be wasted in the drive to the southwest, which was actually a move backward. If stiff resistance were encountered, all chance to capture Moscow in 1941 would vanish. But all these considerations, Guderian finished imploringly, paled into insignificance beside the overwhelming importance of destroying the Moscow army.

Hitler had listened in silence. Now he began to speak. The Ukraine's grain and industry were necessary for the further prosecution of the war. "My generals know nothing about the economic aspects of war," he said, while Keitel, Jodl and the others nodded their heads approvingly at this oft-repeated remark. The Crimea was an unsinkable "Soviet aircraft carrier for attacking the Romanian oilfields" and must be neutralized. Again the heads bobbed. Guderian saw at once that he was up against a master puppeteer and his troupe, and said no more, returning to his Panzer Group with a heavy heart. Within a few days his tanks were clattering south to join Rundstedt's Army Group South in its drive on Kiev.

Wilhelm Pruller's battalion was part of Rundstedt's army group. Pruller was now a lieutenant. He had also been decorated with the Iron Cross, Second Class, for bravery and resourcefulness in action. Pruller had seen much combat since his formation crossed the border at Friedland in Upper Silesia on that fateful June 21, 1941. He was appalled by the carnage of tank warfare, by the sight of the nude and roasted bodies of women—Soviet female soldiers—lying inside or beside burned-out tanks. "An arm there, a head there, half a foot somewhere else, squashed brains, mashed ribs. Horrible!" But he learned nothing by his experience. In him there was no pity, or at least no compassion except for Germans. "Among the Russian dead there are many Asiatic faces, which look disgusting with their slit eyes. Dead women in uniform are lying around, too. These criminals stop at absolutely nothing!"

Pruller was extremely resentful of the atrocities committed on his comrades by the Soviet people. Their reception when they first entered the Ukraine had been so moving. In every village they had been showered with bouquets of flowers even more beautiful than those they had received in Vienna. Many villages had flower-decorated triumphal arches, bearing the inscription in Russian and German: "The Ukrainian peoples thank their liberators, the brave German Army. Heil Adolf Hitler!" But as the campaign wore on it seemed that the Ukrainians were turning against them. Pruller could not understand why.

Pruller was an admirer of Field Marshal Walther von Reichenau, the ardent Nazi who was in command of the Sixth Army. Reichenau was the only high commander who supported Hitler's infamous Commissar Order, the secret command that all captured political commissars were to be summarily executed without trial. He had himself issued an equally base Severity Order, which said in part: "The most important objective of this campaign against the Jewish-Bolshevik system is the complete destruction of its sources of power and the extermination of the Asiatic influence in European civilization. . . . For this reason the soldier must learn fully to appreciate the necessity for the severe but just retribution that must be meted out to the subhuman species of Jewry. . . ."

"Retribution" was to be exacted by members of the "extermination squads," which, like hordes of black vermin, crawled in the wake of the conquering armies. They had been recruited mainly from the ranks of Himmler's special police force, or had drifted in from punishment battalions or psychiatric hospitals. They had been trained at a camp in Saxony in the use of machine pistols on helpless victims, and Reichenau—a lover of detail—had instructed them to use no more than two bullets to kill a Jew. They were dressed in black uniforms, traveling in truck convoys, and became known to the terrified villagers as the Black Crows.

They did not exterminate Jews alone. Village after village fell victim to their homicidal madness. Those who were spared or escaped were left nothing on which to survive: no food, no animals, no homes. Only the death of Reichenau in January 1942 put an end to this wholesale slaughter, but by then the German soldiery in the Ukraine had developed their own taste for blood.

On the slightest pretext prisoners were herded to the wall and shot in the sight of entire villages commanded to watch the execution. Pruller saw such scenes of carnage, but they left him unmoved. So also did the spectacle of trucks rolling toward Germany loaded with Ukrainian women being deported for slave labor. These were the same women who had showered Pruller and his *Kameraden* with flowers; in reward, they had been rounded up by the hundred thousand—married or single, with or without children—and driven into reception centers. There in the coldly clinical German way they had been forced to undergo medical examinations, lining up like so many naked prostitutes on inspection day. *Complete* examinations. The SS doctors who examined them were astonished to find that 99 percent of the unmarried women were virgins. The prettiest and brightest of these were reserved for service in the homes of leading Nazis. But soldiers such as Pruller, capable of locking the populations of whole villages in barns and then setting fire to them, did not find this objectionable. Had not Heinrich Himmler declared:

"What happens to a Russian, or to a Czech, does not interest me in the slightest. What the nations can offer in good blood of our type we will take, if necessary by kidnapping their children and raising them here with us. Whether nations live in prosperity or starve to death interests me only in so far as we need them as slaves for our *Kultur;* otherwise, it is of no interest to me. Whether ten thousand Russian females fall down from exhaustion while digging an antitank ditch interests me only in so far as the antitank ditch for Germany is finished."

It was not only Himmler's SS which turned the Ukrainians against the German invaders. It was also the German soldiery. In Krivoy Rog, Wilhelm Pruller arrested a Russian who was drunk and yelling in the streets. After the man was free, he was found drunk and shouting again, and Pruller calmly had him shot. Next day Pruller found a park with a pond in it. It was a fine opportunity to wash. "It's curious to see the Russian women shamelessly undressing in front of us and wandering around naked. Some of them look quite appetizing, especially their breasts. . . . Most of us would be quite willing to . . . but then again you see the old dirty ones and you want to go and vomit. They've got no morals here! Revolting!"

Ukrainian vengeance was just as savage as German cruelty, perhaps even more ingenious. Sometimes when the partisans caught enemy soldiers, they stripped them naked except for their steel helmets. They tied them together in a long line and threw buckets of water on them until the helmets were frozen to their skulls and their bodies frozen in a solid block of ice, their limbs and faces fixed in every attitude of terror—a hideous mass sculpture for their *Kameraden* to behold when they arrived as rescuers.

Pruller, devout Catholic that he affected to be, naturally enough found such atrocities "horrible," especially when "we harm not a hair of a Russian's head. . . ." He was also indignant at the immorality of starving peasants who looted their own shops. "No people has ever stolen like this one!" Pruller and the *Kameraden* whom he constantly eulogizes in his diaries are brave, loyal and ready to die for *Der Führer,* and they also give living proof of how what is best in man can be perverted in the service of what is worst. Fortitude without justice is the tool of the wicked, Saint Ambrose said—fifteen centuries before the Nazi beast arrived on earth.

The Kiev encirclement was a master stroke. Guderian's panzers drove south across the Russian rear while Kleist's struck north. The two pincers met 150 miles east of the Ukrainian capital with a bag of an estimated 665,000 prisoners. Then Bock's Army Group Center, to which Guderian had returned, surged forward, bringing off another great encirclement around Vyazma with another 600,000 Soviets in the bag. Hitler was jubilant. "I declare today," he told the German nation, "and I declare it without reservation—the enemy in the East has been struck down and will never rise again."

But the enemy in the East had not been struck down; rather, the oncharging Germans had been worn down. Drenching rains had swept over western Russia during September, turning the roads into ribbons of mud and keeping them that way for days on end. Once again the problem of wheeled vehicles arose. They could only advance with the help of tracked vehicles—usually tanks—and because towing was not one of the tasks for which tanks had been designed, they soon wore out. Chains and couplings needed for towing were unavailable. In their place ropes were used, and these had to be dropped in by the Luftwaffe. In the advance on Moscow the single road from Orel to Tula simply disintegrated under the weight of Guderian's armor. Moreover, the Soviets, by long practice now the world's leading experts in demolition, blew almost every single bridge on the line of their withdrawal, and wherever they could had sown either side of the road with minefields. Corduroy roads of felled trees had to be laid laboriously in both directions: to the rear to receive supplies, to the front for the infantry to advance. And they did advance, in a triumph of ingenuity and perseverance, so that by October 20 the German spearheads were within forty miles of Moscow. It was then that Mother Russia's ancient and faithful ally came early to her side.

General Winter.

Moscow was as it had been under Czar Alexander I in 1812: feverish, warlike and patriotic. Just as the czar had successfully appealed to Russian patriotism against Napoleon, Stalin's call to rally to the side of Holy Russia in "the Great Patriotic War" had touched the souls of his countrymen. As it had been 129 years ago, tens upon tens of thousands of women still wearing their city clothes were taken into the mud and slush west of Moscow to dig tremendous trenches and antitank ditches crisscrossing the countryside. The only difference between 1812 and 1941 was that the women did not walk or ride in wagons but were transported by bus, train and truck. The women also extended fortifications clear back into Moscow itself, where barricades of earth, steel and sandbags were raised. The famous Palace of the Soviets, intended to rise as the tallest building in the world, but then only an incomplete steel skeleton, was dismantled for use as raw material for defense. The Moscow Metro, the world's most modern subway system, was reserved exclusively for the movement of troops and supplies. All small shops and factories had switched over to weapon making. A factory that made pots and pans would be turning out hand grenades, one devoted to manufacturing cash registers and adding machines would be producing automatic rifles.

Mass evacuation from Moscow had begun on October 15, triggering three days of panic and stampede. People swarmed into the railroad terminals seeking a seat on a train. Finding none, they climbed onto the roofs of the railroad cars or began walking—grimly walking in growing cold and mounting misery—toward the east. Muscovites, accustomed to short supply and waiting in line for everything, now formed queues of unrivaled length to draw the extra rations of bread, cheese and sausage allotted to the departing evacuees. Engaged couples, even those not so pledged, hurriedly married so that one or the other might be allowed to accompany the person chosen for evacuation. En route to the east, the evacuees passed trainloads or marching columns of reservists arriving from Siberia or Mongolia or other distant provinces for the defense of Moscow. Muscovites were leery of these rough and wild peasants, especially the *Sibirski,* big, blond men said to be even cruder and crueler than the Cossacks. Lavrenti Beria was afraid that the reservists would follow the time-honored tradition of going on a public-menacing vodka binge before leaving for the front. So the chief of the NKVD decided to issue each arriving reservist two liters of vodka and lock them up in unfurnished barracks for a few days guarded by NKVD troops. After they survived the binge, the brawls amongst themselves, and suffered through their hangovers, they were ready to get down to this business of warfare.

Most of the Soviet government was heading east for Kuibyshev. Stalin, however, remained in his Kremlin apartment, concerned with little other than the conduct of the war. He rarely ventured forth, and did not visit the front except on one occasion along the Mozhaysk defense line near Kuntsevo, very far from any fighting. This was immortalized in a painting entitled *Stalin at the Front near Moscow, 1941.* Reproduced at the time on innumerable cards and posters, it showed Stalin much taller than his actual height standing at the edge of a forest swathed in a huge fur coat with binoculars trained on "attacking Germans." Such icons celebrating the bravery of the Supreme Military Leader were of course common throughout Russia in those days, and the fawning poem of the Azerbaijani poet, Samed Vurgun, was being quoted everywhere:

> He is the Bright sun of my country; with his native-born smile.
> He warms the different peoples, and happy is the man
> Who shakes his hand . . . and the high heavens
> Towering over the earth, envy the earth on which he walks.

Surprisingly enough, Harry Hopkins, President Roosevelt's right-hand man, seems to have believed at least some of this official hagiography. Hopkins came to Moscow at the end of July 1941, writing this of his host: "No one could forget the picture of the dictator of Russia as he stood watching me leave—an austere, rugged, determined figure in boots that shone like mirrors, stout baggy trousers, and snug-fitting blouse. He wore no ornament, military or civilian. He's built close to the ground like a football coach's dream of a tackle. . . ." No perception of another man's physical and personal traits could have been more inexact: "His hands are huge, as hard as his mind. . . . His humor is keen, penetrating . . . looking straight into my eyes. . . ." But what matters most is not whence this perception had derived but the unfortunate effect it was to have on Franklin Delano Roosevelt.

Harry Hopkins's report on Stalin helped to convince FDR that he could "handle" the Soviet dictator. During the Atlantic Conference that produced proclamation of the Four Freedoms, William Bullitt, the former ambassador to the Soviet Union, warned Roosevelt against Stalin's postwar designs. "I don't dispute the logic of your reasons," Roosevelt replied. "I just have a hunch that Stalin is not that kind of man. . . . Harry says that he is not." Much to FDR's irritation, Bullitt reminded him that he was not dealing with a high-principled statesman motivated by noblesse oblige, as he thought, but a coldly calculating thief and killer who looked upon anyone who gave him something for nothing as an utter ass. "It's my responsibility, not yours," Roosevelt snapped, "and I'm going to play my hunch." He did, and the wily Koba cynically exploited the American's naive trust to lower the Iron Curtain around Eastern Europe.

Actually, Stalin at the time he met Harry Hopkins was only just beginning to emerge from the state into which he had fallen on the morrow of the German invasion. Gen. P. A. Belov, a corps commander who had not seen him since 1933, was shocked by his appearance in 1941. "Before me stood a short man, with a tired, haggard face. In eight years he seems to have aged twenty. His eyes had lost their old steadiness; his voice lacked assurance." During those three nightmare months when his country seemed to be collapsing around him, Joseph Stalin had indeed endured much. He had been exposed to the most soul-shattering kind of on-the-job training, relying to the extreme on the advice of Marshal Georgi Zhukov. General Belov thought that Zhukov spoke to Stalin in sharp, commanding tones. "It looked as if Zhukov was really the superior officer here. And Stalin accepted this as proper." Gradually, however, these roles were reversed as Stalin's grasp of military matters increased enormously. He still depended upon Zhukov both as an adviser and troubleshooter, but by the time the cold September rains had enmired the men and machines of the Wehrmacht in mud and misery, his heart had lifted, and he was completely in command of the conduct of the war.

At that time also, Stalin was happy to receive the top-ranking Anglo-American supply mission that had arrived in Moscow. The British delegation was led by Lord Beaverbrook, the Canadian press lord who was Churchill's close friend and now minister of aircraft production, and included General Sir Hastings Ismay. Hopkins was ill, so the American side was represented by Roosevelt's roving ambassador, W. Averell Harriman. Stalin at once sketched the gravity of the situation and began to outline his needs. Tanks were at the top of the list in order to counter the German preponderance in that weapon. Without their tanks, Stalin said, the German infantry would be swept away by the overwhelmingly more numerous Soviet infantry. He also wanted antitank guns, medium bombers, antiaircraft guns, armor plate, fighter and reconnaissance planes and all the barbed wire he could get. He was delighted when Harriman cabled Washington and was able to tell him that he could expect 400 tons of barbed wire a month. Stalin was not shy in his demands and not easily put off. But his manner was one of extreme cordiality, especially after he saw that the Anglo-Americans were sincerely interested in helping the Soviet Union. Later he praised the United States for "giving more assistance as a nonbelligerent than some countries in history have given as allies."

The interpreter during this first meeting was Maxim Litvinov, the old commissar for foreign affairs who had been removed in semi-disgrace prior to the love affair with Hitler. Beaverbrook, a keen observer, noticed that behind Litvinov was an open door to another, darkened room, guessing that a second interpreter was inside checking on the accuracy of Litvinov's translations. The following night, Stalin was in a foul mood. At times he seemed discourteous or disinterested. He smoked constantly, either cigarettes or his pipe filled with shredded cigarette tobacco. Three times he made telephone calls, each time dialing the number himself. After each call, he appeared more somber. He did not tell his guests, but he had learned that Guderian had broken through at Orel and was about to take the city. Turning to Harriman, he complained: "Why is it that the United States can only give me one thousand tons of armor plate for tanks—a country with a production of over fifty million tons?" Harriman, who was quite familiar with the steel industry, began to explain the time consumed in raising production capacity. Stalin did not want to hear. With his habit of solving the whole problem with only part of the solution, he snorted: "One only has to add alloys!" But he liked it when Harriman offered him five thousand jeeps. Throughout the war he would justify his demands with the remark: "The United States gives money, Britain gives time —and Russia gives blood."

The discussions with the military were similarly frustrating. General Ismay wrote: "When we tried to elucidate the basis of their astronomical requirements of equipment, we could get no answer out of them. We asked, for example, how many antitank guns were allotted to a division, adding that our divisions had seventy-two. The reply was, "It depends on what sort of division." When we suggested that an infantry division might be taken as an example, the reply was, 'That depends on where it has to fight.' It became obvious that the Soviet generals were not authorized to give information of any kind, and that to try to do business with them was a waste of time." Ismay also did not share Beaverbrook's impression of Stalin as a "kindly old man." Rather, he gave this impression of him at a formal dinner: "He moved stealthily like a wild animal in search of prey, and his eyes were shrewd and full of cunning. He never looked one in the face. But he had great dignity and his personality was dominating. As he entered the room, every Russian froze into silence, and the hunted look in the eyes of the generals showed all too plainly the constant fear in which they lived. It was nauseating to see brave men reduced to such abject servility."

Soured as he was, Ismay did find some divertissement in the plight of his Royal Marine orderly, who, easily the smartest-looking member of the mission in his blue-and-gold uniform, was being constantly saluted by Soviet generals because of the red band on his cap. Ismay, in effect, told the Marine to relax and enjoy himself, and soon the young man became something of a celebrity in Moscow. Winston Churchill was particularly fond of relating the probably apocryphal story of his guided tour of the city. "This," said the guide, "is the Eden Hotel, formerly Ribbentrop Hotel. Here is Churchill Street, formerly Hitler Street. Here is the Beaverbrook Railway Station, formerly the Goering Railway Station. Will you have a cigarette, Comrade?" The Marine nodded, and said: "Thank you, Comrade—formerly Bolshevik bastard!"

On the third night Stalin's disposition had improved. It was, said Beaverbrook, like sunshine after the rain. He smiled affably and listened without a frown while Beaverbrook read to him the list of his demands, checking off those that could not be satisfied and those that would, together with unrequested items being thrown in for good measure. Stalin's face shone with pleasure. He ordered refreshments, the first time he had done so, chuckling even, when Litvinov bounded to his feet and cried:

"Now we shall win the war!"

The effect of the unfamiliar and incredible Russian cold upon the German invaders was paralyzing. In early October heavy snowflakes had begun to fall on the columns of Bock's center group marching onto Moscow. It melted almost immediately upon touching the black soil. But as the day wore on and the late-afternoon frost set in, the softly falling whiteness soon laid a snowy mantle over the countryside. The Germans regarded it uneasily. Everyone—officers and men—thought of Napoleon and his *Grande Armée*. And Moscow still 170 miles away . . .

But the attacks went forward. Sometimes there were night marches to increase the speed of the advance. By day the troops struggled with trucks now mired in mud made of soil mixed with snow. Despite the cold, the bodies of the little *panje* horses used to pull the transport free glistened with sweat. Exhausted soldiers with their legs up to the knees in mud often were too weak to free themselves and had to be pulled out with loud sucking noises. Gradually, ominously, the thermometers sank toward zero . . . below zero. . . .

There was no winter clothing. Hitler had been so confident of victory before the onset of winter that he had scoffed at requests for such provisions. He had even ordered forty divisions disbanded and the men returned to industry. As a result, there were no replacements available for 200-man companies down to sixty and seventy men. And these survivors were weary and fought out. What breath they had left they saved for cursing. Because these soldiers were exceptionally well indoctrinated on their country's strategy and their own objectives, their cursing was of a highly intelligent order. They not only cursed the rains that had slowed them down, but also *Der Führer* for delaying the invasion five weeks. They cursed Mussolini for causing that delay with his witless sally into Greece. They cursed Hitler again for not sending winter clothing, for holding up their advance while following his intuition into the Ukraine, for dismissing the enemy who was battering them daily with the vain vaunt that he was "beaten" and "would never rise again."

Heinrich Haape was with the advanced units. On November 13 he awoke shivering. An icy blast had knifed in from the northeast. Although the sky was clear and dark blue, the sun seemed to have no warmth. Instead of rising during the day, the temperature was falling. By sundown it had dropped to −12 degrees Centigrade (18 degrees Fahrenheit). The soldiers quickly pulled their woolen *Kopfschützer* or "head-savers"—their only piece of winter clothing—down over their ears. But one man marched on bareheaded. Within an hour he came to Dr. Haape with his ears white and frozen stiff. He was Haape's first case of frostbite. Haape gently massaged his ears, taking care not to break the skin, and they thawed out. The soldier was lucky. Within a few days there were 100,000 cases of severe frostbite in Bock's army group. One hundred thousand first-class soldiers had been put out of action as surely as though they had been machine-gunned.

Still the icy winds from Siberia blew colder across the steppes. Temperatures fell as low as the thermometer would go: −24 degrees . . . −36 degrees . . . −48 degrees . . . The men's *Kopfschützer* might protect their ears and faces, but what of their feet? The ordinary army boot was like a block of ice encasing a man's foot. Walking in them was an ordeal. Without winter clothing, fighting or any sudden movement in such cold was likely to end in death. But then, a few days after the Siberian cold whistled in, the winter clothing arrived. The men were jubilant until it was discovered that for the entire battalion of 800 men there were only sixteen greatcoats and sixteen pairs of felt-lined boots! That mean four to each company. There was nothing to do but draw lots for them. The men who won were almost too embarrassed to wear them among their shivering, teeth-chattering comrades. And those who did not win kept a careful eye on these bulkier figures leaning into the wind-driven snow . . . not hopefully, of course, but just in case. . . .

Haape's unit reached the outskirts of Moscow. During a heavy snowfall he and a man named Kageneck walked down the road leading into the city. They saw a trolley station. "Let's walk across and take a look at it," said Kageneck. "Then we can tell Neuhoff that we were only a trolley ride from Moscow." They silently entered the stone shed. They stared at the wooden benches in the waiting room. Haape rummaged inside a wooden bin, pulling out a handful of tickets marked in Cyrillic script, *Moskva.* He and Kageneck left the station and trudged slowly back through the falling snow. "It must fall," Kageneck muttered. "yet I wonder . . . "

Neither man knew it, but they had made their country's deepest penetration on the Moscow front. The date was December 6, 1941, the memorable day on which the Russian bear turned with a snarl on its German tormentor.

Next day Japan awoke the sleeping American giant.

35. The Rise of Modern Japan

TWO EVENTS—the Treaty of Versailles and the Great Depression—were chiefly responsible for the rise of Adolf Hitler and the eruption of World War II in Europe. The same two factors were vastly influential in the emergence of Japan as a world power, eventually to be led by a clique of totalitarian war lords whose imperialist ambitions inflamed the Far East with the fires of the same war.

Less than seven decades before Versailles in 1919 put its seal upon Japan as one of "the Big Five," Nippon had been a hermit kingdom which no foreigner valuing his life dared to enter. True, there had been an interlude of intercourse with the West after a storm drove a China-bound Portuguese ship ashore in 1543. Later ships brought Catholic missionaries. Saint Francis Xavier, the great Jesuit evangelist and a leader of the Catholic Counterreformation, arrived in 1549. Under his influence a large area of the southern island of Kyushu became Catholic. This pleased neither the ruling shoguns—or commanders in chief who had seized power from the emperor—nor the Buddhist priests. The shoguns also suspected that the Catholic priests were the advance scouts or spies for the colonizing powers of Europe. It was remembered that after these priests came to the Philippines, they were followed by Spanish arms, which made those islands possessions of the King of Spain. An uprising by the Kyushu Christians was put down with ghastly severity, and in 1617 a persecution was begun. All Christians, foreign or Japanese, were hunted down ruthlessly, and those who did not recant under torture were executed.

Thereafter Japan sank deeply into isolation. No one could leave the country under pain of death and no ocean-going ships were allowed to be built. Death was decreed for any foreigner entering the country. Every Japanese family was required to register at a Buddhist temple and interest in Buddhist studies was renewed. The naive nature-and-ancestor worship of the ancient Japanese was also revived. This religion was called Shinto, a Chinese word significant of the influence of Chinese culture upon Japan. Shinto was based on a simple feeling of reverence for any surprising or awesome phenomenon of nature: a waterfall, a splendid cloud formation, a mountain, a great tree, even an oddly shaped stone. Places that aroused such a sense of awe became Shinto shrines. At the head of this basically shamanist religion stood a master medicine man: the divine emperor. Japanese tradition claimed that the Imperial family was directly descended from the sun goddess. Actually, this family derived from the Yamato clan, which claimed the sun goddess as its progenitress. During the third and fourth centuries, the Yamato clan's priest-chiefs gained suzerainty in Japan and may be said to have unified the country, although without destroying the rights of the other clans. This ruling family, then, could claim an antiquity to which none of the other ruling families of the world could compare. It also could claim the allegiance of its subjects unto death itself. To fail or to embarrass the emperor was a heinous sin for which there could be no penance other than suicide. This belief in the divinity of the emperor was something cleverly and cynically exploited by the shoguns who ruled the country.

The shoguns came to power after the Imperial armies in the eighth century suffered setbacks at the hands of Japan's original inhabitants, the Ainu. Scorning the Imperial conscripts, the shoguns formed their own smaller but better armed and disciplined forces. These were commanded by a new class of officers drawn from the sons of local clan chiefs. They were called samurai, a hereditary class of professional warriors serving the daimyos, or feudal lords. The samurai were distinguished by their hair, shaven in front and top-knotted, and by the clan badge worn on their kimonos. They lived Spartan lives and were rigorously trained in self-control. A samurai was taught to show "no sign of joy or anger." Nor was he ever to engage in trade or handle money. Like Christian seminarians, he scorned commerce as *infra dignitatem,* beneath his dignity. He was also trained to excel in martial arts, especially swordsmanship. Indeed the two swords—one long and one short—worn by the samurai were another badge of rank. He was expected to become especially proficient with the long, two-handed sword, actually a thick, heavy, single-edged saber. The short one was for decapitating a fallen enemy or for despatching himself by seppuku, more commonly known as hara-kiri, literally, "stomach cutting." A samurai would kill himself to atone for failure or similar disgrace. He would squat on the floor and thrust his short sword into his stomach—turning it in ceremonial disembowelment which, if it became too painful to endure, could be ended by a comrade standing by with the long sword. Indifference to pain, however, was part of a samurai's code of Bushido, "the way of the warrior." With such an inevitably arrogant class of warriors, permitted to cut down any commoner "who has behaved to him in a manner other than he expected," the shoguns ruled Japan. And it was not until more than two centuries after the extinction of Christianity that another foreigner came to Japan and inadvertently ended their rule.

This was Commodore Matthew Perry of the United States Navy, who arrived in 1853 determined to open Japan to Western trade. Both the Russians and the British had unsuccessfully attempted to win entry into Japan, but the Americans were more interested and forceful. They sought Japanese ports for their whaling vessels in the North Pacific and around Japan, and for their clipper ships bound for China they wanted ports to take on water and replenish their stores. With the advent of steamships they desired coaling stations.

Commodore Perry's vessels were steam-powered, and the size and armament of these "black ships," as the Japanese called them, threw the government and people of Tokyo (then called Edo) into fear and confusion. They could not believe the sight of ships moving up the bay against the wind and they knew that their puny shore batteries dared not duel the American cannon. Under the menace of Perry's guns the shogun signed a treaty with the United States opening two ports to the Americans, and in the ensuing years, the first trickle of barbarians through this crack in the isolationist dike soon became a flood. A crisis arose. Conservatives of all callings—the daimyos, the samurai, the merchants—all rallied behind the emperor, who had opposed opening the country to foreign trade. Their cry was, "Honor the emperor, expel the barbarians!"

Paradoxically, this crisis not only ended shogunate power and restored it to the emperor, but the supporters of the Meiji Restoration, as this turnabout was called, promptly embraced the civilization of the hated Western intruders: their science, industry, political institutions, methods of education, business practices, economics, dress and even sports. Never before had any great nation so thoroughly and purposefully made itself over into an exact imitation of a society it had formerly detested. In a sense it was a repetition of the importation of

Chinese civilization a thousand years earlier.

But the outpouring of Japanese envoys and students during the forty-five Meiji years was unrivaled. The Japanese studied and borrowed, copied and assimilated. They went to Britain to study the navy and merchant marine, to France for law, to Germany for the army and medicine and to the United States for business methods.

Sometimes this passion for imitating all things European would seem comical to a Westerner. Although electric lighting had been installed in the Imperial Palace, it was never turned on for fear of fire. When Japanese schoolchildren played ball, they sang to the bouncing of the ball the "Civilization Ball Song," which enumerated the ten novelties most desired by Nippon: steam engines, gas lamps, cameras, telegrams, lightning conductors, newspapers, schools, mailing services, steamships and hansom cabs. And although the ladies of Japan were loath to adopt Western dress, remaining quietly and beautifully adamant in their scarlet *hakama* and raven-black hair combed into wings and mantles, the men rushed to clothe themselves in Western business suits. Unfortunately, these suits were usually far too large, hanging on the smaller Japanese like a scarecrow's tuxedo, the too-long trousers stuffed into boots, top hats pulled down over the wearer's ears or else worn jauntily on the back of the head, and instead of the unmanageable collar and tie, a small bath towel wound around the neck like a muffler. The Japanese were also dismayed to discover that the Westerners whom they were aping were extremely proper about sex. A Japanese, accustomed to striding naked down the street, fresh from his bath with his clothes over his arm, was now required to be clad. Mixed bathing was also banned. The sexes retreated to either side of the bath while a screen was erected between them. In the brothels, the prostitutes were no longer paraded outside in cages; instead, their pictures were.

Under the direction of what was essentially an oligarchy in the hands of fewer than a hundred young men, the government laid special emphasis on creation of a strong army and navy. But the oligarchs also knew that to be truly strong the military needed to be supported by a stable and efficient political system, an educated and technically competent people, a productive industry and a sound economy. Again these fiercely patriotic young revolutionaries—for such they actually were—took everything that they needed from the West: ministries of every description, a prefectural system centralized in Tokyo, the Western calendar, religious toleration, a modern postal system and police force, compulsory education, a standardized system of taxation, a banking system based on American lines, a civil service, a revised legal and judiciary system on a French model, a cabinet on the German plan and finally a Constitution providing for a parliament called the Diet. Japan, then, did not evolve or grow like the great Western democracies it imitated; it was born fully formed like Athena from the head of Zeus. But even though outwardly the new Japan seemed to duplicate the Western democracies, even though there was an open floor on the Diet, the young oligarchs still held the scepter of power, and Japan was still a paternalistic, authoritarian state. Every advance, every modernization, each and every benefit for one and all remained a tool of government.

Japan had had a secret police since the 1600s. Now the new Japan had a Thought Police, censors and spies who, like the samurai of old empowered to kill anyone they caught doing "anything different," were tireless bloodhounds sniffing out sedition and suspicious activity. In classrooms and army barracks young Japanese were taught to glory in Japan's military traditions, to believe that dying on the battlefield for the emperor was the most sublime fate to which a man could aspire. Although the samurai had vanished by Imperial edict, taking the lump-sum compensation granted them to become merchants, professionals or bureaucrats, their famous Bushido code was revived. Soldiers of a mainly peasant army, both officers and men, were taught to think of themselves as heirs of the samurai. Officers wore a so-called samurai saber, much like the two-handed long sword of old. Properly sharpened, it could sever a prisoner's head at a single stroke, and this summary execution of captives was to become one of the less gruesome features of the new Japan's modern army as it took the field in pursuit of territorial conquest and the raw materials in which Nippon was so deplorably deficient.

The islands of Japan were singularly blessed in a happy combination of temperate climate, plentiful rainfall, fairly fertile soil and proximity to other great societies. There were four main islands north to south: Hokkaido, Honshu, Shikoku and Kyushu. They covered the same spread of latitude and range of climate as the Eastern United States. If this chain were to be superimposed on the American East Coast, Hokkaido would approximate New England, the heart of the country from Tokyo west to the Inland Sea would correspond to North Carolina and southernmost Kyushu to Georgia. But as population grew under the Meiji stimulus—it was to shoot up from 30 million in the mid-1800s to 70 million by 1940—it became apparent that Japan could neither feed its people nor take from the bowels of its own mountains the materials required by a modern industrial state. In a word, Nippon needed land.

During the second half of the 1800s a wild scramble for colonies had begun among the Western democracies. Territories in Asia, Africa and Oceania were simply seized to form new empires. Japan eagerly joined the predatory pack. In 1874, she sent a punitive expedition to the big Chinese island of Formosa to punish the natives for having killed Japanese sailors from the Ryukyus. The Chinese were forced to pay an indemnity, which was tantamount to recognizing Japan's claims to the Ryukyus. Next by a show of naval might à la Commodore Perry, Japan bullied the King of Korea into signing a treaty opening the Land of the Morning Calm to trade with Japan. In 1894 the Japanese felt ready for a real trial of military strength, launching a war with China over control of Korea. With surprising ease, Japan drove the Chinese from Korea, overran southern Manchuria, and even captured the port of Weihaiwei (Weihai) in China proper. The war ended in 1895 with China agreeing to pay Japan a huge indemnity, ceding Formosa, the Pescadores and the Liaotung Peninsula at the southern tip of Manchuria.

Although the West was impressed by the emergence of this new Asian power, some European nations were disenchanted by the arrival of a new competitor in the game of "cutting up the Chinese melon," as the raids on the tottering Manchu Dynasty were cynically described. France, Germany and Russia banded together to force Japan to return the Liaotung Peninsula to China. A howl of rage arose in Japan. It was not calmed until the emperor in an Imperial rescript counseled his people to "bear the unbearable." Nevertheless, the military never forgot this "betrayal" made because of "insincere advice" given the emperor by the politicians. They used these charges to compel the government to select its ministers of war and navy from lists of senior generals and admirals. Thus, civilian control of the military, essential to any democracy, had been severely curtailed.

Japan never forgave Russia, its chief enemy and a rival in Manchuria. The Japanese were reluctant, however, to run the risk of arraying the entire West against their country, and accordingly in 1902 made a naval pact with Britain, Russia's old enemy. Then in February 1904, in a sneak attack, the Japanese crippled Russia's Asiatic fleet in Port Arthur. Although Russia was far stronger than Japan, it had to fight a war at the end of a rickety single-track railroad several thousand miles long. Japan quickly bottled up Czar Nicholas II's troops in the ports of the Liaotung Peninsula. In desperation, Nicholas gathered his decrepit European squadrons—"the fleet that had to die"—and sent them creeping out of the Baltic and halfway around the world to the Strait of Tsushima between Korea and Japan, where they were met and annihilated by the entire Japanese navy under Admiral Heihachiro Togo. Although Japan was giving Russia a bad beating, 200,000 of its soldiers had been killed and its treasury was empty. The nation was so exhausted that the government secretly appealed to President Theodore Roosevelt of the United States to negotiate an end to the war. To its delight, he did, and in 1905 the Treaty of Portsmouth terminated the Russo-Japanese War. Russia's embarrassing defeat against the smaller foe was a coffin nail in the rule of the czars.

Japan now confined itself to the ruthless and brutal exploitation of its new possessions in Korea and Formosa. In World War I, as the ally of Britain, Japan immediately declared war on Germany. But it did little fighting, browsing instead among Germany's unguarded Chinese and Pacific possessions, taking Tsingtao and the island chains in the Marianas, Carolines and Marshalls. These were mandated to Japan in 1920 by the Treaty of Versailles, and it immediately, in violation of the mandate terms, began to fortify them.

During the twenties, the Japanese militarist-imperialist spirit seemed to subside. In its place there appeared what seemed to be a trend toward democracy, but was actually a controlling coalition of bureaucrats, politicians and the leaders of big business such as the Mitsui and Mitsubishi families, the *zaibatsu,* or financial clique, as they were called. But the militarists and superpatriots were not dead or even only sleeping. They were merely ignored by a Japanese public which saw no further need for military adventure. Nevertheless a new officer caste largely composed of the sons of officers, or rural landowners, or even of peasants was quietly growing. Most of them were recruited at the age of fourteen and given a narrow, militaristic education. Devotion to the emperor was its keystone. Military glory was its oriflamme. Not until the end of the twenties did the Japanese people become acutely aware that there had risen among them army and navy cliques motivated by a hatred of foreigners and driven by a fanatical patriotism and militarism. Then the Great Depression arrived.

Everywhere there appeared a disillusionment with democracy. The Japanese particularly scorned this form of government as inferior to the dictatorships, whose emphasis on nationalist authority seemed more compatible with Japanese concepts of authoritarian rule. After the collapse of international trade caused by the Depression, there appeared trade barriers in the form of protective tariffs, which presaged disaster for Japan's foreign trade. It became clear that the liberal government's program of prosperity through a growing export of Japanese products had been dependent upon the goodwill of the consuming nations. This was now being withdrawn. Japan, dependent upon other countries for raw materials, upon China, India and the West for markets, was now at the mercy of the tariff policies of other nations. To survive, it would have to accept a lower standard of living and step down as the strong man of Asia. This, naturally enough, it was reluctant to do.

To many Japanese, the answer to the loss of markets through trade barriers was to resume their discarded policy of colonial expansion. Japan should win for itself the sources of raw material and the markets required to make it self-sufficient and invulnerable as a world power. The militarist-imperialists, with the allegiance of superpatriotic terrorist societies excelling in the arts of intimidation and assassination, were back in favor. The agency for launching a career of conquest that would make Japan the richest empire the world had ever known was already in existence in Manchuria: the Kwangtung Army.*

This force was like a law unto itself. By the summer of 1931 it was ready with a plan to seize Manchuria on the pretext of a Chinese plot against Japan. Its officers would do this whether the emperor or the War Ministry liked it or not. They did not like it, but the officers went ahead with the first step. They dynamited the train of Marshal Chang Tso-ling, the Manchurian warlord, inflicting fatal injuries on him. The War Ministry despatched a general officer to Manchuria to halt the plotters. He was taken to an inn where he was entertained by geishas while dynamite planted by the Japanese force exploded on the tracks of the South Manchurian Railway. (The general was too drunk to notice it— though he had approved the plan already, anyway.) Here was the excuse to "restore order" by sending troops into Mukden and attacking a Chinese army barracks. Next, the Japanese overran all Manchuria and landed naval forces at

*Named for the province of China now called Guangdong.

Shanghai to take control of the city. Early in 1932, Manchuria became the puppet state of Manchukuo and 30 million industrious Chinese passed into the exploitation of Japan.

Such naked aggression did not much disturb the League of Nations or the United States. Neither did more than scold, and Japan replied by walking out of the League. Japan described the war to pacifistic President Hoover as "the Manchurian incident." "Incidents," it argued, were not "wars," and the world by its silence seemed to accept this blatant piece of casuistry. Another "incident" was arranged near Peking, and again units of the Kwangtung Army, acting with neither the knowledge nor the approval of the government, went into action. Peking and Tientsin, the chief cities of North China, were captured, as well as large parts of North China and Inner Mongolia.

But now the Chinese led by Premier Chiang Kai-shek were fighting back. This stiffening resistance enraged the Kwangtung Army generals and they determined to take the capital at Nanking. The city fell in December 1937. There then ensued the infamous "rape of Nanking," a full month of murder, rape, loot and mutilation in which the city's gutters literally ran red with the blood of its people. Nothing the Nazis under Hitler would do to disgrace their own victories could rival the atrocities of the Japanese soldiers under Gen. Iwane Matsui. Much as he later protested that he had prohibited "breaches of military discipline and morality," the fact is that while he was himself in the city, his officers made no attempt to restrain their men and that no girl as young as six or seven and no woman however senile was safe from the ravages of howling and drunken Japanese soldiers, who frequently put upon their orgies the climaxing seal of murder and mutilation. Male Chinese were machine-gunned en masse, 20,000 of them in a single day. Others were used for bayonet practice, thrown into pits to be chased and goaded like beasts in a bear garden by bayonet-wielding Japanese soldiers, until, tiring of the sport, they applied the finishing thrust. Soon the surface of the Yangtze River was a human logjam, thick with bobbing and bloated corpses. In this way 200,000—perhaps 300,000—Chinese men, women and children were murdered, while all around them their homes and buildings, deliberately set afire by the Japanese, flamed and crackled and sank into ashes.

Nanking provoked a worldwide outcry of moral indignation but brought no retribution upon the head of Nippon. The Anglo-French, with the Munich sellout only a few months behind them and World War II merely eight months away, were much too preoccupied for any concerted effort on China's behalf. The United States was still so divided by the debate between the interventionists and the pacifist-isolationists that it chose to ignore its Open Door policy guaranteeing the independence of China. It was not remembered until after the Japanese, encouraged by Hitler's string of victories, tried in the summer of 1940 to cut Chiang Kai-shek's supply lines by forcing the distraught Vichy government of France to allow them to occupy ports of Indochina. Next, Japan extracted from beleaguered Britain a promise to close the Burma Road. If it succeeded thus in strangling China, it intended next to bring all of resource-rich Southeast Asia under its control, together with the Philippines, the Dutch East Indies and the islands of Oceania. This was the beginning of *Hakko Ichiu*—"bringing the eight corners of the world under one roof"—and beneath this pagoda-shaped roof Japan would rule perhaps the most populous and certainly the richest empire in history.

President Roosevelt's response to these ominous moves was to place a partial embargo on exports to Japan. In July, Congress passed the Two-Ocean Navy Act, authorizing a shipbuilding program eventually to cost billions of dollars. Next, FDR imposed an embargo on some forms of scrap iron. Japan replied by signing the Tripartite Pact with Germany and Italy. It carved up the world into spheres of influence, recognizing Japan's supremacy in East Asia. It was also aimed directly at the United States, declaring that each ally would help the other "if attacked by a power at present not involved in the European war or in the Sino-Japanese conflict."

Roosevelt now brought heavier pressure to bear on Japan. He froze Japanese assets in America, halted exports of finished steel and scrap iron to Japan and with the cooperation of the British and the Dutch cut off its oil imports. This was nothing less than an economic blockade. Without oil and iron, the blood and bone of war, Nippon could not hope to continue the conquest of China. On the surface, the Japanese people erupted in a paroxysm of rage. Taught to hate Russia, they were now encouraged to hate Britain and the United States. Britain was flogged as a hypocritical nation whose vast empire on which the sun never set eclipsed Japan's colonial possessions. It was maintained that Japan sought only to be the champion of Asiatic peoples long exploited by the white races.

Not many of the peoples of the projected Greater East Asia Co-Prosperity Sphere, aware of the bruises on the faces of Formosa and Korea, were deceived by the sheep's clothing of this new Asiatic wolf. But the Japanese people believed it implicitly. They began to intone such semimystical phrases as "national crisis," "Japanese spirit," "national structure." Western ballroom dancing had already been banned by the war lords as effete, and next golf and other Western sports were condemned as unpatriotic. An attempt was made to stop the use of English scientific and technical words in conversation and writing, while street and railway signs which were once bilingual had the English removed. The United States was excoriated as a racist nation. It was remembered that in 1924 America had abrogated a "gentleman's agreement" with Japan whereby a handful of Japanese immigrants had been allowed to enter the country. But then Congress had classed all Japanese with the other Asiatics all but excluded by law from immigration. The Japanese regarded this as an insult, and in 1940 it was recalled to them with special vigor and venom.

All this was nothing more than the perhaps petty but psychologically powerful way in which a government prepares its people to hate a newfound enemy it may have to fight. But it also suggested that the war lords had made the crucial decision of Japan's modern life.

Two choices were open. One was for Japan to withdraw its troops from

China and settle back to take an economic profit from the European conflict as it had done in World War I. The other was to continue the war in China, thus risking hostilities with America and probably Britain and the Netherlands. The first course was the more sensible, and it was the one advocated by the moderates. But to follow it would be to "lose face" in China and all East Asia and to condemn the policy of the militarists as a failure. This the militarists would not allow. The war lords, by their career of conquest in China without reference to the Diet, had already reduced that body to a timorous and ineffectual debating club. Now, employing the so-called moderate premier Prince Fumimaro Konoye as a foil, and making their customary use of the intimidating arts of the terrorist societies, the war lords strengthened their hold on the government. In October 1941, Prince Konoye resigned, to be replaced by General Hideki Tojo.

36. Hideki Tojo

IN A WAR conducted mainly by small men, Hideki Tojo was one of the smallest. Not quite five feet two inches tall and weighing perhaps 115 pounds, he was physically so scrawny and unprepossessing that his classmates simply could not believe that he had chosen to become an army officer. He was born on December 30, 1884, the son of an army officer and the daughter of a Buddhist priest. Although the Tojo family was not among the higher samurai castes, it had served a northern feudal lord for several generations before the entire caste was abolished. The father, Hidenori, was a dedicated career officer who had joined the Japanese Imperial Army at the age of sixteen. By the childhood death of two older brothers, Hideki became the oldest son, required by the traditions and training of samurai families to become a soldier himself.

The home in which he grew up was simple and severe. Japanese officers were expected to lead austere lives. Although they were highly respected, they were poorly paid. Because of this his mother, known as "a very difficult woman," was given to outbursts of hysteria. Possibly she was no more difficult than many a woman who had given birth to seven children since her marriage at the age of seventeen, who was forced to take in sewing to supplement the meager family finances, and who, because of her husband's prolonged absences at the front, was compelled to rear a large family practically on her own. Nevertheless, she did manage to spoil little Hideki, perhaps for the very reason that he was so puny, and to expose him to a sharply alternating life of indulgence at home and of harsh, unbending discipline at school. Such was not uncommon among young Japanese males.

Small as he was, Hideki Tojo was opinionated, obstinate and quick to pick a fight. Once he got into one, he stayed in it to the end. At school, he was in the beginning no more than an average student, remembered chiefly for his aggressive personality and bad complexion. After he had entered a military preparatory school at the age of fifteen, however, he seemed to have taken to heart the injunction of Ieyasu, the founding Tokugawa shogun: "Avoid things you like; turn your attention to unpleasant duties." He became a prodigy of study and self-denial, excelling above classmates far more intellectually gifted than he was. Such success made him humorless and work-driven. "I am just an ordinary man possessing no shining talents," he was to say of himself. "Anything I have achieved I owe to my capacity for hard work and never giving up." In 1902, he entered the military academy and was graduated three years later and commissioned a second lieutenant of infantry.

That was in 1905, the year Theodore Roosevelt ended the Russo-Japanese War without the customary huge indemnity for the victor: Japan. As had occurred a decade earlier when the Triple Intervention had compelled Nippon to give up the Liaotung Peninsula, the Japanese people rose in a fury of frustration so ugly that martial law had to be declared. Americans were the chief object of their wrath, and the shaken Japanese government never told its people that it was they who had asked Roosevelt to intervene. Young Tojo assimilated much of this anti-American spirit, as much for its racial overtones as for his own frustration at having been denied the opportunity for rapid advancement. After he finished his tour in Manchuria, he entered the War College. He was there when World War I began, being graduated in 1915 and holding routine staff and regimental posts. He was elated when Japan presented China with the infamous Twenty-One Demands, which would have made that great and populous nation a Japanese puppet, and enraged when pressure from Japan's British ally and especially from America compelled it to drop them. Here again, he was convinced, was proof of American hostility to Japan.

After the war he served as military attaché in Switzerland and Germany. He admired the Germans for their toughness in enduring the hardship and suffering of the postwar years. These were qualities worthy of a samurai. He felt entirely differently about the Americans, when he journeyed through their country while returning to Japan in 1922. Here was a rich and powerful nation populated by a people who, in contrast to the formal Germans and ultraformal Japanese, were so casual as to be undignified. They were clever, he thought, but soft and effete, fond of luxury. In battle, he was sure, their material power would be no match for Japanese spiritual power.

In 1922, Major Hideki Tojo looked much older than thirty-eight. He was balding and his clipped mustache was already gray. But his mouth, from habitual compression of his lips, was like a slit, and his eyes were hard behind his horn-rimmed glasses. His slashing tongue earned him the nickname of "Kamisori," or "Razor Tojo." He was not a very military figure, his uniform hanging loosely on his scrawny frame, but it was well known in the army that Tojo was destined for high command. He worked tirelessly, a "twenty-four hour soldier," as he called himself, eating sparingly, drinking nothing stronger than coffee, but smoking incessantly, up to three packs a day. This distressed his wife, Katsu, both for the stink and filthy ashes and the cost. He frequently promised to give up smoking, but finally confessed: "It's the only pleasure I have."

Tojo had married Katsu, the daughter of a small landowner in Kyushu, when she was nineteen. His choice had surprised his parents, because he was marrying for love rather than through the traditional contract made by the parents, and also because Katsu was an emancipated young lady. She had even aspired to higher education. "You could say that I tend to be headstrong," she had said, "and I don't take easily to having my mind changed." Such a willful young lady, Tojo's mother thought, would never be happy in the self-effacing role of a Japanese wife. But she did accept it, gave birth to seven children, and was perhaps her husband's only real friend, certainly his one confidante.

During the twenties, when democratic military forces everywhere were declining in prestige, the Japanese army also sank into desuetude. Disenchantment was so great that it was reduced in strength by four divisions. Only during the Great Earthquake of 1923, when 100,000 Japanese perished and the cities of Tokyo and Yokohama were all but eradicated, did the rescue operations undertaken by the soldiery earn widespread gratitude. So did the enormously generous contributions of the Americans, but a year later this was forgotten with passage of legislation all but excluding the Japanese from immigrating to the United States. Japanese, insulted at being classified as "coolies" like the Chinese, Hideki Tojo among them, renewed their hatred of Americans. Tojo agreed that the law was passed out of jealousy, that Japanese farmers had proved themselves more efficient than the Americans. "It shows," he said, "how the strong must always put their own interest first. Japan, too, has to be strong to survive in the world."

There followed, of course, the Great Depression and the erection of the trade barricades that threatened to reduce Japanese exports to a trickle; and next, in frantic reaction, the Kwangtung Army literally forcing Japan to resume a career of military conquest in Manchuria. That was where the reliable and efficient Hideki Tojo was posted in 1935. Known as a soldier who lived and worked by the book, he was now a major general. His new assignment would put him in command of the Kwangtung detachment of the notorious *Kempeitai:* the Japanese secret police.

In Manchuria, Hideki Tojo did not attempt to make of his military police the same kind of all-powerful, all-insinuating organization fashioned by Heinrich Himmler in Germany. But he did hurl himself into the preparation of dossiers on the activities, private and public, of all those suspected of hostility toward the Kwangtung Army. He was thus ready when, in Tokyo on the night of February 26, 1936, a group of young army officers made a murderous attempt to take over the government.

Led by officers no higher than the rank of captain, assassination squads of soldiers began hunting down their victims just before daylight. They shot or sabered to death anyone who stood in their path, indiscriminately massacring servants and assistants while they killed Viscount Saito, Finance Minister Takahashi, the Lord Privy Seal, and Colonel Watanabe, the inspector-general of military training. They attacked the official residence of Admiral Okawa, the aged prime minister, killing his brother-in-law by mistake while he hid in a cupboard. They also left Admiral Suzuki, the grand chamberlain, for dead—but he eventually recovered. Other victims on the list such as members of the Genro, the advisory council of elder statesmen, were saved from harm by the police. But by daybreak the rebels had occupied the prime minister's residence, the War Ministry, the Diet, law courts, the police headquarters, army and navy buildings and newspaper offices. They issued bulletins denouncing the elder statesmen, parliamentary government and big business as the enemies of Japan, confidently expecting to be joined by the generals and admirals who they knew shared such views. But they never arrived. Instead, on the direct orders of Emperor Hirohito, there came battalions of soldiers to arrest them. Eighteen were allowed to kill themselves, being graciously supplied with sabers for that purpose.

In the meantime, the rebels had sent signals to all the army groups, including the Kwangtung Army in Manchuria, inviting them to join the mutiny. They were confident that General Seishiro Itagaki, the Kwangtung chief of staff, with his fondness for plotting and direct action, would tip the scales in their favor. But General Itagaki knew he could not move without the support of his internal security chief, and he was also aware that Hideki Tojo, with his narrow textbook outlook and simplicist mind, would never raise a hand against the government. So he did nothing, while General Tojo with characteristic efficiency sent his police into action. Within hours they had rounded up all those even remotely suspected of sedition and there was no rebellion in Manchuria.

In Tokyo, at trials conducted in secret, thirteen of the leaders were given death sentences; eighteen others received long prison terms; many others—including NCOs—went to jail for shorter periods; twenty officers were cashiered; and others were shipped to Manchuria, where they were given something of a hero's reception by the men of the Kwangtung Army. Such acclaim was of short duration, however, after Hideki Tojo was gazetted to lieutenant general in early 1937 and replaced General Itagaki as Kwangtung chief of staff.

In 1937 the premiership of Japan became known as one of the briefest and sometimes most dangerous jobs in the world. But a procession of premiers and would-be premiers, all victims of the bullying militarists, seemed to have ended with the appointment in June of Prince Fumimaro Konoye. Hardly more than a week after he took office, on July 7, in another staged "incident" bearing the familiar fingerprints of its predecessors, a Japanese detachment on night exercises at the Marco Polo Bridge near Peking was allegedly fired on by Chinese soldiers. The Japanese struck the Chinese savagely and with superb execution of planning and supply. To the surprise of the Japanese generals, the Chinese fought back stubbornly. China and Japan were once again locked in major conflict, but this time in a war that was to endure for eight more years. Five full divisions had to be rushed from Japan, and General Tojo was ordered to send supporting forces from his Kwangtung Army. On his own, he personally led a Kwangtung force to outflank Chinese troops threatening Japanese near Peking. This, a masterful textbook operation, was Hideki Tojo's only experience of commanding troops in combat. It was also his last, for in 1938 he was summoned to Tokyo for what was to be his first experience in a political office: vice minister of war.

By this time the war lords had become divided over the objectives in Japan's career of conquest. The army favored a "northward" advance, with the Soviet Union as the true target. Hideki Tojo was among those who believed that China was merely a tactical obstacle en route to that strategic encounter. The navy, however, had embraced the concept of a "southward advance," coveting the oil-rich Dutch East Indies, the Philippines and the islands of Oceania. This the generals did not like because it would be a naval war that would make the admirals preeminent and assign to the army a smaller supporting role. In reply, the admirals pointed to the impossibility of Japan's 70-odd million people conquering two great land masses, each with populations several times greater than Nippon's. They reminded the army of what had happened in the Russo-Japanese War, when Japan had almost exhausted itself, suffered 200,000 dead and drained its treasury. Yes, said the generals, but Japan is now much stronger, the Red Army has been emasculated by Stalin's purges and to finish off China will take only four months. To this the sailors gave no answer, if only because the real reply had been given by the Soviets. In the summer of 1938 they had fought the Japanese to a standstill in a pitched battle near Changkufeng on the Manchurian border (now in the U.S.S.R.). In May of the following year another border skirmish had escalated into full-scale war with tanks, artillery and aircraft, and the Japanese had been badly beaten, suffering losses of 50,000 men to the Soviets' 10,000.

These setbacks shook some of the generals, but not Hideki Tojo. Still clinging obstinately to the northward advance, he called together a group of leading industrialists. Barking at them in approved drill-instructor style, "as if he were laying down the law to a company of new recruits," he told them that the Soviet Union remained the chief enemy. He also warned them that if, in the event of this conflict, they placed profits before patriotism, "the Army would find means of seeing that they toed the line in the future."

Furious, the industrialists quickly informed the press of their humiliating treatment, and the incident made headlines not only in Japan but throughout the world, where Tojo's prediction of war with the U.S.S.R. was widely quoted. A few months later, Lieutenant General Tojo was quietly kicked downstairs to the post of inspector general of the air forces. Meanwhile, the war in China brought about the resignation of Prince Konoye. He was succeeded by no fewer than four prime ministers during the period that saw the outbreak of World War II and the string of Hitlerian victories. On July 18, 1940, after the fall of France and amid the tightening of tensions between Japan and the United States, Konoye returned to power. Under the customary pressure of the army he chose as his minister of war the general who had inadvertently helped to undermine him eighteen months previously: Hideki Tojo.

Having finally accepted the southward rather than the northward advance, Tojo was now the darling of the admirals as well as the generals. Therefore, when the gradual transfer of power into the hands of the war lords brought about Konoye's second resignation, it came as no surprise that this son of a samurai family, this colorless careerist but always reliable soldier, his head full of textbook or simplicist solutions and his heart burning with hatred of the United States, should be chosen as the first minister of the divine emperor of Japan.

37. Isoroku Yamamoto and the Planning for Pearl Harbor

ON HIS ASCENSION TO POWER Premier Tojo announced that he would pursue Konoye's policy of "continuation of conversations with the United States." To Tojo, "conversation" meant capitulation to his demands. What he could not get at the conference table he would seize on the battlefield. He did not shrink from war with both Britain and the United States. Hindsight may well condemn him for having challenged the world's foremost industrial nations and its two leading sea powers in what could only be a naval war par excellence, yet in that fateful fall of 1941, war did not seem a bad choice to a nation confronted with a win-all, lose-all situation.

First, the Japanese would be operating on interior lines and would be much closer to the target areas. Second, the enemy garrisons were very weak and could be easily overwhelmed. Third, the oil and minerals seized at the outset would make Japan much stronger militarily. Fourth, Japan's chief Asiatic rival, the Soviet Union, appeared to be collapsing beneath the Wehrmacht's hammer blows, Britain was preoccupied with Hitler, and America, it was believed, would never concentrate in the Pacific so long as Germany remained undefeated.

If Germany won, Japan was safe. If Germany did not, it would at least have distracted the enemy long enough for Japan to crush China and to make its new empire impregnable to counterattack. It would be invincible because the enemy, the Americans in particular, would not have the moral stamina required for a bloody, costly and prolonged sea march to the shores of Nippon. Instead, the enemy, and again especially the Americans, would be eager to accept a negotiated peace that would leave Japan's stolen new empire essentially intact. *Hakko Ichiu*, then, would have been begun.

Japan's faith in German arms in the fall of 1941 was certainly realistic: Britain was at bay, Rommel was rampaging again in North Africa and the Soviets seemed finished. But the belief in American weakness had no basis in fact. Actually, it was just that, belief, superstition even, a religious faith in their own "spiritual power" as being superior to whatever firepower the soft Americans might muster. The Japanese had become, in Arnold Toynbee's phrase, "enchanted with the ephemeral self." They believed their own propaganda, listening only to every isolationist manifesto or pacifist bleat emanating from American shores, reading only of the Ludlow Amendment, seeing nothing but the pacifist-isolationists picketing the White House during the Lend-Lease debate, and closing their minds to any suggestion that the United States was now thoroughly alarmed, rapidly converting its industry to the manufacture of weapons and rearming itself through its first peacetime draft.

Not every Japanese believed that the United States would wage the feeble war assigned to it in the Japanese scheme. Isoroku Yamamoto, the revered "iron admiral" of the Japanese navy, was an outspoken opponent of war with America. On January 26, 1941, he wrote to a friend: "Should hostilities break out between Japan and the United States, it would not be enough that we take Guam and the Philippines, nor even Hawaii and San Francisco. To make victory certain we would have to march into Washington and dictate the terms of peace in the White House." When this letter was discovered by the war lords, they were appalled, deliberately distorting it to mean that Yamamoto believed Japanese victory was certain and then releasing it for publication. This false version was widely circulated in the United States as well, giving the impression that the arrogant Japanese admiral expected to sit in the White House to dictate terms to the vanquished Americans. Actually, Yamamoto's letter was full of biting sarcasm, of which this famous paragraph was merely a sample. He was saying that for Japan to win, it would have to cross the Pacific Ocean, seizing springboard islands en route, invade the West Coast and then march 3,000 miles over great mountains, across scorching deserts and great plains, fighting every inch of the way against a resolute nation of 130 million souls and at the end of a line of communications growing steadily to a length of 10,000 miles. There was no power in the world capable of such a feat of arms. Nevertheless, this sage advice was ignored. Japan was already suffering from "victory fever." It had won limited wars against a Chinese jellyfish and a Russian hollow man and was now quite certain that it could do the same against a big but spineless American playboy. Again, on September 18, 1941, Isoroku Yamamoto had something to say on this score: "It is a mistake to regard Americans as luxury loving and weak. I can tell you that they are full of spirit, adventure, fight and justice. Their thinking is scientific and well advanced. Lindbergh's solo flight across the Atlantic was an act characteristic of Americans—adventuresome but scientifically based. Remember that American industry is much more developed than ours, and—unlike us—they have all the oil they want. Japan cannot vanquish the United States. Therefore we should not fight the United States."

This warning also went unheeded. In a sense, the Japanese leaders had the same low estimate of industry as the sine qua non of modern war that was characteristic of the South during the Civil War, sharing the same misguided belief in the superiority of spiritual power over firepower. Tragically, Japan acted on this miscalculation. Its strategy was to destroy American naval power at Pearl Harbor, after which it would embark on its timetable of conquest. By the time the United States recovered from the Pearl Harbor losses, Japan's new empire would be safe behind a chain of island fortresses. In one of the great ironies of modern history, the planning for this crucial operation—to be a sneak attack like those in 1894 and 1904—was given to the commander who had most steadfastly opposed the war itself: Isoroku Yamamoto.

The child who was to become the Iron Admiral was born April 4, 1884, in the city of Nagaoka in the northwest of Japan's main island of Honshu. His father was Sadayoshi Takano, an impoverished schoolmaster who already had five sons and a daughter. "My age is fifty-six," he said to his wife, "let's call him that." Thus the name Isoroku, written with the characters for five, ten and six. It was then Isoroku Takano, but upon the death of his parents in 1913, he was adopted into the prominent Yamamoto clan. It is still common in Japan for leading families having no male heir to adopt a promising young man to perpetuate the family name.

Little Isoroku led a vigorous outdoor life, gardening and fishing in summer, struggling against the deep winter snows, and absorbing from his father a deep love of learning. He also may have assimilated a hatred of America, according to one biographer, who wrote: "Young Yamamoto began to hate America when his father told him tales of the hairy barbarians, creatures with an animal odor owing to their habit of eating flesh, who had come in their black ships, broken down the doors of Japan, threatened the Son of Heaven, trampled upon ancient customs, demanded indemnities, blown their long noses on clothes which they then put in their pockets instead of throwing them away."

Yamamoto entered the naval academy at Etajima on the Inland Sea, scoring second on examinations taken by 300 applicants. He had by then reached his full height, five feet three inches, small even for a Japanese. But he was strongly built, with broad shoulders and a thick chest. His large, well-spaced, dark eyes shone with intelligence, and his angular jaw bespoke the determined will of a fighter. This was the fledgling navy of the new Japan that Yamamoto had chosen for his career, and he was not the least dismayed to find that during their three academic years at Etajima naval cadets were not allowed to drink, smoke, eat sweets or go out with girls. Yamamoto would always prefer a Spartan life. The fourth year was spent entirely at sea, close to dangerous waters where storms raged and seas ran rough. This also suited Yamamoto, who was graduated seventh in his class, just in time for the Russo-Japanese War. He served aboard the cruiser *Nisshin,* part of the protective screen for *Mikasa,* the mighty battleship that carried Admiral Togo's flag at Tsushima. He wrote of that battle: "I realized no fear when the shells began to fly about me, damaging the ship and killing many men. At 1850 hours a shell hit *Nisshin* and knocked me unconscious. I was wounded in the left leg and two fingers of my left hand were severed. The Russian ships were utterly defeated, however, and their dead littered the sea. When victory was announced at 0200 next day, even the wounded cheered."

Yamamoto congratulated himself on losing only two fingers. One more and he would have been discharged as physically unfit. For the next decade he received the usual peacetime assignments, and spent World War I studying naval aviation and foreign affairs. In 1919 he was sent to Boston to study English, in which he became quite proficient. He also learned to play poker with the best of his American friends, while teaching them Japanese chess. In Boston, Yamamoto developed a passion for the study of oil, which he rightly considered the lifeblood of modern war, and its special relationship to navies. Returning home in 1921, he became an instructor in the Naval Staff College, and in June of 1923 began a nine-month trip through Europe and the United States with the navy vice minister.

In 1924 Capt. Isoroku Yamamoto was obviously one of the most outstanding officers in the Japanese navy. He had become one of its chief theorists on naval aviation, even though he never learned to fly, and was the darling of the pilots, who welcomed his fresh approach to problems and his daring, imaginative decisions. In his boldness Yamamoto was almost unique. Japan had chosen the British navy for its model, and had unfortunately equated the good manners of the gentlemanly British officers with easy affability, thus producing many charming flag officers but not many really bold leaders.

Yamamoto returned to the United States in February 1926 as a naval attaché. Once again his prowess at poker impressed his American friends, who were also surprised to find that under Yamamoto the naval attaché's office in Washington shifted its emphasis from gathering intelligence on tactical and technical data to one of solving the problems of high naval strategy. Adm. Ellis Zacharias, who knew him well, recalled: "I always felt, after Yamamoto was appointed commander in chief of the Combined Fleet and wartime leader of Japan's navy, that the first plans for the Pearl Harbor attack originated in his restless brain right here in Washington . . . great naval strategist that he was, he recognized even at that early stage of sea-air-power development the significance of carriers."

Yamamoto's plan was typically bold and based upon his knowledge of American customs. Sunday morning, the time when the Americans would either be at church services or sleeping off the effects of Saturday night parties, was chosen for the propitious moment. Six aircraft carriers mounting 423 airplanes were selected for the striking force, screened by two battleships, two heavy cruisers and ten or eleven smaller warships, plus the necessary tankers for refueling—a total of thirty ships. Command was given to Vice Adm. Chuichi Nagumo, a sailor with absolutely no experience in aviation. Nagumo was one of those jolly admirals in which the Japanese navy abounded: big, very physical and very hearty, the sort of man who would greet a friend with a shout of welcome and a staggering slap on the shoulder. Because not many specialists had yet appeared in most of the world's navies, he was given the First Air Fleet simply because he was senior to the other admirals. Fortunately for Nagumo, he was able to obtain the services of two rising young specialists in the tactics and techniques of sea-air warfare: Commanders Mitsuo Fuchida and Minoru Genda.

It was these two officers—Genda the creative genius, the idea man; Fuchida, the man of action, the executive putting Genda's proposals into practice—who ultimately solved the appalling problems of the Pearl Harbor operation. First and foremost of these was the shallow depth—forty feet—of the waters there. Japan's aerial torpedoes would undoubtedly bury themselves uselessly in the mud of the harbor floor. Even if the enemy's ships were sunk by other bombing methods, they could eventually be raised. Lahaina Roads, where the American fleet sometimes anchored, was infinitely deeper. At Lahaina, the "fish" would certainly run true and the Americans would never be able to salvage their sunken ships. Fuchida and Genda, however, wasted no time wishing that the attack would be on Lahaina. Instead, they worked tirelessly to solve the problems presented by Pearl Harbor.

Genda experimented constantly with devices to prevent the torpedo at launching from falling below a depth of about thirty-six feet, while Fuchida with unswerving faith put his torpedo-bomber pilots through trial runs at perilously low altitudes. These were conducted at Kagoshima Bay, which, with its smokestacks, cranes and other harbor installations, fairly well duplicated the confined maneuvering space of Pearl Harbor. All efforts failed, however, until the fall of 1941 when a stabilizing fin was attached to the torpedo. Flying high above Kagoshima Bay, Commander Fuchida leaned eagerly out of his cockpit to watch three bombers launch their "fish." One of them sank out of sight, but the other two with their white trails cleaving through the blue water ran straight and true to their targets. Fuchida was elated. Success! Two out of three was a fine percentage. It meant that of forty torpedoes launched, twenty-seven should run true.

The next problem to overcome was the possibility of the American ships being protected by antitorpedo nets. Genda and Fuchida had learned in March 1941 that none had been installed, but there was always the chance that they would be in place at the time of attack. These would greatly reduce the effectiveness of the torpedo-bomber strikes. Also, the American custom of double-mooring its battleships exposed only the outer vessel to torpedoes. What of the inner ship? Genda thought at first that the dive bombers might prevail there. But on reflection he realized that the dive bombers' explosives would not be heavy enough to penetrate the thick armor of the *Maryland*-class battleships stationed at Pearl. He decided to use high-level, horizontal bombers carrying a single bomb adapted from a Japanese battleship's 16-inch shell weighing 1,800 pounds. So the pilots of these craft also were given special training. In the beginning they were taught to fly at about 16,500 feet to avoid antiaircraft fire, but Fuchida insisted that if they came down to 9,800 they would still have enough altitude for the bomb to pierce the armor plate. "The risk is worth running to ensure maximum destruction," he said to Genda, and his colleague agreed.

Fuchida, a daring pilot and resourceful leader, was to command the first wave of fighters and the three types of bombers. It would launch about 230 miles north of Oahu to arrive over Pearl Harbor at about 8:00 A.M. Fuchida's flight would possess the element of surprise and was expected to do the most damage. It would be followed by the second wave of fighters and horizontal and dive bombers launching about 200 miles north of Oahu. Their mission was to give the coup de grace to ships stricken in the first wave's attack and to complete the destruction of United States air power to prevent retaliation against the ships of the First Air Fleet.

Meanwhile—by one of the great ironies of the war—Yamamoto's objective of destroying from one fifth to one fourth of the American Pacific Fleet seemed to be achieved for him as a result of Lend-Lease. Under this agreement the U.S. Navy was to assume responsibility for protection of transatlantic convoys. This was to lead to "the shooting war short of war" whereby American vessels defended themselves against German submarines. It was hardly the proper activity for a neutral, but then the Germans also paid scant heed to international law. In May 1941, one of their U-boats sank the American freighter *Robin Moor* in a neutral zone of the South Atlantic. In that same month, to strengthen the Atlantic Fleet, President Roosevelt ordered the battleships *Mississippi, Idaho* and *New Mexico,* the carrier *Yorktown,* four light cruisers, seventeen destroyers, three oilers, three transports and ten auxiliaries to sail from Pearl Harbor for the Atlantic. During the summer, sixteen more vessels departed for the same waters. The Pacific Fleet had been reduced by about one quarter without Japan firing a shot! It had been weakened to exactly the strength at which it would be unable to interfere in Japanese ambitions in the Far East. Why, then, did Yamamoto continue with his plans for Pearl Harbor? His intelligence there certainly reported the departure of the American vessels. In fact, Roosevelt had practically informed the entire world of this situation in a Fireside Chat of May 27; and it is not very easy for a battleship or an aircraft carrier to sail unobserved through the Panama Canal.

Nevertheless, Yamamoto continued to cling to his plan with an obstinacy that surprised even those who were aware of his strong will, and even after September war games suggested that Japan would lose two or three carriers—a loss that Adm. Osami Nagano, chief of the Navy General Staff, considered prohibitive. Again, why? First, Yamamoto had no way of knowing, in the volatile world of 1941, how long Roosevelt would assign priority to the Atlantic. Moreover, the timetable of conquest drawn up by Japan was so vast and perilous that Yamamoto simply could not risk exposing his eastern flank. In war, it is axiomatic that a commander should not act upon what he thinks his enemy *will* do but on what he has the *capacity* to do. Even at three-quarter strength, the American Pacific Fleet *could* severely chastise the invading fleets, especially in collaboration with British Far Eastern warships. Finally, it seems certain that Yamamoto believed—rather, hoped—that a crushing defeat at Pearl Harbor, with Americans actually dying and ships sinking, would weaken the American will to fight to the point at which the United States government would have to consider Japan's policy of a negotiated peace. Furthermore, the surprise attack had been successful in 1894 and 1904, why not again in 1941? When Prince Konoye had long ago asked Yamamoto about Japan's chances against Britain and the United States, he had replied: "If we are told to fight, regardless of consequences, we can run wild for six months or a year, but after that I have utterly no confidence." The Pacific Fleet at the bottom of Pearl Harbor would provide Japan with a head start for that wild run.

But there are other nagging questions. Did a reduced Pacific Fleet encourage Japan? Probably not. The Pacific Fleet at any strength—full, half or quarter—was no deterrent to a Nippon embarked on a course of war to preserve its standard of living and its standing in the world. It is even likely that Yamamoto would have preferred a much stronger fleet based on Pearl Harbor so that his surprise strike would be even more helpful to the scheduled invasions. The truth is that the war lords knew what they had chosen and where they wanted to go. In Washington, Franklin Roosevelt had not yet laid to rest the ghost of pacifist-isolationism. Most Americans, as anyone who lived through those days will attest, did not believe that war was imminent. All Roosevelt could do was to struggle to keep Britain fighting and to contain the Nazi beast.

Thus Isoroku Yamamoto was urged to complete the plan that would so facilitate the Japanese timetable of conquest. Japanese Intelligence knew full well that American battle plans for the Pacific called for the U.S. Navy to sail to the assistance of the Philippine Islands, which would then become a powerful forward base for operations. But if the American battle fleet was on the bottom of Pearl Harbor, there would be no such rescue. So time was indeed of the essence, especially now that the Philippines were becoming stronger. On July 26, 1941, the day on which Roosevelt closed the Panama Canal to Japanese shipping and froze all Japanese assets in the United States, he also called the Filipino army into American service. Combined Filipino-American forces were to be commanded by an American major general whom he did not name. But the War Department did: Douglas MacArthur.

38. Douglas MacArthur

IN THE YEAR 1825 a ten-year-old boy and his widowed mother arrived in Boston from Glasgow, Scotland. They traveled from there to the hamlet of Chicopee Falls in the lovely hill country of western Massachusetts. There Arthur MacArthur and his mother, Sarah, began a new life in the New World.

They had left behind them a distinguished family heritage, for the MacArthurs had been renowned warriors as far back as the time of Robert the Bruce, the thirteenth-century king and liberator of Scotland. Why the descendants of such a famous clan found it necessary to emigrate is not known, nor are the details of the death of the father. Sarah remarried and Arthur eventually studied law in New York City and was admitted to the Massachusetts bar in 1840. Four years later he married Aurelia Belcher, a descendant of the colonial governor Jonathan Belcher. In June of 1845 she gave birth to a son, Arthur II. By then the senior MacArthur seemed to be prospering through his law practice in Springfield, where he was city attorney; yet in 1849 he left with his wife and son for a relatively unknown city named Milwaukee in the new state of Wisconsin.

In Milwaukee, this big, handsome, affable man, gifted as a wit and raconteur, entered politics as a Democrat. He was elected lieutenant governor, and after his running mate was disqualified because of voting irregularities, served as governor for five days. He became a state judge and then an associate justice of the Supreme Court of the District of Columbia.

Young Arthur MacArthur chose a military rather than a law career. In 1862 he joined the 24th Wisconsin Infantry as a second lieutenant at the age of seventeen, becoming one of the most famous commanders in the Union Army, known as "the boy colonel of the west," and winning the Medal of Honor for leading a victorious charge at the Battle of Chattanooga. After the war he studied law under his father for a few months, but the army was his true love, and he returned to it even though he was reduced in rank to second lieutenant again. By July of 1866 he was back up to captain, and there he stayed for another twenty-three years.

It was during this period that MacArthur met and married Mary Pinkney Hardy, daughter of an aristocratic Southern family. Her father had been a wealthy Virginia planter whose mansion, Riveredge, was confiscated by the Union Army. Four of her brothers were Confederate veterans. But "Pinky" Hardy had eyes only for the dashing Yankee veteran to whom she was introduced at a Mardi Gras ball in New Orleans. They were married at Riveredge in May 1875. He was a month short of his thirtieth birthday and she was twenty-two. It is said that some of her brothers boycotted the wedding of their sister to a "damn-Yankee." It is true, though, that the Hardys and MacArthurs never hit it off.

Nevertheless, Mary was able to return to Riveredge for the birth of their first two sons: Arthur III on June 1, 1876, and Malcolm on October 17, 1878. Douglas would have been born there too, except that he arrived so fast there was no time to journey from the 13th Infantry post at Little Rock, Arkansas, to Virginia. Douglas was born at Little Rock on January 26, 1880.

Douglas MacArthur was the "Army brat" par excellence. From the moment of his birth the sound of blaring bugles and booming guns were as familiar to him as the croaking of frogs to country boys or the shriek of factory whistles to street urchins. MacArthur and his brothers grew up on the frontier. In the summer of

1880 the family of five moved to Fort Wingate, New Mexico. No outpost could have been lonelier or more inimical in terrain, climate and neighbors. "It is a self-evident truth," the Las Vegas *Gazette* reported in November 1880, "that New Mexico has been for years the asylum of desperadoes. Mingled with as good people as are to be found anywhere on the continent is the scum of society from all states. We jostle against murderers, bank robbers, forgers and other fugitives from justice in the post office and on the platform at the depot."

Captain MacArthur saw no exaggeration in this complaint. He had known the badmen of earlier days—the James boys, the Youngers—and the even more picturesque lawmen and scouts such as "Wild Bill" Hickok and "Buffalo Bill" Cody. Indian marauders were not new to him. But at Wingate he had to deal with the likes of Billy the Kid Bonney and Geronimo, the wily Apache leader. To his sons, however, Wingate was a paradise of adventure.

Joined to this stimulation of adventure was the awesome and majestic beauty of their surroundings. Fort Wingate was like a little lost settlement lying on the floor of a valley formed by towering mountains, some of them rising to 11,000 feet. The cold clear headwaters of the Rio Puerco ran nearby. Frequently the boys accompanied the soldiers on the water detail, when they would play in the river. Because there were so few playmates, the soldiers were almost their only companions.

If Fort Wingate seemed like Paradise Recovered to the MacArthur boys, it was like Paradise Lost to their mother. Living there was only less primitive than life as an Indian squaw. But Mary MacArthur bore her burden "with courage and even an heroic gaiety," succumbing to heartbreak only in the spring of 1883 when Malcolm died of measles. Eventually the tragedy seemed to draw her closer to her other two sons, especially Douglas, whom she nursed through attacks of diphtheria, measles, scarlet fever and mumps. In February 1884, Captain MacArthur was ordered to move to Fort Selden on the Rio Grande.

It was only 300 miles, as distances go in the vastness of the Southwest a mere fraction of an inch on a map, but at the slow and slower pace of wagon-speed and walking, it took a solid month. The only thing for which the travelers were thankful at the end of their journey was that they had encountered no hostile Indians. For Fort Selden itself, they had anything but thanks. It was a replica of Wingate, perhaps even lonelier and certainly hotter and dustier. It was tense and anxious, too, after Geronimo and his warriors escaped from their reservation in May 1885. At Selden, Douglas learned to ride and shoot with exceptional skill.

With some help from her husband, Mary began tutoring both boys in the "simple rudiments" of an education. Moral principles ranked highest on the curriculum. "We were to do what was right," Douglas said later, "no matter what the personal sacrifice might be. Our country always was to come first. Two things we must never do: never lie, never tattle." Much as such moral precepts, made stronger by the example of their parents' lives, might form the conscience of the MacArthur boys, they were, on the intellectual side, as Mary MacArthur well knew, no substitute for the three R's. Therefore she and her husband were overjoyed to be transferred to Fort Leavenworth in the early autumn of 1886. Here Douglas attended the post school, which he immediately detested and where he did poorly. He yearned for the wild and carefree life of the frontier. He also chafed at being kept in long curled hair and skirts until he was eight. He was even more unhappy when the family moved to Washington almost three years later. His marks, however, were just a little better than at Leavenworth: about average. Nevertheless, Douglas was elated when in the fall of 1893 his father was transferred to Fort Sam Houston for service on the turbulent Mexican border. MacArthur, now a major, was himself delighted to learn that the Episcopal Church had just opened the West Texas Military Academy near the base. He entered Douglas there in the ninth grade.

Suddenly the spark of ambition, like fire with incense, inflamed the mind of Douglas MacArthur. From an indifferent student with little interest in sports or other extracurricular activities, he became the school's outstanding scholar, and then, in his final two years, its best soldier and athlete. He was the valedictorian of his graduating class. During the final two years he was first sergeant of his company and named to the Crack Squad, an elite drill unit of ten cadets. Douglas also quarterbacked the football team to an undefeated and unscored-on season, won the school's tennis championship and played shortstop for a baseball team that won seven out of eight games one year and was unbeaten the next. A social life was also blossoming. Douglas, already extremely handsome, was dashing in his gray cadet uniform, and he dated many young ladies on the post as well as those at the Episcopal female academy in San Antonio.

In the spring of 1896 Douglas applied for an appointment-at-large to enter the United States Military Academy in June of 1897. Colonel MacArthur and the aging Judge MacArthur prevailed upon many distinguished friends to recommend the young man. President Cleveland received letters from no fewer than four governors, three U.S. senators, two representatives, two generals and two bishops. Unfortunately, all spoke glowingly of Colonel MacArthur and hardly mentioned his son. Douglas got none of the four presidential appointments. But he was undaunted. Having been graduated from the academy, he pursued a course of study that would prepare him for a competitive examination in May of 1898.

The Spanish-American War was barely a month old when, accompanied by his mother, Douglas walked to city hall for the examination. He was nervous and tense, beginning to experience the dreadful nausea that seized him during times of crisis. His mother sought to reassure him: "Doug, you'll win if you don't lose your nerve. You must believe in yourself, my son, or no one else will believe in you. Be self-confident, self-reliant, and even if you don't make it, you will know you have done your best. Now, go to it!"

Douglas was deeply moved by this exhortation, but it was the long, arduous months of study that restored his confidence. When he saw the test questions, his nausea left him. He scored 93.3, sixteen points higher than his nearest competitor, and in June of 1899, still accompanied by his mother, he arrived at West Point.

By the time Douglas MacArthur reached the storied plains above the Hudson River, his father had become famous as the hero of the Philippines. He had helped to defeat the Spanish there, after which, upon the Filipino rising against the United States occupation known as the Philippine Insurrection, he won victory after victory over the *insurrectos* led by Emilio Aguinaldo. His triumphs, his flamboyant speeches and his savage denunciations of his superior officer, the dull and doltish Maj. Gen. Ellwell S. Otis, made him extremely "good copy" for the American correspondents covering the war. On May 6, 1900, MacArthur was a lieutenant general and the military governor of the Philippines.

At the age of nineteen, Douglas showed signs of rivaling his father for brilliance of mind, matchless courage, iron will, striking good looks—and an arrant arrogance approached only by his colossal conceit. It was the arrogance and conceit that decided some of his classmates to shrink his swelling head a little.

At first, resentful sophomores, or yearlings—the official tormentors of the lowly plebes during those days of brutal hazing—were content with forcing MacArthur to memorize great portions of his father's speeches. He was made to stand at attention and recite them. But, Douglas was plainly delighted with the chance to make with the MacArthur manner, so the hazers turned to less harmless pranks.

First, MacArthur was made to eagle—that is, to squat up and down with the arms outstretched. Then, he was forced to hang by his hands from a tent pole, several minutes at a time. Next, he was made to lie face downward on the wooden floor while pumping furiously with his elbows. The ordeal, or "exercising," as it was called, went on for close to two hours. Gradually, all color left MacArthur's face. His body was on fire with the pain of this unfamiliar strain on unused muscles. Repeatedly, the yearling hazers called upon him to give up. He said nothing, but went on jumping, swinging and pumping, until, finally, half in fear of what they had done, half in admiration of MacArthur's doggedness, they let him go.

When the groggy MacArthur dragged himself back to his tent, shared by a plebe named Frederick Cunningham of Utica, New York, he immediately went into convulsions. He sank to the floor and his limbs began to twitch and his feet began to drum on the planking to such an extent that he called out to Cunningham to put a blanket under them "so the company officers won't hear me." Then, his limbs still writhing and twitching, he told Cunningham: "If I start to groan or anything, stuff a blanket in my mouth to stop the noise."

The next day, MacArthur dragged himself from his cot and turned out for drill without a word of what he had endured. Even a year later, when West Point hazing was blamed for the death of a Pennsylvania cadet and became a national scandal, MacArthur was able to shield his tormentors.

Thereafter, his star rose. He would go on to be graduated from the academy as the first in his class with a four-year average of 98.14. This is the highest average in West Point history, though it cannot be compared to any modern cadet's, since MacArthur himself revised the curriculum when he was the academy's superintendent.

After receiving his commission as a second lieutenant, he chose to serve in the engineers, the army elite then, and he sailed for Manila from San Francisco in 1903. He landed at Leyte, and almost immediately came under fire. His surveying party was ambushed by Filipino guerrillas. At the first blast of a shotgun fired at close range, one of his men keeled over. As MacArthur moved to catch him, there was another blast. His campaign hat flew off his head, and a grizzled old army sergeant tapped him on the shoulder and murmured: "Begging the lieutenant's pardon, but from here on in the lieutenant's got nothing to worry about."

"How's that?"

"They just used up the one with your name on it."

This duty was succeeded by a trip through the Orient as an aide to his father, during which he visited Tokyo, then a hitch at home in Milwaukee and four years of study at Fort Leavenworth.

In 1912—the year his father died, collapsing during a speech to members of his old regiment—MacArthur was a captain serving on the General Staff. Though he was by far the youngest, he was by no means the most shy. He did not hesitate to disagree openly in the presence of Maj. Gen. Leonard Wood, the chief of staff —winning Wood's esteem and his seniors' enmity.

General Wood chose MacArthur to be his personal liaison officer at Veracruz, the Mexican port city occupied by U.S. Marines in April 1914 during the near-war between Mexico and the United States. MacArthur quickly perceived that the greatest shortage in the port area was in railroad locomotives. From a drunken Mexican railroad engineer he learned that there were five locomotives available at Alvarado, forty miles away. Although he knew that, for fear of provoking an incident that might trigger a war, American soldiers were prohibited from venturing out of the Veracruz perimeter, MacArthur set out secretly for Alvarado. After all, his orders were from General Wood himself!

MacArthur nearly did start a war, engaging a party of Mexicans who opened fire on him during his return from Alvarado. MacArthur shot back, bringing down a few of his assailants while receiving several bullet holes in his clothing. A friend to whom he related his adventure wrote to General Wood suggesting that MacArthur be awarded the Medal of Honor. Wood did, provoking a bitter division among his staff officers. One side praised MacArthur for his "daring and initiative," the other denounced him for irresponsible behavior that might have wrecked an armistice concluded shortly before he took off for Alvarado. In the end, a special board of General Staff officers voted against the award. And MacArthur protested! He withdrew his objections only upon the advice of General Wood.

MacArthur again opposed the General Staff when the United States entered World War I in 1917. This time, the battle was over the use of civilian-soldiers as opposed to Regular Army men. The General Staff wanted no part of the

National Guard units. Only seasoned soldiers, they said, could be trusted to meet the Kaiser's veterans. But Major MacArthur said it wasn't true. He said civilians were fresh and enthusiastic and would fight well, and he said it so loud and so often that finally one of the General Staff officers snapped: "I can see, major, that you are not interested in pursuing your military career much further."

He was ordered to drop the subject. Instead, he went to War Secretary Newton D. Baker. Enchanted by MacArthur's eloquence, and the force of such arguments as the fine record of the National Guard units fighting for his father in the Philippines, Baker took MacArthur to see President Woodrow Wilson. In the White House, MacArthur unfolded his plan to form an elite division from the crack units of as many states as possible, and at the height of his appeal, he rose in an attitude of exaltation:

"Mr. President, it will spread across the country like a giant rainbow!"

Wilson liked the idea. And that was how the Rainbow (42nd) Division was named and formed. To the self-assertive young major who conceived it and fought for it went the post of chief of staff.

The Rainbow Division made MacArthur one of the most famous American commanders of World War I. Only Gen. John J. (Black Jack) Pershing, the "Iron Commander" of the AEF, outshone the handsome young colonel. Some people thought MacArthur worked hard at making himself conspicuous, and among these was Gen. Enoch Crowder, who made the oft-quoted remark: "Arthur MacArthur was the most flamboyantly egotistic man I had ever seen—until I met his son." Certainly, MacArthur's style of battle dress did much to enhance his glory. It was unique and as nonregulation as any uniform could be. Wearing a garrison hat with just the right amount of wire removed to give it a singular and arrogant cast, his turtleneck sweater peeping above a regulation tunic, a gorgeous and voluminous civilian muffler wound carelessly around his neck, Douglas MacArthur roamed the battlefield as the adored Adonis of the Rainbow's un-shaven, sweat-soaked, mud-caked, lice-infested Doughboys.

His courage was incredible. It was not that he was fearless, which is impossi-ble in an intelligent human being. But he did have his person under control to an extent unmatched, from all reports, by any other officer. He repeatedly stayed erect and refused to take cover during artillery bombardments. Twice, on visits to the front, he was gassed—chiefly because he refused to wear a gas mask, just as he always refused to wear arms. He would not be hospitalized on either occasion. When the Rainbow fought under French command, the famous one-armed Gen. Henri Gouraud told another American officer that he considered "General MacArthur one of the finest and bravest officers I have ever served with."

After the Armistice, Pershing wrote to MacArthur to tell him that he had recommended him for a second star, but that the War Department was now promoting no more general officers. Pershing's headquarters also turned down all nine men from MacArthur's brigade who had been recommended for the Medal of Honor. At the head of the list was the name of Douglas MacArthur.

Between wars, when most generals fade into obscurity, Douglas MacArthur managed to add more and more to his fame. First, as superintendent of West Point for three years, he revised its curriculum and perhaps saved it from abolition at the hands of a Congress that was in a savagely pacifist mood.

While at West Point MacArthur met Mrs. Louise Brooks, an extremely wealthy divorcée who was then acting as Pershing's official hostess in Washington. Indeed it was rumored that Pershing, a widower, hoped to marry Mrs. Brooks. One night at dinner, she whispered to Pershing, "Jack, I'm going to marry Douglas," whereupon Black Jack snapped: "Young lady, if you're not careful you'll be living in the Philippines." She did marry MacArthur—he was forty-two and she was twenty-six—and they did go to live in the Philippines. But the marriage ended seven years later. His wife found Manila dull, and of her husband she has said that he paid court "like a general reviewing a division of troops." For his part, MacArthur has omitted all reference to his first wife in his *Who's Who* biography.

In 1925, at forty-four, MacArthur became a major general, among the youngest commanders to hold that rank in peacetime. And in 1930, Herbert Hoover appointed MacArthur chief of staff. At fifty, he was the youngest man to command the United States Army. Two years later, he was perhaps the most hated man in America. On July 28, 1932, he led the rout of the Bonus Marchers from their shantytown on Anacostia Flats in the Nation's capital.

Trim in leather puttees and fawn-colored riding breeches, in tight-fitting tunic and gleaming Sam Browne belt, his left breast covered with ribbons clear up to the shoulder, with an aide named Maj. Dwight David Eisenhower standing grimly at his side, Gen. Douglas MacArthur stood by as tanks, infantry and cavalry moved in on the 20,000 unemployed veterans who had gathered to besiege Congress for immediate bonus payments to World War I veterans.

Using tear gas and the flat side of their sabers, the troops drove the Bonus Marchers out of the tents and shacks they had erected on the Anacostia mud flats. MacArthur has always called this mission "the most distasteful" of his career, and well he might. He was flogged verbally and in print from one end of the country to the other, and only Herbert Hoover himself could claim a more impressive unpopularity in a nation then afflicted with 15 million unemployed.

Sympathy for the Bonus Marchers was great, even though their expulsion was achieved without serious injury. These were the two main points of criticism: Why was the chief of staff there at all, and why had he swapped the civilian clothes he normally wore for that gorgeous military get-up? In reply, MacArthur said he would not foist the responsibility for such an odious task on any subordinate and that he wore his medals to impress the veterans.

The decision to rout the Bonus Army, of course, was made by President Hoover. At the time it was widely believed that Communist agents had gained control of the Bonus Army. This was absolutely untrue. Douglas MacArthur, however, chose to believe otherwise, and until the day he died he insisted that the Bonus Army was a Communist creation.

The affair of the Bonus Marchers is a landmark in the career of Douglas MacArthur. Until this rout of a body of unarmed, pathetic petitioners, he was one of the most popular men in America. Indeed, because of this very popularity, Governor Franklin D. Roosevelt of New York considered him one of the most dangerous. Among his extreme admirers, his very name had the power to evoke tears. But after the dispersal of the Bonus Army, undertaken, it must always be remembered, on the order of his commander in chief, his name could also provoke jeers. All hero until then, he was a hero-heel, hailed by conservatives, hooted at by liberals. He was and would remain one of the angel-devils of American history.

But he continued to make history, accepting FDR's unprecedented invitation to stay on as chief of staff for a two-year term. In 1937 he married Jean Marie Faircloth of Murfreesboro, Tennessee. She bore him one son, Arthur IV. In that same year he accepted the invitation of President Manuel Quezon of the Philippines to come to the islands to organize their defenses against Japan. With him went Major Eisenhower. At once the liberal press derided MacArthur as "the Napoleon of Luzon," perhaps because of his exalted rank of field marshal (which he chose himself) and the gorgeous uniform which he designed for himself. Unfortunately, this hostility toward MacArthur had the unhappy effect of muting his warnings against the rising power of Japan. Only with the renewal of Japanese imperialism in China was the voice from Manila heeded once more; and after July 26, 1941, the newspapers were full of profile photographs of the handsome general with the squashed hat and the enormous corncob pipe clenched between his teeth.

39. December 1941: "Honolulu Sleeps"

JAPAN HAD NOT YET ABANDONED the diplomatic initiative. Throughout that summer and fall of 1941 its emissaries—Adm. Kichisaburo Nomura and later Ambassador Saburo Kurusu—conferred almost daily with Secretary of State Cordell Hull. They had difficult times with this good gray son of the Tennessee hills. Cordell Hull was a fundamentalist, trained from birth on October 22, 1871, to believe that black was black and white was white and between them there was no gray. A fierce patriot, he had served as a volunteer captain in Cuba during the Spanish-American War. After four years as a backwoods judge, he came to the House at the age of thirty-five, being later elected to the Senate. He was among the first of the New Dealers. Tall and tough, he might have been another Andrew Jackson, another Old Hickory from Tennessee. His manner was direct, and his voice was high and abrasive, delivering only imperatives, softened, perhaps, by the expressive gesturing of his beautiful hands. On March 8 he had put it squarely to Admiral Nomura that his country could no longer sit idly by while Japan and

Germany sought to gobble up the world. When Nomura replied that if the Americans continued their embargoes, Japan would be compelled to resort to force, Hull snapped that the responsibility for such a disastrous course would rest with Nippon. Here was the sticking point: embargoes versus expansion. The United States would not lift its economic blockade until Japan withdrew from China and Indochina; and this, Japan would not—nay, *could* not—do if it wished to remain an Asiatic power.

It seems hard to believe that many Americans in those days were so naive as to believe that at such an impasse war could be averted. But the truth is that the Americans of those days were extremely naive. Foreign policy bored them. Isolationism may have hit the downward curve, but there were still many interventionists who detested the State Department as a school for snobs. They seemed to believe that just by being "the arsenal of democracy," they could defeat the Axis. The problem of war, if ignored, would go away.

The Japanese had no such illusions. Their diplomats were given a pair of proposals, A and B, the first stiff and the second only a less stiff statement of the Japanese position, neither making any concessions and both demanding an end to the economic blockade. The emissaries were told that if one or another was not accepted by November 25, the issue of war would go to the emperor. In fine, there would be war. So the negotiations continued, with the Japanese unaware that in a tour de force of decoding the United States had broken the Japanese code by a secret process called Magic. Thus every time the Japanese conferred with Hull, he knew their instructions in advance. Nomura and Kurusu were also unaware that they were being considered expendable back in Tokyo. At a top-level meeting there, an unknown Japanese leader told Premier Tojo that in order to keep the Pearl Harbor attack secret, "Our diplomats will have to be sacrificed."

Secretary Hull also knew that when Nomura presented Proposal A on November 10, the deadline for acceptance of it was November 25.* This, of course, was the date for Admiral Nagumo to sortie for Pearl Harbor. But no one in the United States attached any significance to it. Indeed, all Roosevelt and Hull wanted was more time. So they began to stall over these obviously unacceptable proposals. As the days ticked off, Tokyo became frantic. On November 15, Nomura received instructions on how to destroy his code machines. A few days later Kurusu arrived in Washington to discover that the United States also wanted Japan to quit the Tripartite Pact. Tokyo then instructed him to present Proposal B. This was also unacceptable. But the Americans, desperate for time, considered countering by offering a three-month truce with resumption of a certain amount of trade. It is doubtful that the Japanese could have been so easily flim-flammed; however, this proposal died a quick death, promptly and understandably torpedoed by Premier Chiang Kai-shek in Chungking.

Now Magic deciphered a chilling message from Tokyo to Nomura: It agreed

*This would be November 26 in the Japanese time zone, just as Pearl Harbor would be December 8. Until the actual commencement of hostilities all dates here are in the Western Zone.

to extend the deadline to November 29, but "This time we mean it, that the deadline cannot be changed. After that, things are automatically going to happen." Alarmed, President Roosevelt met with his "war cabinet." The likelihood of a Japanese surprise attack was discussed, according to Secretary of War Henry Stimson. "The question was how we should maneuver them into the position of firing the first shot without too much danger to ourselves." Next day the Americans were disturbed to learn that a Japanese invasion force numbering about fifty ships had sortied south from Shanghai. They would have been more dismayed if they had also discovered that Admiral Nagumo's First Air Fleet was also sortieing that same day.

On November 26 the United States reiterated its demand that Japan withdraw from China and Indochina and quit the Tripartite Pact. Nomura and Kurusu were stunned. They reported home: "We were both dumbfounded and said we could not even cooperate to the extent of reporting this to Tokyo. We argued back furiously, but Hull remained as solid as a rock." On the 28th another message from Tokyo, again decoded by Magic, indicated that negotiations were to be broken off, but that the two diplomats should give the impression that they were continuing. Now the Americans knew that war was imminent and unavoidable. Their ultimatum, for such it certainly was, had been rejected; their gage of battle had been thrown down and taken up. Messages went out to Rear Adm. Husband E. Kimmel and Maj. Gen. Walter C. Short in Hawaii. Short was warned that hostilities with Japan might begin at any moment and Kimmel was informed, "Consider this despatch a war warning."

Husband Edward Kimmel became Commander in Chief Pacific Fleet (CINCPAC), on a bright, breezy day in February 1941. He was then in his late fifties, a handsome man, blue-eyed with a full head of dark blond hair flecked with gray. He stood ramrod-straight in his dress white uniform, five feet ten inches tall, 180 lean, hard pounds. He had indeed come a long way from the small town of Henderson, Kentucky, where he was born on February 26, 1882. Although his family had a West Point tradition, he was not appointed there, succeeding instead in being admitted to Annapolis. He was graduated thirteenth in a class of sixty-two, rated number 2 for efficiency, excelling in languages, gunnery, navigation and seamanship. Like so many middle Americans born beyond the smell of salt, he was a sailor. Fortunately, once he had departed the banks of the Severn, he shed the nickname "Hubby" and became "Kim" to all his friends.

Kimmel had many friends during his rise up the navy ladder, and also some connections. He married Dorothy Kinkaid, daughter of an admiral whose brother, Thomas, was also destined for flag rank. They had three sons, two of whom became officers in the U.S. Navy. Before realizing every sailor's dream of command of a battleship—the *New York* in 1933—Kimmel distinguished himself at sea and ashore, as a gunnery officer, in staff work and in training men. In 1937 when he became the navy's budget officer, he made a good impression on Capitol Hill through his sincerity and honesty when under questioning. He had also in earlier years been an aide to the then assistant secretary of the navy, Franklin D. Roosevelt. He renewed this acquaintance when he came to Washington. This is not to suggest that influence had gained him command of the United States fleet over many admirals senior to him, although it cannot be denied that knowing the President does have its advantages. Still, Husband Kimmel's file of fitness reports so bulged with acclaim from his superior officers that it seems that in his case he was chosen because he was believed to be the best man for the job.

Like the admiral who was even then planning his fleet's destruction— Isoroku Yamamoto—Husband Kimmel had a terrible temper with an extremely short fuse. Where Yamamoto would stamp his foot until his cabin shook, Kimmel would hurl the nearest book against the bulkhead, and then, if he were really angry, hurl his hat on the deck and jump on it. This had happened so often at sea that messboys kept an old hat handy for the skipper to stomp on.

A few days after Kimmel took command of the fleet, the liner *Matsonia* was sighted off Diamond Head. Twenty-four bombers roared aloft from Hickam Field to salute the liner's distinguished passenger: Maj. Gen. Walter C. Short, arriving in Honolulu harbor to take charge of the Hawaiian Department. Shortly afterward, he was promoted to lieutenant general.

General Short was born in Fillmore, Illinois, on March 30, 1880, and was graduated from the University of Illinois in 1902. He was commissioned in the army in March of that year. Thereafter, during four decades of service, Walter Short's career as an officer was a classic example of how a man may rise by carefully keeping his finger on his number and doing with good grace and efficiency everything he is asked to do. As a captain he did sail for France in June 1917, and was among the first American officers sent to the front. But he held no combat command. His forte was training, in France and later in Germany with the occupying Third Army. During the twenties he studied at Leavenworth, at the Army War College in Washington, spent three years in Puerto Rico, and then another four in Washington again. He returned to field commands during the thirties, winning his first star in 1937, and after the outbreak of World War II was given further command assignments.

General Short and Admiral Kimmel quickly set up a close personal relationship. Every second Sunday they played golf together. Except that they were the same height, they were as disparate physically as two men can be: Kimmel vigorous and radiant, outgoing; Short reserved, slender, almost ascetic, his luminous eyes in his thin small-boned face seemed those of a monk rather than a soldier. Short was certainly a competent officer, neither brilliant nor aggressive, but polished by those four decades of study, travel and a variety of assignments. His subordinates found him something of an enigma. No one knew what he really thought, except that he did have this one passion for training men. Hawaii, however, was the frontier, not a training center.

For secrecy, Vice Adm. Chuichi Nagumo sent his ships debouching from the Inland Sea in groups of twos and threes. All thirty of them would rendezvous in bleak and lonely Tankan Bay in the Kuril Islands. There, Nagumo aboard *Akagi* would await word to sortie en masse, making for Hawaii. The deadline for that signal would be November 26. That date had been chosen, he also knew, for a number of compelling reasons: (1) The United States was daily growing stronger in the Pacific, especially in the Philippines; (2) the Japanese could not wait until February or January to attack Hawaii because the extreme North Pacific winter would make such a voyage impossible; (3) stocks of war matériel, particularly oil, were growing scarce and the invasion forces poised to seize new sources of strategic supplies also could not wait; (4) the phase of the moon had to be such as to give the task force maximum moonlight for night operations; (5) the army wanted to move as soon as possible to avoid having to operate during the monsoon season in the targeted areas; (6) probably most important of all, intelligence agents operating out of Honolulu had reported that the Pacific Fleet, true to Kimmel's custom, would definitely be in harbor on a Sunday.

In his cabin aboard *Akagi*, swathed in a bathrobe against the chill of the thick Kuril fogs swirling about the shadowy steel monster that was his flagship, big and bluff Chuichi Nagumo began to feel misgivings about the operation. Nor had he been able to conceal his uneasiness. It had been apparent to Rear Adm. Matome Ugaki, Yamamoto's cherished chief of staff, the last time Nagumo visited Combined Fleet headquarters. With a kind of happy malice, Ugaki wrote in his diary: "Nagumo appears to be extremely anxious. . . . I hope he will not have nervous prostration before the operation takes place."

A howling gale struck Tankan Bay on the night of November 24. The weather turned bitterly cold. Winter had arrived. Laughing pilots thronged the carrier wardrooms, eagerly "splicing the main brace" with sake, eating, singing. During the following day those aboard *Akagi* listened eagerly to Admiral Nagumo announcing: "This Empire is now going to war with an arrogant and predestined enemy. . . ." He warned of the difficulties ahead, but exhorted his men: "However difficult the situation you may face, don't lose your confidence in victory." Inveterate diarists that the Japanese were, from admirals down to seamen, from generals to privates, many of them wrote down their reaction. "An attack upon HAWAII!" Seaman Iki Kuramoto exulted. "A dream come true!" Aboard *Suryu*, Rear Adm. Tamon Yamaguchi broke the news to his fliers and crewmen assembled on the flight deck. He boasted of the cutting edge of his saber, in the use of which he excelled. In a single blow, he boasted, he had cut a samurai helmet in half. "Cleave the enemy in two," he cried in a passion, breaking into the navy's popular attack hymn, "The Song of the Self-Sacrificing Warrior." The white-clad men massed below him took it up with a roar.

That night Chuichi Nagumo's fears had begun to multiply. He had received a signal from Yamamoto ordering him to sortie next morning. He began to worry about the sea and the weather ahead. A sudden savage wind such as had whirled through Tankan the night before could make vital refueling impossible. A thick fog such as the one that had enveloped Tankan two nights previously might enshroud his carriers just when the planes began returning from the attack, their fuel tanks almost empty. Or the sea could bedazzle him like a treacherous mermaid, lying calm and inviting under bright blue skies, and making his ships as naked to the enemy as flies on a windowpane. He thought of American submarines, of how vulnerable his huge carriers would be to undersea attack. He remembered that at the September war games it was concluded that two— perhaps three—carriers would be lost. Would Chuichi Nagumo be like Britain's John Jellicoe at Jutland in the last war, the one man who could drag his country down to defeat within a few hours? If his airmen did not completely knock out American bombers on the ground, what then? The new B-17s, the Flying Fortresses, were equipped with an incredibly accurate new bombsight. Their flying range far exceeded anything on his own carriers.

By midnight Nagumo found it impossible to sleep. He was distressed to feel his confidence waning, to realize that he was taking counsel from his fears. He almost dreaded receiving the signal that would send him hurrying south to destiny: "Climb Mount Niitake." Nagumo sent for his aide, Lt. Cmdr. Eijiro Suzuki. They talked. Suzuki spoke soothingly of his certainty that the American fleet would be berthed in Pearl Harbor on X-Day. Hadn't Japanese agents in Honolulu emphasized the enemy's habit of returning to base every weekend? Why should this one be different? Reassured, Nagumo shared a glass of sake with Suzuki, and went back to bed.

No such qualms disturbed the peace of mind of the American commanders in Hawaii, even after both of them received war warnings from Washington on November 27. General Marshall's message to General Short declared:

Negotiations with Japan appear to be terminated to all practical purposes with only the barest possibilities that the Japanese Government might come back and offer to continue. Japanese future action unpredictable but hostile action possible at any moment. If hostilities cannot, repeat cannot be avoided the United States desires that Japan commit the first overt act. This policy should not, repeat not be construed as restricting you to a course of action that might jeopardize your defense. Prior to hostile Japanese action you are directed to undertake such reconnaissance and other measures as you deem necessary but these measures should be carried out so as not, repeat not, to alarm civil population or disclose intent. . . .

General Short thought the message was ambiguous. He believed he was being told to be circumspect so as not to give Japan any excuses for starting a war. He doubted that Marshall personally wrote the message because Marshall knew that the navy had the responsibility for the reconnaissance he instructed him to make. Short decided that the message had been written for General MacArthur in the Philippines, where the services had no such agreement.

Admiral Kimmel was also not alarmed when he received from the Navy Department an even stronger message, which said:

This despatch is to be considered a war warning. Negotiations with Japan looking toward stabilization of conditions in the Pacific have ceased and an aggressive move by Japan is expected within the next few days. The number and equipment of Japanese troops and the organization of the naval task forces indicates an amphibious operation against either the Philippines, Thai or Kra Peninsula or possibly Borneo. Execute an appropriate defensive deployment. . . .

Apparently the only thing in the message that impressed Kimmel was that Hawaii was not mentioned. The phrase "war warning" meant to him only that Japan was going to attack some place, but probably not Hawaii. This impression was confirmed when he compared his message to Short's, finding the army warning more cautious. He thought that if the Japanese struck the Philippines, they might coordinate it with massive undersea attacks against his own ships. Accordingly, he ordered that any submarine contacts around Oahu should immediately be depth-bombed. Fortunately, Kimmel later ordered the carriers *Enterprise* and *Lexington* to ferry airplanes to Wake and Midway islands, thus taking the last flattops in his command out of the impact area. Unfortunately, Kimmel did not at once put into effect long-range aerial reconnaissance to the northwest. He did, however, order excellent observation of the southwest approaches, but it was the northwest that was considered vital; and this was indeed the route to be followed by Admiral Nagumo. Short, meanwhile, assumed that Kimmel had done so.

To this tragic error, Short added an equal one of his own: his belief that sabotage of his aircraft represented the greatest danger to Hawaii. There were 160,000 persons of Japanese ancestry residing in the Hawaiian Islands, and Short was quite correct in suspecting that some of them were potential saboteurs. But his fear led him to disarm his airplanes and park them in bunches. This made it difficult for them to be sabotaged, but also rendered them highly vulnerable to air attack.

Much has been made of the so-called ambiguity of these messages from the War and Navy Departments. But in truth any message beginning, "This despatch is considered to be a war warning" can hardly be called vague or susceptible to differing interpretations. The service chiefs in Washington had no way of knowing exactly where Japan would strike. All they could do was what they did, to warn *all* the commanders of the various outposts that Japan could possibly attack. Hawaii was not the most likely; indeed, it was considered by Marshall as probably the least likely, but it was one of them, and it was warned.

But in Hawaii one of the shepherds had left the gate open and the other had massed the sheep in the center of the fold in plain view of the approaching wolves.

A sullen cold light dawned over Tankan Bay on the morning of Wednesday, November 26. Snow fell from leaden skies, melting when it hit the black water. Lookouts peered through the semidarkness, seeing their sister ships only as shadowy shapes in the swirling snow. Suddenly, signal lamps began blinking, stabbing the dark like roman candles. Importunate voices shouted orders. Footsteps pounded on steel decks and made the ladders tremble. Huge anchor chains went clanking up the hawse pipes while enormous turbines spinning in the engine rooms made the propellers churn a white froth beneath the fantails.

The First Air Fleet was sortieing from Tankan. But then *Akagi*'s anchor chain became stuck in the pipe, delaying departure by half an hour. Some of the superstitious Japanese took this for an ominous omen, forgetting it the moment the chain was freed. Now the ghostly great shapes were sliding out of the bay, plunging into the mounting Pacific seas.

The time was 6:00 A.M., Wednesday, November 26, 10:30 A.M. November 25 in Honolulu, and 4:00 P.M. the same date in Washington.

The last deadline had come and gone. Out in the lonely North Pacific, following a route rarely sailed by commercial ships, Admiral Nagumo's fleet sailed steadily toward Pearl Harbor. It was a hideous voyage. Tall black waves shook the ships and washed men overboard. Anxiously, Nagumo awaited word from Yamamoto. It came on December 3: "Climb Mount Niitake." Nagumo was 940 miles north of Midway when he received it. Immediately, he swung his carriers south and sent them steaming toward Pearl Harbor.

In Washington the usual desperation efforts to avert catastrophe, including a personal letter from President Roosevelt to Hirohito, had gone their ineffectual way. The Japanese were already destroying codes and preparing to depart.

From Yokohama a ship named *Tatuta Maru* sailed for San Francisco via Honolulu. Its departure received wide publicity in the Japanese and American press. Ostensibly, it was evacuating Americans from Japan and would bring Japanese home from Honolulu and America. Actually, its captain was instructed to reverse course after the first few days at sea. *Tatuta Maru*'s true objective was to delude Americans into believing that Japan envisioned only a break in diplomatic relations.

On December 6 the first thirteen parts of a fourteen-part message arrived in the Japanese Embassy in Washington. They were intercepted and decoded by Magic and delivered to President Roosevelt. He read them silently, handing the material to Harry Hopkins, who read it also in silence. "This means war!" Roosevelt said. Hopkins nodded, suggesting that since it was inevitable perhaps the United States should strike the first blow to forfend a typical Japanese surprise attack. FDR shook his head. "No we can't do that. We are a democracy and a peaceful people." Roosevelt did not expect Japan to move against American soil. He anticipated fresh aggression in Asia.

On the morning of December 7 the fourteenth part of the message was also intercepted. It broke off negotiations. Roosevelt received it at about ten o'clock in the morning, 4:30 A.M. Pearl Harbor time. Another message came in and was decoded. It instructed Kurusu to present the Japanese reply at exactly 1:00 P.M. that day. That would be 7:30 A.M. in Hawaii, exactly the moment when the emperor's "glorious young eagles" would be swooping down on Battleship Row.

Col. Rufus Bratton, whose duty it was to pass decoded messages on higher, was stunned when he read the intercept. Tokyo had never before specified a precise time for its emissaries to meet Hull. Convinced that the Japanese were planning to strike somewhere in the Pacific at that time, he telephoned General Marshall. But the chief of staff was out on his Sunday-morning horseback ride. Marshall called Bratton later and hurried to the War Department after he learned of the urgency of the message. Marshall wrote out a new warning for all the affected commands:

Japanese are presenting at one P.M. eastern standard time today what amounts to an ultimatum also they are under orders to destroy their code machines immediately. Just what significance the hour set may have we do not know but be on alert accordingly. Inform naval authorities of this communication

Hurrying to save precious time, Bratton got the messages off promptly to MacArthur and other commands. But the one for Hawaii was held up by atmospheric conditions that blocked the channel to Honolulu. The Signal Center thought of transmitting via the navy's apparatus, but decided commercial service would provide quicker and safer transmission. The warning went by direct teletype to Western Union in Washington and thence to San Francisco, where it was picked up by RCA and relayed to Honolulu. It was not received until 7:33 A.M. on the morning of December 7, 1941. But it then had to be deciphered, decoded and delivered—at the fastest, forty minutes.

Japanese luck was still holding.

Throughout December 6 the Foreign Office in Tokyo had been receiving a stream of messages from its consulate in Honolulu. All the reports had been good. There were no barrage balloons over Pearl Harbor, no torpedo nets around the ships, the fleet was safe and snug in the harbor and so far there had been no long-range air patrol. Of course, all the carriers were gone, together with a few cruisers, but there was still an abundance of splendid targets in those eight battleships with supporting warships and auxiliaries, plus those aircraft parked wing to wing. There was one other disappointing report: The American fleet definitely would not be in Lahaina Anchorage. Thus, all hopes of sinking the American ships forever in those deep waters were dashed. But the final message of that momentous Saturday afternoon was certainly encouraging: "It appears that no air reconnaissance is being conducted by the fleet air arm."

Saturday night at Pearl Harbor was the customary party night. Men on shore leave streamed into the fleshpots of Honolulu. The officers held parties in their homes or at their clubs. Many Army Air Corps officers and their wives attended a dinner party at the Hickam Field officers club. Admiral Kimmel and his wife were among the guests at a small dinner given by Rear Adm. H. Fairfax Leary and his wife at the Halekulani Hotel. Kimmel mentioned that the Japanese consul had invited him to drop in for a glass of champagne that night. But Kimmel thought that this was rather not the time to sip bubbly with Japanese officials. True to his custom, Kimmel had but one drink and went home early. So did General Short, who had gone with his wife to the Schofield Barracks officers club for an annual charity dinner-dance. Short drove past Pearl Harbor, ablaze with light, exclaiming: "What a target that would make!"

40. Tora! Tora! Tora!

ADMIRAL NAGUMO'S FLEET had long ago crossed the International Dateline. In the early-morning darkness of December 7, 1941, his ships were closing on Pearl Harbor at a speed of 24 knots. They had not been detected, and Nagumo, having shaken off his fears, was now confident that they would not be.

In the lead was the light cruiser *Abukuma,* followed by four destroyers in fan-shaped formation. These vessels were the eyes of the fleet. About three miles astern were the heavyweights: the mighty battleships *Hiei* and *Kirishima,* flanked on either side by the heavy cruisers *Chikuma* and *Tone.* They were the fleet's defensive screen, alert to break up any unexpected incursion of the American battle fleet. They would fight a delaying action, sacrificing themselves if necessary, to give the six carriers time to escape. The flattops were another three miles to the rear, advancing in two parallel columns. *Akagi* and her sister, *Kaga,* were on the starboard side, while *Soryu* and *Hiryu* sailed to port. Behind them were *Shokaku* and *Zuikaku.* Destroyers sped like giant waterbugs up and down the flanks of the flattops, searching for submarines, while in the rear slipping silently over the sea were a trio of Japanese submarines.

Most of the fleet's pilots had slept well, inducing slumber by drinking a few bottles of beer before turning in. They awoke refreshed, showered and dressed in clean garments so that they might enter battle spotless like the samurai of old. Aboard *Akagi,* Commander Fuchida awoke at five o'clock. He, too, showered and dressed with care. He put on scarlet underwear and a red shirt. He and Lt. Shigeharu Murata had bought the same garments after deciding that if they were wounded the blood would not show and demoralize other fliers. Fuchida found Murata in the officer's mess. He wore full flying togs.

"Good morning, Commander," Murata said gaily. "Honolulu sleeps."

"How do you know?"

"The Honolulu radio plays soft music," Murata replied, waving his chopsticks. "Everything is fine."

After breakfast, Fuchida reported to Nagumo seated in the operations room. He saluted, and said, "I am ready for the mission, sir." Nagumo arose and grasped his hand. "I have confidence in you," he murmured. Next, Fuchida went to the ready room where the pilots awaited him. En route, he encountered Genda in the gangway. The partnership they had so much enjoyed was now ending. It was up to Fuchida to crown it with success. Fuchida grinned, and Genda slapped him on the shoulder in encouragement.

Aboard *Hiryu,* Cmdr. Hidori Matsumura arrived for breakfast wearing the *masuku* or gauze mask with which many Japanese cover the nose and lips to filter out germs. He had worn it since sortieing from Tankan Bay, pushing his food underneath it. Now he took it off, and the mess roared with laughter. Matsumura had secretly grown a mustache under the *Masuku.* "You looked better with the mask on," one of his comrades jeered.

From the cruisers *Chikuma* and *Tone* a pair of reconnaissance seaplanes were catapulted into the sky. They were to reconnoiter Pearl Harbor and Lahaina Roads. They would break radio silence to report. Such procedure, and the very appearance of the scout planes themselves, could end the secrecy so successfully maintained. But Nagumo believed that the need for last-minute, precise information was worth the risk.

At 5:50 the flight decks of all six carriers were roaring with the pulsation of the motors of 185 airplanes. First Air Fleet's flattops were now about 220 miles north of Oahu. The carriers turned into the wind, quivering beneath the onslaught of long, high rollers slapping hard against their hulls, sending spray flying onto the flight deck. The weather and a list of between 10 and 15 degrees would make the takeoffs extremely difficult.

But the pilots seemed unconcerned. They clambered into their cockpits with *hachimaki* (handkerchiefs) bearing the word *Hissho* (Certain Victory) tied around their flying helmets. *Akagi*'s crew presented Fuchida with a special white *hachimaki.* The commander was touched, winding the scarf around his helmet, before he, too, climbed aboard his plane. It was a horizontal bomber, which carried a crew of three: the pilot, bombardier-observer and radio operator. Torpedo bombers had similar crews.

Zero fighters were the first planes launched, and when the first of these roared aloft without mishap, everyone watching sighed with relief. Within fifteen minutes 185 planes had been launched, the fastest launching on record. Only two fighters failed to fly. One crashed on takeoff, but the pilot was rescued; the other had engine trouble and could not take off. As soon as all were airborne, circling the carriers in a huge arc, Nagumo ordered the carriers to turn south again while the plane handlers worked frantically to raise the airplanes of the second wave to the flight deck.

Meanwhile the diminishing specks of the first-wave aircraft vanished from the sky. Cmdr. Mitsuo Fuchida peered ahead of him with rising excitement. The rays of the rising sun seemed to duplicate the alternating stripes of the naval flag of empire. Fuchida half stood up in reverence. He glanced proudly behind him at the huge aerial armada it was his honor to lead. *O glorious dawn for Japan,* he thought. Soon he hoped to speak into his microphone the immortal signal— *Tora* ("Tiger")—that would tell poised invasion forces all over East Asia that the arrogant Americans had indeed been found asleep in their beds.

At Pearl Harbor there had been a submarine alert, involving the destroyer *Ward.* Just after dawn the supply ship *Antares,* with a lighter in tow, was moving toward the port. At 6:30 her skipper, Cmdr. Lawrence Grannis, spotted a suspicious-looking object on the starboard quarter. It seemed to be a submarine, but none like any he had ever seen before, and it was apparently having depth-control trouble. Its conning tower was above water. Grannis promptly notified *Ward.* Lt. (j.g.) O. W. Goepner had the deck. He, too, decided that the object was the conning tower of a submarine of an unfamiliar type. It was obviously trying to follow *Antares* through the opened antisubmarine nets into the port. Goepner called his skipper, Cap. William Outerbridge. Outerbridge sounded general quarters and his crewmen opened fire. The first shot missed, but the second struck the submarine at the waterline, the junction of the conning tower and the hull. It heeled over to starboard and began to sink. Then it passed under *Ward*'s stern (it was a midget submarine) and blundered into a full pattern of *Ward*'s depth charges set for 100 feet. It went down in 1,200 feet of water.

Captain Outerbridge reported his action to the Fourteenth Naval District's watch officer. Now there ensued an exchange of telephone calls—or delays in making them caused by busy signals—which served first to misstate the report and next to cast doubt on its authenticity. The report did reach Kimmel, however —at 7:00, just as he arose—but there had been so many submarine false alarms that he was inclined to believe that the cry of "wolf" was being raised again. If patrols had been sent out immediately or the army had been informed that the navy had sunk a Japanese submarine at the harbor gates, the Hawaiian Department might have moved from Number 1 alert to Number 2 or even Number 3.

But this did not happen. One of Chuichi Nagumo's foremost fears—that one of his own submarines might alarm the enemy—had been realized. But once again Japanese luck had held.

Opana Mobile Radar Station was located on the northern tip of Oahu, 230 feet above the sea. At four o'clock on the morning of December 7, privates Joseph Lockard and George Elliott went on duty. Lockard, experienced at operating the oscilloscope, began instructing Elliott in the use of that instrument. Three hours later Lockard prepared to shut the unit down. The morning's work was ending. Suddenly the oscilloscope showed a disturbing image. It was enormous. Lockard had never seen anything so big, probably more than fifty planes. Elliott suggested that they telephone the Information Center. Lockard at first demurred: Operating hours were over. But then he did telephone.

Pvt. Joseph McDonald, the switchboard operator, took the call. He was impressed by Lockard's report. He called Lt. Kermit Tyler, the pursuit officer. Tyler had begun this assignment only four days previously. It was his duty to assist the controller to order pursuit planes aloft to intercept enemy aircraft. But on this morning Tyler was alone with McDonald. He came to the telephone, listening carefully while Lockard reported "the biggest sightings" he had ever seen. Tyler never dreamed that the mysterious flight could be enemy aircraft. He decided it was the twelve Flying Fortresses due at Hickam Field at eight o'clock that morning. Driving to the Information Center, he had heard Station KGMB playing Hawaiian music, and he knew this was always played to act as a beam for B-17 navigators flying from the mainland to Hawaii. He was correct. The Flying Fortress flight was even then nearing its destination.

But there were only a dozen of them, and Lockard had detected more than fifty blips, though he hadn't reported this to Tyler. For security reasons, the lieutenant did not want to mention the music to Lockard. So he said: "Well, don't worry about it."

Japanese luck was not just holding firm; it was incredible.

Commander Fuchida's pilot was also homing in on that beam of languorous music. Fuchida was himself studying Oahu through high-powered binoculars. The island was a stirring sight. Breaking waves ringed it in a circle of white foam. Its purplish gray mountains were veiled in morning mists that the rising sun was beginning to burn off.

"*Tenkai!*" Fuchida cried into his microphone. "Take attack position!"

Fuchida adjusted his binoculars again, drawing his breath in elation. Beneath him lay the United States Pacific Fleet. *What a majestic sight,* he thought. *Almost unbelievable!*

Eight battleships were neatly moored along Battleship Row. Some of them were side by side. They were *Nevada, Arizona, Tennessee, West Virginia, Maryland, Oklahoma, California* and *Pennsylvania.* The target battleship *Utah* was also in the harbor, along with five cruisers and twenty-six destroyers. Fuchida grimaced. The three American carriers were not there, as he had been informed, plus seven other cruisers. What Fuchida could not see or know was that because it was a Sunday, about one third of the crews were on shore leave. Antiaircraft batteries were only partially manned. Most of the ammunition was in padlocked steel chests. As the Japanese approached, some of the ships were piping the men to morning chow, others were raising the flag. No American patrol craft were aloft that sparkling, sunny Sunday morning. On land all was calm and serene. Church bells were ringing and the messenger with General Marshall's warning was pedaling his way toward General Short's headquarters.

Commander Fuchida swung around Barber's Point just to be sure that the enemy had in fact been caught asleep at dawn. "*Tora!*" he cried in rising jubilation. "*Tora! Tora! Tora!*"

41. Death of a Fleet

FUCHIDA'S ELECTRIFYING SIGNAL confirming the fact that the American giant had been caught sleeping was given at 7:53. The Val* dive bombers had already nosed over to the attack and now the Zeke fighters streaked for the defenseless aircraft bunched together on Hickam Field, the Betty bombers turned into the wind to make their approaches and the torpedo Kates in twos and threes went skimming in low to launch their fish. Precisely two minutes later, Lt. Cmdr. Logan Ramsey stood near a window of the Ford Island command center watching a color guard hoist the flag. He heard the scream of a plane diving over the station, and turned angrily to Lt. Richard Ballinger. "Dick, get that fellow's number. I want to report him for about sixteen violations." Both officers peered out the window to follow the diving plane. "Did you get his number, Dick?" Ramsey asked anxiously.

"No, sir, but I think it was a squadron commander's plane because I saw a band of red on it." Ballinger added: "I saw something black fall out of that plane when it completed its dive."

At 7:57 the center shook with the reverberations of an explosion in the hangar area. "Never mind the squadron commander, Dick!" Ramsey cried. "That was a Jap plane and a delayed action bomb!" Ramsey ran across the corridor to the radio room. He ordered every radioman on duty to flash out in plain English:

"AIR RAID, PEARL HARBOR. THIS IS NO DRILL!"

Aboard *Oklahoma* the same warning cry, though not as famous nor as proper, came blaring over the bullhorn: "Man your battle stations! This is no shit!" But it, too, came too late—and *Oklahoma* was the first to die. Lt. Jinichi Goto brought his torpedo plane down to sixty feet above the water as he dived at *Oklahoma* and launched his torpedo. "*Atarimashita!*" his observer cried. "It hit!" Goto's plane trembled in the shock waves of a huge explosion and a great waterspout shot into the air, drenching the men on *Oklahoma*'s decks when it fell. Two more torpedoes peeled *Oklahoma* open like giant can openers and then two more finished her off. *Maryland,* moored inside, fought back under the protection of *Oklahoma*'s riddled hull. She escaped with only two bomb hits.

Admiral Kimmel was in his quarters dressing for his Sunday-morning golf game with General Short. He was awaiting confirmation of another submarine sinking by the destroyer *Ward* when his telephone rang again. It was Murphy telling him that *Ward* had also stopped a Japanese sampan near the reported sinking site. It was then that Husband Edward Kimmel heard the shrieking of the diving Vals and felt the shock waves of the explosions racking his ships.

*Later in the war, Japanese aircraft were identified by Americans by nicknames, male for fighters and female for all others.

Aboard the minelayer *Oglala,* Rear Adm. William Furlong, who commanded a fleet of service vessels, was strolling along the quarterdeck awaiting a call to breakfast. He heard the roar of aircraft engines but thought nothing of it until he saw a bomb fall from a diving plane. *What a stupid, careless pilot,* he thought, *not to have secured his releasing gear.* But then he heard an explosion, saw a shower of earth rise above Ford Island, and glimpsed the red ball on the fuselage of a fleeing plane.

"Japanese!" Furlong cried. "Man your stations!" At his command, *Oglala* flashed the alarm: "All ships in harbor sortie!"

But the order had come too late. Battleship Row had begun to thunder and blaze. A pall of smoke drifted over the harbor, through which the red-balled enemy planes darted in and out like huge buzzing hornets. Aboard the fighting ships sailors and Marines began battering the padlocks off the ready chests with ringing blows of sledgehammers and mauls. Ammunition was passed out, and at last American antiaircraft guns began to stutter, spitting out shells at the Japanese. Within minutes, five Kates from *Koga* went spinning down in flames. Meanwhile, other men on shore leave came racing back to the docks, on foot, in taxis, on bicycles, jumping into small boats to come bouncing over the waves to their stricken ships. Some of them swam out. And already Commander Ramsay's historic but dreadful warning had been flashed to the United States.

Above the bay now excited Japanese torpedo-bomber observers were crying *"Atarimashita! Atarimashita!* It hit! It hit!" It was the cry Lieutenant Murata had been eagerly awaiting. When it was raised by his own observer, he immediately radioed Nagumo: "Torpedoed enemy battleships. Serious damage inflicted." When Commander Genda heard the report, his heart sang. *Now the attack will be a success!* The new torpedo with its stabilizing fin was carrying the day.

Lieutenant Matsumura led his flight from *Hiryu* against *West Virginia* moored outboard of *Tennessee.* On his second sortie against *West Virginia* his torpedo struck home. He fingered his new mustache in delight, watching in fascination while a waterspout rose gracefully above the stricken ship, falling back like a geyser. He ordered his observer to photograph the sight, but the man misunderstood him, opening fire with his machine gun and wrecking his own antenna. *West Virginia* took five or six more fish, plus two bombs. She capsized, straightened, and sank upright.

Almost all of this occurred while Admiral Kimmel listened to Commander Murphy's report on *Ward.* Murphy was still talking when a yeoman rushed into his office, shouting: "There's a message from the signal tower saying the Japanese are attacking Pearl Harbor, and this is no drill!" Murphy promptly relayed the message to Kimmel, who slammed the receiver down and rushed outside, buttoning his white uniform jacket as he ran. He ran next door to the home of Cap. John Earle, whose lawn commanded an excellent view of Battleship Row. He stared upward appalled while the enemy high-level bombers flew figure eights before dropping their bombs. Each explosion seemed to chip another piece off Kimmel's breaking heart. Mrs. Earle watched him in grief and pity. She had never seen a human being so stricken with horror. His face was "as white as his uniform."

There was small comfort for Kimmel to see that the sky was now dotted with the black puffs of American antiaircraft fire. Sometimes the fire was pepper-and-saltish with the white blossoms of training shells; the gunners were shooting everything they had. But the destruction continued. Lt. Tsuyoshi Nagai off *Suryo* gunned his Kate toward *Pennsylvania* lying at drydock. He saw immediately that the mooring slip would deflect his missile, so he launched it at *Oglala*. It passed beneath Admiral Furlong's shallow-draft flagship and hit the light cruiser *Helena,* crippling both ships. *Pennsylvania,* meanwhile, put up such a cloud of ack-ack that she was racked by only a single bomb hit. *California,* moored alone, blew up when a bomb exploded in her magazine.

Nevada was also moored alone. She was under partial steam when the first wave struck and was the only battleship to get under way. She sailed past the burning *Arizona,* fishing three of her survivors from the water. Heat from the blazing battleship was so intense that *Nevada*'s gunners covered their shells with their bodies for fear they might explode. Above *Nevada,* Commander Fuchida's eyes glowed with delight. A battleship under way making for the channel! He instructed his pilot to bank deeper for a better look. Fuchida thought: *Ah, good. Now just sink that ship right there!* It would bottle up Pearl Harbor. At once the Japanese bombers swarmed down on *Nevada* like bees. She took five hits, but kept on moving. After all, *Nevada* was a battleship. A quarter hour later another hail of bombs racked her. Near misses staggered her. A bomb landing on the forecastle killed many men. Still *Nevada* plowed on, finally running aground in the mud of Hospital Point. The channel remained open.

The full fury of the Japanese attack seemed directed at *Arizona* and *West Virginia.* Just after *Oklahoma* capsized, a fearful explosion sent frightful concussion waves rolling over *Arizona.* They seemed to suck the very substance out of the air. A 16-inch shell had fallen on the number 2 turret, exploding in the forward magazine. It seemed that the great ship would split asunder. Perhaps 1,000 Americans perished in that dreadful moment, among them Rear Adm. Isaac Campbell Kidd, First Battleship Division commander, and *Arizona*'s skipper, Capt. Franklin Van Valkenberg. Bomb after bomb penetrated the sinking battleship, reeling from its wounds like a bull in the ring. *Arizona* sank with hundreds of sailors trapped below decks.

Fickle are the fortunes of war. The bomb that doomed *Arizona* saved the repair ship *Vestal.* She had taken two bombs early on, and was ablaze, but the concussion that racked *Arizona* pinched out her fires like giant fingers. Still, the explosion also rained on *Vestal*'s decks the debris of shell cases, fragments of steel, bodies, severed heads, torsoes, legs, gun barrels—and also blew overboard about a hundred of *Vestal*'s men, including the captain, Cmdr. Cassin (Ted) Young. Those remaining aboard *Vestal* immediately began fishing from the water some of *Arizona*'s horribly burned crewmen. They were given shots of morphine and rushed to hospitals or the hospital ship *Solace.* Suddenly there came the order —from whom it is not known—"Abandon ship!"

Sailors began making for the gangway just as Commander Cassin, dripping water and oil, climbed out of the harbor as though emerging from the primordial mud. "Where the hell do you think you're going?" he bellowed at the officer of the deck.

"We're abandoning ship!"

"Get back aboard ship!" Young roared. "You don't abandon ship on me!"

It was debris from *Arizona* that also doomed *Tennessee*. Seemingly protected by the hull of *West Virginia, Tennessee* was set on fire by a shower of flaming objects from *Arizona.*

Now the red-balled Zeke fighters were taking over, battering the naval air stations on Ford Island and shooting up the sitting ducks at Hickam Field. Eighteen aircraft from Admiral Halsey's *Enterprise* flew into this melee. Lt. Cmdr. Brum Nichol, Halsey's flag secretary, was astounded. "My God," he thought, "the army has gone crazy, having antiaircraft drill on Sunday morning." To his dismay, American ack-ack also thickened the 50-caliber bullets streaming at them from the Zekes. It brought down one American torpedo bomber while the Japanese fighters shot down four more. All the other American planes landed safely.

At Hickam Field the Army Air Corps was awaiting the arrival of the dozen B-17s under Maj. Truman Landon. Officers in the control tower stood ready to guide them in. They sighted airplanes approaching. A cloud of them, coming from the north! The flight divided up and swooped down on the parked aircraft with flaming, chattering wing guns.

Lt. Col. James Mollison had halfway finished shaving when he heard detonations. He threw his bathrobe over his pajamas and rushed outside. He saw Capt. Brooke Allen burst from his home, a bathrobe flapping about his naked body. Allen shook his fist at a departing Zeke, shouting: "I *knew* it! I *knew* the little sons of bitches would do it on a Sunday! I *knew* it!" Allen wasted little more time taking perverse pride in his prophetic powers. He went sprinting for the flight line, impelled by a single thought: Get the Forts flying and strike the enemy. But the enemy bombs and bullets were already chewing up the bombers and killing their crews. A single missile landing in the enlisted men's hall instantly killed thirty-five men. Allen next ran for his own B-17, slamming into the cockpit. Three of its four motors roared into life and Allen taxied the Fort to safety. But he couldn't take off in that rain of incendiary bullets and bombs falling around him.

Colonel Mollison, meanwhile, had called Lt. Col. Walter Phillips, General Short's chief of staff. He told him the base was under Japanese attack. "You're out of your mind, Jimmy!" Phillips shouted. "What's the matter, are you drunk? Wake up! Wake up!" Mollison gritted his teeth in exasperation, holding out the telephone so that Phillips could hear the exploding bombs. "I can hear it. What do you want me to do?" He paused. "I tell you what, I'll send over a liaison officer." Upon that magnificent offer of help, the ceiling of Mollison's office fell down.

General Short was himself merely puzzled by the first explosions. He wondered why the navy was "having some battle practice" on Sunday morning. He was incredulous when Phillips arrived to tell him "that it was the real thing." But he did immediately order Phillips to put into effect alert number 3. This was to dispose his entire ground force in battle positions. Short thought that if the enemy was daring enough to strike from the sky at Oahu, he might attempt a full-scale invasion. He had moved 180 degrees, from defense against mere sabotage to defense against all-out invasion. But Short was still confused, as commanding generals so often are. He knew that Pearl Harbor was under attack, but little else. When he ran into big Lt. Col. George Bicknell, he asked: "What's going on out there?"

"I'm not sure, General, but I just saw two battleships sunk."

"That's ridiculous," Short snapped, and strode away.

But the dead and the dying and the wounded and the wrecked and burning airplanes at Hickam Field were far from being absurd. Half of Hickam's aircraft had been either destroyed or seriously damaged. The dozen Flying Fortresses arriving under Major Landon might also have perished in the holocaust had it not been for the flying skill of their pilots and the bravery and accuracy of their gunners. Landon at first thought that the aircraft flying toward him were from his own Air Corps rising in salute. But then as he banked to land, he heard the control tower warn, "You have three Japs on your tail." Sure enough, they were there, their wing guns spouting flame. And from Hickam's ground forces there rose a hail of shot and shell. But Landon's planes all got through, landing safely all over the island.

Leaving Hickam behind in agony and destruction, the Japanese next struck at Wheeler Field. Of the eighty-two aircraft lined up in tidy rows at Wheeler, under armed guard to prevent sabotage, only fifty-two were modern types. The rest were obsolete. High above Wheeler the Japanese pilots were amazed to see the precise and serried rows of planes beneath them, incredulous to find no storm of flak to greet them, no American fighters roaring aloft to welcome them with flaming guns. They would have been more astonished to learn that the American war birds had no claws, their ammunition belts being removed each night and stored in the hangers. So the Japanese nosed over and came shrieking down to do at Wheeler what they had done at Hickam.

Col. William Flood who commanded there was reading the morning newspaper when he heard "this awful *whang!*" Rushing outside he saw the Japanese "bombing and strafing the base, the planes, the officer's quarters and even the golf course. I could see the Japanese pilots lean out of their planes and smile as they zoomed by. . . . Hell, I could even see the gold in their teeth."

Thus it was the same at Wheeler as it had been at Hickam: By the time army antiaircraft went into action it was too late. Four aircraft in Fuchida's first wave were shot down, not one of them by ack-ack. Flying too close to the ground they came within range of maddened Americans firing ground weapons, machine guns and Browning automatic rifles. Then the second wave broke over Pearl Harbor. *Oglala* was abandoned, *Vestal* went down, ships already in their death throes were punished anew. But no new sinkings were reported. Smoke was everywhere, clouds of it billowing, drifting and eddying, suffused with a pinkish cast by the flames from the burning ships. It was as though the very water were on fire. The smoke made bombing difficult for the second-wave fliers, most of them inexperienced anyway. Moreover, American AA was more intense and accurate, sometimes passing through clouds to score direct hits. Nevertheless, the second wave stirred up a hellish brew, bombs, bullets and blood from which the horrible stench of burning flesh or the acrid reek of gunpowder rose.

Adm. Husband Kimmel watched it all from the windows of his quarters. With him was one of his staff officers, Cmdr. Maurice Curts. Each fresh report of a stricken or sunken battleship seemed to etch a new line of grief in his face. Every time he learned the name of a fallen friend, a groan of anguish broke from his lips. These were the men he had known since Annapolis, or during four decades of service in a tight little navy which was actually one big family bound by shipmate ties. As he stood at the window a spent bullet crashed through the glass, striking him on the chest and leaving a splotch on his white jacket. Kimmel picked up the slug, a .50 caliber. He glanced at Commander Curts and murmured:

"It would have been merciful if it had killed me."

42. America Joins the War

THE DEVASTATION AT PEARL HARBOR had been beyond Yamamoto's dreams of destruction. Eight battleships, three light cruisers, three destroyers and four auxiliary vessels were either sunk, capsized, badly damaged or damaged generally —eighteen ships in all. Ninety naval aircraft were destroyed and the army lost seventy-seven with another 128 damaged. Twenty-four hundred and three Americans were killed or missing while another 1,178 were wounded. By contrast Japan had suffered minimal losses: twenty-nine airplanes, one large submarine and five midgets. Small wonder indeed that Cmdr. Sadamu Sanagi of the Naval General Staff could exult in his diary: "O, how powerful is the Imperial Navy!" Such losses were, of course, not known when Ambassadors Nomura and Kurusu arrived at Secretary Hull's office that same day. They were quite late, having had more trouble than the Americans in deciphering their own messages. It was not 1:00 P.M. but a little after 2:00. As they moved into the waiting room, Hull received a telephone call from President Roosevelt.

"There's a report that the Japanese have attacked Pearl Harbor," FDR said.

"Has the report been confirmed?"

"No," Roosevelt said, and hung up.

The Japanese emissaries entered Hull's office. He stared at them in cold fury and did not ask them to sit down. Nomura apologized for being late. Hull asked him why he had specified one o'clock. Nomura pretended not to know. He handed Hull the note. Hull already knew the contents, of course, but went through the pretext of reading it. Then he fixed Nomura with a coldly contemptuous eye.

"I must say that in all my conversations with you during the last nine months I have never uttered one word of untruth. This is borne out absolutely by the record. In all my fifty years of public service I have never seen a document that was more crowded with infamous falsehoods and distortions—infamous falsehoods and distortions on a scale so huge that I never imagined until today that any government on this planet was capable of uttering them."

Raising a hand as though to cut off any reply, Hull nodded stiffly toward the door. In silence, with downcast eyes, the Japanese made their departure.

The day after the Japanese attack on Pearl Harbor, President Roosevelt addressed a joint session of Congress. "Yesterday, December 7, 1941—a date that will live in infamy," he began, and concluded by asking Congress to declare war on Japan. Congress did, with but a single dissenting vote.

Never before had Americans been so united. Isolationists and interventionists alike burned with anger at Japan's treacherous sneak punch, and only the most indiscreet of cool heads would have dared to suggest that such surprise attacks are common in warfare or that tactically Japan could have done nothing else. In truth, Japan could have done nothing worse. With one blow it had aroused and united a nation that had been dedicated to passivity and torn by dissension. Other factors might gradually have brought America to intervene against the Axis, among them disgust with the dictators, a growing sense of kinship with and admiration for Britain, propaganda from those communist sympathizers who had remained notably silent while Stalin was Hitler's ally, the fact that Americans of Irish or German origin were now a few generations removed from hostility to Britain or loyalty to Germany, the enmity which America's articulate Jewish community bore for Hitler, and even FDR's growing association of his nation's interest with the Allied cause. Yet, if all these generally disparate and unorganized influences had spoken with a single voice, it would have been but a whisper in comparison with the concerted roar of outrage that broke from America's throat in the wake of Pearl Harbor. Washington, Madison, Polk, Lincoln, McKinley, TR, even Woodrow Wilson might well have been envious of how swiftly the problems of leading a pluralist nation at war had been simplified for Franklin Delano Roosevelt.

For Japan, retribution was to be complete. The nation had arrayed against it an immensely superior coalition of powers. It had foolishly believed that the United States would allow it to fight a limited war. It had misjudged the American character, and for the sake of an initial advantage had given that character greater strength and purpose. "One can search military history in vain," wrote the naval historian Samuel Eliot Morison, "for an operation more fatal to the aggressor."

It was unique, then, and perhaps because the Japanese character was unique. Like their soldiers killing themselves in battle rather than accepting the disgrace of defeat or imprisonment, Japan's militarist chieftains preferred a kind of national hara-kiri to a meek and submissive return to the secondary status reserved for it by the Western powers. Nevertheless, it was a "stunned and silent nation" that heard Tojo read the Imperial Rescript declaring war. Too many Japanese had relatives in America or had been there and thus knew its power. But they dared not speak, not in the presence of youths fired by Shinto and samurai, not at the risk of being overheard by agents of the Thought Police or dagger-wielding members of the secret societies.

In Germany there was also much uneasiness. Hitler may have been jubilant to hear that American naval power had been crippled, but on that December 7 his countrymen were stunned. On that day they heard that America was a belligerent and that the temperature on the Moscow front had dropped to 40 degrees below zero. An observer reported: "Unrest grew among the people. The pessimists remembered Napoleon's war with Russia, and all the literature about *La Grande Armée* suddenly had a marked revival. . . . Even the most devoted Nazi did not want a war with America. All Germans had a high respect for her strength. Nobody could help remembering how America's intervention had decided the first world war."

German gloom was matched by a boundless joy in Britain and the occupied countries, where it seemed plain that the Axis could never hope to master the British-Soviet-American coalition. Yet the Führer and the Duce kept faith with Japan and declared war on America, and the United States replied in kind. After Britain declared war on Japan (which the Soviet Union did not do) and Latin America came to the side of the Allies, there were thirty-five nations, representing half of the world's population, engaged in this greatest of wars, a conflict so vast that few of the unengaged half of humanity escaped its effects.

These, then, were the results of the attack on Pearl Harbor. More immediately, this brilliant stroke (for such it was in a military sense) had achieved its purpose of immobilizing the American fleet while the tide of Japanese conquest flowed over Southeast Asia and out across the Pacific. In the Philippines American air power was destroyed on the ground, and on December 10 the first of six landings was made on the big northern island of Luzon. Steadily, the roll of Japanese conquests grew longer: they captured the American island of Guam, subdued Thailand, landed in Malaya to the rear of the great British bastion of Singapore, invaded Borneo in the Dutch East Indies, seized Hong Kong on the coast of China, invaded New Britain, New Ireland and the Solomons in the Southwest Pacific, and sank the British battleship *Prince of Wales* and battle cruiser *Repulse*. With this last blow Japan made itself supreme in the Pacific and Indian oceans, and mighty Singapore, the center of British strength in the Far East, was left helpless.

Yet the island citadel with its garrison of 70,000 men did not consider itself doomed. It was believed that the Strait of Johore to the north or rear of Singapore could not be crossed and that the Malayan jungle still farther north was impenetrable. As a result, like the French with their Maginot Line, the British had sited the guns of Singapore where the enemy was expected to be, in this case to sea. But the Japanese did penetrate the jungle and did cross the strait, and then compelled a capitulation that dealt British arms their greatest check since Burgoyne surrendered at Saratoga.

Only at Wake Island did the Japanese suffer a setback. Here the garrison of 500 U.S. Marines hurled back an invasion attempt, the first and only time in the war that an amphibious assault failed. America was thrilled by the hope that a relief force was at sea and might yet rescue Wake, and it was electrified by the Marines' battle cry: "Send us more Japs!" However, the relief force was recalled, and no one on Wake had or would have sent such a signal. The phrase was gibberish padding for a coded message. After the Marines killed 700 of the Japanese, sank a destroyer transport and damaged four other vessels, while shooting down a few dozen aircraft, all at a loss of 100 men killed and wounded, Wake hauled down the flag.

The Japanese tide of victory rose higher. The East Indies fell after the Allied naval disaster in the Battle of the Java Sea. New Guinea was invaded. Only in the Philippines, where the American-Filipino forces under Douglas MacArthur offered fierce resistance, was the Japanese timetable delayed. Even there, however, it seemed obvious that it was but a delay.

The war lords of Japan might have been surprised to witness the reaction to Pearl Harbor among the effete, luxury-loving Americans. True, there was some fleeting panic and hysteria among a few jittery residents of the West Coast, and there were faint hearts as far east as St. Louis who expected momentarily to see Japanese battleships sailing up the Mississippi River. But on the whole the American people were outraged as never before. Many Congressmen, led by Lyndon B. Johnson of Texas, volunteered for active duty, asking only for a day's respite to cast their votes for war, while across the land recruiting stations were overwhelmed by a flood of patriotic young men eager to enlist. Recruiters and examining physicians in all the big cities worked through the night of December 7 to process these astonishing throngs. At 90 Church Street in New York City, there was standing room only in the corridors of the various services. Red Cross ladies were there passing out free doughnuts and coffee, and cots had been set up for those wearied by standing in line or those needing to sleep off the kind of patriotism that sometimes comes in bottles. These young men came from all over the huge New York metropolitan area, from the states of New York, New Jersey and Connecticut. They represented every race and creed that had emerged from the American melting pot as Yankees. They were to a man mad. Their country had been treacherously attacked, and they were angry. They spoke of the Japanese in terms that were neither complimentary nor printable. At the least, they were "dirty little bastards," or "monkeys without tails." While they waited, these youths chatted or asked the question that was being asked all over America that night: "What were you doing when they bombed Pearl Harbor?" The answers were humdrum and typically American: at church, at the movies, working on the car, bowling, reading the Sunday newspapers, wrapping Christmas presents. One young man from Rutherford, New Jersey, known to his friends as Lucky, said that he was playing basketball. When he got home, his sister opened the door and told him about Pearl. "The dirty little bastards!" Lucky said. His sister said, "That's what Daddy said."

Lucky was a lighthearted youth, just tall enough to meet the Marine Corps minimum of five feet eight inches, but well built, with dark red hair and merry brown eyes. He was two weeks short of his twenty-first birthday and would need his parents' signatures to enlist. He was confident that he would get it, just as he was supremely confident that the Marine Corps would be delighted to accept such a distinguished applicant as himself. In that confidence, he had quit his job as a sportswriter on the Bergen County (New Jersey) *Evening Record* and come over the river to enlist.

Lucky was not aware that even though this throng of eager applicants had brought tears to the eyes of the recruiting sergeants conducting tests for color blindness or eyesight, they, in collusion with the examining doctors, were turning down two out of every three applicants. Or else they were putting them "on hold" for a few months. There was simply no way the East Coast's single Recruit Training Depot—the famous Boot Camp at Parris Island, South Carolina—could accommodate such a flood of trainees. "Try us again next month," they said to applicants whom, only a day before, they would gladly have sent to officer candidate school. Thus the physician who examined Lucky found a defect the young man never could have suspected. Only a day before the doctor would have had it corrected at the Marine Corps' expense.

"I can't let you in unless you get circumcised," he said.

"Circumcised!" Lucky exploded in dismay. "Jesus, Doc, what the hell do you think I'm gonna do to those Japs?"

The doctor grinned, and just as he suspected, Lucky was back four weeks later with the offending organ still swathed in bandages, but freed of sutures and stripped down for action. Fifteen minutes later Lucky lifted his right hand to take the oath and become a United States Marine.

With his newfound buddies, Lucky took the ferry across the Hudson to Hoboken and boarded an ancient wooden train waiting to take them down to Parris Island, 900 miles south. It was a dingy old relic smelling of coal, lighted by kerosene lamps and heated by pot stoves. But the Marines-to-be loved it, singing much of the way and greeting each new batch of recruits picked up at points along the way—Philadelphia, Baltimore, Washington—with the immemorial Marine cry: "You should have been here when it was *really* rough!" At last, weary, filthy, sleepless, they reached the rail terminus at Yemassee and were taken by truck to Parris Island. There the six-foot-four-inch drill sergeant who would be their instructor ordered them to fall in after their sloppy civilian fashion and bellowed at them in a syrupy Southern accent:

"Boys, Ah want to tell yawl somethin'. Give yoah hearts to Jesus, boys, because youah ass belongs to me!"

Sergeant Campbell meant what he said, and he was right. It did belong to him, and he drilled it, marched it, kicked it, shaped it so that in six weeks time (the normal twelve-week course had been cut in half) the sixty boots who formed his training platoon would emerge as Marines. Campbell's most valuable asset was his iron voice. It pulsed with power as he counted the cadence while marching his men in close-order drill.

"Thrip-faw-ya-leahft, thrip-faw-ya-leahft."

It sounded like an incantation to Lucky and his buddies, but it was merely the traditional "three-four-your-left" elongated by the Southern drawl and made sprightly by being sung. Striding along beside his platoon, his great body ramrod-straight and his head canted back, his arms swinging and pumping, his iron voice ceaselessly bellowing, "Thrip-faw-ya-leahft, thrip-faw-ya-leahft," Sergeant Campbell took this ragged remnant and put steel in their slouching civilian spines.

He marched them everywhere: to the quartermaster's where they stripped themselves naked while a cascade of clothing was hurled at them . . . to a wooden barracks staggering under the weight of a seabag stuffed with uniforms . . . to the sick bay for shots . . . to ordnance to draw rifles slimy with Cosmoline, to the water racks to scrub them clean . . . to the barber's to have their civilian locks in four or five strokes of the clippers shaved down to a military fuzz . . . to the marching ground, feet slapping cement, treading the packed earth, coming to a halt with rifle butts clashing . . . To the rear, march! . . . Forr-ward, march! . . . Left oblique, march! . . . Platoon, halt! . . . *clash, clash.* "Right shouldeh, ahms!" . . . *slap, slap* . . . *my fingers! oh, my goddam swollen fingers* . . . "Goddammit, men! Strike youah pieces! Hear me? Strike youah pieces, y'hear? Ah want noise! Ah want bruises! Noise! Bruises! Pre-sent, ahms!" . . . *my fingers!* . . . "Forr-ward, march!" Now again, march . . . march, march, march . . .

To Lucky it all seemed a madness, but gradually he began to see that it was Discipline. He was being made over, being decivilianized, hammered into the image and likeness of Sergeant Campbell. Each day one more bit of his civilian character was being torn from him, as hair and skin cling to peeled adhesive tape. Like all the other drill instructors, Sergeant Campbell had a dozen different devices—sometimes brutal, always humiliating—with which to discipline his recruits. A man who forgot to address him as "sir" would be commanded to clean out the head (lavatory) with a toothbrush. A man who did not shave because he had no beard was ordered to "dry shave," that is, hold a razor in his fingers and scrape his face, usually drawing blood. A man who called his rifle a "gun" was made to sleep with it. Another who dropped his rifle stood high on a second-story platform, holding his weapon at port arms, chanting over and over, "I'm a bad boy, I dropped my rifle," until at last he could barely whisper the refrain.

Once while marching Lucky began to daydream and fell out of step. At once Campbell grabbed him by the ear, almost lifting him off his feet, growling, "Lucky, if you don't stay in step both of us is goin' to the hospital—so's they can get mah foot out of youah ass!"

And so the boots were undone at Parris Island, taken apart, and then they were marched to the rifle range where they were put together again. The rifle is the very special weapon of the United States Marines. True, Lucky and his buddies also fired pistols, went through bayonet drill or fought each other in jujitsu or with sheathed bayonets. But they were out at the rifle range for the very special purpose of learning how to handle that weapon and to "fire for record." Lucky was surprised to see how well the Southerners could shoot and how poorly Northerners like himself. He was also dismayed at the profanity and obscenity with which the noncommissioned officers bullied them into learning how to fire standing, sitting and in the prone position. He had never before been exposed to the full extent of the Marines' cursing facility. There were NCOs on the rifle range who could not put two sentences together without bridging them with an oath. Lucky wondered how they could have developed such facility with mere imprecation. This was no vituperation. It was only cursing, obscenity, profanity—none of which is ever profuse or original—yet it came spouting out in an amazing variety. There was also blasphemy, and those with any depth of religious feeling flushed with anger to hear it, clenching their fingers and yearning to be at the weather-beaten throats of the blasphemers.

Always there was the word. Always there was that four-letter ugly sound that men in uniform have relied upon as the single solution to all difficulties of expression. It was a handle, a hyphen, a hyperbole, verb, noun, adjective, yes, even a conjunction. It described food, fatigue, metaphysics. It stood for everything and meant nothing; an insulting word, it was never used to insult; crudely descriptive of the sexual act, it was never used to describe it; base, it meant the best; ugly, it modified beauty; it was the name and nomenclature of the voice of emptiness, but Lucky heard it from chaplains and captains, from PFCs and Ph.D.s—until, finally, he wondered whether, if a visitor to this planet unacquainted with the English language were to overhear these Marines cursing, he would, in the way of the Higher Criticism, demonstrate by measurement and numerical incidence that this little word must assuredly be the thing for which they were fighting.

At last came the great day when Lucky's platoon fired for record. It was windy and brutally cold. Lucky's eyes ran water all day long. When they fired from the 600-yard range he could barely see the target. He had been conceited enough to believe that he would qualify as an Expert Rifleman—a badge which is to shooting as the Medal of Honor is to bravery—and thus add an extra $5 to his private's pay of $21 a month. But he failed miserably, shooting at the wrong target, shooting too high, getting his windage wrong. But he had fired for record and was now, by some mysterious mystique, a Marine. When Sergeant Campbell marched the platoon back to their barracks, they strode along with a special swagger and a firmer grip on their Springfields.

Arriving in the barracks area, they saw a new group of incoming recruits, still in civilian clothes, unkempt and ragged, bedraggled as boots always are. With one voice the platoon shouted, "You'll be sorree!" Campbell grinned in delight.

Back at the barracks his manner seemed to soften. He had drilled them for six weeks, now. Except for the week on the rifle range, they had never stirred from the barracks save at Campbell's order. They saw no newspapers and heard no radio programs. They knew nothing of the war, had even forgotten about it. The only relaxation of discipline had been for Sunday church services. But Lucky never went back to Mass after he saw to his outrage that the front pews of the chapel were reserved for officers and their ladies, the middle for NCOs and their wives and the back for faceless ciphers such as himself. Lucky was by then aware of the meaning of RHIP—Rank Has Its Privileges—but he also knew that in heaven there was only one King and no colonels. So he never again entered a military chapel.

On the day of departure for the Fleet Marine Force base at New River, North Carolina, Lucky and his buddies swung their seabags onto the trucks that would take them to the train that would transport them to New River. Aboard the train they found discarded newspapers. In them they learned that while they were being made into Marines, the Americans in the Philippines had withdrawn into the Bataan Peninsula, where they still held out under General Douglas MacArthur.

When President Manuel Quezon first broached to Douglas MacArthur the subject of a Filipino army he asked him if, after the Philippines received their independence in 1945, the islands could be defended. MacArthur instantly replied: "I don't *think* the Philippines can defend themselves, I *know* they can." Here was a masterpiece of self-deception. MacArthur was then the chief of staff and what he really *knew* was that the General Staff considered the archipelago with its enormous coastline so indefensible that in the event of a Japanese invasion it was prepared to abandon it. For MacArthur, then, to have so reassured Quezon was incredible; yet this was no mere unfounded optimism springing from his eagerness for a new command. Here was simply the heart giving orders to the head. Douglas MacArthur regarded himself as one of the chief actors in a great historic drama: Through the unprecedented generosity of his own country, which he deeply and sincerely loved, a former colony intimately associated with the MacArthur name was to be reborn as an independent Asian and Christian nation with an economic future rivaling Japan's. Any objection to this vision, any obstacle to its fulfillment, had to be removed.

Therefore he was pleased when this evacuation plan was eventually modified: American land and sea forces would cling to Manila Bay while the Pacific Fleet sailed to the rescue. Most naval planners, however, doubted that the navy could do this in less than two years. But in mid-1941 Anglo-American planners formulated Rainbow Five, the plan for joint war against the Axis and Japan. This called for a defensive stance in the Pacific until Germany was defeated, implying acceptance of the loss of Guam, Wake and the Philippines.

No commander of Douglas MacArthur's ardent and optimistic nature, especially one inflamed by his vision of enacting the Philippine drama, could ever have accepted the passive defeat implied in this plan. Because of his great reputation and experience in the Philippines, he was able to persuade General Marshall, then chairman of the Joint Chiefs of Staff, to believe that the entire archipelago could be held. MacArthur's confidence sprang from a self-induced faith in the Filipino army, in his so-called Mosquito Fleet of torpedo boats and in the B-17 high-level bomber, the famous Flying Fortress. Marshall shared this enthusiasm for the Flying Fort. Three weeks prior to Pearl Harbor, Marshall declared that the thirty-five Forts based in the Philippines represented the world's greatest concentration of heavy-bomber strength! He claimed that the B-17s could defend the Philippine coastline without assistance from sea power and could in a counterattack burn the "paper cities" of Japan to the ground! Here was Douhet unadulterated, maintained a year after its signal failure in the Battle of Britain. Here was another piece of self-deception, because the B-17 simply did not have enough range to fly to Japan and back and because throughout the war it would demonstrate its unhappy inability to sink moving ships at sea. It is nothing short of amazing how many great American commanders in World War II seem not to have observed that when Billy Mitchell's horizontal bombers did indeed sink battleships they were *dead in the water.* To say this is not to sully the fame of this great airplane or the gallant men who flew in them. Against stationary targets or in carpet bombing the B-17 was superb, and the extremely accurate gunfire from its numerous turrets made it the scourge of enemy fighter planes. But high-level, horizontal bombers even when equipped with the astonishingly accurate Norden bombsight simply could not hit ships moving and maneuvering over water. Such accuracy is possible only to dive-bombers swooping down almost to crow's-nest levels or torpedo bombers skimming over the water at the same height.

Still, faith in the Forts as ship destroyers remained strong and every effort was made to get more of them to MacArthur. Only the onset of bad weather, a deterrent often ignored by proponents of air power, prevented their arrival. Other reinforcements were also planned, but the attack on Pearl Harbor canceled the sailing of nine shiploads of arms and men. Nevertheless, by December of 1941 General MacArthur did command a force of about 31,000 Americans, 12,000 Filipino scouts and 100,000 conscripts of the Philippine army. The naval forces assigned to him were small—one heavy cruiser, two lights, four old destroyers, twenty-nine submarines, thirty-two patrol bombers, and a number of auxiliaries —but he did have those thirty-five Flying Fortresses parked at Clark Field outside Manila.

Except for the Forts, these formations were far from being much of a deterrent to any invasion. The Filipino scouts were less than fair and the Philippine army was an ill-trained, ill-equipped mob. MacArthur's only reliable units were the U.S. 31st Infantry Regiment—about 3,000 men—and his tiny navy. Moreover, both he and President Manuel Quezon seemed to share a delusion that Japan would allow the Philippines to remain neutral and therefore were not disposed to vigorous offensive action that might provoke a war. Perhaps worse, there was dissension in MacArthur's top command. Because of his aloof attitude MacArthur had allowed his chief of staff, the autocratic Lt. Gen. Richard K. Sutherland, to make himself a headquarters watchdog. Top-ranking officers resented Sutherland's habit of blocking or limiting access to their chief. This was particularly true of Maj. Gen. Lewis H. Brereton, commander of the Far East Air Force. Although Sutherland's flying experience was limited, he still considered himself an authority on aerial warfare and often interfered in Brereton's orders and plans. MacArthur, in his lofty way, was not aware of this bickering among his lieutenants.

But he had by late November become dubious of the wisdom of leaving his B-17s so far forward and, through Sutherland, ordered Brereton to send them south to the safety of Del Monte Field on Mindanao. But only half departed. Later, Brereton explained that he expected another group of B-17s at Del Monte and that there would not be enough room there for all of the Clark Forts. So eighteen of them were parked at Clark when, at 4:00 in the morning of December 8, Brereton learned of the Pearl Harbor attack. War with Japan had begun and MacArthur's war plan was now in effect. Part of it called for a B-17 raid on Japanese air bases on Formosa, and Brereton went to general headquarters to ask permission to launch it. Sutherland told him the general was too busy to see him. Brereton then asked Sutherland for permission to attack. The chief of staff replied that a photoreconnaisance of the targets must first be made. At 7:15 A.M. he returned to headquarters and again was told that MacArthur was too occupied to see him. About an hour later Brereton called Sutherland to make his third request to launch the air strike and was again refused. Ten minutes later Sutherland telephoned Brereton to inform him that the photoreconnaissance mission had been approved. Now the B-17s that had been marking time aloft were recalled and three of them chosen to make the photo mission while the rest were ordered prepared for an afternoon bombing raid. Eight precious hours had elapsed since the Far Eastern Command had found itself at war, and the priceless B-17s were still parked out in the open when the Japanese struck.

They arrived over Clark and adjoining Iba Field almost without warning and before they departed the Far Eastern Air Force had ceased to exist as a fighting unit. Eighteen B-17s, fifty-six fighters, twenty-five other aircraft and numerous installations were knocked out. So was Cavite Navy Yard a few days later and then the patrol bombers of the Asiatic Fleet. The sky over the Philippines and the air around it belonged to Japan.

Even today it is impossible to fix responsibility for the Clark-Iba catastrophe. Inadequate evidence and contradictory charges exchanged by Sutherland and Brereton, plus MacArthur's steadfast insistence that he knew nothing about any proposal to bomb Formosa, have made it impossible to assign blame to anyone. Brereton has claimed that the Forts were caught on the ground because of Sutherland's refusal to let him see MacArthur, while Sutherland has replied that

Brereton's command was dilatory in conducting the reconnaissance. MacArthur, meanwhile, has maintained that if he had been asked permission to strike Formosa, he would have disapproved it as a mission doomed to disaster. In this he was correct; the Japanese on Formosa expected to be hit and were on the alert, with 500 aircraft and formidable AA. Without long-range escort the B-17s would have been annihilated. However, the Formosa strike had been part of MacArthur's plan and his insistence that he would have prohibited it came a long time after the disaster occurred. If anyone is to blame, it is MacArthur, and chiefly for having assigned so much authority to his chief of staff.

Meanwhile, in the wake of Clark-Iba and subsequent setbacks there was no time to be wasted in acrimony, especially after the Japanese began landing on Luzon.

At dawn of December 22 the spearheads of Lt. Gen. Masaharu Homma's Fourteenth Army began landing at Lingayen Gulf a little more than 100 miles north of Manila. By noon three Japanese regiments with tanks and artillery had easily obtained Homma's first-day objectives. Within a few more days he had put 43,000 men ashore. On the 24th another pincer of about 8,000 soldiers landed at three points on Lamon Bay at Manila's back door. The two forces began driving toward each other, while before them the Filipinos broke and ran. Although shocked, MacArthur immediately abandoned his own plan of defense and returned to the old War Plan Orange-3. This called for American-Filipino forces to withdraw into a redoubt on the Bataan Peninsula and there to await rescue by the U.S. Navy. On the night of the 23rd, MacArthur telephoned Maj. Gen. Jonathan M. Wainwright, commander of the North Luzon Force, and Maj. Gen. George M. Parker, Jr., the South Luzon Force commander, and ordered them to begin withdrawing into Bataan. MacArthur also declared Manila an open city and moved his headquarters to the little rocky island of Corregidor in Manila Bay.

MacArthur's forces executed this double retrograde movement with masterly skill. Using swamps and rivers as shields, fighting tank actions to cover withdrawals and check the enemy's motorized advance, while holding roads and bridges until the moment they had to be blown, they got back to Bataan while their commander installed himself in murky Malinta Tunnel on "the Rock" of Corregidor. By this decision and movement, MacArthur averted immediate defeat, delayed the Japanese timetable by four months, and tied up enemy forces which might have been used elsewhere. Nevertheless, it merely prolonged the inevitable. With the Japanese in control of the air and the sea, it was not possible to reinforce or supply the Philippines. Moreover, most of the fleet that was to fight its way west to the rescue was at the bottom of Pearl Harbor.

In America, a distraught General Marshall called a brand-new brigadier general named Dwight David Eisenhower to Washington and ordered him to do all possible to retrieve the situation.

43. Dwight David Eisenhower

DWIGHT DAVID EISENHOWER was born in Denison, Texas, on October 14, 1890 —the year the American frontier came to an end. His ancestors were Pennsylvania Dutch. They came from the Rhineland, where the name was spelled Eisenhauer, meaning hewer of iron. They were Mennonites, followers of a sect based upon doctrinal pacifism and belief in the Bible as the only authority for mankind. Such convictions were bound to bring them into conflict with any establishment, Catholic, Protestant or otherwise, and they were duly persecuted and forced to flee—first to Switzerland and thence to Pennsylvania in 1741. With arms as strong as their wills were stout, the Eisenhowers prospered at farming, God's work. But after the Civil War the Mennonites wished to put themselves as far as possible from the reaches of a godless government which had not hesitated to adopt that device of the Devil—conscription. So many of them moved to Kansas.

The Eisenhowers settled in Dickinson County, just north of the Smoky Hill River, only twenty miles east of the exact geographical center of the United States. Here, Jacob Eisenhower bought a 160-acre farm, and built a home, a barn, and a windmill—prospering to the extent that he could give each of his fourteen children, daughters as well as sons, a wedding present of a 160-acre farm and $2,000 in cash.

Jacob's son, David, disliked farming. He preferred to tinker with machinery, which led him to believe that he should study engineering. At twenty, David went to a little Mennonite school called Lane University. There he met Ida Stover. She was twenty-two, deeply religious, intelligent, musical and possessed of an incredible memory enabling her to memorize thousands of passages from the Bible. David and Ida were married in 1885 and received from Jacob the gift of a farm and $2,000 in cash. David took the cash, sold the farm and went into partnership in a general store. In 1888—the worst year in Kansas farming history—the store failed. Destitute farmers were unable to pay their debts. David, now as destitute as they were, was compelled to accept employment as a $10-a-week railroad hand in Denison, Texas. It was there that their third child—David Dwight Eisenhower —was born. The baby's baptismal names were reversed because Ida detested nicknames and wanted a name that could not be shortened. Many years later she was appalled to learn that the first syllable of the family name had been converted into "Ike," and that Edgar the oldest was known as Big Ike and Dwight was called Little Ike.

Those nicknames were born in Abilene, Kansas, the town to which the family moved after the Mennonites rallied around the young couple. The church owned a creamery there, and David was hired as a mechanic at $50 a month. This was just enough to live on and to rent a small frame home in which three more children were born: Roy, Paul and Earl (who died in infancy). Now the little house was too small for five healthy, rambunctious boys. But David's brother Abraham rented him a bigger house on the promise that he would take care of their father, the venerable Jacob. If David and Ida would care for Jacob, he would rent them the house at a minimal figure with an option to buy. David and Ida were overjoyed, and in 1898 they moved into what seemed to them their palatial new home.

Family life revolved around the worship of the Almighty. Each day began with the boys on their knees praying and their father reading from the Bible, and each day ended the same way. The Bible was also read before meals, and as the boys grew older, each took his turn at reading from it. Although neither David nor Ida smoked or drank or played cards or swore or gambled, eventually all of their sons would succumb to these vices, and Dwight would become particularly proficient in profanity, as well as a passionate bridge and poker player and a very heavy smoker, consuming, in his maturity, four full packs of Camels a day. Religious and God-fearing as the Eisenhowers were, they were far from being dull. There was much gaiety in the house, what with the irrepressible high spirits of the mother. Ida delighted in playing the piano and leading the singing. David was a typically stern German father. The boys took turns rising at five in the morning to cook his breakfast, at noon carrying his hot lunch to him at the creamery. When David came home from work, his hot supper was waiting for him at the table. At night, his sons gathered around him for the Bible reading, and when he took the clock from the wall to wind it, they knew it was bedtime.

David was far from being an affectionate father. He was very much feared, and the boys sometimes begged Ida to spank them for a piece of mischief rather than inform their father. *That* would mean not a spanking but a fearful beating.

The town that Dwight Eisenhower grew up in was not the famous—or notorious—Abilene of the wild and woolly West. "Sweet Abilene," the cowboys used to sing, "prettiest town I ever seen." That was probably because Abilene meant that the long, wearying six-month cattle drive along the Chisholm Trail from Texas ended at Abilene, the western terminus of the Kansas-Pacific Railroad. Abilene was not pretty in those days. In summer it was hot, dry and dusty, in winter cold, windswept and lonely.

By the time Dwight Eisenhower was in his teens there was hardly a living soul who could recall seeing a herd of cattle clatter into town, still less recall watching a shoot-out. But Dwight and his friends supplied the romantic difference from the pages of those cheap Westerns which were to become Dwight's lifelong love. Actually, Abilene was a pretty dull place. There wasn't even a police force, simply because none was needed in this town of fewer than 4,000 respectable, decent, hard-working Americans. Everybody knew everyone else, and everybody was also of European origin and Christian. A Democrat, as Dwight Eisenhower was to remark later, was just about one social cut above the town drunk.

At Abilene High School there was a tradition of a fistfight among the entering freshman class. The champion of the affluent North Side would meet the champion of the poorer South Side. Edgar, now known as Big Ike, won in his freshman year. In 1904 it was Little Ike's turn against a bigger, stronger, faster boy named Wesley Merrifield. They fought for an hour in what is now hailed in Abilene as "the kid fight of the century." Both boys had bloody noses, cut lips, battered ears and swollen eyes. Neither would quit. Finally, Wesley gasped, "Ike, I can't lick you," and Ike gasped back, "I can't lick you, either."

Dwight had a terrible temper. When he lost it, he trembled and turned beet red. During Halloween of 1900 he had pleaded to go out trick-or-treating with his older brothers, but had been refused. In a rush of rage, he ran outside and began beating his fists against an apple tree, sobbing uncontrollably and unaware that his hands were bleeding and raw. At last his father pulled him away and shook some sense back into him. Running to his room, Dwight cried into his pillow for well over an hour. When he subsided, his mother came to him and put salve and bandages on his hands. She sat silently beside him for a long, long time before she finally spoke: "He that conquereth his own soul is greater than he who taketh a city." Then Ida told her third son that of all the boys he had the foulest temper and would need the most effort to control it, but when he did, he would profit most by his conquest. Dwight never forgot that evening.

Dwight attended the Lincoln Elementary School directly across the street from his home. By his own admission he was not a very good pupil. Spelling bees aroused his competitive spirit, and arithmetic appealed to his logical habit of thought. But on his own he discovered that military history positively excited him. He became so fascinated by it that he began to neglect his other studies and his chores until his mother finally took his history books away from him and locked them in a closet. But Little Ike found the key; whenever his mother went to town, he slipped into the closet and lost himself once again in the clang and clamor of the battles of ancient Greece and Rome.

Sports—especially football and baseball—were the passion of Dwight Eisenhower's young life. At fourteen, Dwight fell and scraped his knee. Since there was no bleeding, he went to school the next day. But an infection set in. That night he was delirious. The family physician, Dr. Conklin, was unable to prevent the infection from spreading. For two weeks, Dwight drifted in and out of a coma. Dr. Conklin saw him two or three times a day. He painted a belt of carbolic acid around his thigh, but still the poison spread. Conklin called in a specialist from Topeka. They agreed that only amputation of the infected leg could save the young man's life.

Through his delirium, Dwight heard his parents discussing the loss of his leg. Quietly and firmly he interrupted: "You are never going to cut that leg off." His distraught parents, who instinctively distrusted surgery, told Conklin of their son's decision. The doctor warned them: "If the poisoning ever hits his stomach, he will die." The poison reached Dwight's groin. His moments of consciousness were fewer and shorter. He called for Edgar and told him, "Look, Ed, they are talking about taking my leg off. I want you to see that they don't do it. I would rather die than lose my leg." Edgar promised. He stayed constantly at Dwight's bedside, even sleeping across the threshold to prevent anyone from entering unobserved. This angered Dr. Conklin. He said the family attitude amounted to "murder." But neither David nor Ida nor Edgar would budge. At the end of two weeks, the poison began to recede. Dwight's fevered body began to cool. Consciousness returned. After a two-month convalescence he was recovered completely. But his prolonged absence from class made it necessary to repeat his freshman year, a development which did not dismay Dwight, if it was not indeed welcomed, since he would be a bigger and stronger freshmen when fall and football came around again.

In 1905 Dwight weighed 150 pounds and was nearing his full height of just a shade under six feet. As an athlete, he was good but a little slow afoot; it was his will to win and his unselfish determination as a team player that earned him the admiration of his teammates and his coaches.

Next to sports, Dwight loved camping and hunting, and often organized such excursions for his classmates. He was a good shot, and was always one of the shooters at the winter wolf hunts when crowds of hooting youths and yelling farmers would drive wolves, coyotes, jackrabbits and other pests into the open to be cut down by waiting marksmen.

In 1909, he and his brother Edgar were graduated from Abilene High School. Although both boys wanted to go to college, Dwight had no specific studies in mind while Edgar wanted to study law at the University of Michigan. Neither had any money. But then Edgar and Dwight conceived of a novel scheme: Edgar would go to Michigan for the first year, while Dwight worked and sent him his money; then Edgar would work for a year to finance Dwight's studies. So Edgar went off to Ann Arbor and Dwight got a job as a night manager at the creamery, working from 6:00 P.M. to 6:00 A.M. seven days a week for $90 a month, almost as much as his father. Except for a few dollars spending money and a few more for shotgun shells and clothing, Dwight sent all his money to Edgar. But when it came his turn to go to school, for some inexplicable reason, he didn't go —and Edgar remained at Ann Arbor.

In the summer of 1910 Dwight became friendly with a young man named Everett "Swede" Hazlett. He had received an appointment to the Naval Academy but had failed mathematics and had come back to Abilene to study for a repeat examination. Hazlett told Dwight that he could get a free education if he were admitted to Annapolis. Then he could play college football, as he dreamed, and become Hazlett's roommate. When Dwight read in a local newspaper that U.S. Senator Joseph Bristow was holding an examination for admission to both West Point and Annapolis, he decided to apply for both, just to be on the safe side. Then he began a cram course under Swede Hazlett's tutelage, and soon, Hazlett confessed, because of "Ike's god-given brain," he was well ahead of his teacher.

Dwight placed second among eight contestants, and was informed by Senator Bristow that he was appointing him to West Point. Both he and Hazlett were bitterly disappointed. Actually, there was nothing Dwight could do: He was now twenty years of age and too old for the Naval Academy. Gradually, however, he began to see West Point in a rosier light, returning to Abilene High School for refresher courses and also, just quite incidentally, to play football. (There were no eligibility standards in those days.) He became the star of the team and studied so hard that he easily passed the examination for the Military Academy in January 1911. In the following June, he was off for West Point.

Dwight Eisenhower fell in love with West Point. It was as though he were walking through the pages of history. Here he lived in the same rooms once occupied by Grant and Lee, by William Tecumseh Sherman; there he strolled through the same corridors they had trod. His passion for military history made him keenly aware of his historic surroundings, and when he could, he was fond of strolling over the plains soaking up tradition, or climbing the cliffs above the Hudson to gaze down at the mighty river, wondering how different West Point's history might have been if Benedict Arnold had been able to betray the post to the British.

Dwight accepted the academy's rigid regimen of civil and military engineering, unchanged since the War of 1812, and its antique style of teaching by rote, as the ordained way of educating officers, just as he had without question accepted the Bible as revealed truth, which ought to be embraced without hesitation. He was also too much of a pragmatist to allow his individuality to be destroyed by a discipline that was deliberately designed to subdue the nonconformist. So far from breaking the law, he merely bent it—like generations of cadets before him. Thus, when he discovered that smoking was strictly forbidden, "I started smoking cigarettes." Rolling his own Bull Durhams, he was frequently caught, ordered to walk punishment hours or to be confined to his room, but he continued to smoke. He was also frequently late for formations, careless in his dress or slovenly in keeping his quarters, receiving so many demerits that, in spite of an academic standing at the middle of his class, he was graduated 125th in a class of 164. But he could not care less and had nothing but disdain for cadets who were mark grubbers or demerit conscious. "Christ!" he exploded upon learning that a classmate had made general, "he's always been afraid to break a regulation."

Eisenhower's grades would probably have been higher had he not loved football so much. His intent in coming to West Point had been simply to get a college education. But what he really liked to do was to play football. He was disappointed in his plebe year to make no better than junior varsity. During the winter, however, he ran on the indoor track, increasing both his starting and sprinting speeds, and worked at gymnastics to improve his coordination. In 1912 he not only made the varsity but emerged as Army's star running back. *The New York Times* called him "one of the most promising backs in Eastern football." But then he twisted his knee against Tufts and later, during "monkey drill" in the riding hall—leaping on and off a galloping horse—his knee buckled when he hit the ground. The tendons and cartilage were so badly torn that the doctors informed him that he could never play football again.

It is an understatement to say that Dwight Eisenhower was brokenhearted. He was so depressed that his friends repeatedly had to talk him out of resigning from the academy, and now his marks really plummeted: As a plebe he had stood fifty-seventh in a class of 212; as a yearling after his injury, he fell to eighty-first in a class of 177. He might just have faded out of West Point had he not been asked to coach the junior varsity. He accepted with great enthusiasm and turned out winning teams. Here, as a football coach, Dwight Eisenhower was able to demonstrate his innate qualities of leadership: his zest, his devotion to the ideal of teamwork, his unflagging interest in the intricacies of what is certainly the most complicated team sport in existence, his capacity for hard work and his ability to get the best from his players. If coaching a football team can be compared to commanding an army—and it certainly deserves to be—then Dwight Eisenhower was unwittingly preparing himself for his future.

The Great War was already ten months old when, in June of 1915, Dwight David Eisenhower was graduated from West Point and commissioned as a second lieutenant of infantry. After four years of obeying orders, he now put his foot on the bottom rung of the ladder of command.

Lieutenant Eisenhower had hoped to do duty in the Philippines, but his first assignment was at Fort Sam Houston, Texas. Here was one of the "country clubs" of army life. Most officers were free by noon, able to hunt or go horseback riding, and in the evening join what seemed an endless social round of dances, parades, parties and poker games. Such a life appealed to Eisenhower's gregarious nature, and he was delighted in the fall when his commanding general practically ordered him to "accept" a job coaching football at a local military academy. In the following year, 1916, he moved up to college coaching, taking a post at St. Louis College, a Catholic school that hadn't won a game for five years. Eisenhower tied his first game, won the next five and then lost a close one for the conference championship.

At this time Eisenhower hoped to join Gen. John J. Pershing's Punitive Expedition into Mexico in pursuit of Pancho Villa, but the War Department rejected his application. This was the first of many disappointments at the hands of what he came to call "that nebulous region." But it was soon forgotten in the great thrill of falling in love. In October of 1915 while still at "Fort Sam" he met Mary Geneva Doud, called Mamie by her friends. She was slender, small, vivacious in a white linen dress and huge floppy black hat. She was only eighteen, the oldest of three girls in a wealthy Denver family. For her part, Mamie Doud thought: *He's a bruiser. He's just about the handsomest male I have ever seen.* When Eisenhower asked her to accompany him on his rounds, she accepted at once. Next day, returning to her quarters, she was told by her maid that a "Mr. I-something" had been calling every fifteen minutes all afternoon. The telephone rang. It was "Mr. I-something" asking for a date. But Mamie was booked for four weeks. However, she did suggest that he might drop in on her some evening at five. Eisenhower was there the next day, and he quickly persuaded Mamie to cancel her four-week booking. They were married on July 1, 1916, in the Douds' fine mansion in Denver.

Eisenhower, now a first lieutenant, hurled himself into his assignment of training the 57th Infantry, a new Regular Army regiment. Mamie devoted herself to pleasing her husband. She loved to entertain, which delighted the outgoing Eisenhower. Their quarters came to be known as the Club Eisenhower, where younger officers and their wives could drink beer and munch pretzels and sing the rollicking ballads beloved of army men the world over while Mamie pounded away on a rented piano. Eisenhower's favorite song was "Abdullah Bulbul Emir," of which he knew no fewer than fifty verses.

After the United States entered World War I in April 1917, Eisenhower continued to train the 57th Infantry. He did so well at it that his ability to train men and form new units, like his skill as a football coach, became a millstone around his neck. Eisenhower wanted to go to France, where the glory was, where an officer could distinguish himself and rise to the top by merit promotion, not by the agonizingly slow process of promotion by class. True, he did make captain, but he wanted combat. The only sunlight that came his way during those days of frustration was the birth of a son, Doud Dwight Eisenhower—nicknamed Icky —in San Antonio on September 24, 1917.

During the six months following the Armistice, the mad rush to demobilize —so characteristic of democracies—resulted in the discharge of 2,608,218 enlisted soldiers and 128,436 officers. By January of 1920, the United States Army had shrunk to 130,000 men, just 30,000 more than Versailles had allowed the conquered Germans. By 1935, the U.S. Army did not have a single combat unit of any size, and it ranked sixteenth in size among the armies of the world.

Eisenhower's rank declined with the army's strength. On July 30, 1920, he reverted to his rank of captain, but three days later rose to major. There he stayed for sixteen years. He had many job offers, as might be expected in a man of his presence and abilities, but he turned them all down. The U.S. Army of the twenties and thirties, publicly scorned as it might have been, was in fact a delightful and entertaining place. Pay and promotion were low and slow, but the Corps of Engineers was ever ready to beautify a post with officers' clubs, golf courses, swimming pools, riding trails and ballrooms, all, of course, at no or minimal cost to the officers, who also did not hesitate to tap the ranks for every conceivable type of servant. Service at these posts was rotated every two years or so, and everyone got to know everyone else, thus creating a binding spirit of fraternity and camaraderie among the officers. Also, the tank and airplane had emerged from the Great War as the most revolutionary new weapons since the introduction of gunpowder, and the challenge of creating the tactical theories for their proper employment was one that a professional such as Eisenhower could not resist.

Eisenhower's experience with tank doctrine at Fort Meade and Camp Colt had placed him in the forefront of the few Americans who foresaw the tank's possibilities. One of these was George Patton, whom Eisenhower met at Meade in 1919. Patton had actually ridden a tank into battle, a fact which impressed Eisenhower far more than his wealth or polo-playing prowess. Except that they were both physically strong and loved sports, two men embarked upon a common cause could not have been more dissimilar. Eisenhower's voice was deep and resonant, and he had the face of a fighter, while Patton's was high-pitched and squeaky and his face, as he frequently complained, would not frighten Little Bo-peep. Much as Eisenhower could swear like a sergeant, his language was clean in mixed company; but Patton, who swore like a drill instructor, made no such concessions to feminine sensitivity. Nor did Patton the loner care very much about what people thought of him, in comparison to Eisenhower's fondness for "laughter and the love of friends." Yet the dogmatic George and the pragmatic Dwight became fast friends, and remained so, bound by their common belief that the tank "was a weapon that could change completely the strategy and tactics of land warfare." Both wrote articles on the subject: Patton for the *Cavalry Journal,* Eisenhower for the *Infantry Journal.* Both called for speedier, heavier, better-armored and heavier-gunned tanks capable of moving both on roads and overland. Both were severely reprimanded. Patton was so angry he transferred out of the Infantry Tank School back to the cavalry. The chief of infantry told Eisenhower not to publish any more of those ideas. He did not recant, but he did shut up.

In 1920 the Club Eisenhower was still in evidence at Camp Meade, where Ike and Mamie still outdid themselves in entertaining friends. A week or so before Christmas, Icky came down with scarlet fever. Eisenhower did everything possible to save his son, even calling in a specialist from Johns Hopkins, who advised prayer. Doud Dwight Eisenhower died on January 2, 1921.

Both Dwight and Mamie were desolated. "For a long time, it was as if a shining light had gone out in Ike's life," Mamie wrote later. For fifty years thereafter Dwight sent Mamie flowers on Icky's birthday, and both arranged to have the child's remains laid beside them in their own burial plot.

Now Major Eisenhower was desperate to get away from Camp Meade, which had for him nothing but unhappy memories. But his commanding general, reluctant to lose such a fine football coach, saw to it that his request to attend the Infantry School at Fort Leavenworth was denied.

In every hierarchical organization an ambitious man needs a powerful patron to help him up the ladder of promotion. Dwight Eisenhower was fortunate in finding four such men, all brilliant, all independent-minded, all forceful—and all generals. They were, in this order: Fox Connor, John J. Pershing, Douglas MacArthur and George C. Marshall.

"Fox Connor was the ablest man I ever met," Dwight Eisenhower was fond of saying to his dying day. He met him at a Sunday dinner in Patton's quarters at Camp Meade. Connor had been Pershing's operations officer in France and had been considered the brains of the American Expeditionary Force. He was then Pershing's chief of staff in Washington. At Meade, Connor asked Patton and Eisenhower to show him their tanks and explain their theories of tank warfare. He listened attentively, asking penetrating questions, and was so impressed that he encouraged them to write their articles on the subject. Then he told Eisenhower that he had been assigned to Panama to command an infantry brigade and would like him to be his executive officer. Delighted, Eisenhower went to his commanding general to request what should have been a routine transfer. It was denied, supposedly because Eisenhower the fine field officer could not be spared; actually because Eisenhower the finer football coach was indispensable. But then Pershing became chief of staff and he ordered Eisenhower to Panama.

Fox Connor and Dwight Eisenhower quickly established a teacher-student relationship. The chores of their command were not very demanding, leaving them ample time for the diversions they both enjoyed—fishing, horseback riding, camping—and above all discussion of military history and its implications. Connor told Eisenhower that he was wasting his time reading dime Westerns and persuaded him to turn to serious biography and history. Major Eisenhower plunged into the memoirs of the Civil War generals, even reading Karl von Clausewitz's voluminous *On War* three times—no small feat of reading, for this most perceptive of military theorists can be very fascinating when discussing war as a social phenomenon or an instrument of policy, but very, very dull when declaiming on the tactics of conducting it. Connor constantly predicted that Versailles would produce another world war, which America would enter earlier than in the last one. He prayed that in the next war nationalist sensitivities should be subordinated to the ideal of a single commander. Dwight Eisenhower profited enormously from his three years in Panama under Fox Connor, and when he returned to the United States, it was with a third Eisenhower: the second son, John Sheldon Doud Eisenhower, born in Denver on August 3, 1922.

Dwight Eisenhower was deeply dismayed when he opened his orders in the fall of 1924. The War Department was sending him back to Camp Meade to coach football again! It seems the army wanted to beat the Marines and to do so was assembling its finest coaches at Meade. Eisenhower was to coach the backfield. Unfortunately, the War Department had ignored the minor detail of talented players, so that Eisenhower and his colleagues went through a horrendous season.
After the last game Eisenhower was ordered to take command of a battalion of tanks. Once again he protested. He wanted to broaden himself and sought admission to the Infantry School. It was denied. Ready to object once more, Eisenhower received a mysterious telegram from Fox Connor: "No matter what orders you receive from the War Department make no protest. Accept them without question." Thus, a few days later, Eisenhower meekly complied with orders to proceed to Colorado for recruiting duty. Mamie was overjoyed. Fort Logan was close to Denver. Meanwhile, Fox Connor was persuading his friends

in the War Department to assign Major Eisenhower to the Command and General Staff School in Leavenworth. When Eisenhower learned of his appointment, he was, in his own words, "ready to fly—without an airplane."

At Leavenworth he was in competition with 275 of the best officers in the army, and although he knew that failure would put a moratorium on his career, he was also aware that success would lead him to the heights. He did succeed: number 1 in his class.

Such a triumph, of course, did not mean immediate promotion, but it did bring him to the attention of General Pershing, who called him to Washington and assigned him to writing a guide to the American battlefields in Europe. It was an enormous project, due to be finished in only six months; but Eisenhower was again fortunate in having his youngest brother, Milton, in Washington to assist him. Milton was one of the capital's rising stars, number 2 man in the Department of Agriculture. He had many influential friends in Washington who could help Dwight, and his own journalistic skill was especially useful in putting the guidebook together on time. Pershing was delighted to receive it and eventually had Major Eisenhower posted to the Army War College at Fort McNair, the final leg of an officer's postgraduate education and the one intended to prepare him for high command. Actually, it was like a sabbatical—no grades, no examinations—a leisurely year in which to listen to lectures by government officials and ranking generals, and to enjoy life. At Fort McNair, the Club Eisenhower was resurrected, and Dwight and Mamie were once again at the center of a circle of old friends. Club Eisenhower was still operative in Paris, Major Eisenhower's next assignment and the one dearest, after Denver, to Mamie's heart. Not long after their return from Paris, Gen. Douglas MacArthur became the army chief of staff.

Much has been written about the alleged animosity between Douglas MacArthur and Dwight Eisenhower. It is true that in the Philippines toward the end of their relationship, both men did become disenchanted with each other, but the fact is that Eisenhower spent seven of his thirty-seven years in the army under MacArthur—as he was also to spend four under Marshall—and these were among the most constructive and rewarding of them all. MacArthur was quick to perceive Eisenhower's abilities. He began to use him to draft speeches or write letters and reports. Eisenhower was the lieutenant par excellence. He was perceptive. He got his work done on time. He attuned his own life to his chief's schedule, to his whims. He was loyal, giving of his criticism freely and honestly when asked, implementing his chief's decisions whether he agreed with them or not. Eisenhower also possessed that rare quality of anticipation, of getting inside his chief's brain to think like him. He also knew instinctively when to make a decision himself rather than pass it on higher. Of him Douglas MacArthur wrote: "This is the best officer in the army. When the next war comes, he should go right to the top." Such unstinting praise surely does not sound like an ungrateful chief who deliberately held Eisenhower back, as has been charged, so that he did not make lieutenant colonel until he was fifty-one. Conversely, Eisenhower was deeply impressed by MacArthur's intelligence. "He did have a hell of an intellect. My God, he was smart. He had a *brain.*" Nor does this reflect the bitterness of an unhappy subordinate. It is probably true that eventually they exchanged the famous gibes: To MacArthur's remark, "Major Eisenhower was the finest clerk I ever had," Eisenhower is said to have replied, "Oh, yes, I studied dramatics under General MacArthur for seven years." But this disenchantment came much later, after Eisenhower's star had risen above MacArthur's, when they were rivals and the European Theater was receiving more support and publicity than the Pacific.

MacArthur's flamboyance and enormous petty conceit, naturally enough, did irritate Eisenhower, as it would any subordinate. But he was circumspect and never attempted to shine before the crowd of reporters who always seemed to flow in MacArthur's wake. In Eisenhower's words, MacArthur "could never see another sun . . . in the heavens." Still, the relationship between the two men was close, sometimes even affectionate; and after MacArthur completed an unprecedented two-year second term as chief of staff under Roosevelt and went to the Philippines to organize the Filipino army, Major Dwight David Eisenhower went with him.

One day in 1936 a beaming Douglas MacArthur strode into Major Eisenhower's office to tell him that President Manuel Quezon was going to make him a field marshal. Quezon also wanted to make Eisenhower and his friend, Maj. James Ord, generals in the Filipino army. Eisenhower turned white. He and Ord had many friends among American officers stationed in the Philippines. Some of them believed that the attempt to create a Filipino army was ridiculous. They would have nothing but derision for "generals" in that army. So he told MacArthur that he could never accept such an appointment. Then he made an egregious mistake. "General," he said to MacArthur, "you have been a four-star general in the U.S. Army. This is a *proud* thing. There've only been a few who had it. Why in the *hell* do you want a *banana* country giving you a field-marshalship? This—this looks like you're trying for some kind of—" MacArthur interrupted and silenced him with a furious dressing-down. "Oh, Jesus!" Eisenhower lamented later. "He just gave me hell!"

Eisenhower's reservations about how American officers would react to such an "un-American" rank was but a reflection of the difficulties that he and Ord were encountering in trying to form a Filipino army. Nevertheless, he pretended to accept MacArthur's explanation that the Filipino mentality was impressed by such exalted titles.

But Eisenhower's relations with MacArthur became steadily more difficult. His only consolation was that his close friend, Major Ord, shared his misgivings; but after Ord was killed in an airplane accident, he had no one to confide in. The difference between the field marshal and the major was that the visionary MacArthur simply could not or would not see the impediments to building a Filipino army that the practical Eisenhower encountered day after day. Money was the chief obstacle. Quezon had allotted only $8 million for defense, but the first budget prepared by Eisenhower and Ord came in at $25 million. MacArthur calmly advised them to cut it in half, which was only possible by halving its strength, paying its soldiers peon wages, cutting their training time from a year to six months, and relying on obsolete or discarded American equipment. There were other problems endemic to the nature of the people that were less easily solved. One was language: A company of conscripts might have soldiers speaking a dozen different dialects. MacArthur thought such diversity of tribe and tongue was an asset because it reflected the character of the people, but Eisenhower knew that in combat it would be rather a communications disaster. It was an immensely relieved Dwight Eisenhower who took ship for home on December 13, 1939. By then, of course, World War II had begun.

In 1940 Dwight David Eisenhower was still a lieutenant colonel and was approaching his fiftieth birthday. As modest as U. S. Grant, who had hoped only for a battalion to command, he told his son John that he expected to be retired as a colonel. "Of course, in an emergency, anything can happen—but we're talking about a career, John, not miracles." The remark came during a conversation about John's application for an appointment to West Point. He had turned down a generous offer from his Uncle Edgar that would have financed his study of the law and given him a lucrative job in Edgar's flourishing law firm in Tacoma. He preferred to follow in his father's footsteps, and his father was delighted when John placed first in a competitive examination in Kansas. "This accomplishment of John's has added two inches to my chest," he wrote. Actually, his chest had expanded, not from pride, of course, but from the physical and outdoor life he was now leading as regimental executive for the 15th Regiment of the 3rd Infantry Division, and commander of the 15th's 1st Battalion. At long last he had obtained field command!

His heart leaped when, in September 1940, he received a letter from Colonel Patton telling him that two armored divisions would soon be formed and that he expected to command one of them. Patton wanted to know if his old friend would like to serve under him. "That would be great," Eisenhower replied immediately. "I suppose it's too much to hope that I could have a regiment in your division, because I'm still almost three years away from my colonelcy, but I *think* I can do a damn good job of commanding a regiment." Patton wrote back: "I shall ask for you either as chief of staff which I should prefer or as a regimental commander you can tell me which you want for no matter how we get together we will go PLACES."

Eisenhower smiled at Patton's serene disregard of punctuation, his heart high again at the prospect of them both working together to prove the theories they had advanced so many years ago. But he soon learned that practically *every* new general in the army wanted Dwight Eisenhower to be his chief of staff. It was a compliment, of course, but he nevertheless still hungered for a combat command and despaired that his very prowess as a staff officer, like his skill at coaching football, might again deny it to him. On March 11, 1940, he was promoted to full colonel (temporary), thus fulfilling his lifelong ambition. Fellow officers who congratulated him predicted that he would soon be replacing his eagle with a star. "Damn it," he complained to John, "as soon as you get a promotion they start talking about another one. Why can't they let a guy be happy with what he has."

Three months later he was on his way to Fort Sam Houston as the chief of staff for the new Third Army, commanded by Lt. Gen. Walter Krueger. Even though what he feared had come to pass, he realized that he had been given a marvelous opportunity, not just a divisional chief of staff or even a corps but an entire army!

Colonel Eisenhower had never dreamed of the breadth of the opportunity awaiting him in his new post. He was to serve as chief of staff to the Third Army during the famous Louisiana maneuvers, the largest such peacetime operation ever conducted in the United States. General Krueger's Third Army was to be the "invader," attacking Gen. Ben Lear's Second Army, the "defender" of the United States. The maneuvers were held in August and September 1941, and just before they began, Eisenhower wrote: "All the old-timers here say that we are going into a God-awful spot, to live with mud, malaria, mosquitoes and misery. But I like to go to the field, so I'm not much concerned about it."

Eisenhower's tent in a bivouac near Lake George soon became "something of a cracker-barrel corner where everyone in our army seemed to come for a serious discussion, a laugh or a gripe." Weary officers who came there went away buoyant, like recharged batteries, leaving their cares behind. They found renewed confidence in the encouragement and wisdom of this remarkable man, whose competence was as plain to behold as his magic grin. And they never forgot the Eisenhower name. Neither did the crowds of young reporters who also made a mecca of Colonel Eisenhower's tent. They loved his frankness, his ability to explain technical details. They laughed at his jokes and frequently included them in their stories, and were delighted by his own gibes at the army's deficiencies, the "tanks" of papier-mâché, or the old trucks careening around bearing the label "artillery." To those following the maneuvers, his name became familiar; soon it became a household word after Krueger's Third Army, operating on plans which Eisenhower helped to draw up, outflanked Lear's Second Army and forced it to retreat. If the battle had been real, the experts wrote, Lear would have been annihilated and the "invaders" securely lodged on United States soil. Credit for this, they wrote, must go to Colonel Eisenhower. With typical modesty, Eisenhower demurred, insisting that the victory was due to Krueger alone. Krueger, however, with a generosity not always apparent in a commanding general, showed that he agreed by recommending him for promotion to brigadier general, which Eisenhower received in late September. "When they get clear down to my place on the list," he wrote, "they are passing out stars with abandon."

On Sunday morning of December 7, 1941, General Eisenhower went to his office to catch up on his paperwork. Mamie had protested, and she was not enchanted when her husband returned so tired that he told her that he was going to take a nap and did not wish to be "bothered by anyone wanting to play bridge." In about an hour, his aide called to tell him that Pearl Harbor had been bombed. Five days later his friend, Col. Walter Bedell Smith, secretary of the General Staff, called from Washington. "The Chief says for you to hop a plane and get here right away," Smith said. "Tell your boss that formal orders will come through later."

Because he believed that Chief of Staff Marshall merely wanted to talk to him about the Philippines, Eisenhower thought he wouldn't be away long and told his batman to pack just one bag. Then he got on an afternoon plane from San Antonio to Washington. Bad weather forced it down in Dallas and Eisenhower continued on by train. Once the train had reached Kansas City and swung east, he realized that he was traveling over the same tracks he had ridden in 1911 en route to West Point. He had been supremely confident, then, that he was on his way. Sunk in thought, preparing for his interview with Marshall, he was much too preoccupied to realize that he was now, like his train, really gathering speed.

PART FIVE

1942

44. Winter 1942: The Fall of the Philippines

MORE THAN ONCE during the train ride east, Dwight David Eisenhower thought of the man he was hurrying to see. George Catlett Marshall's reputation in the army was that of a cold, austere, extremely aloof man who was difficult to impress. He liked people to keep their distance. The first time he met the president, the jovial Roosevelt had called him "George" and tried to slap him on the back. Marshall had demurred, letting the president know that his first name was "General." If the chief of staff had any intimate friends, no one in the army knew who they were. Even in relaxation he was a loner, riding horseback or tending his garden. His lack of humor was legendary, although Eisenhower could remember his quip when he met him after returning from the notoriously soft life of the Philippines: "Have you learned to tie your own shoes again since coming back, Eisenhower?" It would not do to attempt to charm him with the famous Eisenhower grin.

But Dwight Eisenhower also knew that the chief of staff had a highly developed sense of duty. He expected to find the same in his subordinates. If he did, he was intensely loyal to them, perhaps even affectionate, although he would never show it. Like himself, Marshall was a big man with an athlete's build who had played college football; he was ten years Eisenhower's senior, but still remarkably trim and erect. Unlike MacArthur, whose tirades Eisenhower always remembered, Marshall never shouted and only rarely lost his temper.

He was known, however, to be death on certain types. Officers who had "stars in their eyes," consciously seeking promotion, were anathema to him. So were the buck passers or their opposite, the man who tried to do everything himself and never delegated authority. Desk pounders and pessimists also did not impress him. Above all, Marshall detested the publicity moth, the man who loved the limelight. In this, he was probably unconsciously manifesting his hostility toward Douglas MacArthur, the king of the headline hunters. Long ago, in World War I, when Marshall was on Pershing's staff, an order of the day he had written accidentally resulted in MacArthur's being "captured" by American troops. MacArthur never forgot it. When he was chief of staff, he "shanghaied" Marshall to the Illinois National Guard. Marshall, it appeared, would never rise higher than colonel. But in Illinois, Marshall made powerful political friends who led him all the way up to the top.

Such was the man whom Dwight Eisenhower would meet for only the third time in his career, a chief so terrifying to his subordinates that sometimes very able men became tongue-tied in his presence and thus blighted their careers. But

Eisenhower never got tongue-tied in the presence of anyone. At fifty-one, he had never looked better; almost completely bald, but trim and tanned from life in the field, his step springy, his blue eyes as bright as ever, his voice deep and resonant, his habit of speech vivacious and direct, made eloquent by dramatic use of his hands, ticking off points on his fingers as he enumerated them. It is possible that he might have been a little uneasy when his train stopped in Washington's Union Station on December 14, 1941, but he was still serenely confident as he hurried to General Marshall's offices in the War Department (the Pentagon was still under construction). At once the chief of staff fixed his visitor with "that awfully cold eye" and quickly sketched the steadily worsening situation in the Far East, especially in the Philippines. Leaning forward, he asked: "What should be our general line of action?"

Eisenhower was stunned. Without a staff, without familiarity with current Far East war plans, knowing only what he had just heard or had read in the newspapers, he was being asked how to retrieve probably the worst situation in which American armed forces had ever found themselves. Marshall watched him carefully. He was deliberately testing him. He had heard high praise of Eisenhower from officers whom he admired, but he wanted to see for himself how he acted under pressure.

"Give me a few hours," Eisenhower said finally, and Marshall nodded, returning to the pile of problems mounting on his desk faster than he could keep abreast of them.

Eisenhower went to a desk assigned him in the War Plans Division of the General Staff. He wound a sheet of yellow paper into a typewriter. Using his laborious, two-finger hunt-and-peck style of typing, he tapped out the heading: "Steps to Be Taken." Then he sat back and began to think. He knew—as he had known since 1935—that the Philippines could not be saved. Militarily it would be wiser to fall back on Australia, there to build a base for an eventual counterattack. But American honor, American prestige in the Far East, were also at stake, and these political considerations outweighed conventional military wisdom. His first recommendation, then, was to construct a base in Australia from which to reinforce the Philippines. Shipments of planes, pilots, ammunition and other equipment should be started immediately from the West Coast and Hawaii.

Eisenhower listed Australia's advantages as a base: It was an English-speaking country, had modern port facilities and was beyond range of Japanese aerial attack. When he handed his recommendations to Marshall, he told him that everything must be done to help MacArthur, if only because the peoples of the Far East would be watching them. "They may excuse failure, but they will not excuse abandonment." To do so, a strong line of communications must be established between the West Coast and Hawaii and thence to New Zealand and Australia. "In this, we dare not fail. We must take great risks and spend any amount of money required." Marshall nodded. "I agree with you. Do your best to save them." He thereupon placed Eisenhower in charge of the Philippines and Far Eastern Section of the War Plans Division. Marshall again leaned forward, and said: "Eisenhower, the department is filled with able men who analyze their problems well but feel compelled always to bring them to me for final solution. I must have some assistants who will solve their own problems and tell me later what they have done."

During the following two months, Dwight Eisenhower directed all his energy and skill toward saving the Philippines. He was at his desk seven days a week, almost always until ten, frequently until midnight or even later. Hard as he worked, he knew in his heart that he was attempting the impossible. Japan's hold on the area was so strong and its blockade so thorough that he could get only a trickle of supplies into the archipelago—and men not at all. He knew, too, that the islands were doomed, that his many friends there would either die or be taken prisoner. With a heavy heart, all he could hope for was to buy time for some to escape and to strengthen Australia as a base.

"Ships! Ships! All we need is ships!" he wrote in despair in his diary. There were ships on the West Coast, of course, and he had already directed two transports from San Francisco to Brisbane, while diverting fifteen heavy bombers there from Hawaii. But shipping from Australia to the Philippines was almost out of the question. Eisenhower had $10 million in cash to hire blockade-runners. There were so few takers that in desperation he turned to the little vessels that once carried copra from the islands to the mainland. Of six skippers willing to try the blockade, only three got through. Two fast ships carrying a field artillery brigade could get no farther than Darwin on Australia's north coast. Fighter planes he had planned to send from Darwin to Bataan arrived from Hawaii without the necessary combat parts. Otherwise only an occasional submarine could get through. Such frustration was hard enough to bear, but to be accused by MacArthur of deliberately sacrificing the islands was the perfection of anguish, if only because it was basically true.

Angry and desperate, MacArthur was bombarding Washington with impossible demands. He insisted that the navy debouch from Hawaii to break the naval blockade. Eisenhower patiently tried to explain what he was sure MacArthur already knew: that with the Japanese holding Guam, Wake and the Gilberts and Marshalls, their land-based aircraft controlled the air. The navy was helpless. It was Dwight Eisenhower's unpleasant duty to inform his former chief that he would have to fight on with what he had for as long as possible. There would be almost no supplies and no reinforcements.

MacArthur's gallant scarecrows did fight on. During the last week of January 1942, a Japanese regiment had sneaked through a jungle to penetrate American-Filipino lines. They split into two groups which were trapped in the Big Pocket and the Little Pocket, and were almost annihilated in the Battle of the Pockets. Four other Japanese forces which had landed at various points on Luzon were also badly mauled in the Battle of the Points.

By early February, General Homma's forces had suffered such severe losses from combat and disease that he suspended offensive action. He was supposed to have secured the Philippines by the end of January, but he spent almost the entire month of February marking time while reinforcements were sent to him.

At the same time American-Filipino morale began to decline. Soldiers in the front lines heard the enemy's reinforcements arriving, could actually see mountains of munitions and provisions being stacked up within enemy lines. But they had not yet given up hope. They believed MacArthur's reiterated assurances that "help is on the way." Daily their eager eyes searched the skies for signs of those clouds of airplanes flying to their rescue. Lookouts with binoculars swept the seas straining for the sight of masts rising above the horizon. All in vain. Inexorably, food supplies dwindled. Since early January the half-ration for combat troops had included "3.7 oz. rice—1.8 oz. sugar—1.2 oz. canned milk—2.44 oz. canned fish, salmon or sardines—tomatoes when available, basis 10 men per can." On March 2, over the protests of Maj. Gen. Jonathan Wainwright, MacArthur ordered this ration cut to three eighths. Many of the men were by then so weak that they could hardly crawl from their foxholes or lift their rifles to aim them. Many troops lived off slaughtered horses, ponies or carabao. Some dined on the flesh of lizards or monkeys, although one soldier wryly observed that "monkey meat is all right until the animal's hand turns up on the plate." Some units sent out "food patrols" to forage for sustenance inside enemy lines. It was widely believed that it was better to die from an enemy bullet than from hunger or disease. And disease was by then rampant. Diarrhea, beriberi, dengue, hookworm and vitamin deficiencies causing scurvy were so common that a man who could walk to a hospital or sick bay was not considered really ill.

By March 12 at least three quarters of the command was incapacitated in some way. Field hospitals reported 500 to 700 daily admissions of malaria victims. There were days when there was no quinine. Water supplies were so inadequate that thirst-crazed men drank the filthy water of carabao wallows, almost always coming down with dysentery. It was not rare for a man to bathe and shave for an entire week in the same helmetful of water. As has been common in every army since Agamemnon's, while the front-line troops starved and thirsted, the rear echelons waxed fat. The men of the Harbor Defense Command mainly based on Corregidor were issued a ration of 48 to 55 ounces a day, compared to 14 to 17 for the soldiers on Bataan. Sailors aboard U.S. Navy ships in Mariveles Harbor traded a superabundance of food for the war souvenirs brought to them by gaunt fighting men. The great tragedy at Mariveles was that after the surrender there was no more ice cream.

Quite naturally the combat troops came to hate the favored ones in rear areas such as Corregidor, and especially General MacArthur, who certainly could have corrected a situation that was literally destroying his soldiers mind and body. But MacArthur seldom ventured from the safety of Malinta Tunnel on "the rock" of Corregidor; not, of course, because he was afraid, but most likely because he could not endure the sight of his wasted troops, or perhaps even feared to have them read the despair in his own eyes. Nevertheless, they hated him, and their contempt for him was boundless after they learned that he had escaped from the Philippines and arrived in Australia.

At first Douglas MacArthur had planned to disobey President Roosevelt's message of February 22 ordering him to escape to Mindanao and thence to Australia. He thought "of resigning my commission and joining the Bataan force as a simple volunteer." But General Sutherland and other staff officers persuaded him that he could be of much more value to the Allied cause if he could get to Australia to take command of the new Southwest Pacific Theater.

On March 10 MacArthur called for Wainwright and told him of his intention to depart the following night, leaving Wainwright in command. It was an emotional farewell. Both men had been suffering intensely. MacArthur had lost twenty-five pounds and Wainwright—whose West Point nickname was "Skinny" —was so emaciated that he seemed like a walking death's head and might better have been called Bony. In a touching gesture which only men in a starving army can understand, MacArthur gave Wainwright his most precious possessions: a box of cigars and two jars of shaving cream. "If I get through to Australia," he said in a husky, breaking voice, "I'll come back as soon as I can with as much as I can. In the meantime, you've got to hold." Neither man speculated on how long it would take MacArthur to come back, probably because both of them knew that it would not be in time to save the garrison.

At eight the following night MacArthur and his family—including his son's Chinese amah, Ah Cheu—fifteen army officers, two navy officers and an army sergeant began boarding four battered torpedo boats drawn up at the south dock of Corregidor's Bottomside. Because the boats' engines were so badly worn, each of them carried ten 50-gallon drums of gasoline lashed to its deck. Lt. John Bulkeley's PT-41 with the MacArthurs aboard took the lead as the boats roared off into the darkness in diamond formation.

They successfully eluded the Japanese blockade during the night, but became separated next day by storms and engine failures and the absence of seagoing navigational facilities. Rear Adm. Francis W. Rockwell in the trailing boat was astonished to see his young skipper sighting along his finger at the islands he passed. When he asked him how he was navigating, he replied: "By guess and by God, sir."

The four scattered boats pressed on toward a prearranged rendezvous at Tagauayan in the Cuyo Islands at the north end of the Sulu Sea. The skipper of the first boat to arrive there thought he saw an enemy destroyer approaching through the early-morning fog and ordered the gasoline drums jettisoned and the torpedo tubes cleared for action. Fortunately, two army generals persuaded him to hold his fire, for the "enemy destroyer" turned out to be PT-41 with the MacArthurs aboard. Nevertheless, without its extra gasoline, the boat had to be abandoned and its occupants transferred to PT-41 and another craft that had arrived later. These two boats resumed the voyage to the port of Cagayan on Mindanao's north coast. From Mindanao two Flying Fortresses took the MacArthur party to an airfield near Darwin in Australia, and from there a C-47 transport flew them to the tiny frontier town of Alice Springs in the center of the island continent. Weary, bedeviled by clouds of buzzing black flies that got into everyone's ears and nose and sometimes even their mouths, MacArthur and his party boarded a special train for Melbourne. En route, MacArthur learned that he was a national hero in the States, where his daring escape had captured the fancy of a public starving for good news. Already babies and streets were being named for him and the acclaim for Douglas MacArthur had reached the levels enjoyed by Charles A. Lindbergh, General Pershing and Admiral Dewey. Such reports helped to dispel some of his despair upon learning that in all Australia there were only 25,000 American troops, 250 combat aircraft and one regular Australian division. At the railroad station in Adelaide, MacArthur was met by reporters eager for a statement. He told them he had come to their country to build a base from which to launch the American counteroffensive against Japan and the recapture of the Philippines.

"I came through," he said, "and I shall return."

Douglas MacArthur may have been a hero to the American public, but he was a heel to his men on Bataan. "*I* came through, and *I* shall return." That remark stuck in their craw like a fishhook. *I, I, I.* No American commander has ever used the first person singular as often as Douglas MacArthur. Between December 8, 1941, and March 11, 1942—the day he escaped—no fewer than 109 of 142 communiqués issued by his headquarters mentioned only one person: Douglas MacArthur. Fighting units were rarely identified. They were simply "MacArthur's men" or "MacArthur's right flank on Bataan." Some of his more grandiloquent messages—the ones he composed himself—celebrated glorious victories in battles that were never fought. Throughout the war his communiqués were issued under the highly personal dateline: GENERAL MACARTHUR'S HEAD-QUARTERS. His top commanders were terrified of committing the cardinal sin of upstaging the chief. Three-star generals such as Robert L. Eichelberger or Walter Krueger were appalled when the war correspondent Robert Sherrod asked for interviews for a cover story for *Time* magazine. "The cover of *Time?* Do you want me to be sent home?" Because of this monstrous conceit defacing the character of perhaps the most remarkable soldier in American history, he had alienated his men. MacArthur's staff officers might be charmed by his unfailing courtesy, but his men crouching in the mud to eat their pitiful ration of wormy rice, announcing in their rough way their intention to go to the latrine, usually crooked their little finger in derision and simpered: "I shall return." Although all service families had been ordered home, MacArthur had maintained his own in Manila. When he escaped to Mindanao, the necessity of taking his wife, his son and his son's nurse kept three American officers out of the boat.

Behind him General MacArthur also left a legacy of friction that was to overshadow the Pacific War. Under him the army and its semi-autonomous air force were already at each other's throats, and the hatred of the navy and the Marines were guaranteed when, two days before leaving for Australia, MacArthur recommended *all* units on Bataan and Corregidor for unit citations *with the exception of Marine and navy units.* General Wainwright later corrected this deliberate slight, but he could never efface the memory of General Sutherland's pointed remark that the Marines had gotten enough glory in the last war and would get no more in this one.

Still, these splendid scarecrows of Wainwright fought on. Gaunt, sour of heart and stomach, ragged and red-eyed, bombed by day and shelled by night, they fought on and sang their sardonic requiem:

> We're the Battling Bastards of Bataan;
> No mama, no papa, no Uncle Sam,
> No aunts, no uncles, no cousins, no nieces,
> No pills, no planes or artillery pieces.

From both Roosevelt and MacArthur had come orders not to surrender, and MacArthur had ordered a desperation counterattack as a last resort. Fortunately, Gen. Edward P. King on Bataan had the moral courage to see, in Wainwright's words, that "he had either to surrender or have his people killed piecemeal." King surrendered to General Homma's senior operations officer on April 9, 1942. Then there followed the infamous Death March, in which American and Filipino prisoners, without food or water, were clubbed, beaten and bayoneted on the sixty-five-mile route from Mariveles to San Fernando. Then and thereafter, thousands of these American prisoners perished.

Corregidor still remained. Here was Wainwright with a mixed force of American soldiers and Marines. Although under steady aerial bombardment, the Rock held out for another four weeks until the Japanese succeeded in landing there. On May 6, with the Japanese within yards of Malinta Tunnel, while his men spiked guns, smashed equipment, and burned codes, Jonathan Wainwright composed his last sad message to President Roosevelt.

"With broken heart and head bowed in sadness but not in shame," he began, and ended: "With profound regret and with continued pride in my gallant men, I go to meet the Japanese commander. Good-bye, Mr. President."

With the fall of the Philippines, the Japanese order of conquest was complete.

45. Rommel Pushes East

IN JANUARY OF 1942, five months before the fall of the Philippines, Sir Claude Auchinleck in Egypt stood ready to drive Axis forces from North Africa.

Rommel was at El Agheila astride the coastal road, but Auchinleck was confident that the Eighth Army under General Ritchie could move down on him from Benghazi, dislodge him and thrust forward into Tripolitania. But then the reverses which had overtaken British forces in the Far East, and the threat of a fresh Japanese offensive there, began to divert men and munitions away from the Eighth Army.

Two divisions, four light-bomber squadrons and a shipment of antitank guns destined for Auchinleck went instead to the Far East, after which his Middle East Command was required to surrender four fighter squadrons and more than a hundred tanks to that endangered sector. Two Australian divisions followed.

Just as Greece had weakened Wavell a year before and deprived O'Connor of the opportunity to drive the Axis out of North Africa, so the Far East was bleeding Auchinleck and reducing Ritchie's strength. But Auchinleck, ever the gracious and understanding soldier, made no protests. Nevertheless, he was now dubious about the Eighth Army's chances of success in attacking Rommel. He had neither the troops nor the transport to make a fresh advance while establishing a firm base from which to repulse Rommel's inevitable counterattack. Auchinleck was also doubtful about the Eighth Army commander's ability to carry out a sustained offensive. When he had named Ritchie to succeed Cunningham, he had in his own mind considered the appointment temporary. But when Churchill announced the change, he did not say Ritchie was merely a passing chief, and thus both press and public assumed that he was the permanent desert commander. Auchinleck could not now relieve him without damaging army morale and puzzling public opinion. Moreover, to sack two chiefs in three months would seem somewhat excessive, and Auchinleck, in his warm and generous nature—so often a grave defect in a supreme commander—was most reluctant to wound a friend. So he stayed with Ritchie, confident that if he got into trouble he himself could take charge.

This was a serious mistake, as much an error of judgment as his earlier selection of Cunningham, and proof that Auchinleck was unable to guard against his own good nature. Ritchie at Benghazi set to work organizing the offensive, steadfastly ignoring warnings to prepare a defense also on the chance that the Desert Fox might strike first. After all, intelligence had assured him that Rommel had not been reinforced and could not be reinforced in time to forestall any attack on him. These erroneous reports infuriated many front-line commanders, whose troops had actually seen Rommel's new armor. So Neil Ritchie, the handsome, plodding mediocrity stood opposite Erwin Rommel, the tactical genius about to prove himself the equal of Napoleon in speed and Marlborough in maneuver, a mismatch as lopsided and foreordained as a mongoose with a cobra.

In the evening of January 21, Rommel began the prolonged assault that was to make him a field marshal and the very model of the military virtuoso, dazzling in his agility and opportunism. He came at the British and their numerous allied troops in two columns: one moving along the Via Balbia on the coast, the other inland. When the enemy's forward troops were overrun, he quickly concentrated on the coast and pressed forward at the head of his armor. Ritchie thought that

Rommel's thrust was merely a reconnaissance-in-force and that he would retire the next day. But he did not. He pressed on. When some of his tanks ran out of fuel, he deliberately increased his speed to compensate, again employing time as a weapon against the slow-moving British. On January 27, he feinted toward Mechili inland, tricking both Ritchie and Auchinleck into moving their armor to the east. At once Rommel changed direction and drove for the coast, cutting off the 4th Indian Division, which escaped encirclement and capture only by fighting its way out. Nevertheless, Benghazi fell to Rommel two days later, along with all the enormous stores of fuel and supplies which Ritche had collected for the invasion of Tripolitania.

Now Ritchie fell back on Gazala, unaware that Rommel's soaring ambition would confer on him a welcome respite. The Desert Fox now sought a great victory in North Africa, even the prize of Egypt itself. To gain it, he needed more troops and air support. In March, he flew to the Führer's headquarters to plead for it. The German high command was not interested in North Africa; their focus was almost exclusively on the Soviet Union. Nevertheless, it was agreed that in June there should be a joint German-Italian invasion of Malta. Possession of that strategically placed island would enable the Luftwaffe to interdict British shipping in the Mediterranean. Rommel was to stand on the defensive until then. He protested, and was permitted to resume the attack in May.

At Gazala Ritchie had been busy constructing his "mine marsh," a system of "boxes" or independent strong points of men and guns, backed up by armor, stretching inland to Bir Hacheim (now Abyon al Hakīm). This purely defensive posture not only reflected Ritchie's state of mind, it also suggested that he had completely failed to grasp the nature of desert warfare. In a fluid war without front or flanks, devoid of natural features such as rivers, swamps or mountains for protection or as anchors for the flanks, nothing could invite disaster more surely than a fixed defense.

Rommel went around it easily. On the night of May 26, beneath a brilliant moon, his armor began rolling toward Bir Hacheim, lighted like a beacon by Luftwaffe flares. Rommel was again personally in the lead, at the head of 500 tanks. He was not supposed to be attacking, and the soldiers of the Eighth Army believed that *they* were going over to the offensive. Some of them were caught at a leisurely breakfast when the German armor was sighted only a few miles off. "It was the whole of Rommel's command in full cry straight for us."

Rommel swept through the surprised "boxes" and then swung north for Tobruk. At the next garrison half of the men had been given leave to go swimming, and there were not enough soldiers to fire the guns when the Germans appeared. Rommel chewed up this unit, too, hurrying harder north toward Tobruk. Eventually Bir Hacheim fell to him, and the Eighth Army troops in Gazala, now threatened with encirclement, were compelled to evacuate. Thus began the Gazala Gallop. Fleeing troops hastened through Tobruk without stopping in their flight to Egypt.

On June 18 Tobruk stood alone against Rommel, who was already enclosing it in a ring of iron. This was not the old Tobruk that had withstood the Axis flood. Its commander, Maj. Gen. H. B. Klopper, had been a general for a month only. He had no combat experience and felt inferior to the two brigadiers beneath him. His was not a command but a committee. The 33,000 troops holding the fortress lived in an atmosphere of doom. Ritchie had promised Klopper that a powerful force would strike the enemy in his rear. But he did not tell him how slow it would be in coming. Ritchie could never cope with Rommel's speed, could not even imagine it. On the night of the 19th Rommel began attacking. Soon the British were demolishing the huge stores assembled in Tobruk for the British summer offensive. Great columns of smoke spiraled above the town. On the morning of June 21, Klopper hauled down his colors and Tobruk capitulated.

The Gazala battles had cost Ritchie 80,000 men, mostly in prisoners. He had been driven out of Libya and sent reeling back to Mersa Matrûh, the jumping-off point for Richard O'Connor's Desert Gallop almost two years earlier. There he awaited the Desert Fox. But his own career in the desert was nearing its end. On the afternoon of June 25 Auchinleck arrived from Cairo to relieve him and take charge of the Eighth Army himself. At Mersa Matrûh, Sir Claude Auchinleck fought his first battle as a desert field commander, and he too succumbed to the speed and daring of the Desert Fox. Within forty-eight hours Rommel with only sixty tanks and 2,500 foot soldiers routed two British corps with 150 tanks and between 40,000 and 50,000 men and sent them reeling backward toward the Nile. The place where the British turned to stand again was called El Alamein.

It was here that Erwin Rommel struck his final blows in his drive for the prize of Egypt, and it was here that Sir Claude Auchinleck stood firm to deny him. As Auchinleck made his preparations, the news from the U.S.S.R. was dismaying. Von Bock's summer offensive had smashed the Ukrainian front. As commander in chief, Middle East, Auchinleck knew that the vital Persian and Iraqi oil fields were only lightly held. Such a threat to his rear was deeply disturbing. Still, he sought to infect Eighth Army with his own offensive spirit.

For three full weeks the Germans and the British with their Commonwealth allies struggled back and forth in the seesaw First Battle of Alamein. Because the opponents were evenly matched, not only in men and arms but also in rival commanders, it was some time before either chief could sense who was winning. Gradually, however, Auchinleck asserted his superiority over the worn-out Desert Fox, especially after he began to devour Rommel's Italian divisions. Rommel, deeply aware of this strategy, wrote to his wife in despair: "The enemy is using his superiority, especially in infantry, to destroy the Italian formations one by one and the German formations are too weak to stand alone. It's enough to make one weep."

Again he wrote: "It can't go on like this for long, otherwise the front will crack. Militarily, this is the most difficult period I've ever been through." The front did not crack, because Rommel hurried every last reserve to the north to stop the British steamroller rolling south.

The Desert Fox stopped a rout, but his summer offensive was over—and it had failed. First Alamein had tarnished the glory won at Benghazi, Gazala, Tobruk and Matrûh. Afrika Korps lay in his hand like a broken reed; and Rommel was also broken by this sudden defeat, rising like a dark dead end to halt that bright and summery parade of easy victories. He had driven himself, punished himself, in body and soul, and been rewarded with disappointment and despair—an unfailing prescription for bad health. Ahead of him lay a struggle against an infected liver, a duodenal ulcer and desert sores.

Ahead of Auchinleck, it seemed, lay a period of rest: to regroup, repair and retrain. But this was not to be. On top of a message to Auchinleck so unpleasant that it has yet to be published, came another peremptory signal from the prime minister: "The only way in which a sufficient army can be gathered in the northern theatre is by your defeating or destroying General Rommel and driving him at least to a safe distance. If this were accomplished before the middle of September, the Australian divisions could return to their station in Palestine and Iraq. . . ."

By the force of this message Auchinleck as commander in chief was compelled to make a decision which as Eighth Army commander he knew to be both desperate and rash: to send his battle-weary, depleted forces over to the offensive. Within four short days he had prepared a plan and begun to attack Rommel. It seemed to have failed, yet because it had penetrated into Rommel's rear, it forced the Desert Fox to commit the last of his reserves. On July 27 Auchinleck called off the battle. It was the army commander telling the commander in chief that he just did not have the strength to destroy Rommel. But he had stopped him. Rommel himself wrote: "Although the British losses in this Alamein fighting had been higher than ours, yet the price to Auchinleck had not been excessive, for the one thing that mattered to him was to halt our advance, and that, unfortunately, he had done."

Unfortunately for Auchinleck, Winston Churchill never read those lines. What he had read a month earlier was the headlines announcing that his coalition government had lost a by-election through an enormous voting turnaround. It was a shocking criticism of his direction of the war. Churchill had now sunk to the very nadir of popularity during his wartime premiership. Something had to give, someone had to go—and it was Sir Claude Auchinleck, the general who fought the tide-turning battle in the Desert War. The Auk had himself suggested stepping down, and Churchill on August 8 wrote to him that his "high-minded offer" was being accepted. Iraq and Persia would be detached from the Middle East Command and given to Auchinleck (who accepted) and General Harold Alexander would replace him in Cairo.

Command of the Eighth Army would go to a little-known general named Montgomery.

46. Bernard Law Montgomery

BERNARD LAW MONTGOMERY was born in London on November 17, 1887, the fourth of nine children in the family of an Anglican priest. His father was then the vicar of St. Mark's but in 1889 he was appointed bishop of Tasmania, to which island province of Australia he moved his still-growing family.

As a boy, Bernard was extremely willful, always in conflict with his equally strong-willed mother. If she could not find him, she would say to one of the other children: "Go and find out what Bernard is doing and tell him to stop it." He was also hot-tempered and aggressive, once seizing a carving knife to chase a terrified little girl about the house with it. For this, his mother caned him vigorously, evoking not a whimper from Bernard. She seldom could make him cry, and their life together was a constant duel. She was determined to make him toe the line like the other children; he was equally bound to rebel.

Not surprisingly, under such conditions, Bernard worshipped his father. "He was always a friend. If ever there was a saint on this earth, it was my father." This gentle creature, who had become engaged to his wife when she was fourteen and married her one month after her seventeenth birthday, was like the proverbial putty in his wife's hands. She bullied him constantly, perhaps because she could not forgive him for keeping her pregnant during most of their first seven years of marriage, giving birth to five children before she was twenty-five. She doled out his allowance of ten shillings a week—which among other things was to cover the cost of his daily lunches—like a stingy seneschal, haggling with him like a fishwife should he meekly request an extra bob or two. The spectacle of his father pleading with his mother for more of his own money did not dispose young Bernard toward the sacrament of matrimony. Nor did the religious atmosphere in which he was raised instill in him an abiding faith in his father's creed. Ascetic he was indeed, but he was no monk in uniform such as Oliver Cromwell or Stonewall Jackson. Early on his father decided that Bernard was not for the altar.

This was when he was fourteen and the family had returned to London. Bernard was sent to St. Paul's School. Because in Australia most of his education had been by tutors, he had no knowledge of school life. He was also somewhat deprecated as a "colonial" with no experience of the twin passions of British public schoolboys: rugby and cricket. But Bernard was strong and tough and wiry —at maturity he would stand five feet eight inches tall and weigh about 140 pounds—and extremely competitive. Within three years he was the captain of both teams, and had earned the nickname "the Monkey." The school magazine caricatured him thus:

[The Monkey] is vicious, of unflagging energy, and much feared by the neighboring animals owing to its tendency to pull out the top hair of the head. . . . This it calls 'tackling.' . . . To foreign fauna it shows no mercy, stamping on their heads and twisting their necks, and doing many other inconceivable atrocities with a view, no doubt, to proving its patriotism. . . . So it is advisable that none hunt the Monkey.

At nineteen Bernard Montgomery entered the Royal Military College at Sandhurst. Like Winston Churchill before him, he loved the military life. In fact, he was one of those few first-term cadets promoted to lance corporal at the end of six weeks. Lance corporals always became sergeants in their second term, entitled to wear a red sash, and one or two became color sergeants carrying a sword, the highest rank at Sandhurst. This honor seems to have gone to Bernard's head. He became the leader of "a pretty tough and rowdy crowd" in B Company, leading them in combat against A Company cadets on the floor above. Once he and a band of boys burst into the room of an unpopular A Company cadet who was undressing at the time.

"Up against the wall with him!" Bernard cried and the youth was driven backward at the point of a bayonet. "Now, here with that candle!" He set the boy's shirttails on fire. The cadet was badly burned and had to be hospitalized. "Cad" that he was supposed to have been, he never informed on his tormentors. Bernard Montgomery, meanwhile, was reduced to the ranks, never to rise again. Disgrace was good for him. He turned from hazing to study, and left Sandhurst thirtieth in a class of 150. Even so, he was told by one of the ranking instructors there:

"You are quite useless. You will get nowhere in the army."

For the first few years of Montgomery's career, the instructor seemed to be right. The young subaltern posted to India was an obvious misfit in the Kiplingesque army of that day. Unlike Churchill, he had no passion for polo or fondness for a glass. However, just like Churchill, he spurned Ruff's *Guide to the Turf* and began to read military history and theory. Such unsoldierly habits, together with his Spartan tastes and ascetic character, did not endear him to his comrades, and he was once fined for talking shop in the officer's mess. He was clearly approaching cad status.

To prevent it, he entered a point-to-point horse race, even though he possessed neither horse nor horsemanship. Determined as ever, he bought an old regimental packhorse and began training. Came racing day he climbed aboard his mount, carrying considerable weight because he was so light, and promptly fell off. Enraged, he vaulted back aboard. He beat and berated his astonished beast so fiercely that it bolted forward and carried him past the field. At the finish line, Montgomery took another header. But he had won both the race and the esteem of his regiment.

Montgomery's will to win was matched only by his fear of defeat. These two dominant traits in him as a soldier first appeared together in 1911 when the German warship *Gneisenau* sailed into port at Bombay with the Crown Prince aboard. The German sailors challenged Montgomery's battalion to a friendly soccer match, unaware that they were taking on perhaps the best eleven in the

Indian Army. To avoid embarrassing their guests by a lopsided score, Montgomery's brigadier ordered him to field his second team. But he used his first team and the result was a shambles, something like forty to nothing. At once the brigadier called Montgomery onto the carpet.

"Were you not under orders to field a second-class side?" he roared.

"Yes, sir," Montgomery replied, unabashed. "But I was taking no chances with those bastards."

Montgomery was still taking no chances on the Germans when he led a unit of the 10th Brigade into France in August 1914. Again, his was a most irregular attitude. For the majority of the officers in that unit, World War I was going to be "a jolly good show" or something equally British, equally dashing—inevitably ending with the Kaiser overwhelmed by their impetuous charge. When the 10th Brigade met the Germans at Le Cateau, the Kaiser's professionals cut them to ribbons, and Montgomery was one of the few young officers able to maintain some semblance of order in the chaotic disorder of that battle.

There was no plan of attack. Coming to a hill, Montgomery and his comrades were simply told, "Take that hill"—and up it they went, waving their swords and urging their men to follow. The emplaced German gunners shot them to pieces.

Montgomery distinguished himself here and displayed a characteristic coolness under fire, when, with two men, he crawled out under a rain of enemy bullets to rescue his wounded company commander. More important, he was horrified by the consequences of brass-hat stupidity that sent men into battle without a plan, and he never forgot it.

At Ypres Montgomery led his platoon on a bayonet charge against the village of Meteren. They drove the Germans out. But sniper fire still raked them from the houses at the end of the village street.

Standing in the pouring rain, his sword clenched in his hand, the fierce little lieutenant called out to his men to halt their pursuit of the foe. He wanted to regroup them to hold the captured village. Suddenly, he crumpled. A sniper bullet had pierced his back at the right side and passed through his body.

One of his men rushed to his side, but by then, the Germans had recovered and laid down a counterfire in the village street. The man was hit in the head. He swayed, mortally wounded, and sprawled over Montgomery. Others leaped forward to take his place.

"Keep back!" Montgomery shouted. "You fools! They'll kill every one of you. Take cover!"

The men obeyed. For the next three hours, until night fell, Montgomery lay in the mud and the rain, the weight of a dead man's body pressing down on him, the bullets whining about him, and the sensation of life slowly passing from his consciousness. At dark, his men brought him in. It was no effort to sling him in an overcoat and carry him back to the forward dressing station. Even so, it seemed hardly worth it. He looked to be quite dead. In fact, his grave had been started, when a doctor decided that perhaps there was life in him yet. So Montgomery was evacuated to a hospital in England, and when he awoke, he found that he had been made a captain and awarded the DSO.

He survived. One lung was permanently injured. But he recovered in time to get back in action and to reach the rank of lieutenant colonel. But in 1919, at the age of thirty-one, he dropped back to major—and then down to captain. It would take him sixteen years to recover the rank he had held in 1918.

Meanwhile, in the years intervening between World Wars I and II, Montgomery made himself more and more of a student of warfare and more and more of a thorn in the flesh of the pompous. At the Staff College at Camberly, the instructors, speaking out of brass-bound minds and dugout mentalities, regarded him as "a bit of a Bolshevik." With his wasplike humor, his penetrating mind, he and a group of other young rebels had joined in a jeering and derisive attack on the old concept of trench warfare: heavy artillery barrages to be followed by massive infantry assault along a wide front. By this time, Montgomery had already formulated his own theory of how war should be fought. It rested on two poles: mobility and morale.

He had seen trench warfare, and it disgusted him. He believed in offense. Even on defense, he thought, an army should be free to strike when and where it pleased. To sit down behind a big wall was merely to hand over all initiative to the enemy. On the point of morale, he was even more irritating. Having had to attempt to take a hill without a plan, and for no apparent reason, he realized that the worst of all fighting men is the ignorant one. Since it is the foot soldier who wins the battle in the end, he reasoned, then the foot soldier should be told what it's all about and imbued with a creed of victory. Therefore, Montgomery concluded, all of this ceremonial parade, snapping and popping, changing of the guard, was a hangover from a dead past. The best way to train men was to toughen their bodies and instruct their minds—meaning get them off the parade ground and into the fields and the classrooms.

But if Montgomery was a radical to his superiors, he was also a reactionary old bachelor to his subordinates. Perhaps recalling how his mother had bullied his father, he advised his junior officers not to marry. "Marriage is not a good thing for officers," he said flatly. "You cannot be both a soldier and a husband." In 1927, however, reconsidering his strictures against matrimony, Montgomery married the widowed mother of two sons. She bore him his only son, David.

While he commanded a battalion in Egypt in the early thirties, he was repeatedly criticized for his patriarchal interest in both his juniors and his enlisted men. Those who browsed too often in the fleshpots of Egypt might find themselves gazing into those cold gray eyes while that thin, emotionless voice reminded them (with frequent reference to Scripture) of the evils of fleshpotting.

Yet, when Montgomery's men got into the field, they astonished his superiors, who had already taken a dim view of their less-than-soldierly appearance, by the snap and precision with which they went about making monkeys of the other units. Montgomery, too, showed that he had a firm grasp on the art of warfare. Once again, though, he had difficulty concealing his superior knowledge from his superior officers.

In 1937, Bernard Law Montgomery had reached the rarefied heights of independent command. In that year, he was made a brigadier general. In that year also, the great tragedy of his life befell him; his wife died of an infection caused by the bite of a mysterious insect. Montgomery sank into deep mourning. "My married life was absolute bliss," he said later. "The death of my wife was a shattering blow from which I recovered with great difficulty and very slowly." By 1938, however, he had recovered from his loss and led a brigade during invasion exercises in southern Britain. His unit performed so well that when two divisions were sent to Palestine that year to stamp out a savage guerrilla war between Jews and Arabs, one was in command of Maj. Gen. Richard O'Connor, and the other of Maj. Gen. Bernard Law Montgomery.

Montgomery was by now the professional soldier par excellence. He had deliberately deepened himself in his calling, aware that in so doing he had also narrowed his outlook. By his own admission he had no true friends, hobbies or intellectual interests. He had, in one of his favorite phrases, fixed his own ceiling, so that as he traveled up the chain of command his narrow professionalism inhibited his understanding of human nature or of the congeries of conflicts that is humanity itself. His lust to dominate had grown fiercer. One of his students, an admirer of Montgomery's gift for making complicated situations appear simple, also shrewdly observed that when he was presenting a command problem he was particularly clear about what "our side" should do but gave no thought to the "enemy's" intentions. The enemy would and should roll over and play dead, just like that unfortunate German soccer team.

His insatiable egoism, shaping all things to satisfy it, was evident in Palestine. As commander of the 8th Infantry Division he was informed that the much-wanted rebel leader, Abdul Karim, had been killed in the village of Sannûr. Did he wish to view the body?

"Abdul Karim?" he countered. "Who is he? Who is he?"

A colonel explained and Montgomery went off with him to Sannûr. There he found the dead rebel chief surrounded by Palestine policemen and buzzing flies.

"A notebook!" Montgomery snapped.

Taking one of a dozen offered, he wrote rapidly. Then he read what he had written: "Major General B. L. Montgomery at Sannûr, to G.O.C.-in-C., Palestine and Transjordan. Today *my* troops shot and killed Abdul Karim, the rebel leader. *I* have identified the body and pronounced it to be that of Abdul Karim. . . ." (Italics added.)

After the evacuation at Dunkirk, the obsession with himself as the center of the universe reappeared when, as a corps commander, he lectured a group of Home Guard officers. Then he staged a play he had written illustrating the possibility of attack by German parachutists. Four men dressed in German uniforms carrying umbrellas symbolic of parachutes appeared on stage. A shot rang out, and the four soldiers solemnly intoned:

"We'll cut the throat of that bastard Montgomery."

Bernard Law Montgomery was still on Lieutenant General Montgomery's mind when he drove to the airport in London to fly to Egypt to take command of the Eighth Army. Gen. Sir Hastings Ismay was with him. Montgomery was sunk in thought. Then he spoke.

"You know, Ismay, a soldier's life is a tragic thing. He wins a battle and gains promotion. He wins another and becomes famous, a campaign and becomes a national hero. Then, suddenly, defeat—and with it disgrace. He is forgotten."

"But, Monty," Ismay cried, alarmed. "Why should such a thing happen to you?"

"To *me!*" Montgomery repeated in incredulity. "But how could that be? I was speaking of *Rommel.*"

Offensive as such arrogance, such petty conceit, such malice and mendaciousness may be, they were after all only the dark side of Montgomery's outstanding trait: an iron will to win. He was supremely and single-mindedly the dedicated professional soldier. It was this conviction of his own superiority that caused him to disparage all other commanders—particularly Dwight Eisenhower, whom he despised as a warrior without wounds, a commander without combat credentials—just as it was his monstrous egotism that led him to rewrite history to conform to his own self-proclaimed genius. But he did not care about making friends so much as making history. He was a winner, and it was this ruthless driving will to prevail that made it difficult to see how he could be defeated. Certainly not with the flood of men and arms now flowing to the Desert War. The giant American generator had at last got up a head of steam. Out of this iron cornucopia poured a torrent of munitions, among them the superb new Sherman tank with its full-circle swiveling 75-mm cannon. Nevertheless, "he was like a breath of fresh air." In deliberate disobedience he took command of Eighth Army two days ahead of time.

47. Turning Point: The Battle of El Alamein

MONTGOMERY'S BRIEF INTERVIEW with Auchinleck was like a study in mutual dislike. But Monty, as he was now called by everyone, liked the Auk's plans for defeating Rommel very much indeed, so much so that he made them his own and advertised them as such. He also imbued his army with something of his own fighting spirit. At Eighth Army headquarters, he found an officer bent over a field desk.

"What are you doing there?"

"Preparing the plans for retreat, sir."

"Tear them up!"

Next he came upon a group of soldiers digging an emplacement, and said: "You can stop digging. The Germans aren't going to get this far."

That night he assembled his commanders to announce: "The defense of Egypt lies here at Alamein. . . . I have canceled the plan for withdrawal. If we are attacked, then there will be no retreat. If we cannot stay here alive, then we will stay here dead. Two new divisions have arrived in Egypt. . . . With this support, our task is easy. Given a week the situation will be steady. Given fourteen days we will be sitting pretty. In three weeks the issue will be certain. *In due course,* we ourselves will attack. We will then finish with Rommel once and for all."

The phrase "in due course" was somewhat upsetting to Winston Churchill, who wanted an attack in September. But Montgomery stubbornly held out for six weeks in which to train his troops and break in the new Shermans. This was what Churchill had heard from Auchinleck, and his reaction had been to dismiss him. But he indulged Montgomery, even while the delay rose from six to more than ten weeks.

By then Montgomery had caught the fancy of the Allied world as the general in the black beret. He had first exchanged his red-banded general's hat for an Australian slouch hat, on which he had pinned all the badges of the Eighth Army formations. But the slouch hat was too large in the cramped quarters of a tank, so he changed that for a beret offered him by a tanker. Twice, officially, constantly unofficially, the War Office ordered him to remove the beret. But he refused. It was, of course, a calculated stage prop, much like MacArthur's corncob pipe, and it helped dramatize and magnify his legend.

It also helped ingratiate him with the troops, of whom he was sincerely fond. It is difficult to fool a frontline soldier, as MacArthur had already learned, and the only way to gain his affection is to share his hardships. Montgomery, of course, had reserved for himself many more of the amenities of life than had Auchinleck, but Monty riding among the soldiers standing up in his jeep seemed much more down-to-earth than the reserved Auk. They also loved him for his use of sports slang. "We're going to knock the Boche for a boundary six!" he would shout in cricketese, and they would cheer wildly. If he were sighted in his black bonnet, someone would shout, "Hey, there's Monty!" and he would stop, stand up and make an impromptu speech. Then he would pass out cigarettes from the supply he kept beside him on the back seat. He didn't smoke himself, but he did not consider tobacco to be the weed of the Devil.

But while he was establishing his legend he was also alienating some of his senior officers, who were contemptuous of his theatrics and resented the interference of his youthful aides-de-camp. Montgomery seems to have deliberately withdrawn from the society of men his own age, preferring instead the company of these adoring acolytes, whom he seems to have used as his "eyes and ears," in a word, his spies. Rather than visit the messes where he might have to endure the criticisms or suggestions of his peers, he ate his sandwiches in the desert and lived like a monk in his trailer. Eventually, he got rid of those Eighth Army commanders who had not crawled onto the crest of the Montgomery wave, so that there remained not a single senior officer who was not under his spell.

On August 31, two weeks and five days after Montgomery arrived in the desert, his first battle there began. It was called the Battle of Alam al Halfa Ridge, one of two fortified British heights. It had been Auchinleck's plan to lure Rommel's *Panzerarmee Afrika* onto Alam al Halfa and there destroy him. Montgomery improved upon it by digging in his tanks and ordering another division onto it.

Montgomery had no fewer than 767 tanks fit for action, of which 713 were cleverly positioned. One hundred and sixty-four were the heavy American Grants. Rommel had only 200 gun-armed tanks. He was also starved for fuel; he had insisted that without the 6,000 tons promised him he could not think of success. He got 1,800 tons. Moreover all British armored and infantry formations were equipped with the new and efficient 6-pound antitank gun. Montgomery had absolute air superiority. More, he was facing a sick and weary opponent. Rommel's physician had decreed that he could not command a battle without constant medical attention and must have a replacement on the spot. He was so ill with a swollen liver and an infected nose that he could not get out of his Mammoth. Still, he came on, at the head of three veteran German divisions and an Italian division on his left.

He drove steadily eastward, a little more to the inside of Alam al Halfa than he had intended. Heavy British minefields slowed his advance. Soft sand burned up his precious fuel. There was no surprise, and a rain of fire fell on the Germans from the Royal Air Force. Rommel swung north toward the sea, advancing under cover of a sandstorm. But his attacks broke down. They were not pressed with the speed, skill and daring of the old Desert Fox. At night Rommel fell back south into the Ragil Depression. British aircraft and artillery pounded his armor throughout the night. In the daylight of September 1 the Germans again sought to pierce the British defenses, but were thrown back into the soft sand of the Ragil Depression. That night one of Rommel's panzer divisions reported that it was without fuel and could not move. Next day, the Desert Fox called off the attack.

He had been beaten, but he was also in peril of being destroyed. His formations were in chaos, his fuel was gone or going, and he was under constant air and artillery bombardment. Never before had Erwin Rommel been so helpless. One master stroke across his line of communications could have finished him. But none came as he crept cautiously westward away from the battle.

If Montgomery saw the opportunity—and there is no reason to suppose that he did not—he ignored it. In his neat and orderly mind, such strokes did not exist because they were not scheduled. Fond of "tidying up the lines a bit" or "dragging up his administrative tail," he was wary of the unscheduled. Rommel had been scheduled for defeat at Alam al Halfa, and he had been. He was next scheduled for destruction at the Second Alamein. The intervention of Lady Luck was simply not on the program; and so, Second Alamein would go forward as scheduled.

One month and twenty-one days later.

There is no question that Bernard Law Montgomery was the master of the set-piece battle, just as there is no doubt that he would not move until every advantage was his. The last gun had to be emplaced, the last rifle loaded, the last tank fueled and the last soldier counted to assure him of that five-to-one superiority that was his sine qua non. In the weeks following Alam Halfa, he worked tirelessly to train his rapidly expanding Eighth Army in the tactics of his master plan. That is, the absence of tactics. "No more maneuver—fight a battle," he told his commanders. Because he doubted the ability of his army to match the moves of the *Panzerarmee*—like military Rockettes, skillful and synchronized by years of rehearsal and performance—he sought a methodical battle tightly controlled by himself. He had originally conceived a breakthrough followed by a tank battle, but this plan was shelved for one even more straightforward. Two corridors would be cut through enemy minefields, through which armor was to pass or fight its way to open ground in the west. After Rommel's fixed defenses had been broken and his armor destroyed, an armored corps was to pursue and mop up the debris of his ruined army.

Montgomery exuded an incredible confidence in ultimate victory. He infected commanders as low as lieutenant colonels with his unwavering optimism. "He was completely convinced he was going to win the battle. He made everything crystal clear." And why not? Montgomery was aware that there were to be Anglo-American landings in French North Africa in November. The arrival of a large new enemy army in Rommel's rear, considerably closer to his unprotected base at Tripoli than he was, would compel the Desert Fox to fall back rapidly on Tripoli lest he be crushed between two armies both superior to his own. Thus Montgomery *simply could not lose,* and he must have known this. Actually, Second Alamein was tied to Torch, the code name for the Allied landings. It was to be the Torch date minus thirteen days. Thus, Montgomery was insured against defeat. No matter what happened at Second Alamein, Rommel must begin to retreat on the thirteenth day. When November 8 was fixed for Torch, Second Alamein became October 23.

By then Montgomery had achieved an enormous superiority of numbers. In round figures he had 220,000 men to the enemy's 96,000, of which only 53,000 were Germans. In weapons and equipment, his advantage was crushing: no fewer than 1,100 tanks, of which 270 were the splendid Shermans and another 210 the heavy Grants, with another 200 in reserve. Against this the enemy possessed only 200 gun-armed German tanks plus 300 of the Italian "self-propelled coffins." Only the German Mark IV could hope to duel the Shermans or the Grants, and of these Rommel had only thirty. Eighth Army's assault would be supported by a thousand guns of field or medium caliber, amply supplied with ammunition. All formations had the excellent new 6-pound antitank gun, and there were also a hundred 105-mm self-propelled guns. Axis artillery consisted only of old-fashioned, short-range (five miles) Italian field guns, and of the antitank guns only twenty-four were the dreaded 88s. The Royal Air Force owned the skies. With complete control of the air, its aircraft could rove the battlefield at will.

True, Axis forces were cleverly emplaced behind deep minefields, but the extent of their defenses has been grossly exaggerated by Montgomery's admirers, including, of course, himself and Winston Churchill. Actually, the Axis was to deploy about 89,000 men along a front forty-five miles wide, about 2,000 men to a mile. This is by no means an unusually strong array, certainly less than Gamelin's "weak" line of the Dyle in the Battle of France. The Axis defenses, including minefields, were only five miles deep, compared to positions ten or twenty miles deep erected by both sides in the Soviet Union.

Acute fuel shortages also hampered the Axis command. Its armor could not be placed well back to rush to the endangered points like fire brigades. Instead it was stationed close up. Because there was not enough fuel for the armor to move from flank to flank en masse, it was divided, half in the north and half in the south.

Finally, perhaps most advantageous of all to Montgomery, he would not be opposed by Rommel. The Desert Fox was lying sick in a hospital in Semmering. General Georg Stumme had replaced him.

On the night of October 22–23 the assault troops of Montgomery's multinational army moved stealthily into forward concentration areas. Throughout the following day they lay in trenches beyond the British front. Axis air patrols could not detect them there because there were none. It was the RAF that was patrolling Axis airfields. Some 220,000 men were silently poised, waiting for the rise of the moon, the desert "moon of battle." Unwilling to wait for history's verdict on Second Alamein, Montgomery sent them a personal message: "The battle which is about to begin will be one of the decisive battles of history. It will be the turning point of the war."

At a few minutes before ten o'clock that night under the risen moon, some 1,000 Allied guns began to roar. From the Mediterranean south to the Qattara Depression, the Axis troops were battered by a dreadful rain of explosive and steel, a flashing, crashing cataclysm that made madmen of some of them. There was no answering fire because Stumme wanted to conserve his scanty stocks of ammunition. Twenty minutes later the barrage lifted and Second Alamein began.

On the British right 70,000 men and 600 tanks surged forward against the German left center, held by one Italian and one German division. Without counting the armor, the odds were 6 to 1. Following such a mighty artillery preparation, how could it fail? But it did. Too many men and guns and vehicles were packed into too narrow a front. There was no fighting space. The engineers did not clear corridors straight through the minefields, and the armor following the infantry became jammed up in a series of dead ends. Upon this stalled and floundering mass the Axis artillery delivered a heavy and accurate fire.

To the south, a diversionary assault by an armored corps was halted in a similar cul-de-sac. Infantry and armor could not penetrate the enemy minefield and were immobilized by mines that the Germans had cleverly sown between the belts. They remained stuck there until nightfall. The failure of Montgomery's attack, however, seemed to be redeemed by the fact that General Stumme had died of a heart attack. He was replaced by the inexperienced Ritter von Thoma, and then, by a counterstroke of luck, Montgomery heard that Rommel had climbed from his sickbed and was flying to the battle to take command.

Montgomery had issued orders contingent on the very impasse that had halted his assault. If lanes could not be cleared through the minefields, the armor was to fight its way through. Each armored division had three lanes, each wide enough for one tank. In the north, two armored divisions clanked forward, attempting on a six-tank front to force a minefield five miles deep. Some units did pierce the minefield, but not the Axis defense line. The southern attempt across the fireswept Miteiriya Ridge came to a halt at 4:00 in the morning of October 25. There now ensued a dramatic conference in Montgomery's trailer.

He was awakened by three of his generals frantically pleading for him to withdraw his scourged armor. He was told that Maj. Gen. A. H. Gatehouse commanding the stricken division on Miteiriya Ridge had reported that if he succeeded in penetrating the minefield and tried to descend the ridge's southern face, he would be shot to pieces by enemy antitank guns. Montgomery in his *Memoirs* says that he insisted that the armor *must* fight its way out. Gatehouse, who had spent his entire career in armor and had won four decorations for personal bravery, provides a different version. He said he angrily refused the order to continue the attack and called Montgomery on the field telephone. "What the hell's going on?" he exploded, and then, in less than deferential tones he outlined the impossibility of his situation. Montgomery thereupon reduced the scope of the southern assault from six armored regiments to one. It lost all but fifteen of its tanks, and the assault remained enmired in the minefield. Yet, Montgomery years later told a television audience: "The necessary part of the armored division got established beyond the minefields."

In Montgomery's mind *it had to be there.* If it were not, its failure would suggest that after forty-eight hours of fighting against a heavily outnumbered foe, not only had his assault failed but his forces were on the very verge of defeat. Such a conclusion simply could not be allowed. So he blamed the breakdown on the cowardice and foot dragging of his northern armor—as though his northern infantry had not also been halted.

But at this juncture Montgomery proved that if he had planned his battle poorly, he was still a resolute commander. In the field, he was superb. He had the calm and above all the patience to realize that his enemy could in no way match his enormous resources. Like Grant "whittling" Lee in Virginia, he could afford losses. After repelling a piecemeal counterthrust by the inexperienced Thoma, he began attacking again on October 26. Some ground was gained on

Miteiriya Ridge, but the great offensive remained immobilized. Montgomery spent the day in his headquarters, thinking.

But then Rommel arrived on the battlefield. Gathering his armor on October 27, he struck at the British on Kidney Ridge, north and forward of Miteiriya. Here was the Rommel of old, attacking with the setting sun streaming over his shoulder into the eyes of his enemy. But this was not the Eighth Army of old. Rommel was scourged from the air as he assembled a force of fewer than 150 tanks, and then he was beaten off by the British armor and the 6-pound antitank guns. He lost a third of his force. Next day he tried again, but the RAF savaged him once more, breaking up his attack before he reached the enemy. Now his army was almost out of fuel. In such straits, Rommel expected his enemy to launch its decisive attack. But Montgomery remained busy with "stage management" for the next few days, patiently preparing the final blow, which he had given the code name Supercharge.

It began at one in the morning of November 2, with his designated *corps de chasse*—an armored pursuit corps—coming with 700 tanks against Rommel with ninety. Here at Tel el Aqqaqir was fought the last great tank battle of the Desert War, and Rommel rose to the occasion. By the very force of his character, he held his army together. His weary, fought-out veterans did not break beneath the enemy blows. Instead, they rallied to the Desert Fox, cheered by the very presence among them of that familiar stocky figure with the fighting, friendly face beneath the goggled hat. Again and again he struck the oncoming British with counter-strokes aimed at gaining time for the retreat he was preparing, and these blows were so skillfully delivered that they nearly broke through the enemy salient. By the end of the day Supercharge had failed to achieve any of its objectives. Next day the Desert Fox was ready with a rearguard action that held British armor in check while his army began its retreat. This was the most heroic feat of generalship in Rommel's career. Under constant aerial attack and short of fuel, he was going to disengage his vastly outnumbered and mostly immobile army in the face of an enemy possessing great masses of armor and mechanized infantry. That he did so in open country that gave him no natural shields against enemy attack made his withdrawal that much more remarkable. But then Adolf Hitler came to Montgomery's side. On November 3, *Der Führer* ordered Rommel to stand and die at Alamein. Rommel obeyed, canceling his orders to retreat. Without this intervention he almost certainly would have sooner rescued his army from the eager but fumbling fingers of Bernard Montgomery. But he had to wait until nightfall of November 4, while a personal emissary persuaded Hitler to lift his order. This gave Montgomery a gift of thirty-six hours' starting time.

In the meantime, British weight of men and armor finally broke into open desert on November 4. The Second Battle of El Alamein was over.

"Gentlemen," an elated Montgomery announced to the press, "this is complete and absolute victory."

He had paid a stiff price for it: 13,500 dead, wounded and missing and 600 tanks lost, against German losses of 1,000 dead, 8,000 prisoners and 180 tanks, and Italian of 1,000 dead, and 16,000 prisoners. But if in Clausewitz's famous dictum the fruits of victory are to be plucked in the pursuit, Montgomery had dawdled again. Full-scale pursuit was not launched until November 5. Rommel, with a full day's start even after that thirty-six-hour delay, was simply not catchable. All of Montgomery's "traps" in tight little turns toward the coast came up empty. On the night of November 6 a downpour turned the desert into a quagmire. Montgomery offered this as an excuse for his failure to catch the Desert Fox, as though the rain fell only on the Eighth Army. But the fact was that the rain came down only *after* Montgomery had cut into the coastal road four times and *after* Rommel had increased his lead. Rommel himself was not only overjoyed at his masterly getaway, he was also astonished at the ease of it all.

"I wonder why he doesn't hurry," he said to Gen. Fritz Bayerlein. "But it's lucky for us."

When Rommel made this remark, he had only ten tanks, and his little army was intermittently paralyzed by fuel shortages. Why, indeed, did his opponent delay so? Could it have been that he was not too eager to mix it with the Desert Fox? Perhaps he dared not risk sullying "one of the most decisive battles in history" by falling victim to some new stratagem by this unpredictable genius. There seems to be no question that, as a senior officer close to Montgomery remarked, "Rommel's reputation did make an impression on Monty's mind."

One final question: Why was Second Alamein fought at all? It was fought purely for political purposes. Eighth Army need not have wasted itself in those furious frontal attacks, staining the desert sand with the blood of its men and the oil of its ruined armor. Eighth Army should have waited until the Torch landing in Rommel's rear had forced the Desert Fox to withdraw from Alamein and make haste for his base in Tripoli. Then, and then only, Eighth Army could have begun its pursuit. For all his skills, Rommel would have been helpless. He would have been caught between two enemy armies each superior to his own. The Anglo-American landings in the west would form the anvil on which the hammer of the pursuing Eighth Army in the east would have broken him in pieces. Not even the Desert Fox could have conducted an orderly retreat with 90,000 nonmotorized men, a few hundred German tanks followed by a completely mechanized force of 220,000 men, 1,100 tanks and absolute control of the air.

But for Eighth Army to have done this would have been to share the inevitable victory with the Torch forces—with the Americans. This Winston Churchill could not allow. Second Alamein was a battle fought purely for political purposes because Churchill needed a great victory to shore up his collapsing political fortunes. "Ring out the bells," General Alexander cabled from Cairo, accurately reading his chief's mind. They were indeed rung, and the big black banner headlines announced a great conquest comparable to Blenheim or Waterloo. Even though Eighth Army was a multinational force, it was commanded by British generals, and Second Alamein was therefore the last great British victory in the war. It was indeed the very swan song of British military glory. Churchill well knew that, after Torch, the British war effort would be superseded by the

American; and that was another reason why Second Alamein was fought before the Torch landings would have forced Rommel to retreat.

Without Torch, Montgomery still possessed the power to crush Rommel, although it probably would have taken longer; but with Torch, from every standpoint save the political, Second Alamein was an unnecessary battle.

48. Operation Shangri-la, the Battle of the Coral Sea, Midway

THE ANCIENT MILITARY MALAISE known as "victory fever" had seized the Japanese war lords. A career of conquest unrivaled in modern arms, eclipsing even the triumphs of Adolf Hitler, had so exhilarated them and so swelled their self-esteem that, instead of halting to consolidate their gains, they chose to reach out for more.

Japan would take Tulagi in the Solomon Islands and Port Moresby in New Guinea while the Combined Fleet crossed the ocean to destroy the remnants of the American Pacific Fleet and capture Midway Island. This would nail down a defense line from the Aleutian Islands in the north through Midway, Wake and the Gilberts and Marshalls in the Central Pacific. Behind it, meanwhile, New Caledonia, the Fiji Islands and Samoa would be conquered, while Port Moresby in New Guinea and the southern Solomons were seized and Australia was cut off from the world.

Not every Japanese military chief supported this grandiose plan. Some of the more sober-minded admirals saw the danger of overreaching. The army was reluctant also, partly for the same reason, partly from envy of the navy's brilliant successes. Moreover, the army still regarded the Soviet Union as the chief enemy and was still committed in China. However, no one, sailor or soldier, could withstand the now all-powerful influence of Isoroku Yamamoto. Much of the planning for this new scheme of conquest had issued from the mind of the Iron Admiral. He wished to make Japan invincible on the Pacific Ocean. His entire Pacific posture had been based upon his navy's 10 to 7 superiority over the U.S. Navy in big aircraft carriers. Of the American seven, only three were in the Pacific, and none of these was in Pearl Harbor when Nagumo attacked. He had wrecked only the American battleship fleet, but in so doing had demonstrated to the world that the new queen of the waves was the big flattop. The invasion of Midway was intended to lure the entire American fleet with its three big carriers into decisive battle. Midway, then, was to improve upon and rectify Pearl Harbor.

Although Yamamoto's plan was accepted, it was not with unanimous enthusiasm. There were delays, some of them deliberate, and in the interim, on April 18, 1942, the sacred soil of Nippon was desecrated.

When Vice Adm. William (Bull) Halsey sailed into Pearl Harbor and saw the wreckage of the battle fleet, he had snarled: "Before we're through with them, the Japanese language will be spoken only in hell!" His opportunity for revenge came sooner than he had anticipated. Adm. Chester W. Nimitz, the successor to Kimmel as CINCPAC, had an assignment for him. President Roosevelt's desire to bomb Tokyo as a lift to American morale and a psychological blow at the Japanese had received enthusiastic support from Admiral King and General Arnold. Both knew that land-based bombers could not do it, but they agreed that B-25 Mitchell medium bombers based on an aircraft carrier could. Lt. Col. James Doolittle, a distinguished aviator and aeronautical engineer, would lead them.

Nimitz asked Halsey, "Do you think it would work, Bill?"

"They'll need a lot of luck."

"Are you willing to take them out there?"

"Yes, I am."

"Good! It's all yours!"

Halsey conferred with Doolittle and both agreed that they should try to get within 400 miles of Japan before launching the Mitchells. They could not return to their carrier but would fly on to China.

For a month sixteen Mitchells practiced takeoffs from abbreviated runways the exact length of a carrier flight deck. Then they landed on *Hornet,* which sailed to rendezvous with Halsey's Task Force 16, including *Enterprise* and supporting ships. On April 13 they turned west toward Japan.

Although the Japanese exulted in a tide of victory unprecedented in its extent and brevity, there still dwelt beneath the "Banzais!" and the bluster an uneasy sense of peril. With the American fleet crippled and a staggered enemy trying to regroup many thousands of miles away, Premier Hideki Tojo still ordered air-raid drills throughout the islands.

Crowds of Japanese women filled sandbags and stuck them outside each dwelling. They were formed into fire brigades and taught to run uphill without spilling water from their buckets. Outside each house they placed large containers of water and flails looking like huge flyswatters for beating out flames. Smudge pots were set on fire in the low branches of trees, and the women threw pails of water on them to learn how to save a burning structure. Air-raid shelters were dug in backyard gardens. Some families planted flowers on top of them. Each household was required to maintain a pack filled with bandages, first-aid gear, rice, a cooking pan and a thick padded hood to be worn while fighting fires. From these detested hoods would come serious burns when the cotton padding caught fire.

When on air-raid duty, everyone was supposed to wear a kind of uniform. The women were to wear *monpe,* or slacks, although slacks were frowned upon as being too Western. Permanent waves or nail polish were also considered to be in bad taste; but the Japanese women, sleek, coiffed and well groomed, kept their permanents. The men wore "the national uniform," dull khaki with puttees wrapped around the trousers, plus an army cap without insignia. On the 8th of every month, to commemorate the attack on Pearl Harbor, every man and woman was requested to wear the uniform. Those who did not were stopped and scolded; some were sent home to change their clothes.

As the months wore on and no enemy aircraft appeared, the air-raid drills came to be derided as boring and resented as time-consuming. People began to ignore the sirens. In Tokyo on April 18 there was another air-raid drill.

To forewarn Japan against attack, Admiral Yamamoto had established a line of picket boats as far as 700 miles from Tokyo. On April 18 the lookout on one of these boats sighted airplanes overhead. He went to wake the skipper.

"Planes above, sir," he shouted.

The skipper was not interested. There could be no enemy so close to Tokyo. He stayed in his bunk. An hour or so later the lookout stiffened: a pair of carriers was on the horizon. He went below to wake the skipper again.

"Two of our beautiful carriers ahead, sir."

Now the skipper hurried topside, seizing the lookout's glasses. As he studied the approaching flattops the color drained from his face. "They're beautiful," he said. "But they're not ours." He went below and shot himself in the head.

That was the third picket boat that Halsey's ships had sighted, and he and Doolittle agreed that the chance of surprise had vanished. The Mitchells would have to fly 150 miles farther from their target than planned, but they must be launched immediately.

Colonel Doolittle was undismayed. He and his men climbed confidently into the cockpits of the heavily loaded planes while *Hornet* turned into the wind to launch. She was rolling heavily with frothing white water breaking over her bows when the Mitchells took off. Doolittle was first, rising gracefully into the air. The rest of the squadron followed, most of them roaring too fast down the deck. They pulled up, hung by their noses, nosed down again to straighten and roar away.

In Tokyo the Japanese were just completing that boring air-raid drill when the first two American bombers roared over the city at treetop level and released their 500-pound bombs, speeding away unharmed. Twenty minutes later the rest of the bombers appeared. They were met by occasionally heavy but generally inaccurate AA, and because many of them were off course and thus struck from three different points, they confused enemy fighter defenses. Only a handful of Zekes rose to intercept and did little damage. Of the sixteen Mitchells, thirteen reached China. With their fuel exhausted, they either crash-landed or abandoned their planes in flight. Another reached the U.S.S.R., where the crew was interned, escaping fourteen months later. The crew of two other Mitchells were captured by the Japanese in China. They were tried, found guilty and sentenced to death.

Three of five were "graciously" commuted to life imprisonment, and one of them died in captivity. Three others—Lieutenants W. G. Farrow and D. E. Hallmark and Sgt. Harold Spatz—were beheaded. In all, of eighty American airmen involved, seventy-one survived.

The United States was electrified by the news that the enemy capital had been bombed. It was a buoyant FDR who met the press to announce the raid. Asked where the planes had come from, he grinned and replied:

"Shangri-la."*

The Shangri-la Operation horrified Japan. For the first time ever an enemy had struck at the homeland. The ears of the divine emperor had been profaned by the sound of American bombs exploding. Isoroku Yamamoto was so mortified that he put on dress whites and called at the Imperial Palace to apologize to Hirohito. He was not so embarrassed, however, that he failed to see that the raid had put in his hands a stick with which to beat opponents of the Midway Operation. Never again! he thundered. The Americans must be driven so far back that they could never again even think of insulting the emperor. In May 1942, therefore, the first part of the campaign began with invasion forces sailing for Tulagi and Port Moresby.

There was no opposition at Tulagi and Japanese forces quickly seized this tiny outpost in the southern Solomons. Meanwhile, the bigger force sailed serenely against Port Moresby. Vice Adm. Shigeyoshi Inoue expected little opposition at sea, counting, in fact, on surprise. The two carriers reported in the Tokyo raid could not react in time to intercept his fleet, and if the other American flattop attempted to rush north or west to defend Moresby it would be ambushed by his Striking Force stationed to the east. In the event, it was Inoue who was surprised. U.S. Navy code breakers and traffic analysts—experts who drew meaning from enemy messages by studying their location, volume and pattern—had by mid-April concluded that the Japanese planned to invade Moresby.

Admiral Nimitz immediately sent *Lexington* sailing at flank speed to join *Yorktown,* already in the Coral Sea under Rear Adm. Frank Jack Fletcher. Pacific Fleet battleships went steaming for the sanctuary of the West Coast, thus releasing vital tankers and destroyers to refuel and protect the carriers. When Admiral Inoue's invasion force sailed confidently into what appeared to be untroubled waters south of Port Moresby, it was intercepted by *Lexington* and *Yorktown.* Thus began the Battle of the Coral Sea, the first naval battle fought by ships out of sight of each other and by naval and Marine aircraft alone.

The Americans drew first blood. They sank the light carrier *Shoho* in ten minutes, a record for aerial-sea warfare anywhere. *Lexington*'s dive-bomber commander jubilantly radioed: "Scratch one flattop!" Now the invasion force was forced to turn back. Next day, big *Shokaku* and *Zuikaku* came rushing out of

*A mythical Tibetan land in a then best-selling book, James Hilton's *Lost Horizon.*

the east to launch their war birds against *Lexington* and *Yorktown*. They pounced on *Lexington* and gave "Lady Lex" her death blows. But the Americans retaliated by inflicting heavy damage on both Japanese carriers. Thus, the Battle of the Coral Sea ended in a tactical standoff but a strategic American victory. The invasion of Port Moresby was hurled back and two big Japanese carriers were put out of action for the assault on Midway Island—the critical operation for which Admiral Nimitz was even better prepared.

Chester William Nimitz was born on February 24, 1885, in Fredericksburg, Texas, a small town populated chiefly by German-Americans. His father died before he was born and his mother married his father's brother, William. They moved to the nearby town of Kerrville. Here Chester grew up, leading the barefoot, happy-go-lucky life of a small boy in a little American town, or helping in the small hotel owned by his parents. He had little contact with the bigger, outside world, yet he yearned to be educated. Because the family had no money to spare, he applied for admission to the U.S. Military Academy. His congressman told him there were no openings at West Point, suggesting Annapolis instead. Nimitz had never heard of the Naval Academy, but he was delighted to take the examination, and still happier when he passed.

Nimitz was graduated as a passed midshipman on January 30, 1905, coming out six months earlier because of the need for officers in an expanding U.S. Navy. He stood seventh in a class of 114. He was highly regarded by his shipmates. Tall, slender, fair, pink-cheeked and blue-eyed, with a disarming serenity as calm as a sleeping babe, he was eulogized in his yearbook as "A man he seems of cheerful yesterdays and confident tomorrows."

Nimitz's first sea duty was aboard the battleship *Ohio,* flagship of the Asiatic Fleet. He sailed to Japan and met Admiral Togo, the celebrated victor of the Battle of Tsushima. Unlike some of his shipmates, later to be admirals like himself, Nimitz formed a high impression of Togo. Two years later Nimitz was an ensign commanding the decrepit gunboat *Panay,* and a few months later the equally dilapidated destroyer *Decatur.* She had been laid up for years at Cavite. Only by great determination and perseverance was Nimitz able to make *Decatur* seaworthy and manned by a crew that would keep her afloat. But then he ran her aground near Manila and was court-martialed, convicted and reprimanded for "neglect of duty." The sentence, however, was but a dainty slap on the wrist, which had no effect on his career. In 1909 he was a lieutenant (j.g.) and on submarine duty.

Lieutenant Nimitz distrusted the dangerous gasoline engines then in use in the American submarine service. He campaigned vigorously for their replacement with diesels. He studied diesel engines and eventually established a reputation as an expert on them. After America entered World War I, he was assigned as a lieutenant commander on the staff of Rear Adm. Samuel Robison, commander of the Atlantic Fleet's submarine force.

After the war, Nimitz was executive officer aboard the battleship *South Carolina,* and later assigned to the Naval War College in Newport, Rhode Island. Here he met the brilliant, nonconformist Rear Adm. William Sowden Sims. From Sims Nimitz learned to regard the aircraft carrier as the warship of the future. He experimented with the circular formation which in World War II was to replace the traditional line of battle. Although, like Yamamoto, he never learned to fly, his enthusiasm for Sims's theories on air-sea warfare grew apace, and it was with deep dismay that he saw them abandoned after Sims retired and the emphasis on battleships renewed.

Nimitz was happy again from 1933 to 1935 when he commanded the cruiser *Augusta,* the flagship of the U.S. Asiatic Fleet. Aboard her he visited the Philippines, the Netherlands East Indies, Australia and Japan. Nimitz's next assignment was in Washington as assistant chief, Bureau of Navigation, later known as the Bureau of Personnel. Here he learned the facts of political life without which no holder of high command can function. Here, in 1938, he was promoted to rear admiral, later commanding for a brief period a cruiser division and then a battleship division. Back in Washington as chief of personnel, his quiet brilliance eventually drew the attention of the naval-minded Roosevelt. In late 1939, FDR offered him the Pearl Harbor command. He refused, insisting that he was too junior an admiral. The appointment went instead to Kimmel.

When Adm. Chester Nimitz replaced Kimmel in late December 1941, he was nearing his fifty-sixth birthday. His hair was snow white, but he was still a tall, trim figure with pink cheeks and bright blue eyes, a calm and careful sailor with the courage to take risks, and a strange chief indeed in this war of posturing, strutting commanders. Early on, the code breakers of Magic and the Navy's traffic analysts informed him of Yamamoto's Midway Operation.

Almost all of the Combined Fleet was at sea. Isoroku Yamamoto had collected 162 ships and divided them among forces large and small. The small force was to invade the Aleutian Islands in the north and to lure American naval strength in that direction. The large one was meant for Midway, and it included transports carrying troops for an amphibious invasion. Even if the Americans did not take the Aleutians bait, Yamamoto still believed his large force was strong enough to overwhelm them.

The striking force of four big carriers—*Akagi, Kaga, Hiryu,* and *Soryu*—all veterans of Pearl Harbor, was led by Chuichi Nagumo, the hero of that great victory. Far to the rear was the main body, commanded by Yamamoto himself, sailing in his flagship *Yamato,* the mightiest ship afloat.

Because of his foreknowledge of Japanese plans, Nimitz had refused the Aleutians bait and had concentrated his vastly inferior forces of seventy-six ships north of Midway. He planned to hit the enemy carrier forces on their flank. His own flattops included *Enterprise, Hornet,* and the patched-up *Yorktown* with supporting ships. The first two had been the nucleus of Task Force 16 commanded by Admiral Halsey. But Halsey had gone into the hospital suffering from a skin disease. Command was given to Rear Adm. Raymond Spruance, a quiet, modest, but supremely confident sailor, in many ways a seagoing replica of the land-based Nimitz. Nimitz thought so highly of Spruance that he had already selected him for his chief of staff, holding this post in abeyance until Halsey recovered. Task Force 17, including *Yorktown* and her supporting craft, was led by Adm. Frank Jack Fletcher, who had stopped the Japanese in the Coral Sea. Neither he nor Spruance commanded all these forces, both being under Nimitz's control. But Spruance was fortunate in inheriting Halsey's superb air staff, and especially Capt. Miles Browning, renowned throughout the U.S. Navy as the man with the calculator brain.

On June 4—one of the most memorable dates in American military history—the Battle of Midway commenced. Nagumo "began the game" by launching his bombers to strike Midway and soften the island's defenses against his invading troops. Thirty-six Kate torpedo planes and thirty-six Val dive-bombers escorted by thirty-six Zeke fighters roared aloft. Nagumo was confident. He did not anticipate opposition from American carrier aircraft. In this, at least at the start, he was correct. Only a squadron of Marine Corps pilots awaited his war birds. They were at seventeen thousand feet flying their land-based Buffalo fighter planes, perhaps the most hopelessly outclassed American aircraft ever sent aloft. Nevertheless the Marines swooped down gallantly on the attacking Japanese. Some of them deliberately crashed into the red-balled enemy planes or led them into American anti-aircraft fire. The AA was superb. Although seventeen of the Marine planes were destroyed and seven more damaged, one third of Nagumo's 108 aircraft were shot down and many more sent limping back to their carrier decks. Nagumo ordered a second strike.

This was exactly the moment Spruance had hoped for. Captain Browning had calculated that Nagumo would continue to sail toward Midway and would launch a second strike. Browning decided that the time to hit the Japanese would be at this moment, while the enemy flattops were rearming and refueling their planes. This is when a carrier is most vulnerable, with bombs on deck and gasoline lines running. Nagumo's flattops were also in the process of switching from torpedoes to bombs when they learned of the presence of the American carriers. They frantically sought to switch back to torpedoes again, and thus were in a sense disarmed when the Americans sighted them. Also, their fighter cover was off pursuing the remnants of the early American flights they had shattered. So the Americans on this momentous Fourth of June found the Japanese sailing in box formation over a sparkling blue sea beneath a bright blue sky flecked with fleecy white clouds.

In came fifteen Devastator torpedo bombers from *Hornet,* attacking without fighter cover. They were all shot down. Next came fourteen Devastators from *Enterprise,* and ten of these were sent spinning into the sea. A dozen from *Yorktown* followed, and only four survived. For one hundred shining moments it seemed to Chuichi Nagumo that he had won the war for Nippon. But flying high above him, searching for him, were thirty-seven of the peerless Dauntless dive bombers led by Lt. Cmdr. Clarence McClusky of *Enterprise.* McClusky had no fighter protection. He had been flying for an hour and a half and had seen only an empty ocean. His fuel supply was not yet critically low, and he decided to continue searching until he reached the safe limit of fuel endurance. Half an hour later he sighted a Japanese destroyer racing northeastward and throwing up spray. He decided to follow it. Almost simultaneously Lt. J. S. Gray leading a fighter squadron broke radio silence to report that he had sighted the enemy carriers. Moments later McClusky heard the voice of Miles Browning bellowing over the radio telephone: "Attack! Attack!" McClusky replied, "Wilco, as soon as I find the bastards." He did, and soon.

McClusky led half of his dive bombers down on *Kaga* while Lt. (s.g.) Earl Gallaher took the other half hurtling down on *Akagi.* They sank them both.

Next, seventeen Dauntlesses from *Yorktown* under Lt. Cmdr. Max Leslie fell upon *Soryu* and left her a crippled wreck to be finished off later by the submarine *Nautilus.*

In six minutes, Chuichi Nagumo had lost his own flagship and two other carriers. He stood on his bridge in a rage of despair, cursing those officers who implored him to come below and transfer to another ship. Eventually, he was practically compelled to board the cruiser *Nagara,* where he had the satisfaction of hearing that *Yorktown* had been destroyed. But while the bold Kates were breaking through *Yorktown*'s AA defenses, putting three torpedoes into her hull, twenty-four Dauntlesses led by the formidable Gallaher found *Hiryu,* fell upon her and sent her to the bottom.

Far to the rear aboard *Yamato,* Isoroku Yamamoto was engulfed in a black night of despair. Each time a report was handed to him he groaned aloud in anguish. On the following day he ordered a general retirement. For the first time in 350 years Japan had suffered a naval defeat. In a single day's fighting, all the advantages gained at Pearl Harbor lay with his four sunken carriers at the bottom of the sea. Parity in carrier power between Japan and the United States had been restored at 6 to 6, and the cream of Japan's naval aviators had been lost. Admiral Yamamoto remained in his cabin alone and speechless throughout the dirgelike voyage home. Seldom again, if ever, was the word "Midway" spoken in the Imperial Japanese Navy. Premier Tojo was informed of the defeat, but never of the details. Emperor Hirohito heard nothing. The Japanese victory flood had been checked six months after it began. But although the tide had been turned, it was now necessary for the Americans to pursue the advantage on land.

Just as Nelson's sea victory at Trafalgar gave Wellington the chance to destroy Napoleon at Waterloo, Nimitz's triumph at Midway made possible the irreversible tide-turning land battle soon to be fought at a then-unknown island in the Southwest Pacific.

Guadalcanal.

49. Preparations for Guadalcanal

IN THE UNITED STATES NAVY which Adm. Ernest J. King commanded, it was said of this tall, hard and humorless man: "He's so tough, he shaves with a blowtorch." President Roosevelt was fond of repeating this jest in the admiral's presence, hoping thereby to produce that fleeting cold spasm of mirth—like an iceberg tick—which passed as a smile.

If there was little levity in the character of Ernest King, there was also no self-delusion. He knew that he was cordially detested by at least half of the Anglo-American Combined Chiefs of Staff. Henry L. Stimson, the U.S. Secretary of War, hated him with an open ferocity; Winston Churchill, Field Marshal Sir Alan Brooke and Adm. Sir Andrew Cunningham hated him with a quiet, frosted intensity; and not even General Marshall or General Arnold could suppress a certain irritation when their flint-faced colleague raised again and again that most unwelcome cry:

Japan must be checked.

King insisted on this unpopular stance even though he was pledged to accept and implement Anglo-American grand strategy: first dispose of Hitler while containing Japan. But what was *containment*? The drum roll of Japanese victories during the five months following Pearl Harbor sounded more like creeping catastrophe. And what, if anything, had the Anglo-Americans done to Hitler? Japan now looked west toward India and its teeming millions, and if Rommel should beat the British in North Africa, the danger of a German-Japanese juncture in the Middle East would become a dreadful probability. Great China had been cut off and Australia was menaced by a Japanese invasion of New Guinea, while the Anzac lifeline to America was already threatened by Japanese seizures in the southern Solomons.

With grim and exasperating persistence King predicted to his colleagues that the Japanese would reach out for more. They did, of course, at Midway—and after the incredible American victory there, King saw his chance. He proposed that it was now time for America to seize the offensive, and he chose Tulagi-Guadalcanal as the proper place to begin it. But Marshall and Arnold were still cool toward an early Pacific counteroffensive. They were committed to Operation Bolero, the buildup of American forces in Britain. On May 6, Roosevelt had told the Joint Chiefs: "I do not want Bolero slowed down." But that had been a month before Midway. Now, quoting intelligence reports that the Japanese were moving into Guadalcanal, King returned to the attack. Reluctantly, Marshall and Arnold agreed to his proposal.

But who would command? King held out for Nimitz, pointing out that it would be a navy show with Marines going ashore. But the Solomons were in

MacArthur's Southwest Pacific Area, Marshall and Arnold replied. Finally it was decided to include the Solomons in the South Pacific Area commanded by Vice Adm. Robert Ghormley under Nimitz's control. On June 25, the Joint Chiefs ordered Ghormley to confer with MacArthur on the operation. Ghormley was in Auckland, New Zealand. Next day he put in a call for Maj. Gen. Alexander Archer Vandegrift, just arriving in Wellington with advance units of his First Marine Division.

Alexander Archer Vandegrift was of old Virginia stock, the grandson of Confederate soldiers. As a boy in the lovely college town of Charlottesville, where he was born on March 13, 1887, he loved to listen to the stories of the old Butternuts, as the Confederates were known from the color of their homespun uniforms. He always remembered the grandfather who prayed to the God of Battles: "The God of Abraham, Isaac, Jacob, Robert E. Lee and Stonewall Jackson." Very early in his youth Archer Vandegrift decided that he wanted to be a soldier. Unable to pass the physical examination for West Point, he entered instead the University of Virginia not many blocks from his home. Strolling over the lawn or along the Serpentine Way or entering the Rotunda—those famous and enduring features of the great school founded by Thomas Jefferson—gave him a deep sense of tradition. After two years at Virginia he tried again for West Point through a United States senator who was a friend of the family. But there were no openings. There were, however, two vacancies for the Marine Corps examination. With his customary courtesy, young Vandegrift asked what the Marine Corps was. "Son," the venerable senator replied, "if you go into the Marine Corps, you will spend a large portion of your life fighting small wars in the southern American hemisphere."

Vandegrift found this to be the truth indeed. After being commissioned a Marine second lieutenant, he spent many of his thirty-three years in the Corps in Central America. There, he served under General Smedley D. Butler, the celebrated and legendary "Old Gimlet Eye" of the Banana Wars. Butler called him "Sunny Jim" because of the lighthearted way he obeyed an order to ride the cowcatcher of a rickety old Nicaraguan locomotive to "look for mines."

Vandegrift was also one of those Marine officers who, between the wars, refused to accept the doctrine seemingly laid down by the British debacle at Gallipoli in World War I: that hostile and defended shores cannot be seized from the sea. The Marines argued that they could; moreover that it was not necessary to capture ports with all their ship facilities but that invasions could be made over open beaches. Most brass ears were deaf to this absurd doctrine. Many generals, and some admirals, derided Marines as "beach jumpers" unfit to command more than a platoon, let alone discover and evolve new military theories. After all, the Marine Corps was a small auxiliary force of scarcely 20,000 men; it was only, in the phrase of some very famous detractors, "the navy's police force." But the Marines persevered in studying and practicing amphibious warfare. They *had* to. Without a reason for being, they actually *were* nothing but naval police. Struggling for their very existence, they developed the tactics, weapons and equipment needed for amphibious warfare, unaware that they were preparing themselves for the naval war par excellence.

Meanwhile, unlike other branches of the service, they were constantly in action. Fighting the Banana Wars in the jungles of Haiti and Nicaragua, they learned the lessons of jungle warfare that were to be applied on a vaster scale in the island wildernesses of Oceania. Service on the navy's capital ships taught them to appreciate the importance of sea power, as well as of ship-based air power; while duty at troublesome China stations enabled them to study the Japanese at first hand and to learn—most valuable of all—not to underestimate them.

It was from this hard school that Alexander Archer Vandegrift emerged: a big, strong, extremely courteous man, with large blue eyes, thinning sandy hair, a cleft chin and a long belligerent nose, already, by then, afflicted with a night blindness that would in his declining years lead to the loss of his eyesight. On March 23, 1942, Vandegrift received both his second star and command of the First Marine Division then in training at New River, North Carolina. Vandegrift had already been the division's assistant commander, having helped plan and conduct practice landings, one of which was an oddly prophetic exercise at Solomon's Island in Chesapeake Bay. Now in charge, he hurled himself into the task of raising it from a force of 11,000 officers and men to one of 19,000.

From all over the Marine Corps, the old salts and China hands were pouring into the famous "Tent City" at New River. There were NCOs yanked off soft "planks" at the navy yards. There were grizzled old gunnery sergeants—the "schoolmarms of Marines"—who had fought in France or chased "Cacos" in Haiti or "bandidos" in Nicaragua. There were professional privates who had spent as much time in the brig as in barracks. Gamblers, drinkers and connivers, brawlers in starched, creased khaki and natty "pisscutter" caps, they had fought sailors and soldiers of every nationality in every bar from Brooklyn to Bangkok; blasphemous and profane with a fine fluency that would astound a London cockney, they were nevertheless dedicated soldiers who knew their hard calling in every detail from stripping a machine gun blindfold to tying a tourniquet with their teeth. They were tough, and they knew it, and they exulted in that knowledge. No one has described them better than Col. John W. Thomason: "They were the Leathernecks, the old breed of American regular, regarding the service as home and war as occupation, and they transmitted their temper and character and viewpoint to the high-hearted volunteer mass."

Those high-hearted volunteers, the new breed, were also streaming into New River by the Parris Island trainload, and they too were transmitting something of their own character to the old breed: their gaiety and zest.

Private Lucky was among the new arrivals. He was immediately assigned to a machine-gun company: H Company, 2nd Battalion, First Marine Regiment. Everyone on his train landed in the same outfit. In the way of fleshing-out units, H Company had been but a paper formation until that train arrived. Lucky immediately became the buddy of Lew Juergens of Chicago, Bud Conley of

Buffalo, New York, and Bill Smith of Loogootie, Indiana. He also became an assistant machine gunner on the same .30-caliber, water-cooled weapon which, firing 250 rounds a minute, did such bloody work in the last war. It had been strictly a defensive weapon because it was so heavy, but the lightweight, air-cooled gun had yet to be adopted. Lucky carried the thirty-six-pound gun on his shoulder while Juergens had the fifty-one-pound tripod spreadeagled over both shoulders. The other squad members carried the boxed belts and the water can for cooling the gun. Each day they practiced attacking an entrenched enemy. Both Lucky and Juergens cursed wildly while running over uneven ground, the gun grinding into Lucky's shoulders, the tripod banging cruelly against the back of Juergens's head. At a command, they hit the deck to fit the gun together and simulate firing.

From New River they marched out to the boondocks at Onslow Beach on the Inland Waterway. There they practiced climbing down cargo nets from the decks of the "U.S.S. Neversail," a mock-up of the side of a ship. But the wooden Higgins boats into which they jumped were real, and many a Marine became seasick while they rolled and bobbed in the sea swells, vomiting into their helmets, or worse, throwing up to windward to the screeching disgust of their buddies. At Onslow Beach they lived in the pine woods and slept in pup tents and ate a swill of food called chow, but for which they had a more accurate and descriptive four-letter word. For recreation they fought each other in the unpainted shacks that followed them into the woods, where they bought beer for 15 cents a bottle and sang canned patriotic ballads such as "Good-bye Mama, I'm Off to Yokohama," or "Let's Remember Pearl Harbor" for 5 cents per sentimental song. But interfamilial brawling was a good sign. The cubs were cutting their eyeteeth. And then, suddenly one day, a train pulled into New River. The First Regiment was leaving next day.

The Marines who clambered aboard "that New River train" on that bright May morning were astonished to find that this was no crowded, stinking troop train but a row of sparkling clean Pullman cars with a separate berth for each man, a porter for each car and a dining car in which waiters in white jackets served their individual tastes on fine china, silver and starched linen. Very few $21-a-month privates have gone so luxuriously to war. They did so because the Fifth Marine Regiment, which left New River before them, sailing from Norfolk, Virginia, had had a submarine scare as their huge transport, *Wakefield*—the converted liner *Manhattan*—plowed down the Atlantic coast silhouetted at night by the pleasure-as-usual lights of the seashore resorts.

Major General Vandegrift was aboard *Wakefield*.

Wakefield entered the beautiful round harbor of Wellington, New Zealand, on Sunday, June 21. Five days later Vandegrift received Admiral Ghormley's telephone call. Next day he and his staff flew to the capital at Auckland. Vandegrift was astonished when he saw Ghormley. He had known him as a suave and polished diplomat. But now his manner was brusque, and he appeared harassed. He handed Vandegrift a top-secret dispatch. The general read it with unbelieving eyes. The Joint Chiefs were directing him to seize some place called Tulagi-Guadalcanal. He was to land August 1. Five weeks away! Five weeks, with his division fragmented: the Seventh in Samoa, the First at sea, the Fifth here with half of the Eleventh artillery and the other half in Samoa or at sea. Most of his men had not been in uniform six months. His supplies would now need to be unloaded, sorted and combat-loaded. He would need combat supplies such as barbed wire, which had not been included in his inventory for six months of training. Although Ghormley assured him that he would receive the Second Marine Regiment to replace his missing Seventh, this was scant consolation for the most pressing problem of all: He knew nothing of the target area and would have just those five weeks to discover what he could about Guadalcanal.

If General Vandegrift had been commanded to invade the moon, he would have known as much about the target area as he learned about Tulagi-Guadalcanal. All available information was contained in an old marine chart, a few faded photographs taken by missionaries five years before the Japanese landed and a short story by Jack London. Desperate, his Intelligence Section rounded up the same hard-bitten Australian islanders whom Dwight Eisenhower had vainly tried to hire to run the Philippine blockade. They were much more amenable to interrogation, provided that "the Yanks" would slake an elephantine thirst so unquenchable that it made the purchase of Scotch whiskey an acceptable military expense. Some of the information they provided was valuable, some seemed invaluable but turned out to be costly because it was incorrect. So haphazard was this gathering of intelligence and drawing of maps that Vandegrift's staff began to refer to the invasion as Operation Shoestring. Perhaps the only ray of hope in those feverish weeks of pulling a farflung division together and preparing for an invasion on an unknown island 10,000 miles from home was the extra week of grace given Vandegrift by the Joint Chiefs.

The invasion was to be no later than August 7, because the Japanese were coming perilously close to completing an airfield on Guadalcanal. Land-based air could scourge the American invasion fleet. Land-based air could also cut the American-Australian lifeline. That was what Guadalcanal was all about, that was what the island war would be all about: a struggle for air bases, for unsinkable aircraft carriers from which the enemy could be attacked by long-range, land-based air. From Guadalcanal, the Americans would be able to strike at the big Japanese air and sea bases at Rabaul at the northern tip of New Britain, or at Kavieng on the northeastern end of New Ireland.

The coast watchers already had Rabaul and Kavieng under surveillance. They were a unique organization commanded by Lt. Cmdr. Eric Feldt of the Royal Australian Navy. Feldt had trained these men in the use of code and teleradio. They had already been operating, reporting the buildup of the Japanese invasion of the southern Solomons, alerting Port Moresby to impending air raids.

Feldt had chosen his coast watchers from the ranks of the islanders—those hard-bitten adventurers who wore no man's collar and had found the independence they prized in the untamed islands of Melanesia. They were planters, ship captains, goldminers or unmitigated scamps, with here and there a blackbirder or slave trader. They drank hard, loved widely and freely, looked down upon the natives they exploited and spoke a language which, bristling with "bleddy" this and "baastid" that, was unprintable in the extreme, especially when it relied upon that famous four-letter word to modify the nouns of the pidgin English they taught the Melanesians. Missionaries were always shocked to discover that pidgin English was studded with scatology. Ashes, for example, were "shit-belong-fire," and an enemy air raid was described as "Japan he shit along sky."

Whatever their shortcomings, the coast watchers were intensely loyal, brave and clever. They hated the Japanese and their faith in the loyalty of their natives was justified in that not a single coast watcher was betrayed to the enemy during the Pacific War. These were the men who would warn Archer Vandegrift's men of enemy bombing flights headed their way.

Adm. Frank Jack Fletcher stood on the deck of his flagship, *Saratoga,* and gazed unhappily across the sun-dappled sea at the vast concourse of ships he commanded. Besides *Saratoga,* he had the carriers *Wasp* and *Enterprise*—the three flattops representing all of America's air-sea power in the Pacific—the battleship *North Carolina,* heavy and light cruisers by the dozen, and destroyers almost by the score. With auxiliary ships such as oil tankers Fletcher commanded a force of eighty-nine ships plus 19,000 U.S. Marines, the greatest invasion fleet yet assembled.

Yet Fletcher was uneasy. He knew the vital value of the carriers he commanded, and he distrusted the operation on which he was embarked. In Hawaii he had openly predicted that it would fail. He had already lost two carriers to enemy bombs and torpedoes—*Lexington* in the Coral Sea, *Yorktown* at Midway —and he had no desire to enter history as the admiral who had lost five carriers.

Beneath Fletcher in the chain of command was Vice Adm. Richmond Kelly Turner, a man as audacious as Fletcher was cautious. Kelly Turner was a planner and perfectionist who would not hesitate to tell a coxswain how to beach his boat, a man of beetling brows and rimless glasses, of ferocious language and a tongue as caustic as a shaving stick. His job was to command the amphibious force— the troop transports and supply ships—while Major General Vandegrift was to lead only the landing force, that is, the 19,000 Marines who were to seize the objective. When Vandegrift met Fletcher, he was surprised to see how tired and nervous he appeared. Next, he was surprised that the admiral had neither knowledge of nor interest in the Guadalcanal operation. Finally, he was dumbfounded to hear him prophesy failure, and to learn he would only allow two days to unload Vandegrift's Marines. Vandegrift, stunned, told Fletcher this was no mere hit-and-run raid. This was an expedition to take fortified enemy islands. There was going to be a fight. His Marines would need air cover. Five days was barely enough, two was suicidal. Turner agreed, with heat and force. Adm. Frank Jack Fletcher shook his head again. He was leaving on the third day.

"The conference is dismissed," he said.

50. August 1942: Guadalcanal—Part I

IT WAS AUGUST 6, 1942, eight months since Vice Adm. Chuichi Nagumo had turned his carriers toward Pearl Harbor. Now, the American invasion fleet sailed north to Guadalcanal. The skies were overcast, as they had been the day before. Just as storm and fog had concealed the Japanese approach to Pearl Harbor, so low ceilings hid these Americans in their sweep west and north from the Fiji Islands.

Aboard the troopships it was not only the warm moist air that brought the sweat oozing from the bodies of the men on the weather decks, staining the sailors' light blue shirts as dark as their denim trousers, making blotches on the pale green twill dungarees of the Marines. There was tension in the air. Marines squatted on the grimy decks blacking rifle sights or applying a last light coat of oil to their rifle bores. Machine gunners went over long belts of ammunition coiled wickedly in oblong green boxes, carefully withdrawing and reinserting the cartridges into their cloth loops, making certain that they would not stick and jam the guns. Other men adjusted packs, inspected grenade pins or made camouflage nets for their helmets—those exasperating scoops of steel that banged the back of a man's neck at a walk, bumped over his eyes at a run.

Many of these men wondered silently how they would react next day, in the holocaust of battle. Compassionate Marines suddenly became aware that they had no wish to kill, wondering, as they sat alongside cruel Marines carving X's on bullet ends to make dum-dums of them, if they would actually pull the trigger. Sentimental Marines composed that last letter home for the sixth or seventh time.

In the heads the big poker games were played. The money had found its inevitable way into a few skillful hands, and the big winners gathered for show-down games in lavatories deep below decks, places in which the air was such a foul compound of the reek of human refuse and cigarette smoke that a man coughing in revulsion blew holes in those blue clouds.

Above decks on one of the transports a young Marine skipped half dollars across the flat gray surface of the sea. A sergeant raged at him, and the youth replied with a shrug:

"So what's the use of money where we're going?"

Aboard all the troopships platoons of men attended classes on the subject

"Know Your Enemy." For perhaps the twentieth time they listened while lieutenants, none of whom had ever seen combat, read to them from hastily assembled
manuals celebrating those qualities which made the Japanese soldier "the greatest
jungle fighter in the world." Mr. Moto, said the manuals, could swim miles
underwater while sucking air from hollow reeds; he could sneak stealthily
through the jungle on split-toed, rubber-soled shoes; and he could climb trees like
a monkey, often tying himself to the trunks and fighting from the treetops. He
was tricky, capable of booby-trapping the bodies of his friends, and he often cried
out in English to lure the unwary into ambush. At night the Japanese soldiers
set off strings of firecrackers to simulate numerous machine guns and frighten
their opponents into giving away their position, or they signaled to each other by
rifle shot. Finally, this strong, stoic Asiatic, who tortured and slaughtered in the
name of an emperor he believed to be divine, was also able to march farther, eat
less and endure more than any other soldier in the world. Though some of this
was true, much of it was hysterical hokum born of the Pearl Harbor psychosis,
and because they had been fed it so often and in such large doses, many of these
Marines had come to wonder aloud if every last son of Nippon had been suckled
by a wolf.

"All right," said a young lieutenant aboard one troopship, "if a Jap jumped
from a tree, what would you do?"

"Kick him in the balls!" came the answer, almost in concert, and the lieutenant grinned and dismissed his class.

Daylight of August 6, 1942, had turned to dusk.

Among the ships of the American fleet, the motors of the winches and the
landing boats had fallen silent. The open mouths of the hatches made darker pools
in the gathering gloom. Men stood at the rails of their ships, talking in low voices,
gazing at the horizon where the slender silhouettes of flanking destroyers were
rapidly becoming invisible.

"Darken ship. The smoking lamp is out on all weather decks. All troops
below decks."

It had come for the last time, this order. It had been heard for many nights,
by some men for months of nights, but it had never before possessed such capacity
to chill hearts.

They went below, with little of the accustomed horseplay, without the usual
ineffectual insults hurled at the bullhorn that had ordered them down. They
descended to troopholds far below the water line, where five-tiered bunks were
slung from bulkheads and the air could become one with the foul reek of the heads
if the blowers should break down. Many of them took showers, in fresh water
if they were lucky enough to be aboard a ship that could spare it, but generally
in salt water which left their bodies sticky and unrefreshed. Some men gathered
at final Protestant services, others went to confessions being heard by Catholic
chaplains. Weapons were wiped free of excess oil that might gather sand and clog
them. Packs were checked for the last time, filled with mess gear, clean socks and

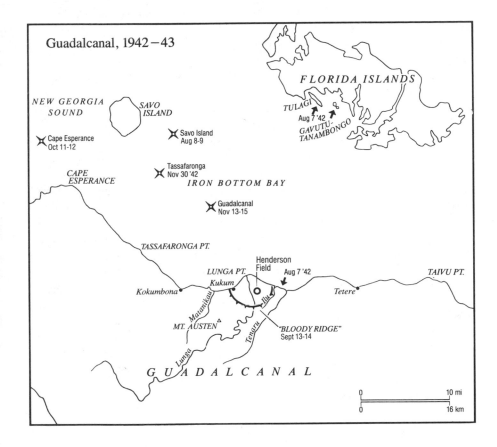

underwear, shaving gear, rations—here a Bible, there a pack of letters-from-home, an unfinished paperback book, a crumpled photo of a pin-up girl—all those individual extras which men put in their packs as whim and character might direct. Now the men were banging the chained bunks down from the bulkheads, crawling into them fully dressed—for no one removed his clothes that night. The showdown games had ended and the ultimate winners were choosing between stowing the money on their persons and sending it home via the ship's post office. Attempts at humor were falling flat and fading into tight-lipped silence; lights were going out below decks, and all was quiet save for the steady throbbing of the ships' motors. Lulled by this and the gentle rise and fall of the ships, the men of the First Marine Division sought sleep.

In the wardrooms above, lights still burned. Shadows formed grotesque patterns on big maps plastered to the bulkheads, and fell in long dark shafts across green-covered tables at which the officers sat with cards and chessboards. Aboard Admiral Turner's flagship, *McCawley,* both Turner and General Vandegrift were grateful for the darkness closing on them as they reached Guadalcanal's back door. They could not know, but they could suspect, that bad weather during the last two days had grounded enemy seaplanes at Tulagi, allowing them to sail along the southern coast of Guadalcanal undetected.

At two o'clock in the morning of August 7, by the light of a moon emerging just as the American force rounded Cape Esperance at Guadalcanal's northwestern tip, men on the weather decks could make out the bulk of Savo Island rising from the mists ahead.

Because of Savo, a round cone which sat like a brooding sentinel at the western mouth of Sealark Channel, the invasion fleet had to split in two. Ships carrying the main body turned immediately east or right to sail between Savo and Guadalcanal and take up stations off the Guadalcanal beaches. The other sailed north or above Savo before making their eastward turn, moving to stations off Tulagi, Florida and Gavutu-Tanambogo.

Both sections were in position before daylight. American cruisers and destroyers opened fire, while the warplanes of Admiral Fletcher's carriers began dropping bombs. The Japanese on both sides of the channel awakened in terror to find their waters covered with enemy ships. Seaplanes in Tulagi Harbor were caught before they could rise and were turned into floating torches. One of them tried to take off and was tumbled back into the water by a cruiser's guns. Fires were started on both sides of Sealark Channel. Marines moving to their battle stations gazed with satisfaction at flickering shorelines to north and south. At shortly after seven o'clock the assault troops of both sections were ready to launch simultaneous attacks.

It was on Tulagi, not Guadalcanal, that the Japanese made their first defensive stand of the war. Tulagi was typically British, the seat of the British Solomon Islands, with a cricket field, a residency and an Anglican bishop. But now this tiny boot-shaped island with its splendid anchorage was Japanese, and its defenders were about to demonstrate that terrible tenacity with which they would cling to every island fortress across the chain of empire.

Against them came the First Marine Raider Battalion, led by Lt. Col. Merritt ("Red Mike") Edson, a slender man of hard jaw and soft voice, of smiling lips and cold pale eyes. Edson's men leaped from their boats into the surf and drove swiftly across the island at a point two thirds up the boot. Another battalion following behind them wheeled left to overrun the lightly defended northwestern third of the island. The raiders attacked three companies abreast. The Japanese responded with a withering sniper fire. Snipers fired from beneath houses or underneath those forest giants with huge buttressing roots three or four feet high. Caves also spat machine-gun fire. Slowly, inexorably, the Americans drove forward, reaching the cricket field at dusk.

That night the Japanese launched the first banzai charge of the war. They came running in bands, their officers leaping and howling before them, waving their long samurai sabers. They might have been drunk—for banzai charges usually were fueled by liberal rations of whiskey—and they screamed in their native language or shrieked those quaint English oaths which, they had been told, would melt the hearts of the effete Americans.

"Banzai!" they cried. "Hurrah!"

"U.S. Marine be dead tomorrow!"

"Japanese boy drink American boy's blood!"

Back with foul-mouthed disdain came the Marine battle cry: "You'll eat shit first, you bastards!"

Firing their rifles as they charged, the Japanese sought to draw giveaway fire, but they were met instead by grenades spiraling silently through the night to go flashing and crashing among them. Sometimes they infiltrated, wielding knives, and where they did, they were met with knives. Five times they charged the Raider position, greeted each time by mortar fire, which thumped and roared among them, breaking up their assemblies and driving them into Raider barbed wire and guns. In the end, they were broken, and just as would occur throughout the Pacific War, the foolish and wasteful banzai charge had also broken their backs. In the morning, the Raiders swept forward against a mere handful, and Tulagi was taken by nightfall August 8.

Big Florida Island directly across the anchorage behind Tulagi fell without a shot being fired. But Florida's eastern offshore flank represented by Gavutu-Tanambogo was not so cheaply won. Both islands rose steeply from the sea and the only landing place was a seaplane ramp on Gavutu. At noon on August 7 boats carrying the First Marine Parachute Battalion headed for the ramp.

They were struck hard by enemy fire. Then they found that naval gunfire had made the ramp a jumble of concrete. The boats veered toward a dock. The Paramarines jumped out, some of them sprinting inland. But most were pinned down in a fierce crossfire. A boat brought a section of mortars to the rescue. Soon the shells were leaving the tubes with a metallic *plop,* landing with a *crrunch-whummp* in enemy trenches. The Americans charged forward to come up against a cliff face pocked with caves. Capt. Harry Torgerson lashed sticks of dynamite to the ends of poles or abandoned planking. He rushed the cave mouths, hurling his charges like javelins. Sometimes he stooped to poke them into narrow cave mouths. Often a bare instant separated his throw and the blast, for these were five-second fuses. Once a quick explosion sent him rolling downhill.

"Goddam, Cap'n!" an irreverent Marine yelled. "You done lost the seat of your pants!"

"Screw the pants!" screamed the singed and denuded Torgerson. "Get me more dynamite!"

Thus was Gavutu taken.

On the morning of August 7 twenty-four torpedo bombers rose from the Japanese airfield at Rabaul and went roaring south to Guadalcanal. They passed over Buin on Bougainville at about 10:30, the thundering of their motors rousing the Australian coast watcher Paul Mason as he sat inside his palm-thatched hut on Malabite Hill. Mason rushed outside to count the red-balled Kates. He ran back inside and flashed the message:

"Twenty-four bombers headed yours."

It was relayed down the Solomons chain, and twenty-five minutes later it was received by the Australian cruiser *Canberra* patrolling the waters between Guadalcanal and Tulagi then known as Sealark Channel, but later, for the ships and airplanes sunk there, to be renamed Iron Bottom Sound. An impersonal voice spoke over the bullhorn:

"The ship will be attacked at noon by twenty-four torpedo bombers. All hands will pipe to dinner at eleven o'clock."

Americans within earshot of that announcement grinned at the suggestion that the Japanese were after "the ship," which was Australian, rather than the entire armada, which was otherwise all American. However, the information was, as the Aussies say, "fair dinkum," and at exactly noon the enemy flight did appear over the bay. It was met with such an incredible storm of antiaircraft fire that the enemy fliers turned away after loosing only three harmless fish into the bay.

The "bonzer boys" up north had given the first of hundreds of priceless warnings.

Just before dusk August 7 the attack on Tanambogo was begun. Dive bombers struck at the enemy while boated Marines came from Gavutu churning toward shore. Destroyers ran in close to rake the island's defenses with 5-inch guns. A Japanese artillery piece was blown high into the air. An oil dump caught fire and was burning furiously. Yet there was no answering fire—until the Americans drew closer.

Then a sheet of fire fell from the crown of a hill. Private Russell Miller, who had been the first American to set foot on Japanese-held soil during the Florida landings, fell dead at his Lewis gun. A destroyer shell dropped short and exploded among the Higgins boats. A stricken coxswain fell from the wheel of his boat, and it veered around, heading back for Gavutu; other coxswains took this to be a withdrawal and followed it. Only three boats penetrated the Japanese fire. A hail of bullets escorted them toward a pier. Here, they were pinned down. Machine gunners trying to set up their guns were silhouetted in the light of the burning oil dump and shot to pieces. With dark, the entire force was compelled to withdraw.

But in the morning another battalion renewed the battle with a land-sea assault, and after some fierce fighting, Tanambogo fell.

When Lucky and Johnny Rivers and their buddies came topside on the *George F. Elliot* the morning of August 7, they caught their first glimpse of Guadalcanal. They paused momentarily, their eyes traveling the length of this slender ninety-mile island. It was beautiful, seen from the sea. Its towering central mountains ran down its spine in a graceful east-west keel. The sun seemed to kiss the timberline, and lay shimmering on open patches of tan grass dappling the green of its forests. Gentle waves washed the beaches white, raising a glitter of sun and water and scoured sand beneath fringing groves of coconut trees leaning languorously seaward with nodding, star-shaped heads.

It was beautiful, but beneath the loveliness, within the necklace of sand and palm, under the coiffure of the sun-kissed treetops with its tiara of jeweled birds, Guadalcanal was a mass of slops and stinks and pestilence; of scum-crusted lagoons and vile swamps inhabited by giant crocodiles; a place of spiders as big as your fist and wasps as long as your finger, of lizards as long as your leg or as brief as your thumb; of ants that bite like fire, of tree leeches that fall, fasten and suck; of scorpions, of centipedes whose foul scurrying across human skin leaves a track of inflamed flesh, of snakes and land crabs, rats and bats and carrion birds and of a myriad of stinging insects. By day, black swarms of flies feed on open cuts and make them ulcerous. By night, mosquitoes come in clouds—bringing malaria, dengue or any one of a dozen filthy exotic fevers. Night or day, the rains come; and when it is the monsoon, it comes in torrents, conferring a moist mushrooming life on all that tangled green of vine, fern, creeper and bush, dripping on eternally in the rain forest, nourishing kingly hardwoods so abundantly that they soar more than a hundred feet into the air, rotting them so thoroughly at their base that a rare wind—or perhaps only a man leaning against them—will bring them crashing down.

Guadalcanal stank. All those Marines who came to her shores on the morning of August 7 cursed and swore to feel the vitality oozing from them in a steady stream of enervating sweat.

Vandegrift's main body, some 10,000 men in two reinforced regiments, had hit Red Beach almost at the center of the island's northern coastline. The Fifth Marines* landed first, two battalions abreast, moving inland before wheeling right, or west, to work along the shore toward Japanese installations near the Lunga River.

A Japanese laboring force of 1,700 men had fled into the rain forest when the first American shells and bombs crashed among them as they sat at breakfast. Marines bursting into their encampment found still-warm bowls of rice on their tables. They also discovered that the airfield the enemy had abandoned was nearly complete: hangars, blast pens and a dirt runway 3,800 feet long. It was promptly named Henderson Field after Maj. Lofton Henderson, who had crashed his airplane into a Japanese warship at Midway. Around the field was a complex of wharves, bridges, ice plants, radio stations and power and oxygen plants. Huge stores of wormy rice—wormy, despicable, gagging rice—were also discovered, and much as the Marines might disdain this enemy staple, it would very soon

---

*Marine regiments are always called "Marines" in the way that army regiments are also known by their arm, as in "4th Cavalry" or "19th Infantry."

stand between them and starvation. Most of this was not immediately captured, although one battalion of the First Marines did take the airfield August 7. The other two continued on south, plunging into the steaming morass of the jungle toward their first-day objective: a high clear height called Grassy Knoll, or Mount Austen, which commanded Henderson Field from the south. But they did not reach it. That night they halted and dug in.

Shortly before nine on the morning of August 8, coast watcher Jack Read stood on a hill overlooking Buka Passage, north of Bougainville, and counted forty-five bombers from Kavieng flying overhead. With the sound of their motors still in his ears, Read ran into his shack and radioed the message:

"Forty-five bombers going southeast."

At noon, counting on surprise, the torpedo-laden Kates came in low over Florida Island to go wolfing among the transports. They were struck by a storm of shellfire that quickly destroyed twelve of them. Only one was successful, dropping a torpedo that pierced the side of the destroyer *Jarvis,* sending it staggering from the battle to be sunk later by Japanese submarines.

Next the dive-bombing Vals came hurtling down, also counting on surprise. But fighters from *Wasp* had taken high station a half hour earlier and were now riding down the Vals, risking the deadly polka-dotting of their own AA to send them flaming into the bay or the jungle.

One of the stricken Vals fell into an open hold of the *George F. Elliott* hours after its troops had gone ashore. The transport with all its combat cargo was set hopelessly afire, scuttled at twilight to become the first American vessel to sink in Iron Bottom Bay.

So the second day of consolidating the airfield or of penetrating deeper into the jungle toward Grassy Knoll went forward, while the second day of unloading was completed. Vandegrift was satisfied. He had all of his Marines ashore and the harbor islands were all but secure. Meanwhile he could count on a few more days of unloading supplies.

But it was not to be. Just like Admiral Fletcher, Admiral Turner was leaving in the morning. The powerful enemy surface force that both of them dreaded was sailing down the Slot.

The Slot was the sea corridor of the Solomon Islands, running 400 miles from Bougainville to Guadalcanal between the double chains of the islands facing each other at near-regular intervals. A force of seven enemy cruisers commanded by Rear Adm. Gunichi Mikawa entered the Slot about noon of August 8. Mikawa's flagship, *Chokai,* led, followed by the heavies *Aoba* and *Furutaka,* two more heavies, then a pair of light cruisers. An American search plane sighted them almost immediately but by 11:30 that night not all the ships in Iron Bottom Sound had been warned.

Cruisers *Chicago* and *Canberra* with their picket destroyers guarded the south gate between Savo and Guadalcanal while the cruisers *Quincy, Vincennes* and *Astoria* held the north gate between Savo and Florida. At midnight, the watches changed. Men of the new watches could see faint flashes of lightning to the west. A rain squall was making up. It would hide Mikawa.

Men on deck heard airplane motors overhead, but thought that they were friendly because the Japanese patrol pilots had boldly switched on running lights. Just before one o'clock in the morning Mikawa's lookouts spotted the destroyer *Blue* to their right. Scores of great guns swiveled around in the dark to aim at *Blue.* Luckily for her, unhappily for her sisters off Savo, she gave no alarm. Mikawa's cruisers sailed on . . . twenty-four knots . . . twenty-six . . . At 1:30 the lookouts sighted Savo rising like a great round tower from the sea.

"All ships attack!"

In five minutes the mathematicians had gotten the range. In one more, the dreaded Long Lance torpedoes went hissing out of their tubes. *Chokai* and her sister cruisers followed them toward the unsuspecting enemy. Now *Chokai* had closed to within two miles of the Americans, still undetected. Finally, from the destroyer *Patterson* came the warning:

"Warning! warning! Strange ships entering harbor!"

It was forty-three minutes past one o'clock in the morning of August 9, and it was already too late.

Eerie greenish flares floated down from the patrol planes and the harbor rocked to "iron tongues of midnight," those 6- and 8-inch guns thundering from *Chokai, Aoba* and *Furutaka.* Marines around the airfield or lying in the dripping rain forest looked fearfully at that baleful light and listened to those explosions, and they knew that it was not a thunderstorm. On Tulagi a dread silence descended upon the conference between Vandegrift and Brig. Gen. William Rupertus, his assistant commander. Then, at once, with a terrible roar, two torpedoes pierced *Canberra*'s hull while a shower of shells fell on her decks. She had been given her death blows. *Chicago*'s bow was blown away. She was helpless to stop the Japanese from swinging north to scourge *Quincy, Vincennes* and *Astoria.* Turning on their powerful searchlight they took the Americans at point-blank range and sank them. Not all went down immediately, but they were finished.

The Battle of Savo Island, which sailors and Marines more accurately called the Battle of the Five Sitting Ducks, wore on fitfully until dawn, when Mikawa went racing back up the Slot. Perhaps he feared the aircraft from Admiral Fletcher's carriers, but they were already withdrawing. A shell hitting the chartroom of *Chokai* also might have influenced him. But he had sunk four enemy cruisers and crippled a fifth, while damaging one destroyer. Like wolves, his ships had killed the shepherds, but unlike wolves had left the sheep alone. Therefore it was a relieved though grieving Richmond Kelly Turner who led his transports and still-unloaded supply ships out of Iron Bottom Bay.

The Marines were all alone.

51. Guadalcanal—Part II

KELLY TURNER stood on *McCawley*'s lower bridge, yelling through a megaphone to Archer Vandegrift standing below him in a tossing small boat.

Turner said the covering force had been badly mauled. He was leaving as soon as he finished fishing survivors from the bay. He did not know when he would be back. He waved and Vandegrift waved, and the general's boat sped back to Guadalcanal where Vandegrift limped ashore.

Vandegrift immediately called a meeting of his staff and all regimental commanders. Colonels, lieutenant colonels and majors, they came straggling through the rain to headquarters. New beards were sprouting patchily on their chins. Their eyes were bloodshot. They drank coffee from C-ration cans. Some of them cursed when the hot metal burned their lips. Others swore when concussions from dying ships shook the palm fronds and sprinkled them with water.

Vandegrift came out of his tent. He spoke quickly and bluntly. They were completely alone and God only knew if or when they would receive support from the sea or air cover. They were open to every form of attack: troops by land, shells from the sea, bombs from the air. Every officer and man in their command must be informed of these facts. But this would not be another Bataan. Marines had been surviving bad situations since 1775, and they would survive this one, too.

Col. Gerald Thomas, the operations officer, spoke next. He said they would now organize the defense of Guadalcanal, get the supplies inland, finish the airfield, patrol. They were going to hold a perimeter roughly 7,500 yards wide from west to east and penetrating inland south by about 3,500 yards. Its northern or seaward front would be heavily defended, for it was here Vandegrift expected the enemy counterattack. Its landward rear would be lightly held, for here there was a jumble of hills and jungle manned by outposts tied together by roving patrols. On the east or right flank was the Tenaru River, on the west or left the Kukum Hills. Inside this thin, tooth-gapped perimeter was vital Henderson Field.

This was the position which the Marines were to hold in isolation against a determined enemy now possessing the initiative and all the ships, airplanes, guns and men required to pursue it. United States Marines, having been trained to hit, were now being asked to hold.

In Japan all was jubilation. Although Yamamoto had privately reprimanded Mikawa for failing to sink the transports, in public Mikawa and his men were hailed as heroes. Headlines announced "great war results . . . unrivaled in world history." Australia had "absolutely become an orphan of the Southwest Pacific." Twenty-four warships and eleven transports "filled to capacity with Marines" had been sunk. The House of Peers directed a certificate of gratitude be presented to the minister of the navy, and English-language broadcasts coyly suggested that there was "plenty room at bottom of Pacific for more American Fleet—ha! ha!"

In America there was silence. Maj. Gen. Millard Harmon, commander of army forces under Ghormley, wrote gloomily on August 11: "Can the Marines hold it? There is considerable room for doubt."

If Admiral King had any doubts, he did not show them. In cold disdain he refused to comment on the exaggerated Japanese reports. When his information officer asked him what he should tell importunate reporters, he snapped: "Tell them nothing! When it's over—tell them who won!"

The Marines themselves were least impressed by the prophecies of their impending doom. When Tokyo Rose* described them as "summer insects which had dropped into the fire themselves," they hooted in derision or made ungallant comment on the virtue of Japan's lady propagandist. Actually, their only interest then was in continuing an ignorantly blissful frolic.

They found and plundered a Japanese warehouse full of delicious Japanese beer and sake, a yellowish rice wine. The day of that discovery Guadalcanal's single coastal road was thronged with grinning Marines balancing cases of beer on their shoulders or pulling rickshas piled with balloonlike half-gallon bottles.

Meanwhile, to conserve dwindling food supplies, Vandegrift put his men on a twice-daily ration consisting chiefly of captured rice. It was a wormy paste, which nauseated some of the daintier palates until they realized that they would have to swallow it—"fresh meat" and all—or starve. Meanwhile, beginning on August 9, signs of their isolation and the enemy's determination to retake the island began to appear. On that date the emperor's "glorious young eagles" began to bomb and strafe the Marines. Twin-engined Betty bombers flying in Vee-of-Vees usually of about twenty-four airplanes began to drop 500-pound bombs that made Guadalcanal shudder and shake and fragmentation grass-cutter bombs that maimed and killed. Soon the Tokyo Express—the name bestowed on the enemy ship traffic up and down the Slot—began to run each night with Japanese destroyers or cruisers entering the bay to shell the Marines cringing in their sodden holes, while submarines surfaced by day to shoot at everything in sight. But by August 12 Henderson Airfield had been pronounced operational, although it received nothing more warlike than a Catalina flying boat.

Lt. Col. Frank Goettge was Vandegrift's intelligence officer. On August 12 a captured Japanese seaman was brought to him. He was a surly little man, but his manners improved after a few shots of medicinal brandy. He told Goettge that

---

*An American citizen of Japanese descent who broadcast Japanese propaganda to American troops in the Pacific, she was tried for treason, served six years, and was pardoned in 1977.

hundreds of his comrades to the west were sick and starving and anxious to surrender. This, coupled with an earlier report of a white flag waving in the same area, led Goettge to form a patrol to go on a mercy mission to Matanikau village, a cluster of native huts. Twenty-five men, the cream of Division Intelligence, plus some of the best scouts from the Fifth Marines, went with him by Higgins boat to the "surrender area." But there was no surrender. Instead, converging streams of machine-gun fire massacred the ill-fated Goettge patrol. Only three Marines survived, escaping by swimming downcoast to the safety of their lines. They staggered ashore streaming blood from flesh torn and slashed by coral. One of them who fled just before daybreak told of turning to see sabers flashing in the sun.

Sabers flashing in the sun.

That was the phrase and the image that transformed Vandegrift's Marines from a merry to a murderous mood. The enemy had chopped up wounded Marines who had come on a mission of mercy to save the false and wretched enemy. So be it. Now let the enemy come, so that these Marines—products of a soft and effete society—could also kill, could also chop up wounded; and with their own sabers.

From that day forward, Marines seldom took prisoners in the Pacific. It was not a considered "policy" ordained from on high. It was to be the arterial response of company-grade officers who, with their men, actually came to grips with the enemy. They had learned now that they must become what they fought.

After the Goettge patrol there would be no quarter.

Lt. Gen. Haruyoshi Hyakutake was annoyed. Imperial General Headquarters had ordered him to squelch the pests in the southern Solomons. Hyakutake was irritated because this would be a distraction from his beautiful new plan for taking Port Moresby by a march overland. Moreover, he had been told that the Solomons must come first. The closest unit of his Seventeenth Army was the crack Ichiki Detachment in Guam. The Ichikis, named for their commander, Col. Kiyono Ichiki, were the elite of the famous 28th Infantry Regiment that had fought the Russians at Nomonhan during the secret border war of 1939. Afterward they battled the Chinese. They had been chosen for the Midway landing, and when they sailed home unrequited, Colonel Ichiki, like Admiral Yamamoto, had stayed in his cabin in despair.

Although there were only 2,000 Ichikis, General Hyakutake thought that would be more than enough to take care of the 2,000 American Marines reported on Guadalcanal. Actually, he thought, it was like sending a man on a boy's errand. So he notified Colonel Ichiki to proceed to Guadalcanal.

> Corpses drifting swollen in the sea depths
> Corpses rotting in the mountain grass—
> We shall die, we shall die for our Emperor.
> We shall never look back.

It was the ancient battle oath, *Umi Ukaba,* now the national anthem. The Ichikis chanted it while boarding ship on August 16 at the great Japanese naval base at Truk, where they had come from Guam with Colonel Ichiki's customary speed. His plan was to send 900 of his best men south on six fast destroyers while the rest of his command and his equipment and heavy guns followed by slower transport.

Two days later the Ichiki Detachment landed at Taivu Point, about twenty miles east of the Tenaru River. General Hyakutake in his orders had cautioned Ichiki not to attack immediately if he thought there would be difficulty, but to await reinforcements. Ichiki, however, a devout disciple of the Spiritual Power school (which more thoughtful Japanese commanders would eventually deride as the school of bamboo-spear tactics), was not even going to wait for the arrival of his second, larger echelon. After all, there were only 2,000 Americans on Guadalcanal. Surely, they would be no match for 900 Japanese as trained and battle-hardened as his Ichikis. Colonel Ichiki was going to attack at night, because he had noticed how the Americans whom he had met in China seemed to believe that the night was made for dancing. Next day he wrote in his diary: "18 Aug. The landing. 20 Aug. The March by night and the battle. 21 Aug. The enjoyment of the fruits of victory."

True, it was only 19 Aug. But Colonel Ichiki could not discount the chance that he might die before he could make the final entry. So he postdated it for posterity, and sent out a detail to lay communication wire.

On the morning of August 19 Capt. Charles Brush led about eighty men on a patrol probing east from the Tenaru. At noon they caught sight of Japanese soldiers laying wire. Brush attacked. In a firefight lasting almost an hour, thirty-one Japanese were killed against three Marines lost and three wounded. Brush sensed something unusual about the enemy formation. He personally searched the bodies and was surprised to find so many officers among the dead. They wore neatly pressed uniforms with rows of campaign ribbons on their tunics. In their map cases were astonishingly accurate maps of the Tenaru, with its weak points clearly marked. Brush hurried back to report to First Marine headquarters. Vandegrift was notified, but he rejected a suggestion to attack east. His mission was to hold the airfield. But he did order the Tenaru line strengthened.

Next day Lt. Col. Alvin Pollock, commander of the 2nd Battalion, First, strengthened his position on the Tenaru. On the left where a sand spit separated the green, sluggish river from the sea, he placed his heaviest concentration: machine guns, riflemen and a 37-mm antitank gun, all dug in behind a single strand of barbed wire. The sand spit was as good as a bridge over the river, so he placed outposts in the coconut grove on the other side of it. On his right he pulled machine guns off the beach front to extend that flank. Among the gunners were Lucky and Lew Juergens, Smitty and Jeff Cochrane. They began to dig a pit for Jeff Cochrane's gun first. Juergens' gun was left standing on the riverbank twenty yards downstream. They dug wide and deep, ten feet square and five feet down, working so furiously that although naked to the waist the sweat streaming from their lean bodies stained their dungaree trousers dark green and made their belts sodden. By nightfall, only the excavation was complete, with a dirt shelf for the gun. They would have to wait until the next day to roof it over with coconut logs and sandbags. In the meantime, they removed the tracers from their ammunition belts, feeling that in night fighting they would give away their position.

She had been the merchant ship *Macmormail,* but now, with a flight deck and guns topside, she was the makeshift aircraft carrier *Long Island,* dignified with the name of a battle and sent into the Pacific.

Off Guadalcanal on August 20 she launched nineteen Wildcat fighters and twelve Dauntless dive-bombers. The planes came skimming over the tops of the coconut trees. Marines below them glanced up apprehensively. Then they saw the American star on their fuselages and sprang to their feet with yells of jubilation. Two of the stubby Wildcats deliberately circled Henderson Field for all to see, and their overjoyed comrades ran shouting along the ridge tops, the riverbanks and beaches, throwing their helmets into the air and hugging each other, cheering wildly for the help that had come at last.

Night fell swiftly as it does in the jungle. A few stray shafts of light seemed to linger, as though trapped between jungle floor and jungle roof, and then it was black and silent except for the small sounds made by the creatures that move at night. Along the Tenaru the men crouching by their gunpits peered uneasily at the narrow dark river gleaming wickedly in the faint starlight, and they felt all those nameless atavistic fears born of darkness and dread clutching at their hearts. A long, widening, rippling V appeared on the surface of the river. At the point of the V was a pair of small, baleful greenish lights. Someone whooped and fired a rifle at the V. From the right came a fusillade of shots. Half of G Company's riflemen seemed to be firing at the apparition. Suddenly, it vanished.

The night darkened and the stars disappeared. One by one the men wrapped themselves in their ponchos and lay down to sleep. They had no mosquito nets because these had been lost when the *George F. Elliott* went down. Only Lucky and Juergens remained on watch. At 1:18 in the morning of August 21, a green flare rose from the coconut grove, a Marine sentry fired a shot—and the charge of the Ichikis began.

They came flowing over the sand spit, sprinting, hurling grenades, howling, sprinting, hurling grenades. "Banzai!" they screamed. "Banzai!" They came blundering into that single strand of barbed wire, and there they milled about in a jabbering frenzy. They hacked wildly at the wire with bayonets. They tried to hurdle it. They slung bangalore torpedoes—long thin pipes packed with explosive —beneath it hoping to blast gaps in it. But then the Marines opened fire, the flare-light faded, and the reenveloping night seemed to reel with a thousand scarlet flashes.

Machine guns chattered and shook. Rifles cracked. Grenades whizzed and boomed. Fat red tracers sped out in curving arcs and vanished. Orange puffs spat from the mouth of the antitank gun. Howitzers bayed in the rear distance and their whistling shells crashed and flashed among the coconuts where mortar missiles had already described their humming loops and were falling with that dull *crrunch* that tears and kills.

On the right flank Lucky and his buddies could hear the battle sweeping up the river toward them like a train of powder. In an instant, they were firing. Lucky jumped into Jeff Cochran's gunpit, although he was not his assistant. His own gun was still out on the riverbank. The screeching of birds arose from the opposite bank, and Cochran fired at it, believing that human intruders had provoked the birds' outcry. Now everyone on the riverbank was firing.

"Tell those clucks to quit firing," Cochran said to Lucky. "Tell them to wait until they hear the birds making a clatter, 'cause a smart man'd try to move under cover of it. That's when they'll be moving."

Lucky was happy to obey. He was not enjoying himself watching Cochran fire. He wanted to do some shooting himself. Outside, Juergens seized his arm and whispered, "C'mon, let's get our gun." They crawled down the riverbank on their bellies, for the night now sang with the angry hum of bullets. Juergens fired, and the gun slumped forward out of his hands. "That yellow belly!" he snarled, cursing a certain corporal who was at the moment cowering in a foxhole. He had set up the gun and done it so poorly that the tripod collapsed at the first recoil. Lucky slithered forward to reinsert the spindle in the socket and tighten the clamps. "She's tight," he hissed, and Juergens sent a burst past his nose.

Lucky and Juergens took turns firing at the sounds of movement across the river. Sometimes they swiveled the gun to fire downstream toward the sand spit. Tracers now came toward them. Out of the river dark they came, bright, dancing, sparkling with the mirth of hell. Time seem to be stretched out, be frozen, stand still, while the silent tracers streamed by and Lucky sought to lean away from them.

"Lew," he whispered, "we'd better move. It looks like they've got the range. Maybe we ought to keep moving. They won't be able to get the range that way. And maybe they'll think we've got more guns than we really have."

Juergens nodded. He unclamped the gun and Lucky lifted it out of the tripod. Juergens lay on his back and pulled the tripod over him, while Lucky laid the gun across his chest. They squirmed backward, almost like backstroke swimmers, to a new position and began firing again.

Downstream the barrel of the antitank gun glowed red in the dark. It was firing cannister muzzle blast straight into the ranks of the charging enemy, sometimes scything them down in squad groups. An enemy potato-masher grenade somersaulted through the night to fall hissing into the antitank dugout, where it exploded. Marine riflemen jumped into the dugout and the gun fired once more.

The Ichiki charge rose in fury. Squad after squad, platoon after platoon, burst from the covering darkness of the coconut grove to dash against the line. They broke it. They came in on holes and gunpits, running low with bayoneted rifles outthrust for the kill.

There were tall shapes mingling with the short ones, figures that closed, merged, became as one grotesquely whirling hybrid of struggling limbs, for now the battle had become that rarity of modern war, the close-in fight of clubbed rifles and thrusting blades, of fists and knees and gouging thumbs. Now there were more tall shapes than short ones, for Pollock had thrown in a reserve platoon, and the guttural cries of "Banzai!" were growing fainter beneath the wild keening of the battle, the crackling of rifles, the hammering of machine guns, the gargling of the automatics and the jumping *wham* of the 37.

The Ichikis were stumbling now over heaps of slain comrades strewn along the sandbar. They were themselves slumping into loose ungainly death, for the Marine fire had been multiplied from upriver where the guns had been swung seaward and trained on the sand spit. The last of the Ichikis were trapped. Marine mortars had drawn a curtain of fire behind them. Bullets ahead, shell bursts behind—forward or backward was to die.

Some chose the river, where American bullets still sought and found them and where crocodiles found them in the morning. Some chose to run the gantlet of guns along the shore, peeling off to their right at the barbed wire, dashing through the surf only to be dropped where the incoming tide would roll their bodies and cover them with sand. Others chose the sea. They plunged into the water. They tried to swim back to the east, but it was now dawn and their bobbing heads were visible targets for those Marine riflemen who had left their pits and thrown themselves flat to fire from the prone position.

"Line 'em up and squeeze 'em off!" roared Pollock, striding among his men. "Line 'em up and squeeze 'em off!"

The remainder of Colonel Ichiki's elite was being wiped out within the coconuts.

"Cease fire!" came the order, up and down the line. "Hold your fire, First Battalion coming through!"

Over the river, green-clad men were flitting through the coconuts. The First Battalion, First, had crossed the Tenaru upriver and had fanned out into a flanking skirmish line. Now they were working seaward.

Downstream, Marine tanks rolled slowly over the sand spit. They reached the coconut grove and turned right.

By nightfall more than 700 Japanese bodies had been counted; there were thirty-four dead Marines and seventy-five wounded. Probably at least a hundred, possibly more, wounded Japanese died of wounds or succumbed to the hunger, black nights and the slow dissolution of the rain forest. It is doubtful if more than fifty of the original 900 survived. They wandered leaderless, for Col. Kiyono Ichiki had already tasted "the fruits of victory."

He burned his colors and shot himself through the head.

52. Guadalcanal—Part III

THE JAPANESE had begun to display fatal tendencies that were to remain with them during the long American sea charge across the Pacific. The first was dilatoriness: during the twelve days following the Battle of Savo Island, they had the opportunity to retake Guadalcanal and drive its defending Marines into the sea. They had the wherewithal to do it—the ships, guns, airplanes and troops—but they did not do it. Failing 2 was the habit of committing forces piecemeal, rather than concentrating them so that they could be defeated in detail. The Japanese were aware of the Chinese proverb "A lion uses all its might in attacking a rabbit," but they ignored it. They preferred to match rabbit with rabbit, as Hyakutake had done with the Ichiki Detachment, and the wrong rabbit won. After the Tenaru the U.S. Marines were invincible. Failing 3 was the habit of writing reports wearing rose-colored glasses. In all the Imperial Army there was no commander more adept at this perverse skill than Lt. Gen. Haruyoshi Hyakutake. He knew all those euphemisms whereby a defeat became a "valiant advance" or a rout reached the ears of the emperor as "a glorious withdrawal of unshaken discipline." But no one had yet coined a euphemism for annihilation, and so it was up to the master to hurdle this temporary impasse with this report to Tokyo: "The attack of the Ichiki Detachment was not entirely successful." Then he drew up another plan for recapturing Guadalcanal.

Still committed to piecemeal reinforcement, Hyakutake would use Ichiki's rear echelon—about 1,500 men—plus another 1,000 from the Yokosuka Fifth Naval Landing Force. He also ordered Maj. Gen. Kiyotake Kawaguchi with his brigade of 5,000 Borneo veterans to stand by for movement to Guadalcanal. It did not occur to Hyakutake to wait for them all to assemble. He still believed that 2,500 men was enough to conquer the 10,000 Marines he now calculated to be on Guadalcanal. He still refused to accept the Americans as worthy foemen. He had faith in the battle report that stated: "The American soldiers are extremely weak when they lack support of fire power. They easily raise their hands during battle and when wounded they give cries of pain." Supporting these troops was the entire Combined Fleet under Admiral Yamamoto. Naval aircraft would soften the Marines by daily bombings while the destroyers and cruisers of the Tokyo Express would bombard them nightly. Three carriers, three battleships, nine cruisers, thirteen destroyers, thirty-six submarines and numerous auxiliaries would cover this reinforcement of roughly 2,500 men bound for western Guadalcanal. Thus, a whale was to escort its whelp to battle.

Such ship movement did not escape the observation of Australian coast watchers and American scout planes. Admiral Ghormley had ample warning. He ordered Admiral Fletcher's carriers (*Enterprise, Saratoga, Wasp*) to protect the sea lanes to the Solomons. On August 23 the three flattops were east of Malaita Island and a mere 150 miles from Henderson Field. Fletcher, misinformed by Pacific Fleet Intelligence that the Japanese forces were still far away at Truk, sent the *Wasp* group steaming away to a refueling rendezvous. It was not his fault, but it was a bad move, for Chuichi Nagumo was already pressing ahead with the big veterans, *Zuikaku* and *Shokaku*.

On the 24th a Catalina flying boat found light carrier *Ryujo* 280 miles northwest of Fletcher's two-carrier force. Yamamoto intended *Ryujo* to be bait for the Americans, just as the doomed *Shoho* had been in the Coral Sea. Fletcher took the bait and with the same results: *Ryujo* was sunk. Now Nagumo launched his own attack groups at *Enterprise* and *Saratoga*. Fletcher was ready for them. Fifty-one Wildcat fighters were stacked above the flattops in three layers. They went wolfing among the enemy, but twenty-four bombers got through. They struck at *Enterprise*, about one every seven seconds. She took three bombs, rupturing her decks, killing seventy-four men, wrecking some of her 5-inch guns. But excellent fire control saved "the Big E." Battleship *North Carolina*, in her Pacific baptism of fire, also was attacked. But she shot down or drove off fourteen bombers. Only *Saratoga* was unmolested, while her own war birds severely damaged the seaplane tender *Chitose*. With losses of only seventeen aircraft, Fletcher withdrew. Pursuing Japanese battleships and cruisers were unable to find him before darkness ended the air-sea phase of the Battle of the Eastern Solomons.

On the following day—August 25—Marine air, now called Cactus Air Force after the code name for Guadalcanal, attacked the invasion force under Rear Adm. Raizo Tanaka. A Dauntless piloted by Lt. Larry Baldinus found Tanaka's flagship, the big cruiser *Jintsu*, and planted a bomb on her forward deck. She went staggering home, asmoke and aflame, while navy and Marine dive-bombers, followed by a flight of Flying Fortresses, fell on the transports. They sank two of them and the destroyer *Mutsuki*. The remaining transports turned north and sailed to the safety of the Shortland Islands, where the troops debarked to board barges for a nocturnal and less ostentatious trip south.

Thus the Battle of the Eastern Solomons had ended in a moderate American victory. One light carrier had been sunk and the enemy invasion force was repelled. Although, as an unfortunate offshoot, *Saratoga* was later torpedoed by an enemy submarine, the ship was saved and returned to action three months later.

Henderson Field, meanwhile, had withstood the aerial assaults which had been planned to make way for these troops. On August 24, the Marine fighter pilots shot down eleven Zero fighters and ten bombers at a loss of three of their own planes. That date marked the beginning of the long epic defense of Guadalcanal's skies, which was to match the stand being made on the ground. From August 24 onward, Marine fliers began shooting down Zeros and twin-engined Betty bombers at a rate of from six to eight kills for every one of their own men lost. They fought, of course, with the almost invariable assistance of navy and army airmen—but the Guadalcanal aerial war was in the main a Marine affair, fought by the self-styled Nameless Wonders of the Bastard Air Force. These men were galled almost nightly to hear the San Francisco radio speak of "navy fighters" or "army bombers" while only the enemy might know who rode the cockpits of "American aircraft" or "Allied planes." And it *was* a Bastard Air Force, for if aerial combat is a gentleman's war, if it is clean, quick and sporting to fight in the clouds with hot meals and soothing drinks and laundered bedsheets awaiting the survivors, this was not so on Guadalcanal. Here the fly-boys were like the footsloggers.

They lived next to Henderson Field, in the very center of the Japanese bull's-eye. They rose an hour before dawn. If they cared to eat that common gruel of wormy rice and canned Spam that passed for meals on Guadalcanal, they ate it standing up, spooning the detestable slop out of borrowed mess gear. They gulped hot black coffee from canteen cups while bumping jeeps drove them through the darkness to the airstrip, where they warmed up planes that had to be towed from revetments by tractor. Then it was dawn, and they were roaring aloft, climbing high, high in the skies, sucking on oxygen. They went to battle in a sort of floating world where the only sounds were the roaring of their own motors and the hammering of their guns; where the only sights were the blind white mists of engulfing clouds, the sudden pain of reappearing sunlight bursting in the eyeballs, the swift dread glimpse of the red balls streaking by.

If the Japanese patrol planes, which came over at night and were called Washing-Machine Charleys for the uneven beat of their motors, failed to kill many of these pilots, they succeeded in keeping them awake. They circled the night sky for hours. When their gas was low and the patience of their victims nearly exhausted, they dropped their eggs and flew home—to be replaced by another Charley, or far, far worse, to be supplanted by Louie the Louse. This was the name for all those scouting aircraft whose swaying flares heralded the arrival of the Tokyo Express off Guadalcanal. Louie's droning motors and his flares were all the warning given. Then the sea-lying darkness flashed and the great naval shells wailed overhead and these pilots who were the very targets of the Japanese ships were flung gasping out of their cots while the roaring air squeezed their bodies like rubber dolls in the hand of a giant.

Only after the warships were gone could the fliers of the Bastard Air Force sleep.

Still they flew on, in patched-up aircraft, flying wing-to-wing in that technique of fighting by pairs which they would bring to perfection. Within a week of their arrival, some of them were aces. By August 30, Maj. John Smith had five little red balls painted on his Wildcat fighter; at nightfall, there were four more.

August 30 was one of those rare days when only the Zeros came down to strike at Henderson Field. Major Smith shot one of them to earth quickly, coming in on the enemy pilot's rear and killing him in his cockpit before he knew he was under attack. Then Smith banked toward a Zero attacking his wingman. The red ball flashed full in Smith's sights. He pressed the button. The Zero flamed and crashed. Now a third Japanese fighter was coming up under Smith. His bullets were sewing stiches up and down his fuselage. Smith nosed over. He came at the Japanese head-on. A bullet struck Smith's windshield and whined past his ear. He kept his thumb on the button. The Zero was coming apart in chunks. The two planes roared toward collision. They tore past each other not fifteen feet apart.

Over his shoulder Smith could see the Zero spinning down, and its pilot bailing out. Then there was no time to watch for the flowering of the parachute, for Smith, running low on gas, had only a few rounds of bullets left for those six wing guns and here he was coming down on top of a fourth Zero hedgehopping along the shore.

Smith skimmed over the coconuts with all guns blazing and the Zero fell into the sea in flames.

So it went into September, while the Bastard Air Force's collective total climbed toward 100, while its fighters also flew the cover under which Major General Vandegrift withdrew the Raiders and other troops from Tulagi to meet a fresh emergency.

The Kawaguchis had slipped into eastern Guadalcanal by night barge and were marching through the jungle toward the gaps behind Henderson Field.

Maj. Gen. Kiyotake Kawaguchi had brought his dress whites to eastern Guadalcanal. They were in a trunk when he landed undetected on September 6. He would not wear them, of course, until that momentous day when, with the Rising Sun again waving above the southern Solomons, with his silk uniform facings gleaming in the sun, his bald head covered by his braided cap and his guardsman's mustache waxed stiffly to attention, he would bow in the direction of the emperor and the photographers.

So Kawaguchi wore pedestrian khaki while he led his men south into the jungle. His trunk remained behind with a rear guard at Tassimboko village. So did his guns.

Red Mike Edson's Raiders found them there when they came ashore at Tassimboko two days later. The Raiders had routed Kawaguchi's rear guards, driving them into the jungle after killing twenty-seven of them at a loss of two of their own killed and six wounded. To their great joy, they found a beer warehouse. To their immense chagrin, it was empty. They burned it down, together with the village and Kawaguchi's supply dump. His guns they towed into the sea, scattering their breech blocks in deeper water. Then they carried Kawaguchi's fancy pants back to Henderson Field in triumph. Two days later they ascended a ridge behind Henderson Field to plug the gap there.

That was where they were on the night of September 13 when Kiyotake Kawaguchi came furiously against the airfield, doubly determined to save his face, now that he had lost his pants.

The ridge held by Edson commanded the airfield, and whoever held the airfield held Guadalcanal. Maj. Gen. Alexander Archer Vandegrift was grimly aware of this when he sent Edson and his men up there. All the signs told him that a payoff battle was impending. New mountain guns still in Cosmoline had been found and seized east of the Tenaru. The supply dump destroyed by Edson had been large. Scores of frightened Melanesians flocking into the sanctuary of the American perimeter told of being forced to help cut "a tunnel" through the southern jungle. (They also reported the murder of Catholic missionary priests and the rape and murder of their nuns.) Finally, enemy aerial and naval bombardment was rising in fury. Something big was coming, and Vandegrift, with but a single battalion in reserve, was powerless to maneuver against it. He had already formed his specialists—truck drivers, pioneers and amtrac men—into rifle battalions and sent them to hold isolated strong points. He dared not strengthen Edson's ridge with Marines drawn from other points already dangerously thin and held by troops melting away with malaria. All depended on Edson and his force of Raiders and Paramarines.

On the 11th there was help. Twenty-four Navy fighters flew into Henderson Field, where they received a welcome from a Cactus Air Force down to eleven planes. That day there had been forty-six enemy aircraft over the airfield. On the same day Edson scouted his front, detecting a buildup, which caused him to bring his men forward and order them to string barbed wire and dig in. Edson knew that his Marines were bitter. They had fought at Tulagi, patrolled Savo, fought at Tassimboko. Here they were in the forward foxholes again. Why was it always them? Why didn't other outfits fight? They cursed Edson for a glory hound who hung around headquarters hunting for assignments that would win him more medals. But they obeyed his orders and dug in.

On the 12th furious aerial battles raged over Henderson Field. Betty bombers flew low to lay sticks of bombs along the ridge. There were casualties. Once the clamor of aerial combat had subsided, the ridge became silent but for the clink of pickaxes, the rasping of shovels, the soft calls between the men who wielded them. The raucous cries of flights of parakeets were fading in the gathering dusk along with the brilliance of their plumage. Night fell clear and moonless. The ridge seemed like an island set in the silent dark sea of the jungle flowing around it. The rippling rapids of the Lunga River to the right were faintly audible. So was the cry of the bird that barked like a dog or the one whose call was a *crrack* like the clapping together of wood blocks.

At nine o'clock a Japanese patrol plane dropped a green flare over Henderson Field. A half hour later an enemy cruiser and three destroyers stood off Lunga Point to pound the ridge with 8- and 5-inch shells. Twenty minutes later a rocket rose on the right or Lunga side of the ridge and the Kawaguchis struck with a howl.

They had marched down the bank of the Lunga, wheeled right toward the ridge, and then, silhouetted in the light of their parachute flares, had come charging forward in waves. Grenadiers came first, followed by riflemen and light machine gunners, coming in columns stretching as far back as the Marines could see. They slapped their rifle butts to a cadenced beat, screaming in a rising, rhythmic chant:

"U.S. Marines be dead tomorrow! . . . *U.S. Marines be dead tomorrow!*"

They broke the Raiders and drove them back. They split Edson's center and sliced off a platoon on the far right flank. Cutting Edson's wire as they came, they moved down the Lunga to attempt an encirclement. Here again, as always, the Japanese penchant for night fighting, either to strike terror into the enemy's heart or to cancel out his superior firepower, dissolved their discipline. Kawaguchi could not capitalize upon the first shattering charge. His men, so far from overwhelming the ridge, now merely flowed up against it, thrashing about in the jungle that had engulfed them, tripped them, confused them, once they had left the straight going of the riverbank. So now the battle was fragmented, man against man, bayonets jabbing or rifles firing against sounds, a mindless melee raging beyond the control of either commander. A fresh Japanese naval bombardment after midnight did nothing to alter the result, falling as it did on friend and foe. Nevertheless, the advantage rested with Kawaguchi. He had driven the Americans back. When daylight came, the Kawaguchis retreated to their assembly areas, spending the 13th preparing for the final blow that night.

Red Mike Edson's men were stunned. They moved like sleepwalkers, lifting their feet as though they were weighted. They had been driven back, and they did not like to remember it. In the morning, they had attempted a counterattack, and this, too, had failed. A relieving battalion had been unable to reach the ridge because of the constant aerial action over Henderson Field. When they did arrive at dusk, they could only take up a supporting position. It was still up to 400 Raider-Paramarines holding a line 1,800 yards long against 4,000 Japanese—one man every five yards against ten of the enemy. Edson sought to tell them how much depended on them.

"This is it," he said softly to a group of them. "It is useless to ask ourselves why it is we who are here. We are here. There is only us between the airfield and the Japs. If we don't hold, we will lose Guadalcanal."

The men returned to their gunpits. But this time there was no cursing.

Kawaguchi was pleased. He had lost more men than he had anticipated, but he had nevertheless broken through that deadly American firepower. His men had proved the superiority of spiritual power. All day long they had exulted in the sound of friendly bombs falling on the Americans. Tonight, he would attack earlier than usual. He wanted to seize the airfield before Admiral Mikawa's cruisers arrived at midnight. Then the honor of retaking Guadalcanal would fall to the army. He also ordered the Ishitari Battalion east of the Tenaru to attack the river line at midnight. Then he, Kiyotake Kawaguchi, would wheel east or right to strike the Tenaru position in the rear. Confident, Kawaguchi sent a radio message to Tokyo. It was not quite as premature or presumptuous as Colonel Ichiki's, but it did suggest that if Radio Tokyo were to announce the recapture of the airfield, Maj. Gen. Kiyotake Kawaguchi would not deny it.

At 6:30 that night he attacked.

"Gas!"

Smoke rolled over the Marine right. Flares swayed down from the black again, again the jabbering and again that precise and un-American voice:

"Gas attack!"

It was, in fact, only smoke, and this typical Japanese trick fooled no one. The Marines kept to their holes, watching while the ghoulish flares made a greenish day of the night. Then, like a monster roman candle, the jungle spat forth hundreds of short tan shapes. They came screaming their dire oaths once more, but this time the Marines answered them with their own coarse epithets. They were firing. Japanese rushing to fire from the hip were falling. Now a full battalion —close to 1,000 men—struck at that fragile right flank held by fewer than a hundred. Again the Japanese fragmented the right.

Individual fights raged. Pfc. Jimmy Corzine saw four Japanese setting up a machine gun on a knob above him. He charged, bayoneting their leader, turning their gun on the rest of them, killing them, and kept on firing until he was himself killed. Capt. John Sweeney's company had been cut into little pockets. He had lost half of his company, and the Paramarines on his left were driven back by a charge supported by mortars.

Captain Torgerson took command of the retreating Paramarines. He rounded up the men drifting rearward, held roll call, singled them out by name and challenged them to go forward. They did. They passed through a shower of enemy grenades to reach a bare slope to set up machine guns, and there they cut down the charging enemy to the ground. But the Japanese replied with another shower of grenades, firing them from so-called knee mortars, the launchers they carried forward strapped to their legs. Sgt. Keith Perkins roved the ridge hunting for ammunition for his two guns. One by one his gunners fell, dead or wounded. Perkins jumped on his last gun, firing it until he, too, perished.

Red Mike Edson was desperate to make contact with Captain Sweeney on the right. He used his field telephone. A voice said primly: "Our situation here, Colonel Edson, is excellent. Thank you, sir." Edson swore. A Goddam Jap! He seized a passing corporal famous for his 50-pound mouth. The corporal ran forward, cupping his hands to his lips to bellow above the bedlam:

"Red Mike says it's okay to pull back!"

Sweeney heard and withdrew. Gradually, Edson shortened his line. He lay on his belly within ten yards of his guns, his arm curled around his field telephone, sometimes lifted and slammed to earth by the mortar blasts. He saw a group of Marines milling aimlessly around. He rushed them in a fury, pointing toward the enemy and screaming: "The only thing they have that you don't is *guts!*" More men were drifting to the rear. With Maj. Kenneth Bailey, Edson went among them, rallying them, taunting them. "*You,* you son of a bitch!" Bailey screeched. "Do *you* wanna live forever?" It was the immortal cry with which Dan Daly had rallied his men in Belleau Wood, and it had gone echoing down the decades to inflame another generation of Marines.

They went forward to dig in once more, to hurl the grenades Bailey rushed to them, and to draw a shallow horseshoe defense atop the ridge, there to await the Kawaguchis massing for the final thrust. But Red Mike Edson had called for artillery. With him to spot the enemy was a corporal named Watson. In the morning he would be Second Lieutenant Watson for the cool skill with which he called down hell from the heavens that night. He marked the enemy's rocket signals and directed a redoubled fire on their assembly areas. He brought the artillery closer and closer to his own lines.

"Closer," Edson whispered. "Closer."

The ridge shook and flashed. A terrible steel rain fell among Marines and Japanese alike. Terrified enemy soldiers dived into Marine foxholes to escape death aboveground. Marines knifed them and pitched them out again. The night was hideous with the screams of the stricken, for artillery does not kill cleanly; it tears men's organs with jagged chunks of steel, it blows off their limbs and burns their faces black.

But now the Kawaguchis were falling back again. They sprinted back into an opaque wall of darkness, jabbering once they had gained cover—for it was the chief failing of these jungle fighters that they could not keep silent in the jungle. At two o'clock they came again behind another mortar barrage, which cut wires to Vandegrift's headquarters and the artillery.

"Marine, you die!" the Japanese shrieked again, but with a notable lack of their former fervor, and the Marines, already exultant with the scent of victory, replied with strings of obscene oaths and streams of bullets as they cut the enemy down.

At 2:30 in the morning of September 14 Red Mike Edson called headquarters and said:

"We can hold."

A rosy dawn was breaking on the left of what was now called Bloody Ridge. It was quiet on the battlefield, save for an occasional shot or the boom of a grenade on a booby-trapped body. Souvenir hunters were already moving warily among the dead. Phil Chaffee was there with his pliers and Bull Durham sack, pulling gold teeth from the mouths of dead Japanese. Mopping up went forward in the jungle and to the Marine rear where there had been infiltrators. Four of them had reached Vandegrift's headquarters, where they were cut down, but only after one of them killed a sergeant with a sword thrust.

There had also been a brief battle to the west where a rare Japanese daylight attack was hurled back at the Matanikau River.

In all, there were only forty dead Marines and 104 wounded, against a death toll of 600 Japanese on Bloody Ridge alone, plus 250 killed at the Tenaru and another 100 at the Matanikau. Many more Kawaguchis died on a retreat crueler even than their bloody defeat. One officer wrote in his diary: "I cannot help from crying when I see the sight of those men marching without food for four or five days and carrying the wounded through the curving and sloping mountain trails. The wounds couldn't be given adequate medical treatment. There wasn't a one without maggots. Many died."

Yet, Bloody Ridge was far from being the end, although it was indeed the end of the beginning. That there would be more battles for Guadalcanal was plainly indicated by that anomaly of the Marines' war: a Japanese prisoner. He stood in splendid defiance among his slain countrymen and said:

"Make no matter about us dead. More will come. We never stop coming. Soon you all be Japanese."

53. The Soviets Fall Back, Ike Becomes Supreme Commander

WHILE THE FATE OF GUADALCANAL hung in the balance and the Desert War raged east and west during that summer and fall of 1942, the Soviet Army became locked in desperate combat with the German invaders.

Adolf Hitler had drastically altered his plan of conquest. He was aware that his strategy to destroy the Soviet armies during the campaign of 1941 had failed. He now sought to destroy the Soviet Union's economic power—that is, to starve rather than kill its armies. This could be done by depriving Stalin of the Kuban cornfields, the Donetz industrial basin and the Caucasian oilfields.

Logical as this plan appeared to be, it was still a mistake not to move on Moscow in 1942, for Moscow was the rail and road hub of the U.S.S.R. If Moscow fell, German air could interdict a critical area between 250 and 350 miles in diameter, thus blocking supplies from Archangel and reinforcements from Asiatic Russia, while all rail movement within central Russia would become chaotic if not halted altogether. By failing to move on Moscow, Hitler was no different from the Germans of 1914 who had failed to occupy the hub of Paris. Nevertheless, the great offensive heaved forward with emphasis on the southeastern front where only the Crimea seemed to stand between the invaders and the rich prize of the Caucasian oil fields.

General von Manstein commanded the Eleventh Army in the Crimea. He had taken Kerch by storm on May 13, and on June 1 he commenced the second Siege of Sevastopol with a furious artillery bombardment. But the fortress of Sevastopol was indeed a tough nut to crack. Twenty miles in its outer circumference, eight on its inner, it was a honeycomb of tunnels and underground arsenals, even underground factories turning out munitions. It was held by 75,000 frontline troops commanded by General Petrov, with perhaps another 90,000 reservists. The Germans hurled 50,000 tons of shells and dropped 20,000 tons of bombs on Sevastopol, but it still held out. Again and again the Soviets sallied forth in attempts to break out. Masses of them shouting "Ourrah! Ourrah!" rushed at the German lines, their arms linked together to prevent anyone from hanging back. Sometimes women and girls of the Communist Youth, themselves bearing arms, took the lead to urge them on. The carnage among the women alone was dreadful.

Ships seeking to supply the city from the Black Sea were pounced upon by Luftwaffe planes and sent to the bottom. Implacable Soviet commissars ordered divers to descend the dark water to retrieve what was lost. Some of them rebelled, affrighted at the sights of piles of horses and dead cavalrymen in the hold, or bodies of dead children rushing at them.

But the commissars pointed out, for the lack of food and bandages other children would die.

The divers went down.

Sometimes when the front fell silent, the Battle of the Loudspeakers would begin. Each announcer talked the enemy's language: The Soviets spoke Romanian and German, the Germans Russian. They came to know each other by voice during the siege. Sometimes they criticized each other's grammar or pronunciation, or accused one another of drinking or exaggeration. The Battle of the Loudspeakers became very popular with the frontline troops, who roared with laughter each time the enemy announcer took the measure of one of their own.

Once from the German side there came the sound of solemn chanting. The Soviets leaned forward to listen to it. It swelled toward the bright blue Crimean sky in a mighty chorus. It was the Romanians praying for victory. Because of the note of despair in their voices, it sounded like the wind wailing in the steppes.

Sevastopol finally fell on July 4. The city was a shambles. Dr. Peter Bamm, a surgeon attached to a medical unit, entered it that day searching for civilian casualties. He found most of them in the Russian Orthodox cathedral. It was cool and murky inside the stone edifice. Bamm saw old men and women, young women and children, lying in piles of straw. A priest knelt among them holding a crucifix aloft. Faint candlelight sparkled on its jewels. The priest was praying for a dying old woman. One of her twisted, arthritic hands was raised, clawing the air. Around her the other victims repeated the priest's prayers in unison. A rattling broke from the old woman's throat, and she died. The priest arose, and the congregation fell silent, their eyes on the dead woman's hand, still poised above her.

Bamm and a sergeant drove out of town to the vineyards. On the southern slopes of Sevastopol the Soviets had abandoned their wounded. Thousands of them lay scattered among the vines. Down below in the valley, Bamm could see 30,000 prisoners crowded into barbed-wire enclosures. He could guess their fate: the labor camps of Germany. Occasionally, a shot rang out in the valley. Bamm

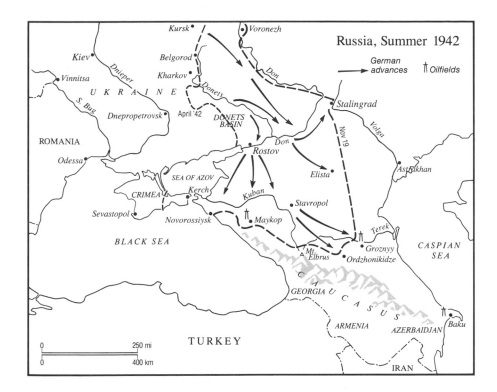

Russia, Summer 1942

turned to the wounded around him. He could see that they had had no surgical attention. They stank and their wounds were suppurating. They had lain in the blazing sun for forty-eight hours without water and were half-mad with thirst.

"*Voda,*" they cried piteously. "Water."

"*Voda, gospodin!* Water, your honor."

Bamm was desperate. There was no water anywhere. Then he remembered the wells down in Severnaya Bay. He selected a number of lightly injured Soviets as supervisors, marking them out by winding gauze around their left arms. They moved among those who could walk, ordering them to form ranks and march down to the wells. They would not move. Enraged, the supervisors yanked the vine-stakes out of the ground and went among them, beating them to their feet and into formation. Leaning against each other for support or hobbling on sticks, they dragged themselves down to the wells. Bamm watched them go with misery in his eyes and guilt in his soul.

They will quench their thirst, he thought. They will gain a little strength. But it will only help them keep going along the dreary route into the realm of the barbarians.

And of that realm we are the frontier.

The capture of Sevastopol gave the Germans the entire Crimea, the gateway to the Caucasus. By then, the mighty attack was going forward all along the eastern front, aiming at the Volga between Saratov and Stalingrad. Victory followed victory. Kursk . . . Shchigry . . . a powerful thrust beyond Byelgorod–Kharkov. . . . Gen. Friedrich Paulus's Sixth Army was driving toward Stalingrad on the Volga. By October it seemed the entire Soviet front would topple. Throughout the summer and early autumn the tone of Stalin's communiqués grew increasingly grave. Soviet radio broadcasts turned anxious. The United States, fearful that the Soviet ally might be knocked out of the war before the Allies could intervene in Europe, began rushing supplies to Stalin.

Three sea routes were chosen, the most famous being "the Murmansk run" along the Norwegian coast and into the Arctic Ocean ports of Murmansk and Archangel. The Murmansk Run was also the most risky. Dreadful shipping losses were suffered at the hands of German U-boats and long-range bombers rising from Norwegian airfields.

The "Persian corridor" was less dangerous. Here, ships sailed around the Cape of Good Hope and up the Persian Gulf to Iran (Persia), after which supplies were carried overland to the U.S.S.R. Eventually, the American-built Trans-Iranian Railway speeded up the process.

The safest route was the result of Stalin's refusal to declare war upon Japan. Ships flying the Soviet flag were unmolested by the Japanese as they sailed to Vladivostok in Siberia through Japanese-controlled waters. But shipment west from Vladivostok via the Trans-Siberian Railway was slow and complicated. Nevertheless, supplies flowed steadily into the Soviet Union from the United States.

Stalin redoubled his cries for a second front in France. He despatched Molotov to Britain and the United States to urge it, and the vocal left wings of both nations redoubled their strident demands for "The Second Front—NOW!"

Undoubtedly, the Soviets had to be rescued. A Hitler gorged with the body of Russia might be unbeatable, or at least so formidable that the democracies, prone to desuetude on the offensive, might grow weary of attacking him. Stalin's demands, then, dovetailed with American plans for building forces in Britain for an early cross-Channel invasion of the Continent.

The American chiefs when they conferred with their British counterparts on the newly created Combined Chiefs of Staff were always enthusiastic about an early cross-Channel invasion. The British were not. They had facts and figures to support their reluctance, but it is likely that they also had at the back of their brains the memory of the dreadful slaughter which followed the stalemate of the last war. Certainly, Churchill did. His physician once advised the exasperated American chiefs that they were not up against illogic but the Battle of Passchendaele. In fine, the British wanted to be absolutely *sure* of successfully forcing Hitler's Atlantic Wall. Three times so far—in France, Norway and Greece—they had been thrown off the Continent. Next time they returned, they wanted to stay.

Eventually, the disastrous Anglo-Canadian reconnaissance-in-force at Dieppe—if such it had been—in August of 1942 would convince them of how much force would be needed to penetrate the French coast. What the British wanted for a Second Front was to invade French North Africa, evict the Axis and cross the Mediterranean into Southern Europe.

The Americans thought the idea was absurd. They thought: Why go thousands of miles to find Germans to kill when there were armies of them twenty-five miles away from Dover? To defeat the Germans in North Africa would not beat Hitler. He was only beatable in northwest Europe. That was the argument advanced by Gen. Dwight Eisenhower.

For six months Dwight Eisenhower had been in daily, often hourly, consultation with General Marshall. He had served him tirelessly and faithfully, showing a remarkable ability to anticipate his chief's desires. He had become Marshall's protégé. Marshall admired Eisenhower for his eager acceptance of responsibility and his efficiency in execution. He had been pleased when Churchill told him that the British chiefs liked Eisenhower and were impressed by his dedication to the Anglo-American Alliance. Marshall believed that Eisenhower could get along with the British better than any other general in the army. In June 1942, he asked Eisenhower to prepare a draft directive for the commander-to-be of the European Theater of Operations, the name which Eisenhower had himself given the London command. In it, remembering his talks with Fox Connor many years earlier, Eisenhower urged "absolute unity of command." On June 8 he gave the draft to Marshall and urged him to read it carefully.

Three days later Marshall appointed Eisenhower to command of the ETO. On June 24, Eisenhower arrived in Britain. For the last time in his life, he received a quiet reception, for on the following day he called the press conference that made him a world figure.

No other man with the possible exception of Franklin Roosevelt ever became so popular with the American press. He became the darling of the British newsmen, too with his good looks, good humor and enchanting grin, his very earthy nickname of Ike—for the way his face reddened with anger when he spoke of the Nazis, or brightened with hope when he talked of the retribution that would overtake them. Ike was just plain folks. London roared when it heard of his reaction to the bedroom of the opulent suite awaiting him at Claridge's: "I feel as though I were living in sin." It applauded his decision to move to a small seven-room house in Surrey only forty minutes from Grosvenor Square, where he could spend his weekends, relax among his intimates playing golf or bridge or singing. Among those at Telegraph Cottage was Kay Summersby, his chauffeur, a pretty and vivacious woman who, it was whispered and then broadcast, had become his mistress. But she had not. It is true that they probably fell in love, but even Kay Summersby herself reported in her book that it was never consummated, if only because except for one night they were never alone together. On that single night they did try to make love, but nothing happened, either because hard work had made Eisenhower impotent, or his morality had subdued his passion.

To the British his most attractive quality was that he was so American. They liked his habit of levying a twopence fine on any Anglicizing American caught saying "Cheerio" or "Here's a go." They were delighted when this chain smoker refused to attend any more formal dinners because no one could smoke until the toast to the king had been drunk. At last his friend Lord Louis Mountbatten prevailed upon him to come to a dinner on the promise that he would not have to curtail his smoking. After the sherry, the party sat down to the soup and after this was consumed, Mountbatten quickly jumped to his feet to cry, "Gentlemen, the King!" Turning to Eisenhower, he said, "Now, General, smoke all you want."

But behind all this ingenuousness and warmth, the former barefoot boy from Abilene with his careful, calculating brain was making a deliberate pitch for the affection of the British public, offering himself as a sort of apotheosis of the American GI and thereby shaping the British attitude toward his army. Dwight Eisenhower would brook no slur upon the British ally. His deep distrust of coalition warfare, even among allies who spoke the same language, was such that he considered any racial insult, however slight, as the start of what could be an important breach in allied unity. He was livid with rage when he heard of an officer who had told his British drinking partner that the Yanks would show the Tommies how to fight. "I'll make the son of a bitch swim back to America!" he swore, and he did send him home by boat. His favorite oath on hearing of such infractions was "I'll send the bastard home by slow boat—without an escort!" Hearing of another Anglo-American fracas, he had the American officer investigated. Concluding that he was guilty, he reduced him in rank and sent him home. The British officer involved protested. "He only called me a son of a bitch, sir, and all of us have now learned that this is a colloquial expression which is sometimes used almost as a term of endearment." Eisenhower did not grin. "I am informed that he called you a *British* son of a bitch. That is quite different. My ruling stands."

One of the results of this fanatic devotion to the principle of unity was that as never before in history the Allied Force Headquarters did work together as a unit. Officers of the British Army, Royal Navy and Royal Air Force worked side by side with officers of the United States Army and Navy and the Army Air Corps. It would be fatuous to suggest that every difference—in slang, accent or practice—was met not with a sneer but an indulgent smile. Yet, this was Eisenhower's ideal, and the men of both nations who worked for him actually did aspire to such perfection.

This devotion to unity, together with his capacity for returning the soft answer to harsh or mocking criticism, was perhaps Eisenhower's greatest asset in organizing and commanding the Allied army that fought the Axis. It also had much to do with keeping acrimony to a minimum when the Combined Chiefs argued over where the enemy should be struck. Eisenhower had prepared a plan for invading France in 1942 called Sledgehammer. It was to be succeeded in 1943 by Roundup, a larger operation. Sledgehammer called for a landing at Le Havre under British command with two American divisions participating. He estimated that the lead division had a 50–50 chance of getting ashore, while the chance of establishing a six-division beachhead was only one in five. Thus, only a 20 percent chance of success. Eisenhower was himself aware that this was much too big a risk for such a limited operation. But, he also wrote and underscored: *"But we should not forget that the prize we seek is to keep 8 million Russians in the war."*

The acerbic Field Marshal Sir Alan Brooke, now the chief of the Imperial General Staff, attacked Sledgehammer. If it failed, it would do the Soviets no good; if it succeeded, it would not draw any Germans from the Eastern Front. Marshall's reply that something had to be done to help the Soviets only gave him the opportunity to reply that "something" à la Sledgehammer would be wasteful, but that "something" in French North Africa had great possibilities. Marshall argued quite cogently that diversion of so much resource to North Africa would make Roundup in 1943 impossible. There would, then, be no invasion of France for two years. The British reply was merely to stick by their guns: no Sledgehammer, North Africa would *not* force a postponement of Roundup.

On July 22 the frustrated Marshall sent Roosevelt a cable admitting that the alliance was deadlocked. Roosevelt cabled back that even though the British would not participate in Sledgehammer, the Americans should cooperate with them in North Africa. A delighted Winston Churchill immediately gave this operation, so dear to his peripheral heart, the code name "Torch." Dwight Eisenhower was brokenhearted. On the following morning, when he sat down to breakfast with his deputy, Maj. Gen. Mark Clark, he told him that July 22, 1942, was "the blackest day in history." But then to his amazement, it was he who was chosen to command Torch. On July 25, as the Combined Chiefs discussed the problem of a commander, Admiral King had said: "Well, you've got him right here. Why not put it under Eisenhower." It was done with pleasure by both sides, and Eisenhower, characteristically, now that he had done his utmost to prevent Torch, plunged with great enthusiasm into organizing it.

Churchill, meanwhile, never a slouch at cloaking bad news in the gay raiment of glad tidings, flew to Moscow to inform Joseph Stalin about Torch.

At seven o'clock in the evening Churchill met Stalin for the first time in the Kremlin. They conferred for nearly four hours, of which "the first two hours were bleak and somber." Stalin's face was glum as he listened to Churchill's arguments against a landing in France in 1942. He frowned when Churchill said that if throwing a few hundred thousand men into France at this time would draw off appreciable German forces from the U.S.S.R., the Anglo-Americans would do it, but if it drew no men away and spoiled the chances of 1943, it would be a great error. By then, he told Stalin, a million American soldiers would be in Britain poised to invade France.

Stalin broke in sharply. Men who did not take risks did not win wars, he said. He asked why the British were so afraid of the Germans. Churchill replied that

Hitler did not try to invade Britain when she was on her knees because he was afraid of the risks. To cross the Channel was not easy. Stalin said this was not a true analogy. Hitler would have been invading a hostile country while the Anglo-Americans would be going into a friendly France. Churchill observed that because of this it was more important not to fail, for a friendly France would then feel Hitler's vengeance. As it became obvious that neither leader was prepared to give in, Stalin concluded by saying that although he could not demand or insist upon a French invasion in 1942, he was bound to say he did not agree with Churchill's arguments. At this point, Churchill unfolded a map of the Mediterranean.

With customary eloquence he began to detail the advantages of Torch. If by the end of the year the Allies could hold North Africa, they could then threaten "the belly of Hitler's Europe." He drew a picture of a crocodile, using it to illustrate the Allied intention of hitting Europe's soft underbelly while also attacking its hard snout.

Now Stalin was impressed. He quickly grasped the strategic advantages of Torch: It would strike Rommel in the rear, it would overawe Franco, it would produce fighting between Germans and Frenchmen in France and it would expose Italy to the full thrust of the war. To these, Churchill, deeply impressed by the Soviet dictator's swift insight, added a fifth: It would shorten Britain's sea route through the Mediterranean. "May God prosper this undertaking," Stalin murmured, his dark eyes glowing. The conference ended in a spirit of goodwill, with Churchill happy that, although Stalin now knew the worst, they had parted friends.

54. Prelude to Operation Torch

NOW THAT EISENHOWER had been given command of Torch, he disagreed sharply with Marshall on how it should be conducted. Marshall, ever cautious about the Mediterranean, was worried about Spain. If the Torch forces sailed "inside" the Mediterranean, as Eisenhower and the British desired, Generalissimo Franco could overrun Gibraltar and close off its western end, thus cutting Torch's line of supply. To forfend against this, Marshall wanted a landing at Casablanca on the Atlantic coast of Morocco. Then there would be two landings inside the Med, at Oran and Algiers. But this plan involved vast distances: it was eight hundred miles from Casablanca to Algiers and another four hundred miles to Tunis. Eisenhower believed that these landings would place his forces too far from Tunis, the ultimate objective. It was at Tunis that the Allied pincers—the seaborne invasions from the west and the British Eighth Army driving overland from Egypt in the east—were to meet and crush Rommel's forces between them. Eisenhower argued that the landings should be much closer to Tunis before the Germans could have time to rush in reinforcements from Sicily slightly more than a hundred miles away. He did not believe that Franco would intervene, while he also doubted that the French in Tunis would fight the Germans. Events were to prove him correct on both counts, but Marshall would not budge. From the start he disliked the Mediterranean operation, not out of spite but because he was convinced that it would lead nowhere. Hitler could only be beaten in northwest Europe. Marshall vetoed Eisenhower's plan for a landing at Bône, a little more than a hundred miles west of Tunis. He insisted there would be three landings —at Casablanca, Oran and Algiers—and there were.

This settled, albeit grudgingly but without rancor, Eisenhower's next problem was what to do about the French army in Morocco and Algeria. Between the Free French of Charles de Gaulle and the Vichy French of Marshal Pétain who garrisoned North Africa, there was open enmity. Put simply, if de Gaulle was right, then the officers who had taken an oath to the Pétain government were wrong. This they could not accept. This was why at the outset de Gaulle was not even considered for a role in Torch, and because of French sensitivity about *l'honneur* it had also been decided to have only American soldiers make the landings for fear that the French might fire on their former ally, the British. But would they also shoot at the Americans? This was the problem that vexed Dwight Eisenhower, and on September 16 he met secretly with Robert Murphy. Since the Franco-German armistice, Murphy had been serving the U.S. State Department in Algeria, negotiating an economic accord there. He had impressed Marshall with his contacts in the French army and his claims that he understood the French mind, and the chief of staff had had him flown to London to meet Eisenhower.

Murphy was a tall, dark, good-looking man, heavy-set, charming and completely confident. Unfortunately, his concept of the French was narrow. De Gaulle said Murphy thought France consisted of the people he dined with in town at night. Nevertheless, Murphy assured Eisenhower that he could cut straight through the squabble between the Free French and the Vichy French, and also gain the allegiance of the French army, if he brought in an outsider. This was Gen. Henri Giraud, a retired officer who had lost a leg to the Germans in the last war and had escaped from a POW camp in 1940. He was then living in unoccupied France. If he were to appear in Algiers, Murphy said, the French colonial troops would rally to him and thus provide an unopposed landing. Murphy said that he had been assured of this by General Mast, chief of staff to the French corps commander in Algeria.

Eisenhower was impressed by Murphy, but he did not believe everything the diplomat told him. He refused to take Murphy's underground organization seriously and rejected Murphy's request for arms for these groups. When Murphy asked for the invasion date, Eisenhower declined to give it to him, instructing him to tell the French it would come in February. Nevertheless, he did tell Murphy to remain in touch with him after he returned to Algiers.

On October 16, Eisenhower received two messages from Murphy. The first was that General Mast had insisted that command of Torch should go to Giraud and that Admiral Darlan's son had told him (Murphy) that his father would cooperate with the Allies. But Mast had also told Murphy that neither he nor Giraud nor the French army would have anything to do with Darlan. Murphy wanted a directive on how to proceed. In his second message, he said that Mast wanted Eisenhower to send a secret delegation to Algiers to meet with him and his fellow conspirators.

Eisenhower was aroused. Jean François Darlan then epitomized all that was odious to the Allies. He hated Britain, and he hated de Gaulle, whom he had branded a traitor; he was an uncompromising Fascist and an eager Nazi collaborator, author of Vichy's anti-Semitic decrees. Yet, Darlan was commander in chief of all Vichy forces, and Giraud commanded nothing. Even with Darlan's repulsive record, the notion of switching to him was tempting, and war makes strange bedfellows. Eisenhower immediately telephoned Churchill, who was spending the weekend at Chequers, the prime minister's country residence. He asked him to come to London. Churchill reluctantly agreed. Accompanied by Mark Clark, Eisenhower met him at 10 Downing Street, surrounded by his lieutenants. Wrote Clark: "There was about as dazzling an array of Britain's diplomatic, military and naval brains as I had yet seen."

Inexplicably, the Darlan question was not the one most seriously discussed. In his best cavalryman's style, Churchill said casually: "Kiss Darlan's ass if you have to, but get the French navy." What appealed most to Churchill's romantic, adventurous nature was General Mast's request for a secret rendezvous. His eye fell with approval on the tall, lean, hawk-nosed Clark—the American eagle, as he called him—whom Eisenhower had already chosen for the assignment. He ordered Fleet Adm. Sir Dudley Pound to have a submarine waiting for Clark that night in Gibraltar to take him to Algiers.

At Gibraltar, Clark and his party boarded the submarine H.M.S. *Seraph,* one of the smaller and slower British undersea boats. Clark had taken off his coat and hat and had about $200 in Canadian gold pieces in a money belt around his waist. Lt. Norman Jewell, the *Seraph*'s commander, welcomed him aboard. He told him he had three British commandos with four foldboats—little, collapsible wood-framed canvas canoes—which would take him ashore at the rendezvous point. *Seraph* got underway, and Clark at once found that a man of his height —six feet two inches—had difficulty moving aboard a submarine. He had to walk with lowered head, and to get into the head he had to crawl on all fours. But he was amused by the ship's crew, all youngsters who said "we're going on a screwy mission with some Americans."

At dawn of October 21, Jewell ran up the periscope and sighted the rendezvous beach. But going ashore in daylight was too risky, so they waited until midnight October 22–23 before putting out in the foldboats. A light showed in a house inland from the beach. It was the signal, and they guided on it, paddling softly over a calm sea, entering a gentle surf, which propelled them ashore. Carrying the foldboats and their gear, they made for the cover of a steep bluff above them. Clark heard movement and stiffened.

"Welcome to North Africa," a voice above them said, and Robert Murphy stepped into view surrounded by Frenchmen.

"I'm damn glad we made it," Clark gasped, climbing the hill and forgetting the fancy speech he had memorized.

They climbed a steep and stony path to the house with the light in the window. It was a typical French colonial villa, red-roofed and built of white stone around a courtyard. It was owned by M. Teissier, a deeply patriotic but very excitable Frenchman. Teissier had sent his Arab servants away for fear that they might report the meeting. Unknown to him, they became suspicious and did report his action to the police. Clark ordered the commandos to hide their boats upstairs and stay there. General Mast and his party arrived at 5 A.M.

They were in full uniform. They had brought bags full of voluminous written information and valuable maps. Clark was highly pleased, and especially impressed by Mast's sincerity. Clark was careful not to let Mast know that Torch was already underway, with some of the leading elements already at sea. In Norfolk, Virginia, ships were being combat-loaded to sail straight to the invasion beaches at Casablanca. During the day both the French and American staffs conferred, at which more priceless information was received. At midday, the telephone rang. Teissier answered it, whirling to shout:

"The police will be here in a few minutes!"

The French exploded, changing swiftly into civilian clothes, stuffing their uniforms into bags and rushing out the doors or popping out of windows to vanish in the brush fringing the beach. Within a few moments, only Teissier, Murphy and his assistant and one French officer, together with Clark and his party remained within the house. Clark ran up the stairs to order the commandos to take to the woods on the beach with their boats. But there was no time! Police cars were entering the courtyard. The commandos fled without the boats, and a shaking Teissier locked the room containing them. Then he led Clark and his party to a trapdoor, opened it—and motioned for them to descend. They did, entering a dank, dark wine cellar, dragging their musette bags stuffed with incriminating French documents behind them. The trap door fell shut. Clark knelt on the stairs, grasping a carbine. He hoped to escape without shooting, but was prepared to fight his way out. Above him he heard the police questioning Teissier.

All four men upstairs had been drinking wine and singing when the police came. Murphy identified himself as the American consul in Algiers. He said that they were having a little party which would be enlivened by the women waiting upstairs, and asked the French not to embarrass him. This satisfied the gendarmes' questions of why the Arab servants were sent away. It also served to allay some of their own suspicions, although they made a great show of stomping about the rooms and looking behind furniture. Every time they approached the trap door, Clark and his companions held their breath. One of them whispered that he was choking.

"I'm afraid you won't!" Clark hissed, taking a wad of chewing gum out of his mouth and giving it to him. The trap door opened.

"They've gone," Murphy said, "but they'll be back."

"How long?" Clark asked.

"Just a little while. Better clear the house."

Clark and his party dragged the bags up the stairs. They brought the fold-boats downstairs. Loaded down, they left—to the immense relief of the frantic Teissier. Down at the beach, Clark was dismayed to see that the sea had risen. It seemed much too rough for the frail foldboats. Still, he tried it. He stripped to his scivvy shorts and OD shirt, fearing that his trousers and money belt full of gold pieces would weigh him down. He rolled the belt inside the pants and put it in the boat. He got in and the first wave capsized him. Clark had lost his pants and his gold.

Now Clark was wet and cold and fearful of being taken captive with all those bags full of Mast's information. He returned to Teissier's house, cutting his bare feet on the stones. The Frenchman was upset. He didn't want Clark near him. The police were coming back. But he gave Clark the pants, sweaters, bread and wine that he asked for. Clark was just tucking the bread and wine bottles under Teissier's too-tight sweaters when the police arrived again. Teissier was terrified. "Please, for God's sake, get out of the house!" he pleaded. Clark jumped the wall on the seaward side, landing painfully on his cut feet. He made his way to the beach again. Now he made radio contact with Jewell aboard *Seraph*. Jewell needed a guide light. Clark sent one of his men to tell Teissier to turn on his light. He had turned it off when the police arrived. Frightened though he was, the gallant little Frenchman obliged. Although still suspicious, the police had departed. Now Murphy and Teissier came down to the beach. At 4 A.M. they stripped and helped Clark and his officers carry a foldboat out through the cold water and past the breakers. The others followed, although one foldboat loaded with papers was lost. Soon Clark saw the dark silhouette of *Seraph* bobbing in the swells. He came aboard, and the others followed.

Clark's elation at his escape was tempered by his fear that the lost foldboat might be found. The papers it contained could implicate Mast and the others in a plot. Worse, it also held secret letters from Murphy to be delivered in Britain. These could reveal Murphy's scheming. But the foldboat was never found. Clark and his party arrived safely in London again, loaded down with excellent maps and valuable military information. Winston Churchill was so delighted at the success of the mission, so eager to hear the details and already chuckling to hear how Clark had lost his pants and his gold, that he invited "the American eagle" to dinner that night.

But Mark Clark was much too tired to accept.

55. Guadalcanal—Part IV

IF THERE WAS ONE BODY OF WATER in the Pacific Ocean dreaded by American sailors it was the 640-mile stretch of the Coral Sea between Guadalcanal and Espiritu Santo in the New Hebrides known as Torpedo Junction. The name was a play on a then-popular swing tune called "Tuxedo Junction." It was a natural for that sun-dappled sea in which enemy torpedoes sometimes seemed as numerous as the flying fish that skipped and skimmed so gracefully over its calm surface.

That was why, when Alexander Archer Vandegrift learned on the morrow of Bloody Ridge that reinforcements were on the way, his jubilation was tempered by his realization that the powerful task force escorting his Seventh Marines had to pass through Torpedo Junction. He was therefore not entirely dismayed when Adm. Richmond Kelly Turner ordered the Seventh's six transports back to Espiritu. A Kawanishi flying boat had been spotted tracking Turner's task force, and he had no desire to risk 4,300 Marines and all their new guns and gear in those treacherous waters.

Deprived of this juicy prey, the Japanese submarines fell on what was in effect most of the American Pacific Fleet: the carriers *Wasp* and *Hornet,* the fast new battleship *North Carolina,* seven cruisers, thirteen destroyers, and the usual complement of auxiliary ships. They put a steel fish into mighty *North Carolina* and sent her hurrying home. Little *O'Brien* staggered after her, but fell apart and sank en route. *Hornet* and the others survived unscathed, but *Wasp* took three torpedoes. She burned brightly, her funeral pyre visible high above the horizons of those cloudless seas, and then, beneath the red glow of twilight on September 15, she sank with a loud hiss.

Under the same red sky in Hinomiya Stadium in Tokyo, cheering thousands heard results of the Torpedo Junction battle announced. They also heard of the "recapture" of the Guadalcanal airfield, and then, interrupted by bursts of thunderous applause, came this announcement:

" . . . and the stranded 10,000 Marines, victims of Roosevelt's gesture, have been practically wiped out."

At Rabaul, Lieutenant General Hyakutake was gratified to hear that his humble part in the victory had not been overlooked. Now he would tidy up his triumph. He would send south all of the Sendai Division—some 20,000 men— to apply the crusher. Hyakutake had shed some of his contempt for the Americans. Reports from the Kawaguchis filtering back to Rabaul suggested that the Imperial Staff manual's estimate of Americans might be off the mark. They were beasts, the Kawaguchis said, the refuse of jails and asylums. They drank blood. They cut off the limbs of their prisoners and staked their bodies to the earth. Then they drove over them in steamrollers. This last was partially true: at both the

Tenaru and Bloody Ridge the decomposing bodies of thousands of Japanese and the millions of buzzing black flies that fed on them presented a health problem. To solve it, huge common graves were dug, the bodies pushed in with bulldozers, doused with gasoline, burned, and then buried beneath small mountains of backfill.

At any rate, Hyakutake would not underestimate his foe again. Advance units of the Sendai would go south in fast destroyer-transports. Lt. Gen. Masao Maruyama, the Sendai's commander, would follow, and then the main body on slower transports would slip down the Slot. Next would come the combined sea and air power of the Imperial Navy, and finally, General Hyakutake himself, who would arrive some time in October to accept the American surrender.

In the third week of September the Tokyo Express began running troops to Guadalcanal again.

There were now about 22,000 Marines on Guadalcanal, for the Seventh Marines had run the gantlet of Torpedo Junction and come ashore on September 18.

Convinced that Vandegrift could not hold without them, or without a valuable load of aviation gasoline he was bringing him, Kelly Turner had turned the Seventh's transports around while they were still at sea and risked the torpedoes again. This time, overcast skies, an attack of army bombers on Rabaul, and Yamamoto's decision to withdraw temporarily to Truk, coalesced in his favor. The Seventh got through.

Vandegrift was elated. Although the Seventh was not battle-tested, it was full of many officers and salty old regulars who were. Chief among them was Lt. Col. Lewis Burwell (Chesty) Puller. At forty-four Puller was already a legend, having won two Navy Crosses in Haiti and Nicaragua. He would win three more in World War II to become the most decorated Marine in history. He was also that very rare bird of war, a man who actually loves combat and who is beloved by his men. Puller's Marines delighted in Pullerisms. Asked why Nicaragua patrols were too slow, he had snapped: "Because of the officer's bed roll!" Shown his first flamethrower, he asked: "Where do you fit the bayonet on it?" Flunked out of Pensacola flying school on the unique report, "Glides too flat, skids on turns, climbs too fast," he was perversely pleased because now he could go back to his riflemen where "all the fightin's on foot." Puller's Marines boasted of his bullhorn voice, and they claimed that his huge rib cage, which gave him his nickname, arching from an otherwise spindly frame barely five feet six inches tall, was capable of repelling enemy bullets. Puller's battle credo contained two articles: conditioning and attack.

One of those enlisted men who adored Puller was Sergeant Johnny ("Manila John") Basilone. Basilone had done a peacetime hitch in the army, serving in Manila. His lurid tales of life on Dewey Boulevard earned him his nickname after he left the army, spent a few years as a civilian, and then joined the Marines in 1940. Basilone's model was Dan Daly of Belleau Wood fame, one of the few

Americans to win two Medals of Honor. Basilone was also an artist with the .30-caliber water-cooled machine gun. He had two of them under his command when he went into the new cordon defense General Vandegrift had ordered.

Hitherto because of a shortage of troops Vandegrift's line had been continuous only on the northern beaches and along the Tenaru to the east. West and south he had held strong points tied together in daytime by patrols with the gaps covered by artillery. Now, he could draw a ring around Henderson Field. It meant spreading a lot of men thin, defending everywhere weakly rather than at selected points in depth or in a series of lines in depth, and it also meant that wherever the enemy chose to attack he could concentrate his most against Vandegrift's least. Such a cordon or circle was as surely outmoded by modern weapons as artillery had made an anachronism of castles. Yet because it was drawn around an object—Henderson Field—the loss or capture of which meant defeat or victory, it was exactly the right military prescription for Guadalcanal.

With bulldozers, barbed wire, axes, shovels, sandbags, and machetes made of cut-down cavalry sabers, Vandegrift's men built his new line with an energy that led a scornful Japanese officer to observe that U.S. Marines were not genuine jungle fighters because "they always cut the jungle down." He was not wrong. In the jungle ravines between the ridges, perspiring Leathernecks hacked out fields of fire up to 100 yards long. In the fields they burned the kunai grass to clear even longer lanes for their bullets. In the coconut groves, axes rang to the gleeful cry "Charge it to Lever Brothers!" a reference to the Australian company that produced copra from the coconuts. After the great trees came crashing down, the trunks were chopped into sections and the logs dragged across holes cushioned with sandbags. Clumps of grass were planted atop the logs and in a few days tropic moisture had fastened them so that the gunpits gave the appearance of low hummocks. Barbed wire was now plentiful, and the Marines strung apron after apron of it until the outer rim of Vandegrift's ring was formed of concentric collars of cruel black lace. Outside this rim mortarmen and artillerists marked all the likely assembly points and trails. All approaches were mined or booby-trapped. Hand-grenade pins were partially withdrawn and fastened to wires intended to trip unwary feet. Inside the rim riflemen dug Japanese spider holes, deep vertical pits in which, if they were not filled with rain, a man could stand and shoot. Machine gunners, meanwhile, interlocked their guns or registered them for night firing. They placed cans of gasoline in trees and pressed cartridges into sandbags under their gun butts to mark the exact spot to fire at night and set the cans afire.

Remember that Death is lighter than a feather,
But that Duty is heavier than a Mountain.

Thus, the motto of the Sendai Division, from the rescript of the immortal Emperor Meiji, the father of modern Japan. The Sendai thought of themselves as "the emperor's own." The division—actually the 2nd—had been founded in

1870 by Meiji himself. He had recruited its men from the town of Sendai to the north of Tokyo. They had fought in the Sino-Japanese War of 1894–95, and in the Russo-Japanese War of 1904–05 had distinguished themselves by capturing Crescent Hill at Port Arthur (now Lüshun, China) during a bloody night attack. They also were distinguished for their ferocity in the Rape of Nanking, had fought the Soviets again at Nomonhan and had won an easy victory in the invasion of Java.

These sturdy young men, the citified descendants of sturdier peasants, could remember receiving their rifles like knights receiving their spurs. "Conscripts," they had been told, "your rifle enables you to serve the emperor just as the sword of the samurai made him strong and terrible in the Imperial service. You will keep its bore as bright and shining as the samurai kept his blade. On the outside it may, like yourselves, become stained with mud and blood, but within, like your warrior's soul, it will remain untarnished, bright and shining." The rifles were taken with a profound obeisance, much like the reverential bow which the Sendai's soldiers made to their mothers on the day of departure for war. Almost all of them wore around their waist a Belt of a Thousand Stiches, given to each by his mother, who had stood in the street begging a stitch of good luck from passersby.

These were the men who were to give the Guadalcanal Marines their first defeat.

General Vandegrift had decided to go on the offensive against the Sendai arriving west of the Matanikau. He wanted to break them up before they could cross the river to menace the airfield with their artillery, and he also wanted to occupy the east or inner bank of the Matanikau himself. So he sent Chesty Puller with his entire battalion to make a reconnaissance-in-force west and south of the perimeter.

With his Crusader's Cross around his neck, his jungle-stained copy of Caesar's *Gallic Wars* in his pocket and his cold stump of a pipe in his mouth, Puller led his men toward the Matanikau. Very soon they came under fire from the Sendai. They faltered. Hard as Puller had trained them, they had marched chiefly over roads, not over the same terrible terrain that had scourged the Kawaguchis, not in the enervating moist heat of the jungle. By nightfall, they were exhausted. Even Puller was out of breath—from swearing at them.

In the morning, the enemy struck again. Capt. Jack Stafford fell, wounded about the neck and face by the explosion of his own rifle grenade. Puller came to his side just as a corpsman gave him morphine. He saw that Stafford was choking in his own blood. He unsnapped a big safety pin from his ammunition bandoleer. Reaching into Stafford's mouth, he seized his tongue and pinned it neatly to his dungaree collar. By this resolute action he saved Stafford's life.

Puller's reports of enemy strength convinced Vandegrift that now was the time to strike the enemy. He fed two more battalions into the area, but in an operation so complicated, so flawed by faulty intelligence and the piecemeal commitment of troops—hitherto only Japanese defects—that he was compelled to withdraw. His casualties were 65 killed and 105 wounded, although his men had definitely given more than they got.

So the month of September ended with the Marines on the ground bruised but far from battered, and with the Marines in the air wresting control of the skies away from the once-invincible Zeros. The Cactus Air Force also had a new commander, Brig. Gen. Roy Geiger. He was a burly white bear of a man, a flying general who had flown as a captain in the last war and had pioneered Marine aviation. He set up headquarters in "the Pagoda," a wooden shack about 200 yards from the main runway.

Soon the gruff and guileless Geiger was known as "the Old Man" to the youthful flying fraternity he commanded. They were actually a band of brothers. They looked so much alike on the ground—their unlined faces obscured by identical long-billed blue baseball caps, the left breast of their identical faded khaki shirts bulky with the same .45 stuffed into the same shoulder holster—that it was not surprising to see them zoom into the blue like wing-joined twins.

Geiger's men had learned never to dogfight a Zeke. The Japanese fighter planes were too fast and too maneuverable. Instead, the Marines depended on the armor and firepower of their stubby Grumman-built Wildcats. Two of them flying together could take on five of the enemy. They watched each other's tails, firing quick six-gun bursts at the flashing Zekes; and because the Japanese planes were so thin-skinned and without self-sealing tanks, they flamed easily. The Marines also avoided striking at a Betty bomber's tail, where the guns were. They made overhead passes on them, flashing past the protecting Zekes with sharp bursts, then diving for safety and a pullout.

Lt. Gen. Masao Maruyama arrived on "Death Island," as the Kawaguchi survivors called Guadalcanal, the night of October 4. Maruyama was a proud man, with a haughty chin and aristocratic nose beneath which ran a thin line of mustache as supercilious as a raised eyebrow. A disciplinarian, he was definitely displeased with Col. Akinosuke Oka for allowing the Kawaguchi wretches to mingle with the splendid soldiers of his 4th Regiment and infect them with their pessimism. He berated Oka for having allowed the Marines to get away so cheaply on September 27. The day after he arrived, Maruyama was given a letter written by a soldier of the 4th and intercepted by his commanding officer. It said:

The news I hear worries me. It seems as if we have suffered considerable damage and casualties. They might be exaggerated, but it is pitiful. Far away from our home country a fearful battle is raging. What these soldiers say is something of the supernatural and cannot be believed as human stories.

Enraged, Maruyama put out the following general order:

From now on the occupying of Guadalcanal Island is under the observations of the whole world. Do not expect to return, not even one man, if the occupation is not successful. Everyone must remember the honor of the Emperor, fear no enemy, yield to no material matters, show the strong points of steel or of rocks, and advance valiantly and ferociously. Hit the enemy opponents so hard they will not be able to get up again.

While awaiting the arrival of his other troops, the 16th and 29th Regiments, his heavy artillery, and a few thousand men of a naval landing force, he began to plan his advance across the Matanikau. He, too, had seized on the importance of its east bank. He would need it as a jumping-off point for his main attack on the airfield. In the meantime, he also searched his map for a suitable place to receive the surrender of the American General Vandegrift.

Vandegrift on that same afternoon of October 5 was also studying his maps, not, however, for suitable surrender scenes but for another strike across the Matanikau. He simply could not allow the enemy to build his forces there. This time he would send five full battalions across the river under Red Mike Edson, now commander of the Fifth, and Col. "Wild Bill" Whaling of the special scout-snipers group.

The operation began smoothly enough, and Edson succeeded in annihilating a trapped enemy unit. But a drenching downpour next day enmired the troops of both sides, and after the coast watchers radioed a warning that a mighty invasion force was making up at Rabaul, Vandegrift was compelled to recall his forces. Nevertheless, he sent Chesty Puller out on reconnaissance again.

That afternoon Puller led his men across a series of grassy ridges until, pausing atop the highest, he saw that a ravine below him was swarming with Japanese. At the same moment he received orders to scout the coastal road toward Kukumbona and avoid combat. He asked and obtained permission to stay where he was, for he had found a whole battalion under his guns.

The ravine became a slaughter pen.

Marine mortars fell with deadly accuracy. They forced the Japanese to come swarming up one side of the ridge into the massed firepower of Puller's men. They fled back down into the ravine, sometimes rolling down in their terror, and went sprinting through that devastating hell of mortar fire in an attempt to escape up the other side. But when they emerged, they were in full view of the Americans and were once again riddled.

Pitifully, pathetically, they ran the same gantlet again, but in reverse, and this time the carnage was thickened by the artillery shells and aerial bombs Puller called down upon them. Fully 700 men fell in that hideous trap. General Maruyama's attempt to seize the Matanikau's east bank had met disaster. Roughly another 200 casualties were inflicted on the 4th Regiment by Edson's and Whaling's converging forces. The 4th was shattered; now Nakaguma's men had horror stories of their own to tell their comrades when they also arrived on Death Island.

Marines withdrawing from the Matanikau—bringing with them their 65 dead and 125 wounded—heard overhead the roaring of massed motors. Glancing up, they saw the Yankee star on silver fuselages. Maj. Leonard (Duke) Davis was bringing Squadron 122 to the Cactus Shivaree. Riding in the cockpit of one of these twenty Wildcats was a blunt-featured, cigar-smoking, high-spirited captain named Joseph Jacob Foss.

"Pistol Pete" was coming to Guadalcanal. This was the collective nickname the Marines had pinned on Maruygama's big guns, those 150-mm howitzers with which he planned to chew up Henderson Field and chastise the Americans. On October 10 four of them went aboard a seaplane tender at Rabaul. Next day they sailed south in the company of destroyer-transports carrying more of the Sendai Division, cargo ships, a protecting screen of destroyers and a division of cruisers with which to shell Henderson and its defenders while the guns, men and supplies were being put ashore.

Waiting for them off Cape Esperance was Rear Adm. Norman Scott with four cruisers and five destroyers of his own.

Once again the island of Guadalcanal quivered like a live thing. Once more the night glowed with the glare of burning ships while concussion waves rolled in thunder across blackly gleaming water. Marines ashore threw aside ponchos or clawed their way out of mosquito nets to rush in frantic, jostling groups for the safety of their gunpits. Alexander Vandegrift went to his headquarters tent to sit there in silent, anguished vigil beneath the light of a single blue electric bulb.

Rear Adm. Aritomo Goto's bombardment and invasion force sailing down the Slot had collided with Scott's fighting force coming up. Scott "crossed the T" —that is put his ships standing broadside to the oncoming enemy so that all his guns were swiveled and trained starboard upon a Japanese column "now visible to the naked eye."

Heavy *Salt Lake City*'s 8-inchers sent ten full salvos shrieking through the black toward cruiser *Furutaka.* They broke her in two and sank her. Heavy *San Francisco* with the lights *Boise* and *Helena,* together with the five destroyers, rained shells upon the others. Big *Aoba,* Admiral Goto's flagship, took forty hits. She staggered out of the battle with Goto dying on his bridge and half his crew dead. Big destroyer *Fubuki* sank to the bottom. Destroyer-transports sank. In the morning, planes from Henderson Field swooped down on big destroyers *Natsugumo* and *Murakama* and sank them. The American destroyer *Duncan* also perished, shot at by both sides. *Boise* had two gun turrets burned out. But Alexander Vandegrift's vigil had ended in exaltation. Colonel Thomas rushed into his tent to tell him that Norman Scott had avenged Savo Island. Iron Bottom Bay was no longer a Japanese lake. The navy was coming back, in strength, and reinforcements were on their way.

But at Kukumbona to the west, General Maruyama gave orders for emplacing four big guns with their tractors. Pistol Pete had survived the holocaust of the Battle of Cape Esperance.

On the morning of October 12 the Marines were astounded to find the army there. The 164th Infantry Regiment had arrived on Guadalcanal from Noumea, just in time for a fiery baptism of fire such as no Guadalcanal Marine had ever experienced.

Because the Australian coast watchers on Bougainville fleeing heavy Japanese patrols were keeping radio silence, there were no advance warnings of three heavy air raids. At noon, twenty-four Betty bombers escorted by Zekes hit Henderson Field before the defending Wildcats could climb to interceptor stations. A storm of bombs and incendiary bullets set stores of aviation gasoline on fire. Two hours later fifteen more bombers arrived unannounced, multiplying destruction and intensifying the 164th's ordeal. Capt. Joe Foss shot down one of the escorting Zekes—his first—took a bullet in his oil pump and came plummeting down from 22,000 feet with a trio of Zekes riding his tail. When the third formation struck, it unloaded on the very coconut grove in which the 164th had bivouacked. To add insult to injury, a swarm of raggedy Marine scarecrows (since August 7 they had suffered an average weight loss of forty pounds per man) who had been unloading ships fell with looting light fingers on the soldiers' duffel bags.

The Doggies had been blooded in more ways than one.

At dusk, Sgt. Butch Morgan was preparing General Vandegrift's dinner. He was frying meat on the upended Japanese safe he used as a griddle.

Crrrrrash!

Sergeant Morgan dropped his spatula, seized his helmet and made for the air-raid shelter. There was another explosion. Vandegrift looked up thoughtfully.

"That wasn't a bomb," he called to the embarrassed Morgan. "That's artillery."

Sgt. Morgan, a veteran of the last war, glanced around him shamefaced. "Aw, hell," he muttered, removing his helmet. "Only artillery."

It wasn't "only artillery," it was Pistol Pete, speaking with enough authority to reach the airfield. For the first time Henderson's runways were subjected to shelling, and Pistol Pete ripped up the big strip with a thoroughness that made night flight impossible. Then he shifted sights to hammer the perimeter, swinging to Kukum to blow up naval stores—and finally falling on the men of the 164th with such rending red terror that a sergeant crawled about begging his men to shoot him.

And then the same terror came upon all the island.

Red flares shot up from the jungle, Pistol Pete roared and roared, enemy aircraft circled overhead—drifting in and out of the crisscrossing searchlight beams that sought them, eluding the flak and dropping bombs—and men stumbled into foxholes, climbed out of them, ran back to them, bracing in expectation of they knew not what.

At 1:30 in the morning Louie the Louse planted a green flare over the airfield, and the Night of the Battleships began.

Mighty *Haruna* and *Kongo* had steamed down from Rabaul. Cruisers and destroyers came with them, some to join the airfield bombardment, others to protect seven transports loaded with General Maruyama's remaining troops.

They slid into the bay, screened by cruiser *Isuzu* and eight destroyers. They awaited the flares of the ground troops, the patrol plane's green light. Then: "Commence firing!"

Star shells rose, horrible and bright, scarlet with the fat red beauty of Hell, exploding like giant ferris wheels to shower the night with streamers of light. And then, the 14-inchers of the battleships, the 8-inchers of *Isuzu,* the 5-inchers of the destroyers . . .

Pah-boom, pah-boom. Pah-boom, pah-boom, pah—

Men in their holes could hear the soft hollow thumping of the salvos to seaward, see the flashes shimmering outside the gun ports, and then the great airy boxcars rumbling overhead, wailing and straining—*hwoo-hwoee*—seeming to lose breath directly overhead, to pause, whisper, and go on. Then the triple tearing crash of the detonating shells and the bucking and rearing of the very ground beneath them.

American troops had never before been exposed to such cannonading and would never be so again. Even the great naval shellings that would one day fall upon the Japanese would not be comparable, for the Japanese would be in coral caves or huge pillboxes of ferroconcrete, while these Americans crouched in dirt holes, within shelters of mud and logs.

Henderson Field's bombers were blown to bits, set afire, crushed beneath collapsed revetments. Shelters shivered, sighed and came apart. Foxholes buried their occupants. Men were killed—forty-one of them, among them many pilots —and many, many more men were wounded. But the overall effect upon men's souls was devastating.

In that cataclysm, when every shell seemed to explode with the pent-up flame and fury of a full thunderstorm, some men might glance at their buddies and see in horror how their features had dissolved in a nerveless idiot mask. Men whimpered aloud. Others burst into sobs and rushed from the pits rather than betray their weakness, if such it was, before comrades. Some men put their weapons to their heads.

The bombardment lasted an hour and twenty minutes, and then *Haruna* and *Konga* and their nine sister furies masked their guns and sailed north.

The bombers remained until dawn.

And at dawn Pistol Pete resumed action.

The airfield was a shambles. The main strip was unusable. Of thirty-eight bombers, only four survived the shelling. But these four went roaring skyward from Fighter Strip 1 to strike at the Japanese transports, which had put Maruyama's troops ashore during the night. They sank one, and flew back to an airfield where Marine engineers and Seabees were already hauling fill to the big strip. Bulldozers were butting earth into yawning shell craters and anxious squadron commanders were conferring with repair officers on the chances of getting airborne.

They patched together ten bombers that day. They filled gas tanks by hand, hauled bomb trailers by hand, and lifted the big eggs into the racks with straining, sweating bodies. They did this while Japanese bombers swept over Henderson Field again and again, for Cactus Air Force must be ready to go by the next day, when the remaining Japanese cargo ships would surely return to unload General Maruyama's supplies.

And then it was discovered that they were running out of gasoline.

Not even the arrival of six more Dauntlesses that afternoon of October 14 raised the drooping spirits of men who heard that news.

General Geiger began issuing orders. He sent a flight of army B-17s back to Espiritu Santo, for the Flying Fortresses drank too much gasoline. He ordered the tanks of wrecked planes drained. He sent out a search party to find a cache of 400 drums of gasoline, which had been buried outside the airfield in the early days. He instructed Marine air transports to fly in nothing but gasoline. He got fast destroyers headed toward Guadalcanal with more drums lashed to their decks. He called off individual fighter sallies to husband his strength, for he wanted to use all that he had at dawn the next day.

But during the night the big cruisers *Chokai* and *Kinugasa* sped down the Slot to enter the bay and hurl 752 8-inch shells into Henderson and its defenders. At dawn, Marines standing atop the southern ridges looked westward to a place called Tassafaronga to contemplate the chilling spectacle of six squat Japanese ships calmly going about the business of unloading supplies.

Behind them on the battered airfield there were but three Dauntless dive-bombers able to fly.

By 10:00 in the morning, after a flurry of single-plane sallies, the patchwork, ragtag Cactus Air Force was rising to the attack. It was incredible. They had no right to be airborne. Departing *Chokai* and *Kinugasa* had assured the transports that American air power was now as defunct in fact as in the communiqués of Imperial Headquarters. But here they were coming with the sun glinting off their wings—Wildcats, Dauntlesses, Avengers, Army P-39s and P-400s, and later Flying Forts from Espiritu. Henderson mechanics had not slept for three days but they had made good their vow to salvage all but bullet holes. Thousand-pound and 500-pound bombs fell among the Japanese ships and beached supplies, bullets flayed and scattered enemy shore parties.

On the night of October 15–16 the heavy cruisers *Myoko* and *Maya* hurled 1,500 shells into Henderson Field on the third straight night of sea bombardment. At daylight of October 16 General Geiger calculated that he had lost forty-one bombers and fighters to Japanese guns in the past three days, plus sixteen more aircraft damaged. He had twenty-five bombers left in flyable condition, once repairs were made to the victims of *Myoko* and *Maya,* but he had only nine fighters. Geiger signaled Efate in the New Hebrides for hurry-up help.

In came nineteen Wildcats and seven more Dauntlesses, led by Lt. Col. Harold (Joe) Bauer—rugged Joe Bauer who had shot down five Japanese aircraft while "visiting Guadalcanal." Bauer's Squadron 212 came in just as the Japanese launched a savage dive-bombing attack on the field and the American ships in the bay. Bauer's gas tanks were nearly empty, but there were eight enemy Vals plummeting down on a wildly zigzagging destroyer.

Bauer went after them alone. He pulled back on the stick and went slashing up through his own antiaircraft fire and then came roaring down again. He shot down four Vals before he landed, and he saved the destroyer. It was swift, as aerial combat goes, but it was then, and has remained, the most extraordinary feat of individual heroism among the Henderson airmen, men who already acclaimed Joe Bauer as the best fighter pilot the Marines had produced. Bauer got a Medal of Honor for it, and it boosted his individual score of kills to eleven.

So ended the six-day ordeal begun with the arrival of Pistol Pete. But Pistol Pete was losing his voice. The airmen had put his shells on the bottom, and this would matter greatly in the tide of battle now flowing back to land.

56. William Frederick Halsey

ON OCTOBER 18 Admiral Halsey led a force of carriers into the harbor at Noumea, New Caledonia. A whaleboat pulled alongside his flagship. An officer came aboard and handed the admiral a manila envelope. It was from Admiral Nimitz. Inside it was another envelope marked SECRET. Halsey ripped it open and read: "You will take command of the South Pacific Area and South Pacific forces immediately."

"Jesus Christ and General Jackson!" Halsey swore. "This is the hottest potato they ever handed me!"

Indeed, fielding hot potatoes, along with a penchant for breaking rules, had been a specialty of William Frederick Halsey, Jr., ever since, as a boy growing up in Elizabeth, New Jersey, he conceived the ambition of following his father into the Naval Academy and thence to sea. In 1897, at fourteen, Halsey wrote to President William McKinley: "I want to ask you, if you have not already promised all your appointments to the Naval Academy that you will give me one." McKinley didn't, but the note was pure Halsey: direct, blunt, unadorned and a little less than regulation English. So Halsey went to the University of Virginia to study medicine, and, more important to him, to play football. As a scrub back he had the distinction of breaking the starting quarterback's leg the day before the big game with Georgetown. As he said later: "They didn't know whether to give me a Medal of Honor or a court-martial."

In the meantime, his mother, with the attorney general of New Jersey as an ally, laid siege to the White House, and her son was finally accepted at Annapolis. But William still thought a man's chief purpose in going to college was to play football. His fondness for the sport, and for "Frenching" into town—that is, shoving off without permission—brought his marks perilously close to the expulsion level. His father urged him to drop football, but William replied that he'd rather "bilge," or flunk. But he did bone up for the impending examination and scored an incredible 3.98, just two decimal points below the 4.0 of perfection. When he announced his grade to his father, that stern sailor scowled at him and shouted: "Sir, have you been drinking?"

In another year, he was graduated from Annapolis, forty-third in a class of sixty-two. As he departed the banks of the Severn, the academy master-at-arms gave him this sour farewell: "Good luck because you'll never be as good a naval officer as your father."

Ensign Halsey's first ship was, oddly enough, the *Missouri*. But this was the "Mizzy" of 12,500 tons, not the awesome "Mighty Mo" of 45,000 tons that would one day be the flagship of his Third Fleet. Still, the *Missouri* was then the most modern ship in the U.S. Navy. It was while he was aboard her that he developed his irrational fear of the thirteenth of any month. On April 13, 1904, during target practice off Pensacola, twenty-six sailors and five officers were roasted alive during a fire in a 12-inch gun turret. Halsey never quite mastered this superstitious dread until Friday, August 13, 1943, when his only son, William Frederick Halsey III, was rescued from a jungle plane crash.

In 1907, Halsey shipped aboard *Kansas,* the newest battleship in the navy. She was the pride of the Great White Fleet that President Theodore Roosevelt sent around the globe to impress the world with emerging Yankee naval power. *Kansas* took Halsey to South America and thence to San Diego, where he marched in a parade. The thin-shanked, thick-chested, beetle-browed and craggy-jawed Halsey was strutting along at the head of his company, when a youngster cried: "Hey, pipe the guy with the face like a bulldog!" The name was apt. Shortened to Bull, it stuck.

Kansas also took Halsey to Japan. There he formed his abiding distrust and hatred of the Japanese people. A man of his directness could not endure their exaggerated politeness. After Japanese sailors had paid Rear Admiral Sperry the peculiar compliment of tossing him gently into the air to soft cries of "Banzai!" Halsey and a few shipmates seized little Togo and heaved him up for what he called "three good ones," that is, way up.

Upon the return of the Great White Fleet, Halsey was promoted to senior lieutenant. More important, he met and fell in love with Frances Cooke Grandy of Norfolk, Virginia. One of her uncles had been the chief engineer aboard the

Merrimac in its historic battle with the *Monitor,* and her relatives were consequently not quite sure they wanted to ship a Yankee sailorman aboard the family
tree. But Halsey persevered in his suit and married her in 1909. They had two
children, Margaret and the third William.

In 1914, after Halsey met the young FDR to begin a lifelong friendship, he
was shocked by the famous Order 99 put out by Navy Secretary Daniels. It
forbade carrying liquor aboard ship, and it sank America's drinking navy, making
it, outside of the Moslem world, the first dry fleet in history. Halsey hated the
order, and said so, though he obeyed it. But he really fractured it shortly before
Pearl Harbor, when he put to sea with 100 gallons of bourbon "for flight surgeons
to issue to pilots." If the issue became as regular as atabrine rations, Bull Halsey
could not care less. He always said: "There are exceptions, of course, but as a
general rule, I never trust a fighting man who doesn't smoke or drink." He would
maintain that belief to the end, throughout Prohibition and in face of the vocal
outrage of the Women's Christian Temperance Union and the Methodist Temperance Board.

During World War I Lieutenant Commander Halsey commanded the Destroyer *Benham,* based at Queenstown in Northern Ireland. He yearned to sink
a German U-boat. But he never did. When he claimed that he had sunk one with
depth charges, it turned out to have been a buoy. For this he was called "the Duke
of Aberdeen," and some of his sailors sang:

> *"Last night over by Aberdeen*
> *I saw a German submarine.*
> *The funniest sight I ever seen*
> *Was old Bull Halsey's submarine."*

Commander Halsey stayed in destroyers after the war, and in 1921 he won
the most resounding "simulated" naval battle in history. He was in temporary
command of a squadron of eighteen destroyers during maneuvers against four
battleships off Long Beach, California, and if he had busted a rule or two before,
this time he splintered the set. He bracketed the battlewagons between his two
columns of destroyers and let go with thirty-six practice torpedoes. Twenty-two
connected, and though they were fitted with soft metal noses to prevent harm to
the target ship, they were fired so close-in and so accurately that they did $1.5
million damage. Halsey had not only enraged the red-faced battleship skippers,
he had infuriated the pinchpenny Congress of that era.

When Halsey left his destroyers to take up his new post with Naval Intelligence in Washington, his relief asked to see his records. Straight-faced, Halsey
handed over "the files"—one folder containing one brief, angry letter addressed
to members of a liberty party who were late getting back to the ship.

"I hate paper work," Halsey explained.

Thereafter, Bull Halsey filled the years between wars as they were being filled
by other professional army and navy officers. There was a tour of duty as naval

attaché in Germany, Norway, Sweden and Denmark, sea duty again as exec of the battleship *Wyoming,* three years as a full captain commanding the Annapolis station ship, a few more years of study at the Naval War College and a year at the Army's War College, and then, in 1934, the big decision of his career.

He applied for flight training.

He was fifty-one years old, he was a grandfather, and he had bad eyes, but he wangled the assignment to Pensacola, swore off drinking for a year—and went winging it into the wild blue yonder.

He did it, of course, in the Halsey manner, that is, against all the rules. Because of his imperfect eyesight, he was restricted to the student observer's course, but in some unknown way, he wound up in the student pilot's course. His instructor, then Lt. Bromfield Nichol, never knew just how the controls passed from his hands into those of Captain Halsey. And, as Nichol recalls, he had an unorthodox approach to flying, distinguished by the fact that "the worse the weather, the better he flew." While at Pensacola, Halsey earned, in addition to his wings, the Order of the Flying Jackass. He won the aluminum breastplate formed like a jackass twice, once for barreling into a boundary light, and again for landing on his back. When another student won this booby prize and Halsey was asked to relinquish it, he replied: "No, I want to keep it. I'm going to put it on the bulkhead of my cabin, and if anybody aboard does anything stupid, I'll take a look at the Jackass before I bawl him out."

The Flying Jackass was installed in the skipper's cabin of the carrier *Saratoga,* which was Halsey's next command. Though the *Sara* would become a famous Pacific ship, and though she was then, with her sister carrier, the *Lexington,* the world's largest warship, Halsey never took her into battle. It was the *Enterprise* that he would make famous. Ten days before Pearl Harbor, with the three stars of a vice admiral on his collar, Halsey set out in his flagship, in command of a carrier force bringing reinforcements of Marine planes and pilots to Wake Island.

Hardly out of signal distance from Pearl, he ordered his ships to arm all torpedoes immediately and to load live bombs and torpedoes aboard their planes. Then he issued what is known as Battle Order I:

1—The *Enterprise* is now operating under war conditions.
2—At any time, day or night, we must be ready for instant action.
3—Hostile submarines may be encountered. . . .

Though Halsey knew of the swiftly worsening relations between the United States and Japan, both nations were still at peace when he issued those instructions. His operations officer, Commander Buracker, thought they were proof that the Old Man had blown his top.

"Admiral," he cried, waving the order, "did you authorize this thing?"
"Yes."
"Do you realize that this means war?"
"Yes."

"Goddamit, Admiral, you can't start a private war! Who's going to take the responsibility?"

"I'll take it!" Halsey snapped. "Let's shoot first, and argue afterward!"

But it was the Japanese who shot first.

When Admiral Halsey sailed back into Pearl Harbor at dusk on December 8, his Task Force 8 was the only American striking force of any consequence left afloat, and he had to put hurriedly to sea the next morning to begin patrol duty off Pearl. Halsey discovered immediately that the enemy was not the Japanese, but the hysteria that had come aboard during that one-day layover in disaster. Lookouts were reporting enemy subs or vessels from every quarter. Every porpoise was a torpedo, every white cap a periscope and every bird a dive-bomber. One day a young officer on the *Enterprise*'s bridge shouted in alarm as a destroyer, riding a big wave off the carrier's beam, dropped out of sight as she dipped into the trough.

"Look!" he yelled to Halsey. "She's sinking! There she goes!"

Halsey whirled on the excitable young man and bellowed, "If you ever make another report like that, sir, I'll throw you over the side!"

There was no more crying wolf. But the spirit of defeatism continued to plague the U.S. Navy in the Pacific. It was up to Halsey to end this, too. On February 1, the ships and planes of Task Force 8 made a surprise attack on the Japanese-held Marshall Islands and on Makin in the Gilberts. The day before the strike, a Japanese patrol plane came within forty miles of the task force, but somehow managed to miss sighting it. Elated, Halsey had this message printed for delivery to the enemy at the start of battle the next morning:

"From the American admiral in charge of the striking force, to the Japanese admiral on the Marshall Islands: It is a pleasure to thank you for having your patrol plane not sight my force."

Frivolous?

No. Halsey hoped the message would bring the execution of the erring pilot and remove one more enemy from action.

The Japanese were completely surprised. Halsey launched no fewer than six strikes, the first flying off just before daybreak beneath a full moon. Again breaking the rules, Halsey brought his carriers close inshore, within sight of the enemy's burning installations. His pilots sank sixteen Japanese ships and damaged two more, shooting fifty planes out of the sky and damaging many more on the ground.

It was a splendid victory. Inevitably, however, the Japanese struck back. Five Betty bombers flying at crow's-nest level came at *Enterprise,* straight at Halsey on the bridge. The admiral ingloriously hit the deck. The enemy bombs were near-misses. Halsey arose, glancing around him sheepishly. A burning Betty came at him again, diving for a row of patrol planes. Again, Halsey dived for cover. The Betty barely missed, striking the edge of the flight deck and toppling into the sea. Halsey came erect to glare at Yeoman First Class Ira Bowman, shaking with laughter at the admiral's discomfiture. Halsey pointed at Bowman and roared:

"Make that man a chief! Any man who can grin like that when my knees are cracking together deserves to be promoted."

Task Force 8 received a hero's welcome back at Pearl, and Nimitz assigned Halsey to a second hit-and-run raid. The target was to be Wake, which had fallen to the Japs. The task force number was 13 and the sortie was set for February 13th—a Friday! Bull Halsey read the orders with horror. He got in touch with Nimitz.

"My God, Chester, have you got it in for me?"

So the designation was changed to Task Force 16 and the date to February 14—and the results were as anticipated. Wake was plastered. Then, on March 4, Marcus Island (now Minimi Tori Shima), only 999 miles from Tokyo, got more of the same. The effect on Japan's ballooning self-esteem was far out of proportion to the damage caused to Marcus by Halsey's ships and planes. It reached all the way to Tokyo, where there was an air-raid alert and a blackout, and no one has ever estimated how much Marcus had to do with disrupting Japan's overall war strategy.

Back home in America, and aboard all the Yankee ships at sea, the effect on morale was enormous. Sinking spirits soared and Halsey became a national idol. He liked the limelight, and he was not unwilling to point out that he had succeeded because he had broken a few rules.

"The reason we brought off these early raids," he was to explain later, "is that we violated all the rules and traditions of naval warfare. We did the exact opposite of what the enemy expected. We did not keep our carriers behind the battle; we deliberately exposed them to shore-based planes. Most important, whatever we did, we did fast."

During the next two months Halsey was in the hospital recovering from dermatitis. Though he preferred to blame it on the sun—he had been practically living on the bridge for six straight months—he admitted that it might also be due to nerves. Between the time when his war birds were launched and the time they returned, Adm. Bull Halsey was always a mighty jumpy man—smoking cigarettes or twirling them nervously, drinking endless cups of coffee, pacing, fretting, refusing to relax. His affliction had already cost him twenty pounds and reduced his sleeping hours to two or three in every twenty-four. So he went on the sick list, and while he recovered, the U.S. Navy fought the crucial Battle of Midway.

Midway was the only major Pacific battle that Adm. Bull Halsey had missed. But now, on October 18, 1942, standing on the bridge of *Enterprise,* he realized that he was in command of a struggle which could have even farther-reaching consequences. For the Japanese, as he well knew, had given absolute and overriding priority to the campaign to recapture the first Japanese-held soil lost to the Americans.

Even the overland campaign to capture Port Moresby in New Guinea, which had begun so promisingly for General Hyakutake, was now on indefinite hold.

57. The Battle for New Guinea

ON JULY 21, 1942, General Douglas MacArthur left Melbourne, Australia, for his new headquarters in Brisbane farther to the north. Brisbane was closer to Port Moresby. This vital harbor, so near to the Australian mainland, had been saved from seaborne invasion by the Battle of the Coral Sea. But Gen. Haruyoshi Hyakutake in Rabaul had already ordered Gen. Tomitaro Horii's elite South Seas Detachment of 16,000 men to stand by for movement to New Guinea. They were to land at Buna on the north coast and march 150 miles overland to Port Moresby.

General MacArthur also had plans for Buna. He wanted to build an airfield there. It would be the first step in the mission assigned him by the Joint Chiefs: to reduce the strategic Japanese naval base at Rabaul by advancing along New Guinea's northeastern coast and up the ladder of the northern Solomons. Before MacArthur left Melbourne, intercepts of Japanese messages had suggested an enemy landing would be made at Buna July 21. But Gen. Richard K. Sutherland, MacArthur's autocratic chief of staff, and Col. Charles A. Willoughby, his fawning intelligence officer, gave no credence to these "rumors."

On that day—seventeen days before the Marines landed on Guadalcanal—MacArthur's special train left Melbourne for Brisbane. The Southwest Pacific commander traveled in a special maroon-colored car. It had been built for the Prince of Wales's visit to Australia and still bore the royal coat of arms. Behind it were two flatbed cars, one for MacArthur's handsome Packard limousine, gleaming in the afternoon sun, and the other for General Sutherland's only less splendid Cadillac. Thus, like Tolstoy's Count Bezukhov going off to fight the French with a manservant and silver samovar, did these two American generals ride closer to the smell of gunpowder.

On the following morning they arrived in Brisbane to be informed that the Japanese had landed on Buna the day before. MacArthur was not terribly dismayed. His staff had assured him (erroneously) that the Australians defending Moresby outnumbered General Horii's troops. MacArthur remembered the Aussies of the last war as brave and daring soldiers. But then the speed of the Japanese advance alarmed him. The first fifty miles from Buna to Kokoda, of course, were not especially difficult. But the final hundred miles over the Kokoda Trail to Moresby was held by the Australians and was over some of the most forbidding terrain on earth.

Not even Guadalcanal's dripping rain forests and jumbles of rock-ribbed ridges could rival the punishing steeps and tangles of the Owen Stanleys. Jagged mountain peaks always shrouded in heavy mists rose to heights of over 13,000 feet. Beneath them were steep rocky gorges down which turbulent rivers flowed

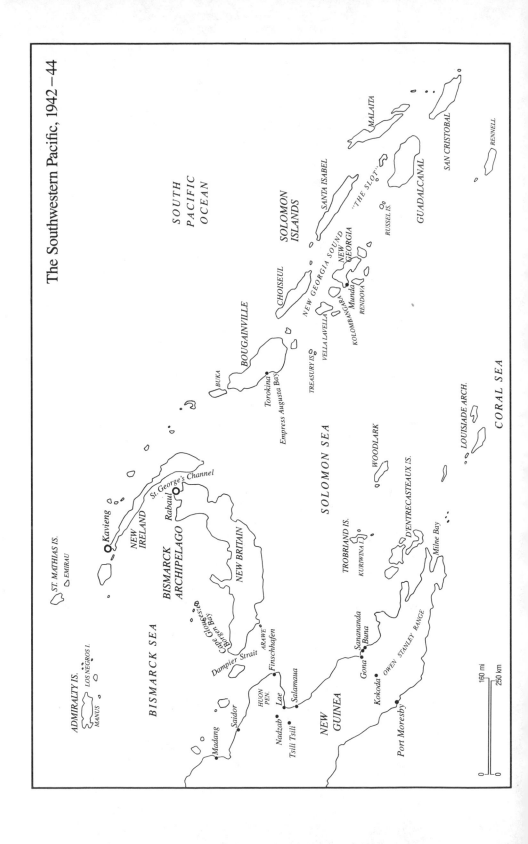

The Southwestern Pacific, 1942—44

in frothing white rapids, leaping and cascading to the sea in spectacular, roaring waterfalls. Everywhere there was the jungle, even on the mountaintops. Almost always there was rain or the jungle's interminable drip. In the monsoon, the downpour was continuous. The so-called Kokoda Trail was nothing more than a primitive track of slippery mud and cruel rock. In some places it climbed the ledges almost vertically. At others it was so narrow that only a single man could pass. "There are mists creeping over the trees all day and sometimes you can't see your hand in front of your face under cover of the jungle," one Australian soldier wrote. "Most of our chaps haven't seen a Jap! You don't see the Jap who gets you!" Seventy-five percent of the troops fighting on the Kokoda Trail never saw a single Japanese.

Nor could the outnumbered Australians stop the enemy advance. Slowly but inexorably the Japanese rolled them back. By mid-September Horii's troops were on the Imita Range in the southern foothills of the Owen Stanleys, the last defensible barrier before Port Moresby.

MacArthur was stunned. Instead of launching his own advance on the enemy bastion at Rabaul, he found himself desperately defending the last Allied foothold on New Guinea. He blamed the Australians. He concluded that they "won't fight." Superficial inspections of "the front" by Sutherland and others—as though this supercilious comfort-loving commander would ever have tried the misery of the Kokoda—reinforced this belief. A staff officer told Admiral Nimitz that New Guinea was "gone." The huge island of New Guinea—second largest in the world after Greenland, 322,000 square miles—gone! And only a hundred miles away was the mainland of Australia itself. It was reiterated that the Australians "won't fight."

General Arnold got the impression that "the Australian is not a bushman, he is not a field soldier. He is nothing but a city slum dweller." Such artful libels on the character of the doughty Diggers, among the bravest, toughest and heartiest troops in the world, were soon to be shown for what they really were—an attempt to transfer blame—when the Japanese tried to land on Milne Bay at the eastern-most tip of New Guinea. Australians based there, assisted by American combat engineers, stopped the enemy dead in a drenching downpour that immobilized even tanks. Then they forced them to evacuate.

But MacArthur was still unimpressed, and he sent General Sir Thomas Blamey north to "vitalize" the allegedly listless Diggers.

In mid-September, while the Japanese astride the Imita Range stood poised for the final push into Port Moresby, the Battle of Bloody Ridge was fought on Guadalcanal, and the slaughter of the Kawaguchi Brigade during that crucial struggle had a direct bearing on the Port Moresby operation. Aware, now, that he must give his undivided attention to Guadalcanal, General Hyakutake ordered General Horii to withdraw as far back as Kokoda. Then, when the deteriorating situation on Guadalcanal brought fears of an American invasion at the coastal village of Buna in Horii's rear, thus trapping him between two forces, some of his units were sent to Buna to take up defensive positions.

Now the Australians launched their own counteroffensive. Reinforced and resupplied, they pushed the Japanese steadily back, recapturing Kokoda by the end of October. At Oivi farther down the trail, they found room for maneuver and turned the Japanese left flank. Driving into the enemy rear they killed General Horii, threw his troops into confusion, captured their food and equipment and pushed them back to the village of Gona.

The Japanese were now concentrated in three of the north coast villages: Buna, Sanananda and Gona. The Australians were assigned the conquest of the latter two while the U.S. 32nd Infantry Division was to reduce Buna. Two regiments—the 126th and 128th Infantry—under Maj. Gen. Edward Harding were moved from Milne Bay and Moresby to the north coast.

The situation was now the reverse of Guadalcanal: The Americans were on the assault and the Japanese were dug in. Invasion from the sea was too risky. There were not enough landing craft, there were treacherous shoals offshore and Buna was within easy range of Japanese aircraft at Lae and Salamaua. Because of these hazards, Vice Adm. Arthur Carpender, MacArthur's naval commander, refused to risk his ships.

Landward approaches to Buna were through dense jungle and swamp passable only along certain trails. The Japanese fortified these with a cleverly concealed network of bunkers. Each of them was "a fortress in miniature. Some are strengthened by great sheets of armor and by concrete. . . . protected from our fire and bombs by sawn logs and felled trees which form a barrier six, ten and sometimes fifteen feet thick. The logs are held in place by great metal stakes and filled in with earth in which the natural growth of the jungle has continued, providing perfect camouflage. . . . From every trench or pit or pillbox, all approaches are covered by wide fields of sweeping fire along fixed lines."

General Harding sent his troops into this formidable labyrinth on November 19, and they were gunned to the ground. They tried again on the 21st and met the same storm of fire. MacArthur ordered Harding to take Buna at all costs. It was a cruel command, made without knowledge of the enemy's advantages and the American disadvantages. Harding had already given three of his battalions to the Australians attacking Sanananda, and he had no heavy artillery, no tanks and no flamethrowers. Most of his supplies had been lost to enemy air attacks. He had only a few light mountain guns and some mortars with which to lay down a preparatory bombardment, and the shells from these actually bounced off the roofs of the Japanese bunkers. Still, Harding sent his men forward, and they failed once again. Angry, MacArthur contemplated bringing up his 41st Division then training in Australia; but then he was stung by General Blamey, who, taking a small revenge, insisted on having Australians "because he knew they would fight." Instead, MacArthur sent Sutherland and a few staff officers to Buna. Their report blamed Harding for poor leadership and said Buna did not fall because "the Americans weren't showing the fight that they should. . . ." Harding, of course, had pleaded in vain for tanks and artillery, and the troops had taken appalling casualties. Nevertheless, Harding was relieved and replaced by Lt. Gen. Robert L. Eichelberger.

MacArthur bade Eichelberger farewell with the cheerful admonition: "Go out there, Bob, and take Buna, or don't come back alive!" He meant every word of it, if only because by then, with his own forces failing in his first offensive on land, the Marines and the Navy had turned the tide at Guadalcanal.

58. Guadalcanal—Part V

ONLY A FEW DAYS BEFORE Admiral Halsey took command of the South Pacific Area, Admiral Yamamoto convened an army-navy conference at Truk. He informed General Hyakutake that in order to retake Guadalcanal, he would receive the complete support of the Combined Fleet: four carriers, four battleships, eight cruisers, twenty-eight destroyers, four oilers and three cargo ships. Hyakutake was no longer displeased with the southern Solomons assignment, and he was in high spirits when he came ashore at Guadalcanal the night of October 17 to take command.

He made straight for Maruyama's headquarters. Maruyama gave him his battle plan. Hyakutake read it carefully. In the dim light, with his thin face and great round eyeglasses, Hyakutake looked something like a lemur. He approved Maruyama's plan. It called for two thrusts—a tank-led assault across the sandbar at the mouth of the Matanikau, and a flanking movement at Nippon Bridge— plus a surprise crusher from the hills south of the airfield. Maruyama not only counted on surprise but also hoped to pierce the enemy line without a fight. The Sendai intelligence officer, Lieutenant Colonel Matsumoto, having failed to obtain information on this sector by torturing a captured Marine, had beheaded the American in the honorable way and then turned to searching enemy bodies. On one of them he found a map showing numerous gaps south of the airfield. Delighted, Maruyama had had Matsumoto's map copied for all of the Sendai officers. Then he and Hyakutake agreed that the American, Vandegrift, should surrender his sword at the mouth of the Matanikau.

News that a fighter had at last taken command in Noumea was greeted with jubilation by the Marines on Guadalcanal. To Alexander Vandegrift news of Halsey's appointment lifted a stone from his heart. A month earlier, while the Battle of Bloody Ridge was raging, Admiral Ghormley had informed him that he could no longer support him. Vandegrift had been so shocked that he had instructed Colonel Thomas to make secret plans for guerrilla warfare from the hills in the event of having to abandon the airfield. Vandegrift wanted neither evacuation nor surrender. Later he had learned that Ghormley had given the visiting Admiral Nimitz the same pessimistic estimate, and Nimitz had flown back to Pearl Harbor shocked by Ghormley's lack of fighting spirit. *But now they had Halsey!* Who better?

Unfortunately, the tenacity and valor of Vandegrift and Halsey and the men they commanded was not shared in Washington. There, the day after Halsey's appointment, Navy Secretary Frank Knox called a press conference. He was asked if the Marines could hold.

"I certainly hope so," the secretary replied. "I expect so. I don't want to make any predictions, but every man out there, ashore or afloat, will give a good account of himself."

Knox's coy little pep talk was received by the Marines on Guadalcanal with that splendid disdain that would always sustain them.

"Didja hear about Knox? He says he don't know, but we're sure gonna give a good account of ourselves."

"Yeah, I heard. Ain't he a tiger?"

Cutting of the Maruyama Road had been slowed considerably. During the first three days, twenty miles of trail had been opened through the foothills of the Lunga Mountains. But then, General Maruyama's pioneers had blundered into a maze of gorges and deep ravines. Only a small patrol could have penetrated this tangle of rock and ridge, creeper and vine, but not a full division loaded down with full marching gear weighing at least sixty pounds, plus the 30-pound artillery shell that each man carried. Handholds had to be cut in the cliffs and the guns hauled up by rope. Many guns were left behind. Rain fell constantly. Advance troops found the going comparatively easy, but they left a churned-up mush for those who followed. Gaps appeared in the column and Maruyama had to call repeated halts to close them. His men weakened daily, barely subsisting on the one-third ration he was compelled to impose after so much of his supplies was sunk. He signaled Hyakutake to ask the navy for a week's postponement. To soften the bad news, he suggested to his chief that General Vandegrift's surrender offer must be accepted at once, and that the American must come to the river mouth alone but for an interpeter.

General Hyakutake was extremely annoyed by Maruyama's slow progress. He was going to order the Matanikau attacks himself. Admirals Nagumo and Kondo had grown churlish. Would soldiers never learn that steamships sailed on oil? The Combined Fleet could not remain much longer at sea. On the afternoon of October 21 Hyakutake at last ordered Pistol Pete to begin pounding the Marines on the ridge overlooking the sandbar at the Matanikau river mouth.

Newly arrived Marine Long Toms—5-inch rifles—answered, and Pistol Pete was badly shaken. Two of the Japanese 150s were silenced and the others forced to change position. When eleven tanks burst from a sheltering tunnel cut in the jungle across the river, followed by Nakagama's 4th Regiment, the Long Toms joined lighter howitzers to destroy the lead tank and send the remaining ten clanking back the way they had come. Nakagama's men swarmed after them.

Hyakutake was furious. Nakagama had not only been mauled, Colonel Oka upstream by Nippon Bridge had not moved. Hyakutake told Oka he had better get across the river to hit the enemy's refused left flank by the night of October 23 or else. Malingerers were to be shot. Hyakutake hoped that by this time Maruyama would be in position to strike. But he wasn't. And Oka was still dragging his feet. Only Nakagama attacked.

Nakagama was one of those "bamboo spear" commanders of whom the Japanese army had an abundance. He would attack under any conditions. He scorned living to fight another day and would look upon death before defeat. So he sent his men into the concentrated fire of ten Marine artillery batteries, into the murderous interlocking fire of machine guns, rifles and automatic weapons. They were like swarms of moths seeking to blot out the light with their exploding bodies. They matched flesh against fire and steel and were torn apart.

General Maruyama was at last ready to attack, and Colonel Oka had finally been goaded into crossing the Matanikau to strike at the exposed Marine left flank there. Both commanders were supremely confident, for both believed that they were moving against a gap in the enemy lines. Maruyama had placed his faith in Matsumoto's map. Why not? How could Maruyama know that the map taken from the dead Marine was actually an American copy of a map taken from a dead Japanese early in August? How could he suspect that the American lettering on it marked positions held by the Japanese before the Marine invasion? How indeed could he have had the slightest inkling that the "gap" he was marching toward was actually a fortified position held by an entire battalion of Marines under Chesty Puller?

At eleven o'clock on the night of October 25 it began to rain in torrents, and the Japanese charged Puller's battalion by the thousands, so many of them that the sodden ground shook beneath their feet. They hit the barbed wire even as Marine guns erupted in a bedlam of firing.

Japanese fell on the wire, others hurled themselves upon it while their comrades used their bodies as bridges.

Colonel Furumiya was at the head of his troops, shouting and waving his saber. He led the color company—the 7th—through a break in the American wire and went racing with them toward the enemy's guns.

Inspired by the breakthrough, willing to follow their colors into hell, the Japanese soldiers flowed toward the gap.

But the Marines closed it. Colonel Furumiya and the color company were cut off from the rest of the regiment.

Now the attack was veering toward dead center. The Japanese hordes were rushing at Manila John Basilone's machine guns. They came tumbling down an incline, and Basilone's gunners raked them at full trigger. They were pouring out 500 rounds a minute, the gun barrels were red and sizzling inside their water jackets—and the precious water was evaporating swiftly.

"Piss in 'em, piss in 'em!" Basilone yelled, and some of the men jumped up to refill the jackets with a different liquid.

The guns stuttered on, tumbling the onrushing Japanese down the incline, piling them up so high that by the time the first enemy flood had begun to ebb and flow back into the jungle, they had blocked Basilone's field of fire. In the lull Manila John ordered his men out to push the bodies away and clear the fire lanes.

Then he ducked out of the pit to run for more ammunition. He ran barefooted, the mud squishing between his toes. He ran into Puller's CP and ran back again burdened with spare barrels and half a dozen fourteen-pound belts slung over his shoulders.

As he did, Furumiya's men drifted west. They overran the guns to Basilone's right. They stabbed two Marines to death and wounded three others. They tried to swing the big Brownings on the Americans, but the guns jammed. They left the pit and drove farther to the rear.

Basilone returned to his pit just as a runner dashed up gasping:

"They've got the guys on the right."

Basilone raced to his right. He ran past a barefoot private named Evans and called Chicken for his tender eighteen years. "C'mon, you yellow bastards!" Chicken screamed, firing and bolting his rifle, firing and reloading. Basilone ran on to the empty pit, jumped in, found the guns jammed and sprinted back to his own pit.

Seizing a mounted machine gun, Basilone spread-eagled it across his back, shouted at half of his men to follow him—and was gone. A squad of men took off in pursuit. They caught Basilone at a bend in the trail and blundered into a half dozen Japanese soldiers. They killed them and ran on.

Then they were inside the silent pit, firing the gun that Basilone had brought, while Manila John lay on his back in the mud working frantically to free the jammed guns.

Beyond the wire in the covering jungle, the Sendai were massing for another charge.

Chesty Puller called Col. Pedro del Valle, the artillery commander, to ask all the support possible.

"I'll give you all you call for, Puller," del Valle said. "But God knows what'll happen when the ammo we have is gone."

"If we don't need it now, we'll never need it. If they get through here tonight, there won't be a tomorrow."

"She's yours as long as she lasts."

Both men hung up and the Marine artillery glowed red again.

It was 1:30 in the morning, and the Sendai were coming again, there was a white breath around the muzzles of the Marine 105s, and Basilone had his guns fixed.

He rolled from gun to gun, firing, exhausting first one belt and then another, while his men worked wildly to scrape the mud from cartridges that had been dragged along soggy trails. And the Sendai rolled forward in even greater strength, with both wings charging, now, punching holes in the Marine lines, forcing General Geiger in the rear—now in command while Vandegrift conferred with Halsey in Noumea—to counter with his reserve, and leading General Maruyama to radio the one signal that all Japan was waiting for:

"Banzai!"

General Hyakutake heard it with elation back in Kukumbona and he relayed it north to Adm. Gunichi Mikawa in Rabaul. Mikawa immediately ordered three large destroyers carrying the Koli detachment to land these troops on eastern Guadalcanal as scheduled.

And Combined Fleet's carriers turned south again.

At 3:30 General Maruyama hurled his third charge at the Americans—and this time his men heard for the first time the eight-round semiautomatic firing of Garand rifles in the hands of American soldiers.

The 164th Infantry was in action.

General Geiger had fed its 3rd Battalion under Lt. Col. Robert Hall into the battle. Hall's soldiers marched from their bivouac behind the Tenaru to the front, sloshing through the streaming darkness guided by a navy chaplain, Father Keough, the only man at headquarters who knew the way.

By seven o'clock in the morning, the Sendai had stopped coming.

Nearly a thousand of them had stopped living. They lay in sodden heaps outside and partly within the American wire. One column of Japanese dead lay opposite a section of antitank guns. They were in perfect formation, each man laying halfway atop the man in front of him—felled in a single sweep like a row of wooden soldiers.

Within the jungle, General Maruyama beheld his survivors: bands of dazed and hollow-eyed men stumbling woodenly back to their assembly areas. Nowhere could Maruyama find Colonel Furumiya. Obviously, the airfield was still American.

Masao Maruyama got off a message to General Hyakutake indicating that he was "having difficulty" capturing the field.

And then Dugout Sunday began.

59. Guadalcanal—Part VI

THAT THUNDERING SABBATH of October 25 was called Dugout Sunday because only those engaged in battle dared to stray from their dugouts. It was set in motion by Masao Maruyama's premature victory vaunt. Although he subsequently modified his "Banzai!" message to an admission of "difficulty" at 7:00 in the morning and then to one of outright defeat that afternoon, the Japanese

Combined Fleet had begun its assignment in the joint land-sea-air attack that was designed to crush the Americans.

Airplanes flew off northern airfields or carrier decks to obliterate the Cactus Air Force and to sink whatever enemy shipping it could find in Iron Bottom Bay. A landing force aboard three big destroyers—*Akatsuke, Ikazuchi* and *Shiratsuyo* —went speeding down the Slot bound for Koli Point on eastern Guadalcanal, while a cruiser-destroyer force made for a point behind Florida Island to enter the battle on call. Admiral Yamamoto, meanwhile, at first electrified by Maruyama's signal, and then irritated by his retraction, kept the remainder of the Combined Fleet sailing a circle 300 miles north of Guadalcanal. He had been made wary by reports of a big American carrier-surface force coming up to the island from southern bases.

So it was the three destroyers carrying the Koli Detachment that opened Dugout Sunday services at ten in the morning. They steamed into Iron Bottom Bay with their guns firing, raking Marine shore installations and sinking the tugboat *Seminole* and other smaller craft. Then, to their surprise, geysers of water began erupting around them, and their ships were staggered by explosions. Marine 5-inch rifles were battering them. Black clouds rose from their burning decks. Sending up a screen of their own smoke, the trio turned and made for home.

At 2:30 the Japanese airplanes flew in, thinking that Henderson had been knocked out. If they had come in the morning, they would have been correct; the preceding night's heavy rains had made a mire of the runways. But hard-working repair crews and a hot, drying sun had made them barely operable by midafternoon. Alerted by the coast watchers, flights of Wildcats thundered down the sodden, soggy runway of Fighter One, their wheels throwing out arcs of spray before they were airborne and climbing for their battle stations. Among them were Capt. Joe Foss and Lt. Jack Conger.

Foss shot down two of three Zekes destroyed in a flight of six. But then, with his fifth Wildcat riddled by enemy fire, he had to go down to get another one. Going up again, he shot down two more Zekes—diving for home with near-empty fuel tanks and fifteen kills to his credit during sixteen days on Guadalcanal.

Jack Conger also shot down a Zero in the second attack. Banking, he went thundering after another. He pressed the gun button. No response. He was out of ammunition. Undaunted, Conger still flew at the Zero. He hung on his nose and brought his propeller under the enemy's tail. The Zero swerved, and broke in two.

Now Conger's plane was going over in a vertical dive. He fought wildly to bring it out. It still fell. Conger strained at his escape hatch. He could see Iron Bottom Bay rising up toward him, growing larger. It was as though a great steel-gray griddle had been catapulted upward, flying up, up and up, expanding until it was a monstrous obliterating roundness. Conger struggled with the hatch. He thought he would never get out, that the huge griddle would shatter him, and then, at 150 feet, he was out in the air, his parachute was blooming overhead, and he was into the griddle, his body jarred as though he had been slammed on the soles of his feet with an iron bar.

Just before he went under, Conger saw his Wildcat crash in the coconuts. Then he was going down deep, only to have his swift descent arrested by his rigging. He surfaced, treading water, slashing with a knife at the smothering shroud of the parachute. Twenty feet away another pilot floated gently down into the water.

He was Japanese.

A rescue boat sped toward Conger. It reached him and reduced speed. Conger was hauled aboard. Then the boat came about and headed for the Japanese pilot. Conger called to him to surrender. The Japanese pilot held his breath and sank out of sight. He came up beside the boat, kicked at it and tried to shove himself away. Conger grabbed a boathook and snared the man by his jacket. The man struggled, snarling with hate. Conger leaned forward to boat him. The Japanese dug his hand under his armpit and whipped out a huge Mauser pistol. His malevolent eyes only inches from Conger's startled ones, he pressed the pistol to his benefactor's temple and pulled the trigger.

Click!

Conger tumbled backward, thinking: *I'm dead!* He was not nor was his enemy who, failing to return death for life, attempted to take his own by placing the pistol to his own head, producing only a second exasperating *click*. Conger seized a water can and slammed it down on the man's head. Unconscious, he was dragged into the boat and taken to Guadalcanal.

Where the two enemies became good friends.

Twenty-six enemy airplanes had fallen to the Cactus Air Force. Besides the three big "tin cans" that had been put to flight, the cruiser *Yura* had been so badly battered—with the assistance of Flying Forts from Espiritu—that she was sunk by her own destroyer, *Yudachi*. Destroyer *Akizuke* had to be beached and abandoned.

Still at sea were two huge naval forces. Most of Yamamoto's Combined Fleet —four carriers, five battleships, fourteen cruisers and forty-four destroyers, less those lost at Guadalcanal—still sailed north of the island. About 360 miles to the southeast were *Enterprise* and *Hornet,* two battleships, nine cruisers and twenty-four destroyers under Rear Adm. Thomas Kinkaid.

Both fleets were confused. Adm. Chuichi Nagumo, still mindful of the debacle at Midway, had gone streaking north with his carriers after an American scout plane was spotted. Admiral Kinkaid, eager for battle, thought he had found Nagumo's ships at noon, but soon lost them in a squall.

Meanwhile, as night fell, the Dugout Sunday battle was renewed again on land.

> *We have a weapon that nobody loves,*
> *They say that our gun's a disgrace.*
> *You crank up 200, and 200 more—*
> *And it lands in the very same place.*
> *Oh, there's many a gunner that's blowing his top,*

Observers are all going mad.
But our love it has lasted
This pig-iron bastard
Is the best gun this world ever had.

Thus the Marine mortarmen sang of their "stovepipes," those harmless-looking tubes that fire looping trajectories, straight up and straight down, putting their missiles down chimneys if need be and dropping them like bombs into enemy pits and holes. Nothing kills men like mortars, and no weapon is more dreaded by foot soldiers. Mortar shells were about the only supplies Chesty Puller was able to get to his lines that reverberating Sunday. He had plenty of them when, at eleven o'clock that night, the men of the Sendai came padding up the jungle trails into assembly areas. Once again, with disastrous indifference to detection, their officers began to whip them into a frenzy. Once more the howling cries were heard: "U. S. Marine you going die tonight. U.S. Marine you going die tonight."

So the Sendai charged and Puller's mortars racked and ravaged them, while small-arms fire finished the survivors who reached the wire.

It was not really a charge but a senseless death swarming. Without artillery preparation of their own, without maps or knowledge of the enemy's position, arrogant in their foolish faith in spiritual power and vainglorious in their desire to look upon death before defeat, Maruyama and his officers sent the emperor's best division into a crucible of fire and steel.

General Nasu was killed, Colonel Hiroyasa was killed, four battalion commanders perished and half of the Sendai's officers were destroyed—and still the Sendai charged.

Colonel Oka was at last attacking.

His men struck hard at the ridge held by Sgt. Mitchell Paige's machine-gun section.

The Japanese came screeching up the hillside full into Paige's guns spitting orange flame a foot beyond their flash hiders. Short shapes fell, but more came swarming in. It was hand-to-hand. Paige saw little Leiphart down on one knee fighting off three attackers. Paige shot two of them. The third killed Leiphart with a bayonet, but Paige killed the killer. Pettyjohn's gun was knocked out. Gaston fought a Japanese officer, parrying saber swings with his rifle, until the rifle was hacked to pieces. Then Gaston kicked at the blade. Unaware that part of his leg was cut away, he kicked high—and caught the officer under the chin and broke his neck.

All over the ridge the short shapes and the tall shapes flowed, merged, struggled, parted, sank to the ground or rolled down the slopes. Everywhere were the American voices crying, *"Kill! Kill!"* the gurgling whoops of the Japanese shouting, *"Bonn—za—ee!"* or screaming "Marine you die!"

Then the short shapes flowed back down the ridge, and Mitchell Paige ran to fix Pettyjohn's disabled gun. He pried out a ruptured cartridge and slipped in a fresh belt of ammunition, just as a burst from a Japanese machine gun seared his hand.

Yelling again, the short shapes came bowling up the hill once more. They could not force the left, where Grant, Payne and Hinson still held out, though all were wounded. In Paige's center they hit Lock, Swanek and McNabb. They moved through the gap, Paige dashed to his right to find a gun to stop them. He found Kelly and Totman beside their gun, protected by a squad of riflemen. He ordered the riflemen to fix bayonets, and led them on a charge that drove the Japanese back. Then he set up the gun in the center and fired it until dawn.

As daylight came creeping over the jungle roof to his left, he saw one of his platoon's machine guns standing unattended on the forward nose of the ridge. Three men in mushroom helmets were crawling toward it. Paige rose and ran forward. . . .

In that same faint light Maj. Odell Conoley saw an enemy force in company strength occupy a ridge between his left flank and Puller's right flank. They raked Conoley's position. He could see vapor rising from their hot gun barrels. Their penetration could be expanded into a breakthrough. Conoley rounded up a ragtag pick-up force: cooks, stretcher bearers, band musicians, wiremen and couriers. There were seventeen of them in all, and they drove the Japanese off the ridge. Then Conoley called for a protective screen of mortars while he consolidated his position and awaited reinforcements. When they arrived, one of the cooks boasted of having brained an enemy officer.

"What'd ja do?" a rifleman jeered. "Hit him with one of yer own pancakes?"

Mitchell Paige reached the gun first.

He dived for it, squeezed the trigger and killed the crawling Japanese.

A storm of bullets fell on Paige, kicking up spurts of dust. Paige fired back. Stat, Reilly and Jonjeck ran to him with belts of ammunition. Stat fell with a bullet in his belly. Reilly went down kicking, almost knocking Paige off his gun and Jonjeck came in with a belt and a bullet in his shoulder. Jonjeck bent to feed the belt into the gun, and Paige saw a piece of flesh go flying off his neck.

"Get the hell back!" Paige yelled.

Jonjeck shook his head. Paige hit him in the jaw and Jonjeck left.

Paige moved the gun back and forth to avoid enemy grenades. He saw about thirty men rise in the tall grass below him. One of them put binoculars to his eyes and waved his hand for a charge.

Paige fired a long burst.

The enemy vanished.

Paige called to his riflemen. He slung two belts of ammunition across his shoulders, unclamped his gun, cradled the searing-hot water jacket in his arm and went down the ridge yelling, "Let's go!"

"Ya-hoo!" the Marines yelled. "Yaaaa-hoo!"

And they went racing down the hill after the dispersing enemy. The officer with the glasses popped up out of the grass and Paige disemboweled him with a burst, and then he and his Marines had burst into the jungle.

It was silent and empty.

The enemy was gone. The battle of Henderson Field was over. General Maruyama had already ordered a full retreat. Colonel Shoji was taking the remnant of the Sendai right wing to the east, Maruyama was leading the reeling left wing to the west. Marine bulldozers were already clanking toward the front to gouge out mass graves in which to inter the reeking carcasses of 2,500 dead. Colonel Furumiya and his companions lay despairing in the bush, and Mitchell Paige and his men were trudging slowly back to the ridge.

They sat down wearily. Paige felt the sweat drying on his body. He watched vapor rising from his machine-gun jacket. He felt a burning sensation in his left arm. He looked down. From fingertips to forearm a long white blister was forming, swelling as thick as a rope to mark the place where flesh had held hot steel.

60. The Battles of Santa Cruz and Savo Island

DENIED HENDERSON FIELD once more, an angry Isoroku Yamamoto sought all the more that decisive battle with the American Pacific Fleet that would redeem both Midway and Guadalcanal. He still had four flattops, five battleships, fourteen cruisers and forty-four destroyers to hurl against what he knew to be an inferior enemy air-surface fleet. He knew *Wasp* had been sunk and that *Saratoga* was being repaired. But he did not know that *Enterprise* was back at sea. With *Hornet,* it formed the nucleus of Fighting Tom Kinkaid's force, which included two battleships, nine cruisers and twenty-four destroyers. In the new battlewagon *South Dakota* with her dozens of new 40-mm antiaircraft guns—and her remarkable skipper, Capt. Thomas Gatch—Kinkaid possessed a formidable weapon indeed. Gatch was a fighter who preferred salty sharpshooters to spit-and-polish sailors. So he ran a "loose ship," concentrating on marksmanship. His men looked "like a lot of wild men," according to one of Gatch's officers, but they could shoot straight, and they idolized their skipper. In the early morning hours of October 26 Kinkaid received plane contacts on enemy carriers only 200 miles away. At about the same time Adm. Bull Halsey in Noumea read his dispatches and studied his operations chart. Struck by the opportunity to strike, he sent Kinkaid the message which began the Battle of the Santa Cruz Islands:

ATTACK—REPEAT, ATTACK!

Enterprise had already launched a search mission, thoughtfully providing each Dauntless with one 500-pound bomb just in case. Two of them did find that target of opportunity: light carrier *Zuiho.* They promptly used their bombs, hit *Zuiho*—and put her out of action for the rest of the battle.

But Vice Adm. Nabutake Kondo's scouts had also found *Hornet,* and he ordered his three remaining carriers to launch strikes against her. Twenty minutes later *Hornet*'s war birds roared aloft. As sometimes happens in air-sea warfare, these hostile flights passed one another, eyed each other apprehensively—and wondered which of them would find a flight deck awaiting them on their return.

Both *Hornet* and *Enterprise* were surrounded by floating gun platforms, the American navy having realized that battleships and heavy cruisers gave far more valuable service as carrier-protectors than as ship killers. Each flattop also had combat patrols stacked high above them. At about nine o'clock, the Val dive-bombers found *Hornet.* They fell out of those fleecy clouds that were the detestation of all ack-ack gunners and staggered the big American. One bomb hit the starboard side of the flight deck aft. The Japanese pilot, crippled by a shell burst, suicide-dived into the smokestack, glanced off and pierced the flight deck where two of his bombs exploded. Now the torpedo-carrying Kates skimmed in to loose their deadly fish. Two of them exploded in the engineering spaces. *Hornet* lost all power. She was now dead in the water, a derelict, a sitting duck. Three more quarter-ton bombs hit the flight deck, and then another suicider, a flaming Kate with a doomed pilot at the controls, plowed into the forward gun gallery.

American aircraft and AA fire protecting *Hornet* had been superb. Only two of the twenty-seven bombers that attacked her survived. Nevertheless, this new and priceless ship was finished. Taken under tow, she was later sunk by two Japanese destroyers. One third of American carrier power in the Pacific thus vanished beneath the waves. If the later expedient of attaching powerful fleet tugboats to task forces had been in practice, she probably would have survived to be repaired.

Nevertheless, *Hornet*'s fifty-two-plane air group commanded by Lt. Cmdr. Gus Widhelm had found the enemy carriers. Lt. James Vose led eleven Dauntlesses screaming down on *Shokaku.* Three to six 500-pounders chewed her flight deck into a twisted, tangled, useless mass. *Shokaku* was out of the war for nine months. So also, for a shorter period of time, was the cruiser *Chikuma,* hit twice with bombs by *Hornet*'s second wave.

Kondo still had *Zuikaku* and *Junyo,* and he ordered them to get *Enterprise.* That unsinkable, lucky lady had already escaped detection by entering a rain squall. Superb ship handling by Capt. O. B. Hardison and some spectacular shooting by *South Dakota*'s "wild men" had also frustrated the enemy. But *Enterprise* did not escape unscathed. Three bombs killed forty-four men, but inflicted no serious damage on the ship.

Thus the decisive battle both Yamamoto and Halsey sought was fought off the Santa Cruz Islands and ended indecisively. Probably, because of the loss of *Hornet,* it was a Japanese victory. But the Imperial Navy had lost the service of one heavy and one light carrier, as well as one light cruiser. They had also lost 100 airplanes against seventy-six Americans destroyed. Santa Cruz, then, was a disappointment to both sides. But neither permitted the standoff to weaken their determination to fight to the end.

Already in the waning days of October, while the Santa Cruz survivors steamed north for Truk or south for Noumea, the Americans were sending more ships to the South Pacific and Marine and army units had been alerted for movement to Guadalcanal.

Back in Rabaul, Lt. Gen. Haruyoshi Hyakutake was reaching for the last shot in his locker: the 38th Division. He had already fed in the Ichiki Detachment, the Kawaguchi Brigade and the Sendai Division, plus a handful of other units. In all, more than 25,000 Japanese ground troops had sailed down the Slot to Death Island. Now roughly another 15,000 were sailing south to the battle.

And then it was November.

In November the Marines of Maj. Gen. Alexander Vandegrift came close to losing their minds.

A bitter aching fatigue had come upon them. They had met the enemy on the beaches, in caves, atop the hills, down in the jungle swamps—and they had defeated him. They had been battered by every weapon in the arsenal of modern war. They had been blown from their holes or been buried in them. They had not slept. They had been ravaged by malaria, weakened by dysentery, nagged by tropical ulcers and jungle rot, scorched by the sun and drenched by the rain. They had met each ordeal with the hope of victory and had survived only to prepare for greater trial. They had come to Guadalcanal lean and muscular young men, and now there was not one of them who had not lost twenty pounds, and there were some who had lost fifty. They had come here with high unquenchable spirit, but now that blaze of ardor was flickering low, and there was a darkness gathering within them and their minds were retreating into it.

All the world was circumscribed by their perimeter. Guadalcanal had become Thermopylae multiplied by ninety days. There might be ninety more, for all they knew, for there seemed no way out, around or through. This was that "feeling of expendability" of which so much has been written, but which, like a toothache, can never be understood but only felt. It was a long shuddering sigh of weariness with which men rehearsed in their minds what had gone before, wondering dully, not that it had been sustained, but in what new hideous shape it would reappear. It was a sense of utter loneliness made poignant by their longing for encouragement from home, which never seemed to be forthcoming, by their hope of help, which was always being shattered. It seemed to these men that their country had set them down in the midst of the enemy and left them there to go it alone. They could not understand—had no wish to understand— that high strategy which might assign a flood of men and munitions to another theater of war, a trickle to their own. They reasoned only as they fought: that a man in trouble should get help, and here they were alone.

So they turned in upon themselves. They developed that vacant, thousand-yard stare—lusterless unblinking eyes gazing out of sunken red-rimmed sockets.

They drew in upon themselves in little squad groups, speaking constantly in low voices to each other, rarely to men of other units. They avoided those top NCOs and officers who might put them on working parties unloading ships. They were not shirking duty, they were saving strength—for the daily patrols, for the ordeal of the night watch with its terrors of the imagination, terrors fancied but real. Some of these men had not the strength to go to the galley to eat, for galleys usually lay in the lowlands behind the lines. Weakened men might get down to the galley, but they could not get back up. Their friends brought them food, just as men brought food to buddies sickened by malaria but not sick enough to occupy a precious cot in the regimental sick bays. Men with temperatures a few points above 100 were not regarded as bona fide malaria cases. There had been only 239 of these in September; there had been 1,941 of them in October—and before November ended there would be 3,200 more.

So these men faced the month of November, forgetting the outside world, forgetting even that they were Americans—mindful only that they were Marines and trying always for those flashes of rough comedy that could nourish their spirit.

Sometimes men stood on the hills and shouted insults at an unseen or nonexistent enemy in the darkened jungle. They called Emperor Hirohito "a bucktoothed bastard." They dwelt at loving length on the purity of his lineage. They yelled unprintables at Premier Tojo while ascribing to him every vice in the book of human depravity. And there came an astonishing night when a thin reedy voice shrilled up at them in outraged retaliation:

"F—— Babe Ruth!"

During November General Vandegrift struck again at enemy forces massing to east and west of him. To the west the Fifth Marines killed 200 Japanese before being recalled while a major battle developed east of the Tenaru. Here a new force on Guadalcanal—the 2nd Marine Raider Battalion under Lt. Col. Evans Carlson—entered the battle. They helped the 2nd Battalion, Seventh, under Lt. Col. Herman Henry Hanneken destroy the Japanese 230th Regiment. Well over 1,000 Japanese were killed and at least three times that many wounded, at American losses of fewer than 100 killed and 200 wounded. But then Vandegrift was compelled to recall these units as well, for Admiral Yamamoto had gathered his forces for that long-sought final and decisive battle.

Admiral Kondo commanded an armada of two aircraft carriers, four battleships, eleven cruisers and forty-nine destroyers, eleven transports and 14,000 men. The troops were to augment General Hyakutake's Seventeenth Army, which at last outnumbered Vandegrift's forces 30,000 to 23,000. Actually, with 4,000 of Vandegrift's Marines on Tulagi, Hyakutake's forces on Guadalcanal were that much larger. Some 3,000 of his reinforcements were from a naval landing force, while the remaining 11,000 formed the main body of the 38th Division. Hyakutake also could expect help from the 51st Division, already alerted to move from China to the South Pacific, and a mixed brigade, also in the Far East.

The 14,000 men immediately coming to him were to land on the morning of November 13, after Henderson Field had been bombarded from the bay both night and day. The first barrage was to be delivered the night of November 12–13 by battleships *Hiei* and *Kirishima,* the cruiser *Nagara* and fourteen destroyers under Vice-Adm. Hiroaki Abe. Gunichi Mikawa with six cruisers and six destroyers would continue the shelling during daylight of November 13 while a convoy of eleven high-speed transports escorted by twelve Tokyo Express destroyers under Tanaka the Tenacious put the soldiers ashore at Tassafaronga.

Meanwhile, Kondo with carriers *Hiyo* and *Junyo,* battleships *Haruna* and *Kongo,* and the remainder of his fleet, would sail in distant support about 150 miles north of Savo. His carrier planes, of course, would join the eagles from Rabaul in pounding Henderson.

Sensing that the truly decisive battle was impending, Admiral Halsey—true to his word to Vandegrift—threw in everything that he had. Six thousand soldiers and Marines were sent steaming north to even the odds that had been against Vandegrift. The Marines arrived first, on November 11 in a convoy commanded by Admiral Scott. Even as they hurried ashore they were savaged by two air raids which ended the aerial doldrums and signaled the beginning of something big. The soldiers—men of the 182nd Infantry Regiment—were in a convoy commanded by Admiral Turner and would arrive November 12. So also, Halsey learned, would the carriers and battleships of Kondo's powerful fleet.

Bull Halsey again threw in everything he had. Crippled *Enterprise* had been in Noumea harbor since her limping arrival from the Santa Cruz battle. For nearly two weeks a battalion of Seabees, all of repair ship *Vulcan*'s specialists and the *Big E*'s own craftsmen had been working furiously to make the carrier shipworthy again. But she still needed ten more days of repairs when Halsey sent her back into action, her decks still shaking and echoing to air hammers, welder's arcs still sparking, with a big bulge in her starboard side forward, one oil-tank leaking and her forward elevator still jammed from the bomb that hit there at Santa Cruz. *Enterprise* sailed back to battle only half a carrier. With her were battleships *South Dakota*—also crippled—and *Washington,* two cruisers and eight destroyers. Outnumbered and outgunned by Kondo's massive fleet, Admiral Kinkaid nevertheless put to sea looking for a fight.

Admiral Turner had arrived at Guadalcanal, quickly putting his soldiers ashore and beginning to unload. At two in the afternoon twenty-four Betty bombers escorted by eight Zekes slashed at him. Turner skillfully avoided their torpedoes while a storm of AA and the slashing attacks of Wildcat fighters shot down all but one bomber and five out of the eight fighters.

The attack, together with those on Scott the day before, aroused Turner's suspicions. When a Catalina sighted and reported the Japanese battle fleet heading south, he realized immediately that the enemy's big push had begun. He did not fear for his transports and supply ships because they were already 90 percent unloaded and he could easily lead them to safety. But he had to protect Henderson Field so that Cactus Air Force would be able to strike at the enemy reinforcements—the soul of the enemy operation—and the planes from *Enterprise* would be able to land there. Moreover, the Japanese fleet must be stopped to give Kinkaid's powerful new battleships enough time to enter the battle.

But to do this Turner possessed only two heavy and three light cruisers and eight destroyers. Nevertheless, he put Rear Adm. Daniel Callaghan in command of this force and ordered him to stop the enemy.

Callaghan had been Ghormley's chief of staff. After Halsey took charge, he went back to sea. He belonged there. Handsome with his thick shock of snow white hair and jet black eyebrows above his dark blue Irish eyes, he might have been an ancient Celtic seafarer. His men loved him and called him "Uncle Dan."

But Callaghan had neither the experience nor the training for this desperation mission. He was chosen because he was senior to Norman Scott, the victor of Cape Esperance, who was also present in his flag cruiser *Atlanta*. Scott's success in crossing the T had inordinately influenced Callaghan, and he formed his ships in column. This was far from being the best formation to confront the night-fighting, torpedo-firing Japanese. But it was chosen because of Scott's success, because it would make maneuvering in the narrow waters of Iron Bottom Bay less risky and because, presumably, it made communication between ships easier. So Callaghan formed his little fleet in column: destroyers *Cushing, Laffey, Sterett* and *O'Bannon* in the lead, heavy cruisers *Atlanta, San Francisco* and *Portland,* followed by lights *Helena* and *Juneau* in the center, and in the rear destroyers *Aaron Ward, Barton, Monssen* and *Fletcher.* Unfortunately, Callaghan did not make proper deployment of his radar ships. *Atlanta* with inferior radar was ahead of *San Francisco* with excellent radar. Finally, no plan of battle was issued.

Nevertheless, for all these oversights and omissions, the Americans led by Callaghan and Scott did possess that single quality which, so often in this desperate struggle, had extricated the unwary or unwise from a defeat of their own devising.

That was their valor.

"Commence firing!" Daniel Callaghan shouted on the bridge of *San Francisco.* "Give 'em hell, boys!"

It was 2:15 in the morning, Friday the Thirteenth of November, and Callaghan's little stopgap fleet drove ahead, straight into the flaming 14-inch guns of the battleships that had sailed south to pulverize Henderson Field. Guns roaring, sterns down, keels carving hard white wakes in the glittering obsidian surface of Iron Bottom Bay, they rushed forward to destruction and glory in the fiercest surface engagement of World War II.

Ashore Marines and soldiers on the beaches, the rivers, the ridges and in the kunai fields sprang from their sleeping holes to make for the safety of their gun pits. On the ridges they could see the battle.

It was as though the world were being remade. It was cataclysm ripping matter apart like paper. Searchlights slashed the star shell-showered night. Gun flashes flitted over water like bolts of summer lightning. The wakes of speeding ships were crisscrossed by the thin bubbling lines of racing torpedoes, blotted out by the flaming geysers of their impact.

Little *Laffey* ran in under great *Hiei's* mighty 14-inch turrets and peppered her bridge. She was so close that *Hiei*'s pagoda towered above her. *Hiei* thundered and *Laffey* began to burn. *San Francisco* dueled *Hiei,* hurling salvo after 8-inch salvo into her superstructure. *Hiei* thundered again. A full salvo screamed into *San Francisco*'s bridge, killing Callaghan and every other man there. *San Francisco*'s gun turrets began firing on local control. But her shells were hitting *Atlanta.* Norman Scott was killed. The hero of Cape Esperance fell to friendly gunfire. But ship silhouettes plunging in and out of the smoke were difficult to identify. Ships of both sides fired on friendly ships.

Now the Japanese firepower was asserting its superiority. Every American ship but *Fletcher* was hit. *Barton* blew up. *Monssen* sank. So did *Laffey, Cushing* —and the cruisers *Juneau* and *Atlanta.*

But the Japanese were running! Every one of them had been staggered. Destroyer *Yudachi* was going down, followed by *Akatsuke.* Abe's ships were streaking north. Following them at a wallowing crawl, like a great stricken sea monster, rudderless, gaping and jagged holes in her hull from the twin torpedoes of bold little *Sterett,* her superstructure a twisted mass from eighty-five shell hits, came great *Hiei.*

Plummeting down on her like shrieking vultures came the fighters and bombers from Henderson Field. Though Callaghan and Scott and many of their men had died, though the Americans had lost six ships, their sacrifice, in what Admiral King called "the fiercest naval battle ever fought," had achieved its purpose. Henderson had not been scratched. Cactus Air Force's fighters and bombers had been preserved, and now they were coming to kill *Hiei.* They shot down the eight Zekes sent to protect her. Maj. Joe Sailer planted a bomb on *Hiei*'s remaining antiaircraft turrets and knocked them out. Capt. George Dooley's quartet of Avengers sent another torpedo flashing into the great ship's hull. Seven Dauntlesses fell upon her with 1000-pounders. Nine Avengers from *Enterprise* joined the assault, and full five more attacks were made that day by pilots now desperate to sink her lest "the admirals start building battleships again." Still the great sea monster wallowed in the swells, glowing cherry red, sailing an aimless circle, now drifting north, now making for Guadalcanal again—refusing to go under.

At night the Japanese scuttled her. By morning only a shining oil slick two miles long marked the sun-dappled seas off Savo where *Hiei* had at last gone down.

But before she did, Henderson Field had been shelled. During the night

Gunichi Mikawa brought six cruisers and six destroyers into Iron Bottom Bay. At midnight, heavies *Suzuya* and *Maya* stood in close to hurl 1,000 shells at Henderson. They might have hurled more, except that a sextet of little torpedo boats crept out of Tulagi's numerous creeks and inlets to launch a spread of torpedoes, hit cruiser *Kinugasa* and drove the rest away.

With daylight, the fliers of the Cactus Air Force were roaring aloft again. Mikawa's shelling had destroyed only two planes and damaged sixteen others. Fighter One had been quickly manhandled into shape. The Marines found Mikawa's ships under a cover of fleecy white clouds. They fell from them to plant bombs on two more cruisers and a destroyer and send torpedoes into crippled *Kinugasa*. Calling for planes from *Enterprise* to finish *Kinugasa* and batter the others, they flew back to Henderson to launch the grisly slaughter of the Nagoya Division known as the Buzzard Patrol.

Gunichi Mikawa had reported the complete destruction of Henderson Field and the absence of enemy surface ships. So the Tokyo Express—eleven transports escorted by twelve destroyers—came down the Slot in a rare daylight run. At a little after noon, the Americans found them. Every last precious airplane from Henderson Field that could struggle aloft was coming after them. Thousand-pound bombs nestled under Dauntless bellies like deadly eggs fell away, described their dreadful yawning parabolas—and fell in showers upon those crowded decks.

Flights came from everywhere: from Henderson, from *Enterprise,* from Espiritu Santo, from the Fijis. They flew in, dropped their bombs, launched their fish, strafed—and flew away, either home or to Henderson for rearming. Zekes flew down from Rabaul to intercept them, but were shot down or driven off by such fighter pilots as Capt. Joe Foss or Joe Bauer. Nor could the Zekes tarry long, fighting as they were at long range. After they left, Marine and navy pilots, the army Lightning fighters recently arrived at Guadalcanal, roared over the stricken ships at crow's-nest level to strafe the defenseless soldiers on their decks.

Even the sea about those listing, sinking transports was incarnadine with Japanese blood. The water was dotted with the bobbing heads of men who had been blown overboard or had jumped to flee the shipboard fires. But water is no shield against bullets and the number of bobbing heads grew fewer. It was merciless, indeed; it had to be merciless. Every enemy soldier who got safely ashore was one more man the Americans must kill. Pilots vomited in their cockpits to see the slaughter they were making. With horrified eyes they could see through the jagged holes in the transports' decks down into troop holds glowing red with heat.

The Buzzard Patrol scourged the enemy until nightfall. By then seven transports were sunk or sinking. The remaining four staggered ashore in flames, beaching themselves there to land a few hundred leaderless soldiers. Then they were destroyed by Marine fliers, the destroyer *Meade* and the 5-inch batteries of the Marine Third Defense Battalion. Of the 14,000 Japanese who had sailed south, not 5,000 survived. Most of these were taken aboard destroyers and carried north. Some reached Guadalcanal by boat. Others were scattered in ragged demoralized groups throughout the central Solomons. As a fighting force, the Nagoya Division had been *zemmetsu,* annihilated.

It was a magnificent victory, and to Vandegrift's Marines it seemed that they had been saved.

But not yet.

Tenacity was the virtue of the Japanese fighting man. But the vice of that virtue was stubbornness or inflexibility. In all the Combined Fleet there was no man more tenacious or stubborn than Nobutake Kondo. On two nights his ships had failed to knock out Henderson Field. Now on the third night—November 14-15—Kondo kept to his plan. He came down the Slot with battleship *Kirishima,* heavy cruisers *Atago* and *Takao* and a flock of nine destroyers. He was loaded for bombardment and was not expecting surface opposition. Only those tiny PT-boats that had buzzed Mikawa were about, and his destroyers would surely make *sukiyaki* of them. Surely the Americans would not risk battleships in the narrow waters of Iron Bottom Bay.

But they did. Rear Adm. Willis Augustus Lee had come north with *South Dakota* and *Washington* and a small screen of four destroyers. He had no battle plans, not even a radio call signal. All he knew was that enemy capital ships were coming south again. Lee was hungry for information as he entered Iron Bottom Bay. He signaled Guadalcanal, using the code name "Cactus." Back came the reply:

"We do not recognize you."

Lee was a personal friend of Vandegrift, who, he was sure, would recognize his Annapolis nickname.

"Cactus, this is Lee. Tell your big boss Ching Lee is here and wants the latest information."

No answer.

Suddenly, over the Talk Between Ships, he heard two torpedo-boat skippers chatting.

"There go two big ones, but I don't know whose they are."

Lee stiffened. The chatter was to his left. He spoke quickly to Guadalcanal again: "Refer your big boss about Ching Lee. Chinese, catchee? Call off your boys!" Then, sharply, to the PT boats themselves:

"This is Ching Chong China Lee. All PT boats retire!"

A skeptical voice murmured: "It's a phony. Let's slip the bum a pickle."

"I said this is Ching Chong China Lee!" the exasperated admiral bellowed. "Get the hell out of my way! I'm coming through!"

Startled, aware that no Japanese impostor could roar and curse in quite such style, the trio of tiny craft roared away with foaming white wakes—and the battleships went through. At 1:16 on the morning of the 15th, Lee's radar screens became covered with approaching pips, and there was a babble of Japanese voices on the radiotelephone.

Suddenly among the Americans there were explosions and giant flames leaping into the sky. Shoals of silently running Long Lance torpedoes had found *Preston, Benham* and *Walke* and sunk them. Enemy searchlights pinioned *South Dakota* like a big bug on a screen. She shuddered under a shower of shells. Her top decks were littered with wreckage and the dead and wounded. But Lee's flagship *Washington* had tracked *Kirishima* and was taking her apart with giant 16-inch guns. Soon *Kirishima* would join her sister battleship *Hiei* beneath the waves. Now *South Dakota* helped *Washington* batter the heavy cruisers *Atago* and *Takao.* They staggered out of the battle and would remain out of action for many months. The light cruisers and destroyers fled after them.

Ching Lee sailed back to Noumea with triumphant *Washington,* valiant *South Dakota* and lucky little *Gwin.* Not for two years would Japanese battleships venture forth again to surface battle. The three-day Naval Battle of Guadalcanal had ended in a decisive American victory.

Next day a jubilant Alexander Vandegrift sent the following message to Admiral Halsey:

"We believe the enemy has suffered a crushing defeat. We thank Lee for his sturdy effort of last night. We thank Kinkaid for his intervention of yesterday. Our own air has been grand in its relentless pounding of the foe. Those efforts we appreciate, but our greatest homage goes to Scott, Callaghan and their men who with magnificent courage against seemingly hopeless odds drove back the first hostile stroke and made success possible. To them the men of Cactus lift their battered helmets in deepest admiration."

Halsey shared Vandegrift's jubilation. Only a few moments before receiving his message, he had told his staff:

"We've got the bastards licked!"

At Buna-Sanananda-Gona, the Japanese were still unconquered. An all-out assault on Buna launched by Eichelberger on December 5 had been broken in blood. The American general wisely decided to postpone such costly attacks until he could receive the tanks and reinforcements Harding had sought in vain. An airstrip completed at Dobadura on the north New Guinea coast had greatly improved Eichelberger's supply situation. Meanwhile, the Australians, reinforced and equipped with a new artillery shell with a delayed-action fuse, had fought their way into Gona on December 9. But they had taken heavy casualties, with 500 men killed.

A few days later Eichelberger received his tanks and an Australian brigade. On December 18 he struck again at Buna. Allied casualties were again heavy. But the enemy was being steadily whittled. His men were battle-shocked and almost starving. Even rifle ammunition was rationed. The tanks and renewed Allied assaults were too much for them. On January 2, 1943, Buna fell.

Sanananda, most formidable of the three Japanese strong points, still held out. For two months its men had stopped the Australians. Now, both Americans and Australians assaulted the village. They gained little ground. But at Sanananda also the apocalyptic horseman of hunger was riding down the Japanese will to fight. By the first week of January they had eaten the last of their rice. Afterward, they existed on coconuts and what they could forage in the jungle. On January 16, the last Allied assault began, and on January 22 Sanananda fell. It had taken no fewer than 3,500 casualties to reduce this coastal position. In all, after six months of bitter fighting, MacArthur's forces had suffered 8,500 casualties—3,000 of them killed—to reconquer an area that might have been his at no cost of time or blood if, during the previous July, he had moved quicker than the Japanese.

Meanwhile, Guadalcanal was also falling.

On December 9, 1942, command at Guadalcanal passed from the Marine General Vandegrift to the army General Patch. Patch wisely waited until he had sufficient force to go out on the offensive against the Japanese. Eventually, he would have an entire corps—the XIV—consisting of the Americal Division, the 25th Infantry Division, the Second Marine Division, and later on, though not committed to battle, the 43rd Infantry Division. With these troops, Patch struck at Hyakutake and the diseased and hungry troops of his Seventeenth Army.

The Japanese resisted with characteristic stubbornness. Nevertheless, they fell steadily backward in the face of a slow, grinding, overwhelming American assault supported by air and artillery. Patch finally dislodged them from their positions west of the Matanikau and pursued them relentlessly toward the sea.

In Tokyo, a debate on whether to hold or evacuate Guadalcanal grew so acrimonious that staff officers exchanged blows. Gradually, the evacuation party led by Premier Tojo gained the upper hand, and on the last day of 1942 it was decided to evacuate.

Once again, swift destroyer-transports swept down the Slot, this time to embark rather than disembark Japanese soldiers. On three February nights, twenty destroyers took off Haruyoshi Hyakutake and 13,000 survivors of his battered Seventeenth Army. On the afternoon of February 9, 1943, a patrol of soldiers from the 132nd Infantry met another patrol from the 161st. They had reached Guadalcanal's west coast and found no enemy. By then, the Marines who had landed on Death Island six months earlier had also departed.

They had begun going out to their ships in late December, these men of the First Marine Division, and their departure would continue through early January 1943. Some of them had been on the front lines for almost five months without relief. All of them were ragged, bearded and bony when they came down to the beach at Lunga Point. Many had barely the strength to wade out to the boats waiting to take them out to the ships. But all of them had visited the Division Cemetery before they left.

It was called "Flanders Field." It was a neatly cleared square among the Lunga coconut trees. Each grave was covered with a palm frond and marked with rough crosses and occasional Stars of David onto which mess-gear tins and dog-tags had been nailed. Surviving Marines knelt or stood before these graves in awe, wondering that there were so few.

In all, 774 Marines of the First Division had died, 1,962 had been wounded and another 5,400 stricken by malaria. Second Marine Division casualties would reach 268 dead and 932 wounded, so that all Marine ground losses would total 1,042 dead and 2,894 wounded. Army casualties would total 550 dead and 1,289 wounded. Navy casualties, never compiled, would certainly equal these, while the much smaller losses among the airmen would never be known.

Yet, the Japanese ultimately lost 28,800 in the ground fighting alone, while many thousands more died at sea, 2,362 pilots and airmen perished, and unknown thousands of sailors also were lost. Probably Japan lost 50,000 men in this vain attempt to recover "this insignificant island in the South Seas," the dreadful green hell where the tide of war was turned against her and sent flowing, with gathering speed, faster and faster toward her own shores.

But victory, as these Marines in Flanders Field well knew, is not always measured by casualties. Nor do casualties describe how victory is gained. Sacrifice and valor, tenacity and skill, these gain victory, and these, though unmeasurable, may at least be described. In their cemetery these Marines found an epitaph celebrating this greatest of Pacific victories and most glorious of American stands. It was a poem. Its words had been picked out on a mess-gear tin with the point of a bayonet. It said:

> *And when he gets to Heaven*
> *To St. Peter he will tell:*
> *One more Marine reporting, sir—*
> *"I've served my time in Hell."*

61. November 1942: Landing in North Africa

WINSTON CHURCHILL was not the only wartime leader who thought of military victory as a political harvest of headlines. When General Marshall informed President Roosevelt that the date for Torch was up to General Eisenhower, FDR held up his hands in an attitude of prayer and said: "Please make it before Election Day." He meant the midterm Congressional elections set for November 3, 1942.

Roosevelt, however, did not fancy himself as a military strategist like

Churchill and seldom interfered with his generals. He said nothing when Eisenhower fixed the date at November 8. On November 2 Eisenhower prepared to fly to Gibraltar, but bad weather prevented the flight, and again on the 3rd. It was still risky on the 4th but an impatient Eisenhower ordered Maj. Paul Tibbets, believed to be the Air Corps's finest pilot, to take off anyway. They flew in the *Red Gremlin,* the same plane that had taken Clark to Gibraltar. Eisenhower was delighted to take command of the Rock, symbol of the British Empire. "I simply must have a grandchild," he wrote in his diary, "or I'll never have the fun of telling this when I'm fishing gray-bearded, on the banks of a quiet bayou in the deep South."

At Gibraltar, he might as well have gone fishing—for there was absolutely nothing for him to do. The fleets were already at sea and the ships were maintaining radio silence. On the afternoon of November 7, fourteen hours short of D-Day (the date set for the landing) Gen. Henri Giraud arrived at Gibraltar in the submarine that had spirited him out of southern France. He came immediately to Eisenhower, demanding to be flown to Algiers to take command of Torch. Eisenhower was astonished by the temerity and hauteur of this tall, austere, one-legged Frenchman: commander of nothing. He asked Giraud to make a broadcast to Morocco and Algeria, urging the French army to cooperate with the invaders. Giraud flatly refused, unless he was given command. Like a man casually changing vacation sites, he calmly proposed to change the target from North Africa to southern France. Eisenhower repeated his request for a broadcast, assuring Giraud that once the Allies moved on to Tunisia, Giraud could have command of the French rear areas. He virtually promised to make him king of North Africa, with all possible American aid. Giraud kept saying, *"Non."* He wanted command. They argued for eight hours, with no results. Giraud excused himself at bedtime with the remark, "Giraud will be a spectator in this affair."

By then the invasions had begun. Eisenhower stayed glued to his radio listening with relief to messages reporting that at Casablanca the surf was down and Patton was going in and that at Oran the landings were going well. There was no news from Algiers. At 4:30 A.M., exhausted, Eisenhower unfolded a cot and went to sleep in his office. He arose at seven o'clock, reading reports and musing aloud about what to do with Giraud. He spoke jokingly of arranging "a little airplane accident," but the French general was still adamant when the discussions were renewed. An exasperated Mark Clark told him bluntly: "If you don't go along, General, you're going to be out in the snow on the seat of your pants." Giraud finally agreed to become commander of all French forces in North Africa and governor general of the area. He made the broadcast written for him by Eisenhower.

And nothing happened.

Not a single French soldier paid the slightest attention to this haughty shadow commander. In Casablanca, the French fought Patton's Americans. In Oran, they put up fierce resistance. In Algiers, Murphy's vaunted underground forces tried to arrest Gen. Alphonse Juin, the French army commander in the city, and were arrested themselves. Murphy rushed to Juin's residence and talked him into joining the Allies. Juin ordered his French troops in Algiers to lay down their arms, just as Admiral Darlan arrived. Juin urged Darlan as Vichy commander in chief to broadcast similar orders to Oran and Casablanca. Darlan refused to do so until he met Eisenhower. He refused to work with Giraud. Giraud told Eisenhower he would have nothing to do with Darlan.

Now the supreme commander was truly exasperated. He complained bitterly of "the petty intrigue and the necessity of dealing with little, selfish, conceited worms who call themselves men." But there was also no escaping the necessity of dealing with Darlan, so he sent Mark Clark to consult with him. In the meantime, Marshal Pétain ordered the French to resist the Anglo-Americans. Shortly afterward, Hitler took over unoccupied France.

But to Eisenhower alone with his fears on the Rock, every minute lost in either combat or negotiation gave the Germans that much more time to reinforce at Tunis and Bizerte; every bullet fired at a Frenchman by an Allied soldier was one fewer to fire at the Germans. Reports that the Americans at Casablanca and Oran were fighting well could not banish a sinking feeling that the chances of strategic success were slipping away from him.

It was noon of landing day on the Casablanca beaches. Maj. Gen. George S. Patton was speeding ashore in a fast boat. Ahead of him he saw an ammunition lighter run aground. Ammunition bearers began heaving cases of bullets onto the sand, leaving the helmsman to his own devices. Roaring with anger, Patton vaulted over the side into waist-deep water.

"Come back here!" he yelled at a pair of ammunition bearers. "Yes, I mean *you! All* of you! Drop that stuff and come back here. Faster than that, goddam it. On the *double!*"

Astonished to see a soaking two-star general put his shoulder to the prow of the beached boat, they came scrambling down to the water.

"Take hold here. You two, over to the other side. Wait for the next wave. Lift and push *Now! Push,* goddammit, *push!*"

With a roar the boat's spinning screw churned the water and the craft backed free.

"Don't you realize that boat has other trips to make?" Patton snapped at the gaping bearers. "How do you expect to fight a war without ammunition? Now go and take that stuff up to the dump. On the *double!*"

Turning toward the town, Patton saw an American soldier lying face down in the sand. His Tommy gun lay beside him. Patton seized it and shouted: "Yeaaaah!"

The soldier rolled over, lifting his arms to shield his face from the sun. "Go 'way and lemme sleep."

The tall figure bending over him did not go away. Instead he pressed the muzzle of the Tommy gun deep into the pit of the soldier's stomach.

"Yeaaaah!"

The soldier's eyes flew open. They traveled incredulously up the length of the cavalry boots, the dripping breeches, the pearl-handled revolver rising to the two gleaming stars on the helmet, dropping again to the cold gray eyes boring into his.

"Jesus."

Patton stepped back, checking the Tommy gun. It was all right.

"Get up, boy," he said gently.

The soldier arose. Patton put his hand on his shoulder. "The next beach you land on will be defended by Germans. I don't want one of them coming up behind you and hitting you over the head with a sockful of shit."

The soldier grinned.

"Here's your gun," Patton said, his voice sharp again. "Now, get going!"

General Clark, again in the *Red Gremlin* with Major Tibbets at the controls, landed at Algiers just as a dozen German Junkers 88s arrived. A Bren-gun carrier met him and took him to the terminal. It was dusk. Clark could see orange ack-ack fire streaming up toward the Junkers from the ships in the harbor. They looked like strings of Christmas-tree lights. Directly overhead two Spitfires shot a Junkers down in smoke. Another Junkers stricken by AA came plunging toward the Bren-gun carrier. Clark glanced around desperately for cover. Providentially, the bomber disintegrated about a thousand feet above him. Relieved, Clark drove from the airport to the Hotel St. George in the city.

Next day he met Admiral Darlan. He was not impressed by the moon-faced little admiral with watery blue eyes and peevish mouth. Clark towered a full foot above him. Darlan kept mopping his balding head with a handkerchief and fiddling nervously with papers as he sat on Clark's left. General Juin was on Clark's right. Robert Murphy acted as interpreter. In full view of a room crowded with French North African officials and generals, Clark lost patience with the evasive little admiral. He had demanded that he order all French troops in North Africa to cease fire; but Darlan had insisted that he could do nothing without approval from Vichy. Clark deliberately began to bully Darlan. He shouted and pounded the table.

"I do not propose to await any word from Vichy," Clark snapped.

"I can only obey the orders of Pétain," Darlan replied.

"Then I will end these negotiations and deal with someone who can act," Clark insisted.

They argued again, and Clark threatened to take Darlan into "protective custody." Darlan asked for five minutes to talk to his staff. Clark consented, warning him that no one was to leave or to attempt to communicate with anyone outside the hotel. During the respite, Juin persuaded Darlan to do as Clark demanded. In return, Darlan was made high commissioner of French North Africa while General Giraud became chief of the armed forces. Darlan also promised that Germany would not get the French fleet at anchor in Toulon. "Under no circumstances will our fleet fall into German hands," he said.

When General Eisenhower flew to Algiers to shake Darlan's hand and the Darlan deal was then announced, there burst upon his head a storm of criticism

—some of it passionate, outright invective—that was unrivaled in the history of World War II. Here, in their first joint offensive, the Allies had made a deal with one of Europe's leading fascists. And it was Eisenhower who approved it. No amount of explanation of the military expediency of concluding such an arrangement, of how it secured the Allied rear for the movement on Tunis, of how it reduced American casualties from an anticipated 18,000 to 1,800, of how it removed from Allied shoulders the burden of policing North Africa, of how it guaranteed the French fleet—nothing could mitigate the intensity of the uproar. Eisenhower was called a fascist or a simpleminded soldier who had gotten out of his political depth. Churchill claimed to be thunderstruck. "There is above all our own moral position. We are fighting for international decency, and Darlan is the antithesis of that." This public stance of moral indignation does not quite square with his private and cynical remark to Eisenhower in October: "Kiss Darlan's ass if you have to, but get the French fleet." Roosevelt was also furious. He indicated that he would repudiate the deal, which meant, of course, that Eisenhower's head would fall. Chiefly because of Eisenhower's misplaced faith in Murphy and Giraud, Torch was already a strategic failure. His campaign thus far had been marked by hesitation and indecision. He was extremely vulnerable.

But not inarticulate. He immediately counterattacked. On November 14 he sent a long cable to the Combined Chiefs stating his position. This, basically, was that Marshal Pétain was the only authority in North Africa. Darlan was Pétain's successor. The French armed forces would obey Darlan, and they had. Without Darlan, he would have had to undertake a complete military occupation of North Africa. This message impressed Roosevelt. Marshall's defense of Eisenhower also helped. Marshall told the American reporters that they had been incredibly stupid in their criticism of Eisenhower and the Darlan Deal. By continuing to criticize and discredit Eisenhower, they were playing into British hands, he said. Eisenhower would be relieved and replaced by a British general, thus severely damaging American prestige in the world. As a result of Marshall's press conference, many newspapers became more discreet about publishing articles filed in North Africa. Most of the intemperate language disappeared. But Eisenhower never forgot this greatest crisis of his career. He never could comprehend why the Fourth Estate would not admit that a conservative could also be an idealist. "I can't understand why these long-haired, starry-eyed guys keep gunning for me. Christ on the Mountain! I'm as idealist as hell!"

In some ways the Darlan Deal was unwise. The admiral did persuade the French in West Africa to join the Allies, and he did stop the fighting in North Africa; but he could not get the French fleet, and he failed to persuade the French in Tunis to resist the Germans, Eisenhower's chief objectives. On November 25 as the Germans planned to board the warships in Toulon, the French admirals ordered their captains to scuttle them. Three battleships, seven cruisers and 167 other ships went to the bottom. In Tunis, the French army withdrew rather than resist the Germans or attempt to halt the reinforcements being rushed there from Sicily. This is true. But the Germans did *not* get the French fleet, as Darlan promised; and it is difficult to see how much damage the thoroughly cowed

French forces in Tunis could have inflicted on their efficient and ruthless German masters. Eisenhower, it should be remembered, hàd always feared that this would happen, and to prevent it had strongly urged Marshall to provide for landings much closer to Tunis. From Darlan he got as much as reasonably could be expected. Giraud was hopeless and de Gaulle dangerous because of the enmity between him and most of the French officers in North Africa. Without Darlan it is likely that Eisenhower would have gotten a bloodbath on the beaches, a French foe rather than an ally, a military occupation with all its enormous dissipation of his resources and—probably—the loss of the French fleet to Germany. These were, of course, short-term considerations. But military commanders seldom if ever can act other than ad hoc. If he had had the inclination, Dwight Eisenhower simply did not have the time to sit down and contemplate the long-term effects of the Darlan deal.

These were indeed formidable and lasting. Stalin naturally wondered if allies so quick to deal with fascists would not also, if pressed, sit down to deal with German generals or even Hitler himself. This suspicion of American fidelity still guides the modern leaders of the Soviet Union, and it might well have influenced Franklin Roosevelt, eager to reassure Stalin, to announce his calamitous policy of Unconditional Surrender at Casablanca two months later. Another adverse effect was on the resistance movements in occupied countries, especially France. If the Allies were going to liberate a country and then deal with collaborationists, why resist? A full year passed before the resistance movements recovered from this blow to their morale, and Charles de Gaulle had not forgotten it when he assumed the postwar leadership of France. These, then, were the far-reaching if unintended consequences of the Darlan deal. The storm of criticism was still raging when, on November 11, Eisenhower ordered an immediate advance on Tunis.

The British First Army under Gen. Sir Kenneth Anderson was driving on Tunis. Actually, Anderson wasn't leading a whole army but only a few thousand men in a reconnaissance-in-force. He reached the Tunisian border November 28, but by then the fast-moving Germans had flown in 15,000 combat troops with supporting armor. There were probably 30,000 German troops in and around Tunis. The Germans also held all-weather airfields, while Anderson did not; and they could supply Tunis by sea as well as by air while Anderson's line of communications ran over narrow dirt roads and a rickety single-track railroad. There was no hope of his taking Tunis by storm.

Actually, the fault lay with Dwight Eisenhower. He had been much too much concerned with politics in those early days of Torch. He also proved in his first field command that he was overcautious. With the British 78th Division he could have landed at Bizerte on Tunisia's northern tip only twenty miles north of Tunis. But he thought it would be too risky and instead landed at Bougie a hundred miles west of Tunis.

The Combined Chiefs were disappointed. They had proposed that Eisenhower invade Sardinia, the big Mediterranean island west of Italy. They realized that it would have to be a shoestring operation, but they pointed out that Sardinia was held by poorly equipped, demoralized Italian troops who would probably not put up much of a fight. Sardinia had immense strategic advantages: It would provide airfields from which to attack Italy, Sicily and Tunis, it would threaten southern France, and best of all it would outflank Italy.

But Dwight Eisenhower had been a staff officer for twenty years, and he was still thinking like one. He had forgotten what his old friend George Patton had told him in 1926: "Victory in the next war will depend on *execution* not *plans.*" To Eisenhower's orderly, staff-school mind, the Sardinia proposal was preposterous, and he rejected it. Without plans, intelligence or preparation, he just could not attempt it. Much like Montgomery, Eisenhower was more concerned with securing his rear. "For God's sake," he complained, "let's get one job done at a time." In those days, Eisenhower was not the Ike that everybody liked. He was, wrote his aide, naval Capt. Harry Butcher, "like a caged tiger." High-ranking visitors to his headquarters were agreed that he was far too much concerned with politics at the expense of waging a campaign. The Combined Chiefs reminded him that large casualties lost in a determined assault were preferable to the attrition of a stalemate.

But then Darlan was assassinated. He was shot by a young Frenchman named Fernand Bournier de la Chapelle, who had once been a member of one of Robert Murphy's underground organizations. He was one of many conspirators eager to kill the high commissioner. A week before his death, Darlan told Murphy: "You know, there are four plots in existence to assassinate me." Bournier was the gunman in one of these, with help from higher-ups. It is still not known why he killed Darlan: to punish him, to promote the Gaullist cause or to restore the French monarchy. General Giraud, who succeeded Darlan, had the assassin tried, convicted and executed within forty-eight hours, after which he destroyed all records. Darlan's removal, however, was providential. General Clark said it was "like the lancing of a troublesome boil."

Dwight Eisenhower saw in it the opportunity to delegate political problems to subordinates and get on with the battle of Tunis.

62. Developing the Atom Bomb

A YEAR HAD PASSED since the United States Government on December 6, 1941, had decided to go "all-out" in the effort to produce the atomic bomb. During that period what had been a dispersed and loosely organized pursuit of this goal by a number of scientists and universities, all acting independently, had coalesced into a unified program under the auspices of the U.S. Army and the harmless-sounding name of the Manhattan Project.

A stocky, bluff brigadier general of engineers named Leslie R. Groves was appointed to command the Manhattan Project. Groves was in charge of all army construction in the United States and its offshore bases, and was also then engaged in building the Pentagon, which he finished in the fall of 1942. Groves was not a popular choice with most of the Manhattan scientists. His brusque manner and his habit of ordering them about like so many private soldiers did not endear him to world-famous physicists and chemists, some of them Nobel laureates. His ignorance of atomic physics appalled them and his indifference to their own knowledge infuriated them. He was not a deferential man. He was also somewhat pudgy, and these for the most part trim young men were convinced that the fat in his paunch and jowls was exceeded only by its concentration above his eyebrows. Their dismay at Groves's appointment was summarized by Dr. Vannevar Bush, director of the Office of Scientific Research and Development, with the wry remark: "We are in the soup."

Fortunately, Dr. Arthur H. Compton of the University of Chicago, himself a Nobelist, did not agree. Compton was a strikingly handsome man, with the grace and strength of an athlete. He saw in General Groves a man able to get things done, and he was not quite so sensitive as most of his colleagues from the halls of academia. He also did not share their distrust of American big business. When Groves decided to assign the engineering, construction and operation of the first plutonium plant to the giant Du Pont chemical firm, many of these liberal scientists vehemently opposed selection of a corporation which they loathed as the epitome of big business in its reactionary opposition to Roosevelt's New Deal. But Compton was able to dissuade all but a few objectors from outright denunciation of the choice. He became a valuable intermediary between the general and the scientists.

"You scientists don't have any discipline," Groves grumbled to Compton after an unpleasant meeting with recalcitrant project leaders. "You don't know how to take orders and give orders."

Compton patiently tried to explain to Groves the difference between the self-imposed discipline of the seeker of truth and the outwardly imposed discipline of the soldier or the industrialist, trained to obey.

"I found myself an intermediary," Compton said, "between those on the one hand who were schooled in self-reliance and to the questioning of all authority and on the other hand the military and industrial men to whom dependence on orders was second nature."

Pearl Harbor had also changed the minds of some scientists unwilling to "do the dirty work" of the military. Among them was Volney Wilson, the brilliant young physicist who had assured Compton that Enrico Fermi was correct in predicting the possibility of a chain reaction. Wilson had then announced that he "wanted nothing to do with" the certain perversion of such enormous new sources of power to military use, and had been transferred elsewhere. Pearl

Harbor compelled him to rethink his crisis of conscience, and he had said he was willing "to go where I am most needed." So he returned to Chicago and was working with Fermi there.

The famous Fermi Five had come to Chicago. At first, Fermi planned to continue his experiments in the Argonne Laboratory to be built in the Argonne Forest some fifteen miles outside the city. But difficulties and delays, many of them caused by labor problems, impeded construction. In November, Fermi came to Compton to suggest that the atomic pile he needed for the final test could be built right in Chicago. It would be foolish to waste weeks waiting for Argonne Laboratory to be completed, even dangerous if the German scientists were as close to a solution as they were reported to be. Compton agreed. But where in Chicago? He thought immediately of Stagg Field.

A half dozen years prior to Pearl Harbor, Dr. Robert M. Hutchins, president of the University of Chicago, had become convinced that intercollegiate athletics, especially football, had become so commercialized that they were a contradiction of the goals of higher education. Accordingly, he led Chicago out of Big Ten sports. In so doing, he made a football stadium—Stagg Field—available for his expanding emphasis on intramural athletics and for scientific pursuits. Under the stadium's West Stands was a slate-walled squash court which no one used. Just the place! No one would suspect what was being done inside it, not even President Hutchins, who might feel obliged to forbid putting it to such dangerous use.

Fermi agreed. Assisted by Wilson and others, he began building his pile. It was intended to be a sphere constructed of carefully machined blocks of graphite, each resembling a long loaf of bread with alternate layers composed of lumps of uranium. On December 1, 1942—the day that gasoline rationing began in the United States—they found to their surprise that only three fourths of the height they had considered necessary was actually enough. Twelve thousand of the 16,000 pounds of uranium metal also sufficed. So they topped the pile off with another layer to shape "an oblated spheroid flatted at the top, i.e., like a door knob."

The next day Compton sat anxiously in his office awaiting a call from the squash court. It came at midmorning. "I thought you would want to know that Fermi is ready to start," Volney Wilson said. Compton hurried to the West Stands, bringing with him Crawford Greenewalt, a Du Pont director. At the West Stands they entered a balcony overlooking the squash court. The pile was at the other end. Above one corner of it was a platform on which stood three men armed with buckets filled with a cadmium solution. This was the "suicide squad." If the reaction were overviolent, it would be their duty to put out the atomic fire. Below them stood George Weill, holding the last of the cadmium-coated rods. All others had been withdrawn.

Fermi greeted Compton and Greenewalt with a smile. Few moments in the history of mankind could have been as tense, but Fermi was glacially calm. He glanced at the 5-inch slide rule he held in his hands to make a quick calculation.

"All right, George," he called easily, "pull it to thirteen feet."

Weill obeyed, carefully measuring the distance with a tape measure. The time was 10:37 A.M.

Again and again the rod was pulled back. The stylus of a recording meter climbed a graph, leveled off, then climbed again. . . . The light of a galvanometer danced back and forth across a scale. . . . From the Geiger counters came an abrupt clicking . . . Compton was amazed at the way the reactor performed exactly as Fermi had predicted. But around noon the emergency control rod, acting automatically, slammed back into its slot with a disturbing crash. Almost immediately Fermi discovered this only meant that the safety point had been set too low.

"It seems like a good time for lunch," he said casually.

Two hours later everyone assembled again in the squash court or on the balcony.

"All right, George," Fermi sang out again.

Weill pulled the rod out by a foot. Then 6 inches . . . another 6 inches. . . . Each time, Fermi made a swift calculation on his slide rule. Calm as he seemed, he drew his lips tighter and tighter, until they were a mere slit. Compton watched him anxiously, sometimes shifting his gaze to the face of Volney Wilson. Anxiety also shone in Wilson's eyes. He stared fixedly at the apparatus he had helped to devise, as though he held a secret hope that the genie would not leap out of the bottle.

At 3:25 P.M. Fermi called to Weill: "Pull it another foot, George. This is going to do it." He turned to Compton. "Now it will become self-sustaining." He pointed toward the recording meter. "The track will climb, and continue to climb," he said softly. "It will not level off."

It did not level off. Minutes passed while the clamor of the Geiger counters rose to a roar. The meters showed a dangerous level of radiation.

"Throw in the safety rods!" Fermi cried quickly.

It was done. The recording stylus dropped, the galvanometer light flitted back to zero and the clatter of the Geiger counters subsided to an occasional click. The genie was out of the bottle. . . . A low cheer rose from the squash court. Eugene Wigner presented Fermi with a bottle of Italian wine and a low bow.

Mankind had entered the Atomic Age.

But the enormous power that had been unleashed could be perverted to evil as well as noble ends. Dr. Compton was aware of this as he returned to his office with Greenewalt. The glow in his companion's eyes as he spoke of the incalculable benefits that atomic energy would confer on mankind was the antithesis of the horror Compton had seen in the eyes of Volney Wilson. Compton realized that atomic destruction would precede atomic constructions. When he was alone, he put through a call to President James B. Conant of Harvard University.

"Jim," he said, striving to keep his voice casual, "you'll be interested to know that the Italian navigator has just landed in the New World. The Earth was not as large as he had estimated, and he arrived in the New World sooner than expected."

"Is that so?" Conant said, also trying to be casual. "Were the natives friendly?"

"Everyone landed safe and happy."

In truth henceforth no one would be safe and an unhappy world would also become uneasy. But war is war, and now the atomic bomb had to be built before Hitler's scientists could build theirs—and something had to be done to erase Hitler's head start.

One of the prizes that fell to Hitler following the conquest of Norway was the Norsk Hydro Hydrogen Electrolysis plant in Vemork near Hardanger Fjord in southern Norway. At the time the Vemork plant was the world's largest producer of heavy water, a substance considered the most efficient for construction of a chain-reacting atomic pile. In May 1940, after the fall of Norway, Germany ordered the plant to increase heavy-water production to the astounding rate of 3,000 pounds a year. In 1942, this was raised to the even more disturbing goal of 10,000 pounds annually. When the Nazis placed an embargo on the export of uranium from Czechoslovakia, British scientists were alarmed. They were almost certain that with enough heavy water and uranium the Nazis could make a chain-reacting pile operate.

Combined Operations began training special forces—both civilian and military—in Britain and later in the United States. Their mission was to pinpoint the Nazi atomic plants and laboratories for either bombing raids or sabotage. Special Forces saboteurs were either members of the local underground or special troops dropped by glider or parachute. In July 1942, the dismaying rise in heavy-water production at Vemork made it imperative to strike there. Special Forces was asked to provide a small advance party for a sabotage attack by troops dropped by glider.

Norway's terrain, however, made glider operations unusually difficult. There were few landing fields. Thickly clustered and steep mountains threw up air pockets and atmospheric currents. Moreover, the Vemork plant was located on top of a high cliff. Its front was inaccessible and heavily guarded there and on both sides. It could be reached only from the rear. A landing would have to be made on a high plateau behind it and many miles away. Then the saboteurs would have to make a preciptious descent into a valley, cross it and climb a steep cliff. Snow could be expected.

Nevertheless, a party of four, code-named "Swallow," parachuted into the area on October 15. They hid half their food and equipment at a base depot to which they hoped to return. Then they set out on a nightmare trek on skis. In high altitude and bitter cold, it was not possible for a man on skis to carry more than sixty-six pounds. Swallow had eight such loads, and thus each man had to make three journeys daily over the same stretch. Sometimes they could advance only a few miles a day. Because the lakes and rivers were not quite frozen, there was slushy water on the surface. The feet of the Swallow trekkers were almost constantly wet, and sometimes they fell through the ice. There was heavy snow about them and those who left the ski tracks sank into it up to their knees. Again and again Swallow tried to make radio contact with London, but were unable to do so until November 9, when they began to make daily transmission of intelligence received from the local underground.

Special Forces was dismayed to hear that the Germans had erected wire barricades around the factory and alongside the penstock lines carrying water down to the factory's dynamos. But the information they received from Swallow enabled them to build a mock-up of the Vemork plant at a training camp in Britain. Troops were drilled in sabotage and the specific demolitions to be used on designated machinery.

On November 19 two aircraft, each towing airborne troops in a glider, arose from a field in Scotland. They headed for Vemork. Foul weather engulfed them, and one aircraft and both gliders crashed on the southwest coast of Norway a hundred miles from Vemork. The men of Swallow held fast, working at 4,000 feet and in temperatures constantly below zero, transmitting their intelligence on an erratic radio. Soon they sickened with fever and stomach pains. Their food gave out, and they began to eat a lichen called reindeer moss. They hunted reindeer, but found none until, just before Christmas, their leader shot one. They celebrated a Merry Christmas.

In London there was no merriment. Airborne troop survivors had been sharply interrogated by the Germans and their objective divined. Vemork's defenses were strengthened. The area was combed for saboteurs and innocent Norwegians arrested. Nevertheless, a second airborne party of six Norwegian soldiers, code-named Gunnerside, left Britain for Norway on January 23, 1943. They actually flew over their country but a heavy mist obscured the dropping point and the lights laid out by Swallow. They had to turn back. On February 10 Gunnerside returned and landed successfully on the frozen surface of Lake Skryken. They were only thirty miles from Swallow but in such formidable country a trek that short was the equal of one 300 miles long elsewhere. Nevertheless, Gunnerside went skiing in search of Swallow.

Thirteen days later they found them. Gunnerside and Swallow were united with "three wild yells of joy." They spent the next four days drawing up a plan of attack. Joachim, the Gunnerside leader, became the chief. All men were instructed that if capture appeared imminent, they were to kill themselves. On February 27, 1943, they moved out in two groups, a covering party and a demolition party led by Joachim.

They waited until 12:30 A.M. the following day to steal up to the plant's railroad gates. One man went forward with armorer's shears to cut the gates' chains. The covering party slipped into the plant yard. The demolition party followed. Next the factory gates were cut open, and the covering party advanced toward the German guard hut to keep it under surveillance.

Joachim led the demolition party toward the factory cellar. They could not open the cellar door. They glanced around nervously, their faces etched in the bright moonlight. The German guards were due at this point momentarily. They began searching for the cable tunnel, becoming separated as they did. Joachim found the opening to it. He and another saboteur crawled inside over a maze of cables and pipes. They could hear the machinery humming through the open door of the high-concentration plant. They stole inside, easily overpowering the surprised Norwegian guard. Joachim began placing the charges while his colleague kept watch. The work went quickly and easily. The models on which he had practiced in Britain were exact duplicates of the real thing. Half of the charges were in position when a window behind him was smashed open. Joachim and his colleague whirled, reaching for their pistols. It was one of Joachim's men. He crawled through the window and helped Joachim place the remaining charges. Then he checked them twice while Joachim coupled the fuses. They lighted both, ordering the Norwegian guard to run upstairs for his life, while they burst through the cellar door and sped away.

Twenty yards away from the factory they heard the explosion.

Three thousand pounds of heavy water, a year's production, had been destroyed. Adolf Hitler's atomic-bomb program had been severely crippled, and the men who had done it returned safely to their base.

63. The Battle for Stalingrad

IN THE SUMMER OF 1942 Adolf Hitler's empire had reached its greatest extent. When the German Sixth Army under Gen. Friedrich Paulus arrived at the Volga a few miles north of Stalingrad, Hitler had conquered almost as much of Russia as Genghis Khan's devouring Mongol hordes in the thirteenth century. The swastika flag now flew from Mount Elbrus, the highest mountain of the Caucasus, a feat that revivified the despondent German people. They realized with jubilation that Germany now ruled Europe from the Pyrenees to the Caucasus.

Hitler's empire was immense. Most of North Africa was in his hands and the Mediterranean was an Axis lake. "Axis" now meant Nazi, for the Italian partner had been reduced to satellite status hardly greater than Romania or Hungary. Central Asia seemed to be opening up and in the far distance the Persian Gulf beckoned. Hitler's insatiable thirst for oil seemed satiated when his forces seized the Maykop oil fields in the Caucasus; but the retreating Soviets had so thoroughly wrecked them that they were for the present useless. Although his troops were within a hundred miles of the Caspian Sea, they never got to the more valuable oil fields at Baku or even those at Groznyy farther west. Nevertheless, Adolf Hitler could quite rightfully compare himself to Genghis Khan or Napoleon. He was another *stupor mundi,* although the quarters in which he now lived were a little short of stupefying.

Der Führer lived near Vinnitsa in the Ukraine. His new headquarters was a collection of miserable huts among the pine trees called Werewolf. It was well named, because Hitler had indeed become a werewolf, snarling at his generals and constantly castigating them. Because he was sleeping badly and had lost weight, he was easily irritated. When General Halder told him on July 23 that the Soviets seemed to be deliberately avoiding battle, he screamed at him in a fury:

"Nonsense! The Russians are in full flight, they are finished, they are reeling from the blows we have dealt them during the past few months."

On that same day Hitler signed a directive ordering renewed offensives on the Groznyy oil fields and Stalingrad. But both these objectives were beyond the strength of the Wehrmacht, as his generals vainly warned him. In late August the offensive in the Caucasus literally ran out of gas. Difficulties of terrain, lengthening lines of communications and Soviet resistance also contributed to its failure.

The German high command was also astounded to discover that the U.S.S.R., like a phoenix rising from its own ashes, was stronger than ever. American supplies were by then flowing to the Soviet Union, but most important of all was the fact that the Soviets had been able to move their industry away from the fighting fronts and as far east as Siberia and Central Asia. Millions of men and women formed into labor battalions had endured the bitter winter cold to construct factories of every description out of range of German panzers and even the Luftwaffe. From this miracle of improvisation came such weapons as the monster new fifty-two-ton tank. A heavily armored vehicle, it mounted 3-inch cannon and machine guns. Smaller German tanks were no match for these KV's, named after Marshal Kliment Voroshilov. But Adolf Hitler remained undaunted. He ordered his southern armies to concentrate against Stalingrad. To the blunder of leaving vital Moscow unmolested, he now added the greater mistake of assaulting a city worthless both strategically and tactically, but yet, because of its name, one sacred to the Soviet mind.

Stalingrad had once been named Tsaritsyn. It was here in 1918 that Joseph Stalin organized its defense against the forces of the White Army, here that the timorous Koba stood poised for flight until he was saved by the arrival of Red cavalry. To commemorate his "victory," he gave the city his own name, and Stalingrad became dear to his heart.

Stalingrad was an ugly, sprawling city, like an American boom town straggling for miles along the western bank of the Volga. It was a place of half a million people, factories, workshops, narrow streets, smokestacks and high-rise workers' apartments looking east over the Volga toward forests and villages. It had no natural defenses. It could have been neutralized by bombing. Holding it could have cut the flow of Groznyy and Baku oil to Moscow, but that could have been done by bridging the river farther down. Stalingrad also could have been starved into submission. But, no, Hitler wanted Stalingrad, and so General Paulus and his Sixth Army of 300,000 men came against it.

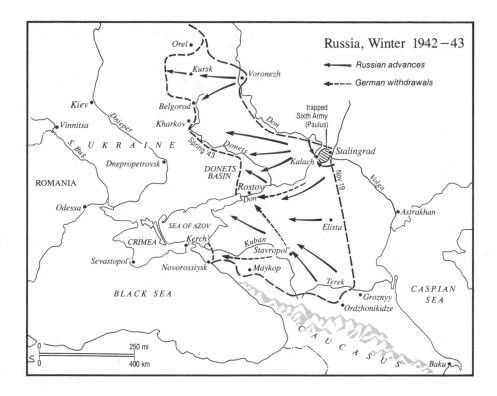

Russia, Winter 1942–43

←——— Russian advances

←- - - - German withdrawals

Their attacks were preceded on September 15 by a fierce artillery and aerial bombardment, which had the effect of turning a city with no natural defenses into a formidable fortress. A city in ruins and rubble is as much a boon to its defenders as it is a torment to its besiegers. Fallen buildings became a labyrinth of caves and sniper holes. When the German soldiers entered, Soviet soldiers occupied every manhole, every shell hole, every drainpipe and every crater around collapsed structures, peering through primitive periscopes. Nothing short of a direct hit could dislodge such hidden, well-protected snipers. German soldiers could not get close enough to their holes to pick them off, and renewed bombing merely convulsed the rubble to provide new shelters.

Stalingrad was indeed a battle among the ruins: of workers' dwellings, schools, stores, factories. Pitched battles were fought for the possession of a warehouse, a bakery or a grain elevator. German soldiers accustomed to maneuvering on the plains, to attacking fortifications built in the open or razing occupied villages, had never before encountered street fighting of such ferocity. The Soviet high command had ordered its soldiers to fight to the death. "Before you die, kill a German—with your teeth if necessary!"

To their growing skill in house-to-house fighting, the Soviets added a phenomenal mastery of the art of infiltration. Every Soviet attack was preceded by small units and individual soldiers slipping through German lines. However carefully the Germans kept their outlying positions under observation, the Soviets got through. Suddenly, there they were, in force, dug in and well armed. It was true that the German front was thinly held, about twelve miles to a division, with very few strong points. Yet, each night, with everyone alerted and wide-awake to the possibility of enemy infiltration, the Soviets somehow got through. In the morning they would be found in strength in the German rear, and they were most difficult to dislodge.

Tenacity and fatalism also marked the defense of Stalingrad. Gen. V. I. Chuikov told his 62nd Army, "You can no longer retreat across the Volga. There is only one road, the road that leads forward. Stalingrad can be saved by you, or wiped out *with* you."

Still the Germans continued with their senseless frontal assaults. Sometimes they gained a small advantage, as when they penetrated into the tractor factory, but these were only local and temporary. The Soviet counterattacks—with the exception of their infiltrations—were hardly better. They were models of rigidity: always the same place, always the same artillery preparation and always a total lack of imagination. Between them the two forces slugged away like artless prizefighters trading roundhouse punches.

In October, Paulus prepared to make his decisive thrust. He moved German troops from his flanks to his front, replacing them with Romanians. This greatly weakened his defenses, but at the time Paulus was not thinking defensively. On the 14th he launched his most massive attacks. Five brand new or newly reinforced infantry divisions and two armored divisions struck on a narrow front less than three miles wide. It was launched following the most hideous artillery and mortar barrage of the entire battle, supplemented by 2,000 Luftwaffe sorties. The roar was so continuous and deafening that it was impossible to register a single explosion or shot. Nothing beyond five yards could be distinguished, the smoke and dust were so thick. In General Chuikov's headquarters the vibration was so great that glasses flew off tables, disintegrating into a thousand bits. It is not often even in modern warfare that an army headquarters suffers casualties, but sixty-three men in 62nd Army's command post were killed and three times as many wounded. Yet, for all of this Paulus's Sixth Army could penetrate no more than a mile, breaking through at the tractor factory. Thereafter, attrition reigned as king of the battlefield, and attrition always erodes the invader the most. Paulus and the intelligent officers and men in this army at the end of a line of supply a thousand miles long knew that they were doomed.

Adolf Hitler didn't. On November 9 he made his annual speech commemorating the Beer-Hall Putsch in the Bürgerbräu keller in front of the Nazi old guard. "I wanted to get to the Volga," he told them, "and to do so at a particular point where stands a certain town. By chance it bears the name of Stalin himself. I wanted to take the place, and do you know, we've pulled it off, we've got it really, except for a few enemy positions still holding out. Now people say: 'Why don't they finish the job more quickly?' Well, the reason is I don't want another Verdun. I prefer to do the job with quite small assault groups. Time is of no consequence at all."

German soldiers on the Stalingrad front heard these incredible words. One of them put his head in his hands and cried in disbelief: "My God, quite small assault groups . . . if he had only at least reached full corporal!"

Hitler had come to Munich by special train. He was accompanied by Albert Speer, now the Nazi industrial czar, General Jodl and members of the general staff. They had left on the afternoon of November 7, delayed en route by the necessity of stopping at many stations to hook up the train's telephone cable to the station's telegraph system. Thus, Hitler got his reports.

In happier days, *Der Führer* was accustomed to showing himself at the window of the special train wherever it stopped, smiling and waving his hand when he was recognized by cheering throngs. On this trip, aware of the nation's somber mood, Hitler did not want to show himself to the people. The shades on the station side of the train were lowered. Late that night, the train stopped at another station. Hitler and his party sat down to dine in his rosewood-paneled dining car. The table was set with shining silver, starched white linen, gleaming blue crystal glasses and beautiful china. Flowers were on each table. A delicious meal with fine wine was served, and as the diners bent to consume it, a freight train came slowly to a stop on the adjacent track.

No one seemed to notice it, or to realize that the shades had not been drawn. The train was returning from the Stalingrad front. It was composed of a string of cattle cars. In them were German soldiers, their faces pinched with cold and emaciated with starvation. Many of them were wounded, blood-stained bandages stark against their filthy uniforms. They stared with pathetic, devouring eyes at that unbelievable other world opposite them, only two yards away. They could not comprehend that the man in the brown uniform with the famous dab of mustache was *Him!* In their lackluster eyes there was not even a hint of resentment at this man who was indeed the author of all their misery.

Hitler glanced up, flushing, and grated out an order to the waiters to draw the shades. Here were German soldiers such as he had been, and he did not lift a hand.

By November of 1942, during sixteen months of fighting on the Soviet Front, the German Army had lost 2 million men killed and wounded, among them their finest troops, veterans who might have been expected to form the nucleus of new cadres. In the six months between June and the end of November 1942, losses in the region of the Don River, the Volga and at Stalingrad had been 600,000 men, 1,000 tanks, 2,000 guns and mortars and 1,400 airplanes. By then the German army was so desperate for new conscripts that it had reached down into the ranks of the sixteen-year-olds.

One of these was Guy Sajer, a native of Alsace born of a French father and a German mother. He spoke both languages and because he was so young, "still playing with my Meccano set," he didn't really care which uniform he wore. But the Germans still held Alsace and the nationality of Sajer's mother was decisive. In July he put on the field gray uniform of the German army.

Because he was so young and not very strong, he was assigned to a supply unit rather than a combat formation. His duty was to help supply Paulus's beleaguered army at Stalingrad. In the fall of 1942, Sajer and his comrades entrained for the Soviet front, bound for Minsk. It seemed to Sajer that he was getting colder by the minute. The train entered a great forest. Then the braking wheels began shrieking, and Sajer saw that the slowing train was being diverted to a secondary track. He got down from his car, beating his gloved hands together and jumping up and down for warmth. He looked down the track.

A locomotive came toward him pushing before it a car loaded with railway materials. The car obscured the locomotive's lights, so that it approached as though through a misty halo. Behind the tender and kitchen with its stack pouring smoke was a high-railed car full of armed German guards. Following it were open flatcars. Sajer and his friend Hals peered at them in apprehension. They could not make out their cargo. Then they stiffened. They were bodies, living bodies. Men in brown coats huddled together, clinging together, crouching together.

"Russian prisoners," Hals said. Sajer nodded, stiffening when Hals said in a voice of horror: "They've piled up their dead to shield them from the wind."

Like huge tumbrils the cars rolled slowly by, each of them carrying a shield of corpses stacked along the sides. Bare frozen feet stuck out from the shields. They had been stripped of their footwear, a soldier's most precious possession. Sometimes three or four of the bodies slipped from the stack and fell sprawling to the roadbed. No one noticed. The cars continued to roll west, to the labor camps or the funeral pyres. . . . Horrified, Sajer and Hals climbed back into their train.

They reached Minsk just as the temperature fell to below zero, and the snow rose to a depth of three feet and more. There they found the *Rollbahn* trucks they would drive, bringing to the front winter clothing and supplies. The Third Reich had not forgotten its soldiers on the Soviet Front this winter. There were huge stores of blankets, special winter clothing made of sheepskin, hoods of double catskin, overshoes with thick insulating soles and uppers of matted hair, felt-lined gloves and portable heaters which could run on oil, gasoline or solidified alcohol. Getting these to the front was an ordeal.

Monstrous ruts in the primitive Soviet roads had been frozen solid. Covering snowdrifts had to be shoveled away to reveal them so that they could be tamped down with snow to level the road or blown up. At night the *Rollbahn* troops sought shelter in peasant isbas, as many as fifty stinking, filthy, lousy men crowding into a hut built to hold a single family. Still they drove east. Nearing Kiev they passed through the litter of bygone battle, landscapes covered with wrecked tanks, trucks, guns and aircraft. They passed cemeteries containing the dead of both sides. There were many more German crosses, even though many more Soviets had died; the Germans were buried individually while there were ten or twelve Russians to each grave. Inside Kiev, they went to the sanitation center where they had their first wash since they left Germany and were deloused and given clean uniforms. A captain in a neatly pressed uniform rode up in a Volkswagen, leaning out the window to deliver the canned exhortation typical of rear-echelon officers.

"Soldiers! Germans! Convoy troops! At this hour when the conquests of the Reich extend across a vast . . ." It went on for ten minutes, to the intense boredom of Sajer and his comrades, ending with the customary peroration: "Never forget that the nation owes you everything, and that in return it expects everything of you, up to and including the supreme sacrifice. You must learn to support suffering without complaint, because you are German! Heil Hitler!"

"Heil Hitler!" the men shouted in unison, and marched back to their trucks to drive east again. Within a few days they heard a rumbling ahead of them. Artillery . . . the front . . . They were held up at a roadblock of Soviet partisans. Jumping down from the trucks, they began to dig foxholes in the snow. Sajer was delighted to fire his Mauser rifle. He fired twelve shots at the unseen foe, thrilled at each report and recoil against his shoulder. German tanks and armored cars clanked up to drive the partisans off. The hundred-truck convoy moved east again. Sajer sat next to his driver with his rifle across his knees. The man was a newcomer who had lost a kneecap in the Polish campaign. He was a veteran with a bagful of the old soldier's tricks and dodges. That night when the convoy stopped in a hamlet, Sajer eagerly opened the truck door to jump down and run to the kitchen truck. The old soldier grabbed his arm. "Don't be in such a hurry, unless you want to be on guard duty tonight. The sergeant doesn't keep records here, you know, the way he does at the barracks. He just grabs the first people he sees, assigns them, and then takes it easy."

Sajer relaxed. He waited five minutes, then alighted and sauntered toward the kitchen trucks. He was amused to see that his friend, the ever-hungry Hals, had been snared by the sergeant. "Shit! They've stuck me for guard duty again."

The thermometer was at 22 degrees below zero, and Sajer was glad he did not have to be outside walking guard. He and the driver approached the cook with extended mess tins. He dug into a tureen with a big spoon and sloshed tepid food onto their trays. "So, you're not feeling hungry tonight?" he asked sarcastically.

A lieutenant came up. "Is the water nearly ready?"

"Just now, *Leutnant.* It's just boiling."

"Good." The lieutenant's eye fell on Sajer and the driver. "You two, take the water to the doctor." He pointed to a lighted doorway.

In dismay, both soldiers closed their mess tins and hooked them on their belts. They would eat the contents later—cold. Each seized a tureen full of boiling water and staggered toward the doorway, careful not to spill the scalding water on their feet. Inside the common room of a Soviet farmer's house the convoy

doctor had improvised an operating room. It was warm, but full of the groans
and moans of wounded men. Two Soviet women took the tureens and began
washing surgical instruments in pans of hot water. The doctor was busy with a
wounded man held down by two comrades. He screamed and jerked his legs
spasmodically as the doctor probed his thigh with a scalpel. He probed and
scraped . . . cut and dug . . . . streams of blood poured from the hole in the man's
thigh.

"Hold his leg," the doctor said softly to Sajer.

Sajer put trembling hands on the man's leg. He could feel himself shaking.
He watched in horror while the doctor cut deeper into the wound. He could feel
the man's leg tensing and untensing in his hands. He looked away. Then he heard
the sound of a saw. The leg suddenly felt heavier in his hands—incredibly heavy.
He glanced up. The man's bleeding stump was a half foot above the leg. Sajer
shuddered and put the amputated leg down on a pile of bandages.

He tried throughout the night to slip away from this room of suffering and
horror. But before he could, the doctor always found another odious chore for
him. At one in the morning, he saw his chance. He made straight for the guard
hut where he warmed his dinner before a blazing fireplace, ate it and fell asleep
on the floor.

In the morning it was so cold it took a good half hour to warm the truck
engines, before the 19th *Kompanie Rollbahn* went rolling east over the Third
International Highway again.

Paulus's mid-October offensive raged for days and nights. At one point the
Germans possessed nine tenths of the city. Paulus wanted the final tenth on a
narrow strip along the cliff above the Volga. The cliff was honeycombed with
galleries containing hidden command posts, hospitals, factories and ammunition
dumps. The Soviets fought ferociously to hold their little "islands" of resistance.
They broke up German massing movements with heavy guns mounted in the
forests across the river. Supplies were ferried over the Volga. Reinforcements
came in the same way. Stalingrad still held.

Now to relieve the pressure on the city, Soviet forces on the Don front began
an offensive on October 19. The Germans were compelled to divert large numbers
of aircraft, tanks and artillery toward the Don. At the same time the Soviet 64th
Army struck Paulus's southern flank. By these timely strokes, the Soviets fighting
under the overall direction of Marshal Georgi Zhukov were able to ease the
pressure on Chuikov's 62nd Army within the city. With this, Zhukov prepared
his own November counteroffensive.

As Zhukov's blows struck deeper wedges into the German flanks, the soldiers there began falling back on Stalingrad. As they did, the second Soviet winter
seized them in its iron grasp. This time, however, they were issued warm clothing
brought to the front by truck convoys such as Guy Sajer's. Nevertheless, the men

froze in their holes. In the morning vapor puffs shot from their mouths as thick as cigarette smoke. Their breath hardened like crystal on the side flaps of their caps. To free the ice from their frozen weapons, they urinated on them. Gradually, there sank into their numbed consciousness the reality of defeat. Victory was no longer possible. Was it worth it even to try to live in this frozen hell of snow and ice?

They struggled on, withdrawing in the face of relentless pressure. Guns were blown up. Munition dumps were set afire and huge stores of clothing and food piled on top of them. Nothing was to be left to the onrushing enemy. Everywhere, alongside roads clogged with stalled tanks and trucks and even sleighs, was the litter of retreat: helmets, gas masks, ground sheets, cooking utensils, entrenching tools. Even rifles and grenades were thrown away either by the wounded or soldiers who now looked upon them as a burden. Icy winds slashing in from the east blew snowflakes as sharp as bits of glass into their unshaven faces. Their skin sagged on their bones as their ragged gray uniforms hung in folds on their shrunken bodies. Men who could go on no longer sank to their knees in the snow and rolled over, dying, to be shaped into white mounds within minutes by the never-ending snow.

Again and again they turned in delaying actions. Some of them had lost so many fingers to frostbite that they had only a little finger to fire their rifles. Or else they held their mugs of ersatz coffee with the thumb and the little finger. For sustenance they had a few slices of bread a day or a thin broth with an infrequent cube of sweetish horsemeat floating in it.

At night they lay in the snow listening fearfully for the Stalin Organs, those dreaded rocket launchers. When they heard them belching sonorously in the distance, they squirmed deeper in the snow, covering their ears against the shriek of the falling rockets and the roar of the explosions spraying fiery red death among them and making the snow seem hot. Then the Soviets would be on them, shouting and singing, and once again the German guns chattered, until the monster KV tanks arrived and a fresh retreat was begun.

Yet, whenever they could, they squatted in the snow and wrote letters home. Most of them were never mailed, taken by the thousands from the unidentifiable remains of men torn to bits by the Stalin Organs. Here is one:

Of the division there are only sixty-nine men still fit for action. Bleyer is still alive, and Hartliebe as well. Little Degan has lost both arms; I expect he will soon be in Germany. Life is finished for him, too. D. has given up hope. . . . All we have left are two machine guns and four hundred rounds. And then a mortar and ten bombs. Except for that all we have are hunger and fatigue. B. has broken out with twenty men on his own initiative. Better to know in three days than in three weeks what the end looks like. Can't say I blame him.

Finally the withdrawing flank troops entered Stalingrad. They took up their positions while the Soviet propaganda loudspeakers intoned with chill monotony:

"Every seven seconds, a German dies in Russia. Stalingrad is a mass grave. Every seven seconds, a German dies. . . ."

On November 19 the Soviet counteroffensive began. Zhukov had skillfully massed perhaps a million troops on three fronts: the southwest on Paulus's left flank, the Don Front in his center and the Stalingrad Front on his right. Almost immediately the Southwest Front armies achieved a breakthrough. The Romanians whom Paulus had sent there to replace German formations broke and ran or surrendered in great numbers. The Don Front armies also broke through. On the following day the Stalingrad Front surged forward, routing the Romanians on Paulus's right. Within a week, the Sixth Army was in danger of encirclement. Soviet armies on their left and right flanks were rushing toward a meeting in their rear at the line Kalach-Sovetskoye. Paulus desperately radioed Hitler for help. None came. Instead *Der Führer* ordered him to stand firm and to transform his position into "Fortress Stalingrad." Once again Richard Wagner's crashing cymbals and wailing horns were in Hitler's ears. But Paulus could not make a fortress of this now-leveled city. He had neither the guns nor the able men. Temperatures were near 30 below and food supplies were beneath subsistence level. Neither could he break out with tanks. There was only enough fuel for each tank to travel twenty miles. On the night of November 23 Paulus radioed Hitler for permission to evacuate the pockets held in Stalingrad by German troops and attempt to break out to the south and west. Hitler replied: "Stalingrad must be held. There must be no breakout." Once again, *Der Führer* was refusing to surrender an inch of conquered ground. But he did promise supplies, a veritable cornucopia to be poured from the skies by the Luftwaffe. On that very day he had received a promise of their delivery from Reichsmarschall Hermann Goering. Goering had conferred with Hitler and Gen. Kurt Zeitzler, the army chief of staff. Zeitzler kept a record of the conversation.

"Goering," Hitler asked, "can you supply the Sixth Army by air?"

"My Führer, I assure you that the Luftwaffe can keep the Sixth Army supplied."

Zeitzler objected. "The Luftwaffe certainly cannot."

"You are not in a position to give an opinion on that subject," Goering replied loftily.

"My Führer," Zeitzler said, turning to Hitler, "may I ask the Reichsmarschall a question?"

"Yes, you may."

"Herr Reichsmarschall, do you know what tonnage has to be flown in every day?"

"I don't, but my staff officers do."

"Allowing for all the stocks at present with the Sixth Army," Zeitzler said, "allowing for absolute minimum needs and for the taking of all possible emergency measures, the Sixth Army will require delivery of three hundred tons per day. But since not every day is suitable for flying, as I myself learned at the front last winter, this means that about five hundred tons will have to be carried to the Sixth Army on each and every flying day, if the irreducible minimum is to be maintained."

"I can do that," Goering insisted.

"My Führer," said Zeigler, "that is a lie."

Hitler knew that it was a lie, and so did Goering; nevertheless Hitler assured Paulus of the cornucopia winging its way to Stalingrad. Actually, Goering never brought more than 100 tons a day to Stalingrad. Sometimes his overworked Junkers brought as little as sixteen tons.

Next Hitler summoned Field Marshal Erich von Manstein from the Leningrad front to take command of the newly formed Army Group Don to relieve Paulus. He was to drive on the city from the southwest. Manstein argued that it would be better for Paulus to try to break out through the west while he struck down from the northeast. Hitler shook his head. Manstein must join forces with Paulus in Stalingrad and hold the city.

Manstein ordered General Hermann Hoth to break the Soviet ring with his Fourth Panzer Army. By December 21 Hoth had driven to within thirty miles of Stalingrad. His forward units said they could see Sixth Army's signal flares. Hoth was astonished. He actually had punched a hole in the Soviet ring. Paulus could escape through it if he wanted to. On that same day Zeitzler tried to persuade Hitler to allow Paulus to make the attempt.

Hitler's reply was incredible: *Paulus could escape if he still held onto Stalingrad.* Zeitzler was horrified. Was *Der Führer* going mad? Manstein composed a clever order to Paulus. It was deliberately vague and could be construed by the general as an order to break out. Later, Paulus could save himself from Hitler's wrath by claiming a misunderstanding. But Paulus, loyal to Hitler, refused to seize the opportunity. Probably, by then he could not have broken out. His troops were dying of frostbite, typhus and dysentery. They had little food, and some of them were suspected of eating their dead comrades. It was not yet an open practice, as it would become among Axis prisoners in the dreadful Soviet prison camps, but the inexplicable absence of limbs neatly severed from dead bodies suggested it. Cavalrymen and some artillery men were tempted to no such aberration, being able to slaughter and eat their horses. With his men in this condition and with no fuel for his tanks and transport, Paulus could not hope to succeed. On December 23, Manstein ordered Hoth to return to the Don Front. By Christmas, the army of the Caucasus was also in trouble, and Hitler reluctantly signed an order for it to withdraw.

Back in Berlin Christmas had not been merry. There were too many wives without husbands, too many mothers without sons, too many soldiers without arms or legs telling their tales of horror. Else Wendel's friend, Edith Wieland, had lost her husband at Stalingrad. Else came to see her, stunned to find a thin old woman in black, not her proud and buoyant old friend.

Edith showed Else her husband's last letter. He spoke of impending, inevitable death. But as long as he felt that his death would serve a purpose, he was ready to die for the Fatherland. Else was shaken, searching her mind for the right thing to say. Her friend began to speak again.

"There is one thing that haunts me. I have heard a rumor that they could have escaped, but that Hitler forbade it."

"No!" Else cried in horror. "Incredible! Hitler never would do such a thing. You know that, surely?"

"I am not so sure," Edith said in a low voice, lifting her head. "I keep rereading that sentence in Albert's letter: 'As long as I feel my death serves a purpose. . . .' That doesn't sound a bit like Albert. It sounds as though his confidence was waning, and he was beginning to doubt."

After General Hoth began his withdrawal from the Stalingrad front and the army in the Caucasus was given permission to retreat, the Soviets opened a drive on Rostov, hoping to cut them off. Among the troops hurrying for that key city was Sgt. Alexei Petrov, a short squat artilleryman. Petrov was eager to liberate the Rostov area, where his family was held captive by the Nazis. The sergeant had heard many horror stories about the Germans: boys and girls deported for slave labor . . . libraries and town halls burned down . . . civilians shot for harboring Soviet soldiers . . . rape without end. . . . He burned for revenge.

But then he met a new and entirely unexpected enemy. Entering a steppes village, he and his gun crew were attacked by peasants wielding pitchforks and hammers. Petrov and his men retreated in confusion. Then they realized that their assailants were Kazakhs, people who hated Russians and Russian rule. "We don't want any Russians here!" they screamed. An officer telephoned division headquarters for advice. Back came the reply: "Destroy them all."

Petrov ordered his men to open fire on the village. Within a quarter hour the homes and buildings made of mud, clay and rough-hewn logs were obliterated. No one was left living, and the pursuit of the Germans was resumed.

Erich von Manstein was a noble soldier. He did not relinquish his attempts to persuade Hitler to allow Paulus to attempt to break out. He sent a personal emissary to him, but after Hitler heard his litany of disaster, he remarked quietly: "Man recovers very quickly." On January 30, Hitler hit upon a ruse which he believed would compel Paulus to fight to the death with *Der Führer*'s name on his lips. Aware that no German field marshal had ever surrendered, he made him a field marshal.

Soviet artillery, however, was more persuasive. It fell mercilessly on Paulus's scarecrows, and even found the new field marshal in his command post in a department store. Paulus was too stunned to make any reply to the Soviet surrender demand. He left it to his chief of staff, Lt. Col. Arthur Schmidt. There was no formal surrender. Instead Paulus and his entire headquarters staff went into captivity, while the various sector commanders made their own arrangements. Thus, twenty-four generals and 180,000 officers and men—the survivors of the original 300,000—passed into captivity. All but the generals were sent by forced marches to the cruel prison camps of Siberia, where almost all of them perished of typhus and cholera epidemics. The Russians were no more tender than the Germans had been. Only 6,000 Axis soldiers are known to have survived the Battle of Stalingrad.

Hitler was shattered by the Soviet broadcast that Sixth Army had surrendered. He had believed Paulus's last message that he and his troops were fighting to the last man and the last round for the glory of *Der Führer* and the Fatherland. The thought of Paulus and his men still alive galled him. He should have killed himself! The whole army should have killed themselves! The Germans should have formed square and aimed their rifles at each other's heads and annihilated one another at a single command. Again and again, Hitler in his rantings in front of Zeitzler alluded to Geli Raubal.

"When you consider," he stormed, "that a woman who has her pride goes out, shuts herself in her room, and immediately shoots herself just because someone has made a few insulting remarks, then I can have no respect for a soldier who is too frightened to do the same thing, but prefers to go into captivity." Hitler was certain that Paulus would be tortured in the infamous Lubyanka Prison in Moscow, along with Schmidt. "The Russians will shut them up in that 'rat cage,' and two days later they'll be so softened up they will say anything. And there's this beautiful woman, a real beauty of the first rank, and she feels insulted by some words, nothing of any importance, and she says, 'Then I can go, I am not needed,' and the man says, 'Get out!' So she goes away, writes a farewell letter, and shoots herself."

Not a word of compassion or admiration for his heroic suffering soldiers fell from the lips of the new *stupor mundi*. He had compared the beautiful niece whom he had driven to suicide to Paulus and the Sixth Army, and found them wanting.

PART SIX

1943

64. Summit at Casablanca

DURING JANUARY 14–24, 1943, President Roosevelt and Prime Minister Churchill with their staffs and war chiefs met at Casablanca in Morocco in the first of a series of wartime summit conferences. It had been hoped that Premier Stalin also would attend the Casablanca conference, but at the time of the invitation in the previous fall, he was much too preoccupied with Stalingrad.

Many problems were solved at Casablanca, and some new ones created. The Americans were clearly suspicious that Churchill's insistence on fresh operations in the Mediterranean was due to his positive colonial intentions. For their part, the British were afraid that Admiral King would press his campaign to exploit the American victories in the Pacific.

As it turned out, Casablanca was characterized by a sense of unity never afterward to be repeated. The British shelved their objections to new Pacific operations, and the Americans agreed to the invasion of Sicily that summer to be followed by landings in Italy. It was also agreed to continue the heavy aerial onslaught on Germany, with the British striking at night and the Americans by day. The British still resisted American efforts to convert them to the policy of daylight bombing, believing that the losses incurred to gain greater accuracy were not commensurate with the increase in destruction. There was no way to dispute this claim at the time; but British bombs by night and American by day meant that Germany's cities and industrial center would quiver beneath a twenty-four-hour rain of fire and steel. The most momentous agreement was to postpone the cross-Channel invasion of France.

Churchill had for some time been unaware that Torch in 1942 canceled out Roundup in 1943. When Eisenhower told him that this was so during dinner at Chequers in the previous September, the prime minister had been stunned. He could not believe it, suggesting that he had paid no attention to Marshall's arguments against Torch, all to the effect that it precluded Roundup. When he was at last convinced, he brought up the idea of an invasion of Norway. But at Casablanca he at last agreed to the French invasion that he would dread until well past the day it began.

At Casablanca Roosevelt announced the Allied policy of Unconditional Surrender. He and Churchill had discussed and concurred in it, but the phrase was not included in the official Casablanca agreements. Roosevelt explained: "Suddenly the press conference was on, and Winston and I had had no time to prepare for it, and the thought popped into my mind that they had called Grant 'Unconditional Surrender' and the next thing I knew I had said it." So casual,

511

so offhand, this drastic new policy ruled out any possibility of negotiation through diplomatic channels and discouraged anti-Hitler conspirators in Germany. It put the steel of desperation into the spines of the Axis warlords, thus prolonging the war and wasting many thousands of lives on both sides. By ruling out any terms for a defeated Germany, it weakened opposition to Hitler within the country, strengthened his hold, and eventually left Germany leaderless and without a law and the Soviet Union supreme on the Continent. As far-reaching as it was to become, it certainly was not born of long reflection and research. Proof that it came as almost an afterthought is that Roosevelt believed that Grant because of his initials U.S. was called "Unconditional Surrender" Grant after he defeated Lee at Appomattox, when in fact the terms he offered there were the most generous of the war. It was at Fort Donelson that Grant refused to offer terms to his former West Point classmate, Simon Bolivar Buckner. Because he held Buckner in low esteem, Grant calculated that he would cave in—and he did.

It has been argued that the real reason for Unconditional Surrender was to reassure Stalin that the Allies would not desert him and that there would be no more "deals" like the Darlan agreement. It may have been born of a deeper miscalculation: a fear that Stalin would make a separate peace with Hitler. Actually, Stalin criticized the policy of Unconditional Surrender. He knew that it would produce a last-ditch desperation in the enemy. As late as May 1945, Harry Hopkins reported that Stalin "feels that if we stick to unconditional surrender, the Japs will not give up and we will have to destroy them as we did Germany." (And if Truman had not modified the policy to allow the Japanese to keep their emperor, he would have been right.)

Goebbels pounced upon the notion of Unconditional Surrender with glee. The memoirs of so many German soldiers, from private to general, bristled with anger when they discussed it. Heinz Guderian wrote: "The effect of this brutal formula on the German nation, and above all on the Army was great. The soldiers, at least, were convinced from now on that our enemies had decided on the utter destruction of Germany, that they were no longer fighting—as Allied propaganda at the time alleged—against Hitler and so-called Nazis, but against their efficient, and therefore dangerous, rivals for the trade of the world."

Unconditional Surrender, though its effects were not then foreseen, proved to be the most formidable of the new problems created at Casablanca. A lesser one was what to do with the Free French. Henri Giraud and Charles de Gaulle detested each other. Both were there, Giraud eagerly in hopes of being proclaimed chief, de Gaulle reluctantly, aware of Roosevelt's hatred for him, unwilling to share his power. Under the goading of Roosevelt, both men agreed to shake hands for the photographers. There they stood, the tall Giraud staring haughtily ahead, the even taller de Gaulle glancing disdainfully down. Nothing came of the "romance"—or "shotgun wedding" as Roosevelt called it. "The day de Gaulle arrived," Roosevelt said, "he thought he was Joan of Arc, and the following day he insisted that he was Georges Clemenceau." Professional politician that he was, FDR could not comprehend that in the hearts of many Frenchmen Charles de

Gaulle *was* the reincarnation of the Maid. He was France, as events would prove; and Roosevelt's gibes were just more American arrows in his heart when he assumed the leadership of the nation whose honor he had upheld.

It was at Casablanca that Dwight Eisenhower became the Anglo-American supreme commander. He seemed nervous when he arrived. "Ike seems jittery," Roosevelt said to Hopkins. He was, indeed, for he had had a harrowing flight over the Atlas Mountains. His Flying Fortress lost two engines and he almost had to bail out. He also had the flu. Nevertheless, he made a masterly presentation, which impressed both Churchill and FDR to the extent that they agreed to put the British Eighth Army under his command when it reached Tunisia.

Other considerations led to the decision. Marshall still supported Eisenhower, which counted heavily with Roosevelt; his devotion to the Alliance and his ability to make the coalition work made him uniquely qualified, and the fact that the French would never serve under a British commander simply ruled out any other candidate. Alan Brooke had a more cynical explanation. Openly critical of Eisenhower's handling of the North African campaign thus far, he declared: "We were pushing Eisenhower up into the stratosphere and rarefied atmosphere of a Supreme Commander, where he would be free to devote his time to the political and inter-allied problems, whilst we inserted under him . . . our own commanders to deal with the military situations and to restore the necessary drive and coordination which had been so seriously lacking."

Eisenhower was not so easily kicked upstairs. He got along famously with his three British deputies: Admiral Cunningham, naval; General Alexander, ground; Air Marshal Arthur Tedder, air. But Brooke's hopes that this anointed trio would ease Eisenhower out of command were quickly dispelled, chiefly by Eisenhower himself. Still devoted to the principle of a single commander, he firmly rejected the British system of command by committee. When the Combined Chiefs issued a directive stating that the deputies would actually control operations, Eisenhower objected with a blistering protest. He was the supreme commander, and he would exercise that authority; and so, for better or worse, his was the responsibility when the rainy season ended in Tunisia and the North African campaign was resumed.

65. Victory in North Africa

FIELD MARSHAL ROMMEL had returned to Germany to plead with Hitler to withdraw the Afrika Korps. He had been appalled by the amount and quality of American war matériel flowing into North Africa and had concluded that all the tactical skill in the world could only delay the eventual collapse of Axis forces there. Hitler rewarded Rommel's fidelity and loyalty to his men by calling them all cowards. Rommel was shocked. He challenged Hitler to come to North Africa to see the situation for himself. "Go!" Hitler screamed. "I have other things to do than talk to you." Rommel saluted and turned on his heel. Hitler ran after him and put his arm around his shoulder. "You must excuse me," he said, "I'm in a very nervous state. But everything is going to be all right. Come and see me tomorrow, and we will talk about it calmly."

Rommel saw Hitler next day, with Goering. "Do anything you like," Hitler said to Goering, "but see that the Afrika Korps is supplied with all that Rommel wants."

"You can build houses on me," Goering replied in the German phrase. "I am going to attend to it myself."

The Reichsmarschall took Rommel and his wife to Rome with him on his special train. For the journey he wore a semicivilian gray suit with gray silk lapels. His tie was held by a big emerald clip. His watchcase was studded with emeralds. On one of his jeweled fingers was the biggest diamond Rommel had ever seen. Goering held up his hand and told Frau Rommel that the diamond was one of the world's most valuable stones. That was when Rommel noticed that his hands were manicured and his nails polished. In Rome, Goering spent most of his time partying or exploring museums on art-looting expeditions. He went to one party wearing a toga. After three days, Rommel told his wife: "I'm doing no good over here—only losing my temper. I'd better get back to the Afrika Korps."

He flew back next day, convinced that Goering was mad and Hitler hardly better. How long could the Fatherland endure such leaders?

Dwight Eisenhower was extremely worried about his American troops. None of the four divisions making up II Corps had had much training and all had been hastily brought up to strength before leaving the States. They were also relatively unblooded, having had only one or two days' action against the French in November. On his inspection tours of the front Eisenhower had found them complacent and undisciplined. Their junior officers were casual. Obviously, they did not take war seriously. One unit had been in position two days without laying a minefield, a vital chore which the Germans accomplished within two hours. Foxholes and slit trenches were not dug, and junior officers failed to carry out orders. Instead of training their men or taking them on long conditioning hikes during slack periods, they let them go frolic in nearby villages.

Eisenhower was concerned because the II Corps was on the southern flank of his front, opposite Rommel holding the Mareth Line on the border with Libya. The supreme commander was even more worried about the II Corps commander, Maj. Gen. Lloyd Fredendall. Fredendall's headquarters were far to the rear in a canyon inside a gulch at the end of a narrow twisting road. To make himself more secure in his hole inside a cave at the end of a tunnel, Fredendall had 200 engineers working to blast out an underground command post. When Eisenhower asked an engineer if he had not first worked on front-line defenses, a young staff

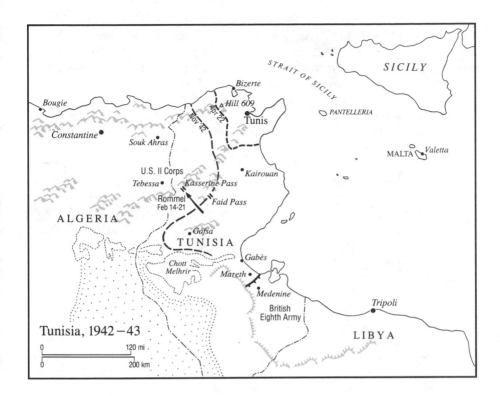

Tunisia, 1942—43

0   120 mi
0   200 km

officer replied for him: "Oh, the divisions have their own engineers for that!" The supreme commander was inwardly furious. The time had come for him to lose that terrible temper and sack Fredendall, but he didn't. The tact that had been his strength in welding the Alliance together was now his undoing as a commander. He was trying to lead in combat by hints and persuasion. Instead of bluntly asking Fredendall, "What the hell's going on here?" he told him instead that "one of the things that gives me the most concern is the habit of some of our generals in staying too close to their command posts." Fredendall did not take the hint and did not leave his private fort.

Fredendall's disposition of his forces was unsound. He divided his 1st Armored Division into two combat commands, A and B. B went north to the Fondouk sector where General Anderson expected the German attack, and A stayed south. Meanwhile, the Desert Fox had been doing some thinking.

The Mareth Line held by Rommel had been built by the French to stop an Italian incursion from Libya. It was an immensely strong position. To outflank it required a turning movement of 150 miles. Rommel correctly concluded that Montgomery in his methodical way would take some time in preparing the customary superiority for an attack. Preferring not to sit down and wait for it, Rommel chose to attack—not the Eighth Army but the Allied First Army.

He had divined the vulnerable spot, the southern sector held by the American II Corps. It was across the Faid plain between Gafsa and Fondouk. North of it was the Kasserine (Qasserine) Pass. On February 14 at the head of about a hundred tanks and supported by Stukas, Rommel debouched from the Faid Pass and fell on the Americans in Command B. He overran them quickly. Many panicked. Rommel drove on toward the Kasserine Pass. By February 21 he had pierced its hastily constructed defenses and driven a big bulge into the Allied line. With his forces still intact, he faced open country. He was in position to turn the whole Tunisian front.

Eisenhower did not panic. He got artillery started on a 735-mile march to the threatened sector, stripped two divisions of equipment to send to Fredendall and cannibalized others. Now it was Rommel who was vulnerable. His long supply line ran through a narrow pass. Eisenhower urged Anderson and Fredendall to strike Rommel's flanks in a counterstroke that would destroy him. They demurred. They insisted on remaining on the defensive, believing that Rommel would make one more attack. But he did not. He quickly saw his danger and began his retreat that night.

Rommel had won a tactical victory. He had lost only nine tanks and a handful of men, while inflicting 5,000 casualties on the Americans—half of them in prisoners—and destroying hundreds of tanks and other equipment. But there had been no strategic gain. Actually, by blooding the Americans he had done Eisenhower a great favor. After Kasserine they were tough, angry troops who now understood, as Sherman said, that war was "all hell." This transformation was so rapid that Rommel himself was to write later: "What was really amazing was the speed with which the Americans adapted themselves to modern warfare. They were assisted in this by their tremendous practical and material sense and by their lack of all understanding for tradition and useless theories."

Eisenhower also turned tough, firing Fredendall and replacing him with Patton. In his first battle he had committed many mistakes. Despite his doubts, he had allowed Fredendall to retrain command; he had permitted a confused command situation to continue; and when he had a chance to trap the Desert Fox, he had allowed the timidity of his commanders to squelch his own offensive spirit.

But the cardinal sin of hesitance he would commit no more.

George Patton arrived at II Corps like an exploding bomb. He sped from unit to unit in his open command car, horns blaring, outriders roaring ahead and behind, standing erect for every soldier to see this tall trim figure with the two stars gleaming on his helmet, his pearl-handled revolver swinging at his hip. To say that he tightened discipline is an understatement. He turned the screws so tight that the men began to wince. "Arrest that truck driver! He hasn't got a tie on!" Ties at the front in North Africa were as ridiculous as they had been at Noumea under Admiral Ghormley. But for all of that Patton gave the II Corps back its pride. The men loved him, calling him Old Blood and Guts. They admired the way he took on the British in the verbal war that erupted after the battle at Kasserine Pass. When some British officers made slighting remarks about American courage, Patton wondered aloud in typically fiery language where "the Brits" were when the stuff hit the fan. Soon the war of words got out of hand. Patton's G-3 issued a report criticizing "the total lack of air cover [a British responsibility] for our units." Air Marshal Arthur Coningham replied that the criticism was an alibi for troops that "are not battleworthy." For once Eisenhower was powerless to stop an exchange of racial insults. Tedder, his air deputy, stepped in, arranging for Patton and Coningham to meet. They shook hands sheepishly, and then, just as the three sat down for a drink, a trio of Messerschmitts strafed the building they were in. Patton grinned in malicious glee. "I always knew you were a good stage manager," Tedder said, staring at Patton morosely, "but this takes the cake." Patton grinned again. "If I could find the sonsabitches who flew those planes, I'd mail them each a medal."

For all of Patton's theatrics, most of which were indeed staged to impress his soldiers, he was a solid commander with a thorough understanding of tank warfare. He was eager to strike Rommel in his rear to cut his communications. But General Alexander, who had taken field command of Allied forces, held him back. He said he was fearful that the Americans would be battered. He was also responding to Montgomery's warning on the Americans: "Don't let them be too ambitious and spoil the show." Alexander, apparently, felt that he was now in the position to implement Brooke's objective of easing Eisenhower out of command.

Disgusted, Patton asked Eisenhower to send him back to Morocco, where he had been planning the invasion of Sicily. Eisenhower complied, and replaced him with Omar Bradley.

Omar N. Bradley was born in Clark, Missouri, on Lincoln's birthday, 1893. Like so many American professional soldiers, he came of modest origins. His father died when he was fourteen and his mother, a seamstress, was forced to provide for him. Like Dwight Eisenhower, he entered the Military Academy because he wanted an education and could not afford one. Again like Eisenhower, he was older than his fellow plebes, having taught for a time before going to West Point.

Bradley was a quiet unassuming man with a soft voice. But his strong jaw and fighting, homely face bespoke an inner determination that would brook neither insolence nor incompetence. His modest bearing and gentle manner was to earn him the sobriquet "the GI's general." But for all his seeming reticence, Bradley was extremely decisive. Once more like Eisenhower, he came early to the attention of General Marshall, who entered his name in his little black book as a soldier destined for high command.

If Bradley lacked Patton's driving force and flamboyance, he was to prove himself a commander of exceptional stability. Men liked and trusted him. Most important of all to Marshall, Bradley could "read" a battle, much like a football quarterback "reading" defenses.

During the Casablanca conference, Marshall had become disturbed that Eisenhower had to handle high-level political and strategic problems while dealing also with units in the line. He suggested that he needed a commander who would be his "eyes and ears," and asked him to name candidates for the post. Eisenhower gave Marshall a list of a dozen officers, from which he chose Bradley.

Later, after Patton returned to Morocco, Bradley became his deputy commander, giving Patton a headstart in working with his officers and men. It was probably well that the unruffled Bradley was about to take charge when Alexander made his final move to deny Americans any combat role in North Africa. He directed that Montgomery come up from the south to join his left to Anderson's right and squeeze II Corps out of the line. In this way the great British victory at Alamein, comparable to Blenheim, would be followed by a second British* triumph at Tunis, comparable, presumably, to Waterloo.

Patton "exploded" when he saw the directive, but Bradley was merely "alarmed." Eisenhower was at last shocked. On April 14 he went to Alexander's headquarters and ordered him to give II Corps Bizerte on the north coast as an objective. Alexander demurred. In a polite but thoroughly demeaning estimate of American military ability, he said that the terrain was difficult and the logistical problems of bringing the Americans out of the line and marching them across Anderson's supply lines to establish a new front were unacceptable. In open insult, he added that the Americans had been beaten at Kasserine and belonged in the rear.

Eisenhower held his temper. He quietly but firmly reminded Alexander of how the United States had unselfishly given its best equipment to the British when they were desperate. He said that if the American public came to feel that its soldiers would not play an important role in Europe, they would turn to the Pacific. Alexander must realize that to beat Hitler, the Allies would have to field armies preponderantly American, and there was no way they could become battlewise by serving in the rear. Eventually, Alexander agreed to send II Corps against Bizerte. But the fact that he needed such a lecture on politico-military grand strategy seemed to suggest that he would not have made much of a supreme commander if Brooke's maneuver had succeeded.

A few weeks earlier, the Desert Fox had fought his last battle of the Desert War.

Rommel thought that he might catch Montgomery still preparing, so he attacked him on March 5 at Medenine. He had waited a few days too long, however, and the British were ready for him. Without barbed wire and with only a few mines to protect them, the British infantry held their positions against two panzer divisions, while their artillery poured a devastating fire on the attackers.

---

*Throughout the war British-commanded armies, composed of Australian, New Zealand, Greek, Polish, Free French, Indian, South African, Canadian, Irish, Scots and British troops, were always "British." Only American formations were all-American.

This was the perfect way to stop tanks, and Rommel lost fifty-two of his 140 tanks before he withdrew.

Once again Rommel had sought to inspire his troops by showing himself at the front. But he was now a very sick man, his throat bandaged and his face covered with desert sores. A week after his defeat, he left for Germany and did not return. Dwight Eisenhower in a rare uncharitable moment said he left "to save his own skin." There were other equally uncomplimentary explanations of the motives of this greatest field commander of World War II, but the truth seems to be that he left to plead once again to save his German troops at the expense of their equipment. *Der Führer* again called him a coward and a defeatist, but this time refused permission for him to return to his men. From this interview and subsequent meetings, Rommel was now firmly convinced that the real enemy of the German people was Adolf Hitler.

Neither of the British armies made much progress against the Axis Bizerte-Tunis line, even though Gen. Dietloff Jürgen von Arnim, now in complete command, was experiencing severe supply shortages. It was up to the U.S. II Corps. On April 30, the attack against Bizerte went forward with the 34th Division moving on Hill 609. The 34th had done poorly at Kasserine, and Eisenhower had ordered Bradley to give it a tough objective. The 34th's soldiers went slowly up the hill, its men falling under a killing cross fire. They took the hill on the following morning, and then threw back a fierce German counterattack.

Now the British armies began to break through Arnim's defenses. On May 7 Anderson's soldiers took Tunis and on that same day the U.S. II Corps entered Bizerte. On May 13 the last Axis forces in Tunisia surrendered. A total of 275,000 enemy troops, more than half of them German, had been taken by the Anglo-Americans, a bag of prisoners even larger than the Soviets took at Stalingrad.

The North African campaign had taken too long and had cost too much: six months in time and 71,810 Allied casualties, of which 10,820 were killed, 39,575 wounded and 21,415 missing or captured. But it was the first complete Allied victory over the Axis; for the first time Hitler and Mussolini had been evicted from a continent. It had landed the Allies, however, firmly in the Mediterranean. They had come there, it would seem, because "something" had to be done against the Axis in 1942 to relieve the pressure on Stalin and to allay Winston Churchill's fears of failure in France, or worse, partial success that would renew the static slaughter of World War I. But because of North Africa there was to be no cross-Channel invasion in 1943, and the Anglo-Americans and their allies would not enter northwest Europe—the one place in which Hitler could be decisively beaten—until thirteen months later. The campaign surely would not have taken so long if Eisenhower had been allowed to land closer to Tunis, as he desired, or if the political problems with the North African French had not delayed him until the winter rains once again bogged him down. But Churchill's shining hopes for a decisive thrust up the Italian peninsula into Hitler's southern flank were never to be realized.

Nevertheless, the Allies had won their first decisive victory, and they had won as allies. Eisenhower had emerged as a true supreme commander. He had made many mistakes born of inexperience, and it is perhaps just as well that they were made in North Africa rather than in France. That, indeed, may have been an unforeseen benefit from North Africa. The Allied coalition from the heads of government through the Combined Chiefs through Eisenhower and his deputies down to the corps and division commanders in the field was now a smooth-functioning machine, as it certainly would not have been in a 1943 invasion of France. Much of this was due to the supreme commander's devotion to the Alliance. It never flagged, never gave way to any consideration, especially not himself.

It was with him even after the campaign was won, after he reviewed a victory parade in Tunis and flew back to Algiers accompanied by Harold Macmillan, his British political adviser who would one day be prime minister. Looking down on the Mediterranean from their Flying Fortress, they saw a huge Allied convoy sailing in serene safety to Egypt. "There, General," Macmillan said, "are the fruits of your victory." Eisenhower turned to him with his quick smile, but with tears in his eyes.

"Ours, you mean," he said—"ours."

66. The U-Boat War

PERHAPS THE MOST far-reaching decision taken at the Casablanca conference was the agreement worded: "The defeat of the U-boat must remain a first charge on the resources of the United Nations." It was made at the peak of the U-boat war, which had taken a disastrous turn in mid-January of 1942. Five weeks after Pearl Harbor, Admiral Doenitz opened a furious undersea attack on shipping off the East Coast of America. The campaign was called Operation *Paukenschlag,* or "Roll of the Drums," and it began with only six U-boats. Yet this scanty sextet of drummers beat out a dreadful dirge for American shipping. They attacked at night, firing their torpedoes from seaward against ships boldly silhouetted by the lights of the East Coast cities behind them. Not until May of that year was a blackout imposed on the American coast, and in the meantime it was "business as usual," with ships sunk and sailors drowned by the light of boardwalks and ballrooms. The vessels themselves were lighted, and even the lighthouses and buoys showed lights. Thus obliged, only barely annoyed by ineffectual antisubmarine tactics, the U-boats grew so confident that they began to attack in daylight. On June 15 thousands of bathers at Virginia Beach watched in helpless horror while a German submarine torpedoed two American freighters. These were the six months of unrivaled success that U-boat crews forever afterward looked back on as "the happy times," and during them they sank no fewer than 568 Allied ships. Alarmed, General Marshall notified Admiral King that shipping losses in the Atlantic and Caribbean threatened the entire American war effort.

Gradually, with the introduction of the convoy system for coastal shipping and improved antisubmarine warfare, the American losses lessened. And Doenitz, resourceful as usual, began to concentrate on the Caribbean. By July 1942, he had introduced the big new submarine tankers, "milch cows," capable of carrying 700 tons of fuel. Meeting U-boats at sea, the milch cows could feed fifty tons of fuel to a medium U-boat, thus widening its cruising range in the Caribbean, or give ninety to a big one and send it ranging as far away from base as the Cape of Good Hope. Toward the end of the year, the wolf packs returned to the North Atlantic.

Doenitz had discovered that air cover for the Allied convoys was given only at either end of a voyage. There was a wide gap in midocean, and this came to be called "the black pit" after the wolf packs began massing there. Ship after ship vanished into it. In November 1942, with many of the escorting warships drawn off to the landings in North Africa, the U-boats sank 117 ships! That was the blackest month of the Battle of the Atlantic, just as 1942 became the black year.

During it the Allies lost 8 million tons of shipping. U-boats sank ships faster than America could build them, and this, of course, imposed a dreadful burden on the American shipbuilding industry. First, it had to replace most Allied shipping losses, after which it was supposed to double the replacement if shipments of munitions to all the fighting fronts were to be doubled as scheduled. Finally, it had to build the warships especially designed for protecting the new merchant fleet.

The response to this dual challenge was magnificent. Newly opened shipyards on both coasts began building Liberty ships. Ugly, slow and uncomfortable for those who sailed them, the Libertys could nevertheless be built very quickly. With amazing speed, American know-how cut construction time from the 244 days required to build the first Liberty in 1941 to an average of forty-two days per ship in late 1942. In all, 2,700 Liberty ships were built, and they carried 75 percent of America's cargo overseas.

Meanwhile, new fleets of destroyer escorts and small escort aircraft carriers called CVEs were built. They were designed to give aerial cover across that deadly gap in midocean. Each CVE carried sixteen fighters and twelve torpedo bombers. Screened by the swift, sub-killing destroyer escorts, the CVEs became the scourge of the wolf packs. Their fighters could strafe surfaced subs or depth-bomb submerged ones, and their bombers struck with torpedoes. Toward the end of the war they launched the Fido homing torpedo. Dropped anywhere near a submarine, it would make for the U-boat's steel hull. Thus, assisted by a growing array of detection devices able to pinpoint the U-boats, the Allies became more and more expert in locating submarines.

In April of 1943 flotillas independent of escort duty were formed to hunt and kill the U-boats, now at their peak operating strength of 230. Gradually, they drove the wolf packs beneath the surface, and then they began to kill them off. In May, thirty U-boats were destroyed. By June shipping losses were at their lowest since America entered the war. Then Allied bombers entered the battle, patrolling the skies over the Bay of Biscay and helping to destroy another thirty-seven U-boats in July.

German shipyards struggled to replace Doenitz's losses. They concentrated on producing a giant new submarine equipped with the new "schnorkel" breathing device, which would enable them to travel farther and faster underwater. What the shipyards could not replace, however, were seasoned skippers and trained crews. One by one the undersea aces failed to return to port, among them Doenitz's two sons and his son-in-law. Meanwhile, Allied shipping had been granted a great breathing spell by the fall of North Africa, which cleared the Mediterranean routes and cut forty-five days from schedules formerly routed around the Cape. But the biggest blow of all was struck with the Allied invasion of France in June 1944. With this the French ports were lost to Doenitz.

Still, he did not despair. He was confident that the new boats with their increased speed and range would revolutionize warfare, and he expected to have 350 of these built during 1945. Shortages of special materials required ruined his plans, however, and in the main he was compelled to carry on with the smaller, older boats, many of which were destroyed in their pens by Allied bomber raids.

In the end, the Battle of the Atlantic was won by the Allies. Some 780 German submarines were lost, of which 632 were sunk at sea. They had accounted for the loss of 14 million tons of Allied shipping, against the losses of 11 million inflicted by their predecessors in World War I. Once again the submarine service, the poor relation of the German military family, had come very close to winning the war on its own. And not until May 28, 1945, three weeks after VE Day, were the United States Navy and the British Admiralty able to issue this joint announcement:

"Effective this date . . . no further trade convoys will be sailed. Merchant ships by night will burn navigation lights at full brilliancy and need not darken ship."

67. The Capture of Sicily and the Invasion of Italy

FOLLOWING THE FALL of Tunisia, Dwight Eisenhower was eager to invade the island of Sicily as soon as possible. But he could not because there were not enough landing craft. Throughout the war the shortage of landing craft in every theater—especially the Pacific, the naval war par excellence in which island after island had to be invaded from the sea—was to be a thorn in the side of the Combined Chiefs. Perusal of the minutes of their meetings and those of the American or British chiefs suggests that no other problem was so persistent or consumed so much of their time.

One good reason for the shortage in 1943 was that Allied production was concentrating on the ships that would end the U-boat menace. Another not-so-good reason was that the proponents of strategic bombing had been so successful that the factories were busier making bombers than landing craft. Thus, a two-month delay in invading Sicily was forced on Eisenhower, and in the interval he decided to strike the island of Pantelleria.

Pantelleria lay between Tunisia and Sicily. With its excellent airfield it menaced any seaborne invasion of Sicily. It was a tiny and impregnable rock held by 11,000 Italian soldiers whose guns were registered on the narrow harbor through which any invasion had to pass. There were no beaches, only steep rocky shores. General Eisenhower thought he could bomb Pantelleria into submission. His British deputies—Cunningham, Alexander and Tedder—demurred. But Eisenhower persisted, convinced that "most Italians had had a stomachful of fighting and were looking for any good excuse to quit." When he added that he wanted the island's airfield, that brought Tedder around to his side. Cunningham followed, after Tedder's air forces had pounded the island and its harbor for three weeks. But Alexander still objected, along with the British general chosen to lead the assault. Both said Pantelleria was a miniature Gibraltar, which not only could not be taken but which also could crucify any invading force. On June 7 Eisenhower joined Cunningham aboard H.M.S. *Aurora,* part of a fleet sailing to bombard the island. The ships ran up to the rocky coast and blasted away, with Cunningham personally directing some of the fire. Only two Italian shore batteries replied, hitting nothing. "Andrew," Eisenhower said to Cunningham, "if you and I got into a small boat, we could capture the place ourselves."

On June 11 the British invasion force set sail, and before a single soldier set foot on Pantelleria, the Italians surrendered. There was one Allied casualty: a Tommy was bitten by a mule.

Eisenhower was elated. No other operation in the war had been so short and sweet and no other command decision so crowned with success. The fact that it had been opposed by commanders senior to him in rank* and experience was a source of satisfaction and balm to his badly bruised self-confidence. Now he was ready for Sicily.

About 180,000 Allied troops would go against 405,000 Axis troops, which would seem like a striking and dangerous reversal of the 3 to 1 superiority usually deemed necessary for a seaborne invasion, except that 315,000 of the enemy were Italians and only 90,000 Germans. Aware that the best of the German forces were concentrated in the west, Eisenhower planned to land in the south and southeast,

*Eisenhower got his fourth star February 14, but his three deputies were all marshals.

after which Patton's Seventh Army and Montgomery's Eighth would wheel away from each other and race for Messina. The objective was not to trap the enemy forces but to clear them out of Sicily. To deceive the enemy, a corpse carrying information indicating landings in Greece and Sardinia was washed ashore in Spain. It fooled only Hitler, who reinforced those areas; but the astute Marshal Albert Kesselring, who commanded Axis forces in Italy, reinforced Sicily.

A vast Allied fleet was gathered, a total of 1,375 ships, the largest amphibious force yet assembled and, on its first day, larger than the cross-Channel invasion of the following year. Some ships sailed to the battle from Britain and the United States. Others sailed from Tunisia, so that Sicily was a shore-to-shore as well as a ship-to-shore operation.

In this mighty Allied armada were the new landing craft produced by Anglo-American ingenuity. Here were the 1,500-ton, 328-foot Landing Ship Tank (LST), the 550-ton, 112-foot Landing Craft Tank (LCT) and the 200-ton, 158-foot Landing Craft Infantry (LCI). The LST, which its disenchanted crew and the troops who sailed it insisted meant Large Stationary Target, was to be the amphibious workhorse of the war. It could run up on a beach, open its bow doors, and lower a ramp down which troops ran and vehicles rolled. It could also do this offshore for amphibious tractors (amtracs) loaded with troops to go splashing into the water to churn shoreward. When the LCIs ran ashore, gangways were lowered on either side for troops to debark. But the LCIs were not very seaworthy troop transports and later became converted into rocket ships. The LCTs carried the tanks and artillery that are vital to support the landing troops in the early hours of an invasion. Troops landing at the water's edge are most vulnerable to counterattack, especially by tanks, and an invasion force required its own tanks and artillery to repel them. Close-up aerial support also can break up tank attacks, but the Sicilian fleet was not to receive the tactical air support it needed. Allied aircraft became too far preoccupied with saturation bombing.

Nevertheless, on the morning of July 10, 1943, Allied soldiers went storming through the roaring white surf of Sicily. Patton's Seventh Army landed on the left, Montgomery's Eighth on the right. They met little opposition. Meanwhile, Allied paratroopers stopped the crack Hermann Goering Division, which came racing out of the west. The airborne troops had been landed during the night. Many had been lost when the gliders were cut adrift too soon and high winds blew them back into the water. Otherwise, the landings were a great success. Montgomery's army began driving north toward Messina while Patton's split into two columns, one pushing west along the coast, the other moving straight north across the center of the island.

Within eleven days American troops had cut Sicily in two and gone rolling into Palermo on the north coast. "As we approached," wrote Patton, "the hills on each side were burning. We then started down a road cut out of the side of a cliff which went through an almost continuous village. The street was full of people shouting, "Down with Mussolini!" and "Long live America!"

So it continued as the Allies pursued the despised Germans, who had gone from being the Sicilians' unloved allies to becoming their hated masters. Flowers were strewn in the path of the liberators and gifts of wine and fruit pressed into their hands. Italian soldiers began to surrender by the thousands. Eventually, both armies joined flanks to advance on a united front. Still, the Germans fought tenaciously, not so much to defend the island as to delay its conquest long enough for them to get safely across the Strait of Messina into Italy. They mined roads and dug tank traps with typical efficiency. They fought as though by timetable, blowing bridges and destroying the narrow roads winding around the cliff faces. Although the Allies were pouring a dreadful weight of metal from the skies, they were bombing open country and did little to deter the Germans' skillful delaying tactics. Allied transport was compelled to press mule trains into service while their engineers clung precariously to the cliffs to build the trestles that supported advancing spearheads. Thus, the Germans were able to get across the narrow strait into the toe of the boot of Italy before Patton's outriders came roaring and clanking into the Sicilian capital. So the Allies had captured Sicily, a most valuable springboard for the jump into Italy; and while Sicily was falling, the father of Fascism also fell.

By the summer of 1943, Benito Mussolini's grip on Italy was weakening. He had believed his generals, or allowed them to persuade him to choose a path he wished to follow, when they had exaggerated the strength of his armed forces, and he had accordingly led his people into an unpopular war. Now Allied air fleets were bringing the mainland under massive bombardment. There were also showers of propaganda leaflets aimed at exploiting the Italian mood of despair. One, signed by Roosevelt and Churchill, declared: "The time has now come for you, the Italian people, to consult your own self-respect and your own interests and your own desire for a restoration of national dignity, security and peace. The time has come for you to decide whether Italians shall die for Mussolini and Hitler—or live for Italy and civilization." Such propaganda gave encouragement to Fascist leaders who were already plotting *Il Duce*'s downfall.

Mussolini was therefore delighted when Adolf Hitler suggested that they meet again. The Italian corporal might not have been so pleased had he known the German corporal's motives. Hitler believed that only "barbaric measures" could now save Italy. He wanted tribunals and courts-martial set up to try suspected traitors. Upon the invasion of Sicily, he saw at once the need to keep Italy out of Allied hands. If need be, he would himself take charge on the peninsula. For these reasons, he asked Mussolini for a conference. Mussolini, insisting that they meet in Italy, chose the little hill town of Feltre north of Venice where the Renaissance palace of a wealthy Fascist senator was located. He flew to it in his own plane, while Hitler arrived in a Junkers surrounded by his bodyguard. A cold and formal welcome made the Germans suspicious. Once arrived at the palace, Hitler's guards cocked their pistols. They did not see the deer nibbling on green lawns or the golden pheasants and brilliant peacocks wandering among the classical statuary, but rather the Italian soldiers lurking behind every tree and bush; and ringing them round, the steep slopes of the Alps. It was a perfect setting for a trap.

Mussolini's advisers had counseled him to present Hitler with an ultimatum: immediate and effective aid to Sicily and large-scale support from the Luftwaffe in Italy, or he would abrogate the Pact of Steel. After the conference began, however, Mussolini had no chance to dictate to Hitler. Nor did he hear any offers of aid. Instead, he had to listen to a catalog of Italy's crimes and omissions. At the head of the list was the Greek fiasco, and Hitler bluntly stated that all his difficulties in the U.S.S.R. derived from Mussolini's ill-fated invasion there. The faces of *Il Duce* and his colleagues darkened. The hands of Hitler's henchmen slid to their pistol butts. Here was an impasse that had never before risen between the two dictators. It was broken when an air force officer ran into the room waving a message slip and shouting that Rome was under massive aerial bombardment.

Mussolini sprang to his feet. Hitler, accustomed to such visitations on his own capital city, calmly remained seated. But then, realizing that he must do something to soothe his friend's shattered nerves, *Der Führer* murmured consolingly of all the assistance he would despatch to Sicily, without, however, going into details. That brought the conference to an end. The dictators shook hands briefly and took each other's leave. Mussolini put on an immaculate white flying suit and hurried to the airport. Turning to face Field Marshal Kesselring and Ambassador von Mackensen who had accompanied him, he snapped to attention and with glowing eyes lifted his fist in the Fascist salute. Once again, he was marching on Rome!

But this time *Il Duce* was rushing into a trap. In his absence, Count Dino Grandi had enlisted a circle of conspirators. Grandi, a former foreign minister and ambassador to Britain, had bitterly opposed Italian intervention. He now welcomed Mussolini back into the Eternal City with a demand that the Fascist Grand Council be convened. It had not met since 1939. But Mussolini's friends were leaving him like rats departing a sinking ship. At their head was *Il Duce*'s son-in-law, Count Galeazzo Ciano. Grandi and Ciano, two men whom Mussolini had made, two men for whom he had secured the coveted Collar of the Annunziata with the right to call the king cousin. And they were there, arrayed against him, when twenty-eight members of the Grand Council dressed in black Fascist uniforms convened on July 24, 1943.

Grandi had proposed that command of the armed forces should be given to the king, an effective end to Mussolini's power. But, before the voting began, the charges and countercharges were exchanged.

The bearded Grandi stood erect, leveling a finger at *Il Duce*. "You believe you have the devotion of the people," he cried, "but you lost it the day you tied Italy to Germany. You have suffocated the personality of everyone under the mantle of a historically immoral dictatorship. Let me tell you, Italy was lost the day you put the gold braid of a marshal on your cap." In anger mixed with pity,

Grandi pleaded: "Take off those ridiculous ornaments, plumes and feathers! Be again the Mussolini of the barricades—our Mussolini!"

"The people are with me!" *Il Duce* shouted furiously.

Grandi gazed at him in contempt. In World War I, he said, 600,000 Italians had died for king and country. "In this war, we have already one hundred thousand dead, and one hundred thousand mothers who cry, 'Mussolini has assassinated my son!' "

"It is not true!" *Il Duce* screamed. "That man is lying!"

Grandi sat down. He stared at Mussolini and with grinding irony quoted his battle cry of 1924: "Let all factions perish, even Fascism, so long as the nation is saved!"

Others rose to excoriate their leader. Then Ciano. With cool detachment he catalogued every treachery of Hitler since the signing of the Pact of Steel. "We have been not so much the betrayers as the betrayed," he concluded.

Mussolini stared into his son-in-law's face with icy loathing. "I know where the traitor is," he muttered.

One by one, to Grandi's rising elation and Mussolini's growing despair, the grand councillors arose to denounce *Il Duce.* The voting began. Nineteen voted "Yes" to give the power to the king, seven voted "No." Two abstained. Mussolini had watched Ciano intently when the proposal was put to him. Ciano returned it calmly. "Yes," he said in a clear voice.

Il Duce arose. He fixed Grandi with the distillate of hatred issuing from his large dark eyes. In a grating voice, he cried: "You have killed Fascism!" Then he left the chamber.

Mussolini, wearing tails, met with the king in the Quirinale. Victor Emmanuel wore a marshal's gray-green uniform with thick red stripes down the seams. He looked like a toy soldier. *Il Duce* was confident that he could persuade his "cousin" to annul the council's decree. He had met him 2,000 times before in this very room and always had his way. But this time, to his surprise, Victor Emmanuel met him with a smile and an extended hand—something that had never happened in twenty years.

Still, *Il Duce* led off assuredly, "You'll have heard, your majesty, about last night's childish prank—"

"Not a childish prank at all," the little king cut in quickly. He began pacing up and down a Turkey-red carpet, while Mussolini raged against the council. "My dear Duce," he interrupted again, "things are not working out in Italy any longer. The army's morale is low, the soldiers don't want to fight anymore. The Alpine Brigade are singing a song that they will no longer fight for you." In Piedmontese dialect, the king chanted a refrain: "Down with Mussolini, who murdered the Alpini." Deliberately, the little monarch led his first minister into a trap. "Today you are the most hated man in Italy. You cannot count on a single friend except me."

Mussolini tried a bluff. "But if your majesty is right, I should present my resignation."

"And I have to tell you," the king said quickly, closing the trap, "that I accept it unconditionally."

Mussolini staggered as though shot. He sank into a chaise lounge. "Then my ruin is complete!" he cried in a hoarse, croaking voice.

It was. He was arrested and jailed in the carabinieri barracks. Marshal Pietro Badoglio, another of his disaffected lieutenants, took over the government. Throughout the night, Fascist leaders still loyal to Mussolini streamed out of Rome headed for Frascati, the headquarters of Marshal Kesselring. Some of them drove past the carabinieri barracks where their fallen leader was pacing the floor, shaking his bald head and rolling his large eyes, crying out, over and over:

"*Ah, il quarantenne, il quarantenne!* Ah, the forty-year-old, the forty-year-old!"

He was lamenting the treachery of his son-in-law, Count Galeazzo Ciano. He had raised him to the height of power and glory, and he had betrayed him. Now, in the black night of his despair, he was thinking of how he could kill him.

Dwight Eisenhower was secretly pleased when he was informed that his old friend George Patton had beaten Montgomery to Messina. But then on the same day Eisenhower's surgeon handed him a report suggesting that the dream was about to become a nightmare.

On August 10 Patton drove to the 93rd Evacuation Hospital. He strode unannounced into the receiving tent, gleaming, starched and salty, and began talking to the astonished wounded, congratulating them on their performance. From the men in bandages and splints General Patton moved with a frown among those seemingly unharmed. The malarial patients he passed by. Then he saw another patient, seated, shaking with convulsions.

"And what's happened to you?" Patton demanded.

"It's my nerves, sir," the soldier replied, tears in his eyes.

Patton stiffened. "What did you say?"

"It's my nerves," the man sobbed. "I can't stand the shelling any more."

"Your nerves, hell!" Patton shouted. "You're just a goddamed coward!"

The soldier began to weep and Patton slapped him. "Shut up! I won't have these brave men here who've been shot see a yellow bastard crying."

Patton struck him again, with his gloves. He called to the receiving officer. "Don't you admit this yellow bastard. There's nothing the matter with him. I won't have the hospitals cluttered up with sonsabitches who haven't got the guts to fight." He whirled on the weeping soldier. "You're going back to the front lines —you may get shot and killed, but you're going back to fight. If you don't, I'll stand you up against a wall and have a firing squad kill you on purpose."

Dwight Eisenhower was deeply dismayed when he read the report of this. He ordered his surgeon to go to Sicily to make a full investigation of the incident, but to keep it quiet. Then he wrote a long, stern and painful letter to Patton, ordering him to apologize to the soldier he had struck and to the hospital staff. Eisenhower simply did not want to lose the services of a commander whom he actually believed was indispensable to the war effort. With that, he considered the matter closed.

But when a general slaps a private in the army of a free-speech society, it is most difficult to hush it up. Three war correspondents—Demaree Bess of the *Saturday Evening Post,* Merrill Mueller of NBC and Quentin Reynolds of *Collier's* magazine—approached Eisenhower offering a "deal." They had the facts, but they would suppress them if Eisenhower sent Patton home. The supreme commander was appalled. With great patience he explained that Patton's "emotional tenseness and his impulsiveness are the very qualities that make him, in open situations, such a remarkable leader of an army. The more he drives his men the more he will save their lives." He told them Patton had made his apologies and had written to him in contrition, declaring: "I am at a loss to find words with which to express my chagrin and grief at having given you, the man to whom I owe everything and for whom I would gladly lay down my life, cause for displeasure with me."

The three newsmen were moved, and Eisenhower thought the incident was closed. However, a radio commentator named Drew Pearson broke the story in a garbled account, and it caused an uproar in the States. Eisenhower very nearly had to sacrifice Patton to a storm of public opinion which, fortunately, subsided almost as quickly as it arose.

Patton's flamboyance never sat very well with the correspondents in Sicily, and they believed that the GI resented Patton's theatrics. But the truth about George Patton is that no commander of his rank ever tried to share his combat soldiers' daily portion of dread and horror as much as he did, because of his belief that the most effective way for a leader to inspire his troops is by assuming an attitude of indifference to death. For this, they loved him; else why did they call him "Old Blood and Guts"?

After Quentin Reynolds remarked, "There are 50,000 soldiers who would shoot Patton on sight," Patton stepped before an audience of several thousand soldiers in Palermo and said:

"I just thought I'd stand up here and let you soldiers see if I'm as big an S.O.B. as you think I am."

They cheered him to the stars.

The fall of Mussolini excited Dwight Eisenhower. He had already made his plans for an invasion of Italy. Montgomery's Eighth Army was to go ashore at Reggio di Calabria across the Strait of Messina from Sicily. Mark Clark's American Fifth Army would land at Salerno, south of Naples. Churchill had argued for a landing farther north, closer to Rome; but withdrew his opposition after Eisenhower explained that his fighter cover could fly no farther than Salerno. But when Mussolini was arrested, the supreme commander saw a golden opportunity to pick off Rome on the run. Although Marshal Badoglio had stated in a radio broadcast, "The war continues," no one—the Germans or the Allies—really believed him. Everyone expected Italy to quit the war. Eisenhower yearned to make a deal with Badoglio that would give him Rome at little cost and perhaps after that the peninsula. But Roosevelt stuck grimly to Unconditional Surrender. "In no event," he told Churchill, "should our officers in the field fix any general terms without your approval or mine." Churchill, more realistic, was inclined to be generous. "Now Mussolini is gone, I would deal with any non-Fascist government which can deliver the goods." Roosevelt stayed firm: Unconditional Surrender. Privately, he told Churchill: "There are some contentious people here who are getting ready to make a row if we seem to recognize the House of Savoy or Badoglio. They are the same element that made such a fuss over [Darlan]."

Eisenhower still burned to make an immediate broadcast to the Italians, offering them an honorable peace and promising to come to Italy as liberators who would free them from the Germans. Now Robert Murphy told him that he had no authority to make such a political offer and must clear it with the two governments. He was right, of course; but Eisenhower sighed for the days of slow communications when the general on the spot could make his decisions and present the home government with a fait accompli. So he submitted the text of his speech to the Combined Chiefs.

Wrangling over the wording delayed Eisenhower's initiative another week. One more passed with no word from Badoglio, while the two governments bickered or bombarded the supreme commander with long cautionary cables, while Eisenhower, in a fury of frustration, read of the flood of German troops flowing into Italy. He complained bitterly: "I do not see how war can be conducted successfully if every act of the Allied commander in chief must be referred back to the home government for advance approval."

It was not until August 17 that the Italians finally approached the Allies. General Giuseppe Castellano arrived in Lisbon and proposed to the British ambassador there a double cross. As soon as the Allies landed in strength in Italy, the Italians would sign an armistice with them and declare war on Germany. Once again, Eisenhower was enthusiastic; but the answer from his superiors was no. It was still Unconditional Surrender.

Although General Castellano was stunned by the Allied insistence on Unconditional Surrender, he did agree to it on September 3. On that same day, spearheads of Montgomery's Eighth Army slipped over the strait into Reggio di Calabria. Now Eisenhower altered his invasion plans. Instead of just the invasions of Montgomery and Clark, he would add airborne operations at the port of Taranto and at Rome. He still yearned to seize the Eternal City before the Germans got there. Actually, he did not have the strength to carry out such widespread operations. The Italians realized this the moment they were informed of the new plans. Marshal Badoglio was so frightened they would fail that he backed down on everything, the armistice included. He would not make his capitulating broadcast scheduled for September 8.

When Eisenhower learned of Badoglio's double cross on that day he was furious. He struggled to contain his rage. Pencil after pencil broke in his hand as he wrote to Badoglio: "I intend to broadcast the existence of the message at the hour originally planned. Failure now on your part to carry out the full obligations to the signed agreement will have the most serious consequences for your country." Reluctantly, Eisenhower decided to cancel the Rome and Taranto operations. But at 6:30 that night he went on the air at Radio Algiers. "The Italian government has surrendered its armed forces unconditionally," he said. "As Allied commander in chief I have granted a military armistice." Next he had the text of Badoglio's proclamation read out. An hour later Badoglio read the same announcement over Radio Rome. Ike had "played a little poker"—and won.

But during the thirty-nine days ensuing between the fall of Mussolini and Badoglio's public capitulation, the Germans had rushed thirteen new divisions into Italy—even withdrawing two SS divisions from the Eastern Front—had begun to take control of Rome and other cities and had accomplished the effective occupation of the peninsula. In the respite granted by stubborn Allied adherence to the policy of Unconditional Surrender, Herr Hitler had turned the "soft underbelly" of Mr. Churchill's crocodile into the crocodile's bristling, armored back. During this period also, Adolf Hitler moved to keep his promise never to forget Benito Mussolini.

In 1938, when Mussolini acquiesced in Hitler's annexation of Austria, *Der Führer* said: "I shall never forget him for this. Never, never, never . . . even if the whole world were against him." The day after *Il Duce*'s fall, Hitler summoned the commando leader Otto Skorzeny to the Wolf's Lair. Skorzeny epitomized Hitler's blond Aryan super race. He stood six feet four inches tall, weighed a muscular 206 pounds and was handsome even though his face was saber-scarred from a duel over a ballet dancer. In a breaking voice, Hitler told him: "Mussolini, my friend and comrade-in-arms was betrayed yesterday by his king and arrested by his countrymen. I cannot and will not leave Italy's greatest son in the lurch. I will keep faith with my old ally and dear friend. He must be rescued promptly or he will be handed over to the Allies."

Hitler did not know where Mussolini was being held. But he ordered Skorzeny to find him and bring him safely into Germany. Skorzeny would have the full cooperation of Maj. Gen. Kurt Student, the chief of airborne troops who had conducted the capture of Crete. Finding the vanished Duce was not so easy. Skorzeny sought him on La Maddalena Island off the Sardinian coast, in Rome, in the towering Abruzzi hills. Conflicting reports sent him rocketing off on wild-goose chases. Mussolini had suffered a stroke and lay dying in a northern clinic. He had committed suicide. He was in Spain under the protection of General Franco. He was in Sicily disguised as a humble blackshirt. Then, by an incredible stroke of luck, he was located. A message to the Italian Ministry of Home Affairs had been intercepted. It said: "Security precautions around Gran Sasso d'Italia have been completed."

In the Gran Sasso were the highest peaks of the Apennines. It was skiing country. A favorite resort was the Hotel Campo Imperatore, 3,000 feet above the village of Assergi on the plain. It could be reached only by funicular railway. Even if rescuers seized control of the funicular, Mussolini's guards would be alerted and prepared to resist by the time they reached the top. Probably, they were under orders to kill *Il Duce* if any attempt were made.

Agents in Assergi reported that many carabinieri had moved into the area. The locals were furious because the staff of the Imperatore had been fired without advance notice. All tourist literature on the Gran Sasso had mysteriously vanished from Rome travel agencies. Because Hitler had forbidden any intelligence operations in the country of his partner, there was not a shred of information available on the area where Mussolini was undoubtedly being held. A hastily taken and smudged aerial photograph showed only that there seemed to be a small airfield where a light Stork scout plane might land, but nothing bigger. The treacherous air currents of the Gran Sasso also ruled out a drop of parachutists. General Student decided that the rescue must be made by Skorzeny's troops mounted in gliders. A Stork to carry Mussolini to safety would land at the same time. The gliders would be wrecked, of course, but Skorzeny's commandos would get away by taking the carabinieri guards hostage.

On Sunday, September 11, twelve towing planes took off from the airfield at Practica di Mare with a dozen frail gliders swaying in the wind behind them. They carried 108 men led by Otto Skorzeny. Thirty miles away a Stork also took off—from a bumpy sheep pasture at Castel Gandolfo, the summer home of the popes. The Stork arrived over Imperatore before the gliders. Its pilot looked around him anxiously. A Stork's flying time was only three and a half hours. But then, with relief, he saw the gliders.

Ahead of Skorzeny's glider the towplane had released the towrope. The glider sank sickeningly downward. Skorzeny and his men straddled the crossbars, the wail of the wind in their ears.

Below was the hotel, squat, white and horseshoe-shaped. Tiny ant men were spilling out of it. With dismay Skorzeny saw that the "landing field" was only a ski run. The pilot tried desperately to brake their fifty-mile-an-hour descent. Terrain rushed up toward them: scrub, parched grass and deadly boulders. They hit the ground, sliding screeching on their belly while the boulders made matchwood of the glider. Sunlight flowed into the wrecked cabin. Skorzeny leaped out, brandishing a machine pistol, and saw the hotel terrace only twenty yards away.

Inside his hotel room Inspector-General Giuseppe Gueli lay stark naked on his bed, taking a siesta. The roar of the towplanes and crash of the gliders awakened him. Lieutenant Faiola burst into the room, shouting: "What do we do?"

Gueli's orders were to kill Mussolini in such an event. But he replied instantly: "Give up without hesitation!" Both men ran to the window to lean out, shouting, "Don't shoot! Don't shoot!" At a second-floor window appeared Mussolini's bald head. "Do not shed blood!" he cried to the commandos sprinting for the hotel.

Skorzeny and a commando saw an open door and ran through it. A carabiniere was bent over a radio transmitter. The commando kicked the man's stool out from under him while Skorzeny smashed the transmitter with the butt of his machine pistol. But the radio room was a dead end. Skorzeny ran outside. A crouching commando offered his back. Skorzeny jumped up on it and scaled a nine-foot wall. He ran into the main building, racing up a staircase three steps at a time. *"Mani in alto!"* he shouted as he ran. "Hands up!"

On the second floor Skorzeny instinctively threw open the door of Room 201. Inside were three frightened men: Gueli, Faiola and Mussolini. It was not the virile strutting Duce whom Skorzeny had seen on the Palazzo Venezia's balcony in 1934, but still, in this broken, balding old man with the eyes huge in his shrunken face, he recognized him.

"Heil, Duce!" he cried. "Duce, the Führer sent me! Duce, you are free!"

Mussolini embraced and kissed him. "I knew my friend Adolf Hitler would not leave me in the lurch."

It had taken Skorzeny four minutes to free Mussolini, and not a shot had been fired. At 3 P.M., over the objections of the Stork's pilot but on the insistence of Skorzeny, Mussolini and his liberator both took off for Practica di Mare. Because of Skorzeny's added weight, they very nearly crashed on takeoff, but the pilot skillfully held the plane steady. When they landed, *Il Duce* took the pilot's hand and said in German: "Thank you for my life."

When Montgomery's Eighth Army landed in Italy on September 3, it wheeled to the right or east, making for the German airfields at Foggia, not far from the Adriatic coast. Six days later, the American Fifth Army under Mark Clark began landing at Salerno on the Mediterranean. At the same time, the Germans took control of Rome, where the Italian government had panicked. King Victor Emmanuel, Badoglio and the chief military leaders fled to the south under Allied protection. Without orders, the Italian armed forces of about 1.7 million men were either disarmed by the Germans or threw away their uniforms and melted into the population. In a trice, Italy had become an occupied country and the Italian army had ceased to exist and was of no use to the Allies.

However, the Italian fleet did sail from its ports, eventually joining the Allies. This left Bari, Brindisi and Taranto open, and they were seized by Admiral Cunningham's ships, thus allowing the British 1st Airborne Division to occupy the heel of Italy.

At Salerno early success was brief. Clark had hoped for surprise but as the assault boats roared toward the beach in the early-morning darkness, a loud-speaker ashore began crackling, and a German voice roared in English: "Come on in and give up. You're covered!" They were indeed, and then made naked by the eerie light of enemy flares floating down from the black. German guns emplaced above the beachhead on both flanks and to the front delivered a plunging fire on them. Nevertheless, the Americans continued to come in, gradually establishing a foothold on those pebbly beaches, and then fighting inland to expand it. Four days later a massive German counterattack came close to hurling the Americans into the sea. General Clark rushed to the fighting front to tell his soldiers: "We don't give another inch. This is it! Don't yield anything. We're here to stay!"

But after Kesselring sent his tanks clanking into the battle, the Americans very nearly did not stay. The German chief had 600 tanks. Had he massed them for a single pulverizing stroke, it is probable that he would have crushed the invaders. But he committed them piecemeal, and the American soldiers at Salerno, assisted by naval gunfire and by close-up aerial support from bases in North Africa and Sicily, held their ground.

Meanwhile, Montgomery's steady drive up the Adriatic coast had unmasked Kesselring's left flank. To straighten his line he had to fall back on Naples. Next the Eighth Army seized the Foggia airfields, providing Allied aerial support right on the edge of the battlefield. Kesselring retreated again, abandoning Naples. Before he did, however, his engineers with customary thoroughness made a blackened, smoking desert of one of the oldest cities of Western civilization. Churches, schools and hospices were put to the torch. Harbor facilities were systematically wrecked. The prisons were thrown open in a deliberate attempt to hamstring the advancing Americans with a horde of criminals; hospitals were looted, and the harbor was sown with sunken ships and the streets mined with booby traps. Yet, within a month the skill and resourcefulness of American engineers had Naples harbor partially cleared and operative. Next, civil affairs officials, representative of that merciful new wrinkle on the ugly face of war, began to provide for a hungry and horrified populace.

Naples and Foggia were the high point of the fall campaign in Italy. After them, Kesselring began to make good on his promise to Hitler that he could hold Italy against all comers. To do so he threw a series of defensive lines across the peninsula, taking advantage wherever he could of its narrowest points. Minefields and demolitions guarded every possible approach to his lines. Mortar and machine-gun positions were dug in and artfully camouflaged to blend in with the countryside. Artillery was registered on every road and trail or bivouac area. Kesselring's was a textbook defense erected in terrain made for the defender. It was a jumble of steep hills, laced with valleys and gorges through which raced swift cold streams fed by mountain lakes. The rivers twisted and turned so frequently that one American division crossed the Volturno so many times a GI burst out in exasperation: "Every damn river in this fool country is named Volturno!"

Painful as the two-pronged Allied advance had become, winter stopped it dead. Torrential rains carried away bridges, washed out roads and turned the earth into mud. The Italian campaign was now almost a repetition of the static trench warfare of the last war. It was once again a front without flanks, leaving no room for maneuver. Tanks were next to useless in such terrain, and when the weather was clear enough for the Allies to take advantage of their aerial superiority, saturation bombing to provide alleys or lanes for penetration was no more effective than had been the massive artillery bombardments of World War I. Why then did not the Allies draw their vaunted amphibious whip and turn Kesselring's flanks with amphibious landings in his rear? There was just not enough sea power and landing craft to do it. There would never be enough to meet the demands of a two-ocean war—given the emphasis on strategic bombing—and most of what had been available had left the Mediterranean for the Pacific. New production was earmarked for the buildup in Britain for the cross-Channel invasion in 1944.

Stalled though the Italian campaign indubitably was, it still had been a boon to the embattled Soviets. By rushing thirteen divisions into Italy—including the two SS divisions from the Eastern front—Hitler caused fatal delays in Operation Citadel. This, like the Battle of Verdun against the French in the last war, was to be an attempt to bleed the Red Army white, thus forcing Stalin to accept a stalemate. It also was intended to slice off a seventy-five-mile salient in the German front in the vicinity of the city of Kursk. It had been scheduled for early May, but because of repeated delays the Battle of Kursk—at once both the greatest land battle and greatest duel of armor in military history—did not begin until July 5.

68. July 1943: The Battle of Kursk and the Soviet Counteroffensive

GERMAN LOSSES at Stalingrad and on the Don and Volga to either side of that city had been so enormous that even Hitler realized that he could not possibly launch a summer offensive in 1943 equaling the attacks of 1941 and 1942. However, it still seemed possible—given probably heavier Soviet losses—to wear down Soviet resistance to the point where Stalin would be willing to accept a stalemate.

Such an objective could not be achieved by switching to static defensive warfare. For one thing, the Wehrmacht simply was not strong enough to hold a line from the Baltic to the Black Sea. German strategists such as Erich von Manstein also were convinced that the Soviets would not go over to the offensive until the Second Front was opened by the Allies in Northwestern Europe. This did not seem likely to happen for another year.

However, Allied success in North Africa made it plain that the Germans would not have much time to strike this bleeding blow to force a draw in the east. It must be completed before the onset of a third Russian winter. It must be a *strategic defensive* implemented by a *tactical offensive,* that is, a series of powerful blows aimed at sapping enemy strength, especially through losses in prisoners. Again, it must be done quickly so as to exploit the still-existing superiority of German troops.

The German high command also had to consider the options open to the

Soviets. Would Stalin sit down and wait for the Second Front in Europe? Or would his growing confidence nourished by the successes at Stalingrad and other fronts decide him in favor of the offensive? From the psychological standpoint, it would not seem wise to mark time and mute the swelling hymns of praise to Holy Russia. Again, would not Stalin be eager to beat his allies to the Balkans, the traditional target of Russian imperialism?

Hitler thus had to choose between two alternatives. He could wait for the Soviets to begin an offensive, probably with a north-and-south pincers movement on the Donetz basin. The Germans would deliberately withdraw before these assaults, luring the enemy westward toward the Dnieper River, where they would strike him so hard on the flanks that they would inflict on Stalin the discouraging defeat that would compel him to accept the stalemate. On the other hand, the Wehrmacht could achieve the same objective by striking the enemy first with a furious but limited blow in the area of the city of Kursk. Hitler chose to attack first. He was still intent upon exploiting the economic benefits of the Donetz basin and feared that any withdrawal westward might be misconstrued in Turkey and Romania as retreat. Most of all, however, *Der Führer* still clung to his determination to fight for every foot of soil won from Stalin in 1941. By so doing, he had assured the German nation, he had "saved the German army from a Napoleonic retreat." He also shrank from the greater risk involved in the tactical difficulties of luring the enemy into exposing his flanks.

Kursk was chosen as the target because this seventy-five mile salient or bulge in the German lines seemed to be begging to be cut off. Because it lay between the German Central and Southern Army Groups, it also could become a springboard for Soviet attacks on the flanks of either of these formations. However, if Operation Citadel, as it came to be called, were begun soon enough, it could catch the Soviets unprepared. They would have to commit armored units already badly battered by the Germans in winter attacks, thereby exposing them to final destruction.

Hitler, his eyes still fixed upon his star, anticipated even greater rewards from Citadel. He actually believed that once his massive armor broke through Kursk, it could roll up and capture Moscow from the rear. His generals, however, were not infected this time by his baseless optimism, anticipating at best that this great pincers movement would stabilize them on a line running from the Gulf of Finland to the Sea of Azov.

In the north, Central Army Group would commit its Ninth Army, consisting of six armored and five infantry divisions, striking down from the north across Kursk's rear, while Southern Army Group would provide two armies, Fourth Panzer and Detachment Kempf, consisting of eleven armored and five infantry divisions thrusting northward.

Citadel was to begin in early May after the mud of the spring thaw had dried. Hitler, however, contrary to the advice of his army group commanders, decided to postpone it until June when the new Tiger tanks and Ferdinand self-propelled guns would strengthen his armored divisions. His war chiefs told him that if there were any more delays, Citadel would have to be shelved. Allied victory in Tunisia suggested an imminent landing on the continent. Moreover, the longer he waited, the more time he gave the Soviets to renew their armor out of their undoubtedly superior tank production. But when delivery of the new Tigers was also delayed, Citadel was postponed again until July.

Two months had been lost while formations that might have been committed to support of Citadel had been despatched to Italy. The whole point of the operation was to surprise the Soviets before they had time to replenish and repair. But now there was absolutely no hope of catching the enemy unawares, while the threat to the flanks of the Central Army Group and Southern Army Group by this diminution of their strength grew greater.

It was not until July 5, 1943, that the Battle of Kursk began.

Marshal Georgi Zhukov with remarkable insight and clarity had exactly divined the German plan. He concluded that the Nazis would launch a major offensive at Kursk with the intention of smashing the Soviet Central and Voronezh Fronts.* As early as April 12, he conferred with Stalin at Supreme Headquarters. Stalin listened in attentive silence, puffing on his pipe, while Zhukov outlined the German intentions. It was agreed to provide a defense in depth in all the threatened sectors, especially at Kursk. Reserves would not be moved toward the threatened sectors but concentrated nearby. In its simplest terms Zhukov's plan was to wear down the German offense with a stubborn defense that was well prepared in advance rather than at the whim of fortune.

As time passed and the ground dried and the German attack still did not come, Soviet confidence grew. The General Staff improved the command structure. Organization tables of fronts and armies were reviewed and improved. Modern equipment flowed to the threatened sectors. There were improved radios and automatic and antitank weapons. New artillery and mortar units were formed. Antiaircraft divisions moved to the various fronts. Artillery brigades, divisions and corps were formed to give the Supreme Command more mobility and higher density of fire. Tank production was increased and armored units received their own new self-propelled guns. By the summer of 1943, Zhukov had at his disposal five full tank armies each consisting of two tank corps and one mechanized corps, somewhere close to fifty armored divisions, as well as special heavy-tank regiments intended to break through the German defenses. This does not take into account the infantry or even the aircraft wings flying improved Yaks, giving each of the four fronts its own air army of 700 to 800 planes. Finally there was a huge pool of motor transport.

Kursk undoubtedly was to be the titanic battle of modern war. Two million

*In the Red Army a "front" was the equivalent of an army group, not a battle line as the word suggests.

men and 6,000 tanks alone, along with uncounted thousands of other vehicles and wheeled artillery, were to be involved when, with a roar of motors and the shrill of whistles, the German armies north and south surged forward.

The German spearheads swept into a sea of mines. Minefields were everywhere. As many as 40,000 mines, each capable of blowing up a Panther or Tiger tank, were sown within a single night. Nevertheless the leading columns plunged deep into the minefields. Following them were cannon-firing Stukas picking off the huge Soviet T-34 tanks. Low-flying Yaks did the same with the German tanks. But the T-34s were more than a match for the Tigers and Panthers, both in arms and maneuverability. Their crews were now just as skillful as the Germans. And there were so many of them! German tankers complained that their enemy counterparts were swarming over the battlefields like packs of rats. Never before or since was so much armor thrown into a single struggle. At Prokhorovka in the south alone there were 1,500 tanks and assault guns skirmishing at the same time. Explosions from stricken tanks came almost as rapidly as machine-gun fire. Frightened peasants screaming in terror ran for the forests with their hands over their ears. At times, the smoke from burning tanks blotted out the sun. Out of that blackened sky fell shrieking, burning airplanes. Almost as many airplanes were destroyed as tanks, and the Germans claimed to have shot down 420 Soviet planes in a single day.

At first, it appeared that the German assault was to succeed. During the first two days the Ninth Army in the north penetrated Soviet defenses to a depth of nine miles. The Soviets counterattacked repeatedly, but never in massive strength. Zhukov was still husbanding his reserves. Meanwhile, his prepared defenses in depth were slowing Ninth Army until, on July 9, the German attack halted before strong positions constructed on a dominant height.

The southern offensive seemed more successful. It got off to a slow start through Zhukov's deeply echeloned positions, but then picked up momentum. The high point came at Prokhorovka in the great tank battle where the Germans broke through. They smashed or badly crippled no fewer than ten Soviet tank or mechanized corps, upward of twenty divisions. By July 13 they had taken 24,000 prisoners, destroyed or captured 1,800 tanks, 267 field pieces and 1,080 antitank guns. At this point, the army commanders were summoned to the Wolf's Lair along with Hitler's other top generals.

Hitler announced that the Allies had landed in Sicily, and it appeared that the island would be lost. The next enemy step would probably be a landing in the Balkans or Lower Italy. It would now be necessary to form new armies for the defense of Italy and Greece. These forces would have to come from the Eastern front. Therefore he was calling off the Battle of Kursk. Much as his generals protested, he made only one concession: Southern Army Group would continue the attack until it had destroyed the enemy's armored reserves. But even this could not be accomplished, for Southern Army Group was compelled to release several armored divisions to the Central Army Group. Thus, the last German offensive in the east ended in failure. The Soviets had lost four times as many men as the Germans, but the Battle of Kursk was a smashing Soviet victory.

Stalin was jubilant when, on July 24, 1943, he signed the order of the day announcing the triumph. "Do you remember how in ancient times when troops won victories they rang the church bells in honor of the soldiers and their leaders?" he asked his generals. Instead of church bells, he proposed artillery salutes. That night from the 124 operable guns in the Kremlin there crashed out a dozen simultaneous salvos signaling the turn of the tide in the U.S.S.R.

To replenish the Kursk losses and to form the new formations for Italy, German recruiters roamed the Eastern front visiting noncombatant units. At Trevda they spoke to three companies of convoy troops, among them Guy Sajer's 19th *Rollbahn*. They were all drawn up on a hillside. Officers stood atop a ruined truck and praised the men of the 19th for their bravery and loyalty. Because of this they were prepared to "honor" any of them who wished to volunteer for combat duty. Twenty men stepped forward. The officers frowned. They spoke at length of German heroism. Fifteen more volunteers took three steps forward, among them Sajer's friend, Lensen. Next the officers promised two weeks leave for those who volunteered. Another 300 did so, but Sajer and big, burly Hals remained motionless. Now a pair of lieutenants mingled among the men, searching for the strongest and healthiest. When they found one, they poked an iron finger into his ribs, inviting him to take the fateful three steps forward while the captain continued his spiel. One of them poked a finger into Hals's ribs and Sajer groaned inwardly. His buddy, his best friend, was leaving him! How could he bear to be without Hals? He watched Hals stride forward, and then to his own surprise, he too "volunteered."

They did not immediately join their designated combat units. While they awaited transfer to them, as a reward for their heroism and as a substitute for the promised leave, they were formed into "burial squads."

Normally Soviet prisoners performed the grisly chore of burying the scores of thousands of men lost at Kursk. But it seemed that they had taken to robbing the bodies. Sajer and his comrades doubted this. They believed that the starving Soviets were searching for food. Every day four of them were asked to share three quarts of weak soup. On some days they were given only water. But every prisoner caught robbing a German body was immediately shot. Usually, officers killed them on the spot. Sometimes they handed them over to Russian-hating thugs. They killed ingeniously. Once Sajer saw one of them tie the hands of three Soviet prisoners to the bar of a gate. Then he slipped a grenade into the pocket of one of them, pulled the pin—and ran. The poor men howled piteously until the grenade exploded.

Most of these murderers had escaped from the hideous Soviet prison camp at Tomvos, where Germans were treated just as cruelly. Four men shared a single bowl of millet a day. Those who did not work got nothing. If there were more prisoners than there was food, the surplus was simply killed. One method of execution was to pound an empty cartridge into the nape of a man's neck.

Sajer shuddered when he heard these tales, but he was even more horrified by the work he was compelled to do. At one point, he and his comrades had to dig out a long tunnel that had been turned into an emergency hospital. Evidently the wounded there had been abandoned to die. By the light of their searchlights they saw a long corridor flanked on either side by rows of three-tiered bunks. Three stiff, blackened, mutilated corpses lay on each of them. They had to pull the cadavers out with hooks.

Sajer was glad when a truck came to take him, Hals, Lensen and the others to the camp of the Gross Deutschland Division, the elite assault unit that had suffered so grievously at Prokhorovka. To his delighted surprise, he was given the promised two weeks' leave.

Sajer spent his leave in Berlin, where he fell in love. The girl's name was Paula. He met her when he went to visit the parents of one of his buddies who had been killed. Paula was blond and slender and very serious. Like so many German girls, she was still infatuated with Adolf Hitler and believed Dr. Goebbels's myths of the invincible Germanic race. "German soldiers never run away," she was fond of saying. Sometimes Sajer, who had run from the Don to Kharkov, blushed when she said this.

But Paula showed Sajer Berlin. He was angry when he saw the devastation wrought by the British and American bombers. He began to hate them as he had never hated the Soviets, particularly the Americans, whose daylight bombing the Berliners feared most of all. "Yankee bastards!" they called them.

Toward the end of his leave Sajer and Paula rode in a little motorcycle taxi out to an open field near Tempelhof Airdrome for a picnic. They climbed to the top of a small hillock from which they could see the network of runways crisscrossing the huge airfield. Both civil and military aircraft used Tempelhof. Sajer and Paula sank into some spongy lichen to watch the Focke-Wolfe fighters climb out of sight with astonishing speed. Suddenly air-raid sirens wailed. It was a raid! Now Sajer understood why so many Focke-Wolfes had roared aloft. They were specially designed to attain great height quickly so that they could swoop down on the attacking bombers.

"Look down there!" Paula cried. "All those people running to the shelter."

"We should get into a shelter, too, Paula."

"But we're perfectly safe here—it's the country. They're going to bomb Berlin again."

But they were also coming at Tempelhof.

The murmuring of many motors grew louder. Soon it was like a continuous roll of thunder. Sajer stared at them. "My God, how many there are! There must be hundreds of them!" Sajer felt afraid for Paula and tried to drag her toward a hollow in the ground beside a big tree.

She shook him off. "Look," she cried, fascinated, "they're coming straight at us. And look at the white trails they make. Isn't it strange?"

Suddenly the German AA opened up. Thousands of guns spoke, hurling shells high into the sky. Puffs of flak blossomed everywhere.

"Come quick," Sajer pleaded, grabbing Paula's hand. "We've got to find a shelter!" He pulled her toward the hollow. Paula glanced upward anxiously. "Where are our fighters?"

"Perhaps they've run away—there are so many planes!"

"You mustn't say that! German soldiers *never* run away!"

"But what can they do, Paula? There must be at least a thousand bombers."

"You have no right to say that about our heroic pilots."

"Forgive me, Paula—you're right. I would be astonished if they ran away."

The deadly eggs could be seen falling from the Flying Fortresses and Sajer could hear them come whistling down on the airfield and the suburban city of Tempelhof. The earth beneath him shuddered and bucked. Paula threw her arms around him and clung to him desperately. Sajer felt the concussion waves kneading his stomach with giant fingers. Before his eyes the ground split open . . . clusters of great trees were uprooted, leaping into the sky . . . houses burst into flame . . . oil tanks caught fire to spread flaming destruction . . . the smoke was so thick it obscured Tempelhof from Sajer's eyes . . . and always the roaring of the aerial engines, some of them stricken and plunging earthward through the smoke, spinning out of control and exploding with a flash and a roar. . . . Sajer held Paula close to him to shield her from the flaming debris falling all around him. Even after the American planes departed, there was still terror in her eyes. She trembled as the earth had trembled.

Explosions from delayed-action bombs continued to erupt on the airfield and in Tempelhof, where 22,000 people died. Parts of Berlin were also in ruins. Berlin's rescue and wreckage-removal services were unable to cope with the devastation. Three quarters of the sky above Tempelhof was black with smoke. Thousands of fires still burned there, on the airfield, along the autobahn and in Berlin. Sajer and Paula crawled from their hole and stood erect. They regarded each other with horror and consternation.

"Willy, I feel terrible," Paula said. "And look at me—I'm filthy."

They began walking slowly down the autobahn. Truckloads of rescue workers were driving down the road toward Tempelhof. One of them stopped. "Come on, you young ones. They need you down there."

The trucks picked up everyone they met. One section of Tempelhof had been abandoned so that the other might be saved. Sajer and Paula worked throughout the night, pulling wounded out of the wreckage. Boys of the Hitler Youth joined them, heroically entering burning buildings to rescue trapped occupants. Many of them died when the buildings collapsed in hissing showers of flame and sparks. Sajer and Paula worked until they were exhausted, finally finding shelter in an apartment that had been three quarters destroyed. They fell instantly asleep.

Paula was with Sajer when his leave ended, and he went to the Silesian station to return to the Soviet Union. Trains for Paris and Smolensk stood puffing in the train shed, their smoke curling upward toward the steel girders. People sending off their loved ones on the Paris train were gay. They laughed and blew kisses and reminded their soldiers what to send home from the City of Light. Those at the Smolensk platform were silent and somber. When the train started, women turned away weeping.

Paula was crying, too, when she said good-bye to Sajer.

"Auf wiedersehen, mein Lieber," she whispered, tears streaking her face. "See you soon, my love."

"Paula, I beg you . . . don't cry . . . please . . . You know I'll be back soon."

The train whistle shrilled. Paula seized Sajer's hand, running beside him as the train chugged slowly out of the station. Then she had to let go.

"See you soon, my love," she said once more.

But they never saw each other again.

Almost nightly now the Kremlin guns roared their salvos, saluting victory after victory as Zhukov's counteroffensive, begun on August 4, rolled forward like the mighty steamroller that it was. At the Battle of Kursk, the marshal had fielded 1.3 million soldiers, 3,600 tanks, 20,000 guns and 3,130 airplanes, but the counteroffensive was even greater: twenty-two full-strength armies, five tank armies and six air armies. Hardly had the troops of Hitler's armies retreated to their start-lines north and south before the Soviets increased the pressure on Orel. Unable to hold, the Germans fell back on Smolensk.

In late August the full fury of the Soviet onslaught struck at the Southern Army front. The odds against Marshal von Manstein there were incredible. In a report submitted August 21 he showed the German high command that he had fifty-two divisions holding a 610-mile front against no fewer than 287 enemy divisions! This, of course, is a simplification, since Manstein's summation spoke of corps, divisions, brigades and regiments of every arm. But during battle it is difficult to learn whether an enemy formation is at half, two thirds or full strength. Even so, supposing that the divisions of both sides at full strength would number roughly 10,000 men, the report suggests a Soviet superiority of 2.87 million men to 520,000! Probably, this estimate is exaggerated, but it is certain that an enemy superiority of at least 3 to 1 and probably 4 to 1 was enough to send Manstein hurrying to the Wolf's Lair to warn Hitler that his group faced catastrophe unless there was a change in the conduct of operations. But *Der Führer,* like a drowning man clinging to the millstone around his neck, insisted on holding the Donetz basin. Only when the Soviets turned Manstein's left flank did Hitler authorize a withdrawal behind the Dnieper River. Even then, he forbade fortifying the river bank, believing, as he always did, that if his generals knew that there was a reserve line, they would immediately fall back there.

Without constructing a defense-in-depth at the Dnieper, Manstein had little chance of halting a Soviet advance. Moreover, there were only five river crossings, meaning that the pursuing Soviets would be able to deliver concentrated hammer blows at the rear of each. The retreat to the Dnieper would only succeed if the Soviets could be delayed.

At once, like Stalin in early 1941, Marshal von Manstein adopted a "scorched earth" policy. He was aware that the Soviet armies, like those of Genghis Khan and Napoleon, made limited use of supply columns, living off the country instead. The most effective means of slowing them down, then, was to destroy everything that might be of use to them. This was done to a depth of fifteen miles east of the river.

By mid-September Southern Army Group was safely across the Dnieper. Its officers and men took comfort in the sight of the broad stream—at its widest some 400 yards—flowing in front of them. Their river bank was higher than the opposite shore, another advantage; although the Soviet side was thick with weeds in which the enemy might hide his boats and conceal his preparations. Marshal von Manstein was aware that Napoleon's very first maxim declared that of all the obstacles to an army's advance—deserts, mountains and rivers—rivers were the easiest to cross.

In mid-October the Soviets struck at the Dnieper line. An incredible artillery bombardment lasting only two hours, during which the ammunition allowance for thirty-six hours was expended, preceded the assault. Each thousand yards of German front was pounded by 290 guns of all calibers. Once the barrage had lifted, the German positions looked like plowed-up fields. Much of their artillery and antitank guns were knocked out. Then the Soviet infantry attacked. They came out of their bridgeheads in long brown waves, uttering fierce cries and followed by low-flying planes strafing German guns that still fired at them. Yet, at no point did the attack gain more than a mile.

Soviet losses were appalling. Yet the attack continued. Riddled divisions were quickly replaced by fresh formations. Always, they attacked over the same ground. Soviet tactics remained rigid. Wave after wave flowed forward even though wave after wave was repulsed with heavy losses. Although the German center held, Marshal Ivan Konev in command was successful on the flanks. To the southeast he seized three bridgeheads near Kremenchug, advancing on the great industrial centers of Krivoy Rog and Nikopol. Dnepropetrovsk fell on October 25. For a time it seemed that the Soviets would take the great bend of the river. Probably it would have been better for the Germans if they had. Hitler's insistence on holding it and in clinging to Krivoy Rog and Nikopol put Manstein in a straitjacket. Still, when he counterattacked as ordered, he flung Konev's columns back toward the river. But in the northwest Marshal Nikolai Vatutin's forces crossed the Dnieper in great strength and closed in on Kiev from two sides. On November 6 Kiev fell, and the Kremlin guns signaled to joyous Muscovites that the ancient and sacred city on the Dnieper, home of the Slavs who made the Russian nation, was once again a part of Holy Russia.

Farther to the south in the Crimea, the Soviets were trying to cut off the Germans who were still there. The morale of German soldiers fighting to escape the trap had sunk very low. There was an epidemic of self-inflicted wounds by men seeking to be flown out of the battle area for treatment. The Soviets learned of it and dropped propaganda leaflets describing exactly how to shoot oneself in the hand without leaving telltale traces of blackened flesh and singed hair. Dr. Peter Bamm knew that this was impossible: No matter where a soldier tries to shoot himself, foot or finger, he will leave powder burns. If caught, Bamm also knew, he would be court-martialed and shot.

Dr. Bamm's first such case was a peasant youth flown to the Crimea from Germany after only a few weeks of training. He was barely eighteen and had yet to shave. Bamm examined the wound in the youth's hand carefully. He touched the serrated edges with a swab and saw that it wasn't dirt. Dr. Bamm had no desire to send this terrified boy to the firing squad. He glanced around at his assistants. They were studying him intently. Bamm was intensely proud of his calling and of his skill as a surgeon. He called his surgeon's knife "the scalpel of Hippocrates." Now his anaesthetist rubbed his mask wryly and said: "Only old Hippocrates can put this right." Without a word Dr. Bamm seized his scalpel and destroyed the evidence—by widening the wound.

The Soviet counteroffensive following the German defeat at Kursk had made three deep penetrations beyond the Dnieper: at Brussilov, Zhitomir-Radomyshl' and Korosten'; but three Russian army groups had suffered grievously. Although reinforcements continued to pour through Kiev en route to these battered formations, the troops were of low quality. The Germans were incredulous to find that half of their prisoners were boys between fifteen and eighteen, some mere children of thirteen, or old men fitter for the fireside than the trenches. The other half were mainly Asiatics, dragooned from the deepest recesses of the Soviet Empire. To flesh out their ordinary infantry divisions, the Soviets seized upon anyone regardless of age or health and sometimes of sex. If a force were cut off, they strove to save only its officers and NCOs. For the ordinary untrained soldier they cared not a fig. Their best men were reserved for the various Guard units or for the tanks and artillery.

The immemorial Russian adage "Our best defense is the living breasts of our soldiers" was again true in the Ukraine. The fatalism undergirding the durability of the Soviet soldiers apparently was simply incomprehensible to anyone who had not witnessed it. They could stand up to the most frightening artillery fire or aerial bombardment, and this was expected of them by a high command that never bothered to keep casualty records. The Soviet soldier actually did not value his own life more than those of his comrades. When ordered to advance into a fiery crucible, he did; when commanded to erect barricades made of the flesh of his friends, dead or wounded, or to drive a tank over them, he obeyed. To such men accustomed to a life of privation, the misery and danger of war entailed only a higher degree of hardship than those of peace. Thus, those long brown waves of shouting, singing soldiers, like the rolling gray waves of a storm-tossed ocean, kept coming at the wearying Germans.

Soviet weapons and their astonishing skills at camouflage and infiltration were also demoralizing the Germans. The multiple-rocket launchers called Stalin Organs were most effective, both in the terror that they inspired and the devastation that they wrought. Multiple and simultaneous detonation blanketing an entire artillery battery or company of infantry was obliterating and terrifying.

In camouflage, they might have been minions of the witch Hecate bringing "high Birnam Wood to Dunsinane Hill." One German battalion commander had for days had the uneasy impression that the wood opposite him was moving closer daily. After a few days it suddenly erupted in a storm of fire. An entire Soviet artillery battalion, concealed behind uprooted bushes and trees, had worked its way up to close range. Again, artificial graves were often gun pits with embrasures for sniper fire.

With an almost inexhaustible supply of such troops and with such tactics and weapons, no fewer than three entire Soviet fronts began the Battle of the Great Bend of the Dnieper. Their objective was to cut off the southern wing of the German armies south of Kiev and force them away to the southwest. They also threatened to overwhelm German forces all but trapped in the Crimea.

Dr. Peter Bamm's division was stationed in the northern steppes of the Crimea. Bamm's unit was in a village inhabited by Bulgarians. Because the Germans paid the Bulgarians for the food they supplied and lent them their horses for harvesting, they did not object to having troops billeted in their homes. Relations were so cordial that Dr. Bamm readily approved a request by the village *starost,* or head man, to be allowed to listen to Radio Sofia along with other *starosts* in the area. Once a week they gathered around a radio in the living room of the *starost*'s home, where Dr. Bamm and other officers lived. Soon Bamm discovered that the Bulgarians were actually listening to Moscow.

To teach them a lesson, he and two other officers burst in upon a radio session brandishing revolvers and shouting, "Hands up!"

The Bulgarians were terrified, except for the local *starost.* He was a tall, strongly built man with an enormous black beard. He might have been a medieval saint stepping out of a stained-glass window. He got calmly to his feet and switched off the radio. With a gentle smile, he said: "*Gospodin* Commandant, what can we do? We are in danger. We have wives and children. *Proshch'te!* Forgive!"

They were forgiven. Soon, however, the *starost* was pleading with Dr. Bamm for permission to lead the entire village back to Bulgaria. He feared that because they were independent farmers, they would be treated like kulaks: torn from their lands and sent to Siberia. Dr. Bamm consented.

For three days the Bulgarians prepared for their departure. They baked bread in a huge brick oven. They slaughtered sheep, boiled the meat, and salted it away in big stone jars. New rims were fitted to their wagon wheels. With quiet dignity and gratitude the peasants accepted the carbines given them by Dr. Bamm for protection against the wolves of the steppes.

At dawn on the day of departure, the horses were harnessed to the wagons and the cattle driven from the sheds. The women and children climbed aboard the wagons. The *starost*'s oldest son came into the village courtyard holding the sacred icon which his great-grandfather had brought from Bulgaria. The whole family knelt while the *starost* began the *Pater Noster.* "Give us this day our daily bread," he intoned, his dark eyes falling sadly on the oven in which the village's bread had literally been baked daily for generations. He kissed the earth which had sustained them. He kissed the icon. Arising, his great beard lifted, he embraced Dr. Bamm, bestowing upon him a fraternal kiss.

Slowly the wagon train rolled out of the courtyard. Lowing cows jostled skittish sheep to the side. Barking dogs ran round and round the wagons. One by one other wagon trains issued out of gates along the wide village street to join the exodus. With sad eyes Dr. Bamm watched them vanish into the infinity of the steppes. At noon the dust clouds marking their progress had also disappeared. But they never reached their native land.

Soviet spearheads forcing back the Germans on the north shore of the Sea of Azov overtook and scattered them. They had given to the steppes that nourished them the sweat of their brows, and now it was joined by their blood and tears.

69. Joseph W. Stilwell and the Fight for Burma

THROUGHOUT THE PACIFIC WAR—except for Australia's small air force and navy and her larger army, which grew even larger with the return of units from the Middle East—the United States fought Japan with no assistance from her European allies. In the Far East, however, considerable British forces of all arms and a large but poorly trained army of Generalissimo Chiang Kai-shek's corrupt Nationalist Government confronted the Japanese. There also the fate of the vast colonial empires of the British, French and Dutch awaited the outcome of the war. The British were determined to hold India against Japanese invasion, and to a lesser degree to recover Burma and Malaya. The French and Dutch, of course, were in no position to do anything except to remind Britain of their own "rights" in Southeast Asia. In his capital at Chungking, Chiang outwardly pretended to be dedicated to evicting the Japanese and to helping the British reclaim Burma, his last land link with the outside world. Privately, he was more interested in obtaining all possible assistance from the United States to stay in power and so deal with his rivals among the Chinese war lords and especially the Chinese Communists in the north led by Mao Zedong.

In the United States, with its traditional fascination for China, it was generally believed that the Nationalist Chinese were struggling bravely against the

Japanese. President Roosevelt said the Chinese had "for four and a half years
. . . withstood bombs and starvation and have whipped the invaders time and
again in spite of superior Japanese equipment and arms." In truth, the Chinese
army had not fought a major battle with Japan since 1938. This so-called army
was not such a cohesive force at all, but rather a coalition of the war lords
commanding twelve "war areas" corresponding to the provinces of old Imperial
China. They exercised both civil and military control. These poorly trained and
worse equipped forces seldom fought the Japanese. Indeed, the war lords were
more interested in enhancing their individual power. Chiang's divisions were far
superior, although they lacked artillery and armor, and many of their commanders were chosen for their loyalty to the generalissimo rather than for any military
prowess.

Like the Soviets, the Chinese soldiers were stoical and capable of enduring
great hardship. Unlike the Soviet troops, they had no sense of patriotism and were
exploited by their commanders in every way possible. The word "primitive" can
hardly describe the Chinese system of conscripting and training troops. American
officers who witnessed it marveled that a conscript could stay alive long enough
to receive training. His pitiful ration of food and clothing passed through so many
larcenous hands that he frequently starved to death before reaching training camp
or arrived a diseased all-but-naked skeleton. One camp inspected by an American
commission found that 100 percent of its recruits were suffering from tuberculosis, beriberi, malnutrition and other afflictions. "The seriously sick replacements
had to cook for themselves in kitchens that were immediately adjacent to latrines.
The dead were lying next to the barely living and left there at times for several
days." Actually, a dead conscript was valuable. His rations and pay were issued
to his commander until his death was reported.

Thus the true Chinese army, and yet, President Roosevelt really had no
alternative but to pour millions of dollars into the China-Burma-India Theater
(CBI), and to waste the skills of thousands of technicians, engineers, aviators and
high-ranking civilian emissaries in a vain effort to turn Chiang Kai-shek's Kuomintang government into a formidable ally against Japan. After all, it was Roosevelt's refusal to acquiesce in Nippon's Chinese conquests that triggered the war
with Japan. American Lend-Lease aid had been flowing to China since the
summer of 1941, arriving in the Burmese port of Rangoon, transported to Kunming over the Burma Road, 700 miles of dirt highway running through mountains and jungles into south China, thence to Chungking, Chiang's headquarters.
There was also an American volunteer group in China, fliers released by the
American services for duty there. Called the "Flying Tigers" for the huge shark
teeth painted on the noses of their airplanes, this valiant small air force was
commanded by Col. Claire Lee Chennault. Thus American assistance was already in place in China, and after Pearl Harbor Roosevelt could hardly have
turned his back on Chiang, even if he had known just how sick the Chinese giant
was.

Even though the Japanese invasion of south Burma had closed the Burma

Road, Chiang was delighted by Pearl Harbor. There was actually dancing in the streets of Chungking. Like Churchill, the generalissimo saw at once that American power doomed the Axis. But then he was disheartened by the Anglo-American grand strategy of defeating Nazi Germany first. As a sop to his prestige, the Anglo-Americans asked him to become the supreme commander, China Theater. He accepted and requested a high-ranking American officer to serve as chief of his joint staff of British, American, Chinese and Dutch military advisers. General Marshall chose Lt. Gen. Joseph W. (Vinegar Joe) Stilwell, an outstanding troop commander whom he had already selected to lead the first American operations in Europe. Stilwell had been expecting this highest command in American history, but he had made the mistake of making himself fluent in Chinese while gaining extensive experience of China itself. He didn't want to go to Chungking but, like a dutiful soldier, agreed to "go where I'm sent."

Stilwell left Washington in early February, not only to become Chiang's chief of staff but also to command all American forces in the CBI, as FDR's personal military representative and controller of Lend-Lease. It was also expected that Stilwell would be offered command of the Chinese troops helping the British fight the Japanese in Burma.

Vinegar Joe Stilwell was aptly nicknamed. This slender, waspish, sharp-featured, bespectacled soldier with the short cropped hair had a tongue as abrasive as emery cloth. He disliked Chiang Kai-shek on sight and thereafter filled his diary with derisive gibes at the character and competence of the Peanut, as he called him (originally a code name). His one desire, it seemed, was "to break the Peanut's face," that is, shake Chiang's normally unshakable aplomb. He proved himself so adept at this perverse skill that the relationship between the two men was, to say the least, adversarial. But Chiang did make Stilwell commander of his Chinese Sixth Army in Burma, and Stilwell was fit to command. Unfortunately, his troops were unworthy of him. After the British on the Sixth Army's right flank collapsed, their troops escaping to India, the Japanese turned the exposed flank and seized a vital juncture on the Burma Road, thus cutting off the Chinese escape route. Stilwell tried to organize an orderly withdrawal, but with many commanders unwilling to follow his orders and their troops panicking, the retreat turned into a rout. Stilwell himself had to lead his staff on a 140-mile mountain march into India. He reached the border without losing a man.

"I claim we got a hell of a beating," he told reporters who met him. "We got run out of Burma and it's humiliating as hell. I think we ought to find out what caused it, go back and retake it." Stilwell cited numerous reasons for the defeat, chief among them Chiang's constant interference and "the British defeatist attitude." What Vinegar Joe did not know at the time was that the British, so far from being able to hold Burma, were having a most difficult time keeping India in line.

For four decades Mohandas K. Gandhi had been the charismatic leader of Indian opposition to British rule. He was almost literally worshipped by millions.

His Indian National Congress was a thorn in the flesh of the British raj. Thus, when Britain took India into the war with Japan without consulting any of her political leaders, "the Mahatma" was enraged. So was his deputy, Jawaharlal Nehru, who wrote: "We want to combat fascism, but we will not have war imposed upon us by outside authority. We will not sacrifice to preserve old injustices or to maintain an order based upon them." Gandhi and Nehru also resented the shipment of a quarter million Indian soldiers to North Africa and Europe. When Britain offered to grant India dominion status at the end of the war, they refused. Instead, Gandhi called for immediate British withdrawal and counseled his people to adopt a stance of nonviolence toward any Japanese invasion. The Anglo-Americans were enraged. Ultimately, Nehru persuaded Gandhi to moderate his position. A "quit India" resolution was prepared, calling for the British to leave immediately but stating that Allied troops might remain for defense of the country. Chiang was dismayed. He could foresee a showdown shaping up. He asked Roosevelt to intervene with Churchill but FDR merely passed his message along to the British chief. Back came the soothing reply: "The Congress party in no way represents India . . . and can neither defend India nor raise a revolt."

One week later—on August 8, 1942—the Congress party adopted the Quit India resolution. Next day the British arrested all the top Congress leaders—and Churchill's impossible revolt erupted with a roar. Enormous demonstrations and riots occurred all over India, punctuated by thousands of acts of sabotage. By month's end 1,000 people had been killed and 100,000 Congress leaders or sympathizers were in jail. By such strong-arm methods British control of India was made secure, but the Quit India resolution and ensuing disturbances had signaled the beginning of the end of British rule.

Because the defeat in Burma had cut Chiang's Burma Road lifeline, India was now almost as important to the United States as to Britain. That was because supplies for China must now take two routes from there. The first was by "flying the Hump." American transports taking off from Indian airfields carried arms and supplies over the 15,000-foot Himalaya Mountains into southern China. For eighteen months these remarkable pilots and their crews worked twelve hours a day seven days a week to keep the Chinese supplied. They flew in rickety non-pressurized transports with oxygen only for the pilots, dodging mountain peaks and Japanese fighters. Every day between six and six when the weather was right, they spent all but two and a half hours in the air. Tired, dirty, drawn, often unshaven, they were a dedicated group of men, interested only in their mission, sleeping wherever they happened to be while their mechanics spent the hours of darkness working desperately to keep their dilapidated planes in flying shape. Much was owed to the men who "flew the Hump."

Much also was owed to the redoubtable American engineers who constructed the second overland route into China, the Ledo Road. This new highway ran from the town of Ledo in the province of Assam in eastern India over the mountains and jungles of northern Burma until it could join the old Burma Road leading into southern China. Although the Americans had at first believed that the British would undertake this project, they found that their allies were not anxious to build roads leading into their empire's eastern frontier. The British also thought it was a nearly impossible job, but the Americans under the indomitable Maj. Gen. Lewis A. Pick successfully built not only their "Pick's Pike" with the labor of Indian, Chinese and Assamese workers, but also constructed two fuel pipelines alongside it. On January 12, 1945, the first convoy left Ledo, arriving in Kunming on February 4.

Although General Stilwell had always been an ardent supporter of the Ledo-Road project, he still believed that the best way to restore Chiang's supply line was to retake northern Burma and link up with the old Burma Road there. He planned to use thirty Chinese divisions trained by Americans in Yunnan Province in China for a thrust from the east, and three divisions trained by himself in Ramgarh, India, for a strike from the west. These last formations were brought into India by Hump transports returning from south China. They arrived without uniforms or weapons, usually in poor physical shape, often sick, and sometimes even naked. They were overjoyed at the food, clothing, weapons and medical attention they received, and Stilwell formed them into the best four divisions ever fielded in Chinese history. But General Wavell, British commander in chief, India, was not interested in such a major campaign. He preferred a limited offensive down the west coast of Burma to capture the island of Akyab with its valuable airfields. But even this was not possible in 1942, with the struggle for Guadalcanal and the North African campaign demanding so much of American resources.

Chiang also was reluctant to commit his troops. He believed with Claire Chennault, now a major general, that Japan could be defeated by air war from India. Chennault told Roosevelt that he could bring down Japan within a year with a force of 105 fighters, thirty medium and twelve heavy bombers. First he would annihilate the Japanese air force, next destroy her shipping and finally obliterate her industrial plant. This with fewer than 150 aircraft! Nevertheless, the immemorial attraction of the "quick fix" and Chennault's skillful public relations campaign made a deep impression on Roosevelt. Only the opposition of the army and the navy—which believed Japan could only be defeated by amphibious operations from the China coast—dissuaded Roosevelt from approving Chennault's request and later ones for 500 planes from Chiang himself.

At the Casablanca conference in early 1943 it was agreed by the Combined Chiefs that a campaign against Burma should be undertaken late in the year following the end of the monsoon. A final decision on the proposal would be made by the Combined Chiefs in the summer of 1943.

Long before then, however, General Wavell's limited offensive toward

Akyab Island launched at the end of 1942 received such rough treatment at the hands of the Japanese that the Combined Chiefs began to have reservations about a long and costly campaign in Burma. Wavell's British and Indian troops under Maj. Gen. W. L. Lloyd made good progress down Burma's west coast until they encountered Japanese fortifications ten miles above Akyab. These were typical lines of concealed log-and-earth bunkers, which the Japanese habitually erected in mountainous terrain. They held up the Anglo-Indians for a month, while the enemy brought in reinforcements. Then the Japanese themselves counter-attacked, moving over ridges the British believed to be impassable to strike their enemy in the rear, rout them and send them streaming back to India broken, racked by malaria and with their morale at its nadir.

This defeat served to dim the earlier successes scored by the 77th Long-Range Penetration Brigade led by Brig. Orde Wingate, a brilliant, ascetic and eccentric soldier. Wingate was a veteran of irregular warfare in Palestine and Ethiopia. With his magnetic personality, he convinced Wavell of the wisdom of forming a force that would operate behind enemy lines to wreck the enemy's communications and demoralize his troops. This was certainly nothing new in warfare, as the Civil War exploits of J. E. B. Stuart and Nathan Bedford Forrest would suggest. In the present war British commandos and American Army Rangers and Marine Raiders had been formed for the same purpose. However, such irregulars usually operate in conjunction with a main body engaged in a major campaign. But the Chinese offensive into Burma had been canceled. There was really no point in sending a diversionary force into action when there was nothing from which to divert the enemy. But in February 1943, Wingate's brigade went into action.

There were 3,000 of these Gurkha and British soldiers, called "Chindits" after the statues of griffinlike creatures guarding Burmese temples.* They operated in seven separate columns and were supplied by airdrop. They attacked enemy outposts and cut the north-south railroad in seventy places, operating for three months and covering 1,500 miles. But they lost a third of their number, and many more were so badly wounded or crippled by illness that they could never fight again. Obviously, it was another of those costly failures that normally overtake such visionary schemes. But the Chindits captured the imagination of an Allied world starved for victories, particularly of the always-fanciful Winston Churchill. "I consider Wingate should command the Army against Burma," he wrote. "He is a man of genius and audacity." Audacious he was indeed, but genius he was not; rather his was the erratic sparkle of eccentricity, which is so often mistaken for the steady gleam of true genius. Nor would he command an army in Burma, for Orde Wingate lost his life in an aircraft crash. His greatest contribution had been to raise Allied morale, for his Chindits had beaten the Japanese at their own game of jungle warfare.

*Actually the correct word is *Chinthe*, but Wingate misunderstood his interpreter.

70. Counteroffensive in the Central Solomons

JAPAN'S STRATEGY in the Pacific War was to erect a chain of island forts around her vast new empire, thus compelling the Americans to fight an island-by-island counterattack. They hoped the eventual cost—especially in blood—would force the Americans to accept a negotiated peace.

Japan had seized many of the islands one by one and believed that the Americans would do the same with these, as well as the islands mandated to her by the League of Nations. But the Americans saw no intrinsic value in the islands, as the land-hungry Japanese had, regarding them only as a means to an end—stepping-stones to the conquest of Japan. Thus Admiral Nimitz and General MacArthur had no intention of falling in with the Japanese plan. Instead, their strategy was to seize the biggest or most important islands while bypassing the others, leaving them "to wither on the vine." If the bypassed islands threatened their lines of communication, then they were to be neutralized by aerial onslaught from carriers or island airfields. Each captured island would become an advanced staging area for the next leap forward toward Japan. Island hopping, then, became a martial game of leapfrogging.

It followed two invasion routes. General MacArthur's was through the Bismarck Barrier formed by the enormous island of New Guinea on the left or southern arm of the advance, and on the right the complex of the Solomons–New Britain–Admiralties. Beyond the Bismarck Barrier lay other island stepping-stones toward the Philippines. Generally, as MacArthur advanced in his Southwest Pacific area his leaps would be limited by the range of his land-based fighter cover, usually about 200 miles.

Nimitz's route was westward through the Central Pacific and the little islands of Micronesia, before swinging right or north at the Marianas and thence onward to Japan. Nimitz's Pacific Oceans Area was by far the larger, a huge watery waste in which the limitless range of carrier-based air gave him the opportunity to take enormous leaps of up to 2,000 miles. Thus Marines staging at Guadalcanal in 1944 were able to invade Peleliu 1,589 nautical miles away. Besides leading this long sea charge on Tokyo, Nimitz eventually commanded vast resources of carrier power, which he used to make punishing raids on Japanese island fortresses that otherwise might have had to be invaded at great cost of life.

MacArthur's march was begun with the conquest of Guadalcanal and Buna–Gona, but after these victories he was compelled to mark time while Allied strength—particularly in shipping—was concentrated in the Mediterranean. In time the South Pacific area reverted to his command along with Admiral Halsey and those forces at his disposal. There were in early 1943, however, several sideshows—if any operation in which men suffer and die may be so lightly described. There was one of a bloodless nature in February when Marines occupied the Russell Islands farther up the Solomons ladder. The following May army infantry reclaimed the Aleutian Islands off the coast of Alaska. American soldiers on Attu fought the Japanese in deep snows, repulsing banzai charges so fanatical that the enemy did not hesitate to arm his sick and wounded and send them to their deaths. Next the Japanese evacuated Kiska and by mid-August the entire chain was again in American possession.

Other than these operations, most of the fighting in the Pacific during the first half of 1943 took place in the air. On March 1, a Japanese convoy of eight transports and eight destroyers sailed from Rabaul to reinforce New Guinea bases in the Lae–Salamaua area. As had become customary, the Japanese depended more on bad weather than on aerial cover to slip their convoys past the striking power of the Allied air forces. Their meteorologists had assured them that there would be cloud cover over Dampier Strait between New Guinea and New Britain, and their intelligence had minimized the growing power of MacArthur's Fifth Air Force commanded by Maj. Gen. George C. Kenney. In fact, Kenney had 205 bombers and 154 fighters stationed in bases on New Guinea's Papuan Peninsula, and another eighty-six bombers and ninety-five fighters in support in Queensland, Australia.

Thus, when large breaks in the clouds appeared on March 1, patrolling Liberator bombers spotted the convoy and reported its location to bases on Port Moresby and Milne Bay. Kenney hurled his land-based air at the unsuspecting Japanese. In a two-day battle, bombers of every description—lights, mediums and heavies, Havocs, Mitchells, Liberators, Flying Forts—roared aloft under the cover of Lightnings and Australian Beaufighters. Before nightfall of March 2 some 350 aircraft had joined the attack, sending all the transports and half of the destroyers to the bottom along with 2,800 enemy soldiers. A jubilant General MacArthur announced a major victory, claiming to have sunk twenty-two Japanese ships and drowned 15,000 men. There now ensued an army-navy squabble of the particularly vicious type that was to disfigure the Pacific War from start to finish.

MacArthur had already angered the navy by declaring that the enemy fleet "completely controlled the Western Pacific," and now his jeering remarks about the superiority of land-based air over carrier-based air stung the admirals further. They questioned MacArthur's and Kenney's figures. Surprisingly, General Arnold ordered the Army Air Forces to make a secret and sweeping investigation of the battle. It was done, and the figure of eight transports, four destroyers and 2,800 soldiers was upheld. MacArthur, coolly challenged the report, sticking to his own exaggerations, like Kenney, to his dying day—even after a postwar investigation in Japan confirmed the lower figures. Nevertheless, for all the American interservice quarreling, the Battle of the Bismarck Sea had indeed struck the Japanese a serious psychological as well as material blow. Never again did they attempt to run the gantlet of American air power without sufficient air cover. Gradually, reinforcement and supply of New Guinea bases was shifted to self-propelled barges. They sailed by night, hiding by day in the numerous coves and inlets of the New Guinea shore. Eventually, the Bismarck barge traffic was also destroyed.

Once again the coast watchers and their faithful Melanesian scouts radioed valuable information on barge movements. They continued to warn Guadalcanal of approaching enemy formations during the widening aerial war and also rescued Allied* airmen shot down in the sea or jungle or shipwrecked sailors. Japanese in similar straits were allowed to surrender, but mostly they were killed. Lt. John F. Kennedy, later president of the United States, was rescued by coast watchers after a charging Japanese destroyer cut his torpedo boat in two.

On Guadalcanal in early 1943 the coast watchers who had occupied the lonely high mountain peaks were being called in. Their work was done. Among them was K. D. Hay, a veteran of World War I and easily the fattest man in the South Pacific. Yet he had continued to operate from the abandoned mining camp known as Gold Ridge. But at last he was coming down, bringing with him the aged nun who was the sole survivor of a Japanese massacre and rape of a Catholic mission. Melanesian bearers carried her down. Hay descended on foot, panting and gasping all the way. When he reached the coastal road, he was near collapse. He sent word to the Americans asking for a jeep, explaining that he was "knocked up." This British slang for exhaustion is, of course, Americanese for being pregnant. When a puzzled army officer drove out to assist Hay, he took one look at his ample belly, clapped his hand to his forehead and swore:

"My God, it's true!"

Fleet Adm. Isoroku Yamamoto had planned a flaming revenge for the loss of Guadalcanal. It was called the I Operation. It was intended to sink American shipping, to whittle American air strength and to make American bases on Guadalcanal and New Guinea inoperable while strengthening Japan's hold on the Bismarck Barrier. Roughly 350 planes—both land-based and carrier—were assembled, a huge force by the Pacific standards of 1943. On April 7, given an early-morning report that four American cruisers, seven destroyers and fourteen transports were in Iron Bottom Bay, Yamamoto let fly. On Segi Point in New Georgia, Donald Kennedy, the coast watcher who had rescued Joe Foss, heard the gigantic humming overhead and ran from his shack to count the enemy. But he couldn't. He could only signal: "Hundreds headed yours!"

In the Russells the radar screens were milky with pips. An earlier warning of "Condition Red" was changed to one never used before or since: "Condition *Very* Red!"

Over Guadalcanal and Tulagi only seventy-six Marine, army and navy

*The word "Allied" here is intended to describe chiefly Australians, some New Zealanders with a Dutchman or two, but no British. Actually, the Pacific War at this juncture was fought almost 100 percent by Americans.

fighters had been scrambled aloft to take on this vast armada. Among them was a Marine boot pilot named Jimmy Swett, who was about to become the most famous greenhorn of the war. Twenty-two-year-old Lieutenant Swett had never been in combat before. With three comrades, he flew his Wildcat toward Tulagi while yelps and rebel yells and cries of "Heigh-ho Silver!" drowned out the fighter director's frantic pleas: "Protect your shipping! Protect your shipping!"

Fifteen minutes later Jimmy Swett had shot down seven enemy bombers. He flamed them so fast he had no recollection of how he did it. First he shoved his Wildcat over and dived into the stream of AA flowing up from Tulagi, shooting down three Val torpedo bombers at three different levels. He cut down to pick-up speed, climbed and went roaring after four more, blasting them into the tall treetops of Florida Island. Finally, with his cooling system destroyed and his face bloodied by flying bits of glass from his shattered windshield, he crash-landed in the bay. For this unique fighting feat, Swett received the Medal of Honor, and, what was perhaps equally rewarding, the knowledge that henceforth Marine boot pilots went into battle eager "to do a Jimmy Swett."

In all thirty-nine Japanese planes were shot down, twenty-eight by Marine pilots at a cost of seven of their own aircraft but no pilots lost. In their jubilation, fliers of all services claimed kills all over the Solomons. Many ack-ack gunners painted little red balls on their gun mounts or the prows or sterns of their ships. All these claims added together would surely have accounted for more aircraft than Yamamoto possessed; yet the American exaggerations were meager in comparison to the reports of the enemy pilots.

Although they had sunk only one destroyer, a tanker and a corvette at Guadalcanal, and two small Netherlands transports at New Guinea in a follow-up assault of similar strength, the Japanese pilots who returned to base reported overwhelming success. Such self-deception, born of the fixation on saving face, was to occur again and again during the Pacific War, to the great benefit of the Americans and the grave detriment of Japan. From the high command reporting directly to Tojo, down to riflemen and sailors coming back from patrol, the Japanese habitually maximized their success and minimized their failure. Yamamoto was so misled by these reports that he canceled strikes planned for the future and scheduled instead an inspection trip to the big Solomon island of Bougainville.

Magic had learned that Admiral Yamamoto was going to fly to Bougainville. A query was sent to the Pentagon: Would it be wise to kill Yamamoto, or would his removal make way for a better chief? Back came the answer: Isoroku Yamamoto has the best military mind in Japan.

Rear Adm. Marc Mitscher, air commander for the Solomons, gave the assignment to the AAF 339th Squadron under Maj. John Mitchell. The 339th's twin-tailed Lightnings were then the longest-range fighters aloft. Sixteen of them took off from Henderson Field on the morning of April 18 bound for Kahili airfield at the southern tip of Bougainville. At about the same time two Betty bombers escorted by nine Zeke fighters arose from Rabaul headed for the same airfield. In the bombers were Yamamoto and his chief of staff, Vice Adm. Matome Ugaki, and the most important officers on his staff.

The slowing Bettys were dropping down for a landing and the Zekes preparing to fly back to base when the Americans arrived.

Capt. Thomas Lamphier and Lt. Rex Barber, among the squadron's best shots, swooped down on the Bettys. Lamphier shot one of them down into the jungle, Barber sent the other plunging into Empress Augusta Bay. Up above, Major Mitchell's triggermen tore into the horrified Zeke pilots. They shot down three of them. Of the sixteen Americans, only Lt. Raymond Hine was lost. The others flew back to Guadalcanal. Their report produced jubilation, which flowed from the Pacific back to the Pentagon. But no announcement was made, for fear of warning the Japanese that their code had been cracked. All elation had to be guarded, like the message Halsey sent to Mitscher: "Congratulations to you and Major Mitchell and his hunters. Sounds as though one of the ducks in their bag might be a peacock."

It was. On May 21 Tokyo announced that the great Yamamoto was lost. He had been aboard the plane Lamphier sent into the jungle and had been killed with his top aides. Admiral Ugaki had been badly injured, but was surviving.

Isoroku Yamamoto, the brilliant proud leader who had planned the Pearl Harbor attack and had indeed "run wild" for more than a year, the emperor's "one and only Yamamoto," was dead.

In May 1943, following the Allied victory in North Africa, the new landing craft that had been so useful there began to appear in the Pacific. The old wooden Higgins boats from which the Marines used to leap into boiling surf were now abandoned in favor of the Landing Craft, Vehicle, Personnel (LCVPs). They were thirty-six feet long, could move at nine knots and carry thirty-six men or a three-ton vehicle or 8,000 pounds of cargo. They had bow ramps, which were lowered the moment they hit the beach, enabling the occupants to run ashore in one of those dry ladylike landings scorned by the old salts. The old amtrac had also been improved. The Marines had had them on Guadalcanal, calling them "Alligators." They had been excellent for crossing swamps or sailing up navigable jungle streams, but they were vulnerable to the corrosion of salt water. Now there was a salt-resistant amtrac coming into the Pacific and eventually it would appear with ramps to the rear, as well as tanks called amtanks and even mounting flamethrowers that could spray tongues of liquid fire 100 feet long.

There was also the new Landing Craft Medium (LCM). Fifty feet long and fourteen feet wide, it could carry a Sherman tank or thirty tons of cargo or sixty-nine men.* LCMs proved to be ideal for the small forays of the Pacific. They

---

*It may appear odd that an LCM could carry seven times more cargo than an LCVP but less than twice the number of men, but the discrepancy is only apparent. Longer and wider assault craft also have higher bows, sterns and sides and therefore more room in which to stack cargo; but you can't stack men in them. This can only be done in much larger troop transports with their below-deck holds crammed with four-tiered bunks.

mounted a pair of .50-caliber machine guns and the ramp could be lowered just enough for the Sherman's 75-mm rifle to fire over it. Roaring inland in support of other LCMs carrying riflemen, they were indeed a terrifying sight for enemy soldiers.

The LSTs were as unpopular in the Pacific as in the Mediterranean. Because they were nine-knot cows, they left for the battle beaches earliest, meaning that they would be exposed the longest to enemy bombing or submarine attack. Invariably, their food and fresh-water supplies gave out (for the troops, of course, never for the crew), meaning that the troops would have to live out of their packs and wash in salt water. Usually, the soldiers and Marines aboard them slept on deck, on cots placed underneath LCTs lashed to the deck or blocks so that they could be launched over the side on D-Day.

The new M-1 or Garand semiautomatic rifle was now the shoulder weapon of the U.S. armed forces. It was carried by the men of the army amphibious divisions now flowing into the Pacific, and also by the Marines. But the men who had fought on Guadalcanal with their beloved five-shot, bolt-action Springfield '03 rifles did not like the M-1 at first. It was not as accurate or durable. However its eight-round clip and its loading mechanism operated by burning powder gases gave it greater and faster firepower, and it was soon accepted by everyone.

For officers and machine gunners and other men firing crew-served weapons, the new carbine replaced the .45 automatic pistol. The carbine was light, firing a clip of fifteen .30-caliber bullets at semiautomatic. The carbine was not too accurate, nor was it tough enough to withstand the corrosion of the sea and the jungle. If fired too long, it would break down. No one who threw away a carbine ever hunted for another one. Instead they searched frantically for an M-1, still the most reliable.

The bazooka, named for the homemade tubelike musical instrument played by comedian Bob Burns, was another new weapon. It was a long-tubed rocket launcher, rested on a man's shoulder to be aimed and fired like a rifle. Its cousin was the flamethrower, also carried by a single man—usually a big one.

New rations had been introduced. The old "C" rations—little cans of meat-and-beans, meat-and-vegetables, meat hash—were replaced by "ten in one" rations containing bacon, cheese, Spam and other processed meats, cigarettes and even tea or coffee, all packed in waterproof cardboard. They were at first popular but actually not as satisfying or as nourishing as the C. With the C rations, a man who liked meat hash could "eat up a storm," trading off one of the other two for two or even three cans of meat hash.

The Army Air Corps had already received the Lightning fighter, the plane in which Maj. Richard Bong was to shoot down most of the forty kills that made him the preeminent American air ace of World War II. Now the navy received the Corsair. Navy pilots, however, swore that the Corsair was "full of bugs," and at least one carrier commander refused to ship them aboard his flattops. Marine squadrons based on land, however, made the Corsair their own. They liked the range and durability of this new reverse-gull-winged, paddle-bladed killer. The Corsair could fly twice as fast as anything Japan had and had a range twice as far as the Wildcat. This was the plane made famous by Maj. Gregory ("Pappy") Boyington and his notorious Black Sheep Squadron.

Boyington was called Pappy because he was already a venerable thirty-one years of age when he burst upon the South Pacific with all the ungentle force of his brash, boisterous, belligerent character. His men called themselves "Black Sheep" because they were a collection of loners, replacements and rejects turned over to Boyington as much to squelch his demands for a squadron as in hopes that he would put one together.

But he did, doing it in less than a month of training on Espiritu Santo. For the captain had found his men, and the men their captain. It was as though a herd of mavericks had gathered to elect a leader, and then having asked themselves who could shoot straightest, fly highest, drink most, care least and make more enemies in high places, had chosen Boyington.

Boyington was a veteran long before World War II erupted. He had left the Marines to join Claire Chennault's Flying Tigers in China and Burma, where he shot down six Japanese planes. After Pearl Harbor he returned home and requested reinstatement. It was denied for "having left the Corps in a time of national emergency." While parking cars in a Seattle garage, he bombarded the Navy Department with pleas for reconsideration and was finally taken back. On Guadalcanal he promptly broke his ankle playing a game of nocturnal leapfrog, and it was after this unsober episode that he was given his squadron and his last chance to redeem himself.

By September he had delivered, and by September 16 the Black Sheep with Pappy in the lead roared aloft in their big Corsairs on their first mission. They were assigned to cover a formation of bombers over Ballale Airfield on Bougainville. They were jumped by about forty Zekes. One of them flew past Boyington's right wing waggling his own wings as though signaling, "Join up." A dismayed Boyington found that his guns were not ready for firing. He quickly corrected this oversight and "joined up" with the Zeke by shooting it down in flames.

Diving down toward the water where the bombers were forming up for the homeward journey, he aimed a burst at another enemy. It blew up, its parts striking Boyington's plane. As the American bombers headed home, Boyington was alone. He nosed over toward a Zero. Sensing a trap, he eased up and caught the enemy triggerman coming at him nose-to-nose. He shot him smoking into the sea. Now Boyington took off after the bombers and found himself above a Zeke also racing home. It was low over the water and a single burst sent it in.

Boyington now had four kills on his first mission, one short of becoming an ace. But he also did not have enough gas to reach his base in the Russells. Heading for Munda, he flew over a crippled Corsair with two Zekes on its tail. He roared down on the closest with chattering guns and sent it down in flames. An ace on his first mission, Boyington landed at Munda with dry tanks and only thirty rounds of ammunition.

The *baaing* of the Black Sheep could be heard all over the Pacific until, on

January 3, 1944, with twenty-two kills to his credit (not counting the six in the Far East), Boyington was shot down near Rabaul and taken prisoner.

The Japanese had decided to rid themselves of Capt. Donald Kennedy of the coast watchers.

Kennedy was among the most daring of all these intrepid Australians. He had kept most of the Melanesians on Rabaul loyal to the Allies, using them to hide downed American flyers in their villages while he signaled for the big flying ships called Dumbos to come get them. Kennedy had also harried the Japanese on New Georgia unmercifully, bursting from his hidden jungle lair at Segi Point to strike surprise blows, then vanishing back into the green tangle. He also waylaid barges laden with Japanese soldiers and massacred them.

Kennedy had only attacked when it became likely that the Japanese might stumble on his hideout and thus unmask the entire coast watcher operation, of which they still had no suspicion. But his strikes had so angered the Japanese that Col. Genjiro Hirata of the 229th Regiment was ordered to kill or capture him. Kennedy ambushed the first force sent against him, capturing the inevitable diary describing Hirata's plans.

Captain Kennedy at last called on General Vandegrift for help.

At dusk of June 20 two companies of the 4th Marine Raider Battalion boarded destroyer-transports *Dent* and *Waters* at Guadalcanal and sped north to New Georgia. At dark the slender craft began to pick their cautious way through the shoal-filled waters off Segi Point. Kennedy built bonfires onshore to guide them in. Once or twice the destroyers scraped bottom, but they worked free and in the morning the raiders came ashore to seize the beachhead, which opened the campaign in the Central Solomons.

The long interlude between the fall of Guadalcanal and Buna–Gona was ending, and the Americans were back on the counteroffensive again.

71. MacArthur Advances North

GENERAL MACARTHUR and Admiral Halsey resumed the counteroffensive in the Pacific in a two-pronged drive aimed at Rabaul. Their directive from the Joint Chiefs instructed them to burst the Bismarck Barrier by taking Woodlark and Kiriwina Islands in the Trobriands, Salamaua, Lae, Finschhafen and Madang on the New Guinea coast, western New Britain and the Solomons as far north as southern Bougainville. This operation was code-named Cartwheel.

On the night of June 29–30, Halsey's III Amphibious Force transported 6,000 troops from Guadalcanal to the Central Solomons. The Japanese were caught by surprise, and landings were made the following morning on southern New Georgia, Rendova and Vangunu. During the next five days two more beachheads were seized by American soldiers on northwest New Georgia.

The objective on New Georgia was Munda, where the Japanese had cleverly built an airfield hidden under treetops. The bottoms of the trees had been cut off and the tops held in place by wires. New Georgia was actually a cluster of islands around the biggest one, New Georgia itself. Northwest of New Georgia was Kolombangara and south of it was Rendova. Because Rendova was lightly held, it was easily secured. At one point, Maj. Gen. Noburu Sasaki, commander of the 5,000 soldiers on New Georgia, thought of boating his troops to mingle them among the Americans in a surprise counterstroke. But he decided instead to await the drive on Munda from Zanana, five miles to the south. Here troops of the 43rd Infantry Division under Maj. Gen. John H. Hester had made the principal landing.

A smaller one—2,600 Marines and soldiers under Col. Harry (the Horse) Liversedge, USMC—was made at Rice Anchorage on northwest New Georgia to block Japanese reinforcements from Kolombangara across the way. Here a brief naval battle was fought. A Japanese destroyer force made a night encounter with three light cruisers and four destroyers under Rear Adm. Walden Ainsworth. As had happened throughout the Solomons, the American radar advantage was canceled out by Japanese skill with their Long Lance torpedoes. The Japanese lost two destroyers, but sank the light cruiser *Helena,* while safely delivering reinforcements to Munda. A week later Ainsworth's task force again met a Japanese destroyer force led by the light cruiser *Jintsu.* Rapid-fire, radar-directed American guns blew *Jintsu* out of the water, but shoals of Long Lances damaged all three American cruisers and sank *Gwin,* the lucky little "tin can" that had survived the Night of the Battleships in Iron Bottom Bay.

Meanwhile, Liversedge's force had marched through the jumbled malarial rain forest typical of the Solomons to surprise and rout the Japanese at Enogai Inlet. They then took up a blocking position on the main trail between Kula Gulf and Munda. But the Japanese on Kolombangara went around the trail block by landing at Bairoko Harbor to the southwest. In the irregular coastline and criss-crossing trails of the Solomons, a blocking position is easily bypassed.

In the south General Hester sent two of his regiments advancing on Munda from Zanana. They quickly ran into trouble from the jungle, the Japanese and themselves. Most of the 43rd's troops were National Guardsmen and all were inexperienced and lightly trained. At one point an entire battalion of Americans were held up for two days by a single enemy platoon, a thousand men against forty. At night the Japanese harassed the Americans with the customary screams, threats and discharge of grenades and mortars. The Americans fired wildly into the jungle, tossing grenades around them recklessly and sometimes wounding each other. At this point Maj. Gen. Oscar W. Griswold, commander of the XIV Corps and Hester's superior, began to have grave doubts about the 43rd. It had had light battle casualties but lost many men to that battle neurosis called "combat fatigue." But there had been little combat to justify any such sort of exhaustion. Yet, a steady stream of sunken-eyed, filthy, bearded, trembling men flowed into the battalion aid stations where they were ticketed as "physically exhausted" and sent to the rear or evacuated. The 43rd looked about ready to collapse, and General Griswold so informed Halsey. At once Halsey sent Lt. Gen. Millard R. Harmon to New Georgia with orders to do whatever necessary to take Munda. Harmon told Griswold to relieve Hester.

At about the same time a great though intangible advantage accrued to the Americans: Adm. Richmond Kelly Turner left the South Pacific for a new assignment at Admiral Nimitz's headquarters. He was replaced by Rear Adm. Theodore Wilkinson. The "loss" of Turner was welcomed by Griswold and his commanders, especially Maj. Gen. J. Lawton Collins. "Lightning Joe" Collins led the 25th Infantry Division on Munda and would distinguish himself in France as a corps commander, going on to become an army chief of staff. Collins attributed many of the Munda campaign's difficulties to the didactic, beetle-browed Turner. With his penchant for playing general, the admiral "studied everything, remembered everything, interfered in everything. . . ." Just as he had brought Vandegrift his reinforcements on Guadalcanal, and then tried to deploy them in hopeless tactical positions, so he also hung himself like a millstone around General Griswold's neck. "It wasn't the navy that was wrong and caused trouble," said one Marine officer who served under him, "it was Turner. Turner was a martinet; very, very gifted, but he was stubborn, opinionated, conceited, thought that he could do anything better than anybody in the world. . . . I challenge anyone to name a naval officer other than Turner with whom the Marines had command difficulties . . . by and large naval officers, they were wary of trying land operations, but Turner, no; no, because Turner knew everything!"

General Sasaki counterattacked, striking at the vulnerable American line of communications from Zanana to the front. He used two regiments, and one of his spearheads penetrated all the way to the 43rd's command post, before it was destroyed by artillery fire. The attack was finally contained, and it seemed to have broken Sasaki's back. Griswold ordered a resumption of the attack on Munda. Once again the enemy clung tenaciously to skillfully constructed defensive positions, but this time, unlike Buna–Gona, the Americans had the élan and the weapons to dislodge them. Air and artillery support was more than adequate, while Admiral Wilkinson's destroyers supplied naval gunfire. Marine tanks also helped, and flamethrowers, in use for the first time, though cumbersome and awkward to employ, turned Japanese pillboxes into crematories. Each assault was carefully preceded by barrages from artillery and 81-mm mortars, which blasted away the camouflage concealing the Japanese strong points, allowing them to be destroyed one by one without a chance of delivering interlocking fire. On August 5 the Japanese were driven from their last positions at Munda and Griswold could tell Halsey that he was "the sole owner" of the airfield. But it still required two more weeks of savage fighting to mop up the remnants General Sasaki had left behind on New Georgia.

Nevertheless, Sasaki managed to transfer most of his troops to Kolombangara, where he impatiently awaited promised reinforcements for his attempt to recapture New Georgia. They came the night of August 6. Four Japanese destroyers crowded with troops for Sasaki entered Vella Gulf about midnight. Awaiting them were six American destroyers under Cmdr. Frederick Moosbrugger. These were radar-directed, torpedo-firing ships, and they had trained together under Moosbrugger since 1941. Their radar picked up the Japanese flotilla at 20,000 yards. Moosbrugger made two daring changes of course to bring his ships within 6,300 yards undetected. A spread of twenty-four fish was launched at the unsuspecting enemy. By the time a Japanese lookout spotted one of them it was too late. *Kawakaze* blew up and *Hawakazi* and *Arashi* were reduced to crippled burning hulks dead in the water where American 5-inchers gave them their death blows. Only *Shigure,* without any troops, escaped—hurrying north with the bad news. Loss of 900 troops and fifty tons of equipment ended Sasaki's hopes of retaking his lost island.

Still, Sasaki had about 12,000 men on Kolombangara, which Halsey had hoped to seize next. Rather than expose himself to another grinding jungle campaign such as Munda, he chose to leapfrog farther up the Solomons chain. It would be risky: Vella Lavella was only sixty miles away from the Japanese airfield at Ballale off southern Bougainville. But for that very proximity it would bring Halsey closer to Bougainville and Rabaul. Counting on speed, surprise and heavy air support, Halsey accepted the risk. On August 15 soldiers of the 1st and 2nd Battalions of the 35th Infantry Regiment clambered down the cargo nets of fast destroyer-transports off Vella Lavella, jumping into the landing boats wallowing in the swells beneath them. They landed unopposed, finding only a few hundred unarmed and starving sailors who had survived the Vella Gulf sea fight. Within an hour troop-laden LCIs arrived, followed by LSTs. It took only half a day for Admiral Wilkinson to put ashore 4,600 men with enough supplies and ammunition for two weeks. Halsey was now poised to spring at Bougainville, the last bastion before Rabaul. Meanwhile, on the left flank of Cartwheel, Douglas MacArthur was also moving toward the same objective.

MacArthur wanted Lae and Salamaua, two coastal villages south of the Huon Peninsula. Lae with a good airfield and anchorage was more important. It also opened on grassy lowlands running northwest 400 miles like a highway to Madang north of the Huon Peninsula. MacArthur needed Madang to secure his left flank while advancing against Rabaul. Although he did not possess the shipping and naval resources available to Halsey, MacArthur compensated with that brilliance of innovation that was his chief virtue as a planner. First his engineers built a concealed fighter base at Tsli Tsli west of Lae and Salamaua. From Tsli Tsli fighters arose to escort Kenney's bombers on a series of heavy raids against the major Japanese airbase at Wewak. More than a hundred enemy planes were destroyed on the ground, leaving the Americans in control of the air over eastern New Guinea. Next the Australian 9th Division was landed twenty miles east of Lae while the U.S. 503rd Parachute Regiment was dropped on Nadzab in Lae's rear. In this first American combat jump of the war, the 503rd seized an airstrip and Kenney's transports ferried in the *entire* Australian 7th Division, a remarkable feat of aerial troop transport. Lae and Salamaua were effectively encircled in a glittering small gem of tactical maneuver. Salamaua fell on September 12, 1943, and Lae four days later.

Now MacArthur speeded up his timetable. A brigade of the Australian 9th Division was landed at Finschhafen on the extreme eastern tip of the Huon Peninsula. The Japanese did not resist at the water's edge but fell back to Sattelberg on high ground north of Finschhafen. After the Australians beat off a foolish Japanese counterstroke from the sea—about 200 Japanese in barges against about 4,000 veterans of North Africa—the force at Sattelberg retreated over inland trails toward Madang and Wewak. MacArthur tried to cut them off with a landing at Saidor much farther up the peninsula but was unable to trap them. Nevertheless, he now held the Huon Peninsula and was ready for fresh amphibious strikes against New Britain itself.

Kennedy the coast watcher had at last "come in from the bush." General Vandegrift on Guadalcanal was insistent that he leave New Georgia, secured on September 25, and come south to his just reward. When he arrived on Guadalcanal, Vandegrift told him he'd like to give him a medal.

"Thanks, no," Kennedy replied. "Give the medals to the chaps doing the flying."

"Captain Kennedy," the general insisted, "there must be something you like."

"If you really insist on wanting to know, then I guess I'd better tell you."

"Captain Kennedy," the general said eagerly, "what would you like?"

"After thirty-six months in the bush I'd like thirty-six beautiful chorus girls arguing over my drunken carcass."

Fleet Adm. Mineichi Koga, who had succeeded Yamamoto as commander in chief of the Combined Fleet, was aware that the American advance was aimed at Rabaul. Koga decided to move carrier-based aircraft from Truk to reinforce Rabaul's air defenses and hold off American assaults. His decision, called *Ro* Operation, coincided with General Kenney's move to use his Fifth and Thirteenth Air Forces to "gain control of the air over New Britain, make Rabaul untenable for Japanese shipping and set up an air blockade of all the Jap forces in that area." Thus was begun a fierce and prolonged air battle. Often hundreds of airplanes fought each other in the struggles over Rabaul, and perhaps the most outstanding feat of flying skill and tenacity involved a Liberator bomber called the *Blessed Event*.

Shells from Japanese fighters knocked out *Blessed Event*'s engine controls and instrument panels. The pilot, copilot, bombardier and nose gunner were wounded. *Blessed Event* flew on to Rabaul. Enemy fire killed the navigator and wounded the top turret gunner, who nevertheless helped to shoot down three red-balled aircraft. Loosing her bomb load, *Blessed Event* staggered homeward with one rudder missing and 120 holes in her. Gasoline streamed from punctured fuel tanks. Her wounded pilot guided her down to an emergency landing, where she collided with a fighter plane. But *Blessed Event* skidded safely to a stop on her belly. One man was dead, another dying and eight were wounded.

Both sides made exaggerated claims of success over Rabaul, but the Japanese did in fact suffer more. Kenney's strikes failed to make Rabaul "untenable," although they did inflict much damage on the fortress. And the air battles had indeed distracted enemy attention from the landings at Bougainville.

72. The Battle for Bougainville

ADMIRAL HALSEY had selected the I Marine Amphibious Corps (IMAC) to invade Bougainville. Alexander Vandegrift, now a lieutenant general, commanded IMAC. Vandegrift decided to land at Empress Augusta Bay about halfway up the west coast of this biggest of the Solomon Islands. The beaches there were not as inviting as those of Guadalcanal, but troops could still come ashore in landing boats. Vandegrift believed that the Third Marine Division under Maj. Gen. Allen Turnage would have no difficulty with the roughly 4,000 men in the landing area. Once a beachhead was established, the density of the Bougainville jungle would make it impossible for the enemy to make a quick overland counterattack.

Vandegrift also ordered Lt. Col. Victor ("Brute") Krulak to land his Marine Parachute Battalion on Choiseul Island farther down the Solomons chain. "Take immediate action," Vandegrift said. "Get ashore where there are no Japs and make as much noise as possible." Krulak, who was called Brute as all the coxswains of Annapolis crews are called, did indeed raise much deliberate hell on Choiseul; so much so that General Hyakutake sent troops from Bougainville and sixty bombers escorted by fighters to Choiseul to strike this "force of about 20,000 men." This diversion, and the distraction of the aerial warfare at Rabaul, enabled the transports carrying the Third and Ninth Marines to sail safely from Guadalcanal to the beaches at Cape Torokina.

November 1 dawned bright and clear, one of those tropic days when the air is soft and caressing and the sea all silvery, glittering in a million points of light dancing in the rays of the rising sun. The air also reverberated to the sound of American cruisers and destroyers bombarding Cape Torokina, which split the landing beaches, and little Puruata Island about 1,000 yards offshore. Smoke rose from both targets. On the right or eastern flank the Third Marines in their landing boats received fire from Puruata to their left and from the shore on their right. Four landing boats were sunk, but the remainder ran up on the beaches to lower their ramps for their occupants to charge ashore. There was stiff opposition from eighteen big pillboxes held by about 300 Japanese, but they were knocked out one by one in savage hand-to-hand, knife-to-knife fighting and their occupants all killed.

On the left or western flank it was not the Japanese but the sea that was the enemy. Although the Ninth Marines came in unopposed, the beaches were too steep for the landing boats to ground the full length of their keels. Many were upended, swamped or filled at the stern, sliding off the beach to sink in deep water. Sixty-four landing boats and twenty-two LCMs were broached before the troops finally floundered ashore. But by noon half the division was ashore and destroyers were racing south to escort the other half up from Guadalcanal. Puruata had been seized by the 3rd Raider Battalion, and the Japanese planes that had been lured to Choiseul had found their true target at Empress Augusta Bay. But they caused little damage, losing twenty-two planes while shooting down four Americans and slightly damaging destroyer *Wadsworth*. They didn't kill a single Marine in the beachhead.

Bougainville was all rain forest. The Marines who landed there had trained in Guadalcanal's steaming jungles and thought of themselves as jungle fighters. But they had not been on Guadalcanal during the rainy season. Before dusk, the rain began to fall. Marines sloshing inland found no lovely beaches of scoured white sand, no pleasant groves of coconuts, for wild and dark Bougainville had never attracted planters. Supplies could only be moved by hand or amtracs, for wheeled vehicles were useless. Wiremen found that it took at least an hour to string a hundred yards of wire. When dusk fell and the Marines prepared to receive the inevitable enemy counterattack, they had to crouch in foxholes filled with water. But nothing came. Instead, CP telephones buzzed with the ominous message:

"Condition Black. You may expect shelling from enemy ships followed by counterinvasion."

Rear Adm. Sentaro Omori had been ordered to take 1,000 soldiers aboard five destroyer-transports down to the American beachhead. But when Omori learned that some of the transports could not make more than twenty-six knots, he sent them back to Rabaul and proceeded toward Bougainville with his fleet of six big destroyers, heavy cruisers *Myoko* and *Haguro* and the lights *Sendai* and *Agano*.

Waiting for him was Rear Adm. A. Stanton (Tip) Merrill. He had already laid a field of mines to protect the beachhead. Now he sent away his transports and prepared for battle. He had eight destroyers, including "the Four Little Beavers" of the audacious Captain Arleigh (Thirty-One-Knot) Burke, and the light cruisers *Montpelier*, *Cleveland*, *Columbia* and *Denver*. At about 2:30 in the morning of November 2, the American radar picked up the approaching enemy.

Battle was joined almost immediately, quickly breaking up into three separate fights: one between the cruisers and two separate destroyer battles. Almost immediately the savage concerted shellfire of Merrill's cruisers struck *Sendai*. It was radar-controlled firing at its best. *Sendai* began to burn brightly, exploding as she burned. Destroyers *Samidare* and *Shiratsuyu* swung violently around to escape the fire that was sinking *Sendai* and collided with one another with a screech of rending steel. They limped home to Rabaul.

Zigzagging violently, making smoke, the American cruiser commanders shifted fire to the Japanese columns centered around *Myoko* and *Haguro*. Again their aim was unerring. The third salvos walked right into them. Destroyer *Hatsukaze* tried to dodge. She swerved between the two big cruisers and shuddered as *Myoko* plowed into her, shearing off two of her tubes, mangling her starboard bow, leaving her to be torn apart and sunk by the American destroyers.

But now Omori's heavies were opening up with 8-inch star shells and patrol planes were dropping white and colored flares. The American cruisers, unscratched for half an hour, began to receive hits. Eight-inch salvos straddled them. *Denver* received three 8-inch hits forward and began to take in water, but she stayed afloat while the battle became a thing of terrible beauty.

Clouds drifting overhead had become suffused with the light of flare and gunflash. They illuminated the battle as though it were being fought upon a theatrically lighted black pond, and all that flashed and glittered and shone seemed to be magnified by the encircling darkness. There was that quality of slow majesty attendant upon night surface action when great ships move at great speed over great bodies of water. Salvos striking the sea threw up huge geysers; they seemed not to leap but to gather themselves upward, to rise in slow-pluming fountains, to catch the red light of burning ships, the green-gold of flame-streaming guns, the jagged orange glinting off swirling black water, to catch it, to make it dazzling with its own phosphorescence—and then to burst apart in a million vanishing sparkles.

It would have been an unreal world, a ghostly one, fantastical, but for the pungent smell of smoke, the constant thundering of the guns and the real crashing of the shells and crying of the stricken.

As the battle continued, Admiral Omori came to believe that he had destroyed three American cruisers. He thought that near-misses, straddling them and raising geysers in the air, had been torpedo hits. When the American cruisers vanished beneath their own smoke, he believed they had sunk—and he sailed home.

Like Mikawa at Savo, Omori had not harmed the American transports. Unlike him he had not sunk an American ship.

Major General Turnage moved swiftly to establish his beachhead line. Inside it the Seabees* worked to build an airfield. Also on the second day the 21st

---

*Naval Construction Battalions were at first called "CBs" and then, because of their efficiency and speed, "Seabees."

Marines, Turnage's reserve regiment, came up from Guadalcanal, followed by the 37th Infantry Division as a corps reserve.

In Rabaul Admiral Koga still clung to the idea of a counterinvasion. He also became infected with General Hyakutake's bad habit of piecemeal commitment. Hyakutake gave him 3,000 men for the strike against an entire American corps of about 35,000 troops. But Koga did have a powerful surface force: seven heavy cruisers—*Takao, Maya, Atago, Susuya, Mogami, Chikuma* and *Chokai*—the old pros, the veteran sluggers of the Second Fleet, together with light cruiser *Noshiro*, four destroyers and a sizable fleet train. They would escort the transports and bombard the American positions. On November 5 this force came into Rabaul to refuel. Koga considered them safe. There were 150 airplanes on the ground and no reports of enemy carriers in the vicinity.

Admiral Halsey in Noumea had been warned by Magic of the enemy plan. But Halsey was almost helpless. All the big warships were preparing for the start of Nimitz's offensive in the Central Pacific. Already, the complications of two commands in the Pacific were becoming apparent. In North Africa Dwight Eisenhower had made single command an article of military faith, but in the Pacific divided command between MacArthur and Nimitz was to hobble the American effort throughout the war.

Although Halsey did not have the surface strength to stop the enemy Second Fleet, he did have available *Saratoga* and the new carrier *Princeton*. With characteristic daring he sent both racing north under cover of darkness to strike the confident and unsuspecting Japanese. On the morning of November 5 Rear Adm. Forest C. Sherman began launching his aircraft. Soon a torrent of American bombers and fighters went thundering over St. George's Channel between New Ireland and New Britain and struck without warning at Rabaul. They flew straight through the flak of the flatfooted enemy ships, breaking up into three groups to begin their work.

Seventy Japanese fighters stacked above them could not shoot down more than ten Americans, and the remainder inflicted enormous losses on Kondo's cruisers. Not a single ship was sunk, but few were left intact. *Takao* was torn apart at the water line, *Mogami* was sent staggering back to Japan for repairs, *Atago* took three near misses, and a bomb fell down one of *Maya*'s stacks and exploded in the engine room. Lights *Agano* and *Noshiro* were also hit, and destroyer *Fujinami* was holed by a dud torpedo and *Wakatsuki* ripped open by near-misses. Then, while navy planes flew back to their ships, twenty-four AAF Liberators and sixty-seven Lightnings came roaring in from the Woodlarks and New Guinea to pound the city itself and tear up the docks. Yet, with the cruiser force put out of action, the Japanese still insisted on sending troops down the Tokyo Express in its first run in nearly a year. Why?

Because Rabaul planes searching for *Princeton* and *Saratoga* thought they had found their quarry between Cape Torokina and the Treasuries. What they actually saw was one damaged LCT covered by an LCI gunboat and a torpedo boat. The three little American vessels not only beat off the enemy but shot some of them down. Next day Radio Tokyo declared:

"One large carrier blown up and sunk, one medium carrier set ablaze and later sunk and two heavy cruisers and one cruiser and destroyer sunk."

Here was the biggest inaccuracy of the Pacific War, the pièce de résistance of the Japanese habit of writing exaggeratedly positive reports. That was why four destroyers escorted 475 barge-mounted Japanese soldiers down the Slot to Koromokina swamp, which gave its name to the brief, bitter battle in which they all died.

Five days later Halsey launched another carrier strike against Rabaul. Reinforced by two big carriers and one light, Sherman's aircraft damaged more Japanese ships and sank a destroyer. They also shot down twenty enemy aircraft over the harbor, and when the Japanese attacked the carriers, another thirty-five were downed. The Americans lost not a single plane.

Counting up his losses, Admiral Koga decided to cancel the *Ro* Operation and sent his carrier aircraft back to Truk. Halsey was jubilant. He had had grave doubts about both operations, especially the first. Of the *Princeton-Saratoga* strike, he wrote: "I sincerely expected both air groups to be cut to pieces, and both carriers stricken if not lost. (I tried hard not to remember that my son Bill was aboard one of them.)"

Yet, General Hyakutake still persisted in sending more men down the Slot. Five destroyers carrying nearly 1,000 soldiers sailed south toward Buka Passage off Bougainville's northern nose. They put them ashore and then were jumped by Captain Burke's Four Little Beavers. A spread of fifteen American fish sank two of the enemy, and then Burke gave pursuit to the other three. It was a wild chase. "I'm riding herd!" the sailor from Colorado shouted over his radio: "Yippee! Yippee-ay!" Finally Burke's ships overtook the fleeing enemy and sank another destroyer in what was the last run of the Tokyo Express.

On Bougainville, meanwhile, the Third Marine Division had expanded and strengthened its perimeter. Inside it the Seabees had wrought another miracle of construction. They had built an airfield in the soup of the Torokina swamp. They began it November 9 and at dawn of December 10 the first Corsair went roaring down the runway. Rabaul was now within range of American land-based fighters. Seabee skill had also made it possible to walk on dry roads instead of slogging through a slop of slime with cold wet mud between the toes. The Marines were so grateful to the Seabees that they paid them the unrivaled compliment of a kind word for another branch of service. On one of the new roads a sign was raised:

> So when we reach the isle of Japan
> With our caps at a jaunty tilt
> We'll enter the City of Tokyo
> On the roads the Seabees built.

It was warm and generous, but it was only a momentary lapse from the customary invective; especially after the Seabees spread the rumor that the Marines never landed anywhere until the Seabees told them that the roads were ready.

Gradually the fighting on Bougainville slowed down to sporadic though still savage combat. In early December, General Turnage decided to occupy a blocking position atop a series of ridges to the right of his beachhead. There were four heights: Hill 600 (so-called for its height), Hill 1,000, a nameless ridge about 250 feet high, and Hill 600A. The Twenty-first Marines struck the nameless ridge, naming it Hellzapoppin' Ridge for the reception they received. It was covered with a dense green tangle in which the Japanese had constructed their customary complex of interlocking holes and bunkers. Giant trees on the hill's summit detonated the mortar shells the Marines tried to drop on its fortified reverse slope. Hellzapoppin' held out for five days, during which the Marines developed the tactic of close-up aerial support, one of their major contributions to modern warfare. Avenger torpedo bombers flew low-level bombing and strafing attacks within unusually close proximity to their own troops. On December 18 the Avengers flew within seventy-five yards of the Marine front to drop their clusters of 100-pound bombs. Then they strafed at treetop level and the Marines rose up in irresistible attack upon the stunned enemy. Hill 600A fell on December 23 and Hill 600 on December 27. Next day General Turnage turned over his Bougainville lines to Maj. Gen. John Hodge, commander of the Americal Infantry Division —the Marines' old friends from Guadalcanal. Control of Bougainville itself passed from IMAC under Maj. Gen. Roy Geiger to Army XIV Corps under General Griswold.

The Third Marine Division had seized an airfield in the heart of a blackwater jungle at a cost of only 423 killed and 1,418 wounded. They had counted well over 2,000 enemy bodies. Probably at least that many more were killed or died of wounds or starved to death. Japanese strength in the Torokina area had been destroyed. As General Vandegrift had calculated, the density of the Bougainville jungle had made it impossible for the enemy to mount a counterattack overland with any speed. It would not be until March of 1944 that they would be able to strike in strength. Long before then Admiral Nimitz's drive through the Central Pacific had begun at a parrot-shaped isle named Betio in the atoll of Tarawa.

73. November 1943: Tarawa—Day One

BATTLE IN THE CENTRAL PACIFIC differed from combat in the Southwest Pacific as heat-bathed coral differs from rain-drenched swamp forest and frontal assault differs from maneuver. In the Solomons and in the Bismarck Barrier, Americans and their allies from Australia and New Zealand had fought prolonged, exhausting campaigns to seize and hold large, heavily forested islands on which maneuver was always possible and the malaria-carrying anopheles mosquito and monsoon rains were enemies nearly as formidable as the Japanese.

But the chains of the Central Pacific were formed by atolls, that is, rings of coral islets enclosing a lagoon. Not every islet in an atoll needed to be fortified. Usually the Japanese selected the largest one, which could hold an airfield, and transformed it into a fortress. On those islands mandated to them by the League of Nations they had begun pouring the concrete for their reinforced pillboxes and bombproofs since 1920, and thus the concrete had had twenty years to become cured to an incredible hardness. On these atolls the seaward coasts bristled with barbed-wire barricades, mines and cement antiboat obstacles. Fortification of the islet beaches fringing the lagoons—where landings could be expected—were even more formidable. Sometimes sea walls four or five feet high would girdle an islet. In these there were firing ports to sweep the narrow beaches, and behind it were interlocking systems of artillery, machine gun and rifle fire. Mortars and artillery were registered on all boat approaches and the water sown with mines so as to channel the boats directly into this fire. Inland were networks of pillboxes mounting antitank guns, again interlaced with small arms and automatic weapons. These positions were sometimes connected by tunnels or trenches. Also inland were the troop reserves and the tanks which were to deliver the counterstrokes aimed at carrying out Japanese battle doctrine of destroying the invader at the water's edge. Obviously, such fixed positions could neither be turned, surprised nor bombarded into submission.

The Japanese defending the forts of Oceania were not the defenders of Pantellcria. Japan's astonishingly successful offensives during the first eight months of the war had given the world the impression that Japanese soldiers were irresistible offensive fighters. Actually, after Guadalcanal put them on the defensive, they developed into tenacious defensive troops. Here was an army perhaps unique in history because so many of its soldiers did fight to the end. (Some Japanese soldiers were so inculcated in their particular war ethic that they remained hidden out in the jungles, carrying out essentially private war, decades after the final surrender was signed.) To overcome such defenses and defenders, Admiral Nimitz relied on the blasting power of his aerial and naval artillery, and the quality of his assault troops. Fortunately, in his opening campaign he found American bravery and dash sufficient to redeem the deficiencies of American bombardment.

This was in the Gilbert Islands, 2,400 miles west of Hawaii. Here Nimitz chose to seize the two chief atolls, Makin (Butaritari) and Tarawa (Bairiki). Makin was only lightly defended, but Tarawa's chief islet of Betio—on the map looking like an upside-down parrot—was then probably the most formidable fixed position in the Pacific. It would hardly have been possible to crowd more guns, men and fortifications onto Betio's 291 acres without reducing the mobility requisite for battle. Every gun in the Japanese arsenal ranging from the .25-caliber Nambu rifle up to 8-inch coastal artillery brought from Singapore was present on Betio. All were mounted in individual pits, pillboxes, blockhouses and huge bombproofs of ferroconcrete two stories high.

These defenses were completed by September 1943, under the direction of Rear Adm. Keiji Shibasaki, commander of the Gilbert defenses. With this, Shibasaki fulfilled his mission in the plan called *Yogaki,* or Waylaying Attack. Under it Shibasaki was to make Betio impregnable while (1) long-range aircraft flew down from Rabaul and Kavieng to bomb the invaders, landing on Gilberts and Marshalls airfields; (2) short-range aircraft flew down from Truk by stages to defend these same atoll chains; (3) Admiral Kondo's powerful Second Fleet arrived to attack American shipping; and (4) a swarm of submarines converged on Betio from all directions.

On September 19 the Americans began to whittle away at this enemy plan. The new carriers *Lexington* and the smaller *Princeton* and *Belleau Wood* made their battle debut at Betio's expense. Their aircraft shot up the boats needed to carry the tetrahedon boat obstacles out into the lagoon and destroyed the cement as well as planes parked on the airfield.

Still, Shibasaki was not dismayed. His fortifications had not been harmed. He had had the time to make Betio's seaward side impregnable and because the waters around Tarawa were now on the neap—the season of the year when tides are lowest—he doubted that the Americans would be able to cross the lagoon reef.

So did the Americans, including a couple of Marine generals named Smith. The first was Maj. Gen. Holland M. Smith, commander of the V Marine Amphibious Corps. He was six feet one inch tall, graying, with a belligerent bald forehead, a dandified white mustache and professorial eyeglasses perched on a big aggressive nose. The Marines called him "Howlin' Mad." In legend he was so named because of the invective he poured out upon the men he led on a record-breaking hike in the Philippines in 1906. More likely it was because the sobriquet fitted both his first name and middle initial as well as his temperament.

The second Smith was Maj. Gen. Julian Smith, commander of the Second Marine Division. He was soft-spoken, gentle-eyed, fatherly. He rarely lost his temper. But he was on the verge of doing so when he learned that he was expected to land his division on Betio during the neap tide. He was so concerned he came to Pearl Harbor with his chief of staff, Red Mike Edson of Guadalcanal, to confer with Holland Smith. He was worried about the tides and the drying reef inside Tarawa lagoon. Although his men would be boated outside the atoll, they would enter the lagoon through a channel on its western edge and have to cross this reef to get to the landing beaches. Julian Smith did not think there would be much water over the reef during the neap. Tarawa was also visited by "dodging tides" —that is, tides that were sometimes irregularly high and sometimes irregularly low. Julian Smith did not share Richmond Kelly Turner's belief that there would be a high dodger when the Marines landed November 20. There *could* be a low one. If there were, the Second's men would never get over the reef in their landing boats. They would have to wade through waist-deep water into a murderous fire. Julian Smith wanted amtracks. Amtracks could crawl over the reef. But he had only seventy-five operable amtracks and wanted 100 more.

"All right," Howlin' Mad Smith said. "I'll get 'em for you."

So Julian Smith and Edson flew back to Wellington while Howlin' Mad Smith spoke to Kelly Turner, who was in command of the Fifth Amphibious Force. Turner said no amtracks. He didn't want them on his ships. Smith replied: "Kelly, it's like this: I've got to have those amtracks. We'll take a helluva licking without them. No amtracks—no operation."

There were 100 amtracks available in California, and of these Turner arranged to rush fifty to Samoa, where Julian Smith could pick them up en route to Tarawa. Meanwhile the admiral and the general decided that Makin Atoll would be taken by another general named Smith: Maj. Gen. Ralph Smith of the 27th Infantry Division. Intelligence believed that Makin was garrisoned by only 500 men; actually the figure was closer to 700.

Intelligence was more accurate in estimating the number of Betio's defenders, using a unique method to count them. Aerial photographs showed numerous latrines built out over the lagoon. The number of holes was carefully marked. Because it was known that the inflexibility of Japanese doctrine extended even to the ratio of holes to behinds, intelligence came up with the remarkably close number of 4,500 men—actually only about 400 short of the true number.

Against them would come the Second and Eighth Marines, about 10,000 men. The Sixth Marines would be in corps reserve for either Makin or Tarawa. All of the Second Division's 18,600 men were aboard transports, however, when they left Wellington in late October. The troops believed that they had embarked for "maneuvers" on Hawkes Bay.

Julian Smith had not forgotten how the First Division had sailed from Wellington fifteen months earlier with the newspapers speculating about an attack on Tulagi. To forestall any breach of security, he took his force out of New Zealand under an elaborate smoke screen. Orders for the "Hawke Bay maneuvers" were drawn up and the New Zealand air force solemnly briefed on its part in them. Marines were told they would be back in camp within a week, and of course they told their girls. Local trucking firms were hired to move equipment back to Wellington from Hawke Bay. New Zealand's governor-general was not informed that the Marines were leaving his country until they were out of the harbor bound for Éfaté in the New Hebrides (Vanuatu).

At Éfaté Julian Smith needed an officer (replacing the ailing commander of the Second Marines) to lead the way into Betio. He named his operations officer, David Shoup, a bull-chested, bull-necked, profane colonel. Smith also conferred with Britishers who had lived in the Gilberts. Someone spoke of the possible difficulty of crossing Betio's lagoon reef during the neap.

"Neap tide!" Maj. Frank Holland exclaimed in incredulity. "My God, when I told you there would be five feet of water on the reef, I never dreamed anyone would try to land at neap tide. There won't be three feet of water on the reef!"

Smith was stunned. A meeting of captains and pilots was called. In spite of what Holland had said, it was concluded that there would be enough water to float both landing boats and LCMs over the reef. This was not true. Whether or not this was a piece of deliberate self-deception is not known, but by then all the plans had been made and there were decisive arguments against waiting until after November 22, when the spring tides would appear. Coincident with the arrival of the spring tides a west wind whipped up a steep, short sea off Betio. Also, the flood of the spring tide would cover Betio's beaches right up to the sea wall. There might not be any place to land, and there would certainly be no place to hide on Betio's extremely flat landscape. Again, each day's delay would mean the flood would arrive an hour later, and because invasions normally must be made at the flood, this meant one hour less of daylight in which to seize the beaches.

Admiral Turner still clung to his conviction—based on what factors no one knows—that there would be a high dodging tide at Betio on November 20. The great invasion force of three battleships, five cruisers, nine destroyers and seventeen troop and cargo ships had already begun to assemble. Naval bombardment officers were already predicting how they would obliterate Betio.

At Betio the Americans were unwittingly tearing the *Yogaki* plan into shreds.

The landings at Bougainville had siphoned off troops intended for Shibasaki to the Solomons. On November 5, Halsey's daring carrier strike had knocked out Admiral Kondo's cruiser screen. On November 11, the American naval planes came again, destroying many planes on the ground and shooting down fifty-five in dogfights. These were the short-rangers from Truk that Koga had called into Rabaul. Now Shibasaki had no aerial cover. Nor submarines, either, the undersea force then being badly depleted. By November 13 when the American fleet left Éfaté, the Gilberts and especially Betio had been pounded regularly from the air and sea. Obviously, the Americans thought they could knock Betio out by bombardment alone. Keiji Shibasaki moving among his 300 headquarters troops inside his two-story bombproof did not. As he had repeatedly assured his men:

"A million men cannot take Tarawa in a hundred years."

At 3:30 in the morning of November 20, 1943, the American invasion fleet stood off Tarawa atoll. Seventeen dark shapes glided into position at the western entrance to the lagoon, a few miles above Betio. These were the transports and supply ships.

Below the lagoon entrance aboard battleships *Maryland, Tennessee* and *Colorado* with their accompanying cruisers and destroyers, gun turrets slowly swiveled toward Betio. The first two had been salvaged from the shallow waters of Pearl Harbor, modernized and fitted as bombardment ships.

A half-moon flitted in and out of fleecy clouds. It was cool. Marines clambering down cargo nets into the waiting landing boats could feel the sweat drying on their foreheads. They had come from stifling galleys where they dined on steak and eggs, an Australian dish which they fancied and which henceforth was to be a traditional battle-morning breakfast among Marines. Some transport surgeons were dismayed to learn what they had eaten.

"Steak and eggs!" a surgeon aboard *Zeilin* exclaimed. "Jesus, that will make a nice lot of guts to have to sew up—full of steak!"

At 4:41 A.M. a star shell rose into the sky above Betio. A half hour later Japanese shore batteries began firing.

Maryland's great long lengths of steel fingered the sky. One of them leaped. Flames gushed from its muzzle. A blob of red streaked toward Betio, visible to Marines in their little, churning amtracks. There was no explosion. Again from *Maryland* the great gob of flame, and still no explosion. But then dawn seemed to burst out of Betio like an erupting volcano. A great sheet of flame leaped 500 feet in the air. The explosion succeeding it sent shock waves rolling over the water. *Maryland* had hurled one of her 16-inch armor-piercing shells into the magazine of the 8-inchers on Betio's western tip. Men were killed by the hundreds. Hundreds of tons of enemy shells were detonated, utterly wrecking the 8-inchers' blockhouse. Now all the battleships were firing in salvos, sending their 1,500-pound missiles sailing through the air, drifting in and out of their own smoke.

Betio was aglow, a mass of fires. Smoke coils snaked into the sky to be suffused pinkish with following plumes of flame. At 5:42 A.M. the American bombardment lifted. An eerie silence came over the atoll. The American Dauntlesses and Avengers covered by the new Hellcat fighters were supposed to strike Betio, preparing the way for the approaching amtracks. But they did not appear, and the Japanese shore batteries began firing.

Shooting at the transports with 5-inchers and those 8-inch guns still operative on the islet's eastern end, they drove them off. Churning after them went the amtracks and landing boats loaded with Marines. For half an hour the transports duck-walked among the exploding shells, and then the bombardment ships resumed firing. Ten minutes later the carrier planes roared over Betio and the islet was once again swathed in shimmering smoke. Surely she would be *zemmetsu* this time. But she wasn't.

Destroyers *Ringgold* and *Dashiell* swept into the lagoon entrance, followed by the Marine boats like baby ducks trailing their parents—and the Japanese artillery opened up again. *Ringgold* was holed twice by duds. Her gunnery officer spotted the flashes of the enemy guns and called for a counterfire that blew up an ammunition dump. At nine o'clock in the morning with the motors of the amtracks rising to full throttle, the clumsy craft went into Betio. Smoke from burning Betio was blown into the Marines' faces by a wind that blew the water flat and thin over the drying reef. But the amtracks crawled over the reef into the inner lagoon just as Betio erupted in a volcano of flame and sound. Amtracks blew up, amtracks began to burn, amtracks spun around, slowing and sinking—for if they cannot move, they sink—and amtracks emerged from the lagoon like prehistoric monsters with water streaming from their sides while Marines in mottled green with weapons held high vaulted from them onto the beaches, sprinting for the sanctuary of that treacherous sea wall; and falling, falling, falling as they ran.

Lt. William Deane Hawkins led his scout-sniper platoon into Betio five minutes before the first wave. Hawk, as he was called, lean and swift like that bird of prey, was a "mustang," an officer who has risen from the ranks. He was as ardent for victory as he was convinced of death. "I'll see you some day, Mac," he told a friend when he joined the Marines, "but not on this earth." Hawkins and his scout-snipers were to seize the pier extending about 500 yards into the lagoon. It split the landing beaches, and from it those numerous latrines, now packed with riflemen and machine-gunners, could rake American amtracks passing to either side.

Hawkins and his men in two landing boats could not cross the reef. They waited for amtracks while mortar shells dropped around them and sniper and machine-gun fire raked their boats. Air strikes were called down on the pier. Drums of gasoline stacked on it were set afire and the pier began to burn. Hawkins got his amtracks and his men swept in to assault the blazing pier. They fought with flamethrowers, with grenades and bayonets, yard by yard, killing and being killed, and they cleared the pier. Then they swept ashore to attack enemy pillboxes.

Hawkins stood erect in his amtrack like Hector in his chariot while it climbed the sea wall and went clanking into enemy defenses spitting flame and steel.

The following waves in landing boats were piling up on the opposite side of the drying reef waiting for amtracks. But few came. Eight had been knocked out in the first wave. Many more were lost in the next two waves and others destroyed when they tried to back off the beach. Fifteen more sank upon reaching deeper water. Maj. Henry Drewes, commander of the amtrack battalion, had been killed. Nearly all the amtrack gunners were dead. Visible and unprotected, they had dueled the entrenched enemy and suffered the consequences.

The Marines at the reef *would have to wade in.*

They clambered out of their boats, crossed the reef and jumped into waist-deep water. Admiral Shibasaki listening to reports from the beaches was grimly satisfied. As he expected, the Americans could not cross the reef. They would never reach shore. But they were trying. Japanese gunners spraying bullets among them were certain they would never keep coming, so many were falling. But they did, wading from a quarter-mile out, a half-mile out. They could not return the fire because they had to hold their weapons over their heads to keep them dry. Sometimes some of them would step into potholes and vanish. But they surfaced again, spitting water, helmetless and weaponless—but they kept coming.

On the leftward beaches Marines who reached them blundered into the point-blank fire of guns poked through sea-wall firing ports. They had waded down avenues of death. Some were hung up on offshore barbed wire and killed. Still they came on, the wounded clinging to the burning pier, working their way inshore hand over hand. They did reach the beaches, even the wounded, even the dying youth who fell on the sand with his chest torn open, crying for a cigarette.

"Here, I'll light one for you," a Marine said.

"No," the stricken youth gasped. "No time . . . gimme yours. . . ."

The cigarette was thrust into his mouth and held there. He sucked in the smoke, let it come curling out his chest—and died.

Col. David Shoup was having trouble getting ashore. Machine-gun fire raked his amtrack. It returned to the pier. A mortar shell hit it, and Shoup was wounded in the leg. The amtrack lurched toward the beach again, at last crunching up on shore. Shoup clambered out, limping. He set up his command post on the left or eastward beach in a hole dug in the sand behind a pillbox full of Japanese. He was fifteen yards inland but could see almost nothing for the dust that hung over Betio. The dust was everywhere, a cloying, caking powder that clogged the nostrils, coarse in the throat and clotted in the corners of the eyes.

With but a single battalion of his reserve uncommitted, Gen. Julian Smith was convinced that the critical point had been reached. At 1:30 he asked Holland Smith up at Makin to release the Sixth Marines to him. If the request were rejected, then Julian Smith was prepared to gather this last battalion, to collect his service people—bandsmen, specialists, cooks, clerks—and to lead them into the battle himself. But Howlin' Mad Smith approved his request. Assured of a three-times-larger reserve, Julian Smith ordered the 1st Battalion, Eighth, to stand by for a landing. The men had been boated since before dawn. All that was needed was to find a proper landing place.

Night was falling and the Marines on Betio clung to two precarious footholds. Some 5,000 assault troops had come ashore and of these 1,500 were already dead or wounded. The remaining 3,500 held a ragged line between the tanks *China Gal* on the left and *Colorado* on the right. Colonel Shoup's command post was inside the left or eastern line. It began about midway of the north coast and ran west for 600 yards. At its farthest penetration it was 250 yards deep, roughly halfway across the airfield. The right or western line was a tiny enclave 200 yards deep held by Maj. Mike Ryan's reorganized force on the islet's extreme western tip—the Betio bird's beak.

Between these two footholds was a gap 600 yards wide filled with Japanese soldiers and guns.

Out on the lagoon, boated since before dawn, was the recently alerted 1st Battalion, Eighth, and those waves of the riddled 3rd Battalion, Eighth, which had been unable to get ashore. West of Tarawa aboard transports was the Sixth Marine Regiment just released to Gen. Julian Smith. There was still no artillery ashore, but the cannon cockers had already begun to break down their 75-mm howitzers to carry them in by hand.

Actually, the lines were not continuous but fragmented. Gaps were everywhere. A group of Marines was dug in here. There they fortified in an abandoned pillbox. Flanks dangled. Inland positions could be measured in feet as well as yards. At some points the enemy needed to advance but thirty feet to throw the Americans into the sea.

It was a situation made for counterattack. As every Marine on Betio knew, the second cardinal rule of Japanese island defense—after the doctrine of destroying the enemy at the water's edge—was to counterattack at night.

Rear Adm. Keiji Shibasaki had planned a nocturnal counterblow. Having held the enemy at the water's edge as he also had planned, he was now in position to finish them off with a night attack. But the dreadful bombardment, which had failed to destroy his fortifications and slaughter his men, had succeeded in knocking out his communications. His men were scattered across the islet in strong points, and there was no way he could reach them with orders for a counterstrike. He could try to communicate by runner, but it was likely the enemy would pick them off. He had dozens of bicycles, but a mounted messenger would be an even larger target.

Shibasaki stood pat within his huge bombproof headquarters. His men lobbed mortars at the entrenched Marines and some of them swam out to the wrecked American boats or the capsized *Saida Maru* to harass them with sniper fire. But there was no counterattack.

Cries of "Corpsman!" or "Blood plasma!" rose throughout the night from the makeshift hospitals under the sea wall. Men wounded during the day, Marines who fought on while wounded, were dying through the night because of a shortage of bandages and blood plasma. Bottles of this precious fluid were tied to bayoneted rifles stuck into the sand. Little rubber tubes ran down from them into the needles piercing the veins of the wounded. Corpsmen talked gently to the stricken men, waving the flies away. Marine sentries guarded the makeshift hospitals, killing Japanese attempting to sneak into them to throw grenades.

Soon the amtracks and rafts carrying the wounded back to the landing boats, passed artillerymen wading ashore with gun parts strapped to their backs. The parts were fitted together on the beaches and long before daylight there were ten short-snouted 75-mm howitzers lined up hub to hub under the sea wall.

They would be firing at dawn.

74. Tarawa—Day Two

THE MORNING of the second day was worse than the first. Because there were only eighteen amtracks left, the replacement Marines had to come up to the reef in landing boats and wade in.

From beach blockhouses and the wrecked hulk of the *Saida Maru* came a steady chatter of machine-gun fire. Marines were scythed to the water. Their buddies dragged those still alive back to the reef and those landing boats whose gallant coxswains had kept them there. But the dreadful wade-in continued, while Marines in the central sector counterattacked furiously against the blockhouses. The Marines' pack howitzers lined up beneath the sea wall leaped and bayed in an attempt to silence that awful fire. But they were using delayed-action fuses intended to explode once the shells had penetrated concrete, and they were firing to a narrow front. They could not silence all the blockhouses. Carrier planes swooped down to strafe and bomb them, but the enemy fire continued. Dive-bombers and mortars ashore pounded *Saida Maru,* reducing but not eliminating its fire. It would eventually take a force of dynamite-throwing engineers covered by riflemen to clean out the *Saida Maru.*

For five full hours the Japanese directed their fire against the wading Marines. They killed 108 of them and wounded another 235, but 600 Marines survived to join the desperate battle raging all over the western half of Betio. At 11:30 Shoup radioed Julian Smith:

"The situation ashore doesn't look good."

Earlier, Shoup had ordered Lieutenant Hawkins to attack an enemy position holding five machine guns. It blocked the central-sector attack with which Shoup hoped to cut Betio in two. The Hawk had always claimed, "I think my thirty-four-man platoon can lick any two-hundred-man company in the world." Now he gathered his men for the attack. They moved from gun to gun with the methodical efficiency in which he had trained them, covering him with their fire while he crawled up to the gun ports to toss in grenades or fire through the embrasure. The guns fell, but not before Hawkins was shot in the chest. He had lost much blood the day before, and now he was staggering. But he still refused a corpsman's suggestion that he accept evacuation. "I came here to kill Japs, not to be evacuated." Three more guns fell to the Hawk and his men, until he was caught in a mortar burst. They carried him to the beach. He was already dying, but Hawkins and his Marines had opened the way for Shoup's cross-island assault.

The attack across the airfield gained momentum. It reached the seacoast by dusk after the Marines occupied enemy positions and beat off two fierce counterattacks. Betio was sliced in two.

On the left flank Marines under Maj. Jim Crowe made slow but steady progress. On the right, those under Mike Ryan took their objective assisted by 5-inch naval gunfire from two destroyers. Colonel Shoup took heart. "I think we're winning," he growled, "but the bastards still have a lot of bullets left." Then he composed a situation report for Julian Smith:

"Casualties many; percentage dead unknown; combat efficiency: we are winning."

Admiral Shibasaki sat within his bombproof in growing despair, reading worse report after bad one. The *Yogaki* plan was shattered. Shibasaki had gotten no help except from a submarine or two. The previous night only one airplane had come in from the Marshalls. He could expect no more. The Marshalls had been neutralized. Tarawa, he knew, was falling. Although his bombproof had resisted the 5-inch fire of American destroyers that day, he knew that when heavier guns spoke, it would be destroyed. Shibasaki composed his last message for Tokyo:

"Our weapons have been destroyed, and from now on everyone is attempting a final charge. . . . May Japan exist for ten thousand years!"

Marines fighting forward on Betio knew better than Admiral Shibasaki or Colonel Shoup that Tarawa was falling. The Japanese had begun to kill themselves.

They had been told that Americans tortured their captives. Worse, to surrender meant the disgrace of a man's family. If a unit surrendered, its colors were destroyed, and its name obliterated in shame. In the final act of atonement to the emperor they chose suicide as the means of immortalizing their souls among the spirits of Japan's warrior dead in Yasakuni Shrine. Japanese soldiers found with bayonets thrust up into their bowels lay beside loaded rifles. Grenade suicides lay in their bunks with missing hand-and-head or hand-and-chest. Others put their rifle muzzles in their mouths and pulled the trigger with their big toe. Many were found in areas where the attack had been only beginning.

Battle on Betio on the third day was businesslike and brutal. It had not the horror and transcending courage of the first day, nor did it possess the desperation of the second, when men fought to avoid defeat. On the third day the Americans fought with a cold, wary, professional precision, to ferret out and destroy an enemy gone to ground.

Priority was given to reduction of the Pocket, that 600-yard gap separating Marine forces. Sherman tanks, bulldozers, flamethrowers and riflemen moved against it in a systematic, synchronized attack. If the Sherman's 75-mm rifles could penetrate a position, riflemen and flamethrowers swept in to destroy its occupants. If the pillbox was too strong, the tank waddled on, leaving it to the riflemen and flamethrowers. If it still held out, a storm of covering fire and flame was laid down while a bulldozer crept toward it, its driver crouching beneath its protective raised blade. Then the bulldozer sealed off the pillbox by burying it in sand. In this way the Pocket fell.

Next came Admiral Shibasaki's bombproof. Jim Crowe's Marines prepared to attack it after a mortar barrage. To their delighted surprise it exploded in a thundering detonation of flame, smoke and somersaulting logs. A puny 81-mm mortar had scored a direct hit on what turned out to be an ammunition warehouse. Next, the tank *Colorado* clanked up to the steel pillbox and destroyed it with three shells. The bombproof now lay open to attack and the Marines moved in on it watching carefully for Japanese suiciders charging forward with magnetic mines strapped to their bodies. They gained the sides of the bombproof and forced their way to the top. Japanese poured out of exits to be cut down by riflemen and the cannister shot of an antitank gun dragged up to the roof. But there were still about 200 Japanese left inside, including Admiral Shibasaki.

Bulldozers heaped sand against the gunports and sealed off the exits. Gasoline was poured down the air vents and grenades dropped in after it. Flames, smoke and screams issued out of the vents, followed by muffled explosions. The Marines moved on.

At night, the Japanese made their customary banzai charge. At four o'clock in the morning with moonshine making a grotesquerie of the hideous litter of the battlefield—its coconut stumps, wrecked and smoking pillboxes, charred vehicles and sprawling corpses—the screaming enemy came flowing against Marine lines. Artillery fire fell only seventy-five yards ahead of the front. It was joined by gunfire from two destroyers. Those Japanese who penetrated this curtain of steel closed with the Americans in hand-to-hand combat. In the light of dawn the Marines counted 325 dead. Probably three times as many more were wounded.

Only the tail of the Betio bird remained in Japanese hands when daylight of November 23 dawned bright and clear. At seven o'clock the first of the American carrier aircraft plunged to attack the tail. They bombed and strafed for half an hour, after which pack howitzers bucked and bayed for fifteen minutes.

"Let's go!" cried Lt. Col. Kenneth McLeod, and the men of the Third Battalion, Sixth, swept forward with crackling rifles.

They were the freshest troops on Betio, spread out on a two-company front to punch down the narrowing tail. Ahead of them lumbered *Colorado* and *China Gal*—those indomitable Shermans still capable of battle—while seven light tanks rolled to either flank. Within minutes the assault penetrated to a depth of 150 yards. The Japanese fired fitfully and then turned their weapons on themselves. On the left one of the companies bypassed the bombproofs and went racing down the ocean flank. Behind them *Colorado* and the flamethrowers went to work. In the biggest of the bombproofs, a door flew open and perhaps a hundred Japanese charged out. *Colorado* fired and killed half of them. The remainder fell to bullets and flames.

To the west in the Pocket, half-tracks moved among the enemy positions blasting with their 75s. Kneeling Marines picked off fleeing Japanese. Others hurled shaped charges and grenades. The Pocket fell.

To the east again a slaughter had commenced. Four hundred and seventy-five Japanese died here at a cost of nine dead Marines and twenty-five wounded. At 1:00 P.M. a dusty, sweating Marine waded into the sea off Betio. Tarawa had fallen.

Admiral Shibasaki had boasted that a million men could not take the atoll in a hundred years. But it was conquered by 10,000 United States Marines in four days.

Next day most of them departed the stench and heat and ruin of Betio. They had killed 4,690 of the enemy, and 991 of their comrades had died or were dying. There were 2,311 wounded, and many of them would never fight again. Bearded and emaciated and filthy, they came down to the beach, and there their sunken old eyes gazing out of young faces blinked in astonishment.

There was no beach.

The spring tides had come, and the sea flowed up to the sea wall. High water on the reef would have meant high water at the sea wall, and there would have been no place to hide.

No one had expected Betio to be easy, but neither Vice Adm. Raymond Spruance, the overall commander, nor Howlin' Mad Smith, the V Amphibious Corps chief, had anticipated any difficulty at Makin. Actually it was not Makin atoll itself that was the objective but Butaritari or Horse Island, its principal islet on which the Japanese had built a seaplane base. Butaritari was shaped like a crutch, thirteen miles in length and never more than 500 yards at it widest. It was held by about 500 Japanese soldiers and more than 100 laborers. They had few heavy weapons and their fortifications when compared to Betio were as paper is to steel. Thus when an assault force of 6,500 soldiers from the 27th Infantry Division landed there November 20, it was confidently assumed that the island would fall in a day or two.

Landings on the west and north shore of Butaritari met little opposition. This was the high point of the invasion. From then on progress was excruciatingly slow. Most of the troops were half-trained National Guardsmen in battle for the first time. They allowed themselves to be pinned down by small pockets of enemy, some of them real, some imagined. At night the curses and screams of the Japanese unnerved them. When the enemy set off strings of firecrackers, the Americans responded with rifle fire, which gave away their positions. At dawn the sight and sound of a soldier running down the beach shouting, "There's a hundred and fifty Japs in the trees!" set off a wave of shooting hysteria.

On the second day, however, the troops began to recover their nerve and to shed their casual attitude toward combat. They drove steadily down the island. On the night of November 22 the Americans dug in and the encounter known as *"Sake* Night" in the 27th Division began.

This was the usual banzai charge—with a new wrinkle. As darkness fell, there came the sound of babies wailing and women shrieking. Out of the shadows came a group of twenty or thirty islanders carrying their belongings. They were herded into the perimeter and ordered to lie down. Ten minutes later another group came down the road, jabbering and trying to wail like babies. The ruse fooled no one, and the Americans opened fire.

At another position, Japanese drunk on sake lurched out of their lines shouting, "Heil Hitler!" or "Long live the Emperor!" They were cut down. Cpl. Louis Lula commanding a 37-mm antitank gun was astonished when he saw a section of Japanese approaching him marching as though on a parade ground, in perfect step and their rifles held stiffly at right shoulder arms. He broke them up with a grenade and then finished them off with cannister shot from his 37. In the morning it was found that the contents of almost all of the slain enemy canteens either smelled of wine or were still partially filled with sake. Japanese losses were more than 200 known dead with probably at least half that many dying of wounds or neglect. That was the end at Butaritari, and Gen. Ralph Smith was able to signal Spruance and Howland Smith: "Makin taken." In all, his division had lost only sixty-six killed and 185 wounded.

But the cost of the 27th's slow conquest of Makin was much higher than that. The escort carrier *Liscomb Bay* was sunk by a Japanese submarine on the last day of the battle at a great loss of life. Bitter naval officers were quick to point out that if Makin had been taken in a day or two, *Liscomb Bay* would have been gone before the submarine arrived.

This was the lesson to be learned from Makin: that quick conquests release forces for use elsewhere and that warships vulnerable to aerial or undersea attack cannot tarry too long in the impact area.

There were also lessons to be learned from Tarawa. Communications, so faulty on Betio, were drastically overhauled. A new dry-cell battery radio called the TBX was developed. So also were Jascos (Joint Assault Signal Companies). Their functions were to go ashore after the landing waves to control naval gunfire and direct it on targets visible to them, to do the same with aircraft and to coordinate beach communications. Jasco units trained beach masters to direct the unloading of supplies ashore as well as shore-party commanders. Studies of the loading and unloading of supplies produced an ingenious technique of layering. Rather than put all the beans at the back of an LST, then the bullets, the barbed wire next and the black oil at the front, all such indispensable supplies were stacked together in multiple rows from front to back, so that there never would be a loss of precious time in getting at one or another suddenly deemed vital.

New command ships were constructed, especially equipped with the gear necessary to direct a land battle from the sea, replacing the battleships and cruisers used formerly, which had proved so woefully inadequate. On gunnery ranges near Pearl Harbor experts built exact replicas of Betio's pillboxes and bombproofs and experimented with ways to destroy them. From these studies emerged such new weapons as the LVT (A) or amphibious tank as well as amphibious flamethrowers. There was also the 2.5-ton amphibious truck or "duck" for lightering supplies from a ship to its destination inland, or to do the same with troops. The Landing Craft Vehicle, Personnel (LCVP), was to become the standard armored assault boat, mounting .50-caliber machine guns and even 37-mm cannon. Perhaps the most ingenious innovation was the use of the Landing Ship Dock (LSD), the big seagoing dry dock used to repair ships at sea. They carried tanks to the battle. The tanks would be preloaded on LCTs, which would steam under their own power into the LSD's flooded dry dock. This would be pumped dry for the run to the battle and then flooded once more and its capacious maw flung open to permit the LCTs to head shoreward with their vital cargo.

The Marine casualties at Betio had the painful effect of agonizing the American public. Americans could not believe that about 1,000 of their countrymen had died and more than 2,000 been wounded during only three days of fighting to take an insignificant islet less than half a square mile in area. War correspondents filed lurid stories, and their newspapers printed ghastly photographs of corpses floating on the tide or bodies piled up on the beaches. Newspaper tycoon William Randolph Hearst seized upon the Tarawa carnage as a stick with which to beat the U.S. Navy and Marine Corps while banging the drum of Douglas MacArthur's presidential ambitions. Hearst and other admirers of MacArthur pointed to his supposedly low casualties and mastery of maneuver as a striking contrast to the "fullback" tactics of the Marines, and from this false premise deduced that his "humane" and brilliant generalship entitled him to be elevated to supreme command in the Pacific. Apart from the obvious fact that a "humane" and brilliant general is a contradiction in terms—as witness McClellan in the Civil War— MacArthur's supporters, indifferent to how they were exacerbating the army-navy rivalry in the Pacific, also ignored MacArthur's very poor tactical performance at Buna–Gona and the vital difference between coral atolls and big forested islands.

Unhappily, to this day there persists the mistaken belief that the shallow water over the reef had caused the carnage at Tarawa. It was indeed the great killer. But so also would have been the spring tide, which came to Tarawa five days later and left no beach under the sea wall. The tragedy was that Tarawa had been scheduled for November 20, 1943, in the conviction that there would be five feet of water over the reef. When it was realized that there might be only three, it was too late to cancel the operation if only because the spring tide was so close. A precious month simply could not be lost. Julian Smith and Holland Smith sought to overcome this unnecessary hazard by requesting more amtracks. Kelly Turner refused, and then, relenting, gave them only fifty of the hundred available. If they had had them all, that horrible wade-in during which most of the casualties occurred might not have happened; and at the end, when they were down to eighteen, they might have had sixty-eight. Tarawa's casualties, then, were the result of a miscalculation and the practice of allowing admirals to command operations which, though seaborne, are to be fought on land. Turner did not want the amtracks aboard his ships, which sounds more like a prejudice than a conviction. He gave the Generals Smith only half of what he could have given them— it appears—to placate them rather than to bow to their superior knowledge of what was needed in amphibious warfare.

That was the true tragedy of Tarawa.

75. Summit at Quebec, Cairo and Tehran

DURING 1943 there were two more important conferences between Roosevelt and Churchill and their war chiefs, and then a third between these two and Stalin. The first of the two Anglo-American meetings was at Quebec during August 17–24. It was code-named Quadrant.

At Quadrant both wartime strategy and postwar policies were discussed. There were arguments about the extent of operations in Italy, but these were overshadowed by the dispute over the invasion of France. Both General Marshall and Secretary of War Stimson had persuaded FDR to insist that Italian operations be limited and that nothing should detract from Overlord, as the cross-Channel assault was called. Churchill naturally enough wanted an extensive Italian campaign. He argued that this was a means of weakening the Axis and of gaining Western influence in Southern Europe and the Balkans to thwart Soviet ambition there. FDR was drawn toward this theory but did not believe he could justify a greater commitment to such operations for political reasons alone. Thus, he extracted from the reluctant Churchill a promise that Overlord would go forward undiminished on May 1, 1944.

But FDR and Churchill were unable to reach an agreement on an attitude toward Charles de Gaulle and his Free French Committee of National Liberation. Roosevelt still hated de Gaulle personally, believing he would make a dangerous military dictator and an opponent of his own plans for postwar decolonization and arms control. With Stimson's solid support FDR refused to approve any use of the word "recognition" in relation to the Free French.

Collaboration on atomic energy was also agreed upon at Quadrant. During the Trident conference in May, Churchill had obtained from FDR informal agreement to a resumption of joint research, but at Quebec they came to a formal compact under which neither would impart any information about atomic development to any third party—meaning the Soviet Union—without the other's consent.

The second meeting took place during November 22–26 at Cairo and was code-named Sextant. Its chief concern was the Far East and the role of Generalissimo Chiang Kai-shek of China in any invasion of Japan. From the start Roosevelt and Churchill were in disagreement. The British chief considered any increase in Far Eastern operations to be a diversion from his own plans for the Mediterranean. Thus he was irked when Roosevelt made China the first order of business. The American chief's objective was to raise Chiang's prestige as a member of the Big Four and to strengthen United States–China relations with an eye toward imposing stability on the postwar Far East. There was talk of reopening the Burma Road as a supply route to China. Chiang said he would support such a project if the United States and Britain agreed to amphibious operations in the Bay of Bengal. Churchill refused. Even Roosevelt was dubious about such plans, and as the conference progressed, he began to become irritated by Chiang's insistent demands. But he did have the conference draw up the so-called Cairo Declaration, committing the Allies to restoring to China the lands taken from her by Japan. There was also an agreement to try to persuade Turkey to enter the war on the Allied side, but the attempt failed. The conference ended with Chiang emerging as a stronger partner in the Alliance and a general agreement for a Far Eastern operation involving Burma. However, Churchill and Roosevelt later agreed to postpone the Burmese project until after the cross-Channel invasions.

The first meeting of the Big Three—the United States, Britain, and the Soviet Union—was held at Tehran, from November 28 to December 1. Roosevelt had planned to stay at the American legation, but reports of a Nazi plot against the Big Three led him to accept Stalin's invitation to stay at the more secure Soviet Embassy. Roosevelt came to the meeting with high hopes of establishing a rapport with Stalin. He had great confidence in his powers of persuasion through personal encounter and believed that he could address political issues concerning the postwar organization of Europe. Thus, he joined Stalin in taunting and teasing Churchill, believing that by belittling one partner he could ingratiate himself into the good wishes of the other. When Stalin at a dinner on the second night began to needle Churchill as desirous of a "soft" peace for Germany, which the Soviet leader, of course, considered at the least abhorrent, Roosevelt did nothing to defend the "former naval person" with whom he had had such a warm and intimate correspondence and relationship for six years. He even sided with Stalin in his barbaric proposal to execute 50,000 captive German officers, rather than to have been aroused by Churchill's noble anger and steadfast refusal even to discuss such an atrocity. At a private meeting of the Big Three on the fourth day, FDR began to tease Churchill about his disposition, his resemblance to the "John Bull" of the political cartoons, his cigars and other habits. By this he thought to have broken down Stalin's reserve and to have established a good relationship with him. History would show that he had done the opposite, that Stalin saw at once that he was dealing with a man flawed by a superficial knowledge of the power politics of Europe.

Roosevelt's plan for controlling the world through "four policemen"—Britain, the United States, China and the Soviet Union—drew Stalin's scorn. He said the Four Policemen would not be welcomed by the small nations of Europe. They would resent China as an enforcer. Stalin also did not think that China would be very powerful after the war. Rather than the Four Policemen Stalin thought that there should be one committee for Europe and another for the Far East, a proposal similar to Churchill's plan for regional councils in Europe, the Far East and the Americas, the three to comprise the Supreme United Nations Council.

There was also much discussion of the Polish question. Churchill, observing that the Allies had gone to war to defend Poland, wanted a strong Poland. He reassured Stalin that the U.S.S.R.'s western frontiers would remain inviolable and that any accretion of land to Poland would have to come from Germany. Stalin, however, was noncommittal in his replies. He also did little to allay Roosevelt's worries about American public opinion in the impending 1944 presidential election. FDR did not wish to alienate the numerous Americans of Polish or Balkan ancestry. Although he agreed that the U.S.S.R. should redefine Poland's borders to satisfy Soviet security concerns, he tried to impress upon Stalin the importance Americans attached to self-determination. In this he received little satisfaction. Both he and Churchill might not have been so agreeable to Stalin's "security concerns" had they known that their partner was already grooming the men of his puppet "Lublin government" (see page 722.) for the eventual takeover of Poland. Postwar plans for a conquered Germany were also discussed, with Stalin pressing hard for a punitive peace. He feared a revival of German nationalism. He was not impressed by Churchill's private proposal that Germany could be controlled so long as Britain, the United States and the Soviet Union remained close friends.

Opening of the Second Front in France overshadowed all other problems at Tehran. On the very first day, Stalin, sitting directly opposite Churchill, came immediately to the point with the question:

"Am I right in thinking that the invasion of France is to be undertaken by thirty-five divisions?"

"Yes," Churchill replied. "Particularly strong divisions."

"Is it intended that this operation should be carried out by the force now in Italy?"

"No. Seven divisions have already been, or are in process of being, withdrawn from Italy and North Africa to take part in Overlord. These seven divisions are required to make up the thirty-five mentioned in your first question. After they have been withdrawn, about twenty-two divisions will be left in the Mediterranean for Italy or other objectives. . . ."

This seemed to satisfy Stalin, although he made it plain that he would not be convinced of Overlord until the western Allies had named its supreme commander. It was perhaps this skepticism that compelled Franklin Roosevelt finally to make up his mind. For months he had wavered between Marshall and Eisenhower for the top command. Just before the Cairo Conference, FDR and Eisenhower had toured Tunisian battlefields together. Roosevelt said that he dreaded the thought of not having Marshall in Washington. But then he said it was only fair that the chief of staff should have a chance to command a great field army. Eisenhower took this to mean that Marshall would lead Overlord. He was positive of it when Admiral King told him: "I hate to lose General Marshall as chief of staff, but my loss is consoled by the knowledge that I will have you to work in this job." Eisenhower said that he took this to be an "official notice."

Marshall to command Overlord, Eisenhower to replace him in Washington, this was indeed Roosevelt's preferred solution to the problem. But this would create an absurd situation: Dwight Eisenhower, the protégé of George Marshall, would become Marshall's boss. He would also be the boss of Douglas MacArthur, whose protégé he also had been. This might be acceptable to Marshall, yearning to command this greatest of modern operations, but never to MacArthur. Roosevelt tried to solve the dilemma by asking Marshall to state his personal preference. Marshall replied like a true soldier of democracy: He would serve wherever he was sent, and would never be his own judge or advocate. Actually, as FDR often said, he knew he could not sleep at night with Marshall out of the country. As the Tehran conference was breaking up, he dictated a note to Stalin: "The immediate appointment of General Eisenhower to command of Overlord has been decided upon."

Stalin was elated, and for the first and last time the Big Three adjourned in apparent harmony.

It is doubtful if Franklin Delano Roosevelt ever made a better appointment than to name Dwight David Eisenhower to the most coveted command in the history of warfare; and it may be that the Western allies owe Joseph Stalin a vote of thanks for hurrying the often dilatory president into making his decision. Obviously, there could have been no other choice. Marshall had made himself too valuable to be spared, even for Overlord. Since command had to go to an American, it had to be Eisenhower.

But there were other reasons, perhaps chief among them Eisenhower's capacity to command a coalition. There is no more difficult way to wage war, and it may be said that much of Napoleon's success may be attributed to the fact that he always fought coalitions. By Eisenhower's devotion to the Alliance and his guiding principle of teamwork he had made a coalition work. When Sir Andrew Cunningham left the Mediterranean to become the first sea lord, he said to Eisenhower: "I do not believe that any other man than yourself could have done it."

Eisenhower also had shown that he was capable of field command. He had made the mistakes of inexperience early on in North Africa, but he had profited by them, as he did again in Sicily and Italy. Canny football coach that he had been, he reviewed his own performance with the same detachment and insights of a coach watching the movies of the preceding Saturday's game. From such self-criticism comes self-confidence, and Eisenhower's belief in himself inspired confidence in him among his subordinates. He was also eminently fair, forever correcting and adjusting, constantly gathering all available information bearing on a decision, and then, having heard what he considered to be the last word, making it.

Above all Dwight Eisenhower was trustworthy. Even Bernard Montgomery, certainly his harshest critic, drew attention to this quality when he said, "his real strength lies in his human qualities. . . . He has the power of drawing the hearts of men towards him as a magnet attracts the bit of metal. He merely has to smile at you and you trust him at once." If Dwight Eisenhower had commanded in another age, it might have been said of him what Macaulay said of Napoleon: "An eye to see and a hand to execute. All men saw that he was king."

76. Famine in Leningrad

WHEN ZHDANOV evacuated almost 400,000 children from Leningrad in June of 1941, it apparently did not occur to him that an unintended effect of this decision was to reduce the number of mouths to feed. If it had, one would think he would have taken immediate steps to remove all nonessential personnel from the endangered city. Leningrad's huge civilian population of 2.5 million simply could not be fed under siege conditions. If the highways and railroad to Moscow were cut —as they were—the only route for food supplies would be a circuitous one to ports on Lake Ladoga's east coast and thence across the lake and up the Neva River to Leningrad. This route would soon be perilous with the advent of the fierce autumn storms, which could make Ladoga impassable for as long as a week at a time. It would be possible to cross it only when the ice was thick enough to support trucks, but this would not happen until late December or later, depending upon the date of the first subfreezing weather. Between June and the end of August when Leningrad first became aware of its peril from possible famine, as many as a million civilians could have been evacuated. But Leningraders had a special affection for their city and, indeed, many famous sons and daughters had *returned* to the place of their birth just to be there during its hour of peril. But it is also true that a Communist commissar is seldom denied, and Zhdanov might have modified the Zhukov Principle to Leave or be Shot. If the firing squad also reduced the number of mouths to feed this probably would not be an unintended effect.

But this was not done and in retrospect it can be seen that this was the gravest Soviet blunder in the siege of Leningrad.

On August 27, with a chill hint of autumn already in the air, it was discovered that Leningrad had on hand the following supplies: flour, exclusive of grain, enough for seventeen days; cereals, twenty-nine days; fish, sixteen days; meat, twenty-five days; dried fish, twenty-two days; butter, twenty-eight days. A telegram was sent to the State Defense Committee in Moscow urgently requesting emergency food shipments. Moscow replied it would provide Leningrad with a forty-five-day reserve of food. In Leningrad it was decided to cut the rations introduced on July 18. The bread ration was reduced to 600 grams daily—about a pound and a quarter—for workers, four hundred grams for office personnel and three hundred for dependents and children under twelve. The meat ration was reduced to three pounds a month, cereals the same, fats to a pound and a half and sugar and candy to five ounces. Lean though this might be, it was still supportable—until the Germans bombed the Badayev warehouses.

These were highly flammable wooden buildings erected cheek-by-jowl and occupying about four acres. They were stuffed with food. The moment they were showered with German incendiary bombs, they burst into smoke and flames. Greasy, blood-red clouds drifted over a horrified Leningrad the night of September 8, marking the city for return raids. Beneath them, all of the city's fire-fighting apparatus—168 units—battled the blazing buildings all night until no fewer than 178 fires were finally brought under control. All of the food was burned. Twenty-five hundred tons of sugar flowed into the warehouse cellars where it sank into the earth, hardening in a molten mass. One day "Badayev earth"—molten sugar shot with dirt dug up by enterprising merchants—would be sold in the Haymarket at outrageous prices. Everyone bitterly blamed Zhdanov and his lieutenants for having concentrated the food supply rather than dispersing it, and this indeed was another serious error.

Next day all the air reeked with the heavy odor of burning oil and flour, the acrid stench of burnt meat, the smell of carbonized sugar. Everyone knew that the Badayev warehouses were the city's greatest. "Badayev has burned," the babushkas wailed. "It's the end—famine!"

Not yet. Into Leningrad from Moscow by air came Dmitri V. Pavlov, one of the most energetic supply officials in the Soviet bureaucracy. Pavlov found the food situation not quite as grim as he had anticipated, but he was appalled when he discovered how many people he would have to feed. In the city were about 2.544 million people, including 400,000 children, and in the environs inside the German ring another 343,000. Military forces defending the city, never precisely counted, were probably about 500,000. So Pavlov had to provide food for 3.4 million souls! He had to do this with a meager, rapidly dwindling supply with absolutely no hope of more than a trickle from "mainland" Russia. He knew that the Ladoga–Neva route as yet had no boats, warehouses, piers, highway or rail facilities to handle huge shipments. To provide them would take time. At once he cut the ration again and began issuing ration cards. Soon he forbade issuing cards to people being fed in hospitals or children's homes. To prevent people from using the cards of relatives who had died or left the city, or from bribing janitors to certify that they lived in empty apartments and thus gain extra cards, or from buying those being printed by the counterfeiters, Pavlov decreed that the cards must be renewed monthly. Soon also he would close all commercial restaurants so that people able to pay could not thus evade rationing regulations. Pavlov's daily dread was that the Luftwaffe would shower the city with fake ration cards. They had already begun to drop booby-trapped valuables such as watches and cigarette lighters, together with counterfeit currency, and Pavlov feared that it was but a short step from rubles to ration cards. In October he persuaded Zhukov to issue a decree providing that all ration cards be reregistered within a period of three days. It was a herculean task, but it was accomplished; and Pavlov breathed much easier in the conviction that whatever had been false or forged was now made useless.

To get extra food, people took their valuables into the countryside, there to haggle with hard-faced muzhiks for vegetables, milk or meat. Soon many Leningrad apartments were bare of rugs or blankets, samovars or silver, and the women no longer wore furs or jewels. Pavlov sought food everywhere; sometimes his foraging parties came under fire as they gathered thousands of tons of potatoes in the countryside before the fields froze. Five thousand tons of oats were seized from a military warehouse. After he closed the breweries, he took their stocks of 8,000 tons of malt to mix with flour for bread. Horses were either slaughtered or eaten after they starved to death. To keep them alive they were fed a food made of bundles of twigs stewed in hot water sprinkled with compressed cottonseed-oil cake and salt. Cottonseed-oil cakes were like coal briquettes, made to burn in ship furnaces. They were considered unfit for human consumption because of all the poisons they contained, but Pavlov found that these could be removed under high temperature, and the cakes also went into the bread—along with sawdust and flour from moldy grain. "We are eating bread as heavy as cobblestones and bitter with cottonseed-oil cake," one Leningrader complained in his diary.

Dependents and children suffered most severely under Pavlov's rigid ration control. For the moment, workers and state employees—and the military—received enough food to maintain their strength. But as of October 1 nonworkers and children received only one third of a loaf of poor quality bread daily and *for the month* a total of five and a quarter pounds of additional food. Even this was laced with unnourishing substitutes—fish or canned goods for meat, candy for oil or fat—and the pastry was sodden and tasteless with noncaloric filling. Soon even these issues fell behind schedule, and eventually Leningrad was living by bread alone. Growing children who needed more nourishment than adults got the least: A boy of sixteen received the same ration as a child of five.

Everyone seemed to have a different regimen intended to make the ration go further. One person might divide his portion into three, eating one slice of bread about as big as a candy bar for breakfast, lunch and dinner. Another might devour the whole issue in the morning so that he or she would have the strength to stand in the food lines or hunt about the city for food. Half the food consumed was not even food. They became ingenious at turning leather shoes or belts into digestible food. Vice Adm. Yuri Paneleyev was astounded when a woman who asked him for his worn leather portfolio sent him a few days later a dish of meat jelly and the portfolio's nickel fittings. She could make food of the leather but not the metal. People tore the wallpaper from the walls and scraped off the paste to eat because they believed it was made of potato flour. Next, they ate the paper, thinking that because it was made of wood it had some nourishment. Like starving wolves gobbling mud to smother the pangs of hunger, they stuffed their stomachs with whatever they could swallow, even knocking plaster from the walls and chewing it. Dogs and cats began to vanish from the streets, and there were no longer pigeons in the squares. In the hospitals and research laboratories the cages for rabbits and guinea pigs were empty. When the snow came, horse-drawn sleighs stood idle. Pets also had to go. A dog might die for a man, but no man was willing to starve to keep his dog alive. Dog legs, it was discovered, made a succulent stew. Many a Leningrader sat in his cold apartment with tears streaming down his cheeks while he munched on the remains of his devoted companion.

Because of the consumption of so many inedible or indigestible substances, diarrhea and dystrophy appeared. They were among the greatest killers. But even an ordinarily treatable affliction such as an ulcer or a bad cold was fatal. The first to die were the undernourished young. The elderly went next, usually quietly in their beds. Men died before women and healthy persons before chronic invalids, a direct result of the unintended inequity in a policy of the same ration for all adults: Men bigger than women needed more food and so did healthy working people compared to people lying in hospital beds.

Starvation, of course, was the greatest killer, although the symptoms differed. Limbs might shrivel into toothpicks and a woman's breasts sag in empty little bags, while skirts or trousers slipped down over the hips; or else the body became bloated, shoes were too small, shirt collars could not be buttoned and the cheeks seemed to be bursting. Always the terrified victims of hunger found depression and growing difficulties rapidly closing around them. Despondency turned into despair. The stairs became too steep to climb, the shelf too high to reach, the apartment too much to clean. "Today it is so simple to die," Yelena Skryabina wrote in her diary. "You just begin to lose interest, then you lie on the bed and you never get up again."

Hunger also suppressed sexual activity to an astonishing degree. Because those physical traits which mutually excite men and women became so shrunken, faded or disfigured that they now mutually repulsive, and because few people had the energy to waste in such activity, the birth rate plummeted. The rate for 1942 was only a third of 1941's, and in 1943 it dropped another 25 percent. From a birth rate of 25.1 per 1,000 persons in 1940, it fell to 18.3 in 1941 and 6.2 in 1942. After the worst winter in the history of Leningrad arrived early in October, few workers had their clothes off for weeks at a time, living or working in buildings where the temperature was near zero. At the public baths the sexes bathed together regardless of whether it was ladies' or men's day.

Once that dreadful winter of 1941–42 arrived in Leningrad on October 14, bitter, subzero cold began to kill nearly as many people as hunger. "Ski Day," the date on which the ground is covered with four inches of snow, was marked on October 31, the earliest advent ever. Normally in Leningrad, the sparkling City of Ice, Ski Day is celebrated with great festivity. In 1941 it was received with foreboding. There was no heat in the great buildings. Would the water pipes burst? They did. Most Leningraders received a monthly fuel ration of 2.5 liters of kerosene in September, but in October and thereafter there was none. There was also no electricity. People went to bed fully clothed and wearing greatcoats, removing only their felt boots before crawling underneath blankets, mattress and pillows. Rising stiff and sore, they put on their boots and heated their tea and food on a tiny grill set on two bricks over a little pile of shavings. People tore down fences and stormed parks to get the wood to burn in their *burzhuikas,* tiny potbellied stoves, which first appeared during similar ordeals in Petersburg in 1919–1920. Probably the burzhuikas caused nearly as many fires in Leningrad as the enemy bombing and shelling. But the people would not give up their only source of heat. They crouched in front of the little stoves numb with cold, shivering, vapor puffs issuing from their mouths. Often in an adjoining room lay the frozen corpses of two or three relatives. Whole families died of cold. A pretty little eleven-year-old schoolgirl named Tanya Savicheva scribbled a record of her family's demise in her notebook:

Z—Zhenya died 28 Dec., 12:30 in the morning, 1941
B—Babushka [Grandma] died 25 Jan., 3 o'clock, 1942

L—Leka died 17 March, 5 o'clock in the morning, 1942
D—Dedya [Grandpa] Vasya died 12 April, 2 o'clock at night, 1942
D—Dedya Lesha, 10 May, 4 in the afternoon, 1942
M—Mama, 13 May, 7:30 A.M., 1942
S—Savichevs died. All died. Only Tanya remains.

But Tanya survived only to die of chronic dysentery in a children's home in the summer of 1943.

One reason why Leningraders allowed the corpses of their loved ones to lie unburied in adjoining rooms was that they had not the strength to take them to the cemeteries, or the food—bread was now the only real currency—to pay someone else to take them. Mostly the corpses were pulled to the cemetery on sleds. There were no automobiles, and the broad, icy, snowdrift-lined streets of Leningrad were thronged with people tugging little children's sleds of bright red or yellow carrying corpses in coffins of unpainted wood or simply swathed in a sheet. Or else they carried the ill and dying to the hospitals. City trucks rolled regularly through the streets, picking up the corpses left outside the apartments, or the lifeless bodies of people who fell dead on the sidewalks, their gas masks still slung over their shoulders. Because it was so cold, the bodies did not decompose or smell; and as the mounds of corpses grew higher at the cemeteries, workers began blasting mass graves in the frozen earth—for if Leningrad survived the winter, its new enemy would be the epidemics issuing from the bodies of the unburied.

By the end of November 1941 an estimated 3,000 persons died daily in Leningrad. The figure would rise, and so would the number of sleds in that charnel swarm moving slowly through the streets on their sepulchral errand, their steel runners slipping over hard-packed snow with sounds like the squeaking of the rats gnawing on the frozen faces of the dead.

Not all the deaths were from hunger and cold: The Nazis had carefully ringed Leningrad's landward front with batteries of artillery and had assigned a special crack bomber echelon—the Hindenburg Escadrille—to destroy the city. Shells and bombs fell day and night in an indiscriminate shower of steel. So many pedestrians were killed or maimed that warning signs were erected: "Citizens: In case of shelling this side of the street is the most dangerous." At work or at home, Leningraders were struck down by enemy fire. Sometimes a line of women standing outside a store patiently waiting for bread or wine to be sold would be hit. There would be screams and limbs and bodies flying through the air. But the survivors stoically picked themselves up and re-formed their queue lest they miss their allotment.

Leningrad could not long endure such decimation. The enemy's iron ring had to be broken. In September 1941, Zhukov had made two such attempts and failed. A third would be made October 20 under Marshal Voroshilov, who had returned to Leningrad. Although the plans drawn in Moscow were grandiose,

Voroshilov could muster only 63,000 men, 475 guns and ninety-seven tanks—fifty-nine of them the huge sixty-ton KVs—with some air support from the Baltic Fleet's air arm. Opposing this force were 54,000 Germans and 450 guns, but also markedly superior aerial support. But the "liberating attack" was doomed even before it started.

Four days before it began, the Germans struck at the hinge of the Fourth and Fifty-second Armies and sent the Soviets reeling back in confusion. Within a few days they were fighting desperately to keep the Nazis from forging a second ring of steel around Leningrad. Next they had their backs to the wall at Tikhvin, the railway station at which supplies could be moved to Lake Ladoga for trans-shipment to Leningrad. If the Germans captured Tikhvin, they would compel the Soviets to supply the besieged city over a 220-mile route along primitive, snow-covered forest trails. Loss of Tikhvin would all but seal the fate of Leningrad, and on November 8 it did fall to the Germans. Rail communications between Leningrad and mainland Russia had been cut. In Munich, a jubilant Hitler declared: "Leningrad's hands are in the air. It falls sooner or later. No one can free it. No one can break the ring. Leningrad is doomed to die of famine."

Der Führer appeared to be correct, and in Leningrad Marshal Voroshilov was doing very little if anything to disprove him. He had already refused the Leningrad Command offered him by Zhdanov, and when the commissar asked him for more supplies, Voroshilov replied that there was plenty of military material in Leningrad. Instead of bringing munitions in from Moscow, he sent them in the other direction. It was now apparent to Zhdanov that the ice road over Lake Ladoga proposed by the Leningrad Military Council on November 3—five days before Tikhvin fell—must now be built. Without it Leningrad would die.

77. The Battle for New Britain

IN LATE 1943 and early 1944 the war in the Pacific swung back to General MacArthur's route to Japan, among the rain forests of the great islands of the Bismarck Barrier. That barricade's outer defenses had already been penetrated by Admiral Halsey's advance up the Solomons ladder as high as northernmost Bougainville on the right flank, and through Lae–Salamaua and Finschhafen by MacArthur's forces in left-flank New Guinea.

Now MacArthur proposed to complete the bursting of the barrier by attacking the western end of New Britain, the long island on which Rabaul was located, and the Admiralty Islands in the northwest. Thus Rabaul would be encircled. To do this he had Lt. Gen. Walter Krueger's Sixth Army, sometimes called "Alamo

Force." Sixth Army should have come under the operational control of General Sir Thomas Blamey, the Australian who commanded Allied Land Forces in the Southwest Pacific. By creating Alamo Force, Sixth Army came under MacArthur's direct command, thus leaving Blamey with little more than Australian troops. This sleight of hand distressed Blamey but it did give MacArthur better control.

On December 15, 1943, the 1st Cavalry's 112th Regiment under Brig. Gen. Julian W. Cunningham went ashore at Arawe, a cape midway on New Britain's southwest coast. The landing was unopposed and the Americans immediately began building a base for torpedo boats. Arawe also would serve as a blocking position between Cape Gloucester on the island's western tip and Rabaul on the northeastern end. Because of the density of the New Britain jungle, probably the foulest in the Pacific, two Japanese battalions counterattacking from distant Rabaul by barge and jungle trail did not strike until the end of the month. They were repulsed, and in mid-January an American counterattack supported by tanks wiped out the last pockets of Japanese in the Arawe area.

The way was now cleared for the larger offensive against Cape Gloucester on New Britain's western tip, where the Japanese had begun building an airfield. The landings would be made by the First Marine Division under Maj. Gen. William Rupertus on the day after Christmas.

Cape Gloucester's importance to both sides lay in the airfield still under construction and the cape's location as the midway point in the Rabaul–New Guinea barge traffic. In the shrinking Bismarck Barrier, it was second only to Rabaul, 370 miles away. There were about 15,000 soldiers and sailors defending the cape under Maj. Gen. Iawo Matsuda. Actually, Matsuda's 65th Brigade was a ragtag, pickup force. War in the Solomons and New Guinea had washed many waifs and orphans onto New Britain's shores, and Matsuda had been made their guardian. His units ranged in size from four men to a 3,300-man regiment. Of his 15,000 troops, Matsuda had about 10,000 defending western New Britain.

For weeks they had been pounded by the big bombers of the Fifth Air Force. Two thousand tons of explosives had been dropped. For the last few nights Liberators had flown over the airfield dropping a 1,000-pound bomb every six minutes. On the morning of December 26, the Marines landed unopposed.

Soon word was flashed to New Guinea to send the second wave of LSTs to Cape Gloucester.

On the cape itself the Third Battalion, First Marines, was driving on the half-finished airfield laid out in a field of kunai grass. They were moving against the Japanese 53rd Infantry Regiment led by Col. Koki Sumiya. Sumiya's soldiers were in a series of deep bunkers holding about twenty men each. They fiercely resisted the Marines, attacking with Sherman tanks, bazookas and flamethrowers. But the tanks became bogged down in a swamp, the bazookas' rockets failed to explode in the sodden earth and the flamethrowers simply would not work. The Marines were mystified by the failure of their weapons. In some places 75-mm howitzers simply sank out of sight. Prime movers vanished with the sound of popping corks. The maps had said nothing of a swamp and the sun was shining overhead. But then by late afternoon they understood what had happened. The sunlight had been a freak, for the sky had turned black and scowling and from the sea there came the sound as of 10,000 machine guns hammering.

The monsoon had come.

It came out of the northwest, an opaque gray wall of water marching over the Bismarck Sea. It came with the sound of rolling drums, millions of raindrops striking the sea in the rattling roar of monster timpani. Within minutes it was over the rain forest, and water was streaming, swishing, gurgling everywhere. Every-one on western New Britain—Japanese defenders, American invaders—was soaking wet within minutes, and they would remain that way for weeks. During the next thirty days there would be twenty-seven hours of sunlight.

In this green hell the fight for Cape Gloucester airfield settled down into a slow, sodden, slugging match.

General Matsuda decided to counterattack. He had already ordered Col. Kenshiro Katayama's 141st Regiment to march to Cape Gloucester from the south coast, believing that the main American thrust had come there rather than Arawe. But he would not wait for Katayama. Instead, he would bring the 2nd Battalion, 53rd, up from Borgen Bay to attack the Seventh Marines enmired in "Damp Flat." Matsuda was acting on two misconceptions: The enemy was only 2,500 strong and his troops were inferior. Actually, General Rupertus had about five times that many Marines ashore, and they had already demonstrated their fighting skill. So Matsuda sent a battalion up against a regiment in a predawn attack December 27 with the foreordained results. When the attack ran down— it was decided in the end by Marine mortar fire "laid in by guess and by God," and the dawn arrival of a special weapons battery—the Japanese withdrew leav-ing 200 dead, with probably three times as many wounded. There were twenty-five dead Marines and seventy-five wounded.

Rupertus marked time the following day, waiting the arrival of the Fifth Marines before resuming the airfield assault. On December 29 the Fifth came in and the assault was renewed. It quickly picked up momentum. Then the rain stopped, and the sun came out. The Marines cheered. Then they laughed. A dog was leading their attack. It was a German shepherd owned by a slain Japanese. Barking happily, undaunted by the blasting of the Sherman tanks and the thunder of artillery, the dog took "the point" of the attack and led the Marines onto the airfield.

There was no one there. Colonel Sumiya had abandoned his positions. He had also withdrawn from a series of bunkers to the south. But that night the Japanese reoccupied them and the Fifth Marines had to clean them out next day in savage point-to-point fighting. But Cape Gloucester airfield was now Ameri-can, and on December 30 General Rupertus could signal General Krueger: "First Marine Division presents to you as an early New Year's gift the complete air-drome of Cape Gloucester. . . . Situation well in hand due to the fighting spirit of troops, the usual Marine luck and the help of God—Rupertus grinning to Krueger."

In the four months following the fall of the airfield, both the Japanese and the Americans on New Britain came to regard both New Britain and the rains as a greater enemy than their human foes. The island itself was a blind, blundering, inconstant place where a man could pass within ten paces of a native village or another man and not see either, where rivers changed their courses during a single night because a dozen inches of rain had fallen within half a day, or where a barricade erected at noon was carried away in the night's flood or collapsed by tomorrow's earthquake. Often soaring mangrove trees with roots loosened by rain would come crashing down during artillery barrages, sometimes blotting out the lives of men crushed beneath them. Twenty-five Marines were killed by these falling "widow makers," and probably that many more among the Japanese. Inside the forest were every manner of creeping, crawling creatures, among them malodorous, poisonous insects, constrictors sometimes growing to a length of twelve feet, huge centipedes which, scurrying across a man's flesh, could leave a trail of rash and huge, furry, red spiders which fell from trees to land sprawling on a man's helmet. Even the vegetation was an adversary. Numberless roots and vines grew across the trails to trip the unwary, and from treacherous tree bark or poisonous weeds came infections so painful that they could only be soothed by morphine.

Nothing could withstand the rain, and when it ceased, the forest dripped on. A pack of cigarettes, though stuck inside a helmet, became sodden and worthless unless smoked that day, lighted with matches kept dry inside a contraceptive; watches recorded the period of their own decay; rain made garbage of the food; pencils swelled and burst apart, fountain pens clogged and their points separated; even rifles slung upside-down under ponchos turned blue with mold and had to be scraped clean. Bullets in the machine-gun belts stuck to the cloth loops, needed to be withdrawn, oiled and reinserted daily—and everything lay damp and sodden and squishy to the touch, including the puckering pulp of a man's flesh, exuding that steady musty reek that is the jungle's own, that individual odor of decay that lurked like a constant presence in a man's nostrils, rising from vegetable life so luxuriant and growing so swiftly that it seemed to hasten toward decomposition from the moment of birth.

With the airfield secured, Rupertus began 1944 by drawing a perimeter around it and ordered his assistant commander, Brig. Gen. Lemuel Shepherd, to destroy the Japanese holding the high ground at Borgen Bay ten miles to the east. Two ridges barred the Marines' path, one an unnamed height, the other Hill 660.

At dawn of January 9, the 3rd Battalion, Fifth, under Lt. Col. Lewis (Silent Lew) Walt, a big, brawny, square-faced man, began a frontal assault on the nameless height. The Japanese, taking advantage of their system of thirty-seven bunkers connected by tunnels with interlocking fire, pinned the Americans down, and Walt called for an antitank gun. It was trundled forward. Walt and his runner put their shoulders to the wheel of the 900-pound gun. "All right," Walt shouted, "who'll give me a hand?" No one came forward and the enraged Walt tore at the gun so furiously that his men leaped to his side to push it forward, firing as it rose. The nameless hill fell and was christened Walt's Ridge. In the morning a fierce enemy counterattack was repulsed.

Now the Seventh Marines took on Hill 660. Enemy fire stopped them the first day. Tanks and mortars were brought up. Covered by their fire, the Marines worked their way around the hill until they discovered an assault route. Riflemen went up it firing as they came, driving the enemy off the height and into the withering antitank and heavy machine-gun fire of a company holding a roadblock between the height and the beach. Cape Gloucester was firmly in American hands.

Nothing was left to do now save destroy the enemy in a series of flanking and entrapping movements directed by General Shepherd, a skillful tactician. Amphibious forces went roaring down the coast to cut off units trying to escape to Rabaul. Patrols penetrated eastward to a depth of 130 miles. General Matsuda, meanwhile, fled by boat to Cape Hoskins more than halfway down the northern coast to Rabaul. Behind him, crawling over the trails, eating native dogs and plundering native gardens, starving and suffering, came the wretched remnant of his 65th Brigade. They had been abandoned. They had been wounded and their flesh stank. Their bodies were covered with fungus infections. Many of them were actually crawling on their hands and knees, for their feet were too rotten to support them. They had little idea of where they were going. When they had no more strength to move, they lay on the trail—waiting. When the point of a Marine patrol appeared, they blew themselves up with grenades. There were others too weak to do this, and the Marines began to take prisoners.

In all, the First Marine Division had killed 5,000 Japanese on New Britain and an unprecedented 500 had surrendered. Many more had been wounded and many of these died of wounds. Marine casualties were 310 killed and 1,083 wounded. New Britain had not only shown how low the Marines could keep casualties when maneuver was possible, but also how well these so-called beach jumpers could maneuver.

Now it was Douglas MacArthur's turn to demonstrate his own daring and tactical skill.

PART SEVEN

1944

78. Taking the Admiralty Islands

THE ADMIRALTY ISLANDS, 217 nautical miles northwest of New Britain, in American hands would effectively close the circle on Rabaul. During January and February of 1944 the Fifth Air Force made regular heavy bombing raids on Admiralty airfields and those at Kavieng on New Ireland to the east. By mid-February General Kenney's airmen reported that they had observed neither AA fire nor troops at the Admiralty airfields.

Actually, although Col. Yoshio Ezaki, the commander in the Admiralties, had no more operable aircraft, he did have 4,000 troops. He ordered them to stay out of sight of American aircraft and to fire no ack-ack at them. Then on February 21 intelligence reported that all aircraft had been withdrawn from Rabaul itself. To this came further reports that Momote on Los Negros was a ghost airfield.

General Kenney at once rushed into MacArthur's office in Brisbane to urge despatch of a reconnaissance-in-force to Los Negros. If there were only light or no opposition, a valuable base could be seized. If resistance were strong, the force could be withdrawn. MacArthur listened intently, pacing up and down with his dead corncob pipe in his mouth. Suddenly he stopped and exclaimed: "That will put the cork in the bottle!"

On February 24 he gave the orders for the invasion to take place February 29. With typical daring and speed, MacArthur had preempted a carefully prepared invasion of Los Negros scheduled for more than a month later. He had also taken a great risk. A fiasco on the beaches of Los Negros could cripple operations in the Southwest Pacific and perhaps end MacArthur's career.

MacArthur took the gamble because he was confident of his ability to make swift reinforcements and counted on the Japanese habit of piecemeal attacks. He was so sure of success that he personally accompanied the task force, going aboard the cruiser *Phoenix* at Milne Bay. His top commanders—from Krueger to Vice Adm. Daniel E. Barbey—were flabbergasted by what seemed a rash decision. Barbey later guessed that MacArthur came along because "he wanted to be present when the decision had to be made whether to continue the assault or withdraw." Krueger argued that "it was unnecessary and unwise to expose himself in this fashion and that it would be a calamity if anything happened to him." MacArthur thanked him with his customary courtesy and said, "I have to go."

MacArthur was on deck the morning of the 29th when the 1st Cavalry Brigade's first waves clambered out of their destroyer-transports and hit the beaches of Hyane Harbor in their landing boats. Japanese 20-mm batteries raked them, but were promptly silenced by the guns of *Phoenix* and other gunfire ships. MacArthur was amazed at their accuracy and became an instant convert to naval bombardment. In the words of Admiral Kinkaid: "He became more royalist than the King."

Five hours after the landings began at eight o'clock, the Americans had captured Momote airfield. There had been little fighting: four troopers dead and six wounded against six enemy dead. But large amounts of abandoned supplies and equipment suggested that there was a numerous enemy somewhere on Los Negros. There was. Guessing wrong that the Hyane Harbor invasion was a feint, Colonel Ezaki had concentrated his troops on the northern side of Los Negros, where he believed the main blow would come.

MacArthur insisted on going ashore, and now, probably, the real reason for his joining the task force became apparent: he wanted to bury for good and all that unjust "Dugout Doug" nickname hung on him at Corregidor two years previously. Scorning helmet and weapon, wearing only his theatrically squashed and braided hat, he strolled casually toward the front to "see what's happening" in the combat area. An anxious cavalry officer touched his sleeve. Pointing to an area fifty yards ahead, he said: "Excuse me, sir, but we killed a Jap sniper in there just a few minutes ago." MacArthur continued to walk in that direction. "Fine," he said, "that's the best thing to do with them."

MacArthur's calm amazed his officers, some of whom later admitted that they wished they were accompanying someone else, but it inspired his soldiery. They fought with great verve against the Japanese whom Ezaki sent against them in the piecemeal attacks MacArthur had anticipated.

With reinforcements that arrived on March 2, the Americans rapidly overran Los Negros. On March 15–19 another brigade from the 1st Cavalry Division landed west of Lorengau on Manus and quickly captured that last pocket of enemy resistance in the Admiralties. By the end of March the Admiralties were in American hands. Momote airfield was in use by then and a new airfield better than Lorengau was being constructed. Seeadler Harbor at Manus would eventually become an excellent anchorage.

By jumping to Rabaul MacArthur had bypassed Kavieng on New Ireland and Wewak and Hansa Bay on New Guinea—and some 40,000 Japanese troops. The Joint Chiefs were impressed, and authorized him to go ahead with the risky 580-mile giant leap up the New Guinea coast to Hollandia.* By then Halsey had easily taken Emirau in the St. Matthias Islands and the days of Rabaul, that once mighty and dreaded enemy bastion, had been numbered.

Lucky lay in an army hospital at Cape Sudest in New Guinea while the fires of malaria ravaged his body. He had been evacuated by plane from New Britain suffering from varicose swelling that made it painful to walk. But the army doctors feared that the required operation would not heal in the tropics. "Okay,"

---

*Jayapura, Irian Jaya, Indonesia.

Lucky had said, "send me back to the States, then." The doctors shook their heads. "No way," one of them said. "Marines don't go home unless they're carried home."

So Lucky awaited transportation back to New Britain. But that night he came down with what was more likely dengue fever than malaria. Lucky had had malaria before but nothing like this bone-breaking fever. To lie on his back was torture, to lie on his stomach a torment. It was as though his bones were in the grip of a giant vise which someone was slowly turning . . . turning. . . . He could not eat or drink—not even hold water. For with the fever had come yellow jaundice and his liver was so distended that a single sip of water had him retching bitter bile. He was fed intravenously for two weeks. If he had been anywhere else but a hospital, he probably would have died, but it was in a hospital that he had been afflicted; probably by a dirty needle. For days he lay baking in the malarial oven, drifting in and out of consciousness like a boat in a fog. He could hear people talking and moving around him, the touch of the nurse's fingers rubbing the blessedly cool but fleeting balm of alcohol on his back, but comprehending nothing. His body was like a bag of aching bones and he yearned for a trickle of sweat to seep from his desiccated flesh.

Then the fever broke. Sweat poured from his pores like a blessed balm. Lucky wanted to laugh or sing, but he had not the strength. The sweat soaked his cot and the nurse moved him to another one which also became sodden. Then came the chills. His body shook uncontrollably. But the shivers made him want to laugh again. It was well over 100 degrees at Cape Sudest but the nurses kept piling blankets on top of his shaking body. At last Lucky had the power of speech again. "It feels so good," he murmured, shivering, "it feels so good."

Gen. Alexander Vandegrift had chosen Cape Torokina for the Bougainville landings because he calculated that it would be three months before Lt. Gen. Haruyoshi Hyakutake's scattered units could march through the island's dense jungle to an assembly area outside the American perimeter. Actually, it took four months. Coming from every direction, hauling field pieces by ropes, carrying artillery shells by hand, the Japanese toiled painfully over Bougainville's green-black mountain peaks. When they had assembled outside the line held by the soldiers of General Griswold's XIV Corps, they were 15,000 strong—but weary from their march. By March 8, 1944, they were ready.

With his old bad habits, Hyakutake underestimated enemy strength at only one division. Actually, General Griswold had two—the 37th and Americal—plus enough support troops to give him a force of 62,000. Thus outnumbered 4 to 1 and on the more vulnerable assault, Hyakutake still believed that he could pierce the American line, destroy the airfields and drive the enemy into the bay. His plan also included the customary detail of when and where Griswold should surrender his sword. Finally, to inspire his troops, he circulated among them a poem written by Lt. Gen. Masatame Kanda, commander of the 6th Infantry Division. It read:

To avenge our mortification since Guadalcanal
Will be our duty true and supreme.
Strike, strike and strike again,
Until our enemy is humbled forevermore.
Brighten with the blood of American devils
The color of the renowned insignia on our arms.
The cry of our victory at Torokina Bay
Shall resound to the shores of our beloved Nippon.
We are invincible! . . .

On March 8 Hyakutake's men fired the opening rounds of the greatest Japanese artillery concentration of the Pacific War. The barrage drove most of the airplanes off the airfields. But the ground attack that followed achieved only a shallow salient into a steep slope called Hill 700 held by the 37th Infantry Division. The Americans counterattacked, but it took three days of fierce fighting to dislodge the enemy from his bulge. Another savage fight raged on the Americal front at an outpost called Hill 260, about 300 yards east of the main perimeter. Here the Japanese seized one of two peaks called North and South Knob. The Americans still holding North Knob launched repeated counterattacks but were repulsed each time. Pulling back, they called for artillery, and some 10,000 rounds were dropped on the Japanese. They withdrew, leaving 560 dead behind them.

Another thrust on March 11 at the American center made only slight gains. Soldiers of the 37th supported by tanks restored the line. Withdrawing his troops from Hills 260 and 700, Hyakutake made one last desperation attack, which was broken up by American artillery. That ended all but mop-up fighting or patrol actions on Bougainville. The long, bloody, toilsome climb up the Solomons ladder, which had begun at Guadalcanal almost nineteen months previously, was over. The Slot was now an American canal. Haruyoshi Hyakutake had issued his last battle order; with the ragged survivors of that Seventeenth Army which he had lost twice over, he was reduced to grubbing for existence in the native gardens of Bougainville.

The securing of Bougainville had little effect on the Pacific War, certainly nothing to compare to MacArthur's Admiralties stroke. But it did cause the Joint Chiefs to issue a new directive for 1944. MacArthur would continue his advance into western New Guinea preparatory to an invasion of the Philippines around November, while Nimitz was to neutralize Truk, take the Marianas in mid-June and seize the Palau Islands in September. Because Hollandia was almost out of range of General Kennedy's fighters, and the Japanese could defend it with their closer air, the Chiefs also instructed Nimitz to provide carrier air support for the operation.

At Hollandia were 11,000 Japanese soldiers but only 500 of them combat troops. All were lightly armed and the command situation so chaotic that leadership eventually devolved on a junior air officer. The Japanese Second Army responsible for the defense of New Guinea had ordered Lt. Gen. Hatazo Adachi to send reinforcements to Hollandia from his Eighteenth Army. But Adachi dragged his feet. He believed the main American strike would come at himself at Wewak. General Eichelberger did all that he could to encourage this mistaken conviction. Heavy bombing raids hit Wewak. Naval gunfire ships bombarded it. Torpedo boats patrolled offshore and Eichelberger's headquarters deliberately spread rumors to the effect that Wewak was next. The ruse worked. Adachi was still at Wewak when the American landings began on April 22.

Complete surprise was achieved at Hollandia and Aitape. The Japanese garrisons fled in panic when the American warships began bombarding. At Tanahmerah Bay the troops were pleasantly surprised to find that the enemy had abandoned carefully prepared fire lanes and half-finished pillboxes in which "a squad could have held up a division." Japanese counterstrikes from the air also failed to materialize. The Fifth Air Force had effectively bombed enemy air power in Northeast New Guinea into impotence.

At last Adachi began counterattacking. His actual combat strength was only about 20,000, of which perhaps 8,000 were trained infantrymen. The others were clerks, service troops, unarmed sailors and artillerymen. Nevertheless Adachi sent them marching on Aitape on half rations and carrying their supplies by hand. Malaria thinned their ranks. It took about a month for them to reach the outskirts of the Aitape defenses, now held by the 32nd Infantry Division under Maj. Gen. William H. Gill. Another month was required for the Japanese to prepare themselves for attack. But they still had only half the small-arms ammunition they needed. By then, the Americans had been reinforced so that five full regiments of infantry—nearly the rifle strength of a corps—and two dismounted cavalry squadrons were emplaced at Aitape.

On July 10 the Japanese attacked. They drove a hole 1,300 yards deep into the American line. Maj. Gen. Charles P. Hall's troops fell back, then counterattacked to restore the line. Adachi now moved around the southern American flank into foothills of the Torricelli Mountains. For two weeks fierce fighting raged around the tiny village of Afua. At the end of July General Hall began his own flanking movements, striking at Adachi's supply lines. The enemy fought with characteristic tenacity. Japanese regiments were whittled to half a company's strength and battalions simply ceased to exist. Most battalion and company officers were dead or wounded. Brave as they were, they could not storm the dreadful American artillery and mortar fire. After twenty-five days of fighting in the Aitape area, Adachi was down to 9,000 men and his Eighteenth Army had ceased to exist as a fighting unit.

Final defeat, however, did not overtake the Japanese until August 1944. By then, Gen. Douglas MacArthur, having entered the Dutch half of New Guinea in mid-April, was already delivering the blows that would complete his approach to the Philippines, and in the Central Pacific the forces of Adm. Chester Nimitz were steadily seizing island after island in the sea charge begun at Tarawa.

79. Storming the Marshall Islands

CONQUEST OF THE GILBERT ISLANDS in November of 1943 had caused the first break in the outerworks of Fortress Nippon. Now, in February of 1944, seizure of the Marshall Islands would start the breakthrough.

The Marshalls sat athwart the Central Pacific about 400 miles north and 650 miles west of Tarawa in the Gilberts. They guarded all the routes to Tokyo. Directly west or behind them lay the Carolines with the monster air-sea base at Truk and the ocean fort of Peleliu. South and west of them lay General MacArthur's Bismarcks–New Guinea route to the Philippines. North and west of them lay the Marianas with Guam and Saipan, the Volcanos with Iwo Jima, and the Bonins.

Japan by now had no real hope of holding the Marshalls. Even though Premier Tojo still expected to wear down the American will to fight, he planned to do it by delaying in the Marshalls while strengthening the inner ring of defenses —especially at Peleliu, the Marianas and the Bonins.

The Marshalls were admirably suited to delaying action because there were so many of them. There were thirty-six true atolls—with perhaps 2,000 islets and islands—in this enormous chain running 650 miles on a northwest-southeast diagonal. They had been in Japan's possession since they were seized from Germany in World War I, but Japan had not bothered to fortify them in any strength until just before the attack on the Gilberts at Makin and Tarawa.

Six atolls had airfields: Eniwetok, Kwajalein, Wotje, Maloelap, Jaluit and Mili. Vice Adm. Musashi Kobayashi, who was in command of the Marshalls, expected the Americans to attack on the eastern atolls, and so began to fortify Jaluit and Mili.

Admiral Nimitz chose to attack the center atoll, Kwajalein.

He chose it because, by knifing right into the heart of the Marshalls, he would bypass the bulk of 28,000 troops and neutralize Kobayashi's work. More, Kwajalein atoll was lightly defended, it had airfields, and its lagoon was the largest in the world, sixty-five miles in length and eighteen miles in width, within an atoll chain forming a shape best described as a flattened pyramid canted on its right-hand base.

A fleet of 300 ships—nearly ten times the force that sailed to Guadalcanal —had been gathered under Admiral Turner to bombard and carry troops to Kwajalein atoll. Among them were one big and ten smaller aircraft carriers and seven old battleships.

To seize Kwajalein Islet in the south and the twin islets of Roi–Namur in the north, Maj. Gen. Howlin' Mad Smith had two full divisions and a brigade.

The 7th Infantry Division would go against Kwajalein and the Fourth Marine Division against Roi–Namur. In floating reserve was a brigade consisting of the orphan Twenty-second Marines and the remaining two battalions of the 106th Infantry. Thus, about 40,000 Americans would be attacking 8,000 defending Japanese, or whatever number survived a preinvasion bombardment planned to surpass anything ever attempted before.

Naval gunfire experts had learned from Tarawa that pillboxes could be knocked out only with direct hits from big shells or big bombs, and that these missiles must be armor-piercing. Old battleships, many of them the salvaged victims of Pearl Harbor, had been found to be ideal for such work. Because it had also been learned that shells or bombs could not take out underwater obstacles and mines, special underwater demolition teams had been organized for this mission. These were sailor "frogmen" trained to swim into enemy beaches to disarm mines or explode underwater obstacles.

Throughout December–January aircraft based on Makin, Tarawa and Apamama had dropped 1,677 tons of explosives on Kwajalein, Wotje, Maloelap, Mili and Jaluit. Carrier-based air also hit these and other atolls with multiplying fury, sinking ships and damaging cruisers, knocking out planes in the air and destroying them on the ground. Seventh Air Force high-level bombers thickened the deadly shower. Next, 6,919 tons of naval shells were hurled against Marshalls targets for three days preceding and during the invasion. Among the bombing victims was Vice Adm. Michiyuki Yamada.

The Fourth Marine Division, brand-new and with no combat experience, was commanded by Maj. Gen. Harry Schmidt, a scowling, dour old China hand who still wore his Chinese sun helmet. With Howlin' Mad Smith he had been a pioneer in the tactics of amphibious warfare, and at the islet of Roi he was borrowing a tactic used by Julian Smith at Tarawa. This was to seize an adjacent islet in order to emplace artillery for the support of troops advancing on the main objective. It was adapted at Roi because a pair of smaller islets guarded the lagoon passage there. Fire from either or both could rake the LSTs sailing *inside* the lagoon with their bowels stuffed with Marines already boated in their LCVPs. At Kwajalein atoll all the LSTs were going to sail *inside* the lagoon, a novel tactic; but at Roi alone there was the risk of enemy fire from these twin specks of coral.

So at eight o'clock in the morning of January 31, 1944, Rear Adm. Richard Conolly ordered the bombardment of them to commence. Carrier aircraft joined in with rockets, and amphibious tanks—those ugly "armored pigs"—wallowed toward them with belching cannon. When a unit of Marines ground up on the beaches in their LCVPs, they found that most of the Japanese defenders had killed themselves. The Marines destroyed the rest and began bringing artillery ashore. At the same time stubby little minesweepers entered all the lagoon passages at Kwajalein atoll to clear them of mines. Aircraft roared low over the Roi–Namur beaches to lay down a covering smoke screen for the invaders. Slowly, like the rising, growling fury of a storm, the bombardment rose to a crescendo.

To the west *Maryland* thundered at Roi. "Move really close in," Admiral Conolly radioed *Maryland,* and the mighty old battlewagon slid closer until she was only a mile offshore. The Marines were delighted. This was the way it should have been at Tarawa, they thought exultantly, and in gratitude they pinned the nickname "Close-in Conolly" on the amphibious commander.

In the morning four battalions of land-based artillery joined the bombardment ships hurling the last of 2,655 tons of shells into Roi–Namur, and the carrier planes struck once more. By the time the Marines hit the beaches not a single Japanese officer of consequence was alive to direct the defense. A 1,000-pound bomb fell on a Namur bomb shelter housing the seven senior officers who had survived the bombardment that killed Admiral Yamada. Namur's Japanese were now leaderless.

On Roi the Marines were able to take the airfield quickly. But on Namur the Marines ran into stiff resistance. They almost immediately lost contact with General Schmidt's floating headquarters. Schmidt depended on information from a Dauntless dive-bomber flying over the battlefield with Maj. Charles Duchein in its rear gunner's seat. A half hour after the 24th landed, Duchein signaled that pillboxes and blockhouses were still standing and fighting back. About one o'clock Duchein leaned out of his seat to examine what appeared to be a huge blockhouse on Namur's eastern shore. Actually it was a warehouse stuffed with torpedo warheads and a platoon under Lt. Saul Stein was already attacking it.

A shaped charge was hurled against one side of the building, opening a hole. Out of it streamed Japanese soldiers. Stein and his men were too startled to fire at them. Instead, Saul cried: "Throw in some satchel charges."

They were thrown in.

"Great God Almighty!" Major Duchein shouted.

Beneath him he thought he saw Namur disappear. His plane shot up into the air like a rocket. Dense clouds of billowing smoke rose toward him. "The whole damn island's blown up!" Duchein yelled.

"Are you hurt?" Headquarters asked.

"Wait a minute," Duchein replied, peering into the smoke. "Stand by a minute."

"Is your plane damaged? Where are you?"

"I'm about a thousand feet higher than I was. But the island's still there!"

It was, but the warehouse stuffed with warheads was gone. Its fragmented ruins were still falling on Marines crouching in shellholes and craters, wondering what had caused that terrible rocking roar. Inky darkness had engulfed them while whole heads of coconut palms, chunks of concrete, bomb and torpedo casings rained down upon them. After the smoke cleared, they saw a great crater filled with water where the warehouse had been.

Lieutenant Stein and most of his men were killed, although one Marine blown 150 feet out into the lagoon was found unhurt. Forty Marines were killed and sixty wounded in the explosion. There were more casualties when the Japanese blew up two blockhouses a half hour later.

In the afternoon the Americans moved through terrain much more difficult than Roi's. Fallen trees and logs were everywhere, providing cover for enemy snipers or soldiers who arose to jump on tanks and drop grenades through the visual ports. At nightfall, the Marines' attack halted and the men dug in.

The inevitable counterattack came under a clear pale moonlit night. It became a man-to-man struggle. Sgt. Frank Tucker lay behind a tree and killed thirty-eight Japanese, firing ammunition brought him by Pfc. Stephen Hopkins, the son of Harry Hopkins. Tucker took bullets through his helmet, his canteen and his field glasses, while young Hopkins received the rifle shot that killed him.

In the morning four medium tanks rolled up to the front to help break the enemy counterstrike with machine-gun and cannon fire. Again, the enemy soldiers celebrated defeat by killing themselves. One of them jumped up on the tank *Jenny Lee*. He produced a grenade, pulled its pin, tapped it on the tank turret to arm it—and then lay down on it.

Enemy resistance crumbled thereafter and within two more days the twin islets of Roi–Namur were in American hands. The Fourth Marine Division on its first battle had buried 3,472 enemy troops while taking 264 prisoners, against their own losses of 190 dead and 547 wounded.

Forty miles to the south the assault on Kwajalein Island had begun. Kwajalein at the southern end of Kwajalein atoll was an island two and one half miles long and about 800 yards wide shaped like an Australian boomerang with one end pointing north and the other west. Because Richmond Kelly Turner realized that Tarawa had not been given sufficient bombardment, he had assembled a huge force of carriers and gunfire ships to strike at Kwajalein.

Heavy rains on January 31 canceled most of the aerial bombardment, but the naval shelling that took place the following day appeared at the outset more than adequate.

Soldiers of the first waves in green dungarees and blackened faces went churning shoreward in their amtracks. It was a perfectly executed amphibious assault, proving what intensive training can do. Maj. Gen. Charles H. Corlett's first waves hit the beaches right on schedule: 9:30 at Red Beach 1, 9:31 at Red 2 a trifle farther away. By four in the afternoon there were 11,000 men ashore. Led by tanks and gunfire from the ships, the two army regiments went forward slowly but methodically. That night the enemy erupted in a relatively mild counterattack that was beaten off.

On February 2 the Americans resumed the advance, again slowly. But with the help of tanks and the gunfire ships the 7th Division's two foot regiments cleared the island in four days.

Kwajalein atoll was a valuable victory. The world's largest lagoon had been seized, and it would eventually become one of the Pacific's great staging areas. The lessons learned at Tarawa had been put to good use. Bombardment techniques were infinitely more effective and casualties much lower: 8,122 Japanese dead against 356 Americans. Next atoll: Eniwetok—"The Land Between East and West."

Eniwetok was truly a dividing land. For centuries the Micronesians had found it a stopping place on their long canoe journeys to and from the Carolines in the West and the Gilberts–Marshalls in the east. Eniwetok was needed for a staging area for United States Armed Forces. Its numerous islets could hold airfields and receive men and within its broad round anchorage ships could find safe harbor. More important, lying nearly 3,000 miles west-southwest of Pearl Harbor, Eniwetok was only 670 miles northeast of Truk and about 1,000 miles southeast of Saipan.

To take Eniwetok, Truk and Saipan would have to be pinned down. Truk being closest would be struck first, and it would be hit by the swelling power of the U.S. Fifth Fleet under Vice Admiral Spruance. Spruance had no fewer than nine carriers commanded by Rear Adm. Marc Mitscher, six new battleships under Ching Lee, ten cruisers heavy and light, three full squadrons of destroyers, plus a special force of ten submarines. All of this would hammer at the mighty atoll known as the Gibraltar of the Pacific.

For years American planners had spoken in awe of Truk, Japan's secret and mighty base in the Carolines. No one wanted any part of Truk—not the navy, not the army, not the United States Marines. Truk was the most perfect island fortress nature could devise and man could improve upon. It was a drowned mountain range inside a coral reef. Its mountain peaks formed the numerous wooded islands within vast Truk Lagoon. On four of these the Japanese had built airfields and on others were naval command and administrative centers. Truk had been safe from surface sea attack because enemy warships were forced to stand outside the coral reef out of range. Assault troops could never cross that encircling reef, if Truk's aircraft ever allowed them to get that close. For years Truk's airfields also had been out of range of land-based American air. Its own land-based air had made American carrier commanders think twice before attacking it. After Torokina and Tarawa, Truk came within range of land-based air, but the flight was a long, long, risky one. After Kwajalein, Truk was open to regular air attack. By early February 1944, the terrible attrition of the Bismarcks and Solomons air battles had destroyed much of Truk's air power. About then, two Marine pilots—Maj. James Christensen and Capt. James Yawn—had flown Liberator scout planes 850 miles to Truk under cover of freak tropical storms. They returned unscathed and with a bag full of the war's first aerial photographs of Truk. The pictures electrified Nimitz's headquarters. They showed the Combined Fleet in Truk lagoon!

That had been on February 4, the day Kwajalein was secured. At once Mitscher's three fast carrier groups went streaking down to Majuro in the Marshalls to refuel. By February 12 they were racing north of Eniwetok to join up with Spruance's enormous Fifth Fleet. But by the time the Americans arrived off

Truk on February 17, the bird had flown. The eight-rayed flag of the commander in chief, Japanese Combined Fleet, could not be found inside Truk lagoon. Nor its ships. Admiral Koga had become alarmed by the presence of the American scout plane and had taken his big ships back to Tawi Tawi in the Philippines. He himself sailed to Japan in 63,000-ton *Musashi,* with *Yamato* the mightiest battleship afloat. But there were still two cruisers, eight destroyers and upward of fifty merchant ships in and around Truk Lagoon, to say nothing of 365 airplanes and those four airfields, when seventy-two Hellcats roared aloft just before dawn and came flashing toward the Pacific Gibraltar.

Forty-five Zekes rose to intercept them, and the Americans shot down thirty of them. One exuberant Hellcat pilot saw a transport plane slip safely into Param Field. Its occupants jumped out and ran for a slit trench. The Hellcat exploded the transport and then tried to rake the slit trench. Fortunately he couldn't, or Maj. Pappy Boyington and his six fellow prisoners might not have lived to cheer the performance of the splendid new Hellcats. The Japanese had been taking the prisoners from Rabaul to Japan via Truk, and their arrival coincided with that of their erstwhile comrades. Boyington and his companions tore off their blindfolds, cheering themselves hoarse while the Hellcats chewed up forty more enemy fighters. They even stood erect to watch the Avengers scattering hundred-pound fragmentation bombs, but when the Dauntlesses arrived with their thousand-pounders, they prudently took cover with their terrified captors.

The Dauntlesses hit everything afloat. Outside the atoll, Spruance in his new flagship, the mammoth *New Jersey,* together with *Iowa, Minneapolis* and *New Orleans* and four destroyers paraded around the reef sinking everything in sight. The Japanese fought back with customary valor, here a destroyer taking on a battleship, there a subchaser battling a destroyer. But the enemy was simply outgunned and outflown. Japan lost two light cruisers, four destroyers, three auxiliary cruisers, two submarine tenders, two subchasers, an armed trawler and an airplane ferry, while twenty-four merchant ships, five of them tankers, were also sent to the bottom. With smaller craft, a total of 200,000 tons of Japanese shipping was sunk. Most of Truk's 365 aircraft were either destroyed or damaged and 75 percent of the base's supplies ruined. Not an American ship was lost, although one Kate did get a torpedo into *Intrepid,* killing eleven men, wounding seventeen and forcing the carrier to retire. With this went twelve American fighters shot down, seven torpedo bombers and five dive-bombers.

It was total defeat, a source of bitter dismay to those Japanese fighter pilots who fought so valiantly during the day taking off, fighting, returning, refueling and rearming and again taking off to fight again. In midafternoon one of them skidded his Zeke into a landing at Param Field. He jumped from his cockpit and sprinted for a bomb shelter while his plane was being made ready again. He passed the slit trench in which the seven American prisoners crouched. He stopped. "I am a Japanese pilot," he said with quiet dignity. Boyington and his companions said nothing. "I am a Japanese pilot," the man repeated. He tapped his pistol holster ominously. "You bomb here—you die!"

The Americans stared at him morosely. Having survived weeks of torture and near starvation at Rabaul, expecting more of it and perhaps death in Japan, they were almost beyond caring.

"With all the goddam trouble we got already," Boyington growled, "ain't you the cheerful son of a bitch!"

There was a momentary pause, and then the rising roar of a Hellcat swooping low to strafe the airfield. Fifty-caliber slugs smacked the coral followed by the tinkling sound of empty, falling cartridges. The Japanese pilot whirled and ran for another bomb shelter, leaving the Americans with another grim joke to sustain them in the eighteen months of cruel captivity lying between the present and the day of their liberation in Japan, a liberation which would bring Boyington the Medal of Honor and find him still the outstanding Marine ace of all time.

Next morning the American planes flew again over Truk, and nothing rose to oppose them. The Fifth Fleet sailed east in jubilation. On that same morning Radio Tokyo announced the dreadful destruction at Truk with unaccustomed candor: "The war situation has increased with unprecedented seriousness," the report concluded, "nay, furiousness. The tempo of enemy operations indicates that the attacking force is already pressing upon our mainland."

There had never before been such an admission. It suggested that Premier Tojo's iron grip upon the emperor and the nation was weakening. Next day there would be more bad news for Tojo and his "Manchuria gang."

Engebi Islet in Eniwetok atoll was falling.

The Twenty-second Marines attacked bomb-pitted, shell-cratered Engebi two battalions abreast. They were met by Japanese crazed by thirst and maddened by the bombardment. The battle split off into small, separate actions. The enemy fought with knives, leaping into Marine holes, or from their own spider holes, lifting the lids after the Americans passed to fire into their rear. The debris of battle inevitably slowed the advance, but by four o'clock the airfield was overrun. General Watson withdrew the Third Battalion for use against Eniwetok the next day. At night, the Japanese crept from their hiding places to rearm themselves with numerous weapons strewn over the battlefield. They launched banzai charges and were destroyed. At dawn, Col. John Walker raised the Stars and Stripes over Engebi while a private blew "To the Colors" on a captured Japanese bugle.

At dawn of February 19 two battalions of the 106th Infantry stormed ashore at Eniwetok Islet. They made slow going at first. Watson sent in his reserve Marine battalion to attack across Eniwetok's waist. The pace of the other battalions quickened. At night, the Japanese spent themselves in individual squad attacks and on the afternoon of February 20 Eniwetok was secured.

Little Parry Islet was next. To bombard it, a reconnaissance unit captured Japtan Islet. Artillery came in and began pounding Parry, assisted by *Pennsylvania* and *Tennessee* standing a half-mile off the little island's beaches. On February 22 the Twenty-second Marines went ashore three battalions abreast. That night their tanks destroyed the enemy's mediums. After naval gunfire knocked out the last enemy pocket, Colonel Walker signaled General Watson:

"I present you with Parry. Request this unit be relieved for reembarkation in the morning."

The request was granted. On February 23 the Twenty-second Marines went back aboard ship, veterans at last. They had lost 184 killed and 540 wounded and destroyed at least 2,000 enemy. Eventually, with the recon boys and the scout company they made dozens of landings to secure the other islets of vast Eniwetok Atoll. Then they enjoyed a brief idyll. They sang hymns with the friendly Marshallese. They stood guard in the bright sunlight wearing only tan GI towels wrapped around their hips like native lap-laps, and they struggled helplessly with those unpronounceable islet names: Ennumennent, Edgigen, Enubuj, Gugegwe, Ennylabegan. When they met and mastered Ennugenliggelap, the campaign in the Marshalls was obviously over.

80. Surviving on the Home Front

By the spring of 1944 the United States, like its enemies and its allies, had also become a "warfare state." But there was one big difference: Its civil population and an astonishingly large percentage of its men in uniform suffered almost nothing in comparison to the civil populations and soldiery of France, Britain, Germany, Italy, Russia and Japan. In the United States, the warfare state was a condition that bestowed an uneasy prosperity on the great mass of the people at the expense of the sacrifice, suffering and death of a relative handful of sailors, soldiers, airmen and Marines.

This novelty was the result of accident rather than design, because the war was two-ocean and global and because internal-combustion engines had conferred upon it an amazing fluidity and variety. Thus the nation's scientific community as well as its young manhood and its industry was subjected to total mobilization. In the military no fewer than 16 million men wore the uniform at one time or another: 11,260,000 in the army, 4,183,000 in the navy and Coast Guard and 670,000 in the Marines, as well as 216,000 women in the various auxiliaries. Yet this great mass of soldiery suffered only 291,000 battle deaths. This is less than half the total for the Civil War and averages out roughly as one man in fifty-five. Such an incredibly low rate is in great part due to a determination to save lives; it is also indicative of how few men actually fought. Except for the Soviet front "fewness" was a characteristic of World War II. If "so few" saved Britain, then it was again so few who fought from American tanks, ships and aircraft or on the mud or coral of the battlefields. Because rotation was not introduced until late in the war, and because seasoned soldiers are an army's backbone, it was the same few who ventured into battle again and again. The same man might also be a casualty more than once, and if the campaigns were new, it was usually the same old ships and divisions that were fighting them. Because of the fluidity of this war, then, and because of the variety of weapons used in it and the vast distances covered, the ratio of combat troops to the number of men in support, training or just sitting on the sidelines was very low indeed. Thus even within its military establishment, the American warfare state exposed relatively few people to the horror of war.

At home, except for the relatives of those truly engaged, the war was not malignant but benign. American cities did not quiver and burn beneath the enemy's bombers, nor was the countryside ravaged as in France, Italy or Russia. At home the war ended unemployment and broke the back of the Depression. American industry performed such prodigies of production that even Joseph Stalin remarked: "Without American production the United Nations could never have won the war." In 1944, the peak year, the United States turned out over 50 percent more munitions than the combined enemy, and actually produced 45 percent of the total arms of all belligerents. In shipping alone, 5,200 vessels totaling 53 million deadweight tons were built, and in aircraft the annual output rose from 2,100 military airplanes made in 1939 to 86,000 in 1943 to 96,359 in 1944. But this was only *half* of the national output, the other half going toward consumer goods. Still secure behind their ocean moats, then, the American people at war were not only prosperous but also able to buy the good things of life. New automobiles were not available, and there was rationing of food, tobacco and gasoline; yet a flourishing black market made it possible for most people to eat well, to smoke and to ride in the family car to a football game or a tavern.

Rationing was also never as severe as it was in Britain, where even labor came under regulation and was treated almost as authoritatively as the military. In the United States, rationing was regulated by the Office of Price Administration (OPA) created in April 1941. As its name implies, it also set prices for goods in an effort to halt the profiteering and inflation which so disgraced the home front in World War I. OPA's first problem had been the shortage of rubber (which Japan had a near monopoly in producing) which resulted in critically low stores of automobile tires. This in turn led to gasoline rationing on the premise that less driving would mean less consumption of tire rubber. The sinking of oil tankers off the east coast by German submarines had also contributed to gasoline rationing, but the tire shortage was the chief reason it was installed in December 1942.

In some parts of the country, especially the East Coast, the gasoline tanks literally ran dry during the summer of 1942. Motorists and even truckers were left stranded. Some stations were "closed" or "out of gas" except to old customers willing to pay a higher price. Gasoline tanker-trucks were trailed by long queues of vehicles, and when they reached their destinations, as many as 350 vehicles would line up for blocks.

Next to be rationed was shoes. A shortage of hides and increased military demands brought shoe rationing for civilians in February 1943. But three pairs of leather shoes a year was not exactly a hardship. In Britain the wartime ration was one leather pair a year, with any additional pairs made of fabric or cardboard.

Food rationing was the most inconvenient and aggravating of all. Sugar was the first item to become scarce. Loss of the Philippines and a shipping shortage, which made transportation of the Caribbean crops difficult, cut supplies of sugar severely. Military demand also reduced the amount available for civilians. Sugar rationing continued throughout the war with consumption only 70 percent of the prewar level. Coffee came next. There was still plenty of coffee in Brazil, but once again not enough ships to carry it to America. All kinds of "ersatz" coffee appeared, brewed from chicory, soybeans or even cracked wheat—all of them awful. FDR's suggestion—rebrew the used grounds—was equally atrocious. Sugar and coffee rationing led to wholesale hoarding, chiefly by housewives, of whatever was canned or imperishable. Even dear old Mom, unassailable as she had been for centuries in her apple-pie fortress, got a black eye on this one—until she explained, "I'm just stocking up before the hoarders get here."

But for fresh fruits and vegetables, people across America started victory gardens. These ranged from farms of several hundred acres operated by war plants growing food for its employee cafeterias to postage-stamp city backyards. It seemed that every backyard or vacant lot in America had a fence around it enclosing a victory garden. At one time there were nearly 20 million victory gardens in the United States, actually producing 40 percent of all the vegetables grown in the country. Some cities had communal gardens in parks or other open lands which they owned. The novelty of growing and eating their own vegetables was a pleasant pursuit in which home-front Americans delighted until the war's end and the appearance of the omni-stocked supermarket. Total production was in excess of 1 million tons of vegetables valued at $85 million.

Oddly enough, victory gardening was encouraged by a shortage of vegetables in—of all places!—the West Coast. There, in the vast, lush Imperial Valley and other agricultural paradises, prices soared to as much as 65 cents for a single head of cabbage or a dollar for a dozen oranges. The explanation was transportation bottlenecks and a labor shortage produced by the flight of farm hands into wartime production. The shortage was also due to the removal of the Japanese-Americans from their farms. They had been so proficient that they raised more than a third of the total California crops.

Of all the austerity programs introduced by the OPA none was more abhorrent than meat rationing. Even though America's pastures and ranges were producing record amounts of meat, the demands of Lend-Lease and the military added a burden of 25 to 50 percent to a civilian demand already swollen by wartime prosperity. Of a total of 25 billion pounds of meat, the military and Lend-Lease took 6 billion.

In the army soldiers were supposed to be fed four and one half pounds of meat weekly, and in the navy sailors consumed seven. This military consumption added to a civilian demand estimated at 164 pounds per person produced a deficit of 3 billion pounds. So it was upon the civilians, of course, that the shortage devolved. Actually, they consumed only about 140 pounds apiece annually.

So meat became scarce. There were substitutes such as horsemeat, which made its debut in March 1943, when 60,000 pounds of this slightly sweetish meat went on sale in St. Louis. In Chicago a meat broker shipped 200,000 pounds of muskrat to San Francisco where it was sold out. Rabbit also was held in esteem, as well as game. Butchers reported difficulty in getting poultry from farmers unless they agreed to tie-in sales of dozens of eggs. Cats were not quite so common in the cities as heretofore, and baby food and dog food seemed to gain in popularity.

Much meat made its way into the black market. After rationing began there was a 75 percent increase in cowhide shipments from unlicensed or uninspected slaughterhouses, with no corresponding increase in meat from them. Although these slaughterers, uninspected by the Federal government, represented only 35 percent of the nation's total, they handled nearly one-half of the country's meat supply. Along with farmers who did their own slaughtering, independent slaughterers were able to divert a significant amount of meat from the regulated market by selling it to friends or local butchers at above-ceiling prices. Much farm-slaughtered meat, about 12 percent of the national total, landed in frozen-food lockers with no ration stamps being passed.

While the meat black market was by far the busiest—and most lucrative—a "red market" in meat also flourished. This was the practice of "upgrading" a low grade of meat and selling it at the ceiling and ration-point price of top grades. Another trick was to sell beef with excess fat, gristle or bone at the top price. Tie-in sales, so common in the liquor black market, were dear to the heart of the wholesalers. In order to obtain top cuts of meat, a retailer had to buy hearts, kidneys and tripe. Some wholesalers completely ignored the OPA and simply sold their meats to the highest bidder and without ration points. A reporter for the Pittsburgh *Post-Gazette* armed with $2,000 in cash was able within three weeks to purchase one ton of top-grade meat without using a single ration stamp. If these had been needed, he could have bought them also—at the going price of $6 a thousand.

Because such a disproportionate share of the meat went to the military or the black-market's affluent clientele, shortages when they occurred punished the underprivileged. Coal miners accustomed to a heavy meat diet were particularly outraged, as much by their low wages as the lack of meat, and they threatened to strike. But it was not until June 1945, with the war nearly over, that the miners' ration was finally doubled.

For the same reasons lumberjacks in Washington State actually did go on strike. Such work stoppages, together with the lure of higher pay in war factories and the increased wartime demands for lumber, produced serious shortages in 1944. A scarcity of paper also arose. To conserve it, publishers of periodicals and books used narrower margins, smaller type and thinner paper. Wartime books were likely to yellow almost as quickly as the daily newspaper.

Meanwhile, the OPA became an ogre and a villain. On the one hand its absurdly complicated regulations infuriated the merchants, and on the other its lackadaisical enforcement tactics enraged the consumer. Many Congressmen cordially hated the OPA, if only because they wanted no controls at all but simply higher and higher prices for their farming constituents. Actually, it is surprising that the OPA was as successful as it was, given its minuscule investigative and prosecuting force. Arrayed against the ubiquitous black marketeers and their conniving consumers were but 3,100 investigators. Each had a territory of about 1,000 businesses. Little help came from the U.S. Justice Department, national, state and local agencies or the courts. Sentences were light and fines ridiculously low. One merchant charged with overcharging $400,000 was fined $30,000.

Eventually, as might be expected, black marketing encouraged unabashed crime. Hijacking became common, mostly in liquor, nylon stockings and shoes. In the West, cattle rustling was revived. Armed gangs descended on the herds like mobile clandestine slaughterhouses. Using sledge-hammers and rifles fitted with silencers they slaughtered the cattle silently. Then they deftly skinned the carcasses and buried the hides in hastily dug holes, loading the beef on trucks for immediate shipment to racketeering butchers and packers in nearby cities. A rancher might ride over his range the following day and not suspect that his herd had been decimated. Sometimes, however, the rustlers were caught in the act and gun battles ensued reminiscent of the old West.

But what, finally, *was* the black market?

Chester Bowles, one of four long-suffering administrators of the OPA, described it as "really any transaction where a sale is made over a ceiling price; or where there is a transaction of a rationed product without passing of rationing currency." But this is to ignore the heart of the matter: *who* operated the black market and *who* were his customers? The answer is that the black market was run by little, independent grocers or butchers or dry-goods merchants who were in yesteryear as decent, circumspect and law-abiding as anyone on the block; and his customers were Americans cut from the same cloth who had been his customers in happier times and who now allowed him to gouge them because they dearly wanted what he had to sell. The impossible demands of an omnivorous military and a work force rolling in the ready cash of high-paid wartime jobs had created shortages which put a premium on items in short supply. Such demand had also demolished moral rectitude. It would have been a saintly merchant indeed who had hewn to the letter of the OPA's frequently naively exacting demands, especially when he was aware that "everybody's doing it."

On the other hand, the phenomenal success of the war-bond sales was a tribute to the American people's faith in their country and their cause. They bought no less than $156.9 billion in war bonds, a sizable share of the total of $389 billion expended by the government between July 1, 1940, and June 30, 1946. When it is considered that 46 percent of the costs of the war were raised by taxation, and the remaining 54 percent by borrowing, it may be seen that 85 million private investors made a substantial contribution indeed. Fund-raising was also expedited by the ingenious pay-as-you-go taxation scheme (the beginning of the withholding tax) proposed by the financier Beardsley Ruml. The national debt likewise soared. It had been $43 billion on June 30, 1940, and six years later it stood at $269.4 billion. Thus the per capita debt had risen from $75 per American at the end of the Civil War to $240 in 1919 to $2,000 in 1946. All but a trickle of this had gone for defense and war, a total of $360 billion of the $389 billion expended.

One of the better features of the war was the restraint exercised by the various departments of the government. True, the old apparatus of alphabetical agencies that had conducted World War I was revived with such improvements as the OPA. But there was no attempt to seize the railroads, as Wilson had done, or to prohibit strikes. Congress also resisted agitation for a bureau that would tell people where to work. Throughout the war Americans were generally free to work when and as long as they pleased, although permission—usually easily obtainable—was sometimes needed to move from job to job. Nor did Congress hang any Joint Committee to Conduct the War around Roosevelt's neck, as was done to Lincoln. Control of the war was left in the president's hands, and Senator Tom Connally of Texas declared: "I am not in favor of Congress undertaking to put on shoulder straps, epaulets, and big hats, and saying 'We are going to run the army; we are going to run the war.'"

The waste, inefficiency and profiteering which would naturally be a concomitant of such a gigantic effort was subjected to the scrutiny of a special committee headed by Senator Harry S. Truman. Hard-working and scrupulously careful not to trespass upon the prerogatives of either business or the military, Truman and his "watchdog committee" were highly successful. Much of Truman's criticism of the military establishment contributed to the unification movement that followed the war.

Because the "sneak punch" at Pearl Harbor had unified the American nation as never before, dissent was not much of a problem during World War II. Moreover, it was a unique American who, for one reason or another, did not wish to see the world rid of Fascism. As a result, criticism was virtually nonexistent. There were even fewer conscientious objectors than in the First World War: a total of 42,500, or less than one fifth of one percent of the 34 million who registered for the draft. That draft, incidentally, was raised from ages twenty-one to thirty-five to ages twenty to forty-four and then lowered to eighteen in 1942. Most of the objectors to it were members of the Quaker, Mennonite and Brethren faiths, which teach doctrinal pacifism. In the main, they were treated fairly, although some Jehovah's Witnesses went to jail because they claimed deferment on the ground that they were all ministers—a tenet of their sect—rather than on a religious horror of war, the only admissible ground. Those objectors who did not wish to serve in uniform as noncombatants were sent to camps to work on important nonmilitary projects. There they suffered much discomfort, but never in any degree comparable to the misery of a frontline soldier's life.

On one occasion only did the nation's desire to defend itself encroach upon constitutional rights. This was during the movement of 80,000 Japanese and Americans of Japanese parentage from the West Coast to inland relocation centers. The excuse for this wholesale invasion of individual freedom—the worst in America since the abolition of slavery—was military security. In retrospect, it does not hold up: all the relocated Japanese and their children were loyal to the United States and the combat record of the American-born Japanese (Nisei) was excellent.

On the other hand, the Supreme Court displayed a strong determination to uphold the right of free speech during wartime. In one decision it refused to halt propaganda to obstruct the draft and encourage disloyalty in the armed services, and in another it threw out government prosecution of twenty-five German-American Bundists on the ground that by counseling refusal of military service, the Bund had merely been awaiting the verdict in a test case on the matter.

America also was highly generous with her men in uniform. A private's pay was raised from $21 monthly to $60, with corresponding raises all along the line, and before the war was over Congress passed the famous GI Bill of Rights, which provided unemployment compensation of $20 weekly for fifty-two weeks for returning veterans, appropriated $500 million for veterans' hospitals, guaranteed half of loans up to $2,000 for veterans' homes or businesses, and gave veterans attending college $500 annually for tuition and books as well as subsistence of $50 monthly for single veterans and $75 for those who were married. The GI Bill was a benevolent and farsighted piece of legislation. It provided the means for millions of youths to make an orderly transition from war to peace, stimulated the economy and created a huge reservoir of technical and intellectual skills.

It is possible that this new American preoccupation with education sprang from an awareness of what science had done for the war effort, for it was in World War II that the fifth revolution—the Scientific—had overtaken modern war. The Democratic, Industrial, Managerial and Mechanical Revolutions had all wrought their changes on mankind's custom of trying to find a final solution in an appeal to arms, and now perhaps the most far-reaching of all was at hand. It was "the battle of the drawing boards," fought between rival scientists—designers, researchers and engineers—in a never-ending struggle to provide their armies with superior weapons. Competition was especially keen in aircraft and tank design, in the velocity of shells, destructiveness of bombs and the accuracy of fire control, guidance systems and detection devices. It grew fiercer at such an accelerating rate that toward the end of the war no new battle was won with the same weapons that won the last. God, Napoleon had said, is on the side of the big battalions, but in this war He seemed to favor the latest models. Probably it was the very fluidity of the new warfare that called forth each successive ingenuity. When General Eisenhower said that the four weapons vital to his success in Africa and Europe were the bulldozer, the jeep, the two-and-one-half-ton truck and the C-47 transport airplane, he was testifying to the fact that this was the communications war par excellence. Not one of these "weapons" had a trigger on it, yet Eisenhower believed that they did most to win the war. In this, then, the multiplication and growing sophistication of weaponry, did World War II differ from its predecessors.

New wars are generally fought with the latest weapons of the old. Thus the tank and airplane, introduced but neglected in the last war, came into their own during this one. But in 1939–45 the ability of the various states to mobilize their scientific and technical skills, as well as to concert them with the military, gave innovation and invention an immediate effect upon the course of battle. Information on flaws or possible advantages detected in combat could at once be routed to a laboratory and thence to the production lines. As soon as the British captured a German magnetic mine, they learned how to nullify it; when the Germans realized the effectiveness of radar, they began to jam it; and two months after the Americans became aware of the vulnerability of Flying Forts to frontal attacks they were fitting the Fort's nose with a power-driven gun turret.

Because the enemy's scientists usually were clever enough to devise a counter to or copy of any new weapon, both sides took pains to keep their inventions from falling into enemy hands. It was a long time before the Americans captured one of Japan's excellent torpedoes, and were able to remedy the deficiencies of their own wretched "fish." But the Japanese never did recover one of America's radio proximity fuses. This remarkable development detonated any antiaircraft shell which merely came near the target, and up until the end of the war it was fired only over water to prevent recovery of a dud. For similar reasons the Americans were mum about having broken the Japanese code through Magic and the British similarly silent about how their Ultra was intercepting and decoding German messages. An elaborate secrecy also cloaked the activity of both sides as they raced to create the most spectacular achievement of all, the atomic bomb.

With spectacular speed and precision American industry seized upon the great secret unlocked in the squash court at the University of Chicago and began to build the massive plants and apparatus to produce large amounts of plutonium. Construction of the first large plant for separating U.235 was begun on February 2, 1943, and the first units were placed in operation on January 27, 1944. Construction of another giant plant for the same purpose began on September 10, 1943, and was operating by February 20, 1945. Work on the first plutonium-production pile was begun on June 7, 1943, and was operative by September 1944. A second and a third pile were in full production by the summer of 1945, producing plutonium on a scale so large that atomic bombs of 1 to 10 kilograms could be made.

In two and a half years time the Americans, again assisted by their British allies and refugees from Fascism, had advanced from a rate of production that would have taken 27 million years for a kilogram of U.235 and 7,000 to 20,000 years for a kilogram of plutonium to a rate at which enough was produced within a few months to end the war in a matter of days. Perhaps in minutes. This greatest scientific gamble in history had cost $2 billion—a truly astronomical figure in those days. Most marvelous of all was this cooperation among the greatest scientific minds drawn from every discipline to which was joined the know-how and unrivaled technical skill of American industry. Equally astonishing perhaps was that this was achieved under the authority of the United States Army by men whose background or convictions had taught them to distrust the military.

Mobilizing industry for national defense and then for war was a complex and controversial task, but one to which Franklin Roosevelt was equal. His old friend turned enemy, Alfred E. Smith, had once said of him: "The Great White Father in Washington throws the alphabet out the window three letters at a time." With this penchant for alphabetical agencies, Roosevelt first created the War Resources Board (WRB) just before the outbreak of World War II and, in January 1941, the Office of Production Management (OPM). Under the leadership of OPM, American production began to shift slowly out of low gear. But by mid-1941 troops still trained with broomsticks instead of rifles and trucks still bore the label "tank." Shortages of steel, copper, rubber and other vital raw materials began to appear. Roosevelt concluded that he could not have both guns and butter and began seriously to curtail production of civilian or luxury items. But war production still dawdled along, and in January 1942, Roosevelt set up the War Production Board (WPB) with Donald Nelson as its chief.

Nelson was a big, heavyset, balding man whose rimless eyeglasses and pink, dewlapped cheeks gave him the impression of being a large Caspar Milquetoast. Actually he was a dynamic, decisive, innovative marketing executive long accustomed to authority. He had just the background for the job. He had been born in Mark Twain's home town of Hannibal, Missouri, and went to the University of Missouri where he studied chemical engineering. Hired by Sears, Roebuck, he became a marketing wizard, yet for all his sales skill he still maintained an interest in science deep enough to enable him to understand such abstruse pursuits as atomic power.

As America's "industrial czar" Nelson had less absolute authority than his counterpart in Britain, Lord Beaverbrook, or even Albert Speer in Hitlerite Germany. But the WPB never awarded contracts or operated factories. Production was always performed by the private sector under contract to the military. Nelson's power to regulate it was in the allocation of vital raw materials, granting of priorities and establishing quotas. One of his first real squabbles in this capacity was when he refused Gen. Leslie Grove's request for top priority for the Manhattan Project. Groves was so irate that he told Nelson that without an AAA rating he would have to abandon his entire project because the WPB would not accede to the President's wishes. Informed scientist that he was, Nelson realized that Manhattan must be as important as Groves said it was and granted the priority.

Nelson also had to act as referee in the squabbles between the army-navy and the big manufacturers. When the army backed by Under Secretary of War Patterson demanded that Lockheed and Douglas be forced to cancel their contracts for between thirty and forty commercial transports, Nelson reluctantly upheld the army. He believed that the manufacturers' claim that the commercial craft were essential to the war effort because they were urgently needed to move increased traffic was not equal to the army's assertion that it had to have aircraft plants *wholly* at its disposal. But he also suspected that the army's adamant stand derived from a lust to dominate.

Labor-management disputes also came across Nelson's desk, and he tried to solve them by setting up labor-management committees in the factories. In the dispute between Big and Little Business he ruefully conceded that Little Business was getting and would continue to get "the dirty end of the stick." WPB's job was to speed up war production, and this could be done only by the award of huge stores of vital raw materials to industrial giants. He also realized that this policy of cooperation would give the giants a greater hold on the American economy, but when he tried in early 1944 to allow small subcontractors to convert from military to civilian peacetime production, the military and big business combined to block the plan. The Pentagon feared a lull in war production might slow the final drive to victory, and big business was afraid of losing its prewar domination of civilian markets.

Conversion was always a sore point. At the start of war production, a corporation holding say 15 percent of the typewriter market was reluctant to convert to making rifles for fear that it would never recover its lost customers. At the end, the same people did not want anyone converting back to typewriters before they did. The argument between craft and mass production was another headache. In general, Nelson had no alternative but to favor mass production, because numbers were just as important as speed. His eye always had to be on the total effort. Thus, he would be compelled to allow certain corporations to freeze airplane design on a new bomber even though a superior design was already off the drafting boards. It simply was not wise to tear apart production lines, thus arresting production, while a new one was put in place incorporating some improvement.

So many Americans in uniform severely strained the labor force. Even with the addition of millions of housewives, older children and elderly men to the work force, unemployment in 1944 sank to 1.2 percent, the lowest in modern times. Competition for labor sent pay rates soaring, from an average weekly wage of $24.96 for production workers in 1940 to $45.70 in 1944. Offers of higher pay caused workers to change jobs frequently. To keep them on the same job the government appealed to their patriotism, and when this failed threatened to put the eligible ones in uniform. Eventually, the difficulty of keeping people on their jobs led to a proposed National Service Act, modeled on the British law. This authorized the conscription and assignment of civilian employees. President Roosevelt was at first reluctant to undertake such drastic invasion of civil liberty, but in 1944 he agreed that some type of legislation was necessary. The House passed such a bill, but with victory over the horizon, the Senate withheld approval.

Even with such difficulties, the American economy rose heroically to the occasion. Under the aegis of the War Production Board and other wartime alphabetical agencies—there were forty-four of them—the production of war goods peaked as early as 1943. This remarkable achievement came in the face of some serious shortages of raw material. In rubber alone, the United States made no synthetic rubber and had very limited stockpiles of the natural material. Japan had conquered most of the rubber-growing areas of the world. Such a shortage threatened to cripple the war effort, but the United States produced 800,000 tons of synthetic rubber by 1944. Aluminum production increased sixfold. Between 1939 and the end of the war 275,000 aircraft were produced.

The war also gave a powerful impetus to medical research. First blood plasma and then whole blood became available on the battlefield itself, thanks to the efforts of medical science and a citizenry willing to donate 13 million pints of blood. The so-called wonder drugs and penicillin were brought to a high peak of development during the war, and with Japan in control of most of the world's quinine, troops in malarial regions were given such effective substitutes as Atabrine. Numerous insect repellents were produced, the most famous being DDT.

These are only a few of the effects which scientism had on modern war, but they are nevertheless indicative of the warfare state's all-encompassing mobilization of every discipline and skill within its purview.

81. The American Fighting Man

IN THE UNITED STATES ARMY one unforeseen and unfortunate consequence of the Scientific Revolution in war was the exaltation of the specialist over the ordinary foot soldier. Nor were the soldierly virtues of obedience and fortitude encouraged as they might have been. By fortitude is meant not only valor but the capacity to endure adversity. There were not enough commanders who understood that the best training for frontline troops is long hikes and short rations. As Napoleon said: "Poverty, privation and misery are the school of the good soldier." This is a hard saying, especially to young men trained to the quest for "the good things of life," but it is nevertheless true. To keep the good things a man must be prepared to put them aside for a time and take up the harsh calling of arms. There were also not enough American commanders who realized that a soldier's pride must be nourished as carefully as his belly, and that any army which snubs its soldiers in favor of its noncombatant specialists is well on the way to suicide. Japan's mistake was to exaggerate the "spiritual power" of her soldiery and to belittle the Americans. If the Americans did not underestimate the enemy, they were yet a bit too preoccupied with firepower and brain power, at the expense of the spiritual. In war there are three, heart, head and hand, and it is an error to exalt any one above the other.

The army was also flawed by an astonishing disproportion of support troops to combat soldiers. At its peak, the American army was a mammoth host 8.5 million strong. But its combat strength was only eighty-nine divisions—sixteen of them armored—as compared with Japan's total of 100 divisions and the U.S.S.R.'s 300, albeit smaller, formations. Eighty-nine American divisions of roughly 14,000 men each comes to about 1.25 million men. With replacements and other combat troops in training, the striking force came to about 1.75 million soldiers. The Army Air Forces received about 30 percent of the army's total, or 2.5 million men. Thus there were about 4.25 million for service, supply, base troops, administration and so on. This figure becomes even larger when it is considered that the Air Corps had an even greater preponderance of noncombatants. In other words, the ratio of support troops to combat soldiers was at least 3 to 1 and probably even higher. Huge reserves of manpower were daily devouring enormous stores of supplies without ever firing a shot. To this surfeit of noncombatants was added a superabundance of officers: no less than 7 percent of total strength compared to 2.86 percent for the German army. Needless to say, most of these soldiers also never heard a shot fired in anger.

To this misplaced emphasis was added the burden of losing "the brightest and best" young men to elite forces such as the Marines, and within the army itself, the airmen, airborne troops and Rangers. But elite formations—shock troops, if you will—do not win great wars fought on land. They may make the decisive penetrations or landings that discomfit the enemy, but they do not roll him up. They may pave the way to ultimate victory, but they do not win it. That is done by the bulk of a nation's armed forces, its army. In the American army of World War II there were not enough of "the brightest and best" of the nation's youth to tip the spearhead, i.e., the rifle battalion. Eisenhower's divisions were going to fight the German army—the most professional and skillful armed force in the history of modern warfare—with the least impressive men America had called to its colors.

To some extent this emphasis on the specialist with its corresponding denigration of the rifleman derived from the ingrained American reliance upon its superior technology. But to a greater extent and for deeper reasons it sprang from America's deep distrust of the military as a threat to freedom. In the United States a military career has never been honorable in the European manner. Among the French, British and Germans, possessors of the world's greatest military traditions, the profession of arms is indeed a noble calling, followed in the main by the well-born. But in America a military career usually has been chosen by the sons of the poor—notably Eisenhower and Bradley—attracted by a free education and the chance to carve out a career without the advantages of birth. The exceptions were a few rich patricians such as Fox Connor or George S. Patton, and Patton has himself declared: "It is an unfortunate and, to me, tragic fact that in our attempts to prevent war, we have taught our people to belittle the heroic qualities of the soldier." It was also a tragic fact that in the U.S. Army a college education or even just a few years of study was a passport to the officer's club. A degree in business administration or modern poetry was more important in the selection of candidates for officer training than those cruder qualities required for leadership in war: toughness of both body and mind, aggressiveness, knowledge of terrain, understanding of human nature, willingness to sacrifice men. Moreover, in the army, work that in the Marines and the armies of Europe was done by sergeants became the preserve of captains. On a military tour with Eisenhower, his aide, Cmdr. Harry Butcher, received this impression: "I am concerned over the absence of toughness and alertness of young American officers whom I saw on this trip. They are as green as growing corn. How will they act in battle and how will they look in three months time?"

Hitler thought he had the answer. "In assessing the military value of the Americans," wrote Albert Speer, "Hitler always argued that they were not a tough people, not a closely knit nation in the European sense. If put to the test they would be poor fighters." This opinion was a natural consequence of his disdain for "mongrel races" as compared to his "ethnically pure" Germans. Hitler's emissary, Konstantin von Neurath, interviewed hundreds of American prisoners captured in the Tunisian campaign, and reported: "Most of them have come over to make money or for adventure, or to see something new, to be in something exciting for once. Not one of them has a political opinion or a great ideal. They are 'rowdies' who quickly turn and run; they could not stand up to a crisis." Hitler read this with delight. "America will never become the Rome of the future," he said. "Rome was a state of peasants."

Although one hardly thinks of the Roman Republic or the Rome of the Caesars as a peasant state, it is certainly true that the Americans were not peasants. Their outlook was perhaps a bit too broad to permit the imposition of absolute regimentation characteristic of European mass armies, especially the Soviet Union's. Moreover the German high command, unlike the perceptive Rommel, never took account of two great American virtues: mobility and knowledge of machinery. It was a rare American soldier indeed who did not know how to drive an automobile. No other race in the world rivaled American mastery of machinery. When to this was added the revival of the frontier spirit provoked by the war, an unprecedented fluidity of movement was conferred on the American army. Vast distances simply did not awe American soldiers; they plunged into the unknown without a qualm. Americans who drove a tank or a truck cared for it with the pride in possession of a cavalryman grooming his horse. Conversely, the German mechanized soldier was usually a peasant who knew little of machinery and cared for it less. As a consequence German armor was frequently worn out prematurely. Thus, the British, Germans or Soviets might put a squad of soldiers aboard a truck and call them mechanized. Actually, they were about as mechanized as a passenger on a bus—externally, but never internally. If the truck broke down, not even the driver would know how to repair it, and the squad would simply climb down and await help. But it is safe to say that as many as two thirds of the twelve men in an American squad would be able, given the tools, to find out what was wrong and repair it. Not until the drive across France was begun would the Germans, and the British as well, be astonished by American mobility and their capacity for swift and bold exploitation.

Much of the German high command's disdain for the American soldier was the result of interviews of prisoners conducted by men like Neurath. But these troops were the victims of the Kasserine Pass debacle. They had had poor leadership from Fredendall on down. They were badly positioned, without supplies or even water. So they panicked. They ran for their lives and threw away their weapons. By the time they were interrogated they were thoroughly demoralized. But then the American soldiers who survived Kasserine were refitted and retrained. They came back, manly enough to be ashamed of themselves. Their junior officers shed their unspeakable casualness, aware, now, that war is not an exhilarating adventure, but a dreadful wearying compound of tedium and terror. Sicily also made the American soldier battle-wise. As Rommel had seen, he possessed a rare ability to learn rapidly from his own mistakes, together with an adaptability unfettered by hidebound military traditions.

It may also be said that the American military in World War II was an "army of surfeits." No other force in the entire history of warfare suffered from such an embarrassment of riches. No warrior ever ate like the American sailor, and after him the American soldier or Marine who was not in combat. Seven pounds of meat weekly for an American sailor and four and a half for a soldier simply flabbergasted both allies and enemies. Even when in Normandy the American soldier received six and a quarter pounds of rations a day, against three and a third for the German enemy. Here was a standard of living unapproached by even the civil populations of the highest societies in Europe. It surely placed an enormous logistical strain on Allied shipping facilities, and when it is seen that the American soldier actually consumed only four pounds of rations daily, at best it was extravagantly wasteful and at worst susceptible to graft.

During early 1944, when American soldiers swamped Britain in a brown flood, their obvious affluence irked their British counterparts. The extraordinary social dominance which they achieved—especially among British girls—was resented. Even the fact that they always seemed to have candy for British children was seen as another sign of Yankee bumptiousness; and the fact that they received three times as much pay—an American staff sergeant earned as much as a British captain—and were thus able to buy up everything in sight or drink every pub dry was only infuriating. Also their fine uniforms. Soon there came this sarcastic assessment of the American soldiers: "They're overfed, overpaid, overdressed, oversexed—and over here."

The camaraderie between the American officers and enlisted men who thronged London's best hotels and restaurants also shocked the British. It did not seem very soldierly, very conducive to discipline. British soldiers, probably because of their country's class system and military traditions, enjoyed snapping and popping, while the Americans hated saluting and saying, "Sir."

Finally, the cold, impersonal character of the Scientific Revolution divested World War II of any glamour it might have had for the Americans fighting in it. Wars, of course, are never glamorous. As Sherman said, they put the glamour in afterward. Nor are wars ever very jolly. Yet there is usually something about a war that makes it seem worthwhile: to fight for independence, in self-defense, for a cause or a crusade, even for booty. However, most American servicemen in World War II did not believe they were fighting for any of these. They were fighting simply because the war was inevitable, and once in it, they had to fight to survive and win. One of Dwight Eisenhower's constant complaints about his soldiers was that "they don't hate the Germans enough." But in World War I the doughboy also did not hate his enemy. Why should the GI? His country had not been bombed and ravaged like Britain or the Soviet Union. His people had not been murdered or enslaved, his wife, or sister or sweetheart raped. GI Joe had come thousands of miles over submarine-infested seas to fight what he sincerely believed was someone else's war. GI Joe in North Africa, Sicily and Europe did not even have the motive of avenging Pearl Harbor that possessed his comrades in the Pacific. In him was little of the lighthearted altruism that had sent the doughboys off to France to make the world safe for democracy. His self-imposed nickname of GI was an abbreviation of the phrase "government issue," and that is what he thought of the army and the war: It was all cut-and-dried, prepackaged, by-the-numbers Government Issue. Every war but his had had a song to sing or a rallying cry. His songs were from other wars, and his battle cry of the Four Freedoms was not very compelling. Noble and idealistic as the freedoms were, they could not move the heart of a man in a foxhole. As Cardinal Newman once said, most men will die upon a dogma but few will be martyr to a conclusion.

Nevertheless, the GIs fought. They had come so far at so little provocation —a splendid demonstration of fidelity to their country that has seldom been celebrated—and by mid-1944 they were fighting so well that the end of this cheerless and deadly chore appeared to be in sight.

82. The Road to Rome: Anzio

THE CHIEF REASON for the invasion of Italy was the Allied desire to draw German divisions away from the Eastern front and to keep them preoccupied when the invasion of France began in the spring of 1944. A lesser reason was the capture of Rome.

The Eternal City was more of a political than a military objective. Its capture would signal the fall of the first Axis capital and herald the inexorable advance of Allied arms. It might also, as Winston Churchill constantly hoped, encourage revolt in the occupied countries. Militarily, Rome was surrounded by useful airfields and was the nerve center of the Italian communication system. Its capture was assigned to Lt. Gen Mark Clark's U.S. Fifth Army, which had landed at Salerno and successfully resisted Kesselring's attempt to drive it back into the ocean. The Fifth moved rapidly up the peninsula's southwest coast—the shinbone of the Italian boot—and took the abandoned though wrecked port city of Naples. Kesselring's decision not to defend Naples was taken by Clark and his commanders to suggest that he would also choose to fight in northern Italy and thus also to surrender Rome. Hitler had indeed tentatively approved this strategy. It had been advanced by Rommel, now commander of northern Italy. Rommel believed that a front across the Po Valley would shorten the supply line to Germany and eliminate the risk of having the position turned by Allied landings to the rear. Because *Der Führer* was disgusted with the Italians and wanted to be rid of them, he leaned in Rommel's direction and even had orders drawn making the Desert Fox supreme commander in Italy. But then Kesselring, commander in southern Italy, countered with the argument that the mountainous south would be easier to defend and to abandon it would bring Allied bomber bases closer to Germany. Rome, he said, was too great a symbol to be so lightly relinquished. The artful Kesselring—"Smiling Albert," as he was called—also played on Hitler's obsessive determination not to surrender a foot of conquered soil. Thus it was his plan that was chosen and himself who became supreme commander. The Fifth Army now must make a fighting march on Rome.

The U.S. Fifth Army was almost as much a polyglot force as Montgomery's British Eighth Army. Of its 100,000 soldiers a little more than a third were Americans, about a sixth were British and the remainder were New Zealanders, Indians, Gurkhas, French, French North African colonials, Poles and even Brazilians. Differences in language, religion and customs multiplied the usual or inevitable difficulties of organizing such a large force for combat. Some of the soldiers from India and North Africa were Moslems who had to be fed a special diet. Two separate supply lines were needed to service disparate American and British ammunition and spare parts.

The Fifth's command structure was perhaps an equal difficulty. At forty-seven, Mark Wayne Clark—always called Wayne by his friends—was not exactly beloved by his subordinate generals. Even the Americans resented him as a brash upstart whose meteoric rise above colleagues much his senior was ascribed to his friendship with Eisenhower. Maj. Gen. Fred L. Walker, commander of the U.S. 36th Infantry Division, had once been Clark's instructor. Under Clark were many non-American officers who measured their battle experience in years while Clark counted his in weeks. Salerno had been his first combat command. Clark also did not have the complete confidence of Sir Harold Alexander, commander of Allied Forces in Italy, nor of Field Marshal Wilson, who would succeed Eisenhower as supreme commander in the Mediterranean. Their understanding of the political consideration Britain had to give its Commonwealth detachments was not matched by Clark, and just because "the American eagle" was the equal of his subordinates in egotism, willfulness and thirst for glory, his dealing with them were not exactly diplomatic.

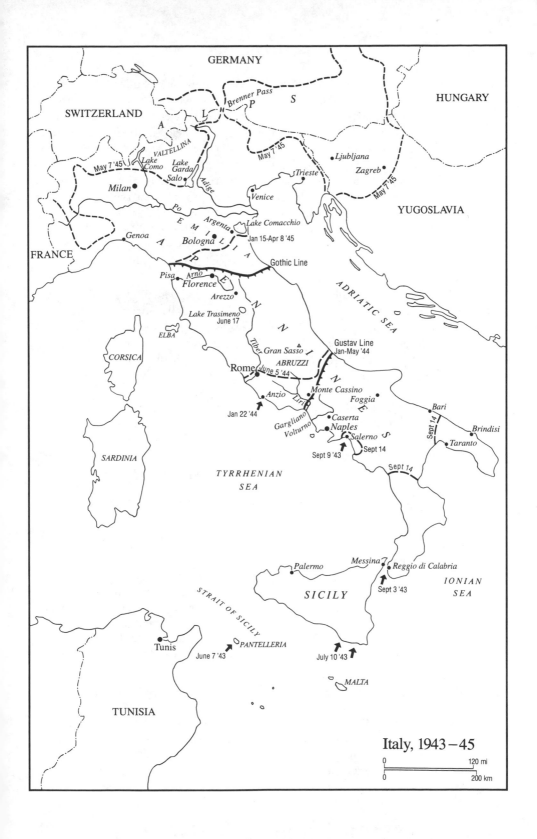

GERMANY

SWITZERLAND

HUNGARY

Brenner Pass

A L P S

Ljubljana

VALTELLINA

May 7 '45

Lake Como

Lake Garda

Salo

Zagreb

May 7 '45

May 7 '45

Milan

Adige

Trieste

Venice

Po

E M I L I A

YUGOSLAVIA

Genoa

A

Argenta

Lake Comacchio

Jan 15-Apr 8 '45

P

Bologna

FRANCE

Gothic Line

A D R I A T I C   S E A

Pisa

Arno

Florence

E N N

Arezzo

Lake Trasimeno
June 17

ELBA

CORSICA

Tiber

Gran Sasso

Gustav Line
Jan-May '44

I N E

ABRUZZI

Rome

June 5 '44

A P E N N

Monte Cassino

Anzio

Foggia

Jan 22 '44

Liri

Bari

Gargliano

Caserta

Naples

Sept 14

Brindisi

SARDINIA

Volturno

Salerno

S

Taranto

Sept 9 '43

Sept 14

Sept 14

T Y R R H E N I A N
S E A

Palermo

Messina

Reggio di Calabria

I O N I A N
S E A

Sept 3 '43

S I C I L Y

STRAIT OF SICILY

Tunis

PANTELLERIA

June 7 '43

July 10 '43

MALTA

TUNISIA

Italy, 1943–45

0   120 mi

0   200 km

Even more formidable than these two difficulties were the terrible Abruzzi Mountains through which the Allies must pass. The Abruzzi cover the southern Italian peninsula from Naples to Rome. From Clark's headquarters at Caserta, they ran 190 miles and there was no way around them. Behind each jagged, rugged hill lay another one at least as daunting. Clark himself wrote: "Each hillside became a small but difficult military problem that could be solved only by careful preparation and almost inevitably by the spilling of blood." Although the Allied air forces controlled the air, they could not prevent the supplying of the Gustav Line, and even their vaunted superiority in artillery was limited or canceled out by the rocky, labyrinthine Abruzzi. During a bombardment of German positions around San Pietro, 206,929 shells were fired, but a party of Germans in an underground bunker in the target area calmly continued to play cards without moving from the table.

Clark had two possible routes: the famous old Appian Way running along the coast of the Tyrrhenian Sea, or Route 6, the equally ancient Via Casilina farther inland. Because the Appian Way passed through the Pontine Marshes, which the Germans could easily flood, Clark selected the Via Casilina. Although its first seventy-five miles from Caserta wound through the Abruzzi, the route then opened on the Liri Valley, from which the path to Rome would be comparatively easy.

Finally, to these three difficulties was added a fourth, the weather. If the prospect of a fighting march on Rome from the south was intimidating in the best of weather, to attempt it in winter was barely short of sheer folly. And as men of the Fifth Army headed north in that October of 1943, the cold downpours of late autumn were already pelting their faces, making seas of mud everywhere, sometimes yellow, sometimes black, and in their rawness hinting at the freezing rains and light snows of the winter that lay ahead. Ernie Pyle, the GI's laureate and among American servicemen probably the most beloved of war correspondents, had this to report of the combat soldiers' ordeal during an Abruzzi winter:

Our troops were living in almost inconceivable misery. The fertile black valleys were knee-deep in mud. Thousands of men had not been dry for weeks. Other thousands lay at night in the high mountains with the temperatures below freezing and the thin snow sifting over them. They dug into the stones and slept in little chasms and behind rocks and in half-caves. They lived like men of prehistoric times, and a club would have become them more than a machine gun. How they survived the dreadful winter at all was beyond us who had the opportunity of drier beds in the warmer valleys.

On both sides of this was mountain warfare at its cruelest. Men fought in small units, often fewer than a hundred, sometimes a handful. Frequently they were isolated from their officers. It could take as long as three hours for one unit to join another only 500 yards away. The danger of shrapnel was multiplied by flying rock splinters, and the roar of the guns was so magnified by echoes crashing and reverberating around the hills that many a soldier would find himself unnerved and unable to fight on. Hot food supposed to be delivered daily to the combatants on both sides was almost always cold when it reached the front. Delivery was usually by mule, the chief instrument of supply in the Abruzzi. Mules were sometimes thought to be more valuable than men, and these poor dumb beasts were often mowed down in droves, or else they fell to their deaths from the narrow paths winding around steep hillsides. Mule transport often became scarce, a shortage which provoked an American sergeant's immortal reply to an officer who requested "pack animals." "If you want pack animals, sir, you'd better teach your men to crap while they walk." If a man were wounded, four others eager to taste the warmth and comparative safety of a field hospital would volunteer to carry him out on a stretcher, thus reducing a fighting force's strength by five. Eventually, both sides learned to have a single man lower a stricken soldier down the hillside by ropes and take him to the hospital on an improvised sled. Thus the Abruzzi fighting wore on through October, November and December of 1943, continuing in mid-January until the Fifth Army at last neared the intermediate objective of the Liri Valley, only to be halted at the Rapido River outside Kesselring's Gustav Line.

The Gustav Line stretched for fifty miles from Minturno near the Tyrrhenian Sea, along the Garigliano River to the Liri Valley, across the valley to Cassino town, thence abruptly upward for five miles along the promontory of Monte Cassino, finally rising still higher into the Abruzzi where it tailed off. Its defense was under the direction of Panzer Gen. Frido von Senger und Etterlin, a tall, athletic, extremely cultivated and charming man, who could converse fluently on the arts and history in three languages. Senger was the child of the petty aristocracy of southern Germany, and had been one of six German students chosen to attend Oxford as a Rhodes scholar in 1912. His education was interrupted by World War I, in which he served with distinction. No admirer of the Nazis, he kept his convictions to himself, rising to top command on the merits of his professional skill. It was Senger's XIVth Panzer Corps of about 75,000 men that had made the U.S. Fifth Army's march on Rome such a bloody ordeal, and now, at the Gustav Line, Senger proposed to stop the Allies cold. His engineers improved enormously on the natural defenses of the terrain, using steel and explosives to fortify the numerous limestone caves in which local peasants had sheltered themselves and their animals. Mindful of Stalingrad, where a city in rubble proved more formidable than one intact, Senger made a fortress of Cassino town by wrecking it. But the keystone of the Gustav Line was the promontory of Monte Cassino, a massive, five-mile ridge rising 1,500 feet to dominate the Liri Valley, as well as the Via Casilina beneath it. And to get at Monte Cassino, Clark must first cross the Rapido.

With the Fifth Army stalled in front of the Rapido, it was proposed to turn the Gustav Line at Anzio, a village on the Tyrrhenian Sea about sixty miles above it. A landing at Anzio might cut Kesselring's line of communications south of Rome, and force him to withdraw north of the city. If not, it might compel him to draw off strength from his right flank and enable Mark Clark's Fifth Army on the Allied left to break through to Rome. Winston Churchill was the most ardent advocate of this plan. Eisenhower was never enthusiastic about it, but then, because he had been named commander of the cross-Channel invasion, he became reluctant to influence a decision in a theater he was about to leave. H. Maitland Wilson of Britain succeeded Eisenhower as Mediterranean chief, and he did not so much approve the Anzio operation as go along with Churchill's advocacy of it.

Anzio was about sixty miles above the stalled Allied left flank, and thirty-five miles below Rome. Anzio had good landing beaches opening on fairly level terrain suitable for maneuver. Good roads led to the Alban Hills some twenty miles inland, and this high ground commanded the entrance into Rome. Seizure of the Alban Hills might force Kesselring to pull all the way back north of Rome.

Anzio would come under the overall command of Mark Clark, who also planned to support the operation with an attack of his own across the Rapido.

The Rapido gains its name from its swift, plunging descent from the Abruzzi Mountains to the level Liri plain, where, joining the Liri River, it becomes the Garigliano, flowing another fifteen miles to the Tyrrhenian Sea. Clark believed that an attack across the Rapido would prevent Kesselring from shifting forces north from the Liri Valley to oppose the Anzio landing. It might even induce the enemy to move troops away from the beachhead, and if the crossing was successful, it might open the road to Rome to Allied armor. The attack would be made by the U.S. 36th Infantry Division, a Texas National Guard outfit, and be preceded by two British thrusts across the Garigliano downstream. The first was near Minturno at the mouth of the river and was intended to draw off troops from the Liri Valley; the second farther upstream was to seize heights commanding the American crossing point.

The first British attack on the night of January 17 caught the Germans by surprise. Minturno was easily taken and a large beachhead established across the river. At once General von Senger appealed to Kesselring for reinforcements. The field marshal sent him his entire reserve—two divisions—a daring move based upon his certainty that no new Allied landings were in the immediate offing. Within three days the new troops evicted the British at Minturno. They also helped to repulse the British attempt on the heights of San Ambrogio across the Rapido. The Germans still looked down the throats of the Americans. Worse, on the Allied side was a heavy minefield a thousand yards wide through which the GIs must pass. Engineers were to sweep corridors through it, and also would bring up the boats for the crossing. After dark the night of the 20th—a daylight attack was considered suicidal—the 141st Infantry's riflemen moved toward the river. A heavy fog engulfed them. They groped their way through muddy fields. At the river, they found that enemy shellfire had destroyed half the boats. Now it fell on them. They scattered for cover, leaving the safe corridors and blundering into the minefields where many were killed or wounded. Still, they pushed out into the river. Some of their boats holed by German shells began to sink. Others capsized. Still more drifted downstream out of control. Only 400 men of the 141st got across the Rapido, and these were eventually isolated. At dawn the attack was called off.

Upriver, the 143rd Infantry fared no better. Hardly a handful of soldiers had reached the farther bank. It was almost certain that they could not advance and doubtful if they could get back alive. At dawn Clark ordered a renewal of the assault—in daylight. He had ordered a frontal assault across an unfordable river into unsilenced enemy guns—in the darkness that usually complicates operations —and now he sought to make good his losses by attacking in broad daylight in full view of an unscratched and confident enemy. The result was foreordained: On the 22nd the attack was called off. The 36th had lost 1,681 men killed, captured or wounded. They would suffer a total of 2,255 casualties in renewed fighting, and the 34th Infantry Division, which joined the battle on the 25th, lost 2,066 men. Eventually, the Rapido was crossed, in part because of the American soldier's tenacity but in greater part because Kesselring now needed his reserve to help hurl the Allies at Anzio into the sea.

A force of 110,000 men—mostly Americans—had been placed under the command of Maj. Gen. John P. Lucas. His orders were to land at Anzio, and if the enemy reacted in strength against him, to take the defensive. If, however, there was a chance for the offensive, he was to move rapidly on the Alban Hills. Such orders leave much to the discretion of the commander, and General Lucas does not seem to have been a very daring leader. He was a professional soldier and a meticulous planner, but he was already fatigued by four months of mountain warfare in Italy and eight days before the operation began he turned fifty-four. "I am afraid I feel every year of it," he wrote in his diary. Again and again Lucas confided his forebodings to his diary. At one point he writes: "These 'Battles of the Little Big Horn' aren't much fun and a failure now would ruin Clark, probably kill me, and certainly prolong the war." At another: "The whole affair has a strong odor of Gallipoli, and apparently the same amateur is still on the coach's bench." In fairness to Lucas, there were shortages of landing boats, the troops assigned to him demonstrated their inexperience during a confused rehearsal, and there was good cause to doubt the success of an operation carried out sixty miles away from support of the main body. Still, Lucas seems to have brooded more over the consequences of failure than to have exulted over the possibilities of success. "They will end up by putting me ashore with inadequate forces and get me in a serious jam," he told his diary. "Then, who will take the blame?"

Yet Lucas's forces were more than adequate when the U.S. Navy began landing them on January 22, 1944. They had taken the Germans completely by surprise and were all but unopposed. An assault force of some 50,000 men and

5,200 vehicles had sailed 120 miles north from Naples and never been detected. What had happened was that Clark's assaults upon the German right flank, especially a bloody attempt to cross the Rapido River, had forced Kesselring to send his reserves south. Lucas had the golden chance to deliver the stroke that might capture Rome. But he did not take it.

Instead of launching a strong offensive toward the Alban Hills, Lucas busied himself building up his beachhead. He feared that if he moved immediately on the hill mass, he might overextend himself and be chopped up piecemeal. But while Lucas waited to grow stronger, Kesselring was recovering from his surprise and organizing a powerful counterattack. Thus began the bitter, seesaw battle of Anzio. Kesselring hurled some 90,000 men, of whom 20,000 were noncombatant troops, against Lucas's 100,000. The German also introduced one of Hitler's secret weapons, a miniature tank called the Goliath. About the size of a big dog, the Goliath was stuffed with explosives and operated by remote control. It was a failure as colossal as its namesake, and the factor that told at Anzio was the dogged valor of Lucas's men, clinging stubbornly to their toehold while naval gunfire in the roadstead behind them scourged the Germans. In this battle also, some of Kesselring's troops behaved badly, one so-called crack regiment of unblooded soldiers actually fleeing in panic to prove, once again, that there are no "crack" units of rookies.

In the end, the Anzio gamble did not succeed. Churchill, with his unflagging faith in such peripheral maneuvers, was understandably bitter. "We hoped to land a wildcat that would tear out the bowels of the Boche," he said. "Instead we have stranded a vast whale with its tail flopping in the water." Kesselring's swift reaction had put the Allies on the defensive there, and Anzio contained was of no use to Clark contained. Worse, having paid such a bloody price to get across the Rapido, he now faced the bristling defenses of Monte Cassino, and at its southern end perched high on the first and steepest hill of the promontory, gleaming gray and yellow in the sun like a sentinel guarding the road to Rome, stood the ancient Abbey of Saint Benedict.

In the year 529, it is said, the wandering Saint Benedict chose Monte Cassino as the site for the monastery that was to become the motherhouse of Western monasticism, as well as one of the most sacred structures in Christendom. Monte Cassino was not only sacred, but also strategic and spectacular. The Italian war college taught that the abbey was the very model of a fortress that should not be subjected to direct assault, and its sweeping view of the Liri Valley was not only breathtaking in an aesthetic sense but from a military standpoint complete. During the Dark Ages Monte Cassino's monks were foremost among the scholars who preserved and added to the learning of previous ages. Music and art also flourished in the abbey. In its multiplicity of chapels and crypts were splendid mosaics and frescoes executed in a severe and formal fashion intended to be a visual counterpoint to Gregorian chant. The Abbey of Monte Cassino was nothing less than an enormous museum of the culture of fifteen centuries. Priceless illuminated scrolls were contained in intricately carved cases, while the walls and corridors were hung with the paintings of the Italian masters of the late Renaissance. To Monte Cassino's own store of treasure had been added much of the art of Naples. After the first Allied bombing of the port, Naples emptied its art gallery and archaeological museum and shipped their contents to Monte Cassino for safekeeping. Some 200 cases arrived, and although they were never uncrated, they were believed to contain irreplaceable artifacts from Pompeii and Herculaneum, as well as paintings on loan for the Naples Triennial Exposition, among them eleven Titians, an El Greco and the only two Goyas in Italy.

As the sound of battle drew closer to the abbey, the monks became worried about the treasure in their care. There was no hope of dismantling the splendid decorations of walls and ceilings, corridors and columns, but the portable wealth of Monte Cassino, along with its invaluable archives, could certainly be transferred somewhere else. Gregorio Diamare, the seventy-nine-year-old abbot of Monte Cassino, had no illusions about the abbey's immunity to the ravages of war. Twice before the Abbey of Monte Cassino had been destroyed: sacked by the Lombards in 580–590; rebuilt in 720 only to be destroyed by the Saracens in 884 and restored seventy years later.

Fortunately, mainly through the efforts of Capt. Maximilian Becker of the Hermann Goering Division, most of the art works were eventually moved to the Benedictine monastery in Rome. Although fifteen cases had been secretly stolen by Goering Division officers, eager to present them to the art-pilfering Reichsmarschall on his fifty-first birthday, for some inexplicable reason Goering did not accept them and the objects were later restored to their owners. Most of the monks also left for Rome, leaving Abbot Diamare with only his assistant, Dom Martino Matronola, and three or four other monks.

Now the great abbey, four stories high and almost as deep below the ground as it was high above it, an immense stone structure covering seven acres, was empty. Even most of its food animals—pigs and sheep and chickens—were gone, taken by the Germans who "recompensed" the abbey for a small fraction of their worth. Abbot Diamare and his handful of monks were now hard pressed to feed a flood of refugees who had fled the wrath of war engulfing their villages or the destruction of Cassino town. Eventually there were from 1,000 to 2,000 refugees inside the abbey, many of them sick and some of them dying. Soon Allied intelligence, along with the Allied soldiery, began to wonder if some of these refugees were not in fact German soldiers.

The problem of the "sanctity" of the Abbey of Monte Cassino revolved around the question of whether or not there were German troops inside the monastery. If there were, they could reasonably be presumed to be fortifying it. Machine guns and antitank guns could easily be mounted in its four-tiered rows of windows. These same openings offered excellent observation posts, the building's ten-foot-thick walls could resist artillery while a headquarters deep below ground would be safe even from 1,000-pound blockbuster bombs. If German soldiers were there, then "military necessity" could certainly dictate the destruction of this veritable fortress. Eisenhower, before he left the Mediterranean Theater, had made this plain in a message to "all commanders" on December 29, 1943:

Today we are fighting in a country which has contributed a great deal to our cultural inheritance, a country rich in monuments which by their creation helped and now in their old age illustrate the growth of the civilization which is ours. We are bound to respect those monuments so far as war allows.

If we have to choose between destroying a famous building and sacrificing our own men, then our men's lives count infinitely more and the buildings must go. But the choice is not always so clear-cut as that. In many cases the monuments can be spared without any detriment to operational needs. Nothing can stand against the argument of military necessity. That is an accepted principle. But the phrase "military necessity" is sometimes used where it would be more truthful to speak of military convenience or even of personal convenience. I do not want it to cloak slackness or indifference.

The Germans, pleased at having scored a propaganda coup by filming the transfer of the abbey's treasures out of the reach of the "barbaric" Allied bombers, were anxious to preserve this new image of the saviors of civilization. Baron Ernst von Weizsecker, the German ambassador, had repeatedly assured the Vatican that there were no "regular German troops" occupying the abbey. The Allies, aware of the Nazi record for veracity, simply did not believe him. Nevertheless, Kesselring on December 11 sent this instruction to General von Senger: "The Roman Catholic Church was simply promised that the Abbey of Monte Cassino would not be occupied by German troops. . . . This means only that the building itself must be spared." Senger interpreted this ambiguous message to mean that he might fortify the surrounding area "right up to the abbey walls if necessary." Devout Catholic though he might be, accustomed to hearing mass at the abbey or to visiting the Benedictine nuns in the valley, Frido von Senger in his profession of arms would seize any advantage available. So he began fortifying the area outside the abbey, even using some caves close to the wall to store ammunition. He also abolished the monastery's "neutral zone," an imaginary circle around the abbey 800 yards in diameter into which no German soldier was permitted to enter. American soldiers pinned down before the abbey for weeks began to complain of enemy artillery fire plunging down on them. They swore it came from the monastery or at least was directed from there. They also chafed at Clark's order banning direct shelling of the abbey, clamoring for it to be lifted. News reports of their dilemma soon began flooding the States. A typical dispatch read: "The Catholics in the artillery battalion would be only too glad to do the firing. 'We could do a job on the abbey in nothing flat,' a Catholic officer said. 'CATHOLIC BOYS ARE DYING BECAUSE WE ARE LEAVING IT ALONE.' "

The American home front was outraged. Military Washington was bombarded with angry protests. "Dear General Marshall: All the stone monuments of Italy, be they 3,000 years old, are not worth the life of one of our boys." Or: "AM A CATHOLIC BUT DO NOT BELIEVE PRESERVATION BENEDICTINE ABBEY WORTH SINGLE AMERICAN LIFE." The White House also received suggestions that FDR, with his eye on a fourth term, was afraid of offending Italian-American or Catholic voters by ordering the abbey's destruction.* The basis of this remarkable outburst was the conviction that the Abbey of Monte Cassino was crawling with Germans. It was a conclusion nourished by the Allied media. Every correspondent who wrote on the subject reported that German troops were using the sacrosanct status given the abbey by Clark to kill Allied soldiers with impunity. But no one in the Allied camp, including the reporters, actually *knew* that there were Germans there. At one point, the Vatican had proposed sending a neutral observer to Monte Cassino to determine the truth of the charge. But nothing came of it. Nor was anything heard from Abbot Diamare, cut off from the world as he was. Lt. Gen. Ira C. Eaker, the American commander of the Allied air forces in the Mediterranean, attempted to verify the German presence. But he was already convinced that it was occupied—"Any soldier would know that the Germans would use it"—when he flew over the abbey in a light plane. Thus the antenna of an abandoned weather station was to him the radio mast of a German observation post, and refugee wash hanging on a clothesline was German uniforms. Maj. Gen. Geoffrey Keyes, commander of the U.S. II Corps, a perceptive soldier who had advocated going around the Gustav Line rather than directly assaulting its center, also flew over the abbey and reported seeing no Germans. So the debate continued, obscuring the fact that if the abbey was in truth a fortified position which by the law of military necessity must be destroyed, by all the laws of military common sense it was also one that could never be stormed by direct assault, not even with aerial bombardment or artillery preparation.

Like Keyes, Gen. Alphonse Juin, commander of the French Expeditionary Corps, seemed to understand that Monte Cassino could not be taken but only turned. He proposed such a movement to Mark Clark back in October, but the American paid little attention to him; probably, Juin thought wryly, because no one had listened to the French since the debacle of 1940. But Juin could remember the carnage of the frontal assaults of World War I, in one of which he received the wound that paralyzed his right arm. He believed that he could get into the German rear by attacking Monte Cifalco high in the Abruzzi on the Allied right flank. He was sure Kesselring had not fortified this "impossible" terrain. If Juin broke through, he could follow a valley into the Liri plain far behind the German line and thus unhinge the Gustav Line. The German position on Monte Cassino would fall without a fight. Juin was allowed to make the attempt, and in the first few days his two divisions fought valiantly, gaining ground into the Monte Cifalco foothills. But then he was recalled by Clark.

*In fact, the Abbey of Monte Cassino was not Catholic property. In 1866, when an anticlerical Italian government dissolved the monasteries, it became state property with the monks as custodians.

83. Breaking the Gustav Line: Monte Cassino

MARK CLARK'S DECISION not to attempt to outflank the Gustav Line was based on his conviction that it would take too long. In early February of 1944, Clark needed quick results. He had been shaken by the defeat at the Battle of the Rapido, and perhaps more so by the bad press that followed. Both he and Field Marshal Alexander were aware of disappointment in London and Washington. Like all commanding generals who do not visit the front to see what the troops are enduring and what they must overcome, both believed that one more strong push would do it. So Clark recalled Juin, and Alexander scraped up another corps from the Adriatic front. This was called the New Zealand Corps, composed of the New Zealand and 4th Indian divisions and commanded by Lt. Gen. Bernard Freyberg.

Freyberg arrived at the Gustav Line with all the force of his explosive personality. Over six feet tall with a splendid physique which—some of his officers suggested with varying degrees of indelicacy—supported a matching brain, he was a national hero at home and one of the largest and most worshiped heroes in Winston Churchill's personal pantheon. Freyberg had studied to be a dentist, but found war to be his true calling. He met Churchill at the start of World War I and shipped out to Gallipoli, where he distinguished himself by swimming ashore to the beachhead. Wounded four times, he won the Victoria Cross, Britain's highest military award, adding more wounds and medals in World War II. Jovial and likable, Freyberg was immensely popular—especially with his men, who loved him for his friendly, joking manner and for the biggest beer bar in the world that he had built for them in Cairo. General Freyberg also had great political influence, which seemed to grow rather than wane after his defeat on Crete. Like all Commonwealth forces, the New Zealand division could be called home at any time, and Freyberg had effectively blocked a move in Parliament to shift it to the Pacific. Thus, he had the power to pull this formation out of Italy. When Alexander told Clark that he was getting the New Zealand Corps, he remarked: "Freyberg is a big man in New Zealand, a big man in the Commonwealth. We treat him with kid gloves, and you must do the same."* Clark now felt himself constricted. Over him were two Britishers and beneath him a New Zealander who need not obey his orders. Also his Americans were almost fought out, and he would have to replace the U.S. II Corps—the 34th and 36th divisions —with Freyberg's corps. "I was the only American in the show," he recalled. Almost immediately Freyberg quarreled with General Keyes, and Clark was soon informing his diary that he was "about ready to agree with Napoleon that it is

*After the war Freyberg became governor-general of New Zealand.

better to fight allies than to be one of them." In this mood, Clark received from Freyberg a request to destroy the Abbey of Monte Cassino by bombing.

Actually, it was Maj. Gen. Francis Tuker, commander of the Indian Division, who first asked that the monastery be bombed. Tuker was a brilliant and aloof man with an intellectual's derisive contempt of less astute men. Thus, Freyberg was "an obstinate dunce," Clark "a flashy ignoramus" and Alexander "an indolent fifth wheel." Like Keyes and Juin, Tuker believed that the Gustav Line should be turned. Once he realized that it was going to be stormed, he began to research the history of St. Benedict's Abbey. He was shocked to discover that it had been converted into a fortress in the sixteenth century and that its walls were sometimes formed by huge blocks of stone twenty feet long and ten feet thick. They had had ten centuries to harden and settle. Obviously artillery could only scratch them and the only hope of destroying the abbey was to drop blockbuster delayed-action bombs from a great height.

When Freyberg made Tuker's request his own, Clark demurred. He was devoted to Eisenhower's directive and had no wish to enter history as the barbarian bomber of churches and convents. His subordinate American generals felt the same. But Freyberg insisted that he could not ask Tuker's Indian Division to assault the monastery without the bombardment. Clark again refused, replying that to bomb the abbey would make it more defensible. Freyberg was not dissuaded by this argument, and he told Maj. Gen. Albert Gruenther, Clark's chief of staff, that destruction of the abbey was a "military necessity." Gruenther also reported, "He stated that any commander who refused to authorize the bombing would have to be prepared to take the responsibility for a failure of the attack."

Failure of the attack. Here was the final clash in an ongoing battle of wills. Here was Mark Clark's head laid under the knife by a subordinate. Clark already had much to answer for: the road to Rome still denied him after so much time and blood, the reverses at Anzio and the Rapido. So also did Harold Alexander, and his head went beneath the knife as well, after Clark—no longer a greenhorn at political infighting—put it there by placing the decision squarely up to his chief. Alexander's reply, quoted years later by Clark, makes clear why Monte Cassino would be bombed: "I would like you to comply with [Freyberg's] request. Remember, Wayne, he is a very important cog in the Commonwealth effort. I would be most reluctant to take responsibility for his failing and for his telling his people, 'I lost 5,000 New Zealanders because they wouldn't let me use air as I wanted.'" Clark asked Alexander to assume responsibility: "I said, 'You give me a direct order and we'll do it,' and he did."

Freyberg's plan was for the Indian Division to attack the abbey immediately after the bombing, while the Germans supposedly inside were still dazed. It was to be made the night of February 14—a daylight assault was unthinkable—and therefore the building would be bombed in the late afternoon. But then the bombing was changed to the morning of the 15th, and that night the Indian

Division was scheduled to strike—not the monastery, but Point 593 or Monte Calvario, the top of the ridge leading to the abbey. Point 593 was not to be bombed, and the assault on the monastery would not be launched until the night of the 16th or even the 17th. Any military advantage to be gained from the bombing was therefore already lost. General Freyberg knew this, but he didn't tell the Indian Division.

On February 14 leaflets were fired into the abbey warning "Italian friends" that the monastery would soon be bombarded and urging them to flee. Dom Martino Matronola, now in charge with Abbot Diamare sick in bed, told his handful of monks to pack their belongings and suggested that they tell the civilians that each should do what he thought best. Some of the refugees accused the monks of arranging for the leaflet as a means of driving them away.

On the morning of the 15th the monks gathered in their refuge beneath the now-empty boy's school. There, in a temporary chapel, kneeling before the altar with the Madonna they had brought from Saint Benedict's tomb, they began to recite the antiphon "Hail, Queen of Heaven." When they came to the words "And for us Christ . . ." they heard above them a terrible explosion.

At 5:45 on the morning of February 15, 1944, 144 B-17 bombers each armed with twelve 500-pound bombs began roaring aloft. They would be followed by eighty-six B-26 Marauder medium bombers carrying four 1,000-pound bombs apiece. After forming formation the Flying Fortresses flew straight up the Via Casilina.

Awaiting them on the slopes of Monte Trocchio three miles across the valley from Monte Cassino—like a holiday throng picnicking in the sun, or a crowd inside a football stadium waiting for the kickoff—were thousands of spectators: dozens of reporters, many of them among the most distinguished correspondents in the Allied media; privates and sergeants, captains and generals; standing on stone walls or perched in trees—all eager to see the show. The entire Fifth Army, it seemed, knew that today was to be THE DAY.

Gradually the murmuring of many motors was heard. The great silvery shapes of the B-17s became visible, their four engines tracing white trails across the bright blue sky. They were in perfect formation, when, out of the bowels of the leading bomber, fell the black shapes gathering speed as they described their parabola. Monte Cassino vanished in a cloud of black and white smoke suffused with flame. Fifteen seconds later the crowd on Monte Trocchio heard the explosions. A great cheer went up. Now as the following bombers made their runs the crowd became as delirious as though they actually were at a football game. "Touchdown!" they cried upon a direct hit. "Bull's-eye!"

Inside the abbey those refugees caught in the open rushed about wildly, screaming, falling, vanishing in the bomb blasts. Those within aboveground structures such as the basilica were often buried beneath collapsing masonry.

Between 100 and 200 civilians—the exact number is not known—died in the B-17 raid and the Marauder attack that followed. None of the monks was scratched. But Monte Cassino aboveground was a pile of rubble, although some sections of its walls were still standing. The great basilica with its sky-blue cupola and monumental stairs had disappeared and the statue of Saint Benedict had been decapitated. In the words of Staff Sgt. Kenneth Chard in the lead Marauder: "Target cabbaged real good."

On the night of the 15th a company of the Indian Division made a probing attack on Point 593. The men were outraged at having been bombed in a friendly raid that had come without warning. "They told the monks and they told the enemy," their commander, Col. J. B. A. Glennie fumed, "but they didn't tell us." Nor had the Germans been bombed, and the assault was hurled back with half the company killed or wounded.

On the following morning almost all the able civilians fled the abbey, leaving behind them the wounded, sick and dying and the few monks who tried to attend to them. In the afternoon Allied bombers came back to Monte Cassino, but they dropped only a fraction of the bombs delivered the previous day. That night the Indian Division again attacked Point 593, this time in greater force, only to be repulsed with twice as many casualties.

On the morning of the 17th sunlight pouring through huge holes in the abbey's tower awoke the monks sleeping there. Matronola glanced up at the ceiling to see with horror that it was sagging and would soon fall. They would have to leave the abbey, the place that was to have been their home for life. A procession formed with Abbot Diamare at its head holding a huge wooden crucifix. Matronola, much taller and stronger, walked at his side to help him over rocks and through bomb craters. Some forty monks and civilians followed. Those who were dying had to be left behind. Others who were sick were carried on ladders used as stretchers. On one of them lay a woman who had lost both her feet. Picking their way through the debris the fugitives came out the monastery gate. They began descending the hill while the monks intoned the rosary and the civilians recited the responses.

"Hail Mary, full of grace . . .

" . . . pray for us sinners, now and at the hour of our death. Amen."

The fugitives were exhausted when they reached the foot of the hill, where a German ambulance awaited them.

General Freyberg had been dismayed at the failure of the Indian Division even to approach Monastery Hill. He ordered two more attacks for the night of February 17–18, one at Point 593, the other at Monastery Hill. Once again, in darkness over unfamiliar terrain, without maps or those grenades so necessary to direct assault, the British, Indians and Gurkhas of this splendid formation moved out. They were greeted with a storm of fire. Two leading companies of Gurkhas sought refuge in a thicket the Germans had cleverly sown with mines. Two thirds of them were cut down in fifteen minutes. At dawn it was clear that both attacks had failed. Some 530 men had been lost, compared to 64 and 130 the two previous nights. Nevertheless, Freyberg wanted to renew the assault, until he was dissuaded by Brig. H. W. Dimoline, who had replaced the ailing Tuker. That same day a New Zealand assault on the Cassino railroad station was repulsed; of 200 men who went forward, seventy returned. With great reluctance, Freyberg called off the attack indefinitely. Two days later German paratroopers occupied the ruins of Monte Cassino.

Destruction of Monte Cassino had harvested headlines all over the world, not only in Allied countries but in neutral lands as well. Reaction everywhere was favorable, convinced as the non-Axis world had become of the presence of German soldiers in the abbey. In the United States Catholic prelates such as the influential Francis Cardinal Spellman of New York hastened into print to support the decision to bomb. No one believed the Nazis' insistence that there had been no Germans in the monastery prior to the bombing. Still less did anyone but Germans pay much attention to Dr. Goebbels trumpeting the theme that the Abbey of St. Benedict, destroyed twice before by barbarians, had been wrecked a third time by the "new barbarians"—the Americans and British.

But the truth was that until after the bombing there had never been German soldiers inside the abbey. Not a single German was in the abbey when it was bombed. A signed statement to that effect was given to the Germans by Abbot Diamare just before he fled his monastery. Yet, for almost four decades the Anglo-Americans continued to maintain the myth of a German military presence in Monte Cassino. Only publication of a diary kept by two monks—Eusebio Grossetti and Martino Matronola—made it clear that *the Germans did not occupy the abbey.* And if this is not sufficient evidence to demolish the Anglo-American deception, why is it that if there were German soldiers among the hundreds of refugees and the half dozen monks inside the abbey, no one in the forty-three years elapsing between the bombing and this writing has spoken of their presence? No one mentioned them because no one saw them.

But it is also true that many Allied officers and men *believed* that they were there. The only soldiers of any rank who were convinced otherwise were Keyes and Clark. General von Senger's decision to fortify the surrounding area "up to the abbey walls" had led everyone else to think that the enemy fire plunging down on the Allied soldiery came from *inside* the abbey, thus giving Freyberg the right to invoke the law of military necessity. To Clark's credit he resisted such pressure until the very end—until Alexander, motivated by political considerations, ordered him to destroy it. True, Clark might have resigned in protest, but that is probably asking too much of any careerist, and it would have changed nothing, while perhaps giving the British the chance to impute all the blame for the slow approach to Rome to Clark. Monte Cassino, then, was not a crime but a blunder, a military mistake made by Clark when he decided to storm rather than flank the Gustav Line. That decision doomed the ancient Abbey of St. Benedict. And the bombing, as Clark and Keyes rightly feared, made the rubble of the now-occupied monastery that much more difficult to storm when the assault was renewed.*

In March the Polish Corps 50,000 strong commanded by Lt. Gen. Władysław Anders replaced the New Zealand Corps and resumed the attack with bloody headlong charges. It was flesh against fire and steel, and the Poles were defeated, just like the Americans, British, New Zealanders and Indians before them. Monte Cassino held out for three months, demonstrating the truth of the Italian war college's doctrine that it should never be subjected to direct assault.

In May a badly shaken Mark Clark at last accepted the wisdom of the flanking movement. But instead of trying the Abruzzi on his right he sent the North African troops of the French Corps through the even wilder Aurunci Mountains on his left. The colonials fought their way through terrain that everyone else considered impassable, and when they seized the high ground overlooking Monte Cassino, the Germans abandoned the abbey. On May 18 the Poles advanced over a silent landscape where bright red poppies grew among decaying bodies, entering the ruins of the abbey to find it empty but for a handful of badly wounded Germans. Monte Cassino had fallen without a fight, just like Rome after Kesselring withdrew even farther north, taking up prepared positions in the Apennines 175 miles above the Eternal City. Meanwhile, the Americans broke out of Anzio and went clattering up the Via Casilina. On June 3 they brushed aside the last German defenses and on the following day entered Rome. With the liberation of the Italian capital, Italy became a theater secondary to the great Channel crossing already being prepared by furious Allied aerial onslaught.

84. Bombing the German Reich

IT WAS THE BRITISH, not the Germans, as is popularly supposed, who were the first to resort to strategic bombing in World War II. The first British bombs were dropped on Freiburg in Baden on May 11, 1940, three months before Hitler opened the Battle of Britain. Thereafter, the RAF steadily increased the tempo

*Monte Cassino was rebuilt a third time by the Italian government. In an invidious half-truth the Italians pointedly observed that it was done without American money, but the fact is that Italy was in receipt of so much American financial aid for other projects that the funds required to rebuild the monastery were thus freed. Today the Abbey of St. Benedict is a great tourist attraction, with streams of buses daily disgorging crowds of camera-wielding visitors.

of its blitz on German industry. Actually, after the fall of France there was very little else that the British could do. Apart from their abortive expedition to Greece, it was three years before they returned to the Continent, and in that long interval they had no intention of allowing the enemy to consolidate and expand.

Neither Winston Churchill nor his military chiefs believed wholeheartedly in strategic bombing's power to win the war on its own. Still, as Churchill said, it was a "well worthwhile experiment," and Sir Arthur Harris of Bomber Command was given a green light.

In the American Army Air Corps strategic bombing was a doctrine central to its being. Most of the leaders of the Air Corps had been the devoted followers of Gen. Billy Mitchell during the twenties, and the Air Corps was embarked on the road to quasi-independence, which was reached when Gen. Henry H. ("Hap") Arnold, chief of the AAF and the army's deputy chief of staff for air, became a member of the Joint Chiefs of Staff.

Unlike their British colleagues, who preferred night bombing because of its relative safety, the Americans favored daylight bombing because of its accuracy; and they adopted the precise Norden bombsight and the tough, long-range Flying Fortress. Some 13,000 of these B-17s were accepted by the A.A.F. between January 1940 and August 1945, and after the Battle of Midway most of them were concentrated in Europe.

After the first American heavy-bomber raid—over Rouen in occupied France, August 17, 1942—the Allied air chiefs agreed that the British would continue to bomb Germany at night while the Americans would strike by day. Thus the enemy would be continuously struck from the skies. Until 1943 most of the American raids were over France or against Doenitz's submarine pens, and the results of daylight bombing were not encouraging. The first really successful mission occurred late in January 1943, when fifty-three of ninety-one bombers reached the target city of Wilhelmshaven and dropped their bomb loads. By that time Churchill and Roosevelt had met at Casablanca and declared the objective of the Anglo-American Strategic Air Force to be "The destruction and dislocation of the German military, industrial and economic system and the undermining of the morale of the German people to the point where their capacity for armed resistance is fatally weakened."

This was a call for all-out strategic bombing, to be known as Operation Pointblank, with the German aircraft industry and the Luftwaffe as the two chief targets. At least this was what Churchill and Roosevelt had envisioned. But they had not reckoned with their air chiefs, still clinging doggedly to the theory of strategic bombing. It is incredible to read today what Air Marshal Sir Arthur Harris, chief of Britain's Bomber Command, wrote to the air commander in chief, Marshal Sir Charles Portal, as early as August 12, 1943: "It is my firm belief that we are on the verge of a final showdown in the bombing war. . . . I am certain that given average weather and concentration on the main job, we can push Germany over by bombing this year."

So confident were these airmen, whom Eisenhower caustically called "the

Bomber Barons," that Operation Rankin was devised to supplement Pointblank. This was nothing less than a plan for the occupation of the continent should strategic bombing, together with dramatic German defeats on the Soviet front, collapse Nazi resistance. It is doubtful if the hardheaded Sir Alan Brooke ever actually put much stock in Rankin, but it is a measure of the naive confidence of the Bomber Barons—especially Harris—that it was even considered. Finally it is even more astonishing that as late as January 1944, when Pointblank obviously was not succeeding, Harris announced his conviction that it would reduce Germany to "a stage of devastation in which surrender is inevitable" by April 1.

Strategic bombing still beguiled the American air chiefs as well. But where Harris sought to force Germany to capitulate by terroristic bombing of its cities, Gen. Carl (Toohey) Spaatz, the American Strategic Air Force commander in Britain, sought to do the same by selective bombing of German industries, especially its synthetic fuel plants. When Overlord was adopted, Spaatz was dismayed. He complained that it would draw off American bombing strength from Germany for two months prior to the invasion, and thus "there will be no opportunity to carry out any air operations of sufficient intensity to justify the theory that Germany can be knocked out by air power." Spaatz's aides were even overheard boasting that they needed only twenty to thirty clear operational days to finish the war on their own.

In the words of its official biographer, by 1944 the AAF was "young, aggressive, and conscious of its growing power. It was guided by the sense of a special mission to perform. It had to justify the expenditure of billions of dollars and the use of almost a third of the army's manpower. It sought for itself, therefore, both as free a hand as possible to prosecute the air war in accordance with its own ideas, and the maximum credit for its performance."

But even with Arnold a member of the U.S. Joint Chiefs of Staff, the AAF had yet to obtain the complete independence achieved by the Royal Air Force as early as 1918. During 1941–1944 when Britain was unable to strike directly at Germany with her ground forces, and after the victory in the Battle of Britain, the prestige of the RAF rose enormously. A vast bomber force had been built during that period and the chance to prove the validity of the theory of strategic bombing came at last in 1944. Each night, up to a thousand British bombers roared aloft bound for Germany. The British populace was heartened to hear of the rain of destruction falling on the cities and industrial centers of the detestable Germans.

In 1943 the Americans appeared with their Flying Fortresses and their own theories of how to make Douhet work by daylight, precision bombing. But the Luftwaffe rose to the challenge. On June 17, 1943, German fighters attacked sixty B-17s over Kiel and shot down twenty-two of them with a loss of nineteen of their own aircraft. This was a defeat for daylight bombing. Another one occurred in August over the Romanian oilfields at Ploesti. Flying from North African fields, a formation of 177 Liberators knocked out 42 percent of Ploesti's capacity, but also lost fifty-four bombers. Most of these losses occurred because the Americans had not developed long-range fighters capable of escorting the bombers to their targets and back. Without protection, the bombers—which were usually only jolted or damaged by enemy ack-ack—were exposed to the swiftly improving tactics of the Luftwaffe.

The German fighters knew where to strike the American bombers and how to attack their formations. They massed for strikes over the target area, usually ganging up on the lead bomber, whose bomb drop was the signal for the others to release. The Germans armed their fighters more heavily to counter the heavy armament of the Forts, and they also tried air-to-air bombing or trailed ropes with bombs attached. Still, the daylight raids continued, and on August 17 the AAF struck a spectacular blow with 516 Flying Forts hitting the twin cities of Regensburg and Schweinfurt. Again there was violent resistance, but the strikes on the enemy's vital ball-bearing plants at Schweinfurt were continued until October 18, when a flight of 228 bombers suffered losses of sixty-two planes destroyed and 138 damaged. Obviously, the daylight raids were becoming prohibitive, even though the Luftwaffe was being whittled, and they were curtailed until December when the long-range P-51 Mustang fighters entered the battle.

Ironically, the very success of the Luftwaffe defensive tactics had compelled the Americans to realize that daylight bombing could not succeed without long-range fighter protection. Thus the marvelous P-51 Mustang fighter was developed. Fitted with long-range drop tanks, it could fly to Berlin and back and outfight anything the Luftwaffe could send against it. After the Mustang came another long-range fighter, the P-47 Thunderbolt. In December 1943, the Flying Fortresses returned to the aerial war.

It was the appearance of the Mustang that signaled the eventual and inevitable defeat of the Luftwaffe. In January 1944, the Germans lost 1,300 aircraft from all causes. The figure rose to 2,121 in February and 2,115 in March during the massive dogfights that raged over the skies of Germany in those two months. Worse than the loss of aircraft was the destruction of Germany's trained pilots, who were being killed far more rapidly than they could be replaced. Now the Americans were consciously attacking targets with the purpose of luring the Luftwaffe into battle to defend them. By June, with direction of Germany's air power still in the hands of the drug-addicted and incompetent Goering, the Luftwaffe had ceased to be effectual.

Meanwhile the Allied Combined Air Offensive was striking night and day. With fighter protection, the American daylight raids had become the most effective. Bombers ranging over the Ruhr and the Rhineland struck telling blows at German industry and particularly at fighter aircraft production. But it did not knock it out. German resilience was amazing. Light industry was dispersed into the countryside or out into East and Central Germany, while workers were housed in bombproof shelters or reinforced cellars or were sent outside the cities to live. Gradually, the Ruhr was emptied of its vitals and transformed into an industrial shell, so that many of the raids upon it did hardly more than convulse the rubble of previous raids. Heavy industry such as coal and steel was not, of course, susceptible to dispersion, and it suffered accordingly. But by September of 1944 most of the industries outside the Ruhr had been supplied with enough coal and steel to continue production. And the attempt to destroy German aircraft did not succeed. In 1944, the knockout year, German aircraft production *rose* instead of falling. The Luftwaffe accepted some 40,000 planes compared with 15,600 in 1942 and about 24,000 in 1943.

Meanwhile, the attempt to break the will of the German people was continuing à la Douhet. In the last week of July the RAF raided the seaport of Hamburg six times by night and twice by day, dropping 7,500 tons of explosives. So many firebombs fell that a dreadful fire storm sprang up and swept howling through the city. Inrushing cooler air, feeding the base of a two and a half mile column of heated air, sucked into it air from outside the perimeter of the fire, increasing its velocity from eleven to thirty-three miles per hour. Soon the temperature was so high that everything burned, and Hamburg was "burnt out." In all, 60,000 to 100,000 people were killed, 300,000 dwellings demolished and 750,000 people made homeless.

Hamburg offered showcase proof of Churchill's determination to make Germany "bleed and burn," but sixty other cities were similarly savaged with the result that 3.6 million houses representing 20 percent of Germany's total residential area were destroyed or severely damaged, 7.5 million people were made homeless, 300,000 were killed and 780,000 injured—and with what result? "The mental reaction of the German people to air attack is significant," the *United States Strategic Bombing Survey* concluded.

Under ruthless Nazi control they showed surprising resistance to the terror and hardships of repeated air attack, to the destruction of their homes and belongings, and to the conditions under which they were reduced to live. Their morale, their belief in ultimate victory or satisfactory compromise, and their confidence in their leaders declined, but they continued to work efficiently as long as the physical means of production remained. The power of a police state over its people cannot be underestimated.

Nevertheless, the strategic air offensive, while falling short of victory through air power alone, did strike extremely effective blows against Germany. If it did not actually destroy the German economy, it undermined it and prepared its eventual collapse. It also denied the enemy fighter aircraft at the time of his greatest need and peril. Goering had gambled that his massed fighter strength could knock the Allies out of the skies in the February-March dogfight. The gamble failed, and the Anglo-Americans in the west were assured of complete control of the air when they began crossing the Channel in June 1944, while in the east the Luftwaffe was powerless to halt the great Soviet winter offensive of 1943–44.

85. Russia Drives West: The Plot Against Hitler

THE YEAR 1943 had seen a remarkable upturn in the fortunes of the Western Allies and the Soviets. Churchill, Roosevelt and Stalin met at Tehran, ostensibly to plan for the reorganization of Europe. Tehran, unfortunately, was an exercise in default by the Western Powers. Marshal Stalin heard not a word—not even one of Churchill's famous "low growls"—to suggest that he could not do as he pleased in Southeastern Europe and the Baltic.

Because of Tehran, a confident Joseph Stalin expanded his war aims from the simple expulsion of Germany from Soviet territory to the conquest of Eastern Europe, the center of which is Vienna and not Berlin. To do this he drastically altered the winter offensive of 1943–44, shifting it to a southeasterly direction both to liberate the Ukraine and to use it as a springboard for the invasion of the Balkans. Thus, the way to Vienna would be thrown open.

In December 1943, Hitler's three army groups were still deployed from the Baltic to the Black Sea: the Northern under Kuchler, the Central under Busch and the Southern under Manstein. The Northern and Central fronts were both stronger than the Southern. They were not only more easily defended by the advantage of natural features, but they had also been held for some time and thus had been fortified. The Southern front under Marshal von Manstein, however, was one huge salient, with its northern and southern flanks exposed to Soviet blows.

The new southern offensive under General N. F. Vatutin was launched on Christmas Eve under cover of a thick early morning fog—a tactic reminiscent of World War I. It overran the German positions on the first day and spread so rapidly that Manstein's counterstrokes were too late to contain it. Within a week the Soviets had retaken Zhitomir and Korosten' and driven even farther south. On January 3, 1944, Soviet mobile forces moving westward captured Novograd Volynskiy fifty miles beyond Korosten' and on the following day they crossed the prewar Polish frontier.

By then Manstein had realized that the Soviets were attempting to cut him off by driving him away in a southwesterly direction. He knew also that he simply did not have enough strength to hold his imperiled position. So he asked the supreme command for permission to withdraw to prepared positions in the west. By halving his front he would save twelve divisions. On January 4, 1944, with his northern or left wing endangered, having received no reply, he flew to Hitler's headquarters to try to persuade *Der Führer* to allow him to make a radical shift of forces from his right to his left wing. He also repeated his plea for reinforcements.

Hitler gave him no satisfaction. He flatly refused to evacuate the great bend of the Dnieper because to do so would result in the loss of the Crimea, thus inducing Turkey to side with the enemy and also increasing uneasiness in Bulgaria and Romania. He could not give Manstein more troops, especially not from the Northern front, because a defeat in the north would cause the defection of Finland from the Axis cause and lose the Baltic. Then it would not be possible to transport iron ore from Sweden, and the vital submarine training areas would be lost. Nor could he transfer forces from the west until an enemy landing there had been repulsed, or until the Anglo-Americans became bogged down in a peripheral operation in Portugal, which he fully expected. From May onward there would be renewed and redoubled submarine warfare employing the advanced new U-boats. By May also the mysterious "secret weapons" would be ready for use against Britain. The time had come, Hitler said, to play for time, in which the uneasy Allied coalition would begin to fall apart, inevitably collapsing under the onslaught of the secret weapons.

As usual, *Der Führer* was indulging in his favorite tactic of overwhelming one of his generals with arguments of high strategy which, if challenged, would provoke the customary and culminating retort that Manstein lacked overall perspective. So the marshal said nothing. But he did return to his oft-repeated plea that a single commander in chief be named for the Eastern front.

"One thing we must be clear about, *mein Führer,*" Manstein said, "is that the extremely critical situation we are now in cannot be put down to the enemy's superiority alone, great though it is. It is also due to the way in which we are led."

Hitler's face hardened. His bulging blue eyes bored into Manstein's with all the will power that they could command. The marshal felt that he had come under the gaze of an Indian snake charmer. He actually felt Hitler's will working through those astonishingly expressive eyes in an effort to crush his own.

"Even I cannot get the field marshals to obey me," Hitler cried in rage. "Do you imagine, for example, that they would obey you any more readily? If it comes to the worst, I can dismiss them. No one else would have the authority to do that."

Erich von Manstein flew back to his command with a heavy heart. He knew that at best he could delay the Soviets with a series of well-timed counterstrokes. But he could not stop them. Hitler, he now realized, was the enemy of the German nation. But to remove him—that is, to assassinate him—would cause the collapse of the German armies in the east, opening his country and perhaps all Europe to communist conquest. This he found no more acceptable than the Allied demand for Unconditional Surrender.

Hitler again had hinted at some all-powerful secret weapon. But Erich von Manstein did not believe it existed.

There were indeed secret weapons in Hitler's arsenal: the V-1 and later the V-2 rockets to be launched against Britain. They were not ready yet, and they were far from being as powerful as the atomic bomb still being sought frantically by the scientists at the Kaiser Wilhelm Institute. But a lack of heavy water had frustrated their quest for the chain reaction. Sabotage of the Norsk-Hydro plant around Vermork in Norway, plus American bombing raids, had so slowed production of that vital element that Hitler finally decided to transport all heavy-water installations and all existing stocks—some 3,600 gallons—from Norway to Germany. Einar, the chief of Swallow Force, learned of this and informed British Intelligence. At a meeting of Churchill and his War Cabinet, it was decided to destroy the equipment and stocks despite the certain danger of reprisals against innocent Norwegians. The Norwegian defense minister in London consented to the operation.

Knut Haukelid, the remaining member of Gunnerside Force in Norway, was assigned to conduct the operation. With his saboteurs, Haukelid slipped into Rjukan on Lake Tinnsjö, where the containers of heavy water had been loaded onto the railway ferry-steamer *Hydro,* for the second stage of a journey to Hamburg.

Carrying concealed Sten guns, pistols and hand grenades, as well as nineteen pounds of explosives in two sacks, Knut and three men boarded the *Hydro.* They heard voices and laughter below. Almost the entire ferry crew were playing poker. The saboteurs slipped into the passenger cabin, where they were discovered by a Norwegian watchman. When they told him they were on the run from the Gestapo, he showed them a hatchway in the deck. Knut and a man named Rolf opened it and descended into the bilge. Standing in a foot of water, they laid their charges in the shape of a sausage under the water. As they worked, they could hardly believe that German security could be so careless. There were SS troops all over the Rjukan valley, but at this one vital point only four guards. Two specially built alarm clocks were linked to the charges, timed to delay the explosion until a quarter of eleven the following morning. At that time, *Hydro* would be over the deepest waters of Lake Tinnsjö. Knut had calculated that an eleven-foot hole would sink *Hydro* in five minutes, thus making it impossible to beach her and salvage her precious cargo. With the charge laid forward, water rushing into the hole would lift the rudder and propeller out of the water. Then railway cars loaded with containers of heavy water would roll forward to vanish in the deep water. By four in the morning the job was finished. Knut hesitated. He thought of taking the friendly watchman with him. He knew that the Nazis had sent the two Norwegian guards from Vermork to a concentration camp. But the watchman might ask questions, might do something—anything!—to arouse suspicions among the *Hydro*'s German guards. Knut could not risk it. With Rolf, he joined the other two who had been covering them and stole down the gangplank. In Oslo next day they read the banner headlines: RAILWAY FERRY HYDRO SUNK IN THE TINNSJÖ

Thus all the heavy water in Norway and the equipment to make more was irretrievably lost, and Nazi science's pursuit of the superbomb had come to a dead end.

At about the same time Hitler lost all hope of producing an atomic bomb, Field Marshal Erwin Rommel entered into a conspiracy to remove him from power. He was recruited by an old friend, Dr. Karl Strolin, a comrade-in-arms from the First World War and now the mayor of Stuttgart. The rape of Czechoslovakia had turned Strolin away from Hitler, and he had been working against the Nazis since 1939. He had been so bold as to draw up a paper demanding an end to the persecution of the Jews and the churches, restoration of civil rights and removal of the administration of justice from the hands of the Nazis. This proposal, tantamount to the demolition of the Party, was sent to the ministry of the interior. Strolin was immediately warned that if he did not keep quiet he would be tried for "crimes against the Fatherland." His name was put on a list of those to be liquidated should any resistance arise in Germany, and his telephone was tapped.

Nevertheless, Strolin persisted in his anti-Nazi maneuvering, giving a copy of the paper to Frau Rommel. She showed it to the field marshal, who was profoundly impressed. His own mind had been working in that direction for some time. Strolin came to Rommel's home in Herrlingen and the two men conferred for five or six hours.

Strolin asked Rommel if he thought there was any chance of winning the war, perhaps by the secret weapons Hitler was bragging about. Rommel said the only thing he knew about secret weapons was what he read in Goebbels's propaganda reports. Militarily, he said, the war was lost—lost from the day Hitler declared war on the United States. Asked if Hitler realized how bad things were, he replied: "I doubt it. In any case, he lives on illusions." Strolin next asked Rommel to try to bring Hitler to reason. The Desert Fox shook his head. "I have tried several times, but I have never succeeded. I don't mind trying again, but they are suspicious of me at headquarters and certainly won't leave me alone with him. That fellow Bormann is always there."

It was decided that Rommel should try, when possible, to explain reality to Hitler. If he could not see him alone, then he should write to him. Failing that, he should attempt "direct action." Rommel said: "I believe it is my duty to come to the rescue of Germany." Strolin was elated. He and a group of like-minded associates were conspiring to jail Hitler and force his abdication. Rommel, they thought, would make an excellent new president of the Reich.

After the conference Rommel returned to France where, under Gerd von Rundstedt, he was improving the defenses of the Atlantic Wall. But his new chief of staff, Gen. Hans Speidel, was already in touch with the conspirators. Strolin had also drawn Gen. Heinrich von Stülpnagel, military governor of France, and Gen. Alexander von Falkenhausen, military governor of Belgium, into the plot. Stülpnagel was on the inner ring of the conspiracy. With Speidel he worked out an armistice agreement which they hoped to present to Eisenhower. It provided for the evacuation of the occupied countries and shortening of the Soviet front.

On May 27 another important meeting of the conspirators was held at Speidel's house in Freudenstadt. It had been called by Rommel, but he did not attend, sending Speidel to represent him. Present among others was Konstantin von Neurath, former German foreign minister and now gauleiter of Czechoslovakia. After Speidel sketched the military situation, Von Neurath said: "With

Hitler we can never have peace; you must tell Rommel that he must be prepared to act on his own responsibility." That was the message which Speidel gave to the Desert Fox at his headquarters in La Roche Guyon.

Erwin Rommel now found himself on the horns of a dilemma; again and again he discussed it with his aide, Vice Admiral Ruge. "To continue the war is crazy," he said. "To what purpose? Merely to make it more certain that Communism will sweep over Europe and bring all the Western Powers down together." But he also knew that he could not attempt to make peace independently until the invasion succeeded. He could not act against Hitler on his own. The troops in the West had suffered nothing like the punishment of those in the East. Intensive propaganda on Unconditional Surrender and the mysterious secret weapons had bound them ever closer to *Der Führer.* Rommel knew that, with the junior officers, they would never rise with him against Hitler. He was like a circus rider balancing himself on two horses, one named Defeat the Invasion, the other Make Peace with the West.

To his great credit, he did perform a remarkable balancing act. He had found Hitler's vaunted Atlantic Wall, guarding Fortress Europe from the Skagerrak to the Spanish coast, a colossal fake. It was built of paper and ink, a propaganda wall, and Rommel went immediately to work to convert it into a fortress of concrete and steel manned by men he had personally convinced of victory.

Virtual destruction of the Luftwaffe's fighter strength by the AAF in the massive dogfight of February-March had conferred the gift of the Russian skies on the Soviet Air Force. Few indeed were the German aircraft bombing and strafing the Red Army as it opened its winter offensive of 1943–44, while the air from the Baltic to the Black Sea was full of Yaks and Ilyushins punishing Hitler's scarecrows stumbling west toward their homeland. Flights of the superior Messerschmitts appeared infrequently.

South of Vinnitsa, Guy Sajer and his comrades of the Gross Deutschland Division had crossed the Dnieper and were withdrawing west toward Romania when flights of Ilyushins caught them in shallow defensive positions dug hastily in the snow and frozen earth. With wild cries of despair the soldiers dived into their holes. Bombs rained down without cease. Sajer found his lips moving in prayer as the earth around him shook and trembled. Air was squeezed from his lungs. Suddenly there was a blinding flash of white light and a terrible roar. Sajer's trench seemed to be lifted into the air. He was slammed against the opposite wall and then a torrent of frozen earth poured on top of him. A terror of the soul seized him. He began howling like a madman. More earth poured over him. Dirt ran down his neck and into his mouth and eyes. He was being buried alive! He wanted to scream but dared not open his mouth for fear he would be choked to death in dirt. Suppression of the effort almost burst his throat. He felt a leg beneath his back kicking and jerking. Struggling to free himself, he shook his head free. Opposite him he saw a soldier with a scarlet face howling wildly. He watched him go into convulsions and die. Somehow he freed himself. Beneath him the kicking man was still . . . inert . . . dead. . . . Two men lay beside him in pools of blood. Another groaned aloud in pain. But then it was still. . . . The Ilyushins were gone. A strange quiet came over the sector . . . and then the night with its terrible, annihilating cold of 20 or more below zero . . . and in the morning the retreat toward Romania was resumed. . . .

Eventually the weather turned warmer, and the snow melted. The Gross Deutschland received orders to clean out bands of guerrillas proliferating in the western Ukraine. Nearing the Romanian border, Sajer saw a dark mass moving over the steppes toward him. It enveloped a group of trucks behind his unit. Gasps broke from the lips of Sajer and his comrades. The mass was composed of 10,000 or 12,000 emaciated and wild-looking German soldiers. They fell on the vehicles like wolves, rummaging through them with howls and animal cries, searching for food and medicine. Sajer could not believe that these were German combat troops.

He followed Lieutenant Wollers as he hastened toward them. Wollers was stopped by a tall, hollow-eyed lieutenant whose tattered tunic, stained with food and oil, blood and earth, hung on his thin body in folds.

"Where do you think you're going?" he snapped.

Wollers showed him his map and the position he was supposed to reach.

"What are you talking about?" the tall lieutenant cried angrily. "What sector? What hill? Are you dreaming? There's nothing left, nothing—do you hear me?—but mass graves, which are blowing apart in the wind."

Sajer was shocked. A German officer openly a defeatist? He stared at the 1935 commemorative National Socialist decoration pinned to his grimy, dust-caked tunic. A Nazi hero to speak so?

"You can't be serious?" Wollers answered in a pleading tone. "You've had a hard time, you're a little light in the head, and you're hungry. We too have been keeping ourselves alive by miracles."

The tall lieutenant lurched closer, his eyes gleaming with hate. "Yes, I'm hungry!" he shouted. "Hungry in a way the saints could never have imagined! I'm hungry, and I'm sick, and I'm afraid, to such a point that I want to live to revenge myself for all mankind. I feel like devouring you, *Leutnant.* There were cases of cannibalism at Stalingrad, and soon there will be here, too."

"You're crazy! If worse comes to worst, we can eat the grass. For God's sake, pull yourself together! You keep going, and we'll cover your retreat."

The tall lieutenant gave a bitter laugh. "You'll cover us, and we can take ourselves quietly away! Tell that to the men you see there. They've been fighting for five months, and have lost three fourths of their comrades. They've been waiting for reinforcements, ammunition, vitamins, food, medicine, God knows what! They've hoped a thousand times and survived a thousand times. You won't be able to tell them anything, *Leutnant,* but you can try."

He lurched toward the mass of human wolves milling around the trucks. Sajer's company put the wounded aboard them. They drove off, away west, toward Romania. . . . Sajer later heard that they had massacred the people of two

Romanian villages and carted away their food. But before they did, thirty of them died of hunger.

In every hungry army only the combat troops starve, while the rear echelons and the higher commanders eat well; and the German army was no exception to this melancholy axiom as it reeled backward through the Soviet Union toward its homeland. By the time Guy Sajer's division had entered Romania, the magnificent but brutal discipline which had held this army together had collapsed. Many formations had disintegrated into bands of stragglers stumbling westward, ever westward, their bellies rumbling with hunger, their minds fixed on the incredible illusion that once they reached Germany, the war would be over. Those who could not accept such monstrous illogic accepted suicide as the only means of avoiding an ordeal ending in oblivion.

Sajer's platoon of roughly forty men was now down to twelve, one of them a replacement named Helmut Frosch. He was one of those boys and middle-aged men that Hitler was now desperately sending East to stop the Soviet avalanche. Sajer had met him when he was in the hospital. He was a gentle, shy youth, an orphan who had worked on a farm before the long arm of the Wehrmacht found him.

Frosch was with Sajer as they trudged through the Romanian hills. Someone up ahead shouted that a truck had fallen into a ravine. Lensen was already climbing down to have a look.

"Watch out!" someone shouted. "It may be a trap."

Lieutenant Wollers joined Lensen while the others drew back, certain that the truck was booby-trapped. Now yells of delight floated up to them.

"A windfall! *Mein Gott,* it's like a whole commissary!"

Now the others came rushing down the ravine.

"Look at that! Chocolates, cigarettes, *wurst* . . ."

"Good God! Here are three bottles, too!"

"So many delicious things," Frosch said in his dreamy voice. "Let's all grab everything we can. We can share it out later, on the road."

Frosch and another soldier took all they could carry and climbed back up to the road. They said they would keep watch. Below, the others loaded themselves down. Suddenly the two lookouts cried, *"Achtung!"* and they heard the roar of a motorcycle. Veteran soldiers that they were, the others vanished into the underbrush. They could hear shouting above them and guessed with sinking hearts that the lookouts had been caught.

"We might as well eat," said Lieutenant Wollers. "I've had enough of giving orders, and sweating, and shitting in my pants like a baby when I'm scared. So let's get started. If we're going to die for it, all the more reason for us to fill our bellies while we can."

They began gorging themselves. They knew that if they were caught with such officer's delicacies in their packs they would be in trouble.

"Let's eat it all," someone said. "They won't slit us open to see what's inside, but it would be just like those bastards to check our shit."

An hour later they climbed back to the road. They commandeered horse-drawn wagons and rode into a village. Next morning they passed a majestic tree with what appeared to be two sacks hanging from its limbs. They stopped and saw Frosch and the other soldier dangling from ropes.

"Don't worry, Frosch," Hals whispered. "We ate it all."

Sajer wept. Other men turned away. Sajer read the placard tied to Frosch's broken neck:

"I AM A THIEF AND A TRAITOR TO MY COUNTRY."

When Marshal von Manstein returned to the Southern front, he found that he must abandon Belaya Tserkov' and Berdichev and fall back on the Bug River and Vinnitsa to cover the chief lateral railroad between Odessa and Warsaw. Here he threw in reserves but was unable to force Vatutin back. The Soviets then drove farther west, capturing the Polish communications center of Rovno on February 5, 1944.

Farther south Vatutin's left wing was merging with Marshal Ivan Konev's right wing to pinch off 60,000 Germans in the Korsun' pocket between Soviet bridgeheads at Kiev and Cherkassy. Hitler's adamant stand-where-you-are orders had left them clinging to forward positions on the Dnieper. Only 30,000 Germans escaped, but without their equipment. Still farther south Nikopol' had to be abandoned. Gradually, inexorably, the Soviet steamroller was grinding down Manstein's enormous and indefensible Dnieper salient.

The deep bulges that they had made in the salient had extended the frontage that the Germans had to cover. Hitler's inflexible principle of holding all captured soil made it impossible to shorten the front by straightening it. The price for such rigidity was a much larger retreat than would have been necessary two months earlier. And that retreat widened and grew faster like a spreading flood. German troops were discouraged by the very size and persistence of the Soviet offensive. The Soviets did not seem to be bothered by supply problems. In the U.S.S.R., at least, they could live where a Western army would have died of hunger. Where a Western army would pause to regroup or wait for communications to be restored, the Soviets flowed on. They were like the tireless riders of Genghis Khan, who had galloped over the same steppes into Hungary. Mounted themselves, they rode in vast hordes behind their tank spearheads. On their backs were sacks stuffed with dry bread crusts and raw vegetables collected from the fields and villages. Their horses lived on straw eaten from the thatched roofs of the isbas. In this primitive, scrounging fashion, the Soviet Union's hardy soldiers could sustain an offensive for three weeks; and when Hitler dismissed Manstein in April of 1944, all hope of checking the flow of this inexorable tide diminished. Germany's greatest strategist had left the war.

86. Leningrad: Lifting the Siege

LAKE LADOGA above Leningrad is the largest in Europe. It is 125 miles long and nearly eighty miles wide at its widest point, more than 700 feet in depth at its deepest and from 60 to 150 feet in the shallow Shlisselburg Gulf at the southern or Leningrad end. Here there was an old branch railroad that could bring supplies into the city. From Leningrad the Ice Road would run twenty to thirty miles over the frozen lake to the old abandoned land road on the eastern shore and thence 220 miles to Novaya Ladoga in the northeast. This was one of the ancient forest tracks of Russia, winding through tamarack swamps, cranberry bogs, little lakes and dense timber. To those familiar with it, it did not seem possible to build a passable road over such a tortuous route in the dead of a Russian winter, and this one apparently the worst ever. But there was no alternative: Build the road or die. The trickle of supplies now coming into Leningrad by air was far too little to replenish the city's dwindling food stocks. In two weeks there would be nothing to eat. So a labor force of peasants, collective farmers, Red Army rear-echelon troops and anyone else unfortunate enough to be impressed into service was set to work on the land route, while in Leningrad a scientist concluded that a minimum of 8 inches of ice was needed to support truck convoys.

Normally, such thickness did not begin to form until November 19, and sometimes as late as early January. Now Leningraders who had regarded the unseasonable cold as an enemy looked upon it as a savior. On November 10 aerial reconnaissance pilots reported that ice was beginning to form in the southern gulf except for one large body of open water cutting across the projected route. But on the 15th a north wind appeared and the open water began to freeze. Soon the temperature had dropped to 8 degrees above zero and was still falling. On November 17 the ice was 4 inches thick, just enough to support a man. On the night of November 19 the desperate Leningrad Military Council at Zhdanov's urging decreed that the ice road must be opened immediately. Capt. Mikhail Murov and the men and horses of his transport regiment were ordered to the bomb-cratered village of Kokkorevo on Ladoga's frozen shore. Twenty to thirty miles across the lake, depending upon the number of detours around open water, was the little port of Kobona—full of supplies awaiting the arrival of Murov's caravan.

Murov was certain that his men could make the trek, even though they were shivering in lightweight jackets and the thermometer stood at zero, but he was not sure of the horses. They were so shriveled and thin it was possible to count their bones. They might make it to Kobona pulling empty sledges, but unless there was hay or oats on the other side, they could never haul loaded ones. Just before the caravan of 350 drivers started out, a commissar arrived from Leningrad. He told Murov that the ration in Leningrad had been cut for the twentieth time to a little more than half a pound of bread daily for workers and half of that for everyone else.

"There are supplies in the city for two more days," said the commissar. "After that there is nothing more. The ice is very young and not very strong. But we can't wait. Each hour is dear."

Murov conveyed the commissar's grim message to his drivers. Their chins lifted in determination, and they urged their horses onto the ice. Between each sledge was an interval of thirty yards or more. The caravan eventually stretched out into a length of five miles. Except for the constant hissing of the sledge runners or the occasional subdued neigh of a horse, the silence on that seemingly endless ice seemed to make it colder. Soon the horses were covered with hoarfrost. Sometimes the ice beneath them cracked, and their driver adjusted his course, or the caravan encountered a crevasse and had to detour. Reaching an island, the caravan halted for two hours' rest. A ration of 800 grams of bread was issued, along with tea with sugar. But there was no forage for the horses, although some drivers shared their bread with them. It was midevening before the column reached Kobona. Again there was food for the drivers: hardtack, sugar, macaroni and cottonseed-oil-cakes. But again nothing for the horses. Murov despaired of their ever making the return journey pulling loaded sledges. But then he saw his men feeding the cottonseed-oil-cakes to the horses. He remembered an old cavalry trick and scraped the snow from the ground to uncover old grass for his beasts to feed on.

In the dark early morning of the 20th Murov's caravan reached the Leningrad side of the lake loaded with supplies. What came to be called the Road of Life had been opened.

Actually, the Ice Road did not immediately save Leningrad from starvation. In its first week of operation it delivered only 800 tons of flour—two days' ration at the starvation rate. Without improvement, Leningrad would only starve more slowly. It had been hoped that when truck convoys began rolling over the thickening ice, deliveries would rise sharply. But this did not happen because the land route being built through the forest would not be completed until December 6, and at some points the road was too narrow for the trucks. It took ten to twenty days to make the round trip from Leningrad to Novaya Ladoga and back. In the first week of truck convoys, forty of them broke through the ice and sank. Gradually, however, the ice thickened to a depth of three to five feet, and the trucks were safe, able to deliver far more food than the horses had been. But they still could not save Leningrad from starvation. The Ice Road would always be supplemental. What was needed was to recapture Tikhvin to reopen communication with mainland Russia and obviate the need for the primitive forest route. On the morning of December 5, Marshal Kiril Meretskov's Fourth Army launched its drive on that vital rail and highway junction.

Meretskov's men fought through snowdrifts five and six feet deep and in

temperatures 20 and 30 degrees below zero. They were helped by a drive from
the north by the Fifty-fourth Army using the KV sixty-ton tanks. Incredibly
enough, the sixty-tonners had rolled safely over Ladoga's ice, having removed
their turrets to reduce their weight. On December 8 the Fourth Army battled into
Tikhvin and on the following day the city was safely in Soviet hands. Its recapture
prevented the Germans from encircling Leningrad with a second girdle of steel
and ended forever Hitler's plan of cutting off Moscow from its rear. Whether or
not the reopening of communication with mainland Russia had come in time to
save the city could not be determined. Leningrad seemed to be on its last legs.
Its millions of walking skeletons, without heat or light, were now also without
transport. On December 9 the Leningrad streetcar system ceased operation except for some lines carrying ammunition. And a new kind of crime had appeared.

Murder for food began with the onset of winter. It was crime that baffled
the Soviet police because it was committed, not by hardened and professional
criminals among whom they had an efficient network of stool pigeons, but rather
by ordinary citizens whom starvation, bombardment and suffering from seemingly every form of privation had driven over the edge. Some of these murdering
thieves killed for bread and ration cards in order to save wives and children dying
at home from dystrophy.

To stop these crimes the Leningrad Military Council transformed the city
courts into military courts and made food and ration-card theft a military crime.
This meant that, when caught, such criminals were summarily shot. Usually the
court was a Red Army firing squad.

Loss of a ration card was almost like a sentence of death. In the beginning
substitute cards were issued, but when the number issued rose from 4,800 in
October to 24,000 in December, Director Pavlov halted the practice. He knew
there were legitimate applications for a substitute, but the figures made it plain
that too many Leningraders were falsifying claims of losing cards by theft or in
fires. For a time only Zhdanov could issue a card. Many people who lost a card
at the beginning of a month simply starved to death. Gradually Pavlov's
draconian rule was relaxed, and a substitute card would be issued if incontroverti-
ble evidence could be produced. Since it was unlikely that many people could
provide testimony from eyewitnesses, building superintendents, the police or
party workers, the vast majority of those who lost cards early in the month simply
lay down in their beds and died.

If their instinct for survival was strong enough, however, and if they could
swallow their repugnance, they might go to the cannibals. They were usually
found in the Haymarket, where they sold meat patties of suspect substance.
Plump, sleek, their hair luxuriant and their eyes bright, among that skeletal
population they were as conspicuous as green trees in a petrified forest. No official
history of Leningrad mentions cannibalism—for pay and otherwise—but survivors have. "In the worst period of the siege," one of them observed, "Leningrad

was in the power of the cannibals. God knows what terrible scenes went on behind the walls of the apartments."

Another Leningrader, walking through the icy streets at night, came upon a bloody snowdrift into which had been hurled the heads of a man, a woman and a little girl with her blond hair still plaited in Russian braids. There were no bodies. Cannibals, obviously, was the only explanation. Many a Leningrader pulling a corpse-laden sled to the cemetery was shocked to see how fleshy parts —thighs and arms—had been cut from the cadavers strewn about the ground. Children began to disappear. Soon terrified parents kept their little ones off the street. It was whispered about in horror that the cannibals preferred children because they were so tender.

On January 25, 1942, it appeared that Leningrad had reached the end. There was no water. A fuel shortage had idled all but one power plant, and there was now no fuel to keep even this one operative. The turbines turned slowly to a halt. The pumps stopped. Without water there would be no bread, and without bread there would be no life.

One of eight bakeries still operating was kept going by fire department pumpers. Another where the pipes had frozen called for help from the Young Communists. About 2,000 of them were organized and sent with pails to the frozen Neva. They cut holes in the ice and bailed out the water, bringing it to the bakery. After the bread was baked, they distributed it to the food shops on children's sleds.

Leningrad's fuel supply had sunk from 120 trainloads a day in peacetime to three or four trainloads of firewood daily. Thousands of Young Communists were sent out into the small forests around the city to chop wood as a substitute for oil or coal. Zhdanov decreed that dilapidated or vacant wooden structures would be knocked down for fuel. In January demolition of 279 houses provided 18,000 cubic meters of wood, and in February destruction of some fewer structures provided 17,000 cubic meters. Eventually Zhdanov authorized the demolition of any structure made of wood, promising that after the war Leningrad would be rebuilt in greater grandeur. But the now demoralized Leningraders had little faith in any "after the war" for them or their city. They began to quote a refrain from the poet Nekrasov:

> In the world there is a czar
> And that czar is without mercy—
> Hunger is what they call him.

Perhaps most depressing of all in that incredible winter of 1941–42 was the failure of the heralded Leningrad offensive intended to break the blockade.

Lifting the Leningrad siege was to comprise one third of a triple offensive also intended to crush the German Army Group Center before Moscow and destroy Army Group South in the Crimea. It was much too optimistic and at that date far beyond Soviet capacity. At Leningrad, two armies under Generals Meretskov and Ivan Fedyuninsky began a slow development of the attack. Both men realized that the Germans were too well fortified to be surprised. They had their own troubles with winter. The attacking Russians had to flounder through deep snows to get to their enemy. On lowered rations themselves, they simply did not have the strength. After months of fruitless assault the winter offensive petered out. Discouraged Leningraders ceased to ask, "When will the blockade be lifted?"

But many of them were encouraged when Zhdanov at last came to the conclusion that the only way to avoid mass starvation was to begin to evacuate civilians from the besieged city. A new Ice Road was built from the railhead at Borisova Griva on the Leningrad end of Lake Ladoga to Lavrova on the mainland side. Some evacuees traveled to the railhead in buses heated by *burzhuiki* with tin chimneys through the roofs. Others went by truck, some of them canvas-covered but most of them open and exposed to icy winds during the thirty-mile trip. Trains took them to the lake, where they boarded trucks again and moved out onto the ice. They passed through white canyons formed by the snow thrown up by snow scrapers. At intervals they encountered traffic officers in white capes, repair shops and white-camouflaged AA positions. Sometimes they saw broken or burned trucks lying in the snow. Frequently they were scourged by the Luftwaffe, or they were buffeted by the *buri,* Ladoga's terrible blizzards. Always the temperatures were at 30 or 40 degrees below zero. Nevertheless, the flood of evacuees grew larger—and also the returning flow of supplies—so that from January 22 to April 15 there were 554,186 persons evacuated from Leningrad.

That meant a great savings in rations to feed those still in the city, and April 15 also meant that even if the blockade could not be lifted, the relief of spring was near at hand.

Spring meant clean-up time in Leningrad. The people were as dirty as their eating halls, and while more and more public baths were opened, the indescribably filthy lunchrooms and cafeterias where most Leningraders were fed had to be thoroughly cleansed. Dishes and tableware had not been washed for weeks. People had been eating with their fingers or lapping up their soup like dogs. But the biggest problem was to clean up the city. In mid-March the streets were still lined with millions of tons of blackened snow shot through with every manner of filth. Every able-bodied person was ordered into the streets to dig and sweep. As the snow melted, it made the task easier; nevertheless between March 27 and April 15, 1942, a million tons of filth was collected and 12,000 courtyards and 3 million square yards of streets cleared. Spring really smiled on the besieged city on May Day. It was sunny and clear. The parks were packed with people, mostly women in tattered old army overcoats and worn-out workers' boots. They clutched little bunches of marigolds, violets or even dandelions. Some grubbed up the green grass and ate it, anxious to obtain any form of Vitamin C to resist the scurvy of winter. Spring also brought a new commander to Leningrad: Lt. Gen. Leonid Aleksandrovich Govorov, a tall, handsome man. Although his name derived from the Russian *govorit,* meaning "to talk," he was extremely reserved. An officer who knew him at the artillery academy said: "Not even two words did he ever squeeze out."

Govorov's assignment was made easier when the Leningrad military council ordered Leningrad transformed into a military city, with only a minimum population necessary to maintain defenses and vital services. This was the decree that should have been made the preceding August. On July 6, the 340th day of the siege, Zhdanov announced that the city should have no more than 800,000 residents. The rest would have to go. To reach that figure was not as difficult as was imagined. No fewer than 1,093,695 Leningraders had been buried during that hideous winter and another 110,000 cremated for a total of 1,203,695 deaths. Thus only 300,000 needed to be evacuated, and there was no dearth of volunteers; not very many people wanted to be trapped inside the city during another winter. Moreover, the bright hopes of spring were fading. The Nazis were on the offensive again and the Red Army was falling back on the Volga. Hitler had replaced Leeb with Col. Gen. Georg von Kuchler, an able and aggressive commander, and was sending him reinforcements. Hitler also had ordered Erich von Manstein to take his Eleventh Army north to reinforce Kuchler.

In September 1942 there were ominous signs that the Germans were going to try to capture Leningrad again. They had massed twenty-one infantry and one tank divisions plus an infantry brigade in front of the city and at nearby Mga and Sinyavino. Stalin ordered a counteroffensive, a spoiling attack, to knock the poised enemy off balance and perhaps even lift the siege. This fourth attempt at breakout was also intended to relieve German pressure on Moscow and Stalingrad. Stalin was so desperate at this point that he even sent Leningrad reinforcements and 20,000 rifles and tommy guns when only 8,000 had been requested. The arms moved by a roundabout route to deceive the Nazis and the men came in closed railroad cars marked "food" or "fuel" or "hay." Tanks also arrived on flat cars covered with hay.

Soviet troops on the Leningrad front forced the Neva River again. Three rifle divisions crossed in broad daylight and under terrible enemy fire. But they got nowhere. Govorov trained more troops for a crossing and brought in amphibious tanks. This fresh assault started September 6 and fared just as badly. Rain began to fall. On October 8 Govorov pulled his troops back north of the Neva.

On the Volkhov front northeast of the city, General Meretskov's command was also stopped. His troops made a small penetration, but on September 20 Manstein began counterattacking, trying to cut off the Soviet spearheads. Meretskov's Second Shock Army became bogged down in marshes. Some units were surrounded. Meretskov bravely plunged into the battle to extricate them. On October 6—the 402nd day of the siege—the Soviet offensive was called off. It had not been a complete fiasco. The new German threat to Leningrad had been removed, and Manstein alone had suffered such severe losses that his men were saying, "Better be three times at Sevastopol than stay on here."

Govorov was undaunted and began planning a fifth counteroffensive to be

code-named Iskra, the Russian word for "spark" and the name of Lenin's revolutionary newspaper. A new army, the Sixty-seventh under the capable General
Mikhail Dukhanov, was to make the Leningrad front as strong as Volkhov.
Leningrad would force the Neva on an eight-mile front from Nevskaya Dubrovka
to Shlisselburg. Volkhov would drive westward on Sinyavino just a few miles east
of Shlisselburg. The objective was a junction which would break the blockade.
The attack was to begin December 27, but because the ice on the Neva was still
thin, the date was changed to January 12, 1943. At 9:30 A.M. on that date Iskra
commenced with a thunderous artillery barrage on both fronts: two hours twenty
minutes at Leningrad, one hour forty-five minutes at Volkhov.

At Leningrad Dukhanov's divisions successfully crossed the ice and stormed
into the German positions. The Nazis counterattacked. But then Meretskov's
Second Shock Army to the east at Volkhov began driving west. Soon the weight
of the Soviet offensive began to wear down the Germans. But the Shlisselburg
garrison was fighting fiercely. Three times Kuchler ordered them to hold to the
last man.

Still, the Soviet offensive was gaining momentum. On January 14 less than
three miles separated the two fronts advancing toward one another. Two days
later it was only a quarter-mile. The night of the 17th Govorov ordered both
fronts to close the gap by any means. Next morning the Germans in Shlisselburg
launched their last counterattack. It failed. A few hours later Leningrad and
Volkhov joined hands. That night the radio announced that the blockade had
been broken. Instantly, almost magically, the streets filled with delirious Leningraders. Music was heard. Red flags were everywhere. Girls danced wildly,
embracing men in uniform. Leningrad radio stayed on the air until three the next
morning. Hastily composed poems celebrating the "liberation" were read.
Speeches were made.

In the morning Leningraders realized that the Germans were still sitting on
their doorstep, still showering the city with their shells. They had been pushed
back, but not routed. About three weeks later—on February 7—train service to
the city was renewed on a new route via the new Shlisselburg bridge over the Neva
and Volkhovstroi. It was again the occasion for great celebration. It seemed to
many Leningraders that this—on the 526th day of blockade—signified the lifting
of the siege. But it did not.

Many more days, many more months, many more trials, remained to be
endured.

Iskra was indeed a spark. It inflamed the Red Army with martial ardor from
Leningrad to Moscow to Stalingrad and south to Kiev and Sevastopol. These
were the titanic battles in which the Soviets, now being heavily supplied by the
Americans, seized the initiative. But Leningrad still suffered, and the tenuous link
between the city and the mainland was always in danger of being severed again.
The Germans mounted heavy artillery on Sinyavino Heights in full view of the
railroad. So many trains were destroyed and so many lives lost that the route was

called the Corridor of Death. During eleven months the Germans cut the railroad no fewer than 1,200 times. During July and August they also raised their bombardment of the city to the mightiest crescendo ever. Nevertheless, the food ration was increased, and in late 1942 American canned butter, Spam, sugar and powdered eggs and milk had begun to appear. But everyone still feared another German attempt to take the city, and when the cataclysmic Battle of Kursk began, they became even more apprehensive. News of the Soviet victory there, however, was a great relief.

Throughout the summer and into September Leningraders were encouraged by the sight of great masses of men and material arriving in the city. There had been the usual sharp arguments between Zhdanov and the Stavka (General Headquarters) over the amount of reinforcement Leningrad needed, but in the end the two fronts had 21,600 guns, 600 AA guns, 1,500 Katyushas, 1,475 tanks and self-propelled guns and 1,500 aircraft. It was probably the greatest concentration of firepower ever assembled by the Soviets, greater even than Stalingrad. Between them the Leningrad and Volkhov Fronts now had 1.241 million officers and men. But the Neva ice again was too thin for a fall offensive and the assault had to be postponed once more, this time to January 14, 1944, the 867th day of the siege.

At 9:30 in the morning, with the battlefield enshrouded in heavy fog, the Soviet guns began bellowing. The earth shook. Plaster fell from walls. Leningraders were delirious, rushing into the streets to listen to the sweetest music they had ever heard. Now it was the Soviet Union's turn to make the heavens roar and the enemy howl. For once Leningrad had a superiority in men and arms: Field Marshal von Kuchler (he had been promoted) had [only] 741,000 men, 10,070 guns, 385 tanks and 370 planes.

Despite the fog the Second Shock Army made fair progress: two miles on a six-mile front. Next morning at the same time the artillery preparation for the attack on Pulkovo began. It lasted 100 minutes while 220,000 shells of all calibers —not counting rockets—screamed into the German "circle of steel." Three air wings bombed the Nazi trenches and forward facilities. The Forty-second Army drove forward on a three-mile front, penetrating the German line from one to three miles. Govorov was not satisfied with the rate of progress, but the fact was that his troops were fighting with great determination. It was the heavy German fire that delayed them.

Next day there was a thaw, and then rain, and the offensive slowed down. But on the 19th the temperature fell sharply, and the pace of the advance quickened. On January 22 there were frontline reports that the Germans were retreating in disorder. This was both true and false; the Germans were indeed withdrawing, but not in panic. Kuchler had wisely decided that he must pull back or be trapped by the Soviet forces punching through both his flanks. So he conducted an orderly withdrawal all the way back to the Estonian and Latvian borders. He stood on a line running south from the Gulf of Finland near Narva to Pskov. This set Leningrad free.

On the night of January 27, 1944, the people of Leningrad stood quietly in the streets, listening to the thunder of guns again, watching the sky expectantly, and when a flight of golden arrows to be followed by a stream of red, white and blue rockets swept over the sword-point spire of the Admiralty and the great dome of St. Isaac's there rose from that battered, broken city a mighty shout of joy.

It was the signal that the siege had been lifted. Leningrad had been liberated! After 880 days—from the fall of Mga on September 8, 1941, to this historic night of January 27, 1944—Leningrad was free again! It had been the greatest siege in modern times, probably in all history. Only two modern blockades are even comparable: the German siege of Paris from September 19, 1870, to January 27, 1871, and the Union Army siege of Vicksburg, Mississippi, between May 18 and July 4, 1863. Noncombatant deaths at Paris due to the blockade were 16,000. Those at Vicksburg for both civilians and the military were 2,500. Leningrad exceeded the Paris deaths any two or three winter days, the Vicksburg rate on any single winter day. Total deaths at Leningrad can never be exactly determined, if only because of Soviet indifference to such statistics, and because of Stalin's postwar denigration of the city's suffering; but the most likely estimate for both civilian and military is between 1.3 million and 1.5 million deaths.

But Leningrad, unlike Paris and Vicksburg, had held.

87. Spring 1944: The Soviets Reach Europe

MARSHAL VON KUCHLER'S new position actually was better than it appeared to be on the map because three fourths of its 120-mile length from the gulf to the bastion town of Pskov was occupied by the two vast lakes of Pskov and Peipus. On the Soviet right Govorov crossed the Narva River but was pinned down there, while on the left Meretskov was stopped at Pskov.

Great as these military victories had been, they were eclipsed by the even greater political success they produced: Finland in middle February entered into peace negotiations with the Soviet Union. It had been this gallant little nation's misfortune to fight its huge Soviet neighbor all alone in 1939–40, and then to be "liberated" by the Wehrmacht's surge across the Baltic and compelled to throw in its lot with Germany and fight the Soviets again. Isolated now, Finland wisely declined a third encounter with the Russian bear. Stalin's terms were remarkably moderate: a return to the 1940 agreement. But the Finns did not trust the marshal and wanted more explicit safeguards, which he refused. The Finns also complained that they were not capable of disarming German forces in Finland, as Stalin wanted, and they were not willing to allow the Red Army into Finland for that purpose. So the discussions were broken off in March, after which Ribbentrop hastened to Helsinki to talk the Finns back into line with a promise of reinforcements. Apart from Marshal Govorov's campaign in the Karelian Isthmus, all that actually occurred was a quiescent renewal of the Russo-Finnish War. However, Finland's brief defection from the Nazi camp had encouraged discontent in the Balkans. It deepened after the Americans launched shuttle-bombing of the region. Flying Fortresses flew their strikes from Mediterranean bases and landed at new airfields in the Soviet Union. Then they refueled, bombed up and struck again en route home.

Meanwhile a sweeping maneuver against the Germans was conducted farther south—west of Kiev—within the Dnieper bend. It was directed by Marshal Zhukov, who had also taken personal command of the group led by Vatutin, who had been ambushed and killed by anti-Soviet partisans. Zhukov's group was on the right while Konev, now a marshal, was on the left with his group. Their first objective was the Odessa-L'vov railroad, which ran parallel to their front.

On March 4 Zhukov attacked on a front of about sixty miles. During the first two days he penetrated fifty miles west, capturing Volochisk on the Odessa-L'vov railroad. On the 9th he reached Ternopol.

Two days later Konev began attacking, moving so swiftly and suddenly that he was able to surprise and capture the great German base at Uman, seizing 500 tanks and no fewer than 12,000 trucks. The Germans, now under Model who had replaced Manstein, broke in panic. Model's inadequate and demoralized forces were completely unable to halt Konev's advance, and on March 27 he had reached the Prut River in Romania.

Meanwhile, Zhukov had turned southward and advanced on Cernauti, the last rail link between the German armies in Poland and the Ukraine. By March 25 he had crossed the Dniester on a front of fifty miles and by the end of the month had taken Cernauti. On the 27th Konev also reached the Prut below Zhukov. By mid-April they held a line running from a little east of Kovel' on the northern flank of their sector to the eastern extremity of Czechoslovakia and thence south and west to Jassy in Romania and bending east to Dubosari on the Dniester. While these great successes were being scored, Marshal Rodion Malinovsky's group even farther south was triumphing in the Black Sea area. On March 13 he captured Kerson and after a fierce battle Nikolayev was taken on the 25th. The great port city of Odessa was undefended and was entered in mid-April by the Soviets. After Malinovsky reached the Dniester, he linked up with Konev's left at Dubosari.

The final movement of the winter offensive was the recapture of the Crimea. The peninsula was defended by the German Seventeenth Army consisting of five German divisions and seven weak Romanian divisions, under General Janecke. To hold it Janecke had strengthened the defenses of the Isthmus of Perekop and the Akmanal Line built by the Soviets in 1942 across the narrowest section of the Kerch Peninsula. Against this position came Gen. F. I. Tolbukhin's 4th Ukrainian Group. Tolbukhin saw that the Sivash Marshes above the Perekop Line were

Russia, 1943—44

→ *Russian advances*

⇢ *German withdrawals*

🌐 *Trapped German pockets*

Boundaries of 1944 are shown

WHITE
SEA

• Archangel

N. Dvina

FINLAND

SWEDEN

Helsinki

Lake
Onega

Lake
Ladoga

GULF OF FINLAND

Stockholm •

BALTIC
SEA

ESTONIA

Narva

L. Peipus

Pskov

Leningrad

• Novgorod

Spring
'44

Spring '43

Volga

LATVIA
Riga

COURLAND
Dec '44

LITHUANIA

Memel •

Dvinsk

W. Dvina

• Moscow

Grodno

Vilnius

Smolensk

Oka

Danzig •

EAST
PRUSSIA

Rastenburg

Minsk

Berezina

Orel

• Berlin

WHITE
RUSSIA

GERMANY

Warsaw •

Vistula

Bialystok

Bug

Brest-Litovsk

P O L A N D

Pripet

Dnieper

Kursk
July 4-23 '43

Prokhorovka

Don

• Prague

Lublin

Rovno

Kiev

U K R A I N E

Belgorod

Spring '43

Donets

Lvov

Zhitomir

Vinnitsa

Cherkassy

Kremenchug

Kharkov

SLOVAKIA

Aug 31 '44

C A R P A T H I A N S

Chernauti

Prut

S. Bug

Krivoy Rog

Dnepropetrovsk

Donetsk

Vienna •

Dec '44

Dniester

Nikopol'

Don

Budapest

Drava

H U N G A R Y

TRANSYLVANIA

Jassy

Spring '44

Perekop

SEA OF AZOV

Rostov

Sava

CROATIA

R O M A N I A

L. Sivash

Kerch'

Belgrade

SERBIA

Ploesti

Sevastopol'

CRIMEA

Danube

Bucharest

Aug 31 '44

BLACK SEA

Sofia

ALBANIA

B U L G A R I A

Istanbul

0   250 mi

0   400 km

GREECE

the weak spot in Janecke's position. He planned to cross them after the lagoons froze, pinch out Perekop town and advance on the Akmanal Line.

However, the winter had been exceptionally mild. When in March it became certain that the Sivash, the waterway between Perekop and the mainland, would not freeze, Tolbukhin decided to ford its shallowest waters and move the bulk of his troops, supplies and heavy equipment across it on barges, rafts and pontoons. Early in the morning of April 8, to distract the enemy, the Soviets began an artillery bombardment of Perekop. Next day, while Kerch on the far German right was being attacked, he struck at the first Perekop line on the far left. Breaking through, the Soviets were stopped at the second line at Yushun. Meanwhile, the Sivash was easily crossed. Because it had not frozen, four Romanian divisions assigned to hold it had moved twenty miles inland at Dzhankoi.

Janecke was so unhinged by this surprise movement that instead of ordering the Romanians to counterattack, he told them to stay where they were. On April 11 the Soviets fell upon them and scattered them, taking Dzhankoi. Now Janecke ordered a general retreat into Simferopol, thus abandoning his outer defenses and throwing open the front and back doors of the Crimea. But Simferopol soon fell and the frantic Germans and Romanians made for Sevastopol. Now, for some inexplicable reasons, Janecke shipped three of his Romanian divisions back to Romania along with some German units. Next Hitler ordered the abandonment of Sevastopol and a movement to Cape Khersonesski on the Crimea's southern tip. There on May 12 the Seventeenth Army surrendered.

Thus ended one of the most remarkable campaigns in history. Most of the German-held lands of Holy Russia were back in Soviet hands. The Red Army stood on the border of East Prussia, inside Poland, on the borders of Czechoslovakia and Hungary, which the Germans had occupied to take advantage of the natural defenses of the Carpathian Mountains, inside Romania and astride the Crimea. But now the spring thaws had come and the offensive came to an end. It would be renewed in June, but the respite still came like a blessed breather to the weary Germans in the East. But the Germans in the West who had seen no combat since the fall of France in 1940 would soon be hearing the rolling thunder of Anglo-American guns.

88. Preparing for D-Day

UNTIL THE VERY EVE of D-Day, Prime Minister Winston Churchill and his war chiefs had the deepest doubts, misgivings and reservations about the Allied invasion of France. British fears first surfaced on October 23, 1943, when Churchill wrote to Roosevelt: "I do not doubt our ability in the conditions laid down to get ashore and deploy. I am however deeply concerned with the build-up and the situation which may arise between the thirtieth and sixtieth days. . . ." In other words, he feared a stabilization of the front and a return to the static warfare of World War I. Churchill also cabled General Marshall: "We are carrying out our contract, but I pray God it does not cost us dear." Again in February 1944, he cried out in anguish: "Why are we trying to do this?" Having already proposed Norway or Greece as better battlegrounds, he then suggested landings in Portugal. On June 5, 1944, the day before D-Day, the attitude of Sir Alan Brooke, chief of the Imperial General Staff and the most outspoken opponent of Overlord, was deeply pessimistic. He wrote: "At the best, it will come very far short of the expectations of the bulk of the people, namely all those who know nothing about its difficulties. At its worst, it may well be the most ghastly disaster of the whole war."

Yet American enthusiasm for the operation remained high and unabated, even rising as D-Day came closer. Why, then, were the British so cautious and the Americans so confident, why did these disagreements remain for so long unresolved among the allies of history's most successful fighting coalition, unsettled indeed until the very last few weeks before the invasion? The answer seems to reside in the differing experience and character of the two peoples.

For a year following the fall of France the British had fought on alone and without any rational hope of victory. Then Hitler's decision to invade Russia in June 1941 sent a ray of hope shining through their dark night of despair. For the remainder of that year Britain struggled against the German submarine force while building a Bomber Command that would retaliate against her tormentor while fielding an army in the only theater in which she could fight: Africa and the Middle East. Then at the year's close came "the miracle" of Pearl Harbor. Such it was, a salvation of joy made surer four days later when Hitler unwisely and with no provocation declared war on the United States. Nevertheless, during the period of roughly a year in which the United States could mobilize its unrivaled industrial might for war and conscript, train and field a mass army of its own, the British continued to suffer. Her strength was waning, her people weary. Production of munitions and equipment had been falling since 1942. By May 1944, the British Army had reached its peak strength of 2.75 million men, while the American Army was at 5.75 million, still far below its peak of 8.5 million. Obviously, the Americans were already dominant in the Grand Alliance. But could the American army defeat the Wehrmacht?

Here was the deep doubt in the minds of Churchill and Brooke. Both were aware of the splendid fighting power of the German army, certainly the most formidable force in modern history. Four years of war against it had taught the British that the Wehrmacht should never be engaged except on the most favorable terms. Throughout World War II, whenever British or American soldiers engaged German soldiers on anything like equal terms, the Germans won. Weapon for weapon German equipment outclassed Allied in every category except artillery and transport. In the air, the Allies were superior. But air power depends on weather, and there was always the consideration that if the weather closed down on D-Day, this great air supremacy on which the entire operation depended would be nullified. This Churchill and his chiefs were reluctant to risk. They also had found their misgivings about Allied troops justified in North Africa and again in Italy, where Kesselring's masterful handling of his forces had thwarted every effort to crush them. And these were line troops, not elite formations. In France the Allies would be facing the SS Panzer divisions, Hitler's finest, and the fanatical Hitler Youth. This fear of the German army, then, was probably the most disturbing doubt reigning at the heart of British reticence to undertake Overlord; and it seems to be safe to say that if it had not been for American enthusiasm for it and insistence on launching it on schedule, the invasion of France might have had to wait until 1945.

British caution and skepticism irked and angered the Americans. They suspected that their allies were too preoccupied with preservation of the Empire and that the gigantic buildup in Britain might be nothing more than a plan to deceive and distract the Germans until continued massive Allied bombing and German losses in the Soviet Union brought about the collapse of the Third Reich, when Overlord would become Rankin, i.e., the invasion force would become an occupying force. American confidence was based upon their faith in their economy and their troops, which was eventually justified, and their fondness for a direct, straightahead dash across the Channel into France. In this the British thought them naive, that in their inexperience they underestimated the vast difficulties in planning, logistics and tactics for such a mammoth operation. There was some truth in this, but then conversely the British were much too prone to emphasize difficulty. They did not understand the American genius for overcoming problems, or appreciate the depth of their energy and abundance. The slogan "The difficult we do immediately, the impossible takes a little longer" was not just another Yankee boast but an expression of reality.

An even sharper disagreement arose over Operation Anvil, the simultaneous invasion of southern France proposed by the Americans. The British opposed it because it would cripple operations in Italy, the Americans wanted it to gain the valuable port of Marseille and for an attack up the valley of the Rhône to join forces with Eisenhower's right flank. For the first time in this continuing squabble, the Americans flatly refused to retreat. They wanted Anvil, later named Dragoon, period. But the old ghost of landing-craft shortages arose to haunt them. Because of the misguided emphasis on aircraft production, the resumption of the Pacific offensive by MacArthur and Nimitz and the demands of the Italian operation, there was simply not enough for both invasions to proceed together. Thus Dragoon was postponed for ten weeks.

But the basic Allied disagreement over Overlord that had begun in the fall of 1943 continued unresolved, and it would remain so until the summer of 1944, with the British cautious and reluctant and the Americans exasperated and eager, until, on May 15, at a briefing of Overlord's top commanders, Winston Churchill approached Eisenhower and declared: "I am hardening toward this enterprise."

Churchill's growing faith in Overlord was probably as much due to his rising admiration of Eisenhower as to any other cause. For the American had indeed fashioned a command structure—Supreme Headquarters, Allied Expeditionary Force, or SHAEF—which even in a single-nation army, let alone a coalition, was a triumph of reason, understanding and generosity of spirit. Eisenhower began by naming three Britishers as his subordinate commanders: Marshal Bernard Montgomery on land, Adm. Sir Bertram Ramsay at sea and Marshal Sir Traffard Leigh-Mallory in the air. He had even named a fourth Briton, Air Chief Marshal Tedder, to be deputy supreme commander. Much as these appointments might have dismayed some American officers, they were a boon to Churchill and gave a great boost to British morale.

Although the supreme commander appreciated Montgomery's abilities, he was not eager to endure his abrasive personality and superior airs, preferring Alexander for his ground commander; but Brooke and Churchill were solidly behind the victor of El Alamein, and so Eisenhower accepted him. Nor did he much admire the "somewhat ritualistic outlook" of Ramsay and Leigh-Mallory. But for Tedder he had the utmost respect and admiration and was on the best of terms with this witty, decisive and able airman.

To have granted four British officers so much authority over Americans was probably Eisenhower's most generous gesture in the interests of the Alliance. Supposedly, he was bowing to British experience and superior military wisdom. This might seem ironic in that Overlord was preeminently an American scheme, springing from their willingness—nay, eagerness—to make the perilous Channel crossing and confront the formidable enemy head-on in an operation which the British chiefs themselves had fought so long to delay or even defer. But it was actually no irony if only because Dwight Eisenhower's generous nature gave him an insight into the hearts of the British people deeper than the intuition of their own commanders. He was keenly aware of the suffering and humiliations they had endured. He gave the top commands after himself to four Britons to harden for battle once again those "hearts of oak" that had begun to wilt beneath five years of frustration. To Eisenhower the psychologist, a Britain renewed and reconsecrated to its determination to return to Europe might have seemed as valuable as sunny skies over France on D-Day.

The true irony in Eisenhower's preparations for Overlord was the difficulty he experienced in obtaining operational control of his own air force. For its success, the cross-Channel invasion depended to the extreme on adroit use of the overwhelming air power assigned to it. Overlord was a direct frontal assault against a fortified position. Hitler's Atlantic Wall was continuous from Denmark to the Spanish coast, so there was no chance of outflanking it. The Germans had the advantages of superior manpower, land communications and interior lines. Eisenhower's advantages were control of the air and the sea, meaning that he could deliver a preinvasion bombardment far greater than the artillery barrages of World War I. Because he was on the offensive, he knew where and when the battle would be fought. Without a line of communications to defend, he could concentrate on a narrow front on the Cotentin Peninsula in Normandy, where the invasion was to take place. Because Rundstedt did not know where the main blow would fall, he had to spread his forces along the Atlantic Wall. Harris's Bomber Command and Spaatz's American Strategic Forces were thus the key to success.

But both air chiefs objected strenuously to Eisenhower's attempt to place them under his operational command during the two months prior to D-Day, now set at June 5, 1944. Specifically, the supreme commander wanted to use the bombers to paralyze the French railway system and thus inhibit Rundstedt from launching his counteroffensive. This was called the Transportation Plan, and its author was Tedder. Spaatz, still clinging to his theories of strategic bombing, offered in its place the Oil Plan, giving priority to the German oil industry, especially its synthetic fuel plants. This, Spaatz argued, would in the long run more effectively paralyze the German army's ground movements—and the Luftwaffe as well—than the Transportation Plan. This was true. But Eisenhower was interested in the *short-term effects.* Spaatz, who seems to have been indifferent to the difficulties of an amphibious invasion, assumed that the Allied host would get ashore easily. Eisenhower knew different. He was aware that the Germans had accumulated large stocks of fuel in France and had cleverly camouflaged them. During D-Day and the few critical weeks thereafter they would have all the fuel they needed in the struggle to hurl the invaders back into the sea. Thus Spaatz missed, or in his strategic-bombing zeal ignored, the heart of the matter.

So did Harris. He argued that Bomber Command had been designed for night raids and blind area bombing and could not possibly achieve the accuracy required to hit marshaling yards, repair centers, terminals and other pinpoint rail targets. Tedder was so exasperated by this piece of casuistry that he openly accused Harris of juggling his figures to support his claims. Like Spaatz, Harris was unwilling to shift from strategic bombing to aerial support of an invasion. Both men simply minimized the importance of getting ashore and staying there.

But the short-term success of Overlord was so vital, such an obvious imperative, it is hard to believe that commanders of such high rank could denigrate it. Hitler *wanted* an attack in the West. In December 1943 he said: "If they attack in the West, that attack will decide the war." He wasn't bluffing. His total forces had sunk from more than 3 million in July 1943 to 2.6 million in December. Another half million had been lost in the Soviet winter offensive. If the Allies could be thrown into the sea, it was inconceivable that they could mount a new invasion for years, if ever. American emphasis would probably shift to the Pacific. Hitler would be free to transfer his fifty-nine divisions in France to the East for a showdown battle with the Red Army. Within the year the rockets and even jet aircraft would be ready, and the Americans were still a year away from perfecting the atomic bomb. Tenuous or far-fetched as this may sound, it was then not impossible and had to be given careful consideration. In short, Eisenhower wanted and needed any help he could get for Overlord, and in fighting for it he showed himself to be the commander *supreme*. He got Tedder on the telephone and told him: "Now listen, Arthur, I am tired of dealing with a lot of prima donnas. By God, you tell that bunch if they don't get together and stop quarreling like children, I will tell the prime minister to get someone else to run this damn war. I'll *quit!*" Next he took on Churchill himself.

The prime minister supported Harris and Spaatz, for humane as well as political reasons. He did not wish to be responsible for the slaughter and maiming of hundreds of thousands of Belgian and French civilians. To avoid a head-to-head confrontation with Eisenhower, he suggested that the bombers should be "attached" to SHAEF for specific operations, subject to the approval of the Combined Chiefs. Eisenhower replied that if he could not receive complete operational control of Allied aircraft, he would "simply have to go home." Shocked, Churchill still sought to stop the Transportation Plan. He consulted Maj. Gen. Pierre Joseph Koenig, de Gaulle's representative in London. Koenig replied: "This is war, and it must be expected that people will be killed. We would take the anticipated loss to be rid of the Germans." Thwarted but not beaten, Churchill turned to Roosevelt with his doubts about "the French slaughters." Roosevelt answered that military considerations must be paramount, and Eisenhower won.

So Eisenhower and Tedder unleashed the vast Allied bombing fleet on the French railway system. By D-Day, 76,000 tons of bombs had been dropped on rail targets. The Seine River bridges west of Paris were virtually destroyed. Based on an index of 100 for January–February of 1944, French rail traffic dropped to 38 by D-Day. There were no outcries from France. Only 12,000 French and Belgian civilians died, many fewer than had been feared.

Having made what he always considered his most important contribution to the success of Overlord, Eisenhower next turned to a familiar family problem: his old friend George Patton had come down with another attack of foot-in-mouth disease.

Patton was the centerpiece of an elaborate deception scheme devised by British Intelligence. It was called Operation Fortitude, and it was the logical companion to the Transportation Plan. Where Transportation was intended to isolate the Cotentin Peninsula from Rundstedt's overwhelmingly superior manpower and logistics advantages, Fortitude would trick the German chief into keeping the bulk of these forces concentrated far away from the Cotentin. A fictitious U.S. First Army Group was created under the command of Patton, the general whom the Germans feared most. Part of it was supposedly stationed in Scotland to give the impression of a diversionary landing in Norway, but the bulk was in Dover opposite the Pas de Calais. The Dover–Calais route was the shortest across the Channel, and Rundstedt was already convinced that Calais was the logical place for the enemy to land. He had concentrated his strongest defenses and the Fifteenth Army, his best, at Calais. To keep him there British Intelligence arranged for a mass of dummy installations—landing craft, vehicles, camps and communications—to be stationed around Dover. Radio signals were sent in a code which the Germans could read to strengthen their conviction that Calais was the place. The British Double-Cross System used German spies (all had been captured and "turned" by the British Secret Service) to send reports in secret writing, specifying the various units and assignments of Patton's fake First Army Group. Ultra intercepts proved that the Germans had taken the Fortitude bait and believed that Eisenhower possessed a total of eighty-nine divisions, when in fact there were only forty-seven, and that Hitler had doubled Norway's defending forces.

To increase Patton's visibility to the Germans, he was instructed to appear frequently in public in the Dover area. He did so. On April 25, at the opening of a club for American servicemen sponsored by British women, he spoke on Anglo-American unity. The two races should work together, Patton said, "since it is the evident destiny of the British and Americans to rule the world, [and] the better we know each other the better job we will do." Of course there was a newspaper reporter present, and Patton's faux pas was flashed around the world, provoking the customary outburst of indignation against this indiscreet and flamboyant commander.

Marshall was furious. He had just sent to the Senate a list of officers for promotion to permanent Regular Army rank, and Patton's name was on it. "This I fear has killed them all," he wired Eisenhower, and ordered him to investigate. He did. Certain that Patton was at fault, but again determined not to lose a commander of his quality, he called him onto the carpet. The general who came creeping into Eisenhower's office at Bushy Park did not in the slightest resemble Old Blood and Guts, but rather a sheepish and abashed small boy anxious for forgiveness. After Eisenhower rebuked him but promised to keep him, Patton burst into tears. A consummate actor, he laid his head contritely on Eisenhower's shoulder. As he did the helmet that he always wore, even in his chief's presence, fell off and rolled across the floor. Eisenhower found the entire performance "ridiculous," but it was now a jaunty Patton, ramrod-straight again, helmet gleaming, leather shining, pearl-handled pistol and all, who returned to Dover where he gleefully informed his diary how he had put one over on his old friend Ike.

Patton's indiscretion, however, had no effect on Fortitude, a deception so successful that when the Anglo-Americans began landing at Normandy, the German Fifteenth Army was still waiting for them at Calais.

The invasion plan developed by SHAEF called for landings on five beaches by six divisions of Montgomery's 21st Army Group. On the right were three American divisions of the U.S. First Army under Omar Bradley, assigned to land at Utah and Omaha beaches; on the left were one Canadian and two British divisions of the British Second Army under Sir Miles Dempsey moving on Gold, Juno and Sword beaches. Once the beachhead was secured and the advance through France begun, Bradley would take command of the U.S. Twelfth Army

Group while Lt. Gen. Courtney Hodges took over First Army and Patton's Third Army followed the First ashore. On the left, the Canadian First Army would come in behind Dempsey's Second British.

The Allied objectives were Bayeux, Caen and the road to St. Lô. Both publicly and in private Marshal Montgomery had announced his intention of taking Caen the first day. When this was done, he would protect the eastern flank of the U.S. First Army as it moved to capture the important port of Cherbourg at the northern tip of the Cotentin. Securing the beach exits was almost as important as landing on them, and to do this Eisenhower decided to employ night drops of one British and two American airborne divisions. In this he encountered the strenuous opposition of Marshal Leigh-Mallory. By letter and in a personal interview, Leigh-Mallory told the supreme commander that the Germans had reinforced the area where the American paratroopers would drop. He thought losses among the 82nd and 101st Airborne Divisions would be as high as 70 percent and said that if the success of the seaborne assault depended on the airborne, "It will be seriously prejudiced." Eisenhower was shocked. He realized that Bradley was counting on the air drops to seize the causeway over a lagoon to the rear of his beaches. After much anguished reflection, he overruled Leigh-Mallory and stuck to his plan.

In contrast to the invincible pessimism of his air commander, Eisenhower got nothing but optimism and the fullest cooperation from his ground commander, Bernard Montgomery. No one did more to raise the morale of the troops of all the Allied nations than Montgomery. His frequent visits to them were all vintage "Monty," beautifully stage-managed from the measured stride down the ranks to the steely stare into the soldiers' eyes and the final order to break ranks and gather round him while he stood on the hood of his jeep, telling them in his sports slang that they were going to knock the Germans "for a boundary six." The enemy was understrength, he told them: "Everything is in the shopwindow. There is nothing 'in the kitty.'" Even Omar Bradley, no admirer of Montgomery, was impressed. "Even Eisenhower with his engaging ease," he wrote, could not excite soldiers like the little general in the baggy pants and black beret.

Thus, as D-Day approached, a massive host and a mighty armada had been assembled in Britain. Men by the millions, ships by the thousands, airplanes and tanks and vehicles by the tens of thousands had been formed into what Eisenhower called "a great human spring, coiled for the moment when its energy should be released and it would vault the English Channel in the greatest amphibious assault ever attempted."

Not all of these men and arms were to make the crossing on the first day. Most would sail after a beachhead had been seized along the sixty-mile Cotentin front and the Allied armies began driving toward Germany from the west while the Soviets launched their summer offensive and rolled toward Berlin from the east. Once ashore, Eisenhower planned to build up his forces before breaking out on a broad front utilizing two army groups. The 21st British on the left would seize necessary ports on its march toward the Ruhr. The 12th American on the right would join the Dragoon force, which was to land later in Southern France. Then, with his left and right joined together again, he would build up his forces once more, cross the Rhine and complete the conquest of Germany.

To contain Eisenhower's host southern England was transformed into a huge armed camp. No fewer than 1,627,000 American soldiers and 53,000 sailors were quartered there, and the roads were thronged with marching men while the air crackled and boomed to the sound of soldiers testing their weapons. At the embarkation ports, the harbors bristled with masts and the wharves were piled high with supplies. Very little was neglected for this great undertaking, which was to be, in effect, nothing less than a large modern city sailing to battle. Divisions of soldiers, and tanks, trucks, guns, rations, barbed wire and medical supplies were the ordinary articles of war, but there were also assembled bulldozers, power plants, radio stations, fleets of buses, hospitals, railroad locomotives, entire telephone exchanges, bakeries and laundries and prison cages and police stations, to say nothing of huge supplies of food, clothing and gasoline and a satisfactory amount of newly minted French money. There were even portable ports called Mulberries, enormous concrete structures which looked like six-story buildings laid on their sides. Two of them, each about the size of the harbor at Dover, were constructed to be towed in sections across the Channel and sunk opposite the invasion beaches. There were also Gooseberries, to be formed by sinking sixty blockships to provide a breakwater, and a submarine pipeline to carry fuel across the Channel.

During the last ten days of preparation, a cloak of secrecy was thrown around Britain. A ten-mile strip of southern England was declared off limits to Britons, all exits to other countries were sealed off, and mail from American servicemen to the United States was held up for ten days. Still, Allied intelligence received an almost electric shock on the day that "Overlord" appeared in a newspaper crossword puzzle. It was not, however, a signal to the enemy but only a coincidence.

For the invasion itself, Eisenhower had 150,000 men, 1,500 tanks, 5,300 ships and 12,000 aircraft; and it was upon this enormous preponderance of air power—a ratio of 30 to 1—that he pinned most of his hopes for success.

Perhaps the most ingenious of the new weapons and equipment were the specialized armored vehicles developed by the British under the direction of Maj. Gen. Sir Percy Hobart. There were bulldozer tanks to clear away beach obstacles, flail tanks called Crabs to beat paths through minefields, petard tanks to hurl charges against enemy fortifications, Crocodiles or flamethrowing tanks, turretless tanks which were actually self-propelled ramps which other tanks could climb to scale sea walls, bridge-carrying tanks to span craters and ditches and, most revolutionary of all, amphibious tanks called DDs (Dual Drive) which could swim ashore by themselves. After British inventiveness had been joined to Yankee production genius, the specialized armor began flowing to Britain by the thousands. When these were demonstrated to Montgomery and Eisenhower, both showed great enthusiasm, but Omar Bradley, who was to command the American

First Army on D-Day, was not impressed. Eventually, he accepted only the DD. Such shortsightedness was to have tragic consequences.

Field Marshal Erwin Rommel—the man who would defend the Atlantic Wall against the Allies—knew full well the awesome might of the enemy air force. He had experienced it in the last days of his desert defeat, and he was aware that it was now much stronger. It was because of this that he had quarreled with his chief, Marshal Gerd von Rundstedt. At his headquarters in Paris the aging Rundstedt planned an orthodox defense. With 3,000 miles of coastline to defend with only fifty-nine divisions—many of them second line and only ten armored —he believed that he must wait until he was certain where the enemy's main blow had come. Then, with the Allies building up for their breakout—the vulnerable point—he would launch his counteroffensive.

Rommel disagreed. His experience with Allied air power had taught him that the rear area's railroads and road networks would be so badly bombed and strafed that there would be no chance of a massive counterstroke ever reaching the fighting front. It was because of this conviction that he had worked so hard to strengthen the Atlantic Wall. Within a few months he had laid 4 million mines, compared to 2 million in the three years preceding his arrival. Given time, he proposed to lay 50 to a 100 million more. He would surround all strongholds with deep minefields and turn "tankable" country into mine swamps. Because he could not get enough mines, he raided depots and arsenals where he found stocks of millions of old shells which he converted into mines. And he planted them in every imaginable variation, overruling his engineers who wanted to lay them by the book.

Because of his strong mechanical bent, he was quick to see the worth or folly of all the gadgetry proposed to him. Among these, beach and glider obstacles— "Rommel's asparagus," as they were called—were beams driven into the beaches below low-water mark, some with mines on top, some with steel-cutters to act as "can openers." There were "nutcracker" mines in blocks of concrete and mined logs with a seaward slope. Obsolete tank obstacles were sunk below the high-water marks to impede infantry. Naval mines were sown in shallow waters with floating lines attached to the horns. Ashore, mined poles were planted in the fields to blow up enemy gliders. Deceptions were everywhere—dummy minefields, dummy artillery designed to draw enemy aerial bombardment, which they did—as well as smoke-making equipment to obscure targets and troops alerted to set the dummies afire once the invasion began and thus draw off enemy gunfire.

Rommel was also anxious to use the V-1 rockets against Allied troop concentrations in the south of England. Hitler refused. Even though many of the rocket-launching sites were ready, *Der Führer* said there were not yet enough to maintain the demoralizing continuous fire he hoped would finally break the British. This was a mistake. Even Eisenhower admitted that if the rockets could have been used "the invasion of Europe would have proved exceedingly difficult and perhaps impossible." It was also a mistake for Hitler to refuse to allow Rommel to place his panzer divisions closer to the coast to evade the Allied aerial threat to movements of his forces. He was allowed to station only one armored division close to the beaches. Yet the Desert Fox remained convinced that the enemy had to be stopped at the water's edge. He knew that the Luftwaffe was now but a broken reed in the limp hands of the drug-addicted Hermann Goering. "The war will be won or lost on the beaches," he told his aide, Capt. Hellmuth Lang. "We'll have only one chance to stop the enemy and that's while he's in the water . . . struggling to get ashore. Reserves will never get up to the point of attack and it's foolish to consider them. . . . Believe me, Lang, the first twenty-four hours will be decisive . . . for the Allies, as well as Germany, it will be the longest day."

Weather would dictate the date of that day. The sea had to be calm for the invasion ships, the tides low to frustrate Rommel's underwater obstacles and the moon bright or the skies at least clear for the airborne night drops. Tides and moon conditions, of course, were predictable. But there was no way of planning for storms. A really violent blow could wreck the invasion. Landing boats would sink in storm-tossed seas. Those soldiers who got ashore might be too seasick to fight. Worst of all, the Allies' only advantages—support from the air and gunfire ships—would be canceled out. If Overlord failed because of the weather, it would take months to plan and mount another invasion. Certainly there could not be another in 1944. If it were canceled in hopes of finding a calm day, the conditions of the tide and moon would have to be just right—and once again, no one could guarantee the weather.

On the night of June 2, RAF Group Capt. J. J. Stagg, Eisenhower's chief weatherman, met with the supreme commander and his deputies in the mess room of Southwick House. Stagg had bad news. The weather on June 5—D-Day —would be bad. It would be overcast and stormy with no way of forecasting more than twenty-four hours in advance. Eisenhower had to make an immediate decision. The U.S. Navy carrying Bradley's troops to Utah and Omaha, the beaches farthest away, had to be notified whether to sail or stay in port. He decided to set them in motion subject to a last-minute cancellation. Final decision would be made next morning.

The same group met again at 4:30 in the morning of June 4. Stagg reported that the sea had abated somewhat but that there would be no chance of using the air force. Eisenhower polled his commanders. Montgomery wanted to go, Leigh-Mallory and Tedder were for a postponement and Admiral Ramsay was neutral. Not to use his air superiority was too great a risk for Eisenhower, and he postponed the invasion for twenty-four hours. Word went out to the American fleet. With superb skill the ships put about and sailed through the storm back to port, refueling there and preparing to sail once more next day. That night another meeting was held. High winds howled around Southwick House. Rain pelted the windows. Captain Stagg was cheerful. "I think we have found a gleam of hope for you, sir," he told Eisenhower. "The mass of weather fronts coming in from the Atlantic is moving faster than we anticipated. We predict there will be rather fair conditions beginning late on June 5 and lasting until the next morning, June 6, with a drop in wind velocity and some break in the clouds."

Cheers burst out in the mess room. Stagg was mildly surprised to hear so much middle-aged high brass cheer that way. Eisenhower began pacing the floor, chin on chest, hands clasped behind his back. His jaw shot out inquiringly at his chief of staff, Walter Bedell Smith. "It's a helluva gamble," Smith said, "but it's the best possible gamble." Eisenhower nodded, dropped his chin again, but then shot it out at Montgomery, huddled in his greatcoat, his face almost hidden. Montgomery returned Eisenhower's gaze calmly. "I would say—go!" Tedder was still dubious. Ramsay told Eisenhower that the American fleet commander must be informed of his decision within a half hour. "If he is told it is on and his forces sail and are then recalled, they will not be ready again until Wednesday morning [June 7]." That meant a two-day postponement, which also meant that tidal conditions would not be right and the postponement would actually be until June 19—with once again no guarantee of good weather. Eisenhower said, "I am quite positive that the order must be given," and Ramsay rushed out to signal the fleets. More than 5,000 ships began making for France.

Eisenhower drove back to his trailer. He slept fitfully. The wind shook the trailer and rain rattled on the roof. He awoke at 3:30 on June 5 and drove through a mile of mud to the last meeting. It was still not too late to call off the invasion. Stagg began speaking. A break in the weather was on the way. There would be a thirty-six-hour interval between the end of this storm and the arrival of another. As Stagg spoke, the rain began to stop and the winds subsided. Cheers rose again in the mess room. For five minutes, Dwight Eisenhower sat on a sofa in profound silence. Should he risk it? If he did not, he would have to wait another two weeks, again with no guarantee of fair weather. A month's delay had ruined Hitler in the Soviet Union. Thirty days lost to the Allies could mean a winter on the Siegfried Line rather than an autumn offensive through it. Another delay of two weeks might cause the Fortitude deception to unravel, make the Atlantic Wall that much stronger. Dwight Eisenhower glanced up.

"Okay," he said briskly. "We'll go."

89. D-Day on Normandy

BY NIGHTFALL of June 5 the great invasion fleet was on its way, converging on the Normandy coast from British ports stretching from Wales to the North Sea. Overhead thundered the transport planes carrying 24,000 airborne troops—one third of them British, two thirds American—who were to land behind German lines and seal off the beachheads. One British airborne division was to secure the Anglo-Canadian left flank, while the American 82nd and 101st Airborne were to seize that wide lagoon to the rear of Utah and Omaha. If they did not and it was held by the Germans instead, the Yankee beaches could become a slaughter pen.

Many of the American paratroopers carried heavy loads of fifty pounds or more, not including their own battle gear and weapons. Fayette Richardson of the 82nd Airborne was one of these. He was a pathfinder, the men who were first to jump, to use radar and beacon lights to guide the following planes to the target area. Richardson had a thirty-two-pound radar set strapped below the reserve parachute on his stomach. Fragmentation grenades were hooked to his harness. Stowed everywhere on his body were gammon bombs, a phosphorus grenade, chocolate D rations, a morphine Syrette, canteen, fighting knife, antitank mine and, curiously, an Armed Forces paperback edition of *Oliver Twist*. Richardson was also supposed to carry a rifle, but that ten-pound weapon seemed a bit too heavy; instead, he strapped a .45 automatic pistol to his boot. So, heavily and clumsily arrayed for battle, the American paratroopers were jammed together in the bellies of their Dakota transports. To talk they had to yell over the roar of the engines, to see out the windows they had to squirm awkwardly around in their clumsy habiliments.

Richardson aboard his Dakota could see the moonlight shining on the Channel waters below. His crew chief waddled to the rear of the plane to pull off the door. Outside were flashes of light. Richardson gaped, puzzled; then realized that these were exploding AA shells. He came to his feet with his comrades and hooked his static line to the overhead cable. Outside streams of light were flashing upward like Roman candles. The green light came on and the paratroopers shuffled rapidly toward the open door. Pivoting sharply they hurled themselves into the slipstream, their wild shouts of "Geronimo!" trailing away with their hurtling bodies.

Richardson's parachute jerked open, and he felt a momentary flash of pain in his neck. Then he was floating down fast on an orchard. He could hear small-arms fire. He let go the front risers of his parachute, just as he missed a tree, and slammed into the ground. Seizing his pistol with one hand, he freed himself with the other. All over the orchard he could hear a metallic *click-clacking*. He *click-clacked* his own dime-store cricket, which was to be used as a recognition signal; one *click-clack* to be answered by two. Gradually his team gathered together. About half of them had survived, with most of the beacon lights and radar sets. The lead radar operator switched on his beacon. In chagrin Richardson watched him take his own set and pull the internal detonator that destroyed it. Only one set was necessary. Only one tripod-mounted beacon was needed, and it was switched on. The other men pointed their lights toward the sky. "Here they come!" someone shouted, and new streams of AA fire flashed upward toward the approaching Dakotas. Richardson and his teammates cheered wildly as they saw the descending blossoms of the parachutes dimly outlined against the sky.

Not all the drops were so successful on that critical night. Many of the Allied Dakota pilots were frightened by German flak and flew badly. Some of them released their human loads as far as thirty-five miles from their targets. But the

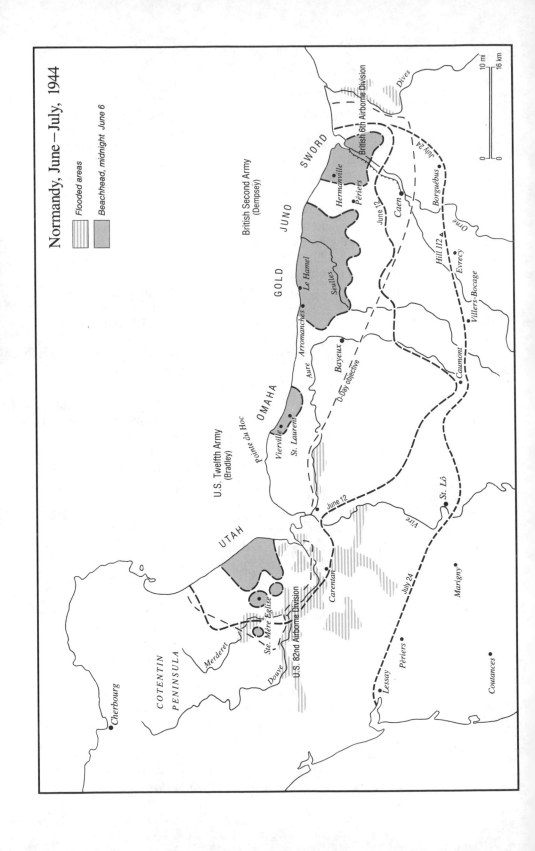

Normandy, June–July, 1944

Flooded areas
Beachhead, midnight June 6

COTENTIN PENINSULA

Cherbourg

UTAH

Merderet
Ste. Mère Eglise
U.S. 82nd Airborne Division
Douve

U.S. Twelfth Army
(Bradley)

Pointe du Hoc

OMAHA
Vierville
St. Laurent

June 12

Carentan

July 24

Lessay
Périers

Coutances

Marigny

St. Lô

Vire

Aure

Arromanches
D-Day Objective

Bayeux

GOLD
Le Hamel
Seulles

Caumont

Villers-Bocage

Evrecy

Hill 112

Orne

JUNO

British Second Army
(Dempsey)

Hermanville
Périers

June 12

Caen

Borguébus

July 24

SWORD

British 6th Airborne Division

Dives

10 mi
16 km

loss of only twenty Allied aircraft proved that the enemy AA was not intense.

By contrast, the glider pilots behaved with great bravery. They crash-landed on their objectives accurately and were of great help to the British 6th Airborne Division as its men seized the bridges over the Caen Canal and across the Orne River to secure Montgomery's left flank. Seventy-one of the 191 glider pilots who landed east of the Orne became casualties. Among the Americans the losses were proportionately higher.

The Americans also suffered more severely from the erratic drops. Jumping into high winds, they were carried far from their objectives, some landing in treetops to be rescued by their comrades or cut down and imprisoned by the Germans. Others, weighted with their heavy equipment, drowned in waters sometimes only three feet deep.

The 82nd under Maj. Gen. Matthew Ridgway had the most concentrated drop. Having the advantage of surprise, three quarters of its leading regiment landed within three miles of the drop zone. Using their crickets to draw together, man to man and squad to squad, they rallied quickly and seized St. Mère Église to block the Cherbourg–Carentan road. But they were unable to hold it in the face of sharp counterattacks by the German 91st Infantry Division, which had been specially trained to repel airborne assault. Airborne troops, for all their bravery and splendid physical condition, are powerless in the face of armor and artillery. Dropping at night in a foreign country, the Americans had no landmarks to guide them. All they had were those insignificant but invaluable little crickets, and their own valor. Thousands of men miles from their targets took on the Germans wherever they met them, spreading bewilderment and confusion among the soldiers of the 91st Division. But because its men were so scattered, the 82nd was unable to seize the bridgeheads over the Merderet River to protect its crossings.

Maj. Gen. Maxwell Taylor's 101st Airborne was more fortunate, its paratroopers landing in an area not so strongly defended. But they too were so widely scattered that by daylight Taylor had been able to concentrate only one sixth of his command. Before then, however, he had been reinforced by a landing of fifty gliders. With these he captured all the exits of all the causeways behind Utah Beach and occupied an abandoned German gun battery.

Although the American airborne divisions had not accomplished all their missions, they had opened the western end of the Cotentin front for movement inland and had so rattled the German 91st that it was forced to give battle in the swamps and orchards of the Merderet Valley rather than to counterattack on the beaches.

German reaction to the Allied air invasion was sluggish indeed. Hitler's intelligence officers had been aware for some time that an Allied signal for a rising of the French Resistance would also proclaim D-Day. The signal was the first two lines from a poem by the Frenchman Paul Verlaine. They were, "The long sobs of the violins of autumn/ Wounding my heart with monotonous languor." On

June 1 the BBC broadcast the first line, which was intercepted and understood by the Germans. On the night of June 5 the second was broadcast and decoded by the German Fifteenth Army at Calais. But it was ignored, probably because the Germans never regarded the French Resistance as anything more than a nuisance, incapable of major operations.

But there was no excuse for many other oversights and omissions. For one, the German navy, convinced that the weather was unfit for invasion, had failed to station patrols in the Channel. Allied minesweeping activity begun with last light of June 5 was ignored. Most detrimental was the absence from headquarters of so many top commanders. No one alerted the 21st Panzer Division, close to the beaches, because no one knew the whereabouts of Gen. Edgar Feuchtinger, its commander. Wherever he was, it was believed that he was accompanied by a lady. Field Marshal Erwin Rommel had gone home to Germany to visit his family and Gen. Friedrich Dollman, Seventh Army's chief, was far away in Rennes at an exercise based on an Allied invasion of France! Gerd von Rundstedt was still in Paris listening to his arteries harden, and his staff refused to alert any of his forces on the coast. Instead, they confined themselves to a general warning that the BBC signal might set off an outbreak of sabotage. Gradually, one by one, the various forces were alerted. But German confusion became compounded by the Allied drop of thousands of dummy paratroops. A regiment of bicyclists sent speeding toward a drop zone found only hundreds of sacks attached to parachutes. So many dummies led to German uncertainty about a possible bluff. It was not until 6:00 A.M. that Rundstedt's headquarters called the German high command to say that a major invasion was taking place and to ask for release of the armored reserve. But no one dared awake Hitler from his drugged sleep, and the appeal was denied. A little later, General von Salmuth, commander of the Fifteenth Army at Calais, having received reports that his forces could cope with any invasion, went to bed. It was not until after 10:30 A.M., following the Allied announcement of the invasion, that Rommel was notified. He at once began driving toward the front at high speed, but did not reach La Roche Guyon until twelve hours later. His "longest day" by then was more than half over.

Most significant was the German uncertainty over whether the Normandy landings were *the* invasion or merely a feint or a diversion. Fortitude had completely deceived them. Even the ferocity of the Allied aerial onslaught failed to remove their doubts, if only because the Calais area was worked over nearly as thoroughly as the Cotentin. A massive air umbrella of thousands upon thousands of Allied fighters and attack bombers ranged over the French interior or swooped down on the invasion beaches to bomb and strafe them. During the night a thousand British heavy bombers struck the coastal defenses, and just before the Omaha landings began, a thousand American bombers roared over the channel to deliver the final blow: a blanket of 13,000 tons of bombs. Unfortunately, almost all of these cascaded harmlessly into the empty hedgerows three miles inland. Because of the smoke and overcast obscuring the beaches, Allied air was reluctant to risk hitting friendly boats and troops and so delayed the drop long enough to guarantee safety but also to cancel out the contribution.

Before dawn, the Normandy coast flickered in the flares and flashes of intensive naval gunfire. There were nine battleships, twenty-three cruisers, 104 destroyers and seventy-one corvettes in the bombardment force, which also gave protection to 6,483 vessels of every description: merchantmen and luxury liners converted into troopships, tank lighters and 4,000 landing crafts and barges to carry troops and guns ashore. The battleships and cruisers stood well out on the Channel to shoot at selected targets. Destroyers with 5-inchers fingering the sky sped inshore to rake the pillboxes. Rocket ships loosed their flights of missiles, and while the minesweepers cleared lanes for the landing craft, frogmen in green rubber suits leaped into the surf to blow up underwater obstacles. Then the bombardment lifted. An eerie silence broken by sporadic gunfire settled over the beaches. Now, as always, it was up to the foot soldier with the hand gun.

At Utah Beach on the American right a strong current swept the 4th Infantry Division's spearheads 2,000 yards south of their designated area. Usually, such a mishap can be disastrous, but at Utah it was fortunate. The Americans came ashore at the most lightly defended sector of the entire Cotentin front. The Germans had thought it unlikely that the "Amies" would land immediately in front of the widely flooded areas behind the beaches there. Of thirty-two DDs assigned to Utah, twenty-eight came successfully ashore.

The Germans defending Utah were almost relieved to see the Americans approach. Throughout the night and early morning they had lain quaking and quivering beneath the Allied bombing, their hands covering their ears. At first light 360 Marauder medium bombers had hit Utah, and then came a remarkably accurate naval bombardment. Many of W-5's bunkers, all its 50-mm guns and its lone 75-mm cannon were destroyed. "Everything's wrecked! Everything's wrecked! We've got to surrender!" an elderly mess orderly cried. But the commanding officer, twenty-three-year-old Lt. Arthur Jahnke, a wounded and decorated veteran of the Soviet front, calmed his men and ordered them to fight. All Jahnke had left was an 88 and the gun of an old Renault tank dug into the sands, plus some machine guns and mortars. To their dismay Jahnke and his men saw that the Americans were landing at low tide. All of Rommel's obstacles and guns were designed or sited for a high-water landing. Now the Americans either avoided or blew up Rommel's clearly visible "asparagus." The Germans also gaped at the sight of the DD Shermans rising from the sea like antediluvian monsters to come against them with flaming 75s. Within a few minutes Jahnke and his guns were both knocked out, and he awoke to find himself and his men American prisoners.

Most of the Germans of the 709th Division defending Utah also surrendered. As the American spearheads mopped up the beaches, the engineers completed demolition of the obstacles. Artillery, vehicles of every description and supplies came pouring ashore. The 4th's soldiers found an undefended beach exit across the flooded fields while the 101st Airborne held four more open for them. Soon the Americans were moving across the floods. By nightfall, 23,000 men of Lightnin' Joe Collins's VII Corps had come ashore at a cost of only 197 casualties. Good fortune and good judgment had combined to make a military miracle. But Omaha, where the 1st and 29th Divisions of Maj. Gen. Leonard T. Gerow's V Corps were landing, had become a fiery crucible.

Omaha Beach gave a dreadful and deadly demonstration of Murphy's Law: All that can go wrong will go wrong at the wrong time. It was at this sector around Vierville and St. Laurent that the American bombers, fearing to hit their own craft and troops, had delayed their drop until their bombs crashed uselessly behind the German defenders. Here also Rommel had stationed the 352nd Division, one of his finest, and British Intelligence's warnings to this effect were all but ignored by General Gerow's staff. Here too the Germans held the strongest natural positions facing the entire Overlord assault: hills and cliffs rising steeply up to 200 feet from the beach and the sea wall above it. At Omaha was the greatest concentration of enemy fire on the sixty-mile invasion front. Finally, Gerow's tactical dispositions and handling of his troops all but guaranteed disaster and were redeemed only by the bravery of his soldiers.

Gerow can hardly be criticized for planning a frontal assault, however; there was no room for maneuver at Omaha. But his staff might have evolved some plan of maneuver for opening the five vital beach exits, and their elaborate timetables were nothing short of an invitation to disaster in even the calmest seas. The V Corps also declined to use all but the DDs of the specialized armor developed by the British. Gerow's soldiers also were boated in darkness twelve miles from the beach, rather than the seven miles used by the British. Even seven is quite a distance for troops in LCVPs to travel, especially in the choppy, ten-knot seas off Omaha. But twelve in those rough waters was either a serious error of judgment or the result of the reluctance of the transports to come in that close. It took V Corps's spearheads three hours to reach the beaches, and by then most of them had thrown up their breakfasts, all were drenched and many were seasick, covered with puke and caked with salt. Finally, Gerow weighed down his soldiers with an incredible load of equipment, much of it unnecessary or useless. Each man carried a gas mask(!), hand grenades, pole or satchel charges, half-pound blocks of TNT, two bandoliers of rifle ammunition, first-aid kit and canteen: a total of sixty-eight pounds. When to this is added his rifle, helmet, bayonet, boots, cartridge belt and clothing, the figure approaches ninety pounds! Even the best-conditioned athletes in the world could not go careening around a battlefield for hours so encumbered.

At the outset at least ten LCVPs were swamped by high waves, drowning most of their occupants. Attempts to land artillery from amphibious trucks called Ducks were a disaster, twenty-six guns lost. Some rockets fired from far offshore fell short among the assault boats. From some unknown incompetent came the order to launch thirty-two DDs three and a half miles out in heavy seas. Five of them reached the beach and the other twenty-seven sank like stones, drowning most of their crews. Without the tanks to take enemy fortifications under fire, the infantry had to storm the beaches themselves, flesh against fire. When the tanks did arrive, they came behind, not ahead of, the eight spearhead companies—1,450 soldiers in thirty-six landing craft.

Heavy machine-gun and mortar fire greeted these men as they waded ashore. Many were wounded before they reached dry land and had to struggle painfully up the beach, heading for the protection of the sea wall. Others still groggy from their seasickness clung desperately to the boat obstacles for protection. A wall of wrecked landing craft and vehicles built up quickly on the beach. Among these, other soldiers sought protection from the scything German fire. Some craft cresting the surf were hurled broadside into the obstacles, creating a logjam, which held up the following waves while gathering more hulks into a swelling barricade. On one of them a soldier with a flamethrower took a direct hit in his fuel tank. The explosion catapulted his dying body into the sea and set the vessel on fire.

A company of 270 specially trained demolition men followed the infantry ashore, planning to blow up the boat obstacles before the tide covered them so that the following wave of 25,000 men and 4,400 vehicles might have an unimpeded path ashore. But German gunfire killed or wounded nearly half of them and most of the survivors took cover. Only a few obstacles were blown that morning. A path to the beach was opened by landing craft ramming the obstacles either by accident or intent, thus detonating the mines and clearing a lane. Toward this headed lighters carrying sixteen armored bulldozers. Only six reached the beach, and of these three more were destroyed.

Among the infantry huddled beneath the sea wall or strewn among the debris, collapse of command followed quickly upon destruction of communications. One regiment lost three quarters of its radios, and its forward headquarters was wiped out by a direct hit. Men landed far from the sector for which they had been trained looked wildly and helplessly around for someone to command them. There were few. Too many of the American junior officers on Omaha that morning had been paralyzed by that same immobilizing dread that had come over their men.

Offshore aboard the cruiser *Augusta,* flagship of Adm. Alan Kirk, the Task Force commander, Omar Bradley sat inside a 20-by-10 steel command cabin constructed on deck. Along one wall was a row of typists while Bradley and his staff huddled around a big plotting table. On the walls were large-scale maps of Normandy and Michelin road maps. Sometimes Bradley left his command post to stand on the bridge with Kirk, his ears stuffed with cotton against the blasting of the big guns, his binoculars trained on Omaha. On Bradley's nose was a bandage covering a nasty boil. The First Army commander's anxiety deepened upon receipt of fragmentary reports suggesting disaster on Omaha. Loss of so many DDs shocked him. He and Gerow had counted heavily on their leading the troops ashore to knock out German defenses. Sinkings, swamping, heavy seas, heavy enemy fire and chaos on the beaches, these were the melancholy reports reaching *Augusta.* When V Corps reported at noon that the situation was "still critical," Bradley considered diverting Omaha's follow-up forces to Utah or the British beaches, where resistance had been far less severe. The bulk of V Corps's assault forces and vehicles were scheduled for the second tide. They *had* to get ashore, if the inevitable enemy counterattack were to be repulsed. Peering grimly through the thinning smoke of battle drifting out to sea, Bradley realized that all depended on "that thin, wet line of khaki" that had struggled ashore and was so desperately clinging to its precarious hold.

To the west or right flank of the Americans on Omaha rose the Pointe du Hoc, a cliff upon which German heavy coastal artillery was emplaced. The guns had a range of nearly twelve miles and could deliver a terrible fire on the ships and craft of the Allied invasion fleet. A force of 200 Rangers under Lt. Col. James Rudder had been trained to scale the cliff and destroy the enemy guns and gunners. They experimented with mortar-propelled grapples used by British commandos to fire scaling ropes over cliffs. They also developed lightweight sectional ladders, which could be quickly assembled and run up the face of the cliff. Four long extension ladders were borrowed from the London Fire Department and mounted on platforms inside Ducks. Rudder's plan was to lead the assault company ashore himself. But Maj. Gen. Clarence Huebner of the 1st Division objected. "You can't risk getting knocked out in the first round."

"I'm sorry, sir," Rudder replied, "but I'm going to have to disobey you. If I don't take it—it might not go."

Rudder led a small force against the Pointe du Hoc. The bulk of his Rangers were boated, awaiting his signal that the cliff had been taken; then they would come ashore to move overland toward the point. But the signal never came. Rudder was delayed by enemy fire. His Ducks carrying his ladders were unable to penetrate a bomb-pitted shelf beneath the cliff. The Rangers began firing their grapples but the water-soaked ropes were too heavy and fell short. Finally a few of them lodged. The Rangers began hauling themselves up hand-over-hand. The enemy dropped grenades on them. An American destroyer swept inshore and cleared the cliff with 5-inch gunfire. The Rangers began bellying over the top.

They found a deserted, bomb-pitted tableland but no big guns. Then patrols pushing inland found the guns intact in an apple orchard. They had been hidden there to escape the American aerial bombardment, but might also have been removed from the sight of the big Allied battleships which their unprotected gunners might have been reluctant to duel. Whatever the reason, Rudder's Rangers disabled them by blowing their breeches, holding onto the Pointe du Hoc against enemy counterattacks until reinforcements reached them two days later.

Meanwhile, the remaining Rangers offshore, receiving no signal, went roaring toward the beaches in their assault boats, losing some of them and taking casualties as they did. They began moving westward toward the base of the Pointe du Hoc, fighting with great bravery and skill, adding their own considerable push to the slowly rising impetus of the American assault.

Although the German defenders at Omaha possessed the power to impede or disorganize the American advance, they were neither numerous nor strong enough to halt or destroy it. Even after the regiment that had gone bicycling away toward the area of the dummy paratroop drop had returned to the cliffs they were not strong enough. Even though eight German battalions instead of a supposed four opposed the American advance, they could not mount those deadly local counterattacks in which the German army excelled. Throughout the battle they fought a static, defensive fight. Thus, whenever the Americans gained ground or seized a toehold, they held it. No Germans attempted to retake it. Like pieces being slowly fitted into a jigsaw puzzle, the Americans steadily expanded their hold. They also were fighting better and with more skill and better judgment.

The commander of eight LCTs bringing a battalion of amphibious tanks into Omaha was appalled when the first five launched sank. He concluded that the seas were far too rough for such operations. He ordered the boats to within 250 yards of the beach before dropping their ramps. The survivors began to take German positions under fire.

Now the battle experience of the veteran 1st Infantry Division on the left began to have its effect. Barely two hours after H-Hour small groups of soldiers from "The Big Red One" had begun to advance up the leftward narrow valleys offering vehicle access from the beach. They mounted local attacks against the Germans in their pillboxes and communications trenches. They fought their way onto high ground and began to hammer the Germans on their flanks. By their valor and rising momentum they gave encouragement to the inexperienced and all-but-paralyzed 29th Infantry Division on their right.

In battle, momentum must be maintained, if only because it can confer mob courage on the men. If it is lost, mob fear takes its place, especially among untried troops. Then the thought uppermost in a soldier's mind is to take cover.

When Brig. Gen. Norman (Dutch) Cota arrived on Omaha with his 29th Division command group at 7:30 A.M., he found chaos and paralysis. He saw a soldier shot down who wept and cried for his mother. He saw another apparently on his knees praying, but when he came closer, he saw that he was dead, his face frozen in terror. Two of his group were killed within three feet of him, while another was hurled twenty feet by a shell blast. Cota moved among his dazed troops, compelling junior officers to lead their men forward, searching for openings from the beach. Coming upon a group of pinned-down Rangers, he asked who they were. "Rangers!" came the reply. "Then, goddamnit, if you're Rangers, get up and lead the way!" Stung, they leaped erect and began blasting paths through the German wire with bangalore torpedoes. Infantrymen lurched through them. The road at the top of the cliff was reached. Americans had gotten behind some of the Germans' strongest positions, killing the enemy or taking them prisoners. By 11 A.M. the 29th took Vierville. Cota found an abandoned bulldozer loaded with TNT desperately needed on the beach to blow obstacles. He yelled angrily for a volunteer to drive it. A red-haired soldier stood up. "I'll do it!" he cried, and climbed into the driver's seat. When Cota found another group of Rangers apparently pinned down, he deliberately walked ahead of them to show that there was no enemy fire. There was, but it didn't kill Cota, and because the Americans had such men—soldiers who did not point the way but cried, "Follow me!"—the near-disaster that had been Omaha was reversed and all along the line the 1st and 29th pressed forward. At 1:30 P.M. a vastly relieved Omar Bradley read Gerow's message: "Troops formerly pinned down on beaches Easy Red, Easy Green, Fox Red advancing up heights beyond beaches."

By nightfall the Americans controlled an area a mile deep beyond Omaha. Offshore, the Navy had loaded ninety Ducks with ammunition. Their exhausted but valiant crews took them ashore to provide enough firepower to repel the anticipated German counterattack. But it never came. Only at the British beaches to the east—where the Anglo-Canadians had achieved encouraging early success —did the Germans strike back.

The assignment which Bernard Montgomery had given to Sir Miles Dempsey's Second Army was an extremely ambitious one. Landing on beaches Gold, Juno and Sword—that is, from west to east—his forces were ordered to seize by evening of the first day the cities of Caen and Bayeux and the road between them while securing an "airborne bridgehead" across the River Orne on the far left or eastern flank. From this firm base, armored columns were to drive inland or south to reach the high ground of Villers-Bocage and Evrecy twenty miles from the Channel coast. This was indeed a bold plan, if not actually a starry-eyed one, which took no account of Rommel's strengthening of the coastal defenses.

Much of Montgomery's optimism sprang from his faith in Hobart's specialized armor. He was aware that Rommel had been convinced that the Allies would attack at high tide and had therefore sown his obstacles and sited his guns accordingly. Consequently, the torrent of defensive fire should fall on the zone between the high-water mark and the sea wall or sand dunes, whichever lay behind whatever beach. In other words, destruction at the water's edge, where men and vehicles would be trapped and scourged in a frightful tangle of blood and steel. Finally, Rommel believed that if his strongpoints were located in casemates of concrete five feet thick they could withstand bombardment from air and sea. Allied assault infantry would have no means of silencing the heavy guns inside them. Thus the foot soldiers would be wiped out before the armor could arrive to support them. However, strongpoints such as the fortress at Le Hamel on the western flank had bought their protection at the cost of narrowing their field of fire. Their machine guns and anti-tank guns were shielded from the sea against naval bombardment so that they could not fire directly seaward and could only hit invading foot soldiers on their flanks.

To offset the German precautions, Montgomery was going to land at *half-tide* and to bring his armor in *ahead* of his infantry. These were not the conventional gunfire tanks, which would have to be ferried ashore by vulnerable LCTs, but Hobart's Crabs and the DDs, which could be launched out of range and swim ashore themselves. This reversal of infantry and armor in an amphibious invasion had not been needed at Utah, where the beaches were lightly defended, while at Omaha the rejection of all but the DDs among the specialized armor had had tragic consequences.

But the British beaches were also storm-tossed. A fifteen-knot wind whipped up waves four feet high. Many of the Tommies in their landing boats also became seasick, despite their antiseasickness pills and their much shorter run-in. Offshore the wind had turned the water into one vast concourse of careening and colliding ships, like an enormous watery "Dodg'em" arena. The big "Rhino" rafts for ferrying trucks had broken loose from their towns and were drifting among the wildly dodging smaller boats. So strong was the wind that the tide was being driven ashore a half hour ahead of time. Commanders of the DDs wisely decided, unlike the inflexible fools at Omaha, not to try to "swim" them ashore but to land them behind the infantry. When the spearheads of the British 50th Division did come ashore at Gold Beach, they found that the specialized armor had landed ahead of them and was already engaging the enemy.

Not all the Crabs and Petards survived German gunfire, but one Crab that did immediately began pounding lanes through the minefields. It was like an apparition to the Germans as it waddled forward, its great clanging proboscis flailing the sands, detonating mines that exploded harmlessly in front of its heavy armor, its 75-mm cannon belching flame and smoke. Under its onslaught two companies of infantry were able to work their way around to the rear of Le Hamel.

Another assault battalion landing out of range of Le Hamel's guns was more fortunate. Here the specialized armor operated like a textbook exercise, clearing mines, smashing concrete fortifications and filling craters. Within an hour armored assault teams had cleared three exits and the jubilant Tommies rushed through them toward the heights beyond. At the eastern end of the 50th's front Crabs also cleared the way, but a German 88 in a pillbox knocked out two Petards, whereupon a Crab, taking advantage of the enemy's limited traverse, moved off to its blind flank to "post a letter" through its embrasure at a range of 100 yards. When the pillbox fell, the German defense also began crumbling. By evening, the 50th Division held a beachhead six miles wide by six deep.

At Juno the wind and the tide created worse complications for the troops of the 3rd Canadian Division. Treacherous offshore reefs forced a delay of half an hour until the water was high enough for the assault craft to float over them. But this also put them on the crest of a swiftly flowing incoming tide that floated them directly into Rommel's Asparagus. Many of the craft foundered and sank. One battalion lost twenty out of twenty-four boats. Even so, casualties were surprisingly light. Once ashore, the assault troops were supported by DDs launched only 800 yards out. Within an hour the waterfront strongpoints were overwhelmed, but there was difficulty in gaining exits from the beaches. Reserves could not reach them because the narrow beaches behind them were choked with armor, guns and transport. It was an hour and a half before they could force a passage, and this delay took some of the momentum out of the attack.

Farther east progress was swifter, although one company was cut to half-strength after it landed by mistake in front of a well-armed strongpoint. Only the bold intervention of a flak ship, which almost ran aground to take the German position under fire, saved this formation from annihilation. By the time a regiment of French-Canadians arrived, the German beach guns were wiped out and only snipers remained to contest it. Beach exits were seized and by nightfall the Canadians were seven miles inland. They probably would have penetrated deeper if the wind and the fast-flowing tide had not made such a hopeless confusion of Second Army's complicated timetables, while creating traffic jams so enormous and tangled that many a beachmaster was left choking and incoherent with helpless rage. Eisenhower's roadbound habits of thought, shared by every Allied top commander, had stuffed into the Allied beaches such a surfeit of vehicles— so many of them unnecessary—that it was simply impossible for reserves to struggle forward to reinforce the assault or for the engineers to detonate the obstacles in time for the arrival of the second wave coming in on the second tide. Even so, by nightfall the 3rd Canadian Division's spearheads were in sight of Caen. Two battalions were only three miles from the city's northwestern outskirts. But they got no further and this was the deepest penetration of the day.

At Sword Beach the attacking British 3rd Division was supported by ferocious predawn bombardment by Flying Forts and Liberators, followed by medium bombers and fighters ranging up and down the coast seeking targets of opportunity. It made a strip of coast three miles wide and a half mile deep tremble and shake. When it ended, the British troops went in behind their special armor to strike the dazed German defenders. There were twenty-five DDs swimming ashore. A flotilla of LCTs blundered in among them. They rammed and sank two and might have struck more if a salvo of rockets had not fallen short among them and scared them away. But twenty-one DDs emerged on the beach. They covered British infantry quickly clearing the foreshore. Within an hour three exits for tanks had been opened from the beaches. The assault moved rapidly inland for a mile and a half and by 9:30 A.M. Hermanville had been captured. The way seemed clear for a dash to Caen.

But here traditional British Army caution intervened, and the attack lost its impetus. British armor moving toward Périer Rise was driven back into Hermanville by the 88s of the 21st Panzer, and the assault was stalled. A renewed but still cautious assault was held up by two German strongpoints called Morris and Hillman. Morris surrendered at 1:00 P.M. after a heavy bombardment, but Hillman—a network of positions 600 by 400 yards—held out stubbornly, delivering a furious fire at any British formations attempting to move inland south of it. Hillman was not reduced until late that evening when two squadrons of Shermans led infantry against it. But the damage had been done. German positions inland had been remorselessly whittling the strength of British forces moving on Caen.

Gradually it became apparent to Maj. Gen. T. C. Rennie, commander of the British 3rd Division, that he could not make that bold dash upon Caen that would prove to be of such great strategic value to the Allied invasion. To make it, he needed armor, not infantry; massed, swift-moving armor. This was available in Rennie's 27th Armored Brigade comprising 190 Shermans and thirty-three light tanks. But two thirds of 27th Brigade's strength was too deeply entangled in the fighting on the beaches to be available for the dash on Caen. Tanks attached to the various infantry formations were also so engaged. Rennie, though an able, thorough soldier, was extremely cautious. He did dispatch some infantry supported by some tanks and self-propelled guns down the road to Caen, but it was a foregone conclusion that they would never reach the city. In Rennie's mind a more urgent priority was to reinforce the "airborne bridgeheads" across the Orne and the Caen Canal; and so, Montgomery's dream of a dash on Caen gradually sank into the category of the unfulfilled.

Meanwhile, General Rennie was anxiously asking himself, Where is the 21st Panzer Division? It was between Caen and the British, preparing to attack. Gen. Erich Marcks told Colonel von Oppeln-Bronikowski, the commander of the 222nd Panzer Regiment chosen for the assault: "If you don't succeed in throwing the British into the sea, we shall have lost the war." But Oppeln did not. Heavily gunned Shermans and emplaced British infantry hurled Oppeln back with a heavy loss of tanks. Then a simultaneous fly-in of 250 gliders of the British 6th Airborne Division to reinforce the Orne bridgeheads on the extreme left flank so unraveled Marcks that he fell back on Caen.

Thus D-Day—the historic June 6, 1944—came to an end. The failure to take Caen may have been important, but nothing could obscure the great victory that was achieved on this date. Not enough credit has been given to the German defenders—so many of them youths or middle-aged men equipped with outmoded weapons—who fought so valiantly against the best the Allies could hurl at them. They did all that Rommel could have desired.

D-Day demonstrated the decisiveness of Allied air power. Throughout the day the Luftwaffe put fewer than a hundred fighters aloft. Outnumbered 55 to 1, the German pilots did next to nothing to halt the Allied invasion, though with only three times more planes they possibly would have stopped it.

Erwin Rommel's "longest day" had been long enough for the Allies to come back to France.

90. Normandy: D-Day Plus 34

AT CAEN the Anglo-Canadians lay fifty miles closer to the heart of France than the Americans, and had the chance to break out into open tank-fighting country while gathering in airfields and airfield sites to support the attack. Precious fighting room might be captured before the German army could be committed to battle. But it didn't happen. On June 7 a British brigade's attempt to force a way into the city through Lebisey was stopped cold. Canadians also attempting to break out encountered elements of the formidable 12th SS Panzer Division newly arrived on the battlefield. Soon units of the Hitler Youth appeared as well as Gen. Fritz Baylerlein's redoubtable Panzer Lehr Division, probably the finest German formation in France. Rommel now shielded Caen with two superb and one good armored divisions, together with the Hitler Youth and those various line formations that had defended the sector on D-Day.

Their dispositions were typical of the German genius for war, their adaptability to any situation and their matchless skill in combining and coordinating the efforts of infantry, armor and artillery, and this in the face of that dreadful Allied aerial superiority. In preparation for the Battle of Villers-Bocage June 9–11, General Bayerlein of the Panzer Lehr sent all his half-tracks to the rear, realizing that he would not move far or fast in any direction. He dug in his tanks as mobile strongpoints, cleverly camouflaged with only a foot or two of turret visible above the ground. Tank tracks, made approaching the front, were carefully swept away at night before daylight brought the spotter planes. Infantry were deployed among the tanks or in ditches or ruined roadside houses. Against these and other forces Montgomery sent two veteran divisions of his old Eighth Army: 51st Highland and 7th Armored Divisions. "You don't send your best batsmen in first," he had said when asked why these units were not D-Day spearheads, but now he was putting them into the game.

They fared hardly better than their predecessors. Massive aerial strikes and fearful artillery bombardments by both British and American planes and guns sometimes helped them to make gains, but the Germans always counterattacked to regain lost ground. Gradually there began to appear among Second Army units, especially the British, a disturbing caution. Ranking officers began to suspect that Montgomery's "best batsmen" were not the high-spirited warriors that they had been in the desert. Many veterans acted as though they believed that they had done more than their share of fighting in the Mediterranean and should not be called upon to go to the fatal well of combat "just once too often." There were indeed many brave and valiant soldiers in the Anglo-Canadian forces, but the spirit and élan which had animated many of them on D-Day had begun to wilt in the fiery crucible of the Caen battles. Too few of them fought with the fervor of the enemy soldiers, each man convinced that upon him depended victory or defeat. Here was a great paradox of World War II: Allied soldiery fighting in a noble cause was usually no match for the German marching under an evil banner.

Excessive caution had also begun to characterize the conduct of battalion and company commanders, who had quietly reserved to themselves the judgment of whether or not an operation justified going all-out. Appalling carnage among the troops had shocked officers who, having trained their units in Britain for four years, knew every man by name; and they sometimes thought more of husbanding lives than of taking objectives. A survival psychosis also appeared among officers as well as men; they had lasted nearly five dreadful years and now, with the end in sight, they were reluctant to take risks that formerly never daunted them. Veterans seldom win medals. So "nontrying" became a constant problem for corps and division commanders, and even these generals, in the opinion of no less a critic than Sir Alan Brooke, were unworthy of their command. "Half our corps and divisional commanders are totally unfit for their appointments," he wrote. "If I were to sack them, I could find no better! They lack character, drive and power of leadership. The reason for this state of affairs is to be found in the losses we sustained (sic) in the last war of all our best officers who should now be our senior officers."

Brooke himself as well as Churchill, Montgomery and all the other British war chiefs can hardly escape criticism for their own deep concern over casualties. Almost the last uncommitted manpower and material reserves of the British Empire had been sent to the continent in the British Second Army. It would be joined by another Commonwealth army, the First Canadian, and that would be the last. American divisions would continue to flow into France throughout 1944, but there would be no more from the British Commonwealth. To risk great casualties similar to those of World War I would be to risk Britain's status as a world power. So these two armies had to be hoarded to preserve the U.K.'s influence in the peacemaking. British caution becoming evident at Caen was nothing less than an infection spreading from the top down. It is, of course, absurd to suggest that a British Tommy anxious to take care of himself would ever be motivated by such lofty strategical considerations; and yet, when there is something in the air, one does not need to identify it to catch it. Meanwhile, as the Battle of Villers-Bocage ended in a standoff, the American First Army on the Allied right flank also seemed to be bogged down in an incredibly difficult tangle of terrain called the Bocage.

The Bocage is a hilly region extending almost as far south as Brittany. Hedgerows—earthen parapets from three to twelve feet high and a foot to three feet thick—are everywhere. They were planted centuries ago by Norman farmers as boundary markers or to protect fields and flocks from cold winds. Out of them grow a tangle of hawthorn, brambles, vines and trees up to fifteen feet in height and also adding to the width. These hedgerows divide the entire Bocage into enclosures sometimes as big as a football field but usually much smaller. They gave the Germans natural earthworks for defense and in the bushes excellent concealment for small arms and machine guns. Apart from the main roads, passage through the Bocage was by wagon trails, in effect sunken lanes. These were often overarched by the hedges, forming covered ways and making of the Bocage a labyrinth of covered ways. Such terrain was ideal for a defending army and a nightmare to an attacker. Only rarely could a tank penetrate the hedgerows. American mechanized forces moving along the main roads came under constant enemy fire, which could only be silenced by riflemen on foot. The German army holding the Bocage, though much inferior to the forces around Caen, including in its ranks dragooned Poles, Serbs and Russians anxious to surrender, was thus given a defensive advantage canceling out the Americans' superior mobility and air power.

It fell to General Collins's VII Corps to clear the Bocage. Collins was already something of a legend in the American army, and his nickname "Lightnin' Joe" was gained by his speed and energy. The tenth child of a poor Louisiana family, Collins was another of those underprivileged Americans who went to West Point to gain a free education. He had also stagnated between wars and did not make lieutenant colonel until he was forty-four and the army had begun to expand. At one time he considered leaving the service to become a lawyer. Cultivated in his love of literature and the opera, sophisticated from his wide travels, he was nevertheless a hard driver who did not hesitate to relieve officers who did not meet his standards.

Collins had two good infantry divisions in the 4th and 9th, but his other formations—the green 90th and 79th—were sluggish and skittish. When spearheads of the 90th left Utah, they encountered an approaching column of German prisoners and opened up with all their weapons. Of the 79th, Maj. Harry Herman of the 9th had this to say: "They were almost a cruel laugh. They had one regiment attacking through our assembly area whose commander could not read a map, and they lost more men than I've ever seen through damn recruit tricks. It is quite evident that they are not prepared for combat—a shameful waste of good American lives." Some units refused to attack. After General Gavin of the 101st Airborne showed the 325th Gliderborne Infantry where they were to strike, their battalion commander suddenly felt ill and had to be relieved. The moment his men hit German resistance, they halted and would not advance. In the Bocage German tactics of infiltration were eminently successful against such troops, forcing them to panic or to withdraw because they were "outflanked." Although the Germans did not launch any large-scale counterattacks, they hurled a succession of local assaults in battalion or regimental strength against the Americans. Fortunately for Collins he had the help of the airborne divisions. Though lightly armed, and without the support of armor, the paratroopers fought valiantly to hold onto the passages through the floods so vital to Collins's breakout. They also redeemed the failures of the inexperienced units, and showed themselves the equal of any formations in France. It was the 101st that took Carentan on June 12 assisted by the 2nd Armored Division. On the 13th the units from Utah and Omaha were finally in contact across the great expanse of wetlands that had divided them. The way was now clear for Collins to move on Cherbourg, the great port at the tip of the peninsula. On the same day Hitler's "secret weapons"— self-propelled rockets—began falling on Britain.

The first V-1 rockets—small, pilotless, self-propelled bombs—fell on London a week after D-Day. They did not appear to be very frightening, and the British immediately called them buzz bombs or doodlebugs. But there was nothing comical about their successors, the one-ton V-2s, which buried themselves deep in the ground before exploding. Flying at 3,000 miles an hour, the V-2 could not be heard approaching. The only warning was the roar of its explosion on impact. In all, the V-2s killed 8,000 British—nearly as many as the entire blitz of 1940 —before this new threat to Britain was ended by Allied capture of the launching sites in the north.

Meanwhile, General Collins had begun his assault on Cherbourg.

Cherbourg's defenses had been designed to repel an attack from the sea. Its landward fortifications were not strong. In May, a German exercise had demonstrated their vulnerability at exactly the points Collins chose to hit. Moreover, the defending troops were not the best; actually a ragtag of sailors, supply troops, clerks, Luftwaffe ground personnel and other rear echelons mixed in with second-line infantrymen, all beneath the command of Gen. Karl-Wilhelm von Schlieben. Collins was astonished but pleased to discover that Schlieben was not making a stand on the high ground outside the city but had retired to its inner forts. At 2:00 P.M. on June 22, following a heavy aerial bombardment, the Americans attacked.

Though Cherbourg's defenders were poor quality troops, they were inside huge concrete bunkers from which they could deliver a withering machine-gun fire. Such conditions can stiffen a soldier's spine, and in the beginning the Germans fought savagely. They compelled the Americans to conduct a house-to-house street-fighting campaign. One by one the German bunkers were reduced by American infantry firing rifles, hurling grenades or crawling up to the gun embrasures to fix pole charges there.

General von Schlieben directed the defense from an underground command post at St. Sauveur on the southern outskirts of the city. Each day the positions of the advancing Americans on his wall map showed that he was losing the battle. On June 27, American tank destroyers began firing point-blank into the tunnel entrances above him. With 800 of his men, Schlieben surrendered. Maj. Gen. Manton Eddy, commander of the 9th Division, hurried to the command post. To his astonishment a tall, dignified officer detached himself from a group of prisoners and came to him, saying: "I am von Schlieben." Eddy took him to lunch, but an infuriated Bradley declined to join them, angered as he was by the German's protracted defense at a cost of so many American lives.

Eddy's delirious soldiers, meanwhile, had discovered Cherbourg's vast stocks of champagne and cognac. He tried to restrain them, but they paid no attention to him. "Okay," he cried in despair, "everybody take twenty-four hours and get drunk."

Cherbourg had fallen but in name only; the port was gone. Or so it seemed to Schlieben before he finally surrendered. Col. Alvin Viney, who planned to reopen it, claimed that "The demolition of the port of Cherbourg is a masterful job, beyond a doubt the most complete, intensive and best-planned demolition in history." Estimates of how long it would take to make it operational again—based on a similar predicament at Naples—were three days. It took closer to three months. The Germans had blocked all port basins with sunken ships, sown the harbor with a variety of mines, destroyed all cranes, demolished the Gare Maritime, housing the port's heating plants and electrical control system, and blown 18,000 tons of masonry into the deep basin that had housed transatlantic liners.

Nevertheless, the redoubtable American engineers set immediately to work restoring the port, while on the eastern Allied flank the British Second Army made its third attempt to take Caen.

On the morning of June 19 the worst storm in twenty years broke on the Channel coast of France. It tore apart one of the Mulberries off the Allied beaches and destroyed 140,000 tons of supplies. This was the very day on which D-Day would have come, had Dwight Eisenhower not taken his gamble to land on June 6. A message from Group Captain Stagg reminded the supreme commander of this. "Thanks," Eisenhower scribbled at the bottom of the message, "and thank the gods of war we went when we did."

The storm continued until June 23, bringing unloading to a standstill and delaying the third assault on Caen until June 26. Three of the British Army's finest divisions—14th Scottish, 11th Armored and 43rd Wessex—were to take part as the VIII Corps under Lt. Gen. Sir Richard O'Connor. The hero of the early desert warfare had escaped from an Italian prison after two years of confinement and been welcomed back to the war by his old friend, Bernard Montgomery. O'Connor was attacking on a four-mile front with 60,000 men and 600 tanks supported by 700 guns. The plan was to get around Caen's western flank by gaining the thickly wooded banks of the River Odon. In the rainswept early morning of June 26 the attack began.

A furious artillery bombardment helped the British to achieve early penetrations. But once the barrage lifted, the Germans began firing back. Operation Epsom, as the assault was called, was Passchendaele all over again. "It was pretty unimaginative," a young platoon commander wrote, "all the things that we had learned to do at battle school. A straightforward infantry bash." It was certainly not a plan worthy of the brilliant tactician of the Western Desert, and it came just as the II SS Panzer Corps—the 9th and 10th SS Panzer Divisions—arrived from the east. Again, reminiscent of World War I, it was a vicious, grinding, yard-by-yard advance until in the pouring rain of June 29 British tanks at last crossed the bloody Odon to gain the heights of Hill 112. At this point, General Dollman of Seventh Army, in his last order before he killed himself, pleaded with General Hauser of II Panzer Corps to hurl both his armored divisions against the British right. He did, and the Germans were thrown back. In probably the finest fighting of the British in Normandy, superbly supported by Allied air, the German counterstroke was stopped cold. Unfortunately, General Dempsey misread the battle. Believing that Hauser's Panther tanks would strike again, fearful for O'Connor's exhausted troops east of the Odon, he ordered the 11th Armored to withdraw to the west bank. With this Montgomery closed down Operation Epsom, and the third attempt to take Caen also failed.

In more than a month of fighting, the British Second Army still had not captured Caen. In desperation, Montgomery and Dempsey launched a massive aerial attack on the city the night of July 7, hoping it would clear the way for an assault the following morning. Some 450 heavies of Bomber Command dropping mostly delayed-action bombs droned over the stricken city in wave after wave. Hundreds of thousands of Allied soldiers cheered as a great pall of smoke and dust rose above the steady rumble of explosions. It seemed to them that the German defenses must have been obliterated. But once again the airmen, fearful of hitting friendly troops, had delayed their drops too long. Instead of wrecking the German defenses, they all but destroyed the ancient city of Caen.

At the urging of the Germans and the local prefect, about a quarter of Caen's citizenry fled the city before the bombing. Most remained in the phlegmatic conviction that "to evacuate is only to escape Germans to meet other Germans, to avoid bombs and shells to meet other bombs and shells." But even this aplomb was shattered by a devastating attack so much fiercer than anything experienced before. After the bombers departed, a great silence fell upon the city, broken only by the cries of the wounded and the shudder and collapse of buildings. Because water mains had burst all over the city, firemen struggled hopelessly to draw water from the Orne. Caen was still burning when the British and Canadian divisions attacked the next day.

Dismayed to find the Germans still full of fight and their path still blocked by the magnificent 12th SS Panzer, the Anglo-Canadian soldiers nevertheless sustained a steady advance. In two days of savage combat, some battalions lost as many as 25 percent of their men. But they finally fought their way into Caen, while on the west the 43rd Wessex Division crossed the Odon to retake the commanding height of Hill 112—retook it only to lose it once more to elements of the 12th. It would exchange hands once more before, on July 10, Caen finally fell.

It was captured thirty-four bloody, costly days after Bernard Montgomery had confidently predicted he would take it, and now a storm of criticism fell upon the proud head that wore the black beret. It was certainly not deserved, but Montgomery kept his unshakable, unflappable poise. A less self-disciplined commander might have allowed his own disappointment or dismay to have infected his forces. But the Tommies and Poles and Canadians of the Second Army showed an amazing confidence in their senior officers.

Eisenhower was furious at the delay, frittering away the time he had gained by his great gamble to go on June 6. He was also enraged by the cutting criticism of himself in the American press and repeated suggestions that he fire Montgomery. He probably would have if he could have, but he dared not risk disrupting the Alliance or going head-to-head with Montgomery's faithful patron, Sir Alan Brooke. Churchill certainly would have approved; he was already beyond patience with his cold and controversial little commander, and on the night of June 6 had furiously denounced him to Brooke, who just as vehemently defended his protégé. Tedder also distrusted him, wondering aloud if the chief of 21st Army Group really understood the importance of time, the urgent need to get across the River Seine before autumn. But no one moved against him, probably because of the great blow his removal would strike at British pride.

How much concern for casualties contributed to Montgomery's caution is not known. Commander Butcher, Eisenhower's aide, wrote that one of Montgomery's American staff officers told him that "Monty, his British Army commander Dempsey, the British corps commanders and even those of the divisions are so conscious of Britain's ebbing manpower that they hesitate to commit an attack where a division may be lost. When it's lost, it's done and finished. . . . The commanders feel the blood of the British Empire, and hence its future, are too precious for dash in battle."

Such concern perforce had to be like a straitjacket on Bernard Montgomery's undoubted high skill as a military professional, and it is also likely that the storm of argument still raging about his performance in June–July 1944 might not have erupted if he had loved the truth a little more than his own glory.

But dash in battle does not necessarily bring on a bloodbath. Speedy conquest can reduce casualties by cutting the length of a campaign or even of a war. The truth of this, apparently ignored by the bogged-down Allies in France, where the specter of a stalemate and the attrition of static warfare was again haunting the high command, was being given clear and repeated demonstration in the reeruption of the Pacific War.

91. The Central Pacific: Assault on the Marianas Islands

BEFORE ADM. CHESTER NIMITZ could turn north toward the Marianas and Japan, he had to complete the destruction of Truk to the south or rear of that sea assault. On April 28, 1944, flights of Hellcats flew over the dreaded fortress of the Carolines. They tangled with sixty-two Japanese fighters and shot most of them down. In two days they destroyed fifty-nine in aerial combat and knocked out thirty-four on the ground. Truk was left with twelve planes. Then the bombers did their job.

All the ships of any size in the lagoon were sunk. Everything aboveground on the airfields was knocked down. So thorough was this obliterating blow that the Americans could rescue their downed airmen in Truk lagoon. Of forty-six Americans shot down, more than half were rescued.

Truk was through. Task Force 58, which had finished it, was already wheeling and steaming north to give Marianas bases a foretaste of the storm that would soon blow up the northwest route to Tokyo.

Guadalcanal, New Georgia, Choiseul, Bougainville, Tarawa, Kwajalein, Eniwetok, New Britain—all those fights in the air, in water, on earth—were now history. Kavieng, Rabaul, Truk—the three terrors of the Pacific—were penned in and chained up.

"The seasons do not change," wrote Vice Adm. Chuichi Hara, the commandant at Truk. "I try to look like a proud vice admiral, but it is hard with a potato hook in my hands. It rains every day, the flowers bloom every day, the enemy bombs us every day—so why remember?"

Even as the greatest amphibious force ever assembled was preparing to cross the twenty-mile English Channel to the beaches of Normandy, an enormous procession of ships was gathering to take the Marianas Islands. In all 800 ships carrying 162,000 men were sailing a total of 3,700 miles from the Hawaii staging areas and 2,400 miles from those in Guadalcanal. Their targets would be Guam, Tinian and Saipan. Saipan would be the first.

Saipan, an island fourteen miles by six, had caves like Tulagi's, mountains and ridges such as those of Guadalcanal and Bougainville, a reef like Tarawa's and a swamp like Cape Gloucester's—while also possessing such novelties as cities, a civilian population of Japanese and Chamorros (natives of the Marianas), and open plains where maneuvering would come under heavy artillery fire. Saipan did not look appealing, and it sounded specially repugnant to those men of the Fourth Marine Division who listened to their battalion surgeon explain some of the island's other defects.

"In the surf," he said with solemn relish, "beware of sharks, barracuda, sea snakes, anemones, razor-sharp coral, polluted waters, poison fish and giant clams that shut on a man like a bear trap. Ashore," he went on with rising enthusiasm, "there is leprosy, typhus, filariasis, yaws, typhoid, malaria, dengue fever, dysentery, saber grass, hordes of flies, snakes and giant lizards." He paused, winded, but rushed on: "Eat nothing growing on the island, don't drink its waters, and don't approach its inhabitants." He stopped, smiled benignly and inquired: "Any questions?"

A private's hand shot up. "Sir, why'n hell don't we let the Japs keep the island?"

Those islands—which an angry Magellan had named *Los Ladrones* ("The Thieves") in honor of light-fingered Chamorro natives, and which a priest had renamed Las Marianas, in honor of Spain's Queen Maria Anna—were important to the Pacific strategy because possession of them would cut off Truk irrevocably, would pierce Japan's second line of defense, would provide a base to bomb Japan with those huge B-29s now coming off the assembly lines and might lure the Japanese fleet into all-out battle.

Saipan was the chief target because it was 1,500 miles from Tokyo and already possessed a good air base in Aslito airfield to its south and a new one being built in the north at Marpi Point. It was the heart of the Marianas, the headquarters of Japan's Central Pacific Fleet commanded by Admiral Nagumo as well as of that Thirty-first Army which Japan had formed by siphoning off battalions from its celebrated Kwantung Army in China. On Saipan were 30,000 troops under the command of Lt. Gen. Yoshitsugu Saito.

General Saito was an aged and infirm man. He had taken over on Saipan after the Thirty-first Army's commander, Lt. Gen. Hideyoshi Obata, had departed on a far-flung inspection tour. Saito did not get on with Nagumo, for the hero of Pearl Harbor had been powerless to prevent the steady sinking of Marianas-bound ships by American submarines.

On February 29 the submarine *Trout* sank the transport *Sakito Maru* bound for Saipan with 4,100 troops. Only 1,680 men survived to be shipped on to their destination at Guam. It went on intermittently, this submarine attrition, and as late as June 6 the submarines *Shark, Pintado* and *Pilotfish* sank five of seven ships bringing 3,463 soldiers to Saipan, causing the loss of 858 men. Almost as bad was the loss of cement and construction steel with which Saito hoped to emplace his numerous coastal guns. Of this he complained bitterly to Nagumo: "The situation is unbearable."

Nagumo did not think the situation unbearable at all. He did not think the Marianas would come under attack before November. He was positive, as was Japanese Imperial Headquarters, that the Americans' next step would be along the New Guinea–Philippines axis, probably in the Palaus. For this reason Japan had spent most of her material and energy in fortifying the Palaus, especially a postage stamp of an island named Peleliu. Adm. Soemu Toyoda had assembled the Combined Fleet at Tawi Tawi in the Sulu Sea, preparatory for a dash to the Palaus to engage the American invasion fleet in the all-out battle he sought as much as had Togo before him and, before him, Yamamoto.

And so, while General Saito got his abundant artillery in place in the hills, grumbling over his inability to emplace coastal guns to carry out his plan "to destroy the enemy at the water's edge," Vice Adm. Chuichi Nagumo, like almost everyone else in the army and navy, kept his eyes fixed on the Palaus.

Lieutenant General Smith, in command of all Marianas ground troops, planned to attack Saipan on June 15. Three days later Guam would be assaulted. Tinian would be taken a few days after the fall of Saipan. That was the overall plan.

The plan for Saipan called for a two-division assault on the island's western side just south of the coastal city of Garapan. The left or northern beach would be hit by units of the Second Marine Division, now commanded by Thomas Watson, who had earned his second star after Eniwetok. The Fourth Marine Division, still led by the Stolid Dutchman—Maj. Gen. Harry Schmidt—would strike the right or southern beach. In floating reserve would be the Army's 27th Infantry Division under Maj. Gen. Ralph Smith.

Holland Smith's assaulting force of about 50,000 men with its attached elements held far less than the 3 to 1 superiority in numbers usually required for an amphibious assault. However, because the Marines had reorganized their rifle squads, they now had far greater firepower than their numbers suggested. Each squad now had three BARs, compared to one previously. Each platoon had a special assault squad armed with a bazooka, demolitions and two flamethrowers. The divisional flamethrower strength had been increased from twenty-four to 243, and there were twenty-four long-range flamethrowers for mounting on light tanks. Each tank battalion now had forty-six Shermans.

While some 700 amtracks carried the assaulting battalions ashore, another force drawn from the Second Division would make a feint at the heavily defended beaches north of Garapan.

Four days before this attacking force dropped anchors off Saipan, the planes and guns of the fast carrier fleet began striking the culminating blows of the preliminary bombardment. Three days later, on June 14, the carrier force sent two smaller groups racing north to pin down enemy aerial strength at Iwo Jima and at Chichi Jima and Haha Jima in the Bonins.

That same June 14 Adm. Chuichi Nagumo changed his mind. "The Marianas," he wrote, "are the first line of defense of our homeland. It is a certainty that the Americans will land in the Marianas group either this month or the next."

But a tank officer named Tokuzo Matsuya figured the ships offshore meant something more immediate, and he filled his diary with bitter lamentation.

"Where are our planes?" he wrote. "Are they letting us die without making any effort to save us? If it were for the security of the Empire, we would not hesitate to lay down our lives, but wouldn't it be a great loss to the 'Land of the Gods' for us all to die on this island? It would be easy for me to die, but for the sake of the future I feel obligated to stay alive."

And on June 14 the commander of Task Force 58, Vice Adm. Marc Mitscher, got off an exuberant message characteristic of all bombardiers or artillerists captivated by the sound and fury of their cannonading.

"Keep coming, Marines!" he signaled. "They're going to run away!"

92. The Invasion of Saipan

SAIPAN BURNED fitfully beneath a drifting pall of smoke, and yet she did not seem menacing. She was, along with Tinian, absolutely ringed round by American warships. They sailed back and forth, firing, and some of them lay in the strait between Saipan and Tinian to hurl broadsides at Saipan's southern tip. Others in the strait fired along the beaches which would soon be swarming with American Marines.

Above Garapan the Marines of the diversionary force had boarded their landing boats. They were roaring inshore, drawing off only a regiment of General Saito's force. The aged defender of Saipan had guessed that the true effort was coming at Chalan Kanoa's beaches, and he had prepared his artillery for it. His guns were emplaced behind Mount Fina Susa, the ridge overlooking Chalan Kanoa. They were firing with skill, for they had the water between beaches and reef thoroughly registered, and they had sown it with little colored flags to mark the range.

Counterbattery shells screamed seaward. *Tennessee* was hit. Shells burst on the decks of the cruiser *Indianapolis,* the flagship of Admiral Spruance. The American warships lashed back. Dive-bombers shrieked down on both islands. The shore batteries were silenced, a flight of 161 navy bombers came down a staircase of clouds to pound Chalan Kanoa once more—and the LSTs had run in close to the fringing reef and were disgorging amtracks filled with Marines, discharging also those amphibious tanks or "armored pigs" which would lead the assault in flaming V's.

Halfway inside the 1,500-yard run to the beach, the amtracks began to take hits. Officers and men could almost guess the caliber of the next enemy barrage by the color of the flags they passed.

On the right sector attacked by the Fourth Marine Division, riflemen were vaulting from the amtracks and running in low toward Chalan Kanoa. Shells were exploding among them. Some of the combat teams remained aboard their amtracks, fighting from them as they swayed inland. But the amtracks were targets for the enemy artillery, as were the amtanks, and soon the Marines preferred to advance on foot toward Chalan Kanoa.

On the left the Second Marine Division passed through a rhythmical, flashing hell of artillery and mortars. Every twenty-five yards, every fifteen seconds of their ride to the beaches, a shell exploded among the amtracks. On Afetna Point in the center of the landing beaches an antiboat gun began clanging. Shore batteries opened up again. Close-in destroyers roared back at them, silencing them. But there were amtracks smoking and burning, there were bloody Marines writhing on their twisted decks. And the antiboat gun was driving the amtracks farther and farther north, forcing some of the battalions to land on the wrong beaches.

Within a few minutes of the arrival of the Marines on the leftward beaches, every one of the commanders of the four assault battalions had become a casualty. Maj. William Chamberlin re-formed a battalion and wheeled it to the right to strike south at Afetna Point, the men blasting away with shotguns issued especially for close-in fighting. They knocked out the antiboat gun and also reduced those batteries that covered the reef channel where the tanks had been held up.

But by nightfall Afetna Point had not fallen. It was a Japanese pocket almost in the center of the beachhead.

Back on the beaches the accuracy of Japanese artillery fire was crowding medical aid stations with casualties. Never before had the Marines encountered such deadly artillery fire, and with about 8,000 men put ashore by nine o'clock in the morning, there was a plenitude of targets for the enemy gunners.

Within the Fourth Division's zone, men dug foxholes to shelter the wounded. One man was brought in with his leg almost blown off between hip and knee. A battalion surgeon amputated it without bothering to remove him from his stretcher. By nightfall the Second Division alone had 238 men killed and 1,022 wounded—and of 355 reported missing few would be found alive. The Fourth Division, though not so badly hit, had already exceeded its casualty rate for the Roi–Namur campaign.

But by nightfall there were something like 20,000 Marines ashore on Saipan. They held a beachhead about four miles wide from its northern down to its southern flank and a mile at its deepest inland or eastern penetration. Within the perimeter, which had both flanks bent back to the sea, were tanks and artillery, as well as Generals Watson and Schmidt, both of whom came ashore in the afternoon.

However, neither division had reached its first day's objective. The Afetna Point pocket still stood between both divisions at the sea, and there was another bulge inland in the unconquered Lake Susupe region. So the Americans lay down that night in the ruins of a sugar refinery.

Opposite them the enemy was stirring. The counterattack was preparing. The men of Gen. Yoshitsugu Saito were in high spirits. For everyone in the Marianas seemed to know that the Combined Fleet was coming to the rescue. Admiral Nagumo had told General Saito so. As far away as Guam, Lt. Rai Imanishi was writing in his diary: "The Combined Fleet is about to engage the enemy in decisive combat. . . . The enemy has already begun landing on Saipan. Truly, we are on the threshold of momentous occurrences. Now is the time for me to offer my life for the great cause and be a barrier against the enemy advancing in the Pacific Ocean."

Although he would have to wait a month or more for his chance on Guam, Lieutenant Imanishi was right. The Combined Fleet was indeed coming. Adm. Soemu Toyoda had bitten hard on the Saipan bait.

On the morning of June 15 word of the Saipan invasion was flashed by Nagumo to Admiral Toyoda at his headquarters on Japan's Inland Sea. At 8:55 that morning, Admiral Toyoda sent this message to all his commanders: "The Combined Fleet will attack the enemy in the Marianas area and annihilate the invasion force."

Five minutes later, suddenly mindful that it was close to the thirty-ninth anniversary of Admiral Togo's destruction of the Russian fleet at Tsushima, Toyoda bethought himself of Togo's words on that occasion and flashed them to the Combined Fleet: "The fate of the Empire rests on this one battle. Every man is expected to do his utmost."

It was, to the Japanese mind, the tocsin of total battle. It brought the carriers of Adm. Jisaburo Ozawa up from Tawi Tawi to the narrow waters of San Bernardino Strait, bound for their Philippine Sea rendezvous with a battleship force led by Vice Adm. Matome Ugaki. It brought the Japanese fleet out fighting for the first time since Guadalcanal.

Exhilarated by the great news, the Japanese on Saipan attacked all along the line. From dark until dawn there was hardly a moment when enemy shells were not falling on the Marines or the enemy was not probing for the weak spot against which he would launch his full fury. At about eight o'clock on the night of June 15, the Japanese thought they had found a hole on the front held by the command-riddled 2nd Battalion, Sixth.

At that time, the Japanese began moving down the coastal road from Garapan. They came in columns of platoons, riding tanks, trucks, anything that rolled —coming with the customary clamor of a traveling circus. At ten o'clock they were close enough to attack. Flags were unfurled. Samurai sabers flashed and glinted in the moonlight. Someone made a speech. A bugle blared—and the Japanese charged.

A Marine officer picked up a telephone and spoke two words: "Illumination requested."

It came so swiftly it stunned the Japanese. They had not calculated on the American warships still cruising up and down the west coast. They found themselves outlined from their puttee-taped ankles to the round tops of their mushroom helmets, and they were rapidly cut to pieces in a horizontal hail of bullets, cannister shot, mortar and bazooka shell fragments. They broke and fell back, and then the naval gunfire and Marine artillery burst among them.

The counterattack downroad from Garapan cost General Saito 700 soldiers. It also cost him Garapan, for in the morning General Watson asked the warships and planes to flatten this enemy staging place.

General Saito's plans for driving a wedge into the gap between the Marine divisions was also doomed. Some 200 Japanese who emerged from the gloom of Lake Susupe and struck for the Chalan Kanoa pier collided with the men of Lt. Col. John Cosgrove's Third Battalion, Twenty-third. They were destroyed. So also was a three-tank attack launched down the Garapan road just before daylight. June 16 dawned with the Marines still holding what they had seized the day before and preparing to expand it. That same day Admiral Spruance hauled back on the line holding the Saipan bait.

93. Defeat of a Japanese Fleet

SPRUANCE KNEW that Ozawa had sortied from Tawi Tawi. Throughout the afternoon and night of D-Day, he had been receiving submarine reports of the Japanese approach. At 4:30 the sub *Flying Fish* sighted the Japanese carriers debouching from San Bernardino Strait into the Philippine Sea, making dead east for Saipan. An hour later *Seahorse* spotted Ugaki's battleships racing north to the rendezvous area.

On the morning of June 16, Spruance conferred with Admiral Turner and

Gen. Holland Smith aboard Turner's flagship *Rocky Mount.* He ordered Mitscher's Task Force 58 to intercept the Japanese, postponed the Guam invasion, promised Smith only two more days of unloading operations, launched prolonged air searches for the enemy, and alerted the old battleships to make nocturnal patrols twenty-five miles west of Saipan to block any Japanese ships that might elude Mitscher.

In the meantime the escort carriers would continue to give the Marines on Saipan aerial cover, and Ralph Smith would commit the 27th Infantry Division that very day. The conquest of the island was to be pushed forward as rapidly as possible.

Satisfied, Spruance prepared to return to his own flagship, *Indianapolis.* Smith stopped him.

"Do you think the Japs will turn and run?"

"No," Spruance said. "Not now. They're out after big game. If they'd wanted something easy, they'd have gone after MacArthur's operation at Biak. But the attack on the Marianas is too great a challenge for the Japanese navy to ignore."

With fifteen batteries of the Fourteenth Marines ashore, Saipan should have been the pushover that artillery duels with the Japanese had always been. But it was not. Four batteries were knocked out, although the division ordnance company had them back firing before dusk. One howitzer named Belching Beauty took a direct hit, which killed or wounded every member of the crew but one. It was repaired and firing an hour later. Two others were blown to bits, and the ordnance man gathered up the pieces and made a new gun from them.

Gradually, the Marine artillery asserted its superiority. One by one, the enemy guns were silenced. At 12:30 the Fourth Division moved out. It slugged ahead slowly. The battalion commanders began calling for tanks. As the Shermans moved up to the front, the Japanese 75s erupted again.

The tanks pierced that shower of shells and the attack went forward slowly, but by dusk the Marines' lines were firm all along the beachhead. The Fourth Division had a penetration of 2,000 yards across its 4,000-yard front. The Second Division had contented itself with cleaning out the Afetna Point gap, with patrolling and with consolidating its own left flank facing north toward Garapan. At dusk, while the 27th Division's 165th Infantry began to come ashore, Saito ordered the first night tank attack of the Pacific War.

Up in the blackened rubble that was once the city of Garapan, Colonel Goto unbuttoned the turret of his regiment's leading tank. He stood erect. He raised his saber and flourished it over his head. The turrets of the following tanks came open. The commanders, among them that Tokuzo Matsuya who had written so fiercely in his diary two days before, stood erect. They flourished their sabers.

Colonel Goto struck the side of his tank a resounding clank. His junior officers spurred their metal-mounts forward with similar saber slaps. The turrets were closed.

The 9th Tank Regiment swept forward.

At 3:30 A.M. Capt. Claude Rollen heard what he thought was a tank attack coming. He requested illumination.

Fifteen minutes later the squeaking, rattling Japanese mediums—the kitchen sinks, as the Marines called them—burst into Rollen's sector in two waves.

The first wave carried riflemen or light machine gunners sprawled on the long trunk of the engine compartment or hanging on to the guide rails like firemen. Crewman led the tanks forward on foot, although here and there a commander stood erect in an open turret, shouting orders and flashing his saber in the crashing glare of the star shells. Behind the second wave of tanks the bulk of Colonel Ogawa's 136th Infantry Regiment came trotting forward.

The tanks drove into a roaring caldron of explosions and flashing light. As they were hit and set afire, they illuminated other tanks farther back. Sometimes the tanks to the rear stopped. An officer jumped out, waved his saber, made a speech and climbed back in again. A bugle blared. The tanks came on and the Marine bazookamen tore them apart.

Some of the tanks penetrated, but they were destroyed by bazookas and half-tracks roving the battlefield like wolves. A destroyer knocked out the last one. Colonel Goto had lost all but twelve of his forty tanks and 700 men.

By the morning of the second day the Marines had already suffered 3,500 casualties, but the attack went forward with the army's 105th Infantry Regiment entering combat on the right flank of the Fourth Marine Division. The 105th was to take Aslito airfield in southern Saipan the following day. Meanwhile the Second Marines under Col. Walter Stuart moved upcoast until they were 1,000 yards below Garapan. There they would sit until southern Saipan had been cleared and the final drive north was begun.

Out on the ocean Kelly Turner was already taking the transports and cargo ships away from Saipan to empty blue seas many, many miles to the south and east. There they joined all the ships and men of the Guam invasion force, circling, circling, circling, to the extreme disgust of the troops, until word arrived of the victory or defeat of Mitscher's Task Force 58.

At a point about 500 miles east of the Philippines, the fleets of Admirals Ozawa and Ugaki rendezvoused and refueled, and were now speeding for Saipan, their scout planes conducting searches many hundreds of miles before and around them, hunting for the American fleet.

Tracking the Japanese for Admiral Spruance was a submarine called *Cavalla.* She was making her first cruise. She had sighted Ozawa's carriers astern at dusk. Cmdr. Herman Kossler had quickly put 15,000 yards between them and *Cavalla.* It turned dark, but Kossler could still see the vast silhouette of a monster carrier.

"Christ!" Kossler swore. "It looks like the Empire State Building."

Then Kossler had been forced to take *Cavalla* down. She submerged 100 feet and Kossler and his men tried to count the screws of the ships passing overhead in a half-hour-long procession. They counted fifteen, but Kossler thought that was too low.

Cavalla surfaced and got off her report to Spruance. She went down again for two hours. When she surfaced, shortly before midnight, she had lost contact.

Cavalla was going down again. A night-flying Japanese plane had sighted the American sub and Commander Kossler was submerging. It was three o'clock in the morning of June 19.

At seven o'clock *Cavalla* was up once more—but another enemy plane spotted her and drove her down. Something was stirring, Kossler could guess it from the number of enemy planes abroad. At ten o'clock he brought *Cavalla* up. Again the Japanese planes menaced him.

Cavalla went down. Kossler decided to wait fifteen minutes. . . .

Albacore was cruising at periscope depth and Cmdr. J. W. Blanchard was peering into the glass.

He started. There was a big carrier, a cruiser and the tops of other ships about seven miles away—and that carrier was big! It was *Taiho,* the carrier Commander Kossler had first sighted and the biggest flattop that Japan was able to float. She was 33,000 tons, brand-new, and she flew the eight-rayed, single-banded flag of Admiral Ozawa. She was launching planes, for Ozawa's attack on the Americans had already begun.

Commander Blanchard retracted his periscope and made plans to attack. He calculated the range and ordered a spread of six torpedoes prepared. Then something went wrong with the torpedo data computer. The "correct solution" light refused to flash—and *Taiho* was fast moving out of range.

Blanchard upped periscope and fired by sight.

Then he sent *Albacore* plunging down deep and awaited the arrival of both the enemy destroyers and the sound of a torpedo explosion.

They came swiftly—three destroyers and one great explosion.

Blanchard was disappointed. He could never hope to sink the biggest enemy carrier he had ever seen with a single torpedo.

The quarter hour had passed and *Cavalla* was up to periscope depth.

There were four planes on the starboard bow. But they did not molest *Cavalla.* Kossler watched. He saw the mast of a destroyer over the horizon. He moved to his right. He saw the mast of a carrier. She was taking on planes. She was not as big as the monster he had seen last night, but she would still rate around the 22,000-ton *Shokaku* class. Wanting to be sure she was Japanese, Kossler came in closer.

"Goddam!" he exploded when the ship's flag came into view. "It's the Rising Sun—big as hell!"

Cavalla began firing torpedoes. She got four off in rapid succession and another pair as she began to submerge.

Going down, Kossler heard three of his fish hit. And then he heard and felt the wrath of the Japanese depth-charges. For two hours the enemy worked *Cavalla* over, while above the surface mighty *Shokaku* was a holocaust of burning gasoline and exploding bombs.

At about three o'clock in the afternoon *Cavalla*'s sound gear picked up monstrous water noises. Kossler and his crewmen heard great concussions.

"That damn thing is sinking," Kossler said.

He was right. One of *Shokaku*'s bomb magazines had exploded, and the big ship fell apart and sank.

A single torpedo hit did not alarm Admiral Ozawa, nor should it have. *Taiho* was much too big, much too modern, to be so easily knocked out.

But aboard her was a damage-control officer who was not very experienced, and after *Albacore*'s fish had ruptured one of *Taiho*'s gasoline tanks, he ordered all ventilating ducts turned on full blast while the ship tore ahead at twenty-six knots. He hoped to blow the fumes away, but he only succeeded in distributing them. He filled *Taiho* with gasoline fumes, and also the vapors of the crude petroleum then being used for fuel, and he turned her into an enormous floating gas bomb. All that was needed was friction.

It came at 3:30. *Taiho*'s flight deck blew up, her hangar sides blew out and her bottom blew down. She rolled over on her left side and sank by the stern, taking with her many airplanes and all but 500 of her 2,150 officers and men. Among those who survived were Admiral Ozawa and his staff.

Carrying the admiral's flag and a framed portrait of the Emperor, Ozawa and his staff were ferried by lifeboat to the destroyer *Wakatsuki*. Soon he was to learn that not only was *Taiho* lost and *Shokaku* sunk, but his airplanes and aviators were being torn to bits in the battles that the Americans would nickname the Marianas Turkey Shoot. That day alone Ozawa lost 330 planes, against thirty American craft destroyed—the most resounding single day's defeat in the history of aerial warfare. Next day he lost a third carrier, *Hiyo*, plus two tankers, and seven more of his ships were damaged. The airfields on Guam were turned into rubble by the American bombers. He himself was forced to flee toward Okinawa, with Admiral Ugaki following.

There was no rescue at Saipan. In the log of the commander who opened battle June 19 with 430 aircraft on his decks, there was this ominous entry on the night of June 20:

"Surviving carrier air power: 35 aircraft operational."

The disaster had been even greater. With scout planes and land-based air losses added in, Japan's defeat in the Battle of the Philippine Sea totaled 476 airplanes destroyed and 445 aviators killed. American losses were three ships damaged and 130 planes lost—eighty of these during night landings at the conclusion of the pursuit of the Japanese—and seventy-six airmen dead.

"The enemy has escaped," Admiral Mitscher's after-action report declared. Capt. Arleigh Burke who drafted the report claimed that "we could have gotten the whole outfit. Nobody could have gotten away if we had done what we wanted to." This is debatable. Annihilation at sea is even rarer than annihilation on land. It is claimed that if Spruance had sailed farther west away from Saipan, he would have put Mitscher's search planes in range of the Japanese by morning. He chose rather to protect the forces off and on Saipan. It is said that he risked his carriers rather than Saipan, which is not exactly true, and that "the loss of a few transports" would have been nothing in comparison to the calamitous loss of his carriers. Sunk by whom? Certainly not the remnant of carrier air power left to Ozawa. And there were much more than a few transports at Saipan, close to 100,000 American soldiers, sailors and Marines. Destruction of this force would have been a disaster at least equal to loss of Spruance's carriers. Spruance's first charge was protection of the Saipan forces, not to risk them in the interest of annihilation. He was faithful to it, while also dealing a terrible blow to enemy naval air strength.

No nation had ever been so badly beaten in the skies above the seas. But Tokyo was already telling the world of the customary magnificent victory, just as Saito had been telling Tokyo of the splendid successes being achieved in the hot, shell-blasted hills south of Mount Tapotchau.

94. The Fall of Saipan

ON JUNE 22 Holland Smith launched his all-out assault against northern Saipan. Three divisions attacked abreast, the Second Marine on the left, the Fourth Marine on the right and between them most of the 27th Infantry. The 27th's terrain was through Death Valley, flanked on both sides by high fortified hills, sheer cliffs and mountains. But as the Second Marines climbed up the side of Mount Tapotchau, Saipan's highest peak, they were urged on by their hard-driving, profane commander. At one point Watson bellowed at a hesitant commander: "There's not a goddam thing up on that hill but some Japs with machine guns and mortars. Now get the hell up there and get them!" They did, while the Fourth on the right also advanced steadily.

In the center the 27th might have profited by such prodding. Its progress was painfully slow, and even worse on the following day when one of the regiments got lost on the way to the front, blundered into another regiment and got the division off to a late start. After two days of fighting Holland Smith's line was bent back in a U with the 27th at the bottom of the U about 1,500 yards to the rear. Thus the flanks of the two Marine divisions were dangerously exposed. Exasperated, Holland Smith conferred with Turner and Spruance and then relieved the 27th's commander, Gen. Ralph Smith. Army Maj. Gen. Sanderford

Jarman, who was to have been Saipan's military governor, took his place.

Thus was triggered the bitterest and nastiest interservice dispute of the war. Prior to Saipan five army generals had been relieved of command in the Pacific, but this was decidedly different: Holland Smith, a *Marine* general, had booted Ralph Smith, an *army* general.

Inevitably the press took up the quarrel. From the army side came the charge that Ralph Smith had been sacked because of his refusal to sacrifice lives in the speedy advance characteristic of the Marines. The Marine side responded that the army had raised a brouhaha intended as a smokescreen to conceal the poor performance of the 27th Infantry Division.

While the two services were thus engaged in vilifying one another, the attack to the north was resumed. By the end of June, the 27th Division had at last fought its way through Death Valley and linked up with the Second on its left. While the assault continued up the narrowing island, the Second was gradually pinched out of line and sent into reserve. The west coast flank was now the responsibility of the 27th while the Fourth moved through the center and east coast. By July 5, when this change was completed, all the airfields and chief towns were in American hands. Even the little airfield at Marpi Point on the island's northern tip had been destroyed. "General Saito is not going to get away in an airplane if I can help it," Howlin' Mad Smith said, ordering his artillery to wreck the airstrip.

On the following morning the aging Saito gathered his staff in his cave. His hair was long and matted. His uniform was stained. His strength was almost gone. He wrote out a final message to the remnants of his command, urging them to make one final banzai charge shouting the battle cry *"Shichi sei hokoku!"* That is, each would take "Seven lives to repay our country!" Finishing his message, Saito sat down to a final meal of canned crabmeat and sake. At ten o'clock, he wiped his lips and arose. "It makes no difference whether I die today or tomorrow, so I will die first. I will meet my staff at Yasakuni Shrine."

Saito walked slowly to a flat rock. He cleaned it off fastidiously and sat down. Facing the misty east he bowed gravely. He raised his glittering samurai saber and cried, *"Tenno Heika! Banzai!"*—pressing the point into his breast. The moment he drew blood his adjutant shot him through the head.

In another cave on Saipan at the same time, Chuichi Nagumo, once the idolized hero of Pearl Harbor, sent a bullet into his brain. That night the surviving Japanese would follow their leaders' orders without their leaders.

That same day Howlin' Mad Smith visited 27th Division headquarters, where he warned Maj. Gen. George Griner—the division's newest commander —that a banzai would probably come against him that night or in early-morning darkness. Smith had long anticipated a strong enemy counterstroke on his western flank. He believed it would come now because the low-lying Tanapag Plain to Griner's front was ideal for counterattack and because the enemy, hemmed-in and desperate, could be counted upon for this unfailing reaction. Smith also cautioned Griner to be sure his battalions were tied tightly together on their flanks.

But the battalions of the 105th Regiment—2nd, 1st and 3rd from left to right —were not buttoned up. Between the 1st in the center and the 3rd on the right was a gap of 100 yards. Above it, the Japanese began to mass, singing the funereal anthem *"Umi Yukaba."*

Down the coastal plain they swept, screaming. They swept through the gap, 3,000 of them, wheeling to their right to overrun the 1st and 2nd Battalions. Army artillery and Marine guns returned fire constantly. Some of them shot so many Japanese that their fields of fire were clogged, and they had to move their guns. Others shot themselves out of ammunition and fled.

The Japanese who had shot the gap burst in a howling flood on Marine artillery batteries farther down the coast. The startled Marine gunners lowered their 105s to point-blank range: 100 yards . . . fifty yards . . . forty . . . twenty . . . . Disarming their guns, the Marines formed a ring-defense and fought on with pistols and carbines. With daylight they could see three to four hundred bodies strewn around them. With morning also the Japanese hospitals disgorged, and the banzai became a ghoul's parade.

They came down the plain hobbling and limping, amputees, men on crutches, walking wounded supporting one another, men in bandages. Some had weapons, most brandished "idiot sticks"—knives lashed to poles—or bayonets. Behind them some 300 others who had been unable to move had been put to death. Their crippled comrades came down Tanapag Plain seeking to die themselves—and they were requited.

By nightfall of July 7 the beaches of Tanapag Harbor were stacked with enemy dead. By then also Holland Smith had given up on the 27th. A regiment sent to rescue the two riddled battalions—they had lost nearly 700 men—had stopped for the night because its commander feared Japanese in his rear. The soldiers of the trapped battalions had to be evacuated by destroyers and amtracks. Smith ordered the entire division into reserve and swore he would never use it again. In return, army generals vowed they would never serve under Smith again. Thus, in mutual recrimination, the Saipan campaign was coming to an end. All that remained was for the Japanese civilian population to make the final gesture to the emperor.

Marpi Point was a high plateau. It rose 220 sheer feet from the shore above a clutter of cruel coral rocks. Its seaward face was honeycombed with caves. At Marpi Point had gathered half of Saipan's Japanese civilian population, together with the surviving remnant of its military defenders, and here, throughout the afternoon and night of July 9, throughout the following day, there occurred an orgy of self-destruction which sickened those Americans who were powerless to halt it.

Surrender pleas broadcast from sound trucks, the entreaties of the Marines themselves, the pleading of prisoners—both civilian and military—nothing could deter these Japanese civilians from the horrible slaughter of themselves and their families.

Men and women jumped hand in hand from the cliff onto the rocks. Fathers stabbed or strangled their babies to death, hurled their tiny forms over the cliff and threw themselves after them. Soldiers prodded groups of civilians out of the caves, posed before them and blew themselves apart. Cowed, the civilians also committed suicide.

On the beaches below, one boy of about fifteen paced irresolutely over the rocks. He sat down and let the water play over his feet. A roller gathered out on the sea. He awaited it stoically. It broke over his body, it swept him away. He lay face down in it—and then, suddenly, frantically, unable to restrain the youth of his life, his arms flailed the water.

But it was too late. He lay inert. His trousers filled with water, and he sank.

Not far away, three women sat on a rock combing their long black hair. They stood erect. They joined hands and walked slowly out into the sea.

A father, mother and three children had also walked into the water. But they had come back to the rocks. A Japanese soldier in one of the caves shot the father. The soldier fired again and hit the woman. She dragged herself along the rocks, but the sea seized her and floated her out in a spreading stain of blood. The sniper took aim on the children. A Japanese woman ran across the beach and carried them away.

The sniper strode out of his cave and crumpled under the concentrated firing of a hundred Marine weapons.

When the Marines were able to rescue a child, an entire squad of men would rush about for dried milk to placate the squalling infant. One big Marine squatted in the road, brushing flies from the face of a dazed six-year-old girl, while the tears streaked his earth-stained cheeks.

Eight days after this ultimate expression of the horror of Bushido, the very high priest of the cult—Premier Hideki Tojo—was himself fallen. The loss of Saipan, the catastrophe of the Battle of the Philippine Sea, had broken the power of the man who led the Empire into the war. He was forced to resign on July 18, and shortly afterward tried to kill himself by firing a pistol into his heart. Because he was left-handed he could not take proper aim and missed, living to be convicted as a war criminal and hanged.

Saipan had cost a total of 14,111 American casualties—3,674 soldiers, 10,347 Marines—while destroying all but 1,000 prisoners of the island's 30,000 defenders. But Saipan also caused changes as important as the fall of Tojo. After Saipan, Japan was within bombing range of air bases which she could not neutralize, as she would do in China; she had no more carrier air power, and the inner works of Empire lay open to attack. The force of the blow struck by the Americans was measured in anguish by Fleet Adm. Osami Nagano, supreme naval adviser to the Emperor. Hearing of Saipan's fall, Nagano held his head and groaned:

"Hell is on us."

95. The Battle for Guam

GUAM HAD BEEN United States territory for forty years, until the Japanese captured it December 10, 1941. It would be the first American soil to be reclaimed in the Pacific. This peanut-shaped island, thirty-two miles long and four to eight miles wide, was the biggest and most populous of the Marianas. Its Chamorro inhabitants were intensely loyal to the United States, for which fidelity—including their reluctance to learn Japanese or to call their home *Omiya Jima,* "Great Shrine Island"—they had come under fierce persecution, their schools and churches closed, their Catholic priests tortured and murdered, their men beheaded for so much as a smile at the approach of an American airplane.

All of Guam's objectives were on its west coast: the former U.S. Navy Yard at Piti, the old Marine barracks and airfield on Orote Peninsula, Apra Harbor and the coastal city of Agana.

Against Guam's 19,000 defenders under Lt. Gen. Takeshi Takashina came 40,000 Americans of Maj. Gen. Roy Geiger's III Amphibious Corps: the First Marine Brigade, Third Marine Division and 77th Infantry Division. While Geiger awaited the arrival of the 77th from Hawaii, Guam was subjected to fourteen days of naval and aerial bombardment, the heaviest preparation of the Pacific War. Geiger planned to land just as the Japanese had, to either side of Apra Harbor: Marines of the Third Division on the left or north, those of the First Brigade on the right. On July 21, blessed by a light wind and a calm sea, the landings commenced.

The Marine Corps really wanted Guam. Some of the NCOs and officers descending to the waiting landing boats had been buddies of the 153 Marines captured there. To recover Guam would heal an old hurt. At eight o'clock the men of the Third Division's first wave transferred from landing boats to amtracks and went roaring inland. A half hour later the Marines had returned to Guam, but already the sands beneath the bleak white face of Chonito Cliff were splotched red with blood.

About six miles to the south, the 1st Marine Brigade attacked with both regiments abreast. Heavy as the Guam bombardment had been, Japanese 75s and 37s were firing as the men of the 4th and 22nd Marines rode inshore in their amtracks. Before the amphibians had waddled up on the sand, twenty-four of them were knocked out. Casualties mounted, and there was no one to care for them. Doctors and corpsmen were the heaviest hit. One battalion's aid station took a direct hit from a 75, which killed and wounded all but one man.

Corpsman Robert Law saw a shellburst spread eight Marines around him. One of the men had a shattered leg and his life's blood was spouting carmine from it. Law gave the man morphine. The man smiled and asked for something to hold. Law shoved clods of earth into his hands. He pulled out his combat knife and began to amputate the leg. The Marine squeezed the clods of earth to dust. But he made no sound. Law bandaged the stump. When he glanced up, the Marine smiled at him again. Then he sank into unconsciousness.

Col. Alan Shapley's Fourth Marines drove toward Mount Alifan, about 2,000 yards inland. They passed through a grove of palm trees and concealed snipers. Sherman tanks led them through a maze of pillboxes and blockhouses. They sprinted through the slippery muck of a rice paddy, leaping across its myriads of tiny interlacing streams. They ran the gantlet of machine-gun fire and mortar shells, threaded the strong points of Alifan's foothills while the lumbering tanks bucked and roared and sealed off cave after cave, and by nightfall they held a beachhead a mile deep.

Behind that beachhead, the Old Bastards were wading ashore.

They were not really so old, these soldiers of the 77th Division's 305th Infantry Regiment. But they were in their late twenties, something like an average of four to six years older than their youthful comrades in the 1st Marine Brigade.

They had to wade into the southern beaches from the reef simply because the Marine amtracks had suffered heavy losses, and they had none of their own. Fortunately, the young bastards ahead of them were busily cleaning out the enemy. The soldiers had only the discomfort of waist-high water and occasional potholes to hinder their walk ashore. The entire regiment was on land by nightfall, the last to arrive being its commander, Col. Vincent Tanzola, who was saved from being stranded on the reef when a rubber boat drifted by. He grabbed it and paddled ashore.

The southern force had the situation in hand, and while the northern force battled slowly inland the Marianas campaign shifted to the island of Tinian.

Tinian had to be taken. Its seizure together with the recapture of Guam would consoldiate the American hold on the Marianas; but more important, this island of five by ten and a half miles had an excellent airdrome with three more under construction and enough level ground to make it the chief air base of the giant B-29s, or Superforts.

But Tinian, visible to the naked eye across a strait three and a half miles south of Saipan, had very few suitable landing beaches. Those fronting Tinian Town on the island's southwest coast, though accessible, were heavily defended. Reconnaissance troops found two narrow unfortified beaches on the west coast. One was sixty yards wide, the other 150 yards.

It did not seem possible to land two big amphibious divisions on such abbreviated beaches, but Maj. Gen. Harry Schmidt decided to land there.

His daring plan was to put the Second Marine Division aboard transports and make a feint at the heavily defended beaches off Tinian Town. Meanwhile the Fourth's men in amtracks would deliver a rare shore-to-shore assault mounted from Saipan's beaches. Schmidt made a battering ram of the Fourth, giving it the Second's tanks and artillery with all of Saipan's guns in support. If the feint succeeded, the Fourth would have enough power to penetrate deep inland, after which the Second would land behind it. Schmidt was so confident that Tinian would be short and sweet that he ordered his men to leave all cumbersome equipment behind on Saipan. Besides their weapons, all they carried was one can of rations, a spoon, a pair of clean socks and a bottle of mosquito lotion, all weighing not a pound and stuffed inside a single pocket.

"Hell's bells!" one Marine swore when he received his ration. "It's a silly picnic kit!"

General Schmidt's confidence might have been greater if he had known that an army-navy service rivalry on Tinian as bitter as *l'affaire* Smiths on Saipan had divided its defenders. Col. Kiyochi Ogata, commander of the 50th Infantry Regiment, rarely spoke to Capt. Goichi Oya, chief of the 56th Naval Guard Force. Each acted independently of the other. Captain Oya had fortified Tinian Town himself. All of Tinian's coastal guns, being naval, belonged to him —and he sited them all to fire seaward. He was positive the Americans would come at him when the panoply of American martial might ringed Tinian round on July 24.

Battleships and cruisers, five escort carriers and three of the big ones, army and Marine fighter squadrons, army bombers already operating from renamed Isely Field on Saipan, and 156 big fieldpieces massed hub to hub and firing from southern Saipan—all this was arrayed against the lovely flat checkerboard of canebrakes and rice paddies that was Tinian. Some planes were dropping America's newest weapon, napalm bombs made of tanks of jellied gasoline called "hell jelly." Gushing flame clouds were mushrooming everywhere through the smoke, setting the canebrakes afire, flushing out concealed Japanese while burning down buildings.

To the south at Tinian Town, Captain Oya ordered his 6-inchers to open fire on the American warships offshore. They were guarding boated Marines of the Second Division heading shoreward in a feigned invasion. Oya's gunners had a splendid target in old *Colorado,* only 3,200 yards offshore, and they hit the big battleship twenty-two times before she could get out of range. *Colorado* lost forty-three men killed and 198 wounded. Six hits on the destroyer *Norman Scott* killed her skipper, Cmdr. Seymour Owens, and eighteen other sailors while wounding forty-seven more. But then the Japanese guns were spotted and knocked out by a rain of American salvos.

Still, Captain Oya was elated. He had stopped the Americans. He could see their landing boats veering, turning, churning back to their mother ships. The enemy Marines were reboarding their transports. They were sailing north with their warships.

It was then about nine o'clock, and it was then that Captain Oya received word that the Americans had landed up in the northwest and were pouring over narrow beaches there in incredible speed and volume. And all of Captain Oya's guns were sited to fire to seaward. He was out of the fight. From now on, it was up to Colonel Ogata.

Colonel Ogata had also been hoodwinked by that feint off Tinian Town. By the time he had realized that the true landing was being made over those un-defended northwest beaches, it was too late for him to move troops there.

Battalion after battalion of the Fourth Marine Division burst from the bellies of the LSTs and went racing shoreward. Full 533 amtracks—all the III Corps could muster—brought them inland while the LCI rocket boats raced ahead and darkened the sky with showers of rockets. Even the 140-mm cannon that Colonel Ogata had set up in Faibus San Hilo to the right or south of the beachhead were knocked out by battleships, which fired armor-piercers into the cliff face above them and tumbled both guns and emplacements into the sea.

Only land mines, which the Japanese had concealed between high- and low-water marks, survived to defend these narrow beaches against the attacking Americans. Three amtracks were demolished by these, and many others were forced to bring their boatloads around to the coral ledges.

Throughout the afternoon, Colonel Ogata sought desperately to reinforce his surprised northern sector. He tried rushing up small party after small party from the south, but the American planes spotted and scattered them. By late afternoon the Fourth had established a beachhead about a mile deep and a little less than twice that wide. It had been seized at a cost of seventy-seven Marines killed and 470 wounded, and it held nearly 16,000 men. Colonel Ogata ordered an attack at 2:00 in the morning. About 600 screaming Japanese struck at the left flank, where they were annihilated by the Twenty-fourth Marines.

A half hour later the first of a series of strong thrusts began against the 25th Marines in the center. About 200 Japanese found an opening at the boundary between this regiment and the 24th. They poured through. They met muzzle-blasting artillerists and counterattacking riflemen. They were killed to a man.

At 3:30 the third and final assault fell on the Twenty-third Marines to the right. The attackers were blown to bits. Five tanks were destroyed. At dawn, astonished Marines saw Japanese bodies flying fifteen feet into the air. The wounded were blowing themselves up with magnetic mines—an end at once more powerful and spectacular than the customary hand-grenade suicide.

That dawn was also the end of Colonel Ogata's defense of Tinian.

Strewn all around the Fourth Division's perimeter were the bodies of 1,241 Japanese soldiers and sailors. At least another 700 had been wounded. With a single stroke, Ogata had deprived himself of perhaps a quarter of the best troops that had survived the first day's assault. He could do nothing else but fall steadily south until he and all but 255 of his command were destroyed.

That took seven more days, with the Second Marine Division joining the attack. On July 25, the Second moved in behind the Fourth. It cleaned out the northern end of Tinian, then wheeled to move down the eastern half of the island. Second on the left, Fourth on the right, General Schmidt's attack rolled south with the impetuosity which had not been possible on Saipan. On July 31, Tinian was declared fallen. On that night, Colonel Ogata himself fell—machine-gunned to death on Marine barbed wire—while leading the last banzai.

There was mopping-up to follow, and also a smaller replication of the suicidal horrors of Marpi Point. But Tinian had been taken at a loss of only 327 men killed and 1,771 wounded. As a masterpiece of maneuver, Tinian was as close to perfection as the cruel standards of war allow. It was a tiny price to pay for what would turn out to be the most valuable air base in all the vast Pacific.

It was only by four days of the most savage fighting that the Third Marine Division was able to establish the northern beachhead on Guam. Weakened by long debilitating weeks aboard ship, gasping for breath in the intense heat, its men had to fight their way up the steep heights above the sea. On the left the Third Marine Regiment was riddled by a plunging machine-gun fire from the face of Chonito Cliff. No fewer than 815 Marines were killed or wounded on that terrible ascent. But by the fourth day they had penetrated to about a mile on a front four miles wide. To the south, the First Marine Brigade had turned its sector over to the 77th Division and marched north to seal off the Orote Peninsula.

By then Lieutenant General Takashina was satisfied that the Americans in the north had all their supplies and equipment ashore and that he could now destroy them at one blow. He had already sent his suicide troops out to infiltrate the Marine lines and hide in the area's numerous caves. They were human bombs, with explosives wound around their waists or stuffed inside their packs.

"The time has come," Takashina told his commanders, "to solve the issue of the battle at a single stroke with an all-out counterattack."

The Marines on Guam had been taught everything they needed to know about the island, except that it was the Japanese liquor locker for the Central Pacific. Guam had whisky by the pond, rivers of sake and lakes of beer by the uncountable case. It had, in this sea of intoxicants, the answer to a question that had puzzled Marines since the first enemy banzai at Tulagi on the night of August 7, 1942:

Are they drugged or are they drunk?

On Guam the night of July 25 they were clearly drunk, especially on the Orote Peninsula, where the First Brigade had cornered an enemy force under Cmdr. Asaichi Tamai. At 11:00 that night an indescribable clamor arose in a mangrove swamp opposite the Americans.

"Lissen at 'em," a Marine hissed to his foxhole buddy. "Damn if it don't sound like New Year's Eve in the zoo!"

The Japanese were screaming, singing, laughing, capering—they were smashing empty bottles against the big mangroves and clanging bayonets against rifle barrels.

Hoarse voices cried, "The Emperor draws much blood tonight!" Some tossed grenades, yelling, "Corpsman! Corpsman!" or "K Company withdraw!" If they had hoped to unnerve the Marines or to goad them into giveaway fire, they had less than success. Their uproar only helped artillery observers call down a restraining fire on the edge of the swamp, while carefully registering all the Japanese avenues of approach with the combined guns of the brigade, the corps, and the 77th Division—as well as with the light and heavy mortars and 37s of the front-line companies.

At 11:55, a Japanese officer staggered out of the swamp. He waved a saber in one hand, a big flare in the other. Stumbling into view behind him, wielding their rifles and light machine guns, as well as pitchforks, idiot sticks, baseball bats and broken bottles, came his sake-mad followers. A Marine spoke into a telephone:

"Commence firing!"

The ground shook. Flares cast their ghostly light. Puttee-taped legs, khaki-clad arms, went flying through the air. The ground to the left front became a slaughter pen. Within it the Japanese began to run amok. They screamed in terror. Those who survived fled back into the mangroves, where the Marine artillery pursued and punished them. Between midnight and 2:00 in the morning, 26,000 shells were poured into the swamp.

Forty-five minutes later another banzai began on the far right flank with the cry of "Marines, you die!"

The Japanese rushed in among the Marine foxholes. Flares and star shells displayed them in all their drunken madness. They reeled about. They tossed grenades into foxholes with the giggling cry "Fire in the hole!"—and lurched crazily on. They clambered over heaps of their own dead to jump into the holes with the Marines, to kill or die there. Waves of attackers following them were caught in a crossfire and cut to pieces. Morning showed 400 Japanese bodies strewn in front of this position. On the First Brigade's left, a single platoon killed 258 Japanese without the loss of a single man.

Commander Tamai's attack had failed utterly.

But up in the north, Lieutenant General Takashina's counterattack was breaking through.

Takashina's grand banzai came in three columns, and it was only the first —and strongest of these that had no success.

This stroke was made around midnight by the full force of the 48th Brigade on the left of the American line, the sector held by the Third Marines reinforced by the Second Battalion, Ninth Marines. It was against this last battalion that the 48th Brigade struck.

But the 48th never got through.

Seven times the Japanese attacked the American left, and seven times they were hurled back.

The fight raged for ten hours and was not spent until around 9:00 in the morning of July 26. Before it was over the Second Battalion, Ninth Marines, was cut in half—but its men had killed 950 Japanese.

Takashina's second column was formed by the 2nd Battalion, 18th Regiment, led by Maj. Chusa Maruyama. He struck a soft spot held by only fifty Marines. At 4:00 in the morning of July 26, hurling grenades, they broke through. Marine companies on both sides bent back their flanks as the enemy rushed through the hole. Many were human bombs and the rain-swept darkness was broken by flashes of light as the American fire detonated their explosives. But they got through in strength, sweeping down on Marine tanks parked in the rear.

They attacked the tanks with their bare hands. They kicked them, beat upon them with their fists, backed off and fired futile shots against them, while the Marines inside calmly shot them off each other's tanks. Other Japanese attacked a battalion command post, where, with the arrival of daylight, they were destroyed by a pick-up force of clerks, cooks and wiremen. Behind them a company of Marine engineers and three weapons platoons plugged the hole that had been opened, and when Maruyama's reserves struck it in a second wave, they too were wiped out.

The left-center of the Marine line was safe.

On the right center the 3rd Battalion, 18th, under Maj. Setsuo Yokioka found a huge gap 800 yards wide in the American line and poured through, heading for the division hospital near the coast. Many of them were also suiciders. One group stumbled out of a cave, where they had spent the night singing and drinking, unaware that they had been sitting on top of a Marine who gradually lost his mind. Swigging the last of the sake in their canteens, screaming and hurling grenades, Yokioka's men ran down a hill to fall on the hospital. Patients and corpsmen seized weapons and fought back from behind cots and cartons of blood plasma. Patients unable to find arms ran for the beach. A doctor absorbed in an operation glanced up as shrapnel whizzed through his tent. He sent his corpsmen out to fight while continuing the operation.

At Division Headquarters another pick-up force of Seabees, MPs, combat correspondents and truck drivers was rounded up by Col. George Van Orden to attack the Japanese at the hospital. Gradually the Japanese were driven back into the hills. Then Van Orden's men began to mop up all the enemy between the sea and the front. Their work was made easier by the Japanese penchant for suicide, this time with a new wrinkle. Enemy soldiers removed their helmets, placed a primed grenade atop their heads, replaced the helmet and waited with folded arms for obliteration.

By noon General Takashina's "single stroke" had been broken. Thirty-five hundred of his soldiers had died and the drugged-or-drunk debate was a dead issue.

Two days later Takashina was himself dead, machine-gunned by Marines driving up the island. Soldiers of the 77th Division also came up north, took Mount Tenjo and linked up with the Third Division on their left. General Shepherd's First Brigade, meanwhile, cleared the Orote Peninsula. Their dead and missing numbered 431 and their wounded 1,525, but they had killed 3,372 Japanese and even taken three prisoners. Finally, they took a fourth, the last living Japanese on Orote. He was a forlorn sparrow of a man, small even for a Japanese. His uniform was much too big for him. His eagerness to surrender puzzled his captors. Usually a rare bird of a Japanese prisoner scowled and asked for a knife to commit hara-kiri.

"Why did you surrender?" a Marine interpreter asked.

"My commanding officer told us to fight to the last man."

The interpreter's eyebrows rose. "Well?"

"I *am* the last man."

Guam's chief city of Agana was empty, ruined by American bombardment. The Chamorro population had fled into the bush as American leaflets had advised them. But at a place called Yona the Americans did come upon a concentration camp filled with about 2,000 cheering, weeping, laughing, singing Chamorros.

They had been living in lean-tos and thatched huts built in the mud to either side of a sluggish stream. They had had little food, no medical care. They were clothed in rags. They were weak, racked by continual coughing fits—victims of malnutrition, malaria and tuberculosis. Their bodies were sticks of bones and their olive skin was drawn drum tight. But this July 31 was the day they had awaited for nearly three years. When they saw the American soldiers coming through the trees, they hobbled to their feet with glad cries.

They sang "The Marines' Hymn"—for they remembered the Marines—but the soldiers of the 3rd Battalion, 307th Infantry didn't mind that at all. The Chamorros then began to sing a song of their own underground, composed especially for this date and memorized in face of every threat of reprisal.

> Early Monday morning
> The action came to Guam,
> Eighth of December,
> Nineteen forty-one.
> > Oh, Mr. Sam, Sam, my dear Uncle Sam,
> > I want you please come back to Guam.
> Our lives are in danger—
> You better come
> And kill all the Japanese
> Right here on Guam.
> > Oh, Mr. Sam, Sam, my dear Uncle Sam,
> > I want you please come back to Guam.

Soon the Chamorros were streaming south where a Civil Affairs Section had been set up to care for them. Stockades were built, captured Japanese food was issued and clothing passed out. Some Chamorros came south just to eat and regain strength, after which they seized machetes to slip into the jungle bent on revenge.

Guam had fallen. It had cost 7,800 Americans killed and wounded—839 soldiers, 245 sailors and 6,716 Marines—but Uncle Sam had indeed come back to Guam.

96. The Russian Summer Offensive of 1944

ALONG THE ENTIRE FRONT from the Baltic to the Carpathian Mountains during June 1944, the Soviets were visibly preparing to attack. The Germans looked for them to strike south of the Pripet Marshes, for here they were already deep into Poland. A three-month pause waiting for the spring thaws to dry had given Marshal Zhukov the time to repair rail communications in this sector.

Instead, the Soviets surprised the Germans by attacking north of the Pripet Marshes, in White Russia (Byelorussia) where the enemy still held much of their soil. Soviet communications here were excellent and gave the assault early momentum. No fewer than 166 divisions in four "fronts" or army groups moved against the German Army Group Center, now under Gen. Field Marshal Ernst von Busch, who had taken over after Kluge was badly injured in an automobile accident. Once again the extent of the German front was its undoing. Busch asked Hitler for permission to withdraw ninety miles west to the line of the Berezina River. Such a step back could have taken the momentum out of the Soviet offensive. As usual, Hitler refused.

All that space in the center of the sector was to the advantage of the Soviets with their newly increased maneuvering skill. The value of American supplies was also evident in the hosts of motorized infantry following on the heels of the tanks, including the new Joseph Stalins. A breakthrough was achieved immediately and within another week an advance of 150 miles had been made. Moving in a giant pincers with converging horns north and south, a maneuver strikingly similar to the one executed by the Germans in the other direction three years earlier, the Soviets virtually destroyed Army Group Center with a loss of over 200,000 men. By mid-July the Red Army had not only driven the Germans out of White Russia but had recaptured Minsk and overrun half of northeastern Poland. Its most westerly spearheads were deep into Lithuania and not far from the East Prussian frontier.

West of Minsk the retreating Germans made a momentary stand. But they had not enough troops to cover a front growing progressively larger as the Soviet bulge expanded. Red Army units always found the space to penetrate between the towns to which the Germans clung or else to bypass them. Their advance was now a semicircle of spearheads radiating outward north, center and south, thrusting toward Dvinsk, Vilna, Grodno, Byalistok and Brest-Litovsk.

At the same time—July 14—the Soviets launched their long-expected summer offensive in the sector south of the Pripet Marshes, between Ternopol and Kovel'. Now the Soviets were attacking on a vast front. On the same day Stanislav in the Carpathian foothills was captured, Byalistok in northern Poland fell, Dvinsk in Latvia was taken, and Siauliai junction on the railroad from Riga into East Prussia was seized. Farther south the Red Army swept into Lublin only thirty miles from the Vistula and 100 miles southeast of Warsaw.

On July 31 the Germans were forced out of Siedlce and a Soviet column entered Praga, a suburb of Warsaw on the east bank of the Vistula. On the same day the Red Army began cutting the escape corridor of the trapped German Army Group North, capturing an important junction on the Gulf of Riga after a fifty-mile night advance and occupying Kaunas, the capital of Lithuania.

Now the Red Army was on the Vistula, within ten miles of Warsaw. Its tanks were probing the suburbs of the capital city. Here the Soviets paused. They had moved 400 miles in little more than a month and their momentum had taken them farther and farther from their supply bases, so that now the offensive was coming to a halt. It was also necessary for Marshal Zhukov to begin repairing wrecked railway lines in his rear. The Germans had first converted the railroads to the narrower European gauge and then demolished them during their retreat, so that the Soviets also had to restore them to their original width. Encouraged by their presence, urged to turn against the Germans by the Moscow Radio, the Polish Underground in Warsaw rose in revolt.

Gen. Tadeusz Bor-Komorowski had about 40,000 men in his Polish Home Army. General Bor had heard the sound of the Soviet guns across the Vistula and seen the bombs exploding on German positions in the city. He had taken great heart from the Moscow radio broadcasts calling upon him to rise and promising help. On August 1 at five o'clock in the afternoon thousands of windows flashed as they were thrown open in the sun and a hail of bullets riddled German soldiers on the streets below. Civilians cleared the street and then the Polish freedom fighters poured out of their houses to launch the attack. Within fifteen minutes an entire city of about a million inhabitants was engulfed in battle.

The Germans threw five full divisions against the Poles. Three more— including the veteran Hermann Goering Division—were rushed to Warsaw from Italy. From London the Polish government-in-exile appealed to the Allies to aid their soldiers fighting with only one week's supply of food and ammunition.

Stalin ignored all appeals to go to the aid of the Poles, whether from Churchill or Roosevelt, or General Bor or Premier Stanislaw Mikolajcyk of the Polish government-in-exile, who flew from London to Moscow to plead with Stalin. The Soviet chief called the Warsaw rising "a reckless and fearful gamble" made by a "handful of power-seeking criminals." Their uprising, of course, was exactly what he wanted. Bor's Home Army was filled with Polish patriots as fiercely anticommunist as they were antifascist. With Koba's simple cunning, he intended to allow his German military enemies and his Polish political enemies to kill each other off. So the Red Army marked time in the suburbs, while this mutual slaughter continued.

It was a violent street-by-street battle. Sometimes German tanks herded hundreds of Polish women and children together and drove them in front of them as a shield. Because the only means of communication between the Polish-held sectors was through the sewers, much of the fighting was underground. German soldiers dropped grenades into the manholes or jumped into them to give hand-to-hand battle. Poles and Germans struggled to the death standing waist-deep in filth. Men perished by the knife or were drowned in slime. The uprising continued for two months, and at the end of each day the Warsaw Radio broadcast the notes of the Polish patriot Chopin's famous *Polonaise*. Gradually, the German's overwhelming weight of numbers pressed the Poles to the ground. On the last day the Warsaw Radio broadcast the sorrowing strains of Chopin's *Death March* to signal that the Polish Uprising had ended in defeat and death. In its last broadcast, Radio Warsaw said:

"This is the stark truth. We were treated worse than Hitler's satellites, worse than Italy, Romania and Finland. May God, who is just, pass judgment on the terrible injustice suffered by the Polish nation, and may He punish accordingly all those who are guilty. Your heroes are the soldiers whose only weapons against tanks, planes and guns were their revolvers and bottles filled with gasoline. Your heroes are the women who tended the wounded and carried messages under fire, who cooked in bombed and ruined cellars to feed children and adults, and who soothed and comforted the dying. Immortal is the nation that can muster such universal heroism. For those who have died have conquered, and those who live on will fight on, will conquer and again bear witness that Poland lives while the Poles live."

Nearly a quarter of a million Poles perished in the Warsaw Uprising, and when the Red Army's formations at last crossed the Vistula, they entered a ruined city whose streets were littered with the reeking, rotten corpses of the unburied dead.

While the Polish Uprising was in the full flame of battle, Soviet grand strategy shifted to the extreme south for the master stroke of the 1944 summer campaign. This was the area between the Carpathians and the Black Sea, a sector of 300 miles held by twenty-seven German and twenty Romanian divisions. The destruction of German reserves on the central and northern front had left Hitler with no strategic reserve here. Most of his armor was also north of the Carpathians, nor could he reinforce the south across this mountain barrier. On August 20 the Soviets attacked and quickly brushed aside the unreliable Romanian divisions. Within three days they had crossed the Prut, captured Jassy and all but surrounded the German armies facing them. On the 23rd King Michael of

Romania arrested Marshal Ion Antonescu and dismissed his government. That night the king broadcast the immediate cessation of hostilities and accepted an armistice offered by the Soviet Union, Britain and the United States.

So completely had the German southern front collapsed that Marshal Malinovsky's motorized columns were able to sweep down on the precious Ploesti oilfields before the Germans had time to destroy them. On August 31 the Soviets marched into Bucharest and on the following day reached the Danube on the Bulgarian border. Bulgaria, meanwhile, had already defected from Hitler and Finland also asked for an armistice in September.

Within less than two weeks, in the most dazzling offensive of the German War, the Red Army had overwhelmed and almost wiped out two of Hitler's armies, had deprived him of three of his allies, captured his chief source of oil and reached the northern frontier of Yugoslavia while gaining control of the Lower Danube. Soviet victories had also made it possible to supply and reinforce their armies in Romania by a new route across the Black Sea and up the valley of the Danube. This would be of great consequence in future Balkan offensives and in the future of postwar Europe. Even if Stalin at this point had the strength and the supply lines to move through strong German forces in Poland en route to Berlin, which he did not, he would still have preferred to press the southern offensive. Stalin's primary purpose now was to gain complete control of southeastern and central Europe before the war ended. His true objective was Vienna, not Berlin. Stalin also expected to invade Yugoslavia that fall, looking for assistance from a veteran Marxist revolutionary whom the world was to know as Marshal Tito.

97. Josip Broz and the Yugoslav Partisans

JOSIP BROZ, who was to be called Tito, was born in May of 1892 in the little village of Kumrovec in Croatia, then part of the Austro-Hungarian Empire. After the Treaty of Versailles Croatia became a northern province of the new nation of Yugoslavia. Josip was the seventh of fifteen children born to Franjo and Marja Broz. Of these only seven survived the hard life of a peasantry exploited in turn by Austrian and Hungarian rulers. Still the Croats were a proud people, stubbornly clinging to their Slavic language, their Catholic faith and their ancient traditions. Franjo Broz's forebears had lived in Kumrovec for centuries. He shared a low, solid, whitewashed house with his cousins. Each family had two rooms and half the kitchen, in which there were two fireplaces and two stoves. Josip and his brothers and sisters slept where they could, and often fought each other for the last scraps of the simple meals served them by their mother, a tall, fair-haired, blue-eyed woman whose determination to rear her children properly compensated for her hard-drinking husband's inability to earn a living out of the ten-acre farm he had inherited.

Josip was Marja Broz's favorite child, not so much because he had her curly fair hair and bright blue eyes, but because he was a great help around the house, as he was to his father in the fields. He was small, good-natured and determined —but he also could be fierce, quick with his fists and the leader in fights with boys in neighboring villages. Because Marja was a devout Catholic, Josip became an acolyte in the little white St. Roko's Church above the village. He loved to put on his white surplice and red cassock, or to swing the heavy incense censer on its chain or make the Latin responses in the liturgy. Once, however, a priest new to St. Roko's, a big, surly man, boxed Josip's ears for being slow while helping him divest. Josip never went back to mass unless his mother made him go.

At twelve Josip left school. His record was "very good" to "excellent." He got a job as a waiter in a café in the nearby town of Sisak, after which he put in three years as a locksmith's apprentice. Eager to see the world he left Sisak for Zagreb, the capital of Croatia, where he got a job as a mechanic. From there he traveled on to Trieste, Mannheim, Pilsen, Munich and Vienna, sometimes out of work and sleeping in barns, but always determined to improve himself, learning German and Czech as well as how to waltz to the music of Johann Strauss and Franz Lehar. By the time he reached twenty-one, he was employed as a skilled mechanic and test driver at the Daimler works outside Vienna.

By then he was also eligible for two years of service in the Austrian Army. As a member of an underprivileged minority, Josip detested the empire and Emperor Franz Josef. But he became a good soldier, rising to the rank of sergeant major within a year. Soon after the outbreak of World War I he became a warrant officer. On the morning of Easter, 1915, he was in the trenches on the Eastern front when the Russians launched a heavy attack. Wildly screaming troopers of the famous and dreaded Circassian "Savage" Division came pouring over the parapets, brandishing their horrible two-pronged lances. Two of them attacked Josip. He fought one of them off with his bayoneted rifle but the other stabbed him in the back, leaving him lying unconscious in the mud. He was lucky he was alive, for the spearpoints had entered his body just below his left arm, barely missing his heart and inflicting a deep and serious wound. Taken to a prison hospital near Moscow, Josip required a year to recover from it, as well as from the pneumonia and typhus that followed it.

Josip came to like his captors, adding Russian to his repertoire of languages. After the outbreak of the Russian Revolution, he joined the Red Army and fought with it from 1917 to 1920. Returning to his homeland, he joined the outlawed Yugoslavian Communist Party, and was imprisoned from 1928 to 1933. Freed, he went to Paris, where he organized recruiting for Communist formations during the Spanish Civil War. In 1937 he became secretary-general of the Yugoslavian Communist Party and was now known as Tito.

After the German invasion in 1941, Tito at once began to organize a resistance movement among his 12,000 communists. He insisted on Croatian-Serbian cooperation against the hated occupying countries—Germany, Italy, Romania and Bulgaria—as well as the Ustachi, as the collaborating native terrorists were called. He also came into conflict with and fought the Chetniks led by Draza Mihailovich.

Mihailovich had been a colonel in the Royal Army of the ousted King Peter II. He later became the minister for the army and navy of Peter's government-in-exile, and he soon embraced the royalist policy of husbanding strength for a postwar restoration of the monarchy. Tito hated Mihailovich and called him a traitor. He also detested the monarchy and had no desire to see it return to power to resume its tactics of dividing and ruling the country's diverse ethnic groups. He urged his countrymen to abandon their fratricidal enmity and unite behind him against the invaders. Fortunately for Tito, Hitler's invasion of Russia in June 1941 left only four German divisions occupying Yugoslavia. Tito's partisans scored victory after victory in their guerrilla warfare against them. Nevertheless, the British continued to support Mihailovich, even though the Chetnik leader came to an agreement with the Germans on November 11, 1941. But Tito the tenacious fought on, so inspiring his countrymen that many of them did unite behind him. Tito also impressed a British mission sent to his headquarters, reporting to London that it was Tito who had done most against the occupying powers and that Mihailovich had in fact defected to the Axis.

But it was not until 1944 that the British, supported by the Americans, transferred their military assistance from the Chetnik chief to the Communist commander of the partisans. Thus it was that Tito was ready to assist the left wing of Stalin's southern forces when it approached Yugoslavia's eastern frontier in the fall of 1944. On October 20 Tito's army entered Belgrade in triumph. Stalin, who had unaccountably urged Tito (whom he distrusted) to cooperate with Mihailovich and had sent him few supplies, now came to Tito's side, expecting that he would lead his country into the Communist camp and thus, with the exception of Greece, complete Communist conquest of the Balkans. Tito accepted Stalin's support, and he did, on March 7, 1945, set up a Marxist state with himself at its head. But Josip Broz was still fiercely independent, and he alone among the Communist leaders of Southeastern Europe kept his nation outside the Soviet orbit.

98. The Attempt on Hitler's Life

THE IMMENSE AND GROWING material power of the Anglo-Americans had convinced Erwin Rommel that his balancing act had come to an end. He had failed in his first obligation: to throw the Allies into the sea. The deception of Fortitude, Hitler's refusal to release the armor in the early, critical hours, Rundstedt's insistence on keeping the panzers well back and the incredible might of the Allied air forces were too much for him to overcome. Once the Allies were safely ashore and beginning to build their forces, he knew, as he had long suspected, that the war was lost. He must now keep his pledge to Dr. Strolin: to inform *Der Führer* that there was no hope. On June 12 he wrote a long and deeply pessimistic letter to that effect to the high command, requesting that it be shown to Hitler. A few days later Rundstedt managed to persuade *Der Führer* to confer with him and Rommel near the front. Hitler's response to their pleas to withdraw into a new defensive line received the unfailing reply: no retreat. Rommel also angered Hitler by protesting a so-called incident at Oradour-sur-Glane. There the infamous SS Das Reich Division, in reprisal for the killing of a German officer, had driven the women and children into a church, and then set the village on fire. Men and boys emerging from blazing buildings were mowed down by machine-gun fire. The church was blown up and all 600 women and children inside murdered. Hitler was unmoved when Rommel also told him that there were two villages named Oradour and that the SS had massacred the wrong one. He demanded permission to punish Das Reich. "Such things bring disgrace on the German uniform," he said. "How can you wonder at the strength of the French Resistance behind us when the SS drive every decent Frenchman into joining it?"

"That has nothing to do with you!" *Der Führer* snapped. "Your business is to resist the invasion."

Undaunted, Rundstedt and Rommel then boldly broached the subject of peace overtures to the Western Allies. With that, Hitler adjourned the meeting and left. But the marshals he left behind still clung to the hope of peace. In early July, Keitel called Rundstedt from Berlin with the desperate question: "What shall we do?" Rundstedt roared back: "Do? End the war, you bloody fools!" For this and other signs of "defeatism," he was relieved of command in the West and replaced by Field Marshal Gunther von Kluge, who had recovered from his injuries on the Soviet front.

Undeterred by this warning to defeatists, Rommel decided to make one more appeal to Hitler. In consultation with Speidel, who wrote the draft of his letter, he wrote even more pessimistically, concluding: *"Our troops are fighting heroically, but even so the end of this unequal battle is in sight."* Kluge, who had come to France believing he could turn the tide but had quickly changed his mind, forwarded Rommel's letter to Hitler with an even gloomier covering letter of his own.

Before *Der Führer* could reply, Erwin Rommel on July 17 began his daily tour of the front. With him was his aide, Capt. Helmuth Lang. In late afternoon they began driving back to La Roche Guyon. Because the air was full of Allied aircraft, the driver took the back roads. Suddenly two British Typhoons appeared behind them flying at great speed only a few feet above the road. Rommel shouted at the driver to hurry and make for a side road about 300 yards ahead. Before he could reach it the leading enemy plane opened fire. The first shell struck the left side of the staff car. The driver's left shoulder and left arm were shattered. A shower of flying windshield glass struck Rommel's face. He was hurled against the windshield's steel support, the impact causing a triple fracture of his skull. He immediately lost consciousness.

With the driver so badly wounded, the car spun out of control. It struck a tree stump, skidded to the left side of the road and turned over in a ditch. All the occupants, including Rommel, were thrown onto the ground, where the second British aircraft tried to bomb them.

Lang and a sergeant carried Rommel, still unconscious, to safety. He was taken to a Catholic hospital, where a French doctor attended to his numerous facial wounds, especially cuts around his left eye and mouth. The doctor did not believe that the marshal would live. Later Rommel and the driver were taken to a Luftwaffe hospital about twenty-five miles away. That night the driver died, but a few days later Rommel was transferred to the care of a specialist in his hospital at St. Germain.

The man whom the conspirators against *Der Führer* hoped to proclaim as president of the Reich still lay unconscious and close to death when, on the following day—July 20, 1944—they moved to kill Hitler.

Col. Klaus Philip Schenk, Count von Stauffenberg, was the sort of German aristocrat with whom Adolf Hitler never felt at ease. He was the descendant of a long line of Swabian noblemen. One of his ancestors was Gen. Count von Gneisenau, who fought on the British side in the American Revolution and at Waterloo and became one of the Prussian army's most famous field marshals. Stauffenberg was a devout Catholic, a brilliant scholar, a musician, a superb horseman and something of a poet. His was the unconscious grace and ease of manner that always put the nose of the self-conscious Adolf Hitler badly out of joint.

Although an aesthete and an intimate of the German poet Stefan George, Stauffenberg surprised both his family and friends by deciding in 1925 to enter the army. Ten years later he came to the attention of Gen. Ludwig Beck, then the chief of the German General Staff. Beck, a small, frail man with an iron will, was by then distrustful of Adolf Hitler. He feared what would happen when he came to power and the German army fell into his hands. After *Der Führer* did become the dictator of Germany and began to rebuild its armed forces, Beck drew around him a circle of conspirators. Stauffenberg was one of them, and most of the others were like him, intelligent, high-minded aristocrats. Some were high-ranking commanders. At a meeting in the Paris office of Franz Halder, another former chief of the German General Staff, there were no fewer than three generals present. All openly discussed the necessity of killing Hitler before his lust for power destroyed Germany. But as *Der Führer*'s incredible string of victories lengthened, their opposition gradually subsided. Even Halder became intimately involved in planning the early triumphs, especially on the Eastern front. Only after disaster overtook the Wehrmacht there did he and the others renew their determination to remove "the enemy of the German people." However, none of them possessed that ruthlessness and organizing genius without which no conspiracy can succeed. None—to kill Hitler—could stoop to Hitler's level.

Nor was Hitler easy to kill. He wore a bulletproof vest and in his military cap were three and a half pounds of laminated steel plate. His bodyguards were all sharpshooters, and he himself was a marksman who always carried a revolver. His traveling timetables were well-kept secrets, which he always changed at the last moment. He boasted that he had a sixth sense for danger, but what had actually protected him was that he rarely appeared where he was expected to be.

Beck and his conspirators decided against trying to shoot Hitler because they knew that if the first shot missed, there would not be a second one. So they chose time bombs. Because they were such amateur assassins, it did not occur to them that there were other means: hand grenades, contact bombs, poison, acid to squirt into his eyes blinding him, a poison dart or even a knife. Of the five or six recorded attempts on Hitler's life, all involved time bombs.

Stauffenberg had been chosen as the assassin because he had direct access to Hitler. He belonged to the organizational department of the German high command and traveled extensively in the conquered territories. He reported regularly to his superiors and on several occasions to Hitler, standing within three feet of him. In North Africa in April 1943, the count was severely wounded by a strafing enemy airplane. He lost an eye, his right hand and two fingers of his left hand. Making a painful recovery in a hospital, Stauffenberg resolved to kill "the enemy of the world." Hitler, with his hero-worshiping admiration of brave men, much as he might surround himself with toadying desk soldiers such as Keitel and Jodl, was impressed with Stauffenberg's wounds and remembered him.

Stauffenberg had offered to sacrifice himself to be certain of killing Hitler. But it was refused because he had been chosen to direct the uprising that was to follow *Der Führer*'s death. Thus the sine qua non of successful assassination had been ruled out. It is also likely that Stauffenberg had been chosen because Rommel, the man whose popularity was expected to give momentum to the movement, now lay at death's door. Though not as famous, the count's family name and aristocratic origins would count for something among the German people.

The bomb he was to carry weighed two pounds. It would explode after a glass capsule containing acid was broken and the acid ate away the wire holding back the firing pin from the percussion cap. It took exactly ten minutes for this to happen, and it was done silently. The explosive was hexite, which gives off no fumes.

Actually, Stauffenberg made four attempts to kill Hitler. On December 23, 1943, he was summoned to a headquarters conference. He had a bomb in his briefcase, but Hitler did not appear as scheduled. On July 11, 1944, the count flew to the Berghof carrying a bomb, but although Hitler was present, he did not act because Himmler was not there. Four days later another meeting was set for the Berghof, but before it took place Hitler flew off to the Wolf's Lair. July 20, then, became *Der Tag*.

On that day Stauffenberg came to the Wolf's Lair to report. In his briefcase was a time bomb. He immediately encountered changes. The conference would not be at 1:00 P.M. as he and his coconspirators expected, but a half hour earlier because Mussolini was due to arrive at 3:00 P.M. and Hitler wanted extra time to prepare for him. This was no real obstacle, but the change of location was. Instead of being in Hitler's underground bunker, where the bomb would explode in a confined space and kill everyone, it was to be in a prefabricated wooden building aboveground. Because it was a hot day the windows would undoubtedly be open, thus dissipating the concussion. There would be survivors, Stauffenberg thought unhappily.

Stauffenberg met Keitel and explained what he intended to say. Keitel, always fearful of his master's wrath, nodded nervously and said: "Yes, but above all be brief." Stauffenberg excused himself and went into Keitel's lavatory where he broke the acid capsule with a pair of pliers. Three minutes later he was in the conference room where Hitler sat at the middle of a big rectangular table surrounded by about two dozen officers and stenographers. On Hitler's right Gen. Adolf Heusinger was on his feet reporting. To Heusinger's right sat his aide, Col. Heinz Brandt. Stauffenberg stood between and behind Heusinger and Brandt. He put his briefcase on the floor resting against one of two huge oaken supports that upheld the table. There, its blast would flow directly toward Hitler, probably blowing off his legs. Excusing himself, Stauffenberg went outside. He went to the telephone exchange to tell the sergeant major there that he expected a call from Berlin and wanted to be notified the moment it came in. The sergeant major nodded. Stauffenberg strolled nonchalantly toward the office of Gen. Erich Fellgiebel, a coconspirator. At the sound of the explosion he would drive at top speed for the airport and fly to Berlin to sound the tocsin of revolution.

Inside the conference room Colonel Brandt reached down to place Stauffenberg's briefcase on the *other* side of the support. Exactly why is not known. Perhaps it was in his way. Whatever his reason, the bomb was now *away* from *Der Führer,* who was leaning across the table, studying a map. General Heusinger was concluding his report on the Eastern Front:

"If the Army Group around Lake Peipus is not withdrawn immediately, there will be a catastrophe—"

A blazing sheet of flame flashed out from beneath the table followed by a horrible, rocking roar. Waves of concussion flattened the men around the table, and the table itself was lifted into the air and hurled into a corner. The walls and ceiling were torn to shreds and blocks of concrete from the building's outer shell rained down. Wood splinters flew about like bullets, bloodying and burning everyone. For some reason everyone's hair stood on end. An SS general's thick hair stood erect capped with flames. Screams and moans came from the stricken. "Murder! Murder!" one officer cried. "Where is *Der Führer?*"

He was on the floor, pinned beneath a fallen beam, but he was still alive. Four men—including Colonel Brandt—had received their death wounds while all the others were either shocked or wounded in varying degrees; but Hitler suffered only temporary paralysis of his right arm and a punctured eardrum. He had been saved by the tabletop and the support, both the results of chance, that ageless nemesis of the incomplete plotter.

Outside Stauffenberg heard the explosion and saw smoke and the flying debris. He assumed Hitler had been killed. He leaped into a waiting automobile driven by Lt. Werner von Haeften and sped away for the airport. It was now up to General Fellgiebel to shut down or destroy all communications from the Wolf's Lair. He ran toward the smoking and wrecked building and saw Keitel and Hitler staggering about outside, each supporting the other. Fellgiebel was stunned. If he had sent a coded message to the Wehrmacht headquarters in the Bendlerstrasse saying that the plot had failed, he would have saved many conspirators, perhaps most of them. But he was so paralyzed by terror at the sight of a live Führer that he did nothing. Hitler was able to get in touch with Himmler, whose headquarters were twenty miles away, and the grim gray executioner hurried to the Wolf's Lair to begin an investigation that lasted for weeks. Then Hitler shut off communications and no message reached the Bendlerstrasse.

Now the revolt and counterrevolt degenerated into what might be called a comedy of errors were there not so much at stake. Stauffenberg arrived at the Bendlerstrasse to find that next to nothing had been done. With his friend, Gen. Friedrich Olbricht, he began telephoning as many commands as he could to report that the revolt had begun. He was only successful in Paris, Vienna and Munich, where open uprisings arose. Meanwhile, Gen. Friedrich Fromm, the commander of the reserve army and a coconspirator, telephoned the Wolf's Lair and was told by Keitel that Hitler was alive and Stauffenberg was suspected of planting the bomb. To save his own skin, Fromm tried to arrest Stauffenberg and Olbricht. They not only refused to surrender, they arrested Fromm. But they did not place him under guard.

Stauffenberg still believed that Hitler was dead, and that the revolution had arrived. Yet he did nothing concrete to organize it, except to speak into a battery of telephones. He did not go on the air proclaiming revolt, and he did not move to take over the radio station, the telephone and telegraph or the post office—the vital nerve centers of government and therefore of antigovernment. He did not even put a guard around his headquarters; anyone could come and go as he pleased. Stauffenberg was in a state of constant euphoria produced by the sight of that liberating bomb blast, and he actually believed that all the military installations in Berlin, including the all-important Battalion of Guards, were on his side. But they were not. When Stauffenberg ordered Maj. Otto Ernst Remer of the guards to arrest Goebbels, this devout Nazi merely notified Goebbels and requested instructions.

The conspirators worked into the night telephoning, telephoning, telephoning. Nothing concrete was undertaken by Beck, Stauffenberg, Olbricht, Gen. Erich Hoepner, Col. Merz von Quirnheim and Lieutenant von Haeften, the six men at the heart of the conspiracy. They were still at work when a handful of SS soldiers under Lt. Col. Franz Herber broke into the War Ministry and started shooting. Stauffenberg was wounded in the left arm. All were arrested, and General Fromm emerged from hiding to conduct a brief court-martial. Beck and Hoepner were given the opportunity for honorable suicide. Beck shot himself but Hoepner declined, unwisely—as he might have suspected. He was arrested and reserved for a more agonizing end. Stauffenberg, Quirnheim, Olbricht and Haeften were taken out in the courtyard and shot. Stauffenberg's last words were: "Long live our sacred Germany."

At the Wolf's Lair Hitler's paralyzed arm had been placed in a sling and his ear stuffed with cotton. Wrapping himself in a great coat, even though it was a warm day, *Der Führer* rushed off to Rastenburg Station to greet Mussolini. Of the two, Mussolini actually looked the worse. Gone was the old arrogance and the jutting jaw. His cheeks were sunken and his hair snow white. *Il Duce* knew that he had become Hitler's plaything, the puppet ruler of the Salo Republic, the Fascist puppet state set up for him in northern Italy. Even the mayor of Salo had more actual power, and Mussolini had said of his citizenry, "They call me Benito Quisling."

But the Duce was startled when *Der Führer* shook hands with his left, stunned when he swept open his coat to reveal his wounded arm and singed clothing. Then they embraced.

"An infernal machine has just been set off!" Hitler cried. "At me! Look! Trousers ruined, hair scorched. My buttocks are like the backside of a baboon. I can tell you how it feels to be tattooed. But I survived. That's the important thing. A miracle!" Leading his old comrade to an automobile, Hitler drove with him back to the Wolf's Lair to show him the damage. "Frankly, Duce, I regard this event as the pronouncement of Divine Providence." Mussolini had recovered from his earlier shock. He glanced around him with feigned wonder. Actually, he was secretly pleased, chortling to himself: "Even to him. It can happen to *him!*" Aloud he said: "A marvelous escape. Truly marvelous."

"*Marvelous?* It's more than that. It's God's intervention. Look at this room, at my uniform. When I reflect on this, I know nothing will happen to me. Clearly it is my divine task to continue on and bring my great enterprise to completion."

One overpowering consideration in Hitler's "great enterprise" was vengeance. Because these noble but inept conspirators had left a trail as wide as a bear bolting from a camper's tent, some 7,000 suspects were rounded up, implicated by an incredible volume of letters, address books, records of conversations, proclamations and personal memoranda. Prisons and torture chambers were as crowded as in the days of Jewish persecution, and the SS treated them with the same merciless ferocity. Surprisingly, only 2,000 of these unfortunates were convicted and sentenced to death, by a judge whose taunts and mocking gibes were crueler than the prosecutor's. Hitler ordered the guilty to be hanged. "I want them hung up like carcasses of meat," he said.

Taking their cue from this request, the SS stripped them naked and hung them from meat hooks with piano wire. Cameramen dutifully recorded the convulsions of their final agonies, and the rushes were hurried to the Wolf's Lair.

Hitler's hold on the German people, made tighter by Unconditional Surrender, was now by the failure to kill him made unbreakable.

To the astonishment of his colleagues, Benito Mussolini had been keeping to one mistress for more than eight years. She was Clara Petacci, daughter of a prominent Vatican physician. Clara was very pretty in a fresh-faced way, much like Hitler's Eva Braun. She had curly brown hair and dark blue eyes. She was warm-hearted and impetuous and had been infatuated with the Duce since she was eight years old. She showed it when she threw a stone at a workman who had heard a donkey bray and sneered: "There speaks the Duce." At night she slept with Mussolini's picture under her pillow; at school, she kept it inside her French dictionary. As she grew older, she sent him poems of adulation wrapped in the Italian tricolor. When she went swimming she wrote "Duce" in the sands and in cooking school wrote it in the icing on top of the cakes she baked.

Clara never saw Mussolini in person until April 24, 1932. She was then twenty, riding in a limousine with her mother and sister and fiancé, Air Force Lt. Riccardo Federici. From behind them came the harsh and imperious sound of a horn. A scarlet Alfa-Romeo roared by in a cloud of dust. Crouching at the wheel in a blue beret was Benito Mussolini. Careening after him came a limousine packed with bodyguards. Claretta was transported. *"Il Duce!"* she cried, springing to her feet. *"Il Duce!"*

Mussolini must have noticed the pretty girl in the open touring car for he slowed down and began to play vehicular tag, slowing and speeding, slowing and speeding. Finally he pulled over and stepped out of his car. His bodyguards' car stopped, and his police ringed him round. Claretta demanded that the Petaccis' chauffeur stop also. Her fiancé objected. Claretta ignored him, exclaiming: "I'll go and introduce myself. I'll never have another chance like this." She did, followed by the glum Federici.

Mussolini was the soul of propriety, although courtly. He pretended to have read Claretta's poems and inquired after the health of her father. Then he roared away. Two days later he called the Petacci residence. Clara's nine-year-old sister Myrian answered the telephone. "Oh, God!" she cried. "It's *him!*" There followed a series of chaperoned meetings at the Palazzo Venezia with Claretta still dazzled and *Il Duce* still correct. But the flirtation seemed to have ended in 1934 when the impulsive Clara married Lieutenant Federici. Violent quarrels, sometimes in public places, brought about their separation, and Clara returned to the family apartment. It was then that Mussolini summoned her mother to the Palazzo. "Signora," he asked, "have I your permission to love Clara?"

Signora Petacci was aware how dangerous it could be to thwart this "godlike" dictator, nor did she ignore the golden chance for the Petacci clan to make a nice thing out of such an arrangement. So Claretta became the mistress of her sincerely adored Duce. For once Mussolini was discreet, and Donna Rachele actually knew nothing of her husband's relationship with Clara until the night he was arrested.

Thereafter, however, she brooded upon it and, because she had her own powerful friends, began to make inquiries into the activities of the Petaccis. This resourceful clan had already enriched itself via Claretta and were now believed to have dark political ambitions. Donna Rachele feared both for her family and the republic. She also resented Clara's well-known habit of calling her husband —Donna Rachele's—"*my* Ben." After the Duce was rescued and took up residence with his wife at Lake Garda, Donna Rachele was angered by his daily visits to the Villa dei Morti where Clara had been established. One night in August after Mussolini returned from the Wolf's Lair, she told him that she was going to pay a call on Claretta. "If you must," Mussolini said with a deep sigh eloquent of his conviction that once they start on you, they leave you nothing.

Accompanied by the plump little Secretary of State, Guido Buffarini-Guidi, Donna drove to the Petacci villa in her own little car. An SS officer refused to admit them. Enraged, Donna Rachele began shaking the tall wrought-iron grilles protecting the windows. She rattled them so vehemently that the startled SS officer returned and allowed them to enter. They were conducted to a small room where Clara sat guarded by two SS men. At the sight of her, Donna Rachele burst into a furious tirade. Claretta paled. Donna Rachele asked her if she were married or single. Claretta said married. Donna Rachele told her to go back to her own husband and leave hers alone. She said her presence at Lake Garda was sapping her husband's physical and mental strength and was a scandal to the Italian people. Leave him! she commanded.

Claretta fainted. The distressed Buffarini hurried off in search of brandy. Clara recovered and counterattacked. She spoke feelingly of how charmingly "my Ben" had always spoken of Donna Rachele. It was a serpentine stab, which aroused Donna Rachele into full fury. Claretta closed her eyes, as though about to swoon again. Then she stabbed deeper.

"My Ben can't live without me."

Like an avenging fury the corpulent and aging Donna Rachele leaped to her feet and began a verbal vivisection of her young and beautiful rival.

"You'll come to a bad end!" she shrieked. "Everyone hates and despises you! I warn you!"

Claretta was dissolved in tears. She buried her face in a crumpled handkerchief and then she fainted again. Donna Rachele, the avenging Spirit of the Romagna, retired from the field.

Victorious.

99. Breakout from Normandy

BY JULY THE ALLIES had not only secured and extended their beach lodgments and taken Cherbourg, but had brought into France an enormous number of troops and supplies. On Bradley's forty-mile front there were now two airborne, two armored and eleven infantry divisions, while Montgomery's front of the same width held eleven infantry and five armored divisions. In the three weeks succeeding D-Day, the allied navies had ferried no fewer than a million men ashore together with 560,000 tons of supplies—enough to fill a freight train 190 miles long. Here was a logistics feat heretofore unmatched in military history.

The objective now was to break out of the lodgment in which the German Seventh Army still held them contained. To do this, Montgomery at Caen was to be the pivot on which the entire Allied line was to swing eastward toward the Seine and Paris. Bradley's First Army was to provide the impetus for this assault with an attack on the westernmost end of the line. The Americans were to sweep south of the Cotentin past Avranches and at that point cut off the Brittany peninsula at its neck. Next Patton's Third Army was to plunge into Brittany in quest of its valuable deep-water ports. With the American right anchored on the Loire River, the remainder of the Allied line would make the dash for the Seine. Behind the Seine the retreating Germans would probably reorganize for a stand, while the pursuing Allies paused to regroup and receive supplies.

On July 3 Middleton's VIII Corps attacked south toward Coutances–St. Lô–Caumont. They made little progress. Next day—the Fourth of July—Middleton's men received novel support from First Army's artillery. Bradley and General Gerow had been discussing the army's tradition of firing a forty-eight-gun salute to mark Independence Day.

"Just forty-eight guns?" Gerow asked.

"No, hell no, Gee. We'll fire every gun in the army."

Thus 1,100 massed guns of every caliber fired a single shell at the Germans, each timed to explode on the split second of noon. All arrived on the German front together, exploding with a single thunderclap that not only shook the Germans but also killed and wounded many of them. Nevertheless, Middleton's advance was slow. After twelve days of fighting, his forces had suffered 10,000 casualties and gained only seven miles. It sounded like World War I all over again, and thus Bradley's dream of a breakout and a dash for Avranches ended in "a crushing disappointment to me personally."

Three basic problems had combined to contain the Coutances drive: the Bocage country, the fighting spirit of the German soldier and the lack of it in the ordinary American rifleman. It is difficult, however, not to sympathize with the plight of GI Joe. Unlike the glamorous airmen who received medals and rotation home for flying a specified number of missions, with or without combat, the ordinary footslogger in France during 1944 saw nothing in sight but the next hill and beyond that the next river. Although rotation home had begun for servicemen with a minimum of twenty-four months overseas, in July of 1944 this applied chiefly to troops in the Pacific who had been out there since the spring of 1942 and earlier. Even Bradley's veterans of North Africa and Sicily would have to wait until November for rotation home. Only a wound or death could relieve GI Joe from his constant companion: the fear of death. Bradley himself wrote: "Sooner or later, unless victory comes, the chase must end on the litter or in the grave."

So it was perhaps inevitable that even the bravest American conscript soldier, his valor eroded by a war-weariness that has to be felt to be understood, should seize upon the pretense of "combat fatigue" to liberate himself from the specter of the foolkiller waiting for him on the other side of the river. In varying degrees, all the armies of World War II realized that a soldier can be disabled by combat fatigue, the shock and strain of continued battle, just as completely as by bullets, concussion or shrapnel. But the American army was easily the most permissive. By July 10,000 cases of combat fatigue were treated daily. Between June and November 1944, a staggering 26 percent of casualties were combat fatigue. Throughout the war the U.S. Army recorded 929,307. How many of these were authentic can never be established, but the fact was that by July a veritable epidemic of combat fatigue was eroding Bradley's army.

Desertions were another problem for the Allies. By July the Allied rear areas were fairly well populated by deserters. Those who were British were dealt with far more harshly than the Americans were. British military police who returned American deserters to their units were astonished to find them welcomed back like heroes. In a sense, they were; for a time at least they had "beaten the system," had "had themselves a ball" by imbibing a little French ooh-la-la with perhaps even a willing mademoiselle to comfort them. To be court-martialed meant nothing to them. They knew well enough that even a life sentence in an army prison would be commuted to pardon and a bad-conduct discharge after the war. So what were a few years in prison compared to death or a life in a veterans' hospital as a basket-case? Service in the infantry in France was everywhere regarded almost as a sentence to death or wounds, and many rear-echelon outfits or the ground units of the AAF used the threat of it as a disciplinary device. Finally, no American serviceman anywhere in the war feared execution.

But the German soldier did. Not all of the German soldier's fighting spirit derived from loyalty to Hitler or to soldierly pride. In the seven months between January and September 1944, the Wehrmacht executed nearly 4,000 soldiers, 1,605 of them for desertion. Since punishment is always read out to a guilty man's unit, it is likely that even veterans of years of combat—like those Eastern front soldiers said to have been there so long that they forgot how to speak German—would calculate that the risk of certain death in desertion was even greater than in battle. Inasmuch as most of the other executions were for cowardice, running away was also rather risky. But in all the American armed forces of World War II there was only one execution, and even today the execution of Private Slovik remains a cause célèbre.

Bradley was also having difficulty with his senior officers, having sacked no fewer than five two-star division commanders since D-Day. Numerous regimental and battalion leaders had also felt the axe, but in no place did the relief of a commander improve the fighting quality of his unit, just as the sack of two successive commanders of the 27th Division in the Pacific had done nothing to make it battleworthy.

Bradley's third problem, however—the Bocage—seemingly the most difficult to overcome, was solved by Yankee ingenuity. No tanks—Allied or German—were capable of penetrating the hedgerows. All of Bradley's armored units addressed themselves to the problem. In the U.S. 2nd Armored, a soldier named Tennessee Roberts asked, "Why don't we get some saw teeth and put them on the front of the tanks and cut through these hedges?" His buddies burst into laughter, until Sgt. Curtis Culin said, "Hold it! Maybe he's got an idea." Culin welded a set of steel tusks to a Sherman's nose. Experiments showed that this was the answer. The tusks of the "Rhinoceros" bit into the hedgerows to secure the Sherman to it, after which the tank literally exploded through both dirt and roots. When Bradley saw the Rhino demonstration, his homely face glowed with delight. He ordered lengths of steel from Rommel's Asparagus to be brought secretly from the beaches and had welding equipment rushed over the channel from Britain.

The value of Sergeant Culin's invention can hardly be exaggerated. It restored maneuverability to Bradley's armor. Now his tanks could move through the Bocage and the Germans could not. They had to stay on the roads while the Shermans, blasting through the hedgerows, now had the power to outflank them. Bradley's next move was to cancel out the German soldier's fighting skill: a massive aerial bombardment of the German front by thousands of aircraft, what came to be called carpet bombing. Before it began, First Army's forward units would withdraw to reduce the risk of short bombing, or creep back, as the British called it. Afterward the breakout from St. Lô—Operation Cobra—would begin.

Cobra had one great though unsuspected advantage: The enemy expected the main push to come from the Anglo-Canadians on the left or eastern flank at Caen. Marshal von Kluge had gone there himself to direct a battle of fourteen divisions against the same number of Anglo-Canadians. On the west he had only eleven divisions to oppose fifteen American. Gen. Paul Hausser's Seventh Army staff in the west also confidently expected the big Allied push to be in the east. They were surprised when on July 24 some 1,600 aircraft were ordered aloft over St. Lô, just as the weather closed in. Many were recalled or refused to risk bombing through the overcast. But enough loosed their bombs to kill twenty-five Americans and wound 131 more in the sector of the 30th Infantry Division. Some soldiers were so enraged that they turned their guns on their own aircraft, a not-uncommon reaction among all armies in World War II. Footsloggers despised "fly boys," chiefly for the luxurious life they led between missions or the way their absurd Air Medal, passed out for every ten missions, cheapened the infantry's own hard-earned decorations. Foot soldiers joked obscenely about the AAF's "Bad-Chow Medal" or "Inclement Weather Cross," or regaled each other with such stories as the airman who saw the film *The Battle of Britain* and came out of the theater with another cluster pinned to his Air Medal.

Next day the weather cleared and the bombardment began in earnest. At Fritz Bayerlein's Panzer Lehr headquarters a message was received: "American infantry in front of our trenches are abandoning their positions." Kurt Kauffmann, the operations officer, rejoiced. "Looks as if they've got cold feet. Seventh Army is right after all." But then Bayerlein began to receive other reports.

"Bombing attacks by endless waves of aircraft. Fighter-bomber attacks on bridges and artillery positions." For twenty minutes the fighter-bombers blasted the German front. At about ten o'clock 1,800 heavy bombers of the U.S. Eighth Air Force thundered toward their targets. Bradley had asked the Eighth to fly out of the sun and bomb along the east-west axis of the St. Lô-Périers road. *It was a straight road, and if the bombers flew parallel to it, they could not mistake the American front to the north of it for the German front to the south of it.* For unknown reasons of their own the bombers came in on a north-south axis. Below, tens of thousands of American soldiers in foxholes and tank turrets gazed upward in an awed confidence tinged with fear. Soon they realized that the bomb carpet was not unrolling forward but creeping backward toward them! The bombardiers high above them were aiming their releases at the smoke line, but a gentle breeze was blowing the smokeline back toward the Americans! Slowly, inexorably, that horrid black cloud crept toward the American lines until it finally flowed over them.

The ground was shaken and rocked as though by an earthquake. Men were beheaded, split in two, buried alive. Even those underground felt as though they were being clubbed. One hundred and eleven American soldiers died and 490 were wounded in that horribly inaccurate bombardment. Among the dead was Lt. Gen. Lesley McNair. Now that Patton was scheduled to come ashore to lead the Third Army, someone was needed to "command" the fictitious "1st Army Group" which still kept the Germans concentrated at Calais. McNair, who had trained the Stateside army, was chosen. He had come to St. Lô to observe. To maintain the fiction, he was secretly buried two days later. News of his death was suppressed until a new "commander" of the 1st could replace him.

Nevertheless after the bombers left, the attack got going. All along the line officers were rallying their shattered units and ordering them to move out. "You've gotta get going! You've gotta get going!" Men moving slowly forward were dismayed to discover that the enemy had not been devastated. Some German units had occupied the air-safety zone evacuated earlier by the Americans. Fighting was savage. Panzer Lehr soldiers had dug their tanks hull down and were battling stubbornly from them. Yet, the Eighth Air Force's performance on both days had succeeded in fragmenting the German lines. Lightnin' Joe Collins, a fine battle reader, sensed that the fiercely resisting Germans were not manning a continuous line. Gaps could be penetrated to outflank or bypass separated units. The customary defense-in-depth was not evident.

Even the matchless Panzer Lehr had been pulverized. When Kluge sent a staff officer to Bayerlein with orders to hold the St. Lô-Périers line to the last man, Bayerlein replied with anguished sarcasm: "Out in front everyone is holding out. Everyone. My grenadiers and my engineers and my tank crews—they're all holding their ground. Not a single man is leaving his post. They are lying silent in their foxholes, for they are dead. You may report to the field marshal that the Panzer Lehr Division is annihilated." To punctuate his remark, the explosion of a huge ammunition dump hit by fighter-bombers shook the ground they were standing on.

On the afternoon of the 25th, Collins ordered his mobile columns forward. Bradley had given him six divisions for the breakout, all among the finest in the U.S. Army: the 1st, 4th, 9th and 30th Infantry, the veteran 2nd and 3rd Armored. By nightfall American units had pierced the German line and were outside of it at Marigny. In the morning across the entire front American formations began to shake free of the tenacious Germans. Resistance was crumbling, and the American army's matchless mobility was turning the Seventh Army's retreat into a rout. Tank columns, waiting only a few minutes for the Rhinos to cut paths through the hedgerow, went speeding by the road-bound German armor, easily flushing lightly armed enemy infantry from their concealment in the Bocage.

On the 26th Middleton's VIII Corps joined the assault on the western or right flank, the 8th and 90th Divisions leading the way. Their progress on the first day was disappointing but at first light of the 27th, they found that the German left was crumbling and the enemy had been forced to give way. They left behind them immense minefields, which only delayed VIII Corps's pursuit.

A sense of exhilaration had seized the American soldiers. *Breakout!* Pockets of resistance met at crossroads were eliminated by the infantry jumping down from halted tanks, and then the pursuit was renewed. Exultant riflemen rode on the hulls of the tanks or waved from their troop carriers at the cheering, weeping, singing, kiss-blowing French, who greeted them like gods as they roared through their villages. Everywhere along the road abandoned and blackened German vehicles testified to the terrible, wide-ranging scourging of the American fighter-bombers. Even the German *Panzergrenadiers* accustomed to mechanized movement could not believe the speed of the American advance, especially by the two armored divisions.

Sgt. Helmut Gunther was one of these. He had recovered from wounds and returned to his company when the VII Corps assault began. Ordered to fall back, he found the roads so thronged with American traffic that he had to take to the fields. Always and everywhere it seemed that the Americans were ahead of them. More and more men of his unit slipped away to surrender. Later he would receive their letters from prison camp in America. Once he ran into a staff car and told the officer inside where he was going. "Are you crazy?" the officer cried. "The Americans are there already!" Gunther ran into a paratrooper who told him that all the men in his unit had tried to surrender but had been killed. Coming to a farmhouse, he and his men found a pig and killed it and cooked it. They put a bedsheet on a table and put the pig on it just as a Luftwaffe man burst in shouting: "The Americans are right behind me!" Gunther and his men grabbed the corners of the sheet with the pig inside it and threw it into a staff car, roaring off as the first of the Shermans clattered into the farmyard. "I had been on the first retreat from Moscow," Gunther wrote, "which was terrible enough, but at least units were still intact. Here, we had become a cluster of individuals. We were not a battleworthy company any longer."

Nor were many battalions, regiments or even divisions. General Hausser of Seventh Army reported that ten of his divisions had disintegrated. Scattered bands of stragglers roamed northwest France without equipment or leaders. Most of them were motivated by a single thought: survival and *Heim ins Reich*—home to Germany. All of them dreaded the ubiquitous Allied fighter-bombers, those British Typhoons and American Thunderbolts and Mustangs, each powerful enough to carry 2,000 pounds of bombs. They roamed the countryside behind the German front, actually bursting upon the surprised enemy from behind tall trees.

One day in late July a New Zealand group captain named Desmond Scott took off in a Typhoon on an early-morning mission. Over the German rear area he found the roads jammed with vehicles—tanks, trucks, half-tracks, even ambulances and horse-drawn wagons—all hurrying frantically to the east before the rising sun brought down on them the deadly whip of enemy air. Scott sped to the head of a mile-long column, just as hundreds of German soldiers began to take cover in the fields beside the road. Scott zoomed up sharply over a plowed field where a platoon of Germans were sprinting for a clump of trees. Out of nowhere came a Mustang, which sickled them to the earth. Now Scott turned on the convoy, led by a half-track. Hurrying to strike it and block the road he launched all eight rockets at once. He missed but hit the following truck. It leaped from the road, bodies flying out of it, and fell back on its side. Two other trucks behind it rammed into it, and the column was stalled.

Meanwhile, another fighter-bomber had sealed off the end of the column with a similar strike. Suddenly Allied fighter-bombers from seemingly everywhere converged on the stalled column like vultures, while their radios called in the Spitfires to the ghastly feast. Rockets and cannon shells streamed into the stalled German vehicles. Ammunition trucks exploded like miniature and multicolored volcanoes. Wildly neighing teams of horses stampeded and galloped across the fields dragging their wagons behind them. Some were strafed, rearing on their hind legs and screaming before they fell in tangled, kicking heaps. Others tried to jump the fences and were impaled upon the stakes. Thus the dreadful, recurring ordeal of an unprotected army in retreat, relieved only by the blessed fall of night or arrival of a concealing rainstorm.

Bradley's close-up air support was provided by Maj. Gen. Elwood ("Pete") Quesada, a pioneering airman of innovating intelligence. Quesada was that rare war bird, an aviator who understood that in the final analysis Germany could only be defeated on the ground. Almost all the others, especially the Air High Command—from Tedder to Spaatz to Leigh-Mallory to Harris—were possessed of a deep-seated prejudice against the idea that the services of the air and the sea must be subordinated to this purpose. Quesada not only established a close and warm working relationship with Bradley, but also did much to develop air-ground cooperation at the front. For the first few weeks following D-Day, Allied forward air control was clumsy and inefficient. The technology was available, but there were not enough forward air control units up front with the troops. Requests for air support had to be forwarded to a rear staff and then passed along to the squadrons with only a map reference for a target. Montgomery's Goodwood Offensive failed in great part because of the destruction of a single RAF vehicle carrying all the forward air control for his central forces.

It was Quesada who suggested mounting aircraft radio on American tanks at the beginning of Cobra, and it is a measure of the mutual distrust between the services that he was flabbergasted when Bradley agreed to give them to him. With aircraft radio in spearheading tanks, the American armor could call down fighter-bombers on enemy targets. If the pilot were too cramped in his cockpit to read his map, the controller would sometimes call down artillery smoke bombs on the target. Inevitably, the clever enemy began to fire his own smoke inside American lines. On such occasions the controller's only recourse was to scream "Pull out! Pull out!" to the Mustang or Thunderbolt pilot diving on his own troops. GI Joe came to admire the fighter-bomber pilots with the same ardor with which he detested the heavy-bomber bombardiers. Probably, he relied upon them a little too much for support and expected the impossible of them. Sometimes, just to encourage ground troops, the controllers would direct the fighter-bombers to attack empty countryside. Such aggravated risk infuriated the pilots, well aware that low-level attacks gave them absolutely no chance to bail out if they were hit. Close-up air support was dangerous work indeed, and when the RAF hoped to solve a shortage of Typhoon pilots by asking for volunteers from the Spitfires, they got none and had to "volunteer" them. By one of the ironies of war there was no longer much work for the splendid Spitfire interceptor, because there were no longer very many Luftwaffe aircraft aloft. Because the speedy Spitfire was lightly armed and therefore easily flamed, and could carry only 1,000 pounds of bombs, it could not be converted to close support. Yet, the RAF had amassed an immense force of Spitfires for a mission already accomplished. As a result, and because the Mustangs and Thunderbolts were superior to the Typhoon, the British 2nd Tactical Air Force was not the equal of Quesada's IX Tactical Air Command.

Nevertheless, both units were of great assistance to the Allied ground forces: the 2nd on the east flank where the 2nd British Army continued to pin down more than half of Kluge's forces, the IX in the west where Bradley's First Army had at last reached Avranches and "turned the corner" into Brittany. There they were surprised to receive unexpected support from the Maquis of the French Resistance.

100. The Rise of the French Resistance

A MONTH BEFORE D-DAY, General de Gaulle placed General Koenig in charge of the French Forces of the Interior, a formal organization to direct and supply those various clandestine units of heroic French who operated independently against the Germans in a movement called the Resistance. These men and women were writers, intellectuals, scientists, lawyers, nurses and doctors, even high-ranking sympathizers within the Vichy Government, and the officers and men of guerrilla warfare formations called Maquis. This is a French word for wild, bushy land, and it was in such terrain—in Brittany, the mountains of the Jura and the Vosges, and the great stretches of guerrilla country in southern France—that the Maquis units were active.

After the fall of France in the summer of 1940, there were not many Maquisards. A few more, on the run from the Gestapo or the Vichy police or dodging the German forced-labor net, arrived in 1941. In 1942, after the invasion of French North Africa provoked Hitler into occupying Unoccupied France, there was a fairly large influx of French soldiers fleeing the German incursion. In 1943 and 1944, however, recruits flowed steadily into the Maquis camps. Most of them were high-minded boys, prepared to suffer and die for their country. They responded to such stark appeals as the one below:

Men who come to the Maquis to fight live badly, in precarious fashion, with food hard to find; they will be absolutely cut off from their families for the duration; the enemy does not apply the rules of war to them; they cannot be assured any pay; every effort will be made to help their families, but it is impossible to give any guarantee in this matter; all correspondence is forbidden.

Bring two shirts, two underpants, two pair wool socks, a light sweater, a scarf, a heavy sweater, a wool blanket, an extra pair of shoes, shoe laces, needles, thread, buttons, safety pins, soap, canteen, knife and fork, flashlight, compass, a weapon if possible, and also if possible a sleeping bag. Wear a warm suit, a beret, a raincoat, a good pair of hobnailed shoes.

You will need a complete set of identity papers, even false, but in order, with a work card to pass you through roadblocks. It is essential to have food ration tickets.

For security reasons Maquis units were never more than sixty men and usually only thirty. For food they depended on friendly farmers or raided German warehouses. Weapons and clothing were similarly obtained, or else air-dropped to them by the American Office of Strategic Services or the British Special Operations Executive. OSS and SOE officers also parachuted into camp as weapons instructors or demolition experts, often bringing orders for specific missions. Maquis chieftains were constantly demanding arms and money from the Anglo-Americans and De Gaulle's French Special Service. Because money was only infrequently forthcoming, the Maquis turned bandit, robbing banks, railroad stations and post offices for the cash needed to buy weapons and supplies. At St. Claude about $25 million was stolen from the Banque de France and another $400 million from a Banque de France armored car near Clermont-Ferrand. Most sensational of all was the holdup of a railroad train carrying nearly $1 billion in gold at the unoccupied town of Neuvic. The Maquisards who pulled off this train robbery without firing a shot were unaware that their sensational coup had been stage-managed for them by a Vichy prefect named Callard.

The Maquisards not only dwelt in misery, they also lived in dread of capture by the enemy. German soldiers, especially the SS, hated these French "terrorists" who killed and tortured their *Kameraden.* Thus, they came up with "the seesaw." A pair of Resistance victims, having been tortured in the conventional manner, were dragged to a suspended beam and tied by the throat to either end with their toes a few inches above the ground. Whichever one managed to touch the ground, to relieve the pressure on his own throat, began to strangle his comrade. Such exquisite sport might continue for half an hour until both men were dead, a culmination made more hilarious by the ingenious twist compelling the Frenchmen to kill each other.

Perhaps worse than the SS was the Milice, the last of the various anti-Resistance forces fielded by Marshal Pétain. In the Milice were about 25,000 muscular young Vichy Frenchmen trained in infiltrating Resistance movements to uncover their members. The Milice was a fully equipped organization with an excellent spy service. As auxiliaries of the German army, its soldiers were licensed to kill, which they did with an élan that the SS found pleasantly surprising in Frenchmen. Because no one kills like brothers, the Miliciens and the Maquisards, hating each other as traitors, conducted a ferocious civil war which, made hideous by mutual atrocities, soaked the soil of a sorrowing France with fresh outpourings of blood and tears.

Nevertheless, neither the Wehrmacht nor the Milice was able to exterminate the Maquis, and in November of 1943 they were actually powerless to prevent probably the most stirring and daring act of defiance in the history of the Occupation. November 11—Armistice Day—is a date sacred to French memory and despicable to the German mind, for it marks the anniversary of the German humiliation in World War I. The Germans had explicitly forbidden its observance, but a Maquis colonel named Romans (real name Petit) decided to wave the French flag in their face. He would celebrate the Armistice in the town of Oyonnax. To deceive the Germans, Romans had provocative posters announcing the observance plastered all over the neighboring town of Nantua. The police chief there, a member of the Resistance, demanded reinforcements, thus decoying police away from Oyonnax.

The Oyonnax police chief was also in the Resistance, helping Romans organize a full-dress parade on Armistice Day. Truckloads of men in the Maquis of the Départemente de l'Ain rolled into town. All the men were in uniform, wearing their medals. The color guard wore white gloves. At a trumpet call they formed ranks before the post office. Most of Oyonnax's population of 15,000 people flocked to the square. The trumpet blew again.

"*Le Maquis de l'Ain,*" Romans cried. "At my command, attention!"

The crowd howled in ecstasy. "*Vive le Maquis!*" they cried. "*Vive de Gaulle! Vive la France!*" They made such a joyful commotion that the Maquisards could not hear the order to march. When the crowd became quiet, they strode off to the crepe-draped Monument to the Dead, trumpets sounding, drums beating. The crowd followed. Romans laid a flowered Cross of Lorraine at the base of the monument. It was inscribed: "To the victors of yesterday from those of tomorrow." The men saluted. Bugles blew "To the Fallen." All sang "La Marseillaise."

Now the crowd fell upon the soldiers, weeping, kissing them, pressing money into their hands. But the Maquisards could not tarry to taste their hospitality. They re-formed ranks, marched to the trucks singing "La Marseillaise" again, clambered into them—and drove off.

All of Gaullist France was thrilled and inflamed by this defiance of both the hated Germans and the only less-despised Vichy French. Now the tide of recruits flowing into the Maquis camps became a flood, and all was in readiness for the great uprising timed to coincide with the Allied landings in Normandy. The signal was to be given in the broadcast of Verlaine's couplet. The Germans had learned of the plan, and were alerted when the first line was broadcast on June 1, 2 and 3. But when the second line—which was to trigger the uprising—was broadcast the night before D-Day, no one in high command paid any attention to it.

But the Maquis did. In Brittany, home of probably the most defiant and durable men in France, railroad lines were blown apart, tunnels were blocked, factories were emptied, lights went out and telephones were stilled. German troops ordered to Normandy from Brittany were forced to move on bicycles or on foot. One formation marched the entire 125 miles to the front on foot, harassed by Maquisards all the way, arriving in the battle zone riddled and too exhausted to fight. The Das Reich Division was ordered to Normandy but could not find a single train running in the five départementes of Brittany. Moving over the roads, they were attacked by Maquis guerrillas and blasted by Allied bombers. They, too, arrived in Normandy too weak to fight. All over France troop trains moving to the front were sabotaged or delayed. The Resistance had been asked to wreak two weeks' worth of transportation havoc, and they had. One day General Marshall would salute the Maquis with these words: "The Resistance surpassed all our expectations, and it was they who, in delaying the arrival of the German reinforcements and in preventing the regrouping of enemy divisions in the interior, assured the success of our landings."

101. Patton Drives East: Counterattack at Mortain

ON AUGUST 1, 1944, the American ground forces in France became the equal of the Anglo-Canadian-Polish forces in Montgomery's 21st Army Group. U.S. 12th Army Group was made operational under command of Omar Bradley. It was composed of the First Army, now under Lt. Gen. Courtney Hodges, and the newly activated Third Army commanded by Lt. Gen. George Patton. Bradley had expected that he would be an autonomous equal with Montgomery, but Eisenhower could not make that change yet. This was because he was still in

Britain, unable to take direct command of the battle, when he would no longer need a deputy ground commander. However, the Allies had not yet captured a French city capable of housing SHAEF's huge administrative facilities. So Montgomery became the *temporary* overall ground commander, but with no real authority over Bradley and his Americans except to arrange for coordination and draw boundaries. Bradley did not object to the arrangement because his relations with Montgomery had so far been cordial, even at times friendly. After having been granted a free hand, while the testy little general was the actual ground commander and he was only an army chief, Bradley did not anticipate any interference at 12th Army Group.

U.S. equality in command with Montgomery's 21st Army Group had been agreed upon in the Overlord plan months before D-Day. At no time did Eisenhower ever consider continuing him as ground commander. The United States was to provide for two thirds of the Continental ground forces, and it was unthinkable that they should be commanded by a Briton. Nevertheless, because of Eisenhower's unwillingness to offend either Montgomery or the British public, news of the changeover was censored. Yet an American reporter broke the story two weeks later. A great furor was raised by the British press over the "demotion" of their war hero, which was decried as a rebuke and an insult to the British people. It was nothing of the sort, although it did signal the end of the British media's habit of referring to all Allied troops as "Montgomery's forces," just as American daylight bombing raids were described as "Allied" attacks while Bomber Command's nocturnal strikes were indeed "British." Also the British media and public apparently did not understand that Montgomery's passive role at Caen on the eastern flank had been long planned. He was to contain the enemy while the Americans in the west were breaking out. The more forces he drew against him the better he was fulfilling his mission. It was too much, of course, to expect the ordinary Tommy or even his lieutenants and captains, as well as their relatives, to understand such a relatively unglamorous role. Eisenhower might well have calmed the storm by explaining the situation; but he said nothing, probably out of his reluctance to offend Montgomery or the British public. Montgomery certainly could have silenced it by explaining all to the British media. But he did not, probably because he didn't want to.

On August 31, the same day that 12th Army Group was removed from Montgomery's command, Montgomery was made a field marshal. If this promotion was to take the sting out of his so-called demotion, it was not successful; for British resentment had risen still higher at the spectacle of George Patton's Third Army racing through Brittany with a speed and dash that made even the celebrated German blitzkrieg appear like slow-motion war.

On August 1 Patton's Third Army exploded out of the Cotentin Peninsula and charged into the narrow Avranches corridor. Because only two roads led into Avranches and only one out of it, the spearheading armor followed by motorized infantry became stalled in a bumper-to-bumper bottleneck. Patton personally

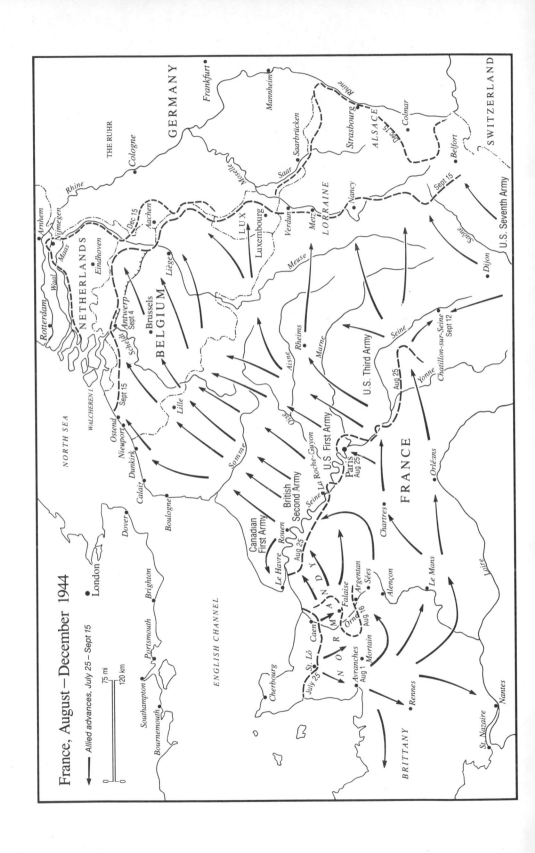

France, August–December 1944

→ Allied advances, July 25 – Sept 15

75 mi
120 km

uncorked it. He was everywhere up and down the line in his jeep,* clearing the way for his tanks with the cry: "Let my killers through!" Sometimes he marched in ranks with a column of foot soldiers moving into line. Or he pulled an officer out of a ditch, screaming at him in his high-pitched voice not to infect his troops with his fear. Again, he excoriated another officer for taping over his insignia. "Inexcusable! Do you want to give your men the idea that the enemy is dangerous?" In Avranches Patton's jeep was blocked by a hopeless snarl of trucks. Again the general in the pink breeches and star-studded helmet, wearing the white pistol and the gleaming leather boots, sprang from his jeep to enter an empty police box in the center of the square. For an hour and a half he directed traffic, unsnarling it and sending the trucks flowing west again. Occasionally, his white teeth flashed in a grin at the expressions of incredulity on the drivers' faces. Within twenty-four hours he had successfully passed two armored and two infantry divisions through the corridor, and sent them dashing west into Brittany. "If the greatest study of mankind is man," he said, "surely the greatest study of war is the road net."

Patton actually loved war. To be bombed or strafed or machine-gunned or shelled exhilarated rather than frightened him. Even the debris of war, so far from depressing him, actually exalted him. Coming out of Avranches he drove with his aide, Lt. Col. Charles R. Codman, along a road lined on either side with masses of smashed trucks, half-tracks, ambulances and the reeking rotting corpses of German soldiers. On either side were ruined farms: crumbled buildings, fields blackened with burnt grass, the stiff-legged and bloated carcasses of cows sprawled everywhere. "Just look at that, Codman," Patton shouted. "Could anything be more magnificent?" From a clump of bushes a concealed battery began bellowing. "Compared to war," Patton cried in a trembling voice, "all other forms of human endeavor shrink to insignificance." He paused. "God, how I love it!"

Not all of Patton's commanders had the same fondness for combat. Some of them dreaded the arrival of the Old Man to hear him shrilly inquiring why they had not advanced farther.

"But my flanks, General."

"You have nothing to worry about. If anything develops—and it won't—our tactical air will know before you do, and will clobber it. That will give me plenty of time to pull something out of the hat." Again the dramatic pause followed by a pat on the shoulder. "Get going now. Let the enemy worry about his flanks. I'll see you up there in a couple of days."

So goaded and driven, under such impetus, Third Army came bursting out of Avranches at a forty-mile-a-day clip, seizing all the roads and gathering in prisoners by the tens of thousands. It was a sensational dash, indeed, although not actually the stupendous feat of arms it seemed then. Much of Brittany's defending forces had been withdrawn by Kluge for use against Bradley and

---

*Patton always called his quarter-ton open car a peep, but everyone else in the U.S. Armed Forces called it a jeep.

Montgomery. The peninsula itself was largely in the hands of the Maquis and many German formations on their own volition had hastened into the sanctuary of the fortified ports of Brest, Lorient and St. Nazaire. Brest did not fall until September 19 and the other two held out until the end of the war. Thus, Patton did not take his primary objective, the deep-water ports to the west. But there are other fruits of victory which fall to the impetuous. One was the growing intoxication of Patton's troops, riding through Brittany on their tanks and trucks with their helmets pushed back jauntily on their heads; another was the harvest of headlines which so gratified an electioneering Franklin Delano Roosevelt; and a third was that when Patton swung his Third Army west to join in the attempt to encircle the German Seventh Army, his reputation helped to induce Hitler to issue perhaps his most stupid order of the war.

"We must strike like lightning," *Der Führer* told Field Marshal Gunther von Kluge. "When we reach the sea, the American spearheads will be cut off. Obviously they are trying all-out for a major decision here, because otherwise they wouldn't have sent in their best general, Patton. . . . We must wheel north like lightning and turn the entire enemy front from the rear."

This was Hitler's fantastic reaction to the threatened encirclement of his Seventh Army. It was not that he saw that Kluge's left flank was open and dangling, but rather that he saw a chance to strike north toward Avranches to trap the Americans in Brittany, and then wheel east to roll up the entire Allied line from its rear. It was as far from reality as a demented mind may retreat and conceived as far from the battlefield as safety would permit: the Wolf's Lair on the edge of the Soviet avalanche. If Kluge had been Rommel, he probably would not have obeyed the order; but he was Kluge, merely another of those high German commanders who seemed to lose their sanity under Hitler's spell. So he obeyed. Reduced to 650 tanks from the 1,400 committed to battle in Normandy, he scrounged what he could from the eastern front at Caen and formed five panzer and SS divisions into the hammerhead of his counterattack at Mortain.

It began August 6, coming in the main against the 30th Division, which had just relieved the 1st. Because the 1st had still been fighting while preparing its positions, they were not in sufficient depth. Within a few hours the German attack had penetrated the 30th's lines. The 2nd Battalion, 120th Regiment, was overrun and cut off. But it hung on doggedly, refusing for six days to submit to German demands for surrender. Its only request was for medical supplies. After half of the parachuted supplies fell within German lines, the 30th stuffed semifixed artillery shells with morphine and sulfa and lobbed them inside the gallant formation's perimeter—now a wall of German bodies.

Kluge's attack on the second day looked hopefully for bad weather. But the skies cleared and Quesada's fearful Thunderbolts, supported by Typhoons, fell on German armor like avenging furies. Promised help from the Luftwaffe never arrived. Every sortie was intercepted and shot down or turned back. A pall of flame-flickered smoke rose from the burning German tanks. So far from relieving the threat of encirclement, Hitler's maniacal decision had driven his divisions deeper into the American noose.

Omar Bradley saw that the Mortain counterattack gave him two choices: he could throw in his four uncommitted divisions to help Hodges's First Army hold at Mortain, or he could hope that the enemy would drive deeper into Mortain and thus allow these four formations to move through Kluge's open left flank and thus destroy the Seventh Army. Bradley could be cautious and contain the enemy before resuming the painful slugging match across the face of France, or he could be daring and win the Second Battle of France at a stroke. Knowing that Montgomery had already ordered his Twenty-first Army to advance to the Seine, he chose the gamble. Kluge's transfer of forces to the west had produced a noticeable loosening of the forces opposite him. Crerar's Canadians were to drive down the Caen road to Falaise and pivot northwest toward Rouen. Dempsey's British were to follow the arterial road that ran to Argentan, twenty-five miles south of Falaise. Thus, Bradley planned to have Patton swing north to Argentan behind Kluge and there meet Montgomery's forces moving south.

"We'll go as far as Argentan and hold there," Bradley told Patton. "We've got to be careful we don't run into Monty coming down from Falaise."

Secretary of the Treasury Henry Morgenthau was visiting Omar Bradley's headquarters when the Mortain counterattack began. "This is an opportunity that comes to a commander not more than once in a century," the exultant Bradley said. "We're about to destroy an entire hostile army." Morgenthau, who was fond of playing soldier, looked skeptical and Bradley continued: "If the other fellow will only press his attack here at Mortain for another forty-eight hours, he'll give us time to close at Argentan and there completely destroy him. And when he loses his Seventh Army in this bag, he'll have nothing left with which to oppose us. We'll go all the way from here to the German border."

Kluge did continue to drive deeper into the trap, while Patton sent his XV Corps under Maj. Gen. Wade H. Haislip driving hard north from Le Mans to Argentan. It was not until August 11 that Kluge conceded that the foolhardy attack should be canceled. He requested permission to withdraw to the Seine. For the first time, Hitler agreed to a withdrawal. But he specified that Kluge must first clear his left flank and rear before he pulled back! Here was madness compounded by idiocy. As Bradley said, with XV Corps nearing Argentan in Kluge's rear, "Hitler might more reasonably have ordered his field commander to reverse the downstream flow of the Seine."

But Montgomery in the north was moving with slackening speed. After five days his Canadian pincer had only moved halfway to Falaise. Thus when Haislip reached Argentan on the night of August 12, he found the Anglo-Canadians stalled in the north with an eighteen-mile gap between him and them. Patton was exasperated. He phoned Bradley.

"We've got elements in Argentan. Let me go on to Falaise, and we'll drive the British into the sea for another Dunkirk."

Bradley ignored still another intemperate Pattonism and said: "Nothing doing. You're not to go beyond Argentan. Just stop where you are and build up on that shoulder . . . the German is beginning to pull out. You'd better button up and get ready for him."

Meanwhile Bradley's reports to SHAEF had created great excitement in the Allied world. Eisenhower, Churchill, Roosevelt and even the phlegmatic Brooke were jubilant. Correspondents who had been writing so gloomily of the impending stalemate on the Western Front, now remembered November 1918 and wrote euphorically of the impending German collapse. Everywhere people were talking of a German surrender by September. When reporters asked Eisenhower on August 15 how many more weeks until the German capitulation, he was furious. He reminded them that Hitler could only expect death if he surrendered, that whereas the Kaiser in 1918 had President Wilson's generous Fourteen Points to persuade him, *Der Führer* contemplated Unconditional Surrender. Nevertheless, in New York City the stock market tumbled in anticipation of an early peace.

In France, Montgomery's progress remained slow. His troops were faced by stiffer resistance than Haislip's Americans had met on the road to Argentan, but a fuming Bradley still thought that he might have speeded his advance to stem the flow of Germans escaping through what was now called "the Falaise Gap." Bradley still hesitated to send his own forces into Falaise. Any head-on junction between two friendly armies can become a dangerous and perhaps uncontrollable maneuver. If the field marshal could not reach Falaise, he might better shift his weight to the east at Chambois and close the trap there. Meanwhile, nineteen German divisions were backpedaling frantically to escape the trap. By day in clear weather, they were fair game for the Allied fighter-bombers, but they still could move at night and during bad weather, and many of them were escaping.

"Hell, by now they've all gotten out," Patton complained to Bradley. "Instead of waiting here for Monty, we ought to be moving again. There's nothing out front, nothing at all between me and the Seine."

That was exactly one of the options Bradley had been considering. He could hold where he was until Montgomery arrived; he could move northeast ten miles to Chambois and close the trap there himself; or he could leave part of his forces at Argentan and make a dash for the Seine and Paris. If Patton could seize a bridgehead there, he would thwart the enemy's last chance of forming a defense behind the Seine River line. Kluge would then certainly have to go all the way back to Germany, 350 miles to the east. Bradley knew the Seventh Army could escape if he did not go to Chambois. But he decided to abandon orthodoxy in the quest for greater prizes, and he sent the Third Army dashing for the Seine.

Shortly after he did, Montgomery called to propose that Bradley extend his pincer from Argentan to Chambois. He said he had already diverted his Polish Armored Division toward that objective.

"I agree with you, sir," Bradley said. "We ought to go northeast. In fact, I've just sent two divisions northeast—northeast to the Seine."

The silence at the other end was like a thunderclap. Montgomery said nothing and hung up. His dream of being first to the Seine, of being the great British architect of a great British victory, had been shattered. It was still not until August 19, twelve days after Kluge attacked at Mortain, thirteen after he had begun his own movement, six days after Patton reached Argentan, that Montgomery's forces entered Chambois and closed the trap. Four days later Patton's Third Army crossed the Seine and drove to Troyes about thirty miles farther east.

To complete the destruction of the enemy, Bradley asked General Dempsey if he would like to take two British divisions over Patton's path through Avranches and wheel north with a pincer up the Seine's left bank. "We'll get you the trucks to make the move," Bradley promised.

"Oh, no thanks, Brad," Dempsey said, pulling a straw through his teeth, "we couldn't pull it off. I just couldn't spare two divisions for so wide an end run."

"If you can't do it, Bimbo," Bradley said, "have you any objection to our giving it a try? It'll mean cutting across your front."

Dempsey had no objection, nor did Montgomery, and Bradley began an extremely difficult maneuver of marching 80,000 men across his ally's front, aware that he would have to march them back again while the British were themselves driving for the Seine. But the maneuver was highly successful. Four American divisions rolling north penetrated all the way to Rouen and panicked the enemy retreating from Montgomery's advance. They were forced into a narrow river crossing near the mouth of the Seine. There they were punished by Allied air, roaring in to bomb and strafe them, and by American artillery firing for two days. Now there was absolutely no possibility of Kluge re-forming behind the Seine. East and west, he was beaten—and Army Group B was in full retreat. But Gunther von Kluge by then was dead.

On August 15 his staff car had been strafed and his radio destroyed. He was out of contact with his own forces and the high command. Hitler suspected that he was secretly negotiating with the western Allies. On the 16th Kluge refused to obey the high command's order for a counterattack and instead ordered a withdrawal. Hitler relieved him the following day. On his way back to Germany, Kluge poisoned himself. "You have fought a great and honorable fight," he wrote Hitler. "Now show yourself great enough to put a necessary end to a struggle that is now hopeless." Thus another ranking German commander chose suicide rather than risk trial. Kluge was replaced by Field Marshal Walter Model, a Nazi fanatic but also an extremely capable general.

Model's order to escape came much too late. The Germans lost 60,000 men in the Argentan-Falaise Pocket: 50,000 prisoners and 10,000 dead. How many of the wounded died of wounds or were left unfit for combat is not known. Usually the wounded figure is four or five times the number of dead. Between 20,000 and 40,000 men escaped carrying only their personal weapons, but there is also no figure on the number who actually survived passage through hostile country or the knives and guns of the Maquis. Also, it was the support units that got out first, often on a division's direct commands, so that most of those who escaped were noncombatants.

Inside the pocket the sticky-sweet stench of rotten flesh—both human and equine—was nauseating. Many men marching through it put on their gas masks to avoid becoming sick. The roads were choked with wrecked vehicles and bodies. No fewer than 1,800 horses had been killed. Many of the victims had been dead for days, and their bodies were already moving white masses of maggots. Before these swollen corpses were burned Allied soldiers fired into them to release the dangerous gases gathering within them. Bits of uniform and shreds of flesh clung to the blackened hulls of tanks while human remains—hands, heads and limbs—hung from the branches of the hedgerows. Dwight Eisenhower, who arrived at Falaise while the cleanup was in progress, thought the scene "could be described only by Dante. It was literally possible to walk for hundreds of yards at a time, stepping on nothing but dead and decaying flesh."

More than any other event in the Battle for Normandy, the Falaise Gap created a bitter and enduring controversy between the British and Americans, in the beginning by the commanders on the spot, today by the military historians who write about it.

British historians write of an "Allied" failure to close the gap, as though Bradley were as much to blame as Montgomery. With unfailing caution, 21st Army Group—particularly the Canadians—started for Falaise a day before Bradley ordered Third Army to Argentan, and they did not close the gap until five days after Patton arrived at his appointed place and was ordered by Bradley to stay there. If there is any fault at all, it would seem to have been in Montgomery's 21st Army Group, guilty of the same cautious progress that took it thirty-four days rather than one day to get to Caen. Some critics say that Bradley himself could have pushed his forces eighteen miles to Falaise. But Bradley simply did not have the strength to do it. Patton with four divisions was already blocking three escape routes through Argentan, Sées and Alençon. If he had stretched himself to Falaise, he would have been so thin that the nineteen German divisions struggling to escape would have overwhelmed him. Bradley himself wrote: "I much preferred a solid shoulder at Argentan to the possibility of a broken neck at Falaise." He was right. Falaise, as agreed upon, was *Montgomery's* responsibility. Moreover, Bradley might have been thinking like the wily old Kutusov pursuing the retreating Napoleon from a careful distance. Why bring to battle an army dying of winter and scorched earth? Why need Bradley bring to battle desperate men struggling to escape, skilled soldiers who might inflict upon him a humiliating defeat? Why indeed when they were being whipped and lashed from the skies like no army before or since? If the wounded bear is dying in the thicket, why go into it to give him superfluous death blows?

All this happens to ignore the German soldier. The question should not be why the Allies did not close the trap but could they have? From D-Day up until the dramatic American breakout at St. Lô, whenever the Americans or the Anglo-Canadians, and the Poles as well, met the Germans on anything like equal terms, the Germans prevailed. It was only after an enormous attrition had worn them down that Bradley and Montgomery, with a tremendous assist from their air forces, began to make progress. Both commanders were deeply conscious of the enemy's superior soldiery, just as their own troops were very much aware of their own immense advantages in matériel and counted upon this more than on themselves to tip the scales. To denigrate the German soldier because he fought in an evil cause is as rational as disqualifying the powers of their Führer because he was the devil incarnate. Saint Ambrose's already quoted dictum that fortitude without justice is the tool of the wicked is indubitably true; but it is also true that it can pack a wicked wallop, and the German army was undoubtedly the finest that the world has ever seen. It lost because Hitler misused it and made too many enemies.

Omar Bradley read the battle correctly. Choosing to allow Kluge to penetrate, hoping he would penetrate in the interests of encircling him, was the master stroke of the campaign in the West. Sending Patton across the Seine and four divisions up the river's left bank across the Anglo-Canadian front was another masterly maneuver, which sent the Germans scurrying for the safety of their West Wall.

Thus the Battle for Normandy ended in a great Allied victory. It had cost the German Army 450,000 men, of whom 240,000 were killed or wounded. Also lost were 1,500 tanks, 3,500 guns and 20,000 vehicles. More than forty German divisions had been destroyed. Army Group B's eight surviving panzer divisions numbered as few soldiers as a battalion or less, some without even tanks or artillery. Seventh Army had been destroyed and of the 100,000 men of the First Army facing the Bay of Biscay, only 65,000 got safely east of the Seine. Only what was left of Fifteenth Army retiring from the Pas de Calais possessed any semblance of organization. All this was accomplished at a cost of 209,672 casualties, of which 36,976 were killed. Some 28,000 Allied airmen were also lost, either over Normandy or during the massive bombardments preceding it.

Germany's Nineteenth Army stationed in the south also was compelled to retire.

102. The Death of the Vercors Maquis

As LATE AS JUNE 28, 1944, the day Rome fell, Prime Minister Winston Churchill and his war chiefs were still reluctant to undertake Operation Dragoon, as the invasion of southern France had been renamed. They insisted that the best way to help Overlord was to concentrate in Italy. Thereafter an amphibious strike in the vicinity of Trieste at the head of the Adriatic would enable the Allies to debouch through the famous Ljubljana Gap into Austria and Hungary and strike at Germany on her unguarded southern flank.

The purpose of this operation was political, and probably rightfully so: Churchill wanted to keep the U.S.S.R. out of the Balkans. The Baltic states, Poland, Czechoslovakia and Romania were already all but won for the hammer and sickle, and Churchill hoped to forestall the loss to communism of Austria, Hungary, Yugoslavia, Greece and Bulgaria. In this he was adamantly opposed by the Americans, including President Roosevelt. On the 28th in a telegram to FDR, Churchill reopened the argument for movement into the Balkans. Roosevelt's prompt reply reminded Churchill of the "grand strategy" of Tehran, which was to minimize operations in the Mediterranean and concentrate Anglo-American strength in the West. Also FDR had just been nominated for a fourth term, and the president made his position plain with the observation: *"For purely political considerations over here, I should never survive even a slight setback in Overlord if it were known that fairly large forces had been diverted to the Balkans."*

That seemed to settle the matter and preparations for Dragoon went forward, until on August 4, with the St. Lô breakout history and Patton rampaging through Brittany, Churchill again asked Eisenhower to abandon Dragoon. Instead he wanted to use the forces to capture Brest and push harder in Italy. Eisenhower refused. Five days later Churchill pressed the point again, this time under cover of his complaint that the United States had become a "big, strong and dominating partner." The supreme commander found the prime minister surprisingly "stirred, upset and despondent." With all his considerable tact he refuted the charges of American bullying and said, "I am sorry that you seem to feel that we use our actual or potential strength as a bludgeon."

Eisenhower told Churchill frankly that he thought that his purpose was to get Allied troops into the Balkans ahead of the Soviets. If this was true, then Churchill should take his arguments to Roosevelt. Eisenhower added that he fully understood that wars were fought for political objectives, such as thwarting Soviet ambitions in the Balkans, and that if the heads of government should decide to support such a change, he would "instantly and loyally adjust plans accordingly." But on strictly military grounds, Eisenhower said, Churchill was wrong. The prime minister denied having such political objectives, insisting that the correct military policy was to avoid the barren Dragoon campaign in favor of capturing Brest and pushing on in Italy. On such grounds, Eisenhower again refused, adding that he doubted that Charles de Gaulle would allow the French forces in Dragoon, though armed and equipped by America, to fight anywhere but in France.

There is no doubt that Churchill was indeed motivated by political considerations, and history has shown him to have been right. But he pressed the point no longer, having already received FDR's unbending reply, knowing full well that the American war chiefs disliked serving "political" motives, which they considered tainted and ulterior, rather than "military" grounds, which they believed to be honest and straightforward. So Churchill's far deeper understanding of European reality and of the Stalin's czarist ambitions was ignored. Yet, neither Eisenhower nor Roosevelt can be faulted. FDR was only expressing a melancholy truth when he said that, with the German army then on the run, the naive American public would never have accepted a diversion to the Balkans. So the last disagreement which had threatened to shake the Anglo-American coalition came to a painful end in what Eisenhower later described as his most difficult discussion ever with Winston Churchill, and Operation Dragoon went forward as planned —with splendid assistance from the Resistance in southern France.

Most of the Maquis of the south had gathered on the Vercors, an Alpine plateau thirty miles long by ten miles wide in the southeast fourth of France. Three rivers shape it like a primitive arrowhead pointing north, with a notch in its southern base. Its steep sides rise a half-mile from the river flats below and on its surface are plains and valleys, peaks and cliffs, with here and there a tiny village. The Vercors is a natural citadel, a redoubt, and so it was intended to be in the summer of 1944. Four thousand Maquisards had gathered there by then in the largest concentration of guerrillas in the war. They intended to hold their redoubt against any German attacks, waiting until the Americans and French landed in southern France, when they would explode like a bomb in the enemy rear.

The Maquisards of the Vercors, of course, had not the armament to have such an effect upon the Germans, disorganized though they might be from the shock of the Allied landings. Many of their weapons were relics of World War I given them by farmers, or even older pieces taken from museums. Modern rifles and artillery, as well as a formation of trained soldiers, was to be provided by Force C, an airborne group to be landed on the Vercors by gliders. This was the original plan, called Operation Montagnards. But somewhere in its progress from tray to tray in the paper-shuffling offices of London and Algiers, Montagnards suffered strange mutations.

On the Vercors, however, the changes were not known. Everyone—including the overall commander, a Grenoble café owner named Eugene Chavant— believed that Force C, having been adopted by de Gaulle, would go forward as planned. In early June, the Germans attempted to storm the Vercors, but were beaten back, not, however, before they burned the little village of St. Nizier to the ground, hauling the Maquis dead out of the mortuary and hurling them into the flames. When the Germans did not return to the attack, there ensued the remarkable month of "the Republic of Vercors." There was food distribution for the civilian population. Pensions and family allowances were paid out and all civilian functions continued to operate. Free World media sang the praises of Chavant. Volunteers flocked to the redoubt from as far away as Paris. Airdrops brought in modern weapons and instructors. On July 11, General Koenig saluted the Vercors in his order of the day: "You fly the French colors over a corner of the French earth." Next a twenty-man American combat team arrived by air, and then Mission Paquebot, a team of five French officers assigned to clear and maintain a landing ground for Force C. On July 14—Bastille Day, the French Fourth of July—there was a traditional military review and a mass for the St.

Nizier dead. American bombers put on a dazzling aerial display, dropping hundreds of red-blue-and-white parachutes. Five days later the Germans attacked with two divisions, 20,000 men, the exact number which the Vercors Maquisards believed they could withstand—with the arrival of Force C.

Encirclement of the redoubt began on July 19, but the assault upon the Vercor's sheer steeps did not begin until dawn of the 20th. Rain began to fall, but the Maquisards held grimly in place, glancing eagerly into the sky, their ears cocked for the thrumming sound of motors. They heard them. Then they saw the tiny specks growing larger. Twenty gliders! Cheers rang out on the Vercors plateau. Force C was coming! Down through the scudding mists skimmed the gliders, bearing 400 *poilus* with mortars and heavy machine guns. The men tumbled out. The Maquisards froze.

They were *Germans!* The enemy was inside the redoubt!

Still, the Maquisards did not panic. They fought back. But more enemy glider troops arrived, and the issue was no longer in doubt. Message after anguished message was fired off to London. Where was Force C? There was no answer. Finally, Colonel Huet, the Vercors military commander, ordered his men to disperse and to fight for themselves. He signaled London: "We are bitter at having been abandoned, alone and without support in the hour of combat." Chavant's final message read: "If you don't send help now, we will agree with the population in saying that you in London and Algiers have understood nothing of our situation here, and we will consider you criminals and cowards, repeat, criminals and cowards." But there was no help, and the victorious Germans, with tremendous ferocity, began to massacre the civilian population and the valiant Maquisards who had tried to protect them.

For many years the destruction of the Vercors redoubt remained a bitter memory in the minds of the French. De Gaulle was blamed for having abandoned his gallant countrymen in their hour of need. It was hinted that he had allowed the Vercors Maquis to perish because its ranks included too many communists. It is true that de Gaulle distrusted the communists in the Resistance, but not even the Reds suggested that the Free French chief was guilty of such treachery. General Eisenhower was also criticized, yet the supreme commander in London was far too preoccupied with the Normandy stalemate to succor a few thousand Frenchmen on a faraway plateau. What probably happened was that the Vercors Maquisards made far too much noise on their plateau, causing the Germans to take thought and decide to destroy them before they could attempt whatever they planned to do. Why Force C was never organized and sent to the rescue is not known, nor is the identity of the officer who sent Mission Paquebot to clear the airfield used by the Germans and not Force C. This mystery might conceal treachery, but there is no evidence to prove it.

Yet all the Maquisards who fought at the Vercors did not die. Many escaped to join other guerrilla units. Among them was Col. Henri Zeller of the Committee for Military Action. He was taken to de Gaulle, who was so impressed by his report that he sent him to U.S. Gen. Alexander Patch in Italy. Patch commanded the army scheduled to invade the South of France. Zeller told him that his timetable was too slow, that it ignored the considerable Maquis strength in the region. Patch changed his plans accordingly, and thus when the Americans and French began landing in Provence in August 1944 they found their progress speeded by the action of Maquis saboteurs and guerrillas.

103. The Invasion of Southern France, the Liberation of Paris

ON AUGUST 15 A HUGE ARMADA of 1,800 ships, including seven British and two American carriers, appeared off the French Riviera between Toulon and Cannes. They carried the U.S. 6th Army Group under Lt. Gen Jacob L. Devers. His spearheads were from the U.S. Seventh Army, commanded by Lieutenant General Patch, and the French First Army, under General Jean de Lattre de Tassigny. American paratroopers were also aboard.

As soon as they were ashore, the invaders were joined by French Forces of the Interior. Although only lightly armed, the Maquis knew the countryside and were of invaluable assistance in scouting and in rounding up French collaborators. The first objectives were the Mediterranean ports of Toulon and Nice and the huge port of Marseilles. They were taken with little difficulty. Germany's weak Nineteenth Army, holding a hundred-mile front, had been as badly deceived as the fifteenth at Calais. Even two weeks of concentrated aerial and naval bombardment had failed to shake its belief that the Allies were planning another leapfrog attack in Italy, this time at Genoa. In two days of fighting Allied casualties were only 1,800 men and the Germans were in flight.

After securing their beachheads and the vital southern ports, the Americans and French burst out in pursuit, pushing rapidly north through the Durance Valley and west toward the Rhône. In ten days they were driving through Avignon, the ancient city of the captive papacy. Opposition continued to be light. All was swept aside as the onrushing armies pressed due north toward Lyon and Dijon. Other units in the east moved northeast on Grenoble, taking thousands of prisoners daily. On September 11 the left flank reached Dijon. Both flanks then wheeled east to await a linkup with Patton's Third Army, speeding down from the north. All the Allied armies now formed a continuous front from Switzerland to the North Sea.

Marseilles was the great prize. From September through December 1944, Marseilles unloaded more tonnage than any of the other ports available to the Allies. During the last three months of the year, one third of all supplies shipped to Europe came in from the southern ports. Marseilles remained the chief port until Antwerp was taken in November, and even afterward nearly one quarter of the ammunition and weapons entering Europe came over its wharves.

Eisenhower was elated with Dragoon. It had been even more fruitful than he had anticipated, and with fewer casualties. His next biggest problem after the landings was what to do about Paris.

While the Allies raced through France—Montgomery's 21st Army Group along the coast toward Belgium, Hodges's First and Patton's Third Army heading east toward Paris and beyond—Dwight Eisenhower pondered the question of liberating the City of Light. He did not want to attack it and provoke street fighting that might desecrate and destroy the most beautiful city in the world, a monument to Western Civilization. He had already issued stern orders that no fighting should take place in areas containing important historical or religious landmarks, explaining that in great measure they represented what the Allies were fighting for. But Paris could become a severe logistics burden. To feed its 2 million residents would require 4,000 tons of supplies daily, the equivalent needs of seven full divisions.

On August 19, however, a rising of the Resistance all but forced Eisenhower's hand. It appeared that there might be fighting between them and the German forces under Lt. Gen. Dietrich von Choltitz. Choltitz commanded about 5,000 soldiers, fifty light and medium guns and sixty airplanes. But he also was anxious to ignore Hitler's order to burn Paris to the ground. That night he concluded what was to be an uneasy armistice with the Resistance. On the 21st Charles de Gaulle accompanied by General Koenig called on Eisenhower. They asked him to detach Maj. Gen. Jacques Le Clerc's 2nd French Armored Division from the First Army and rush it into Paris. Eisenhower politely declined, whereupon an angry de Gaulle withdrew. There was no animosity between the two men. They respected one another. But there was no warmth. De Gaulle next sent Eisenhower a note saying he might have to order Le Clerc into Paris on his own. Eisenhower, still undecided, scribbled on de Gaulle's note: "It looks now as if we'd be compelled to go into Paris." Finally, the Resistance leaders begged the supreme commander to send troops into the city before the Germans broke the armistice.

Paris with all her glamour was now like a magnet drawing everyone in the Allied camp to itself: de Gaulle, Le Clerc, Eisenhower, his own commanders eager to claim the honor of liberation and especially his combat soldiers. Remembering the song their fathers sang—"How you gonna keep 'em down on the farm, after they've seen Paree?"—they were eager to taste the delights of the fabled city. At last Le Clerc started for Paris on his own and Eisenhower decided to send the American 4th Division and a British contingent along with him. The French got there first—on August 25—and de Gaulle arrived shortly thereafter, appointing Koenig military governor and taking control of all government buildings himself. On the following day, de Gaulle led a parade down the Champs Elysées. It was, in effect, a Roman triumph, without, of course, "tributaries to grace in bonds his chariot wheels" but just as effective. Choosing the humble "we" of kings and popes, de Gaulle described it himself: "Since each of all these here had chosen Charles de Gaulle in his heart as the refuge against his agony and the symbol of his hopes, we must permit the man to be seen, familiar and fraternal, in order that at this sight the national unity should shine forth." Yet who would say that Charles de Gaulle was not worthy of such glacial grandeur? Throughout the dark night of France's travail, he alone among her leaders had upheld her honor and preserved her worldwide interests. France knew this, and Paris. With all the emotion of her ardent heart, Paris gave a delirious, weeping welcome to that tall, stern figure.

Even Eisenhower and Bradley had been unable to resist the allure of Paris. On the following morning, a beautiful, sunny Sunday, the two generals slipped into the city. But everyone was not "sleeping late," as they had thought. The boulevards were thronged and the two men quickly recognized. They were mobbed, grabbed and kissed. Eisenhower was embarrassed. "I prefer camps to cities," he wrote to Mamie.

Next day Eisenhower visited de Gaulle surrounded by the Garde Républicaine in their gorgeous uniforms. The practical Frenchman was worried about the number of communists in the Resistance. He asked Eisenhower for a show of force—a parade that would demonstrate American military might. Eisenhower asked Bradley what could be done. He replied that since he was planning to attack east of Paris, he could parade his men in full battle gear and with all their equipment straight through the city on their way to the front. De Gaulle thought it an excellent idea, and so did Eisenhower, now eager to show the Parisians that America had had something to do with their liberation. On August 29 Maj. Gen. Norman Cota led his 28th Infantry Division down the Champs Elysées. Eisenhower, de Gaulle, Bradley and Gerow took the salute from a reviewing stand formed by an upside-down Bailey bridge. Paris went wild again, with the same singing, shouting, kissing fervor with which it had welcomed the doughboys of the U.S. 1st Infantry Division twenty-six years previously.

After four years of darkness, the City of Light had been liberated.

104. The Capture of Biak: Politics at Pearl Harbor

ONE OF THE CHIEF REASONS for General MacArthur's Hollandia operation had been to provide air bases for heavy bombers supporting Nimitz's drive through the Marianas and MacArthur's own return to the Philippines. But MacArthur was disappointed to learn that Hollandia's soil was too soft to support a heavy-bomber strip until extensive engineering work was completed. Rather than delay his timetable, the Southwest Pacific commander decided to seize Japanese bases farther up the northern coast of Dutch New Guinea.

These were west of Hollandia at the town of Sarmi, on the coastal island of Wakde and on Maffin Bay between Wakde and Sarmi. Even here the soil was too soft for big bombers. For a good hard crust MacArthur needed the island of Biak in the Schoutens about 300 miles west of Hollandia. The Wakde-Sarmi airfields would be used for fighters supporting the Biak invasion.

On May 17 the 41st Division's 163rd Regiment—the same soldiers who had taken Aitape a few weeks earlier—landed at Arare on the New Guinea mainland four and a half miles across a strait from Wakde. There was little opposition, and within a few hours the Americans took the village of Toem directly opposite Wakde. Next morning the 163rd's 1st Battalion shoved off from Toem for Wakde. A trio of LCI rocket ships pinned down the Japanese gun positions on Wakde's beaches, and the Americans landed with light casualties. Within an hour they had reached the southern end of the airfield. There were two more days of fighting on Wakde, but before it ended, army engineers and aviation technicians were already at work enlarging and improving the airfield. In another twelve hours it was operational. A week later Liberators taking off from Wakde made the first aerial reconnaissance of southern Mindanao in the Philippines.

Sarmi, about sixteen miles east of Toem, was the headquarters for the Japanese 36th Division under Lt. Gen. Tagami Hachiro. Intelligence reported that Hachiro was preparing to attack the Wakde area and General Krueger of the Alamo Forces intended to hit him with a spoiling attack. Krueger also believed that Sarmi's defenses were weak. Actually, they were very strong. At Lone Tree Hill, a 175-foot rise on the coastal plain, they had constructed a maze of caves, pillboxes and bunkers in which 75-mm mountain guns were concealed. When the 158th Infantry Regiment attacked Lone Tree, the Japanese hit them with a storm of fire, hurling the Americans back with 300 casualties. It was not until a month later that the assault was resumed by the 6th Infantry Division. Two battalions of the 20th Infantry, supported by artillery and fighter planes, finally fought their way to the top of the hill, where they were cut off and surrounded. But they held out, ultimately cleaning out the Japanese at a cost of 1,000 casualties. The Japanese at Sarmi, however, remained unconquered until the end of the war.

Meanwhile Krueger had moved against Biak, his ultimate objective. Biak was a large island east of the Vogelkop Peninsula at New Guinea's western extremity. Bosnek (Bosnik) on the coast was its principal town. It was another martial honeycomb of caves, bunkers and pillboxes—held by about 11,000 troops under Col. Kuzume Naoyuki. Naoyuki disdained the doctrine of destruction at the water's edge, with its back-breaking corollary of nocturnal banzais. He deliberately allowed the Americans to land with little opposition so that they might stroll unwarily into his ambush. This was what happened to the spearheading 162nd Regiment of the 41st Division. When the soldiers of its 3rd Battalion landed at Bosnek May 27, they advanced to within sight of the airfield before they realized they had walked into a trap.

From roadside caves came a storm of bullets from machine guns and automatic weapons. Hidden mortars began their deadly hiccuping, dropping shells among the surprised Americans. It was nightfall before the 3rd Battalion covered by the 2nd could extricate itself from the trap. But the 2nd was isolated. In the morning, Colonel Naoyuki threw his tanks against it. These were the thin-skinned nine-tonners mounting 37-mm guns that had been and still were the dread of the lightly armed Chinese. But on Biak they came up against the far more formidable Shermans firing 75s and were destroyed. Nevertheless, the 2nd was still cut off. Its soldiers repulsed three attacks before they were withdrawn by amtracks arriving under cover of darkness.

Now Maj. Gen. H. H. Fuller commanding the 41st appealed to Krueger for reinforcements. He got two battalions, which he sent into the jungle on a turning movement behind the Japanese-held ridges. A stronger force backed by artillery and aircraft moved down the coastal road again. Biak's enervating heat and humidity took a toll almost as great as enemy gunfire. Biak had very little water. Although the Japanese, aware of this, had been able to stock supplies, the Americans were forced to draw from scattered water holes. Most American soldiers had to fight on one canteen of water a day. Some died crawling to the water holes at night.

After a week of hard fighting the Americans under General Fuller seized Mokmer airfield. But the enemy still held the ridges commanding it and poured down an inhibiting fire on engineers seeking to rebuild it. Now Krueger's and Fuller's seething dislike for one another boiled over. Irritated by Krueger's constant prodding, Fuller asked to be relieved. Krueger, under pressure from MacArthur to get Mokmer Airfield operative as soon as possible, readily obliged, replacing Fuller with Eichelberger.

At this point the Japanese high command prepared to intervene at Biak. The navy had been expecting Nimitz's attacks in the Marianas and had planned to sail there in force in search of decisive battle. But an American-held Biak flying off heavy land-based bombers could strike the Combined Fleet sortieing from the Sulu Sea in the Philippines bound for the Marianas. So the navy persuaded the army to send its 2nd Amphibious Brigade of 2,500 men to Biak under a strong naval escort. The convoy was spotted by a Liberator flying from Wakde, just as a Japanese scout plane mistakenly reported an American carrier force off Biak. That was more than enough to compel the Japanese armada to return to the Philippines.

But the Combined Fleet was still determined to hold Biak. Admiral Koga assembled a powerful force, including the giant sisters *Musashi* and *Yamato*. Just as it was prepared to sail for Biak, reports were received of Admiral Spruance's great fleet heading for the Marianas. That was when the Imperial Navy canceled Biak and headed for Saipan and the disaster of the Marianas Turkey Shoot.

It has been said that this change in strategy was a "striking illustration of the mutual interdependence of the Allied Southwest and Central Pacific Areas." It was indeed, but only accidentally so. If the Japanese had persisted in their determination to strike at Biak, it might have been instead "a striking demonstration" of the folly of dividing the Pacific War into two independent commands. Such division of forces gave the Japanese the opportunity to concentrate superior forces against one part of the American advance—MacArthur's. Combined Fleet could have sent the handful of American cruisers and destroyers at Biak to the bottom of the sea, brought the Americans on the island under a terrible sea and air bombardment and put decisive reinforcements ashore. Biak could have been an American disaster that would have wrecked the Pacific timetable, and even, by the mutual recrimination which certainly would have succeeded it, so unraveled army-navy unity that conquest of Japan would have been delayed a year or even longer.

Fortunately for the United States, the Japanese navy submitted to its obsessive desire for decisive battle, thus dooming its forces on Biak. But it took several more weeks for the Americans to capture the remaining airfields and even longer to blast and burn Colonel Naoyuki's stubborn soldiers out of their caves and bunkers. In the meantime, General MacArthur received a mysteriously vague order from General Marshall to proceed immediately to Pearl Harbor for an "important conference with the President."

In Chicago that summer the Democratic Party nominated Franklin Delano Roosevelt for an unprecedented fourth consecutive time as its candidate for president. Even before the convention ended, Roosevelt boarded the cruiser *Baltimore* in San Diego and set sail for Pearl Harbor. Although FDR never explained his reasons for this "important conference," a good explanation came from Rep. Everett Dirksen of Illinois, campaign manager for Roosevelt's opponent, Governor Thomas E. Dewey of New York. "MacArthur," Dirksen said, "is no longer a fourth-term threat. But he is still exceedingly popular in America. And in an election year it's a good idea to be seen as much as possible with as many popular people as possible."

MacArthur had no illusions, either. Flying toward Hawaii in his B-17, the *Bataan,* he fumed at being made a pawn in his chief's political strategy. At one point he exclaimed: "The humiliation of forcing me to leave my command to fly to Honolulu for a political picture-taking junket!" But by the time he landed at Hickam Field he had calmed himself and was thinking of a way to upstage the president. Going immediately to Fort Shafter, he met his old West Point friend, Gen. Robert C. Richardson, commander of army forces in Nimitz's theater. He asked him to find him the most spectacular automobile in the islands. There were two huge and well-known open touring cars in Honolulu, Richardson said; one belonged to the madam of a brothel, the other to the fire chief.

MacArthur chose the chief's fire-engine-red convertible. Then he delayed his arrival at the dock where the *Baltimore* was moored, waiting until he could be sure that he appeared alone, sharing neither the photographers nor the crowd's plaudits with any one.

Aboard *Baltimore,* the president was obviously annoyed. Nimitz, Halsey,

Richardson and about fifty other high-ranking officers were there. Where was MacArthur? No one knew. But the publicity-minded FDR, very much aware of MacArthur's own penchant for the front page, had his suspicions. They were confirmed when a wild shriek of sirens arose from the dock. Led by the President in his wheelchair, everyone rushed to the quarter-deck rail.

Below, a huge crowd behind a two-acre cleared space was cheering wildly while a fire-engine-red open touring-car drove around and around behind a wailing motorcycle escort. Seated in the back seat alone, dashingly handsome in an aviator's leather jacket and his squashed hat—both nonregulation—was Douglas MacArthur, smiling broadly and waving airily to the crowd. The car stopped at the gangplank and MacArthur got out. He smiled, trotted halfway up, and turned to acknowledge another ovation. Then he went to the quarter-deck to meet the president.

"Hello, Douglas," Roosevelt said in grudging admiration. "What are you doing with that leather jacket on? It's damn hot today."

"Well, I've just flown in from Australia. It's pretty cold up there."

MacArthur was well aware that when Brisbane feels a snowflake, there'll be ice on the Equator, but he was still undismayed by the palpable falsehood of his retort. He was enjoying himself, even chuckling when his commander in chief snapped:

"Douglas, I'm taking that car."

He did, dashing about in it next day for six hours on an exhausting but well-photographed tour of military installations, followed faithfully by Nimitz, MacArthur and their entourages in less spectacular vehicles. The following evening, after a sumptuous meal in a palatial mansion overlooking the beach at Waikiki, Roosevelt turned to the supposed purpose of the conference: to plan the next phase of action against Japan. He picked up a long bamboo pointer and touched it to the Philippines on a huge wall map.

"Well, Douglas, where do we go from here?"

"Leyte, Mr. President," MacArthur replied immediately. "And then Luzon."

Although Nimitz agreed that the southern or central Philippines should be seized, he insisted that Formosa should be invaded before Luzon. MacArthur thereupon delivered an impassioned plea for the liberation of all the Philippines. The United States had a "moral obligation" to free the oppressed Filipinos and American servicemen imprisoned there. Not to do so would make the American name a stench in the nostrils of Asia, he warned, pointedly suggesting that if the archipelago were bypassed, an angry American public would register its displeasure at the polls in November. Roosevelt seemed impressed. On the whole, the conference was extremely amiable. MacArthur flew back to Brisbane confident that he had "sold it." He was also distressed by the physical appearance of the president. His skin had the grayish pallor of the very sick. "I had not seen him for a number of years," MacArthur said, "and physically he was just a shell of the man I had known. It was clearly evident that his days were numbered."

Upon his return to his command, MacArthur found that his drive along the coast of Dutch New Guinea was still proceeding smoothly. Biak had fallen before he left Brisbane and so had the island of Noemfoor about sixty miles farther west. Brig. Gen. Edwin D. Patrick's 158th Regimental Combat Team, which had fought at Lone Tree Hill, captured Noemfoor along with three fine airfields. An overwhelming aerial bombardment of 8,000 tons of explosives left the Japanese defenders so dazed that there was little opposition.

Throughout the rest of the summer MacArthur's forces completed the reduction of the Vogelkop Peninsula. Airfield sites were taken near the villages of Sansapor and Mar. The final stepping-stone in MacArthur's approach to the Philippines was Morotai Island in the Moluccas between the Vogelkop and Mindanao. The 31st Infantry Division landed on Morotai unopposed on September 15.

Douglas MacArthur had completed a masterful advance with a minimum of casualties. It had taken him six months to retake Papuan New Guinea from the Japanese. Nine months had been needed to burst the Bismarcks Barrier. But in less than three months he had advanced 1,400 miles from the Admiralties to the Vogelkop and into the Moluccas. The Philippines were now only 300 miles away. A few hours after Morotai fell MacArthur arrived on the island. He stood on the shore gazing intently toward the northwest, as though he actually had Bataan and Corregidor in view.

"They are waiting for me there," he said softly. "It has been a long time. . . ."

105. The Allied Drive for the Rhine

AT MOSCOW IN THE FALL of 1943, U.S. Secretary of State Cordell Hull, British Foreign Minister Anthony Eden and Soviet Foreign Minister Vyacheslav Molotov had agreed upon creation of an international security organization. But they did not specify its nature. This was left to another council of diplomats from the United States, Britain, the Soviet Union and China, which gathered in the Dumbarton Oaks mansion in Washington from August 21 to September 29, 1944. In that order the representatives were Edward R. Stettinius, Jr., Sir Alexander Cadogan and Viscount Halifax, Andrei Gromyko and Wellington Koo. They were to make "tentative proposals," and they did make these recommendations:

1. The world organization would maintain international peace and security, take effective collective security measures to prevent and remove threats to the

peace, suppress acts of aggression or other breaches of the peace, and by peaceful means bring about adjustment or settlement of international disputes.

2. Develop friendly relations among nations and take other appropriate measures to strengthen universal peace.

3. Achieve international cooperation in solving international economic, social and other humanitarian problems.

4. Create a center for harmonizing the actions of nations in achieving these common ends.

Although the framework for the United Nations had thus been hammered out, there were many areas of disagreement. One of them was the fact that the Soviet Union was not at war with Japan and therefore the Soviet and Chinese emissaries did not meet together. But the chief discord arose when Gromyko blandly proposed that each of the Soviet Union's sixteen republics should have a seat in the General Assembly. This, wrote Cordell Hull, "left Stettinius and Cadogan breathless." Gromkyo also demanded that in the Security Council the Big Three should have the right to veto any proposals except procedural ones. Both Britain and the United States had wanted the Security Council to hear the grievances of the smaller nations, but Gromyko stood firm with the remark: "The Soviet position on voting in the Council will never be departed from!"

In other words, it appeared that the Soviets envisioned the United Nations as the instrument through which the Big Three would rule the world—an attitude which raised grave misgivings in the mind of Franklin Delano Roosevelt.

Within three months after D-Day, the Allies poured 2 million men into France. They also poured in 3.5 million tons of supplies. With every mile of advance, the need for food and gasoline grew more critical, if only because it took the spearheads that much farther away from the supply ports. One answer was the Red Ball Express, a circular one-way trucking route running from Normandy to the front and back. But logistical problems were soon to dictate military decisions.

Eisenhower had enough supplies at the beginning of September to hurl one army group into Germany, and thus perhaps destroy the enemy before he could turn and recover. Naturally enough, both Montgomery and Bradley saw this clearly, and each argued that his own line of advance should be given priority. Montgomery's was "the long envelopment," that is the longer in distance but the one more likely by boldness and daring to achieve success. It was the northern route across the Rhine between Holland and Germany, knifing down through the northern German plains into the industrial heartland of the Ruhr and thence into Hitler's heart in Berlin. Bradley's was called "the short envelopment" driving east across the waist of Germany to cut the country in two and perhaps come up on Berlin from the south.

There were two very strong arguments favoring Montgomery's northward movement up the Channel coast: the need to overrun the launching sites for the new V-2 rockets soon to fall on Britain, and the even greater need for the huge Belgian port of Antwerp, third largest in the world. The overtaxed Channel ports —Calais, Dunkirk, Nieuport, Ostend—were actually hardly more than river mouths transformed into small harbors by artificial locks and basins. The enormous effect that Marseilles had had on the logistics problem was argument enough for Montgomery to move on Antwerp. During the two months following the appearance of the first V-1 bombs over Britain, more than 5,000 people had been killed and 35,000 injured with some 30,000 buildings destroyed. Efforts of Harris's Bomber Command and Spaatz's Strategic Air Forces had failed to knock out the launching sites. Introduction of the 435-mile-an-hour British Tempest fighter planes had had some appreciable effect; the Tempests eventually exploded 630 V-1s by attacking them over the Channel. But the V-2s offered no such targets. They were rocket-launched ballistic missiles rising to a height of up to eighty miles and hurtling to earth noiselessly at five times the speed of sound. They could not be seen, heard or intercepted. Obviously the only defense against the V-2s was to capture their launching sites. Here, too, was a powerful argument, which convinced Dwight Eisenhower at the beginning of September, that Montgomery's 21st Army Group should have supply priority. Bradley's 12th Army Group, however, was to build up east of Paris and "prepare to strike rapidly eastward."

As Eisenhower tried to reach a decision, the warp and woof of the Alliance began to come apart under the plucking, tearing, me-first tugging of his fractious commanders. Meanwhile Patton gleefully kept his Third Army spearheads rolling eastward. On August 30 they had crossed the Meuse River and were more than a hundred miles east of Paris, almost that close to the German border. But then they literally ran out of gas. On that day they received only 32,000 gallons of the 400,000 they consumed daily. When one of his corps commanders complained that he was low on fuel, Patton told him to keep going "until the tanks stop, and then get out and walk."

On September 2, Eisenhower—now in complete field command—met with Bradley, Hodges and Patton at Versailles. Patton in high spirits told Eisenhower that his patrols were on the Moselle and (untruthfully) in Metz. "If you let me retain my regular allotment of tonnage, Ike, we could push on to the German frontier and rupture that goddammed Siegfried Line. I'm willing to stake my reputation on that."

"Careful, George," Eisenhower replied teasingly, "that reputation of yours hasn't been worth very much."

Patton grinned impishly. "That reputation is pretty good, now."

Nevertheless, the persuasive Patton got Eisenhower to give him more gasoline and to allow him to move on Mannheim and Frankfurt. Eisenhower also agreed to Bradley's request that First Army stay on Patton's left.

Montgomery exploded when he heard Patton was getting more fuel and Hodges had been detached from his right flank. There were not enough supplies for two offensives, he protested. He insisted on retaining priority for his "fullblooded thrust." He even went as far as to suggest that Eisenhower come to

Brussels to confer with him. This peremptory summons of his superior, like a cardinal calling a pope from Rome, was typical "Monty" arrogance. Montgomery also knew that Eisenhower had injured his old football knee and was in great pain, barely able to walk. Because his B-25 broke down on his return to Granville from Versailles, he had continued on in a small L-5 single-passenger plane. A storm arose and the pilot, running low on fuel, landed on a beach. Eisenhower jumped out to help the pilot push the plane above the tide mark, slipping in the wet sand and badly twisting the bad knee. It was weeks before the knee healed, yet, in his desire to mollify Montgomery, the supreme commander practically crawled aboard his B-25 to fly to Brussels. Getting off it was out of the question, so Montgomery came aboard. Assuming a pedantic air he at once launched into a discussion of basic tactics, like a professor lecturing a plebe. Eisenhower began to redden, yet as Montgomery's language approached invective, he contained himself with superhuman calm. Putting a hand on Montgomery's knee he said: "Steady, Monty. You can't talk to me like that. I'm your boss." Montgomery flushed. "I'm sorry, Ike," he murmured, and changed the subject to his new plan that he said promised great results. It called for a daring crossing of the Lower Rhine at Arnhem in Holland to turn the German right flank. It would be done by the British Second Army and the Allied Airborne Army.

Eisenhower approved it. He was eager to use the Airborne Army and wanted to get across the Rhine before his offensive lost momentum. Thus was born Operation Market-Garden.

Montgomery's plan was a good one, but if there was anyone preeminently unqualified to execute it, it was Bernard Law Montgomery. Omar Bradley himself has written: "Had the pious teetotaling Montgomery wobbled into SHAEF with a hangover, I could not have been more astonished than I was by the daring adventure he proposed." Bradley went on to describe the plan as "one of the most imaginative of the war." But Montgomery to lead it? No. Market-Garden called for a bold opportunistic leader with the style of George Patton, not a careful, methodical master of the set-piece battle like Montgomery. At hand was Patton, Old Blood and Guts, the commander whom even an admiring Hitler called, "that crazy cowboy general." But if Eisenhower ever considered Patton, or even Bradley—and there is no evidence that he did—he could never have made the change.

Eisenhower would also find that he had, to his eventual great distress, ignored the importance of Antwerp. The great Belgian port was of paramount importance. It had to be seized if any attack on Germany was to continue. Cherbourg was not yet operative, Marseilles was taxed to the limit and the French railroads were not yet running from Normandy and the Channel ports. Antwerp had to be taken without delay, and Market-Garden was a delay. Both Montgomery and Eisenhower also ignored a second critical factor:

The resilience of the German army.

After the Battle for Normandy, it appeared that the Wehrmacht had suffered almost irreparable losses in both the East and West. It had lost 450,000 men in the West and in the East a staggering 900,000. Yet at the beginning of September there were still 3.421 million troops on the rosters of the *Feldheer,* or field army. Of these about 2 million had to be committed to the Soviet front. The remainder would go to Model defending the Siegfried Line.

Throughout September Hitler worked with great skill to provide Model with more troops. Because he could count upon an inexhaustible reservoir of slave labor to man his industries, he could impress all Germany's able manhood into the Wehrmacht. In late July he ordered the creation of eighteen new divisions earmarked for the West. He also transformed 100 infantry fortress battalions in rear areas into replacement battalions for Model. In mid-August *Der Führer* ordered activation of twenty-five reserve divisions to be called *Volksgrenadier* divisions and thus become the foundation of a new People's Army to replace the old one, which had betrayed and tried to kill him on July 20. The eighteen divisions formed in July also were called *Volksgrenadier* and all would receive their indoctrination and training from Reichsführer Heinrich Himmler and his SS.

The fragments of armored forces battered in the East were organized into ten new panzer divisions, and some were ready for action in the West by mid-September. Hitler also decreed that German tank production must match Allied quantity and quality. Production must be concentrated on the formidable Tigers and the peerless Panthers, both of which were more than a match for the Shermans. Hitler also ordered that the West be given priority on the new ironclad killers and that they should go to the new armored divisions, rather than to the depleted panzers. Although this seemed to ignore the experience of the veteran formations, it made certain that the new ones would be built around a battalion of forty Panthers each—a most formidable armored force indeed. Also the unwelcome defeats on both fronts had conferred a logistics gift on the Wehrmacht: As the amount of conquered territory shrank, so did the fronts and supply lines.

So when Market-Garden commenced on September 17, it was not against an enemy in disarray as so many Allied soldiers of all ranks, motivated by their the-war-is-won attitude, actually believed, but against forces rearmed, reequipped and reinforced in what the Germans called "the Miracle of the West."

106. Operation Market-Garden

BY DRIVING A SIXTY-MILE SALIENT into the German right or northern flank in Holland, Market-Garden would outflank the Siegfried Line and carry Montgomery's forces across the lower Rhine and down the shortest route to Berlin. Five major water courses crossed Montgomery's path between Antwerp and his objective of Arnhem in Holland. The first two were canals north of Eindhoven. The third was the Maas River—or Meuse—twenty-four miles farther on. Eight miles farther was the Waal River, flowing under an arched bridge at Nijmegen, and finally the end of the salient twenty miles farther east at Arnhem on the lower Rhine. Here it was assumed the German forces were light.

Three airborne divisions—the U.S. 82nd and 101st and the British 1st—were to seize bridges and crossings around these points and thus roll out a carpet for the following infantry and armor of the Second British Army. This would be the first daylight drop of the war and the largest airborne assault or "vertical envelopment" in all history. Some 16,500 paratroopers and 3,500 glider troops would be involved, practically all the strength of the Allied Airborne Army under Maj. Gen. Lewis Brereton. Operational command on the ground went to Lt. Gen. Browning. This was an unfortunate choice. Browning was just the sort of supercilious British aristocrat that Americans detest. Nor was he the equal of Gen. Matthew Ridgway commanding the U.S. XVIII Airborne Corps. When Bradley heard of the selection, he exploded: "Christ, why don't they use Ridgway? He's a fighter and knows more about airborne than all of them."

Ridgway certainly never would have allowed Maj. Gen. Paul L. Williams's U.S. IX Troop Carrier Command to drop the Red Devils of the British 1st Airborne so far from their objective at Arnhem. Because of the immobility of airborne troops, it is doctrine that they must be dropped as close to their objective as possible. When the British 6th Airborne Division secured the Orne bridgeheads on D-Day, they were dropped almost on top of them. But Williams so feared German ack-ack that he was going to drop the Red Devils eight to ten and a half miles from their objective, the bridge over the Rhine. Although British Maj. Gen. Robert Urquhart commanding the 1st Airborne had misgivings about this decision, he was an infantry officer with no airborne experience and therefore felt himself unqualified to protest. In all such disputes, the airmen prevailed. The division commanders wanted two lifts on D-Day in order to consolidate their strength by sundown. General Brereton sided with Williams, ruling that because of the necessity for repairs and "resting" the crews, there would be one lift a day, with three and a half divisions being carried to the drop zones by the end of D-plus-2 (two days after the campaign opened). This made three or at least two days of good weather an imperative requisite, one that the meteorologists refused to guarantee along the English Channel at the approach of autumn.

On a sunny Sunday morning 1,545 transports and 478 gliders, together with 371 British fighter escorts and 548 Americans thundered over the Channel carrying the first waves to Belgium and Holland. They followed in the wake of an Allied bombardment force that had struck during the night at enemy fighter bases and AA installations. The Luftwaffe flew only 100 to 150 sorties and shot down but a single Allied fighter. General Williams's fears about enemy flak were almost baseless. Only sixty-five transports and forty-three gliders were lost, all but five of the gliders because of broken tow ropes. The British lost not a single aircraft to enemy action. For all units the drops were the most accurate ever conducted, either in combat or in training.

But then Market-Garden began to come unraveled. The Red Devils landed first, but by extreme bad luck almost all of the armored jeeps of the division's reconnaissance squadron were aboard the crashed gliders. The jeeps were to compensate for dropping the paratroopers so far from their objective. Instead of dashing to Arnhem in them to seize the railway and highway bridges, the British had to march there on foot and four vital hours were lost en route.

North of Arnhem was high ground commanding the bridges. One battalion of paratroopers was sent to seize it, but was stopped by armed patrols of the 9th SS Panzer Division. A second battalion moving on the bridge was halted by other elements of the 9th SS. Only Lt. Col. J. D. Frost's 2nd Parachute Battalion was left to assault the bridges. As they neared the railway bridge, it blew up in their faces, seeming to curl into the air toward them. But they did find the highway bridge intact and captured its north end, the one debouching toward the German plain. Frost tried to take the entire bridge during the night by frontal assault and men crossing the river in rowboats, but was stopped each time.

General Urquhart could not break through to Frost because he had to hold open his landing zones for the rest of his division due to arrive during the next two days. He had pleaded for enough air lift to land his entire division on D-Day —his was the most exposed sector, at the tip of the Allied spearhead—but he had been denied. Next day fog over Britain delayed the D-plus-1 reinforcement until 3:00 in the afternoon.

More misfortune befell the Allies. The presence of another SS panzer division, the 10th, was discovered near Arnhem, and complete operational orders for Market-Garden had been captured. It had been taken from an American officer, who had foolishly and improperly carried it with him into battle. His glider was shot down, and he was taken prisoner. Within a few hours, the plan was on the desk of Field Marshal Model in his headquarters fortuitously located almost within the Red Devils' drop zone. Model saw at once that he could contain the British spearhead and slow the advance of the following infantry with well-timed counterstrokes.

At the southern end of the airborne corridor, the U.S. 101st Airborne under Maxwell Taylor also landed within its drop zone on D-Day, concentrating quickly to move against the highway bridge over the Wilhelmina Canal at Son and thence to their objective at Eindhoven. Two battalions of the 506th Parachute Regiment were held up by enemy 88s, and when they came in sight of the Wilhelmina Bridge, it rose into the sky with a roar. Two officers and a sergeant waded into the canal and swam out to the bridge followed by a larger party in rowboats. The center trestle was still standing and American engineers, led by Dutch civilians to a cache of black-market lumber, were able to build a footbridge across the canal. By midnight the entire regiment was across, the next day its soldiers took Eindhoven and captured four bridges over a local river and a canal. Still, General Taylor worried about where the following British ground forces might be.

They were behind him. German roadblocks had held up the Irish Guards spearheading the advance of Montgomery's leading XXX Corps. They did not reach Eindhoven until seven o'clock in the evening of the second day. But the tanks of the Guards Armored Brigade could not reach Eindhoven until the makeshift bridge over the Wilhelmina Canal was strengthened. British engineers did erect a Bailey bridge, but it was daylight on D-plus-2 before the first tank crossed it. Lt. Gen. B. G. Horrocks's XXX Corps was now thirty-three hours behind schedule.

In the middle of the airborne corridor around Nijmegen Gen. James Gavin's 82nd Airborne faced more difficult problems. The 82nd had to capture the highway bridge over the Maas at Grave and next the great 650-yard highway span over the Waal. But seemingly more important to General Browning, the Airborne Army commander, was the 300-foot high Groesbeek Ridge commanding both and supposedly held by the enemy. He wanted Gavin to take the ridge first. Gavin's paratroopers did, but found no enemy. Having lost valuable time there, still not moving against the Nijmegen bridges, they next captured the Grave bridge and another bridge over the Maas-Waal Canal. But now the Germans were pouring into Nijmegen, and it seemed to Gavin that the opportunity to capture the Nijmegen bridges over the Waal was flowing away as swiftly as the river current. He was heartened, however, by the arrival of the Guards Armored Division in the morning of D-plus-2. At Nijmegen both the highway and railway bridges were held by about a battalion of reservists armed with abundant artillery. They beat back attacks by the American paratroops and British guards. Gavin conferred with Horrocks, who had arrived in the area. He asked him if his corps had any assault boats. Horrocks said that there were thirty-three available—but they could not be brought to the front until the following morning. In the morning, the time was pushed back until noon. Gavin realized that he could not schedule his assault until 2:00 P.M. Once again time was working against him. Worse, reinforcements scheduled for the day before had been held up by more bad weather. It also kept the Polish Airborne Brigade from reinforcing the embattled Red Devils at Arnhem. Such delays had worked in the Germans' favor. Paratroopers and panzer units from the Reichswald in nearby Germany—all elite troops—had been arriving in the area. If they attacked the Groesbeek Ridge, they could cut Market-Garden neatly in two, to say nothing of how they would strengthen the reservists on the bridges.

At three o'clock in the afternoon of September 20, Gavin's paratroopers began moving toward the launching point on the quarter-mile-wide Waal. They had only twenty-six boats—not thirty-three—and had not seen them until twenty minutes before they moved out. They were about twenty feet long with canvas sides and plywood bottoms. Such frail craft would be like cockleshells tossed on the Waal's swift ten-knot current. Nor could they be launched from concealment but in full view of the enemy on the bridge towers and about 200 yards of open shore across the river. But Gavin's brave soldiers waded far into the shallow south shore before throwing themselves and their weapons into the assault boats. As soon as they reached deep water, the current took them and spun them around like flotsam. Without paddles, the Americans propelled themselves with their hands or rifle butts. Half the boats reached the north bank. Nauseated and vomiting, the paratroopers waded ashore and fought their way to a diked road three quarters of a mile inland. A second wave came over. Now, with the Germans concentrating on the Americans who had crossed the river, more of Gavin's men with infantry and tanks from the Guards approached the southern end of the highway bridge. As they did, they saw the Stars and Stripes go up across the Waal. It was flown from the railway bridge, but Gavin's Anglo-Americans assumed that it rose from the highway bridge and entered it. They came immediately under fire, but the Guards tanks fired back, aiming at the towers, and reached the span's northern end, where they were greeted by three soaked, grimy but grinning American paratroopers. The vital Nijmegen bridges had been captured, and one day General Dempsey of the British Second Army would seize James Gavin by the hand and say: "I am proud to meet the commander of the greatest division in the world today." Nevertheless, even the valor of these splendid troops had not been enough to take the spans before nightfall of the fourth day of Market-Garden. It would take XXX Corps another day to resume the advance.

There was more bad timing when the Polish Brigade was flown from clearing British skies on D-plus-4, only to encounter bad weather over Holland. Of 110 troop carriers, only fifty-three dropped their loads. And those Poles who did arrive could not cross the Rhine to the 1st Airborne because the Germans sank the ferryboat. They had to wait for assault boats. Meanwhile, the Red Devils' hold on the northern end of the Arnhem bridge had been broken. They had been driven back. Tanks and guns of the II SS Panzer Corps had rolled over the bridge bent on reinforcing the Nijmegen area. Although the bridges fell before they arrived, they set up a roadblock between Nijmegen and Arnhem. Meanwhile the British VIII and XII Corps, advancing on the right and left respectively of XXX Corps, moved forward with what Montgomery called "depressingly slow" movement. They got no farther than Eindhoven, where the men of Taylor's 101st Airborne were fighting in American pioneer fashion, forming circles to fend off the counterattacking Germans. Horrocks tried to send a turning movement to his left over secondary roads to reach the Red Devils, but it bogged down in the area's soft polderland.

The Red Devils fought on with legendary valor. But it was a hopeless fight. Steadily, remorselessly, the numbers of the paratroopers in their bright red berets shrank. Their ordeal lasted for nine days and nights. Each day German counterstrokes cut them up into smaller groups. With no armor and little artillery they fought with rifles and pistols against enemy armor, air and artillery. Food rations were cut to a sixth. Even ammunition was rationed. Finally, Field Marshal Montgomery brought Market-Garden to its melancholy close. Of the 9,000 Red Devils who had jumped so gallantly and confidently into a fiery crucible, some 2,000 were withdrawn to British lines. About 6,000 had been captured by the Germans, and half of these were wounded. The rest were dead.

Bad luck, bad weather and bad intelligence had plagued Market-Garden from the beginning. Montgomery himself blamed the weather for the operation's failure. But bad weather had to be anticipated in that time and place, and bad luck must always be expected in battle. If the 1st Airborne's invaluable armored jeeps had not been lost aboard crashed gliders, then it might have been some other critical load like the airborne headquarters shot down in a transport. Bad intelligence gave no indication of all the armored strength on Model's supposedly weak right flank. Nothing, of course, could have been unluckier than capture of Montgomery's operational order.

Still, tactical boldness was the missing ingredient in the execution of Montgomery's bold strategic plan. The movement of Dempsey's three corps was altogether too cautious, and the delay in the attack on the Nijmegen bridges altogether too long. If Urquhart with all his forces had been close to the bridge, he might have held it until XXX Corps arrived and prevented the II SS Corps from getting across it to block the path between the Waal and the Rhine. So Market-Garden progressed according to plan, but not according to timetable.

In deep disappointment, and after some very exasperated prodding by Supreme Headquarters, Field Marshal Montgomery turned to what should have been his prior purpose: the seizure of Antwerp. Although the British 11th Armored Division had entered Antwerp as early as September 4, capturing it with almost all of its docks intact, strong German positions around Walcheren Island at the mouth of the Scheldt Estuary made it impossible to use this magnificent port until they were cleaned out. This laborious operation undertaken by Canadian troops was not completed until November 26. By then it was depressingly clear that the war would not end in 1944.

107. The Battle for Peleliu

ON SEPTEMBER 11, 1944, Prime Minister Churchill and President Roosevelt with their top military advisers met again in Quebec in a conference code-named Octagon. The meetings were friendly, conducted in a buoyant atmosphere of imminent victory.

Plans for completion of both the European and Pacific Wars were made. One big change was to remove the American Strategic Air Forces from Eisenhower's command and return them to General Spaatz, thus assuring a rise in American bombing of Germany's synthetic fuel plants. Spaatz had begun striking them as early as May 12 when 935 heavy bombers of the U.S. Eighth Air Force launched the first raid—which, said Albert Speer, Germany's industrial czar, "meant the end of German armaments production." At Quebec Roosevelt also somewhat precipitately accepted Churchill's offer of the British fleet and air forces for use in the Pacific. Admiral King and other military advisers had strongly opposed the proposal. So far the American Joint Chiefs had had a free hand in the Pacific, and they did not wish to see British imperial political objectives encroaching upon their grand strategy of absolute concentration on defeating Japan.

Although there were no disputes between the Allies, the extremely controversial Morgenthau Plan was put forward by U.S. Secretary of the Treasury Henry Morgenthau. It proposed to convert the highly industrialized German nation into an agricultural one. Its critics called it a plan for starving the Germans to death. Germany had never been able to feed itself, depending upon imports for its food, which it bought with money obtained from the sale of its manufactures. When Churchill first heard of the plan, he was shocked, saying that he looked upon it "as he would on chaining himself to a dead German." He reversed himself the following day, probably because of Morgenthau's generous promise that Britain would receive an additional $3.5 billion of Lend-Lease between the fall of Germany and the defeat of Japan and another $3 billion for nonmilitary materials after that. Churchill's revision of the plan concluded: "This program for eliminating the war-making industries in the Ruhr and in the Saar is looking forward to converting Germany into a country primarily agricultural and pastoral in its character."

Secretary of State Cordell Hull, who was not in Quebec, was horrified when he heard of the Morgenthau Plan. He called it "a plan of blind vengeance," one sure to breed in the heart of the Germans a matching ache for revenge. Secretary of War Stimson, also not in Quebec, attacked it as bound to have a depressing effect on the postwar European economy. Once news of the plan was leaked to the press, a storm of public criticism arose, with surprisingly little favorable comment. In Germany, of course, Dr. Goebbels gleefully informed his countrymen that where "the Jew Roosevelt" through his policy of Unconditional Surrender hoped to make slaves of them, his treasury chief preferred to starve them to death. Goebbels was also careful to point out that Morgenthau was a Jew. Eventually, the public outcry and the protests of Hull and Stimson compelled Roosevelt to reconsider, and the Morgenthau Plan was quietly shelved.

At Quebec it was also agreed that General MacArthur would land in Mindanao in the southern Philippines that November, and that in the following month MacArthur and Admiral Nimitz would jointly invade Leyte in the central Philippines. But then the Joint Chiefs received an electrifying message from Admiral Halsey reporting that his carrier aircraft had found Japanese air defenses in the Philippines surprisingly weak. Halsey recommended the invasion of Leyte in October. MacArthur agreed and the chiefs made the authorization. Thus, in a remarkable demonstration of interservice cooperation and flexibility at the summit, the schedule was advanced two months and the landing site moved up closer to Japan.

It was a bold and brilliant decision. By attacking the center of the archipelago, the Americans would split the 225,000 Japanese there, giving MacArthur the opportunity to defeat them in detail: first on Leyte, next on Luzon and finally on Mindanao. This was the kind of maneuvering in which MacArthur exulted and excelled. If the Japanese attempted to establish a continuous front in the Philippines, they would have to commit their fleet—an eventuality dear to the heart of Admiral Nimitz.

Actually, Nimitz was already moving to protect MacArthur's right flank by attacking the Palau Islands. There he hoped to gain the air bases and anchorage necessary to support the Leyte landings. These were at Angaur, Ulithi and Peleliu. They would be seized by the III Corps under General Geiger. The army's 81st Infantry Division would take Angaur and Ulithi while Peleliu—the most formidable fortress in the Pacific, held by about 15,000 men—would be taken by the First Marine Division.

The Palau Islands formed a string of volcanic islets within a coral reef seventy-seven miles long and twenty miles wide. They provided the Japanese with anchorages and bases lost in the destruction of Truk. At the southern end lay little Peleliu, an islet about six miles long and two miles wide at its broadest. It was shaped like a lobster's claw, and was in fact a pair of peninsulas joined together by a causeway. On the east coast were shoals and mangrove swamps, on the west accessible beaches heavily fortified and defended in the accustomed manner. In the south was Peleliu's excellent airfield, which had been in use since before the war. It was said that the famous American aviatrix, Amelia Earhart, was forced down over Peleliu to be tortured and executed there. Commanding the airfield and running north for about two miles was a low wooded ridge, which the Japanese called the Momji Plateau, which the Micronesians called Umurbrogal Mountain and which the American Marines would call Bloody Nose Ridge.

Actually, the Umurbrogal was neither ridge nor mountain nor plateau but an undersea coral reef thrown above the surface of the sea by a submarine volcano. Sparse vegetation growing on its thin topsoil had concealed its crazy contours from the aerial camera's square eye. It was a place that might have been designed by a mad artist given to painting mathematical abstractions: all slants, straights, jags, steeps and shears. None of its heights rose more than fifty feet before splitting apart in a maze of peaks and defiles cluttered with boulders and machicolated with caves. For the Umurbrogal was also a monster Swiss cheese of hard coral limestone pocked beyond imagining with caves and crevices. They were to be found at every level in every size, crevices small enough to hold one sniper, caverns big enough for a battalion.

Defense of Peleliu was in the care of Col. Nunio Nakagawa. By the end of August, Nakagawa had fortified 500 caves, most of them connected by interior tunnels. Barricades protected the entrances, while the tunnels turned sharply after a few feet to escape both direct gunfire and the terrible American flame-throwers. Some of the caverns were five and six stories deep, containing barracks and kitchens. If the top of the Umurbrogal were lifted off, it would reveal great H's or a series of E's laid back to back. This would be repeated for five and six levels down.

Within these caves Colonel Nakagawa placed all of his artillery except his coastal guns, all of his mortars and also the new 200-millimeter rocket-launchers just received from Japan. The guns fired from cave mouths equipped with sliding doors of armored steel. They could hit the beaches to the west, the airfield to the south and the offshore airfield-islet of Ngesebus north of them. They were protected by squads of riflemen and machine gunners firing through the slits of the crevices. All of these strong points were mutually covered by interlocking fire. Americans attacking one of them might draw on themselves the fire of two or three others, to say nothing of those which would remain silent to allow the Marines to advance under the impression that they had knocked out the entire system. Then, as Hercules had discovered with Hydra, they would find the beheaded stump sprouting two fresh heads to bite at them.

It was this height that made Peleliu so adaptable to the evolving new Japanese battle doctrine of defense-in-depth. Destruction at the water's edge had gone the way of its suicidal advocates, and the new tactics first used at Biak called for allowing the invaders to come ashore and then punishing them from high ground. A new warrior had been trained by Nakagawa, who had also abolished the banzai. Japanese soldiers on Peleliu were instructed to stay underground during aerial and naval bombardment, and not to return enemy fire. Perhaps this was why Rear Adm. Jesse Oldendorf, commander of the bombardment force off Peleliu, jubilantly signaled Geiger:

"We have run out of targets!"

Peleliu lay blinking and winking and smoking beneath a fiery Moloch of a cloud. It grew bigger and bigger, fed by the smoke and dust of naval shells exploding beneath it, the swoooosh-crashing of the rockets and the whuffling thump of the bombs. Aboard his transport Col. Chesty Puller prepared to go over the side.

"Coming back for supper?" the ship's skipper called out cheerfully.

"Why?" Puller growled.

"Hell, everything's done over there. You'll walk in."

"If you think it's so easy," Puller snapped, "why don't you come on the beach at five o'clock? We could have dinner together and maybe you could pick up a couple of souvenirs."

Most of Puller's First Marines were aboard LSTs, boated in their amtracks inside their great bays. The air was filled with the roar of motors and exhaust smoke. *It's like sailing to battle in the Lincoln Tunnel,* Lucky thought, crouching in his amtrack over a .50-caliber machine gun. Then the bow doors swung open and the amtracks with a rising concerted roar went waddling ahead, plunging into the water and churning shoreward. Before them was the great fiery cloud. Above and around them was the sound of thunder, like a ceiling and walls of noise. Lucky turned to look at his LST. The bow rail was black with sailors shaking their fists at Peleliu like football fans. Lucky swung his .50 caliber around, raised it and fired a burst over their heads. The bow was cleared instantly.

"Come and get me, you cheerleading swabbie sons of bitches!" Lucky yelled into the wind.

The men of this veteran division had never gone into battle so cheerfully. General Rupertus had said Peleliu would take only four days, and they held up four fingers to each other or sang songs like "Give My Regards to Broadway." On Lucky's right his buddy Bill Smith was on a machine gun with Lew Juergens and Bud Conley beside him. Smitty held up his hand touching thumb and forefinger in the gesture of perfection and Lucky grinned. Then there was an odd bumping noise as his amtrack crawled over the drying reef and then the naval and aerial bombardment lifted and all around him the lagoon was blossoming with geysers of water and the sides of the amtrack clanged and reverberated to ricocheting shrapnel. Lucky let go of the gun and ducked below the gunwales.

All along Peleliu's beaches the amtracks were coming ashore, taking mortar shells and losing men as they did. On the reef some amtracks were burning under the guns of Colonel Nakagawa's thousand-eyed mountain. Survivors were wading ashore or trying to rescue the wounded. High on the Umurbrogal a steel door swung open, and a gun was trundled out. It spoke again and again, and more amtracks began burning. Aboard the cruiser *Portland* a gunnery officer directed 8-inch armor piercers against the cave just as the gun vanished and the steel doors swung shut again. The hillside blazed and smoked but the gun came out again. Four times the exchange was repeated until the gunnery officer gave up and said:

"You could put all the steel in Pittsburgh on that thing and still not get it."

In the center the First Marines were held up by beach defenses. Mortars pinned them down together with machine-gun fire from an outpost the enemy had blasted out of a coral promontory jutting into the lagoon. Demolition men crawled up to it to hurl their charges into the rear entrance. A storm of small-arms fire swept into it. Flamethrowers arched their hissing, flaming liquid through it. Enemy soldiers began pouring out the entrance, jumping into a tunnel. They were as quick as rabbits, vanishing in their underground warren. But the last man was too slow and too fat. His uniform was stuffed with rice. As he appeared a sheet of bullets hit him, and he erupted in a shower of flesh and rice. With the fall of the bunker the First Marines moved forward to the airfield.

On the right the Seventh Marines had entered a deadly subsea garden sown with antiboat mines, antitank mines, antiboat barriers and antitroop mines— above which sprouted a wicked black tumbleweed of barbed wire—all planted to channel the invaders into preregistered mortar and artillery fire. From reef to shore, smoke and flames rose from stricken amtracks while exploding ammunition popped and crackled around them. On the beaches hastily dug foxholes were filled with Marines in mottled green dungarees and camouflaged helmets. Limbs and heads and pieces of bodies flew through the air. Men staggered about in the last throes of death, the crimson spouting from riddled faces or severed limbs. Files of men wading ashore from their wrecked amtracks vanished under obliterating shellbursts. But then the Sherman tanks began coming ashore, taking the enemy positions under fire, outdueling them with their heavier 75s going against 37s. One of the tank commanders led the following Shermans ashore by trailing toilet paper out his turret. Rallying, the men of the Seventh left their foxholes, running low and drove eastward before wheeling to the right to close off Peleliu's southern tip—just as Colonel Nakagawa launched his tanks against the left-center juncture of the Fifth and First Marines.

The little nine-tonners came in a cavalry charge, emerging from a cluster of reinforced concrete bunkers serving as Nakagawa's headquarters at the northern edge of the airfield. Guns on the Umurbrogal laid down a supporting fire ahead of them. Gathering speed, they reached thirty miles an hour, unwisely leaving their following infantry far behind. Thirteen of them went whizzing across the front of the Second Battalion. Snipers rode their hoods or were slung on their rear in camouflage nets. American riflemen picked them off one by one. The snipers fell off, and those in the nets were left lolling like dolls in a Christmas stocking. Marine bazookas opened up, and the tanks began to flame. One of them butted an amtrack and was in turn butted in its own rear by another amtrack and trapped between them. Its emerging crewmen were shot down. When the Shermans arrived, supported by an Avenger skimming low over the airfield, Nakagawa's armor was annihilated.

To the Seventh Marines fell the dubious distinction of being first to discover that the targets which Admiral Oldendorf imagined to be eliminated were still intact and active. Assigned to clear the south of the island, the Seventh's men received fire from still-standing pillboxes, casemates, bunkers, rifle pits, trenches and here and there a steel-reinforced concrete blockhouse. Using Nakagawa's tactics of "passive infiltration," the Japanese took refuge in their underground labyrinth, waiting until the Marines swept over them before reoccupying positions supposedly knocked out. They struck the Americans from the rear or popped out of unsuspected cave mouths. Where they held high ground, they ran out entrances on one side of their height to escape enemy flame and dynamite entering the other side, then ran back in again to resume fighting.

The attack south became a grinding, three-day push, which might have been longer and costlier had not Colonel Hanneken been able to strike the enemy on his flank and rear. At last the Japanese remnants were herded into a pair of tiny, pillbox-studded promontories. Converging fire struck them. Many of them jumped into the water, attempting to swim to the islets on Peleliu's lower prong, but they were picked off. Hanneken reported to Rupertus:

"The Seventh Marines' mission on Peleliu is completed."

On the left and center the mission of the Fifth and First Marines advancing across the airfield beneath the Umurbrogal was only just beginning. The temperature was 110 degrees. Heat rose from the crushed-coral surface of the runways in visible, shimmering waves. To deflect it the Marines had pulled their camou-

flage cloths free of their helmets to hang like little capes over their necks. There
was no water. Some incompetent cretin of a supply officer had floated water
ashore in drums from which the residual oil had not been cleansed. Those who
drank this foul mixture sickened of water poisoning. Still the line went forward,
advancing into a storm of bullets plunging down from the height already nicknamed Bloody Nose Ridge. By nightfall of the first day, the Marines were just
short of it.

Puller's Second Battalion was the first to begin climbing Bloody Nose Ridge.
Up, up, and up they struggled, climbing in 112 degrees, crawling over the cruel
slashing coral, flopping behind boulders, gasping for breath, shinnying up the
pinnacles, rolling down the steeps to escape enemy bullets and grenades, but then
struggling back up again to re-form and reattack. All around was a clanging hell
of enemy artillery and mortars, punctuated by the cries for water and blood
plasma, and over and over again: "Corpsman! Corpsman! Stretcher-bearers!"

Repeatedly Puller's men took a height only to find another above them, or
sometimes having to slide back down again to a "fallen" peak, which had erupted
once more with enemy fire. Nakagawa's fierce resistance had cut Puller's battalions down to half the size of companies and some companies down to squads.
When the remnants of his First Battalion were joined to the survivors of the
Second, the combined force numbered barely 100 men—out of about 2,400.
Casualties in the entire regiment of 3,500 men numbered 1,749 men—and many
more had been made noneffective by heat exhaustion, water poisoning, combat
fatigue or blast concussion. But the First had killed 4,000 Japanese—about two
fifths of Peleliu's defenders—and taken one third of its fortifications. Still Puller
ordered his men to attack, and they did; but after the First-Second Battalion
drove deeper into the Umurbrogal, they had only twenty-seven effectives left.
Puller now had only his understrength Third Battalion.

General Geiger was appalled by reports of the slaughter under Bloody Nose
Ridge. On September 21 he went to Rupertus's headquarters and told him to
relieve the First Marines with the 321st Infantry Regiment of the 81st Division.
Two other regiments of the 81st had landed unopposed at Ulithi and met only
light opposition on Angaur. Rupertus protested, but Geiger overruled him. The
321st's soldiers came ashore at Peleliu on September 23 and relieved the First
Marines. They, too, went into line against the Umurbrogal, they too felt the fire
of Nakagawa's hidden guns. But now the Americans had a new weapon against
the enemy, napalm. Marine squadron 114 led by Maj. Robert Stout had landed
their white-nosed Corsairs on the airfield at Peleliu. They ranged over the Umurbrogal to bomb and strafe it and launch their tanks of jellied gasoline. They were
so effective that Nakagawa observed: "The enemy plan seems to be to burn down
the central hills post to ashes by dropping gasoline from airplanes." Eventually
the remnants of the Seventh Marines relieved the 321st Infantry and joined with
the battered Fifth in a drive against 1,000 Japanese remaining in what was called
the Pocket. By October 15 they had cut their number in half, and on that date

Delivered from Evil

command on Peleliu passed from Rupertus to Maj. Gen. Paul Mueller of the 81st Division. Yet it would be another month before the Pocket was reduced, and this mainly in a battle fought with bulldozers, dynamite charges and bombs more than foot soldiers with hand guns.

Speed was no longer necessary, for the Palau airfields and anchorage were already operational. Five days after Mueller took command, MacArthur began landing on Leyte with his right flank thus secure. By then a stream of the new huge B-29s began landing on airfields at Saipan. On November 24 the first Superfortress bombing raid was launched against Tokyo. On that same night Col. Kunio Nakagawa killed himself, signaling the end of the Battle of Peleliu.

But his gallant men had inflicted a total of 6,526 casualties on the First Marine Division—the most veteran American formation in the Pacific—of whom 1,252 were killed. They had also killed 208 American soldiers and wounded 1,185. Most of the casualties were among the veterans of Guadalcanal. The inexorable law of averages cannot be denied its toll. All 11,000 of Nakagawa's command had perished. In proportion of the number of men engaged, Peleliu was the fiercest, bloodiest battle of the Japanese war. No tribute to the fallen foe could be greater than the one coming from the weary, filthy, hollow-eyed Marines who climbed up the cargo net of Colonel Puller's transport. Sailors crowded around them eagerly, among them the skipper who had confidently assured Puller of a "walk-in."

"Any souvenirs?" the skipper asked.

One of the Marines stared at him contemptuously. "I brought my ass outta there, swabbie. That's the only souvenir I wanted."

108. The Invasion of Leyte

"LEYTE," SAID GEN. DOUGLAS MACARTHUR, "was to be the anvil against which I hoped to hammer the Japanese into submission in the Central Philippines —the springboard from which I could proceed to the conquest of Luzon, for the final assault on Japan itself."

Leyte was an island about 115 miles long ranging from fifteen to forty-five miles in width. It had a native Filipino population of about 915,000 people, although the capital of Tacloban on the northeastern coast was only 31,000. Leyte is mostly mountainous and rugged terrain, although there are two plains in the north holding most of the island's population: the highly cultivated Leyte Valley in the northeast and less populous Ormoc Valley in the northwest. MacArthur hoped to develop an enormous complex of air and supply bases in the Leyte Valley to support future operations. He also wanted the island's six airfields,

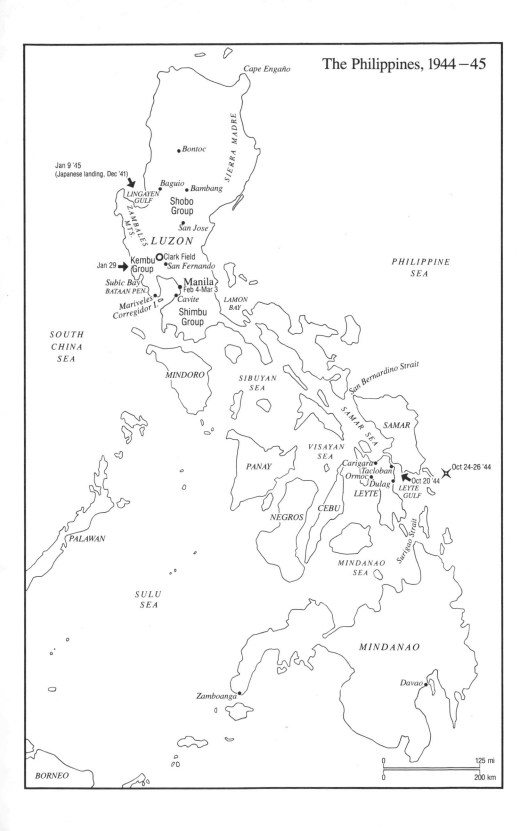

The Philippines, 1944–45

Cape Engaño

SIERRA MADRE

• *Bontoc*

Jan 9 '45
(Japanese landing, Dec '41)
LINGAYEN
GULF
Baguio • *Bambang*
Shobo
Group

ZAMBALES MTS.

San Jose

LUZON

Jan 29 → Kembu
Group
O Clark Field
• *San Fernando*

Subic Bay
BATAAN PEN.
Manila
Feb 4-Mar 3
• *Cavite*
Shimbu
Group

Mariveles
Corregidor I.

LAMON
BAY

PHILIPPINE
SEA

SOUTH
CHINA
SEA

MINDORO

SIBUYAN
SEA

San Bernardino Strait

SAMAR SEA

SAMAR

VISAYAN
SEA

PANAY

Carigara •
Tacloban
Ormoc •
• *Dulag*
LEYTE
Oct 20 '44
LEYTE
GULF
✕ Oct 24-26 '44

NEGROS

CEBU

Surigao Strait

MINDANAO
SEA

SULU
SEA

PALAWAN

MINDANAO

Zamboanga •

Davao •

BORNEO

0   125 mi
0   200 km

especially Tacloban where land-based army planes could support Leyte ground operations. Finally, the spacious anchorage available in Leyte Gulf would provide an excellent base for MacArthur's Seventh Fleet commanded by Adm. Thomas Kinkaid and greatly facilitate supply of the invasion itself. This was to take place at the northern head of the gulf on two excellent beaches between Dulag and San Jose and near Tacloban. These beaches were among the most easily accessible of any crossed so far in the Southwest Pacific.

Nor were they heavily defended. The doctrine of annihilation at the water's edge, so quietly and effectively shelved at Biak and Peleliu, was now officially abandoned by the Japanese high command. Instead, Nakagawa's defense-in-depth became the new battle doctrine. It was embraced by Gen. Tomoyuki Yamashita when he arrived in Manila on October 9 to assume command of his 225,000-strong Fourteenth Area Army. However, Yamashita was guided by Imperial General Headquarters' conviction that the south and central islands should be equipped to fight only holding actions, and that the all-out defense of the Philippines should take place on Luzon. Accordingly, he concentrated there. Only the four-division Thirty-Fifth Army under Lt. Gen. Sosaku Suzuki held the south and center from Mindanao to Cebu and Leyte. On Leyte there were only about 23,000 soldiers, most of them in Lt. Gen. Shiro Makino's 16th Division. Few of them were on Leyte's east coast where MacArthur intended to land. The bulk were at Ormoc on the opposite coast or had been withdrawn to escape the furious American naval and aerial bombardment.

Much of this was delivered by Halsey's Third Fleet. Actually, since the summer of 1944 a unique arrangement had been worked out between Halsey and Adm. Raymond Spruance. When Halsey was aboard his flagship, the powerful new battleship *New Jersey,* this force was designated Third Fleet. When Halsey and staff went ashore to plan their next operation to be replaced by Spruance and his team, it was called the Fifth Fleet. Whatever it was called, it was the most powerful, immense and awesome naval striking force ever assembled. It was also almost completely air-oriented. An excellent seagoing supply system could keep it at sea for weeks at a time. Thirty-four oilers, together with ammunition ships, aviation supply ships and refrigerator ships kept the Third-Fifth Fleet more than adequately supplied with beans, bullets and black oil, while specially assigned escort carriers brought in replacement aircraft.

Aviator admirals had also taken precedence over battleship admirals. Almost all carrier task force commanders were now aviators. Moreover, Admiral King had decreed that in all carrier groups the carrier admiral would always be in tactical command, even if other admirals in the fleet commanding the cruiser or battleship screen were senior to him. Since 1942, 70 percent of the captains promoted to rear admiral had been aviators. King had also ruled that if a fleet or task force commander were a nonaviator, he would have to have an aviator as his chief of staff. If they were aviators themselves, then their chiefs of staff had to be nonaviators.

Since September the Third Fleet under Halsey had been launching heavy strikes against Japanese bases in the Philippines and nearby bases from which the enemy could support his Philippine forces. On September 9 and 10 his airplanes raided Mindanao, on the 12th they hit the Visayas and on the 21st and 22nd they assaulted Leyte. The Japanese did not oppose the raids, holding their aircraft in reserve. But many of them were destroyed on the ground and the installations themselves badly damaged. These were the attacks that prompted Halsey to suggest stepping up the Philippine timetable.

Returning on October 10 to strike Luzon, Okinawa and Formosa, the Americans found themselves locked in what Halsey called "a knock-down drag-out fight between carrier air and shore-based air." The Japanese suffered severely, for these, after all, were no longer "the emperor's glorious young eagles" who had known victory at Pearl Harbor and in the Indian Ocean. They were new recruits, many only teenagers, who had never before flown in formation. Many of them had learned about aerial combat only by watching training films.

Adm. Shigeru Fukudome commanding both army and naval air on Okinawa was well aware that he dared not send such pilots against the American carriers. Still, he thought they could defend their own airfields. But when he saw them spinning earthward in flames, he observed sorrowfully that "our fighters were nothing but so many eggs thrown against the stone wall of the indomitable enemy formation." Fukudome lost more than 500 planes against American losses of fewer than a hundred. His slightly more experienced pilots of the night-flying Typhoon Attack Force were more successful, badly damaging the cruisers *Canberra* and *Houston.* Yet, because their lack of experience prevented them from telling an oiler from a battleship, they claimed wildly exaggerated victories. Radio Tokyo jubilantly broadcast destruction of the Third Fleet with the loss of nineteen carriers along with several battleships, cruisers and destroyers. Emperor Hirohito issued a special rescript commemorating "the victory of Formosa" and celebrations were held throughout Japan.

Hearing these exaggerations, Halsey decided to provide a trap for the enemy. Using the crippled cruisers as bait, he stationed one of his carrier groups between them and Japan. Taking the bait, the Japanese sent Vice Adm. Kiyohide Shima's cruiser-destroyer force out to sea to finish off the Third Fleet. But when Shima's scouts saw all those American carriers still afloat and undamaged, the admiral wisely sailed back to the Inland Sea. Although disappointed, Halsey issued the sarcastic report: "All Third Fleet Ships Recently Reported Sunk by Radio Tokyo Have Been Salvaged and Are Retiring at High Speed Toward the Japanese Fleet."

The "victory of Formosa" was to have grave consequences for the Japanese. Since the admirals did not bother to tell the generals that the victory was a sham, Imperial General Headquarters made some unwise changes in tactics. They stopped fortifying Luzon, which had the best supply system and was big enough for a defense-in-depth. Instead, the army planned to reinforce Leyte and there to fight the decisive battle.

When Douglas MacArthur arrived at Hollandia aboard the cruiser *Nashville,* Admiral Kinkaid signaled him: "Welcome to our city." Hollandia anchorage was indeed a floating metropolis. Ships were visible everywhere, to the horizon and beyond. They would carry 160,000 men to the battle, along with 1.5 million tons of general equipment, 235,000 tons of combat vehicles, 200,000 tons of ammunition and 200,000 tons of medical supplies. For every month thereafter, 332,000 tons of supplies would be required. So great were the logistical difficulties for the landings alone that nine staging bases across the Southwest and Central Pacific were used: Oro Bay, Finschhafen, Biak, Morotai, Manus, Hollandia, Noemfoor, Guam and Oahu. Altogether the Central Philippine Attack Force numbered 738 ships. Its total naval strength was slightly less than the cross-Channel invasion but had much greater firepower. Halsey's Third Fleet alone numbered 105 major war vessels, including eighteen big carriers. Nimitz had also informed Halsey that if the chance should arise to destroy all or "a major portion" of the Japanese Combined Fleet, "such destruction becomes the primary task." It was an order that could have been—a week later—a prescription for disaster. However, neither Halsey nor MacArthur expected the enemy fleet to challenge them at Leyte. Luzon, so close to Japanese bases in China, Formosa, Okinawa and Indo-China, seemed to be a far more vulnerable area. Indeed, Halsey felt so secure that he sent one of his four carrier groups to Ulithi for rest and replenishment. The battleships supporting the landings in the Third Fleet carried only 25 percent armor-piercing shells (the kind used in ship-to-ship fights) in their magazines. The rest was for bombardment.

Just after midnight on October 20, 1944, the ships of the invasion fleet entered the channel leading into Leyte Gulf. They were guided by navigation lights erected by soldiers of the 6th Ranger Battalion, who had captured the channel islands on October 17. The sun rose behind heavy clouds to the fleet's rear. Its rays shone faintly on *Nashville*'s bridge, where Douglas MacArthur stood peering to the north, or right, toward Tacloban. "It had changed little since I had known it forty-one years before on my first assignment after leaving West Point," he wrote. "It was a full moment for me." Sight of his native land was also a full moment for Sergio Osmena, the new president of the Philippines. He had succeeded Manuel Quezon, who had died August 1, comforted in the knowledge that on July 4, 1946, the United States would return to the Philippines its independence.

At 6:30 the bombardment force opened up. Dust, smoke and flames soon obscured the landing beaches. But there was no answering fire. At ten o'clock MacArthur's assault force began landings, four divisions abreast. On the left were Maj. Gen. A. V. Arnold's 7th Infantry Division and Maj. Gen. James L. Bradley's 96th Infantry Division, on the right the 1st Cavalry Division (Dismounted) under Maj. Gen. Verne D. Mudge and the 24th Infantry Division commanded by Maj. Gen. F. A. Irving. There was only light opposition. Fewer than fifty Americans were killed on A-Day (assault day). By nightfall Leyte's northeastern shore was securely in American hands. The 1st Cavalry stood on the outskirts of Tacloban holding the airfield and surrounding high ground, while on the far left the 7th Infantry had captured Dulag and was moving on the airstrip. All of A-Day's objectives and more had been secured.

MacArthur was so elated by the good news coming from the beaches that he decided to go ashore early. At one o'clock in the afternoon he appeared on deck in a set of freshly pressed suntans, his famous braided hat, sunglasses and his equally familiar corncob pipe in his mouth—a sight calculated to set flash bulbs flashing and popping. With General Sutherland and others he descended a ladder to a waiting motor whaler.

"Well, believe it or not, we're here," he said to Sutherland. En route to the beaches, President Osmena came aboard the whaler. MacArthur had chosen to land at the 24th Division's sector, where the stiffest resistance had been encountered. More than half the casualties for both sides had been inflicted there. Mortar and rifle fire could be heard. Four landing craft hit by Japanese mortar shells were burning. Another had been sunk. Enemy sniper fire could be heard pinging off boat hulls. Such sights and sounds seemed to exhilarate MacArthur. But he was dismayed when it was discovered that the whaler drew too much water and could not run up on the beach. A lieutenant telephoned the beachmaster to request a small landing craft. But that worthy charged with directing the unloading of supplies on a crowded and confused beach was too harassed by importunate coxswains and the whine of sniper bullets to be impressed by this august request. "Let 'em walk in!" he snapped, and hung up. It was a grim-faced Douglas MacArthur who stepped off the whaler into knee-deep water and waded ashore followed by his equally unhappy entourage and President Osmena. But he had walked straight into a photographers' lens and the ensuing picture became world famous.

Soldiers on the beach gaped to see this little party of celestial rank come splashing ashore. A flabbergasted sergeant cried, "Button up! Button up!" With splendid bad grace his grumbling men put their T-shirts back on.

"Who's those two guys?" a soldier asked.

"They're the generals."

"What the hell are they doing up here?"

"Damfino. They just come around, I guess."

A weapons carrier fitted with a portable radio transmitter was brought to the beach. The portable was linked to the *Nashville*'s master transmitter capable of broadcasting on several wave lengths. MacArthur seized the microphone just as a fine rain began to fall. "People of the Philippines," he began, his hoarse, throaty voice trembling with emotion. "I have returned! By the grace of Almighty God, our forces stand again on Philippine soil. . . . Rally to me! Let the indomitable spirit of Bataan and Corregidor lead on. As the lines of battle toil forward to bring you within the zone of operations, rise and strike! For your homes and hearths, strike! In the name of your sacred dead, strike!" His hands now also trembling, MacArthur concluded: "Let no heart be faint. Let every arm be steeled. The guidance of divine God points the way. Follow in His name to the Holy Grail of righteous victory!"

MacArthur's speech was received in some parts of the American media with angry protests. It was either "sacrilegious" or "in bad taste" or else "flamboyant" or "proof of MacArthur's supreme egoism." In Western ears it was indeed grandiloquent, but not in those of the Filipino people devoted to the MacArthur name and guided by deep religious fervor; and they did indeed rally to him.

Criticism of his speech, however, was far less intense than the howls of derision greeting the photograph of him wading ashore. It was scoffed at as a fake, a piece of typical MacArthur stagecraft. Even General Yamashita thought it had been staged in New Guinea. If he had suspected that MacArthur was on Leyte, he said, he would have avenged Yamamoto by hurling suicide troops and planes against the American commander. In truth, however, it was an accident, happening exactly as described; although it is also true that MacArthur, having found the scene so productive of publicity, actually did make planned wade-ins at later landings.

During the next two days the Americans steadily expanded their beachhead. First Cavalry troops entered Tacloban on the afternoon of the 21st. To the south soldiers of the 96th and 7th Divisions sloshed through swamps toward airstrips of the southern Leyte Valley west of Dulag. Opposition was still light. On the 23rd a ceremony was held on the steps of the capitol in Tacloban, where MacArthur and Osmena announced President Roosevelt's restoration of civil government in the Philippines. At opposite ends of the building the American and Filipino flags were thrown to the winds. Far, far out at sea the battle flags of the Japanese Combined Fleet were also unfurled.

109. The Battle of Leyte Gulf

TO ADM. SUEMO TOYODA, the American invasion of Leyte presented the opportunity for the annihilating battle that he had sought since he became chief of the Combined Fleet. When on October 18 his scout planes reported a vast concourse of enemy ships converging on the Philippines, he devised the plan called Operation Sho-1. It was based on his strength and his weakness. His strength was the largely undiminished power of his battleships. Of the ten with which Japan began the war, seven were still afloat and undamaged, and had been joined by the gigantic sisters, *Yamato* and *Musashi.* His weakness was in his carriers. With few aircraft and fewer pilots they were all but helpless. But Toyoda would use the useless carriers as bait to lure Admiral Halsey's Third Fleet away from Leyte Gulf. Then three forces of fighting ships would thread their way through the

Philippine inland straits to debouch upon the unprotected American escort carriers and transports. They would be like starving wolves falling on unguarded sheep. They would not only give Japan a fighting chance to hold the Philippines but also might even turn the tide that had begun to roll against her since the defeats of Midway–Guadalcanal.

The three gunship fleets were two Southern Forces under Vice Adm. Kiyohide Shima and Shoji Nishimura, which were to slip through Surigao Strait while the mighty Center Force commanded by Vice Adm. Takeo Kirita moved through San Bernardino Strait. The Northern Force under Vice Adm. Jisahuro Ozawa was to sail off Cape Engaño far to the north, where Halsey's scout planes would find it and hopefully make the reports that would bring "the Bull" tearing north from his patrol off Leyte.

At 1:15 in the morning of October 23 the submarines *Darter* and *Dace* were on surface patrol in Palawan Passage when Cmdr. David McClintock of *Darter* received radar contact of a big enemy force 30,000 yards away. It was indeed big: Kirita's five battleships, ten heavy cruisers, two light cruisers and a dozen to fourteen destroyers. They were in three columns. McClintock seized his megaphone and yelled to *Dace*'s Cmdr. Bladen Claggett:

"Let's go!"

They sped off toward Kirita, submerging when they came within range. Five hours later at a mere 980 yards, McClintock ordered his torpedomen to fire *Darter*'s six bow tubes at heavy cruiser *Atago*, Kirita's flagship. Next McClintock swung hard left to allow four more fish to go flashing away from the four stern tubes toward the next heavy in column, *Takeo*. Swinging his periscope back on *Atago* he saw "the sight of a lifetime."

Kirita's flagship was a mass of billowing smoke and leaping flame and was already going down by the bow. Kirita transferred his flag to mighty *Yamato*, where he was met by that inveterate diarist Rear Admiral Ugaki. *Takeo*, meanwhile, was limping home—her rudder and two propellers blown off and three engine rooms flooded. Then *Dace* sent four torpedoes speeding toward heavy cruiser *Maya*. The explosions and horrid crackling noises that followed were so fierce that *Dace* herself trembled as though hit. *Maya* blew up. "After the spray and smoke had disappeared, nothing of her remained to be seen," wrote Admiral Ugaki. Kirita had now lost two heavy cruisers sunk and a third ruined without having seen or harmed the enemy. Worse for him, *Dace* and *Darter* had informed Halsey of the Center Force's location and a hotter reception awaited Kirita when daylight of October 24 dawned over the Sibuyan Sea. By afternoon, three American fast carrier groups were launching their war birds for the hunting there.

From Luzon to strike the carriers came Japanese naval planes in three flights of fifty to sixty each. They were all shot to ribbons by Hellcats scrambled aloft to intercept them. No serious loss would have been suffered from the Japanese counterattack except that a Judy bomber dropped a 550-pound egg on *Princeton*, which plunged through three decks before exploding in the bakeshop. *Princeton* was soon a floating litter of twisted steel and blackened dead and wounded.

American destroyers fired torpedoes into her to send her to the bottom.

But then the Marine and navy bombers found Kirita's Center Force. Mighty *Mushishu* was sunk, heavy cruiser *Myoko* was forced back to Borneo and battleships *Yamato, Nagato* and *Haruna* were damaged, although left in operation. But only eighteen American airplanes were shot down. "The small number of enemy planes shot down is regrettable," wrote Admiral Ugaki. In dismay, Admiral Kirita reversed his course to the west.

As the sun of October 24 began to sink, this was the situation: Kirita was retiring west and Nishimura's 1st Striking Force was steaming steadily toward Surigao Strait, followed by Shima with the 2nd Striking Force. Off Samar sailed the American Escort Carrier Group—sixteen escort carriers, nine destroyers, twelve destroyer escorts—under Rear Adm. Thomas L. Sprague. To the south inside Leyte Gulf, the waters off the invasion beaches were crowded with transports and supply ships. To the north at Cape Engaño was Ozawa's decoy force with four carriers—*Zuikaku, Chitose, Chiyoda* and *Zuiho*—together with supporting warships and the two flight-deck battleships *Ise* and *Hyuga.* Ozawa had only 110 planes left after the destructive Formosa battles. He was also disappointed that his force had not yet been detected by the Americans. To guarantee discovery he sent *Ise* and *Hyuga* farther south, where they were spotted by American search planes around 4:00 in the afternoon. To Admiral Halsey here was "the one piece missing in the puzzle." With such huge enemy forces appearing in the Philippines, he had known that there had to be carriers around somewhere. Now he had found them!

Until this moment Halsey had been preparing to fight Admiral Kirita should he reverse course and enter San Bernardino Strait. To do so he had formed Task Force 34—four battleships, two heavy cruisers, three lights and fourteen destroyers—under Vice Adm. Willis Lee of Guadalcanal fame. Nimitz in Hawaii was notified of this provision and Kinkaid at Leyte was delighted when he learned of it because now his Seventh Fleet could concentrate on Surigao while Lee was guarding San Bernardino. But when Halsey received reports of Ozawa's fleet, he signaled Kinkaid: "Am proceeding north with three groups to attack carrier forces at dawn." Kinkaid assumed that a fourth group—Lee's Task Force 34— was still watching San Bernardino. But it wasn't. That powerful surface fleet force had not yet been detached from the Third Fleet and was steaming north with Halsey.

San Bernardino was wide open without so much as a pistol raised to defend it. If Kirita did change course, he could sail through it untouched and burst with his hungry wolves upon the sheep of Sprague's Escort Carrier Group off Samar. If Nishimura and Shima could fight their way past Kinkaid's surface force holding Surigao, the slaughter would include the transports and be complete.

Nishimura had battleships *Yamashiro* and *Fuso,* the heavy cruiser *Mogami* and five destroyers when he entered Surigao. He calculated on reaching Leyte Gulf about 4:30 in the morning of October 25. In high spirits he steamed straight ahead—into a trap.

Adm. Jesse Oldendorf's battleship force was planning "to cross the T." This is the centuries-old maneuver by which one fleet forms in battle line horizontal to the enemy approaching in vertical column. This enables the first fleet to fire broadside, that is, bring all its guns to bear on the advancing column able to fire only its forward guns. If the broadside fleet's shells miss the other's leading ships, they can hit the following ones. Thus the horizontal line has by far the fairest targets, and Nishimura's fleet was also a very small vertical column in comparison to the huge horizontal line being formed by Oldendorf. In the trap Kinkaid had ordered him to set, Oldendorf had six battleships—*Mississippi, Maryland, West Virginia, Tennessee, California* and *Pennsylvania*—five heavy cruisers, two lights, twenty-eight destroyers and a flock of torpedo boats. For the last time in naval history the T would be crossed, and Oldendorf felt as though the ghosts of all the great sea captains—the galley admirals of Greece and Rome, Don Juan of Austria, John Paul Jones and Horatio Nelson—stood at attention on his bridge to watch the final battle of the dreadnoughts.

But first the fleas of the seas—the torpedo boats—struck Nishimura. For three hours they churned around him, zigzagging in the light of his powerful searchlights, making smoke, firing their torpedoes "hot, straight and normal"— but they didn't hit a thing. Nishimura was a canny night fighter, and he drove them off, hitting ten and sinking one.

Next came the destroyers. Just before three o'clock in the morning of October 25, Squadron 54 under Capt. Jesse B. Coward sighted the enemy at 12,800 yards. *McDermut, Monssen, Remey, McGowan* and *Melvin* swept down on the Japanese, launching torpedoes as they came. A spread of perhaps three dozen fish streaked toward Nishimura, who was only then forming battle formation: destroyers ahead, cruisers next, battleships last. It would be eight minutes before the success or failure of the torpedo strikes would become known. In that interval Coward's destroyers turned and fled. Japanese searchlights came on. *Remey* was caught and held in one beam, making its crewmen feel "like animals in a cage." Enemy shells began falling among the wildly maneuvering Yankees. Star shells exploded overhead to illuminate them. But they got away.

Now came great flashes and roars. The American torpedoes had struck. Battleship *Fuso* slowed down, out of the fight. *Monssen* and *McDermut* came back to the battle, firing as they came. Nishimura turned away in evasive action —straight into the path of the enemy fish. *Yamagumo* blew up and sank. *Michishio* began to sink and *Asaguma* limped to the rear with her bow blown off. All three had been hit by *McDermut*. Now *Monssen* delivered a parting hit on battleship *Yamashiro,* though it failed to stop her. Nishimura was at last alarmed. He got off messages to Shima and Kirita to the effect that he was not alone in Surigao Strait. He sailed on and ran into two more splendid destroyer attacks from squadrons commanded by Capts. K. M. McManes and Roland Smoot. Now the battle had become general. Big *Yamashiro* exchanged haymakers with the heavies of the American battle line. Star shells from both sides illuminated the darkly shining seas. Geysers from exploding shells erupted everywhere and the surface was crisscrossed by torpedo wakes. Above it all rose the clamor and thunder and flashing of the big guns. Streams of huge 14- and 16-inch tracers went arching through the night like strings of lighted freight cars. After four o'clock, the American destroyers pulled out, leaving the fight to the battle line.

Six battleships, five of which had been sunk and salvaged at Pearl Harbor, now bellowed in revenge for that Day of Infamy. Within sixteen minutes these monsters, supported by cruisers and destroyers baying away, finished off all but one of Nishimura's remnant. On the left flank Oldendorf's cruisers sent an incredible 3,100 rounds screaming toward the foe. Battleship *Yamashiro* was a floating holocaust. After Oldendorf gave the cease-fire, she sank, turning over with a horrible hissing roar to carry all hands and Admiral Nishimura down with her.

The score: two Japanese battleships, one heavy cruiser and four destroyers sunk, one destroyer damaged for the Japanese, against one American destroyer damaged. Oldendorf now prepared to receive the 2nd Striking Force. But Admiral Shima was no fire-eater like the gallant but perhaps foolhardy Nishimura. He had entered Surigao with two heavy cruisers, one light and seven destroyers—bending it on at speeds up to twenty-eight knots. But after he saw the flashes and heard the explosions ahead of him, after he had passed the burning hulks of *Fuso* and *Yamashiro* and had his own light cruiser *Abukuma* crippled by a torpedo, after he had even ordered torpedo attacks on "enemy ships" which actually were the Hibuson Islands, he discreetly turned and fled. The islands did not sink, nor did Shima get clean away. He lost *Abukuma* and two destroyers in later engagements in this far-flung battle. And his retirement ended the third phase of the Battle of Leyte Gulf, the Battle of Surigao Strait.

Early in the morning of October 25 a highly satisfied Kinkaid conferred with his staff. He turned to his chief of staff, Capt. Richard H. Cruzen. "Now, Dick, is there anything we haven't done?" Cruzen replied: "Admiral, I can think of only one thing. We have never directly asked Halsey if Task Force 34 is guarding San Bernardino Strait." Kinkaid immediately signaled Halsey: "Is TF 34 GUARDING SAN BERNARDINO STRAIT?" Back came the reply: "NEGATIVE. TF 34 IS WITH ME PURSUING ENEMY CARRIER FORCE." Twenty minutes later Kinkaid received word that a powerful surface force was attacking the escort carriers.

Admiral Kirita had reversed course. A message had come from Admiral Toyoda: "All forces will dash to the attack, trusting in divine guidance." More fearful of a tongue-lashing from Toyoda than he trusted in the divine Kami of the Shinto cult, Kirita entered San Bernardino Strait. He was not aware that it was wide open and there would be no toll to pay. Even his seamen marveled at their tranquil passage, but Kirita was apprehensive that he might be sailing into a trap like Nishimura. When he debouched into Leyte Gulf and saw the silhouettes of the American escort carriers over the horizon, he feared that they might be big carriers. Nevertheless, he steered toward them.

The hulls he had seen were those of the sixteen escort carriers and twenty-five destroyers in Admiral Sprague's group. An escort carrier, or CVE, is a shrimp in comparison to the whales of naval warfare, the big fast carriers. Actually a CVE was only a converted merchant ship with a flight deck added. It had no armor, only fair AA armament and a single 5-inch popgun on its stern. Escort carriers had been built for antisubmarine duty in the Atlantic and only latterly had come to the Pacific to provide close air support for invasions. Coming against them was mighty *Yamato* with 18-inch guns, the biggest warship afloat, 3,500-pound shells against the CVE's 100-pounder, as well as three other battleships, ten heavy cruisers, two lights and a dozen destroyers.

Sprague's group was divided into units called the three Taffies. Taffy 1 was led by Sprague himself, Taffy 2 by Rear Adm. Felix Stump and Taffy 3 by Rear Adm. Clifton ("Ziggy") Sprague. All three Taffies had launched their covering aircraft when Ziggy Sprague's lookouts reported antiaircraft fire to the north. Sprague was astounded. What could it be? Bull Halsey was up there guarding San Bernardino. Then his radio watch reported "Japs gabbling" on the inter-fighter direction net. Next a navy pilot gave him the complete rundown on Kirita's approaching fleet—all of it. Finally, lookouts on Sprague's flagship *Fanshaw Bay* sighted the swaying pagoda masts of Kirita's heavyweights. Even the rawest recruit was aware that American naval architects do not design ships that look like Shinto shrines.

But Kirita was cautious. Still fearful of big carriers ahead, he deployed into a circular antiaircraft formation. When he at last realized that the enemy was the defenseless force it actually was, he gave the order, "General Attack!" But instead of sending his destroyers ahead as a torpedo-firing screen behind which his behemoths could pick off the Yankees at leisure, he rather touched off a ship-for-ship melee that gave Ziggy Sprague his chance to escape.

Sprague made smoke, launched his planes, made all speed east and radioed for help. Sprague hoped to outsail Kirita, to keep him from encircling him.

But Kirita's guns were walking their fire into Taffy 3. Three 14-inch salvos straddled *White Plains,* making her buck and twist violently. Huge colored geysers of water rose into the air. The Japanese had loaded their shells with dye to mark their accuracy. All around Taffy 3 the ocean seemed to be sprouting shimmering plumes of color. Aboard *White Plains* a seaman shouted: "They're shooting us in Technicolor!"

All of Sprague's ships were firing their stern popguns. But they were also taking big-gun hits. They shuddered and leaped, but there were no explosions. The Japanese were firing armor-piercers, which went right through the thin-skinned CVEs like arrows through paper. But such luck could not last. The enemy inevitably would make the correction to high-explosive. Ziggy Sprague gave himself five more minutes—until a rain squall arose across his bow. Taffy 3 sailed into it and gained a fifteen-minute respite from Kirita. Now Ziggy Sprague made his big decision. Hoping for help in the gulf, he ordered his carriers to steer for it. If help did not materialize, at least they would put distance between themselves and the enemy. In the meantime, he ordered his three destroyers to attack Kirita. Out of the funnel smoke and the sheeted gray rain they came: *Hoel, Heerman* and *Johnston*—a trio of snarling sheep taking on the wolves of Kirita's battle line. Aboard *Johnston,* barrel-chested, deep-voiced Cmdr. Edward Evans told his men: "Stand by to attack major portion of Japanese fleet." *Johnston*'s main battery of 5-inchers peppered the heavy cruiser *Kumano* with 200 rounds while she launched all ten of her torpedoes. Evans grinned when he heard the underwater explosions where his fish had flashed into *Kumano,* setting her afire. But thirty seconds later a battleship and a cruiser made a wreck of *Johnston.* One blast stripped Evans naked to the waist and tore two fingers from his left hand. *Johnston* staggered out of the fight.

   Hoel, flying the flag of the division chief, Cmdr. W. D. Thomas, took on mighty *Kongo.* Within 9,000 yards of the battleship she launched four torpedoes. But they missed, and *Kongo* hit *Hoel* again and again. Her rudder jammed hard right, the little American inadvertently was headed straight for the big Japanese. Somehow she passed through *Kongo*'s shower of 14-inch shells and turned on heavy cruiser *Haguro.* Badly overmatched, she began to flee, "chasing salvos" by heading for those distinct purplish or yellowish splashes where enemy shells hit, knowing that a Japanese salvo would not come that way again. But *Hoel* was finally finished off by *Kongo* and two heavy cruisers.

   Heerman, the last of the three, was challenging *Haruna,* the battleship so often reported sunk. Her 5-inchers bayed and three torpedoes flashed away from her, but *Haruna*'s answering fire was too destructive and *Heerman* retired. Now mighty *Yamato* with Kirita and Ugaki aboard entered the battle. Her 18-inchers belched away at the darting, heeling Yankee gadflies—for there were more in the battle after Ziggy Sprague committed his still-smaller destroyer escorts. *Yamato*'s lookouts reported torpedo tracks, and Kirita ordered evasive action. The maneuver put the big battleship squarely between two spreads, four to starboard, two to port—all chasing her from astern. Mighty *Yamato* fled for ten full minutes until the American fish had run their course, and when Admiral Kirita looked back, he found himself out of the battle. "This was a highly unfortunate maneuver," Admiral Ugaki informed his diary.

   Far to the north Bull Halsey was receiving frantic calls for help from both the Spragues and Kinkaid. For some reason he ignored them. Lee twice informed Halsey that he was certain Kirita was coming through San Bernardino but received only a "Roger" in reply. Halsey was still mindful of Nimitz's instruction that he should regard any "major portion" of the Combined Fleet as his "primary task," and he grimly pursued it. Carriers *Chitose* and *Zuikaku* plus one destroyer were already sinking when he received the signals from the south. He still refused to reverse course to fight Kirita. He had formed Task Force 34 but was using it to finish Ozawa's damaged ships. But he did order Vice Adm. John S. McCain's Task Force 1, still bound for Ulithi to rest and rearm, to turn and go to Kinkaid's aid. But McCain would need two hours to reach Kirita.

By then Nimitz in Hawaii and King in Washington were deeply concerned. Although Nimitz customarily allowed his admirals to fight their own battles, the situation was so serious that he sent a coded inquiry to Halsey: "Where is Task Force 34." It went with the usual padding, beginning "TURKEY TROTS TO WATER" and ending "THE WORLD WONDERS." But the yeoman who sent the message added a "repeat" for emphasis and left in the final padding. At 10:00 A.M. Halsey received this message; "WHERE IS, REPEAT, WHERE IS TASK FORCE 34? THE WORLD WONDERS." Halsey was infuriated by this seeming insult, but after another hour's delay, he detached Lee and one of the fast carrier groups to sail south at top speed. Kinkaid, meanwhile, had ordered some of Oldendorf's battleships to sail to Samar from Surigao. But they were three hours away, and it appeared that the Taffies would definitely not live that long.

Two hours had passed since Ziggy Sprague had launched Taffy 3 on its fighting flight. Many ships from the other Taffies had also been committed. All of them had sent their war birds aloft. Hellcats, Wildcats and Avengers dived on the enemy vessels with chattering guns. They ran the gantlet of the ack-ack, banked, climbed and dived again. When their ammunition was gone, they flew daring "dry runs" to divert Japanese fire from the ships. Some of them with remarkable accuracy blew up enemy torpedoes from aloft. Little *Heerman* was twice saved from certain destruction by the tactics of these gallant airmen, once while swapping salvos with *Chokai* and and again with *Tone.* One of *Chokai's* 8-inchers tore into the destroyer's storage locker packed with navy beans. Fierce heat instantly changed this hated Saturday-breakfast staple into a hot paste. It was sucked into the uptake, spurting up the stack to fall—to the everlasting honor and glory of Japanese gunnery—on the head of the supply officer.

At last Kirita launched the torpedo attacks with which he should have opened his assault, just as the destroyer escort *Roberts* began to sink with half her crew of eight officers and 170 men. Light cruiser *Yahagi* and four destroyers began to close on Taffy 3's carriers. They had a clear path because all the ships of Sprague's screen were engaging the enemy cruisers then battering *Gambier Bay* to her death—all but *Johnston.*

Plunging out of the smoke, *Johnston* attacked the five Japanese. It made little difference to Commander Evans that his torpedoes were gone, one engine was lost and many of his men were dead or dying. He sped toward *Yahagi* with smoke and flame spitting from his 5-inch guns. Both ships exchanged hits. *Yahagi* turned away! Now Evans tried to "cross the T" on the remaining four enemy destroyers! They too veered away. From a good distance they launched their spreads of torpedoes. The enemy fish ran their courses without a single strike and one of them was exploded by an Avenger. Evans strutted up and down his bridge in justifiable pride. "Now I've seen everything!" he cried. "Now I've seen *everything!*"

But he had not. *Yahagi* and the four destroyers returned, formed a circle and sailed around the *Johnston,* shooting into it until it sank. Of its 327 sailors only

141 were saved. The fierce Evans was not among them. But he and the men who had perished with him received their epitaph from the Japanese destroyer captain who stood on his bridge at attention, saluting *Johnston* as it went under.

With *Gambier Bay* gone, Ziggy Sprague still had five escort carriers: *White Plains, St. Lo, Fanshaw Bay, Kalinin Bay, Kitkun Bay.* Kirita's ships were still attacking them individually in his foolish ship-for-ship tactics. *White Plains* was dueling big *Chokai* with her stern popgun. *Chokai* closed. "Hold on boys," yelled Chief Gunner Jenkins. "We're drawing the bastards into forty millimeter range!"

Aboard *Fanshaw Bay* a signalman cried, "They're gettin' away!" Although this magnificent malapropism was not exactly accurate, Kirita was indeed retiring. He called his wolves off at the very moment when the mighty Center Force could have sunk the Americans and burst into Leyte Gulf. True, he was under constant air attack and had already lost three cruisers to this pack of paperweights, but Center Force's battleships were only bruised, and he had plenty of cruisers and destroyers left. In U.S. Navy slang, Admiral Kirita really didn't know whether to sweat or draw small stores. Ziggy Sprague's daring tactics had bewildered him. He still couldn't make up his mind about the Americans' strength. All morning he had been intercepting those frantic messages to Admiral Halsey in the north. Halsey could burst upon him at any moment, and he still had unhappy memories of the losses he had suffered from *Dace* and *Darter* and in the Sibuyan Sea. Until the war was over, Kirita would never know that he could have spent the entire day chewing on the Taffies. Lucky for the American invasion force and Admiral Halsey that it was the diffident Takeo Kirita and not the fire-eating Shoji Nishimura who was on the bridge of *Yamato* that day. So Kirita headed for San Bernardino Strait, his biggest problem now being the preparation of a suitably roseate report for Admiral Toyoda.

So ended the fourth and crucial phase of the Battle of Leyte Gulf. Now the kamikazes entered history, those suicide planes so named for the Kamikaze, or Divine Wind, which rose off Japan to destroy the invading Mongol fleet in 1281. They came from land bases on Davao, Mindanao. Adm. Thomas Sprague's Taffy 1 was the first to be struck by them. A kamikaze crashed the port side forward of the escort carrier *Santee*. But its bomb did not explode. Another suicider, however, crashed *St. Lo* of Taffy 3 and sank her. Many more ships reported coming under attack by this typically Japanese desperation weapon. At last in this fifth phase of the Battle of Leyte Gulf, the answer had come to that exasperating question: "Where's the Bull?"

He was hurrying south aboard *New Jersey,* leading a powerful rescue force. Behind him his carriers were devouring the last of Ozawa's bait. Halsey arrived off Samar after Kirita had made his exit, and in fairness to the Japanese admiral it may be asked what would have happened to Center Force if he had tarried to taste more Taffy. Halsey was unabashed when he learned of the close call off Samar. To his dying day he defended "the Battle of Bull's Run" by insisting that if he had been allowed to remain off Cape Engaño, he would have destroyed all of Japan's remaining carrier power.

The Battle of Leyte Gulf, the greatest naval battle of all time, was now sputtering out after raging for five full days and nights over 500,000 square miles of Western Pacific. Its final blows were struck by American submarines closing in on Ozawa's remnants. In all, Japan lost three large carriers, one escort carrier, three light carriers, four battleships, fourteen cruisers, thirty-two destroyers and eleven submarines for a total of sixty-eight ships. American losses were one light carrier, three escort carriers, six destroyers, three destroyer escorts, one high-speed transport and seven submarines for a total of twenty-one ships. In tonnage, however, Japan lost far more than this deceptive ratio of slightly more than 3 to 1. Half of the sixty-eight vessels sunk were capital ships, while only one of the Americans was. In tonnage, the ratio could have been 10 to 1. Once again the sailors and Marines of the United States Navy had shown themselves invincible in pitched battle, not so much by tactical skill or technological superiority as by simple guts and boldness.

Ashore on Leyte now, General MacArthur's soldiers were free to secure the island without fear of attack from the rear.

110. The Battle for Leyte

IT WOULD SEEM THAT the great victory in the Battle of Leyte Gulf would assure the Americans of control of the seas and doom the approximately 23,000 men in the Japanese 16th Division there. But this did not happen. From Mindanao, from Cebu, from Panay and most especially from Luzon convoy after Japanese convoy quietly threaded the dangerous narrow waters of the Philippine archipelago to bring reinforcements and supplies to Ormoc on the west coast of Leyte. By mid-November the 26th and the elite 1st Division had arrived there. Japanese strength rose to 55,000 men and another 10,000 troops would land in December.

As at Guadalcanal, the Americans had shown themselves powerless to halt night traffic, especially concealed movement by coastal barges. American air power on Leyte was relatively weak, and the escort carriers had been badly battered off Samar. Halsey's big carriers were low on fuel and would shortly be needed for Iwo Jima. Land-based air from Gen. Ennis Whitehead's Fifth Air Force was expected to substitute for weakened naval air, but the airfields from which they were supposed to fly were all but useless.

Four captured airstrips at Bayug, Buri, Dulag and San Pablo were turned into mud sinks by the incessant October monsoon, raining as much as an inch a day. Army engineers, working up to their knees in water and muck, were unable to make them operational, and all but Dulag were abandoned. Construction was begun on new sites with firmer soil and better drainage, and the strip at Tacloban was improved enough to receive Lightning fighters on October 27.

But the Japanese were able to reinforce their Philippine air bases with their own planes from Formosa and Japan, even though this weakened home defenses. Both the Japanese army and navy had not committed so much air to decisive battle since Guadalcanal, and although they failed to wrest control of the air from the Americans, they fought for it until almost the end of the Leyte campaign. In response, MacArthur asked Nimitz to send his fast carriers back to Leyte. Nimitz agreed, and three of Halsey's groups returned to Philippine waters after refueling at Ulithi. In November they destroyed an entire Japanese convoy carrying 10,000 soldiers to Ormoc. Land-based air joined the assault, but again like Guadalcanal, the Americans were never able to cut the enemy supply line completely.

General Yamashita in Manila was reluctant to relinquish his Luzon troops for action on Leyte. He complained to Field Marshal Hisaichi Terauchi that his defenses were being eroded by a sideshow. Terauchi refused to stop reinforcing Leyte, although he did promise Yamashita more troops. Actually the Japanese practice of celebrating defeat with a hymn of joy had convinced most of Yamashita's officers that Leyte Gulf had been a victory for the Imperial Navy. The chief of staff of General Suzuki's Thirty-fifth Army actually drew up a plan to capture MacArthur and demand the surrender of the American army.

This was in late October, after Gen. Walter Krueger had almost all the 160,000 men of his Sixth Army ashore. General Sibert's X Corps on the right and General Hodges' XXIV Corps on the left had pushed out of their beachheads. On the left or southern flank the Americans moved through the rain into the mountains and captured the important junction town of Dagami. One battalion of the 7th Division farther south, marching over dreadful terrain which the Japanese considered impassable, seized the town of Baybay on the west coast. On the right or north, the 1st Cavalry and 24th Infantry divisions were advancing toward the vital town of Carigara fronting the Bay of Carigara. The Japanese wanted Carigara, too, hoping to use it as a base for an attack across the Leyte Valley that would drive X Corps into the sea. But the Americans got there first. Now General Suzuki, who had come to Leyte from Cebu, decided to make a stand in the mountains west of Carigara and astride the American route to Ormoc.

Krueger unfortunately did not seize this high ground himself before Suzuki could get to it. Instead he ordered X Corps to dig in on the Carigara beaches and deploy to receive a seaborne invasion. Why he did so remains a mystery. Certainly his intelligence reports suggested no such operation. Japanese convoys were all going to Ormoc. For the battered and shrunken Imperial Navy to recover quickly enough and in strength enough to mount such a large-scale seaborne assault did not seem possible. Yet, Krueger delayed at Carigara, and while he did, Suzuki's crack 1st Division seized the western heights. With their usual skill in fortifying a defense, the Japanese made a formidable but concealed fortress out of this convoluted mountain terrain. When the American soldiers of the 24th assaulted "Breakneck Ridge," they found themselves raked from front and side by thousands of unseen guns and automatic weapons. The bloodiest fighting of the Leyte campaign occurred here. Japanese defenders were just as numerous as the American attackers and were inferior only in the number of artillery pieces. It looked like a bloody stalemate, until two of the 24th's battalions moved east over unoccupied high ground then swung west by sea to come in behind the enemy and set up a blocking position on Kilay Ridge. From here they commanded the Ormoc Road, thus cutting the Japanese supply line.

Still the enemy 1st Division held out, and the exhausted 24th had to be relieved by the 32nd Infantry Division coming out of reserve. At this point Krueger thought of coming up on Ormoc from the south. More units of the 7th Division crossed southern Leyte to Baybay on the west coast and began attacking north toward Ormoc. Krueger actually had hoped to take Ormoc with an amphibious hook, as he had done so often before in New Guinea. But there was not enough shipping available, until MacArthur postponed his operation against the island of Mindoro just south of Luzon. This released Rear Adm. Arthur D. Struble's Amphibious Group 9 to take aboard the 77th Infantry Division—General Bruce's Guam veterans—and make for Ormoc Bay.

While they were at sea, the Japanese launched their own offensive, called the *Wa* Operation. The 2nd Parachute Brigade tried to capture the three American airstrips around Burauen, hoping the 16th and 26th Divisions would link up with the parachutists to secure them a day later. The Japanese were apparently unaware that these fields had been abandoned. But after a preattack raid launched by airborne commandos to put the Burauen airstrips out of action, three of the four transport planes crashed on the beach at Dulag and the fourth was shot down with the loss of all aboard. In the wreckage the plans for *Wa* Operation were discovered. Krueger immediately notified his commanders to be on the alert for airborne attacks. But most of them around Burauen were convinced that the raid had been merely a suicide attack and expected no further attacks. They were completely surprised when units of the 16th Division burst from the jungle around Buri airfield at dawn of December 6 to overrun the bivouacs of supply troops and engineers. Sleeping Americans were blown to bits by grenades or bayoneted in their beds. But the 16th had jumped the Japanese timetable, attacking twelve hours before the paratroopers were to land at Buri and San Pablo airfields supported by aircraft.

These dropped just before dusk that evening. But they were actually a confused, disorganized mob, shooting wildly, setting off flares, calling out, "Hello, Hello, where are the machine guns?" or "Surrender, Surrender! Everything is resistless." The response among the mostly supply and service troops at the airfields was just as confused, wild and leaderless with everyone shooting at shadows and hitting as many friendly troops as enemy. In the morning two battalions of American infantry arrived to expel the Japanese and restore the airfields to American control by December 10.

By then the 77th's soldiers had landed unopposed above and below Ormoc. The Japanese rushed reinforcements to the endangered city, but AAF and Marine aircraft intercepted a convoy and drove its ships away from Ormoc and into San

Isidro harbor on Leyte's northwestern tip. On December 10 the Americans laid down a bombardment from artillery, mortars and rocket launchers, following which Bruce's soldiers attacked Ormoc and took the city. Bruce signaled Hodges and Krueger: "Have rolled two sevens in Ormoc." With this, the Leyte campaign came to an effective end. The Japanese were now fragmented and dispersed, cut off from supply and reinforcements. It would take a few more weeks to end all opposition, but on December 15 Leyte was declared secure.

The Americans had returned to the Philippines to stay.

111. Rommel's "Reward"

ON OCTOBER 14, 1944, Field Marshal Erwin Rommel received his final reward from a grateful Führer. In early August Rommel had returned to his home in Herrlingen to convalesce. He had not been a good patient, had even bitten a surgeon major general who had told him to keep quiet. Unknown to Rommel, his colleagues in the conspiracy inadvertently had begun to implicate him deeper in their clumsy plot.

Gen. Heinrich von Stülpnagel, the commandant of Paris, on that fateful July 20 had ordered the arrest of the Gestapo there. Although he released them upon hearing of the failure to kill Hitler he shortly received a notice to report to Army headquarters in Berlin. Like Kluge after him, Stülpnagel understood the dread meaning of that summons. Driving east, he had his driver stop at the Meuse Canal. He got out, waded into the water, drew his pistol and shot himself in the head. But the bullet did not kill but only blinded him. His driver pulled him out of the canal and took him to a hospital. While recovering he repeatedly moaned one word, "Rommel!" Gestapo officers standing around his bed removed him to Berlin where he was tortured and eventually hanged. No one knows what he might have said under duress.

At Herrlingen the weeks passed quietly until, on September 6, Rommel's chief of staff, General Speidel, came to see him and informed him that he (Speidel) had been removed from his position and ordered to report to Guderian in Berlin next day. But Speidel never saw Guderian. At six o'clock the following morning, the Gestapo knocked at his door and took him away. He was twice interrogated, perhaps tortured, but he did not talk.* Rommel wrote a letter of protest to Hitler, but heard nothing from him. Next there came to Herrlingen his old friend, Dr. Strolin. Fearing that the Gestapo might have planted a microphone in Rommel's study, they conversed in whispers. Strolin asked Rommel what he wanted with

---

*Actually, Speidel survived the war.

the pistol on his desk. "I'm not afraid of the English or the Americans," Rommel replied, "only of the Russians—and the Germans." Strolin left, never to return, after Frau Rommel telephoned him to say that the house was being watched.

Rommel's next visitor was a man named Maier, the local party leader from Ulm. He told the field marshal that the SS chief in Ulm had informed him that Rommel no longer believed in victory. "Victory!" Rommel exclaimed. "Why don't you look at a map?" When Maier mentioned Hitler, Rommel cried: "That damned fool?" Maier was aghast. "You should not say things like that, Herr Field Marshal. You will have the Gestapo after you—if they are not after you already." It is said that Maier returned to Ulm to write a damaging report on Rommel.

Rommel's last visitors were two toadying Nazi generals named Wilhelm Burgdorf and Ernst Maisel. Burgdorf was known as "a drunken, foul-mouthed butcher who should never have been a general," and Maisel: "If there was any dirty, underhand work going on, you can be sure Maisel was somewhere at the bottom of it." They arrived October 14, asking to see the field marshal in private. Rommel took them into a downstairs room while his distraught wife hurried upstairs. Nearly an hour later Rommel entered his wife's room. There was on his face a strange and terrible expression that she had never seen before.

"What is the matter with you?" she exclaimed in alarm. "What has happened? Are you ill?"

"I have come to say good-bye," he replied, gazing at her tenderly. "In a quarter of an hour I shall be dead. They suspect me of having taken part in the attempt to kill Hitler. . . . They say that von Stülpnagel and General Speidel have denounced me. It is the usual trick. I have told them that I do not believe it, and it cannot be true. The Führer has given me the choice of taking poison or being dragged before the People's Court. They have brought the poison. They say it will take only three seconds to act." Frau Rommel begged her husband to go before the court. "No," Rommel replied firmly. "I would not be afraid to be tried in public, for I can defend everything I have done. But I know that I should never reach Berlin."

Rommel said good-bye to his wife, and also to his son, who had come into the room. He went downstairs to take his leave of his devoted aide, Captain Aldinger. Aldinger pleaded with him to attempt to escape. But Rommel said there was no hope. The house was surrounded and the roads blocked off. He could not risk retribution against his wife and son. If he killed himself, at least Frau Rommel would receive a pension and there would be a state funeral. If he chose the court, the situation would be seriously different. "I have spoken to my wife and made up my mind," he said. "I will never allow myself to be hanged by that man, Hitler. I planned no murder. I only tried to serve my country, as I have done all my life, but now this is what I must do. In about half an hour there will come a telephone call from Ulm to say that I have had an accident and am dead."

Rommel got into the car with the two generals and drove off. A few hundred yards from the house the SS driver stopped the car. Burgdorf gave Rommel the poison, saw him take it, and got out of the car. Death did not come in three seconds. For more than five minutes Rommel lay doubled up, convulsed and sobbing in the back seat, practically unconscious, until life at last left him.

Late that afternoon a stricken Frau Rommel and her son were taken to the hospital where Rommel lay, supposedly dead of a stroke. Broken-hearted and grieving, Frau Rommel was nevertheless startled by the expression on her husband's face.

His lips were twisted in a grimace of utter contempt.*

112. Planning the Ardennes Counteroffensive

ADOLF HITLER NEVER REALLY RECOVERED from the effects of the July bombing. His figure was stooped, his puffy face had the pallor of death, his left arm twitched uncontrollably much as he tried to conceal it and when he walked, he dragged one leg behind him. Yet, when he uttered the frequent and enigmatic remark, "My time will come in the mists and snows of winter," his generals were amazed at how his bulging blue eyes shone once again with the old evangelical fervor. But it was not until September 16, 1944, when the high command gathered with him in the Wolf's Lair, that his top generals understood his mystifying prediction.

Gen. Alfred Jodl, chief of operations, was summarizing the situation on the Western Front when he observed that the Americans were attacking in the Ardennes and that the Germans had little there to stop them. At the word "Ardennes," Hitler's eyes shone again, and he cried: "I have made a momentous decision! I shall go over to the offensive! That is to say," his hand fell on the map before him, "here, out of the Ardennes, with the objective Antwerp!"

The high command was astounded. After three months of fighting on both fronts, the Wehrmacht had suffered a million casualties, almost half of them in the West. Where would *Der Führer* find the men, weapons and fuel for such a massive counterstroke? Perhaps as many as thirty divisions would be needed, with a third of them armored. Where would all this come from?

Hitler's situation was desperate, and desperate men try desperate remedies. His plan was to strike through the wooded, hilly terrain of the Ardennes where the Allies were weakest on their broad front and dash for the port of Antwerp about a hundred air miles from the German Siegfried Line. By seizing Antwerp

---

*It may seem incongruous that a man dying as Rommel did would be able so to express his detestation of Hitler and his murderers. But it is possible that it occurred just as he began to sink into unconsciousness. Certainly Rommel's wife and sister were impressed by the expression and mentioned it to Desmond Young, Rommel's biographer. It is also evident on Rommel's death mask.

he would trap the Allied armies in the north and compel them to sue for a separate peace, or at least replace the implacable policy of Unconditional Surrender with a more amenable attitude. Hitler hoped to put a chink in the strangest coalition in military history: the Big Three. If he could destroy the British and Canadian armies, Britain would not be able to make good her losses, and Canada would be most reluctant to send another force to Europe. Catastrophic losses would so shock the United States that she would leave the European war altogether and concentrate on her true enemy, Japan. Thus, Nazi Germany would be able to turn with all her still formidable resources on Red Russia and crush her.

When Hitler spoke of "the mists and snows of winter" he meant that his counteroffensive would be launched in the bad weather that enshrouds northwestern Europe in November and December and thus cancel out the Anglo-American air superiority. He counted heavily on speed and surprise and actually expected to be in Antwerp within a week. To command Operation Watch on the Rhine, later changed to Autumn Mists, he brought the aging Gerd von Rundstedt out of retirement. Because he hoped to deceive the enemy as thoroughly as they had deceived Rundstedt with Operation Fortitude, he at first told this wizened but still venerated old soldier that he was to defend outside the Siegfried and then fall back into the fortifications for the decisive battle. Only later at his own choosing would he reveal his true design.

This was to assign the Schwerpunkt or main effort of the thrust to the four armored divisions of the Sixth SS Panzer Army to be led by his old Nazi crony, the hard-drinking but faithful Josef ("Sepp") Dietrich. He deliberately chose the SS for the point of honor to humiliate the regular army which had tried to kill him. Dietrich on the right flank was to be supported by the Fifth Panzer Army under General Hasso von Manteuffel, another trusted general brought in from the East. On the left or southern flank would be the infantry divisions of the Seventh Army under Gen. Erich Brandenberger, who would protect the southern flank of the penetration. Once it had been made, infantry divisions would fan out to secure both flanks.

A special force commanded by Otto Skorzeny, Hitler's favorite Aryan and the man who had rescued Mussolini, was to precede the main attack. Dressed in captured American uniforms and riding in captured American vehicles, the troops were to take the bridges over the River Meuse before they could be blown and thus block the drive on Antwerp. They were also to cut telephone lines, kill American military police directing traffic, so that Germans in Yankee uniforms could direct forces in the wrong direction, shoot up radio stations and sow panic and confusion on the American rear by making false reports of heavy American losses and passing false orders. The Wehrmacht was combed for troops who spoke the American "dialect." There were many volunteers, so that Skorzeny eventually had 3,300 men in his 150th Panzer Brigade, but few of them knew the dialect and—as events would show—none of them knew much about the private lives of Americans sports and film stars or could light and hold a cigarette in that special American way.

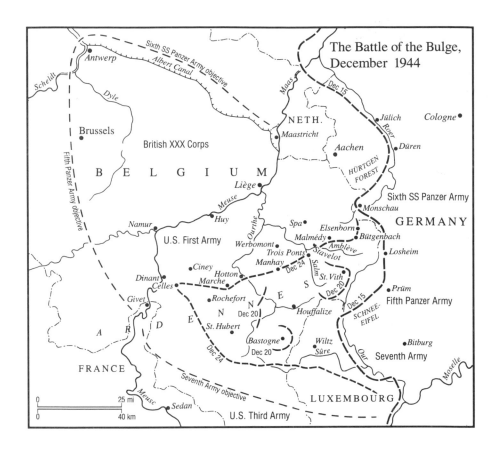

The Battle of the Bulge, December 1944

The code name, *Greif,* could mean a griffin, a mythical creature that was somehow to rule the world for Germany, and also "grasp." One of Skorzeny's lieutenants told him that he had deduced the unit's mission from this word: to race to Paris to seize and kill Dwight Eisenhower. With a straight face Skorzeny, who did not want his men to learn of their mission prematurely and perhaps give it away, made the clever young man promise not to tell anyone of the secret. Skorzeny went to bed that night confident that by morning every man in the 150th would be certain that Paris and the amiable "Ike" of the "Amies" was the unit's objective.

Ultimately there would be thirty divisions, eighteen infantry and twelve panzer, or panzergrenadier, committed to Autumn Mist. In fire support would be no fewer than twelve artillery corps, ten rocket-launching brigades and five motorized antiaircraft regiments. There would also be 2,300 tanks and self-propelled assault guns plus general support troops such as engineers and signal battalions. Although no one believed Reichsmarschall Hermann Goering, now openly derided in the Wehrmacht as "the fat boy," when he promised 3,000 airplanes, even Hitler was delighted when the Luftwaffe came up with half that number.

As he had done in "the Miracle of the West," Adolf Hitler had reached deep into the cupboard and again found it far from empty. In five years of war Germany had lost almost 3.75 million men, and yet, for all these enormous losses, the Wehrmacht still stood at close to 10 million men, including 7.5 million in the army. Although these 260 divisions were indeed far-flung, Hitler raised new levies by inducting heretofore-deferred students, men with less than crippling illnesses or defects, nonessential government workers, hospital convalescents, sailors and airmen converted into foot soldiers and by extending the draft at either end to run from sixteen to sixty. Few of these beardless youths and old men, of course, were conscripted into battle formations. Nevertheless, they could relieve noncombatant soldiers for combat.

Even more surprising, the will of the German people to fight on was still strong by late 1944. Unconditional Surrender and the threat of the Morgenthau Plan had bound them closer to their Führer and even the regular thousand-plane raids on their industry had not shaken their faith in him. Indeed, strategic bombing had not prevented German industrial production from reaching its peak at this time. Small industries were dispersed, especially to the East where the Soviets had few big bombers. Although Germany never did go into round-the-clock production or fully utilize its women workers, a sixty-hour work week was decreed, impressed foreign workers were driven harder and production of civilian or luxury goods drastically curtailed. More and more Jews and other "undesirables" were shipped in cattle cars to provide slave labor at concentration camp-run factories and mines.

All the planning of Autumn Mist had been in secret. Hitler was so fearful of its discovery that he would not entrust any of its details to be transmitted to anyone by the use of Enigma. By October he was at last ready to inform Gerd von Rundstedt of the plan. The "old man" was by then ensconced in Ziegenberg Castle east of the Rhine, from which he rarely ventured. Indeed, he quickly divined that he was to be a figurehead for Hitler's secret and ambitious operation and that Field Marshal Walter Model, one of his three army group commanders, was to be the true chief. Rundstedt, like almost all Prussian Junkers, did not like Model, finding him rough in manner and sometimes unethical in method. But the two men agreed heartily that Hitler's plan, as Model said, "hasn't got a damn leg to stand on." It was far too ambitious. Rundstedt said that "all, absolutely all conditions for the possible success of such an offensive were lacking." Between them Rundstedt and Model drew up an alternative plan, called the Small Solution in comparison to Hitler's Big Solution. Its objective was only about half the distance to Antwerp: a crossing of the Meuse at Huy about midway between Namur and Liège to be joined by a simultaneous attack from the north. This would trap the Americans around Aachen in a double envelopment costing them from ten to fourteen divisions. Hitler's response: He called for Autumn Mist to begin the morning of December 16. The final plans were marked "not to be altered."

In December of 1944, following the fierce and costly fighting in the Battle of the Hürtgen Forest, Dwight Eisenhower had sixty-five infantry, armored and airborne divisions covering a front of 500 miles stretching from the North Sea to Switzerland. His problem was that he had few reserves. Almost every unit was committed. Aware of Frederick the Great's admonition, "He who defends everything, defends nothing," he decided to concentrate his forces in two areas most conducive to continuing the offensive. One was north of the Ardennes region pointed toward the Ruhr, the other south of the Ardennes aimed at the Saar. In the Ardennes itself, that region of eastern Belgium and western Luxembourg through which the German blitzkreig of 1940 had passed, he deployed minimal forces. But he still had no reserve with which to contain any possible enemy penetration.

Under this alignment the British 21st Army Group composed of the First Canadian and Second British armies and commanded by Montgomery was watching the Ruhr. To the south chiefly in Alsace was the U.S. 6th Army Group under General Devers. In the center was Bradley's 12th Army Group: Ninth Army led by Lt. Gen. William H. Simpson in the north on Montgomery's southern flank, Hodges's First Army in the center around and south of Aachen and Patton's Third Army opposite the Saar. Hodges was also responsible for the Ardennes.

Most of this was held by the three infantry divisions of Gen. Troy Middleton's VIII Corps, backed up by an armored division. Middleton's front ran sixty miles from a point southeast of Luxembourg City in the south to the Losheim Gap in the north. Usually three divisions would cover only half that frontage. Middleton was stretched so thin that he had to commit his mechanized reconnaissance force and one combat command of the 9th Armored Division, and was thus almost without reserves. His inexperienced 106th Infantry Division was entrenched on a ridge called the Schnee-Eifel inside the Siegfried Line. North of the Losheim Gap to Monschau for another twenty miles was held by an infantry division of Leonard Gerow's V Corps. Eighty miles defended by only four foot divisions supported by a single armored division! The Ardennes was thus an Achilles heel, and Hitler knew it.

The German plan was for Dietrich's 6th SS Panzer Division to capture Monschau and Bütgenbach in the north and open the way for three infantry divisions to protect his northern flank from counterattack. Skorzeny's "Americans" would then dash ahead of him to seize the Meuse bridges. In the center the key objectives of Manteuffel's Fifth Panzer Army were the important road junctions of St. Vith and Bastogne. He would get to St. Vith by enveloping the Americans inside the Siegfried Line along the Schnee-Eifel. South of the Schnee rival forces held either side of the little River Our marking the boundary between Germany and Luxembourg. Here Manteuffel's special forces of infantry and engineers were to seize river crossings, building bridges over them for the passage of Manteuffel's armor, bound for Houffalize and Bastogne. Once they were taken, the Fifth's armor would strike out for the Meuse. In the south Brandenberger's Seventh Army's chief function was to protect the southern flank of Manteuffel's rampaging armor. It was a good plan, depending on surprise, speed and bad weather; but its most attractive feature was that it was directed against the Ardennes.

The Ardennes itself is rolling wooded terrain, broken by steep and twisting narrow river valleys. Many roads connect the numerous tiny villages, but few of them are good. The good roads run to the southwest, but the Germans would be moving west and northwest, advancing against the grain over narrow roads winding through woods and steep valleys, over ridges and rivers. In the spring of 1940, in good weather and lunging southwest over the good roads, it still took the Germans three days to reach the Meuse. Model was well aware that the campaign that was to be known as the Battle of the Bulge would be a fight for roads and especially for road junctions such as St. Vith, Houffalize and Bastogne. Although he knew that he would never reach Antwerp, he was confident that he would cross the Meuse, chiefly because he did not think the Americans would recover quickly enough from his opening blows.

Model was also certain of surprise. An elaborate deception was designed to lull the Americans in the Ardennes into a feeling of false complacency. Its theme was that all German troop movements were geared to an anticipated enemy offensive against the Siegfried Line. To that end all orders began, "In preparation for the anticipated enemy offensive . . ." After the Sixth SS Panzer Army was reorganized and refitted, it moved, not into position opposite its Ardennes objectives, but onto a plain before Cologne in full view of enemy intelligence operatives. Among the Fifteenth and the Twenty-first Armies and the Fifth Panzer Army names were exchanged and aliases assumed to create both an impression of confusion and the belief that Manteuffel's panzers were headed for Aachen to defend against American armor. But they were scheduled instead for the center of the Ardennes. On the southern flank Brandenberger's Seventh Army remained in place where it had been for some time and where Allied intelligence expected it to remain. Who would think that the Seventh had a new mission?

As late as December 12, four days before the battle was to begin, Bradley's intelligence officer, Brig. Gen. Edwin L. Sibert, observed: "It is now certain that attrition is steadily sapping the strength of German forces on the western front and that the crust of defenses is thinner, more brittle and more vulnerable than it appears on G-2 maps or to troops in the line." Bernard Montgomery's intelligence chief, Brig. E. T. Williams, was equally optimistic: "The enemy is in a bad way . . . his situation is such that he cannot stage a major offensive operation."

On December 15 Montgomery wrote to Eisenhower saying he would "like to hop over to England" on Christmas to see his son. The supreme commander replied that he had no objection and added, "I envy you." But Eisenhower was looking forward to an earlier celebration next day, when his aide Mickey McKeogh would marry a WAC sergeant, the Senate would give him his fifth star —making him Montgomery's "equal" at last—and he would be able to tell Kay Summersby that his friend the prime minister was going to give her the British Empire Medal. For these three—a ring, a star and a medal—there would be a champagne reception.

Although life for the troops in the Ardennes was not quite that good, it was also really not that bad. Except when they were on front-line duty or attacking, soldiers had warm, dry places in which to sleep: houses, cellars, or bunkerlike squad huts built of logs from the area's numerous big fir trees and covered with sandbags. Some were heated by stoves "procured" from the villages. There was almost always hot food, and there were occasional forty-eight-hour passes to regimental or divisional recreation centers in the rear, where a soldier could take a shower, sleep on a clean cot, drink a watered beer or hot coffee served to him by smiling Red Cross girls and even watch a movie or a USO show. They might also find one of those hideous stand-in-line brothels where men were serviced with assembly-line precision, emerging embarrassed and unsatisfied and perhaps also infected by one of a truly astonishing variety of venereal diseases ranging from "the Big Joe" to hard and soft chancres.

The Ardennes front was also something of a combination nursery and nursing home. Old divisions came there to rest after heavy fighting, new ones to be "blooded," that is, exposed to a light treatment of combat. Some of these units were so new that their men arrived in France with their unfired rifles still thick with Cosmoline (storage grease). In the north the 99th Infantry Division, like so many other newly formed formations arriving in Europe in the fall of 1944, had been raided for replacements before boarding ship. It had been fleshed out again with men from AAF ground troops, AA units and those pampered "geniuses" of the ill-considered and ill-starred Army Specialized Training Program (ASTP). These were draftees with high IQs who had been enrolled for technical training in colleges and universities. This was the ultimate in the United States Army's policy of exalting the specialist over the soldier, and it came to a sad end if only because these untrained youths, accustomed to an easy campus life, were the first to be thrown into the breech helter-skelter under pressure of mounting battlefield casualties.

The 106th Infantry Division in the center suffered from replacement levies, losing all told 7,000 soldiers or 60 percent of its enlisted personnel formations. They were replaced by 1,200 men from the ASTP, 1,100 air cadets, 1,500 from other divisions—usually misfits or unwanteds dragooned from prison stockades —and 2,500 from various disbanded small units, usually from service and supply. Many of the 106th's soldiers arrived at the front wearing neckties, and at least one of them was found standing watch rigidly at attention with his rifle at right shoulder arms. It was thought that green divisions such as the 99th and 106th would receive a kind of on-the-job training in the quiet Ardennes. Apart from desultory exchange of shelling and patrols searching for prisoners—and the ever-present fear of the unknown—life in the Ardennes was a boring bunt.

Not so on the German side, where an atmosphere of expectation had excited the soldiery. Although the troops were to be told nothing until the night before the jump-off, they could tell that something big was brewing. Units moving into position marched only by night, taking cover by day in the forests and cooking with smokeless charcoal fires. Patrolling on the existing front line was restricted only to trusted veterans, who would not be tempted to desert by what they saw. Ethnic Germans from the border regions such as Alsace were combed from combat units for fear that they might go over to the enemy with whatever small but potentially dangerous knowledge which, when fitted together, might make a pattern. Artillery fire was kept to normal. Security troops were on the lookout for camouflage violations. Formations moving to the front marched by stages: on the first night twelve miles, the second six and the third two. On the last two nights, while noisy tanks and mechanized artillery drew closer to the front, airplanes flew low over the Ardennes to drown the sound of their approach. On the third night and just before dawn of the fateful 16th, their progress was again covered by the roar of V-1 rockets flying low toward Liège and Antwerp.

Amid such mystery and martial movement the German soldier could not fail to become excited. Many were openly enthusiastic. "There is a general feeling of elation, everyone is cheerful," wrote Pvt. Klaus Ritter. He and his friends were "euphoric—in four weeks they would actually be in Paris." Others were more interested in battlefield booty than glory, eager to get hold of a pair of the "Amies'" good leather boots, or to be compelled to make that marvelously difficult choice between smoking Camels and Chesterfields. The SS troops were exalted. One of them wrote to his sister: "I write during one of the momentous hours: before we attack. . . . Some believe in living but life is not everything! It is enough to know that we attack and will throw the enemy from our homeland. It is a holy task." On the back of his envelope he scribbled: "Ruth! Ruth! Ruth! WE MARCH!"

113. The Battle of the Bulge

BEFORE DAWN OF DECEMBER 16 fourteen German divisions began moving through the misty forests of the Eifel. They were illuminated in the eerie light of giant searchlights bouncing their beams off the clouds above them. Hitler had gotten his bad weather. Overcast skies would ground Allied air for eight days. The sound of this massive movement was again drowned by the roar of the V-1s overhead bound for Liège and Antwerp. At 5:30 A.M. 2,000 German guns commenced a furious bombardment. It was not an especially shattering barrage, more frightening than devastating, especially so to untrained troops unaccustomed to the screeching sound of "the Screaming Meemies," missiles fired by the *Nebelwerfer,* a multiple-barreled, electrically controlled rocket launcher. The Americans, still thinking of the Ardennes as a quiet sector, were mostly puzzled by the shelling—until they saw the Germans in their coal-scuttle helmets emerging from the morning mists.

On the River Our the 28th Infantry Division stretched out on a front of nearly thirty miles was overwhelmed by the attack of five divisions. That night, once more in the light of searchlights, Manteuffel's panzers surged west of the Our with orders to continue the advance through the darkness. On the Schnee-Eifel two regiments of the 106th Division were rapidly outflanked. Although they held their ground, they were surrounded the following morning, opening the way to St. Vith.

In the south the 4th Division held firm and in the north Gerow's V Corps units upset Dietrich's timetable. At Monschau his attack was stopped short, and the lunge toward Bütgenbach made scant progress, even though Dietrich committed his 12th SS Panzer Division to reinforce the slow-moving infantry. South of Bütgenbach, however, the 1st SS Panzer Division found a soft spot: a mechanized cavalry group holding the junction of the VIII and V Corps. These troops, untrained and unequipped for battle, were quickly overrun and the spearheads of the 1st SS penetrated six miles.

Everywhere else the Americans were fighting with bravery and determination, for it was in this great Battle of the Bulge that their military virtues of tenacity, mobility and resilience came to the fore. Even the heavily outnumbered troops on the Schnee-Eifel gave the Germans as good as they got, preventing them from obtaining their first-day objectives.

General Gerow in the north was the first to realize that the enemy assault was far from local but rather "something big." He asked Hodges for permission to call off his attack against the Roer dams and withdraw as soon as possible to the Bütgenbach Ridge. Hodges refused both requests, chiefly because he didn't appreciate the scale of the assault or realize that there had been penetrations to the south. His information was scanty at best. Skorzeny's "Americans" had cut most of the telephone lines that had survived the artillery barrage. Reports reaching Middleton at his headquarters in Bastogne were also conflicting and confused. By nightfall all of Middleton's reserves were committed or about to be. It would be a full twenty-four hours before he got any reinforcements.

At Versailles the champagne reception was over when Bradley arrived in late afternoon. He had come to complain about the replacement situation, which was not keeping abreast of the casualty rate. As he spoke to Eisenhower, word was received that the Germans had launched an attack in the Ardennes that morning and had penetrated at five points. Bradley said it sounded to him like a spoiling attack aimed at drawing Patton's forces away from the Saar. "That's no spoiling attack," Eisenhower said, observing that the Ardennes itself was of no strategic value; therefore the Germans were after something bigger. "I think you'd better send Middleton some help," he said. Studying a map, the supreme commander saw that the Ninth Army's 7th Armored was out of the line and that the Third's 10th Armored was also uncommitted. He suggested giving them to Middleton. Bradley hesitated. He thought that Hodges and Patton would be upset at losing these formations, especially Patton, whose 4th Armored was his favorite unit. Eisenhower lost his temper. "Tell him that Ike is running this damned war!" he snarled. Bradley got Patton on the telephone. As he expected, Patton howled his protests, insisting that the Ardennes was only a spoiling attack. But Bradley overruled him. The 10th Armored went to Middleton's southern flank and the 7th to St. Vith in the north.

As Bradley hung up, Bedell Smith entered the room. "Well, Brad," he said, putting a hand on Bradley's shoulder, "you've been wishing for a counterattack. Now it looks like you've got it."

"A counterattack, yes, but I'll be damned if I wanted one this big."

That night over a fine dinner, Eisenhower, Bradley, Smith and Maj. Gen. Sir Kenneth S. D. Strong, SHAEF's intelligence chief, discussed available reserves. The 82nd and 101st Airborne were both resting and reequipping near Rheims while the 17th Airborne, 11th Armored and 87th Infantry divisions were available in Britain. No one thought of committing the formations in Britain. If needed, the units at Rheims could be rushed to the front. But they were not alerted.

After dinner the four generals opened a bottle of scotch and sat down to play five rubbers of bridge.

Throughout the 17th Dietrich's Sixth SS Panzer Army drove west toward Stavelot, spearheaded by a powerful force called Battlegroup Pieper after its commander, Lt. Col. Joachim Pieper. That night when this force reached Stavelot it was twenty miles inside Belgium and only eight miles from Hodges's First Army headquarters at Spa. But on Pieper's right or northern flank the 2nd and 99th divisions stood firm along the Monschau–Elsenborn line. Even a parachute landing to their rear the night of the 16–17th failed to unsettle them. At Bütgenbach the 12th SS was thwarted once more, this time by a regiment of the 1st Division moving south by night from the Roer region over the road that the German paratroopers were supposed to block. The Americans got to the commanding Bütgenbach ridge before the Germans did and held out during the night until the rest of their division joined them.

At St. Vith the Germans ran into more trouble. A combat command of the 7th Armored Division under Brig. Gen. R. W. Hasbrouck—one of the heroes of the Bulge—arrived at this vital junction in early afternoon, and the rest of the division appeared at dark. This was a remarkable achievement. Twice Hasbrouck had to swing west to avoid Pieper's plunging armor. At a place called Malmédy one of Hasbrouck's units blundered into Battle Group Pieper.

Battery B, 285th Field Artillery Observation Battalion, was not actually a part of 7th Armored. It was a technical unit trained in the sound-and-flash detection of enemy mortars. Its men also did mapping and surveying. When the 7th was ordered south from the Aachen area, so was Battery B, 285th. There were about 140 soldiers in Battery B commanded by its executive officer, Capt. Roger L. Mills. They rode south in thirty-three open trucks. They were armed only with M-1s and carbines and were not trained fighters. As the convoy neared Malmédy, it began to sleet. Those men who had tarpaulins covered themselves with them. Entering Malmédy they found the town's narrow, winding streets jammed with military vehicles, all going in the opposite direction. Townspeople ran alongside Battery B's trucks shouting, *"Boche! Boche!"* and pointing ahead in the direction Battery B was going. Warned that there had been a German breakthrough at Bütgenbach and advised to change direction, Captain Mills demurred. If he lost his position in the march column, it might be difficult to get back in. He continued on, his trucks climbing a hill toward a road junction known as Baugnez. On a road parallel to them was Battle Group Pieper's powerful spearhead: tanks, half-tracks, armored cars, artillery. The Germans spotted the American truck convoy and came charging across an open field, firing as they came.

Tank shells and mortar shells rained down on the Americans. Machine-gun bullets raked them. Trucks exploded or crashed into roadside ditches. The kitchen truck caught fire. Captain Mills and 1st Lt. Virgil Lary vaulted into a ditch. Some Americans tried to fight back with their puny weapons but the Germans came on. Others ran for a nearby wood and were cut down. An American jeep drove up and braked to a screeching halt. Its driver was Colonel Pieper. He was infuriated. All that ammunition wasted on such a helpless target! "Those beautiful trucks, which we needed so badly, all shot up." With some difficulty, Pieper stopped the firing. Now the Americans emerged from the ditches with their hands up. They were herded together while SS soldiers eagerly relieved them of their rings, watches, cigarettes and gloves. The gloves were a particularly welcome prize. Colonel Pieper drove away. About 130 Americans were drawn up in eight rows within the fields with their hands upraised. Their arms became numb with the effort and their hands numb with cold. A German officer later identified as Maj. Werner Poetschke—probably because he was later killed and made a convenient fall guy—ordered two Mark IV tanks to cover the prisoners. Then he ordered them to open fire. Americans began to fall.

"Machen alle kaput!" someone cried. "Kill them all!"

Machine guns on both tanks began to chatter. Americans fell screaming. Others flung themselves to the ground, burying their faces in the mud and squirming to get below the level of the bodies around them. For fifteen minutes the tank machine guns were swiveled back and forth on this huddled mound of bodies. Screams, cries, groans of agony rose from it "almost like a lowing." Then the Germans drove away with a roar. An awful silence descended on that bloody field. No one moved, not even the survivors. Passing German formations amused themselves by firing into the mound. It was too dangerous to risk that fire. But then the silence was broken by German voices and footsteps. The 3rd SS Pioneer Company had arrived to finish off the living. They waited silently beside the bodies for telltale moans or movements. Then they fanned out for the final shots. One German killed five Americans by shots through the heart. "I was sure I killed each man at whom I fired," he said later.

Lieutenant Lary lay still while a man next to him was shot in the head. He was sure he was next. "I lay tensely still, expecting the end. Could he see me breathing? Could I take a kick in the groin without wincing?" But the German moved away. Eventually, the executioners took their departure. Frightened and agonized, almost all of them wounded, dozens of survivors began to whisper among themselves. "Let's go," one man said. "They'll be back." "No, no, wait until dark," another urged. Lieutenant Lary wanted to wait until dark. But Pfc. James Mattera wanted to flee. "Let's go!" he cried, springing to his feet. About twenty men followed, a dozen of them making for a roadside café. "Head for the woods!" Mattera shouted, but the rest ignored him. Mattera disappeared in the wood and would survive. So would Lieutenant Lary and forty-one others—testifying to the poor marksmanship of the German ghouls who tried to kill them all—but the men who sought refuge in the café were massacred. Returning Germans set the café afire, and when the Americans emerged to escape the flames, they were cut down.

Eventually details of the hideous Malmédy Massacre—the most vicious crime visited upon American troops in Europe—were published throughout the American army. In the hearts of those American soldiers embattled in the Ardennes and those coming to their rescue there burned a horrible ache for revenge.

That night General Hasbrouck positioned his combat command in a loose horseshoe around St. Vith. Within it he re-formed the remnants of those units that had withstood the first shock. Hasbrouck transformed St. Vith into a rock upon which the German tide broke and became divided into a northern and southern channel. The northern channel opened by 1st SS became a narrow salient twenty miles long and only five wide. Within it was only one east-west road, a narrow, winding trail following the valley of the Amblève River. Battle Group Pieper followed this road on December 18 but found itself too confined to maneuver. Halted in his drive westward, Pieper swung north, probing for an opening. But each of his thrusts were parried by First Army pickup forces organized from headquarters troops. One of his spearheads reached the edge of the great American fuel dump containing 3 million gallons of gasoline for which the panzers thirsted. But the Germans were sent reeling back by walls of flame after the Americans set up a roadblock of burning gasoline drums. Pieper was left squirming helplessly in his narrow river valley while the U.S. 30th Infantry Division marched out of the Roer sector to strike at his northern flank and recapture Stavelot. Pieper's supply line was cut, and there was no way Dietrich could get to him with reinforcements. At this point the German hope for a rapid thrust to the Meuse was dashed.

Unfortunately, Hodges with his incomplete information was not aware of this. He was also alarmed by reports that Pieper was advancing on his headquarters at Spa. He knew only that there was now a good concentration of American forces at St. Vith but that the situation west and south of Stavelot was unknown. Hodges had planned to put General Gavin's 82nd Airborne at Houffalize between St. Vith and Bastogne. But now, thinking that Pieper had a clear field before him west of Stavelot, he ordered Gavin to Werbomont farther west of him. Gavin did reach Werbomont, where he established a blocking position. But between St. Vith and Bastogne in the vicinity of Houffalize facing the German southern channel there was a wide-open gap.

By the morning of the 18th—the third day—General von Manteuffel's Fifth Panzer Army had opened a hole twelve miles wide south of St. Vith. Into it he ordered Gen. Heinrich von Luttwitz's XLVII Corps composed of three armored and one infantry division. The 116th Panzer made for Houffalize while the 2nd Panzer and Panzer Lehr with an infantry division struck out for Bastogne fifteen miles away. Nothing lay between this force but the remnants of a weak American armored command that the Fifth Panzer had battered the day before. Von Luttwitz urged all speed. An intercepted American message had informed him that the two American airborne divisions had left Rheims, and he presumed that they were heading for Bastogne.

There were no American troops in Bastogne except Middleton's headquarters and stragglers from the 28th Division streaming back from the defeat at the Our. American communications were so bad that Middleton had no instructions to hold the town and had no idea of what reinforcements were on the way. The closest units were the 101st Airborne at Rheims 100 miles to the southwest and Combat Command B (CCB) of the 10th Armored forty miles to the southeast of Luxembourg City. Between these two forces and Luttwitz's spearheads there now began a race for the town that was the key to the defense or capture of the southern Ardennes.

Tenth Armored's CCB got there first, arriving at dusk of the 18th. Immensely relieved, Middleton quickly ordered this force to block the three roads leading into Bastogne from the east and northeast in hopes of holding off the onrushing German armor until the 101st Airborne arrived. Middleton now knew that this formation was on its way. Although he was still out of contact with Hodges, he had managed to obtain from Bradley orders to hold Bastogne.

It was a close call. By ten o'clock that night Luttwitz's Panzers were only five miles from the town. Panzer Lehr commanded by Gen. Fritz Bayerlein was in the lead and had slipped between two of CCB's roadblocks. Bayerlein hoped to gain the prize by a quick thrust under cover of darkness. He might have made it had he not listened to some "friendly" Belgians who told him of a side road. It turned out to be a quagmire, and by dawn of the 19th Panzer Lehr was still two miles short of Bastogne. Worse, the 101st had arrived during the night and joined battle with Panzer Lehr at daybreak.

Throughout the 19th the Germans made no headway, although they did menace Bastogne by capturing Houffalize to the north and Wiltz to the southeast. From Hasbrouck's loose horseshoe at St. Vith to Dietrich in the south, a distance of about twenty-five miles, only Bastogne stood in the path of Manteuffel's panzers. Although the Fifth Panzer Army commander had been surprised by the speed and aggressiveness of the American reaction, he still intended to strike west for the Meuse. Accordingly, he ordered Luttwitz to contain Bastogne with his infantry and send his armor racing west, appealing to Model for reinforcements.

Manteuffel's request put Model in a bind. He was well aware that Hitler wanted Dietrich's Sixth SS Panzer Army to reach the Meuse first and thus humiliate the Wehrmacht. This decision had induced him to put his armored reserves—two SS and three Wehrmacht panzer divisions—behind Dietrich to exploit his anticipated breakthrough. But now it was obvious that Manteuffel had made the most progress and had the best chance, so Model asked *Der Führer* for permission to release the armored reserves to Manteuffel. Hitler refused to transfer the two SS panzers, insisting that Dietrich be given another chance, but with great reluctance he did agree to release the three Wehrmacht formations to Manteuffel. Model was delighted. He was now certain that the Americans had little to check the advance of this powerful armored force through the hole torn open by Manteuffel.

When an army's communications break down, rumor takes charge, followed by its unlovely and unruly offspring, panic. Behind the American lines in the Ardennes, rumors were multiplying. There were reports of German tanks deep in the American rear, German paratroopers dropping everywhere although they only jumped at Monschau, German saboteurs and fifth columnists at work in every town from the Our to the Meuse. Conflicting reports and lack of information also helped to unsettle corps and even higher commanders. Among some troops, always the noncombatants, panic ensued. They abandoned their equipment and took to the roads, thus blocking reinforcements rushing to the front.

But there were other gallant noncombatants who stayed to fight, most especially a party of engineers engaged in operating sawmills. West of Stavelot they blew two bridges in the faces of Battle Group Pieper. Other resolute service troops demolished more bridges or threw up roadblocks. How much they delayed the advance of the 1st SS or slowed Panzer Lehr in the race for Bastogne can never be calculated, but it certainly was a factor. Nevertheless Operation Grief's objective of spreading confusion and alarm behind the American lines had succeeded far beyond Hitler's expectations.

Skorzeny's "Americans" had slipped through the crumbling front on the first two nights, and some of them actually reached the Meuse before they were stopped. The others were busily cutting telephone lines, intercepting liaison officers and dispatch riders, shooting up radio stations and killing military policemen assigned to direct traffic. One of them even took over a traffic booth to direct a reinforcing regiment down the wrong road. Despite this atmosphere of confusion and uncertainty, the Americans were far from broken. Many small units fought with great bravery, usually without any direction from above. Middleton's corps, though battered, was far from destroyed. Bastogne and St. Vith still held out on Manteuffel's flanks. By December 18, the date by which Rundstedt had hoped to reach the Meuse, his timetable was badly off schedule. Dwight Eisenhower now ordered Bradley, Devers, Patton and others to meet him at Verdun on the 19th.

The generals met in a cold, damp squad room in a Verdun barracks on the site of the greatest battle ever fought. Faint heat issued from a single pot stove. Aside from Patton, everyone seemed depressed and embarrassed. Observing this, Eisenhower opened the meeting with the remark: "The present situation is to be regarded as one of opportunity for us and not of disaster. There will be only cheerful faces at this conference table." Patton pounced on the theme. "Hell, let's have the guts to let the sons of bitches go all the way to Paris. Then we'll really cut 'em off and chew 'em up."

Eisenhower replied with a grin that he wasn't *that* optimistic. The line of the Meuse had to be held. But he said he was not thinking defensively. He saw in the German decision to venture out of the Siegfried Line the chance to chew up their panzers. He asked Patton how long it would take him to shift his attack from east into the Saar to north in a counterattack on the German southern flank. "Two days," Patton replied, and the others chuckled at this latest Pattonism. But Eisenhower knew that there was no one on the Allied side who could equal Patton in rapid deployment of troops. He told him to take an extra day to make his attack stronger. Then he would abandon the Saar assault and turn north to relieve Bastogne and hit the German left. Devers was advised to prepare to retreat to shorten his lines and make units available for Patton. Eisenhower also said he would ask Montgomery in the north to organize an attack on the German right. By December 19, then, on the fourth day of the Battle of the Bulge, before the issue was resolved in Bastogne or on the Meuse, Dwight Eisenhower had prepared the counterattack designed to destroy the Germans in the Ardennes.

When Eisenhower returned to Versailles that night, he found that the situation had deteriorated seriously. Although the southern and northern shoulders of the breakthrough appeared to be holding firm, the enemy seemed to be advancing unchecked everywhere else. Bastogne would certainly be encircled, and there were no reserves to fill the twenty-mile gap between the 101st Airborne there and the 82nd at Werbomont. Through that hole a German flood was pouring, heading for the Namur-Dinant-Givet sector of the Meuse. It appeared that the Germans would be on the river in another twenty-four hours. Model's six panzer and panzergrenadier divisions yet uncommitted could then be thrown into the battle and press on to Antwerp.

Except for the divisions withdrawn from the Roer and being withdrawn from the Saar, Bradley had no reserves. SHAEF's only reserves were those divisions back in Britain, and they could not be brought over in time to affect the result. If the Germans crossed the Meuse, the only reserve that could stop them would be the four divisions of the British XXX Corps. This was already being moved by Montgomery into the danger area between the Meuse and Brussels. Perhaps worse was the obviously imminent breakdown of Bradley's command. The American front had been split in two, and there was no communication between Bradley in Luxembourg City and Hodges now near Liège. Bradley had refused to move back to Verdun to control the battle, insisting that it would be dangerous to both military and civilian morale. But Eisenhower realized that the moment was fast approaching when his old friend would simply be unable to oversee the battle from Luxembourg City.

At SHAEF, Bedell Smith proposed to Eisenhower that the only solution to this problem was to place all the forces north of the breakthrough under Montgomery. He was in the proper place with all the reserves and the organization needed to deal with the crisis. Thus, Bradley would have command in the south of the German penetration and Montgomery to the north. Such a step would solve the very serious communications problem. Eisenhower agreed. He asked Smith to tell Bradley. Although Bradley did not disagree, he told Smith the shift would bring discredit on the Americans. "Bedell, it's hard for me to object," Bradley said. "Certainly if Monty's were an American command, I would agree with you entirely." Nevertheless when Eisenhower called Bradley next morning he found him utterly opposed to the change. It was an insult to himself and an affront to the American people. "By, God, Ike," he roared, "I cannot be responsible to the American people if you do this. I resign!" Eisenhower reddened with anger. He took a deep breath, and replied: "Brad, I—not you—am responsible to the American people. Your resignation therefore means absolutely nothing." Bradley protested again, but with no threats, and Eisenhower said calmly: "Well, Brad, those are my orders." Eisenhower next called Montgomery, but the connection was unfortunately poor, and the supreme commander's words were garbled. But Montgomery heard what he wanted to hear—that he was in charge—as well as other things he had not. He told Brooke that Eisenhower had called, and said: "He was very excited, and it was difficult to understand what he was talking about. He roared into the telephone speaking very fast." Such panic was so unlike Dwight Eisenhower, especially when dealing with the troublesome "Monty," that it can only be construed as the fancy of a commander who believed he had been called upon "to save the Americans." Certainly, when Montgomery conferred with Hodges and Simpson that same day, one of his own officers said "the field marshal strode into Hodges's HQ like Christ come to cleanse the temple." Remarkably enough, Hodges and Simpson were eagerly cooperative. Montgomery wanted Hodges to shift his weight westward. Simpson's Ninth Army would take over the entire Roer River front, thus freeing roughly half of Collins's VII Corps for a defensive front west of Stavelot to Marche. To provide Collins with more strength, Montgomery suggested that Hodges provide the forces by shortening his line on the northern shoulder. At this point, Hodges politely but adamantly demurred. For the first time Montgomery found himself up against the United States Army's extremely sensitive sense of honor, and he did not press the proposal.

Unfortunately, Hodges and Simpson did not seem to understand what Montgomery was trying to do, which was to channel the Germans away from the vital point between Malmédy and Marche, where the only good roads ran northwest to the Meuse, and into the network running away from the river to the southwest. He had no fear that the Germans would get across the Meuse because he had troops holding the other side of the river as well as the bridges on this side. Although he would later intimate that he had taken charge of a critical situation, this was not true. It was only Bradley's inability to communicate with his two northern armies that had put Montgomery where he was. This was serious, indeed, but in no way critical. The Americans were far from panicking, but rather angry and out for German blood. Montgomery's patient, methodical approach was not for them, and therefore they were unwilling to withdraw to satisfy his understandable anxiety for straightening out his lines. In the situation then existing, the Americans were wrong—wrong perhaps for the right or honorable reasons but nevertheless wrong. And they would continue to balk at further directions to withdraw.

At this point—Hodges's demurral—a letter arrived in his headquarters from Hasbrouck in St. Vith, informing him that he had not only his own 7th Armored but also a combat command of 9th Armored plus two infantry regiments "in bad shape." Hasbrouck said that the right flank of his horseshoe was "wide open" and that two German divisions were at that moment attacking it. "I can delay them the rest of the day *maybe* but will be cut off tomorrow." In the light of this dire news, Montgomery decided to straighten his line not by pulling back but by hurrying to Hasbrouck's side. He ordered Ridgway's XVIII Airborne Corps to cross the River Salm "to restore the line Malmédy–St. Vith–Houffalize." To do this Ridgway had only Gavin's 82nd Airborne and a weak combat command of 3rd Armored.

Ridgway moved out immediately. That night 82nd Airborne reached the Salm, closing the ring around Battle Group Pieper and making contact with the western edge of the St. Vith horseshoe. Pieper was now forced to escape overland and at night with the 800 men remaining from his battle group but without any of his equipment. In the morning, however, the 82nd Airborne found that its western flank had been turned by a new and powerful German force, and before it could be dealt with St. Vith fell. Hasbrouck, however, in a brilliant tactical maneuver, succeeded in extricating his forces and getting across the Salm. But the Germans had gained a clear route from St. Vith to Houffalize—which fell on December 20—to St. Hubert, west of Bastogne. Bypassed, Bastogne still held out. Manteuffel was now determined either to storm it or choke it to death.

If Manteuffel's panzers had won the race to Bastogne, they would have had an open run to Dinant and Namur on the Meuse. There were then only light

American forces between the Ourthe and the Meuse. But the Americans in Bastogne had reacted so aggressively that it took 2nd Panzer and Panzer Lehr three days to work around the town, while a third panzer—the 116th—also had been stopped and diverted. All this delay had taken much of the momentum out of Manteuffel's drive and had given Hodges time to set up defenses on the Ourthe as far west as Marche. This move compelled Manteuffel to make a wider westward sweep than he intended, which caused him further delay. At last the diminutive German general realized that Bastogne was too important to bypass. He would choke it to death—compel its capitulation—by drawing an iron ring around it.

On the 21st Luttwitz's forward units began the encirclement of the town. But when they began probing for weak spots through a series of piecemeal attacks, they found fierce resistance at every point. They had found an American ring of iron, and Luttwitz next tried to bluff the Americans into surrendering. He sent an English-speaking emissary into the town with a message which said that the only possible way to save the American troops from annihilation was surrender. The note was brought to the officer commanding the battle in Bastogne, Brig. Gen. Anthony C. McAuliffe. It was read by his chief of staff, Lt. Col. Ned D. Moore.

"What does it say, Ned?" McAuliffe asked.

"They want you to surrender."

"Aw, nuts!" McAuliffe exclaimed. Annoyed, he tried to think of a suitably defiant and derisive reply until Lt. Col. Harry Kinnard remarked, "That first crack you made would be hard to beat."

"What was that?"

"Nuts."

Seizing a pen, McAuliffe wrote, "To the German Commander: 'Nuts!' From the American Commander."

When Col. Joseph Harper, commander of the 327th Glider Infantry, brought the reply to the Germans, they were mystified.

"If you don't understand what 'Nuts!' means," Harper snapped, "in plain English it is the same as 'Go to Hell!' And I will tell you something else: If you continue to attack, we will kill every goddam German that tries to break into this city."

The Germans snapped to attention and saluted. "We will kill many Americans," said 1st Lt. Helmuth Henke. "This is war."

"On your way, Bud!" Harper snapped, and then, before he could restrain a remark he always regretted: "And good luck to you."

McAuliffe's reply delighted the heart of the American public and remains enshrined in a high place in United States military history. It also infuriated Manteuffel, who considered Luttwitz's bluff a threat which, without extensive artillery, he could not enforce. To save face he called upon the Luftwaffe to bomb Bastogne.

The hearts of the defenders were lifted by reports that George Patton was already on the way to lift the siege. Although the Germans had been astonished at the speed with which Patton had disengaged in the Saar and wheeled north, they had been warned of his approach by monitoring the extremely careless radio network that controlled American traffic. Roadblocks were put out to receive him. So prepared, they upset Patton's timetable of driving swiftly to the relief of Bastogne and thence on to retake St. Vith. The German blocking forces were strong and because of the surrounding terrain—rugged and heavily wooded—they could not be bypassed. One of Patton's columns came within five miles of Bastogne but was temporarily halted.

McAuliffe was dismayed by Third Army's slow progress. His meager supplies of ammunition were almost gone. By December 23 his artillery was down to ten rounds per gun. But by then the weather had begun to clear. Supplies were air-dropped. Even though this did not replenish ammunition stocks, the airdrop boosted American morale for the heavy attack that came that night.

The Germans pierced the southeastern side of the perimeter in their heaviest assault so far. They took possession of a commanding height, and some tanks even broke into the streets of Bastogne. But each one was destroyed and their supporting infantry repulsed. By morning the breach had been restored.

Manteuffel was desperate. With Model he realized that early capture of Bastogne was essential to the new plan which they had submitted to Hitler. By then German forces were sixty miles inside Belgium, but slowing down. They were also literally running out of gas. The huge American stocks, which would have replenished their own dwindling supplies, had not been captured. Although Hitler had promised enough fuel for 300 miles of normal running, he had actually given them only a third of that amount. This had been consumed by armor and transport crawling through the tortuous side roads of the Ardennes, a necessity forced upon them by the delay in taking St. Vith and the failure to seize Bastogne and Malmédy.

The new plan was simply a revision of the Small Solution. A firm western flank would be established on the east bank of the Meuse followed by a drive north. Having swept the east bank, this force would drive on to Aachen while another force would attack southward out of the Roer sector. This would wipe out the Allied salient at Aachen. Units for the Roer thrust would be provided if Hitler would call off his proposed offensive in Alsace.

At that point, *Der Führer* demurred. He said the Alsace operation would compel Patton to move south again, thus relieving pressure in the southern Ardennes and freeing Model for the northern drive. Although he had not abandoned hope of reaching Antwerp, he knew he could not strike for it until the Liège–Namur sector of the Meuse (actually called Maas below Namur) had been secured. So he accepted the plan, with the insistence that Bastogne must first be captured.

Manteuffel had three full divisions against McAuliffe's forces half that size.

He decided to strike northwest of the town, where defenses had not yet been tested. In fact, this was McAuliffe's strongest sector. Throughout his command that Christmas Eve his men were convinced that the end of their ordeal was at hand. It was now do-or-die. Many of them shook hands for what they thought was the last time. At three o'clock on Christmas morning, the Germans attacked. One penetration was made before dawn, and another hole opened at the first light. Eighteen German tanks roared up to exploit the breakthrough, blundering into the American tank destroyers, which McAuliffe had wisely sited in anticipation of just such an attempt. All the tanks were knocked out and their following infantry destroyed to a man. By midmorning the line was restored. Another assault was launched the next day, but before it could gain momentum, one of Patton's relief columns burst through the enemy's containing ring.

Bastogne had been relieved. One of the most gallant and dramatic stands in the history of the U.S. Army had inflicted on Manteuffel a severe defeat that would have disastrous repercussions on the Meuse.

On Christmas morning the spearheads of the 2nd Panzer Division stood on a ridge above the Meuse, impatiently awaiting the arrival of the fuel and reinforcements they needed to plunge down the Ardennes' western slope to the gleaming river below them. They had been waiting there for thirty-six hours, and they were alone. The rest of the 2nd was occupied in trying to capture Rochefort and Marche. Rochefort, garrisoned by a single gallant American battalion, held out for two nights and a day before falling on Christmas. Now the 2nd's main body was driving west toward Dinant. To the left rear of Dinant, Panzer Lehr was still engaged at Bastogne. On the right rear the 116th Panzer had been checked between Marche and Hotton. None of the three reserve armored divisions Hitler had given Manteuffel would reach Dinant. Still, Manteuffel ordered the 2nd Panzer to press on to Dinant.

By Christmas morning reconnaissance forces had detected a screen of British armor along the Meuse, and there had been reports of clashes with American tanks around Ciney. The Germans did not suspect that these were the advance units of General Lightnin' Joe Collins's 2nd Armored Division rolling down from the north. One American combat command intercepted and turned back reinforcements heading for Rochefort while another encircled the woods around Celles where the German advance guard was entrenched. Without fuel, the Germans had to fight where they stood while the Americans maneuvered freely over frozen ground. By nightfall of December 27, 1944, the 2nd Panzer's remnants were reeling back toward Rochefort, leaving behind them that river which they had seen but never reached.

On December 23 the weather over the Ardennes suddenly lifted, at last giving Allied air power the chance to strike at the roadbound Germans. Having crowded the roads by daylight in the conviction that they would still be protected by gloomy skies, and having burdened themselves with hundreds of empty American trucks they had taken along as plunder, they were concentrated targets, which the Allied airmen had not seen since the days of the Falaise Gap. Between them the Anglo-Americans flew 15,000 sorties. They not only struck the narrow river crossings and crooked defiles around Houffalize and St. Vith but also at roads, railroads and airfields throughout the Rhineland. Model's railheads in the Eifel were knocked out, making his forces dependent on supplies brought over roads from distant depots. Because Hitler for security reasons had ordered that all the big dumps for Autumn Mist should be located east of the Rhine, the interdiction of roads and railways had left him powerless to deliver the tonnage necessary for the maintenance of Model's armies. Certainly the defunct Luftwaffe could not lift it, anymore than it could protect the Wehrmacht from Allied air.

Now it appeared to Eisenhower that he could make good on his earlier prediction: "By rushing out of his fixed defenses, the enemy may have given us the chance to turn his great gamble into his worst defeat." Bradley had already proposed that the three divisions now in SHAEF reserve be given to Patton to strengthen his thrust against the German southern flank while Hodges struck from the north. Montgomery disagreed. He wanted to wait until the Germans had exhausted themselves before attacking. This annoyed Bradley and Patton, both of whom thought that Montgomery was letting the Americans do all the fighting. They wanted him to use the four divisions in his reserve. He was reluctant to do so because he did not want to commit them until the Germans had thrown in their own reserves. Montgomery was also looking beyond the Ardennes. American divisions were arriving constantly in France, but no British. He wanted to keep his XXX Corps intact for the imminent battle for the Rhineland. The dispute was finally resolved by agreeing that if the German attack were not renewed, First Army would begin its counteroffensive on January 3.

Gerd von Rundstedt, meanwhile, had been trying to persuade Hitler to drop the Ardennes offensive before the enemy counterattacked. Hitler refused. He still wanted to reach the Meuse, but only after he had launched an attack in Alsace.

On New Year's Day 1945, eight German divisions struck southward from the Saar. This time the Americans were ready for them. The main German drive west of the Vosges Mountains toward the Saverne Gap was stopped cold before it had gone ten miles, thus preventing any attempt at exploitation by armor. East of the Vosges—on Eisenhower's express orders—Gen. Alexander Patch skillfully withdrew his Seventh Army from its penetration into the Siegfried Line in the face of the advancing Germans. A jubilant Hitler took this for retreat—as Eisenhower intended—and ordered in his reserves. They blundered into a re-formed American front at the Maginot Line and were repulsed. An attack from the Colmar Pocket also failed, even though Heinrich Himmler, still thirsting for military glory, waved his baton over it. The grim gray little executioner found how difficult it could be to execute people who also carried weapons.

At one point Eisenhower for strategic reasons had thought of abandoning Strasbourg, a city sacred to French memory. De Gaulle, however, protested vehemently, insisting that to do so would provoke a political crisis in France. So

Eisenhower ordered Devers to hold Strasbourg at all costs, and he did—at so little cost that it was not necessary to divert any divisions to him. In this way Hitler's Alsatian adventure failed at the loss of valuable forces he might better have employed elsewhere.

In the Ardennes, meanwhile, Patton was driving deeper and deeper into the German left flank, so much so that Hitler was forced once again to dip into his dwindling reserves. Three infantry divisions were rushed west from Germany while four armored divisions were transferred from Dietrich to Manteuffel, who was ordered to capture Bastogne and thus harden the southern flank.

Perhaps remembering the Japanese success at Pearl Harbor on a Sunday morning when half the Americans were bedridden with hangovers and the other half on their knees in church, Hitler decided to risk what remained of the Luftwaffe in an early New Year's Day raid on Allied airfields. This would prevent enemy fighter-bombers from interfering in Manteuffel's attack on Bastogne.

Over the Netherlands that morning the pilot of an artillery observation plane yelled incredulously into his radio: "At least 200 Messerschmitts flying low on a course 320 degrees!" But what he saw was only the vanguard of formations of 1,035 Focke-Wolfe bombers and ME-109 fighters coming to strike twenty-seven Allied airfields, where row after row of fighter-bombers stood unprotected. There was no warning—not even from Ultra—of what the Allies later called the Hangover Raid. The Germans destroyed 156 planes, including Montgomery's personal C-47. Heavy as these losses were, they could not compare to the Luftwaffe's loss of more than 300 aircraft with their irreplaceable pilots and crewmen. Most Allied losses were on the ground, with no loss of personnel. Worse for Hitler, he had squandered the Luftwaffe's remaining strength in raids that were unneeded: When Manteuffel began attacking January 3, bad weather grounded all aircraft.

Manteuffel's heaviest and best-coordinated attacks were on January 3–4, 1945. They triggered the fiercest fighting of the entire Ardennes campaign. Denied air support, Patton's Americans fought with exceptional bravery and skill, and even the untried divisions he had to commit west of the town surprised him by their tenacity. Artillery was used so effectively against the Germans that many attacks were broken up before they could get started. On the 5th German momentum weakened, and two days later stopped altogether when Montgomery launched his counteroffensive from the north.

How to conduct the Allied counteroffensive in the Ardennes provoked another Anglo-American dispute. Patton wanted to trap all the German forces in the Ardennes. While he assumed the defensive in Bastogne, he would launch Manton Eddy's XII Corps on a drive northeastward across the Sûre and Our rivers to Bitburg and Prum inside Germany. There they would be joined by the First Army striking southeastward from Elsenborn Ridge. Model would be caught and caught easily, because, as Patton explained: "If you get a monkey in the jungle hanging by his tail, it is easier to get him by cutting his tail than kicking his face."

Hodges approved Patton's plan "in principle" but voiced doubts about moving masses of armor over the road network southeast of Elsenborn. Here, of course, Model might have given him a resounding second. But Lightning Joe Collins thought he could solve that problem and still cut the base of the German salient: move his VII Corps behind Malmédy and drive southeast on St. Vith while Patton moved north up Skyline Drive on the Schnee-Eifel. When Montgomery came to Collins's headquarters, he said it would be impossible to supply an entire corps over a single road. Collins replied: "Well, Monty, maybe the British can't, but we can."

Unfortunately, now that the Germans had effectively lost the Battle of the Bulge, the supreme commander turned conservative again. He did not try to knock the feet from under an enemy inside a bulge sixty miles deep and forty miles wide at its base but rather approved Montgomery's typically cautious plan to strike him at the waist. This would hurt him and drive him from his bulge, but it would not trap him. Nevertheless, that was the objective of the Allied counteroffensive, which began on January 7.

Using the overwhelmingly American forces at his disposal, Montgomery attacked from the west with the British XXX Corps and the U.S. VII, XVIII Airborne and V corps in that order right to left. Driving up from the south came Patton with his VIII, II and XII corps in that order left to right. Once again foul weather deprived the Allies of their air support and gave the Germans the chance to exploit the winter-fighting skills they had learned on the Eastern front. They entrenched themselves strongly in the bare timbered ridges, their positions camouflaged by a thick carpet of snow. Better-equipped and better-trained for fighting in the bitter cold, they made their enemies pay dearly for every yard. Allied riflemen floundered in the deep drifts and tanks skidded off the icy roads into ditches. Many blew up on German mines cleverly laid loose in the snow. It took the Americans driving on Houffalize five days to cover five miles. They were helped by a new artillery shell designed to explode in air bursts triggered by radar. This was enough to persuade Model to demand—not request—permission to withdraw from the western Ardennes. On January 9, Hitler consented, realizing that he was in danger of losing his last remaining armor on the Western front. With that the great Battle of the Bulge ended in an Allied victory.

Inevitably, the Battle of the Bulge was succeeded by what might be called the Battle of the Bilge. Charges and countercharges were exchanged between Bradley and Montgomery, although it must be observed that Bradley conducted himself with infinitely more dignity. As usual, Eisenhower said nothing, even though he was being violently and unjustly criticized in the chauvinistic British press. The supreme commander was so rudely castigated that Winston Churchill found it necessary to write Franklin Roosevelt to state that "His Majesty's

Government have complete confidence in General Eisenhower and feel acutely any attacks made on him."

Much of this witch's brew was stirred up by Bernard Law Montgomery, affecting to come to Eisenhower's side and sing the praises of the American soldier. At a press conference January 7 he did state that he was "perturbed" about what was being said of his chief and declare that the GI was "basically responsible for Rundstedt not doing what he wanted to do." Montgomery would "never want to fight alongside better soldiers." With such remarks, all would have been well, except that Montgomery added his own analysis.

Rundstedt, he said, had driven "a deep wedge into the center of the United States First Army and the split might have become awkward" but "As soon as *I* saw what was happening *I* took certain steps myself to ensure that if the Germans got to the Meuse they would certainly not get over that river." *He* took "precautions," *he* was "thinking ahead." Yet, "the situation began to deteriorate." Still, "the whole Allied team rallied to meet the danger, national considerations were thrown overboard; General Eisenhower placed me in command of the whole Northern Front." (No ameliorating explanation of why.)

Next: "*I* employed the whole available power of the British Group of Armies," bringing it "into play very gradually," so as not to disrupt American communications. "Finally, it was put into battle with a bang and today British divisions are fighting hard on the right flank of the United States First Army." They were alongside "American forces who have suffered a hard blow. This is a fine Allied picture." (Emphasis added.)

So much of this is so palpably untrue that it must be regarded as being the lowest blow struck in the Battle of the Bilge. Because he needed to husband his strength for the drive into Germany, Montgomery had moved British troops into reserve positions, where they would be spared casualties. There were no British "divisions" fighting hard on the First Army flank but rather a brigade, two battalions and one division, assigned to move the Germans back from the tip of their penetration—as if they were not already backpedaling—but to move cautiously to forfend undue casualties. This was far from being "the whole available power of the British Group of Armies" and certainly not a commitment "with a bang."

With typical self-adulation masquerading as modest understatement, Montgomery had found the battle "most interesting . . . possibly one of the most interesting and tricky" he had ever "handled." He had decided first "to head off the enemy from the tender spots and vital places," and then "rope him in and make quite certain that he could not get to the places he wanted, *and also* that he was slowly but surely removed away from those places."

What, actually, did Montgomery do?

1. He wanted to withdraw from Elsenborn Ridge even as the battle there was almost won, until Hodges objected.

2. He wanted to withdraw also from St. Vith, giving the Germans early use

of a vital road junction, until Hodges insisted that that decision was up to Hasbrouck—the man on the spot.

3. He ordered the 82nd Airborne to pull back from the Salm River to the Trois–Manhay line, but Ridgway had already directed Gavin to prepare for such a withdrawal.

4. He ordered abandoning the Manhay crossroads, so that Hodges, realizing that this gave the Germans another route to the Ourthe, had to order Manhay retaken.

5. He ordered Collins to assemble for attack, but when Collins's units became involved in the defensive battle, authorized withdrawal. Instead, Collins on his own initiative attacked and stopped the Germans short of the Meuse.

6. In reducing the German salient, Montgomery moved so slowly—if indeed "surely"—that the Germans were able to mount a fierce fresh attack on Bastogne unhindered by First Army.

All these points, made by the historian Charles B. McDonald, who carries the high credentials of having fought in the Bulge as a twenty-two-year-old captain in the 2nd Infantry Division, clearly indicate that Montgomery's chief contribution to the victory was to have taken charge in the north when the breakdown in American communications had made it impossible for Omar Bradley, far to the south in Luxembourg City, to control his northern First and Ninth Armies. But this decision was made by Dwight Eisenhower. Montgomery executed it, indeed, and he had also anticipated it by moving his XXX Corps behind the Meuse.

It would have been a supernatural being indeed who would have remained calm under such an ill-considered shower of slings and arrows, and Omar Bradley was merely human. He immediately telephoned Eisenhower to protest Montgomery's remarks and also SHAEF's failure to state that the transfer of command had been temporary. Even though he was sure that Eisenhower would not make Montgomery overall ground commander again, he said, "After what has happened, I cannot serve under Montgomery." If Montgomery was to be overall commander, Eisenhower "must send me home." Patton, he said, felt the same way. Not until two weeks later did the Battle of the Bilge come to an end, when Winston Churchill rose in the Commons to state unequivocally that the Bulge was almost exclusively an American battle. "The Americans have engaged thirty or forty men for every one we have engaged and they have lost sixty or eighty men for every one of us." The Bulge was "the greatest American battle of the war and will, I believe, be regarded as an ever-famous American victory."

Eisenhower helped to calm the tempest when he remarked, with characteristic magnanimity, that the decision to take a calculated risk of spreading Ardennes defenses thin had been his. "If giving him [the enemy] that chance is to be condemned by historians, their condemnation should be directed at me." Nevertheless, it was Eisenhower's, perceptions and decisions that won the Battle of the Bulge, and there was no other time when he rose to such greatness and showed so clearly the qualities of a true supreme commander.

But the real hero of the Bulge was GI Joe, *Combat* GI Joe. Whenever in the Ardennes the American soldier met Jerry the Kraut on anything like equal terms, he overcame him. The Americans fought when fragmented and leaderless, often on their own with no promise of help—high soldierly virtues—and in bitter cold and darkness while looking at death and defeat. The Ardennes was GI Joe's finest hour.

PART EIGHT

1945

114. Preparing to Drop the Atom Bomb

BY THE FALL OF 1944, the scientists of Manhattan Project were absolutely confident that the atomic bomb could be produced by the summer of 1945. Thus, long before its first test on a barren stretch of semidesert fifty miles from Alamogordo, New Mexico, preparations had to be made for using it against Japan.

This required the training of special crews to carry it to Japan, making modified models of the B-29 designed for greater speed and safety and preparation of an advance base on Tinian, then the closest island to Nippon.

In the fall of 1944 a highly secret air base was established at Wendover, Utah. It was for the 509th Composite Group, 313th Wing, 21st Bombing Command of the Twentieth Air Force. The 509th was commanded by the veteran Col. Paul Tibbets, generally regarded as the AAF's most outstanding pilot and the flier who had once flown for Mark Clark and Dwight Eisenhower. Under Tibbets were assembled seventy-five of the most daring fliers in the AAF, together with an equal number of distinguished NCOs and ordinary airmen. They made up fifteen crews of nine men each, four of whom were officers. In addition there was an enormous ground crew of 1,700 men skilled in servicing of Superforts. All of these airmen had been assembled from far-flung bases in the States and the various battlefronts.

Only Tibbets knew what the 509th's mission was. All of the others had been asked to volunteer for an outfit that was "going to do something different." Throughout the winter of 1944–45 and the spring of 1945, these men trained incessantly on the bleak Utah desert. Secrecy was so complete that even the top-ranking officers and scientists of the Atomic Bomb Project were unaware of their existence. Inasmuch as the effectiveness of the bomb was not yet known, it had been decided not to guide it to its target by radar but to bomb visually. It also had to be dropped on the exact center. This meant that the bombardiers had to be chosen for their accuracy. An exact model of the atomic bomb was dropped over selected desert targets. It had the same weight and shape as the eventual A-bomb but was packed with ordinary explosive. The perfectionistic Colonel Tibbets trained his crews to take off and arrive at their targets at the exact scheduled minute. He had no patience with those who missed the deadline.

On Tinian construction was begun on the secret atomic bomb base there. It was actually an island within an island. Its inhabitants were completely isolated from the world around them. There were fewer than 2,000 of them, of whom 1,850 were aviation personnel. The others included twenty-seven civilian scientists, eleven naval officers, nine army officers and twenty-one enlisted men, of whom all but three were scientists. They worked in an even more isolated part of the island, within a small cluster of Quonset huts containing testing laboratories. One building was air-conditioned, and here a staff directed by Dr. Norman F. Ramsey of Columbia University would one day assemble the atomic bomb and prepare it for delivery.

When Colonel Tibbets and the 509th Group arrived at this secret base on Tinian in the spring of 1945, they were subjected to considerable needling from other units who were puzzled by their training tactics and their seeming detachment from the war. Every day the beautiful silvery Superfortresses would take off in huge formations for missions against Japan, many failing to return, others coming back crippled with wounded and dead crewmen. But every day all the 509th's fliers did was to form tiny, three-plane formations, drop a single missile somewhere in enemy territory and then return. Even the 509th's airmen were unaware that the purpose of their practice runs with these comparatively harmless models of the atomic bomb was to condition the Japanese home islands to the sight of three-plane formations dropping bombs that did little damage. Surprisingly, the Japanese saw nothing suspicious in these unusual tactics. But the other American airmen on Tinian did. Some unknown satirist among them expressed his comrades derision in verse entitled "Nobody Knows."

> Into the air the secret rose,
> Where they're going nobody knows.
> Tomorrow they'll return again,
> But we'll never know where they've been.
> Don't ask us about results or such,
> Unless you want to get into Dutch.
> But take it from one who knows the score—
> The 509th is winning the war.
>
> When the other Groups are ready to go,
> There's a rundown on the whole damned show.
> And when Halsey's Third shells Nippon shore,
> We hear about it the day before.
> Where MacArthur and Doolittle give out in advance,
> With the 509th we haven't a chance.
> We should've been home for a month or more—
> The 509th is winning the war.

When Tokyo Rose took to poking fun at the 509th, Colonel Tibbets was not exactly upset, knowing full well that the final and dreadful reply would be his to make—but his still-mystified airmen felt a little disenchanted with this mission that was "something different."

115. The Battle for Italy

BECAUSE OF FIELD MARSHAL Albert Kesselring's skillful defense of Italy, Hitler had changed his mind about defending only the northern half of the peninsula and chose instead to reinforce Kesselring for a defensive stand in the south. Kesselring's plan was to slow down and wear out the Allies by a series of delaying actions throughout the summer, after which he would withdraw to his strong Gothic Line for the winter. About eighty miles north of Rome there was a natural line of defense near Lake Trasimeno, where Hannibal had trapped the Romans in 217 B.C. It offered a good position for the first stand, and German engineers improved it considerably with their demolitions.

On June 5, 1944, the day after the Americans entered Rome, the Allied advance began. After two weeks of crosshatch fighting, that is, battling against the grain in difficult mountainous terrain laced by numerous swift rivers, the Allies were brought to a standstill before Trasimeno. Kesselring had ably stabilized what had appeared to be a potentially dangerous situation. He was greatly assisted by the fact that Field Marshal Sir Harold Alexander commanding in Italy had had to relinquish seven of his divisions and the larger part of his aerial support for use in France. During the two months succeeding the stalemate before Trasimeno, Alexander's units fought a frustrating and disappointing war. Battles were a series of isolated corps actions between the Germans—with their Italian Fascist troops raised by Mussolini—and the Allies. German policy was to hold a position until it became clear that the enemy was massing for an all-out assault, and then fall back to the next obstacle line. Thus, after Alexander's units got past Trasimeno, they were checked at the Arezzo Line in the beginning of July and, after they pushed through there, stopped at the Arno Line two weeks later. This position ran from Pisa on the west coast through Florence to the Adriatic. Here the Allies were held in check until a massive autumn offensive pierced the Arno Line north of Florence, whereupon Kesselring ordered most of his formations to withdraw into the Gothic Line farther north. Mark Clark's U.S. Fifth Army on the left tried to burst the Gothic, but found itself bogged down in fierce mountain warfare where the advance measured a mile a day. On October 27 Clark abandoned the offensive, and the Allies prepared to mount a final assault in the spring of 1945.

Meanwhile, the supreme commander, Mediterranean, Field Marshal Sir Henry Maitland Wilson, was transferred to Washington to be replaced by Alexander, while command of the Fifteenth Army Group fell to Mark Clark.

In March of 1945, Field Marshal Kesselring was recalled to the Western Front, replacing Rundstedt. His place in Italy was taken by General S. von

Vietinghoff. In Army Group C, Vietinghoff had some 491,000 Germans and 108,000 Italians, while Clark's Fifteenth Army Group had 536,000 soldiers, mostly American, along with the British and their Commonwealth troops, Poles and French, plus 70,000 Italians. Although troop strength appeared about even, the Allies were 2 to 1 in artillery and over 3 to 1 in armored vehicles. Clark was also assisted by the presence of some 60,000 partisans, and possessed overwhelming aerial superiority. Allied strategic bombing—especially of the fuel plants— had had a paralyzing effect on German troop movement. Even if Hitler had so ordered it, they could not possibly have been moved out of Italy to other theaters. Nor could Vietinghoff's fuel-starved motorized formations move quickly to close gaps, as they had done under Kesselring, or carry out fast-moving delaying actions. Hitler, by then half demented in his bunker beneath the Reich Chancellery, was even less inclined to permit strategic withdrawals.

During the interval of the winter lull, Clark's troops had undergone a great change in spirit and outlook. The relatively battle-free months below the Gothic Line had improved their morale, and they could feel that the end of fighting was imminent. They also had seen the arrival of an abundance of new weapons: improved and heavier-gunned Sherman and Churchill tanks, "Kangaroo" armored troop carriers, flamethrowing tanks and tank-dozers, amtracks and new bridging equipment, together with enormous supplies of ammunition. In contrast the Axis troops were downhearted, certain at the worst of death or wounds, at best imprisonment. To make the assault on the Gothic, Clark had the British Eighth Army under General R. L. McCreery on the right or Adriatic flank and the U.S. Fifth Army commanded by General Lucian K. Truscott on the left or Mediterranean side.

On the right, while a flanking maneuver against Lake Comacchio on the coast had drawn Vietinghoff's attention to that sector, his front was subjected to a massive aerial and artillery bombardment. On April 9 some 800 heavy bombers and 1,000 medium or fighter-bombers dropped a series of five concentrations, each of forty-three minutes duration. Because there was an interval of ten minutes between each raid, designed to draw the enemy aboveground, the attacks were called "false alarm" bombardments. At first the Germans were too stunned to resist the attacking Allied infantry, or to repel the terrifying flamethrowing tanks. Gradually, however, resistance stiffened. By the 18th the British overran the formidable Argenta Gap near the coast and the Poles in fierce fighting pushed back the elite German 1st Parachute Division.

Bad weather on the left delayed the attack of Truscott's Fifth Army until April 14, also depriving the Americans of close air support. Progress over two mountain ranges between them and Bologna was slow, until a record 2,300 tons of bombs were dropped on the 15th. Two days later the U.S. 10th Mountain Division achieved a breakthrough, debouching on the plains before Bologna. Racing north they made for the vital Route 9, the celebrated Via Emilia. Vietinghoff's front was collapsing. Three Allied armored divisions in two sweeping moves had cut off and surrounded most of his forces. The time to talk surrender had come.

Surrender negotiations between Gen. Karl Wolff, SS chief in Italy, and Allen Dulles of the U.S. Office of Strategic Services (OSS) had begun as early as February. Wolff hoped to avoid further senseless destruction and death in Italy, and also wished to repel communist forces there by joining the Allies. Dulles shared these motives. Wolff had great power because of his control of the SS and those regions in Mussolini's Salo Republic which Hitler hoped to turn into an Alpine redoubt.

The talks were complicated on the German side by Vietinghoff's replacement of Kesselring—who sympathized with Wolff—and on the Allied side by Soviet demands to participate in them. By the end of March, however, the negotiations had made good progress—until Himmler learned of them in early April and ordered Wolff to cease and desist. But then Vietinghoff and Wolff conferred on April 23 and decided to ignore Berlin's orders to continue to fight and to negotiate a surrender. Wolff also ordered his SS troops not to resist the Italian partisans, unaware as he was that most of them fighting the Fascists in the civil war raging inside the Salo Republic were communists.

116. The Murder of Mussolini

CLARA PETACCI WAS URGED to flee to Spain or Portugal. "Never!" she replied fiercely. "I loved Benito when times were good. I shall love him even more now that times are bad." When *Il Duce* left Lake Garda on April 18 and came to Milan, he thought he had left Clara in a safe place. But she followed him to Milan, where she arrived in tears. She stayed with him in the Palazzo Monforte, where, with his Fascist lieutenants, Mussolini planned a mass address to rally the Milanese behind him. But on April 21 he learned that Mark Clark's Americans had taken Bologna and were moving on Milan. Next he was informed that he could negotiate nothing with either the new Italian government or the Allies. He must accept Unconditional Surrender. Mussolini was enraged and then infuriated when he was told that General Wolff was not only preparing to surrender to Clark but promising to disarm his Fascist allies. In his old voice of thunder he shouted: "For once we can say Germany has stabbed Italy in the back! They have always treated us like slaves. And at the end they betrayed *me!*"

Il Duce conceived a new, grandiose plan. He would raise a force of 300,000 men and retreat with them to Val Tellina, there to make a last stand. He expected to hold out six months while thrilling the world with radio messages of indomitable defiance. Mussolini had already sent emissaries to Ravenna to disinter the bones of Dante and bring them to Val Tellina as the symbol of his resistance. When he broached his plan to Ildefonso Cardinal Schuster, archbishop of Milan, the devout little Benedictine shook his head. He did not think *Il Duce* could raise even 3,000 men. "More like three hundred, Mussolini." But Cardinal Schuster was unable to dissuade *Il Duce.* Nor could his lieutenants and ministers, even when it was pointed out to him that his path to Val Tellina would be through country dominated by communists who had sworn to kill him. His son Vittorio urged him to stay in Milan, where he could hold out against the communists until the Americans arrived. "And be put in a pillory in the Tower of London?" his father shouted in a rage. "Or in a cage like a wild animal in Madison Square Garden?"

Benito Mussolini did leave Milan for Val Tellina, but not in hopes of raising 300,000 blackshirts, or even 3,000. Nor 300, either: There were twelve faithful Fascists with him when he departed in his Alfa-Romeo, holding a machine-pistol he did not know how to use. He had hoped to elude his SS guards, who had seldom left him out of their sight during his 600-day rule of the collapsed Salo Republic. But they took control of his motorcade. *Il Duce* realized with a sinking heart that they were taking him to Germany, him and Claretta, for she had joined him once again over his objections. His first stop would be the German embassy at Merano.

A communist roadblock halted the German convoy near the village of Musso. After threats were exchanged, the communists agreed to allow the Germans to proceed to their homeland, but all Italians must stay behind. The Germans accepted because they had already put Mussolini in a German soldier's uniform and Clara in men's overalls. The convoy moved on to the village of Dongo. There *Il Duce* in his ridiculously long soldier's coat and coal-scuttle helmet was recognized by a sailor who had seen him face to face. Mussolini might disguise his body, but he could not conceal those staring eyes. He and Clara were taken prisoner, and spirited away to a peasant farmhouse in Moltrasio just north of Lake Como. Mussolini still wore a gray-green soldier's jacket, but Clara had changed to a brown corduroy suit and high heels. A mink coat hung carelessly from her shoulders. Now it was the communists who feared to lose their prisoner to Fascists or those partisans who hated both the Red and the Black. It was decided to disguise *Il Duce* as a "wounded" partisan. Bandages were wound around his head until only three slits remained for his eyes and nose.

In pouring rain the convoy moved into Moltrasio. Across Lake Como rockets rose into the night sky. Machine-gun fire could be heard. Mussolini's communist captors were concerned to learn that the U.S. 1st Armored Division was approaching. They knew that the Americans wanted Mussolini as much as they did. Once again, he was hidden—this time in a tiny farmhouse. For the first time since their affair began, Benito and Clara spent an entire night in bed together. Late on the following day Mussolini had more visitors. One of them was Walter Audisio, a swaggering thirty-six-year-old colonel of communist partisans. During the Spanish Civil War he had fought with the International Brigade and been known as Colonel Valerio. With him was Aldo Lampredi, a bespectacled, middle-aged carpenter. Audisio said later that he sought to allay *Il Duce*'s suspicions by saying, "I have come to liberate you," and that Mussolini replied: "I will give you an empire." But Lampredi said no such dramatic exchange took place. "Mussolini knew perfectly well his time had come."

Mussolini and Clara were put into a Fiat. Clara held her personal belongings in a scarf. Her other hand was in Mussolini's. The car moved slowly with Lampredi walking in front of it and Audisio standing on the running board holding his machine pistol. Outside the high iron gates of the Villa Belmonte, Audisio ordered the driver to stop. He told *Il Duce* and Clara to get out of the car. Audisio pronounced the death sentence: "By order of the high command of the Volunteer Freedom Corps, I have been charged to render justice to the Italian people." Claretta screamed. "You can't kill us like that! You can't do that!"

"Move aside, or we'll kill you first!" Audisio snarled.

Sweat was pouring down Audisio's face when he pulled the trigger. But the gun wouldn't fire. He tore his revolver from his holster. But this too misfired. Audisio took a machine pistol from one of his men and lifted it. Mussolini unbuttoned his gray-green jacket. "Shoot me in the chest," he said calmly. Audisio fired, just as Clara seized the gun barrel. The first shot entered her heart. Then the communist executioner triggered a burst of nine bullets into Benito Mussolini and killed him.

The corpses were taken to Milan—the city in which Mussolini had become famous and from which he had launched the March on Rome—and thrown onto the pavement of the Piazzale Loreto. *Il Duce* lay with his head on Clara's white blouse. A huge throng gathered around them. Soon the crowd became a howling, hissing, jeering, spitting, kicking mob. They began to dance and caper around the bodies. A woman rushed up with a pistol, firing it into *Il Duce*'s carcass. "Five shots!" she screamed. "Five shots for my five murdered sons!" Other bereaved mothers rushed at the body of the man who had once made women hysterical when he bathed in public. Lifting their skirts they squatted over him to urinate on his face. At last only the intervention of Cardinal Schuster prevented this maniacal mob from tearing the bodies to pieces. Mussolini and Clara were hoisted into the air by their heels. Like the kindly English soldier who held up a cross for the eyes of Joan of Arc at her burning stake, a decent partisan fastened Clara's skirt to her legs. Only a glimpse of her light blue lingerie was visible at the hem. A woman gazed up at her and murmured:

"Imagine—all that, and not even a run in her stockings."

117. Hitler's Predicament: The Soviet 1945 Offensive

THE CONSEQUENCES OF HITLER'S costly gamble in the Ardennes were more immediately apparent in the East than in the West, for it was the Soviets who were first to benefit from *Der Führer*'s reckless expenditure of his mobile reserves.

During the waning days of 1944 the Red Army had lain quiescent on a vast front from the Baltic to the Carpathians. Zhukov could not continue his advance through Poland until he had repaired and widened the wrecked railroads of the Ukraine and White Russia, and because his master was still far more interested in Balkan fruit than in Berlin plunder. By Christmas Eve 1944, with the Germans only four miles from the Meuse, Stalin had succeeded in exploiting the Romanian defection to the extent of putting communists in power in Bucharest and Sofia, while in Hungary he made no move to take the capital of Budapest, merely encircling it and installing Red rule in the conquered sectors. Thus the U.S.S.R. now menaced Hungarian bauxite, so necessary for the aluminum which was the basis of aircraft industry, and Hungarian oil, Hitler's chief supply after loss of the Ploesti airfields and American demolition of his homeland fuel plants.

Guderian, now army chief of staff, pleaded again and again with Hitler to call off the Ardennes offensive and send the panzer divisions engaged there to the East. He argued that it was not possible to reach Antwerp, but that the Ardennes offensive had already done great service by disrupting the Allied timetable, the most it could actually do. Guderian wanted strong mobile reserves assembled in Poland before the Soviets resumed their offensive. He insisted that Allied air had paralyzed the Ruhr and that the center of German industrial production was now in Upper Silesia. If it should be conquered, Germany would fall within a few weeks. "All of this was of no avail," Guderian wrote. Hitler not only persisted in the Meuse adventure but also moved a panzer corps from Warsaw to Hungary. To mix metaphors, by rolling snake eyes on the Meuse and chasing a wild goose on the Danube, he in effect measured the Wehrmacht for a coffin on the Vistula.

His attitude was not entirely fatuous. Even though his empire had shrunk drastically he could rightfully claim that he still held an area "which is essentially larger than Germany has ever been, and that there is at our disposal an armed force which even today is unquestionably the most powerful on earth." There was some truth in this last remark. Hitler had 260 divisions in the field, twice as many as he had had in 1940. However, they were so widely dispersed that it was not possible to concentrate either in West or East a force as formidable as the one that conquered France and invaded the Soviet Union. Such dangerous dispersal was a direct result of Hitler's conqueror complex. Always eager to enter history greater than Alexander, the Caesars or Napoleon, he could not abide relinquishing an inch of the soil he had conquered. A strategic withdrawal was anathema to him, even if it was the soul of military wisdom—as it was—and would by shortening his line thicken his defenses and leave the enemy off balance. To this in early 1945 was added the conviction that he might weary the western Allies, or at least compel them to relax their demand for Unconditional Surrender, by holding them at the Siegfried Line until he could surprise them with his "new weapons." These were jet aircraft already under production and the electrosubmarine which, equipped with the *Schnorkel* breathing device, freed of dependence on fuel oil, could make wide-ranging sorties while remaining submerged indefinitely and moving at fifteen knots, a speed faster than any merchantmen or their escorts. It was for this reason that he clung to Hungary for bauxite for the jets and to Denmark for bases for the new U-boats.

This was also the reason for *Der Führer*'s growing dependence on the judgment of Grand Adm. Karl Doenitz. Doenitz had been a U-boat commander in the First World War, and in the Second as chief of the Submarine Command had devised the dreaded wolf pack tactic whereby his U-boats attacked Allied shipping in devastating groups. Tall, stern and shrewd, Doenitz was an ardent admirer of Adolf Hitler. He was not a sycophantic toady like Keitel, but an officer of his own convictions, who would not hesitate to disagree with his Führer. On becoming commander in chief of the navy in January 1943, he had not hesitated to challenge Hitler on the dispute that had cost Grand Adm. Erich Raeder his job: Hitler's intention to scrap the High Seas Fleet. But Doenitz's opposition was not of the querulous, abrasive quality so often exhibited by Hitler's generals, but rather a combination of patience and tact that eventually changed *Der Führer*'s mind. Because of this and his promise to Hitler of recovering the initiative in the West through the revolutionary new submarines, Doenitz was granted a much wider sphere of independence than any of the generals possessed. In a word, Hitler listened to his admiral alone, and not at all to his generals.

When Guderian urged him to yield the eastern Baltic to hold the shortest possible line between the Bay of Danzig and the Carpathians, Doenitz argued that the western Baltic was too close to Allied air and mining operations and that to surrender the eastern Baltic would be to "paralyze naval warfare and especially U-boat operations." Hitler "agreed entirely." Thus some forty German divisions —nearly one third of the forces opposing the Red Army—continued their useless watch in the eastern Baltic, contributing nothing to the defense of the Reich just to sustain Doenitz's naval prejudice and Hitler's vainglorious delusions.

As the historian Chester Wilmot has so aptly observed:

The history of the Second World War affords no more striking example of the interplay of naval, air and land power, or of the interrelationship of the Eastern and Western Fronts or, for that matter, of the grotesque miscalculations and wild hopes that governed Hitler's strategy. Because the German Air Force was unable to protect the U-boat bases and training waters in the Western Baltic, the German Army was obliged to hold the Eastern Baltic against the Russians so that the German Navy might build up a new U-boat fleet capable of inflicting a severe defeat on the Western Allies, and especially on the hated British whose refusal to capitulate in 1940 had made inevitable this war on two fronts which had already destroyed most of Hitler's empire and was in the process of destroying the Third Reich.

To this day the Soviets insist that what they call "The Great Patriotic War" was won largely by themselves, that the Western Front was but a sideshow in comparison to the great holocaust of the East. From the standpoint of numbers alone, this might be true. Such a simplistic view, however, ignores many facts: the Soviet absence from the Pacific War; the enormous amount of supplies shipped to the U.S.S.R.—first by the British and then in far greater volume by the Americans—with attendant and horrifying losses in shipping to the German

U-boats and Focke-Wolfe bombers attacking the Murmansk-bound convoys off the coast of Norway; the destruction of Luftwaffe fighter power by the Western Allies which conferred on the Red Army the gift of control of their own air and the interdiction of German industrial capacity by the same force; the weakness of the Soviet Air Force, supplied with aircraft so inadequate and pilots so poorly trained that Erich Hoffman, the chief German ace, could record no fewer than 352 kills; the Allied campaigns against the Axis in North Africa, Greece, Sicily and Italy; the unsuccessful but nonetheless erosive sea, air and land battles of 1939–41 when the U.S.S.R. was Germany's ally; and finally the massive Western front itself which, though indubitably not the equal in numbers or area or weapons of the Eastern, nevertheless did draw off Wehrmacht forces from the East, especially after Hitler's foolish expenditure of his mobile reserves in the Battle of the Bulge. So far, *Der Führer* had not once weakened the West to strengthen the East. All of the transferrals of forces were in the other direction. In the air alone the disproportion is staggering. By the end of 1944, 1,756 of 2,276 day fighters were deployed in support of the Western front or defense of the Reich together with 1,242 of 1,289 night fighters. Protection of German industry against Allied air caused a gigantic diversion of manpower and productive facilities. Some 900,000 German soldiers were deployed in antiaircraft units, and of all German guns one third were AA. According to the United States Strategic Bombing survey "the threat and the effect of strategic bombing reduced the labor force available for other purposes by at least 4.30 to 5.45 million persons." Thus the comparative forces Hitler arrayed against his enemies in the air; on the sea, one can hardly compare puny Soviet naval power to the mighty American armada, and between Soviet naval strength and the combined might of the Anglo-Americans at sea it is comical even to suggest comparison. Put simply, there was effectively no Red Navy.

The state of German unpreparedness in the East was the theme of the melancholy report given to Hitler by Guderian upon his return from a tour there. He reported that "the Russians had vast forces ready to attack and that the German troops in the East could not hold them." Once again he pleaded for massive strategic withdrawals, to abandon Italy, Norway, the Balkans and the Baltic and to concentrate these dispersed troops to keep the Soviets out of Germany. But Hitler refused. Even though he had just then called off the Ardennes offensive, he was still preoccupied with the West. He had sent 2,300 new tanks and assault guns to Rundstedt and only 921 to the East. Two thirds of the Luftwaffe's strength was still deployed against the Anglo-Americans.

The Western allies were then engaging 100 German divisions, seventy-six in the west and twenty-four in Italy. Another twenty-seven were arrayed in outlying strategic areas and ten more in Yugoslavia and seventeen in Scandinavia. Against Russia, where Hitler once had 157 divisions opposing the Red Army, he now had only 133. Even these were not deployed in strength to stop the main blows of the Red Army in Poland. On the northern flank in Courland and Memel thirty German divisions were cut off with their backs to the Baltic. On the southern wing guarding Hungarian oil and bauxite were twenty-eight, including half of Guderian's armor. In Poland and East Prussia Hitler had only seventy-five divisions opposing 180 Soviets. Admittedly, a Soviet division was much smaller than the Allied or German division, and was not so well equipped or supported from the air; but *Der Führer* still had far too little to hold a front 600 miles long against a force probably about twice the size of his own. As Guderian had anticipated Hitler simply refused to accept reality. "He had a special picture of the world, and every fact had to fit into that fanciful picture. As he believed, so the reality must be; but in fact it was a picture of another world." After Guderian had made his dismaying report, Hitler said: "The Eastern Front has never before possessed such a strong reserve as now. That is your doing. I thank you for it." Incredulous, Guderian replied: "The Eastern front is like a house of cards! If the front is broken through at one point all the rest will collapse!" It was a true prophecy.

On the morning of January 12, 1945, the Red Army offensive was launched on the frozen plains of southern Poland. Konev's army group burst out of its bridgehead on the Upper Vistula between Cracow and Sandomir and almost immediately broke through the thin defenses and weak reserves there. This was the first blow in the greatest offensive of the war. Stalin assembled at the points which he wished to strike a superiority in men and armor that was threefold and even sixfold. Reports reaching Hitler were so distressing that he returned to Berlin to set up his command post in the massive bunker deep beneath the Reichs Chancellery. Rarely did he emerge from this safest place in the city, although once he did visit the Goebbelses for tea. Rarely also could there be a clearer picture of the cloud-cuckoo-land in which *Der Führer* and his Nazi henchmen lived. When Hitler arrived, Joseph and Magda Goebbels stood smiling at the door. Goebbels gave a brisk Nazi salute and the little girls curtsied. Hitler fondled them and remarked on how much they had grown since he was there last five years earlier. His chauffeur and SS bodyguards brought in his own tea and cakes. At the table Hitler spoke with enthusiasm of the great city—more beautiful than Paris even—that he and Speer would erect on the ruins of Berlin after the war. After he had consumed his cakes with the customary lip-smacking, finger-licking relish, washing them down with cup after cup of sugary tea, he kissed the little girls and took his departure. At dinner that night the Goebbelses spoke touchingly of how much *Der Führer* had enjoyed his visit. "He wouldn't have gone to the Goerings," Magda said proudly.

Zhukov had gone over to the attack. He crossed the Vistula on both sides of Warsaw, isolating it, and on January 17 stormed it from the rear. In the north Rokossovsky broke the line of the Narew and struck northwest to the Bay of Danzig. Next he drove deep into the defenses of East Prussia while Marshal Ivan Cherniakovsky's army group shattered them in direct assault. Within a week the entire Eastern front was collapsing westward and the Soviet armor plunged 100 miles closer to Berlin.

The front had been breached in so many cases that there was simply no chance of restoring it. Still commanded by Hitler to yield no ground, the German units were destroyed where they stood or so fragmented that they had to seek shelter in fortress towns bypassed by the Red Army. Guderian's reserves were too weak to check an offensive on so vast a scale. Most of his mobile reserves were engaged in Hungary in a futile attempt to relieve Budapest. His twelve panzer divisions in Poland and East Prussia were too short on fuel to make those aggressive, local counterattacks in which the Wehrmacht usually excelled. Fuel shortages also prevented effective delaying actions.

At last on January 22 Hitler sought to strengthen his reserves by evacuating all his forces in Memel. But he still refused to abandon Courland because Doenitz still insisted that the U-boat training areas in the Gulf of Danzig must be maintained. For the first time *Der Führer* took troops from the West, ordering Dietrich's Sixth SS Panzer Army to move to the Eastern front. In his heart Hitler realized that he could not stop the Soviet avalanche. "There is no point in hypnotizing myself into a state of mind by saying, 'I need something here, therefore it must materialize.' In the last resort I have to deal with things as they are. The deployment of really effective forces from the West cannot take place in less than six to eight weeks."

Even this was an optimistic estimate, if only because Hitler could no longer take advantage of his central position, giving him interior lines between East and West. Allied air power had destroyed his mobility. German railroads were moving only a third of the traffic they had been handling six months earlier. The vaunted autobahn highway network, which ran across Germany from the Oder to the Rhine, was all but worthless. Hitler had boasted of how the autobahn he had built would allow him to shift forces rapidly to and from either front, but without fuel and under constant Allied surveillance, it was of no help. It was his enemies who would make use of it. Moreover, all of the concrete, steel and labor he had expended in building these roads might have been put to better use constructing an eastern defensive system similar to the Siegfried Line. The Soviets had no such fortifications in their path as they bore down on Berlin in giant strides.

During the second half of January Rokossovsky in the north reached the Bay of Danzig and cut off twenty-five divisions trapped in East Prussia. In the south, Konev broke into Upper Silesia from Cracow and menaced Breslau. The Soviets were now in the only corner of Hitler's empire that had not felt the wrath of Allied air. Because of the decline of coal production in the Ruhr, the Silesian mines had become Germany's chief source of supply, providing full 60 percent of production in December of 1944. Now they were lost at a time when Germany's railroads, power plants and factories had stocks for only two weeks more. This, Speer reported to Hitler, had created "an unbearable situation." Because of this loss Speer said that he could provide only a quarter of the coal and a sixth of the steel produced a year ago. Capture of Silesia had also given the Soviets possession of those factories which Hitler had moved east to escape destruction from Allied air. They even seized three synthetic fuel plants just starting production.

In the Soviet center, meanwhile, Zhukov was driving rapidly through central Poland bound for Berlin. He advanced 220 miles within two weeks. By January 27 he had crashed through the German frontier and was only 100 miles from the Nazi capital. Within the city and on the same day Hitler, with Goering and Jodl, began a self-mesmerizing conversation. Hitler asked: "Do you think the English can be really enthusiastic about all the Russian developments?" Jodl replied: "No, certainly not. Their plans were quite different. Only later on perhaps will the full realization of this come." Goering added: "They had not counted on our defending ourselves step by step and holding them off in the West like madmen, while the Russians drive deeper and deeper into Germany." Hitler explained how he had begun to play on British nerves. He had ordered a report planted among the British to the effect that the Soviets had infected 200,000 German prisoners with communism and were sending them into Germany. "That will make them feel as if someone has stuck a needle into them," Goering agreed. "They entered the war to prevent us from going into the East; not to have the East come to the Atlantic." Eventually all three came to the comforting conclusion that the Soviet offensive was a good thing because it would compel the western Allies to compromise rather than see Western Europe fall to communism. "If this goes on," Goering predicted confidently, "we will get a telegram in a few days."

But they would not. Instead they would hear that Roosevelt and Churchill were en route to the U.S.S.R. to confer with Stalin. The conference would be at Yalta on the Black Sea.

118. Yalta: Stalin's Greatest Victory

A CONFERENCE OF THE BIG THREE was first proposed by Franklin Delano Roosevelt in November 1944 after his reelection victory over Thomas E. Dewey, but it was not convened until February 1945, and then only according to a timetable carefully contrived by Stalin. Ambassador Andrei Gromyko told FDR that Stalin was much too busy directing the war personally—that is, nailing down the military conquest of southeastern and central Europe—to leave the Soviet Union. Thus it was not against a backdrop of the successful Anglo-American drive to the German border or the great victory in the Battle of Leyte Gulf that the Big Three conferred, but rather in the wake of the death of Stalin's anticommunist enemies in Poland during the Warsaw Uprising, the Red Army's dazzling winter offensive already penetrating German soil and what appeared to have been an American defeat in the Battle of the Bulge.

The need for such a conference was obvious. Germany was collapsing, and there were as yet no agreements about what to do with her after her defeat. Roosevelt was also eager to obtain from Stalin the precise date and extent of Soviet participation in the war against Japan and to iron out with Churchill and Stalin the problems of the United Nations left unsettled by Dumbarton Oaks. Most important of these was the Soviet insistence that the three Great Powers should have in the Security Council a veto amounting to the power of ukase. Finally, there was the question of postwar Poland.

Poland was a particularly disturbing problem for Britain because it was for Poland, after all, that she had gone to war. British honor was obliged to guarantee the restoration of a free, independent and sovereign Polish nation. But for a year Churchill had struggled unsuccessfully to reconcile Stalin with the London-based Polish government-in-exile. Stalin insisted that the Soviet-Polish border should be the old Curzon Line* established in 1919 by the Supreme Allied Council. Churchill was inclined to agree with Stalin, if only because it was through Poland that Napoleon and Hitler had invaded Russia. A buffer composed of Poland's eastern territories did not seem to him an unreasonable demand, especially since Stalin had promised that in recompense Poland would receive all of East Prussia and other German territory up to the Neisse River. The London Poles, however, demurred, and their refusal gave Stalin the excuse for setting up in Lublin his own National Committee of Liberation composed of his own communist creatures. Churchill now feared that if the Red Army occupied Poland, the bargaining power of the London Poles and the mediating influence of the Anglo-Americans would be fatally weakened, and he tried even harder to persuade the London Poles to come to an agreement with Stalin.

In October 1944, when Churchill visited Moscow a second time, it appeared that Polish Prime Minister Stanislaw Mikolajczyk was willing to accept the Curzon Line if Poland could retain the Carpathian oilfields and the ancient city of L'vov. But when Mikolajczyk's colleagues in London refused to accept this proposal, the prime minister resigned and power passed to the intransigents. Nevertheless, both Churchill and Roosevelt hoped to resolve the impasse at another meeting with Stalin.

Churchill and Roosevelt, unfortunately, were not the warm, cohesive, friendly partners working together in unmatched harmony that so much popular history has portrayed them to be. Rather there reigned at the heart of the Anglo-American alliance a mutual distrust far greater than any suspicion which either chief might hold for Stalin. There can be no better means of expressing this disagreement than Churchill's famous remark in November 1942, "I have not become the King's First Minister in order to preside over the liquidation of the British Empire," and Roosevelt's lesser known admonition, "Winston . . . you have four hundred years of acquisitive instinct in your blood and you just don't

---

*Roughly from Grodno in the north to Przemyśl in the south, today's border between the U.S.S.R. and Poland.

understand how a country might not want to acquire land somewhere if they can get it. A new period has opened in the world's history and you will have to adjust yourself to it."

In Franklin Roosevelt's vision of a postwar world of international peace and self-determination for all peoples there was simply no room for colonialism. He regarded colonialism as the root of all international evil. "The colonial system means war," he told his son Elliott. In contrast to this idealistic, if not simplistic, concept of the nature of nations and empires was Churchill's realistic albeit self-interested understanding that nations are less likely to commit the imperialist sin of aggrandizement if they are restrained by a balance of power preserved by alliances. Although he was not anti-Soviet by nature, his last visit had suggested to him that "it would be a measureless disaster if Russian barbarism were to overlay the culture and independence of the ancient states of Europe." He had become sensitive to the Soviet Union's enormous military power and believed that it could only be counterbalanced by a strong British Empire, a firm Anglo-American alliance and a United States of Europe. To Roosevelt balance of power and alliances were the abhorrent tools of colonialism. Worse, Roosevelt's detestation of imperialism and naive faith in the Soviets was shared by every top-level member of the New Deal as well as its war chiefs. Six months after Yalta, Harry Hopkins wrote: "We know, or believe, that Russia's interests, so far as we can anticipate them, do not afford an opportunity for a major difference with us in foreign affairs. We believe we are mutually dependent upon each other for economic reasons. We find the Russians as individuals easy to deal with. The Russians undoubtedly like the American people. They like the United States. They trust the United States more than they trust any other power in the world . . . above all, they want to maintain friendly relations with us. . . . They are a tenacious, determined people who think and act just like you and I do."

If, four decades later, it is difficult to credit such misjudgment, listen to Dwight Eisenhower in the same vein: "In his generous instincts, in his love of laughter, in his devotion to a comrade, and in his healthy, direct outlook on the affairs of workaday life, the ordinary Russian seems to me to bear a marked similarity to what we call an 'average American.' " Eisenhower went on to state that both peoples "were free from the stigma of colonial building by force." It was thus that the American entourage came to Yalta more suspicious of its British ally than of Stalin.

Franklin Roosevelt was also disarmed by Stalin's eagerness to enroll the Soviet Union in the world peace organization, which was his greatest goal, and his desire to bring the U.S.S.R. into the war against Japan as soon as possible. Edward Stettinius, who had succeeded the ailing Cordell Hull as secretary of state, has written of "the immense pressure put on the president by our military leaders to bring Russia into the Far Eastern War. At this time the atomic bomb was still an unknown quantity and our setback in the Battle of the Bulge was fresh in the minds of all. We had not as yet crossed the Rhine. No one knew how long the European War would last nor how great the casualties would be." Stettinius said that the Joint Chiefs had told FDR that without the Soviet Union it might cost the United States a million casualties to conquer Japan. This was, of course, mistaken. But Marshall and King believed it, and they had Roosevelt's ear. In truth, MacArthur and Nimitz—the commanders on the spot—had assured Roosevelt at Hawaii that Japan need not be invaded but could be beaten and starved into submission by aerial and naval bombardment and naval blockade. General Arnold of the Army Air Force also was convinced of this, and his Superfortresses were already taking off from Saipan and Tinian to bomb Japan's home islands. Nor was there any need for airbases in the U.S.S.R.'s Maritime Provinces. The so-called shuttle bombing of Hitler's Europe had shown Arnold how useless they could be. What was true is that the Joint Chiefs, having so badly underestimated Japan at the start of the war, were now even more grossly over-estimating her. No one can blame Roosevelt for accepting their judgment, even if it did weaken his bargaining position and make him less ardent than he should have been in support of Churchill's fight for a free Poland.

At the opening session of the Yalta Conference, held on February 4, 1945, in the opulent Livadia Palace overlooking the Black Sea, Stalin proposed that Roosevelt should take the chair. By this tactful tactic he brought the American halfway to his side, or at least halfway away from Churchill's. To his great annoyance, the prime minister now had to present the Anglo-American positions alone. By his ready acceptance of the role of mediator, Roosevelt also uninten-tionally gave the Soviets an exaggerated perception of the warmth of his friend-ship toward them. However, FDR really did favor the role of arbiter because it gave him freedom of action and enabled him to hear both sides before committing himself.

Partition of Germany was the first order of business. Stalin wanted a Three Power occupation with the Reich cut up into separate states and Germany deprived of 80 percent of her heavy industry and forced to pay an astronomical (for those days) reparation of $20 billion, half of which was to go to the Soviet Union. Churchill objected. He did not wish to see Germany become an economic basket case nor so weak that Britain would have to depend on France alone "to guard the Western approaches to the Channel." This oblique reference to a new European menace was not lost upon Stalin.

However, in all discussions of Germany's future, both in the plenary sessions and the meetings of foreign ministers, three viewpoints finally emerged. Stalin wanted partition and the huge reparation, Churchill wanted no commitments either way and Roosevelt suggested that dismemberment should be mentioned in the surrender terms but without any binding power. He also favored Stalin's reparation demands as a "basis for discussion." Churchill wanted France to have an occupation zone and a seat on the Allied Control Commission, Stalin wanted neither and Roosevelt said that France should have a zone but no seat. Eventually France got both and with China became one of the Big Five permanent and veto-wielding members of the UN Security Council.

The question of the veto power in the Security Council now arose. Some have claimed that FDR accepted the veto as a concession aimed at inducing Stalin to join the United Nations. This is not true. The Big Three were firmly agreed on the veto and none wanted to subordinate its own affairs to the interference of an international organization. Roosevelt was haunted by Wilson's failure with the League of Nations and realized that the U.S. Senate would never surrender to an international agency the right to send American troops into battle. Churchill himself remarked that he would never consent "to the fumbling fingers of forty or fifty nations prying into the life's existence of the British Empire." Stalin held similar views. It was only on the issue of seats in the General Assembly for each of the Soviet Union's sixteen republics that he was adamant; and here, just as in his eventual acceptance of a zone and seat for France in the Allied Control Council, it may now be seen that Stalin's intransigence was actually a skillful diplomatic tactic. He could originally stand firm on issues that did not really disturb him so that he might later give way in a "concession" for which he expected to be repaid. Thus, he later softened the demand for sixteen seats to three, one each for the Soviet Union, the Ukraine and White Russia, while offering three seats to the United States. Churchill found this acceptable, if only because with the United Kingdom, four of the Dominions and India each having a seat, the British Empire would in effect have six seats. Roosevelt, of course, was not interested in Stalin's offer; but he and Churchill were delighted at this expression of Stalin's willingness to join the United Nations. Neither of them could foresee how the Soviet Union would abuse the veto power. It seemed to them that Anglo-American diplomacy had won a great victory. Yet, the issue of Poland and Stalin's imperialist ambitions in the Far East had still to be resolved.

President Roosevelt opened the Polish question by stating that he would accept the Curzon Line, if Stalin would agree to let Poland keep the city of L'vov and the adjacent oilfields. These last, his advisers had told him, were essential to the Polish economy. Churchill had already accepted the Curzon Line, but he reiterated his desire for a fully representative Polish government pledged to holding free elections. This, he said, was a matter of honor to Britain. Stalin disagreed.

"For the Russian people," he cried passionately, "Poland is not only a question of honor but also a question of security. Throughout history Poland has been the corridor through which the enemy has passed into Russia. . . . It is in Russia's interests that Poland should be strong and powerful, in a position to shut the door of this corridor by her own force." He demanded acceptance of "the line of Curzon and Clemenceau," crying: "You would drive us into shame! What will be said by the White Russians and the Ukrainians? They will say that Stalin and Molotov are far less reliable defenders of Russia than are Curzon and Clemenceau." It was then that he said he favored extending Poland's western frontier all the way to the River Neisse in Germany.

Stalin also rejected Roosevelt's suggestion that a new Polish government be formed from the country's five chief political parties, including members of the government-in-exile in London. He said that he did not trust the London Poles and would recognize only his own Lublin leaders already in power.

Churchill responded by saying that Britain would never accept the Lublin Committee since it didn't represent even a third of the nation. He also would not agree to extending Polish territory deep into Germany in recompense for reestablishment of the Curzon Line. Dryly reminding Stalin of how Hitler used the "ethnic Germans" to yank into his sphere those Versailles-created states in which they lived, he said: "It would be a pity to stuff the Polish goose so full of German food that he will die of indigestion." On this discordant note, the Polish issue was temporarily dropped.

But that night Roosevelt sent Stalin a conciliatory note in which he said: "The United States will never lend its support in any way to any provisional government in Poland which would be inimical to your interests." He added: "I am determined there shall be no breach between ourselves and the Soviet Union." With this he indicated, whether consciously or not, that if Stalin insisted on having his way in Poland, the United States would not oppose him.

So the Polish issue lay dormant, not to be reopened until there appeared the glow of goodwill among the Anglo-Americans created by Stalin's "concessions" on the sixteen Soviet seats in the General Assembly and his promise to join the United Nations. When the glow arrived, Stalin merely reiterated his earlier position. His only concession was that the Lublin Committee might be enlarged to include some democratic leaders among the London Poles. Inasmuch as Mikolajczyk, chief of the Polish Peasant Party, was not considered to be a "democrat," this was a concession made of air. By this intransigence Stalin made it clear that although he might join the United Nations, he relied upon his own power to subjugate Poland and the Balkan Peninsula, excepting Greece, to Soviet interests. His troops were already in possession of Poland, and his Lublin Poles—the "Polish Provisional Government"—had taken power at the points of their bayonets. That was the status quo on Poland, and that was how it would remain.

Turning next to the Far East, Stalin and Roosevelt held secret discussions about the Soviet Union's entry into the war against Japan. Roosevelt had requested that Churchill not attend this meeting, and he did not. Neither did Stettinius, FDR's own secretary of state. Besides the two chiefs, the only other persons present were two interpreters and Molotov and Ambassador to the U.S.S.R. W. Averell Harriman. None of these has written a word concerning what was discussed. Adm. William D. Leahy, Roosevelt's personal chief of staff, and FDR's biographer, Robert Sherwood, have each written accounts of it, but these are all second-hand and therefore not entirely reliable. What was decided, however, may be deduced from the terms of the agreement subsequently signed by Roosevelt, Churchill and Stalin. Under it the Soviet Union agreed to take the offensive against Japan "in two or three months after Germany has surrendered." But only under certain conditions: that Soviet domination of Outer Mongolia was to be preserved; that the Kurile Islands north of Japan were to be "handed over to the Soviet Union"; that the U.S.S.R. was to regain possession of the naval base at Port Arthur, the "international port" of Dairen (Luda) and southern Sakhalin; and that although China was to "retain full sovereignty in Manchuria," the chief Manchurian railways were to be operated by a joint Soviet-Chinese company which was to protect "the preeminent interests of the Soviet Union." Apart from promising to attack Japan, Stalin conceded nothing in writing. Orally, he offered Roosevelt bases in the Maritime Provinces, but never actually gave them. Stalin referred to the Russo-Japanese War of 1904: "I only want to have returned to Russia what the Japanese have taken from my country." Roosevelt agreed. "That seems like a very reasonable suggestion from our ally. They only want to get back what was taken from them."

It is surprising that Churchill, so often on his feet and growling whenever British sovereignty was menaced, should not have made some protest against these claims. The Kuriles had never belonged to Russia. Russia's preeminence in Manchuria during the last century was only one of the many raids on the corrupt Chinese carcass made by all the predatory and colonizing nations of Europe. They had been nothing more than extraterritorial privileges obtained by force or the threat of it. Russia never had any more true rights in China than Japan did. Yet, with Anglo-American agreement, the Soviet Union was now to be made the political heir of Japan in Manchuria and by extension North China. All this was to be achieved without the consent of China, the nation so to be robbed. Stalin even extracted from Roosevelt a promise not to inform Chiang Kai-shek of what had occurred at Yalta until he was ready to strike Japan. Further, FDR promised to persuade Chiang to accept the concessions. As Robert Sherwood has observed, "If China had refused to agree to any of the Soviet claims, presumably the U.S. and Britain would have been compelled to join in enforcing them."

Why, then, did Roosevelt and Churchill thus betray the Chinese ally? In Roosevelt's case the answer is that he signed probably out of gratitude for Stalin's having joined the United Nations and in reward for his promise to strike Japan. It is almost certainly untrue that these concessions were wrung from a sick and weary Roosevelt by a forceful and importunate Stalin. Robert Sherwood has said that FDR was indeed tired and ailing but that he had been "prepared even before the Tehran Conference . . . to agree to the legitimacy of most if not all of the Soviet claims in the Far East." Churchill, under constant pressure from Anthony Eden not to sign, probably did so because he believed that "the whole position of the British in the Far East might be at stake." Having been excluded from the Stalin-Roosevelt discussion of the Far East, he had good reason to fear that he also might be barred from future negotiations about the Japanese war if he failed to go along with his American ally. As Admiral Leahy pointed out, Churchill might also have realized that a Roosevelt who so easily gave away China's territory would be shorn of any moral support in reforming the British Empire.

So the deal was done, and in defense of it and in an effort to fend off the storm of criticism that erupted once the details were known, Edward Stettinius has written: "What, with the possible exception of the Kuriles, did the Soviet Union receive at Yalta which she might not have taken without any agreement?"

Here is might-is-right at its baldest, here is double-speak in its pristine impurity: "Nothing is lost, save honor." What indeed could Stalin have taken without violating the basic principles of the Atlantic Charter and the United Nations to which he had subscribed? Whether or not he would or could have achieved his designs in Asia by force is not at issue. The point is that the Yalta Agreement gave him the moral cloak to do as he pleased. Worse for the Anglo-Americans: Roosevelt, by agreeing to break the promise he had given to Chiang Kai-shek at Cairo in 1943, left himself in no position to protest when Stalin moved to drop the Iron Curtain around the Balkans. Principles that he had abandoned in Asia could not be resurrected in Europe—not in the face of so wily and astute a negotiator as Joseph Stalin.

After settling the Far Eastern problem, the conference renewed its discussion of Poland. Here, also, Stalin achieved every objective. Nothing more was said about L'vov or the oilfields, and the Curzon Line was accepted with the question of Poland's western frontier left to the Peace Conference. Rather than accept the Anglo-American proposal of an entirely new government formed by "all democratic and anti-Fascist forces," Stalin held stubbornly to his proposal merely to "enlarge" the Lublin Committee. That is, add a few "acceptable" so-called democrats for window dressing of what was actually the mixture as before. The Soviets accepted the Western demand for free elections but refused to have them supervised by the foreign ministers of the Big Three. This, said Molotov with a straight face, would be "an affront to the pride and sovereignty of the independent [Polish] people." Eventually, the ministers hammered out this formula: "The Provisional [Lublin] Government which is now functioning in Poland should be reorganized on a broader democratic basis with the inclusion of democratic leaders from Poland itself and Poles abroad." Once again the mixture as before, with the mere substitution of "reorganized" for "enlarged." Even Roosevelt had some doubts about this vague formula, especially after Leahy said to him: "Mr. President, this is so elastic that the Russians can stretch it all the way from Yalta to Washington without technically breaking it." Nevertheless, it was approved.

So also eventually was Stalin's demand for $20 billion in reparations from Germany, half of which was to go to the Soviet Union. Roosevelt agreed with Eden's argument (correct as it turned out) that to do so would so ruin Germany economically that the Allies would have to feed and finance her. Even Stalin's impassioned description of the vast damage done to his country by the Germans failed to budge the British from their position, and a Soviet-British deadlock appeared to have ensued—until Harry Hopkins intervened. "Mr. President," he said to FDR in a note, "the Russians have given in so much at this Conference that I do not think we should let them down. Let the British disagree if they want to—and continue their disagreement at Moscow." So a suffering Roosevelt, weary of argument, agreed with Stalin that the reparations committee should accept the Soviet position "as a basis for discussion." Although the British refusal to accept any figure was duly recorded, it had no ultimate influence. Stalin had won again.

It was no difficult verbal feat for the double-speaking Molotov to leap from "basis for discussion" to mean "accept in principle" and thence a mere sidestep to "President Roosevelt had agreed at Yalta that Soviet reparations should total at least ten billion dollars."

In defense of Roosevelt and Churchill, it must be stated that they could not have foreseen that Stalin would distort and misinterpret the Yalta Protocol as he saw fit, and would promptly and consistently violate those principles of the Atlantic Charter and the United Nations to which at Yalta he had given solemn reaffirmations. Even Churchill was elated by what appeared to be the great diplomatic victory of the Western Allies. Both he and Roosevelt were pragmatists who made the mistake of taking Stalin at face value. They could never imagine the extent of his perfidy, begun only a few days after the Yalta Protocol was signed amid expressions of mutual trust and good will.

On the day that Winston Churchill in Parliament extolled the honesty of Stalin and his lieutenants, remarking, "I believe also that their word is their bond," the Soviet Union gave King Michael of Romania two hours to dismiss Prime Minister Radescu, the leader of an all-party government. On the day that Franklin Delano Roosevelt told a joint session of Congress that Yalta signaled the end of colonialism and all the failed systems of unilateral action, spheres of influence and balances of power, the Soviet Union ordered King Michael to appoint as his prime minister Petru Groza, the leader of the Romanian Communist Party.

Yalta had not ushered in a brave new world but had rather set the stage for the fall of the Iron Curtain.

119. The Liberation of the Philippines

"WITH MY EIGHTH ARMY off the southern coast of Luzon," General Douglas MacArthur told his staff, "I will threaten landings on . . . southern ports and draw the bulk of the Japanese into the south. This done, I will land the Sixth Army in an amphibious enveloping movement on the exposed Northern Shore, thus cutting off the enemy's supplies from Japan. This will draw the enemy back to the north, leaving the Eighth Army to land against only weak opposition on the south coast in another amphibious movement. Both forces ashore, with but minor loss, will then close like a vise on the enemy deprived of supplies and destroy him."

Thus, MacArthur's plan for reconquering Luzon and recapturing Manila, the capital of the Philippines, and although this delicately balanced plan of feinting south to draw off forces for an invasion north, and then striking north to lure them away from a landing south was skillfully executed, it was not "with but minor loss." There would be heavy losses in the Philippines, on land, on sea, and in the air.

Because MacArthur did not have enough land-based air within range of Japanese bases on Luzon, Formosa and Japan, he needed new bases north of Leyte. Unless he got them, he would still have to rely on naval air support, Kinkaid's escort carriers which had been borrowed from Nimitz and Halsey's big flattops of the Third Fleet. However, the escorts had been battered in the Battle of Leyte Gulf, and Halsey's ships also needed replenishment and repair. MacArthur's date of December 20 for the Luzon landings had to be postponed until January 9, 1945.

Before then, MacArthur decided to invade Mindoro just south of Luzon. He hoped to build airfields there for land-based air to support the Luzon landings and to protect the shipping that would supply the operations. Mindoro was invaded on December 15, and it was a true walk-in. At sea, however, the kamikazes reappeared. One suicider exploded his plane on the cruiser *Nashville,* killing 130 men and wounding 190. Others destroyed two LSTs and damaged two other ships. Nevertheless, Mindoro was like an unexpected bonus. Within five days hardworking American and Australian engineers constructed one airfield there and took thirteen to build another—a week ahead of schedule. From these not only could the Luzon operations be supported, but the kamikazes could be struck at their bases and enemy shipping between Formosa and Japan interdicted.

MacArthur's first objective on Luzon was Lingayen Gulf, halfway up the west coast. It had excellent landing beaches and was close to the best rail and road network in the Philippines, running through the central plains straight south of Manila. The Lingayen area also provided room for maneuver and to receive the large forces MacArthur commanded. There were ten divisions and five regimental combat teams in his Eighth and Sixth Armies, making the campaign the largest thus far in the Pacific, even bigger than those in North Africa, Italy and southern France.

In Manila, General Yamashita prepared to fight the Americans, deprived, as he had been, of so many troops sent to Leyte. Yamashita had no intention of defending either Bataan or Manila. He decided instead on a series of delaying actions designed to inflict the costliest casualties on the invaders. To do this he formed three groups and withdrew them into mountain strongholds. The strongest was his own *Shobu* Group responsible for all of northern Luzon east of Lingayen. Within it was the fertile Cagayan Valley, which would feed this force. The much smaller *Kimbu* Group held the mountains to the west of the central plains and the vital airfield complex around Clark Field. The third force, the *Simbu* Group, occupied the mountains east of Manila, where it could control the city's water supply.

On January 2 Admiral Oldendorf's bombardment force of battleships, cruisers and destroyers, together with his air-supporting escort carriers, sailed from

Leyte Gulf. Two days later the troop transports and supply ships with their escorts followed. MacArthur was with Oldendorf, aboard the cruiser *Boise*. Bareheaded, in suntans and wearing dark glasses, his blackened corncob pipe clenched in his teeth, he strode back and forth, gazing at this vast concourse of ships. There had been persistent rumors that Yamashita was still out to "get" MacArthur to avenge Yamamoto's death. Suddenly bugles blared over the bull-horn sounding general quarters! "All hands man your battle stations! Prepare for submarine attack!" MacArthur glanced to port where a stream of white bubbles streaked toward *Boise*. With a sudden surge of speed, the cruiser turned to starboard and the torpedo sped harmlessly by. A destroyer dug her bow into the water to hasten to the area and drop depth charges. A Japanese submarine surfaced, rolling like a baby whale. The destroyer rammed and sank it. Once again the bugles blared. "All hands to your battle stations! Prepare for air attack!" A Val dive-bomber came plummeting down to release its deadly egg. Mac-Arthur stood watching it fall into the sea between *Boise* and the destroyers. Another bomber appeared and was sent spinning into the dark blue sea by the guns of eight warships. MacArthur resumed pacing the deck, still puffing on his pipe. Soon Oldendorf's forces were off Luzon. MacArthur stood at the rail watching all the familiar landmarks slide by: Manila Bay . . . Corregidor . . . Mariveles . . . Bataan. . . .

Coming off Lingayen Gulf the American fleet was attacked by every shot the Japanese had left in their locker. There were only 200 aircraft still operable, and all took to the skies to fend off the invaders. A kamikaze crashed through the escort carrier *Ommaney Bay*'s flight deck, turning her into a hopeless, flaming wreck which eventually had to be sunk. Next day the kamikazes struck again, diving relentlessly through streams of AA to damage escort carriers *Manila Bay* and *Savo Island* and destroyer *Stafford*. Entering Lingayen Gulf at dawn of the 9th to take the identical position assumed by the Japanese invasion fleet almost three years before, Oldendorf's ships were again staggered. The kamikazes flew low along the crest of the hills and inside the valleys surrounding the gulf to avoid radar detection. They maneuvered wildly to distract AA fire and confuse their target ships. Many of them were shot down by the fleet's combat air patrol or ack-ack, but enough of them got through to inflict serious damage on Oldendorf 's flagship *California* and to damage heavy cruisers *Louisville* and *Columbia,* battleship *New Mexico,* the Australian cruiser *Australia* and sink destroyer escort *Long.*

Oldendorf was dismayed. He had protested that the little escort carriers simply were unequipped to intercept enemy airplanes and bomb their airfields. He warned that without the protection of Halsey's big carriers or land-based Allied air the following transports would be risking disaster at the hands of the kamikazes. But the Japanese had shot their bolt. They had suffered severe losses in sinking twenty-four American ships and damaging sixty-seven others, and there were few red-balled aircraft aloft when the Americans began going ashore at Lingayen at 9:30 in the morning. Like Mindoro, it was a walk-in. There were no Japanese defenders because Yamashita had decided on delaying tactics inland. Even so Douglas MacArthur came wading ashore again, still puffing on his pipe, his head covered by his squashed, scrambled-egg hat. But this dramatic "return" to the fabled island of the MacArthur family saga was such palpable stagecraft that many newspapers back home declined to print it.

Within a few days General Krueger had 175,000 men of his Sixth Army ashore on a beachhead twenty miles wide. On the right was XIV Corps under Lt. Gen. Oscar W. Griswold, while the left was held by I Corps led by Maj. Gen. Innis P. Swift. I Corps was supposed to protect the rear and flanks of Griswold's corps as it drove south for Clark Field and Manila. I Corps was also assigned to strike north and east to seize an important road junction. But its route passed through rugged mountain country which the Japanese had fortified with their customary skill. Artillery, mortars and machine guns concealed in caves slowed the advance to a crawl.

XIV Corps met little opposition as it probed south through flat and open farmlands. Nevertheless, Krueger held it in check until I Corps could secure its left flank. This upset MacArthur, who urged Krueger to push on to Manila immediately. He wanted the all-weather airfields around Clark and Manila's extensive port facilities. Krueger thought he also wanted to enter Manila in time to celebrate his sixty-fifth birthday on the 26th. He ordered Griswold to drive south without delay, and on January 18 the XIV Corps struck out for Manila. Five days later its soldiers reached the forward defenses of the *Kembu* Group guarding the Clark Field complex. But it took a week of fierce fighting to clear General Tsukada's troops out of the area. Once the Clark complex was in American hands, the XIV took to the road to Manila again, leaving its 40th Division behind to guard the airfields. But it would take three more weeks to break the *Kembu* Group.

Meanwhile on January 29 General Hall's XI Corps landed unopposed on the Zambales coast northwest of Bataan. Because the major units of the *Kembu* Group were still fighting the XIV Corps, Hall's soldiers were unimpeded as they began to seal off Bataan. Next day the 11th Airborne Division under Maj. Gen. Joseph M. Swing landed unopposed at Nasugbu on the Batangas coast south of Corregidor. With this, MacArthur had fulfilled his prediction, landing in force almost unopposed in the north and in lesser strength without opposition in the south. Much of the success of these maneuvers, of course, was the result of Yamashita's decision to defend in his three fortresses.

MacArthur was dissatisfied with the progress toward Manila. He made a personal jeep reconnaissance along Highway 13 toward San Fernando, where the 37th Division was fighting. Upset by what he saw, he signaled Krueger: "There was a noticeable lack of drive and aggressive initiative today in the movement toward Calumpit." Stung, Krueger called upon Griswold to urge the 37th on. MacArthur also called upon the 1st Cavalry Division to join the race for the capital. "Go to Manila," he told General Mudge. "Go around the Nips, bounce off the Nips, but go to Manila." First Cavalry was ideally suited for such a dash.

Smaller and more lightly equipped than the infantry divisions, it could move faster. Mudge formed a pair of flying columns under Brig. Gen. William C. Chase. Each was composed of a cavalry squadron (dismounted), a company of tanks, a 105-mm howitzer battery and enough vehicles to carry the troops. A third unit entered the race when two regiments of the 11th Airborne moved out of Nasugbu to capture an important bridge before the Japanese could blow it and went speeding north along Route 17. They were joined by Swing's third regiment jumping into 17. Now the entire regiment rolled toward Manila, roaring through towns and barrios filled with cheering Filipinos.

Their path was blocked at the little town of Imus on the river of that name. The Japanese occupied an old stone building from which they delivered a heavy fire. Light 75-mm howitzers were unable to knock the building down. Tech. Sgt. Robert Steele climbed atop the building's roof, battered a hole in it and poured in gasoline which he set afire with a phosphorus grenade. Emerging Japanese were cut to the ground. But on February 4 the 11th's paratroopers were halted at the Parañaque River, just four miles south of the capital. They had run into a line of camouflaged steel-and-concrete pillboxes—Admiral Iwabuchi's main defensive position south of Manila.

The race for Manila was now between the 1st Cavalry and the 37th Infantry. At the start, the 37th was closer to the prize. But its path was impeded by unspanned or unfordable streams. The 37th had to halt and either ferry its tanks and trucks across them or wait for the engineers to erect bridges. There was no such problem for the dismounted troopers. Their progress was over bridged or fordable rivers. Soon the race became one between the two flying columns. Sometimes they hit speeds of fifty miles an hour over primitive gravel roads trying to beat each other to the capital.

Near the town of Talipapa a few miles northeast of Manila the troopers of the 5th Cavalry Regiment almost collided with a Japanese supply column emerging from a side road. The Americans boldly waved the Japanese to a halt, and the astonished enemy obeyed. Then as each of the 5th's vehicles rolled past, the Americans poured bursts of roadside fire into the enemy, just like Oldendorf's battleships "crossing the T" in Surigao Strait.

But it was the 8th Regiment that was in the lead on February 3. Its troopers were barred only by the steep gorge of the Tuliahan River just above the city. As they arrived, the Japanese were preparing to blow the bridge over it. They opened fire on the Americans and lighted a long fuse running to a large dynamite charge in the middle of the span. Naval Lt. James P. Sutton, a demolitions expert, dashed through enemy fire to cut the burning fuse before it could trigger the charge. Over the bridge clattered the 8th's triumphant tanks and trucks. That night they were in Manila's northern suburbs. A tank butted down the gates of Santo Tomás University, where some 4,000 Allied civilian prisoners were interned. Their guards were quickly routed and the prisoners freed.

When MacArthur arrived at Santo Tomás and alighted from his car, he was greeted by a thunderous roar. Inside the main building thousands of people mobbed him. Shouting, weeping, the liberated civilians tried to kiss him or embrace him. Those who threw their arms around him had to be gently pried loose. At Bilibid Prison, 800 people who had barely survived on a diet of wormy rice, corn and soybeans were joyfully liberated.

Within the military section of Bilibid a profound silence broken occasionally by a stifled sob greeted the Southwest Pacific commander. Emaciated and unkempt men—scarecrows of rags and bones—stood silently at attention beside their cots. Here was the captured remnant from Bataan and Corregidor. As he moved among them, he was greeted with murmurs of "You're back" or "You made it" or "God bless you." In a shaking voice hoarse with emotion, MacArthur replied: "I'm long overdue. I'm long overdue."

A soldier in filthy long drawers and a torn undershirt hobbled forward to introduce himself as a major who had fought at Bataan. "Awfully glad to see you, sir," he said. "Sorry, I'm so unpresentable." MacArthur shook his hand. "Major, you never looked so good to me."

The prison receptions were a foretaste of the tumultuous greeting MacArthur and his liberating Americans received when they entered Manila proper. Men, women and children swarmed through the streets shouting, "Veektory!" or "*Mabuhay!*" (Tagalog for "Hurray!"). Filipinos stripped of all their possessions by the lords of the Greater East Asia Co-Prosperity Sphere broke into Japanese-owned stores, shops and breweries, drinking and singing and seizing everything in sight, joyous loot which they tried to press upon their liberators. MacArthur was overcome, although he insisted on a simple ceremony, merely a salute to the colors. Shaking General Chase's hand, he said: "I'm a little late, but we finally came."

The Americans had moved swiftly on Manila, but recapture of the city was to be a grinding, bloody ordeal. With a population of 800,000 the capital was one of the largest cities of Southeast Asia. Its buildings of ferroconcrete designed to resist earthquakes and its old Spanish stone fortifications were ideal for defense. Its numerous wooden structures and the thatched-roof houses of the barrios made it highly flammable. This last was one of the reasons why Yamashita had decided not to defend Manila. He also could never feed its huge population while under fire or defend its vast, flat metropolitan area. That was why he had directed Gen. Shizuo Yokoyama of the *Shimbu* Group to destroy the bridges over the Pasig River, dividing the city into northern and southern halves, before evacuating.

But General Yokoyama was *Shimbu* commander in title only. Because of the army-navy rivalry and the peculiar way in which might became right, possession of 16,000 of the troops in the 20,000-man garrison gave actual command to Rear Adm. Shanji Iwabachi. With reluctance, Yokoyama agreed to help Iwabachi defend Manila. Although the admiral's sailors had no training or experience as foot soldiers, they did have an abundance of weapons and naval guns salvaged from ships in the harbor.

Upon the arrival of the Americans, Iwabachi withdrew south of the Pasig, demolishing the bridges and as much as he could of the military facilities and supplies in the port area. Flames from the demolitions spread to the highly flammable dwellings of the slums, and American troops lost two days fighting fires. Meanwhile, MacArthur's headquarters with typical optimism issued a bulletin announcing the imminent retaking of the city. MacArthur's staff began planning a victory parade. But there would be no such celebration for a month, and then not very much left of Manila to parade through. Crossing the Pasig, MacArthur's soldiers encountered stubborn resistance from Iwagachi's sailors. Eleventh Airborne driving up from the south was even more fiercely engaged, for the admiral had expected the attack from that direction and had fortified it more.

Fighting in Manila was street combat at its most vicious: building by building, block by block. Americans accustomed to battle on beaches or inside dense jungles quickly learned the skills that their brothers had acquired in the cities and towns of Italy, France and Germany. To conquer a building, they entered from the top. Squads of soldiers worked their way from roof to roof, chopping holes in each of them to descend downward, floor by floor, with grenades and flamethrowers.

MacArthur forbade air support of his troops for fear of inflicting casualties on Filipino civilians. Nevertheless, civilians died in large numbers because of the use of artillery by both sides. Japan's brutal soldiery multiplied the dead and wounded by murdering, beating, raping and even burning innocent Filipinos caught within their lines. In all, 100,000 Filipinos were killed—almost six times the number of soldiers killed on both sides—and probably three or four times that many were wounded. On March 3 General Griswold reported that the last enemy resistance in the city had ceased. Of Allied cities only Warsaw had suffered more devastation than Manila, and the ruined city joined the ghostly, ghastly company of the Polish capital, Stalingrad, Dresden and Nanking.

The restoration of Manila was to preoccupy both MacArthur and Osmena for months to come. Epidemics had to be prevented, shelter found for the homeless, succor for the sick and wounded, law and order restored, port facilities and utilities rebuilt or repaired and commerce revived. For months possession of Manila would be more of a liability than an asset, a great drain upon the resources needed for operations in Luzon. But to Douglas MacArthur the reconquest of Manila was the fulfillment of a sacred mission. On February 27 a ceremony celebrating the restoration of the Commonwealth government was held in Malacañan Palace. Osmena and MacArthur were present. MacArthur gave a brief and moving speech retracing the history of the loss of the archipelago to Japan followed by the days of despair in the Pacific and then the counteroffensive and triumphal return. He was himself deeply moved as he spoke, his voice again hoarse and trembling. He paused many times as though unable to continue. Addressing Osmena he said: "Your country thus is again at liberty to pursue its destiny to an honored position in the family of free nations. Your capital city, cruelly punished though it be, has regained its rightful place—Citadel of Democracy in the East. Your indomitable—" MacArthur's voice cracked and broke. He could not finish. Instead he asked the assembly to recite with him the Lord's Prayer. Later, he explained why he had broken down: "It had killed something inside me to see my men die."

While XIV Corps had been advancing on Manila, General Swift's I Corps had removed the Japanese threat to the Sixth Army's rear and flanks. It had also captured the key town of San Jose, gateway to Yamashita's mountain fastness inside *Shobu* Group, while destroying much of his armor. XI Corps under General Hall had had little difficulty in its opening operations on Bataan, easily capturing Olongapo on Subic Bay. But when it started eastward along the base of the peninsula, it ran into rough going in Zigzag Pass. Here the Japanese were entrenched in strong, camouflaged positions. Because they were invisible, it was thought there were not many of them. Piecemeal attacks based on that mistaken assumption proved to be costly. One regiment of the 38th Division lost so many key officers and NCOs that it had to be withdrawn from combat. Hall promptly relieved the division commander, replacing him with General Chase, whose flying columns had been first to enter Manila. Chase did not immediately change the situation. It was not until after he was reinforced and received aerial support from a newly completed airfield that the 38th Division finally cleared Zigzag. After that XI Corps had little difficulty taking the remainder of Bataan, where there were, in fact, only 1,400 defenders.

Corregidor fell to a masterly airborne-seaborne assault. Because the tadpole-shaped island was so small, it was at first feared too little to risk airdrops. But then it was decided that to hit Corregidor from the sea right after it was assaulted from the air, would greatly reduce the risk. Paratroopers from the 503rd Regimental Combat Team leaped into the sky over what once had been the island's golf course and parade ground, a slope about 350 yards by 200. Less than an hour later assault troops landed on the southern beaches near the foot of Malinta Tunnel. They rapidly began to root the Japanese out of their American-built warrens inside Malinta. On the morning of February 26, the Japanese defenders, either by accident or design—it would never be known—exploded the tons of ammunition and explosives stored in the tunnel. A series of mighty blasts shook Corregidor. Scores of Americans and hundreds of Japanese were killed by concussion or flying debris, buried in rockslides or hurled unconscious into the sea where they drowned. With that, "the Rock" was once again American.

Even before the fall of Manila, Bataan and Corregidor, MacArthur had ordered General Eichelberger's Eighth Army to launch the liberation of the remaining islands of the archipelago. He had no authority from the Joint Chiefs to do so, and especially not from the Combined Chiefs. The British had been assured that these islands would be cleaned out by Filipino guerrillas. But MacArthur, since September 1944, had been determined to liberate the entire archipelago on his own. For some mysterious reason still unexplained the Joint Chiefs let him do as he pleased.

Actually seizure of these islands could have little if any effect on the defeat of Japan. It might be that the conquest of Palawan Island and the Zamboanga peninsula at the southwest corner of Mindanao, as well as some islands in the Sulu archipelago, could be justified as bases for aerial support of a projected Australian invasion of Borneo. But the fact was that by 1945 destruction of the Japanese navy and the far-ranging operations of American submarines had severed Japan from communication with Borneo. Even the Borneo operation, therefore, was of no strategic value. Neither were the southern islands of the Philippines. If they were anything at all, the operations there were wasteful because MacArthur used five full divisions to liberate these lightly held islands, leaving Krueger's Sixth Army seriously weakened in his battle against Yamashita's powerful forces.

Although the Southwest Pacific commander never thought it necessary to explain why he undertook this useless, wasteful campaign, it seems likely that he was motivated by a mixture of humane, personal and selfish considerations. Certainly the barbaric treatment of Filipino prisoners by the Japanese would be reason enough to liberate as many Filipinos as possible. Also there had emerged a pattern of growing brutality among Japanese guards in proportion to the advance of the liberating Americans. On Palawan they had massacred 140 American and Filipino captives. MacArthur might have feared wholesale slaughter as Japan came closer to defeat. Such is indeed a humane consideration, but nonetheless a nonmilitary motive. Civilian populations in occupied countries all over Europe were exposed to Nazi wrath because of the Allied decision to concentrate on the defeat of the Wehrmacht rather than to be distracted by campaigns of liberation. If such judgment appears callous and inconsiderate, so is war.

MacArthur's other motives are not quite so pure. There is no doubt that he wished to be known as the liberator of *all* the Philippines. Thus the personal consideration. The selfish one is the deliberate commitment of the Eighth Army, the 11th Air Force and much of the Seventh Fleet to an unproductive campaign so that these formidable forces would not be transferred to Nimitz. Such dodges are, of course, commonplace. Patton during the Bulge deliberately ordered Manton Eddy to get the 4th Armored Division engaged before Bradley, who had already taken his 10th Armored, could snatch away this formation also. But to have held out on Nimitz after the Central Pacific chief had been so generous to him at Leyte does indeed suggest that MacArthur operated on a one-way street.

Whatever the motivations for the campaign, it was carried out by Eichelberger with an élan and despatch that reminded MacArthur of Stonewall Jackson in the Shenandoah Valley. Eichelberger was ably assisted by the ships and airplanes of Admirals Kinkaid and Barbey, by the Marine pilots whom Halsey had lent to MacArthur at Leyte and by the "webfoots" of the Engineer Special Brigades. Landings were made on Palawan, Zamboanga, Panay, Mindanao and Cebu. In all there were fourteen major and twenty-four minor amphibious operations in the southern islands. In all of them the Japanese withdrew inland where they were left to the tender mercies of the Filipino guerrillas. Although they were not completely subdued until the end of the war, the chief towns, roads and airfields that they had abandoned were all in Allied hands, and by June civil government was in operation. Brilliant as the campaign and its splendid air-sea-land cooperation had been, much of the success was also due to the flaming new aerial war which the American Superfortresses had brought to Japan.

The first American strike on the home islands was at the iron and steel works of Yawata on Kyushu June 14, 1944. In Washington jubilation was so great that both the House and Senate suspended deliberations to hear the announcement of the raid by Maj. Gen. Kenneth B. Wolfe, chief of the 20th Bomber Command, as well as his prediction that destruction of Japanese industry was now imminent.

But Wolfe's forcast was premature. There were not yet that many Superforts, and they were distracted from stepping up their attacks by the necessity of flying their own fuel over the Hump from India. Also the big bombers were new and still suffered from mechanical bugs. When General Arnold called Wolfe from Washington to order more strikes on Japan, Wolfe tried to explain these difficulties to him. As a result, he was relieved of his command and replaced by Maj. Gen. Curtis E. LeMay.

LeMay was only thirty-nine, a big, husky, full-faced man who had commanded B-17s in Europe. His exasperating habit of speaking in low, indistinct and sometimes garbled tones was complicated by the inveterate cigar or pipe clenched between his teeth. But LeMay was a driver. He worked to improve the accuracy of radar bombing—as yet not too successful an innovation—and increased the size of the basic bombing formation. But for all of this, the 20th's bombers were not nearly as effective as the wildly exaggerated stories the Stateside press reported. The Superforts flew only about two sorties per month against the enemy, only half of which were against Japan itself. Pinpoint bombing of industrial targets in Manchuria had been more successful, but actually of no real strategic value because Japan's vanishing merchant marine was unable to carry Manchurian products to the home islands. But then the B-29s struck Hankow (Hankou) in support of Chinese efforts to halt Japanese offensives of November–December 1944. They also hit Formosa to support MacArthur's invasion of Leyte.

The Hankow raid was significant because incendiary bombs were used with encouraging results. Firebombing seemed to be the answer to the thus far disappointing results of the B-29 daylight precision-bombing raids. For decades the U.S. military had known how vulnerable to fire the cities of Japan were. As far back as 1919 a Marine officer had proposed building high-speed cruisers to carry seaplanes armed with fire bombs to Japan. In 1939 Admiral Yamamoto had said: "Japanese cities, being made of wood and paper, would burn very easily. The army talks big, but if war comes and there were large-scale air raids, there's no telling what would happen."

With the results of the Hankow raid in mind, LeMay began to experiment with incendiaries. On February 4, 1945, his Superforts raided Kobe, Japan's sixth largest city, dropping only firebombs from high altitudes. Results were good. Five of the twelve chief factories were damaged and production at the two largest shipyards was cut in half. Tokyo was hit by a second high-altitude, incendiary raid on February 25. Probably because LeMay now had 200 B-29s, the results were even more impressive than the Kobe strike: 28,000 structures were destroyed.

With the bad weather ahead precision bombing would become less effective as visibility was reduced. Such difficulties, however, would not limit incendiary bombing as much, especially if the bombs were dropped in area attacks. Fire-bombing would be even more successful if done from low altitudes. This would avoid the strong winds over Japan, which buffeted the big bombers at high altitudes. It would also allow the planes to carry a heavier bomb load. Low-altitude attacks, of course, would increase the danger from Japanese AA fire, but LeMay thought it would be worth the risk. He was convinced when, early in March, one of his group commanders flew a huge B-29 over Tokyo at night and at low altitude and returned to base unharmed.

On March 8, 343 Superforts, armed with incendiaries only, took off from Marianas bases to bomb Tokyo at night from as low as 4,900 feet. Even their machine-gun ammunition had been removed to provide for heavier bomb loads. The planes were to bomb individually from wide, loose formations. Such new tactics took the Japanese completely by surprise. A rectangular target area more than four times as densely populated as the average American city quickly burst into flames fanned by a moderately heavy wind. Almost sixteen square miles of Tokyo were completely burned out, including 18 percent of the industrial area. Some 267,000 buildings were destroyed in this most destructive bombing in history.

The Japanese in Tokyo were completely unable to cope with such new tactics. Their fire-fighting equipment was primitive and their firemen untrained. The flames rapidly raged out of control. Dwellings made of paper or packing-case wood flared and vanished like matches. Water in the canals began to boil. Clouds of steam rose into the air to mingle with thick drifts of smoke and soot. Charred bodies were strewn all over the city and in the end 83,000 people died and another 41,000 were injured.

For the rest of the war American strategic bombing was modeled on the March 9 raid on Tokyo. By early June, Japan's six chief cities—Tokyo, Nagoya, Kobe, Osaka, Yokohama and Kawasake—were devastated. Forty percent of the structures in these cities were razed to the ground. Millions were homeless. Now, with 600 B-29s available, LeMay turned to firebombing Japan's lesser industrial centers, hitting fifty such selected targets. Next his bombers began to mine Japanese home waters. Because of American submarine warfare the Japanese had been forced to confine their shipping to the Inland Sea and coastal waters. But this too came under interdiction when American bombers, trained by navy mine experts, began sowing mines in Shimonoseki Strait between Honshu and Kyushu. Strategically, this was almost as effective as the firebombing. At Kobe tonnage shipped dropped from 320,000 tons in March to 44,000 in July. LeMay had become so confident of bringing Japan to her knees that he ordered his pilots to drop leaflets warning Japanese civilians of impending raids. Such disdain for Japan's ability to defend her people had an enormous psychological effect.

Never before in the history of warfare had the retribution overtaking an aggressor nation been so terrible and complete. Once again the American people had shown that to arouse them was to turn loose the dreadful demon dwelling within them, as well as all other men. After Pearl Harbor, in a thickening mood of revenge, Americans embraced every and any weapon, however horrible, however contrary to their normal peace-loving instincts, if it would satisfy their vengeance. It was because of this that Japan lay prostrate, her cities desolated, her people scourged and homeless, all but a thin shred of her communications with her stolen empire cut fast away, and her soldiers in the Philippines left to fight on without hope of help from home.

Tomoyuki Yamashita was the ablest commander that the Americans had faced so far in the Pacific. By his skill in delaying tactics he exacted from Walter Krueger's Sixth Army the maximum in casualties and turned his campaign to clear Luzon into a grinding, wearying, frustrating, bloody battle. Sixth Army began its mission already depleted by troops assigned to Eichelberger's operations in the south. Its first objective after the fall of Manila was to subdue the *Shimbu* Group astride the city's water supply to the northwest. To do this troops of Griswold's XIV Corps moved into the Marikina Valley to secure the Wawa and Ipo dams, believed to be the source of Manila's water supply. A bitter two-month struggle for Wawa dam was almost at an end when MacArthur discovered that Wawa was no longer in use and that Ipo dam was Manila's source of water.

Ipo was easier to take. Fifth Air Force fighter-bombers dropping napalm, and the assistance of a regiment of valiant Filipino guerrillas, helped the Americans capture the dam. This victory ended resistance from the *Shimbu* Group, whose soldiers withdrew deep into the Sierra Madre mountains, where they were harassed by Filipino guerrillas and whittled by the twin grim horsemen of war, starvation and disease.

Griswold's conquest of the *Shimbu* Group was far less difficult than Swift's war of attrition against the *Shobu* Group commanded by Yamashita himself. Swift's XI Corps had been so badly depleted by MacArthur to reinforce Eichelberger that he was outnumbered almost 2 to 1, enormous odds for any attacking force, especially one striking against well-fortified and well-defended mountain positions. Shipping shortages also ruled out an amphibious hook into Yamashita's rear. So it was straight-ahead slogging and slugging against a triangular defense marked by the towns of Baguio, Bontoc and Bambang.

At first the assault on Baguio, Yamashita's headquarters and the former summer capital of the Philippines, moved slowly. Units of the 33rd Infantry Division under Maj. Gen. Percy Clarkson found that Route 11—the best road to Baguio—was strongly defended. Other 33rd formations, however, moving north and east from the coastal town of Caba encountered surprisingly little resistance. Clarkson's troops captured Bauang on the coast and then turned inland to take Naguilian. They were now in Yamashita's rear, and Clarkson eagerly signaled for permission to dash west along Route 9 and come down on Baguio from the northeast. There was no immediate response, but the 33rd continued to move along Route 9. Within a week its soldiers were halfway to Baguio. It was then that Krueger was able to relieve the 37th Infantry Division from a mopping-up mission in Manila and send it into line behind the 33rd. By then air strikes and the forays of Filipino guerrillas had so mauled Yamashita's supply lines that his men were on starvation rations. Yamashita had already ordered all civilians and the Filipino puppet government out of Baguio, and he himself later departed for the Bambang sector. There were not many Japanese defenders left in the Baguio leg of the triangle. These made their last stand in the Irisan Gorge of the Irisan River. They held out for six days, finally withdrawing to join the other remnants of the Baguio command in the rugged mountainous terrain of the rain forests.

Although Baguio had fallen, Bambang and Bontoc remained unconquered. Until the end of the war the Japanese defenders in north central Luzon still held the Americans off. MacArthur had been simply unable to overcome Yamashita's skillful delaying tactics. The Japanese commander had taken advantage of every feature of the terrain lending itself to defense, and had compelled his American counterpart to fight the most costly kind of warfare: crosshatched, cross-grained combat. MacArthur's admirers speak of the campaign on Luzon as "the achievements of a great strategist." But tactics and terrain, not strategy, were the decisive factors in the campaign against Yamashita, and they redounded to the enemy chief's advantage. The same might be said of Kesselring in his masterly defense against Clark in Italy. For some inexplicable reason, where Clark has been roundly criticized for taking so long in a contest actually settled by attrition on the Western and Eastern fronts, MacArthur, fighting in the same kind of terrain against the same kind of quality commander and with identical results, has not. MacArthur's strategy in the Philippine landings was superb, and well executed by Krueger and Eichelberger. The dash on Manila was also masterly. But the decision to liberate the entire archipelago with the consequent depletion of Krueger in the north to reinforce the empty but showy triumphs of Eichelberger in the south contributed to Yamashita's stubborn defense. Why, it may be asked, was it necessary to conquer *Shobu* Group? Yamashita could have been contained. All the ports and airfields and sites for the invasion of Japan were already in MacArthur's hands. Yamashita so far from the sea and unable to build airfields, caught in a cup of his own devising, certainly could not expect help from either element. His lines of supply and communication were cut. Unless he chose to sally forth in a suicidal banzai, he could only wither on the vine. Yet, MacArthur, who would later criticize Nimitz for his "awful" handling of the campaign on Okinawa, had ordered the same sort of useless attacks with identical "sacrificial" losses.

MacArthur also welched on the promise to Nimitz to return to him by

January 19 those naval forces he had borrowed for the Lingayen Gulf landings. Nimitz needed them for the Iwo Jima assault scheduled for February 19. MacArthur replied that he still required them for Eighth Army's landings in southern Luzon. Nimitz agreed to allow MacArthur to retain some of the borrowed ships, including four old battleships, for three more weeks. But MacArthur and Admiral Kinkaid insisted on holding six battleships and twenty-six destroyers. In reply, Nimitz, who had cooperated generously at Leyte and was still allowing Halsey's Third Fleet to operate in the Philippines, consented to retention of four battleships, two cruisers and twenty-two destroyers—but even this angered MacArthur. In the end, he did not release any of the borrowed warships for use against Iwo Jima. His intent upon occupying Manila had become so obsessive that it blocked out all considerations of the Central Pacific commander's legitimate requirements; and thus there were fewer enemy guns destroyed when the U.S. Marines came ashore on the warm black sands of Iwo Jima.

120. The Battle for Iwo Jima

BY THE END OF 1944 it became apparent that Iwo Jima in Japan's Volcanic Islands 760 miles south of Tokyo must be seized as soon as possible. The B-29 Superfortresses, which had begun to bomb Japan in late November, were suffering severe losses. Japanese antiaircraft fire was intense. Japan had many fighters left to defend the home islands, and those which could not shoot down a Superfort would ram one. There was no chance of surprise raids because Iwo-based radar warned the homeland in time to fly off fighter protection.

Worst of all was the long 1,500-mile flight home to Saipan and Tinian. Crippled Superforts unable to fly more than a few hundred miles from their target cities fell into the sea and were lost with their crews. Those that fell between Iwo and their bases might be reached by Dumbo rescue planes, but if the crews were saved, the enormously expensive B-29s were lost.

With Iwo Jima in American hands, the Superfortresses could fly much closer to Japan undetected, they could be escorted over the targets by Iwo-based fighters and airmen shot down off the very shores of Japan could hope for the arrival of Iwo-based rescue craft. With the eventual use of Iwo Jima as a regular stop-off on return flights, smaller gasoline loads would provide for larger bomb loads. Iwo's own raids on the Marianas would cease, releasing Marianas-based fighters for use elsewhere, while possession of the island would nail down the eastern flank of the invasion of Okinawa to follow. Such was the importance and urgency of Iwo Jima as 1944 gave way to 1945. Seldom before had an objective been so obviously necessary, and perhaps never before had so much counted on such a no-account place.

Iwo Jima, or Sulfur Island, was only four and a half miles long by two and a half miles wide. It was a loathsome little cinder clog, a place of volcanic ash, black and charred, shaped like a lopsided pork chop. Maj. Yokasuka Horie thought Iwo was an abomination, "only an island of sulfur, no water, no sparrow and no swallow. . . ." He detested it so thoroughly that he suggested to its commander, Lt. Gen. Tadamichi Kuribayashi, that the best way to defend it was either to sink it or cut it in two. Kuribayashi was so unimpressed that he transferred Horie to Chichi Jima 160 miles to the north. Kuribayashi was like that: curt, stern, cold—one of those moon-faced pudgy men who are all energy and driving ruthlessness. He did not look like a warrior, but then, neither did Narses, the great eunuch general of the Eastern Roman Empire. Kuribayashi's soldiers did not like him. He provided no girls from the "comfort troops," not even sake. They said he was a martinet, but he was really something better, a perfectionist whose credo was one harsh word: duty.

Tadamichi Kuribayashi began his career in the cavalry, then the Japanese elite arm. He moved from success to success, even meeting the emperor—an honor rarely bestowed on anyone below cabinet rank—when he reorganized the Imperial Guards Division. Then in June of 1944 he was given command of Iwo Jima, another honor because Iwo was within the very Prefecture of Tokyo.

His command was the customary Japanese mixture of army and navy troops numbering about 21,000 men, of which his own 109th Infantry Division formed the nucleus. Iwo's new chief began his tenure by sending all civilians back to Japan and setting all troops to work turning their unlovely little black isle into a fixed position surpassing even Peleliu. His 21,000 men gave him the great advantage of proportion—just enough men in the right place—and thus spared him the confusion and carnage of a crowd. He had guns by the thousands, some of them bizarre. His monster 320-mm spigot-mortar fired a 675-pound shell bigger than the firing cylinder, fitting over and around it. Its life was no more than a dozen rounds, and its erratic projectiles were feared as much by its crew as by the enemy. Yet, with 60,000 U.S. Marines eventually crowded onto tiny Iwo, it would be difficult for even this unpredictable weapon not to do some damage. His rockets, varying in size from 550 to 200 pounds, were also more noisy than nasty, but otherwise Kuribayashi had a ferocious armament, which he judiciously emplaced in an elaborate complex of caves and concrete blockhouses.

Where Peleliu had had 500 caves, Iwo Jima had 1,500. Where Tarawa had had blockhouses and pillboxes of ferroconcrete, Iwo also had them—walls five feet thick, ceilings ten feet high, sandbagged, humped around with fifty feet of sand and piggybacked with machine-gun turrets—and they were invisible. Kuribayashi's underground tunnel system surpassed even the Umurbrogal. To build it his men had worked wearing gas masks to filter out the fumes from the island's numerous sulfur wells. Some of them were so hot that the men could cook

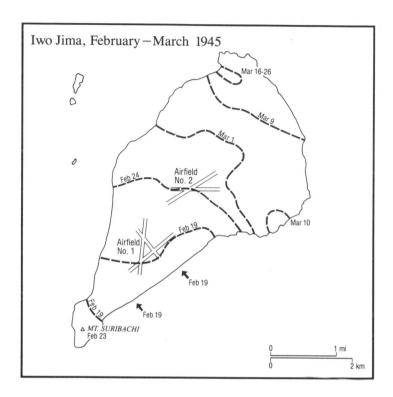

Iwo Jima, February–March 1945

their rice over them in twenty minutes. Kuribayashi had also constructed two formidable defenses. They were a mile apart, reaching from shore to shore, and thus could not be flanked. Nor could Iwo be taken by an amphibious thrust at its rear where steep cliffs rose from the sea. Its only accessible beaches were those on the lower half of the island on either side of the pork chop tail. They looked peaceful enough. From the sea all that could be seen were terraces of volcanic ash, which the wind and the sea had piled inland at heights up to fifteen feet. Otherwise there was just barren flatland dotted with hummocks of sand. Usually these innocent-appearing humps concealed gun positions. Iwo's fantastic terrain had made concealment easy. The island had no bottom and could receive massive underground installations. One of these was Kuribayashi's communications center located in the north just above the unfinished Airfield Number 3. It was a fortress 150 feet long and seventy feet wide, with five-foot walls and a ten-foot roof. It could be reached only by a 500-foot tunnel seventy-five feet underground. Kuribayashi's gunners and riflemen firing from these positions would not be the usual bad shots that the Americans had encountered across the Pacific. They were not marksmen equal to the Marines, but their commander had made them the best in the empire, prepared to execute the slaughter celebrated in the Iwo Jima Garrison Song:

Where dark tides billow in the ocean
A wink-shaped isle of mighty fame
Guards the gateway to our empire:
Iwo Jima is its name.

We brave men who have been chosen
To defend this island strand
Filled with faith in certain triumph
Yearn to strike for Fatherland.

Oh, for Emperor and homeland
There's no burden we won't bear.
Sickness, hardship, filthy water
These are less to us than air.

Officers and men together
Work and struggle, strive and trust,
Till the hated Anglo-Saxons
Lie before us in the dust.

Anglo-Saxons?

Though there were indeed many men of that racial strain in the force forming for Iwo Jima, the Japanese who had mistakenly assumed at the war's outset that their chief opponents would be the British army and navy had again erred in identifying the foe.

They were *Americans.* There were indeed Anglo-Saxon names such as Cates or Chambers, but there were others such as Schmidt or McCarthy or Stein or LaBelle or Basilone, and there was that commonalty of the Smiths that could be any or all of these. Chief of the Smiths was old Howlin' Mad, now a gruff lieutenant general at sixty-three. He was commander of the troops mounting out for Iwo but the position was purely titular. Kelly Turner commanded at sea and Maj. Gen. Harry Schmidt would be in command ashore once his V Corps had landed. "I guess they brought me along," Smith quipped, "in case something happens to Harry." Actually, it was the admirals who wanted him—to lean on his experience. Schmidt, who had brought off the master maneuver at Tinian, would have no such opportunity against Kuribayashi's steel labyrinth. His three Marine divisions—Third, Fourth and Fifth—would have to storm their way through it. Schmidt's only choice was between the eastern and western beaches. He chose the western ones for supply and the eastern for the landings. In assault would be the Fourth Marine Division on the right with the Fifth on the left and the Third in reserve.

Maj. Gen. Keller Rockey commanded the fledgling Fifth. He had been assistant commandant of the Marine Corps before taking over the newly activated Fifth in January 1944. Although big Keller Rockey's formation was new to battle, neither he nor many of his men were. Rockey had fought in Belleau Wood and was entitled to wear the French fourragère.

Maj. Gen. Clifton Cates—the oldest "salt" of them all—commanded the Fourth Division. This calm Marine with the smooth aristocratic features had also been in Belleau Wood, coming out of France loaded with French and American decorations. He had commanded the 1st Regiment at the Tenaru on Guadalcanal and the Fourth Division at Tinian. His was the toughest assignment, landing on the right in the heart of enemy defenses. "You know," he said to a war correspondent, "if I knew the name of the man on the extreme right of the right-hand squad of the right-hand company of the right-hand battalion, I'd recommend him for a medal before we go in."

Graves Erskine's Third Division would not "go in" immediately, waiting in floating reserve. This was not the sort of mission to enchant Erskine. Like Rockey and Cates, he had fought in France and had once taken a thirty-eight-man patrol into no-man's-land and returned with only four. He was ordered: "Go back out there and throw a rock at that machine gun so it will shoot at you and then we can knock it out." Erskine threw the rock. Strong-willed and intelligent—he had been Smith's chief of staff—Erskine was also an unusually handsome man. But he was stern. On Guam he had court-martialed artillerymen for firing short rounds at riflemen. His men called him "the Big E." These were the "Anglo-Saxons" mounting out for Iwo, and as they sailed to battle they sang a sardonic little ditty diametrically different from the fire-eating Iwo Jima Garrison Song. To the tune of "McNamara's Band" it went:

Right now we are rehearsing for another big affair,
We'll take another island, and the Japs will all be there.
And when they see us steaming in, they'll take off on the run.
They'll say, "Old pal from Guadalcanal, you didn't come here for fun!"

February 19, 1945, was a bright, clear day.

Superforts were bombing, Hellcats were strafing, all the warships and rocket ships were thundering, but Iwo Jima lay still and deathlike—Mount Suribachi squatting toadlike to the south, the black beaches and hummock-dotted sands silent and foreboding in the center, the jumble of ridges and hills vaguely visible to the north. It was a day made for invasion, and the Marines went roaring in.

They hit the beaches at about nine o'clock, and within an hour both divisions had all their assault battalions ashore and fighting.

One hour.

That was all that Tadamichi Kuribayashi gave the Americans. Then his gunners struck them with all the fury of their formidable armament. Shells shrieked and crashed among the invaders, every hummock spat automatic fire while the beaches erupted with land mines showering sand, flesh and blood on the survivors. But the Americans had had the chance to move inland from 200 to 300 yards and that was all that they needed. On the left flank the Fifth Division was attempting to drive across the island.

"C'mon, you guys," yelled Manila John Basilone. "Let's get these guns off the beach."

His gunners shouldered their weapons and sprinted up the beach toward the terraces, their feet sinking to the ankles in that hot, loose sand, the soles of their shoes turning warm, their calf muscles straining—but Manila John would never see Dewey Boulevard again. A mortar shell exploded in his very footprints, and he died with four of his men. Now in the ears of all those crawling, sprawling, sprinting Americans was the sound of battle that would not subside for forty-five days: the constant crashing of enemy shells, the whisper and sigh of bullets, the soughing of big projectiles and the whizzing of shrapnel. Concussions lifted men and slammed them down. Foxholes frantically dug in the beaches filled in almost instantly with sliding buckshot sand. No hummock could be trusted. A captain sat down on one and was knocked unconscious by the blasting of a 5-inch gun beneath him.

Still on the left Tony Stein was fighting one of the most incredible personal battles of the Pacific War. He had devised his own weapon, an air-cooled machine gun, taken from a navy fighter, which he called "the Stinger." Weighted with his ammunition and his Stinger, Stein covered his entire company when it landed. He struck at pillbox after pillbox, killing twenty Japanese. When he ran out of ammunition, he threw off his helmet, shucked his shoes and socks and ran to the rear to get more. He did this eight times, pausing each time to help a wounded Marine to an aid station. At last the enemy forced his platoon back. Stein covered the withdrawal. Twice his Stinger was shot from his hands, before the inevitable bullet found him, and he died.

It was with such men that the Fifth drove across the island, cutting off Mount Suribachi to the south. But behind them both beachheads were bloody, smoking, burning shambles. Kuribayashi's gunners had raised their sights to the beaches. Only a few landing craft were able to penetrate that curtain of fire drawn offshore and on the beaches. Tanks in lighters, amtanks or amtracks sank or blew up on the beaches. Others duelled the enemy's shore guns.

On that extreme right for which General Cates had shown such respect, the "ghouls" of Jumpin' Joe Chambers fought into their Gethsemane. They called themselves ghouls for the ghostly antiflash cream they had smeared on their faces in anticipation of heavy demolition work. But cream does not ward off bullets. Although Chambers's men took the high ground on the right, beating off repeated enemy counterattacks, there were only 150 frontline survivors out of a battalion of more than a thousand when they were relieved that night. But the right flank was nailed down and on the far right Cates's men had reached the edge of Airfield Number 1.

Reinforcing regiments coming ashore came in riddled, forming on a battlefield more horrifying than any in the memory of the oldest salts. Death had been violent on Iwo Jima. Few indeed were the corpses not mangled. Some were cut in half. Legs and arms lay everywhere, sometimes over fifty feet away from the bodies from which they had been wrenched. It was as though the owner of a toy store had gone berserk and strewn handfuls of heads and limbs over a miniature island. Except for the puttee tapes of the Japanese and the yellow leggings of the Americans, it was difficult to identify the fallen of either side. From it all rose the intensifying sticky-sweet stench of death and decay.

The Marines incurred 2,420 casualties the first day, to secure a beachhead 4,000 yards wide from south to north, 1,000 yards deep where the island had been crossed on the left and 400 yards deep on the right. Of these casualties more than 600 were dead and more were dying.

There were more casualties during the night and no respite from the noise of battle. The huge enemy rockets appeared, although they turned out to be harmless, invariably overshooting their targets and falling uselessly into the sea. But at first they terrified the Americans, passing overhead with a horrible blubbering sound and trailing tails of red sparks. Soon the Americans grew contemptuous of them, calling them Bubbly-Wubblies. But they had the deepest respect for the artillery fire coming from Iwo's highest ground to the south on Mount Suribachi.

Big Col. Harry (the Horse) Liversedge had led a Raider battalion on New Georgia, and on Iwo he led the Twenty-eighth Marines against Suribachi. On February 21, the second day on Iwo, Liversedge attacked south with two battalions abreast. Warships, artillery and rocket ships pounded Suribachi's approaches. They knocked out some pillboxes, but merely unmasked most. The Marines had to take them with flamethrowers and dynamite. Navy and Marine fighter planes strafed Suribachi's slopes and dropped tanks of napalm. But the firebombs merely flamed and flickered out. There was nothing to catch fire. Harry the Horse's men gained only 200 yards and took heavy casualties. The wounded were taken to the beach aid stations where wine-colored bottles of whole blood hung like bougainvilleas from bayoneted rifles stuck upended in the sand.

At night the men of the Twenty-eighth dug in. They did not like the sight of the flares rising from Suribachi. The commander there had signaled, "We should rather like to go out of our position and choose death by banzai charges." Kuribayashi curtly answered, "No," and told him to mark the enemy positions with flares. In their light a storm of Japanese artillery fire fell on the Americans, making the night almost as bad as the day had been.

Next day the Twenty-eighth resumed the assault, supported by fighters and bombers, tanks, half-tracks, naval gunfire and field artillery. By nightfall all of Suribachi's lower pockets had been cleaned out. "At dawn," said Harry the Horse, "we start climbing."

They started at dawn and went right up.

Sgt. Sherman Watson and Pfcs. Ted White, George Mercer and Louis Charlo climbed to the summit without spotting a single Japanese. Watson reported back. Lt. Col. Chandler Johnson of the 2nd Battalion made a decision. He rounded up a forty-man patrol under Lt. Harold Schrier.

"If you reach the top," Johnson said, "secure and hold it." He handed Schrier an American flag. "And take this along."

Schrier's patrol picked its way up the northern or inner slope of the volcano. They climbed through the debris of shelled positions, through an eerie silence.

Battle sputtered to their rear, but here there was no sound. They worked past the Japanese defenses and came to the crater where they spread out and charged.

Nothing—nothing but the lava pit yawning beneath their feet.

Suribachi had fallen.

At 10:30 the American flag was raised above it, flown from a hollow pipe someone had found and jammed between rocks. It was raised by Schrier and Sgts. Ernest Thomas and Henry Hansen, by Cpl. Charles Lindberg and Pfc. James Michels. It fluttered while Sgt. Louis Lowery photographed the event, and Pfc. Jim Robeson snorted, "Hollywood Marines!" and wisely kept a wary eye peeled for Japanese.

They came. Even as the tiny flag brought forth a cheer from the Marines below, an enraged Japanese jumped from a cave to heave a grenade. He was shot dead. An officer charged waving his sword. He was shot into the crater.

"Let's go!" Schrier called. "We haven't got any time to waste around here. Let's get back to work."

For the next four hours fierce fighting raged at every level of Suribachi, but by 2:30 the volcano was fairly secure, and it was then that the most dramatic picture of World War II was recorded.

From below Suribachi the Marines could barely see the little 54 by 28 inch flag. One of them went aboard LST 779 beached near the eastern base of the volcano. He borrowed a big flag, 96 by 56 inches, and took it up Suribachi. Joe Rosenthal of the Associated Press saw him going, and followed with his camera. When Rosenthal reached the summit, he saw six men raising the new flag. They were Pfc. Ira Hayes, Pfc. Franklin Sousley, Sgt. Michael Strank, Corpsman John Bradley, Pfc. Rene Gagnon, and Cpl. Harlon Block. Rosenthal photographed them, and the great battle photograph of American arms had become history.

The flag had risen at Iwo Jima, and although scoffers have called the event "a phony," there was very little fakery about the deaths that shortly overtook Sergeant Strank, Corporal Block and Private Sousley, or in the wound of Corpsman Bradley. Nor was the first flag raising a piece of stagecraft any more than the subsequent deaths of Sergeants Hansen and Thomas and Private Charlo, or the wounds suffered by Privates Robeson and Michels. The flag went up in the first place because the sight of it would cheer Marines below who knew that the Japanese looked down their throats so long as they held the highest land on Iwo. When the first flag proved too small to be seen, a second and bigger flag went up. This raising was photographed by Rosenthal with no attempt to stage it—why was everyone facing away from the camera and thus unidentifiable for the newspapers?—and it turned out to be superb. The fact that the famous flag raising was the second, not the first, no more affects its place in history than the fact that the Suribachi flag raising was itself intermediate to the first flag raising on Guadalcanal and the last on Okinawa. The facts were that Suribachi fell because American Marines suffered and died to conquer it, and that some of them raised flags above it to proclaim the victory.

It was the second, famous flag which was seen by Secretary of the Navy

James Forrestal, stepping on the warm soil of Iwo Jima just as it was caught and flung by the strong north wind whipping Suribachi's crest. Forrestal had followed the battle aboard the command ship *Eldorado.* Standing on the battleground, with General Smith beside him, he saw the flag unfurling, and he turned to Smith. "Holland," he said, "the raising of that flag on Suribachi means a Marine Corps for the next five hundred years."

To the Marines slowly slugging into the First Belt in the north, the news came over the loudspeaker used by the beachmaster to direct unloading operations. The speaker blared:

"Mount Suribachi is ours. The American flag has been raised over it by the Fifth Marine Division. Fine work, men."

Those who could turned dust-rimmed staring eyes to their rear. They squinted and saw the flag. They looked to the north once more, the loudspeaker blared again:

"We have only a few miles to go to secure the island."

The young-old eyes blinked.

"Only," one Marine repeated. "Only . . ."

All but three of the twenty-six Medals of Honor awarded to Marines and their navy corpsmen on Iwo Jima were won in that dreadful up-island battle which began the day the Twenty-eighth Marines swung south on Suribachi and the remainder of the assault troops slugged north against Kuribayashi's first line. On the right flank the Fourth Division fought a fierce battle to overrun Airfield Number 1 as well as to penetrate deeper into the cliffs north of it. On February 23, the fourth day, Cates's units made their biggest gains. They broke into the ridges at the point where the pork chop bellies out. They thought they had pierced the enemy's inner line, but they had actually only reached the Meat Grinder. It was then that the Marines began to suspect that they had seized no beachhead on Iwo because Iwo was all beachhead. The familiar rhythm of break-in, break-out, break-through was not to be repeated, and Howlin' Mad Smith was not to be favored with that blessedly stupid counterattack: "That is generally when we break their backs."

In the center the Twenty-first Marines of Erskine's Third Division had been committed. They tried to cross Airfield Number 2. But each penetration seemed to become a disaster. Units were raked from the flanks, chewed up—sometimes wiped out. Tanks were destroyed by interlocking fire or were hoisted into the air on the spouting fireballs of buried mines. Engineers crawled through the sands on their knees searching for these kettle-shaped killers, which the Japanese had sown so abundantly, but they couldn't find them all. Nor could flamethrowers or dynamite knock out all the pillboxes. There were 800 of them in this sector 1,000 yards wide and 200 deep. Nevertheless when Erskine came ashore on February 23 with Gen. Harry Schmidt, he ordered the Twenty-first Marines to move forward "at all costs." They did, and then they were ordered, "Hold at all costs." This they did also, and on the following day the Third Division's spear-heads flowed through the hole they had punched in Kuribayashi's first line, fighting with a bravery that drew from Admiral Nimitz his famous salute: "On Iwo Jima, uncommon valor was a common virtue." But on the left flank the Fifth Division had been brought up short in an evil pocket known as Hill 382, while the Fourth had entered the Meatgrinder.

The Hill, the Amphitheater and Turkey Knob were the three knives of the Meatgrinder. Within this complex was Iwo's highest ground and its huge under-ground communications center. Tanks buried to their turrets guarded all natural approaches. Antitank guns poked their muzzles from cave mouths. Antiaircraft 75s and twin-mount artillery pieces lowered to fire point-blank were everywhere, together with an abundance of heavy and light machine guns. Because these three strongholds were mutually supporting, capable of bringing down fire on each other, they had to be attacked at once. Up against the Hill went the Twenty-third Marines, the Twenty-fourth took on the Amphitheater and the Twenty-fifth assaulted Turkey Knob.

At the Hill the Marines reached the summit with ease—only to be struck down by a murderous converging fire, much of it coming from the rear where they had passed hidden pillboxes without noticing them. Under cover of a smoke-screen, the Americans came back down. A similar reception awaited the Marines at the Amphitheater and Turkey Knob. They could take these heights at will, and then regret it. Each time it became clear to the Japanese that they could not hold, they withdrew and called for artillery and mortars. When the Americans with-drew at dusk, the Japanese returned.

For seven days—from February 26 to March 3—the Fourth Division was chewed and torn on the knives of the Meatgrinder, taking so many casualties that 400 pints of whole blood were used on a single day. Casualties among the naval doctors and corpsmen were also severe. Gradually, the persistence of the Ameri-can attackers whittled the Japanese. Caves were sealed off, observation posts destroyed, blockhouses blasted into rubble. Amtanks following the paths cut by bulldozers squirted liquid flame through holes made by demolition men, pack howitzers were dragged to the front to fire point-blank. On March 3 the Meat-grinder was utterly broken. By then the Fourth Division had lost 6,591 of its men killed or wounded, and its fighting capacity was down by 30 percent.

On the left at Hill 362 men of the Fifth Division met just as fierce resistance. Here the Marines flushed the enemy out of their caves by rolling drums of gasoline into them and shooting them aflame, or by lowering explosives by rope —which the Japanese sometimes cut—or bringing up rocket trucks to launch flights of missiles on the hillside. Hill 362 held out to the last man. On March 1 a Japanese came out of a cave to tap his grenade on his helmet to arm it. The Marines opposite him ducked. Then they raised their heads. The Japanese was crouching with the grenade to his ear, as though listening. He tapped it again and listened. No sound. He tapped it a third time. This time it went off.

"I am not afraid of the fighting power of only three American divisions," General Kuribayashi signaled Tokyo, "if there are no bombardments from aircraft and warships." On March 4 he called for his own aircraft and warships. "Send me these things, and I will hold this island. Without them I cannot hold."

He would not get them, although Imperial General Headquarters had tried. On February 21 the kamikazes made a major attack on American shipping off Iwo. The escort carrier *Bismarck Sea* was sunk, big *Saratoga* so badly damaged that she was forced to return to Pearl Harbor, and the escort carrier *Lunga Point,* an LST and a transport slightly damaged. All of the suiciders perished.

That was all the help Iwo received from a homeland beginning to reel under the massive raids of the Superfortresses. On March 4, the very day that Kuribayashi appealed for help, a Superfort was desperately trying to raise Iwo on its radio. At last Sgt. James Cox heard a voice.

"This is Iwo. What is your trouble?"

"We are running low on gasoline. Can you give us a bearing for Iwo?"

"Course 167 for 28 miles. Do you prefer to ditch offshore or try to land?"

"We prefer to land."

Cox switched off his radio. He watched the tiny black cinder drawing closer. Lt. Raymond Malo circled the flashing, smoking little island twice before making a perfect landing on the runway. Malo and Cox grinned to hear the cheering of the Marines outside.

The first B-29 had made an emergency landing on Iwo. It was the forerunner of 2,251 Superforts with 24,761 airmen who made emergency landings on Iwo. This is not to suggest that all these planes and men actually were "saved." At the time there were only 600 Superforts in the Marianas bases. Obviously the same plane and the same crew were preserved more than once. Nevertheless, rarely in warfare, with the outcome of the battle still in doubt, has the value of an objective been so quickly demonstrated.

General Erskine had come to realize how skillfully the Japanese had adapted to American attacks. When artillery and naval gunfire began the bombardment preceding an attack, they scampered down to their deepest caves to wait it out. When it lifted, they sprinted back to their guns to receive the Marines. Erskine decided to make a surprise flanking attack on stubborn Hill 362-C at night and without a preparatory barrage. In the early morning dark of March 7, the Ninth Marines attacked. A whistling wind and a cold rain dashed against the faces of the men of the left flank battalion stealing silently up the hill. Behind them were the center and right battalions who would move out in daylight. The left-flank Marines found the enemy asleep in their positions and destroyed them to a man. They were jubilant, reporting that they had taken Hill 362-C. But they had not. In the darkness they had mistaken Hill 331 for their objective. Now it was daylight, and the center and right battalions had been spotted and pinned down. They fought back savagely. The men in the center were crucified. Some companies had been reduced to squad strength. Lt. William O'Bannon commanded fewer than ten men, all that remained of a 200-man F Company. When tanks came to the rescue to straddle them and drag them inside the escape hatches, there were only five left. It appeared that Erskine's surprise attack had ended in disaster.

But it had not. The center and right actually had penetrated the outer works of a formidable bastion. On the left the men who had taken Hill 331 fought doggedly on to take their original objective, Hill 362-C. They took it, but only because their surprise capture of Hill 331 had destroyed the enemy's heaviest concentration. By nightfall all of the highest ground on the Motoyama Plateau was in American hands—and from it the end was in sight. On the following night some unknown enemy commander obsessed with martyrdom disobeyed Kuribayashi's prohibition of the banzai and led a force of 1,000 suiciders against the Fourth Division on the right. They hoped to penetrate Airfield Number 1 to destroy aircraft and installations with the explosives wound around their waists. But they were themselves blown up. The Marines easily killed 784 of these human bombs in what was the only mistake in Kuribayashi's skillful and valiant defense.

On the following day, March 9, a patrol of the Third Division reached the northern end of Iwo Jima. The men clambered down the rocky cliffs to the sea, filling a canteen with water and sending it back to General Schmidt with the inscription: "For inspection, not consumption." Iwo Jima had been traversed in eighteen days. But there were still many Japanese holding out in pillboxes and blockhouses. To exterminate them required the most grinding work in this grim-mest battle in the history of the United States Marine Corps. One blockhouse withstood endless shelling and demolition attempts with forty-pound shaped charges. After surrounding supporting positions were cleaned out, the Marines bypassed it, leaving it to tank-dozers to seal off its air vents and collapse it with 1,600-pound dynamite charges.

On the night of March 21, General Kuribayashi signaled Major Horie on Chichi Jima: "We have not eaten or drunk for five days. But our fighting spirit is still running high. We are going to fight bravely to the last." Three days later Horie's radio crackled again: "All officers and men of Chichi Jima—good-bye."

On the following night some 300 shadowy figures rose from the ruins of positions in the enemy's last northwest pocket. Many carried samurai sabers, for there were many officers among them. Most of them carried explosives. For once they did not shriek and howl but slipped silently down to the western beaches where they fell on the AAF's VII Fighter Command. They had chosen the only troops on Iwo untrained to fight on foot and in the dark, and they executed a fearful slaughter among them. Then they attacked the Fifth Marine Pioneer Battalion where they were annihilated in a counterattack. The Marines searched eagerly for the body of Tadamichi Kuribayashi, for they had heard that it was he who had led this last lash of the Japanese tail. It was never found. But there were the bodies of more than 5,000 Marines to be buried in grim testimony to the skill and tenacity of Tadamichi Kuribayashi. Nearly 20,000 more were wounded. Of the twenty-four battalion commanders who had landed with their men, nineteen were killed or wounded. Yet, against what may have been the world's strongest fixed position, the Marines had killed all but a few wounded survivors of Kuribayashi's 21,000 men. Here was a dramatic reversal of the 3 to 1 adverse casualty ratio usually accepted by a force invading from the sea, and this was the theme of General Erskine's speech dedicating the cemetery of the Third and Fourth Divisions.

"Let the world count our crosses!" he cried.

"Let them count them over and over. Then when they understand the significance of the fighting for Iwo Jima, let them wonder how few there are. We understand and we wonder—we who are separated from our dead by a few feet of earth; from death by inches and fractions of inches.

"The cost to us in quality, one who did not fight side by side with those who fell can never understand."

But even to the victors a battlefield is a sad and tragic place. Carved on those rows and rows of white crosses, punctuated here and there by Stars of David or the plain headboards of the "unchurched," were epitaphs written by the buddies of the fallen. One of them, in a single, stark cry of anguish, synthesized all the folly and waste of war itself:

BUT, GOD—FIFTEEN YEARS IS NOT ENOUGH!

121. Preparing for Okinawa

NEITHER THE JAPANESE nor the Americans expected Okinawa to be the last battle. To the United States, this chief and largest of the Ryukyu Islands chain was to be the last stepping-stone to Japan, an excellent staging area of airfields and anchorages within less than 400 miles of Kyushu in southern Japan. To Nippon, Okinawa was to be the anvil upon which the hammer of a Divine Wind was to destroy the U.S. Navy.

Destruction of American sea power was still the chief objective of Japanese military policy. Sea power had brought the Americans through the chain of island fortresses as far as Iwo Jima within the Prefecture of Tokyo and now to within a few hours' flying time of the home islands. Only sea power could bring about the invasion of Japan, something that had not happened in 3,000 years of Nippon's recorded history.

The last attempt was made in 1281 when the Mongol Emperor Kublai Khan massed a huge invasion force on the Chinese coast. Japan was poorly prepared to resist the Mongols, until a terrible typhoon—the *Kamikaze* or "Divine Wind" —sprang up and demolished the enemy fleet.

In early 1945, nearly seven centuries later, a whole host of Divine Winds was blowing out of Japan. These were the suicide bombers of the Special Attack Forces, the new kamikazes who had been so named because the Japanese seriously believed that they too would destroy an invasion fleet. They first appeared on October 25, 1944, at the beginning of the Battle of Leyte Gulf. But many of them missed their targets and many of them were shot down. Of 650 kamikazes launched in the Philippines, about a quarter of them scored hits—but mainly on small ships. But the high command, still writing reports in rose-colored ink, still carefully keeping the national mind empty of news of failure, announced hits of 100 percent. Privately, the high command estimated the percentage at between 12 and 50 percent, while stoutly maintaining that all the ducks were geese: carriers, battleships and cruisers. Nor was it admitted that the Special Attack Forces were needed because Japanese bombers could not penetrate the American fighter screens or AA barrages.

So the kamikaze corps was born in a great outburst of national enthusiasm and anticipated glory. Emperor Hirohito gave it his reluctant approval, and it was organized under the sure hand of Vice Adm. Matome Ugaki. By early 1945 it was an integral—if not the dominant—part of Japanese aerial strategy. So many kamikazes would be ordered out for an operation joined by so many fighters and so many bombers. The fighters were to protect the suiciders and the bombers to guide them to their targets.

They needed to be guided because they were usually a combination of old, stripped-down crates, from which even the instruments had been removed, and young, hopped-up pilots. Ugaki did not use his best planes or his best pilots, as Vice Adm. Takejiro Onishi had done in the Philippines. Ugaki considered this wasteful. The white flying scarf wound around the suicider's head—the badge of the kamikaze—would inflame them with the spiritual power needed to compensate for their lack of flying skill and outmoded aircraft. To this end they were hailed as saviors: wined and dined, photographed and fondled. Many of them attended their own funerals before climbing into the cockpit on legs made wobbly by the sake drunk at farewell feasts. It did not seem to occur to the Japanese that the bottled spirits thus imbibed might inhibit the purpose—to say nothing of the aim—of the kamikaze corps. Nevertheless, it was this very real faith in the success of the suiciders that dictated to the high command how the Battle for Okinawa would be fought: sink the enemy fleet at sea so as to cut off and isolate the invading army, which would then be destroyed. These were the orders which Maj. Gen. Isamu Cho brought to Lt. Gen. Mitsuru Ushijima on Okinawa in January 1945.

Ushijima and Cho were a team much in the mold of the great German duo of Hindenburg and Ludendorff in the First World War. They had served together in many stations, and they were as unlike as two commanders can be. Ushijima, chief of the Thirty-second Army, graying, in line for full general, was a man of great presence and serenity, capable of inspiring his subordinates and of judging his own incapacities. To fill these he had chosen Cho as his chief of staff. Fifty-

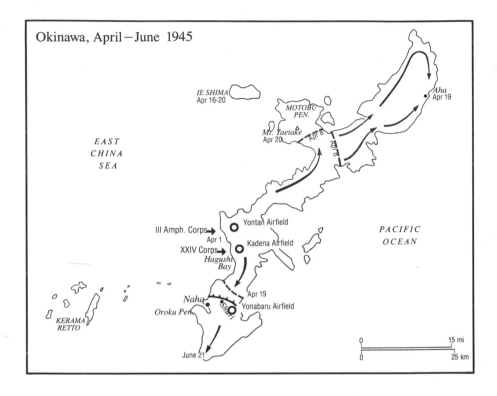

Okinawa, April–June 1945

one, also in line for promotion, Cho was a firebrand and an organizer, strict but resourceful, aggressive and so invincible in argument as to be unpopular. Between them, the two men laid down the rules for defending Okinawa:

One Plane for One Warship
One Boat for One Ship
One Man for Ten of the Enemy or One Tank

Fulfillment of the first stricture depended on the kamikaze corps, for Ushijima had few aircraft remaining on Okinawa's five airfields. The second would be handled by nautical Divine Winds of the Sea Raiding Squadrons. These were enlisted youths fresh out of high school, brainwashed like the kamikaze and trained to ram enemy warships with explosive-stuffed motorboats. There were about 700 suicide boats hidden in the Ryukus, and half of these were about fourteen miles west of Okinawa in the islets of Kerama Retto. The third stricture was directed to about 100,000 soldiers of Thirty-second Army, of whom about

20,000 had been conscripted from an Okinawan population of roughly half a million people.

Ushijima's strongest fortifications were in the south, where a fantasia of cliffs and caves made excellent defensive terrain. Here he built a line facing north like a broad arrowhead. It was anchored at Naha on the left or west coast and Shuri and Shuri Castle in the center-right to Yonabaru airfield on the right or east coast. Along a twelve-mile front it sealed off the southern quarter of Okinawa's 485 square miles. Holding it was the bulk of Ushijima's forces: the 62nd and 24th Infantry Divisions, the 44th Independent Mixed Brigade. To the west of Naha on Oroku Peninsula were 3,500 sailors and 7,000 civilians under Vice Adm. Minoru Ota. Roughly 3,000 soldiers of the 2nd Infantry Unit under Col. Takehiki Udo held the wild and uninhabited half of northern Okinawa—that part which Ushijima at the urging of Cho would hold only lightly. Nor would he defend the excellent western beaches opposite the Hagushi anchorage. He would hold the southern beaches to his rear and strongly defend his fortified line and the approaches to it. Like Yamashita and Kuribayashi before him, Ushijima was going to use delaying tactics to fight a war of attrition. Even Yontan and Kadena airfields east of the Hagushi beaches were to be abandoned, destroyed the moment the Americans arrived by a special force drawn from the *Boeitai,* the Home Guard which Ushijima had ruthlessly drafted from Okinawan males between twenty and forty. The wrecking crew was called the *Bimbo Butai,* or Poor Detachment, by those Japanese soldiers whose loathing of Okinawa and all things Okinawan had already become a problem for General Ushijima.

There was indeed little to love about the Great Loo Choo, as Okinawa was called when Chinese influence was strong enough to give the entire chain the name of Loo Choos, or "bubbles floating on water." Japanese military might and difficulty with the L sound changed this to the Ryukyus in 1875, but even the Divine Emperor could do nothing about the "bubbles." No place in the world is more humid than Okinawa, from whose skies as much as eleven inches of rain can pour in a single day. Its people of mixed Chinese, Malayan and Ainu ancestry are among the most docile human beings, with no history of war, neither making nor bearing arms (a fact which would fill Napoleon Bonaparte with furious contempt). Most Okinawans were poor and primitive farmers, working their tiny plots of sweet potatoes, sugar cane or rice. Their religion was a kind of animism, the chief feature of which was the worship of the bones of their ancestors. These were kept in urns within lyre-shaped tombs strewn over the plains and low hillsides. Ushijima had found the tombs ideal for concealing machine guns and cannon.

Many of Ushijima's soldiers filled their diaries with complaints of the lack of fresh vegetables, a result of taking so many males off their farms. To compensate the Thirty-second Army commander issued each man a pint of sweet-potato brandy, proclaimed a temporary amnesty for drunkards and promised another ration around mid-April. Before then, however, the aircraft of the American Fast

Carrier Forces began hammering Okinawa to an extent for which no extra issue of brandy could compensate. One Japanese superior private wrote in his diary:

While some of the planes fly overhead and strafe, the big bastards fly over the airfield and drop bombs. The ferocity of the bombing is terrific. . . . What the hell kind of bastards are they? Bomb from six to six!

They were "hard-nosed bastards," these Americans, converging on Okinawa in the greatest amphibious force ever assembled for the most furious battle of the Pacific War. Ten old battleships, ten cruisers and scores of destroyers and gunboats—the heaviest bombardment concentration of the war—would cover the landings on the Hagushi beaches, as well as the far-ranging new battlewagons and big fleet carriers of the Fast Carrier Forces, the flying buffer of the British task force in the southern Ryukyus, the U.S. Navy's minesweepers and underwater demolition teams, the big B-29 bombers of the Twentieth Air Force and the Tenth Army's own Tactical Air Force made up chiefly of Marine pilots and commanded by Marine Maj. Gen. Francis Mulcahy.

Okinawa was to be the biggest single battle of the Pacific with 548,000 Americans of all services involved, and also history's greatest amphibious assault —an attacking force of 183,000 men, of which 154,000 were in the actual combat divisions.

Tenth Army was commanded by Lt. Gen. Simon Bolivar Buckner, Jr., the son of the famous Confederate general of the same name and rank. Called "the old man of the mountain," Buckner was a big man, ruddy-faced, white-haired and devoted to the physical conditioning of troops. He had spent four years in Alaska and the Aleutians and had hoped to lead the invasion of Japan from the North Pacific, until that thrust was canceled in favor of the strike from the center, which Buckner was called down to join. His Tenth Army was only a new name for seven veteran divisions: the 7th, 27th, 77th and 96th Infantry Divisions of Maj. Gen. John Hodge's XXIV Corps and the First, Second and Sixth Marine Divisions of Maj. Gen. Roy Geiger's III Corps.

On March 26, 1945, the 77th's soldiers began taking the islands of Kerama Retto, destroying the lairs of Ushijima's suicide boats. Other islets were also occupied to provide bases for the 155-mm Long Toms of the 420th Field Artillery group, which laid down a galling fire on the Hagushi beaches.

These beaches were to be taken by the soldiers on the right or south and the Marines on the left or north. Maj. Gen. Archibald Arnold's 7th and Maj. Gen. James Bradley's 96th were to drive east across the island's waist to capture Kadena airfield and then wheel south to attack abreast. Maj. Gen. Lemuel Shepherd's brand new Sixth Marine Division and the First Marine Division now commanded by Maj. Gen. Pedro del Valle would move on Yontan airfield before swinging north to overrun that half of the island. Meanwhile, the boated Second Marine Division still under Maj. Gen. Thomas Watson would make a feint off the southern or Minatoga beaches, which Ushijima had so carefully fortified. By the end of March the American armada was off Okinawa, its troops listening in amusement to a Radio Tokyo broadcast announcing the sinking of enemy battle-ships and cruisers by the dozen and destroyers by the score. An American-educated voice with a faint singsong inflection simpered:

"This is the Zero Hour, boys. It is broadcast for all you American fighting men in the Pacific, particularly those standing off the shores of Okinawa . . . because many of you will never hear another program. . . . Here's a good number, 'Going Home' . . . it's nice work if you can get it. . . . You boys off Okinawa listen and enjoy it while you can, because when you're dead, you're a long time dead. . . . Let's have a little juke-box music for the boys, and make it hot. . . . The boys are going to catch hell soon, and they might as well get used to the heat." A few more days of jocular references to "bottom half of ocean occupied by U.S. Navy" and dire predictions of the varieties of dreadful deaths awaiting the fighting troops, and Radio Tokyo had lost its audience. "The boys off Okinawa" had gone ashore.

That was on April 1—Easter Sunday, April Fool's Day, or L-Day as it was officially called. The L stood for "landing" but the Americans who hit the Hagushi beaches with hardly a hand raised to strike them had another name for it.

They called it Love Day.

122. The Battle for Okinawa: Death of a President

THE BIMBO BUTAI broke and fled at the first salvo of American naval guns. Airfields at Yontan and Kadena were abandoned, and only the inevitable confusion of putting 50,000 men ashore on a beachhead eight miles wide hindered the invasion of Okinawa. Otherwise the landing was going forward with incredible speed all along the line.

The honeymoon following Love Day had been brief for the soldiers of the U.S. Army's XXIV Corps—hardly more than a weekend. On April 2, while the Second Marine Division made another feint off the south coast, the XXIV's spearheads raced across the island. Next day they turned south, 7th Division on the left, 96th on the right. Their advance seemed to be effortless. But on April 4 they found resistance "stiffening." It grew stiffer daily until, on April 8, "greatly increased resistance" was reported. The Americans had come into the outerworks of Ushijima's barrier line. Three days later they were stopped cold under one of the Pacific War's most furious and skillful artillery barrages. A regiment of the 27th Division—now ashore after the Second Marine Division sailed back to Saipan—was ordered to reinforce the 96th on the right.

On April 12 the Japanese launched a land-air counterattack. While another massed kamikaze raid struck at American shipping during the day, at night the Thirty-second Army attacked all along the line. The Japanese were repulsed, but they came again the following night, when they were stopped again. Total losses were 1,594 dead.

It seemed to General Hodge that the moment for a breakthrough had arrived. He scheduled a powerful thrust with three divisions abreast for April 19. In the meantime, the 77th Infantry Division, assisted by Maj. Jim Jones's Marine Reconnaissance Battalion, moved to seize Ie Shima just off the western tip of the Motobu Peninsula. It was a good-sized island and had an airfield. The 77th's dogfaces landed on April 16 and fought a fierce four-day battle in which 4,706 Japanese were killed as against only 258 Americans dead and 879 wounded. One of the dead was the most famous and beloved civilian of all the United States services; the war correspondent Ernie Pyle.

Throughout the campaigns of North Africa, Italy and France, Pyle had been the chronicler of the glories and miseries of GI Joe. It was he who had fought for recognition of the ordinary mud-slogger and had single-handedly compelled Congress to give the combat soldier extra pay and the Combat Infantryman's Badge (a raise and an honor refused by the Marines on the ground that all their men were combat troops). He had left Europe to march with the GI Joes of the Pacific and had chosen to land with the First Marine Division at Hagushi. Before he left Ulithi, another newsman called out jokingly, "Keep your head down, Ernie," and Pyle had snorted, "Listen, you bastards—I'll take a drink over every one of your graves." But he had fallen among the fighting men whose cause he had championed, and over his grave on Ie Shima his new comrades of the Pacific placed the inscription: "On this spot the 77th Infantry Division lost a buddy, Ernie Pyle, 18 April 1945."

Next day the XXIV Corps launched its all-out attack.

For the Marines moving north on Okinawa, Love Day was succeeded by a series of lovely days. Barely opposed, whooping as they rode bareback on shaggy little Okinawan ponies, the men of the Sixth and First Divisions might have been going to a football game. By nightfall they had taken two airfields and secured all their objectives at a cost of only twenty-eight killed, most of them victims of two kamikaze attacks. But all objectives which were expected to take three days or more to seize at the cost of many lives were now in American hands. At dusk on Yontan airfield, bulldozers were already clearing away Ushijima's wrecked planes, along with his clever dummies of sticks and stones. Already an airplane was touching down. But it had a red ball on its fuselage. Marines eating their rations stood quietly erect and sauntered toward it with unlocked rifles. The Zero pilot clambered out of the cockpit and came toward them. He stopped. Between the moment when he reached for his pistol, and the next when he sank to the runway, riddled, an expression of indescribable horror had twisted his face.

A Marine looked down at him ruefully, and said: "There's always some poor bastard who doesn't get the word."

On April 19, with the 7th Division on the left, 96th in the center and 27th on the right, with six battleships, six cruisers and nine destroyers firing on call, 650 Marine and naval aircraft flying close-up support, twenty-seven battalions of artillery firing everything from 75-mm to 8-inch shells, the XXIV Corps attacked.

And it began to measure its advances by the yard. The army infantry had come to its own Tarawa or Peleliu or Iwo Jima. It had come into defenses against which enormous massed bombardment from land, sea and air were hardly more than smokescreens. Barrages might get them close to such positions, but only ardor could overrun them. Only the impetuous foot soldier, slashing in with his hand weapons and using tanks, explosives and aimed flame, can succeed in such combat with armed and resolute moles. The naval shell's flat trajectory, the bomb's broad parabola, the artillery projectile's arc or even the mortar's loop cannot chase such moles down a tunnel. If they can occasionally collapse the tunnel and the whole position with a direct hit—a rare feat—only one spoke in the wheel has been destroyed and the wheel continues to turn. In the absence of that military miracle—direct hits *on call*—the rifleman has to go in. With his tanks, if he can.

But Okinawa's terrain and Ushijima's tactics made this almost impossible. In the 27th's sector a company of thirty tanks ran into a trap at Kakazu Ridge. Without covering infantry they were helpless against antitank guns and hurled satchel charges. Only eight survived. In one day, the 27th had lost two-thirds of its armor.

During twelve days of seesaw fighting against the Naha–Shuri–Yonabaru Line, the XXIV had advanced only two miles.

Within three days of "fighting" the First Marine Division had severed the island and reached the eastern sea wall overlooking the bay and the Pacific Ocean. This, at a cost of three dead and eighteen wounded. The division wheeled north to follow in the trace of the swift-moving Sixth. Now the Marines' chief problem was in caring for the Okinawan civilians who clogged the roads.

There were so many of them: women with babies at their breasts; children without parents; grizzle-bearded ancients hobbling along with bent backs, leaning on staffs and carrying pitiful small bundles representing all that the war had left them, that terrible war which had also robbed them of the authority of their beards and had exposed them to Japanese mockery and American pity; and the old white-haired women who could not walk, who merely squatted in the road, shriveled, frail, hardly bigger than a monkey, waiting to be carried, waiting for the kind Marine who might stop and stick a lighted cigarette between their toothless gums.

They were a docile people, and now they were terrified because the Japanese had told them the Americans would torture them. They were frightened also because they knew that among them were Japanese soldiers disguised as civilians. But their fear vanished with gentle treatment, with the policy of carefully searching all males between fifteen and forty-five—to discover many a knife or cartridge belt beneath a smock—and of placing all of these within prisoner-of-war camps. Soon the Okinawans were speaking openly of their hatred for the Japanese, their loathing for the Reign of Radiant Peace.

"*Nippon ga maketa,*" they said. "Japan is finished."

But Nippon was neither *maketa* nor *zemmetsu.* Nippon had at last recovered from the American carrier strikes at the homeland and was about to hurl her thunderbolts with characteristic suicidal fervor. On April 6 hundreds of kamikaze came roaring down from the north, and trailing after them in the spreading white majesty of her mighty bow wave came nothing less than a suicide battleship.

She was the *Yamato,* the mightiest warship ever built, the most beautiful battleship afloat and the last capital ship left to Japan.

Yamato had survived Leyte Gulf where her sister ship, *Musashi,* had not. *Yamato* could outshoot anything in the U.S. Navy. She had nine 18.1-inch guns firing projectiles weighing 3,200 pounds a distance of 45,000 yards, compared to the 2,700-pound shell and 42,000-yard range of the American 16-inchers. She displaced 72,809 tons fully laden, and drew thirty-five feet. She was 863 feet long and 128 in the beam. She could hit twenty-seven and a half knots at top speed or cruise 7,200 miles at sixteen knots. And she was sortieing out of the Inland Sea for Okinawa with only enough fuel in her tanks for a one-way voyage.

If soldiers and tanks, fliers and airplanes, sailors and boats could be enrolled in the ranks of the suiciders, it was logical that admirals and dreadnoughts should follow. There were three admirals coming with *Yamato,* and the light cruiser *Yahagi* and eight destroyers. There might have been more of them and more warships, but Admiral Toyoda could scrape up only 2,500 tons of fuel for the venture. Toyoda also had only 699 planes, half of them kamikaze, to hurl against the Americans in the aerial phase of the attack. He had hoped to have 4,500, but American strikes on the homeland had crippled aircraft production and had also destroyed many planes on the ground.

Still, Toyoda hoped for great things from the *kikusui,* or "floating chrysanthemums," which was the name given to ten massed kamikaze attacks planned for Okinawa. His hopes for the Surface Special Attack Force led by Vice Adm. Seichi Ito aboard *Yamato* could not have been other than forlorn. He gave the great ship only two fighter planes for cover.

Yamato shoved off from Tokuyama at 3:20 on the afternoon of April 6, exactly twenty minutes after the first of the *kikusui* dived on the American ships off Okinawa.

The kamikaze and other Japanese aircraft attacked the forest of American masts in Hagushi anchorage and the Fast Carrier Forces in the northern Ryukyus. At Hagushi destroyers *Bush* and *Calhoun* were sunk, plus a minesweeper, an LST and two ammunition ships. Nine other destroyers were damaged, along with four destroyer escorts and five minesweepers. Up north the carrier *Hancock* and two destroyers of the Fast Carrier Forces were hit.

Although it was an impressive first day for the first sally of the *kikusui,* the Japanese had lost 135 aircraft.

At ten o'clock in the morning of April 7, *Yamato* entered the Pacific Ocean. Admiral Ito planned upon pouncing on the Americans off Okinawa at dusk the following day. Overhead his pathetic pair of fighter escorts turned to fly back to Japan. Submarine *Hackleback* was sighted by destroyers and driven off. But *Hackleback* had alerted Admiral Spruance. Patrol planes took off from Keramo Retto to shadow the mighty dreadnought, now sailing in the middle of a diamond-shaped destroyer screen with cruiser *Yahagi* following. At 10:30 Rear Adm. Morton Deyo was ordered to lead a force of six battleships, seven cruisers and twenty-two destroyers north to intercept *Yamato.*

Kelly Turner signaled Deyo: "Hope you will bring a nice fish back for breakfast." Deyo seized a pencil to write, "Will try to—" just as an orderly handed him a message that scouts of the Fast Carrier Forces had found the enemy. Three air groups totaling 380 planes were preparing to strike. "Will try to," Deyo concluded, "if the pelicans haven't caught them all!"

The "pelicans" had. At 12:30 the American war birds were over the targets and diving. Two bombs struck *Yamato* near her mainmast, a torpedo pierced her side. At the same moment destroyer *Hamakaze* stood on her nose and slid under. *Yahagi* shuddered under a bomb and a fish and went dead in the water. At 1:30 the Americans came again and planted five torpedoes in *Yamato*'s port side. A half hour later the final attack began. Hellcats and Avengers fell from the skies to strike at the helpless giant. Bombs and torpedoes shook and staggered *Yamato.* Waves of roaring air were flung across her torn and twisted steel decks, jumbling sailors together in heaps. Admiral Ito emerged from such a struggling mass, bowed solemly to his chief of staff, and strode calmly into his cabin, either to embrace death or await it—the world never knew which.

Mighty *Yamato* was dying slowly. Her decks were nearly vertical, her battle flag almost touched the water, explosions racked her monster frame and her own ammunition began to explode. All around her, her sister ships were in their death agonies. At 2:23 P.M. on April 7, *Yamato* sank beneath the sea, a full day's steaming from Okinawa.

Japan had lost her once mighty navy, her suicide battleship had failed, and now it was up to the kamikaze and Ushijima's men on Okinawa.

In the north of that sixty-mile-long island the Sixth Marine Division had cornered the remaining 2,000 Japanese soldiers of Colonel Udo's northern defense force on Motobu Peninsula. "Cornered" in the sense that one may so isolate a hornet's nest. All of the enemy's concealed caves seemed to spit fire from scores of heavy Hotchkiss machine guns and hundreds of Nambu lights. "Jesus!" a Marine yelled, "they've all got Nambus, but where the hell are they?" By April

12 they had driven Udo's survivors to the crest of Mount Yaetake and were preparing to launch a pincers against them: three battalions from the west, two from the east. Suddenly they heard a bullhorn blaring at sea:

"*Attention! Attention all hands! President Roosevelt is dead! Repeat, our supreme commander, President Roosevelt, is dead!*"

The pallor and obvious ill-health of Franklin Delano Roosevelt which had so shocked General MacArthur in June of 1944, and which had become an issue in FDR's presidential campaign in the following fall, had begun to become obvious to many perceptive Americans. Photographs of him showed a gaunt and hollow-eyed man whose once magnificent physique seemed to have shrunk. At Yalta it seemed astonishing that a man who once had towered over the diminutive Stalin and the only slightly taller Churchill should appear hardly bigger, should seem slumped in his chair. Nevertheless, most Americans did not suspect that their president was in fact dying.

Roosevelt himself was careless about his health. He disdained all health regimens or prescriptions, discouraging even talk about health. He liked his personal physician, Rear Adm. Ross T. McIntire, the surgeon general of the navy, because McIntire was an eye, ear, nose and throat specialist who concentrated on the president's recurrent sinus affliction. Anne Roosevelt Boettiger, the president's daughter who lived with him in the White House during the last year of his life, had no confidence in McIntire. Yet, no one suspected tragedy when FDR boarded his special train in April for a brief vacation at the Little White House, his summer cottage in Warm Springs, Georgia. With him were his cousins, Laura Delano and Margaret Suckley, and his mistress, Lucy Mercer Rutherford. Mrs. Roosevelt was not present.

On April 12 the president was sitting for a portrait by the watercolorist, Elizabeth Shoumatoff, who had done earlier paintings of him. His cousins and Mrs. Rutherford were with him. At 1:00 P.M., apparently in a reference to lunch, FDR said, "We've got fifteen minutes left." Exactly a quarter hour later the president collapsed in his chair, never to regain consciousness. Margaret Suckley later said she saw him rub the back of his neck and heard him say, "I have a terrific headache."

At 3:35 that afternoon Roosevelt was dead. He was sixty-three years old. The cause of death was a cerebral hemorrhage probably resulting from arteriosclerosis. This could not be substantiated by Admiral McIntire's records, because they disappeared from navy files and were never found. Reference to this disease came from Fred Patterson, funeral director of H. M. Patterson and Son in Atlanta. He said: "On starting the embalming it was shortly discovered that he had been a victim of arteriosclerosis, which seemed to have seriously affected all of his arteries."

No president since Lincoln was mourned as deeply as FDR. As his funeral train moved out of Warm Springs bound for Washington late in the morning of April 13, the train moving slowly at thirty-five miles an hour passed through the small towns of the Carolinas and Virginia. The stations were thronged with mourners, who had stood for hours waiting for it. Mrs. Roosevelt, who had flown to Warm Springs from Washington, was aboard her husband's favorite car, the *Ferdinand Magellan*. She wrote of its progress: "I lay in my berth all night with the window-shade up, looking out at the countryside he had loved and watching the faces of the people at the stations, and even at the crossroads. . . . The only recollection I clearly have is thinking about 'The Lonesome Train,' the musical poem about Lincoln's death. I had always liked it so well—and now this was so much like it. I was truly surprised by the people along the way. . . . I didn't realize the full scope of the devotion to him until after he died. . . ."

No one was more shocked by FDR's death than Vice President Harry S. Truman. When he met reporters and was asked how he felt, he countered: "Did you ever have a cow fall on you?" But he quickly recovered, sent for the Cabinet and prepared to take the oath as the thirty-third president of the United States. Many Americans when they heard of FDR's death had paused, and then cried: "Oh, my God, *Truman!*" It seemed a terrible prospect. This neat little man in the bow tie and rimless glasses seemed to be the essence of mediocrity, chosen by Roosevelt as his running mate because of his ability to get along with Congress. FDR had treated him almost like a fifth wheel, confiding in him little. On such things as the atomic bomb or the agreements at Yalta, Truman was completely in the dark. He always said the first months of his presidency was "on-the-job training."

But he learned quickly. Because of his very simplicity, his direct mind uncomplicated by subtlety or nuance or guile, he was among all high-ranking Americans the quickest to see the blood on Koba's hands. It was chiefly due to Truman's simple courage and decisiveness that the Red flag did not fly over Western Europe and Japan.

Marines and soldiers, airmen and sailors fighting on, above and around Okinawa were stunned by the news of the death of Roosevelt. Many of them wept, most of them prayed. So many of these youths had known no president other than Franklin Delano Roosevelt. Having voted for him overwhelmingly in the last election, they had shown how they truly loved him, had depended on him—how much they did not realize until he was dead. For those at sea or on the airfields, there was the opportunity to show their grief by flying flags at half-mast or half-staff. For the Marines on Motobu there was only that brief, sorrowing pause —and then the attack once more into those nasty nests spitting death. It was four more days before Udo's last bastion fell, and not until April 20 that the rest of Motobu was secured.

In the meantime, the First Division had been enjoying what was called "Lilac Time." This was not battle as the First had known it in three years of tramping around the Pacific. Many battalions had built bivouacs with showers and mess halls. The men made shanties with sliding panels from abandoned Okinawan homes. Everyone had a pet: a pony, goat, even one of those multitudinous Okinawan rabbits that might have escaped the pot. Adept as ever at brewing jungle juice from their own garbage, they drank it out of "borrowed" Okinawa lacquer ware—one of the island's few crafts. But then they were ordered south to join the attack on Ushijima's barrier line. Two miles to the front, in a dimly lighted tunnel beneath Shuri Castle, the Japanese command was debating Isamo Cho's proposed counterattack.

Ushijima and his top commanders sat on canvas chairs at a rough flat table. Around them the stones of the tunnel glistened with sweat. Water from the moat surrounding medieval Shuri Castle seeped through every crevice and dripped on the earthen floor. Dim light glinted off the glasses worn by all present or danced on their collar insignia. An argument had begun between the fiery, arrogant Isamo Cho, now a lieutenant general, and the calm, unbudging Col. Hiromichi Yahara, the Thirty-second Army's chief of operations. Unimpressed by either the eloquence or the rank of Isamo Cho, it was Yahara who had raised the single protest against Cho's abortive counterattack of April 12–13.

Now Cho proposed a full-scale assault supported by the kamikaze and followed by massed artillery fire. It would not be a foolish banzai but a carefully prepared attack. The fresh 24th Division would strike the American center, opening a hole for the 44th Brigade to rush through in a thrust to the west coast. Then the 44th would wheel south and the First Marine Division—the hated butchers of Guadalcanal—would be isolated and annihilated. Twenty-fourth Corps would be rolled up. Counterlandings on either flank would be made, a strong one to the rear of 7th Infantry Division on the east coast. Even Yahara thought that the plan was a good one, detailed and "realistic." Actually, it was highly complicated, but involved operations were dear to the Japanese military mind. Yahara felt that it was Cho's strategy that was bad.

"To take the offensive with inferior forces against absolutely superior forces is reckless and will only lead to certain defeat. . . ." Yahara said. "Moreover, our forces will inflict but small losses on the enemy, while on the other hand, scores of thousands of our troops will have been sacrificed in vain as victims of the offensive."

Nevertheless, it was the impetuous Isamo Cho, not the reflective Hiromichi Yahara, to whom the impassive Mitsuru Ushijima gave his approving nod.

Ushijima's aerial assaults began at 6:00 P.M. May 3. Betty bombers striking at the ships in Hagushi anchorage encountered a storm of AA. Thirty-six were shot down. Only the kamikazes broke through, sinking destroyer *Little* and an LSM, while damaging a few smaller ships. After midnight, about sixty Bettys struck Tenth Army headquarters. They flew in, scattering "window," streamers of metal foil designed to cover radar screens with blips of nonexistent aircraft. Terrible, crisscrossing antiaircraft fire streamed upward, forcing the enemy to remain at high altitudes and to bomb aimlessly. An hour later Marine amtanks opened fire on troop-laden barges off the west coast, driving them into the annihilating guns of B Company, First Marines. Soldiers of the 7th Division did the same to the attempted landing on the east flank.

At dawn the main attack began. It went straight to the doom forecast by Colonel Yahara. Wave after wave of 24th Division soldiers sprinted forward to their deaths on that gray morning. To get in closer to the Americans, the Japanese moved among their own artillery shells—but the soldiers of the 7th and 77th divisions held firm. Offshore naval shelling and the massed firing of sixteen battalions of division artillery and twelve battalions of heavier corps artillery flashed and crashed among the Japanese to break up their charges or scatter them in their assembly areas.

Across the island, kamikazes dived again at the Hagushi ships, falling once more on the luckless small vessels of the radar picket screen. With them were the *baka* or "foolish" bombs. These were piloted, rocket-fired suicide missiles carried slung beneath the bellies of the Bettys. When a *baka* pilot sighted his victim, he was released from the mother plane. The *bakas* were well-named. Clumsy, with low fuel capacity, flown by poorly trained suiciders, they seldom hit anything. But the kamikazes sank two more destroyers, *Luce* and *Morrison,* as well as two more LSMs, while damaging carrier *Sangamon,* cruiser *Birmingham,* another pair of tin cans, a minesweeper and an LCS. But they again failed to hit the supply ships and they lost ninety-five planes.

Isamo Cho's counterattack, meanwhile, had been broken in blood. Geiger ordered the First Marine Division to strike on the right while the 7th and 77th held firm on the left. In three days of fighting the Marines penetrated nearly a mile, and Ushijima called off his assault. He had lost 6,227 dead and many, many more wounded. Combined army losses were 714 men killed or wounded while the Marines suffered 649 casualties in the more costly business of attack.

It was a tearful Ushijima who assured Yahara that he would henceforth listen to no one but him. Isamo Cho, meanwhile, sank into a sullen silence.

It was on May 7 that the Great Loo Choo's skies opened with rains that men of the First Marine Division found at least the equal of the New Britain monsoon. The downpour brought battle to a standstill and gave Ushijima a respite in which to improve his positions, and it also made the notorious Okinawa mud. It was everywhere, in the ears, under the nails, inside leggings or squeezed coarse and cold between the toes. It got into a man's weapons, it was in his food and sometimes he could feel it grinding like emery grains between his teeth. Whatever was slotted, pierced, open or empty received Okinawa mud. Also wounds. Men prayed not to get hit while rain fell and made mud. It stalled the bulldozer and turned haughty tank troops into pick-and-shovel men. Some days it denied the Americans the use of roads altogether, so that they could only be supplied by airdrop. Two strides and a man's shoes were coated, two more, and they seemed as though sheathed in lead, another two and it was wiser to shuck one's shoes and walk barefooted. Engineers working on the airfields threw away their shoes and labored with their feet inside sacking tied at the knees.

Obnoxious as the ordeal of Okinawa mud had become, it was a trifle in comparison to the suffering of the sailors of the ships on picket duty. Here the kamikaze and the *baka*s, probably mistaking destroyers for battleships and minesweepers for cruisers, attacked in massed hundreds. Men were burned horribly or blown into the ocean, either to drown or pass agonizing hours awaiting rescue. Those who survived the kamikazes' screaming dives went for days without sleep, their nerves exposed and quivering like wires stripped of insulation. Sailors in the boiler rooms worked in fierce heat. The superheaters designed to give quick pressure for high-speed maneuvering were often kept running three or four days at a time, though they had been built for only intermittent use. They had to be that way, for naval-air war off Okinawa was war at a moment's notice. To the aid of these suffering sailors came those Marine Corsairs that had been brought to Okinawa for close-up ground support. Their pilots fought the kamikazes until they ran out of ammunition, and then the big gull-wingers rode the suiciders down, forcing them away from the ships and into the water if possible—going after them with their whirling propellers, even.

Still the kamikaze scourge continued, and ship after ship sank or became a cripple to be towed away to the port facilities and landing-ship docks of Kerama Retto. After more than a month of such losses, the navy began to become concerned over the army's careful and slow tactics. "I doubt if the army's slow, methodical method of fighting really saves any lives in the long run," said Admiral Spruance. "It merely spreads the casualties over a longer period. The longer period greatly increased the naval casualties when Jap air attacks on ships is a continuing factor. . . . There are times when I get impatient for some of Holland Smith's drive. . . ."

Such comparison was really not fair to Buckner, simply because there was no room for maneuver. He was fighting the same kind of mountain warfare that had bogged down Clark in Italy and Krueger in Luzon. Why, indeed, was it necessary to annihilate Ushijima's remaining 60,000 men? Tenth Army had already secured and improved all the air and port facilities available on Okinawa. Why not contain the cut-off enemy and let him starve, or whittle him with aerial, naval and ground artillery bombardment, perhaps thus goading him into a desperation, backbreaking banzai? Undoubtedly, he would not remain completely contained but would sally forth in typical night forays aimed at spreading terror and destruction. But this could have only minor success. It could not inflict casualties on the Americans to the extent that they suffered in straight-ahead assault.

Nevertheless, at the urging of Kelly Turner, also impatient at the battle's slow progress with its attendant shipping losses, General Buckner did launch a straight-out four-division assault on May 10. Once again, the advance was measured by the yard. Showers of shells and bombs upon these human moles had the usual negligible effect. They had to be dug out of their holes. Tank-infantry teams were needed, but even these were skillfully thwarted by Ushijima's tenacious soldiers. A tank's direct cannon fire or aimed flame could be very effective, but the enemy also could knock out the tank with antitank guns or satchel charges. Tanks needed riflemen to support them, but riflemen were often reluctant to cover men protected by armor plate while the only thing between a rifleman and enemy fire was his khaki shirt.

Surprisingly, there is nowhere among the reports and accounts of the Battle for Okinawa the slightest suggestion that an amphibious strike in Ushijima's rear was even considered. Perhaps these fortified southern beaches were scouted and found too formidable to force. If this is so, then, because of Nimitz's ill-considered decision to take Okinawa by storm, there was indeed no other way for Buckner but straight ahead into the sausage machine. In the end, Okinawa did not fall until June 21. Some 7,000 Americans were killed ashore and another 5,000 died at sea, the worst losses suffered by the U.S. Navy in any naval campaign. Some 70,000 Japanese soldiers died and also 80,000 Okinawans, most of them civilians.

On June 15, Simon Bolivar Buckner, Jr., came to Mezado Ridge to watch an attack by a regiment of the First Marine Division. Buckner watched the assault for about an hour.

"Things are going so well here," he said, "I think I'll move on to another unit."

As he spoke, five enemy shells struck Mezado Ridge. They filled the air with flying coral. A shard pierced Buckner's throat, and he died ten minutes later in the realization that his forces were at last prevailing.

Replacing Buckner was Roy Geiger, about to be made a three-star general. It was fitting that the grizzled white bear of a general who had been in on the beginning at Guadalcanal should command at the end on Okinawa.

Six days later a patrol of the Sixth Marine Division reached a small mound atop a spiky cliff. Beneath them mingled the waters of the East China Sea and the Pacific Ocean. Okinawa had fallen.

The following night, Ushijima and Cho sat inside a cave shaken by the explosions of American grenades above it. Cho, precise to the end, wore the white kimono required for the ceremonial rite of hara-kiri. Ushijima had put on his full dress uniform. They sat down to their last meal. Behind them at the mouth of the cave moonlight shimmered upon the sea. They finished eating and drank off final toasts of scotch whisky. They arose.

"Well, Commanding General Ushijima, as the way may be dark, I, Cho, will lead the way."

"Please do so. I will take along my fan, since it is getting warm."

They strolled out to a ledge above the ocean, Ushijima calmly fanning himself. They bowed in reverence to the eastern sky and the Imperial Palace in Tokyo. They sat on a white sheet spread over a quilt. A hundred feet behind them were the Americans still hurling grenades.

First Ushijima, then Cho, bared their bellies to the upward thrust of the ceremonial knife, while the adjutant stood by with his saber, awaiting the first sign of blood. Two shouts, two saber flashes and it was done—and the moon began sinking beneath a polished black sea.

123. The Allied Drive into Germany

THE DECISION OF THE BIG THREE at Yalta to persist in the policy of Unconditional Surrender guaranteed that Germany would not be defeated until the armies of the Anglo-Americans in the West and the Soviets in the East met in the heart of Europe. By February of 1945 it was clear that this moment was now imminent.

The Wehrmacht could no longer be fed and fueled by German industry. Soviet forces had captured the new industries of Upper Silesia, and the Ruhr lay in ruins. The "new weapons" upon which Hitler relied so heavily were simply not forthcoming in sufficient numbers to make a difference. February production of jet aircraft was only 283, and few of these were able to zoom aloft because their special airfields with unusually long runways were easily identified and bombed into futility. Hitler's attempt to neutralize the great port of Antwerp and thus delay Eisenhower's spring offensive also failed. With an output of only 1,500 V-1s and 600 V-2s a month, a steady volume of fire—the sine qua non of this operation—could not be maintained. Five thousand V-bombs falling on Antwerp had not done more damage to installations there than one conventional raid of 100 heavy bombers.

Doenitz's promise of recovery at sea had also been a delusion. Although 126 of the new electro U-boats had been commissioned by mid-February, only two of them had put to sea. Prospects of getting the remainder into service were all but eliminated by the Red Army's advance on Memel and the Bay of Danzig. U-boat bases in the eastern Baltic were now within range of Anglo-American air power. Even though Doenitz had managed to amass no fewer than 450 U-boats of all types by this time—the largest number that Germany ever possessed—they were no longer of any strategic value. Anglo-American naval and air power was successfully protecting the vast stores of supplies and troops steadily increasing Eisenhower's strength. New divisions were now arriving at the rate of one a week, and the losses suffered in the Bulge had been made good long ago.

Hitler's refusal to yield had brought him to the verge of renouncing the Geneva Convention so that he might slaughter captured Allied prisoners and thus "induce the German people to resist to the utmost" while discouraging his own troops from deserting for fear of retaliation in kind. He was dissuaded from this mad and evil policy only by Doenitz's convincing arguments that "the disadvantages outweighed the advantages." Nevertheless, *Der Führer*'s unbending stand was approved by the vast inarticulate mass of the German people. They not only feared the anarchy that would erupt upon any internal collapse, but dreaded the prospect of having their homeland overrun by Soviet soldiers no more tender in their mercies than the German soldier had been. They hoped then that the Soviets could be held at the line of the Oder while the Anglo-Americans crossed the Rhine and penetrated deeper into Germany.

Although Hitler still thought of holding firm on both fronts, the reality of the threat to Berlin compelled him to give priority to the East. Confident that the Anglo-Americans could not recover from the Ardennes campaign in time for a winter offensive, he stripped the West of more than half of its panzer divisions and in February sent 1,675 new or repaired tanks and assault guns to the East in comparison to only sixty-seven in the West. In this *Der Führer* again underestimated the resilience of the Americans.

Dwight Eisenhower had no intention of sitting still until spring. Having repulsed the enemy's winter offensive, he wanted to launch one of his own. He believed that "one more great campaign, aggressively conducted on a broad front, would give the death blow to Hitler Germany." But once again, however, he found himself having to deal with the conflicting proposals of his British and American commanders. This divisive debate which had begun in August and had been exacerbated by the failure of Market-Garden in September and then boiled over into bad blood between Montgomery and Bradley after the Bulge, was still unresolved. Everywhere in the American army there was a deep and burning resentment of what Montgomery had said at his post-Bulge press conference. It surfaced again when British Brig. Gen John F. M. Whiteley of SHAEF had called Bradley, who was at Patton's headquarters, to tell him that Eisenhower wanted him to lend several divisions to General Devers for an attack in Alsace. Patton wanted these formations for his own offensive in the Eifel. "We would be giving up a sure thing for a sideshow!" Bradley roared, his grip on the telephone so tight that his knuckles turned white. Then he began screaming at the startled Whiteley: "Go ahead and take all the corps and divisions! There is more at stake than the mere moving of divisions and corps. . . . If you feel that way about it, then as far as I am concerned, you can take any goddam division and/or corps in the 12th Army Group, do with them as you see fit, and those of us that you leave back will sit on our ass until hell freezes!" Calming himself, Bradley concluded: "I trust you do not think I am angry. But I want to impress upon you that *I am goddam well incensed!*" In the background Patton shouted loud enough to be heard: "Tell them to go to hell and all . . . of us will resign."

That had been in late January, and Eisenhower had relented, telling Devers that he would have to make do with his own 6th Army Group units. But the incident had impressed upon the supreme commander how unified his Americans were in their resistance to the British proposal to stop Bradley and Devers in their tracks while allowing Montgomery to keep Bradley's First and Ninth armies for a single, massed crossing of the lower Rhine north of the Ruhr. When the Americans insisted upon bringing their own armies under their own command up to the upper Rhine, he listened to them.

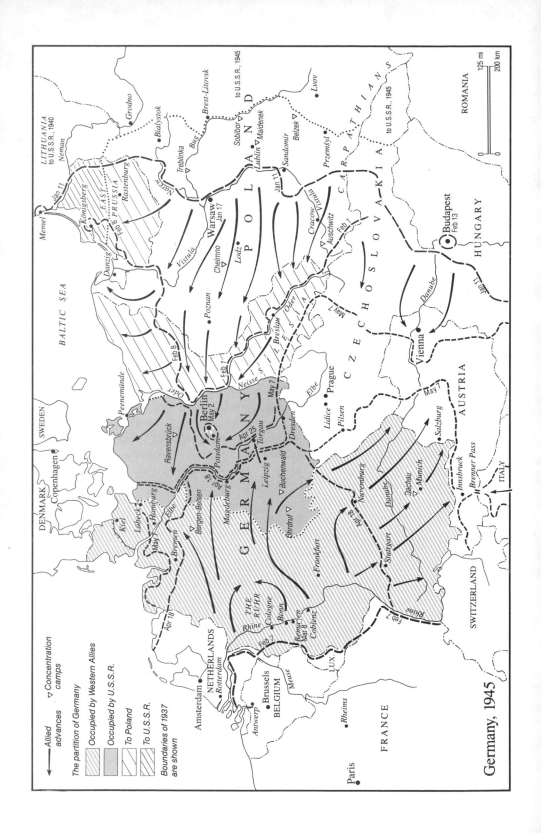

Germany, 1945

Allied advances ▽ Concentration camps

The partition of Germany

Occupied by Western Allies

Occupied by U.S.S.R.

To Poland

To U.S.S.R.

Boundaries of 1937 are shown

125 mi
200 km

Thus, he chose a double thrust, with crossings of both the lower and upper Rhine. He suspected that Hitler's conqueror complex would lead him to order his forces to hold fast west of the Rhine, and this would give the Anglo-Americans the chance to kill or capture large numbers of German soldiers. Brooke and Montgomery were most unhappy with this decision. They didn't want to fight *any* battles west of the Rhine. They wanted the supreme commander to give the 21st Army Group everything he had and to allow Montgomery to lead it on a drive to Berlin. Obviously, they had forgotten Montgomery's too-tidy tactics in Market-Garden. Even General Whiteley at SHAEF was appalled. He said that the feeling among everyone at Supreme Headquarters "was that if anything was to be done quickly, don't give it to Monty. . . . Monty was the last person Ike would have chosen for a drive on Berlin—Monty would have needed six weeks to prepare." There was another, ulterior motive for Brooke's insistence on concentrating on the single "full-blooded" thrust in the north: the British wanted to get to the ports and bases of Northern Germany before the Red Army did. But they did not mention this for fear the Americans would suspect them once more of "political" motives. So the debate continued to rage, a disagreement becoming so violent that in the end Marshall had to tell the British chiefs that if the SHAEF plan were not accepted, he would "recommend to Eisenhower that he had no choice but to ask to be relieved of his command." With this British resistance came to an end. Eisenhower's double-thrust aimed at encircling the enemy and patterned on the double envelopment of the Romans at Cannae by Hannibal— the supreme commander's boyhood hero—was to commence on February 8, 1945.

Throughout early February the weather favored the Germans. A thaw had melted thick snows, turning rivers into torrents and flooding the soft polderland through which Montgomery's northern thrust must pass. Nevertheless, on February 8, the extreme left or northern flank, the British Second and Canadian First Armies attacked following a heavy bombardment. One of the bloodiest battles of the war ensued. Bad weather and soggy terrain negated Montgomery's armor, and his infantry became bogged down. Still the Germans were pushed back steadily. By February 21 the Anglo-Canadians had reached the Rhine, and the Germans retreated east of the river and blew the bridges.

At this point the Anglo-American air forces combined for the fiercest aerial preparation of the war. The U.S. Twelfth and Fifteenth Air Forces in Italy, the U.S. Eighth and Ninth Air Forces in the West and the entire Royal Air Force combined for an all-out assault on enemy communications. On two days, February 22–23, more than 16,000 sorties were flown and 20,000 tons of bombs dropped.

The U.S. Ninth Army under Simpson was poised on the Roer River on Montgomery's southern flank. The Americans planned to cross in floating assault bridges. But the desperate Germans destroyed the penstocks to produce a calculated flow to swell the river four feet above its normal level and flood large areas in the Düren–Jülich area. Simpson's soldiers had to wait two weeks for the waters to subside before crossing the Roer. By March 13 all the northern half of the west bank of the Rhine was in Allied hands.

In the center Bradley's First Army under Hodges and the Third Army led by Patton also closed on the Rhine. Hodges took Cologne on March 7 and the Germans retreated across the river, again blowing bridges. Patton reached the Rhine near Coblenz while below him Devers with his American and French forces linked up with his southern flank.

Eisenhower's double-thrusting broad advance had been a brilliant success. The enemy had lost 250,000 men taken prisoner, in addition to untold scores of thousands killed and hundreds of thousands wounded. The Rhineland lay at the feet of the Allies. Tanks rolled through the streets in town after town to find the windows of all the houses shuttered with white sheets of surrender hanging from them. Whole units of enemy soldiers emerged from cellars with their hands held high. But even as the Anglo-Americans closed on the historic broad Rhine, they heard and saw scores of bridges rise into the air and fall into the river in pieces. Eager as Eisenhower had been to take a Rhine River bridgehead, it appeared that the Germans would leave none standing. On the orders of Hitler, any commander who allowed a bridge in his sector to be captured intact would be shot. Not since Napoleon in 1805 had an enemy crossed the Rhine in war. In the center between Cologne in the north and Bonn in the south the river was an especially formidable barrier. Peaks rising from the east side gave the Germans the opportunity to deliver a murderous, plunging fire on anyone attempting to cross below. Great as Eisenhower's campaign had been, it appeared that, in an opposed Rhine crossing, he faced extremely costly, perhaps even prohibitive losses. But then in the gray, drizzly daylight of March 7, the 9th Armored Division, spearheading the advance of Hodges's First Army against the Bonn–Cologne center, split into two columns, one under Brig. Gen. William M. Hoge made for the Ahr River in hopes of capturing a bridge there, the other drove toward the Rhine intent on capturing the town of Remagen on the west bank.

In that raw drizzle the American soldiers of Capt. Karl Timmerman's company saw in Remagen the hope of finding a warm fire and perhaps a glass or two of schnapps. Timmerman and his men stood on a height above the town looking down on the Rhine. They saw a bridge there. It was the Ludendorff Railway Bridge, and it was still standing! At the moment the enormous significance of that intact span did not dawn upon Timmerman. He saw German soldiers pouring over it to the east bank and also civilians urging cows and horses along. His first thought was to plaster them with mortars, but then he decided to call for Colonel Engeman, his commanding officer. Engeman thought of bringing down artillery on the bridge and requested it. But the artillery was afraid of hitting friendly troops in the vicinity, so Engeman decided to take Remagen first and take care of the bridge later.

At that point Maj. Ben Cothran, General Hoge's operations officer, arrived in Remagen in his jeep looking for Engeman. He found him and also saw that incredibly intact bridge across the Rhine.

"Don't you think we ought to bring some artillery down on that?" Engeman asked.

"My *God!*" Cothran cried, ignoring the question. "I've got to get the Old Man."

Racing back to his jeep, he radioed Hoge, who left the Ahr and made for Remagen. He arrived at one o'clock, raging at Engeman to take the town. Speed! Speed! Speed! Timmerman's company drove rapidly into Remagen.

Hoge studied the bridge. On the other side he could see German soldiers frantically laying cable and fastening charges to the beams. At that point he received word that German prisoners captured at the Ahr claimed that the Remagen bridge was to be blown at exactly 4 P.M. It was then 3:15. He turned to Engeman: "I want you to get that bridge as soon as possible!" Engeman bristled: "I'm doing every damn thing possible to get that bridge!" Below there was a rumble and a roar. The bridge swayed and then was obscured by smoke. When it cleared, the bridge was still standing! There was a crater at the western end but the catwalks could be crossed. Captain Timmermann and his men eyed the span nervously. They had been ordered to cross it.

"What if the bridge blows up in my face?" Timmermann asked Major Deevers, his battalion commander. Deevers looked away. "All right," Timmerman called to his platoon leaders. "We're going across." The platoon led by Sgt. Alex Drabik led the way. Machine-gun bullets hummed among them, and they began to run.

Above them General Hoge was stunned by a message from 9th Armored headquarters ordering him to link up with Patton's 4th Armored with all possible speed. Should he obey and abandon the prize, probably the biggest windfall of the war? If he obeyed, nothing would happen to him. If he disobeyed and succeeded, he would surely be decorated, even promoted. If he disobeyed and failed, losing as much as a battalion caught on the bridge when the Germans blew it, he would certainly be court-martialed. But none of these considerations applied, Hoge thought: The opportunity was simply overwhelming, and he stayed where he was.

Drabik's men were shouting wildly as they ran toward the startled Germans at the eastern terminus of the bridge. Drabik urged them to run as fast as they could to make difficult targets of themselves. Other Americans climbed the bridge towers where the machine guns were sited, capturing both guns and gunners and throwing the guns into the river. Drabik's men reached the end of the bridge, routing the retreating Germans, fanning out to take the height above them. Behind them came Army engineers cutting fuses and cables and dropping the charges into the water. The main charge of 500 pounds of TNT had not been detonated, probably because a tank shell had severed its wrist-thick cable. More and more Americans were pouring over the bridge, climbing the heights to repel any enemy counterattack.

The Rhine had been crossed and an intact bridge was in American hands.

That night Gen. Omar Bradley sat in his headquarters at Namur with Maj. Gen. Harold ("Pinky") Bull. General Bull had arrived from SHAEF with a proposal to divert four of Bradley's divisions to Devers. Bradley was not happy to see him. Suddenly his telephone rang. It was Courtney Hodges.

"Brad, we've gotten a bridge."

"A bridge? You mean you've got one intact on the Rhine?"

"Yep. The Ninth Armored nailed one at Remagen before they blew it up."

"Hot dog, Courtney! This will bust him wide open! Are you getting your stuff across?"

"Just as fast as we can push it over. The navy's moving in now with a ferry service, and I'm having the engineers throw a couple of spare pontoon bridges across to the bridgehead."

"Shove everything you can across it, Courtney, and button up the bridgehead tightly. It'll probably take the other fellow a couple of days to pull enough stuff together to hit you."

With a grin, Bradley hung up and turned on Bull. "There goes your ball game, Pink."

Bull blinked behind his rimless glasses. "Sure, you've got a bridge, Brad, but what good is it going to do you? You're not going anywhere down there at Remagen. It just doesn't fit into the *plan.*"

Bradley's long jaw dropped in incredulity. He stared at Bull, the eternal staff officer so serenely certain that all things must go according to *plan,* that improvisation must never interfere with *plan:* the *Plan,* the whole *Plan* and nothing but the *Plan*—so help you Karl von Clausewitz.

"What in hell do you want us to do?" Bradley yelled, "pull back and blow it up?" Bull did not answer and Bradley called Eisenhower, who was overjoyed. "Hold onto it, Brad. Get across with whatever you need—but make certain you hold that bridgehead."

It was held, despite fierce German efforts to send it to the bottom of the Rhine. But these came too late, after American combat engineers had restored the heavy planking and supporting beams to allow trucks, tanks and trains to cross. Within twenty-four hours there were 8,000 American soldiers east of the Rhine, while two temporary pontoon bridges were thrown across it within less than forty hours. It was against these that the Germans finally struck in fury. The Luftwaffe sent twenty-one of its new jets to dive-bomb it; all but five were shot down. Eleven V-2 rockets fell harmlessly nearby. The Americans clung to their bridgehead, again displaying their great virtues of mobility, initiative and exploitation. It was ten days before the German counterstrike at last collapsed the center span into the Rhine. But by then the penetration of the Rhine had been made and widened. "While the bridge lasted," said Walter Bedell Smith, "it was worth its weight in gold."

The German high command was appalled by the Remagen disaster. Hitler ordered four officers considered chiefly responsible to be court-martialed and shot. Gerd von Rundstedt was removed from command again and replaced by Field Marshal Albert Kesselring. But then the American engineers showed a technological speed and skill that left their proud German counterparts filled with awe and envy. In a matter of days, 75,000 American engineers built sixty-two spans—forty-six pontoon, eleven fixed highway and five railway bridges—across the river. Using the Remagen bridgehead as a fulcrum, seven Allied armies went over the Rhine all along the north-south line of the great river. They crossed in every conceivable way, Treadway and Bailey bridges, pontoons, aboard the navy's amphibious ducks or sea mules and landing craft. By March 25 all seven armies were over the Rhine, together with the greatest concentration of tanks ever assembled, all poised for another double-envelopment—this time of the Ruhr.

On that same day there surfaced what was to be the last great Allied controversy of the war.

On March 25 Eisenhower went to Montgomery's headquarters to confer. Churchill and Brooke were there. Churchill showed the supreme commander a typically arrogant note from Molotov charging that the West by negotiating a German surrender in Italy was dealing "behind the backs of the Soviet Union, *which is bearing the brunt of the war against Germany.*" Eisenhower was infuriated at this insult and also the exaggerated claims of Hitler's former partner. He told Churchill that he would always accept surrenders in the field. If political questions arose, he would consult the heads of governments. To this Churchill replied that the Allies ought to make a definite effort to beat the Soviets to Berlin and to hold as much of eastern Germany as possible "until my doubts about Russia's intentions have been cleared away." Eisenhower politely but firmly refused. He believed—as he had always believed—that his mission was to conquer Nazi Germany as soon as possible and that he was to be guided by military considerations only. As he had once said to Churchill, and would say again in this latest controversy, if the heads of government should decide that political considerations now took precedence over military ones, he would gladly and immediately adjust his strategy to suit.

The supreme commander had a very real fear that Hitler would conduct a guerrilla war from an Alpine redoubt and that he must crush the Nazis before this could happen. SHAEF Intelligence had reported that the best SS divisions were moving toward Berchtesgaden, where impregnable positions were being prepared. It concluded: "This area is, by the very nature of the terrain, practically impenetrable. Here, defended by nature and by the most efficient secret weapons yet invented, the powers that have hitherto guided Germany will survive to reorganize her resurrection; here armaments will be manufactured in bombproof factories, food and equipment will be stored in vast underground caverns and a specially selected corps of young men will be trained in guerrilla warfare, so that a whole underground army can be fitted and directed to liberate Germany from the occupying forces." Eisenhower was not alone in believing what can now be seen as a military fairy tale. German forces falling back before the 12th Army Group were being drawn toward Innsbruck and Salzburg. The supreme commander wanted to occupy the Alps. To him they were a more important military objective than Berlin.

He had not felt that way in September 1944 when he had agreed to Market-Garden and told Montgomery: "Clearly Berlin is the main prize." But that was before Yalta had delineated the occupying zones with Berlin well within the Soviet sector, and also while the Soviets were still outside Warsaw more than 300 miles from Berlin and the Allies were about the same distance away. Berlin, then, because of the thrust through the Ruhr to get to it and its still glamorous allure, was a military as well as a political prize. But in March of 1945 the Allies were still 200 miles away while the Red Army was within thirty-five miles. Berlin itself was a hollow shell with a demented Führer cowering beneath it in command of a phantom army.

Advice from Bradley, upon whom Eisenhower greatly depended for counsel, also helped to dissuade him from a dash on the German capital. Bradley had pointed out that even if Montgomery should reach the Elbe River before the Soviets reached the Oder, he would still have to move through fifty miles of lowlands studded with lakes, crisscrossed with streams and interlaced with canals. Bradley also said it would cost 100,000 casualties, and added: "A pretty stiff price to pay for a prestige objective, especially when we've got to fall back and let the other fellow take over."

By March 1945, Dwight Eisenhower was completely fed up with Montgomery. He said later: "Montgomery had become so personal in his efforts to make sure that the Americans—and me, in particular—got no credit, that, in fact, we hardly had anything to do with the war, that I finally stopped talking to him." In this he was echoed by even the British generals at SHAEF. Said the acerbic Whitely: "Monty wanted to ride into Berlin on a white charger." Brooke felt the same way. But such base, ulterior motives could never be attributed to Winston Churchill. He had fought a losing battle at Yalta and had come to regret some decisions which, granting Roosevelt's defection, he could hardly have avoided making; and he knew now that Stalin's appetite for small nations was insatiable. But he could not dissuade Eisenhower from deciding to make his main thrust in the center with Bradley's 12th Army Group aiming toward Dresden. To strengthen Bradley, Simpson's Ninth Army was returned to him. Eisenhower did, however, direct Montgomery to cross the Elbe and move on Lübeck. This would seal off the Danish peninsula and prevent the Red Army from turning Denmark into still another "Soviet republic." The same might have happened to Czechoslovakia when Patton reached its border and requested permission to move on Prague. Eisenhower, however, refused, and here it became clear that, for all his protestations and disclaimers, the supreme commander was indeed motivated by political considerations of his own.

Dwight Eisenhower yearned to get along with the Soviets and had no desire to offend them by racing them to Berlin or preempting them in Prague. Lübeck was first and foremost a military objective and the fact that it would also save Denmark for democracy was a bonus. Eisenhower like all other Americans had absolutely no experience of the Soviets and their own dictatorial apparat. Even Harriman in Moscow saw only what he was supposed to see. Thus Eisenhower was deeply distrustful of all those commanders—like Patton and Montgomery—who wanted to disarm the Germans in such fashion that they might be immediately rearmed to join the Allies in driving the communists back to Russia. He considered this dishonorable and self-defeating. He wanted to work with the Soviets to build a brave new world. In this he was also motivated by his abomination of the Germans. What he saw in visits to the Nazi concentration camps deepened his hatred of them. He thought that the Nazis and their people were devils incarnate beyond redemption, but that the communists were not. To his sorrow as a two-term president of the United States, he would learn that Soviet communism in its merciless grip upon its brainwashed people and in its use of any means however foul to obtain its end of world dominion was just as inimical to his dream of a better and peaceful world rising from the ashes of the one he had helped so much to destroy.

This, then, was the supreme commander's true motive in disdaining "political" objectives and sending his seven armies crashing into Germany in pursuit of purely "military" goals.

On March 24, Simpson's Ninth Army struck the Ruhr's northern rim above Essen and Dortmund, bound for Lippstadt. From Remagen Hodges's First drove around the eastern flank with the same objective. On April 1 the wings of these two great pincers met at Lippstadt to encircle the Ruhr. Model's troops were caught in a circle eighty miles in diameter while the Ruhr itself was split in two. Some 400,000 German prisoners were taken, while Model stood in a lonely wood near Duisburg and shot himself to death.

Although Eisenhower on the last day of March broadcast an appeal to the German soldiers and people to surrender, there was no response. Senseless as it was to prolong the struggle, there was actually no way that the Allies could stop it. The soldiers themselves had to surrender individually. This they began to do, until their numbers overflowed the prison cages. When they could, the Germans stampeded to the West to surrender there rather than to the dreaded Soviets. Throughout April Eisenhower's rampaging forces broke through the cracked and buckling Reich.

In the north Montgomery's 21st Army Group stormed into Holland and the north German coast, sealing off Denmark. In the center Bradley's 12th Army Group raged eastward. The Ninth and First Armies moved so fast that the Ninth's 2nd Armored Division sped fifty miles in a single day to throw a bridgehead over the Elbe River at Magdeburg on April 15. South of them Patton's Third Army moved fastest of all. His tanks rumbled over Hitler's prized autobahn like racing cars to reach the Czechoslovakian border by April 23.

On the far southern flank Devers's Sixth Army Group also thrust eastward. On April 20, its Seventh Army took Nuremberg—the shrine of Nazism—and captured Hitler's beloved Munich on April 30. All along the great Allied front, now, the British, Americans, Poles and French began to slow their advance in accordance with the agreement reached with the Soviets at Yalta, awaiting the historic juncture that would end the war.

They met on April 25, 1945, at Torgau on the Elbe, about seventy-five miles south of Berlin. Patrols of the 69th Infantry Division of General Gerow's V Corps greeted vanguards of the Soviet 58th Guards Division in the group commanded by Marshal Ivan Konev. There was a wild celebration. "It was like the finale of a circus," reported one eyewitness. Regardless of rank, the soldiers of all nations embraced each other and exchanged toasts in captured German schnapps and wine. "Today," a Soviet major cried, "is the happiest day in all our lives. The most difficult for us were those days when the Germans were at Stalingrad. Now we meet one another and this is the end of the enemy. Long live your great leader! Long live our great leader!"

124. The Death of Hitler

HITLER HAD TURNED FIFTY-SIX on April 20. But he looked much older. His face was ashen, his hands trembled, his shoulders were stooped and his eyes were lackluster. He was a man grasping at straws, placing his hopes for salvation in the wildest fantasies. One day it would be death rays, the next—incredibly enough —Greek fire! The death of Roosevelt also was seized by him as an augury of deliverance. He compared himself to Frederick the Great, whose fortunes changed upon the death of the Czarina Elizabeth.

In his bunker deep beneath the Reichs Chancellery—the safest place in Berlin—he sent out order after order to armies destroyed long ago by his enemies rushing at him from East and West. He called for a program of demolition and destruction that would result in obliteration of the German nation. When Albert Speer came to him with a memorandum of protest, he told him in icy tones: "If the war is lost, the people will be lost also. It is not necessary to worry about what the German people will need for elemental survival. On the contrary, it is best for us to destroy even these things. For the nation has proved to be the weaker, and the future belongs solely to the stronger eastern nation. In any case only those who are inferior will remain after this struggle, for the good have already been killed." A few days later he answered Speer's protest with the order: "All military, transportation, communications, industrial and supply facilities, as well as all resources within the Reich" were to be destroyed. Wholesale destruction of the means of livelihood in Germany was to be carried out by the gauleiters. Speer was through. If the order had been carried out—and it was not—there would have been no electricity, gas, pure water, fuel or transportation in Germany. All railroad facilities, canals, locks, docks, ships and locomotives were to be destroyed. Such was the paranoia of Hitler's last days. The German Reich was his; he had made it, it had proved unworthy of him and now he would destroy it. Once again in his ears were those wailing horns and shrieking violins of Richard Wagner. Siegfried was preparing to lie down alongside Brünnhilde on the self-immolatory fires.

Haggard though he was, he was still capable of inspiring fear, of falling into raging "carpet chewing" tirades. On April 25, he received a message from Goering: "*Mein Führer:* Since you are determined to remain at your post in Fortress Berlin, do you agree, that I, as your deputy . . . assume immediately the total leadership of the Reich . . ." Goaded by the Goering-hating Martin Bormann, *Der Führer*'s eyes bulged with fury. "Nothing is spared me!" he screamed. "Nothing! Every disillusion, every betrayal, dishonor, treason has been heaped upon me!" Ordering Goering arrested and stripped of all titles, he next heard that Heinrich Himmler had begun to negotiate with the enemy. "Now Himmler has betrayed me!" he shouted, and issued the same orders for the destruction of the weak-chinned little mass murderer. Hitler now executed his last general: Hermann Fegelein, Eva Braun's brother-in-law, and Himmler's representative in the Berlin Bunker. His guilt was one of attainder; he was found and led out into the garden for execution.

By then Dr. Goebbels and his wife Magda and six children were living in the bunker. They had a tiny room and slept on the bare floor. Magda was careful to keep the children quiet and not to disturb "Uncle Adi." Sometimes the children were perplexed to hear their mother weeping. She knew that her husband had decided to kill himself and all of them. But Goebbels was happy to be *Der Führer*'s confidante during his last hours. It was he who provided a justice of the peace when Hitler declared that he wished his marriage to Eva to be proper and legal. Walter Wagner, the man who had married the Goebbelses, was found serving in a *Volkssturm* regiment on the beleaguered Friedrichstrasse. Soviet artillery battering Berlin could be heard when he was brought to the bunker. He still wore civilian clothes with a *Volkssturm* armband. Wagner made out an official certificate listing Goebbels as the witness for Hitler and Bormann for Eva.

Both Adolf and Eva swore that they were of pure Aryan descent with no disease precluding their marriage. Wagner turned to Hitler and said: "*Mein Führer*, Adolf Hitler, are you willing to take Eva Braun as your wife?"

"I do," Hitler replied in a sonorous voice.

"Fräulein Eva Braun, are you willing to take our *Führer*, Adolf Hitler, as your husband?"

"I do," Eva said, and Wagner concluded: "I declare that this marriage is legal in the eyes of the law."

The wedding feast followed. Eva became a little giddy with champagne, but Hitler sipped his quietly, talking to Goebbels about his own marriage when *Der Führer* was the best man. "That was a happy day," he said pensively, and then, bitterly: "It is all finished. Death will be a relief to me. I have been deceived and betrayed by everyone."

The date of the marriage was April 28, 1945, although it had actually taken place a few minutes after midnight on the 29th. Hitler had had to wait that long for Wagner to be found. In the interval he composed his last will and testament, in which he formally expelled Goering and Himmler from their posts, replacing Goering with Grand Adm. Karl Doenitz as president of the Reich and commander of the armed forces. There was not very much left to command. Hitler's empire had shrunk to a few streets in Berlin defended by old men and boys and a detachment of 300 impressed Frenchmen who had fought on the Eastern Front. It annoyed Hitler that he should be protected at the end by Frenchmen.

Hitler spent the 29th in the usual series of conferences with his generals, including the odious General Burgdorf who had carried the message of death to Rommel. Phials of potassium cyanide poison were passed out to those who requested them. Dr. Goebbels took eight. No one could be positive that the poison would really work and Hitler ruefully consented to test them on his favorite dog, the wolfhound Blondi. It was done and *Der Führer* was told: "Death was very nearly instantaneous." The rest of the day was spent once again issuing orders to nonexistent units. He still clung to hopes of rescue. Even when he was told that the capture of the Reichs Chancellery was only a few hours away, he delayed his suicide, going to bed about midnight. At 2:20 A.M. on April 30, he arose to say good-bye to everyone, walking gravely along a line to shake hands but saying nothing. His color was deathly white, and he was trembling.

Certain that *Der Führer* was now about to kill himself, the people of the bunker gave themselves up to unrelieved gaiety. They played records, sang, danced, joked, smoked cigarettes—and in the SS guard rooms there was a jolly little orgy with naked girls. Such conduct might have meant death a few hours earlier; even so, Hitler did order the noise to stop, again delaying the final gesture.

Hitler ate his last meal at midday of April 30. It was spaghetti with a light sauce prepared by his vegetarian cook, Fräulein Manzialy. Eva ate nothing. She was surprisingly radiant, dressed in a dark blue polka-dot dress, nylon stockings and her favorite brown shoes made in Italy. On her wrist was a diamond-studded watch. She embraced the women and smiled at the men. Hitler said nothing. Together they walked into a small room in which hung a portrait of Frederick the Great, Hitler's favorite picture. They closed the door and sat on a couch together. Outside the door a huge guard named Otto Guensche stood watch. Everyone within earshot tensed, waiting for the sound of a shot. There was none, only a faint odor of gunpowder. Guensche flung open the door and rushed inside.

Adolf Hitler sat slumped on the couch. A hole the size of a dime was in his forehead. Blood trickled from it. At his feet was his 7.65 Walther revolver. Beside it was Eva's smaller 6.35 pistol. She had discarded it, taking potassium cyanide instead. Her head lay on Hitler's shoulder. They might have been the babes in the woods. On Hitler's chest was the silver-framed photograph of his mother which he took everywhere with him. Someone took a photograph, and then the bodies were carried up the stairs and out into the garden. Gasoline was sloshed over them and set afire. When the flames subsided, fresh fuel was added, until even the bones had turned to ashes. After this makeshift cremation lasting two and a half hours, just an hour before midnight April 30, 1945, the ashes were gathered up and buried in an unknown place in the garden.

All that was mortal of Adolf Hitler, the vilest tormentor of mankind, was now but a handful of dust.

125. The Holocaust

IN MID-APRIL OF 1945, with his armies driving into Germany, Dwight Eisenhower decided to visit a Nazi concentration camp. He did so with reluctance, for the stories he had heard of the atrocities which his troops had begun to uncover as they overran the camps had filled him with fear of the horrors he must witness. Yet, he chose deliberately to visit Ohrdruf, near the XX Corps headquarters at Gotha, "in order to be in a position to give *first-hand* evidence of these things, if ever, in the future, there develops a tendency to charge these allegations to 'propaganda.' " George Patton went with him.

Ohrdruf was an extermination camp which sometimes received victims of Hitler's infamous *Nacht und Nebel* (Night and Fog) Decree. It was promulgated by Keitel on December 12, 1941. Under it people suspected of "hostility to the Reich" or of Resistance sympathies vanished without a trace, their whereabouts remaining unknown forever to their family and friends. The usual procedure was to arrest them in the middle of the night and spirit them to prisons and camps hundreds of miles away from their homes. There they were "interrogated"— matches burned beneath their fingernails, tongues pulled out, eyes gouged, testicles crushed with nut-crackers—and in the end despatched to the camps of Natsweiler and Gross-Rosen specially reserved for them, or sometimes to the extermination camps at Ohrdruf or Buchenwald. They were given neither trials or explanations. In rare cases where there was a trial and the suspect was not condemned to death, *Nacht und Nebel* decreed "the disappearance of the accused without a trace." And: "No information whatsoever may be given about their whereabouts and their fate."

Nacht und Nebel victims who proved stubborn under such questioning were frequently murdered by methods which showed the SS rising to the very heights of evil genius. A Frenchman suspected of being in the Resistance was stripped naked and spread out on an opened dining-room table with his private parts dangling between the sections. Laughing SS men slowly pushed the table together. In Lyon, four girls suspected of helping the Resistance were stripped and beaten. But this was pedestrian torture, standard procedure which in this case produced no information, until an innovative SS guard noticed that one of the girls was having her monthly period. He removed the sanitary pad, dipped it in gasoline, replaced it—and lighted a match. The other three girls were treated the same way with cotton batting soaked in gasoline. The last of them took four days to die.

Eisenhower and his entourage had heard these stories and they were therefore apprehensive when they pulled up outside Ohrdruf, sprawling like an ugly growth in the bright spring countryside. A double enclosure of barbed wire surrounded rows of hideous barracks. A pale and shaken XX Corps officer came outside the gate and said: "They tried to eliminate the evidence before we arrived, but as you see, they were not successful."

The Americans moved in silent horror through barracks in which the naked and emaciated bodies of the starved dead had been piled up to the ceiling. Lying all over the camp were the corpses of recently murdered inmates, usually killed by bullets fired at close range into the base of the skull. There were gallows contrived to produce a slow, agonizing death; whipping racks and butcher blocks for smashing jaws to remove gold teeth or fillings. At the crematories there were still-smoking ovens the insides of which were coated with charred flesh. Over all floated the reeking, sticky-sweet stench of death. Quickly, the color faded from the cheeks of the veteran soldiers in Eisenhower's party. Patton became so sick he had to rush outside a barracks to throw up.

Before Eisenhower left Ohrdruf, he addressed the officers around him in tones of cold fury: "I want every American unit not actually in the front lines to see this place. We are told that the American soldier does not know what he is fighting for. Now, at least, he will know what he is fighting *against.*" Eisenhower later arranged for British MPs and American Congressmen, reporters and photographers, to be brought to the camp. Some of them arrived in time to visit Buchenwald, the next one to be liberated by the XX Corps.

Buchenwald's prisoners were dying daily by the hundreds. General Patton quickly despatched hospital teams, medical supplies, food and transportation to Buchenwald. But he declined to visit it, sending his aide, Lt. Col. Charles Codman, instead. Codman had been at Ohrdruf, and he thought he was prepared for what he would see—until he entered Barracks 61. Inside a room 150 feet by 30 were four tiers of wooden shelves inclining slightly toward a central corridor. Here were crammed 2,300 "nonworkers" whom tuberculosis, dysentery, pneumonia or starvation had left incapable of enduring the daily 12-hour shifts at the armament factory or nearby quarries. They were stuffed onto the shelves to die, after which they would be stripped of their clothing and their bodies thrown out on the pavement to be picked up by the crematory-bound death carts. To Codman, all this deliberate horror seemed pointless, and he asked a freed inmate, Professor Richet of the *Académie de Médecine:* "If extermination is their object, why haven't they just wiped you all out once and for all?"

"The system is not pointless," Richet replied. "It is carefully thought out. In this camp are twenty-five thousand Russians, Poles, Czechs, French, Belgians and others who are in disagreement with the tenets of the Reich. True, they must disappear, but before they go they contribute their bit. On arriving here they are put to work. . . . A workingman requires a diet of two thousand or twenty-five hundred calories per day. Here he is put on a diet of eight hundred calories per day—a diet calculated to produce death by starvation in a certain period of time. That period may be lengthened or shortened in accordance with available replacements. If the replacements are ample, the quota of non-workers sent to what are frankly known as extermination camps, such as Ohrdruf, are increased. There the principle is the same, but the tempo is accelerated."

Richet next explained that extermination camps were useful to spread the number of deaths "from natural causes" in a way that would satisfy German public opinion. But all camps did their own exterminating as well. At Buchenwald during January, February and March of 1944 there were 14,000 deaths.

Codman, who had been a flier in World War I, also met Colonel Hertaux, the French flying ace whom he had known slightly. Hertaux had been accused of organizing resistance, spying, sabotage and hostility to the Reich, but the Nazis had been unable to prove any charges. Instead of executing him, they had sent him to Buchenwald. Hertaux explained that the whole concentration-camp system was carefully worked out.

To the French colonel the horrors and sadism of the SS interrogations were almost as nothing compared to the prolonged ordeal of the concentration camp, where the Nazis were diabolically ingenious at breaking down morale. When a contingent of prisoners was to be shipped to Ohrdruf, it was not the Germans who selected the victims. Rather, they made the chiefs of the various prisoners' committees do the choosing. They were told: "You will this evening submit a list of a hundred prisoners to be ready to leave for Ohrdruf at five o'clock tomorrow morning. When it has been approved, you will call the roll and announce the names to your section and have them ready at the appointed time."

Obviously, the only fair basis on which a committee chief could make his ghastly "selections" was to choose inmates closest to death, even if they happened to be friends or relatives. With the same artful evil, the Germans assigned prisoners to the burial detail, the flogging detail or the cremation detail. Any ruse or stratagem that might excite hatred, distrust or bitterness among the inmates was employed, usually with startling effect. Yet, even this mad malevolence in the German camps could hardly be compared to the Jewish extermination centers in Poland.

Hitler's early conquests and his invasion of Russia had indeed presented him with a problem: What to do with the millions of Jews in his clutches? At the outset it was decided to enforce the laws existing in Germany. Because these had defined who was a Jew, it was therefore easy to begin the persecutions by excluding Jews from public office, the professions and the universities and seizing their property. They also were forced to wear a yellow Star of David. Similar measures were enacted in the satellite states of Romania, Bulgaria and Hungary, and milder ones in unoccupied France. In these nations Himmler set up a tight network of Security Service (SD) units and police.

During the invasion of Poland five mobile SD units followed the advancing troops. Their mission was to exterminate intellectuals and others thought capable of arousing opposition. Many of these were Jews, and some SD detachments actually specialized in the murder of Jews. Such atrocities did indeed adumbrate the systematic extermination that would be adopted, but at the time the Nazis had not decided on a concerted course of action. Hitler spoke vaguely of deporting four million Jews to the island of Madagascar off the coast of East Africa, and also of putting that many aboard ships and taking them out to sea and sinking them. This last, given the Reich's dearth of shipping, could hardly have been more than a joke or an empty threat. A proposal to put the Jews on a reservation between the Vistula River in Poland and the Bug in Russia also came to nothing. But *Der Führer* was still determined to clear Jews out of his empire. He thought of expelling all of them from Europe and locating them in the Russian interior, until the Wehrmacht failed to win the quick victory he had anticipated. Still obsessed by his desire to "cleanse" his empire of the race he hated, in September 1941, he ordered all German Jews deported to Poland. They were sent to ghettos in Lodz and Riga, where their presence complicated the chaos existing in both cities. Gradually, the ghettoes began to be replaced by concentration camps. In December 1941, the first of these was opened by the SS at Chelmno near Lodz, where Jews were murdered upon arrival. Thus was born the killing center, and there would be many more of them after the "final solution" of the Jewish question was begun by Reinhard Heydrich.

Reinhard Heydrich was the son of a Dresden music teacher. In 1919, when he was fifteen, he joined one of Munich's numerous Free Corps and became enamored of Nazi racial theories. He went into the Navy, but was discharged in 1931 for "conduct unbecoming an officer and a gentleman," that is, the seduction of a shipyard director's daughter. He became a Nazi and soon attracted the attention of Heinrich Himmler, who eventually made him his right-hand man. Tall, slim and blond, with deep-set blue eyes, proud in bearing and ruthlessly cool in conduct, he was the apotheosis of the Nordic hero of Nazi mythology. A fine athlete—a superb fencer, an excellent horseman and a skillful pilot—he was also an accomplished violinist.

Heydrich came to be known as "the Blond Beast." He stopped at nothing —torture, death, denunciation, intrigue, treachery—to weave his spider's web of power throughout the Third Reich. Eventually, he became chief of the SD. Heydrich was also the author of the forged documents planted on Stalin to compromise Tukhashevsky, and was therefore ultimately responsible for the purging of the Soviet generals in 1937. A year later he turned his arts against German generals. Werner von Fritsch, commander-in-chief of the Wehrmacht and an almost painful puritan, was accused of homosexuality and ordered into retirement. It was Heydrich who organized *Kristallnacht,* and after the conquest of Poland in 1939 it was to him that *Der Führer* gave his "housecleaning" assignment: the removal by execution or imprisonment of "undesirable" Poles and deciding the fate of three million Polish Jews who came with Hitler's half of Poland. Heydrich began with the Jews by deporting them to German labor camps, but in his first report to Hitler he used the now notorious and chilling phrase, "the final solution" of the Jewish problem. Heydrich next ordered the concentration of Jews in ghettoes and the formation of "Jewish councils," a characteristically treacherous way of inducing Jewish communities to collaborate in their own destruction. Under his brutal hand, the black-clad SS began to terrorize small towns by shooting leading citizens. They unjustly rounded up thousands of other innocent Poles and put them in prison. In Poznan alone, five thousand persons were crammed into an ancient citadel fit to hold at most two thousand. The Poznan prison actually became a Gestapo training school in torture. Within its freezing confines during the coldest winter in nearly half a century, trainees played two games. In "dog," prisoners scurrying about on all fours were whipped senseless. In "rabbit," those hopping down the corridors were shot to death. In some cities, men and women were beheaded. Lodz had a gallows and people were burned alive in Lublin. There are, of course, no accurate or documented figures on the extent of the German atrocities, but it has been estimated that in the last months of 1939 between fifty and a hundred thousand Poles were exterminated under Heydrich's hand. Eventually, "the Blond Beast" became the chief of the Reich Security Office (RSH), the agency charged with executing the Final Solution. As yet, no direct instruction had come from Berlin on how the mass extermination was to be achieved, but on July 31, 1941, six weeks after the invasion of the Soviet Union, the order was given. It came—not from Hitler—but from Goering. At no time did *Der Führer* ever commit his evil intention to writing. Yet the Nazi hierarchy, like the milkman's horse that knows where to stop, knew exactly what he wanted: *Es ist des Führers Wunsch*—Hitler wishes the Jews destroyed. Thus Goering wrote to Heydrich:

Complementing the task that was assigned to you on 24 January 1939 which dealt with carrying out emigration and evacuation, a solution of the Jewish problem as advantageous as possible, I hereby charge you with making all necessary preparation with regard to organizational and financial matters for bringing about a complete solution of the Jewish problem in the German sphere of influence in Europe.

Wherever other governmental agencies are involved, they are to cooperate with you.

I request, furthermore, that you send me before long an overall plan concerning the organizational, factual and material measures necessary for the accomplishment of the desired solution of the Jewish question.

Here was the order that triggered the destruction of the Jews of Europe. However, Goering's vague letter did not immediately suggest to Heydrich that Hitler had shifted from a policy of deportation to one of elimination. Heydrich did not at once order construction of killing centers. Instead, on January 20, 1942, five months after receipt of Goering's order, he called a conference of sixteen top Nazis at Wannsee, a wealthy suburb of Berlin. There he proposed that the Jews should be worked to death while building roads into Russia.

This would kill two birds with one stone: eliminate the Jews while providing the invading Wehrmacht with a modern road network. Those Jews who survived a combination of insufficient diet and endless hard labor would be put to death lest they "become the seedbed for a new efflorescence of Jewry." Heydrich also declared that mixed marriages should be annulled so that the Jewish spouse could be sent to a concentration camp. Part Jews still in the Reich would be sterilized. Also: "In the course of the final solution, Europe will be raked over from west to east."

This recommendation seems to have been in line with Hitler's desire for a mass exodus of the Jews to the east. But as far as a Final Solution was concerned, nothing was said at Wannsee. Such vagueness about how the Final Solution was to be achieved persisted among the Nazis. To the very end the program was sometimes a conflicting collection of differing approaches. But Heydrich, with his authority from Goering, eventually saw it as a program of mass murder. He authorized construction of more extermination centers: Bergen-Belsen in March 1942, Sobibor in April, Auschwitz in June, Treblinka in July, and Maidanek in the autumn. By then, Heydrich had left Poland for Czechoslovakia.

In the previous spring, Hitler had appointed Heydrich as Governor of the Protectorate of Bohemia and Moravia. Shortly after his arrival in Prague, two young Czechs—Josef Ganchik and Jan Kubis—trained by the British for the express purpose of assassinating Heydrich, parachuted into the Prague area. On May 29, they ambushed Heydrich as he drove toward Prague, throwing a bomb into his open Mercedes and giving him his death wounds. Both men took refuge inside a crypt in a Prague church. But their associates broke under SS torture and revealed their hiding place. They were seized and executed, after which a wave of terror engulfed the protectorate. An enraged Hitler bent on avenging the death of the man whom many Nazis believed would be his successor decided that the Czechs must suffer a signal chastisement. Calling for a map of Prague and its environs he put his finger on the village of Lidice and ordered it destroyed. All of the men—most of them steelworkers—were rounded up and murdered, the women were sent to a concentration camp at Ravensbruck and the children despatched to Gneisenau in Germany to be reared as Nazis.

After the death of Heydrich, Himmler chose Ernst Kaltenbrunner to take his place as chief of RSHA. Kaltenbrunner was born in 1903 at Inn, near Adolf Hitler's birthplace at Brannau, Austria. He joined the Nazi party in 1932 and became one of Himmler's most loyal police officers. Unlike his chief, Kaltenbrunner took pleasure in bloodshed and proved himself a dedicated murderer, devoted to developing new methods of execution. A skillful liar and an alcoholic, he was also a giant of a man—nearly seven feet tall with huge shoulders and arms and a coarse brutal face covered with scars from his student dueling days. Kaltenbrunner's deputy was SS Lt. Gen. Heinrich Müller, the de facto chief of the Gestapo and much admired by Himmler for his blind obedience and willingness to accept such "delicate" assignments as the framing of generals or the denunciation of Himmler's enemies. Beneath Müller was a mouselike little minotaur who might have been Himmler's double, an obscure SS major named Adolf Eichmann.

Adolf Eichmann was born in Solingen on March 19, 1906, although the family later moved to Linz, where the young Eichmann became the boyhood friend of Ernst Kaltenbrunner, whose family had also moved there. Although the Eichmanns were a solid bourgeois family engaged in mining enterprises, the young Eichmann was a shiftless drifter, flunking out of engineering school and moving from job to job. His father could find no better employment for him than as a laborer in his mines. In 1934, after a succession of lost jobs, this scrawny sparrow of a man with surprisingly Semitic features moved across the border into Bavaria, where he joined the exiled Austrian Legion and served 14 months military duty. In 1934 he found an opening in Himmler's SD, where he discovered that he was a born bureaucrat. By 1935 he had become the SD's expert on "the Jewish question," acquiring a smattering of Hebrew and Yiddish and briefly visiting Palestine in 1937 to study the possibility of the emigration of German Jews to the Holy Land.

Eichmann was useful in preparing the way for Hitler's *Anschluss* in Austria. As a reward he became chief of the Office for Jewish Emigration set up by the SS in Vienna. From issuing exit permits for Austrian Jews he rose to the position of the Nazi expert in "forced emigration." In December 1939, after distinguishing himself in assembling, registering and deporting both Austrian and Polish Jews to the killing centers in Poland, Eichmann was transferred to the RSHA's Amt IV (Gestapo) to become chief of *Referat* IV B4, dealing with Jewish affairs and evacuation. Although not present at the Wannsee Conference in January 1942, he was by then the accepted "Jewish specialist" of the RSHA, and Heydrich formally assigned to him the mission of implementing the Final Solution.

Although never known as a fanatical anti-Semite, always maintaining that he had nothing against Jews "personally," Eichmann nevertheless became one of the great murderers of history. He shipped Jews by the millions to the killing camps, gathering them in from every corner of the new German Empire. His industriousness was matched only by his indifference to the suffering and humanity of his victims. He was so icily detached that he might have been shipping sausage to the front rather than human beings to their death. He complained constantly about such loopholes in the Final Solution as the free zone in Vichy France, or of the laxness of the Italians or other German allies in expediting their Jews to Poland. He was incapable of rage, only of pique or pout, especially when, after arranging for a train to carry Jews to a concentration camp, he had to cancel his orders because an insufficient number of victims had been rounded up. Yet he never reported incompetence to Müller or his friend Kaltenbrunner for fear that the ultimate blame would fall upon him.

Eichmann's creed was the Nazi cardinal virtue of obedience. No matter how hideous the consequences of an order, he told a friend, "I will obey, obey, obey." Although, like Himmler, he shrank from violence personally and was sickened by the sight of blood, his attitude of indifference to the nature of his work was probably an affectation. He told the same friend that the extreme satisfaction he received from murdering five million Jews would cause him to "leap laughing into my grave." Even when, in November 1944, a Heinrich Himmler terrified by the Russian advance through Poland issued his "no gassing" order, Eichmann continued to kill Jews. And yet, until approximately that time, the name of this shrinking sparrow-man with the blood-soaked soul was unknown to his victims and most of the Free World.*

Among all the human abattoirs supplied by Adolf Eichmann, the one at Auschwitz in Poland 30 miles west of Cracow was the largest and foulest. It had been chosen by Heydrich for its isolation and easy accessibility by rail. Until the spring of 1941, Auschwitz contained 12,000 prisoners, about as many as the earlier camps at Dachau and Buchenwald. But just before Hitler's invasion of Russia, Himmler ordered it expanded to hold 130,000 prisoners, 100,000 of them to be captured Russian soldiers. At first, Auschwitz, again like the other camps, was to provide slave labor for adjoining industries. They were, of course, to be worked to death, so that the Reich might profit from their labor while satisfying its leader's vengeful hatred of both Russians and Jews. Of 12,000 Russian captives detailed to work on camp expansion in December 1941, only 150 survived the winter. Gradually, as the real meaning of the Final Solution became clear to the camp commanders, Auschwitz and its companion centers became more concerned with killing than with supplying slave labor. Most of the victims were Jews.

Nevertheless, the need for slave workers persisted. They were drafted according to the needs of the camp. If an epidemic or a severe winter had reduced the number of inmates, or it was summer and farm laborers were needed, as many as 30 percent of the prisoners in an arriving train might be spared. When bodies were plentiful, as few as 10 percent would be so chosen. These survivors arose at three o'clock every morning and were marched off to work at four. There was a half-hour break at lunch when each worker received a bowl of filthy soup made from carrots, cabbage or turnips. Work ended at six and supper consisted of an ounce of bread—a little more than one slice—after which they were marched

*Eichmann only became notorious after the war when he was captured by American troops, but escaped and fled to Argentina. Israeli agents found him there in May 1960 and secretly abducted him to Israel, where he was tried for crimes against humanity, convicted and executed on May 31, 1962.

back to their "barracks." These were windowless structures with steeply pitched roofs. Along the walls inside ran tiers of balconies honeycombed with cubbyholes two and a half feet high shared by three men or women each.

Each week a third of the prisoners died. Sick or injured inmates were taken to the infirmary, where they were allowed two or three days in which to recover. If they didn't, they were "spritzed"—given a fatal injection of phenol straight into the heart.

To survive, a prisoner had to become part of the camp administration, which all the commandants needed to keep functioning. They could become nurses in the infirmary, or join the various squads for burial or cleaning the freight cars after their cargoes of human misery had been unloaded, or rise to the position of block elders or camp clerks. This prison bureaucracy was joined in unholy alliance with the SS through the cement of a chance to survive. Through them, the commandants were able to operate their charnel houses or squelch the surprisingly frequent—though small and ineffectual—rebellions. To escape, of course, was to work a miracle. Getting beyond the two rings of electrified wire was difficult enough, but to move through a hostile population with shorn heads and prison clothes was even more daunting, especially when pursued by soldiers and SS guards combing the woods with baying hounds. If someone did escape, some of those left behind paid for his freedom with their lives. Rebellions also triggered bloodbaths.

Executions at first were by firing squads or hanging, although no one ever deterred an enraged or sadistic guard from beating or stabbing someone to death. Eventually, some "scientific" form of mass murder was needed. The first of these was the "gassing vans" developed at Auschwitz. They were at first primitive and not entirely satisfactory. An SS *Untersturmführer* named Dr. Becker has given an incredibly clinical report on his assignment to inspect the vans. First, he is distressed because when it rains the vans skid off the roads, so that they can only be used in dry weather. He deplores the place of execution because it is difficult to reach from the highway. He complains that "the persons to be executed get restless" when they see the van or are unloaded at the slaughtering ground. To avoid this, he camouflages the vans as house trailers by putting window shutters on their sides. To his chagrin, he does not fool the local Poles, who immediately call the vehicles "death vans." Next, he is concerned for the health of his SS men who suffer headaches from the carbon monoxide gas leaking from the vans. This also wastes fuel, he reports, but he has solved both problems by having the leaks soldered. Dr. Becker is also worried that the driver of the van steps on the gas pedal too hard, causing "death by suffocation and not death by dozing off as was planned." However, this problem also has been solved, he proudly reports: "My directions now have proved that by the correct adjustment of the levers death comes faster, and the prisoners fall asleep peacefully. Distorted faces and excretions, such as could be seen before, are no longer noticed."

Thus, the perfectionist; and yet, to chide a murderer for seeking a more efficient form of murder is no more logical than to rebuke a thief for stealing from the church poor box. The difference is not in kind, but only in degree. What is monstrous is that the murders do not spring from the human instincts for hatred, revenge or gain, but because they are perceived as necessary for the good of the Reich—the only acceptable moral standard—and they are only revolting because of the detached, clinical way in which they are carried out. Eventually, the crude vans were replaced by the more sophisticated gassing showers. Jews who had gone without bathing for weeks were taken naked and en masse to what seemed to be shower rooms. But it was not water that came hissing from the shower head but the exhaust from diesel trucks. Later in 1942, a prussic acid derivative made by I. G. Farben and called Zyklon B was used to provide a more efficient form of lethal gas.

Mass murder, of course, raised the problem of what to do with all the bodies. The Nazis might make soap from human fat, or extract from corpses gold teeth and fillings to be melted down for bullion, or shave them for the hair with which to stuff mattresses, or even make lampshades from their skin, but these at-best marginal means of turning a profit out of murder did not solve how to dispose of so many corpses produced by a program in which at Auschwitz alone 10,000 Jews died daily. At Auschwitz after the first hundred thousand corpses had been dumped in narrow trenches dug in the spongy earth of surrounding fields, the decomposing bodies caused the ground to rise like yeasty dough. Nauseating gases bubbled to the surface, spreading noxious fumes for miles. Rats multiplied and swarmed in packs. Fish died in the rivers. The camp's water supply became polluted. The immediate solution was to dig huge pits, filling them with wood, placing the bodies atop the wood and burning them in open pyres. For weeks towering clouds of greasy black smoke rose above Auschwitz and its environs, drifting as far away as Cracow or the Vistula River.

After the incineration the skulls and bones were pulverized by prisoners using hammers and the powder, together with the ashes, was either thrown into the nearby Vistula River or used to fertilize farmlands. Eventually, a bone-crushing machine was developed and the camp was equipped with four huge crematories capable of daily reducing 12,000 people to ashes. With these, and with the zealous Eichmann's trainloads of victims arriving almost daily, there developed among the camp commanders a ghoulish rivalry. They sought to outdo each other in killing Jews, especially after a Wehrmacht defeat. They knew that an exceptionally large butcher's bill would help console *Der Führer.*

After the disaster at Stalingrad, Hitler ordered SS General Juergen Stoop to destroy the Jews in the Warsaw Ghetto. He attacked with 3,000 SS soldiers using tanks, armored cars, artillery and flamethrowers. To his surprise the poorly armed Jews rose in wrath against their tormentors. Stoop had been ordered to reduce the Ghetto in three days, but it took four months. Although 56,065 Jews died, they had chewed up a formation that could have been put to better use on the Russian front.

Hitler was always preoccupied with the problem of how to prolong the death agonies of the Jews. He asked Himmler how best to do it. Himmler ordered his scientific advisers to make a recommendation. They reported that stuffing Jewish prisoners inside freight cars coated with dehydrated calcium oxide—quicklime—would produce excruciating burns. And it would take at least four days for the prisoners to die. Even better, the freight cars could be left standing on some forgotten siding. With freight cars, it would not be necessary to send Jews to the already overworked camps; and eventually the freight cars were used in addition to the camps.

Himmler's SS guards, like Heydrich's SD men, were the scum of the German earth: thieves, rapists, murderers, misfits, torturers and perverts, all of them deeply streaked with sadism. They took ghoulish delight in contriving the vilest punishments for "capital" crimes of attempting to escape, stealing a potato or smiling in ranks. The perpetrators were taken to a basement and placed beneath hooks sunk in the wall eight feet above the floor. Slip nooses were placed over their heads and they were lifted up to the hooks and hung there. If their death writhings were too prolonged and became boring, the guards beat out their brains with long-handled clubs looking like potato-mashers.

When they could, the guards gleefully relieved themselves in the prisoners' food, or drowned their babies in buckets of water. Jewish women in early stages of pregnancy were aborted on arrival. Once at Auschwitz, a new doctor ordered that Jewish women be allowed to keep their babies; but after two months of this anomalous amnesty, orders came from Berlin to kill them and they were all taken to the gas chamber. Again at Auschwitz, when the gas showers ran out of Zyklon B pellets, the children were thrown alive into the furnaces. Grotesquerie was always in fashion at the extermination camps where the guards sought to banish boredom by playing games. Thus a tall handsome woman would be ordered to mate with an ugly dwarf in full view of everyone in the area. Afterwards they were shot for having commited a "crime." The fact that the crime was ordered under pain of death by an SS guard was irrelevant. It was also great sport to order Jewish men to lower their trousers and run around the camp. Those who sought to pull them up were shot.

Some of these sick creatures found sexual satisfaction in torture. A female guard named Irma Greis was fond of seeking out shapely women to strip them and cut their breasts open with whiplashes. She then took them to a doctor who sewed them up again without anesthesia while Irma watched, swaying rhythmically, cheeks flushed and foaming at the mouth.

Although the camp commanders later claimed that such cruel "sport" was not deliberate policy but was rather, in the words of Rudolph Höss, the Auschwitz chief, "excesses committed by individual leaders, subleaders and men who laid violent hands on internees," this is palpably untrue. Heinrich Himmler himself, during visits to Auschwitz, at least twice ordered inmates murdered. The first time he became upset to learn that a dozen boys aged eight to fourteen had been brought to Auschwitz for stealing coal and were assigned to various men's barracks. Fearing that they might be sexually assaulted, he ordered them killed —thus preserving the camp's "morality." He was also shocked in August 1944, when he beheld the dreadful deterioration of some 4,000 survivors of 16,000 Gypsies confined at Auschwitz. Because of the filth and starvation in which they existed they had been ravaged by diseases unknown since the Middle Ages. Seeing these pitiful creatures without noses, and teeth growing through their cheeks, he ordered them exterminated as a "humanitarian solution" to their problem.

Wilhelm Boger, the SS chief of security at Auschwitz, devised the infamous "Boger Swing." Victims were trussed up like a pig and tied on a pole between two bars with their heads hanging down. They were then beaten on the sides and buttocks until their bones were crushed or until they "confessed." The victims could plead to any crime, committed or not. It was the "confession" that satisfied Boger. He also introduced the "Boger salad." This was a plate of highly salted and spiced herring forced upon inmates being starved to death in tiny standing cells reminiscent of the Medieval "little ease." Consumption of it added the agony of thirst to the slow torture of starvation. Cutting off the breasts of beautiful women and allowing them to bleed to death was another common and condoned practice at Auschwitz. And yet, as the flood of Hitlerite hate rose higher, there sailed upon its surface (to borrow an image from Sholem Asch) a small ark carrying a band of Christian saints guided by the Judeo-Christian commandment to love God and their fellow man.

The huge area of Europe seized by the Nazis and their allies held approximately 8,300,000 Jews. Of these an estimated 6 million perished. Of the surviving 2,300,000 perhaps 1 million escaped by flight or evacuation before the Axis troops entered their homeland. That more than a million others remained alive while dwelling in the very heart of the Hitlerite crucible was a miracle of selfless love: the fearless devotion of those Christians who risked and often lost their lives to save them.

It will never be known exactly how many of the roughly 300 million Europeans who lived at one time or another under the heel of the Nazi jackboot actually resisted the persecution. Numbers, however, are irrelevant; what matters is that there were enough of them fired with the belief that the Jews were their brethren and that they themselves were indeed "their brothers' keepers."

The extent of this resistance varied according to the nature of the countries and to the number of Jews dwelling in them. Some, such as the Western and Scandinavian democracies with a long history of freedom and with fewer Jews in their midst, tended to be more solicitous of the safety of their threatened breathren. In Norway and Denmark in 1938 there was only a total of 8,500 Jews, and of these less than 800 were murdered. France, with 270,000 Jews, yielded but 60,000 to the executioners. Many Greeks, Czechs and Bulgarians also tried to help the Jews. Most victims came from the countries of Eastern Europe, with their long history of drudgery and oppression at the hands of foreign invaders, and in the case of Czarist Russia and its satellites, serfdom and official anti-Semitism. Of the 3,300,000 Jews living in Poland an estimated minimum of ·2,350,000 or a maximum of 3,000,000 perished. Death came to a minimum of

700,000 Russian Jews or a maximum of 900,000 out of a total of 5,000,000, but these were murdered only in those lands west of Moscow, comprising only a small fraction of the vast Soviet Union. Here, though the number of heroic Christians was comparatively smaller, it was nevertheless significant.

Everywhere in Christian Europe there were Good Samaritans. In Poland a cattle dealer named Jozefek who had sheltered thirty-five Jews was hanged in the public square of Lwow and left rotting at the end of a rope for days as a warning to those who might try to emulate him. In Vilna Benedictine nuns hid Jews in their convent and dressed them in their own habits to allay suspicions. Pastor Vergara, a German Protestant minister, forged a Gestapo order to secure the release of seventy Jewish children whom he distributed among Gentile families. For this his wife was tortured, his son-in-law murdered and he himself driven into hiding. The heroism of Eduardo Focherini, editor of the Bologna Catholic daily, *Avvenire d'Italia,* in protecting Jews did not cause his own death but sent seven of his children into a Fascist concentration camp where they all perished. And from Archbishop Jules-Gerard Saliege of Toulouse came this defiance delivered into the teeth of the Nazi occupation authorities: "There is a Christian morality . . . that confers rights and imposes duties. These duties and these rights come from God. One can violate them. But no mortal has the power to suppress them. The Jews are our brethren. . . . No Christian dare forget that . . . France, which cherishes in the conscience of all its children the tradition of respect for the individual . . . is not responsible for these horrors."

If sheltering Jews was heroic, the art of hiding them was ingenious. Double walls and hanging ceilings were built behind which Jews lived for years. Cellars and attics were camouflaged. Annexes of abandoned office buildings came into use. One of these in Amsterdam hid the family of Anne Frank, the girl whose immortal diary now belongs to world literature. Jews were hidden in cemetery graves, stables, haystacks, pigsties and cowsheds, to the great exasperation of Gestapo agents, who sometimes swore that the Jews had vanished into the earth like moles. Hiding places were often so cramped that the occupants took turns lying down or were forced to stand immobile for hours. A Jewish woman in Warsaw lived for eighteen months in a standing position and required hospitalization for her benumbed legs after her liberation. There are also two recorded cases of Jews existing in pigeon houses. Hospitals were known to accept hunted Jews as bogus patients, though their staffs might be terrified in the knowledge that if the Gestapo discovered a circumcised male it meant the end for all. Those Jews in hiding in remote woods or fields were often fed by members of the Polish underground. In one celebrated case a Polish gardener named Wolski hid Emmanuel Ringelblum, the Warsaw historian and archivist, together with his family and another twenty Jews, in an underground bunker over which he had planted a greenhouse. They might have stayed there until the end of the war had not an informer turned them in to the Gestapo, which promptly shot Wolski and executed Ringelblum and the others.

Informers were the Gestapo's chief allies. They were either professionals seeking a monetary reward, drunks out for brandy or vodka, collaborationists or anti-Semites. They were usually paid a quart of brandy, four pounds of sugar, a carton of cigarettes and a small amount of money roughly the equivalent of two or three U.S. dollars. Ordinary gossips chattering away about the suspicious things they had seen or heard were just as dangerous and just as feared by the hidden Jews or their hosts. Because of this, certain techniques evolved. A couple planning to shelter Jews first had to be sure of the cooperation of like-minded friends who would receive them if a raid were imminent. Members of a Jewish family often were distributed among several hosts. Frequent movement and changes of hiding places were also necessary. Thus the saving of even a single Jew often required the cooperation of many Christians. It was learned that hiding Jews in private homes in large cities usually ended in disaster. There were too many curious eyes and wagging tongues. Increased food purchases in the local markets might immediately arouse suspicions. Because most homes did not have inside toilets, the problem of surreptitious disposal of waste also arose. A guest becoming sick or dying or a pregnant woman delivering her child created other obvious difficulties. Small children were a great risk and they were often fed tranquilizers to keep them quiet, or else they were stuffed inside stoves, garbage cans or boxes. One six-year-old Jewish boy so incarcerated for a long time could not walk and was almost totally blind when he was freed. But he lived to recover.

Sometimes parties of Jews chose to leave the care of their benefactors lest they incriminate them. "We are trailed and hunted," wrote Francisca Rubinlicht of Warsaw. "We can no longer find a place to hide. Our money is gone. We cannot stay here any longer because we have been threatened with being reported to the Gestapo. If this happens, our protectors will suffer as well. We cannot commit suicide in this place because our protector will be victimized. So we have decided to surrender, in the knowledge that we can swallow the [suicide] pills that now constitute our only, our priceless possession."

Here was the sublime self-sacrifice, suicide born not of despair but conceived in faith and hope and a love that did indeed pass all understanding. How such mutual and heroic love between the persecuted Jews and the Christians who sheltered them can be weighed in the scales of God's justice against the enormously greater evil engulfing Europe is not known to man. But it did exist, and it was in the darkness of that hate that the light of this love was magnified.

Like pain, the overwhelming sense of horror that engulfed the Jews in the extermination camps is impossible to describe. All of them upon arrival knew at once that they were there to die an indecent death. And before that, hope would perish. All those people and places, family and friends, home and hearth, old haunts and familiar sights, the things like love and laughter that nourish hope were never to be seen or heard again. Instead there was the daily drudgery of the early-morning roll call, twelve hours of rewardless labor, disgusting food and sleepless nights made hideous by screams and the leaping flames of the crematories. Death might almost be a relief from such madness, and the Jews did go to their death with a quiet dignity that confounded their murderers.

Indifference to the suffering of the prisoners could be as much a torment as deliberate torture. At Auschwitz one tap of water served 12,000 women inmates. Sometimes the water was not flowing or was unfit to drink. To get to it, the prisoners had to pass through a washhouse occupied by female German guards who beat them horribly. Prisoners could go as long as three months without changing their clothes. If it was winter they would melt snow to wash in. In spring, they drank from roadside puddles, and then washed their clothes in them. Always their throats burned with thirst never slaked by the half cup of herbal tea issued twice daily. Like soldiers, the prisoners found that their most precious possession was their shoes. But the mud and ice of the fields in which they worked soon demolished footwear, forcing some inmates to work barefoot. Foot sores and frozen feet were common. Usually the prisoners slept with their muddy shoes on for fear that they might be stolen, and many a 3:30 A.M. reveille began with the anguished cry: "My shoes have been stolen!" Ubiquitous lice were another affliction. They swarmed over cots like ants and it was a fortunate prisoner indeed who escaped typhus. Rats as big as cats were everywhere, gnawing on corpses piled up in the courtyards and even attacking the dying.

Auschwitz could also claim the crown of having put torture in the service of "science." It was, of course, pseudo-science that was served in all the diabolically inhuman "experiments" that were conducted there. Every level of duration or toleration could be tested: how long a man could endure torture, or go without sleep, or without food, or suffer indignity, or respond to every manner of chemicals injected into his veins. Although at Auschwitz there were any number of these coldly curious creatures who, in the name of this utterly worthless research, would vivisect a Jew or infect him with some agonizing debilitating disease, there was among them, a nonpareil of evil. This was Dr. Josef Mengele, known to the inmates as "the Angel of Death" because of his unlined face and mild manners.*

Mengele was the son of a wealthy German manufacturer of farm machinery. In 1935, at the age of twenty-four, he joined Hitler's Brownshirts. In 1938 he received his degree from the Frankfurt Medical School. He had also studied anthropology and zoology—the beginning of his interest in genetics—at the Universities of Munich and Vienna. In 1940 he joined the SS and rose to the rank of captain, and in 1943 he was sent to Auschwitz as a camp physician. Five feet nine and well built, Mengele had a dark complexion, chestnut hair and blue eyes of striking beauty. Even those Jews who came to fear him and his dreadful "experiments" were impressed by how handsome he looked in his neatly pressed black SS uniform. "He had the face of an angel," said Orna Bierenbach, a Hungarian Jew who survived Auschwitz. "He did not look like an angel of death, like a Satan. I always wanted to see his hands," she said, referring to his practice

---

*Josef Mengele was one of the most sought-after Nazi criminals. He escaped to South America where he lived for 40 years under a variety of aliases. It was discovered that he drowned in 1979 while living in Brazil.

of wearing white gloves. "I was sure he had very dainty hands, the hands of a pianist."

It was Mengele's custom to welcome each new trainload of prisoners. He sat on a platform in the station with his hand pressed palm inward on his chest. As prisoners stepped off the train, he indicated by a flick of his thumb to right or left who was to be gassed and who spared for experiment. Mothers with babies were paraded past a firepit, their infants torn from their arms and hurled into the flaming maw of a modern Moloch. Identical twins were confined in a yard-square cage, where they crouched in their own refuse awaiting injections by the Angel of Death, who then stood by, notebook in hand, waiting to see which one died first. Other children were led by him on a tour of his pathological laboratory so that he might record their reaction to his collection of human eyes glued to shelves like so many butterflies.

Once he sent a message to the women's barracks saying that pregnant women could sign up for a special milk porridge. Many did, including the nonpregnant, and everyone who did was sent to the gas chambers. He "solved" an epidemic of scarlet fever caused by lice by sending about 600 of the 700 women in one barracks to the gas chamber so that he could disinfect the building. Prisoners in adjacent barracks were then forced to wade through a disinfectant bath to enter the cleansed structure. Mengele was widely praised for having gotten rid of the lice, and of course the report on his success made no mention of his irrelevant murder of 600 women. In all, it is believed that he was responsible for the death of 400,000 Jews.

Such was the incompetence of the SS murder machine, like an enormous apparatus designed to burn down a barn to roast an egg. Unknown hundreds of millions of marks were spent on the men, buildings, food and material and the railroads specially built for the extermination camps. Although it is not known how many men were wasted in conducting this slaughter of defenseless human beings, it must have been at least 200,000—the equivalent of an army of about twenty divisions. Certainly this large force of troops might have been put to better use elsewhere, especially on the Eastern Front so close to Poland. But once again the whim of Adolf Hitler prevailed over practical military considerations. It may also be asked why did not Adolf Hitler yoke these millions to the wheels of the Wehrmacht? The young men certainly could have been compelled to wear the German uniform, just like the French, Poles, Russians and others impressed into Hitler's armies; and they could have been controlled by SS officers and NCOs. They certainly could not have been trusted in combat, especially not against the Western Allies; but they could have been used to release other units for battle; or, granted *Der Führer*'s indifference to law, morals or the sanctity of human life, as the Soviets used their Mongols and other despised minorities: to pass on foot through minefields and thus detonate corridors for the following regulars. The labor of the unskilled, or of those too old or too young to serve, might also have been valuable, to say nothing of the huge reservoir of Jewish technicians—

scientists of every discipline, architects, physicians, builders and designers—that could have served the Reich under the pain of execution. Even the noblest among them would have hesitated to refuse if their wives and families were to be held hostage. The Jews might even have been worked to death as Reinhard Heydrich proposed, but in this Adolf Hitler would have taken no pleasure. The former acting corporal from the Linz Barracks wanted mass murder. Despite Nazi protests to the contrary, he wanted vengeance from the very start: the Jews were to die in agony and degradation. That is why the vaunted German efficiency did not appear in the Final Solution, except, as in the case of the quicklime freight cars, to inflict more pain.

It has been said that Hitler's failure to use the Jews was one of his greatest mistakes. Rather it seems to have been a bad choice: between allowing the Jews to live in his service while holding his revenge in abeyance, or immediately satisfying his hatred. He chose the latter, a typically emotional response. So the Final Solution went forward. All over the German-occupied territories the killing centers and mobile execution squads made martyrs of the Jews for their twin "crimes" of blood and creed. Here, in a scene described by a German engineer named Hermann Graebe, is a typical execution squad at work in a death-pit near the small industrial city of Dubno in the Ukraine:

Without screaming or weeping these people undressed, stood around in family groups, kissed each other, said farewells, and waited for the sign from the SS man who stood beside the pit with a whip in his hand. During the fifteen minutes I stood near, I heard no complaint or plea for mercy. I watched a family of about eight persons, a man and a woman both of about fifty, with their children of about twenty to twenty-four, and two grown-up daughters about twenty-eight or twenty-nine. An old woman with snow-white hair was holding a one-year-old child in her arms and singing to it, tickling it. The child was cooing with delight. The couple were looking on with tears in their eyes. The father was holding the hand of a boy about ten years old and speaking to him softly; the boy was fighting his tears. The father pointed to the sky, stroked his head and seemed to explain something to him.

At that moment the SS man at the pit started shouting something to his comrade. The latter counted off about twenty persons and instructed them to go behind the earth mound. Among them was the family I have just mentioned. I well remember a girl, slim with black hair, who, as she passed me, pointed to herself and said, "twenty-three." I walked around the mound and stood in front of a tremendous grave. People were closely wedged together and lying on top of each other so that only their heads were visible. Nearly all had blood running over their shoulders from their heads. Some of the people shot were still moving. Some were lifting their arms and turning their heads to show that they were still alive. The pit was nearly two-thirds full. I estimated that it already contained about a thousand people. I looked at the man who did the shooting. He was an SS man who sat at the edge of the narrow end of the pit, his feet dangling into the pit. He had a tommy-gun on his knees and was smoking a cigarette. The people, completely naked, went down some steps which were cut in the clay wall of the pit and clambered over the heads of the people lying there, to the place to which the SS man directed them; some caressed those who were still alive and spoke to them in low voices.

It is not possible to describe more strikingly the two characteristics of the Hitlerite pogrom: the quiet nobility of the Jews juxtaposed against the hateful brutality of their murderers. Here the oafish guard nonchalantly sprays his bullets knowing full well that he is only wounding some of his naked victims who will soon be buried alive. Thus the Jews must not only perish but also die in agony and ignominy. But the Jews do not quail but rather comfort each other. They embrace or caress the afflicted. There is also a unique submissiveness by which they accept death on the orders of but two guards. Why such docility? One answer comes from the Jewish historian Raul Hilberg, who maintains that so many millennia of persecution had taught the Jews to abhor violence. "In two thousand years they had deliberately unlearned the art of revolt. They were helpless." He is probably right. Once a race of warriors who had seized and held their homeland by force of arms, worshiping a God of Battles who had enjoined them, "And when the Lord thy God shall deliver (the city) into thy hands, thou shalt slay all that are therein of the male sex with the edge of the sword," the Jews had learned in those unhappy centuries of dispersion the supreme folly of matching their small violence against the superior violence of the Roman Empire or of the host European kingdoms in which they dwelled. And because they had become a migrant people they were no longer motivated by that territorial imperative which impels all creatures—human beings included—to fight fiercest in defense of their own nest, lair or homeland. Perhaps the males were unwilling to revolt for fear of some new and more hideous torture that might be inflicted on their women and children in retaliation. Even their nakedness could have inhibited them, for the Nazis stripped their victims before killing them, probably more to induce a sense of helplessness than to rob them of their clothing.

And so European Jewry all but perished, consumed like a burnt offering— the word for which is Holocaust.

126. The German Surrender

GRAND ADM. KARL DOENITZ saw in Hitler's suicide an opportunity to split the Big Three. He believed that the Anglo-Americans would now be ready to regard Germany as a bulwark in the anticommunist alliance. To detach West from East he resorted to piecemeal surrender to the Western Allies only. First, Reichsführer Heinrich Himmler sent an agent to Sweden to try to arrange for the Wehrmacht's capitulation to the West alone. President Truman replied that the only term acceptable was Unconditional Surrender. This left Himmler with no alternative but his own suicide.

In the West, meanwhile, German soldiers were surrendering in hordes and so were men from the East hurrying to be taken captive by the Western Allies. German civilians in the East also sought to flee to the West. The Germans facing Montgomery's 21st Army Group wanted to surrender not only themselves but also those formations still fighting the Soviets. Eisenhower ordered Montgomery to refuse the latter offer, and on May 4 only those Germans opposite 21st Army Group laid down their arms. A similar attempt was made by the Germans opposite Hodges in the center. They tried to surrender their own armies as well as those battling the Soviets in Czechoslovakia and Austria. The Americans rejected this proposal and forbade German civilians to cross to the west bank of the Elbe. No attempt was made to enforce this prohibition, and thousands more Germans fled to the West.

On May 4 Doenitz made another attempt to split the Big Three, sending Adm. Hans von Friedeburg to SHAEF to request permission to surrender the remaining German forces in the West. Eisenhower replied through Bedell Smith that a general surrender in the East and the West had to be simultaneous. The supreme commander refused to see any German commander until the documents of Unconditional Surrender were signed. At last Doenitz capitulated, and at two o'clock in the morning of May 7, Generals Bedell Smith, Morgan, Bull, Spaatz, Marshal Tedder, Gen. François Sevez of France and Gen. Ivan Susloparov of the Soviet Union and other ranking commanders gathered in the second-floor recreation room of a dismal little red-brick schoolhouse for boys in Rheims. Actually, it was SHAEF's war room. The walls were covered with maps studded with pins and arrows and other symbols testifying to the absolutely overwhelming defeat of the Wehrmacht in the West. The room was so small that the Allied officers had to squeeze past each other to gain their seats around a heavy oak table.

Field Marshal Alfred Gustave Jodl, chief of the German General Staff, strode into the room followed by two aides. Tall, ramrod-straight, bald, immaculately dressed and resplendent in all his decorations, his monocle in place, Jodl was the personification of the Prussian Junker. In another room Eisenhower waited, pacing the floor and smoking.

It took almost forty minutes to complete the surrender. When it was signed and done, Jodl arose and in a breaking, almost sobbing voice made a plea for the German people. "In this hour, I can only express the hope that the victor will treat generously with them." There was no reply, and Bedell Smith led Jodl into Eisenhower's presence in the adjoining room. The supreme commander sat at a desk, grim-faced, those cornflower-blue eyes cold and hard. In a clipped voice he asked Jodl if he understood what he had signed. *"Ja,"* the German replied, and Eisenhower said: "You will, officially and personally, be held responsible if the terms of this surrender are violated, including its provisions for German commanders to appear in Berlin at the moment set by the Russian high command to accomplish formal surrender to that government. That is all."

Jodl saluted and left.

Eisenhower came into the war room and slumped wearily into a seat. He sighed and said, "I suppose this calls for a bottle of champagne." Someone fetched a bottle and opened it to faint and unconvincing cheers. The bubbly was flat, but not nearly so flat as the supreme commander. He felt even worse when, just before he went to bed, the Soviets sent him a message refusing to accept the surrender signing at Rheims and demanding another in Berlin. This was done next day in an elaborate ceremony from which the Soviets made a splendid film documentary celebrating the victory of the Red Army in the Great Patriotic War with Germany.

Dwight Eisenhower saw the film some months later and was not a little disturbed to find that it failed to mention Rheims.

127. Burma: A Slow Road Back

IN WASHINGTON THE STRUGGLE over air power in China between General Stilwell and Generalissimo Chiang Kai-shek supported by General Chennault had ended in victory for Chiang. However, Stilwell and Marshall had been correct in their observation that any air attack strong enough to damage the Japanese would provoke a Japanese ground offensive to destroy the airfields, just as the Japanese had done after Doolittle's Shangri-La raid on Tokyo, when they went rampaging through eastern China to erase every airfield in sight. President Roosevelt, urged on by Harry Hopkins, was determined to try the aerial war, if only to placate the ever-restive, ever-complaining Chiang. Chennault was given command of an independent air force, the Fourteenth. This freed him from serving as part of the Tenth Air Force under Gen. Clayton Bissell, whom he openly despised. Some of Chennault's aviators hated Bissell so fiercely that they hired and trained a non-English-speaking Chinese to shout at all arriving Tenth Air Force personnel: "PISS ON YOU, BISSELL!" Chennault was to be reinforced and to receive the first 4,700 tons of all supplies flown over the Hump each month. The remaining pittance would be left for Stilwell for his Burmese operation, which, Vinegar Joe observed, was like "trying to manure a ten-acre field with sparrow shit." This decision also severely delayed construction of the Ledo Road. General Pick's supplies and engineers were diverted to improving Chennault's airfields or building new ones.

Fourteenth Air Force achieved little. Chennault's fighters were never strong enough to wrest control of the air from Japan, and they were eventually driven from their east China bases by Japanese bombing. Many of the aircraft promised him failed to arrive, and those that did complicated his chronic fuel-shortage problem. Big B-24 Liberator bombers could not be serviced in China and had to carry their own supplies from India, thus reducing their bomb loads. Although Chennault claimed that his bombers sank 40,000 tons of Japanese shipping in the summer of 1943, the true figure was 3,000 tons.

Meanwhile, Wavell had become viceroy of India, while General Sir Claude Auchinleck replaced him as Indian commander in chief. Because Auchinleck would have no responsibility for operations against the Japanese in Southeast Asia, a supreme commander for that area had to be named. Churchill chose Vice Adm. Lord Louis Mountbatten. Tall, handsome ("He has the curliest eyelashes," Vinegar Joe informed his diary), and a close relative of the royal family, Mountbatten had distinguished himself in the Mediterranean as a commander of a destroyer flotilla. He was a man of immense charm with a flair for public relations. Some senior admirals considered him a lightweight, perhaps because at forty-two he was the youngest vice admiral in British history. Although he and Stilwell outwardly professed mutual admiration, privately their relationship was only a trifle friendlier than Vinegar Joe's vendetta with Chiang. His Anglo-American staff was flawed by petty racist bickering and backbiting and was nothing like Eisenhower's smooth-functioning SHAEF. The Americans said that SEAC—the initials for the Southeast Asia Command—stood for "Save England's Asiatic Colonies." Despite all this squabbling and haggling, mutual distrust and the exasperating delays or cancellations of projected campaigns—all so characteristic of the CBI—Stilwell at the end of 1943 was able to launch his long-planned offensive to reopen northern Burma.

His objective was the town of Myitkyina with its airfield. Myitkyina was also a vital communications hub. South of it, the Ledo Road could hook up with existing tracks leading to the old Burma Road. Hump traffic could use this much shorter, safer route to China. To take Myitkyina Stilwell planned to use three of his Ramgarh-trained divisions of Chinese, spearheaded by the first American ground troops to be committed in the theater.

Surprisingly enough, the Joint Chiefs of Staff—orthodox realists like Marshall and King—had been beguiled by the glamour of the Chindits. Wingate had so impressed them that they formed the 5307th Provisional Regiment, code-named Galahad. It was to be an elite force of seasoned jungle fighters. There were indeed some of them in Galahad, particularly soldiers from the Americal Division who had fought on Guadalcanal. There were also brave volunteers from other outfits. But as frequently happens when a new unit is being formed, it receives the dregs of other formations cleaning their misfits and malingerers out of the stockades and the hospitals. Many Pacific veterans who volunteered for Galahad had chronic psychiatric or malarial problems and hoped to get better medical care. Others thought that volunteering for a dangerous assignment would bring them home leave. It didn't. Instead it brought them swiftly and secretly to India where they were placed with the Chindits.

Stilwell at once asked Mountbatten for them, and the supreme commander agreed "because it seemed to mean more to Joe than the bickering was worth." Wingate, displaying a surprising command of the American idiom, advised Galahad's temporary commander to "tell General Stilwell he can take his Americans and stick 'em up his ass." Stilwell did indeed take them, appointing Brig. Gen. Frank Merrill, who had been with him on the jungle trek out of Burma, to command them. A reporter promptly christened them Merrill's Marauders and so they were called thereafter.

Stilwell did not use the Marauders until after his offensive in north Burma had slowed down. His Chinese 38th Division had entered the Hukawng Valley at the end of October and won its first victory ever over the Japanese in a small engagement at the village of Yubang Ga. Minor though it was, it finally convinced the Chinese that they were a match for the Japanese. Nevertheless, Stilwell was dissatisfied by their lack of speed. From the 38th's headquarters he tried to envelop the Japanese 18th Division in a series of wide swings. But his Chinese moved so slowly—one unit took an entire week in "preparation"—that they were never able to close the trap. So in February Stilwell decided to use the Marauders in a blocking position across the Japanese line of withdrawal, thus trapping the Japanese between the advancing Chinese and the blocking Americans.

Lt. Gen. Shinichi Tanaka, the 18th's commander, divined Stilwell's plan and decided to hurl himself against the Marauders and destroy them before the slow-moving Chinese could close up. But the Americans dug in along a river and repulsed his attacks. Then a force of Chinese tanks under U.S. Army Col. Rothwell H. Brown forced a passage through two of Tanaka's regiments and began blasting his headquarters. Shaken, Tanaka abandoned his attacks on the Marauders and began marching south for safety. Although he lost 800 men, he managed to elude Stilwell's trap. The Chinese-Americans were nevertheless exultant. Merrill told his troops: "Between us and the Chinese, we forced the Japanese to withdraw farther in the last three days than they have in the last three months of fighting."

Stilwell tried to trap the withdrawing enemy again, sending the Marauders on another wide swing to cut off Tanaka's retreat to Kamaing while his Chinese continued their frontal advance. About twenty miles above Kamaing the Marauders set up a block. The Japanese came at them so fiercely that Merrill withdrew into the surrounding hills. Tanaka tried his own turning movement, sending a force to flank the Chinese. With this Stilwell ordered the Marauders to the village of Nphum Ga to cut the trail the enemy flankers would have to follow. Once again the exhausted Americans were compelled to make another grueling jungle trek. Yet they reached Nphum Ga in time to set up another block. Merrill put one battalion on a hilltop near the town and another three miles away on an airstrip that was his only means of supply and communication with Stilwell.

No sooner had the Marauders dug in than the Japanese came against them fiercely, pounding them with artillery and mortar fire. Eventually, the Japanese cut the trail to the airstrip and captured the hilltop battalion's water hole. Allied aircraft dropped enough water for the Marauders to keep fighting. Gradually, the two battalions fought toward each other. At one point Sgt. Roy Matsumoto, a Nisei interpreter, overheard the enemy discussing a plan of attack. He warned his comrades, who booby-trapped their foxholes and then withdrew. When the Japanese attacked, they charged into well-aimed fire from the waiting Americans. They dived into the empty foxholes for cover and were blown to bits. Then Matsumoto bellowed "Charge!" in Japanese and another unit was destroyed. Finally, the Japanese exhausted themselves in fruitless frontal attacks and withdrew.

Now it would seem that the weary Marauders would be granted a well-earned rest. They had come into Burma lean and hardened men but by March they had suffered an average twenty-pound weight loss. They were down to less than half their original strength, and many of the survivors were sick. General Merrill had suffered a heart attack at Nphum Ga and was relieved by Col. Charles N. Hunter. However, Stilwell had been reinforced by two more Chinese divisions flown into north Burma, and the Marauders also received Chinese replacements. Stilwell also had five Chindit brigades. He resolved now on a daring march across the mountains to capture Myitkyina. For a spearhead he needed a formation he could rely on, and that meant the fought-out and worn-out Marauders. Once again they began a jungle march—over the 6,000-foot Kumon Mountains—on an end run to Myitkyina. And they took the enemy there completely by surprise, seizing the airfield with ease. Stilwell was exultant, writing in his diary: "WILL THIS BURN UP THE LIMEYS!" Churchill sent Mountbatten a petulant cable demanding to know how "the Americans, by a brilliant feat of arms, have landed us in Myitkyina."

But Myitkyina was not so easily held. Instead of flying in food, reinforcements and ammunition, the first planes brought in engineers and an AA detachment. The Japanese quickly rushed their own reinforcements to the area, taking the town and holding it against Chinese assaults. Then the monsoon arrived and the battle for Myitkyina settled down to a siege reminiscent of the jungle stands of the Pacific. Stilwell was unable to relieve the miserable Marauders, some of whom were so severely sick of dysentery that they had cut away the seats of their pants to free themselves for action. At one point he even ordered Marauders hospitalized with fatigue or illness back to the battle. But he also ordered construction troops on the Ledo Road to seize rifles and join the fight. Stilwell had no choice. Constantly pressuring Chiang for more troops, while keeping equally fought-out British Chindits in the line, he could not afford to appear sparing of American troops. Nevertheless, he might have been more concerned for the Marauders. Of his indifferent attitude Colonel Hunter wrote that up until Myitkyina "no member of Galahad had received a combat decoration, no member had received a promotion, a candy bar, a bag of peanuts, an issue of cigarettes, a can of beer, a bottle of whiskey, or a pat on the back from anyone." Such bitter words are surely a damning indictment of a commanding general. Not even a *medal?* Death and wounds, hardship and privation are indeed the portion of combat troops, but it would seem that Stilwell might have tried to make their ordeal seem worthwhile by passing out a little glory. Yet, it is a melancholy fact that commanders in love with glory themselves are often loath to share it with their men.

So the siege of Myitkyina continued, with the Japanese sitting strangely still in their positions instead of sallying forth to sweep the Chinese-Americans away. Probably they overestimated the enemy forces. Their situation deteriorated after the Chinese in a rare display of skill and determination drove the Japanese 18th Division out of the Mogaung Valley to cut off the Myitkyina garrison's chief source of supply. It was not until August 3, 1944, that the town of Myitkyina finally fell. Before then, however, Hump air transports began using the airstrip to make their shorter, safer runs. From 13,700 tons delivered to China in May, the figure rose to 25,000 in July and would go increasingly higher. And construction on the Ledo Road was at last resumed.

Meanwhile, far to the southwest on the Indo-Burmese border—around the towns of Imphal and Kohima—the decisive battle of Southeast Asia was being fought. Here the Japanese had begun their campaign to cut off the British forces in Burma and sever communications to the province of Assam in India, the base for both Stilwell's army and the Hump air traffic. In the beginning, using their customary tactics of infiltrating around and behind British units, cutting off their supplies and forcing them back, all went well for the Japanese. But they were surprised and shocked by the speed with which the British were able to airlift new supplies and forces to threatened areas. In one engagement an entire division was shifted to a danger point within eleven days. British and Indian troops at Kohima fought stubbornly, but even so the garrison appeared ready to collapse until a relief column broke through with reinforcements and supplies.

Further south a war of attrition reminiscent of the battles of World War I erupted on the Imphal plain. But the Japanese had overextended their supply lines, and the Anglo-Indians gradually forced them back until they were compelled to withdraw across the Chindwin River into Burma. With this decisive victory, the Japanese hold on Burma was pried loose and the way cleared for the final blow. This came under General Sir William Slim, probably the most competent general in the CBI. Slim's Fourteenth Army crossed the Chindwin and pursued the Japanese as far as the Irrawaddy, which the enemy had made his new line of defense. At this point, part of Slim's air transports were taken from him for use in China. In road-poor, rain-soaked Burma no piece of equipment was of more value than a flying troop transport. Slim was understandably outraged to lose his aircraft. Nevertheless, still possessing complete control of the air and an overwhelming superiority in armor, he decided to cross the Irrawaddy by feinting north to draw off Gen. Hoyotaro Kimura's forces, and then cross south. To deceive Kimura he set up a dummy corps headquarters in the north and sent another corps moving secretly south. The plan worked perfectly. After Kimura rushed reinforcements north, the southern corps forced the Irrawaddy.

Slim was now prepared to move on Rangoon, the capital and chief port of Burma. But another distress call arrived from China, where the Japanese were also attacking, siphoning off Slim's Chinese divisions and threatening to take his air transport. Slim appealed frantically to Mountbatten who signaled Churchill. A limited concession was wrung from General Marshall: Slim could keep his transports until the monsoon came, but when the rains arrived, he would lose them, whether or not he had captured Rangoon.

Slim put his men on half rations to make more room for fuel and ammunition in their vehicles. He exhorted his tank commanders to press on with all speed. "I told them that when I gave the word for the dash on Rangoon, every tank they had must be a starter and that every tank that crossed the starting line must pass the post in Rangoon. After that they could push them into the sea if they wanted!"

Moving rapidly through Japanese opposition at—for Burma—the astonishing rate of up to ten miles a day, the Anglo-Indians were within forty miles of Rangoon by the end of April. And then the monsoon came—two weeks early. The rain only slowed but did not stop Slim's fired-up forces. On May 2 a landing was made south of the city. On the same day a pilot flying over Rangoon looked down on a big sign saying: "JAPS GONE." Next morning Slim's triumphant but sodden spearheads sloshed into Rangoon—and the so-called "impossible" conquest of Burma had been accomplished.

But to the east in China it appeared that Chiang Kai-shek's Nationalist Government was doomed.

As General Stilwell had predicted, the Japanese refused to sit still for the raids of Chennault's Fourteenth Air Force on their supply lines. Instead they launched a series of offensives in China called *Ichigo* for the purpose of knocking out Chennault's airfields, and also to stop the more dangerous raids on Japan by the new American Superforts based in east China.

Ichigo began in April 1944 with a thrust into Honan Province between the Yangtze and Yellow rivers. It achieved immediate and spectacular success. Thirty-four Chinese divisions opposing the Japanese collapsed so completely that positions held by a thousand or more Chinese were overrun by a hundred or fewer Japanese. An offensive into Hunan Province achieved almost the same results. The Chinese Fourth Army holding Changsha abandoned the city without a fight, although the Tenth Army at Hengyang held out for six weeks, valiantly supported by Chennault's fliers. Nevertheless, the so-called Chinese army was a hollow giant dying under the attack of the old diseases: incompetence, divided command, corruption and incessant interference by Chiang. Some of the commanding generals were Chiang's old enemies, and he had no desire to send military equipment to potential postwar rivals. However, for Chiang and China there did not appear to be any postwar, after the fall of Hengyang on August 8 cleared the way for assault on Chennault's airfields at Kweilin and Liuchow.

Chennault sent frantic and fruitless appeals to the Joint Chiefs for more supplies and diversion to him of material intended for the B-29s, while demanding that Stilwell reinforce the threatened areas. Stilwell's reply was a smirking "I told you so" and an equally fruitless attempt to get the Joint Chiefs to relieve Chennault. Still the Japanese steamroller rolled on. Roosevelt replied to Chiang's appeals with a sharp note calling for appointment of Stilwell, now a full general, to complete command of Allied forces in China "including the communist forces." Chiang was appalled. He had no intention of allowing any foreigner to command his armies, or to befriend his war-lord enemies, or make some unpalatable deal with Mao in the north. Yet, he knew he could not refuse outright, and so he stalled, hoping that a distracted FDR would forget about China. The ruse bought him two months grace until Stilwell learned of his intention to pull back the forces intended to help clear the last sections of the Burma Road. Aghast, Stilwell radioed Marshall that the Generalissimo was about to "throw away all efforts" to free China. A response over Roosevelt's signature directed Chiang to place Stilwell in command at once and reinforce him. Here was the spark that ignited the powder keg.

Stilwell interrupted a conference between Chiang and Maj. Gen. Patrick J. Hurley, FDR's personal representative, and "handed this bundle of paprika to the Peanut." Chiang froze. Hurley thought Chiang "had been hit in the solar plexus." But the Generalissimo simply murmured, "I understand."

What Chiang understood was that the time had come to rid himself of this —to him—contrary and contumacious general. Through Hurley he demanded Stilwell's recall. To his incredulous surprise, his request was granted. Stilwell was replaced by Maj. Gen. Albert C. Wedemeyer, chief of staff to Mountbatten. What Chiang did not understand was that he had picked the least propitious moment for playing his ace. Capture of the Marianas bases for B-29s and Stalin's promise at Tehran to declare war on Japan after Germany fell had made China in 1944 much less important than in 1942. Admiral King would persist in his desire for bases on the China coast until the war ended, but the conviction that China would be needed for operations against Japan was no longer widespread. MacArthur was already preparing the Leyte landings and Nimitz was looking hard at Iwo Jima and Okinawa. So Wedemeyer arrived in Chungking, intending to supplant Stilwell's "vinegar" with his own "honey." But he was soon sending signals as acerbic as Vinegar Joe's.

Meanwhile, the Japanese captured Kweilin and Liuchow with their invaluable airfields. Chiang's forces, which he had assured Wedemeyer would hold out for at least two months, abandoned both key cities without a fight. Panic reigned in Chungking. Kuomintang officials inquired at the U.S. Embassy about facilities for evacuation by air. Its generals actually withdrew forces defending precious Kunming at the end of the vital ground and aerial supply line from India for defense of themselves and their families in the capital. China appeared to be finished.

But then the fortuitous, which so frequently alters the fortunes of war, spared Chiang and the Kuomintang. Just as the death of Genghis Khan had saved Western Europe from the Mongols, withdrawing from the gates of Vienna to return home to elect a successor, so the Japanese at the end of a perilously long and precarious supply line, caught in the grip of a bitter Chinese winter and daunted by the rising threat to the China coast represented by American victories in the Philippines, decided to bring *Ichigo* to a halt.

In this respite, Wedemeyer conceived a plan for a drive to that very coast in 1945. It seemed desirable because of the current belief that if the Japanese home islands were overrun, the enemy might try to make a stand in China and Manchuria. Accordingly, Wedemeyer launched a program of training Chinese forces under American instructors. He also cast covetous eyes north toward the armies of Mao Zedong. Mao's Communists had developed an effective guerrilla warfare against the Japanese. By living with the peasants and sharing their hardships, they had built a basis of solid support among them. For the "wars of liberation" of the future the guerrilla would be "the fish, and the peasant would be the water in which he swims." Some American leaders had already called for a coalition of Communist and Nationalist forces in the face of common danger. Chiang had even given his reluctant consent to a mission of American soldiers and diplomats to Yenan in July 1944. But nothing came of it. General Hurley, now the United States Ambassador, was against it, and it is doubtful if either Chiang or Mao could ever bury the hatchet except in each other's skull. Still Wedemeyer's preparations continued, and attacks were begun in July 1945. But then came word of the Japanese surrender.

The campaigns in the CBI (split in two after Stilwell's recall) actually contributed little to the defeat of Japan, while siphoning off a disproportionate amount of American men and matériel, especially those priceless air transports and their pilots.

Indubitably such resources might have been put to better use in Europe, except that, as has already been observed, it was politically and psychologically impossible for the United States, which had gone to war for China, to abandon China. Britain, of course, also found the CBI a terrible drain upon her resources; but then, Britain was fighting there to defend her empire and to recover what had been lost. After Burma fell, Mountbatten was prepared to invade Malaya.

Ineffectual on the course of the war, the CBI was nonetheless enormously influential upon the peace. Asian colonies had seen an Asian race conquer their heretofore invincible European masters and also had been given a heady, if limited, taste of self-government under the Southeast Asia Co-Prosperity Sphere. They had not loved these Japanese, far more brutal and exploitative than their British, French and Dutch predecessors, nor did they fight for them. But they had received a measure of military training and arms, and they were not inclined to lay these down to welcome back their old rulers. In Edmund Burke's phrase, "War never leaves a nation where it found it," and war in the CBI was the beginning of the end of imperialism in the world. China-Burma-India, then, may be said to have been the birthplace of the movement for freedom and self-government among all oppressed and exploited peoples of the world.

128. U.S. Submarines Against Japan

THE STRIKING AMERICAN VICTORY on Okinawa seemed to have been a disaster for the Japanese. They had lost a whole army from their ground forces, already badly depleted by either battlefield defeats or isolation among the far-flung islands of the new empire; the sinking of *Yamato* had signaled the symbolic destruction of their navy and the loss of hundreds upon hundreds of aircraft suggested the doom of their air power was imminent. Yet, the Joint Chiefs of Staff were far from being elated. Rather Okinawa raised the disturbing question: If a base in the Ryukyus cost so much to seize, what would be the price of an invasion of Japan?

Even before Okinawa the navy and the army disagreed over the way to bring Nippon to her knees. Naval strategists supported by Admiral King believed that seizure of portions of the south China coast would provide the bases for aerial bombardment and naval blockade, which would bring about the collapse of Japan without an invasion. Army strategists replied that operations on the south China coast would not necessarily be less costly than direct invasion of Nippon, while the subsequent war of attrition might take years to be effective. MacArthur shared this conviction. He also observed that bombardment alone was no guarantee of Japanese surrender any more than the strategic bombing of Germany had brought about defeat of the Nazis. MacArthur urged an early assault of the southern island of Kyushu followed by an invasion of the main island of Honshu. When Nimitz agreed with him, King withdrew his opposition, and the plan known as Operation Downfall was approved.

Downfall had two parts: the first, Olympic, was the invasion of Kyushu in the fall of 1945, and the second, Coronet, landings on Honshu in March of 1946. Gen. Walter Krueger's Sixth Army was charged with conducting Olympic. He would have eleven army and three Marine divisions—about 650,000 ground troops, some of them staging from as far away as Hawaii. Three corps of three divisions each would assault southern Kyushu at as many different points while a fourth of two divisions would make a diversionary move off Shikoku. On Kyushu the Americans hoped to develop the air and naval bases for the subsequent invasion of Honshu.

In a meeting with President Truman on June 18, 1945, the Joint Chiefs presented this plan for his approval. Truman showed himself deeply concerned about casualties. He did not want to see another Okinawa from one end of Japan to the other. The Joint Chiefs conceded that casualties would be high, but no higher than any assault anywhere else. A direct invasion of Japan, they said, would demonstrate to the Japanese the American determination to conquer them. Admiral Leahy told Truman that the Okinawa casualty rate was 35 percent, from which he could expect among a total force of 767,000 Americans total losses of

268,000 dead and wounded. This was an unintended but nevertheless actual exaggeration if only because Okinawa "casualties" included combat fatigue and many other nonbattle disabilities. Shocked, Truman had no other recourse but to accept Leahy's estimate.

In Japan the ever self-deceiving enemy was actually jubilant. It was believed that loss of Okinawa not only brought decisive battle right to the shores of the home islands—where the material advantage of interior lines and the spiritual factor of fighting for home and hearth would be of incalculable value—but also that the toll taken by the kamikaze among American warships had seriously crippled the U.S. Navy. About 2,000 aircraft—not many of first-line vintage— had been carefully husbanded to repeat these highly exaggerated losses of 50 percent. Japan's strategists expected the battle for Kyushu "to be fought under conditions incomparably more advantageous to the Japanese."

In fact, the estimates of both sides were wildly off the mark. Japan was beaten. With her navy, army and air force gone or going, cut off from the food and fuel once flowing to her from her stolen empire, she could not possibly last beyond November 1—with or without an invasion—and certainly not beyond December 1, 1945. Already the Imperial Palace was receiving in the mail hundreds of index or trigger fingers chopped off by Japanese males in a grisly protest characteristic of the Japanese mind. The truth was that the strategists of both sides—the Japanese deliberately, the Americans unconsciously—had ignored the destruction of Japanese merchant shipping by the depredations of the U.S. Navy's Submarine Service.

In 1920 Captain Thomas C. Hart, a veteran of American submarine duty in the First World War, delivered a lecture on undersea warfare to the Naval War College. He said: "I shall pass over the inhumane features of German submarine warfare because their ways were characteristic of their race. Any nation that attempts commerce destruction by submarines will tend toward certain of the same practices that the Germans arrived at; how far it will go depends on its racial characteristics and, very likely, by how hard it is pressed." Captain Hart was a true prophet, and as Admiral Hart, commander of the U.S. Asiatic Fleet, he was one of those who after Pearl Harbor received this message: "Execute Unrestricted Air and Submarine Warfare Against Japan."

Neither the American nor the Japanese submarine fleets actually were prepared to carry out such a directive. All their training had ignored the German policy of attacking enemy sea commerce, rather emphasizing the use of undersea craft as scouts and ambushers serving the main battle fleet. Submarines were to lie in wait off the enemy's bases or in a naval action strike the enemy from beneath the waves. Capital warships were considered the U-boats' true quarry, and the Japanese navy went to the extent of specifying how many torpedoes should be launched against what size ship.

Between the wars both navies sought to develop a bigger, faster submarine able to remain abreast of the battle fleet at a surface speed of seventeen knots. By

1941 the U.S. Navy had exceeded this goal in its *Tambor*-class submarine, displacing about 1,500 tons with a top speed of twenty-one knots and a range of 10,000 miles. They could crash-dive to periscope depth in thirty-five seconds and once submerged were quiet and easy to handle. With powerful, dependable engines, sturdy lightweight hulls and ample torpedo storage space, *Tambor*-class submarines were the finest afloat.

Japanese submarines were much inferior. The I-class craft, although bigger and carrying heavier deck armament, were cramped, unwieldy when submerged, took a longer time to dive and were so noisy beneath the surface that they could be easily tracked.

Both services were an elite: volunteers specially selected for those qualities of steady nerves and team spirit enabling them to endure a dangerous life in quarters that can only be described as floating telephone booths. Because the Japanese were smaller, their facilities were marvels of inadequacy. Even the roomier American boats, with their amenities of air-conditioning and a delicious diet, were claustrophobic. Half of a crew of about eighty men slept in quarters no larger than a small dining room. Others bunked down among the torpedoes. The officers' wardroom was about the size of a restaurant booth and the crew's mess hall—in which they ate in shifts—was even smaller. In submarines everywhere under the sea in World War II was that pervasive stench of diesel oil.

American submarine commanders were all graduates of Annapolis and the quality of the seamen so high that 50 percent of the prewar force became officers before the war ended. Scrutiny of submarine officers, especially the skipper, was intense. So much depended on the skill, nerve and judgment of the commander, who almost always operated alone, directing the attack from his periscope, that shy or excessively cautious types could not be tolerated. Once the war began it was easy to detect who was unfit to command: the skipper with the worst results. Almost 30 percent of all submarine skippers were removed for this reason in World War II. The Submarine Service was also reluctant to give command to a reservist; only seven reserve officers received combat commands throughout the war.

At the start of the conflict neither side proved to be efficient. The Americans, who had the world's greatest concentrations of submarines in the Philippines, could do nothing to prevent their fall. Japanese boats were almost as bad at Pearl Harbor, where the midget submarines—as typically Nipponese as the kamikaze or the *baka*—almost gave the attack away. For the Americans there was really no overall tactical doctrine except that concentration should be in narrow shipping lanes where the most targets abounded. There were no priorities for any specific ships—especially not the vital, vulnerable tanker—and the emphasis was simply on "tonnage sunk." In 1942, American submarines sent about 725,000 tons of enemy ships to the bottom. Japan was able to replace all but 90,000 tons of this and even to expand her tonnage in tankers. Worse, imports from Southeast Asia were not reduced. Success against enemy fleets was nil. Japanese carrier forces were well screened and moved too fast.

The chief reason for such modest success was the defective American torpedo. Where the Japanese Long Lance was one of the best in the world, the U.S. Navy's Mark-14 was perhaps the worst. Outwardly, the M-14 had appeared to be superb. It was equipped with a magnetic exploder designed to erupt under a ship's keel rather than against its side as old "contact" torpedoes did. Changes made by a steel-hulled ship in the earth's magnetic field triggered the explosion. Each of these triumphs of American technology cost $10,000 and because they were so expensive the Bureau of Naval Ordnance never tested the Mark-14 with a live warhead. Instead exercise warheads filled with water were used. Because no one ever saw or heard a Mark-14 explode, its serious defects were not even suspected until the war began.

The first of these was the Mark-14's habit of running deeper than its setting. Set to run at, say, ten feet it might go down to twenty or even twenty-five feet below the surface and thus pass uselessly under the quarry's hull. Tests conducted by Rear Adm. Charles A. Lockwood in his command at Fremantle, Australia, demonstrated the failing. Yet, the always-haughty Bureau of Naval Ordnance refused to accept Lockwood's report until Admiral King, a former submariner himself, ordered the mechanism corrected.

It was also discovered that the magnetic exploder was defective. It was found that a ship's magnetic field varied in shape relative to its position on earth. Near the Equator the shape was quite different from those on the waters off New England, where the device was developed. Next, the contact exploder, which triggered any "fish" striking a ship's side, was found to be imperfect. The impact was supposed to release a spring, which pushed the firing pin between a pair of guides into the fulminate cap. But this complicated procedure was frequently fouled by the force of a direct hit jamming the firing pin against the guides. After this, too, was corrected, the American submariners possessed a peerless weapon. An abundance of targets became assured after code breakers at Pearl Harbor were able to transmit the schedules and routes of Japanese merchant-marine convoys. Instead of ranging far at sea in search of quarry, American submarines could be directed squarely into the path of slow-moving enemy convoys. Finally, beginning in 1943, submarine admirals in Pearl Harbor and Australia adopted Doenitz's enormously effective wolf-pack tactics; and in July 1944, the new Mark-17 torpedo, which left no telltale wake, replaced the Mark-14.

With these new weapons and tactics, the Americans submarines began to ravage Japanese shipping to an extent with which the enemy navy was totally unprepared to cope. The Japanese before the war had not considered the transport of fuel and food to the home islands to be a problem. This was because they had not believed that the Americans could penetrate their island barriers. They thought American U-boats inferior to their own and American submariners to be the same soft, effete, luxury-loving men they had expected to encounter everywhere else. They anticipated losing about 800,000 tons of shipping during the first year of war, with a sharp drop in the following years. American failures in the early months of the war reinforced that conviction.

But by the middle of 1943 losses were a grave problem. In 1944 American submarines, now also operating from New Guinea, the Marianas and the Admiralties, sank more than 600 enemy ships for a total loss of 2.7 million tons. This was more than the combined total of 2.2 million tons for 1941, 1942 and 1943.

An equally serious miscalculation by the Combined Fleet aggravated the problem of defense against this onslaught. Admirals from Yamamoto to Toyoda demanded the best destroyers for Combined Fleet action. The oldest and slowest and most ill-equipped ships went to the Grand Escort Service. Protection of convoys was thus inadequate. Moreover, the best of the I-class submarines were being used as transports to supply farflung Japanese outposts rather than as wolves to launch a counteroffensive against American shipping. The submarine admirals protested, but their influence over the Combined Fleet's decisions was nil. In direct neglect of both protection and counterattack, the Japanese navy began to build a new type of cargo-carrying U-boat. Many of these were sunk by American warships notified of their location by code intercepts.

Thus the U.S. Submarine Service's assault upon Japanese shipping was one of the most decisive factors of the war. In proportion it was the most decisive, for only 2 percent of the U.S. Navy's personnel and less of its ships had accounted for 55 percent of Japanese shipping losses. More than 1,500 enemy ships were sunk by these intrepid but unsung heros of the "silent service," among them a battleship, eight aircraft carriers and eleven cruisers. By the end of the war American submarines had so isolated Japan from her overseas possessions that they had literally run out of seagoing targets and were sinking ferryboats in the Inland Sea. By then, Japan was also compelled to face another new weapon: the mightiest and most destructive ever to spring from the mind of man.

129. Alamogordo: Testing the Bomb

IN THE MIDDLE of the New Mexican Desert about 125 miles southeast of Albuquerque lies Alamogordo Air Base. On the slope of a hill at the base's northwestern corner was a complex about twenty-four miles long and eighteen miles wide. It was called Trinity, a code name not quite congruous with the work being conducted within. Here was the headquarters of the Atomic Bomb Project. Here on the dark night of July 15–16, 1945, a plutonium bomb called the "Fat Boy" sat atop a steel tower 100 feet high.

Ten miles away was the base camp for what might be called the Scientific High Command under Prof. Kenneth T. Bainbridge of Harvard University. Here had been erected barracks and other facilities for that brilliant company of atomists gathered under the leadership of Prof. J. Robert Oppenheimer of the

University of California. Among them were Dr. Enrico Fermi, the Nobel Prize winner who might be said to have pioneered the project or at least labored longest and hardest to bring it into being. Pres. James Bryant Conant of Harvard was also there, along with Dr. Vannevar Bush, director of the Office of Scientific Research and Development. Also at Trinity was Sir James Chadwick, who had won the Nobel and been knighted for his discovery of the neutron, the key that unlocks the atom. So was Prof. Ernest O. Lawrence, also of California, another Nobel Prize winner who had discovered the cyclotron. Prof. Edwin M. McMillan of the same school was one of the discoverers of plutonium, the new atomic energy element. There were many other similarly distinguished scientists, and, of course, Brig. Gen. Leslie R. Groves, commander of the Atomic Bomb Project, and his deputy, Brig. Gen. T. F. Farrell.

Of all the posts inside Trinity—each of them about six miles away from Zero, where the Fat Boy sat atop his tower—the most important was S-10. At this point Dr. Oppenheimer and his field commander, Dr. Bainbridge, issued orders and coordinated the assignments of the other posts. Bainbridge would give the signal that would set in motion a complex of mechanisms which would begin when Dr. Joseph L. McKibben, also of California, would activate a master robot. This would set off other robots and send strategically spaced electrons toward the proper place at the proper split second. At forty-five seconds to Zero, set for 5:30 A.M. in the cold predawn drizzle of July 16, 1945, Dr. Bainbridge gave that signal and Dr. McKibben activated his robot.

Silence reigned on the desert. Observers not at S-10 lay down in assigned trenches dug in a dry abandoned reservoir, "faces and eyes directed toward the ground and with the head away from Zero." They waited. A voice like the voice of the Creator spoke from above the black clouds: "Zero minus ten seconds!" A green flare exploded in the darkness, illuminating the clouds before it vanished. "Zero minus three seconds!" The silence deepened. In the east was the first faint pink blush of dawn. And then out of the bowels of the earth there shot into the sky the herald of another dawn, the light not of this world but of many suns in one. Within a fraction of a second it flashed to a height of more than 8,000 feet, a great greenish glare rising ever higher until it pierced the clouds, lighting the desert with a pure brilliance never before witnessed by human beings. It was a great ball of fire a mile in diameter. Shooting upward, ever upward, growing wider as it rose, it kept changing colors like a giant chameleon, changing shape like a monster genie, first an enormous mushroom and then—fleetingly—a Statue of Liberty magnified many times. At last it reached its apex 41,000 feet above the earth, 12,000 feet higher than the highest mountain in the world, seeming to lean slightly to gaze down upon the pygmy peaks of the Sierra Oscuro Range.

Having seen the flash, transfixed with awe and wonder, the men gathered on the desert that momentous morning next heard the sound. It came with a mighty roar like the simultaneous explosion of thousands of blockbusters. Its thunder reverberated among the Sierra Oscuros and made the desert floor shake as though convulsed in the grip of an earthquake. Suddenly some of the scientists and science writers began to caper and dance, like primitive man celebrating the discovery of fire. They laughed and clapped their hands. "The sun can't hold a candle to it," someone said. Another felt it was as though the Creator had said: "Let there be light." To Prof. George B. Kistiakowsky of Harvard it was "the nearest thing to doomsday that one could possibly imagine. I am sure, that at the end of the world—in the last millisecond of the earth's existence—the last man will see what we have seen."

But perhaps the most intuitive and ominously prophetic remark came from Dr. Oppenheimer. A scientist of the West who had helped to produce this greatest and most fearful achievement of Western scientism, he retreated into the Eastern mysticism which had nourished another side of his extraordinary intellect. A student of Sanskrit, the ancient language of India, he quoted two passages from the Bhagavad-Gita, the sacred epic of Hinduism. The first: "If the radiance of a thousand suns were to burst into the sky, that would be the splendor of the Mighty One. . . ." The second: "I am become Death, the shatterer of worlds."

130. Summit at Potsdam

PRESIDENT TRUMAN was at the Potsdam Conference held in that German city from July 17 to August 2, 1945, inside the Cecilienhof—twentieth-century imperial palace—when he received word from General Groves that the atomic bomb had been tested successfully. Although Churchill, Chiang Kai-shek and Stalin were also there, Truman told only Churchill of the terrifying, awesome fireball and mushroom cloud that had risen over Alamogordo. The British prime minister was both jubilant and awed. "It's the Second Coming," he growled, "in wrath!"

That was perhaps the last important event in the long and incredible career of Winston Churchill. On July 26 he left Potsdam to return to London—a private citizen once more. He and his Tories had suffered a stunning defeat in the British general election held on July 5. The class-conscious British Labour Party got rid of "old Church" and his class with a resounding 2 to 1 landslide. Churchill was replaced at Potsdam by the new prime minister, Clement R. Attlee, who had served in the War Cabinet.

On August 1 the Big Three (Chiang did not participate in discussions of Germany's future) issued a 6,000-word communiqué outlining the demilitarization, denazification and decentralization of Germany. The Nazi Party with all its evil works—its racist laws, its religious persecution, its judicial murders, its lying press and its mocking courts—was to be abolished. The new Germany, divided into American, British, French and Soviet zones, would be a democracy based on freedom of speech, press and religion. In actuality, of course, this did not occur in the Soviet zone, later to be known as East Germany.

All living Nazi leaders charged with having authorized or committed atrocities or war crimes were to be rounded up and tried, thus providing for the famous —or notorious—Nuremberg trials.

There would be Allied controls to carry out programs of industrial disarmament, to assume the costs of occupation, to insure a balanced economy in the four zones, to handle international financial transactions and to control all German agencies connected with the economy. Germany was to pay reparations "to compensate to the greatest possible extent for the loss and suffering she caused the United Nations and for which the German people cannot escape responsibility." The lion's share of these payments, of course, was to go to the Soviet Union on the ground that the U.S.S.R. had suffered most. The Soviets also were permitted to remove from their zone vast amounts of German industrial equipment to satisfy part of their reparations claims. In addition they were to receive from the Western zones 25 percent of all metallurgical, chemical and machine-manufacturing facilities considered "unnecessary" to the Germany of the future. Fifteen percent of this was to be paid in an equivalent value of commodities— this equivalent to be estimated by the Soviets—while the remaining 10 percent was to be transferred to the Soviets "without payment or exchange of any kind." To the Soviet Union also came complete control of German assets in its own zone as well as German assets in Bulgaria, Finland, Romania and eastern Austria. Poland's claims would be satisfied out of the Soviet share of reparations. Claims of other countries plus those of the United States and the United Kingdom would be met from the Western zones.

The insatiable Stalin also extracted other concessions: "tentatively"—whatever that meant—the northern portion of East Prussia, including the great port of Königsberg, while communist-controlled Poland would receive the rest of East Prussia, including the port of Danzig, as well as the district of East Germany running to the Oder and Neisse Rivers and to the Czech frontier, pending the final peace conference. There would be an "orderly transfer" of the ethnic *Volksdeutsche,* Germans who had lived in the Slavic countries for many centuries, driven out by the Poles and pressured out of Hungary and Czechoslovakia. Here was Stalin's only error in a masterful swindle of his two willing, war-weary partners: the loss of a quarter of Germany's 1937 territory affected only communist East Germany, while the departure of the Germans there swelled the population of West Germany until it stood—in 1987—at 70 million to 17 million in East Germany.

Nothing was said publicly about the Soviet territorial claims on the Baltic, where Estonia, Latvia and Lithuania were eventually to be made into Soviet republics, and Finland, like Poland and all of Southeastern Europe except Greece, was to be one of the communist satellite states within the Iron Curtain. Privately, there were disagreements, but none strong enough to dissuade the Soviets from that intransigence that ultimately led to the Cold War.

The Soviets said nothing about Japan, having still not declared war upon the

Empire, but Truman, Attlee and Chiang issued a joint warning that the alternative to instant and unconditional surrender by the Japanese was "complete and utter destruction." This, of course, was backed by the existence of the atomic bomb. Truman, eager to induce Stalin to join the Pacific War but nonetheless wary, only hinted that America now possessed a new and extraordinarily powerful weapon. Stalin was not interested, and he vacillated again on the question of fighting the Japanese. It was because of this that President Truman ordered Groves to put the atomic bomb to use against Japan as soon as possible.

131. Hiroshima

GROVES AND HIS DEPUTY, General Farrell, got to work immediately. A large batch of the atomic material was rushed to San Francisco, where it was loaded aboard the new and ill-fated cruiser *Indianapolis* and carried to Tinian. (Four days after *Indianapolis* unloaded its precious cargo, it was torpedoed by a Japanese submarine and sunk with the loss of almost all hands.) A trio of B-29s flew the last quantities of the active material to Mather Field at Sacramento, the embarkation point for Superforts. At Mather, disaster nearly overtook the *Laggin' Dragon* piloted by Capt. Edwin M. Costello. Just after he took off for Tinian, when the plane was only fifty feet up, the life-raft door blew open and wrapped itself around the right elevator. By then the *Laggin' Dragon* had already crossed the end of the runway and was nosing over. Costello and his copilot, 2nd Lt. Harry B. Davis, pulled on the wheel with all their strength to raise the elevator. But the huge plane was trembling so violently they could barely hold onto the wheel.

Costello and Davis finally managed to raise the weight of the raft and to climb to about 300 feet. At that point, the raft was blown free. Costello signaled the control tower and was told to remain aloft until his weight was down to 120,000 pounds, when it would be safe to land. But the plane's weight was 132,000 pounds, one ton heavier than the allowable limit at Mather Field. Costello now noticed a flutter in the tail. Chunks of the elevator had been blown away and more pieces were unraveling. Costello told the tower he had to come down for an emergency landing. He ordered his crew of nine and ten passengers to assume crash positions, hands behind their heads. Everyone braced for the worst—until Costello brought *Laggin' Dragon* down in a perfect landing.

After the damaged elevator was replaced by one cannibalized from a worn-out B-29, the trio of great aircraft again took off for Tinian, arriving safely this time.

General Farrell followed, stopping off at Guam to confer with General LeMay and arrange the details for the atom-bombing of Hiroshima, and later, if necessary, of another target city. Farrell also spoke to Fleet Admiral Nimitz, who was now also at Guam. Nimitz promised to station rescue submarines along the route the atom-bomb aircraft would take to Japan, should the crews be forced to bail out. Nimitz also drew Farrell to a window and pointed to an island offshore.

"That island over there is Rota," he said. "There are about three thousand Japanese on it. They bother us a great deal. They have radios. They know what we are doing. They are sending out information. Haven't you got a small bomb you can drop on Rota? I don't feel it warrants an amphibious invasion at this time. But they do bother us."

Farrell shook his head. "Unfortunately, Admiral, all our bombs are big ones."

Farrell arrived in Tinian at the end of July. On August 5 good weather was predicted for the following morning. Farrell ordered the bomb prepared for immediate loading. But Capt. William S. Parsons, a navy ordnance expert who was fully responsible for assembly and use of the bomb, was worried. The night before he had seen four B-29s in a row crash and burn at the end of the runway.

"You know," he told Farrell, "if we crack up at the end of the runway tomorrow morning and the plane gets on fire, there is the danger of an atomic explosion, and we may lose this end of the island, if not the whole of Tinian with every blessed thing and person on it."

"We will just have to pray that it doesn't happen," Farrell replied.

"If I made the final assembly of that bomb after we left the island, it couldn't happen."

"You mean, if the plane cracks up and burns, we just lose the airplane and the bomb and the crew and you—but we don't lose the island. Is that right?"

"Yes."

"Isn't that nice? Have you ever assembled a bomb like this before?"

"No, but I've got all day to try it."

"Go ahead and try," Farrell concluded.

Captain Parsons spent hours studying how to assemble the bomb. By afternoon he was confident he could do it aloft. In late afternoon the partly assembled bomb was rolled out of its heavily guarded air-conditioned hangar and hung in the bomb bay of the *Enola Gay,* the B-29 named after Colonel Tibbets's mother. The bomb was covered with ribald messages to Emperor Hirohito, including one from the now-dead sailors of *Indianapolis.* That night Tibbets assembled six selected crews for briefing. Everyone was silent. There was none of the jesting camaraderie usually present at such gatherings.

"Tonight is the night we have all been waiting for," Tibbetts told them. "Our long months of training are to be put to the test. We will soon know if we have been successful or failed. Upon our efforts tonight it is possible that history will be made. We are going on a mission to drop a bomb different from any you have ever seen or heard about. This bomb contains a destructive force equivalent to twenty thousand tons of TNT."

A gasp of incredulity arose. But there were no questions, and Tibbetts outlined the mission's tactics. Three airplanes would take off an hour ahead of the other trio, at 1:45 the following morning. Each would fly over one of three previously selected targets to report the weather there. An hour later the other three B-29s, one of which was the *Enola Gay* piloted by Tibbets, would take off to assemble over Iwo Jima about fifteen minutes after daybreak. They had to enter the target area together because the Japanese had by then been conditioned to seeing flights of three Superforts dropping a single missile. The target was Hiroshima, selected from a list of four chosen on the basis of proximity, military value and weather. The others were Kokura, Niigata and Nagasaki.

That night *Enola Gay* was illuminated by batteries of lights for picture taking. It was an unnecessary risk. Like Nimitz's island of Rota, the hills of Guam were full of Japanese equipped to communicate with Japan. But the photographers had to be served. At exactly 2:45 on the morning of August 6, the three huge aircraft roared down parallel runways. *Enola Gay* was in the middle with Tibbetts at the controls. Captain Parsons was aboard armed with an automatic pistol. He was the only man present familiar with all of the mysteries of the atomic bomb, and if something should happen to *Enola Gay,* he was determined not to be taken alive.

Tibbetts kept *Enola Gay* to the ground until what appeared to be the last foot of the runway. Observers remembering what had happened to the four Superforts the preceding night held their breath in anxiety. "We were almost trying to lift it with our prayers and hopes," said Farrell.

Then the great silvery aircraft pointed its nose toward the night sky, roaring aloft to vanish from sight within seconds. Very few people in Farrell's command slept easily that night. There were so many dreadful possibilities: Parsons might not be able to assemble the bomb correctly, the weather might be poor, *Enola Gay* could develop engine trouble or be intercepted and shot down, the bomb might not even explode and be captured. . . .

In the morning time dragged its leaden feet. Everyone's eyes were on the clock. *Enola Gay* was scheduled to arrive over Hiroshima at exactly 9:15 A.M. By ten o'clock Tibbetts should be out of enemy territory. At 9:20 A.M. on that fateful morning of August 6, 1945, Parsons flashed two words across the Pacific: "Mission successful!"

Hiroshima means "the broad island." It was built on the delta of the Ota River flowing down from Mount Kammuri. Seven arms of the Ota—seven streams—pour into the Inland Sea, enclosing Hiroshima in an almost perfect triangle: harbor, factories, warehouses, oil refineries and an arsenal. With a population of 250,000, Hiroshima was the seventh largest city in Japan. One hundred and fifty thousand soldiers of the Second General Army and headquarters of the Western Command were also stationed there.

August 6, 1945, dawned a cloudless blue day with a light breeze blowing from the south. Visibility was almost perfect for ten or twelve miles. At 7:07 in the morning an air-raid siren blared. Four B-29s were visible high in the sky. The air-raid shelters filled quickly. But then two of the Superforts flew away and the other pair seemed to vanish. At 7:31 the all-clear sounded. People quickly left the shelters, secure in the belief that this was one of those strange but frequent appearances of three or four Superforts dropping but a single almost harmless missile.

Suddenly an unearthly light of a whitish-pinkish cast engulfed the city, followed by an awful blast like a hundred simultaneous thunderclaps. A horrible, howling wind arose, succeeded by a wave of suffocating heat. Within a few seconds the center of the city vanished. Thousands of people on the streets or in the parks and gardens were instantly killed. Thousands more lay writhing in their death throes. Everything standing in the path of the explosion—walls, houses, apartment building, temples, stores, everything—was swept away and annihilated. Trains loaded with commuters were hurled from the tracks. Trolley cars were flung from the streets like gigantic toys. For three quarters of a mile from the center of the blast nothing was left erect or alive. What had been living beings—animals as well as humans—were frozen in attitudes of indescribable agony. Trees were uprooted and flung into the air like flaming spears. Green rice plants turned tan and the grass became straw.

Beyond the central circle of death even the most solidly built structures collapsed in simultaneous rows, and falling debris of beams and bricks, glass and girders, were seized by the wind and hurled about the city like missiles, killing and wounding many thousands more. Other homes built of wood and straw simply flamed and fell. Almost everyone inside these buildings died or was wounded. Those who escaped perished two or three weeks later from the delayed effects of deadly gamma rays.

Reservoirs and rivers were stuffed with corpses. People unable to bear that awful heat rushed into them hoping to cool their bodies, only to be boiled to death. Everywhere were dead and dying soldiers. They must have had their coats off before the explosion because they were burned from the hips up. Beneath the burned-off skin the flesh was wet and mushy. They also must have been wearing their military caps: the black hair on their heads was unsinged, making it appear as though they wore black-lacquered bowls. But their faces were hideous. Their features had been burned off and their ears melted off. It was not possible to tell which way some were facing. Some were left with only their white teeth protruding, as though bared like those of a horse. Everywhere among those still living there arose a piteous crying for water. Chaos reigned at those hospitals that had survived the blast. The corridors were jammed with mothers seeking their children, husbands searching for wives, their anxious cries mingling with the screams of the afflicted. Some hospitals caught fire in the general conflagration that swept the city and had to be evacuated.

Half an hour after the explosion, beneath a still-cloudless sky, a gentle rain began to fall. Some Japanese believed that the gods had intervened. But the rain had been caused by the rise of overheated air to a great height, where it became condensed and fell back as water. The rainfall lasted but five minutes, after which the wind rose again and the fires spread with frightening speed.

By nightfall, the flames began to subside. But there was really not much left to burn. Sixty percent of Hiroshima had been destroyed and 150,000 people died or received their death wounds.

Thus the Atomic Age had dawned, not in the benign brilliance of a thousand radiant suns, but in the malignance of a black mushrooming cloud and a wrathful, spreading fireball. Death, the shatterer of worlds, had come upon the Earth.

132. Nagasaki and the Surrender of Japan

ON AUGUST 8, 1945, two days after the atom-bombing of Hiroshima, the Soviet Union declared war on Japan. On that same night a second atomic bomb was dropped on Nagasaki, leaving it in ruins with another 35,000 dead to be added to the total of 150,000 or more at Hiroshima. Although Kokura had been selected for the second bomb, bad weather over the city prevented a drop and the Superfort carrying the missile flew on to Nagasaki. Clouds were also encountered there, until a parting of them gave the bombardier his opportunity.

Only a few hours before this second bombing, Foreign Minister Shigenori Togo, one of the earliest and sharpest critics of the war, had convened a meeting of the Supreme Council for the Direction of the War to discuss the Potsdam Declaration. Bitter argument continued for hours, with the military stubbornly insisting that the declaration was unacceptable. The ghastly death and destruction at Hiroshima and Nagasaki apparently had made little impression on them. No conclusions were reached, but on the following night Emperor Hirohito announced that Japan should accept the Potsdam terms with the sole reservation that the imperial institution be preserved.

The Americans were surprised by this unexpected shift. Truman met with Stimson, Forrestal and Byrnes. The president said that during the past twenty-four hours he had received 170 telegrams, of which 153 urged him to impose the harshest terms on Japan. One Congressman told him to "let the Japs know unqualifiedly what unconditional surrender means. Let the dirty rats squeal." Byrnes seconded the sentiment, although not the language, whereupon Stimson observed that to allow the Japanese to keep their emperor would prevent "a score of bloody Iwo Jimas and Okinawas." He said only imperial authority would induce the unconquered Japanese armies in Southeast Asia, China and Manchuria to lay down their arms. On reflection, Byrnes drafted a compromise reply which declared: "From the moment of surrender, the authority of the Emperor and the Japanese Government to rule the State shall be subject to the Supreme Commander of the Allied powers who will take such steps as he deems proper to effectuate the surrender terms." Byrnes's message also repeated the Potsdam assurance that "the ultimate form of the Government of Japan shall be established by the freely expressed will of the Japanese people." Upon receipt of the approval of the British, Chinese and Soviet governments, the reply was forwarded to Switzerland.

The Allied answer provoked another bitter dispute in the Japanese Supreme Council. Once again the hard-line militarists were against accepting it. Togo and the Foreign Office were for it. Prime Minister Suzuki vacillated. On August 14 American aircraft showered Tokyo with propaganda leaflets giving the full text of the Japanese surrender offer and Byrnes's reply. This tactic had a decisive effect upon Marquis Koiso Kido, the lord privy seal who was also Hirohito's political adviser. He urged the emperor to summon another Imperial Conference and break the deadlock himself. Before stunned and sorrowing cabinet ministers, Hirohito arose and insisted that the terms be accepted. "We demand that you will agree to it," he said. "We see only one way left for Japan to save herself. That is the reason we have this determination to endure the unendurable and suffer the insufferable." Hirohito also demanded that an imperial rescript announcing the surrender be prepared for him to broadcast to the nation. By this he hoped to forestall any violent moves by firebrands and hardliners to prevent the surrender.

The emperor's precautions were justified that very night when a group of fanatical army officers seized control of the Imperial Guards Division, murdering its commander and breaking into the palace grounds and the radio station in search of recordings of the emperor's message. They found none, and the revolt was suppressed when senior officers refused to join it, instead bringing in troops to clear the palace. On the same day Gen. Korechika Anami, the war minister who had so bitterly opposed surrender but who had refused to join the conspiracy, committed suicide rather than hear the imperial broadcast. During the next day plots to assassinate Kido, Suzuki and other moderate leaders failed. In further precautions, Suzuki's government issued separate rescripts to the armed forces ordering them to lay down their arms, while emissaries of the imperial family were sent overseas to persuade top commanders to comply with Hirohito's wishes. A new government headed by Prince Toshihiko Higashikuni, Hirohito's uncle-in-law, replaced Suzuki on August 17, and the danger of revolt among the superpatriots was removed.

Debate still rages over whether or not the atomic bomb should have been dropped on Japan. To his dying day, Harry Truman insisted that he "never had any doubt" about the necessity of so doing nor any regret or guilt at having given the order. However, recent discovery of his private papers disclosed a letter to his sister in which he said, "It was a terrible decision," and he confided in his private journal that "even if the Japs are savages, ruthless, merciless and fanatic, we as the leader of the world for the common welfare cannot drop this terrible bomb on the old capital or the new [Tokyo]."

By "old capital" he meant Kyoto, the sacred center of Japan's historic, cultural and religious heritage. Although AAF planners had singled out Kyoto as the likeliest target for technical and military reasons, Truman and Stimson agreed that it should not be touched. Their reasons may have been humanitarian, but they certainly could not have excluded the effect destruction of such a national shrine would have on Japanese resolution to fight on or to rush into the arms of the Soviet Union.

The question also arises over whether or not the bomb was needed at all. There is much evidence to suggest that Japan was already beaten. The U.S. Strategic Bombing Survey, which Truman created to assess the effects of Allied bombing in World War II, probably the most authoritative voice on the subject, declared: "Based on a detailed investigation of surviving Japanese leaders involved, it is the Survey's opinion that certainly prior to 31st December, 1945, and in all probability prior to 1st November, 1945, Japan would have surrendered, even if the atomic bomb had not been dropped, even if Russia had not entered the war, and even if no invasion had been planned or contemplated." No judgment could be more unequivocal. Why, then, was it dropped? From some critics comes the explanation that the thickening mood of savagery which had seized the American public demanded satisfaction. Also the atomic bombings certainly kept the Soviet Union out of Western Europe and compelled her to walk softly in Asia. This was indeed a strategic consideration of the highest order, one that no statesman could refuse to balance against the terrible loss of life which would ensue and the certainty that American declarations of peace and prosperity for all peoples would henceforth have to be read in the light of those terrible fireballs. The atomic bombs did indeed keep the communists out of Western Europe and limited their ambitions in the Far East, but henceforth the Soviets would hold a powerful psychological stick with which to beat the free world.

To these considerations was added the belief by many navy and AAF commanders that Japan could be bombed, shelled and blockaded into submission. This is probably true, although it can never be definitely proved. What is also true is that such horrible attrition would probably have caused greater losses in life and property, and because it would have taken so much longer, would have given Stalin the chance to enter the war for much longer than six days, thereby clothing him in the customary mane of the lion roaring for his "rightful" share. There is, however, no question that the bombings did severely shock the peace faction and brought Hirohito to their side; and also no doubt that the *second* bombing at Nagasaki was unnecessary. Hiroshima was dreadful enough to bring Togo and Suzuki and Kido out into open defiance of the unmoved war lords. Moreover, Nagasaki came too close after Hiroshima to affect any decision. All that can be said for it is that it might have shown dubious Japanese that the United States possessed more than one bomb, and, presumably, could produce many more.*

Out of all such speculation there seem to emerge two probabilities: Japan was beaten and would have surrendered before an American invasion three months later, and Harry Truman—granting his growing distrust of the Soviets leading to that Cold War confrontation now entering its fifth decade—dropped both bombs almost as much to frighten Stalin as to finish off Japan.

Sunday, September 2, dawned gray and overcast in Tokyo Bay. Sailors and Marines aboard mighty battleship *Missouri,* surrounded by a fleet of smaller ships, began to appear on deck scanning her masts and yardarms and gun platforms for a likely place from which to watch the surrender proceedings. On the admiral's veranda deck, an ordinary mess table covered with a green baize cloth was set up. Surrender documents in Japanese and English had been laid upon it. At Morning Colors the flag that had flown over the Capitol on December 7, 1941, was flung to the breeze. After Fleet Admiral Nimitz came aboard shortly after eight o'clock, his five-starred flag was broken at the main. Three quarters of an hour later it was joined by the same ring of stars flown by General of the Army MacArthur. A few minutes before nine, the Japanese delegation came aboard, headed by Foreign Minister Mamoru Shigemitsu. Having lost a leg to an assassin's bomb many years ago, Shigemitsu had difficulty coming up the ladder. Like the other Japanese civilians he wore formal morning dress—frock coat and striped pants—and a top hat. The Japanese took their appointed places behind the table. A naval chaplain delivered an invocation over the bullhorn, followed by a recording of "The Star-Spangled Banner." A Soviet photographer tried to position himself at the table, but was removed to his proper place.

Admirals Nimitz and Halsey and General MacArthur came on deck. MacArthur approached a battery of microphones. To the rear and either side of him were Lt. Gen. Jonathan Wainwright, who had surrendered the Philippines in 1942, and British Lt. Gen. Sir Arthur Percival, who had surrendered Singapore the same year. MacArthur spoke:

"It is my earnest hope—indeed the hope of all mankind—that from this solemn occasion a better world shall emerge out of the blood and carnage of the past, a world founded upon faith and understanding, a world dedicated to the dignity of man and the fulfillment of his most cherished wish for freedom, tolerance and justice."

Observers watching the Japanese saw that they were visibly relieved. One of them felt that the battleship's quarterdeck was now "a true altar of peace." MacArthur pointed to the surrender documents. Shigemitsu hobbled to the table to sign, but seemed puzzled. Actually, he was in deep pain from climbing the ladder on his artificial leg. MacArthur cried to his chief of staff: "Sutherland, show him where to sign." It was done. The Japanese signed, then MacArthur for

---

*Actually, the United States then possessed only two.

all Allied powers—Britain, China, France, the Soviet Union, Australia, Canada, the Netherlands and New Zealand—finally Admiral Nimitz supported by Admirals Halsey and Sherman, for the United States of America. MacArthur spoke again:

"Let us pray that peace be now restored to the world and that God will preserve it always. These proceedings are now closed."

Overhead the sun broke through the clouds. Sunlight danced on the waters of the bay where a single Japanese destroyer—all that was left of Japan's once-mighty Combined Fleet—testified to the retribution that had overtaken unconquerable Nippon. A flight of 450 carrier aircraft followed by about half as many AAF planes roared over the *Missouri*.

Fifty million human beings had died—many of them civilians—but now mankind's fiercest struggle had come to an end.

Bibliographical Note

———— ◆·◆ ————

Because of space limitations and because I have attempted to write a swiftly moving narrative, I have decided not to include footnotes, which might have delayed and detoured it. Nevertheless, I feel obliged to say a word or two about my sources, if only to forfend the charge of writing what the U.S. Marines call "sea stories." Thus: "I know this story is true because I made it up myself!"

Quotations are usually from the speaker's own memoirs, such as Dwight Eisenhower's *Crusade in Europe* or Omar Bradley's *A Soldier's Story*— an excellent and surprisingly lively narrative—or biographies of them, such as Stephen Ambrose's magnificent *Eisenhower* or Desmond Young's smaller though equally enthralling *Rommel: The Desert Fox*. Among the numerous biographies of Hitler, Robert Payne's *The Life and Death of Adolf Hitler* was the deepest mine of information on *Der Führer*, and the same may be said of *Duce!*, Richard Collier's penetrating and engaging biography of Mussolini. Although studies of Stalin also abound, few were as useful to this writer as Edward Ellis Smith's *The Young Stalin*.

On a less exalted level are the first-person accounts of Wilhelm Pruller, a German lieutenant from Poland in the beginning to Berlin in the end; or Charles B. MacDonald, a twenty-two year old captain who led his company into the Third Reich; and Dr. Peter Bamm, a cultivated and compassionate German army surgeon whose conscience could not let him forget the Nazi atrocities in the Soviet Union. At the cannon's mouth similar dramatic scenes and quotations are taken from the memoirs of front-line footsloggers: Guy Sajer, who shows us in *The Forgotten Soldier* the incredible suffering of the men who fought for Hitler on the Eastern front, as well as the Wehrmacht's hideously brutal discipline; my own attempt to chronicle the humor and horror of the Pacific War in *Helmet for My Pillow*; or Hans Habe's melancholy account of the disintegration of the French will to fight in *A Thousand Shall Fall*. In *The Taste of Courage*, a massive anthology put together by Desmond Flower and James Reeves, there resides a veritable treasure trove of dramatic incident and anecdote gathered from hundreds of participants such as Else Wendel, a German *Hausfrau*, and Ivan Krylov, a Soviet staff officer.

So many military historians emerging from the holocaust known as World War II have contributed to the history of the subject that, once again because of space limitations, there is no place to name them except in the Selected Bibliography that follows. Yet I must admit my debt to the extraordinary diligence and perception of two of them: Max Hastings in *Overlord*, a complete and stirring history of D-Day and the Battle for Normandy, and the afore-mentioned Charles B. MacDonald for *A Time for Trumpets*, a similarly thorough and human narrative of the Battle of the Bulge, in which he himself fought.

Official histories are usually dull, more about maps than chaps, geography than biography, but those written on World War II, at least on the American side, are often first class: the enormous ninety-six-volume *History of the U.S. Army in World War Two* written by competent or better professional historians, usually civilians, under the aegis of the Office of the Chief of Military History; Samuel Eliot Morison's monumental fifteen-volume *History of United States Naval Operations in World War II,* on which this book depended for details of the great sea war; seven unusually thick volumes narrating the role of *The Army Air Force in World War II;* plus the Marine Corps Historical Section's fifteen monographs on the Leathernecks' Pacific War campaigns.

Once more lack of space makes it necessary for the following bibliography to be selective. There are so many books on World War II! Many more will come, so that, as Saint John says about Jesus at the end of his Gospel (21:25), "The world itself, I think, would not be able to contain all the books that should be written." In my own library alone there are about 700 titles on the subject; and I possess only a few dozen of the hundreds upon hundreds of unit histories—about divisions, squadrons, submarines, air forces, aircraft carriers and so forth—that are extant. So I have restricted the list to those histories, memoirs and accounts of operations that produced most of my material.

Selected Bibliography

Ambrose, Stephen E., *Eisenhower*. New York: Simon and Schuster, 1983.

Antonov-Ovseyenko, Anton, *The Time of Stalin: Portrait of a Tyranny*. New York: Harper & Row, 1981.

Arnold, H. H., *Global Mission*. New York: Harper, 1949.

Aron, Robert, *De Gaulle*. New York: Harper & Row, 1966.

Baldwin, Hanson, *Battles Lost and Won: Eleven World War II Campaigns*. New York: Harper & Row, 1964.

————*Great Mistakes of the War*. London: Alvin Redman, 1950.

Bamm, Dr. Peter, *The Invisible Flag, Memoirs of a German Army Surgeon*. London: Faber & Faber, n.d.

Barnett, Correlli, *The Desert Generals*. Bloomington, Ind.: University of Indiana Press, 1982.

Bell, Kensil, *Always Ready: The Story of the U.S. Coast Guard*. New York: Dodd, Mead, 1943.

Belote, James H. and William M., *Corregidor, Saga of a Fortress*. New York: Harper & Row, 1967.

————*Titans of the Seas: Development and Operations of Japanese and American Carrier Task Forces*. New York: Harper & Row 1975.

————*Typhoon of Steel; The Battle for Okinawa*. New York: Harper & Row, 1982.

Benoist-Mechin, Jacques, *Sixty Days That Shook the West: The Fall of France, 1940*. New York: Putnam, 1963.

Blumenson, Martin, *Anzio: The Gamble That Failed*. Philadelphia: Lippincott, 1963.

————*The Duel for France 1944*. Boston: Houghton Mifflin, 1963.

Boyington, Col. Gregory, USMC, *Baa, Baa Black Sheep*. New York: Putnam, 1958.

Bradley, Gen. Omar N., *A Soldier's Story*. New York: Holt, 1951.

Brendon, Piers, *Winston Churchill*. New York: Harper & Row, 1984.

Browne, Courtney, *Tojo: The Last Banzai*. New York: Holt, Rinehart and Winston, 1967.

Bryan, J., III, *Admiral Halsey's Story*. New York: McGraw-Hill, 1947.

Bryant, Arthur, *The Turn of the Tide, 1939–1943, A History Based on the Diaries of Field Marshal Lord Alanbrooke, Chief of the Imperial General Staff*. New York: Doubleday, 1957.

————*Triumph in the West, 1943–1946*. New York: Doubleday 1959.

Buchanan, A. Russell, *The United States and World War II*. New York: Harper & Row, 1964.

Bullock, Alan, *Hitler.* New York: Harper & Row, 1963.

Butcher, Harry C., *My Three Years with Eisenhower.* New York: Simon and Schuster, 1946.

Carell, Paul, *Invasion—They're Coming, German Side of D-Day.* New York: Dutton, 1963.

Carver, Field Marshal Sir Michael, ed., *The War Lords, Military Commanders of the Twentieth Century.* Boston: Little, Brown, 1976.

Chalfont, Alun, *Montgomery of Alamein.* New York: Atheneum, 1976.

Chapman, Guy, *Why France Fell: The Defeat of the French Army in 1940.* New York: Holt, Rinehart, Winston, 1968.

Churchill, Winston S., *Memoirs of the Second World War* (an abridgement of his six-volume *The Second World War*). Boston: Houghton Mifflin, 1959.

Clark, Mark W., *Calculated Risk: The Story of the War in the Mediterranean.* New York: Harper, 1950.

Codman, Col. Charles R., *Drive, Memoirs of Aide to Patton.* Boston: Little, Brown, 1957.

Collier, Basil, *The War in the Far East.* New York: Morrow, 1969.

Collier, Richard, *Duce! A Biography of Mussolini.* New York: Viking, 1971.

Conot, Robert E., *Justice at Nuremberg,* New York: Harper & Row, 1983.

Cook, Don, *Charles de Gaulle, A Biography.* New York: Putnam, 1983.

Craig, William, *Enemy at the Gates: The Battle for Stalingrad.* New York: Bantam, 1982.

Craven, Wesley Frank, and James Lea Cate, *The Army Air Forces in World War II,* 7 vols. Chicago: University of Chicago Press, 1948, 1949, 1950, 1951, 1953, 1955 and 1958.

Crisp, Robert, *Brazen Chariots: Tank Warfare in the Western Desert.* New York: Bantam, 1978.

Davis, Burke, *Marine! The Life of Chesty Puller.* Boston: Little, Brown, 1962.

Davis, Kenneth S., *Experience of War: The United States in World War II.* New York: Doubleday, 1965.

DeChant, John, *Devilbirds, The Story of U.S. Marine Corps Aviation in World War II.* New York: Harper, 1947.

Deighton, Len, *Blitzkrieg: From the Rise of Hitler to the Fall of Dunkirk.* New York: Knopf, 1979.

Divine, David, *The Nine Days of Dunkirk.* New York: Norton, 1959.

Doenitz, Adm. Karl, *Memoirs.* Cleveland: World, 1959.

Dollman, Dr. Eugen, *The Interpreter: Memoirs of Mussolini's Interpreter.* London: Hutchinson, 1967.

Dugan, James and Carroll Stewart, *Ploesti: The Great Air-Ground Battle of 1 August 1943.* New York: Random House, 1962.

Ehrlich, Blake, *Resistance: France, 1940–1945.* Boston: Little, Brown, 1965.

Eisenhower, Dwight D., *Crusade in Europe.* New York: Doubleday, 1948.

Eisenhower, John S. D., *The Bitter Woods: Hitler's Ardennes Offensive.* New York: Putnam, 1969

Erickson, John, *The Road to Stalingrad.* New York: Harper & Row, 1975.

Farago, Ladislas, *The Tenth Fleet: Untold Story of U.S. Anti-Submarine Operations.* New York: Obolensky, 1962.

Feis, Herbert, *Churchill, Roosevelt, Stalin.* Princeton, N.J.: Princeton University Press, 1957.

Feldt, Cmdr. Eric A., RAN, *The Coast Watchers.* New York: Oxford, 1946.

Fergusson, Bernard, ed., *The Business of War: The War Narrative of Sir John Kennedy.* New York: Morrow, 1958.

Fitzgibbon, Constantine, *The Winter of the Bombs: The Story of the Blitz on London.* New York: Norton, 1957.

Flower, Desmond, and James Reeves, eds., *The Taste of Courage: The War, 1939–1945.* New York: Harper, 1960.

Friedman, Philip, *Their Brothers' Keepers.* New York: Crown, 1957.

Froman, James, *Code Name Valkyrie: The Plot to Kill Hitler.* New York: Phillips, 1973.

Fuchida, Capt. Mitsuo, and Masatake Okumiya, *Midway: The Battle That Doomed Japan.* Annapolis, Md.: U.S. Naval Institute, 1955.

Fuller, Maj. Gen. J. F. C., *The Second World War.* New York: Duell, Sloan & Pearce, 1962.

Galland, Adolf, *The First and the Last, The Rise and Fall of the Luftwaffe by Germany's Commander of Fighter Forces.* New York: Bantam, 1982.

Gibson, Hugh, ed., *The Ciano Diaries.* New York: Garden City, 1945.

Goebbels, Joseph, *Diaries.* New York: Putnam, 1978.

Graham, Otis L., and Meghan Robinson Wander, eds., *Franklin D. Roosevelt, His Life and Times.* Boston: G. K. Hall, 1985.

Greenfield, Kent Roberts, gen. ed., *The United States Army in World War II.* 96 vols. Washington, D.C.: Office of the Chief of Military History,

Grew, Joseph C., *Ten Years in Japan.* New York: Simon & Schuster, 1944.

Griffith, Brig. Gen. Samuel B. II, USMC, *The Battle for Guadalcanal.* Philadelphia: Lippincott, 1963.

Guderian, Gen. Heinz, *Panzer Leader.* Washington, D.C.: Zenger, 1952.

Habe, Hans, *A Thousand Shall Fall.* New York: Harcourt, Brace, 1941.

Hapgood, David, and David Richardson, *Monte Cassino: The Day American Bombers Destroyed the Great Abbey.* New York: Congdon & Weed, 1984.

Hara, Capt. Tameichi, *Japanese Destroyer Captain.* New York: Bantam, 1961.

Hastings, Max, *Overlord, D-Day, June 6, 1944.* New York: Simon and Schuster, 1984.

Hayashi, Saburo, in collaboration with Alvin D. Coox, *Kogun: The Japanese Army in the Pacific War.* Quantico, Va.: The Marine Corps Association, 1959.

Heiden, Konrad, *Der Fuehrer.* New York: Houghton Mifflin, 1944.

Hersey, John, *Into the Valley: A Skirmish of the Marines.* New York: Knopf, 1963.

Hilberg, Raul, *Destruction of the European Jews,* New York: Harper Colophon Books, 1961.

Hough, Maj. Frank O., USMCR, *The Island War: The United States Marines in the Pacific.* Philadelphia: Lippincott, 1947.

Hough, Lt. Col. Frank O., USMCR, Ludwig, Maj. Verle E., USMC, and Shaw, Henry I., Jr., *Pearl Harbor to Guadalcanal: History of U.S. Marine Corps Operations in World War II,* Vol. I, together with fifteen monographs covering Marine campaigns in the Pacific. Washington, D.C. Historical Branch, G-3 Division, Headquarters U.S. Marine Corps, 1947 to 1955.

Huie, William Bradford, *Can Do! The Story of the Seabees.* New York: Dutton, 1944.

Hull, Cordell, *Memoirs,* vol. II. New York: Macmillan, 1948.

Hunt, Frazier, *The Untold Story of Douglas MacArthur.* New York: Devin-Adair, 1954.

Hunt, George P., *Coral Comes High, Two Days in Hell on Bloody Peleliu.* New York: Signet, 1957.

Hyde, H. Montgomery, *Stalin: The History of a Dictator.* New York: Giroux, 1961.

Inoguchi, Rikihei, Tadashi Nakajima, and Roger Pineau, *The Divine Wind: The Story of the Kamikaze.* Annapolis, Md.: U.S. Naval Institute, 1958.

Irving, David, *The Secret Diaries of Hitler's Doctor.* New York: Macmillan, 1983.

————*The War Path: Hitler's Germany 1933–1939.* New York: Viking, 1978.

Ito, Masanori, *The End of the Imperial Japanese Navy.* New York: Norton, 1956.

James, D. Clayton, *The Years of MacArthur.* 3 vols. Boston: Houghton Mifflin, 1973, 1975, 1985.

Kemp, Lt. Cmdr. P. K., RN, *Key to Victory: The Triumph of British Sea Power in World War II.* Boston: Little, Brown, 1957.

Kenney, Gen. George C., *The MacArthur I Know.* New York: Duell, Sloane & Pearce, 1951.

King, Fleet Adm. Ernest J., *A Naval Record.* New York: Norton, 1952.

Knox, Donald, *Death March: The Survivors of Bataan.* New York: Harcourt Brace Jovanovich, 1981.

Lang, Jochen von, *The Secretary: Martin Bormann, the Man Who Manipulated Hitler.* New York: Random House, 1979.

Lang, Jochen von, and Sibyll, Claus, eds., *Eichmann Interrogated, Transcripts from the Archives of the Israeli Police.* New York: Farrar, Straus & Giroux, 1983.

Laurence, William L., *Dawn over Zero, The Story of the Atomic Bomb.* New York: Knopf, 1946.

Layton, Rear Adm. Edwin T., with Capt. Roger Pineau, USNR, and John Costello, *"And I was There," Pearl Harbor and Midway—Breaking the Japanese Secrets.* New York: Morrow, 1986.

Leahy, Fleet Adm. William D., *I Was There: Account of Experiences as Aide to FDR.* New York: McGraw-Hill, 1950.

Leckie, Robert, *Strong Men Armed: The U.S. Marines Against Japan.* New York: Random House, 1964.

————*Helmet for My Pillow, The Humor and Horror of War by a Machine-Gunner and Scout in the First Marine Division.* New York: Random House, 1957.

———— *The Battle for Iwo Jima.* New York: Random House, 1967.

———— *The Story of World War II.* New York: Random House, 1964.

———— *Challenge for the Pacific: The Struggle for Guadalcanal.* New York: Doubleday, 1965.

———— *Great American Battles.* New York: Random House, 1968.

———— *The Wars of America,* rev. ed. New York: Harper & Row, 1984.

Lee, Clark, and Richard Henschel, *Douglas MacArthur, Biography.* New York: Holt, 1952.

Liddell Hart, B. H. *History of the Second World War.* New York: Putnam, 1971.

Lingeman, Richard R., *Don't You Know There's a War On? The American Home Front, 1941–1945.* New York: Putnam, 1970.

Lochner, Louis P., *The Goebbels Diaries, 1942–43.* New York: Doubleday, 1942–1943.

Long, Gavin, *MacArthur as Military Commander.* London: Von Nostrand Reinhold, 1969.

Lord, Walter, *Incredible Victory, The Battle of Midway.* New York: Harper & Row, 1967.

Lucas, James, *War on the Eastern Front: The German Soldier in Russia.* New York: Bonanza Books, 1979.

MacArthur, Gen. Douglas, *Reminiscences.* New York: McGraw-Hill, 1964.

MacDonald, Charles B., *A Time for Trumpets: The Untold Story of the Battle of the Bulge.* New York: Bantam Books, 1984.

———— *Company Commander, A Twenty-Two-Year-Old Captain Leads His Men into Germany.* New York: Bantam, 1978.

Macmillan, Harold, *The Blast of War, 1939–1945.* New York: Harper & Row, 1967.

Majdalany, Fred, *Cassino: Portrait of a Battle.* New York: Longmans, 1957.

Manstein, Field Marshal Erich von, *Lost Victories.* Chicago: Regnery, 1958.

Marshall, S. L. A., *Night Drop: The Blazing Story of U.S. Paratroopers on the Night Before D-Day.* New York: Bantam, 1962.

Mayo, Lida, *Bloody Buna: The Campaign That Saved Australia.* New York: Doubleday, 1974.

Merillat, Capt. Herbert L., USMC, *The Island, Story of Guadalcanal.* Boston: Houghton Mifflin, 1944.

Miller, Francis Trevelyan, *History of World War II.* Philadelphia: Universal Book and Bible House, 1945.

Miller, Thomas G., Jr., *The Cactus Air Force: The Handful of Fliers Who Saved Guadalcanal.* New York: Harper & Row, 1969.

Montgomery, Bernard L., *Memoirs.* Cleveland: World, 1958.

Morison, Samuel Eliot, *The Two-Ocean War, A Short History of the United States Navy in the Second World War.* Boston: Little, Brown, 1963.

———— *History of United States Naval Operations in World War II.* 15 vols. Boston: Little, Brown, 1947–62.

Mosley, Leonard, *Hirohito: Emperor of Japan.* Englewood Cliffs, N. J.: Prentice Hall, 1960.

Murphy, Audie, *To Hell and Back, Memoirs of Most Decorated American in World War II.* New York: Bantam: 1982.

Nagatsuka, Ryuji, *I Was a Kamikaze.* New York: Macmillan, 1972.

Newcomb, Richard F., *Iwo Jima.* New York: Holt, Rinehart, Winston, 1965.

———— *Savo: The Incredible Naval Debacle off Guadalcanal.* New York: Holt, Rinehart, Winston, 1961.

Nicolay, Helen, *MacArthur of Bataan.* New York: D. Appleton-Century, 1942.

Nimitz, Fleet Adm. Chester W., and E. B. Potter, eds., *The Great Sea War: The Dramatic Story of Naval Action in WW II.* Englewood Cliffs, N. J.: Prentice-Hall, 1960.

O'Donnell, James P., *The Bunker: The Last Days Inside Hitler's Underground Hideout.* Boston: Houghton Mifflin, 1978.

Ogburn, Charlton, Jr., *The Marauders, American Guerrillas in Burma.* New York: Harper, 1956.

O'Sheel, Capt. Patrick, USMCR, and Staff Sgt. Gene Cook, USMCR, *Semper Fidelis, The Stories of Marine Corps Combat Correspondents.* New York: Sloane, 1947.

Padfield, Peter, *Doenitz: The Last Führer.* New York: Harper & Row, 1984.

Patton, George S., *War As I Knew It.* New York: Houghton Mifflin, 1947.

Payne, Robert, *The Life and Death of Adolf Hitler.* New York: Praeger, 1973.

Peers, William R., and Dean Brelis, *Behind the Burma Road: Guerrilla Warfare in the CBI.* Boston: Little, Brown, 1963.

Pogue, Forest C., *George C. Marshall, A Biography,* 3 vols. New York: Viking, 1963, 1965, 1973.

Prange, Gordon W., *At Dawn We Slept: The Untold Story of Pearl Harbor.* New York: McGraw-Hill, 1981.

Pratt, Fletcher, *The Marines War.* New York: Sloane, 1948.

Pruller, Wilhelm, *Diary of a German Soldier.* New York: Coward, McCann, 1963.

Reischauer, Edwin O., *Japan: Past and Present.* New York: Knopf, 1964.

Reynolds, Clark G., *The Fast Carriers: Forging of an Air Navy.* New York: McGraw-Hill, 1968.

Ridgway, Matthew, *Soldier.* New York: Harper, 1956.

Rings, Werner, *Life with the Enemy: Collaboration and Resistance in Hitler's Europe.* New York: Doubleday, 1982.

Roosevelt, James, and Sidney Shalett, *FDR.* London: Harrap, 1960.

Roscoe, Theodore, *United States Submarine Operations in World War II.* Annapolis, Md.: United States Naval Institute, 1949.

——— *United States Destroyer Operations in World War II.* Annapolis, Md.: United States Naval Institute, 1953.

Ryan, Cornelius, *The Longest Day, June 6, 1944.* New York: Simon and Schuster, 1959.

Sajer, Guy, *The Forgotten Soldier, Memoirs of a German Soldier.* New York: Harper & Row, 1971.

Salisbury, Harrison, E., *The 900 Days: The Siege of Leningrad.* New York: Harper & Row, 1968.

Schoenbrun, David, *Soldiers of the Night: The Story of the French Resistance.* New York: Dutton, 1980.

Seaton, Albert, *Stalin as Military Commander.* New York: Praeger, 1976.

Shactman, Tom, *The Phony War, 1939–1940.* New York: Harper & Row, 1982.

Sherrod, Robert, *Tarawa: The Story of a Battle.* New York: Duell, Sloane & Pearce, 1944.

——— *On to Westward: War in the Central Pacific.* New York: Duell, Sloane & Pearce, 1946.

Sherwood, Robert, *Roosevelt and Hopkins.* New York: Harper, 1948.

Shigemitsu, Foreign Secretary Mamoru, *Japan and Her Destiny.* New York: Dutton, 1958.

Shirer, William L., *The Rise and Fall of the Third Reich.* New York: Simon and Schuster, 1960.

——— *The Nightmare Years, 1930–1940.* Boston: Little, Brown, 1984.

Sims, Edward H., *The Greatest Aces.* New York: Harper & Row, 1967.

——— *Greatest Fighter Missions.* New York: Harper, 1962.

Smith, Denis Mack, *Mussolini: A Biography.* New York: Knopf, 1982.

Smith, Edward Ellis, *The Young Stalin.* New York: Farrar, Straus & Giroux, 1967.

Smith, Gen. Howland M., USMC, *Coral and Brass: Memoirs.* New York: Scribners, 1948.

Snyder, Louis L., *The War: A Concise History, 1939–1945.* New York: Messner, 1960.

Spector, Ronald, *Eagle Against the Sun: The American War with Japan.* New York: Free Press, 1985.

Speer, Albert, *Inside the Third Reich.* New York: Macmillan, 1970.

Sykes, Christopher, *Orde Wingate, a Biography.* Cleveland: World, 1960.

Taylor, Fred, ed., *The Goebbels Diaries, 1939–1941.* New York: Putnam, 1983.

Toland, John, *Battle: The Story of the Bulge.* New York: Random House, 1959.

——— *But Not in Shame: The Six Months After Pearl Harbor.* New York: Random House, 1961.

——— *The Last 100 Days: The Final Fighting in Europe.* New York: Random House, 1966.

——— *The Rising Sun: The Decline and Fall of the Japanese Empire, 1936–1945.* New York: Random House, 1970.

Truman, Harry S., *Memoirs,* Vol. I, *Year of Decisions.* New York: Doubleday, 1955.

Tsuji, Masanobu, *Singapore: The Japanese Version.* New York: St. Martin's, 1960.

Turner, E. S., *The Phony War, Britain's Home Front 1939–40.* New York: St. Martin's, 1961.

Vandegrift, Gen. A. A., *Once a Marine.* New York: Norton, 1964.

Ward, Geoffrey C., *Before the Trumpet, Young Franklin Roosevelt, 1882–1905.* New York: Harper & Row, 1985.

Weigley, Russell F., *Eisenhower's Lieutenants: The Campaigns of France and Germany.* Bloomington, Ind: University of Indiana Press, 1981.

Werth, Alexander, *Russia at War.* New York: Dutton, 1964.

Wheeler, Richard, *The Bloody Battle for Suribachi: How a Few Marines Took the Site of the Famous Iwo Jima Flag-Raising.* New York: Crowell, 1965.

———— *A Special Valor: The U.S. Marines and the Pacific War.* New York: Harper & Row, 1983.

White, Theodore H., ed., *The Stilwell Papers.* New York: Sloane, 1948.

Whitney, Maj. Gen. Courtney, *MacArthur: His Rendezvous with History.* New York: Knopf, 1956.

Willoughby, Maj. Gen., Charles A., and John Chamberlain, *MacArthur: 1941–1951.* New York: McGraw-Hill, 1954.

Willoughby, Malcolm F., *U.S. Coast Guard in World War II.* Annapolis, Md.: United States Naval Institute, 1957.

Wilmot, Chester, *The Struggle for Europe.* New York: Harper, 1952.

Winterbotham, F. W., *The Ultra Secret: How the British Broke the German Code.* New York: Harper & Row, 1974.

Wistrich, Robert, *Who's Who in Nazi Germany.* New York: Macmillan, 1982.

Wright, Robert, *Dowding and the Battle of Britain.* London: McDonald, 1969.

Young, Desmond, *Rommel: The Desert Fox.* New York; Harper, 1950.

Zhukov, Georgi I., *Marshal Zhukov's Greatest Battles.* New York: Harper & Row 1973.

Index

Index

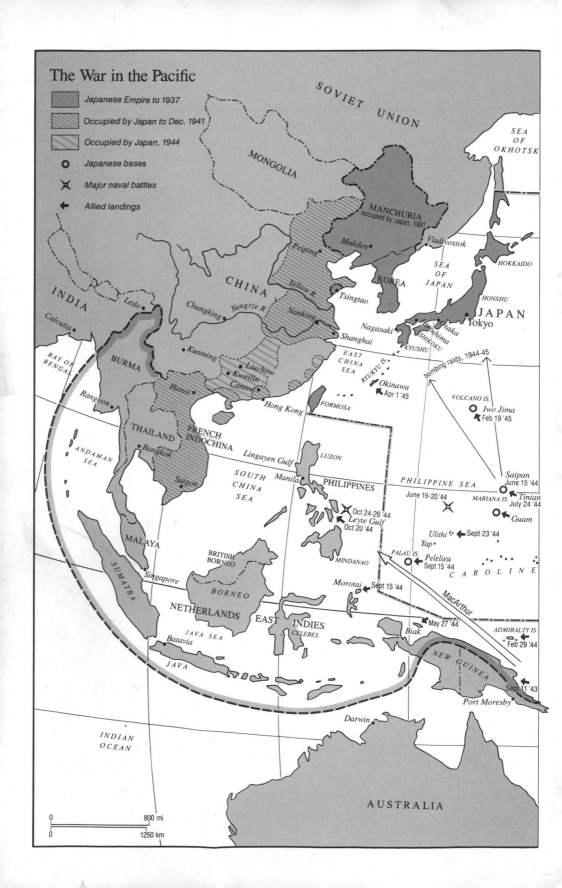

The War in the Pacific

- Japanese Empire to 1937
- Occupied by Japan to Dec. 1941
- Occupied by Japan, 1944
- ○ Japanese bases
- ✕ Major naval battles
- ← Allied landings

SOVIET UNION

SEA OF OKHOTSK

MONGOLIA

MANCHURIA
occupied by Japan, 1931

Mukden

Vladivostok

HOKKAIDO

KOREA

SEA OF JAPAN

HONSHU

Peiping

CHINA

Yellow R.

Tsingtao

Nagasaki

Osaka
Hiroshima
KYUSHU
SHIKOKU

JAPAN
Tokyo

INDIA

Ledo

Calcutta

Chungking

Yangtze R.

Nanking

Shanghai

EAST CHINA SEA

bombing raids, 1944-45

BAY OF BENGAL

BURMA

Kunming

Liuchow

Kweilin

Canton

Hong Kong

Hanoi

FORMOSA

RYUKYUS IS.

Okinawa
Apr 1 '45

VOLCANO IS.

Iwo Jima
Feb 19 '45

Rangoon

THAILAND

FRENCH INDOCHINA

ANDAMAN SEA

Bangkok

Saigon

Lingayen Gulf

LUZON

Manila

PHILIPPINES

SOUTH CHINA SEA

PHILIPPINE SEA

Saipan
June 15 '44

June 19-20 '44

MARIANA IS.

Tinian
July 24 '44

MALAYA

SUMATRA

Singapore

BRITISH BORNEO

MINDANAO

BORNEO

NETHERLANDS EAST INDIES

CELEBES

Leyte Gulf
Oct 20 '44

Oct 24-26 '44

Ulithi

Sept 23 '44

Yap

PALAU IS.

Peleliu
Sept 15 '44

CAROLINE

Morotai

Sept 15 '44

MacArthur

JAVA SEA

Batavia

JAVA

Biak

May 27 '44

ADMIRALTY IS.

Feb 29 '44

NEW GUINEA

Sept 11 '43

Port Moresby

INDIAN OCEAN

Darwin

AUSTRALIA

| 0 | | 800 mi |
| 0 | | 1250 km |